Desert Temples

Sacred Centers of Rajasthan in Historical, Art-Historical, and Social Contexts

Desert Temples

Sacred Centers of Rajasthan in Historical, Art-Historical, and Social Contexts

Lawrence A. Babb
John E. Cort
Michael W. Meister

RAWAT PUBLICATIONS
Jaipur • New Delhi • Bangalore • Mumbai • Hyderabad • Guwahati

ISBN 81-316-0106-4

Published by
Prem Rawat for **Rawat Publications**
Satyam Apts., Sector 3, Jawahar Nagar, Jaipur 302 004 (India)
Phone: 0141 265 1748 / 7006 Fax: 0141 265 1748
E-mail: info→rawatbooks.com
Website: www.rawatbooks.com

New Delhi Office
4858/24, Ansari Road, Daryaganj, New Delhi 110 002
Phone: 011-23263290

Also at Bangalore, Mumbai, Hyderabad and Guwahati

Typeset by Rawat Computers, Jaipur
Printed at Chaman Enterprises, New Delhi

Contents

Part III
PILGRIMS AND PATRONS

Part IV
SOCIAL IDENTITIES

Acknowledgments

Fieldwork by all three of us, as well as other activities, was funded from 1996 to 1998 by a Senior Collaborative Research Grant from the J. Paul Getty Trust. The Center for the Advanced Study of India (CASI) at the University of Pennsylvania funded a thematic seminar in 1995, "Ethnography and Art History", that contributed to the intellectual development of the project. Some of the papers from this seminar were published in Michael W. Meister (ed.), *Ethnography and Personhood: Notes from the Field* (2000). The application to the Getty Trust was sponsored by CASI and the University of Pennsylvania History of Art Department. The subsequent Getty award was ably administered by Elyse Saladoff, then Administrative Coordinator, History of Art Department. A post-fieldwork workshop at the University of Pennsylvania in April 1999 was funded from the Getty grant and by funds from the History of Art Department. We also conducted preliminary and subsequent research in India while there on grants for other projects funded by the American Institute of Indian Studies (Babb), the Asian Cultural Council of the Rockefeller Foundation (Cort), and the University of Pennsylvania Research Foundation (Meister). The Department of the History of Art Publications Fund at the University of Pennsylvania provided a subvention to make a larger format and higher quality plates possible for this publication.

In Jaipur we were affiliated with the Institute of Rajasthan Studies, whose founder and director, Professor Rajendra Joshi, was an enthusiastic supporter of this project. In Jodhpur we benefited from the gracious hospitality of the Singh family at Indrashan: Chandrashekhar, Bhavna, Ba, and Yasho. Prabhu Singh Rathore drove us safely throughout Marwar.

In our research we have benefited from the assistance, advice, and collaboration of a number of people on several continents. While this list is not inclusive, we would like to thank the following. Jodhpur: Lalit Bhandari, Shanti Chand Bhandari, Girdharilal Daga, Prem Vallabh Dadhich, Vardhmanchand Goliya, Sheolal Jain, Shiv Narayan Joshi, Mahavirji Kanstia, Komal Kothari, Naval Krishna, Sayarmal Mehta, Chandalal Salecchа, and Makkhan Lal Varshney. Jaipur: Buddhi Prakash Acharya, Ganpat Acharya, J.N. Asopa, Ashok Bhandari, Surendra Bothara, Navratanmal Dugar, Rajendra Joshi, Nirmala Joshi, Varsha Joshi, P. D. Kudal, and Surjit Singh. Osian: Mohanchand Dhadha, Javaharlal Deshlahra, Bhanu Prakash Sharma, Vimal Sharma, and Om Prakash Sharma. Ahmedabad: Lalit Kumar, Ajit Parekh, and Rabindra Vasavada. Bikaner: Brigadier J.S. Rathore and Ajay Nahta. Balotra: Bhanvarlal Vaishnav. Borunda: Prakash Detha. Salasar: Mahavir Prasad. Mumbai: Kanak Mal Dugar. New Delhi: Romila Thapar. United States and Europe: Vivek Bhandari, Paul Dundas, Anne Feldhaus, Steve Heim, Darielle Mason, Sam Parker, Cynthia Talbot, and Guy Welbon.

Earlier versions of chapter one appeared in *Res: Anthropology and Aesthetics* 27 (1995), 118–32; and John E. Cort (ed.), *Open Boundaries: Jain Communities and Cultures in Indian History* (Albany: SUNY Press, 1998), 111–38.

Chapters two and seven were delivered at the American Council for Southern Asian Art Symposium in Charleston, SC, in November 1998. They were also delivered at a workshop at the University of Pennsylvania in April 1999. They appeared in slightly different forms in Michael W. Meister (ed.), *Ethnography and Personhood: Notes from the Field* (Jaipur: Rawat Publications, 2000), 193–222 and 165–92.

Chapter four was presented at and appeared in *South Asian Archaeology 2003* (Bonn: Deutsche Archäologische Institut, 2005), 577–84.

Chapter five was delivered at a seminar "Shangar and Sringar" in Mumbai, Dec. 1998–Jan. 1999. It appeared in Lawrence A. Babb, Varsha Joshi, and Michael W. Meister (eds.), *Multiple Histories: Culture and Society in the Study of Rajasthan* (Jaipur: Rawat Publications, 2002), 232–53.

Chapter six was delivered at a seminar "Vital, Mutual, and Fatal Attractions: The Sharing and Contesting of Sacred Space in South Asia," at the University of California, Santa Barbara, April 2000. A different version of it, entitled "Devotees, Families and Tourists: Pilgrims and Shrines in Rajasthan," appeared in Carol Henderson and Maxine Weisgrau (eds.), *Raj Rhapsodies: Tourism, Heritage and the Seduction of History* (Hampshire: Ashgate, 2007), 165–81.

Chapters three, eight, and nine were first delivered at the Annual Meeting of the Association for Asian Studies, Chicago, April 2005. Chapter nine was also presented to a seminar at Le Centre d'Etudes de l'Inde et de l'Asie du Sud (EHESS) in March 2006. Chapters three and eight have not previously appeared in print. A different version of chapter nine will appear in *The Anthropologist and the Native: Essays for Gananath Obeyesekere*, edited by H. L. Seneviratne.

Note on Language

Much of our fieldwork was conducted in Hindi (and a lesser amount in English). We have used written sources in Hindi, Gujarati, and Sanskrit, in addition to English. The use of multiple Indic languages presents a problem of transliteration into English. In Hindi and Gujarati a final short *-a* is generally silent, whereas it is pronounced in Sanskrit. Similarly, in many cases in Hindi and Gujarati a medial short *-a-* disappears, whereas it is pronounced in Sanskrit. A word is therefore transliterated into English differently depending upon its Indic source language. For example, the same word is spelled Upkeś when it is originates from Hindi and Gujarati sources, but Upakeśa when those sources are in Sanskrit. We have used both styles of transliteration—vernacular Hindi and Gujarati, and classical Sanskrit—depending upon the cultural and intellectual milieu of the source. This is usually a Hindi or Gujarati milieu, but in places a Sanskrit one. We hope that the differences in spellings do not cause confusion, but there is no simple way to address this issue without losing the linguistic flavor of our many sources.

We have given English spellings of certain words that have come into English, such as Brahman (rather than Brāhmaṇ or Brāhmaṇa). We have spelled the names of deities with full transliteration, and the names of major deities in their Sanskrit forms; thus, Kṛṣṇa, Mahāvīra and, Śiva. We have used standard English spellings for all place names, as found on current maps of India. We are confident that a careful reader will find instances in which we have been inconsistent, for which we beg their indulgence.

List of Plates

Architectural and site documentation at Osian in 1998 was carried out with assistance from a team organized with the help of Anu Mridul, architect, Jodhpur. Two principal participants from his office were Rajendra Roop Rai and Ajay Ramavat. To these we extend our thanks. The pencil drawing of Sacciyā Mātā hill used in Plate 17 was drawn on-site by Ajit Parikh, architect, Ahmedabad. Earlier ground plans of Osian temples were drafted with assistance from Nadeem Shafi and used in the *Encyclopaedia of Indian Temple Architecture* (Meister 1991c–e). Photographs and final drawings are © Michael W. Meister unless otherwise credited.

Plate 1. Khed, Raṇchoḍjī temple: mirrored ceiling in *gūḍha-maṇḍapa*; view into north ambulatory corridor; Osian, Sacciyā Mātā temple, view of *gūḍha-maṇḍapa* looking toward the eighth-century Sūrya shrine.

Plate 2. Raṇchoḍjī temple: forecourt in the 1920s and 1998; Osian, Mahāvīra, and Khed temples: ground plans with enclosed ambulatory paths (*sāndhāra*) and balconies (bottom).

Plate 3. Raṇchoḍjī (top) and Dadhimatī Mātā (bottom): temple compounds extended in the nineteenth and twentieth centuries.

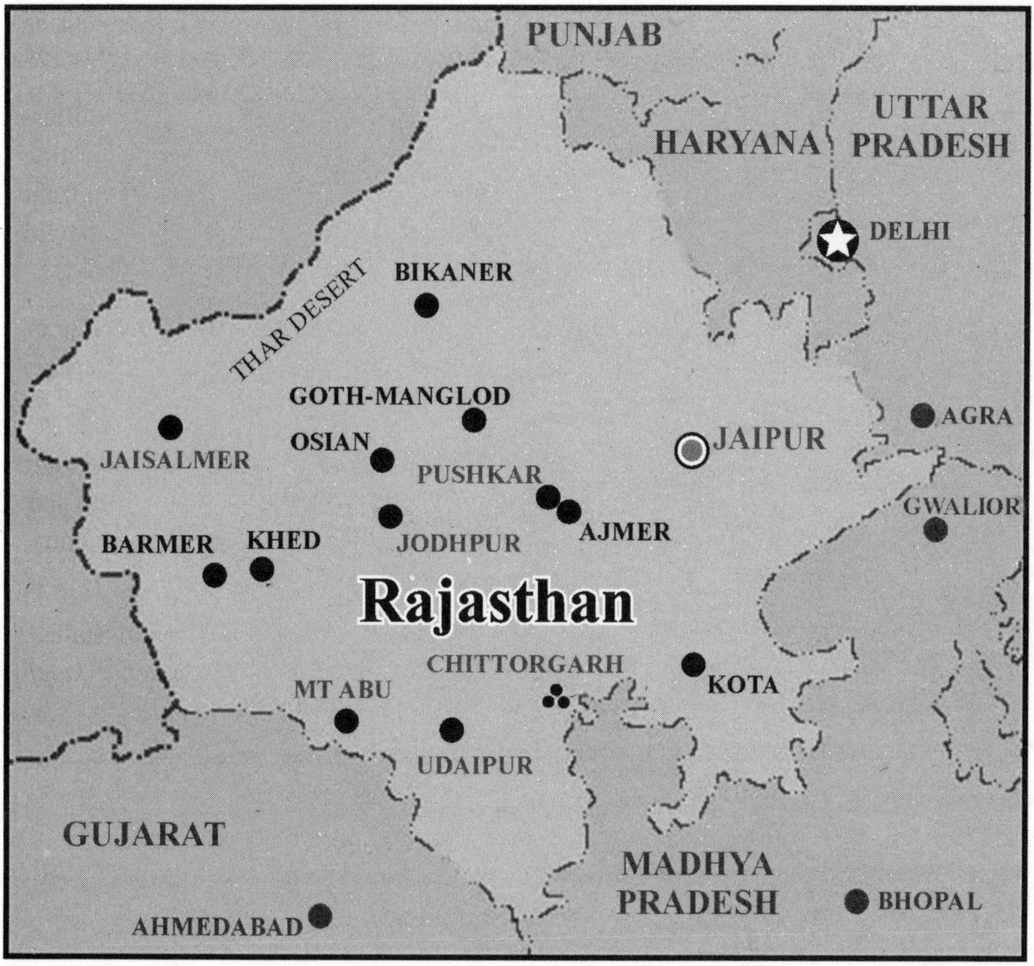

Map
Sites in Rajasthan

Introduction

LAWRENCE A. BABB, JOHN E. CORT, AND MICHAEL W. MEISTER

What is a temple? A building? An institution? Like everything in life, it depends—it depends on regional, historical, and cultural contexts, as well as the idiosyncrasies of the particular temple or cluster of establishments in question. What, then, is a temple? This is, as readers will see, a more complex question than first appearances might suggest. In their heterogeneity, the essays presented in this book reflect this difficulty, but they also—or so the authors hope—convey something of the excitement of pursuing this question in what was, for each of them, a new way and a new frame of reference.

The essays represent some of the fruits of an interdisciplinary study of four temples in Rajasthan conducted by the three individuals listed as the authors of this volume: Lawrence A. Babb, John E. Cort, and Michael W. Meister. The four temples were the Mahāvīra and Sacciyā Mātā temples of Osian, the Dadhimatī temple located between the villages of Goth and Manglod in Nagaur district, and the Raṇchodjī temple at Khed near Balotra. The temples we chose shared one crucial characteristic: they are functioning temples today that are also of very great antiquity. As we discovered, this does not necessarily mean they have been continuously functioning throughout their existence, but it does mean they have long and complex histories that raise crucial questions about the conditions under which temples can sustain life. This issue was the point of departure for our study. Our work was framed at the start by what we called "continuities of community patronage." As we learned more about our temples, however, we came to recognize that in many ways discontinuity was more salient than continuity in their institutional lives.

The disciplines we brought to our task were three. Michael W. Meister is an art historian whose career has been dedicated to the study and analysis of India's sacred monuments. He has researched these four temples intermittently for over four decades starting in 1964. John E. Cort and Lawrence A. Babb brought into play the insights and techniques, frequently overlapping, of religious studies and social anthropology respectively. At the time of our research, Cort had already done extensive field research on the Jains, especially in Gujarat, and Babb had studied Hindu ritual and religion in both rural and urban contexts, and more recently had done research on the Śvetāmbar Jains of Jaipur. At the same time, as we explain below, all three of us have been shaped by the interdisciplinary premises of area studies. In our individual research we each ask questions pertaining to South Asia as a historical and cultural area, and are committed to an approach that employs and intertwines insights from diverse conventional disciplines as they bear on and illuminate our inquiries.

Our question, "what is a temple?" is not just a matter of academic pedantry. It is also a sharply contested question in contemporary India. This became a serious issue in Jaipur in the late 1990s because of a recent law banning the worship of Satī Devī (associated with the self-sacrifice of widows) within a temple. Advocates of her worship said this meant in or in front of the sanctum. Opponents argued that her worship was banned anywhere in a temple complex. The most successful argument was, perhaps, that of practice: in practical terms, a temple begins where worshipers first feel the need to take off their shoes.

The Project

Our joint endeavor was many years in planning and execution. If one were to trace it back to a moment of inception, it probably was when Meister first began working on Osian in the 1960s and also read about the Dadhimatī temple in Nagaur district and its seventh-century inscription. A remarkable thing about this temple was that it appeared to have been in continuous use over thirteen centuries of its existence. This fact, extraordinary in the history of historical monuments in India, gave rise to a range of questions centering on what factors or forces underlie the lives of temples as institutions. Certainly religious impulses are critical, but just as important are the kinds of social constituencies a temple generates and the sorts of patronage by which it is supported. Temples such as the Dadhimatī temple that enjoy long spans of life can be seen as exceptionally useful laboratories for the investigation of these issues.

As best we can remember, we first began to discuss these issues as a threesome during preparation for a conference on Jainism organized by Cort and hosted by Amherst College in 1993. (This conference led to a volume of essays that addressed issues of social and religious identity in Jainism [Cort 1998a], in which an earlier version of Meister's chapter one first appeared.) Planning for a joint project began in the fall of 1994 as part of a thematic seminar on "Art, Ritual, and Patronage" sponsored by the Center for the Advanced Study of India (CASI) at the University of Pennsylvania. These discussions culminated in a decision to pursue a joint investigation of Dadhimatī and three other temples that shared Dadhimatī's combination of deep antiquity and continuing contemporary use. These were the Mahāvīra and Sacciyā Mātā temples at Osian and the Raṇchoḍjī temple at Khed near Balotra. A successful application for a multi-year interpretive research grant from the J. Paul Getty Trust, undertaken in collaboration with CASI, set the project in motion.

Our work unfolded in stages. All three of us visited India for the purpose of laying the groundwork for our project and conducting preliminary interviews, including a joint visit to Jaipur, Jodhpur, and the four temples in December 1996 and January 1997. Our extended joint field research period was from January to May 1998. In India, our official affiliation was with the Institute for Rajasthan Studies, founded and directed by Professor Rajendra Joshi in Jaipur. We were headquartered in Jodhpur, which was a central location convenient for excursions to our four temples and also the venue of some of our most important interviews. In addition to our primary quartet of temples, we visited many others in the region that were relevant to our work, often repeating our visits. These included Gāṅgāṇī, Kāparṛā, Nākoṛā, Sālāsar Bālājī, Pādāmātā (near Didwana), and a number of temples in Jodhpur and Jaipur.

Interdisciplinary Research

A foundational concept of our project was the idea that no single academic discipline can adequately deal with something as complex as a large and functioning Hindu or Jain temple. This is not to say that we devalue the disciplines, for in fact the three of us are enthusiastic practitioners of our very different fields. At the same time, we recognize that the traditional disciplines have both strengths and weaknesses. Their main strengths lie in their narrowness of focus, which is conducive to analysis in depth in an uncluttered field of view. But this very strength is also the source of a notorious weakness, which is that traditional disciplines do not engage well with the study of complex social and cultural institutions, or at least they do not do so when they operate in isolation. The social and cultural world is not only very complex, but there is an entangled and seamless quality to its complexity that the traditional disciplines, owing to their tendency to focus narrowly, either miss or represent poorly.

It is hard to imagine a more dramatic illustration of this truth than the great and little temple pilgrimage centers of India. To return to the question with which we began—What is a temple?—we knew from the outset that functioning temples are many things at once. At one level, they are purely physical things. But even here, we must consider context. To borrow a concept that anthropologist Leslie A. White (1959) once made famous in relation to cultural things, a temple is part of a thermodynamic system. It is, that is to say, a crystallization of, as well as a continuing sink for, energies made available by agricultural surpluses and mobilized by a highly stratified society. Simply to construct and maintain in functioning order these extraordinary physical structures requires an extremely complex array of people acting in specialized occupational roles: architects, artisans, priests, potters, and many others. And this requires the support of a political system that possesses the authority to extract surpluses from both countryside and cities and the organizational capacities to organize and coordinate the building and maintaining of temples. It also requires an economic order with the capacity to funnel those surpluses into temple construction and maintenance. Indeed, temples often play a vital role in constructing the authority of the rulers and communities that support them. The historians Burton Stein (1960, 1961) and George Spencer (1969; also Hall and Spencer 1980) have shown that precisely because temples worked efficiently to mobilize and develop economic resources, the construction of temples was an essential element in the ruling kings' expansion of control into less-developed hinterlands in medieval Tamilnadu.

But of course there is more. Functioning temples are confluence points for social relationships of virtually every sort. Deities are emblems of social groupings of all kinds—lineages, clans, castes, and even village or regional communities. By supporting particular deities, and by making them a part of their life-cycle rituals, groups enact their own sense of themselves as social entities, and also project their identities into public space. Temples are also idea systems rendered in stone; they are physical substrates, that is, upon which Indian civilization deposits layers upon layers of meanings. Temples reflect cosmological and soteriological ideas that are centuries old, that have complex histories, and that are embedded in regional and even subcontinental social and cultural webs. They are also things of beauty, and in this respect must be seen as expressions—and in the case of India, one of the most important expressions—of a civilization's aesthetic principles and values. The beauty of a temple serves to demonstrate the sophisticated "taste" of a patron who paid for it. It is also created to please the deity who resides there. And so, we must remember, in the eyes of pilgrims and other devotees, the temples we studied are also where a god (or gods, or simply God) lives.

Now it is the office of the traditional disciplines to disengage these various things from each other and examine them in depth. But to study a functioning temple, especially one with a long history and a large and varied clientele, one must put them or keep them together. We tried to keep this holistic ideal always in sight during the course of our investigations. We were not always as successful in transcending the limitations of the disciplines as we had hoped, and our chapters clearly indicate the extent to which we continue to be grounded in our separate disciplines. Moreover, bringing in the insights of still other disciplines—economics, political science, geography, or environmental studies—in a systematic fashion would have added to our analyses still more features that we inevitably overlooked. Still, it can be said that necessity required us to weave in and out of our disciplinary perspectives, and to this extent religious studies, social anthropology, and architectural history became the fields of all three of us. We hope that some of the excitement of this widening of outlook is preserved in the papers presented in this volume.

Method

Our methodology was a somewhat eclectic mixture of approaches reflecting the interdisciplinarity of our project. All three of us, however, participated in all phases of the work.

A major focus of our labor, and in some ways the foundation of everything else we did, was an archaeological and art-historical assessment of the temples. Under Meister's supervision, a team of young local architects created a preliminary set of survey drawings of the temples at Osian and Goth-Manglod. This was quite a substantial and time-consuming undertaking. The Sacciyā and Mahāvīra temples at Osian had never adequately been surveyed in this manner before, nor had nineteenth- and twentieth-century modifications of the Dadhimatī temple. After our return to the U.S., Meister scanned and digitized these preliminary drawings and produced others, expanding the analysis and reconstructions potential in our data. There now exists a portfolio of over twenty-five such drawings that have been exhibited in the Architectural Archive at the University of Pennsylvania. Much of this material is available for use by scholars through the image collection of the University of Pennsylvania library as well as in our published reports.

We also spent much of our time conducting interviews. Our interviewing was done both individually and as two- and three-person teams, and ultimately we talked to hundreds of people: pilgrims, priests, craftsmen, monks, trustees, genealogists, politicians, intellectuals, and ordinary men and women. Some of our interviews were target-of-opportunity encounters in the temples themselves or with members of the relevant communities met in other contexts. Much of our interviewing, however, was of a more formal character. We conducted lengthy formal discussions with priests, individuals prominent in temple and community affairs, and ordinary people at the temple sites and in Jodhpur, Jaipur, Nagaur, Salasar, Borunda, Bar, Balotra, Bikaner, Malpura, Mumbai, Ahmedabad, and Patan.

Above all, our investigation of the ritual life of these temples required on-the-spot observation of the sort that anthropologists call "participant observation." All three of us were deeply involved in this sort of work. We made several extended visits to the Dadhimatī, Sacciyā, and Mahāvīra temples, often in conjunction with important annual festivals to which hundreds and thousands of pilgrims came from surrounding villages, other Rajasthani cities, and as far away as Mumbai, Kolkata, and Chennai. We also made many shorter visits to these temples to observe day-to-day ritual activities. This aspect of our research obviously overlapped with our interviewing and reading, as it involved many conversations with pilgrims and priests, and the reading and translation of relevant pilgrim pamphlets, ritual manuals, and hymns.

In order to reconstruct the nineteenth- and twentieth-century histories of our temples, and also to understand their cultural and social contexts, we found it necessary to examine an extensive and extremely heterogeneous body of written materials. We read relevant writings in Hindi, Gujarati, Sanskrit, and English, almost none of which is available in the United States or Europe. We were extremely fortunate in being able to gain access to private and community libraries in Jodhpur, Jaipur, Bikaner, Osian, and Gangani. Some of these libraries had been closed for many years. We have had the further good fortune to be able to photocopy selected materials from each of these libraries, and in some cases to obtain rare publications that we subsequently turned over to the Van Pelt Library at the University of Pennsylvania.

The on-site phase of our work ended in May of 1998. This was not, however, the end of our work together. After the fieldwork phase of our research, we have remained in communication about our project, and on three occasions made joint formal presentations of some of our materials. The first was at a workshop at the University of Pennsylvania organized by Meister that contributed to the production of a preliminary volume, *Ethnography and Personhood, Notes From the Field* (Meister 2000a). The three of us formed a panel at the American Council for Southern Asian Art (ACSAA) Symposium in Charleston, SC, in November of 1998. Finally, we organized a panel at the spring 2005 meeting of the Association for Asian Studies in Chicago entitled "Constructing Tradition: Ideal Communities and Temples in Modern Rajasthan." Some of the essays in this volume were written for these three settings. We have also included some essays emerging out of the joint research written by Cort and Meister for other occasions, including a volume to honor Rajendra Joshi, *Multiple Histories: Culture and Society in the Study of Rajasthan* (Babb, et al. 2002). Material we collected from this project has also contributed to the on-going individual scholarship of each one of us. This volume represents the fruit of our continuing collaboration for more than a decade.

The Temples

As noted already, our four temples share an impressive antiquity, but in other respects they are quite different. Of the four, two stand out as a natural dyad; they are physically close together and in both myth and reality they have deeply intertwined histories. These are the Mahāvīra and the Sacciyā Mātā temples located in the busy market town of Osian. The former is a Jain temple dedicated to Mahāvīra, the twenty-fourth and final Jina of this era. The latter is dedicated to the goddess Sacciyā Mātā (also spelled Saccikā), who is worshiped by both Jains and Hindus. A highly significant feature of this location is that Osian is the putative place of origin of the Osvāl caste, and both temples play roles in a version of the Osvāl origin myth retold by temple priests and also in the writings of Jñānsundar, a Jain monk whose writings figure prominently in this book and who was a tireless promoter of Osian and the Osvāl caste. This myth, as will be seen later in this book, unites the two temples in a single narrative. The Mahāvīra temple was founded in the eighth century CE and appears to be the oldest extant Jain temple in western India. The Sacciyā Mātā temple, located on the summit of a nearby hill, possibly also dates from the eighth century, although the present central structure is a product of the twelfth century. Both have been reconfigured a number of times since then, and our visits have frequently been accompanied by the sound of stone carvers hard at work making still more additions and changes.

The Osvāl origin myth—as retold at Osian—asserts that Sacciyā was instrumental in the "awakening" of the inhabitants of ancient Osian to the truths of Jainism, which was how the Osvāl caste was created. Originally the ferocious and bloodthirsty Cāmuṇḍā, she became vegetarianized into Sacciyā Mātā shortly after the townspeople became Jains. The same body of myth maintains that the Mahāvīra temple was built at that time, and credits the goddess with the creation of the image now enshrined in the Mahāvīra temple. Sacciyā occupies the role of clan goddess for many Osvāls today, though by no means all. As a practical matter, this means that those who venerate her as clan goddess have their childrens' tonsure rite performed at her temple and also perform a rite known as "giving *jāt*" (*jāt denā*) as a postlude to marriage.

Whatever its connection with the Jain Osvāls, the Mahāvīra temple is indisputably a Jain temple. The social and religious complexion of Sacciyā is a more complex issue. It would be easy to be misled by the prominence of the Osvāl origin myth in the affairs of the temples into a belief that Sacciyā is essentially an Osvāl goddess. As we learned, however, Sacciyā is a regional goddess with many caste constituencies, most of which are not Jain. Indeed, the Jains who are most prominent in the temple's affairs today are Terāpanthīs from Shekhawati, a region in the north of Rajasthan, who do not worship images in Jain temples and many of whom do not regard her as their clan goddess.

The handsome main image of Sacciyā in the temple (Plates 5 and 26) clearly relates her to the pan-Indian goddess Durgā Mahiṣāsuramardinī. Her head is slightly bowed and facing to her left (the viewer's right), as she looks down upon the demon Mahiṣāsura whom she is in the process of slaying. Her upper right hand holds a prominent sword, with which she is about to smite the demon. The rest of the image is usually covered by the extensive and expensive ornamentation of precious gems, silver coverings, colorful silks, and garlands of flowers which her many devotees lavish on her, and so the iconography is invisible to the sight of a worshiper. While one author (Rāṭhoḍ 1948:97) has written that the image depicts her riding on her lion—the standard iconography of Durgā Mahiṣāsuramardinī—he appears to be mistaken. Only the upper half of what we assume was the original, complete image is visible. The extant Sacciyā image is an incomplete one, and in this it bears a striking similarity to the aniconic image of the goddess Dadhimatī, which is also understood to be incomplete.

The story of why the image of Sacciyā is "incomplete" does not play as significant a role in the mythic history of the temple as does the story, related by Babb in chapters two and nine, of why the image of Dadhimatī is "incomplete." Whereas the latter is recounted in several written sources, the former we heard only when we asked a temple official about the apparent incompleteness of the image. He replied that as a matter of tradition, established by the goddess herself, only the *pujārī*s of the temple can see her entire image. The image is affixed to the very rock of the mountain with cement, underscoring the way that, as with Dadhimatī, the goddess, her image, and the very rock of the place are all inextricably one. Our informant then gave two accounts, seemingly contradictory, to explain the incompleteness.

On the one hand, he simply said that it would be inappropriate for anyone other than a *pujārī* to see the lower half of the image, which depicts the nudity of the goddess. The presence of many other complete images of "naked" goddesses in the temple undermines the credibility of this explanation (see chapter five).

His second explanation is so similar to the Dadhimatī account that we obviously are dealing with a mythic theme that is widespread in the region (and probably South Asia). He said that only half of the image had emerged from the mountain (but did not explain why, therefore, the *pujārī*s can see all of the image). A small boy was tending his cows on the mountain when the image started to emerge. He was told by an invisible voice that if he said anything, the image would not emerge. Nonetheless, he uttered a fearful cry in response to the loud roaring of the mountain breaking apart, and so the image stopped emerging when it was only halfway out of the mountain.

The Dadhimatī temple is situated approximately thirty-eight kilometers to the east of Nagaur between the villages of Goth and Manglod. It appears to have originated as a shrine of some kind built in the seventh century, although the present structure dates from the ninth century. It houses an aniconic image, a featureless stone normally covered by a face-like mask of the goddess Dadhimatī. She is a Hindu goddess, with no connections whatsoever with Jainism. The affairs of this temple are almost totally dominated by a regionally important Brahman caste known as the Dādhīc or Dāhimā Brahmans. (Depending on context, both designations are used in this volume.) Just as Sacciyā is mythically connected with the origin of the Osvāl caste, Dadhimatī is the origin goddess of the Dādhīc Brahmans, and all Dādhīc Brahmans regard her as their clan goddess. In effect, she is a caste goddess for the Dādhīc Brahmans. The fact that Dadhimatī is so closely connected with these Brahmans singles this temple out from our other three temples, because the others have close contemporary links with trading castes. As we learned, however, she is not exclusively a goddess for Brahmans.

The story of recent changes affecting the Dadhimatī temple can be seen as exemplary of changes in the caste system in modern times. An inscription found at the temple and dating from 608 CE shows that the shrine was then patronized by a Brahman community named Dadhya. (Unfortunately, the present location of this inscription is unknown, although a copy was made that remains in the temple.) Contemporary Dādhīc Brahmans believe this community to have been ancestral to theirs, a claim that has played an important role in supporting their case for proprietary rights in the temple. These Dādhīc Brahmans were once concentrated in Dadhimatī's hinterland, but, in accordance with a common pattern, they have mostly migrated out of the area, both to the cities of Rajasthan and well beyond, a process that appears to have begun in the late nineteenth century. They nevertheless continue to return to the temple to perform the rituals normally associated with clan goddesses. But more than that, their relationship with Dadhimatī figures centrally in the efforts of Dādhīc Brahman elites to reconfigure their caste's identity, as this volume's final chapter will show.

Our fourth temple, the Raṇchoḍjī temple at Khed, a Vaiṣṇava temple initially constructed in the ninth century, was the outlier of our sample of four. Its main image is a form of four-armed Viṣṇu known as Raṇchoḍjī or Raṇchoḍrāy. While the derivation and even precise meaning of "Raṇchoḍ" is a matter of scholarly speculation—it literally means "the one who fled (*choḍ*) the battlefield (*raṇ*)," but may instead be taken to mean "the one who takes away (*choḍ*) faults or wrong-doings (*ṛṇa*)"—images of Viṣṇu as Raṇchoḍ are fairly common in western India. They represent a historical level of Viṣṇu worship in Rajasthan and Gujarat that predates the large-scale penetration of the region by devotional Kṛṣṇa worship (*bhakti*) in the past five hundred years (Mallison 1983).

Our initial interest was primarily in the Osian and Dadhimatī temples. As we developed our proposal, we added the Khed temple as an equally old structure that, to the best of our initial and scant knowledge, had been patronized largely by neither Jains nor Brahmans, but possibly founded by kings. As our research progressed, however, we were unable to give it the same attention or develop the same level of detailed understanding as with the other three. Although it has undergone extensive renovations in the twentieth century, it appears to have, as Meister puts it, "a somewhat constricted contemporary life." It is, nonetheless, of considerable archaeological and historical interest. A local Agravāl community centered in the nearby town of Balotra has dominated its affairs late in the twentieth century. The Agravāls, like the Osvāls, are a merchant caste, but although there are Agravāl Jains, the caste is numerically dominated by Hindus.

Our limited study of the Raṇchoḍjī temple and its present social setting did highlight both important continuities and discontinuities with the other three, and we are confident that our research would have been enhanced had we had more time and resources to devote to it. In a similar vein, many other temples in Rajasthan could have greatly enriched our research. We make no claims for our research either as conclusive or comprehensive, or that these are the only interesting temples in Rajasthan to study. The reader will find our language often tentative and speculative, even after studying these temples and their social contexts for many years. But the very unboundedness of our enterprise—the ways our research at times seemed to take us far away from the physical structures that generated the project, and the realization that every insight opened up yet more avenues of exploration—is, we feel, one of the most important strengths and "findings" of this project.

Temples in Time

The physical fabrics of these ancient temples have been analyzed and described in the *Encyclopaedia of Indian Temple Architecture* (Meister and Dhaky 1991) and phases of their construction discussed in other scholarship (Dhaky 1968; Handa 1984; Meister 1989). Often, however, these descriptions stop at a point deemed an appropriate historical horizon—when the structure is perceived to have been "completed"—rather than a "horizon of expectation" as predicated by reception theory (Iser 1978; Meister 1995b). The social sources and consequences of changes—the "reception" of the monuments, their lives—have not been explored.

In the eighth century, temples not supported by direct royal patronage remained human in scale, small by the standards of later monuments and built for use by particular sects and for individuals to approach the deity directly. With the passage of time, increasing wealth of patrons and changing public functions of the temple led to enlarged temple establishments. Temple rituals shifted from esoteric practices, privately performed by Brahman sects for the benefit of kings and other wealthy patrons who were not present, to public forms of community and family worship (Inden 2000; Davis 1991). These included increasingly popular *bhakti* practices, pilgrimage, and public festivals, which still were able to validate royal sponsors. Craft guilds perfected the technologies of stone construction, halls were added, and shrines were incorporated into larger compounds and social institutions (Meister 1985; 1991a). This enlargement of compounds and temple complexes occurred during the medieval period when kings and communities overlapped in their uses of temples. The trend continued in the modern period, but with different sets of agendas.

The pattern of multiple agendas and multiple communities of use is strongly exemplified by our materials. Establishing the Mahāvīr Jain Vidyālay, the boarding school attached to the Mahāvīra temple, early in the twentieth century was intended to restore an Osvāl population in Osian. Its compound physically doubled the space occupied by the temple as an institution. Four courtyards added around the Dadhimatī temple at Goth-Manglod in the middle of the nineteenth century also enlarged and redefined that temple, while providing a place for pilgrims to stay. In the twentieth century, the Dadhimatī temple has been further enlarged and has had decades of lawsuits first establishing and then gradually shifting control away from a local Dādhīc Brahman community toward a broader *bhakti* agenda. In the mid-twentieth century, priests of the Sacciyā temple at Osian began to plan to build shrines to Nine Durgās in order to increase patronage and support. More recent pilgrims' patronage, based largely on different agendas, has added large Osvāl and Māheśvarī *dharmśālā*s (pilgrim rest houses). Changing laws that make donations to temples run by Public Trusts tax deductible have also altered the way these institutions run themselves.

Some of these ancient and modern agendas we have been able to parse, some we have not. However, the patterns of change and use we find in our four examples—varied even for desert temples in Rajasthan—help frame questions elsewhere. Problems of where do the barbers sit or who drinks alcohol and where may seem particular to our local context, yet the survival of temples has depended in part on the engagement of communities of users with such issues. Government regulations have changed the way worshipers, patrons, and temples interact in an independent and modernizing India, as we discuss in chapters three and seven, but not yet in ways that reject the past. From such events as Jñānsundar's labors in the twentieth century, the establishment of the All-India Dāhimā Mahāsabhā, and the hasty scramble to set up public temple trusts in the 1970s, living temples emerge.

Organization of the Book

Our work together resulted in a common pool of data from which each of us has drawn in the course of pursuing writing projects of his own. We hope that all of the papers included in this book demonstrate something of the interdisciplinary sensibility that we fostered during our fieldwork together. They are, however, separately authored, and to this extent they reflect our specific individual interests, opportunities, and proclivities. We have done some re-editing of the papers, but the editorial hand has been light in order to preserve their integrity as stand-alone essays. We have tried to attain a degree of stylistic uniformity, but we have not attempted to project a single authorial voice. The circumstances of the origin of the chapters as independent essays have presented problems for the organization of this book. How should we organize papers written for highly diverse venues into chapters of a single but multi-authored volume? We have tried to group them into sections in a way that makes sequential sense, but there is a considerable amount of overlap and even repetition among the chapters.

The papers we have brought together are nine in number and we have grouped them into four sections. These sections reflect what seem to us to be the major categories into which our work naturally fell.

Part One: Histories

We start the book with two chapters that investigate how the Osvāls and the Dādhīc Brahmans themselves have thought about these temples. Both castes have had long-standing, intimate relationships with the physical structures and the sites where they are located, because they also have close—and in the case of the Dādhīc Brahmans, genealogical—relationships with the deities who reside there. These two chapters show that temples and their deities play key roles in the ways that people think about themselves as social units. Whatever else the temples may be, for Osvāls and Dādhīc Brahmans they have been the locus of intense and sustained thinking about who they are as caste communities, a matter to be explored in detail in the final chapters of this volume. Questions of identity are always also questions of history: part of the answer to the question "Who are we?" is found in the answer to the question "Where do we come from?" Part of what makes a temple live and allows it to survive for as many centuries as these have, is that the temple is embedded in a community's self-understanding as expressed in historical or mythohistorical ideas. People narrate their own history, and because a temple is central to that history, they travel to, worship at, and maintain that temple. These histories, told over and over, with many variants, became central to our research.

An earlier version of Meister's "Sweetmeats or Corpses?" served in part as a position paper that outlined some of the basic questions we wanted to investigate. The version here was revised and strengthened in light of the subsequent joint research. His focus is the special relationship, from the Osvāl point of view, between the Mahāvīra and Sacciyā temples and the Osvāl's own history and destiny as a caste community. There are, as the chapter shows, two "histories" of the temple complex. One is the sort of history researched and written by modern historians and art-historians. This is history as concerned with the on-the-ground facts that explain who, what, where, when, and why. The other is the sort of mythohistory or narrative that serves as a charter for, among other things, the identity and often the internal structure of social groups. Meister brings these two narratives into contact, drawing the mythic version from the *Upakeśa Gaccha Paṭṭāvalī*, and although the two narratives are certainly in tension, they also mesh in interesting ways.

The crux of the Osvāl origin myth is the monk Ratnaprabhasūri's conversion of the townspeople of Osian from the worship of bloodthirsty Cāmuṇḍā into non-violent Jains. Sacciyā Mātā is a local goddess, associated with the Great Goddess Durgā in this myth. Cāmuṇḍā, an early fierce form of the Goddess, however, is not the principal form by which Sacciyā is known at Osian (Meister 1986b). Within the frame of this story, Meister focuses on the subsequent conversion of Cāmuṇḍā (in the form of Durgā slaying the buffalo demon Mahiṣa) into a vegetarian goddess suitable as an object of worship for Jains. Transmogrified, she becomes Sacciyā Mātā, who is patrilineage goddess for some Osvāl clans and also serves somewhat diffusely as a symbol of Osvāl caste identity.

In "Time and Temples," Babb relates the theme of social identity to the way origin mythology manipulates time. If modern scholars, and indeed modern people, measure time in isometric units, the narratives that serve as charter myths for social groups construct a very different picture of historical duration. Time as measured in isometric units is "metrical time." The timescape of origin myths, however, is what Evans-Pritchard (1940) famously called "social time," which is time as a reflex of social proximity and distance—of "social space," that is—as expressed in myths about how groups and relationships between groups once came into being. The Dadhimatī, Mahāvīra, and Sacciyā temples are, as we see in this essay, situated in social time as well as the metrical time of the modern historian.

Babb first examines the officially sanctioned origin myth of the Dādhīc (or Dāhimā) Brahmans; this he compares with the Śvetāmbar mendicant Jñānsundar's story of the origin of the Osvāl caste. The Dādhīc origin myth establishes three levels of Dādhīc identity—as generic Brahmans, as Dādhīc Brahmans, and as members of specific patriclans—each with its own social timescape. Somewhat more complex is the Osvāl case, in which the disciplic descent of mendicant lineages intersects with the physical descent of worldly lineages, a pattern that may be characteristic of social identity of Jain groups generally. The Osvāl myth, moreover, exists in a tension with the timescape of modern historians, a difficulty we do not see in the Dādhīc case.

Part Two: Structures

We move in the second section from the narratives people have told about the temples to a focus on the temples as designed, ornamented, and geographically situated physical structures. Meister's "Building a Temple" provides a detailed survey of the four temples from archaeological, architectural, and art-historical points of view. In the process, he gives a sense, consistent with the limitations of our data, of how these temples have changed in time. Our knowledge of the evolution of the temples as physical structures is reasonably good, but of course our grasp of their changing social and political contexts is limited to what archaeology and limited epigraphy can provide. From our standpoint, a recoverable history of our temples emerges into the full light of day only in the nineteenth and twentieth centuries.

In this chapter Meister also introduces a theme that was of great importance to our project and one that informs much of the material presented later on in this book. This is the necessity of patronage, of whatever sort, to what Meister calls (in specific reference to the Osian temples) a "pattern of replacement, reformulation, and rededication." The analysis of such social and political support is key to understanding how temples that succeeded in staying alive over centuries survived the natural processes of decay and the vicissitudes of history. He also introduces evidence from legal history that helps explain significant differences between behavior of communities who established temple trusts early in the twentieth century and the functioning of Public Temple Trusts today.

In "Water in a Desert Landscape," Meister shifts the spotlight to the natural environment, with specific reference to Osian's past. There are several ancient temples at Osian as well as a spectacular step well. Of these temples, the Mahāvīra and Sacciyā Mātā temples are of greatest historical and contemporary importance; the other structures, however, are evidence of the great significance of Osian as a religious center in ancient times, for it must have been a major population center and source of patronage in those days. The paper highlights the importance of water to understanding why Osian flourished as it did. Water in adequate supply made possible the physical existence of the populations that built and maintained these temples, to say nothing of supplying the needs of the thirsty crowds of pilgrims that must have been a part of the picture from the time the temples were built. The story of the decline early in the twelfth century of another city in Marwar, Bhinmal (Shrimal)—whose ancient history is tied to that of Osian in many ways—is that the majority of its inhabitants had to leave after a long drought (Cort 2000a:109-10). Although the history of the Osvāls is certainly one of total emigration from Osian, as far as we know the town of Osian itself faced a fate similar to that of Bhinmal only early in the twentieth century, before the building of the Rajasthan canal.

One day we had a conversation with one of our principal informants—Om Prakash, an employee of the Sacciyā temple whose family had been *pujārī*s there for generations—about the ways that the economy of the region had been transformed by the arrival in Osian of water in significant quantities due to the Indira Gandhi canal. We remarked that there must have been some similar source of water in ancient times, when Osian was described as a great capital city, as evidenced by the many ruins and still extant ancient temples that dot the landscape. He took us into the hills several kilometers outside of town, and showed us the faint outlines of what was once a significant water storage system built to capture and retain rainwater needed to support the town. This centered on the wells described by Meister, drawing on a scant available water table (annual rainfall is less than five inches a year) and thus enabling such a sacred complex to flourish in the desert.

But water is more than a mere fluid; it also possesses great symbolic significance in South Asian cultures. Following Coomaraswamy, Meister notes that water is a key symbol in South Asian cosmologies and that one can see this visually reflected in prints of Osian's origin story found in books and in paintings we saw mounted on the walls of many Jain institutions in Rajasthan. These almost inevitably depicted Ratnaprabhasūri seated in a verdant landscape filled with waterfalls and rivers. Osian is an apt example of the ability of water, however hidden, to "empower" the sacred, especially in the desert.

The next chapter, Meister's "Light on the Lotus," directs attention to the Dadhimatī temple. In this chapter he discusses both patronage and the manner in which the temple relates to the social identity of the Dādhīc Brahman caste. He also provides a sketch of the ninth-century temple and the development of its compounds in the nineteenth and twentieth centuries in historical and art-historical terms. A particularly interesting point documented in this essay has to do with a neighboring ninth-century temple located near Didwana that, though again in use today as a goddess temple, has not been a continual worship or pilgrimage center comparable to that of Osian or the Dadhimatī temple. Part of the ornamentation of this recently resurrected shrine depicts a goddess in the form of Durgā Mahiṣāsuramardinī emerging from the ground in the presence of herdsmen and their cattle. According to contemporary local myth, the aniconic stone representing Dadhimatī emerged—as noted earlier—from the earth in the presence of a frightened herdsman and his cows, and a similar story is told of Sacciyā Mātā. This image and stories of Dadhimatī and Sacciyā suggest the existence of a myth-motif that is both ancient and deeply embedded in contemporary regional culture.

Part Three: Pilgrims and Patrons

If there is a selection process by which some temples succeed and others fail at the test of staying alive over centuries, continuity and/or discontinuity in their relationships with the individuals and communities that provide their support is its primary basis. A key variable is, of course, the nature of this support, which was a major focus of our work. Cort's "Pilgrimage and Identity in Rajasthan" introduces these issues in the context of a study of Osian as a pilgrimage center. A pilgrimage center is, as Cort points out, "a sacred complex, an elaborate network of shrines and subshrines," with a physical layout that interacts with religious symbols and practices in complex and fluid ways. Multiple deities mean multiple things to multiple constituencies, some very local and some far-flung.

Cort distinguishes three ways in which the significance of deities (often the same deities) is understood by worshipers. Some deities are what he calls "family lineage deities"; these are deities, usually goddesses, specific to lineages and sometimes castes, and are closely connected with the theme of social identity to be explored later in this volume. Second, "place deities" have to do with geographic as opposed to the social hinterlands, although these principles usually overlap in practice. Third and finally, "adored deities" refers to deities worshiped as objects of devotion in the context of *bhakti* ideology; this, too, is clearly a category that can overlap with the other two. All of these patterns are manifested at Osian, as they are at all major pilgrimage centers.

The multiplicity of relationships between deities and their human constituencies provides a convenient bridge into another area of intense focus of our research, which is patronage and proprietary rights. A temple cannot live without support, and, if it has support, a temple is likely to live. Indeed, the Mahāvīra temple of Osian might be said to have been revived from near death because of miraculously restored patronage. But the extent to which it has support is in a feedback loop with an array of relationships that communities and individuals have with deities and the temples that enshrine them.

In "Patronage, Authority, Proprietary Rights, and History," Cort makes the point that although a one-time visitor might conclude that a temple is a "fixed entity," historical and sociological perspectives show that temples are fluid entities at every level. This is even true of temples as physical objects, which—in the case of temples that have lasting ritual lives—are typically subject to repeated renovations during the passage of deep-historical time. And these changes, in turn, point to the crucial importance of the kinds of people and groups that have interests in the temple, whoever or whatever they may be. Over the course of time, these interests clash and claims of authority over temples are challenged. In the body of this paper, Cort anatomizes the sources of legitimacy in terms of which groups claim proprietary rights in temples. These include the claims of priests, of locally dominant castes, of *jajmānī* patronage, of special connections (such as descent) to the deity, and the influence of charismatic renouncers in establishing or reviving a group's special interest in a temple.

Cort's "Patronage" essay provides a transition to an issue that became the leitmotif of the sociological dimension of our work. With the possible exception of the Raṇchoḍjī temple (about which our information is insufficient), each of our temples in one way or another remains connected with the social identity of multiple groups, and this defines a major focus of our inquiries. One of the most significant of our discoveries, if that is the right word, was the realization of how layered this phenomenon actually is. Perhaps overly influenced by the claims of groups currently dominant in the affairs of the Sacciyā and Dadhimatī temples—claims articulately and forcefully promoted in the literature produced by these groups—we began with the tendency to see these temples and the deities they contain as intertwined largely with the social identities and internal affairs of single groups: the Osvāls in the case of Osian, the Dādhīc Brahmans in the case of Dadhimatī. As it turned out, this was much too simple a view, as Cort's "Patronage" essay shows.

All of our temples have multiple constituencies, even the Mahāvīra temple if one distinguishes properly between different Jain constituencies, and timelines of changing patronage. In this sense, temples can be seen as confluences of social relationships. They are arenas in which groups, especially caste groups, come into close juxtaposition, and the ritual life of temples often has the theatrical function of displaying intercaste relationships in a particularly dramatic way. Indeed, a temple can even be said to sanctify the intercaste and intergroup relationships that converge so densely on its premises.

But even if this is so, some groups take temples and the deities therein as having a special relationship with their own histories, internal composition, and social identity; they see them as *their* deities and expressive of their own unique identity. Indeed, this can bring the group making such claims into conflict with others who have interests, ritual or material, in the temple in question.

Cort's discussion shows just how many different human actors enter into the life of any one temple. In significant part this is because temples are important economic institutions, and so control over the temple gives one access to pilgrim income, the movable and immovable wealth of the temple, and any land that is in its endowment. In the context of our research, Babb and Cort spent several days in the small town of Borunda, known to have had a significant population of Dādhīc Brahmans at one point. Here they also visited the local Jain temple. No image-worshiping (Mūrtipūjak) Jains have lived in Borunda for many generations, but the local congregation of Sthānakavāsī Jains—a sect that rejects the ritual culture of images and temples—carefully maintained the temple and paid for a *pujārī* to conduct daily rituals in it. One of the trustees of the temple, when we asked why he supported an institution that in theory he should have theologically rejected, answered quite simply that the congregation had to maintain the temple in order to retain control over the land that belonged to the temple (and probably its modern Public Trust).

But temples are equally important as social and cultural institutions. A list of the different categories of people who might have a vested interest in any given temple makes this clear. There are the pilgrims from afar and the local worshipers. There are priests—and in some places in India, this means also both the state-run schools that train the priests and the local union to which the priests belong. Since temples in contemporary India are registered legal entities, there are elected and appointed trustees, some of whom reside locally, and some of whom reside in distant cities. In part, the category of trustee can also overlap with that of patron and donor. These patrons and donors, of course, include not only those who are alive and active in the life of the temple today, but those who were responsible for the life of the temple in previous decades and centuries. Some temple trusts include appointed government officials, so the life of a temple intersects with various governmental agencies at the local, regional, state, and national level—and in the case of those few living monuments that have been recognized by UNESCO as part of the world heritage of all humanity, even international agencies. None of the temples we studied has yet generated a duplicate outside of India, nor the sorts of transnational networks now attached to some of the wealthiest temples of India. But a Jain firm in England uses a photograph of the Mahāvīra image in Osian in the advertisements it regularly places in global Jain periodicals. We will not be surprised when, in a few years, one or more of these temples hosts its own homepage on the internet. As mid-2007 only the Dadhimatī temple has a limited, non-interactive web site, as part of the home page of the Dādhīc Brahmans (www.dadhich.com/dadhimati_temple.htm).

Temples are built structures, and so there are past and contemporary architects, stone masons, and sculptors who have left their imprint upon them. Temples are religious institutions, so inevitably there are religious leaders involved, some of whom gain their interests through inherited or appointed positions, others through charisma and personal devotion. Many sites with temples are the goals of pilgrims, both from within India and from abroad. Sand dunes opposite Osian are now the location of an expensive desert tourist camp, where people from Europe and America can live in tents, eat exotic desert cuisine, ride a camel, sip cocktails, and possibly visit the temples. Several years after we completed our joint fieldwork, when Cort was in Jaipur on a different research project, he was asked by the director of an American museum who knew of this project to spend several days in Osian explaining the temples to a special tour of art aficionados. This should remind us that among those we need to include in our portrait of people involved even at the local level are global scholars. Meister has been studying the temples at Osian intermittently for nearly four decades, and several informants readily referred to his earlier visits or published scholarship. The *Encyclopaedia of Temple Architecture* (or some "foreign scholar's opinion") is often cited to give credence to local claims of a temple's antiquity and current stature. Meister was asked by a future-thinking District Collector to attend a community meeting he had called with local Māheśvarī and other residents of Osian to discuss the need for an archaeological park.

Finally, as the pilgrims and devotees again would remind us, there are the deities themselves. As scholars we cannot study deities directly; we can study them only through the human actions and responses to their presence. But they are who "really matter" for most people who come to the temples or festivals that surround them. To borrow a phrase from Richard Davis (2000), it is important when researching a religious institution to remember to try to "write as if icons are really alive."

Part Four: Social Identities

The final section of the book indicates some of the ways that our research, taking the built structures of the temples as our physical and spatial starting point, spiraled out into a wide array of other questions. Many of these were not questions that a narrowly defined art-historical project would necessarily have investigated, but they became germane and even central given our multidisciplinary approach. The two chapters in this section look at how the construction—taking "construction" to mean an intellectual and social project as much as a material one—and maintenance of temples are tied to the construction and maintenance of social groups. We look at two groups in particular, one voluntary and the other ascriptive: a Jain mendicant lineage, and a Brahman caste. We could have conducted similar studies of other groups—the caste of Śākadvīpī Brahmans, also known as Bhojaks, who serve as priests at the Mahāvīra and Sacciyā Mātā temples is an obvious choice. But these two chapters suffice to demonstrate how our multidisciplinary methodology allowed us to see these temples as nodes within rich and complex webs of social and historical signification.

Cort's "Constructing a Jain Mendicant Lineage" greatly deepens the Osian story. The paper traces the early twentieth-century career of Jñānsundar, a sternly ascetic and unbending Jain monk. He was a tireless promoter of the Osvāl caste from which he came, of Osian as an Osvāl pilgrimage center, and of a once-important but now mostly defunct mendicant lineage known as the Upkeś Gacch that he attempted to reconstruct. Cort gives us a thorough sense of the character and outlook of this extraordinary individual. A large part of this story has to do with the politics of Śvetāmbar Jain mendicant traditions and lineages. Jñānsundar attempted to create a unified vision of social identity. At the foundation of this concept was his insistence that an Upkeś Gacch *ācārya* was responsible for creation of the Osvāl caste, a version of Osvāl origin promoted at Osian and retold in Babb's "Time and Temples" but at variance with other versions. At the core of this origin story are the two temples, Mahāvīra and Sacciyā, and Cort shows how—in Jñānsundar's construction—Osvāl identity comes as part of a package that includes the Upkeś Gacch and its lay ritual culture, the temples at Osian, and the "true" version of the caste's history seen in the context of the "true" version of Jainism's history. The result was a vision in which the mendicant community, the lay community, and the Osvāl caste become a single unified whole, with Osian and its temples as the physical and spiritual anchor points of this grand conception. This was a vision, however, that fit poorly with on-the-ground realities, whether early in the twentieth century or at other times in Jain history.

The volume's final chapter, Babb's "Cleaving to the Goddess," examines the Dadhimatī temple in the context of historical changes of great importance in the late nineteenth and twentieth centuries. This was a period in which caste elites all over India were, in response especially to changes related to urbanization and the emergence of new economic opportunities, revising their sense of themselves as caste communities and their notions of the nature of caste as a social institution. This trend was certainly apparent among the Dādhīc Brahmans. When they migrated away from Dadhimatī's rural hinterland, they found themselves in need of burnished Brahmanical credentials and, in the face of their increasing geographical dispersal as a caste, a symbolic focus for caste unity. The paper traces the ways in which Dādhīc elites polished their Brahmanical pedigree by manipulating their caste genealogy. It also describes how they reshaped their caste's origin myth in such a way as to support their claim that Dadhimatī has a unique relationship with the Dādhīc Brahmans as a caste community. Such a claim has little basis in regional tradition—for she was always the goddess of many communities—with the result that the Dādhīc Brahmans came into conflict with others over control of her temple, a contest that non-local Dādhīc Brahmans have won for now but has yet to play out fully.

Lessons Learned

So what is the moral of our story? We suggest that it is best expressed by two words: discontinuity and multiplicity.

As for discontinuity, we began our work with the idea of exploring what we called, in our original proposal, "continuities of community patronage," but as we gained knowledge our confidence in this idea weakened. The continued existence of the temples implies some degree of continuities of patronage, but our data did not indicate similar corresponding continuities of patrons. As Cort shows in his "Patronage" chapter, the Mahāvīra temple was apparently abandoned (or nearly so) in late medieval times only to be reclaimed from the desert sands and renovated in the nineteenth century. Some Dādhīc

Brahman accounts make it also seem likely that the Dadhimatī temple was in a state of near desuetude in the early nineteenth century. And as Cort also shows in the same chapter, if the Sacciyā temple is largely patronized by wealthy Osvāls today, and if its Temple Trust was set up consciously to represent all communities, it was being run by Bhojak priests until recently and supported by the patronage of local Rājpūts and Māheśvarīs. There is also a discontinuity between the intentions of those who set up the Temple Trust in the 1970s and the growing recent history of Terāpanthī pilgrimage and patronage. That is, there are even multiple discontinuities in the histories of the past thirty years, as Meister has pointed out. On the basis of these and related points, Cort concludes that far from exhibiting continuities of patronage, the temples in our study demonstrate histories of discontinuities and "contestations of patronage, worship, and control" involving "differing understandings of the relationships between the deity and castes, between worshipers and worshiped, and between donor and donated."

Cort's "Constructing a Jain Mendicant Lineage" can stand as a cautionary tale about discontinuity and continuity in the world of our temples. In a manner reminiscent of the fantasies of some functionalist social theorists, Jñānsundar believed that a perfectly seamless social order is possible—a social order in which ritual, social structure, and culture more generally, form an internally interconnected and mutually reinforcing plenum. This vision ran aground on the reality of social life as it actually exists in Rajasthani Jain communities and indeed in all communities. Reality presents a picture of difference, disagreement, and struggle. Manyness, not oneness, is the essence of social life, and to the extent that the life of temples is an extension of social life, it is bound to reflect this fact.

More than a structure of stone, a temple is a place where relationships join and touch—a multiplicity of relationships, heterogeneous in the extreme. To extend Babb's notion of social space and time somewhat, there is a sense in which social space and social time curve in the gravitational field of temples, bringing relationships of all kinds into a converging pattern and pulling the past into alignment with the social and cultural exigencies of the present. The participants in these relationships include objects (temples, shrines, images, ritual implements, etc.), places (defined geographically, historically, mythologically, etc.), persons (worshipers, priests, scholars, politicians, even tourists), and groups (communities of many sorts). We must also count the patrons of the present and the past, and the architects and artisans who created and modified these structures. And there are so many others: community leaders, agents of the state, and even (in recent times) law-makers, politicians, and foundation bureaucrats. But above all, we must include the individuals and groups who have ritual and spiritual relationships with the temples and the deities or forces they enshrine.

What then is a temple? It is, as we knew from the outset but have come to appreciate more deeply than before, a multiplicity of things, and it is all of those things at once. A successful temple—a great temple that functions and lives—is the sum of its relationships with its contexts. To the extent that the chapters of this book with their multiple authors reflect a sense of this reality, they will have succeeded in conveying the main lesson that emerged from our joint research.

Part I

Histories

1

Sweetmeats or Corpses?

Community, Conversion, and Sacred Places

MICHAEL W. MEISTER

This chapter is about the multi-layered life of things. It is—in part intentionally—neither linear nor consecutive. In it I attempt to combine narrative evidence from one text, standing monuments, available inscriptions, and ethnographic observations made by many passers-by over time. If these speak with multiple voices, it is their multiplicity that I wish to record. If they overlap in significant ways, I wish that significance to rise only slowly to the surface.

If there have been indeed "open boundaries" for Jains (Cort 1998a)—interstices in the categories of traditional India—there also are boundaries open for history as a whole. The very origin of many lay Jain communities, through "conversion" by a mendicant Jain teacher at some time in the past, is one such interstice. Evidence may always resist a single narrative. The many valid perceptions of history require that multiple, conflicting narratives not be reconciled, but explored.

The site I will explore in this chapter is one temple-place—the town of Osian in the Rajasthan desert—that is of particular importance to Jainism in Western India. I will look not only at what survives at the site, but at the history of the site's use, re-use, and re-formation over time. In exploring the continuing role of the monuments at Osian, I have drawn on three bodies of evidence: first, the archaeological record, of both monuments and inscriptions (Bhandarkar 1907:36–37; Bhandarkar 1912; Nahar 1918; Dhaky 1968; Meister 1991c–e); second, a seventeenth-century text called the *Paṭṭāvalī of the Upakeśa Gaccha* or the "List of Pontiffs" of Osian's (ancient Upakeśa's) lineage (Hoernle 1890);

and third, a body of minor ethnographic observations recorded by visitors to Osian in this century. In doing so, I hope in part to provide an object rooted case-study for testing the definitions of "ritual culture" provided by L. A. Babb (1996, 1998b).[1]

Archaeological Remains

D. R. Bhandarkar (1907) was the first archaeologist to report on the monuments at Osian. He was informed, as he approached the site over the desert (Bhandarkar 1912:101), that "there were only two temples at Ōsiā that would be archaeologically interesting, *viz.* the temple of Mahāvīr and the temple of Sachiyā Mātā, which have been referred to in both the Hindu and Jaina accounts." He went on, however, and found, instead, a site rich in archaeological artifacts: "On my visit I found that the place was studded with the ruins of many old fanes" (Plates 10–12).[2]

His first information was correct in terms of then current ritual practice and patronage. Today at Osian there are still only three ancient temples in active worship, both of those mentioned by villagers in 1904–05 and a third, a recently renovated small Śiva shrine (Meister 1991c:189–91). Two other of the archaeologically protected shrines, Viṣṇu no. 1, called Kesariyā Kaṅvar by recent worshipers, and Pīpalā Devī, have been coopted in recent years for occasional ritual use by specific communities (Plate 29). The villagers (as well as the Archaeological Department's watchmen) still use the other archaeological remains for storage, denying that they are temples (*mandir*s).[3] Instead they call them *bhūta-gṛha*s (houses for ghost-spirits) (Meister 1989).

The Mahāvīra temple at Osian of circa the late eighth century CE, in fact, is the oldest Jain temple surviving in Western India today (Dhaky 1968:312–27; Meister 1991c:182–89). This now serves as an important temple for many among the broad dispersed merchant community of Osvāl Jains, some of whom send their male children to the attached Jain school (Vaśiṣṭh 1988). This temple does not serve, however, as "origin" temple for the Osvāl Jains (that is, as the shrine of their *kul devī*, or lineage goddess). That role today is reserved, for a small number of Jain *gotra*s, for the larger pilgrimage temple to Sacciyā Mātā (mother Sacciyā) on the hill at Osian (Plate 9). In this connection, Lawrence A. Babb (1993:9) cites Osvāl origin myths—what he calls "the Osiyā legend"—both as told to him by priests (*pujārī*s) of the Sacciyā Mātā temple in 1991 as well as from printed sources, but does not make the distinction, as had Dhaky (1967:64), between Brahmanical and Jain versions. He describes Sacciyā Devī (goddess Sacciyā, i.e. Sacciyā Mātā) as "a Jain goddess enshrined at a famous temple at Osiyā, and clan goddess (*kul devī*) to many Osvāl Jains" (Babb 1993:9 n. 9). She is so, however, as our more recent research has shown, for only some communities of Jains, and she remains a multivalent goddess—serving multiple communities of Hindus as well as Jains—today.

Both the Sacciyā Mātā and Mahāvīra temples at Osian have had interesting histories of use, transformation, and re-use (Meister 1989). The Mahāvīra temple had been in the hands of Brahman ritual functionaries (*pujārī*s) for many centuries before its return to a committee of the Osvāl community within the twentieth century. The present Osvāl Jain school was established only early in the twentieth century, in 1915.[4] The present *pujārī* at the temple (Plate 25), who confirms that he is "Brahman, not Jain,"[5] identifies the reestablishment of the temple and the founding of the community school with patronage from a devout lay Jain from the town of Phalodi.[6] This is supported in the *Jain Tīrth Sarvasaṅgrah* (Śāh 1953), where it is stated that no Jains resided in Osian at that time and that the temple was then managed from Phalodi.

New patronage for the extensive conservation and rebuilding of this earliest of Western Indian Jain temples in the late 1970s and 1980s, however—carried out in part, I suspect, in response to M.A. Dhaky's pioneering scholarship in the 1960s identifying the temple's historical importance to the present Western Indian Śvetāmbar Jain community (Dhaky 1968)[7]—has come instead from the Āṇandjī Kalyāṇjī trust in Ahmedabad, which had also taken on responsibility for many other major Jain pilgrimage temples throughout Gujarat and southern Rajasthan following independence.[8]

The Sacciyā Mātā temple's complex on the hill at Osian began with a shrine with an image of the goddess Kṣemaṅkarī (one of the Nava-Durgās) early in the eighth century CE (Dhaky 1967).[9] This small shrine seems to have been rebuilt as a much larger temple, with a cult image of Durgā-Mahiṣāsuramardinī late in the twelfth century (circa 1178 CE), then converted in part to Jain use, then or at a slightly later date.[10] Through all of these transformations, the local goddess, Sacciyā, was identified with whichever image was in the sanctum, regardless of its changing iconography or form (Plate 26). Inscriptions, as well as a much later text, the *Upakeśa Gaccha Paṭṭāvalī*, can give us some layered (if also veiled) information on these periods of temple use and reformulation (Bhandarkar 1912; Hoernle 1890; Nahar 1918).

Both temples have been the focus of considerable patronage by a variety of communities in the last forty years, leading to their restoration, expansion, rebuilding, and, to some degree, to a transformation of their roles. Whether this has led to a change in the "cultural" rather than "social" functions of these two temples depends in part on the view-points both of those who participate in and who analyze them.[11]

"Sweetmeats or Corpses?", my essay's title, refers to the story of Sacciyā Mātā's "conversion" from one ritual community to another, as reported both in inscriptions and in the Osian legend, and to the sounds of her "crunching"—first on corpses then on sweetmeats—heard throughout Osian's village in both Brahmanical and Jain myths (Hoernle 1890:237–38).[12]

As an art historian, I would argue that the courses of renovation and expansion in these two temple compounds are integral to our understanding of these structures as social and ritual as well as archaeological monuments—not simply a matter of chronology—and also that the renovations of recent decades are of an importance equal to the archaeological layering of earlier periods (Meister 1972; 1989).

The Sacciyā Mātā Temple Complex

M. A. Dhaky (1967) was the first to postulate an eighth-century temple—dedicated to an image of a benevolent form of the Goddess, Kṣemaṅkarī—on the hill at Osian, of which only the shrine image has survived (Plate 26).[13] Dhaky based his identification of this form of the Goddess on a description of the Nava-Durgās in the *Aparājitapṛcchā* as well as on other early surviving images. His speculation that this was "the original Saccikā Devī of the Pratihāra age" (ibid.:67) can be contrasted with two dated sculptures—an inscribed image of the fierce active goddess, Mahiṣāsuramardinī, from Juna dated 1180 CE (VS 1237) (Agrawala 1954a, 1954b), and an image in a San Francisco collection dated 1179 CE (VS 1236) (Bhattacharya 1992)—which for the first time clearly identify Sacciyā Mātā with Durgā through an image of a fierce rather than pacific form of the Goddess (Dhaky 1967:64).

An inscription of 1177 CE (VS 1234) is important because it gives us a date for the replacement of the older Kṣemaṅkarī shrine by the sanctum and superstructure of the present Durgā temple. It is located on the east wall of the sanctum, in the ambulatory, next to a *bhadra* image of Durgā as slayer of the demon, Mahiṣa; two other fierce goddesses, Śītalā and Cāmuṇḍā, fill corresponding central niches on the north and south walls of the sanctum (Dhaky 1967:66). This inscription refers to the wall-frieze of the *Śrī Saccikā-devi-prāsāda* as ornamented with five *pratimā* (visible-image) forms of the Goddess. These are, as cited in the inscription: "Caṇḍikā, Śītalā, Saccikādevī, Kṣemaṅkarī, and Kṣetrapāla" (Handa 1984:222). The present cult image placed in the sanctum takes the form of Durgā-Mahiṣāsuramardinī. Subsidiary Mahiṣāsuramardinī images also appear on the walls of many of the other Saura and Vaiṣṇava shrines at Osian in the eighth and ninth centuries (Meister 1991c–e) (Plate 26).

Also representing the first phase of architectural construction on the Sacciyā Mātā hill is the entry-hall and small rebuilt Satya Nārāyaṇa temple located to the northwest of the present Sacciyā Mātā temple-complex on the hill's western scarp (Meister 1983, 1991e:128–32). These two early structures are, in fact, slightly out of alignment with the east-west axis of the later complex and may represent an earlier approach to the hill (Plates 12, 18).

Contemporary with the now missing eighth-century Kṣemaṅkarī temple and standing just south of the present Sacciyā Mātā temple's sanctum is a shrine dedicated to the sun-god Sūrya based on his image placed in the central niche of its back wall (Meister 1991e:132–7). Other images on the walls of this shrine, however, suggest a Śaiva connotation, and Śiva perhaps would have been the more appropriate cosmic occupant, paired with the Goddess, for a set of eighth-century shrines.[14] The shrine is ecumenical, with Śaiva images on its north wall, Gaṇeśa on the central wall projection (*bhadra*) on the south, and the Jain Supārśvanātha flanking Sūrya on the west. The ceiling of the entry pavilion is marked by the entwined bodies of snakes (*nāga*s) and is ringed by Kṛṣṇa-līlā scenes, with images of Balarāma and Kṛṣṇa over the large guardian figures (*dvārapāla*s) flanking the door (Meister 1973).[15]

Dhaky (1967) in his scholarship has presented a clear verbal reconstruction of the Sacciyā Mātā temple's complex as it existed in the early 1960s, with the west-facing Sūrya shrine embedded in the larger temple's mirrored hall, the eighth-century Kṣemaṅkarī image lying loose by its side (Plate 19).[16] He also has outlined several intermediate phases of enlargement and rebuilding that added a late-tenth century north-facing Vaiṣṇava sub-shrine attached to the south of the present pillared hall and two south-facing Vaiṣṇava sub-shrines of the eleventh century on the north, the placement of which would indicate an earlier main sanctum located where the twelfth-century Sacciyā Mātā shrine now stands (Plate 21). All of these subsidiary shrines thus preceded the construction of the present main shrine.[17]

Dhaky (1967:67), by his association of these Vaiṣṇava sub-shrines with an earlier main shrine, first questioned whether the original temple could have been Vaiṣṇava and the Goddess worshiped not Sacciyā Mātā but "Durgā as a Vaiṣṇava śakti." He concluded, however, primarily on the basis of the surviving eighth-century Kṣemaṅkarī image, that the original Sacciyā Mātā temple was a Kṣemaṅkarī shrine, replaced by the present Mahiṣamardinī sanctum in 1178 CE: "Why could it not be the cult image, the original Saccikā Devī of the Pratihāra Age?"

Ethnography and Conversion

Archaeology provides a frame but not the canvas for an exploration of patterns of social conversion and ritual culture at Osian. Written sources provide color and detail. Ethnographic observations (or at least their few recorded fragments) help define the ground (Meister 1995c). Yet it is discrepancies in these sources that help make the picture whole.

Bhandarkar (1907:36) was the first to report what he identified as a Brahmanical tradition that Osian (in this source founded under the name Melpur Pattan) was abandoned and re-peopled after a period of devastation by a Paramāra prince who took refuge (*osla*, here claimed as the etymology for Osa-nagari, i.e. Osian) under "the Pratīhāra rulers of Marwar": "It was this Uppaldev who built the temple of Sachiyā *mātā*." According to Bhandarkar's field information, this goddess at Osian was then considered "the tutelary goddess of the Sāṁkhlā Paramāras."

According to the *Upakeśa Gaccha Paṭṭāvalī* ("List of Pontiffs") (Hoernle 1890:233), on the other hand, the founding of Osian and of its "ancient Jain temple with a miraculous figure of Mahāvīra"[18] was attributed instead to a person named Ūhaḍa, who "migrated from a place called Bhīnmāl with a large following of Jain relatives and friends" (ibid.:233–34). In the story that follows, conversion of the Brahmanical population is associated with the arrival of the Jain sage, Ratnaprabhasūri, with 500 followers. These, the text says (ibid.:236), "stayed for a month in the wilderness, and wandered about in the exercise of their calling . . . but did not obtain any alms, for the people who lived there were unbelievers."

The description of this conversion seems to me particularly significant for any decoding of the multiple histories of the Sacciyā Mātā temple and its monuments. According to its translator (ibid.), "at another time Ratnaprabha-Sūri returned to that place, when he was advised by his tutelary goddess (*śāsaṇadēvī*) to stay four months, after which he would be successful."

Ūhaḍa's young son, bitten by a snake, was pronounced dead, then brought back to life by Ratnaprabha. (Brahmanical sources attribute this to a Jain ruse: Bhandarkar 1912:100; Dhaky 1967:63–64.)[19] Ūhaḍa, then, according to Hoernle (1890:236) "placed before the *Guru* a large quantity of gems, pearls, gold, cloths, and other things, and asked him to accept them. But the *Guru* said that he had no need of them, and exhorted the *Sēṭh* to adopt the Jain religion, which already numbered one *lākh* and a quarter (125,000) adherents."[20]

In response, according to the text,

> At first the *Sēṭh* began to build a magnificent temple for *Nārāyaṇa* [my emphasis]; but what he built in the day, fell in the night. He questioned all the people who saw it; but none was able to suggest a remedy. Then he asked the *Āchārya* Ratnaprabha the reason why his temple fell down every night. The *Guru* enquired, in whose name he was building it. The *Sēṭh* replied, in the name of *Nārāyaṇa*. The *Guru* said,—"that will not do; make it in the name of Mahāvīra; then you will succeed."[21]

Only after Ūhaḍa had begun to build such a temple did Ratnaprabha's "tutelary goddess"[22] tell him that (ibid.:236) "she had begun to make an image of Mahāvīra, worthy of that magnificent building, on the hill called after the salt-lake, towards the north of the temple." This seems a particularly ambiguous statement, given the geography of present-day Osian. The Mahāvīra temple, set on the plain, has the Sacciyā Mātā temple on the most prominent hill to its east-northeast. Does this translation suggest that the image should be worthy of that "magnificent building, on the hill"—the Sacciyā Mātā (Kṣemaṅkarī) temple northeast of the newly constructed eighth-century Mahāvīra temple—or that the tutelary goddess's newly made image, suitable for a magnificent new Mahāvīra temple, would be found south of the Sacciyā Mātā hill, near the smaller Luṇādrī hillock where Ratnaprabhasūri had first descended from the sky (Plate 30)? The latter seems more likely, given that Hoernle was not familiar with the site.

It should be clear from this description, however, that Ratnaprabha's own Jain guardian goddess (*śāsaṇadēvī*) was by no means the same goddess as Osian's Sacciyā Devī (nor that all Osvāls—the residents of Osian—had yet become Jains).[23] After the Jain temple's magical consecration, in fact, during which Ratnaprabha was said to have been in two places at the same time, only "*some* [my emphasis] of the relatives of the *Sēṭh* were converted from their unbelief to the profession of a *Śrāvaka* (Jain). *Then* [my emphasis] they were made to adopt the true faith (*samyaktva*) by the *Āchārya*" (ibid.:237). Only *then* does he say to them:

> O ye faithful, ye should not go to the temple of Sachchikādevī [Sacciyā Mātā]; she is merciless, and incessantly delights in hearing the sound of the breaking bones and the killing

of buffalos, goats, and other animals; the floor of her temple is stained with blood, and it is hung about with festoons of fresh skins; the teachers of her devotion, rites, and service are cruel men; she is altogether disgusting and horrible.

The guru's guardian goddess (*śāsaṇadēvī*), identified by other sources as Cakreśvarī, and Sacciyā Mātā, goddess of the place, serve separate roles. The goddess temple on the hill in the *Paṭṭāvalī*'s narrative preceded by a significant period the newly built temple on the plain for Mahāvīra, a chronology that, in my account, becomes somewhat intermixed.

The Mahāvīra Temple Compound

The Mahāvīra Jain temple at Osian is located on the desert west and slightly south of the Sacciyā Mātā hill. It faces north, set on a high basement, and was originally approached through a two-storied covered pavilion (*valānaka* or *nāl-maṇḍapa*). This compound entryway was renovated in the tenth century when a sub-shrine was added on the west; late in the eleventh century when a large ornamented ceiling was added over the stairway (Dhaky 1968);[24] and then late in the twentieth century when the hall was completely re-formed and the ceiling reinstalled (Plates 22–24, 34).

A long inscription dated 956 CE (VS 1013), was set into a niche on the north wall in this *valānaka* (now removed to the back aisle of the compound's colonnade). This inscription records that the father of a man named Jindaka had made additions to the entry-hall; that his wife, a follower of Jainism, had also made a contribution; and that Jindaka himself, on behalf of the temple committee, had been responsible for adding a small shrine (*jinadeva-dhāma*) during this important period of reformulation (Handa 1984:217–18).[25]

Because of this inscription's reference to Osian's existence in the time of Vatsarāja Pratīhāra, archaeologists have tended to use it to date all of the early group of temples at Osian, and particularly the Mahāvīra temple, to the late eighth century (Bhandarkar 1912; Dhaky 1968). Many later Jain sources, however, have instead attributed the founding of the present temple to the tenth-century, the date of this historical inscription and of the renovations that it records.[26]

In the last quarter of the twentieth century, this same entry-pavilion was substantially dismantled, then reconfigured and rebuilt using new as well as old materials. Eighth-century pillars taken from the front of this hall have been re-utilized to enlarge the fronting aisle (*mukhālinda*) of the main temple, making it into a much larger open hall.[27] Modern craftsmen (at a cost of circa Rs. 8,000 per pillar in 1989) have copied new columns from the style of the older ones (using photographs to make stencils). These have then been installed both to reshape the *valānaka* as well as to extend the hall for the main temple (Plate 24).[28]

If Dhaky (1968) can demonstrate that there were several archaeological layers to the "re-freshening" of this temple in ancient times, to approach the reasonings behind such reshapings in any period we benefit by turning to contemporary ethnography. John Cort

(1991:215 n. 5), for example, has reported on a recent renovation (*jīrṇoddhār*) of a Jain temple in Patan,

> Feelings about the renovation were mixed. Most people agreed that the new, spacious, marble structure will lack some of the *bhāv* of the old temple. But renovating a temple is a highly meritorious deed, and people admired the spirit of devotion which motivated the man who organized, and in part paid for, the renovation. . . . Everyone admitted that the existing structure was in need of extensive repairs, and not to have repaired the temple would have been an *āśātnā* (moral fault).

I would hypothesize that very little may have changed in these aspects of the ritual culture of Jain donors since the time of Jindaka and his family's renovations of the Mahāvīra temple at Osian in the tenth century CE.

An elaborately ornamented gateway (*toraṇa*) was added in front of the main temple's entry stair in 1018 CE (VS 1075) (Plate 23).[29] This had been moved to the north side of the compound, in order to accommodate the vast enlargement of the temple's pillared hall, where it served for a decade as a site for wedding photos (Vasavada 2001). More recently it was moved into the old Jain school's compound to act as entry to the temple compound for pilgrims staying there. Several elegant sub-shrines on the east and west were added at the same time as this tenth-century renovation as well as in the next century (Dhaky 1968:319–23). Inscriptions in the compound show that continuing activity occurred through the fourteenth–fifteenth centuries, when the present superstructure for the main shrine was first constructed (Handa:220–27).[30] An inscription dated 1188 CE (VS 1245) (only a decade after the rebuilding of the Sacciyā Mātā temple's main sanctum) on a pillar behind the Sacciyā Mātā temple's fortress-wall refers to a shed, to which Yaśodhara made a gift, for housing Mahāvīra's golden chariot (Handa 1984:223–24).

Each of these archaeological intercessions can be seen as a trace of a ritual culture working itself out in real time. That these past remediations are difficult to unpack is as much due to limited perspectives as to limited sources.

Accounts in the *Paṭṭāvalī of the Upakeśa Gaccha*

In this regard, what can we make of the references in the *Upakeśa Gaccha Paṭṭāvalī* to the building of a temple to the Tīrthaṅkara Mahāvīra at Osian? The text involved was published in an abridged translation by Rudolf Hoernle in 1890. Of the historical applicability of this text (or what he perceived as its lack of one) the Jainologist Walter Schubring (1962:68) wrote, "the fabulous *paṭṭ'āvalī* of this Gaccha probably written in the 2nd half of the 17th century, proves as an exception to the rule that these chronicles are mines of reliable dates regarding the history of Jain Orders and writings." Such a text, however, can preserve appropriations, re-appropriations, and re-formulations as complex as those found in the monuments themselves.[31] It provides a series of embedded clues to significant periods of transformation in the Jain community's perception of its monuments as well as a fantastic and fabulistic account of Osian's origin.

The Mahāvīra temple that stands dates both much later than the text's claim that Ratnaprabha "consecrated it in the 70th year after Mahāvīra's death" (Hoernle 1890:234) and many centuries earlier than the historical dates for Ratnaprabha, who probably was active in the twelfth century (Dhaky 1967:68).[32] First, this seventeenth-century text tells an interesting story about the sanctum image—repeated in other sources—that relates in an interesting way to the present image (Hoernle 1890:236–37). Today, the image is said to be made of clay and milk.[33] In the *Paṭṭāvalī* (ibid.), Ūhaḍa

> learned from the talk of the cowherds that at the place [where Ratnaprabha-Sūri's *śāsaṇadevī* was preparing the image] there was something that caused the cows to drop their milk. . . . [He], being impatient to see it, dug it up a few days earlier, when an image of the size of a lime with two nipples on its breast was found. The *Āchārya* said that it was still not quite finished, and advised him to wait [for its installation]; but the *Sēṭh* replied that the touch of the *Guru's* hand would complete it.[34]

The present image does indeed have knobs in odd places (Handa 1984:plate 136)—as nipples, at the throat and heart, and on shoulders and knees—that can best be explained by reference to contemporary ritual (Plate 30). Cort (1991:218) describes the beginning of the "eightfold *pūjā*" in the following way:

> After carefully cleaning the image, (the worshiper) bathes it with water and milk, and then dresses it. . . . Using the ring finger of his right hand, he performs the nine-limbed sandal-wood-saffron *pūjā* to the *mūl-nāyak*, dabbing the sandalwood-saffron paste onto the (1) two big toes (2) two knees [etc.] . . . Many images have small silver knobs at these thirteen places, so the worshiper will not in any way damage the actual image.

The *Upakeśa Gaccha Paṭṭāvalī* (Hoernle 1890:237) records that Ratnaprabhasūri, following his installation of the found (*svayaṁbhū*) image, taught Ūhaḍa "the rules of the whole course of daily worship of the image of Mahāvīra which was in Upakēśapura (the rite of the daily eightfold *pūjā*); how to bathe it, and adore it, and so forth." In speaking of later *ācāryas* in the lineage, however, it also tells a different tale about "the rites connected with the bathing of Svayaṁbhū-Mahāvīra, and when and why they were instituted" (ibid.:238):

> At that very time, a festival which lasted eight days was held by the people in the temple. Among them were some young men to whom the evil thought suggested itself, that, as the two knobs on the breast of the blessed Mahāvīra were only an eyesore to the worshippers, there could be no harm in removing them. . . . The old people tried to dissuade them. . . . But they disregarded the old men's advice and bribed a carpenter to cut away the two knobs.

As might be expected, there were dire consequences to such an act: "At that very instant the carpenter died, and from the place where the two knobs had been cut away, there issued untold streams of blood. Great distress befell the people."

Other communities of Jains have told tales of decline, as at Bhinmal, attempting to use a mythic past to explain conditions of the present. The absence of Jains in Osian—that pilgrims should not stay the night—is rooted by the myth. Here, it is hard to believe, as a Westerner who has read both Freud and Wendy Doniger (O'Flaherty 1973), that stories of milk and blood do not also have to do with psychological issues of conception and birth (that is, with the origin of the community as well as its decline).

After Kakkasūri, the then living guru of the Upakeśa Gaccha, had fasted for three days, according to the *Paṭṭāvalī*, his *śāsanadēvī* (*not* said to be Sacciyā Mātā[35]) appeared (Hoernle 1890: 238–39) and "told him that the young *Śrāvakas* had committed an outrage in mutilating the image and depriving it of its round parts (*kalā*)." As a result of this act, she asserted (ibid.:239) that "the town of Upakeśa would gradually become deserted, a schism would arise in the *gachchha* and quarrels among the *Śrāvakas*, and the guilds would be dispersed in all directions." To stop the blood, she demanded that all the *gotra*s (lineages of Jains) gather, fast for three days, and then bathe the image of Mahāvīra in butter, curds, sugarcane juice, milk, and water—a special *snātra pūjā* discussed further by Babb (1996:153–5).

These descriptions of one Jain community's origination and dispersal from Osian in a seventeenth-century *Paṭṭāvalī* might support the passive/violent dichotomy of Jain/Hindu relationships proposed by Babb (1993:8) in the conversion myths of Jains he found in Rajasthan: "In this sense, Rājpūts and Jains are fundamentally 'other' to each other. But, at the same time, there is a point at which Rājpūt and Jain identity merge, at least from the Jain perspective." This may also seem most clear in the merging of what Cort (1987:249), following A. K. Ramanujan (1999b–c), calls "Breast" and "Tooth" Mothers in the story of Sacciyā Mātā's conversion.

Sacciyā Mātā's Conversion

I have used my own observations and interviews over the past forty years; those of D. R. Bhandarkar (1907, 1912) who, as an archaeologist, visited Osian early in this century; those of M. A. Dhaky (1968, 1975), who visited in the 1950s; and those of my colleagues John Cort (1987, 1991 and personal correspondence) and Lawrence Babb (1993) in recent years, to form an ethnographic frame for changes in the Jain community's perceptions of, and relationship to, the Osian monuments in the twentieth century. Bhandarkar (1907:36), for example, had recorded Brahmanical rather than Jain versions of the Osian legend early in the century, at a time when no Jains were living in Osian. He reported that Sacciyā Mātā was thought to be the "tutelary goddess of the [Hindu] Sāṁkhlā Paramāras." Dhaky (1967:63), in the l950s, found that "Oswal Jains of Saurashtra [in the neighboring western Indian state of Gujarat] have lost [all] memory of the goddess at Osia."

The form of Sacciyā Mātā as Kṣemaṅkarī, the original cult goddess on the Sacciyā Mātā hill, represented the great Hindu Goddess, Durgā, in a transcendent and beatific mode, comparable in the passivity (and power) of her presentation to that of a Jain sage

(Plates 26, 31). In its telling of the legend of Sacciyā Mātā's conversion, the *Upakeśa Gaccha Paṭṭāvalī* records (Hoernle 1890:238),

> the Devī entered the body of a maiden who was standing near, and thence replied,—"O Lord, I wanted one sort of thing to crunch and munch, but you have given me another sort." [Ratnaprabha] said that what she wanted was an animal sacrifice, but that it was neither proper for him to give, nor for her to take it. He then gave some further religious instruction, the result of which was that Sachchikā-dēvī [Sacciyā Mātā], who was still in the body of the maiden, was converted, in the presence of all the people who were there, becoming a follower (*bhakta*) of Mahāvīra in the city of Upakēśa, and a believer in the true faith; so much so that, letting alone flesh, *she could not even bear the sight of a red flower* [emphasis mine].

In this account the Goddess has become capable of offering protective services as does a *kul devī* (ibid.:238):[36]

> The Goddess (*satī*), by the mouth of the maiden in whose body she had entered, now said to her followers, "Listen; whoever of you shall worship the image of Svayaṁbhū-Mahāvīra which is set up in the city of Upakēśa, and shall follow the *Āchārya* Ratnaprabha, and shall serve his disciples and the disciples of his disciples, with him I shall be well pleased, his evils shall I remove, and his worship I shall heartily accept." In consequence of these words of Sachchhikā-dēvī, spoken by the maiden in whose body she had entered, a large number of people, in the course of time, adopted the profession of *Śrāvakas*.

If "the serene, supple bodied goddess" Kṣemaṅkarī (Dhaky 1967:67)—perhaps the fair maiden in this story?—could, by her own conversion to Jainism, have won back to herself those of her Hindu worshipers who had also been converted, what role was there for changing the cult image to a fierce, active form for Sacciyā? Why was Kṣemaṅkarī's temple rebuilt in 1178 CE, with an image of Durgā as the slayer of the demon Mahiṣā replacing that of Kṣemaṅkarī in its sanctum? Had Jainism chosen to give up a passive view of the Goddess (*vide* Vāc, the goddess of speech; Meister 1976) in order to counterbalance Brahmanical Durgā's fiercer aspects (Plate 26)?

Sacciyā Mātā's Challenge

When Ratnaprabha urged Ūhaḍa's relatives to refrain from the blood and gore of Sacciyā's temple (Hoernle 1890:237), they replied: "What you say, O Lord, is quite true; but if we do not go to worship that cruel Dēvī, she will slay us and her families."[37] The Goddess then challenged Ratnaprabha's theft of her followers, pricking his eyebrow, but he "resolutely replied that he would repay her the injury by his own power." Frightened, she "humbly said to him": "It is not seemly, O lord, for great sages, like yourself, to dispute and quarrel; if you will give me something to crunch and munch, I will remove your pain and be your servant, as long as the sun and moon endure." The *Ācārya* then went to her temple early in the morning with "two heaps of various kinds of cakes and sweetmeats, together with camphor, saffron, and other nice things" (ibid.:238). "Then having made worship apart from the *Śrāvakas*, and crushing a quantity of cake with both his hands . . . he said to the Dēvī,—'I have given you something to crunch and munch, henceforth you must be a follower (*upāsakā*) of me'."

This de-fanging of the goddess—her conversion from *aghora* to *sāttvikā*—requires, it seems to me, that her "ambiguous duality"[38] be preserved. Sacciyā Mātā is both Jain and not Jain, Breast Mother and Tooth Mother. Dhaky (1967:69) has pointed out that an image of Mahiṣamardinī from the site of Juna, dated 1180 CE (VS 1237), for the first time labeled this fierce form of Durgā with the name "Saccikā" and that this image was the donation of a Jain nun. Sacciyā Mātā's fierce re-dedication to non-violence (*ahiṁsā*) can also be attested by an inscription of 1598 CE (VS 1655) that refers to Ratnaprabhasūri's conversion of Cāmuṇḍā (an even fiercer, wilder form of Durgā) to the Jain goddess, Sacciyā (Reu 1948:10).[39]

Community Conversion

Although many Jain sources repeat the claim that Ratnaprabhasūri consecrated the temple of Mahāvīra "seventy years after Mahāvīra's death" (Hoernle 1890:234), Dhaky (1967:68) must be closer to historical reality in stating that "there is no point in attaching a very early date to Ratnaprabha-suri. [The] one prominent figure of that name . . . flourished in the twelfth century."

What this must mean is that the settlement of some Jains in Osian from Bhinmal—and their establishment of the Mahāvīra temple in the eighth century—had little historically to do with the conversion of Sacciyā Mātā on the hill to vegetarianism. Yet their stories have been conflated in ways meant to reinforce changing meanings in the nature of Jain identity. Dhaky (1967:68), referring to the rise of Solaṅkī patronage of Jainism in the twelfth century, concluded, "It is not easy to tell whether Ratnaprabha-suri invoked the temporal power or used [his own] persuasive means to stop the sacrifices at the altar of Sacciyā." He points out that the Solaṅkī ruler Kumārapāla had, in the twelfth century, "stopped the animal sacrifices at the altar of Devi Kantesvari whose shrine was founded in the eighth century at Aṇhilapātaka . . . and who was the kulāmbā [lineage goddess] of the Cāpotkatas and subsequently of the Solankis of Gujarat."

Handa (1984:47) has suggested that the Mahāvīra temple at Osian was dedicated originally to Pārśvanātha in the eighth century, then rededicated to Mahāvīra, perhaps at the time of the structure's renovation in the tenth century.[40] All that is certain is that the structure was both renovated and expanded in the late tenth and eleventh century at a time when substantial patronage was also being expended on the building of the Vaiṣṇava sub-shrines for the original Sacciyā Mātā temple.

Brahmans were still worshiping in the Sacciyā Mātā temple late in the twelfth century, after the rebuilding of its main sanctum in 1178 CE, as attested by an inscription on a pillar in the *maṇḍapa* dated VS 1247 (circa 1190 CE) (ibid.:224) and by other inscriptions (Bhandarkar 1912:110). And one should not forget that in "the Osiyā myth" presented by the *Upakeśa Gaccha Paṭṭāvalī*, Ūhaḍa first attempted to build a temple to Viṣṇu in the form of Nārāyaṇa (Hoernle 1890:236), not a Jain shrine.

The Epigraphic section of the Archaeological Survey of India *Annual Report* for 1921-22 (ASI 1924:119) reported on a series of inscriptions at Osian, which date from VS 1135 to 1524 (1078–1467 CE), found on the backs of brass images from Jain temples:

> They mention the names of donees, the year of gift and the names of Jain teachers who performed the consecration ceremonies. Various castes including the Balāhī (*sic*) are also mentioned. As Mr. Ojha says that the Balādis are at present an untouchable caste among Hindus, the mention of the name as a class in the Ukesa caste is proof of the story of the wholesale conversion of the town of Osian [Ukesa] to Jainism.

The *Upakeśa Gaccha Paṭṭāvalī* itself would seem to suggest, not so much the mass conversion of Osian's population to Jainism, as its gradual conversion and initiation into Jain practices and rituals. The placid goddess Kṣemaṅkarī may have seemed too little "other"—that is, too lacking in the fierce qualities of Durgā that were in need of changing—to emphasize this process. Cāmuṇḍā and Mahiṣamardinī better could represent Sacciyā Devī, the local goddess, who gave up corpses for sweetmeats (as illustrated and named by the Juna image dated 1180 CE, given by a Jain nun).[41] Whether the temple's major rebuilding in 1178 CE and its rededication to an image of Durgā slaying Mahiṣa—but given the name of Sacciyā as at Juna—was then meant in part to serve Jain purposes is unclear, yet through "the Osiyā myth" of Sacciyā's conversion from meat to sweetmeats, this image could still make the temple available to both communities. Only a decade later the wife of Yaśodhara, according to the inscription, would provide a shed for Mahāvīra's chariot (Bhandarkar 1912:110).

Babb (1996, 1998b) makes clear a triangular relationship in the ritual culture of Jains that anticipates the geographic relationship of the Mahāvīra and Sacciyā Mātā temples at Osian for pilgrims (as well as, in part, the need for Sacciyā Mātā's accommodation to Jainism). In his view, deities are the model worshipers in Jainism; Tīrthaṅkaras the non-responsive focus for worship; and patrons the reflexive recipients through ritual of the deflection of what is unclean. What better exchange than to have the Goddess receive sweetmeats from the Jain sage; become a devotee of the Tīrthaṅkara; and her purified temple to act as one ritual axis for Jain pilgrims, who otherwise focus on the Jina represented in the Mahāvīra temple (except for those who, as we subsequently found out, do not worship Jina images at all).

Community Use Today

Bhandarkar (1912:101), during his visit in 1907, was able to record the Brahmanical myth that Ratnaprabha, by faking a snakebite, had forced "the king and his subjects" to embrace Jainism:

> This enraged Sachiyā Mātā, as she could no longer obtain any living victims. She cursed the people, and defied them to stay there. . . . [The Osvāls] had to flee in all directions. But they

prayed to the goddess, and propitiated her to the extent of allowing them to present offerings to her after the performance of marriage rites. And no Osvāl now passes at Osiā the night of the day on which he pays homage to the *mātā* for fear of being overtaken by some calamity.

Of the temple, he says (ibid.:109):

It is a sacred place in Mārwāṛ, and people from even as far south as Pālanpur come here to worship the goddess. It is, however, the Ōsvāl Jainas, who regard her with particular reverence. They bring their children to the temple for the tonsure ceremony, and invariably present offerings to the goddess after the performance of marriage rites. The worshipers dare not pass the night at Osiā after paying their homage to the goddess, for if they do so, they are sure to be overtaken by some calamity or other.[42]

This prohibition certainly no longer seems to be the case. Not only was the Jain Higher Secondary school founded and the Mahāvīra temple itself restored in the last century, but the Sacciyā Mātā temple also has, in the last few decades, increasingly been the recipient of lay Jain support (but primarily of non-temple-worshiping Jains). The present pilgrimage shrine on the hill of Sacciyā Mātā is still visited by both Hindus and Jains, and its trustees are both Jain and Hindu.[43] Since the end of the nineteenth century, its expansion, re-formation, and redefinition have not stopped.

Between Bhandarkar's and Dhaky's visits, for example, local craftsmen carefully rebuilt the demolished superstructure of the Sūrya temple next to the Sacciyā Mātā temple's sanctum out of ancient pieces.[44] Colored glass and white marble were used to ornament the sacrificial hall of the Sacciyā Mātā temple in which "coconuts, fruits, flowers, and sweets; no meat" are now offered by either of the two user communities (Plates 8, 11).[45]

Up to the early 1970s, this temple's ancient compound had stood in splendid isolation on its hill, approached by a long flight of steps on the west, with only a few rooms for pilgrims alongside (Plate 9). In recent years, however, an increasing flood of Jain pilgrims have come to the temple (Plate 31). The results of their patronage can be seen in the compound's rapid expansion. Nine new Goddess temples are under construction that ring the older structure's compound wall.[46] New facilities for pilgrims increasingly cover the hill, and a series of elegant gateways (*toraṇas*) now march up the staircase, each with its own set of dedicatory inscriptions (Plate 18).

Conclusion

What I think we are seeing in recent years is a specific contemporary reclamation of Osian by lay Jain pilgrims. The Mahāvīra temple, now recognized within the Jain community as Western India's oldest Jain temple, has received substantial institutional support, attention and funds from the Āṇandjī Kalyāṇjī trust in Ahmedabad for the past thirty years, from the mid 1970s. It now receives as many as 20,000 Jain visitors a year from all parts of India. Sacciyā Mātā, therefore, it seems to me, has, in relatively recent times, changed from being a local personal goddess serving a variety of resident communities in Marwar more specifically into a restored *kul devī* (origination goddess) for certain of the extended communities of Osvāl Jains.[47] If Bhandarkar (1907:36, 1912:100) in 1907 could record only Brahmanical versions of the Osian myth at the site and Sacciyā Mātā was then thought to be the "tutelary goddess" of the Hindu Sāṁkhlā Paramāras, by the 1960s Dhaky (1967:63) found her instead to be the "patron goddess of the Oswal banias who are mostly Jainas."

Published lists of sacred sites (*tīrthas*) for Jain pilgrimage focus largely, at Osian, on the temple of Mahāvīra, but A.P. Śāh (1953) reports that the handwritten *Osval Utpatti* says that Ratnaprabhasūri, after enlightening the goddess Cāmuṇḍā Devī, gave her the name "Sacciyāyaka Mātā" much as the Jain nun who had a sculpture of the fierce form of Durgā slaying the demon Mahiṣa dedicated at Juna had that image inscribed with the name of Sacciyā (both reclaiming the goddess from Hindu and local uses for Jain ones).

The seventeenth-century *Upakeśa Gaccha Paṭṭāvalī* (Hoernle 1890) makes clear, however, that the *śāsaṇadēvī* who assisted Ratnaprabhasūri was not the Goddess he converted; that converting the Goddess had, in fact, its risks for the community; and that her temple continued to welcome all residents of Osian, whether Hindu or Jain. That Vaiṣṇavas and Jains had interacted in a "ritual culture" that made this possible is signaled by the monuments that have, over many centuries, ringed the Sacciyā Mātā hill, and by the ritual life at Osian today.

The temple that verified early Osvāl conversion to Jainism, however, was not that dedicated to Sacciyā Mātā, but that built for the *svayambhu* image of Mahāvīra that was created, according to the *Paṭṭāvalī of the Upakeśa-Gaccha*, by Ratnaprabhasūri's *śāsaṇadēvī*. Yet—first built in the eighth century CE and then renovated or re-founded in 956 CE—the real existence of this temple must demonstrate a strong Jain presence in Osian many years before Ratnaprabha's historical time. It may thus, indeed, have been the *re*-formulation of *Sacciyā's* temple, not the building of the Mahāvīra temple—from one with an image of Kṣemaṅkarī to one of Durgā-Mahiṣamardinī (yet by doing so from meat-eater to a cruncher of sweets)—that Ratnaprabhasūri precipitated on his arrival at Osian in the twelfth century.[48] If so, his re-imagining of ritual culture at Osian was one across "open boundaries," not closed ones.

Recent lay patronage at Osian of the Sacciyā Mātā temple also fits well into the re-imaging of present-day Rājpūt Jains in Jaipur recorded by Babb (1993). The local warrior Goddess, Sacciyā, as slayer of demons, suits the need to define a "proper" Rājpūt *kul devī* origin (Harlan 1992:52–90) for at least one lay Jain community.[49] Such an interpretation, as at all periods in Osian's past, however, also represents non-linearity of use and of interpretation—that is, the lack of a single way to tell the story—inherent in both history and scholarship. Contested and multivalent as history may be, it would be unwise to conclude that a modern community's assertion of its origin need reflect documentable history more than its longing for an "embedded" past. As Romila Thapar (1986:354–5) wrote:

> Each version of the past which has been deliberately transmitted has a significance for the present, and this accounts for its legitimacy and its continuity. The record may be one in which historical consciousness is embedded: myth epic and genealogy; or alternatively it may refer to the more externalized forms: chronicles [etc.]. . . . There is no evolutionary or determined continuum from one form to the other and facets of the embedded consciousness can be seen as part of the latter, whether introduced deliberately or subconsciously.

Jains, Hindus—Indians, humans—share porous boundaries. Brahman *pujārīs* hereditarily serve in the Mahāvīra and other Jain temples; Jain pilgrims patronize the Sacciyā Mātā temple's many shrines, but Vaiṣṇavas and other Hindu communities still worship there. One temple demonstrates no greater fluidity than the other. Both seem able to serve a deeper ritual culture that Babb (1998:161) can characterize as "neither Hindu nor Jain" but "simply South Asian." Local Muslim and Hindu craftsmen continue to carry out renovations on these temples; those on the Mahāvīra Jain temple are now supervised in part by Sompurā Brahmans employed by Jains in Ahmedabad (yet more recently they have also been employed to renovate the Sacciyā Mātā compound and by the State Archaeological Department to reconstruct other desert shrines). Such permeability denies no boundaries, only opens them.

Notes

1. Of the ritual culture of Jains, Babb (1998b:150–51) wrote, "The fact that the object of worship is an apotheosized ascetic generates much of this ritual culture's distinctive structure and spirit."
2. The Archaeological Survey of India's Western Circle Annual Reports located in Harvard's Widener library are bound with the original sketch plans drawn by D. R. Bhandarkar of the compounds of the Sacciyā Mātā and Mahāvīra temples (Plate 8).
3. Bhandarkar (1907:37) describes their use as public latrines.
4. Personal communication from the *pujārī*, Bhanuprakash Sharma, in 1990.
5. Bhandarkar (1910:63) records that the *pujārīs* in the Jain temples in Merta were "of the *sevak* Brāhmaṇa caste," and an inscription of VS 1405 ordained that "only those Brāhmaṇas, who were descended from Lokeśvara" could serve in the temples of "Pārśvanātha and Phalaudhī."
6. This town is Pokaran-Phalodi, not Merta-Phalodi, where there also are Jain temples. According to Cort, this same family has served the temple for the past three generations, or circa 100 years (personal communication 1988).
7. Dhaky traveled to the Osian temples early in the 1960s and left a record of his estimate of the importance of the Mahāvīra temple as well as a plea for more attention to its conservation in the visitor's book at the entrance to the Jain school.
8. Cort (personal communication 1988) records that "money for *jīrṇoddhar*" at the Mahāvīra temple in 1987 was "coming from Āṇandjī Kalyāṇjī." The present *pujārī* reports also on Kasturbhai Lalbhai's involvement in the restoration of the temple begun more than thirty years ago and of Kasturbhai's son Shrenikbhai today. Cort reports, however, that no money for the expansion of the Sacciyā Mātā temple had come from the Āṇandjī Kalyāṇjī trust but rather some "money from individual Jains." See Cort 2000a.

9. M. C. Joshi (1994:206) questions Dhaky's identification of Kṣemaṅkarī and sees the form of this goddess as associated with the Hellenic and Hellenistic warrior goddess Cybele.
10. Handa (1984:224), in reference to an inscription of VS 1246 (CE 1190), states, "it seems that in the thirteenth century and later, the myths about the *en masse* conversion of people to Jainism were evolved."
11. Babb (1998:143, 150) points out that the deities "are Jainism's paradigmatic worshipers." The focus of worship, however, must be "a Tīrthankar or one who is like a Tīrthankar" and the relationship of patron to ritual is both "displaced" and "reflexive." Babb (1996:16) wrote, "In the materials to be presented here, ritual emerges not just as theater-like, but as a theater of soteriological and social identities."
12. Hoernle (1890:237 and note 23), translates *kaḍaḍa-maḍaḍa* as "something to crunch and munch" and refers also to Gujarati *kaḍ'kaḍ'vuṁ*, "to crack."
13. Initially lying as a loose image in the temple compound on the southwest next to the *jagatī* of the Sūrya subshrine (Dhaky 1967), this image has now been "enshrined" in a locked cage in the southeast corner of the Sacciyā Mātā temple's large *maṇḍapa.*
14. A similar set of paired shrines, with Śiva and the Goddess, exists at Menal in eastern Rajasthan (Meister 1991b:277–83).
15. A similar ecumenism is shown by the superstructure of the Satya Nārāyaṇa temple (Meister 1991e:128–32).
16. He misses the presence of the Satya Nārāyaṇa shrine and gateway but does record a number of eighth-century sculptural fragments within the Sacciyā Mātā compound and documents the inscription of 1178 CE that dates construction of the present main Sacciyā Mātā sanctum and tower.
17. An inscription of VS 1247 (1190 CE) in the enlarged pillared hall records that "*brāhmaṇas* continued to worship her" (Handa 1984, 224). Other inscriptions show that screens were added to the earlier sub-shrines in VS 1421 (1364 CE) (ibid.:225).
18. Cited in Hoernle (1890) from Muni Ātmārāmjī's *Ajñāna-timira-bhāskara*, pt. 2, p. 16.
19. O'Flaherty (1973:26) writes, "Snakes represent death and the underworld, but also rebirth (for they slough their skins and are reborn)."
20. Babb (1993:9) cites Bhūtoṛiyā's account instead (1988:70–71), where the *ācārya* "said that he would restore the prince's life only if all the people would accept Jainism. The people agreed, the prince was revived, and 125,000 Rājpūts became Jains."
21. Perhaps significantly, most of the eighth-century shrines at Osian, as well as the tenth—eleventh century sub-shrines in the Sacciyā Mātā complex, are dedicated to Viṣṇu.
22. According to John Cort (personal communication 1988; see also Cort 1987) Jain *śāsanadēvīs* are *yakṣīs* who preside over "the *śāsana* established by each Jina. Since the Upakeśa Gaccha claims to be descended from the *śāsana* established by Pārśvanātha, the *śāsanadevī* would be Padmāvatī. But nowhere does the text name her."
23. Babb (1993:9), following a version in Bhūtoṛiyā's history (1988), says, "Saciyā Devī appeared in person and begged [the *ācārya*] to teach Jainism to the people." This seems to be a confusion; both it and subsequent details suggest that Bhūtoṛiyā's version conflates Brahmanical with Jain sources.
24. A number of inscriptions on pillars in this *nāl-maṇḍapa* of VS 1231 (circa 1174 CE) (Handa 1984:221–22) can suggest an alternate date for this elaborate ceiling.
25. Handa (1984:69) speculates that the *devakulikā* no. 5 attached to the *nāl-maṇḍapa* on the east "may have been the '*Jinadeva-dhāma*' constructed by Jindaka in A.D. 956."

26. Śāh (1953:173–74, 315–16) says the temple was built in VS 1013. He also reports that the *Osiyā Vīr Stavan*, written in VS 1712, records the *pratiṣṭhā* of the image in the sanctum in VS 1017 and that a handwritten manuscript entitled *Osvāl Utpatti* records that "Osa vaṃśa was established in V.S. 1011 at [the] pleasure of Osiyā Mātā, and in V.S. 1017 [the] temple was built."
27. The decision to open up the *maṇḍapa*, according to the present *pujārī*, was made "primarily to help the pilgrims so that their heads wouldn't be hit" (a reference, perhaps, to the lower-storey entrance through the original *nāl-maṇḍapa*, now destroyed).
28. This work has been done with the guidance of Bachhubhai Sompura from Ahmedabad, but many craftsmen have been locally trained and employed. The carving for pillars and a new *toraṇa*, however, was done in Palitana (Krishan Chandra Sompura, personal communication).
29. Bhandarkar, Ojha, and Dhaky have given this date; Handa (1984:219), following Nahar's printed transcription, gives VS 1035. The style of the *toraṇa* corresponds better with the former reading.
30. Dhaky (1968:326) first dated this *śikhara* to the time of the *toraṇa*, but has since changed his mind. Bhandarkar (1912:108) recorded that "I gathered from the villagers that it was in ruins a hundred years ago, and was rebuilt of the fallen pieces."
31. For "recent theoretical discussions on the relationship between facticity and the principal historical genre of narrative" see Cort 1998b. Schubring (1962:68 n. 4) states that the complete text of the *Paṭṭāvalī* can be found in Jinavijaya, *Jain Sāhitya Saṃśodhak* I. This was reprinted by Muni Darśanvijay in 1933.
32. Dhaky (1967), while insisting that Ratnaprabhasūri "flourished in the twelfth century," adds that "he was not the disciple of the illustrious Hemacandra as Brahmanical legend purports to say, but of Hemacandra's senior contemporary Vādi Devasuri" who had two works completed "in A.D. 1277 [and] A.D. 1282." (These dates seem to be a mistyping. Vādidevasuri was active early in the twelfth century.)
33. Cort (personal communication 1988) cites a *pujārī* for this information who also gave the date of the image as "Vīr Saṁvat 72."
34. Such a miraculous origin for a found image has wide currency (Eichinger Ferro-Luzzi 1987), as do other magical tales surrounding the temple (Granoff 1990, 1993).
35. The account of a still later guru of the Upakeśa Gaccha, Kakkudācārya (Hoernle 1890:239–40), does have "Sacyakā" in attendance, when violence is part of the outcome: when a landholder named Somaka mistakenly suspects the guru of misbehavior ("capable of indulging in sensual pleasures after the manner of prostitutes"), the Goddess boxes his ears "and he began to vomit blood."
36. See Harlan 1992:118–20.
37. Schubring (1962:69–70) refers to traditions from other Gacchas that permit the worship of "Cāmuṇḍā and other local deities."
38. Babb (1993:13) uses this phrase to characterize the identity of all Rājpūt-origin Jains.
39. This sixteenth-century inscription is the first to record Ratnaprabha's association with the story of Sacciyā's conversion. The importance of the fifteenth century's "renascent" Hinduism—producing also such major Jain temples as the one at Ranakpur—needs emphasis (Dhaky 1965–66).
40. Evidence for this is slim. Handa refers to an image of Pārśvanātha dated VS 1035 now in the Jodhpur Museum, to Supārśvanātha on a lintel in the *gūḍhamaṇḍapa* and to the image of Supārśvanāth on the northeast corner of the Sūrya temple south of the Sacciyā Mātā temple.
41. It is also true that many Vaiṣṇava communities had already taken a similar path.
42. Dhaky (1967:63–64) repeats this story in Bhandarkar's words, but does not confirm whether he found any such prohibition still in place.

43. An inscription of VS 1236 refers to "Śrī-Saccikā-devī-dvāraṁ *Bhojakai*," of which Handa writes (1984:223), "the family of Bhojakas mentioned in the inscription still serves as the priests of the Saciyā, the Mahāvīr and other temples."
44. Bhandarkar (1912:plate 44b) shows this superstructure in ruins; Dhaky, who took its authenticity for granted, was told by local craftsmen that it had been "built" by their grandfathers.
45. Cort (personal communication 1988) also records that the temple's food-hall serves only vegetarian food "but also potatoes," i.e. a root vegetable eaten by Vaiṣṇavas but not by proper Jains.
46. Are these the Nava-Durgās of whom Kṣemaṅkarī is one?
47. Babb (1993:9 n. 9), refers to her as "clan goddess (*kul devī*) to *many* Osvāl Jains" (my emphasis). Dhaky (1967:63), on the other hand, had pointed out that Osvāls of Saurashtra, by the 1950s, had lost all memory of this goddess. After our fieldwork we have developed a fuller understanding of the dissimilar processes by which these two temples have received funds for renovation over the past three decades, as is explored in this volume.
48. Dhaky's comment (1967:68) is that "the general atmosphere of the age which favour[ed] non-violence under Jaina influence and piety of the great Jaina Sage may have ultimately helped compel the animal killers at the door of Sacciyā to stop their violent acts."
49. Babb (1993:20) elegantly concludes his discussion of Jain devotees worshiping a Dādāguru by saying "they are kings and queens in need of healing, and are invoking an old bargain."

2

Time and Temples

On Social and Metrical Antiquity

LAWRENCE A. BABB

A temple can be many things: a venue for ritual, a locus of sacred power, a crystallization of social energy, an object (sometimes) of beauty, and much else. This chapter treats temples as physical substrata for the deposit of historical ideas. The temples in question are three in Rajasthan: the Dadhimatī temple at Goth-Manglod (near Nagaur) and the Mahāvīra and Sacciyā Mātā temples at Osian. Everyone agrees that these temples are very old. From a modern-historical point of view, the Osian temples date from the eighth century CE (though not the current Sacciyā Mātā structure) and the Dadhimatī temple possibly from as early as the seventh century CE (though, again, not the current structure) (Meister 1991c:182–91; 1991d:252–54; 1991e:128; also, chapter three in this volume). But this is not the only possible point of view, for there are also indigenous interpretations of the antiquity of these structures, and—as will be seen—these interpretations are very different from those of modern historians. This difference is our subject. What do people mean when they say a thing is very old?

Timescapes

The canard that the Indic world has no sense of history surely deserves a decent burial. It is true that India has produced cyclical visions of time's passage, and it is at least arguable that these visions are, in and of themselves, inhospitable to the sense of the importance of linear sequence that seems so crucial to historical reasoning (cf. Eliade 1971). But as John Cort (1995) has shown for the Jains, the cyclical timescape is by no means the whole story, for in India we also find genres of historical writing—Cort calls them "localized histories"—that are conceived and formulated within linear timescapes. So much for India's lack of historical consciousness; linear time, it seems, has an honored place in the Indic world. Still, this does not necessarily mean that all linear visions of time's passage are alike, and this brings us to the important issue of how Indic constructions of history might differ, if they do, from those of modern historians.

The question of what distinguishes the modern historian's craft is a vexed one, and far beyond the scope of this chapter. So instead of trying to grapple with such a large question, I would like to focus on a particular point of difference that relates directly to the question of the meaning of antiquity. This is the issue of how time is measured. Let us stipulate at the outset that, among many other things that might be said of them, modern historians operate within a timescape that is scalar in the sense that it is divisible into equal and countable units, and thus exactly measurable. I call this timescape *metrical time*. There is nothing in the least arcane about metrical time in India; Indian civilization has produced several scalar dating systems. But in India (and not only in India) metrical time coexists with another scheme, one that is linear but not scalar. I call it *social time*, and it will be the focus of much that follows.

There is nothing new about the idea of social time. It is a theme in the work of Pierre Bourdieu (1977:Ch. 3), but the idea is probably most famously expressed in E. E. Evans-Pritchard's discussion, in his study of the political institutions of the Nuer (1940:94–138), of the relationship between social structure and space and time. Social relationships among the Nuer, he says, take the form of closeness or distance in "structural space" in a way that is only partly related to physical reality. From the standpoint of a metrically-minded outside observer, it is as if space is somehow distorted by social forces. Time is similarly malleable (ibid.:94–104; 198–201), and this is most dramatically illustrated by the way the Nuer trace patrilineal descent. Were genealogies mere records of begettings, they would obviously grow longer with every generation. Nuer genealogies, however, maintain a constant depth over time. This is because they are records of the past that express the social relations of the present. Social distance (i.e. distance in structural space) is expressed by means of the temporal depth of common ancestry, and as long as social distance stays the same, so does lineage depth. Constant lineage depth is made possible by a selective amnesia in which the Nuer remember only those ancestors who are the starting points of lineages or lineage segments, with others dropping out of the system. This is social time, linear but not metrical.[1]

It should be stressed that social time is not simply metrical time badly or incompletely reckoned. It is, rather, a timescape that allows the social present to be invested with certain kinds of meaning. Thus, while metrical time passes at the rate of one year per annum, social time elapses at a rate determined by the relationships of which it is a temporal expression. Moreover, metrical time is a universal framework. Although different cultures have different metrical dating systems (thus the year 2000 was not everybody's millennium), mutual conversion is a mere matter of arithmetic. Social time, however, is relative time; events within it take on significance only in relation to specific groups or communities.

In this chapter I want to show how indigenous thinking about the antiquity of our three temples occurs against the backdrop of social time expressed in a genealogical format. Here, too, Cort has blazed our trail by showing the crucial importance of this format to Indic historiography in a linear mode (1995:180–85). I turn first to the Dadhimatī temple at Goth-Manglod. The indigenous timescape on which this temple is located is, in essence, simple genealogical time. I then turn to the more complex case of the temples at Osian; here we see that genealogy is a loose format that is susceptible to interesting variations. At the end of the chapter I look briefly at how social and metrical ideas of the temples' antiquity are currently interacting.

Social Time and the Dadhimatī Temple

The Dadhimatī temple belongs to a class of temples that might be called *origin temples* (as do the Osian temples). These are temples that are associated with the creation of specific social groups, in this case, the Dāhimā Brahmans (also known as Dādhīc Brahmans), a Brahman caste prominent in Rajasthan. For them, the temple is the actual site of the creation of their community and the shrine of their caste goddess (*kul devī*), whose name is Dadhimatī. The connection between the temple and the caste's origin is emphasized by a tree-shaped caste genealogy (*vaṃś vṛkṣ*) conspicuously displayed on one of the temple's inner courtyard walls. The origin account was originally transmitted (probably in many variants) by the caste's genealogists (known as Rāvs); more recently it has appeared in a more systematized form in a Sanskrit composition of uncertain origin called *Dadhimathī Purāṇa* (hereafter referred to as the *Purāṇa*). This text was first published in book form with a Ḥindi translation early in the twentieth century and again in 1981; it appears to be the basis (or part of the basis) for other versions subsequently presented in various caste publications and is the source of the summary given here.[2]

The Origin of the Dāhimā Brahman Caste

The tale opens (leaving aside certain framing-story preliminaries) with the birth of Brahmā from a lotus growing from the sleeping Viṣṇu's navel. (The *Purāṇa* story is retold in greater detail and from a slightly different angle in chapter nine of this volume.) Brahmā fathered the sage Atharvā (Skt. Atharvan). Atharvā married a woman named Śānti, who bore him a son and daughter. The daughter was a goddess named Nārāyaṇī Devī (later Dadhimatī), and at a later point the text describes how she destroyed Vikaṭāsur, a demon who threatened the sovereignty of the gods. The son was a great sage named Dadhīci, who is revered by the Dāhimā Brahmans as their common ancestor.

The precipitating cause of the caste's origin was the gods' difficulty with another demon, the famous Vṛtrāsur. Finding themselves unable to defeat him, the gods sought the advice of Viṣṇu. He sent them to Dadhīci, famed as an ascetic, to obtain his power-charged bones out of which to fashion a thunderbolt-weapon (*vajra*).[3] They did so, and in the end were victorious.[4] Now, when the gods were on their way to Dadhīci's hermitage to get the bones, he knew they were coming. Wishing to leave his wife with a son, the sage deposited some semen in a cloth that he gave to her for washing; she thereupon went to the Ganges, and when she entered the water with the cloth, she became pregnant. Only after returning to the hermitage did she learn of Dadhīci's sacrifice. Brahmā told her of the son she carried, so before becoming a *satī* she cut out her womb and gave it to Brahmā, who placed it in the custody of a pipal tree. Because of the boy's association with the pipal tree, he came to be known as Pipplād. In time, Pipplād became a great sage and the father of twelve sage-sons;[5] in time they also produced twelve sons each, who became sages of great renown.

The story now turns to a king named Māndhātā.[6] In order to conquer the three worlds, he sponsored a great sacrifice, and on the advice of Vaśiṣṭh, he invited Pipplād's 144 grandsons to officiate, making them into "*ācārya*s." It was a vegetarian sacrifice directed at the goddess Dadhimatī, and was conducted at the site of the Dadhimatī temple, which the text refers to as *kapāl piṭh*. Pleased by the sacrifice, the goddess herself emerged from the sacrificial pit (*kuṇḍ*). The 144 priests asked her to be their clan goddess (*kul devī*) and to fulfill the king's desires, which she agreed to do. She ordered that her sacrifices should never involve the killing of animals, and described various benefits that would result from bathing in the pit. She then stepped into the pit and vanished. Although (as the text makes clear) the 144 sages were not of the sort to make material demands, they nonetheless accepted payment (*dakṣiṇā*) from the king in the form of a village and a bride for each of them (given with pipal leaves). The text then describes how Māndhātā prospered as a result of his worship of the goddess. It closes with a description of the benefits of her rites of worship together with instructions for their performance.[7]

The *Purāṇa* says nothing of the building of the temple itself. Rather, the physical focus of the tale (insofar as it relates to the temple) is the sacrificial pit, which Dāhimā Brahmans believe to have become the bathing *kuṇḍ* adjacent to the temple today; Dadhimatī herself, they say, filled it with power-charged water (Plate 34). As for the building of the temple, a widely known and constantly retold legend maintains that the goddess's image—and in some tellings the temple itself—emerged from the earth (a theme we shall encounter again). The goddess had warned a herdsman that there would be a great commotion when she came out from the ground and that he should not be afraid. But when the moment came, he forgot the warning and fled from the spot (or, in another telling, shouted "stop mother!" in order to recall his fleeing cows [Plate 28]). As a result, only the goddess's skull (some say knee) had enough time to appear, which explains the dome-shaped, aniconic image that is the temple's principal object of worship. Some say that the temple emerged from the ground at this time. Another telling holds that Māndhātā actually built the temple at the goddess's direction, but that it was hidden until she emerged from the earth (Jośī n.d.:4).[8]

Analysis

Among other things to be sure, this text is about the establishment of a line of descent. The text shows how the Dāhimā Brahman caste consists of patriclans descended from the 144 sons of the twelve sons of Pipplād.[9] His father was the great sage Dadhīci, who was descended, through Atharvā, from the creator deity Brahmā. All Dāhimā Brahmans are thus shown to be agnatically related and to share a distinguished Brahman pedigree. The text attaches the goddess Dadhimatī to the genealogy as Dadhīci's sister, thus providing the scaffolding for a perpetual relationship between her and Dadhīci's progeny.

The assertion of common patrilineal descent for the Dāhimā Brahmans raises the obvious question of how caste endogamy is possible. I discussed this issue with various individuals. Most respondents immediately recognized the point of my query, but seemed to believe that the relationship is simply too distant to matter. One acquaintance, a Dāhimā Brahman journalist, responded that King Māndhātā gave the twelve sages (I think he meant the 144 sages) Kṣatriya wives, but it is not clear how this would make any difference because the progeny of the sages would still be agnatic kin.[10] This is clearly not a matter to which Dāhimā Brahmans give much if any thought—or if they do, it is socially repressed. The dilemma is probably intractable; if you wish to trace your descent as a caste to one individual, than you must avert your eyes from the issue of incest. So important, it seems, is the contention of common descent from Dadhīci that it trumps everything else, including this problem.

Another key element in the tale is the image of a group being created by means of a ritual transformation. The ritual that plays this role is Māndhātā's sacrifice, and this exemplifies a general Indic association between the sacrifice and creative power, a pattern we shall see again.[11] Why is a transformation needed? It is because although Dadhīci's progeny are indisputably Brahmans, they are not yet a Brahman caste. Their position is actually liminal, somewhere on the boundary of the social order, for the text describes them as hermit sage/priests, living in the "deep forest" (*Purāṇa* 22.14). Such sages can have wives, but are never quite householders.[12] The ambiguity of their status is illustrated by Dadhīci's relationship with his wife. It is true he is married, but as a renouncer he cannot physically and socially reproduce himself in the normal way; thus, the semen on the cloth and all the rest.[13] There is a profound dissonance between the world-renouncing, forest-dwelling manner of life of sages and the requirements of fully socialized domesticity.

When Pipplād's grandsons participate in the sacrifice, they enter the social order; in effect, for them the sacrifice is a rite of incorporation (Van Gennep 1960). They do so in the classic role of Brahman priests serving a Kṣatriya patron, and his payment to them, taking the form of wives and land, cements the deal; now they are family men with property. The most significant gift is not the wives; after all, sages do have wives, although the nature of sages' sexuality is always an issue. More crucial is Māndhātā's gift of land, for this not only cements the Brahmans to the territorial order of the state, but shifts the focus of their identity from common Brahman descent, as such, to that of a bundle of related but distinct patrilineages. The text's suggestion that the Brahmans are domesticated by means of grants of land is consonant with the fact that actually existing lineages of the caste are identified with the villages from which most of them take their names.

A third essential element in the story is the goddess. This exemplifies a widespread myth-model in which goddesses provide crucial assistance at the birth of social groups with which they then maintain permanent ties. Lindsey Harlan (1992) has described the pattern well in connection with Rājpūt clans, but it can be found in many other contexts. In the Dāhimā case, we see that the goddess comes to the aid of the caste's ancestors-to-be by guaranteeing the efficacy of Māndhātā's sacrifice; this, in turn, produces the gifts with their consequences. She then binds herself to the group (and the group to her) by a pledge of perpetual protection.[14] When Dāhimā Brahmans come to the Dadhimatī temple they are reconnecting themselves to these events and thus reactivating the goddess's ancient pledge.

What sort of temporal framework provides the background of these events? Let us begin with the obvious, namely that cyclical time is present in the tale but hardly central to it. Its sole appearance is at the beginning of the story with the emergence of Brahmā from the reclining Viṣṇu, an event that is cosmically recurrent. This is not an incidental detail, for it has the function (I suggest) of connecting the entire narrative to a transcendental reality, thus investing it with a sort of cosmic significance. Cyclical time is therefore a very important context for the story, but a context that lies at its far periphery.

Social time, not transcendental time, is the true timescape of this narrative. Its format is genealogical, and thus its directionality is linear; where it ends is different from where it began, and the present is a consequence of the past. Nothing, however, is said of actual dates, and from the standpoint of a strictly metrical historical sense, the story has no temporal framework at all. Māndhātā's sacrifice seems to have occurred in the *satyug*, but this is less a matter of dating than a way of dramatizing the deep antiquity of the event.[15] And that antiquity is social antiquity, having less to do with measurement than with the Dāhimā Brahmans' desire to establish a Brahman pedigree extending back to the beginning of the present creation.

The narrative accounts for three levels of social segmentation: Brahmanhood in the widest sense, the Dāhimā Brahman caste, and the caste's constituent patriclans. These segmentations are differentiated in relation to a genealogical sequence. Brahmanhood itself takes the lineage back to Atharvā and the creator deity Brahmā. The text implies that Atharvā is one of the mind-born sons of Brahmā, and Brahman tradition proclaims these sage-sons to have been the progenitors of various Brahman lineages (*gotra*s). The text then defines the Dāhimā Brahmans as a particular *kind* of Brahmans whose identity is defined by common descent from the sage Dadhīci, their own apical ancestor. Finally, the text distinguishes the constituent patriclans of the Dāhimā Brahman caste, called *śākhā*s (branches), whose apical ancestors are Dadhīci's grandsons. The group's differentiation into intermarrying descent groups completes the origin of the caste as such, and it is precisely at this moment that the goddess Dadhimatī and her temple (or at least the sacrificial pit) come into the picture as embodiments (one metaphysical, the other physical) of the social identity of the Dāhimā Brahmans.

As we know, the production of the patriclans from Dadhīci was a three-step process: first one (Pipplād), then twelve, then 144.[16] Why the differentiation occurred in this way is not entirely clear, but it seems possible that Pipplād is inserted in the sequence in order to avoid having to explain how superascetic Dadhīci could have multiple offspring. We have seen that he had problems enough producing one. The subsequent squaring of twelve represents the inflationary epoch of the tale; one becomes many in a mere (social) instant, allowing the caste to become completely formed within a scant five generations of the creation of the world.

It should be noted that, apart from the patriclans, the Dāhimā Brahman caste is also divided into twelve supposedly exogamous units called *gotra*s that trace descent from Pipplād's twelve sage-sons. The pattern for this is an ancient Brahmanical tradition of tracing patrilineages (called *gotra*s) to founder sages, for which the seven sages (listed variantly) are the prototypes (see Mitchiner 1982).[17] In the Dāhimā case, however, this is a pseudo-segmentation, for although the *gotra*s are listed in the caste's literature and are known to some respondents, they do not actually regulate marriage or anything else. I suspect, in fact, that most Dāhimā Brahmans do not clearly understand the difference between the *gotra*s and the *śākhā*s. Some say the *gotra*s were once exogamous but have lately fallen into disuse, but I know of no evidence to support this contention. I suspect that they were tacked on to an already established system of patriclans in an effort to make the entire system seem more Brahmanical.

Because the formative moments of the Dāhimā Brahman caste are pushed back into the deepest antiquity that can be imagined, the temporal foreground between those long gone days and the present is largely undifferentiated. It is a hazy middle ground, offering no particular temporal landmarks in relation to which other events might be dated. This explains an interesting phenomenon. An inscription dated VS 1908 (1851 CE) describes how the King of Udaipur financed the then just completed creation of the temple's current courtyards at the behest of a trusted Dāhimā Brahman advisor named Viṣṇudās. Many Dāhimā Brahmans subsequently came to believe that the King of Udaipur was in fact the builder of the temple.[18] Indeed, one highly educated respondent, a man very well versed in caste affairs, informed me that a certain king Māndhātā "of Udaipur" sponsored a sacrifice at the site of the temple. But from the standpoint of the socially relevant events, it matters little which king built the temple. If the event in question passes beyond the horizon of the present, then it is likely to end up in the remotest past, and Māndhātā and the King of Udaipur merge into a kind of anyking at the beginning of social time.

Hybrid Antiquity: Osian

We now move to a somewhat more complicated case, that of the Mahāvīra and Sacciyā Mātā temples of Osian. Here, as before, our temples are linked with an account of a caste's origin, in this case the Osvāl caste (see also chapters one and eight of this volume). Also as before, the master metaphor is genealogical, but it is employed in a more extended sense and against the background of a more differentiated timescape. A big difference is that in this case social and metrical time are entangled with each other. The religious context is also very different, for the Osvāls are mostly Jains, and their origin story reflects that fact. Monks belonging to a Jain ascetic lineage known as the Upkeś Gacch (now nearly defunct) appear to have been the primary transmitters of the version summarized here.[19] What follows is based on a historically recent retelling of this version published early in the twentieth century (1929) by a distinguished monk named Jñānsundar who was the last-but-one fully initiated monk of this lineage. Of Osvāl origin himself, he was a tireless promoter of Osian and the Osvāl caste.

Osvāls

Jñānsundar's account of the origin of the Osvāls (this portion summarized from his Ch. 3) is, as is our Dāhimā narrative, organized around a genealogy. In this case, however, the descent in question is disciplic, not patrilineal. The tale begins with the inception of an ascetic lineage issuing from Pārśvanātha, the twenty-third Tīrthaṅkara and Māhavīra's predecessor. This is the Upkeś Gacch, which Jñānsundar refers to as Pārśvanātha's "progeny" (*santān*). He traces lineage succession from Ācārya Śubhdatt (one of Pārśvanātha's *gaṇadhar*s), to Haridattsūri, Āryyasamudrasūri, Keśīśramaṇācārya (who lived during the period of Mahāvīra), and finally Svayamprabhsūri, Pārśvanātha's fifth successor. Except for the reference to Mahāvīra's period, the narrative is dateless.[20]

Although all these *ācārya*s are represented as great proselytizers of Jainism, identifiable convert-castes enter the picture only when we get to Svayamprabhsūri. Once when he was at Mount Abu with his followers he met some businessmen from Shrimal City (subsequently known as Bhinmal). They told him that hundreds of thousands of innocent animals were being killed in sacrifices there—a horrendous state of affairs to Jains—and invited him to the city. He arrived at a time when preparations were being made for a great sacrifice. When his disciples entered the city in search of alms and saw how matters stood, they returned empty-handed, saying that the city was an unfit source of food for Jain ascetics. Svayamprabhsūri thereupon gave a sermon that convinced Jaysen, the king of Shrimal, and his subjects to release the animals and become Jains, and their descendants became the Śrīmālī caste. Then came news that a similar sacrifice was about to be held at Padmavati (a city near Abu). Svayamprabhsūri went there with the same result, thereby creating the Porvāl caste.

Ratnaprabhsūri, Svayamprabhsūri's successor, was the creator of the Osvāl caste. He came on the scene in the following fashion. One time when Svayamprabhsūri was giving a sermon to the goddesses Cakreśvarī, Ambikā, Padmāvati, and Siddhāyikā, a wizard by the name of Ratnacūḍ was flying overhead. His celestial vehicle came to an abrupt stop over the great monk's head. Then, in order to pay proper respect, Ratnacūḍ descended and listened to Svayamprabhsūri's discourse, after which he requested and received initiation. Later, in the fifty-second year after Mahāvīra's liberation, he became an *ācārya* himself—thus acquiring the name Ratnaprabhsūri—and ultimately succeeded Svayamprabhsūri as head of the ascetic lineage.

Now, in the meantime, important events had occurred at Shrimal City. One of Jaysen's sons, Bhīmsen, had become king; he was a non-Jain, and all the Jains had left the city in order to escape persecution. Bhīmsen had two sons, one of whom was named Upaldev. Because of a quarrel with his elder brother, Upaldev left the kingdom; his companion was Uhaṛ (the Ūhaḍa of chapter one), the younger brother of Bhīmsen's minister. After many a twist and turn, they found their way to a spot north of Mandor in present-day Rajasthan where they founded the town known as Osian today.[21] In time, large numbers of people from Shrimal City followed the prince to settle there, and it became a large and flourishing city.

In the four-hundredth year before the start of the Vikram era, and at the urging of the goddess Cakreśvarī, Ratnaprabhsūri journeyed to Osian with 500 disciples. The monks made camp on the hill known as Luṇādrī (a short distance from the present day Sacciyā temple). There they completed a month-long fast, at the end of which a few of them went into the town in search of food. The inhabitants of the town were meat-eaters, drinkers of alcohol, and devotees of the ferocious goddess Cāmuṇḍā. As a result, there was no food suitable for Jain monks available, and Ratnaprabhsūri decided to move on. But Cāmuṇḍā was quite distressed when she heard about their impending departure, for it would be disgraceful not to receive with proper hospitality a distinguished monk sent by Cakreśvarī. She therefore asked him to remain for the rainy season retreat, saying that his stay would be highly beneficial. He did so with thirty-five of his hardiest disciples.

Then one night a snake bit King Upaldev's daughter's husband (in fact the son of Uhaṛ, now Upaldev's minister) as he was sleeping. He appeared to be dead, but when the king and his subjects were carrying the body to the burning grounds, they were accosted by a Jain monk—the goddess Cāmuṇḍā in disguise—who asked why they were about to burn a living person. The monk thereupon vanished, but the people then remembered that there had been a group of monks on the hill outside the city, so they all went there with the body. There the boy was brought back to life by means of Ratnaprabhsūri's footwashings. As a result of this miracle, Upaldev and the others agreed to become Jains. Using sanctified powder (*vāskṣep*) supplied by Cakreśvarī herself, Ratnaprabhsūri initiated the king, his minister and others as lay Jains. Rājpūts, but also Brahmans and Vaiśyas, were converted, all coming together in a single "Mahājan Saṅgh." This group much later became known as the Osvāl caste.[22]

At the time of the conversion, Minister Uhaṛ had been in the midst of building a temple for the god Nārāyaṇa (Viṣṇu). But whatever he built each day would fall that night. The problem was finally solved when he changed his project into a temple for Mahāvīra in mid-construction, and this is the Mahāvīra temple in Osian today. The image of Mahāvīra was fashioned underground from sand and milk by the goddess Cāmuṇḍā herself. Unfortunately, the eager new Jains unearthed the image before it was fully formed, with the result that there were two lemon-shaped, knot-like flaws on its chest.[23]

Despite her central role in these events, Cāmuṇḍā was left in the lurch. She had been present at, and was much pleased by, the conversions to Jainism. At that time, however, she had asked Ratnaprabhsūri if the conversions meant that she would have to give up her beloved animal sacrifice, and his answer was ambiguous. The people became very anxious as the date of the autumn *navrātrī* came near. This is a festival at which Cāmuṇḍā would expect animal sacrifices, which as Jains they would be unable to provide. In the end, Ratnaprabhsūri intervened, with the result that Cāmuṇḍā gave up meat and liquor, accepted vegetarian offerings, and became a proper Jain goddess (Plate 31).[24] Ratnaprabhsūri renamed her Saccikā Devī (Sacciyā) because she had spoken truthfully when she told him that a rainy season stay in Osian would prove beneficial. For her part, Cāmuṇḍā promised to protect her devotees in the town (by implication the inhabitants at that time and their descendants) who worship the image of Mahāvīra in Osian's Mahāvīra temple and who serve Ratnaprabhsūri and his descendants (by which she meant the Upkeś Gacch). She also became the protective goddess of the Mahāvīra temple.

These events culminated in the consecration of the Mahāvīra temple. As it happens, the 465 monks who had not stayed with Ratnaprabhsūri at Osian had gone to the town called Korantpur for their rainy season retreat. The people there (whom Svayamprabhsūri had originally converted) had also built a Mahāvīra temple, and its consecration had been set for the same day as that of the Osian temple. Because he was a wizard, Ratnaprabhsūri was able to preside bilocationally at both consecrations, which occurred in the year Vīr 70. He had done so, however, in his *nij* (true) form only in Osian, and when the people of Korantpur came to know of this they were quite angry. In their pique they conferred *ācārya* status on one of the monks who had spent the rainy season retreat with them, and this was the origin of the division between the Upkeś Gacch and the Koranṭ Gacch.[25]

Later, King Upaldev built a Pārśvanātha temple. According to Jñānsundar, this same temple is currently Osian's Sacciyā temple. He believes (ibid.:91, f.n.) that the temple's principal goddess image was originally located in a shrine outside the main temple and was put in Pārśvanātha's place after the Jains had begun to abandon the town (below). Jñānsundar probably feels he needs to make this point because it would seem odd indeed for a Pārśvanātha temple never to have been built in a place to the history of which the Upkeś Gacch is so important.[26]

There is an important sequel to the conversion story (given in ibid.: Ch. 5; see also chapter 1 of this volume). In Jñānsundar's narrative, the thread that connects this sequel to the occurrences just described is a line of disciplic succession, for the context in which the story is given is an account of the career of the Pārśvanātha's thirteenth successor, an *ācārya* named Kakksūri. In Vīr 373 (that is, 303 years after the original consecration), some young men of the town were doing *pūjā* in the Mahāvīra temple when they noticed the flaws on the image's chest. They foolishly had them chiseled off. The goddess was infuriated, and blood immediately began to flow from the image. Word of this was sent to Kakksūri, then at Girnar, and when he arrived he began a fast. On the night of the fast's last day, the goddess appeared and explained what had happened, adding that the "*jāti*" would be destroyed as a result of the outrage. The *ācārya* was able to mollify her, and in the end she agreed to end the disturbance, but said that a special rite, a *śāntipūjā* (a peace-inducing rite), would be required.

At this point there occurs an extremely interesting interlude (ibid.:99–102). Noting that there are many different kinds of *śāntipūjā*s, Kakksūri asked the goddess of what sort it should be. He added that it should use locally available materials. The goddess responded by saying that he, Kakksūri, could use only *vāskṣep* powder to bestow peace, but that this rite should be one in which others (meaning laypersons) could take part. The great ascetic replied that it would be inappropriate for him to teach any such new rite without support from the scriptures, and thereupon sent her to Mahāvideh Kṣetra to obtain instructions from Sīmandhar Svāmī.[27] This she did. It was a bathing rite, and the text includes instructions for its performance. Under Kakksūri's supervision, the lay participants were arranged by their patriclans (*gotras*), of which there were eighteen; nine were stationed to the image's left and nine to the right. When the rite was performed the flow of blood stopped. The text then lists the attending patriclans.

Other versions of the Osvāl story, including those told by the Sacciyā temple's *pujārī*s as well as the *Upakeśa Gaccha Paṭṭāvalī* (Hoernle 1890:239), maintain that the Osvāls ultimately had to leave the town as a result of the goddess's curse. The *pujārī*s have a clear interest in promoting such an idea, for its effect would be to keep meddlesome Osvāls at a distance, and they may well be the main transmitters of the diaspora story. By contrast, Jñānsundar, who wanted to promote Osian as an Osvāl center, rejects the diaspora story as baseless (ibid.:102–03f.n.).[28]

Two Histories Compared

The Osian narrative clearly belongs to the same genre as the Dāhimā Brahman story. In neither case are we dealing with histories of temples as such; rather, both are histories of social groups that have the temples as physical foci. In a sense, the sheer existence of the temples and their obvious antiquity are visible testimonials to the truth of the narratives; in a reflex of this, the antiquity of the temples is defined in social-temporal terms. The basic elements of the Dāhimā and Osvāl narratives are also the same: genealogy, rites of sacrifice, a goddess. The way these elements are treated in the Osvāl case, however, reflects a distinctively Jain point of view.

Let us begin with genealogy. There is a striking contrast in the way the two stories begin. The Dāhimā story starts with Brahmā, who is the point of origination of a line of patrilineal descent that connects the moment of creation to the present day. Pārśvanātha plays a similar role in the Osvāl story. He does not create the world (for the Jains possess no such concept), but he originates a line of descent that provides the spine of the subsequent story. The difference is that this line of descent is disciplic, not patrilineal. His teachings become a kind of spiritual seed equivalent to the more purely physical continuity established by the Dāhimā Brahmans' descent. It was also from this seed that the Osvāl clans, which in our narrative are portrayed as lay offshoots of an ascetic lineage, were produced.[29]

There is a sense in which it is impossible to transmit Jain identity purely by means of patrilineal descent. Brahmanhood is different; to borrow Marriott's phrasing (1976), Brahmanhood is in essence a biomoral quality that is transmitted from the very beginning of things by means of physical reproduction. In contrast, no Jains emerge at the moment of creation. For the Jains there was no such moment, but in any case Jains are cultural, not natural, creations. That is, for Jains to exist, someone must be "converted," a process begun by self-enlightened Tīrthaṅkaras who introduce Jain teachings into the flow of time. These teachings are not transmitted by physical descent, but through the teacher-disciple tie. Membership in an ascetic lineage, conferred by initiation, is the behavioral marker of adherence to such teachings for ascetics. A Jain laity, in turn, consists of those who manifest reverence for Jain ascetics, or a particular lineage of ascetics, who transmit Jain teachings.

Thus, there is necessarily a deep social discontinuity in the Osvāl story. The Dāhimā Brahmans were Brahmans at first and always. The Osvāls, by contrast, were warlike Rājpūts before they become nonviolent Jains, and their transformation was therefore truly fundamental. In a sense, they have no past—or perhaps a minimal past—outside of Jainism. Having become Jains, their significant past becomes that of Jainism and the ascetic lineages through which Jain teachings are socially transmitted and reproduced.

The radicality of the change is expressed in the way the sacrificial metaphor is employed. For the Dāhimā Brahmans, the sacrifice plays a ritually inclusive role. Their story is an account of how a preexisting identity, that of Brahmanhood, is fully realized socially when sages are given wives, property, and a social function (that of royal priests, which is to say, an institutionalized position in the sacrifice) in exchange for a fruitful sacrifice. In the Osvāl story, the sacrifice plays the opposite role of ritual exclusion, propelling the group in question out of one social order and into another. The Dāhimā Brahmans maintain continuity with their original identity; the new Jains, in contrast, completely sever themselves from their past identity. Their ancestors were Rājpūts, sponsors of blood sacrifices. Because of their abhorrence of violence, Jains cannot sacrifice; therefore, when Rājpūts become Jains they must expunge their relationship with this rite and the Brahmans who perform it.

Jñānsundar presents non-violence as the principal reason for the Jains' break with the sacrifice, but an equally important reason is surely the need for a break with Brahmans. After all, one can sacrifice non-violently, as we see with the Dāhimā Brahmans. Brahmans must perform sacrifices in order to be Brahmans; vegetarian Brahmans must thus, perforce, believe in the possibility of vegetarian sacrifice. Osvāls must break with the social order for which the sacrifice is a dominating metaphor; for them, therefore, a belief in the possibility of non-violent sacrifice is ruled out.

Their links with the past having been cut so completely, the Osvāls must then—in effect—exchange one set of ancestors for another. The Dāhimā Brahmans venerate the sage Dadhīci as their common ancestor, and in fact he is represented by an image in a side-shrine at the Dadhimatī temple (Plate 28). In contrast, no patrilineal ancestors from pre-conversion days are objects of worship at Osian.[30] Rather, in the Osvāl case (or at least in our narrative) the pattern of venerating ancestral figures is shifted to the Tīrthaṅkara (technically Pārśvanātha but generically Mahāvīra) and his spiritual successors in the Upkeś Gacch.[31] As represented in the narrative, this is the true "ancestor cult" of the Osvāls.

An implication of these points is that a Jain caste is actually incapable of socially reproducing itself. The Osvāl caste is a social group like any other that, at the most basic level, reproduces itself physically and socially in the normal manner. But not all Osvāls are Jains, and "Jainness" is a non-biomoral quality that is transmitted in the form of teachings and initiation. These belong to the domain of ascetics. This suggests that even after the Osvāl caste is created, it becomes a sort of shadow of the ascetic lineage of which it is the offshoot, for without sustained contact with the ascetic lineage, the caste is not capable of transmitting its essence—as Jain Osvāls—to the next generation.

As in the Dāhimā Brahman case, a goddess is central to our Osvāl tale, but with a difference having mainly to do with the sacrifice. For the Dāhimā Brahmans, her relationship with the rite is positive, which is made possible, at least in part, by the Dāhimā Brahmans' belief that non-violent sacrifice is possible. For the Osvāls, her relationship with the rite is colored by the assumption that sacrifice is forever and always blood sacrifice. New Jains are created when sacrificers become non-sacrificers; in parallel with this, the goddess Cāmuṇḍā becomes a goddess suitable for Jains only when she no longer receives sacrifice.

This is deeply linked with that most ubiquitous of themes in Jain life: diet. The conversion process begins when Jain ascetics cannot find food. This leads to the transformation of Osian's Rājpūts into Jains, which in turn makes possible a sustainable commensal relationship between an ascetic lineage and a lay community. But now the tables are turned, for Cāmuṇḍā cannot be properly fed (i.e., with meat) by Jains. She, too, must undergo a transformation, a change of name and diet. She remains a clan goddess to her original worshipers, pledging her protection to them. But her primary relationship has shifted to Mahāvīra and the Mahāvīra temple (as evidenced by her fury over the desecration), just as the new Jains themselves have relinquished a Rājpūt past for a totally new kind of pedigree.

As a clan goddess of Rājpūts, Cāmuṇḍā participates in their nature as a warrior community. The vegetarianization of this community occupies the same ritual-logical niche as a rite of separation, severing them from their previous condition. But until Cāmuṇḍā's nature is changed, the transformation is incomplete, leaving the community in a liminal state. Seen against this background, the establishment of the community's new ritual relationship with the goddess, based on vegetarian offerings, becomes the functional equivalent of a rite of incorporation.

The social timescapes of our two narratives are similar, but with interesting differences. Both accounts reach backward to connect with cyclical time—the Dāhimā Brahmans to Brahmā, the Osvāls to Pārśvanātha. Although Pārśvanātha's individual biography situates him in the stream of social time, he is eternally recurrent in the sense that his Tīrthaṅkara career is, in its most significant essentials, exactly the same as that of any and all Tīrthaṅkaras. Like Brahmā, he is a genealogical uncaused cause, not because he creates the world, but for the simple reason that he is spiritually autonomous and without a teacher. The twenty-four Tīrthaṅkaras of each cosmic half-cycle are a mere series, not a lineage. He thus embodies a reality beyond history, but one that is brought into the stream of history by his individual persona, and then preserved within the flow of historical time by means of disciplic succession.

Once launched in the stream of time, this spiritual lineage produces segments, both mendicant and lay, and these moments of subcreation are the main temporal markers of the Osvāl narrative. The relative complexity of the segmentation results in a somewhat more complex social timescape than we see in the Dāhimā Brahman case. There are three principal lay offshoots, the Śrīmālīs, Porvāls, and Osvāls. Using a modified idiom of segmentary descent—i.e., one in which patrilineal descent is grafted on to its disciplic parallel—Jñānsundar's account registers the fact that all three castes, though different, are quite similar in their social customs and adherence to Śvetāmbar Jainism. By assigning a separate creator-*ācārya* to the Osvāls, the narrative adds additional social distance between the Osvāls and the other two castes (who in any case figure marginally in the story).

But why trace descent to Pārśvanātha in particular? As far as I am aware, all other Śvetāmbar ascetic lineages treat Mahāvīra as their apical ancestor. This being so, it seems possible that tracing descent to the earlier Pārśvanātha had the purpose of differentiating the Upkeś Gacch from other ascetic lineages in a decisive way, perhaps in the context of rivalry with other Gacchs for the allegiance of lay Jains. The date assigned to the creation of the Osvāls is a crucial consideration, and this is a matter to which Jñānsundar gives careful attention (ibid:Ch. 4, 1–40). He considers three alternatives—Vīr 70, VS 222 and the tenth century of the Vikram era (the latter the most plausible by the standards of modern historians). As we know, he favors the Vīr 70 date, which seems to be the general Upkeś Gacch preference.[32] This date would render implausible any claim by another Gacch to have converted the Osvāls; that is, it creates the temporal depth required for the Upkeś Gacch to lay exclusive claim to the Osvāl caste as a lay segment.

The later mutilation of the image is a puzzling aspect of the tale. The story seems to struggle with the ostensibly outrageous idea that the goddess herself is somehow embodied in Mahāvīra's image. She was the source of the milk from which the image was partly made (dropped from a cow on the spot). The two flaws on the image's chest reiterate the milk/breast theme, which is further reinforced by the blood (or, in one telling, a mixture of blood and milk[33]) that issues from the flaw (or flaws) when the desecration occurs. It is as if she herself were the victim of the foolish mutilation. But whatever its symbolism, the episode represents a rebirth or second birth of the Osvāl caste complete with a transformative ritual (the *pūjā*) and an *ācārya* who tames the goddess.

Just why there should be a revisiting of this idea, a whiff of "eternal return" in the midst of a linear narrative, is unclear. Of course for those who believe in the goddess's permanent curse (not Jñānsundar), the second creation explains the Osvāl diaspora, but this could be done without a separate creation. Perhaps the two creations are a simple artifact of the Upkeś Gacch disciplic genealogy. Kakksūri might have been a central figure in some different Upkeś Gacch tale of Osvāl creation, a story that would naturally enter the main narrative at a time corresponding to Kakksūri's position in the genealogy. But the second creation might also be compelled by ritual logic. While the converted Rājpūts of Osian worked out a proper ritual relationship with the goddess at the time of their original conversion, they had apparently not yet established an equivalent ritual relationship with the Tīrthaṅkara. Or at least this is suggested by the fact that, although the Mahāvīra image was clearly in worship at the time of the mutilation, Kakksūri and the goddess nonetheless had no clue at all about what a lay ritual to quell the disturbance should actually be until they consulted Sīmandhar Svāmī. This slight vestige of liminality in the Osvāls' status is finally resolved by the *pūjā*, an occasion in which they emerge for the first time as a completely formed caste, subdivided into named exogamous patriclans.

Commensurablity

Thus far our concern has been solely with group histories and their social-temporal frameworks. Recently, however, something new has entered the situation: a rapidly thickening layer of modern historical interpretation. This is constructed against the metrical timescape that is at the foundation of modern historical study and that posits a very different kind of antiquity for the temples, one that is less a reflex of social structures and more a response to imperatives of measurement for its own sake. What this development portends for future understandings of these temples and the caste histories with which they are associated cannot yet be said. Still, some interesting developments need to be noted.

Basic to this whole issue is the question of commensurablity. Systems of time reckoning are not necessarily commensurable at all. For example, typical Indic constructions of cyclical time are incommensurable with most linear schemes[34] to the extent that it is possible for cyclical and linear timelines to overlap without conflicting with each other. That is, just as it is possible for a geometrician to ignore the earth's curvature when working with small figures, linear time can be part of a cycle and yet retain its linearity, so long as the cycle is very long. The temporal cycles of the Indic world are long indeed.[35] But the matter is very different with regard to metrical and social time, which are now on a potential collision course. As long as social time remains entirely relative—that is, entirely sequestered within a narrative that never includes a date relevant to any other group—it can be serenely indifferent to potential historical disconfirmations. But in our era this is increasingly difficult to do.

In the case of the Dadhimatī temple, metrical time intruded into the situation with the discovery of an inscription bearing a date of Gupta Saṃvat 289 (608 CE) that appears to associate Dāhimā Brahmans with the temple at that date. This, however, does not seem to challenge traditional history in any significant way, which is probably because the metrical date falls more or less in the featureless middle ground of Dāhimā Brahman social time where it contradicts nothing of importance. In fact, it has been folded into caste-historical materials (such as Jagatnārāyaṇ Jośī n.d.) with enthusiasm, probably because it demonstrates a respectable metrical antiquity for Brahman association with the temple, a useful fact in arguing for Dāhimā proprietorship over the temple in modern courtrooms (see chapter seven of this volume).

The situation at Osian is more complex, for here social and metrical timescapes have already had to interact for a considerable period of time (speaking metrically). As an example, the Upkeś Gacch/Osvāl genealogy has had to take into account the metrical dating of Mahāvīra's career on earth. As noted, the Upkeś Gacch narrative appears to have made constructive use of this metrical (and thus universal) temporal landmark in its effort to establish its own exclusive claim to the creation of the Osvāl caste. And in any case, given the metrically dated landmarks of Jain history, it is hard to see how any history of a Jain community could be totally enveloped in social time. But having conceded the necessity of metrical landmarks, Jñānsundar seems to have tried to re-relativize Osvāl history. He did so by introducing the concept of a new dating system, *Osvāl samvat*, for which the zero date was Vīr 70, which he regarded as the date of Osvāl origin. He used this dating system on many of his publications, but it never caught on.

More recently the problem of reconciliation has become less tractable. Jñānsundar, for example, attempted with might and main to refute the historians who opt for a tenth or eleventh-century dating for Osvāl origins (1929:Ch. 4, 1–40), but the strength of his conviction was offset by the total lack of plausibility of the date he preferred, which was the much earlier Vīr 70. And of course his placing of the Sacciyā and Mahāvīra temples in this period is simply preposterous by standards that, willy-nilly, have come to prevail among educated people. If nothing else, Jñānsundar's struggles illustrate the fact that once social time is de-relativized, it becomes fair game for modern historical and/or art historical challenge.

But the sky has not fallen at Osian. Rather, the modern timescape appears to have been absorbed and coopted in a new and highly creative reaction to the confrontation between old and new. While the Sacciyā temple continues to function as a goddess temple for both Osvāl and non-Osvāl constituencies (prospering greatly in this role), the Mahāvīra temple has become the focus of a shifting frame of reference. It has become the object of extensive renovation and preservation activities of a major Śvetāmbar Jain trust. This, in turn, is linked with a view of the temple in which the Osvāl *caste* has receded from the picture while the image of a wider and socially more encompassing *Śvetāmbar Jain* community has moved to the foreground. Exemplary of this outlook is Dhaky's (1968) analysis of this and other temples in which scrupulous metric dating lies at the foundation of a warm (and scholarly) appreciation of Śvetāmbar tradition. The trend is obviously in the direction of the universal. The Śvetāmbar community's current engagement with the temple projects a definition of the community as a group worthy of the custodianship of a great cultural treasure. This mildest of parochialisms points beyond itself, for the value of that treasure is, finally, not merely social—at any level—but civilizational and human.

Notes

1. Social time can be cyclical. An example is the Nuer use of their age-set system as a frame of reference for the dating of some events.
2. It should be understood that I am concentrating on one version of the origin story here, and that other versions exist, both folk and printed. My summary is drawn from the Hindi translation; it is a partial plot summary and excludes a number of details.
3. The *Purāṇa* puts the emphasis on Dadhīci's ascetic powers. Other versions, however, tell of how the gods had left their divine weapons with Dadhīci for safekeeping; he absorbed the weapons' power in his bones, and then discarded them (see, e.g., Jośī n.d.:8–9). In a variant the author and John Cort heard from a genealogist in Borunda village, Dadhīci used a *vajra* (apparently gotten from Śiva) to grind his *bhāṅg*; over a five-thousand-year period the weapon had worn down and the resulting particles had entered the sage's bones.
4. Tradition proclaims (though not the *Purāṇa*) that the gods brought the Kāmdhenu cow to lick off his flesh; apparently only the cow could absorb the sin of Brahmanicide. This episode is represented in a frequently reproduced picture of the sage (Plate 28).
5. Their names: Vṛhadvats, Gautam, Bhārgav, Bhāradvāj, Kaucchas, Kaśyap, Śāṇḍilya, Mahābhāg Atri, Parāśar, Kapil, Garg, Laghuvats (elsewhere also known as Mam).
6. The text identifies Māndhātā as the son of a sun-line king named Yuvnāśva. Tod (1990:1629–630) describes a legendary Pramār king by this name who ruled from Dhar and Ujjain. Quite by chance, I came across a reference to a king named Māndhātā, son of a king Yunāśva, in a history of the Jāṭ caste (Vidyālaṅkār 1992:207); here he is said to be the apical ancestor of a Jāṭ patrilineage called Gaur. I suspect that he figures in the origin stories of other groups as well. There is also reference to a King Māndhātā in the *Mahābhārata* (Vana Parva 126.1–40) and in early Buddhist Sources.
7. In this respect the text resembles a *vrat kathā*.
8. Cort reports a version in which the temple bursts forth from the ground when Viṣṇudās (below) arrives on the scene.
9. Tradition proclaims that the descendants of one of Pipplād's sons, Laghuvats, became *mlecch* and left the Brahman fold. This is not reported in the *Purāṇa*. The number 144 is pure convention. On the basis of a comparison of several modern compilations, J. N. Asopa (1988:43–67) lists a total of 146 *śākhā*s (branches, or "surnames" as he calls them), most of which have been fitted into the *gotra* scheme (below) but many of which have not. He includes information on the villages after which they are named (e.g., village Pāṭodā for the Pāṭodyas). However, a survey of registrants at a marriage introduction convention (*Dadhimatī* 1994:10–24) reveals that only a dozen or so of the listed *śākhā*s occur commonly; the remainder are rare or possibly non-existent. I suspect that there has always been uncertainty about whether particular lineages are original *śākhā*s or segments of them, but that this became a problem only when efforts to systematize the clan and lineage system began early in this century. This topic is addressed in chapter nine of this volume. Despite the existence of published lists, I suspect the system remains somewhat open-ended to the present day.

10. When asked how Dāhimā Brahmans could be Brahmans in view of the fact that their ancestors had non-Brahman wives, he responded with the seed theory of descent in which descent is carried exclusively by the seed that is planted in the mother by the father.
11. See also Babb 1998a and 2004.
12. A status whose ambiguities are registered by the double character (hermits with wives) of the *vānaprastha āśrama* (Biardeau 1994).
13. Pipplād's story is similar. After 88 years of meditation (*smaraṇ*) with his wife, he divided his semen into twelve parts and put them into his wife's womb, then becoming passionless.
14. As it happens, Dadhīci himself had already done *tap*, at the suggestion of Śiva, in order to get her to become the *kul devī* of his progeny (*Purāṇa* 18.2–4).
15. There is, in fact, some ambiguity on the matter of dating. The *Purāṇa* places the Vikaṭāsur incident in the *satyug* (6.4), but I am unable to find any specific statement about the era of the sacrifice. This would not be an issue were it not for the fact that at least one source (Jośī n.d.:4) places the sacrifice in the *tretāyug*. This makes no chronological sense if the 144 presiding priests are, as the tale proclaims, Dadhīci's grandsons. The myth, with its many versions, is a jerrybuilt structure that shows various seams. The essential point about the dating of all of these incidents is that, in social time, they occur in deep antiquity.
16. Readers might wonder why Atharvā needs to be interposed between Brahmā and Dadhīci. The answer seems to be that Atharvā and Dadhīci are present as a pair in the Ṛg Veda, and thus cannot be severed from each other. Dadhīci is identified with Dadhyañc, who is the son of an Atharvan priest. He was given a horse-head through which he taught the Aśvins; Indra then severed this head, after which the Aśvins restored Dadhyañc's original head (see O'Flaherty 1981:183–85). This episode is also included in the *Purāṇa* (18.12–26). Interestingly, in the genealogical tree displayed at the Dadhimatī temple (and frequently reproduced in caste publications), Dadhyañc is interposed between Atharvā and Dadhīci. The tree's creator has clearly not gotten the message about the identity of this figure and Dadhīci (on which point see Asopa 1988:Ch. 2).
17. The *pravaras* represent an additional complication; they are sometimes listed with Dāhimā *gotras*.
18. This belief may have developed rapidly, for the text of a frequently reprinted *stuti* (O. Dādhīc 1996:12–14) composed in 1853 CE seems to credit the king with the building (as opposed to renovation) of the temple (see chapter seven of this volume). Dāhimā tradition also credits Viṣṇudās with a crucial role in the coming to the Mewar throne of this particular king (Svarūp Singh) (see Jośī n.d.:5; also S. R. Dādhīc n.d.:6).
19. As far as I am aware, the lineage is currently represented by a single *yati* (a type of ascetic whose vows are less onerous than those of full ascetics) who lives in Bikaner.
20. No dates are given for the above *ācāryas*, either here or on a succession chart provided on p. 95.
21. It was then known as Uespaṭṭan or Upkeśpur.
22. Most accounts of the creation of Jain castes stress their Rājpūt origin, and that is definitely an emphasis in Jñānsundar's writing. Nonetheless, he includes Brahmans and Vaiśyas as well. His intent, I surmise, is to stress the complete elimination of the *varṇa* system and the Brahmanical/sacrificial order with which it is associated. Elsewhere in the book (Ch. 4:34) he says that the Osvāls mostly come from "pure Kṣatriya *varṇa*." In the same chapter he also says that the Osvāl caste does not have any Śūdra ancestry. Also, he attributes the *vīrtā* (heroism, courage) of the Osvāls to their Rājpūt ancestry (Ch. 4:46). But he also wants to push the line that the conversion freed the converts from the bondage of caste and *varṇa*.

23. The Minister's cow was dropping milk on the spot below which the image was being formed, and the image was discovered when a herdsman followed the cow. Similar stories are widely known in connection with other images.
24. Non-Jains, however, have sacrificed animals at (or outside) this temple until—apparently—quite recently.
25. Later Ratnaprabhsūri went to Korantpur and a reconciliation took place.
26. The assertion that the Sacciyā temple was originally a Pārśvanātha temple is not present in Hoernle's (1890) translation of the *Upakeśa Gaccha Paṭṭāvalī*.
27. According to Jain teachings, no Tīrthaṅkaras are now present in our region of the cosmos. Sīmandhar Svāmī is a Tīrthaṅkara currently teaching in a mythical region called Mahāvideh Kṣetra (see Dundas 2002:305–06, n. 75).
28. To begin with, he says, the caste was known as Upkeśvaṃś in those days, not Osvāl, and the town was called Upkeśpur; in any case, rich merchants of the Upkeśvaṃś were living in Osian until the tenth to eleventh centuries (VS). Business declined when the "sea" (*samudra*) receded from the city, thus driving the business community elsewhere, and a famine in the fourth century (VS) also caused people to move out. But nowhere, he says, is there any mention of the people all leaving suddenly.
29. In this respect, the lay sublineage of Osvāls resembles somewhat the matrilaterally differentiated lineage segments of the Nuer. Sacciyā occupies the same structural position as the co-wife whose son's children become a new lineage segment.
30. There are, of course, doctrinal reasons for the Jain prohibition of the *śrāddh* (Jaini 1979:302-04). But one has to wonder if the prohibition might also reflect a shift of ancestry to disciplic lineages.
31. Ratnaprabhsūri is represented by a footprint image in a *dādābāṛī* (a shrine where deceased Jain ascetics of note are worshipped) on Luṇādrī Hill.
32. This is the date given by the *Upakeśa Gaccha Paṭṭāvalī*.
33. This was a version given by one of the Sacciyā temple's *pujārīs* to me in 1991.
34. At least in the form in which we have encountered them here. Modern scientific cosmology may represent another sort of challenge.
35. An exception is the historical cosmology of the Brahmā Kumārīs, and here problems of conflict do arise (Babb 1986:Ch. 5).

Part II

Structures

3

Building a Temple

MICHAEL W. MEISTER

Building a temple begins, not with construction but with finding a spot where sacrality exists. And no temple is ever finished—but exists and is tangible through the skin of its use. It is not a person but a lineage—ever a shape-shifter—renewed through time and its continual remaking. Such a process of restoration, reoccupation, and self-preservation of sacred sites we have been privileged to approach through this shared multi-disciplinary project.

As test (and taste) of this process of *jīrṇoddhār* (transformation, rebuilding), the four pilgrimage temples we studied in western Rajasthan have helped frame certain ongoing art-historical issues:

1. archaeological/art-historical reconstructions of phases of building and rebuilding are possible, but insufficient;
2. an historically framed continuity of reconstruction through time is impossible, but perhaps unnecessary;
3. the materiality of a temple and the sociology of its use must be combined to reclaim the process by which it exists in space and time.

Laws in modern India that govern a legal definition of a temple state the following (K. N. Shah 1997:93; HREC 1962:3):

> a temple is a place of worship where people congregate to approach an embodiment of the Supreme, to worship Him and offer prayers and gifts. Theoretically speaking, this can be done at any place and at any time, but temples provide . . . a special environment and traditional

facilities for arousing a feeling of devotion. . . . Thus, temples may be described as *occult laboratories* where certain physical acts of adoration coupled with certain systematized prayers, psalms, mantras, and musical invocations, can yield certain physical and psychological results.

Khed, Raṇchoḍjī Temple

Of four temples we chose to study, the Raṇchoḍjī temple at Khed—a few miles west of Balotra—built first by the mid-ninth century, has a good possibility of once having had royal patronage (Meister 1991d:254–8; 2000b:24–5), yet its current condition suggests a somewhat constricted contemporary life (Plates 1–3). The Jain temple complex at Nakoda not far away flourishes with a continual rush of pilgrims because of its wish-granting Bherū (Vinayasāgar 1988). What we found at the much more ancient temple at Khed was a tentative, continuing, contemporary patronage (one group of visitors characterized the temple as an "Agravāl *sthāna*" or place of merchants) and limited ongoing daily life, with little evidence of multilayered use.[1] On the other hand, when I first visited it in the early 1970s, the lovely sculpted walls of the main sanctum were still carefully (and expensively) polychromed,[2] much as the pillars of the Mahāvīra Jain temple at Osian were in 1968. A generation apart, the Mahāvīra Jain and Raṇchoḍjī temples share a regional, open-balcony, circumambulatory plan (Plate 2) and both seem to have fallen largely out of use by the nineteenth century, maintained as active temples into the twentieth century by a handful of priests. The gate to the larger compound at Khed has an inscription with a date of VS 1993 (1935–6 CE), suggesting one period of semi-expanded use and reclamation early in the twentieth century.[3]

When we revisited the temple at Khed in 1997, recent patronage had ornamented the interior of the enclosed front hall (*gūḍha-maṇḍapa*)—first renovated in the eleventh century by the addition of four elaborately carved central pillars and a new ceiling—with elaborate glittering glass (Plate 1).[4] Over its long life the Khed temple has clearly been valued—its hall was reconfigured and a large new marble image installed in the sanctum in the eleventh century, its carved walls re-polychromed in the early twentieth century—but a contemporary purpose for worshiping this pre-*bhakti* form of Viṣṇu today, freed of its royal connections, has largely been forgotten.

Local individuals still cherish the site and its heritage; yet much recent attention and patronage has shifted to the construction of a new mirrored temple to Brahmā built nearby (the rarity of a Brahmā temple in modern India seen as one of its popular virtues).[5] Large annual festivals still occur, however, and a Temple Trust established in about 1976 has reconfigured the temple's outer compound and provided amenities that can be compared to those at other temples in this study (Plate 3). We were told that the Trust consisted of 20 or 21 elected members. Little printed material was available, save for painted signs with donors' lists, of which a majority were Agravāls and Māheśvarīs from Balotra.

This temple can act as an interesting control for our study. It is patronized locally by merchant castes, seemingly with little of the national draw of our other temples, although there are some donors listed from Mumbai and elsewhere. According to Bhanwar Lal Vaishnav, temple trustee and author of a book on *Kheṛ Mandir* (Vaiṣṇav 1973), the Temple Trust has recently drawn up a twenty-year master plan (interview, 13 February 1998). "Plans so far are to move out the walls of the temple chowk, so one can see the main temple more clearly; to put in new flooring in the chowk; to build a meditation hall; and to build new *dharmśālā* facilities with attached bath and latrine."[6] As John Cort observed (notes 18/ii/98), "some in the trust are interested in raising the status and visibility of this temple; from a temple of purely local interest, they want to raise it to being a temple of some more regional interest." In Cort's words, the temple today still can demonstrate the many "opportunities for *jīrṇoddhār,*" which he has defined with precision as "the lifting up of the old to make it current and fit as the site of worship." The most compelling definition of Khed's current weakened position, however, was L. A. Babb's, that "there is no [current] crystallizing of identity around this temple."

Goth-Manglod, Dadhimatī Mātā Temple

Let me describe three other temples we have studied through fieldwork as examples of temples transformed over time—and in recent times—and perhaps as suggestive of methods for understanding them and their survival. The first—the Dadhimatī Mātā temple near Nagaur (Plate 4)—existed in the seventh century perhaps as no more than a sacred rock with a shelter—much like one now sacralized beside a road near Udaipur (Plate 5). We know from an inscription of Gupta Saṃvat 289 (608 CE), discovered late in the nineteenth century, of grants to this local goddess by a community of "Dadhya" (Dāhimā or Dādhīc?) Brahmans,[7] "meditating on the feet of Dadhimatī" and "protected by the feet of (the king)" according to the seventh-century inscription (Ram Karna 1911–2).[8]

In the ninth century, a stone Nāgara-style temple was built around this sacred rock, but clothed in the imagery of high Brahmanism—the Goddess (in the form of Mahiṣāsuramardinī) placed on the fronton of the *śikhara* and an eclectic array of images on the outer walls of the sanctum: celestial female attendants (*apsaras*es), Dikpāla guardians on the corners; Gaṇeśa (south), the beautiful goddess Kṣemaṅkarī (west) and Pārvatī performing penance (north) on the central projections (Meister 1991d:252–4; 1995e) (Plate 6). In the recessed necking underneath the tower (*śikhara*) are a clockwise set of Rāmāyana narratives starting from the south (Giri and Tiwari 1989).

For the ninth century, under Pratīhāra royal hegemony, these images and the Nāgara stone-temple structure itself proclaimed an established orthodoxy for local praxis, yet the image in the sanctum remained the aniconic stone, and the goddess Dadhimatī remained a local goddess, only stitched into the trans-regional ethos of the *Devī Māhātmya*, Vālmīki's *Rāmāyaṇa*, and the *Purāṇa*s.

From the ninth to the nineteenth century we can reconstruct little of the life of this temple: only that many local communities—Brahman, Jāṭ, and Māheśvarī, even eventually Muslim—utilized the sacrality of the *sthāna*.[9] In the twelfth century there are records of *satī*s being performed within the temple's compound (Somani 1981; 1983:62,

78–9, 110).[10] In the mid-nineteenth century, however, the temple took on a new configuration: four courtyards (*cauks*) were built around the stone structure. This was done under patronage from the Mahārāṇa of Udaipur, at the instance of the Dāhimā Brahmacārī, Viṣṇudās, with work carried out between 1849-51 (Plate 4).[11] A contemporary inscription records both this patronage and that the craftsman (*kārīgar*) was Pīrā Mālīthā of Nagaur (G. N. Śarmā 1915).

How these compounds (and myths) were woven into the identity of a twentieth-century community is a part of L. A. Babb's story of the Dāhimās in this volume. The discovery and publication of the seventh-century inscription, however, helped precipitate formation of an All-India Dāhimā Brāhmaṇa Mahāsabhā early in the twentieth century,[12] and a Temple Trust suitable to recent laws governing public trusts was first established in the 1970s. An additional large compound for pilgrims was added south of the four nineteenth-century *cauks* by the Mahāsabhā, and the current Trust has drawn up plans for a much larger hostel (*dharmśālā*) to be built nearby (Plate 7).[13]

These *cauks* now define the present temple. Rituals followed in worship no longer take into consideration the images on the stone sanctum's outer walls; but move from the image in the *cella* to an aniconic Bherū at the back (underneath the ignored Kṣemaṅkarī statue); then from the small Śiva shrine in the forward *cauk* to a Bherū in the outer *cauk*; and to a recent cella set up in the northwest corner of the temple's *cauk* with an image of the lineage originator, Dadhīci Ṛṣī (Plate 28).

In notes I took during Gupt Navarātrī, 2–3 February 1998, on the issue of how space is used in the present temple, I observed that while the sanctum with Dadhimatī Mātā herself centers the temple ritually, the expanded temple serves much as a house does, with all the flexibilities and layerings of use one finds in a pol, haveli, or palace. At the Dadhimatī Mātā temple, the back veranda was being used to prepare food; the court near the sanctum as the *bhojanśālā* (place for preparing food); the south veranda for administration, singing, and sleeping. In the *maṇḍapa*, the flow of people past the sanctum was in part controlled by a barrier, but a variety of approaches was possible—*darśan* from a distance, circumambulation within the *maṇḍapa* and around the temple, *pūjā* with a priest standing at the sanctum door, etcetera. Individual use of the *maṇḍapa* included recitation, meditation, and so forth. Group use included taking over the central aisle as a place for chants and singing. The deity could be moved outside of the sanctum to a bed in the hall for sleep; and the group of worshipers could be moved from the *maṇḍapa* to the space in front of the entry porch for a final ceremony and for distribution of *prasād* after the temple's sanctum was shut for the night.

Cort commented that this kind of multiple use of temple *cauks* is changing, with much more segregation of functions at more highly populated centers such as Sacciyā Mātā temple or Sālasār Bālājī. This sort of timed flexibility, however, I think is characteristic of the temple's compound as it evolved in early modern India: Cosmic space = the *mūl prāsāda*; ritual space = the *maṇḍapa*; domestic space = a variety of *maṇḍapas* and compounds at different times during the day; pilgrimage space = movement through the *cauk*s, compound, and the surrounding land outside, including the *kapāl kuṇḍ* (see chapter five).

The historical roles of the Dāhimā Brahmacārī, Viṣṇudās, and the Mahārāṇa of Udaipur, Swarūp Singh, in the nineteenth century in making the temple's modern courtyards are conflated in pilgrims' books available at the temple with the myth of the temple's founding in a much much older period, still by the Mahārāṇa, but during the rule of the first (mythic) universal king, Māndhātā.[14]

In spite of this ever-receding historical horizon found in the present, we have been able to recover a reasonably fine-grained history of the reclaiming of this temple and its meanings in the nineteenth and twentieth centuries, fascinating as a model for other transformations that we cannot now recover from a more distant past.

Osian, Temples and Step-well

The Sacciyā Mātā and Mahāvīra temples at Osian, however, provide overlapping and in part archaeologically recoverable histories, both in the distant past and recent present. The many monuments at Osian have been known since D. R. Bhandarkar visited them in 1906–7 and published his reports for the Archaeological Survey (Bhandarkar 1907:36–7; 1912) (Plate 8). Scattered across the desert, these are framed by two living shrines: the Mahāvīra Jain temple, the oldest structural Jain temple surviving in India, and the Sacciyā Mātā temple on the hill, dedicated to a local goddess who converted to Jain ways (Plate 9). The orientation of the site links another hillock, that known as Luṇādrī in the Osvāl myth of the goddess's conversion, on which a Jain sage is said to have settled seventy years after the death of Mahāvīra, leading (at least in this foundation myth) to the building of the Jain temple (Meister 1998; chapter one). This hillock has a small modern structure, a *dādābāṛī,* sheltering a plaque of a twelfth-century sage's footprints (Handa 1984:232) (Plates 28, 29).

Eighth-century Vaiṣṇava, Saura and Śaiva temples stretch from the Luṇādrī hill to the location of the Mahāvīra shrine and the Jain school established early in the twentieth century (Plates 10–12). The north-facing Mahāvīra Jain temple to the south is oriented at right angles to the east-west axis of the Vaiṣṇava temples. The Sacciyā Mātā hill to the left is oriented to the southwest as if in deference to the location of the Mahāvīra temple. In the catchment area between the Mahāvīra temple and the Sacciyā Mātā hill, a large tank and step-well, as part of a larger system to capture and retain water, was constructed late in the eighth century shortly after the original Sacciyā Mātā temple and the Mahāvīra temple had first been built (see chapter four Plates 13–16).[15]

Osian, Sacciyā Mātā Temple and Hill

One part of my research involved reconstruction of phases in the life of these temples, both in the distant and the recent past. I can compare, for example, the Sacciyā Mātā temple's compound as I saw it in 1972 to how one sees it today, transformed by its new festival and ritual use and by new patronage (Plates 17–20, 32). The process of transformation, however, has been both longer and continual.

A small shrine to the northwest on the Sacciyā Mātā hill, for example, was a Vaiṣṇava shrine facing the entry to the hill in the eighth century. It was in ruins at the time of Bhandarkar's visit (Plate 8), and was remade into a practicing "Śrī Satya Nārāyaṇa" temple in the 1920s. Its archaeologically interesting entry pavilion (Meister 1991e:130) was dismantled in the 1970s, its pillars reused elsewhere in the compound. It has now been replaced by a new Sītā-Rāma shrine (Plate 21).

Another significant temple on the hill survives from the eighth century, the Sūrya temple set to the south of the Sacciyā Mātā temple's sanctum (Plate 8). This had partly collapsed at the time of Bhandarkar's visit and was rebuilt by the grandfathers of priests and workmen who are still active at the site today (Plate 11). Three more sub-shrines were added in the tenth and eleventh centuries, and the principal shrine to the goddess was rebuilt by circa 1177 CE by a banker named Gayapāla, replacing an earlier eighth-century structure (Plate 21).

This pattern of replacement, reformulation, and rededication has been part of a process by which this temple has survived—from the eighth to the thirteenth, to the sixteenth, and into the twenty-first century. This was true for both the Sacciyā Mātā and Mahāvīra temples. The Sacciyā Mātā compound today is surrounded by nine newly if only partly constructed shrines for the nine Durgās. The hill is approached up a stairway sheltered by ten new stone gateways (*toraṇas*), built about thirty years ago and more recently adorned with aluminum ornaments (Plates 18, 21) (as Cort had concluded of the current condition of the Raṇchoḍjī temple at Khed, these demonstrate the "many opportunities for *jīrṇoddhār*"). Further *toraṇas* are still being added to define the terrace in front of the Sacciyā Mātā temple's older compound.

The idea for Nava-Durgā shrines had been formulated by the community of hereditary priests (Jugrāj *sevak*, the family of Jugrāj Śarmā, then head priest, who began pressing for renovation of the temple as early as 1959–60) before the present Sacciyā Mātā Temple Trust was established (interview, Makhanlal Varshney, 7 March 1998) (Plate 33). Jugrāj argued that to have all forms of Durgā available for worship at one place would make the temple unique in India. (When the Trust was set up in 1976, Jugrāj was made its Secretary.)

New laws governing temple management and ownership have led to substantial reformulation of the Sacciyā Mātā temple and its mission since the establishment of a Temple Trust. A rapidly developing interest in the healing powers of Sacciyā Mātā by a diaspora of non-image worshiping Osvāl Jains has to a degree eclipsed (or stands parallel to) management by local *pujārīs* and Māheśvarī shopkeepers. This diasporic community has poured large resources into the hands of the local ecumenically organized temple trust.[16] This new patronage has in part created a "new" temple, responsive to modern taste and pilgrimage, a "place" increasingly rediscovered by a Jain community dispersed through

India and now more able easily to come on holiday or pilgrimage (Meister 2000b) (Plate 32).

This, interestingly, was not the expected outcome of the transformation of management in the 1970s when, according to a past headmaster of the Jain School, "the [Sacciyā Mātā] temple was simply in the hands of the *pujārīs* until the Temple Trust was set up in 1976. . . . We made [them] fear that the temple would go to the Government unless we got it registered [as a Public Trust]" (interview, Makhanlal Varshney, 7 March 1998).

At the turn of the last century, the Sacciyā Mātā temple was much more self-contained (Plate 19). Bhandarkar (1907:36) was told that the goddess was then the tutelary deity primarily of "Sāṁkhaḷā Paramāras." Her priests lived in a set of rooms to the northeast, within the temple's fortress-like compound, probably configured in the late Mughal period, which Bhandarkar had not been able to document in his early sketch plan (Plate 8; compare Plate 19). The festival reach of the modern shrine has now reoriented the compound's austere facade, made new paths for large crowds to wend their way through on major occasions like the festival of Navrātrī, and, outside the earlier fort-like compound, has provided opportunities for clients to build facilities for pilgrims and additional shrines (Plates 18, 20).

Osian, Mahāvīra Temple

As a measure of the dimension of change in the twentieth century, we found one printed advertisement in the library of the Jain school from the second decade of the twentieth century urging temple-worshiping Jain pilgrims to take the opportunity to visit the newly refurbished Mahāvīra temple—as well as the goddess temple at Osian—now that the newly built narrow-gage rail line from Jodhpur to Pokaran, which had a stop at Osian, had made such a journey much less demanding for pilgrims. That the story of Osian, its temple, and the conversion of its goddess was known in the nineteenth century, however, is supported by an illustrated *paṭṭāvalī* now in a collection in Gujarat (but with a set of photographs kept by the Jain school) (Plate 30).

The Mahāvīra temple has also undergone numerous transformations, in the past as well as in the last thirty years (Plates 22–24). The temple had been left almost abandoned early in the nineteenth century, with no Jains living in Osian itself, and nearby Jain communities committed to Sthānakvāsī practices, i.e. not worshiping images in temples. Only the priests of the Sacciyā Mātā temple kept the Jain temple's compound alive (they still speak of the two structures forming one temple today), perhaps then as now serving other communities who come to honor the Bherū spirit located on the west exterior wall of the temple's sanctum.

The Mahāvīra temple was first built late in the eighth century, yet in 956 CE the compound was partly reformulated and rededicated, as reported in a long historical inscription once mounted in the rebuilt entry hall to the compound (Handa 1984:216–8). Several sub-shrines, gates, pillars, and a large ceiling for this entry hall (Plate 34) were contributed to the compound in subsequent centuries and the sanctum's superstructure was replaced in the fifteenth century, suggesting a continual process of rebuilding and renewal over a long period (Dhaky 1968).

In 1878, Mohanlāl, a Jain mendicant wandering through Osian with his followers, discovered the Mahāvīra temple (he saw the spire while he was urinating on the desert according to one source) and urged neighboring Jains in Jodhpur and Phalodi to pay for its restoration and rededication. This period of *jīrṇoddhār* lasted from 1879 to 1894.

In 1915, Muni Ratnavijay came to Osian. Seeing that there was no Jain population there to care for the Mahāvīra temple, he suggested starting a Jain school, and requested Phulcand Guleccha of Jodhpur to raise funds to do this. The Śrī Vardhmān Jain Vidyālaya was inaugurated in Osian on July 17, 1915.[17]

Ratnavijay converted the Sthānakvāsī mendicant Jñānsundar to temple worship and requested him to direct the Jain school, help preserve the temple, and return a Jain population to Osian. Jñānsundar dedicated the rest of his life trying to reestablish a lineage of Jain sages from Osian (Plate 28). He died only in the 1950s (see Cort, chapter eight, this volume).

Modern Remakings

In the last thirty years, the Mahāvīra temple again has undergone reformulation, with funds from the Āṇandjī Kalyāṇjī Trust in Ahmedabad.[18] This post-1972 restoration has changed the Mahāvīra temple in significant ways. In order to accommodate activities of boys attending the Jain school, and a growing community of pilgrims and tourists coming in groups, the shallow open entry portico of the temple's *prāsāda* was substantially expanded, adding pillars taken from the compound's two-storied entry pavilion on the north (Plates 22–24). This had been built first in the eighth century, then reformulated in the tenth and twelfth and more recent centuries.

The two-storied entry pavilion (*valānaka*) of my earliest visits, however, no longer stands (Plates 22, 23), but has been replaced by a lower single-storied open entry-hall used now largely to welcome groups of tourists (Plate 24).[19] One part of my work has been to retrace the process of recent patronage and renovation, and to recover evidence of these transformations and their motivations.

Plans and sections before and after the renovations of the past thirty years show starkly the changes made to the compound and this entry hall (Plates 22–24). The compound has been expanded and a single-storied open entry placed at the same level as the courtyard, allowing groups to enter directly and the school boys to have a place to perform.[20] This hall no longer can provide, however, the intimate private eye-level view of the Mahāvīra image that the older two-storied pavilion once gave to small groups of devotees who sat within it (Plate 22).

Of this remaking of the compound's entry pavilion and reformulation of the temple's entry, the school master, Makhanlal Varshney (interview, 7 March 1998), said that they had decided to raise "the door from the outside" that led up to "the entry-hall inside the building"; to lower the floor-level to make it common; and that in order to do this they had needed to re-set the dome, make a new gate from the outside, and make the half and full pillars taller by adding extensions at the base.[21]

The Jain temple today—much like the Dadhimatī Mātā temple and its *cauk*s—can only be fully understood in relation to the Jain school attached to it, which, when it was built, doubled the temple's compound early in the twentieth century (Plate 10). That institution, established in 1915 and added to further over the years, even more radically has transformed the temple than previous revisions, redefining the orphaned shrine as part of a larger living community institution. The original school's cool courtyard now acts as an office and as a place for Jain pilgrims and ascetics to stay; new student dormitories and a government-supported school have recently been built nearby (Plate 12).

The Jain school itself has shifted several times into larger facilities, most recently to the Government-built buildings in the 1970s. These new buildings of the Government school (not precisely the same thing as the community-supported school before) have, however, helped re-establish and re-assert the ancient relationship of the Jain community and the Sacciyā Mātā temple, which is visually framed on axis and seized by the new school's courtyard (Plate 12). In part this assertion is the accidental product of old orientations embedded in the site; but in part it is ironic, given the recent great power of the Sacciyā Mātā Temple Trust.

There continues a standoff between the goddess and Mahāvīra, and between those Jains who worship in Jain temples and those who do not, yet visit the goddess for her miracle cures. I have written elsewhere (Meister 2000a:40) that "a temple is not simply a structure, of one period or even one community. It moves through time, collecting social lightning and resources. It must be repositioned constantly to survive. . . . Both temples and the communities they serve continually redefine their pasts and renegotiate the present."

The goddess Sacciyā Mātā resides above Osian today, still a mystery to multiple communities, her presence continually remade, reclaimed by new and diverse clientele. Sacrality at such sites survives, but its social settings change. Can archaeology learn from living temples? Can a sequence of monuments be fitted into a framework of changing use? The archaeological layering of a monument that once lived can better be understood, it seems to me, if one has also experienced living monuments and their changes.

This essay so far has been about buildings and my documentation of them, and how changes over time are carried out by individual people to suit multiple and diverse human uses (Plate 25). There is a further issue, however, that ties these institutions to the "lawyers and bureaucrats" of Cort's tale (chapter seven, this volume) of twentieth-century modernization, that of the nature of temple trusts. These temples—and the communities who have used and tried to manage them in the twentieth century—have been affected by the evolving laws, first of a colonial state, then of a new democratic nation. These need to become part of this discussion.

Trusting Temples

Early Hinduism focused on rites of sacrifice; temples to shelter images of deities began as instruments of cults. To patronize cult communities became a means to extend kingship; and through such royal and community patronage, temples gradually became public institutions. Arjun Appadurai (1978:48) wrote, "In classical Indian thought, generosity to Brahmans, codified as the 'law of the gift' (*dānadharma*), was an important element of the role of kings":

> [I]n the late seventh and early eighth centuries, a fundamental change occurred in the conception of what constitutes sovereignty: the giving of gifts, which was previously only one element of the basic definition of kings as *sacrificers*, now became the central constituent of sovereignty. This shift . . . coincides with the beginnings of temple-building associated with Purānic deities.

Ronald Inden (2000:46) also has outlined a shift in this same time period in North India from sacrificial to image-worshiping liturgies that led to the substitution of temple rituals for those of sacrifice.

How temples have functioned as institutions—leaving aside the commonalities of their symbolic architectural vocabularies (Meister 1986a)—has varied widely over the long history of temple Hinduism, adapting in remarkable ways to social change (Stein 1978). That this is as true in the last few decades as in past centuries for the temples we studied is part of our conclusion.

In the nineteenth century, the temples we have studied in Rajasthan seem by default largely to have been run by communities of hereditary priests (*pujārīs*, *sevaks*).[22] Temple lands in Rajasthan had largely been divided among Sevaks' families.[23] In the twentieth century, however, user communities began to identify temples and myths of origin as sources for reformulating self-identity (Babb 2004). Both local and transnational, these "subaltern" histories have not been easy to recover, and before independent India they were—as in the case of the Dadhimatī Mātā temple—worked out largely in piecemeal and litigious ways. These can seem as petty as the struggle of local Dāhimās for the keys to the *bartan bhaṇḍār* (storeroom for ritual implements). Yet they represent how temples stay alive. In the histories presented in this volume, some of the texture of that daily struggle we hope may have been captured.

New Frames

To the above I would wish to add a note on the changes wrought in the second half of the twentieth century by laws of independent India. Underlying the fabric of changes we have observed and the development of community management in the form of Temple Trusts is a significant shift in India's laws.[24]

Early in the century, as with the local trust for the Jain School and Mahāvīra temple at Osian, established in 1915, or the *All-India* Dāhimā Brāhmaṇa Mahāsabhā (Calcutta,

1924), single communities found common cause. In the 1960s, these were replaced by multi-community boards of trustees in the form of Public Trusts, which were required to register with a Devasthanam office set up by the State. Some significant shifts in management and patronage we found at Khed, Osian, and Goth-Manglod fit a chronology matching shifts in the application of these laws.

Social Legislation

The beginning of new India's approach to temples and the communities who used and managed them can be found in the Bombay Public Trusts Act, 1950, "*An Act to regulate and to make better provision for the administration of public religious and charitable trusts*" (K. N. Shah 1997). The preamble to this Act deserves extensive citation (ibid.:3; S. L. Gupta 1990:77):

> There are instances of how Mahants, Pujaris, Bhatjis and Acharayas who have lived on the temple income for years and flourished fat on the earnings of the Holy shrines have the hardihood of asserting their proprietary rights over such shrines and attempting to devour and appropriate the deity and donations to themselves. Though they may have for generations held out to and invited innumerable devotees for *Darshan*, and hundreds of devotees may have openly come for *Darshan*, and worshiped the idol for years, and though donations, offerings and emoluments may have been begged, asked for, offered and received uninterruptedly, when it comes to registration of the Temple as a Public Trust and accounting for its income, they would not stop of claiming exclusive rights of ownership not only over the income but the idol, the deity of the temple too. They, the preservers of the deity and the spiritual heads, the supposed saviours of the souls of sinners & the sanctity of the holy shrine would go to any length to perjure themselves, if they could not establish their ownership over the endowment and its property, and derive the material benefit of getting its income. Such instances are not few.[25] The richer the endowment, the greater the temptation to swallow the same. To such impious Pujaris, Managers and Mahants, nothing matters: considerations neither of this world nor the next, if they could only serve their selfish end. Such instances, justify the passing of and the utility of this act.

The Bombay Public Trusts Act was adapted and modified through the 1950s, and became the model for the Rajasthan Public Trusts Act, 1959 (S. L. Gupta 1990:73–212) and laws in other states. It is no accident that the head priest at Osian, Jugrāj, took interest in the establishment of the Sacciyā Mātā Temple Trust, or that he was joined by merchants in the community.

Public/Private

According to the Bombay Public Trusts Act, 1960 (K. N. Shah 1997:97), "The distinction between a private temple and public temple is now well settled. In the former case the beneficiaries are specific individuals; in the latter they are indeterminate or fluctuating general public or a class thereof." Rajasthan's "Rules for the Cash Grant-in-aid to Temples and Other Religious and Charitable Institutions" (S. L. Gupta 1997:617–18) makes one factor crucial to a Public Trust clear.[26] While these "apply to all cash grant-in-aid given by the Devasthan Department of the State," they are only "admissible to the temples and other religious and charitable institutions so long as they are open to all classes of public without any restriction of caste or creed."

That temples like Dadhimatī Mātā and Sacciyā Mātā now serve multiple communities is to their advantage. That the Dāhimā Brāhmaṇa Mahāsabhā fought throughout the last century to establish one community's control over management is not, and has led to numerous trips to law courts and the Devasthanam Department to settle disputes.

The law's distinction between Public and Private gives importance to subtle negotiations among users and to good management (S. L. Gupta [1997:111], citing the case of *Goswami Shri Mahalaxmi Vahuji vs. Rannchhoddas Kalidas,* 1970): "the origin of the temple, the manner in which its affairs are managed, the nature and extent of gifts received by it, rights exercised by the devotees in regard to worship therein, the consciousness of the manager and the consciousness of the devotees themselves as to the public character of the temple are factors that go to establish whether a temple is a public temple or a private temple."

Private temples can still be owned by families and run as businesses. Nirmala Joshi's family, for example, has had a Hanuman temple in its village allotted to it from Mughal times, but she pointed out that revenues from such family-owned temples are now fully taxable as income in modern India, at circa fifty percent.[27] In a case such as that of the Moti Dungri Ganesh (Gaṇeśa) temple in Jaipur, owned and managed by a Dāhimā Brahman family, the family can hire *pujārī*s to carry out daily rituals, and such temple expenses are tax-deductible; or "a temple charitable trust can be set up, which gives considerable tax shelter."[28]

Implementation

A Public Trust is for religious or charitable purposes. It is not the same thing as a Society, which comes under a separate act and is limited to science, education, etc. Law Books warn about mixing the two. Public Trust Acts define how a new public trust can be set up or an existing one recognized, and make it a matter of law for Government to keep a register of such trusts, but do not make it obligatory for an existing trust to register immediately.

Rajasthan Local Laws, sec. 17.[3] (S. L. Gupta 1990, 138), however, adds a dated addendum: "*Registration is compulsory.*—It has been made compulsory on the trustees of a public trust under the Act for the registration of the public trusts within the specified time lest the trustees be liable for disabilities," citing a 1972 decision "*Jagannath vs. Satya Narayan, 1972 RLW 491; 1972 RLW 709.*"

It no longer seems strange to me that the Sacciyā Mātā, Mahāvīra, and Dadhimatī Mātā Temple Trusts all finally appear to have been registered in the early 1970s, although modern Public Trust Acts existed a decade or more before that. (Note that "*Jagannath vs*

Satya Narayan" cited above was only settled in 1972.) This flurry of reorganization—in the case of Osian's Jain school and the All-India Dāhimā Brāhmana Mahāsabhā, involving separation of a Temple Trust from previously existing charitable Societies—was the result of pragmatic compulsion.

An appendix in K. N. Shah (1997: 941–1010), entitled "Public Charitable and Public Religious Trusts Taxation and Exemption of their Incomes from Income-Tax Act, 1961," has a long "Table Showing Applicability of Provisions for Different Assessment Years." This makes explicit that for Assessment years 1962–63 to 1970–71 there was an "unconditional exemption"; for 1971–6, Public Trusts were still "Unconditionally exempted": "However . . . Any income which is not applied to the purposes of trust during the previous year to which it relates or which is not *deemed* to have been applied . . . will be liable to tax as if such income were the total income of an association of persons."

For assessment year 1976–77, Trusts were only exempt "if 75% of the income is applied to the purposes of the trust. . . ." A section in a Table on "Accumulation of Income" breaks down this same crucial time-period as follows:

> 1962–71: exempt, subject to conditions [75% has to be invested in Government securities];
>
> 1971–76: same, but extended to other approved securities;
>
> 1976– : Failure to fulfil conditions will result in taxability of accumulation in excess of 25% of income (inclusive of non-corpus *voluntary contribution*).

Basically, for existing trusts in 1962, there was a ten-year tax exemption, then they got socked with regulations. According to K. N. Shah (1997:967):

> In order that the concessional [tax] treatment . . . is available to a trust . . . it is necessary that it must have made an application for its registration . . . to the concerned Chief Commissioner or the concerned Commissioner of Income-tax. . . . The application has to be made before 1-7-73 or before the end of one year from the date of creation of a trust or institution, whichever is later.

In other words, to apply for income-tax exemption an existing trust had to get itself registered—or at least an application filed—by 1 July 1973.

Significance

The Rājpūt vice-president of the Sacciyā Mātā Temple Trust, then a Member of the Legislative Assembly, N. S. Bhati (interview, 30 January 1998) told us, "in the early days of the Trust there were problems with the *pujārī*s. Before the trust, all the money and ornaments offered to the goddess went to the *pujārī*s, but now this is controlled." (He stressed several times that the Trust is on the whole well and responsibly managed in terms of finances.) He believed that "the Trust was formed in response to the requests of pilgrims for a regularized organization to which they could give donations." Both Annual Reports of the Trust and records kept by *pujārī*s suggest such regularized organization is indeed in place.

Perhaps the Raṇchoḍjī temple at Khed, the least successful of the living temples we've studied, does act as a foil for the varied successes of others. Cort (notes 13.ii.98) had commented on "the Balotra baniyās, for whom looking after the temple is part of their larger portfolio of charitable works" and concluded (17.ii.98):

> At Khed we have, I think, something a bit akin to the Rotarian or Fraternal approach to temple management: the local merchants view it as part of their overall portfolio of publically visible charitable giving, but it is not important enough to consume too large a part of any one person's portfolio, and again the lack of either a charismatic holyman or wonder-working deity takes away the *puṇya* factor in giving.

Each one of the temples we've studied, in its own way, location, and from its own history, within the laws of modern India, has found ways to accommodate itself to India's contemporary commodity society.

Notes

1. There are two festivals a year, with up to a lakh of pilgrims; neither is special to any single caste. Local fairs are held on full-moon nights. According to a conversation with Purushottam Gupta, temple trustee (Cort's notes, 13/ii/98), "the two big annual fairs are Kartik Purnima and Radhastami. The latter is the anniversary date of the establishment of the temple."
2. Vaiṣṇav (1973) attributed this painting of the *garbha-gṛha* to Māndās Vaiṣṇav and other renovation over the past sixty to sixty-five years to Balotra residents.
3. Bhanwar Lal Vaishnav, temple trustee, interviewed on 13 February 1998, referred to *jīrṇoddhār* "by one Mukundcandji about 40 years ago," but gave a date of VS 1980 (1923 CE).
4. We were told that this mirror work was done about ten or eleven years before; one old man insisted it was 250 years old.
5. This temple was set up by Chandmal Chandak, a Māheśvarī trustee of the Raṇchoḍjī temple.
6. Similar facilities also have been part of recent additions to the other three temples in our study.
7. "Dāhimā" can be used to refer to multiple communities from the area of this temple; "Dādhīc" relates the lineage of "Dāhimā" Brāhmaṇs to the legend of an ancient sage, Dadīchi (Meister 1998). The shift of designation toward "Dādhīc" in this century is discussed by Babb, chapter nine. The inscription speaks of "Dadhya" Brahmans, now taken to be the present community.
8. Bhandarkar (1907:31), who studied the original inscription where it was stored in the Historic Office in Jodhpur, recorded that this "inscription was removed from an old temple of Dadhmat *mātā*, the tutelary deity of the Dāhimā Brāhmaṇas, lying between the villages of Goṭh and Mānglod in the Nagaur district." A copy of the inscription by Ram Narayan Asopa, with an additional history of the Dāhimās upto the present, has been mounted to the left of the doorway in the temple's hall (Ram Karna 1911–2).
9. During an interview, 7 January 1992, with Jagdish Chandra Bhatt, Dāhimā *rājguru* of the City Palace temple, Jaipur, his son, Ravi Das Sharma, reported that some "Muslim Dāhimās" come to the temple who "treat it as a *pīr*."
10. Somani cites inscriptions dated VS 1232 and 1249 (1175 and 1192 CE) and the *Annual Report of Indian Epigraphy 1965–66*, B-487.

11. Jośī (n.d.): "According to an inscription of samvat 1908 [1851 CE] in the temple, at the instructions of Brahmacārī Viṣṇudāsjī of Buḍhādeval, Mahārāṇā Svarūpsingh of Udaipur built outside the temple the *cauks*, gates, pilgrim rest-house, well, Shiv temple, etc., and renovated the Kapāl Kuṇḍ" (trans. Cort). For this inscription, mounted to the right in the front entry porch, also see G. N. Śarmā 1915.
12. Vaidya Buddhi Prakash Acharya (interview, 25 December 1991) reported that the All-India Dāhimā Brāhmaṇa Mahāsabhā began circa 1920–24. D.R. Bhandarker had invited Pt. Ram Karna Asopa to teach in Calcutta in 1919, and Asopa was president of the "15th annual meeting of the Akhil Bhāratvarṣīya Śrī Dāhimā Brāhmaṇ Mahāsabhā," Calcutta, in 1924 (G. Asopa 1940; I. Āsopā 1993:90–94). The fourteenth, and I believe all previous ones, had been held at the temple, making this the first "All-India" session.
13. The many wells outside the compound represent the many communities who use the temple (each with its own source of water). Representatives of both the Dāhimā Mahāsabhā and the local and public trusts that have managed the temple have emphasized that the Goddess serves multiple communities, however, and that disputes have been over management.
14. For the story of King Māndhātar contained in the *Divyāvadāna* 18 and the Kah-gyur, see Schiefner (1906:1–20).
15. K.C. Jain (1972:468), citing Jñānsundar (n.d.) as his source, reported that Kakkasūri, writing in his 1336 CE *Nābhinandanajinoddhāra*, had recorded "tanks and a wonderful stepwell called Vidagdhā at Osiā." See also Handa (1984:232).
16. "When we made the Trust we took new members from all different communities: Vaiṣṇav, Jain, Rājpūt, Māheśvarī, Jāṭ (Chaudrī), Sonī, Khatrī, Sevak, etc." (interview, Makhanlal Varshney, 7 March 1998).
17. This narrative is incorporated into volumes of printed annual reports of the temple trust, from VS 2002–18, and the school trust, from VS 1993–2008, provided us at the school, and in the school's diamond jubilee commemoration volume, 1988 CE.
18. Āṇandjī Kalyāṇjī Trust involvement in renovation at Osian was from 1976 only (interview, Amrat Lal and Krishna Chandra Sompura, Ahmedabad, 28 July 1996).
19. M.A. Dhaky observed of the then existing two-storied *valānaka* (Dhaky 1968:312–14) that it "is also known as Nālamaṇḍapa by virtue of its construction above the principal stairway of the Jagatī."
20. Bhanu Prakash, *pujārī* at the temple, explained this change as needed so that pilgrims didn't "bump their heads."
21. Krishna Chandra Sompura of the Āṇandjī Kalyāṇjī Trust, Ahmedabad, (interview, 28 July 1996) reported that in 1976 the Mahāvīra temple's entry "was like Kumbhariya, that is, you went up into the entry hall, then down into the temple. The ground level had shifted."
22. Bhanu Prakash, interview, 8 February 1996, reported that "seventy-five years ago, before the school, the Mahāvīra temple was managed by the village *pujārī*." Vaidya Buddhi Prakash Acharya, interview, 25 December 1991, said of the Dadhimatī Mātā temple that for the "last 200 years the temple was in the hands of priests [who were] not Dāhimā Brahmans but *sevaks*. In 1924, Dāhimā Brahmans went to court to establish ownership. They couldn't provide security money. They then tried to get the temple taken over by the Antiquities Act. The reply [in 1928?] says that the temple was [to be] turned over to the community. The Management Committee includes persons of other castes."
23. Nirmala Joshi, interview, 18 January 1998.
24. Rajendra Joshi first pointed out to me the importance of the post-independence Devasthana Act, which took revenue land away from priests, and to the incentives it gave to communities (collectively) to take control of temples at a party for Komal Kothari, Jaipur, 4 January 1992.

25. S.L. Gupta (1990:77), misquotes this as "Such instances are few."
26. The manager of the temple at Khed (interview, 12 February 1998) had said, "for development of the temple, one need only give the Government a 'master plan' and the Government will give seventy percent."
27. Interview, 18 January 1998.
28. According to Nirmala Joshi, "the Ganesh temple has a weekly income of circa one lakh, much of which is then used for the money-lending business. Understandably there was a tax raid the year before."

4

Water in a Desert Landscape

MICHAEL W. MEISTER

The high rolling sand dunes of India's Thar desert begin at the edge of the village of Osian[1] (Handa 1984; Meister 2003a) and march west toward Pokaran, Jaisalmer, across the Rajasthan canal, and on to Cholistan (Mughal 1997). To Osian's east lies what can best be called scrub desert, stretching beyond Jodhpur and the great Salt Lake, even beyond the city of Jaipur, Rajasthan's state capital, where tigers once roamed forests in living memory—the result of relatively recent desertification. At Osian, circa forty-one miles north-northwest of Jodhpur, a group of seventh-to-twelfth-century temples of some reputation have been studied, if intermittently, for over a hundred years (Bhandarkar 1912; Viennot 1976; Kalia 1982; Handa 1984; Meister 1991c–e), yet their liminal position in this high desert landscape has hardly been noted.

The oldest extant Jain temple in western India (Dhaky 1968) lies at Osian—the Mahāvīra temple, first established in the eighth century—as well as a goddess temple dedicated to Sacciyā Mātā, perhaps founded as early as the eighth century but rebuilt in the twelfth. The Sacciyā Mātā temple retains national as well as regional importance for pilgrims. Remarkable changes have occurred to both monuments as pilgrimage centers since my first visit in 1965 (Meister 1995c).

Both have been transformed by new conservation and construction. The Mahāvīra temple's entry hall and court have been reformed and the levels changed. The Sacciyā Mātā temple's presence for pilgrims has been expanded by the addition of a series of gates leading up the hill and by a ring of nine newly built shrines for the Nava-Durgās.

The foundation myth of Osvāl Jains and of the lineage of the Upakeśa Gaccha records an ancient visit by a passing sage, Ratnaprabhasūri, who settled on a hillside at Osian from the air as he was flying by (Hoernle 1890; Jñānsundar 1929). By performing miracles and through conversations and instruction he was able to convert both a large part of the population of Osian—and the goddess Sacciyā Mātā herself—to Jainism. The otherwise nondescript Luṇādrī hill to the southeast at Osian is still marked by a small white-washed shed with two votive foot-print plaques within, one inscribed in 1189 CE (Handa 1984:224, 232).[2]

As this volume records, John Cort, L. A. Babb, and I have studied these shrines as part of an on-going project addressing "continuities of community patronage" at pilgrimage temples in Western India. A dozen other temples were built at Osian from the seventh to twelfth centuries, oriented in different ways, but clustered, in my analysis, around Osian as a catchment area for water in this high desert landscape (Plate 13).

A large multi-storied step-well and tank placed at the core of the sacred center acts as the most formal expression of this function, but two other temples nearby seem also to have had small tanks.[3] Outside of Osian to the east there are also remnants of multiple dikes (*bands*) used to dam and collect water linking hills that border the town. In a region with an average rainfall of under five inches in a year, these must primarily have slowed down runoff, reduced evaporation and promoted the absorption of rainwater into the local water table (from which the tanks in Osian were sometimes filled) (Agarwal and Narain 1997).

This paper draws on documentation carried out at Osian by a multi-disciplinary team, but directs that documentation toward the link between landscape and temple symbolism to answer a question that I, as the art historian on the team, was frequently asked: "Why were all of these temples built here?"

Located midway in the sacred zone, the large well, step-well, and tank complex at Osian was still substantially buried when I first visited it in 1965 and 1971 (Plate 13). (At present it is surrounded by dense thorn thickets planted by the Government to keep the desert sands away.) Two ornamented pavilions, with broad niches at the back and pillars with beautifully carved capitals, once acted as viewing platforms half-way up the height of the cistern.

This vast tank has been excavated in recent years to a depth of seven levels and in part restored under the auspices of the Rajasthan State Department of Archaeology and Museums (Plate 14). Local sculptors and artisans were called upon to do this work (one, Chuna Ram Prajapat [Plate 25], is a leading local sculptor also called upon to carve replacements for damaged images at the Mahāvīra temple). The rebuilt tank unfortunately is still not appropriately maintained. (At my last visit sewage from nearby habitation trickled in from the northwest corner, producing a mass of plant-growth and slime.)

At the tank's center, the rectangular basin has seven stepped layers of steep stairs (*ghāṭ*s) on north, west, and south, to provide access to water (Plate 16). On the east, there were once two, narrow, L-shaped, stairway-corridors that allowed users to descend from ground level to doors into the two balconies. These viewing pavilions over-looked a central gap or sluice-gate that allowed ground water from the shaft of a deep draw-well behind to flow or be transported into the tank. As in other step-wells, accommodation of drought or flood conditions was considered, so that water could be obtained from several levels (Mankodi 1991).

At desert level on the east there are remains of a gatehouse that enclosed a circular space perhaps meant to allow oxen to draw up skins of water from this deep well (Plate 16). Placed in relation to the Mahāvīra Jain temple and the Sacciyā Mātā hill, and with two other later temples with remains of tanks (*kuṇḍs*) nearby, this giant water-construction marks not merely public works and public service, but a rationale for Osian as a *tīrtha* or holy place marked by many temples.

On the east side of the step-well's *kuṇḍ* and exposed by recent excavation, two massive masonry buttresses look like shrines, with ornamented curvilinear *śikhara*-like superstructures, yet they had no *sancta* nor housed a deity. They rather frame the gateway channel through which water from the sacred earth entered into the tank.

Water was the origin of Osian's sacrality and temple building, as water was the "source of all things" in India's ancient cosmology (Coomaraswamy 1993). In this desert landscape, to locate water and to create access was to open up the cosmos. In its presence, local goddesses or Jain sages could take up residence as witnesses on hills nearby; land and hills themselves were conceived as stemming from cosmic waters, to which Osian's *tīrtha* gave a gate.

Osian's sacred landscape subtly nestles into the scenery, desert seeming to deny the water that lies beneath (Plate 13). The original line of temples built on the desert through the eighth century stretched from the Luṇādrī hill on the east to the present Jain temple and school on the west (beyond this, dunes of the high desert begin). It is precisely the almost unperceived dip in the desert between that captures available groundwater and makes it accessible to wells and tanks temple builders made to mark the site. To the northwest, Sacciyā Mātā's hill appropriately deflects to the south-southeast, the direction of this sump, seeming even to bow to this source (Plate 12). (The earliest shrine surviving on Sacciyā Mātā's hill—the present to Satya Nārāyaṇ temple and its gate—is oriented fully northwest and the last temple built on the desert below in the ninth century—the present Viṣṇu temple no. 2—to the southeast.)[4]

That temples have tanks or should be located near sacred waters is a cliché of texts on temple building from the time of Varāhamihira in the sixth century CE (Meister 2003b:255), yet the empowerment of water—its capacity to make the sacred—is nowhere more apparent than at Osian. A similar large tank-and-well was built in Rajasthan near the Vaiṣṇava temple at Abaneri early in the ninth century, but the tank there should be seen as the ground for the temple, not the temple the rationale for the well (Meister and Dhaky 1991:237). Perhaps, by its location on axis with the temple's sanctum, the remarkable rectangular water tank built in the eleventh-century in front of the Sun temple at Modhera in Gujarat (Herdeg 1967; Lobo 1982; Hegewald 2002) more fully pronounces its sacred (as well as secular) functions; but both root the temple to the earth. (At Modhera there is also a small step-well outside the temple compound.)

As a result of recent conservation carried out at Modhera, this tank now mostly remains dry. This is because a mistake was made by sealing the rebuilt well, thus making it waterproof when its stones were replaced. What this has done is to seal the groundwater *out*, making clear why similar tanks, as at Osian, needed no drains. They are designed as filters, to pull natural groundwater in. Existing water makes the temple possible.

That water underlies growth and maturation of the cosmos, its differentiation, might seem a logical position in India's ripe agrarian landscapes; yet to see water under the desert, as at Osian, sets an extreme frame for understanding India's "water cosmology" (Coomaraswamy 1993). I am struck, going back to early-twentieth-century illustrations of the story of Jain conversion at Osian, that the sage Ratnaprabhasūri is shown most often in a water-filled landscape, not a desert landscape like that of Rajasthan.[5] In one of these images from Osian's narrative, labeled "Ratnaprabhasūri meets Svayamprabhasūri," Svayamprabhasūri is shown seated on a lotus, its stem growing up from water (Plate 14). (A portrait of Jñānsundar, Osian's great twentieth-century promoter, also shows him in front of a painting of a water-filled landscape [Plate 28].)

That so powerful a mythic world has persisted into twentieth-century sources is a testament to a world-view that can see beyond the desert's veil and could tap water that was actually present without having to build a concreted Rajasthan canal (a leaky branch pipe-line of which is the reason for the Osian village's considerable recent urban growth) (Agarwal and Narain 1997).

At Mandor, near Jodhpur, a small ancient L-shaped step-well (Plate 14, bottom right) was cut through solid rock and bears an inscription dated VS 742 (685 CE) (Meister 1991e:125). Carved to either side were two sculpture panels, one with the seven mothers dancing with Gaṇeśa and Naṭeśa, and one to the left of cosmic Śiva seated on a lotus, much like Svayamprabhasūri in the print from Osian, its stalk growing up from the waters flanked by snake-devotees (Plate 14, bottom). It is this same cosmically centered model that early twentieth-century illustrations invoke, as does the site of Osian.

It is from the presence of very real water, hidden by desert sands, that Osian's temples spring; their deities embody cosmic creation, not merely cultic diversity. Because of this water Osian *tīrtha* exists. It is the water of the cosmic ocean that twentieth-century images invoke to portray the reality of Osian—invisible water made visible by temples sprouting in a desert landscape.

Notes

1. 26ºE18'N, 73º1'E.
2. "Now people generally believe these foot-prints to be those of Ratna-prabha as is also borne out by a recent renovatory inscription of these foot-prints" (this inscription was installed at the instructions of Muni Jñānsundar in 1909 CE) (Handa 1984:232).

3. The Sūrya-Viṣṇu and Pīpalā-devī temples (nos. 9 and 12, Plate 12).
4. These are numbered 2 and 14 in Plate 12.
5. Both illustrations from Jñānsundar (1929) are signed "D.C. Mali"; the one on the left is dated 1928. Jñānsundar helped found the Jain school at Osian early in the century and did much to recreate the myth of Osian for Jains (see chapter eight). He installed an inscription concerning renovation of the foot-print shrine on Luṇādri hill in 1909 CE (see note 2).

5

Light on the Lotus

Temple Decoration or Essential Form?

MICHAEL W. MEISTER

Sometime by the seventh century, a goddess partly emerged from the earth near Manglod, startling a herdsman who halted her emergence by his cries. All that marks her presence is her knee or elbow, emerging—as is the case with many other local goddesses in Rajasthan—as a natural stone (Plate 5).[1] Such stones are ornamented by ritual, silvered, dressed with color and flowers. Around this goddess, who took the name Dadhimatī Mātā, local Brahmans built a *sthāna* or sacred platform early in the seventh century.[2]

The seventh-century inscription that records their donations also records that this community of Brahmans were called "Dadhya," now taken to be the present community of Dāhimā Brahmans who still worship Dadhimatī as their clan goddess or *kul devī* (Ram Karna 1911–2).[3]

The present stone temple to Dadhimatī, located between Goth and Manglod villages in Nagaur district, replaced the original *sthāna*; it was built perhaps in the second quarter of the ninth century, on the basis of art-historical evaluation of the temple's architectural form and stone decoration (Meister 1991d:252–54) (Plate 6).

The sanctum floor of this enclosure is at the level of the original shrine, sunk several feet below the present hall's level.[4] In one published photo, the stone is covered with a silver mask and ornamented as it was worshiped in circa 1989 (Meister 1993:fig. 35). Today a new mask, ritual implements, and shelter have replaced those (Plate 5).

The myths of the Dāhimā Brahmans connect their lineage to the sage Dadhīci, who gave his bones to Indra to make a *vajra* powerful enough to slay an earth-threatening demon (*Dadhimathī Purāṇa* 20.19–23; *Bhāgavata Purāṇa* VI.9–10). Only a cow could lick away his flesh to free that essential substance (Plate 28, bottom). Dādhīc Brahmans today trace their lineage to this sage and to his protective relationship with their goddess (J. N. Asopa 1988), including a medieval branch that "left true practice," perhaps even becoming Muslim.[5]

A shrine to this sage Dadhīci was installed in the court (*cauk*) surrounding the Goddess's shrine several decades ago (Plates 4, 28).[6] His image has also been set up in public places (primarily traffic circles) in Jaipur and Jodhpur in recent years to reinforce the identity of the community.[7] In the village of Borunda, however, we encountered a less reverent folk version of the story of Dadhīci and Indra.[8] In that version, Indra had left his most powerful weapon in the sage Dadhīci's care. By using it as a pestle, Dadhīci over time absorbed all of its essence through the herbs he ground for his own consumption. In the words of this village bard, "he had drunk the rolled *bhāṅg* of *vajra* for 5,000 years (which was given to him by Śiva)," thus inspiring Indra's request for his bones.[9]

The sculptures that ornamented the shrine in the ninth century (Plate 6) show that this local goddess, Dadhimatī, was then being clothed by associations with the deities of Puranic Hinduism (Meister 1991d:252–54). On the high *śukanāsa* fronton facing the temple is an image of what we normally identify as Durgā slaying a buffalo demon. This same typological form of the Goddess, however, can often be seen used elsewhere in Rajasthan as the visible image for a number of other locally powerful goddesses like Dadhimatī, such as Pādāmātā or Osian's famed Sacciyā Mātā, in both her guise as a Hindu and as a Jain goddess (Dhaky 1967).

Over the sanctum's doorway also sits an image of the goddess with Śiva above. On the lintel in front of the foyer to the sanctum that frames the space that shelters the goddess's immediate worshipers, the long narrative of the slaying of the buffalo demon is portrayed once again.

Images on the sanctum's outer walls show *dikpāla*s guarding the directions on the corners. The central offsets show Gaṇeśa on the south, a beautiful form of Durgā as Kṣemaṅkarī on the west and Pārvatī performing yogic austerities (herself "burning as the fifth flame") on the north. Above, below the *śikhara*, is a necking with a long sculpted narrative with multiple scenes from the epic *Rāmāyaṇa* (Giri and Tiwari 1986:161–74) (Plate 6).

Clothed in this ecumenical web of Brahmanical Hinduism, this local goddess, however, remains also herself, worshiped by many other communities as well as by the Dāhimā Brahmans who take her name.[10] A community of nearby Jāṭs from Bidyasar (Ratav) also take her to be their local protective goddess, telling a tale of mayhem and murder solved by her intervention at the beginning of their lineage.[11]

These communities have returned to the temple over many centuries, reusing and elaborating it as a form of ornament to the goddess. In the mid-nineteenth century in particular, a Dāhimā sage who was an advisor to the king of Mewar was rewarded by him by having the temple substantially repaired and its compound enlarged.[12] He added the four large open courts that now encase the historical structure, to which a fifth was added to serve as a much larger *dharmśālā* by the Dāhimā community in the twentieth century (Plate 7).[13]

This entire set of compounds must be understood as being the temple today. The legend of the Mahārāṇā of Udaipur's patronage has been conflated in community myth with vague knowledge of the sanctum's seventh-century foundation inscription, and pamphlets state that the temple built by the Mahārāṇā was built by him in a much more ancient mythic time.[14]

Each encasement of the goddess is a new decoration and a new manifestation. Form itself is the ornament (Meister 1995a). A "temple" is best understood as decorated by its worship and worshipers, as threads adorn the pillar next to the sanctum at Dadhimatī. These are tied by pilgrims who believe that to do so gives them powerful benefits (*camatkār*). Community memory says this pillar floated above its base until a generation ago as a symptom of its magical power.[15]

Without such memory, ornament loses meaning (Meister 1990). The ninth-century sculptures that I, as an historian, can interpret have largely lost their identity in the present temple.[16] Few worshipers even look at them. Ritual ambulation at the temple now goes from worship of the mask in the sanctum to a Bherū placed below the west *bhadra*, then to the shrine in the temple's compound set up to honor the ancestral sage, Dadhīci (Plate 4).[17]

Worship moves from the centrality of the goddess's shrine out to newer shrines in other *cauks* set up to honor Śiva, Hanumān, a second Bherū, as well as Dadhīci (Plate 28, bottom). Like the temporary mask that covers her autochthonous elbow in the sanctum; like the implements and adornment of ritual; like the sculpted images that clothe the historical sanctum and the expanding architectural compounds that made the temple new; it is this life of worship that makes the goddess's presence real. It is this "ornament" that gives the image, the temple, the lives of the devotees form (Meister 1995a) (Plate 27).

Finally, of course, within the calendrical cycle of ritual, the goddess is ritually placed within a temporary image kept in an early twentieth-century painted palanquin within the *maṇḍapa*, moved to a modern horse-drawn chariot mounted on a jeep, and taken in procession by worshipers to celebrate the decorating spirals of worship in real time (Plate 34, bottom). She is returned to the front of the temple's podium for group worship in the evening, then her presence returned to the permanent object in the sanctum within. Carrying out such seasonal festivals is as much a part of ornament as of her rituals.[18]

There is also an exceptional and archaeologically related ninth-century temple in nearby Didwana, now re-dedicated to a local goddess called Pādāmātā, that has had very little of this ritual life woven around it through the passage of time and the vicissitudes of its history.[19] Perhaps the elaborate sculptural ornamentation preserved on this temple's walls can better represent what we usually talk of as "temple ornament," more than the ritual life of the Dadhimatī Mātā temple on which I have chosen to focus this essay (Plate 27).[20]

Yet in the case of this wall, if I choose to read its iconography carefully, I come back to its physical ornament as a marker of manifestation.[21] On this temple's north wall, in the necking at the top beneath the *śikhara,* for example, to the left under the shadow of the *maṇḍapa*'s awning, is a startling depiction of a goddess, in her form as slayer of the buffalo demon, emerging from the earth in the presence of cattle and herdsmen (Plate 27, bottom). This contemporaneous ninth-century "vision" of a goddess becoming physically manifest can only take us back to the continuing local myth of Dadhimatī Mātā's emergence near Goth-Manglod (Plate 28, bottom).[22]

Along this necking around the temple are a series of other depictions of Puranic goddesses and gods, while on the central *bhadra* of the wall below Durgā again presides in her iconic reality as buffalo slayer (Plates 6, 27). The miscellaneous narrative cycle under the *śikhara*, however—as with *Rāmāyaṇa* scenes on the Dadhimatī Mātā temple—would seem to be about the necessary rooted reality of ornament as representing the process of manifestation within time and history (Meister 1996).

The life of ritual marks and makes the temple live.[23] At Dadhimatī Mātā, while I was there for the celebration of spring Navrātrī, as the procession brought the temporary form of the goddess out to be worshiped on the edge of her tank, a great spring rainstorm blew across this desert *tīrtha*, as if the goddess were ready to spring forth from the earth again (Plate 34).[24] Few of the gathered worshipers were surprised.

In Mumbai, Kolkata, Bangalore, Chennai—even Los Alamos and New Jersey—the Dāhimā diaspora in the twentieth century has carried this goddess, her home shrines and her worship to distant places.[25] The circles of encasement spread out from that point near Manglod where a simple herdsman first heard the sound of her emerging from the earth. Each shrine and worshiper ornaments her manifestation; they give her form. She is adorned by worship. Decoration is the residue of worship.[26] A temple is a god's embodiment (Maxwell 1982). As a made stone image must be carved with its adornment of jewels and garments, it also must then be garbed in real cloth and flowers (Plate 30). So the temple must be wound about, not only by images but by ritual (Waghorne and Cutler 1985). Worship, as the ultimate ornament, is the deity's intimate final form in time.

In India's world of worship, ornament is thus essential. It is the light on the lotus. It makes the flower visible in all its ephemeral beauty. There is no body *and* ornament. Body *is* ornament. What is adorned is somewhere invisible deep inside.

A Note on the Date of the Dadhimatī Temple Inscription

D.R. Bhandarkar (1907:31) studied the original stone inscription when it was stored in the Historic Office in Jodhpur and reported that it had been "removed from an old temple of Dadhmat [*sic*], the tutelary deity of the Dāhimā Brāhmaṇas, lying between the villages of Goṭh and Mānglod in the Nagaur district." The inscription was soon published in *Epigraphia Indica* (Ram Karna 1911-12), where a date of Gupta Era 289 was proposed.

Bhandarkar (1914:71–74; 1983:182, no. 1336) supported this dating and placed it in his "List of North-Indian Inscriptions." Ram Narayan Asopa mounted a copy of the inscription—which is still in the temple—to the left of the *maṇḍapa*'s doorway, adding to it his own history of the Dāhimā Brahmans up to the early twentieth century (Śarmā 1915).

V.V. Mirashi (1961; 1964), however, in a scattered series of articles attempted to read the date as 189, rather than 289, and to place it either in the Harṣa or Bhāṭika era (either 795 or 813 CE). These dates have not commonly been accepted by archaeologists or architectural historians, nor by the Dāhimā community (Meister and Dhaky 1991:252; Handa 1984:6). Because the Dadhimatī inscription refers to "a verse nearly identical" to one in the *Devīmāhātmya* (11.9), however, it has recently reentered a debate about the date of that important religious text (Yokochi 2004:21, n. 42); Yokochi has pointed out that there is "a considerable possibility that the verse was not quoted from the *Devīmāhātmya*" and that "this inscription cannot provide a definite *terminus ante quem* for the *Devīmāhātmya,*" even as she accepts Mirashi's dating.

However this text-based debate will work itself out, in the context of our project the sunken floor of the stone temple's sanctum still suggests the existence of an earlier *sthāna* that preceded the ninth-century temple with its overlayering of Puranic iconography. As Babb has written earlier in this volume (pp. 56–57), the dating of this inscription "does not seem to challenge traditional history in any significant way, which is probably because the metrical date falls more or less in the featureless middle ground of Dāhimā Brahman social time where it contradicts nothing of importance."

Notes

1. This stone, however, also gets interpreted as her "skull" and ornamented with her face. One telling of the myth connects the *kapāl kuṇḍ*, the large circular tank outside the temple compound (Plate 34), with the emergence of her head from the ground (Plate 28, bottom).
2. At the seminar on "Shangar and Sringar" in Mumbai where I first presented this essay, I was struck by Harsha Dehejia's characterization of *śṛṅgār* as three different things—love, adornment, and *bhakti*—but not *prem* nor *alaṁkāra* precisely.
3. Gehlot et al. (1988:235) cite a nineteenth-century publication of this inscription (Devīprasād 1894:7). Bhandarkar (1907:31) saw this inscription in the "Historic Office at Jodhpur, capital of the Mārwār State," where it had been moved.
4. The folklorist Ram Prasad Dadich, Jodhpur, 3 January 1998, claimed that the whole "inside" temple (I take this to mean the interior sanctum, i.e. its natural floor) came out of the earth with the Goddess.
5. This branch is shown on the lineage tree painted on the south wall of the temple *cauk* at the Dadhimatī Mātā temple and reproduced from time to time in *Dadhimatī* magazine. A signboard lists twelve branches of Dāhimās, stating that the twelfth *gotra* "became *mlecch* due to bad conduct (*anācār*)." Nagauriya Muslim "Dāhimās" still live in Udaipur, Tonk, and elsewhere in Rajasthan, although they have no memory of the Goth-Manglod temple. Rajendra Joshi, however, carried out an interview with a community genealogist in August 1998 in which a Brahman link was acknowledged (personal communication).

6. Interview with Nityanand Shastri, Nagaur, on 10 March 1998, who claimed its establishment. The Dadhīci image in the shrine has an inscription below of VS 198[x] (1923–32 CE); an inscription on the decorated floor of the shrine says it was installed in this location in 1976.
7. There is also a Dādhīc Lane in Mumbai. The Dāhimā Mahāsabhā lobbied for years for a commemorative postage stamp and a special 60 paisa stamp to honor "Maharshi Dadhichi" was finally released in Jaipur on 26th March 1988. The first-day-cover brochure from the National Philatelic Museum, New Delhi, identifies the sage Dadhīci as a Vedic saint: "about 5,000 B.C." who "Taught men to make fire. Conferred bones on Indra, to destroy Vrttra."
8. Sung by Ghisu Maharaj for John Cort and L. A. Babb in Borunda on 25 March 1998.
9. Ghisu's version is quite explicit as to why Dadhīci's bones were essential to Indra; that of the *Bhāgavata Purāṇa* is quite a bit less so.
10. In an interview with Vaidya Buddhi Prakash Acharya, secretary of the All India Dāhimā Mahāsabhā from circa 1945–48, Jodhpur, 25 December 1991, Buddhi Prakash parsed the multi-community worship of Dadhimatī by saying the goddess could be perceived as Mahā Kālī by Jāṭs, Mahā Lakṣmī by Baniās and Sarasvatī by Brahmans.
11. This extended narrative was retold to L. A. Babb and Michael Meister by Prem Prakash Bidyasar, based on the story he had heard as a boy from his family's genealogist, no longer alive, in an interview in Jodhpur on 4 May 1998. In an earlier interview recorded by John Cort and Vivek Bhandari at the Dadhimatī Mātā temple on 3 January 1997, Shrikisan *Pujārī* identified *gotras* of Jāṭs who view Dadhimatī as *kul devī* as "Renuā, Bhidosar, and Indriyā."
12. A large stone inscription now mounted to the proper left of the east entry to the temple's hall records that "additions to the temple were made by a Dāhimā Brahmachāri named Viṣṇudāsajī in V.S. 1906" according to Ram Karna 1911–12 (reprinted in J. N. Asopa [1988:71 n. 2]), who goes on to report that "further repairs to the temple are being executed [circa 1913] by the Dāhimā-mahāsabhā, by raising subscriptions from the whole community of Dāhimā Brāhmaṇas residing in all parts of India. Nearly Rs. 10,000 has already been collected and spent for this purpose." This inscription has been published by Śarmā (1915).
13. Kathābhaṭṭ (1990) reported that the Dāhimā Mahāsabhā was founded at the Caitra Navrātrī of VS 1967 (April 1910) at the Dadhimatī Mātā temple. According to the account published in the first issue of *Dadhimatī*, all present at this meeting accepted that the Mahāsabhā should be based in Dadhimatī *kṣetra* and its main work should be *jīrṇoddhār* (renovation) of the temple and publication of a monthly magazine. Several structures have been built against the east wall of the five *cauks*: a Māheśvarī *pyāu*; a Dadhimatī *pyāu*, VS 2005 (1958 CE); and a "Śri Viśvakarma *pyāu*" (itself a large *dharmśālā*), VS 2010 (1963 CE). Plans for a large new two-storied *dharmśālā* building separate from the temple compound have been drawn up by Shilpankan architects in Jaipur and a fund-raising campaign has been launched by the current president of the Mahāsabhā, Mahavir Prasad (color brochure, October 1996) (Plate 7).
14. Omnārāyaṇ Dādhīc (1996) writes that this temple was first built by Viṣṇudās about 2000 years ago. Jośī (n.d.) more accurately reports that "according to an inscription of samvat 1908 [CE 1851] in the temple, at the instructions of Brahmacārī Viṣṇudāsjī of Buḍhādeval, Mahārāṇā Svarūpsingh of Udaipur built outside the temple the *cauks*, gates, pilgrim resthouse, well, Śiva temple, etc., and renovated the Kapāl Kuṇḍ." This current construction of the temple's antiquity suggests three levels: 1) a structure founded by the king of Ayodhya, Māndhātā, in the *treta yug* when he came to the *kapāl pīṭh*; 2) the *sthāna* constructed when the goddess emerged to the view of the cowherd; 3) the present temple as it was reformulated by Viṣṇudās.

15. References to this "*adhar thambh*" are common in guidebooks and interviews, and its decoration can be observed today. Striking, however, are the memories of it hovering in past decades, repeated by many worshipers.
16. Tivārī (1997:21–23) comments that "possibly the invasions of Mohammad Ghazni or Aurangzeb reached here, and damaged images on the four sides of the *śikhar*." He also notes that one branch of Rājpūts was known as Dādhīc and that there is a Dāhimā sub-caste of Muslims.
17. Observed on the seventh day of *gupt* Navrātrī, 2 February 1998.
18. Observed on the eighth day of the spring Navrātrī festival, 4 April 1998.
19. This temple is located near the old salt factory, on the banks of a salt lake, in a compound remade by the salt mines to provide a few *dharmśālā* rooms, two bathing rooms and a small mosque in front to show the harmony of the two communities. The *pujārī* on our visit on 3 February 1998 said the temple's present goddess functions as *kul devī* for some local groups of Jāṭs and other communities. I thank Vijay Verma, Shadaja Centre for Art and Culture, Jaipur, for directing me to this important structure.
20. See Coomaraswamy (1995), his seminal article on ornament.
21. Kramrisch (1946) uses the pregnant phrase that the temple is a "monument of manifestation."
22. As in a booklet bought at *gupt* Navrātrī from a stall outside the temple gate (S. Dādhīc n. d.:5–6) (Cort's translation): "At that time he heard a voice from the sky, a lion's roar which frightened the cattle, and the cowherd cried out 'Oh! What is coming forth?' Mahāmāyā's head emerged from the ground, and the goddess said, 'Those who worship my head will get happiness and peace.'"
23. This is not to say that the integrity of the temple as symbol cannot exist without ritual. For the complexity of conservation and worship, see Meister 1995d; for the complexity of a "synchronic sample," see Meister 1990.
24. This procession occurred on the eighth day of Navrātrī, 4 April 1998.
25. Ravi Bhatt, son of Jagdish Chandra Bhatt (Jagdishchandra Sharma Kathabhatt), former Rājguru of Jaipur State, for example, worked for NASA in the U.S. for nine years (interview, 6 January 1992). Other near relations live in Los Angeles and New Jersey.
26. Kramrisch (1946:45) cites sources that make all building (*vāstu*) the "residue of sacrifice": "The Universe is in the Residue. Heaven and Earth, all Existence is in the Residue (*AV*. [*Atharva Veda*] XI.9.1–2a)."

Part III

Pilgrims and Patrons

6

Pilgrimage and Identity in Rajasthan

Family, Place, and Adoration

JOHN E. CORT

Why do people go on pilgrimage? The simplest answer is that a person goes to a specific place, a shrine that is holy for a special reason: it is the site of a special image or icon, a sacred relic, or where an important event occurred. One goes to a pilgrimage shrine to partake of direct access to something that is holy, or to engage in the memory of a sacred event.[1] In India, pilgrims usually go to temples.[2] One can then ask: Why do Hindus and Jains in Rajasthan go on pilgrimage to temples? The simple answer is that the pilgrim has a special relationship with a deity who is located or resides in that temple in the form of an image, either iconic or aniconic.

Most temples are homes to multiple deities, however. There is the main deity in the central sanctum, after whom the temple is usually named. There are other deities, too, often numbering in the dozens. They reside both on the central altar and subsidiary altars. Furthermore, many pilgrimage temples attract subsidiary temples. Some of these are newly built to share in the glory of the main temple, and others are older nearby temples that are pulled into the orbit of the sacred power of the shrine. A pilgrimage shrine is thus a sacred complex, an elaborate network of shrines and sub-shrines.[3] This multiplicity further distinguishes the experience of one pilgrim from another. Pilgrims travelling from different distant places will have different experiences. But we must also distinguish between pilgrims from afar and local residential pilgrims. If we define pilgrimage as the act of going from one place to another for a religious reason, we must include in our discussion the residents of the city or town where the pilgrimage shrine is located. Some pilgrims travel a great distance to arrive at the shrine, and many go only once in a lifetime. They travel by plane, train, bus, car, and bullock cart. In former times, they would have travelled many miles on foot. Others live nearby, and so can go every day. They can easily walk the five or ten minutes to the temple. For the former, experience of the sacred goal is of something new and out of the ordinary; for the latter, of something familiar. Nor can we assume that pilgrims' relationships with deities are all of the same type. In practice, pilgrims go on pilgrimage for multiple reasons, go to different circles of shrines at any one pilgrimage site, and have differing relationships with the deities there.

Does a pilgrim have a relationship with one, a few, or all of these deities? Does a pilgrim come every time to fulfill a relationship with the same deity, or on different visits does a pilgrim interact with different deities? Are the pilgrims' intentions uniform, or do they vary? If the intentions are variable, what factors shape them? Some people visit a temple as part of the long-distance ritual of pilgrimage. Others who visit a temple are residents of nearby neighborhoods and villages. Do intentions also vary for these different groups of pilgrims? These were some of the questions that underlay our interdisciplinary research project.

We were interested in understanding the social factors that enable some temples to survive as functioning entities for many centuries. Scholars often know why a temple was built; either the sponsor has left us a dedicatory inscription detailing his (or more rarely her) intention, or there is a narrative text telling the story of the temple. But these founding intentions rarely if ever account for the survival of a temple, and the thousands of ruined and abandoned temples in South Asia, as well as those which we know only from texts, are eloquent evidence of this. For a temple to survive for more than a generation or two it needs to be maintained and periodically renovated or restored. This happens only if people have an ongoing relationship with the deity who resides in the temple. This brings us back to the question with which I started: Why do Hindus and Jains go on pilgrimage to a temple? The answers to this question go far toward explaining why some temples have flourished for centuries, while others have quickly subsided into insignificance and eventually become ruins.

Given the multiplicity of temples, deities, pilgrims, and intentions associated with any pilgrimage shrine, we must see it as the locus of complex interlinkings and disjunctions. Multiple intentions mean that there are multiple relationships between humans and deities expressed in a single shrine. A pilgrimage shrine therefore does not have a single "meaning," so we also have to understand the deities who reside at a shrine in multiple ways. In discussions with pilgrims, trustees, and temple officiants, three key concepts emerged by which they explained differences among deities at Osian.

Some deities are "family lineage deities" (*kul devatā*), specific to a particular social group. This is either an entire caste (*jāti*) or a patriclan (*gotra*). This deity often has a special role in the history of the kin group. Members of the group worship the deity in the context of life-cycle rituals, especially marriage and birth, as part of a relationship based on shared descent.

Some deities are "place deities" (*sthānīya devatā*), who are specific to a place. Their names are often synonymous with the place, as in the Mother Goddess of Osian (Osiyā Mātā), the Bherū of Osian (Osiyā kā Bherū), and the Mahāvīra Who Adorns Osian (Osiyā-Maṇḍan Mahāvīra). Most if not all people who reside in the place worship these deities on specific annual occasions as part of a relationship based on mutual residence.

Some deities are "adored deities" (*ārādhya devatā*). They are worshiped because of a relationship of adoration (*ārādhanā*) that provides meaning and spiritual sustenance in the lives of the devotees. This worship is not necessarily tied to a specific liturgical schedule, as it can occur whenever the devotee feels a need or a calling ritually to activate the relationship.

These three categories arose most clearly in discussions concerning Sacciyā, but all of the deities I discuss in this chapter can be fitted into this typology. They are not mutually exclusive categories, but highly elastic ones which easily slide into each other. Scholars of Hinduism will recognize them, for they are similar to a tripartite categorization of Hindu deities into family deity (*kul devatā*), village deity (*grām devatā*), and chosen deity (*iṣṭa devatā*).[4] I should underscore that the three categories arose only slowly out of the analysis of the fieldwork material, not out of any pre-fieldwork assumptions.

Deity as Family Protector and Progenitor: *Kul Devatā*

Traditionally almost all Hindu and Jain families in north India had a relationship with a particular deity, a family lineage deity (*kul devatā*), who was understood to be the protector or progenitor of a specific caste or other kin group. In the vast majority of cases this deity was a goddess. Some contemporary Hindus and Jains have lost knowledge of their family deities as a result of migration, urbanization, and secularization, and some "reformist" and more monotheistically oriented sects among Hindus and Jains have encouraged their adherents to abandon the worship of family deities. Some family deities are specific to a particular caste or patriclan, but most of them, such as Sacciyā, are shared among multiple castes. While Sacciyā historically has had a special connection with the Osvāl merchant caste, she is also the family deity for lineages of Jāṭ peasants, Rājpūt landowners and warriors, Māheśvarī merchants, and others.

Osvāls comprise one of the largest Jain caste-clusters in western India, with Jains from northern Rajasthan to southern Gujarat identifying themselves as Osvāl.[5] Osvāl Jains from an area stretching from Palanpur in north Gujarat to Godwar, the belt of southernmost Rajasthan bordering on Gujarat, exhibit a greater awareness of Osian than Osvāls in many other parts of western India. Most of the Jains in this area are Mūrtipūjak (Image Worshiping), but they come to Osian primarily to worship Sacciyā, not at the temple of Mahāvīra. Osvāls from this area, from towns such as Sirohi, Balotra and Bhinmal, make up the second largest group of donors according to the recent inscriptions at the Sacciyā complex. Sacciyā is their lineage goddess, and so they come on the occasion of first tonsure (*jhaḍūlā*) of sons.[6] Inscriptional evidence indicates that Sacciyā has been the lineage goddess for some Osvāl patriclans since at least 1315 (Handa 1984:17). While many of them go first to Mahāvīra to take the auspicious sight (*darśan lenā*) of the image of the Jina, and may stay overnight in the Mahāvīra rest-house, the tonsure ritual at Sacciyā is the occasion for the visit. In several cases, we also saw daughters being tonsured, and on one occasion even the father had his head shaved.

Another group of pilgrims who come from afar to Osian are non-Jain peasants, especially Jāṭs from the area southwest of Jodhpur around Barmer. They come to perform *jhaḍūlā* to sons, and also to perform the post-marriage rite known as "giving *jāt*" (*jāt denā*), in which the deity witnesses to the sacred transformation in the couple's status.[7]

In "giving *jāt*" the newly-married couple present themselves to the goddess for her to witness their new state as auspicious householders. Both the bride and groom wear tinsel crowns to appear as a princess and prince. The groom also wears a prominent turban, and the bride her wedding sari or skirt-and-blouse. One end of the bride's sari or blouse is tied to the end of the groom's turban. They briefly go before the deity and make an offering (Plates 30, 31). Some of the offering they receive back as *prasād*, a tangible and often edible divine blessing. When giving *jāt* at Sacciyā, most couples are guided through the rite by a barber (*nāī*), who also rents them the tinsel crowns. Some couples purchase 125 auspicious coconuts outside the temple. (Throughout India one-and-a-quarter is an auspicious number, signifying open-endedness and therefore a continued flow of worldly well-being.) As they walk up the steps of the hill to the temple, one barber makes an auspicious red dot on each step, and another barber places a coconut on the dot. As soon as the couple has passed each step, another barber grabs the coconut, places it in a burlap bag, and at the end of the ceremony resells the coconuts to the vendor who had originally sold them to the couple (Plate 32). The central act in giving *jāt* is not significantly different in action from any other visit to a temple to worship the deity. It consists of the sacred dynamic viewing (*darśan*) of the deity. Hindus understand this act to be as much a case of the deity viewing the human worshiper as the humans viewing the deity.[8] As part of the ritual worshipers also make offerings of flowers, sweet foodstuffs, and incense, and may wave a lamp (*āratī*) in front of the deity.

A corner of the Sacciyā temple compound is reserved for tonsuring (*jhaḍūlā*). On busier days there is a crowd of barbers in the area, and evidence of hair clippings is strewn about the compound floor. The specifics of the ritual vary from family to family, patriclan to patriclan, and caste to caste, but there is a basic order common to all. The barber shaves all the hair on the child's head. Osvāls from the Palanpur region place some of the hair inside rolled-up chapatis, which are offered to an image of Sacciyā in the corner of the barber's compound. The barber eventually throws the hair in a body of water such as a well, or in some other way disposes of it ritually in a safe manner.[9] The chapatis are given to the barber; this seems clearly to be a prestation in which the patron passes on any inauspiciousness to a lower-caste recipient (Raheja 1988). The barbers in turn pass on the inauspiciousness by feeding the chapatis to dogs. If the child is wearing special clothes for the occasion, these might also be gifted to the barber. The family makes a cash payment to the barber; the amount ranges from several rupees for poor peasants to several hundred rupees for wealthier businessmen. The family then makes offerings of sweets (almost always the hard white sugar-candy known as *makhāṇī*, purchased from vendors outside the entrance gate to the temple compound, sometimes also the cooked wheat and molasses dish known as *lāpsī*), coconut, and flowers to the goddess, part of which are received back as *prasād*. The temple officiant (*pujārī*) at the main altar marks an auspicious *svastik* in sandalwood paste on the child's shaved head. The barber, as we saw, is responsible for disposing of the cut hair, although some peasants keep a small amount of it for offerings at other shrines.

In many cases both these rituals are performed by Jāṭs in one visit. The couple gives *jāt* to the goddess to have her witness their marriage, and then performs *jhaḍūlā* to one or more young sons who are the fruit of the marriage. Oftentimes these life-cycle rites are performed in the context of a pilgrimage to Ramdevra, as Osian is directly on the road from Jodhpur and Barmer to Ramdevra. Ramdevra is the site of the tomb of a deified medieval Rājpūt hero, whose Hindu-Muslim syncretic cult is widespread throughout western India.[10] An employee of the Sacciyā temple informed us that while the largest number of pilgrims comes to Sacciyā during the eight days of the autumnal and vernal "Nine Nights" (Navrātrī), the day that sees the next largest number of pilgrims is Rāmdev Dauj, the day of a big annual fair at Ramdevra in the fall.

Deity as Place: *Sthānīya Devatā*

For people who reside in and around Osian, Sacciyā is *their* goddess. In the words of some informants, she is the *sthānīya devī*, the "place goddess." They are just as likely to call her Osiyā Mātā, "The Mother Goddess of Osian," indicating the degree to which the goddess is central to local identity. Some residents of Osian visit Sacciyā daily, and most visit her at a minimum during the two major annual goddess festivals, the autumnal and vernal Nine Nights. During Navrātrī many people from Jodhpur also make the one-and-a-half hour trip to Osian by car or bus for *darśan* of Sacciyā, and photographs of the ornamented image of the goddess appeared in Jodhpur newspapers. But she is not the only deity in Osian.

Pilgrims to Sacciyā circumambulate the inner sanctum, stopping briefly to bow to the three goddesses enshrined in the outer niches of the shrine: Śītalā to the north, Sacciyā (as Durgā Mahīṣāsuramardinī) to the west, and Cāmuṇḍā to the south. Many also take *darśan* from and bow to the images of Bherū and Gaṇeśa located in niches on either side of the sanctum. After that pilgrims can proceed for *darśan* to some of the other deities in shrines in the immediate vicinity of the main sanctum: Gaṇeśa, Śiva, Sūrya, and Lakṣmī-Nārāyaṇa.

Pilgrims who have come from afar to give *jāt* to Sacciyā usually stop at this point. For locals, however, she is merely one of a circuit of local deities to whom *jāt* is given. Some of them worship Sacciyā as their lineage goddess. But for many people Sacciyā is not their lineage goddess, as the lineage goddess is only one of several deities to whom people give *jāt*. Each resident caste has its own circuit of local, place-specific deities to whom *jāt* is given. Giving *jāt* to the lineage goddess confirms the new couple's transformed status within the lineage, from celibate youths to married and potentially fertile householders. *Jāt* is also given to place deities to establish the couple's new identity in their place of residence.

The Bhāṭī (also spelled Bhaṭṭī) Rājpūts are the former *jāgīrdār*s (estate-holders) of Osian, who held this *jāgīr* (estate) from the king of Jodhpur.[11] According to one Bhāṭī informant, Sacciyā was one of seven sister goddesses (Sapta Mātṛkā) in the Jaisalmer area, and the lineage goddess of many Bhāṭīs. The founder of the Osian branch, who lived about a dozen generations ago, brought her from Jaisalmer to Osian when he was given the *jāgīr* in reward for his heroism in fighting the Moghuls. Those Bhāṭī Rājpūts who view Osian as their native place worship Sacciyā as their lineage goddess, even if they have subsequently migrated elsewhere. They also try to come to Sacciyā at the time of *jhaḍūlā*. The cut hair is wrapped in a cloth and offered to the goddess; if for some reason the people cannot come to Sacciyā, they can still send the hair to be offered.

Two Bhāṭī Rājpūt informants, both of whom were important senior members of the clan, described different circuits of place deities to whom *jāt* is given. This indicates the extent to which giving *jāt* is a highly family-specific custom.

One informant, for whom the Jaisalmer roots of the family were more important, said that in his family they give *jāt* in Jaisalmer in addition to giving *jāt* to Sacciyā in Osian. They still have sacred connections with their place of "origin." In Osian, his family gives *jāt* at the shrine of a deified heroic ancestor named Pratāp Singh, located on the outskirts of the village. According to this informant, Pratāp Singh was a nineteenth-century Robin Hood, who robbed from the rich and gave to the poor, and was killed in an encounter with policemen from Jodhpur State.[12]

The second Rājpūt informant, the head of the other *jāgīrdār* family and a member of the Sacciyā temple trust, said that in his immediate family the couple gives *jāt* at two other shrines besides Sacciyā. One of these is located in a small garden a ten-minute walk from the Jain temple. Here are three marble plaques, each depicting a sword-bearing hero riding a horse. These are memorial images to deceased heroic ancestors of the family. The inscription on one of them identified the deified ancestor as Cain Saudjī Bhāṭī Bhomyā. A *bhomyā*, or *bhomiyā*, is an ancestor who died protecting the place (the *bhūmi*).[13] A painted sign on the outside of the garden identified the principal deity—and the one mentioned by our informant—as Jhunjār Singhjī Dādosā. *Dādosā* literally means "honored grandfather," and is used to refer to any deified and worshiped ancestor. A *jhunjhār* is also a heroic ancestor, who died defending the village.[14] The usual story of a *jhunjhār* is that he mounted his horse to chase cattle rustlers. In the course of battle he was beheaded, whereupon two eyes sprouted from his chest, and he fought on until all the foes were killed. He then returned to the village, where he was pacified by women sprinkling indigo water on him. In many cases, the *jhunjhār* is memorialized in three places: where his body fell, where his horse fell, and where his head fell. The Osian shrine represents the first of these.

The other shrine mentioned by the second Rājpūt informant was that of the most important Bherū in Osian, known as Roivāle Bherū, "Desert Bherū." His importance for the entire area, and his relationship to Sacciyā, is seen in his other two names: Osiyā kā Bherū (Osian's Bherū) and Sacciyā kā Bherū (Sacciyā's Bherū). Almost every village in Marwar has a particular Bherū who is responsible for protecting the village, and to whom the inhabitants perform rituals on a number of annual, crisis, and lifecycle occasions.[15] In addition, there is a strong relationship between Bherū and the goddess: every goddess has a Bherū who assists her, and most every Bherū is therefore associated in some fashion with a goddess.[16]

There are two shrines of this Bherū. One is an altar on the side of the Mahāvīra temple, and the other several miles north of town. Together these two images make up the totality of the deity. Bherū images are frequently bilocational in Rajasthan. In many places there is both a Gorā (Light) Bherū and a Kālā (Black) Bherū (Bharucha 2003:120). The former, located within the residential area, receives vegetarian offerings; the latter, located in the desert or jungle outside the inhabited area, receives offerings of meat and liquor. While some informants at Osian verbally denied that the two images of Roivāle Bherū represented a Light and Dark Bherū, the ritual practice clearly points to such a distinction. The bilocational nature of Roivāle Bherū is also expressed at the Jain temple itself, for there are two images of Roivāle there. One is an aniconic stone on the small altar on the wall of the temple itself. The other is an aniconic stone leaning against the outside of the compound wall. While legally all people are allowed entrance into the temple compound, some untouchables still prefer to make offerings at the outside image, where in former times all untouchables had to worship.[17]

We heard from several informants variants of the following story concerning how this Bherū came to be in two parts. A Māheśvarī (member of a Hindu vegetarian merchant caste) had noticed that childless couples (one informant specified Rājpūt) sacrificed buffalos to the Bherū and in return received sons. So he vowed to offer (but not sacrifice) a buffalo if he received a son. When he was blessed with a son, he brought a buffalo to the Bherū image, and tied it to the stone that was the image. The buffalo became hungry, pulled at and broke out the stone, and started to run, dragging the top half of the stone behind him. (In some versions, Sacciyā came to meet the buffalo and released him from the stone.) When the rope broke, people decided that was the location chosen by Bherū. The original site was at the Mahāvīra temple, and the second site in the desert outside of the village. (Some tellings had the desert shrine as the original site, and the shrine at the Mahāvīra temple as the second, chosen site.)

The Rājpūt, and some other higher-caste informants, go only to the image at the Mahāvīra temple (Plates 30 and 31). Being attached to a Jain temple, this image of Roivāle Bherū receives only vegetarian offerings of flowers, coconut, incense, vermillion paste, in line with the Jain ethical imperative of *ahiṃsā*, non-harm.[18] People in some castes at the time of *jhaḍūlā* also offer a lock of the boy's hair. The image outside of town, in an unpretentious brick structure built fairly recently, receives offerings of goats and liquor. Several informants said that due to the bilocational nature of Roivāle Bherū, one should make half of one's offerings at each location; since meat and liquor obviously cannot be offered within a Jain complex, this requirement is met by splitting one's monetary offerings in half.

The Bhojaks are the hereditary officiants of both the Sacciyā and Mahāvīra temples. They are the officiants in many, perhaps even a majority, of the larger temples throughout Rajasthan and Gujarat.[19] They claim originally to be not from India, but instead from Śākadvīp, a continent to the west. There they were priests or servants (*sevag*) at temples of the sun god Sūrya. One therefore will find references to the Bhojaks as Sevag or Śākadvīpī Brahmans. According to their own myths, they were brought to India by Kṛṣṇa when he instituted Sūrya worship to cure his son Sāmba of leprosy.[20] While they view themselves as Brahmans, they share neither food nor marriage with other Brahmans in western India, nor are they included among any of the lists of the *che nyāt*, the "six castes" comprising the orthoprax upper stratum of Rajasthani Brahman castes. In their relatively low status they are similar to temple priestly castes throughout India.[21]

We received from Bhojak informants several lists of deities to whom Osian Bhojaks give *jāt* at the time of marriage. Two of these we have already encountered: Sacciyā and Roivāle Bherū. At Sacciyā, many Bhojaks also give *jāt* to Mundiyāṛ, another goddess located in the main sanctum. She is the lineage goddess of the patriclan of the majority of the Bhojaks in Osian. They claim to have been brought to Osian from the village of Mundiyar near Nagaur, a connection maintained through this goddess. Some Bhojaks also give *jāt* to her at Mundiyar. For most pilgrims, the focus of the main sanctum is the centrally located and elaborately adorned image of Sacciyā.[22] There are other images in the sanctum, as well as a variety of ritual instruments—but in the brief time a pilgrim has for *darśan*, these are part of the background blur of the shrine. I myself did not take cognizance of Mundiyāṛ for many visits, until an interview with a Bhojak called her to my attention, and I asked a priest at the sanctum to point her out to me.

Bhojaks give *jāt* to other goddesses. Some give *jāt* to Bāyosā (also Bāyāsā and Bāyāṅsā) Mātā. Her shrine is a small, recently constructed and unpretentious brick structure on a small hillock just outside the village behind the Mahāvīra temple. Inside are seven goddess plaques, for Bāyosā Mātā, literally "Revered Little Girl Mother," is the name in Rajasthan for the Seven Sisters (or Seven Mothers, Sanskrit Sapta Mātṛkā). This is a pan-Indian conception of the goddess as a local protector, although the specific names are usually highly localized.[23] This shrine also houses two images of Bherū. In a small wall niche inside the shrine is a Bherū stone covered with red foil, and giving evidence of frequent offerings of oil (a common offering to Bherū). Bhojaks and other high and middle castes give *jāt* to Bāyosā and to this Bherū. Outside the temple is another Bherū stone, to which lower castes offer liquor and goats.

Some Bhojaks give *jāt* to Pīplā Mātā, whose temple is an ancient goddess temple near to the Mahāvīra temple (Plate 29). Pīplā is *kul devī* for several Bhojak patriclans, and they seem to be the people who most patronize her shrine.

Bhojaks also give *jāt* to two male deities. One of these is shared with many other castes in Osian (and Rajasthan), whereas the other is specific to the Bhojaks of Osian.

Kesariyā Kaṅvar (Saffron Prince), also known as Gugā or Gogā (and Ghoghā in Gujarat), is an important deity worshiped throughout Rajasthan, Panjab, and north Gujarat.[24] His local shrine is one of the early temples important to archaeologists and art historians and labeled by them as Viṣṇu Temple Number 1 (Plate 29). Inside this temple is a plaque of the dog-headed serpent deity. Michael Meister did not see it when he first visited Osian in the 1960s, nor did either D.R. Bhandarkar or M.A. Dhaky make written note of its being there. I have a slide of it from a visit in 1987, so this is a relatively recent reuse of this ancient temple.

The other male deity is a Dādosā (Honored Grandfather) or Bhomiyā who is specific to the local Bhojaks. His shrine is located on the side of the hill on which the Sacciyā temple is located, in an area formerly inhabited by Bhojaks. There are two images here of the Dādosā, plaques depicting a man holding a sword in his downturned right hand and a flower garland in his upturned left hand. The more recent image has an inscription dated VS 1880 (1823 CE). We were told the following story concerning this Bhojak Dādosā. The only well for this neighborhood was outside the village, so when going to it most people took a sword or staff for protection. A Bhojak went to the well with his son one evening, at the particularly dangerous liminal time right after sunset, when one needs to be doubly careful about ghosts and other malevolent spirits. The man heard a sound, which he took to be a ghost. He pulled out his sword, and as he did so he accidentally decapitated his young son, who thereby became a Dādosā, a Bhomiyā.

The Nāyaks are a formerly untouchable caste of Rajasthan.[25] The Nāyaks give *jāt* at Roivāle Bherū, at Kesariyā Kaṅvar, and at a Nāyak *bhomiyā* located near the Kesariyā shrine. They also give *jāt* at Sacciyā. Previously they did not give *jāt* to her at the main image in the temple, for they were forbidden entrance into the temple. As a result they gave *jāt* to her at an old pillar outside the entrance to the temple. Many still give *jāt* here as a matter of customary practice. On one occasion when we observed an untouchable family giving *jāt* at this pillar, we asked if they also planned to go inside the main temple. They answered in the affirmative, as if to show that they had as much right to enter the temple as members of higher caste; but when they entered the temple, and became disoriented in the complex set of shrines and levels, it was obvious that they had never been inside the temple before.[26]

These surveys of the circles of deities to whom members of three local castes give *jāt* by no means exhaust the list of deities who reside in Osian. On a stone platform on one side of the main pavilion of the Sacciyā temple is an image of the goddess Śītalā, the "Cool One." Most of the time she is ignored by worshipers, but on the day of Śītalā Eighth (the eighth of the dark half of every month) she is the focus of worship by many young women of Osian and the surrounding area.[27] Young women also come to the temple on the springtime festival Gaṅgaur, a day when they fast to obtain a good husband. A portable metal image of the goddess Gaṅgaur is set up on the platform near the Śītalā image for worship.[28] In the past two decades a set of temples to the Nine Durgās has come up on the hill surrounding the Sacciyā temple. As of 1998 the set was unfinished and consequently received relatively little attention from worshipers, but the amount of pilgrim attention may well change once they are all completed.[29]

One of the old temples on the plain has been reclaimed as a temple to Śiva sometime before the 1960s, and receives a low level of regular attention. On the Sacciyā Mātā hill an ancient temple was renovated, probably in the second quarter of the twentieth century, as a temple to Satya Nārāyaṇa, a form of Viṣṇu. On the main alley running from the Mahāvīra temple to the Sacciyā temple is a temple of Viṣṇu in his cosmic four-armed form as Caturbhuja (containing some medieval images relocated into a more modern structure) that also receives a low level of regular attention. Near the Pīplā Mātā temple next to the Mahāvīra temple is a small shrine of Bālājī, visited by local Māheśvarīs on the occasion of giving *jāt*.[30]

There is a small Jain shrine containing stone footprints of two deceased Jain mendicants on Luṇādrī hill, to the east of the hill on which the Sacciyā temple is located. Luṇādrī hill is important in the Jain history of the site, for supposedly this is where Ratnaprabhasūri stayed while he converted Cāmuṇḍā into Sacciyā and converted the Rājpūts into Osvāl Jains. The shrine is what is known as a *dādābāṛī*. The term *dādābāṛī* (literally "grandfather's garden") is used by Śvetāmbar Mūrtipūjak Jains in Rajasthan to refer to any shrine in a "garden" outside of a residential area. The footprint images are of an otherwise unknown late-thirteenth-century monk named Kanakaprabha,[31] and Ratnaprabhasūri, the ancient monk central to the Jain story of the conversion of both the inhabitants of Osian and Sacciyā herself to Jainism (Plates 28 and 29).[32] As far as we could ascertain, this shrine is visited only by the officiant of the Mahāvīra temple, who comes daily to apply a small amount of sandalwood paste on the toes as veneration.

Undoubtedly there are other shrines which either we did not notice or did not investigate. We studied those temples and shrines to which our attention was called by informants. Nor in our research did we ascertain the perspectives on all these Hindu and Jain temples and deities of the Muslims who live in the neighborhood at the southwest base of the Sacciyā hill.

In giving *jāt* a couple is establishing its relationship as a new child-bearing unit with the deities of that place. In India *who* one is is very much a matter of *where* one is.[33] But where (and therefore who) one is involves elements of both geographical and social location. All Hindus in Osian bear a relationship with Sacciyā, the goddess of the town, and Roivāle Bherū, her Bherū. The centrality of these two deities to the religious life of residents of Osian is underscored by their alternate names of Osiyā Mātā and Osiyā kā Bherū. But each caste also has relationships with deified heroic ancestors, lineage goddesses, and other deities who are specific to that caste (or smaller social unit). The differing circles to whom members of different castes give *jāt* shows how residential identity is social as well as geographical.

Deity as Personally Adored: *Ārādhya Devatā*

Pilgrimage to Sacciyā

The largest number of the Jains who come to Sacciyā are Osvāl Terāpanthī Jains from the Shekhawati region of northern Rajasthan. Terāpanthīs for the most part do not perform *jhaḍūlā*, nor do many of them come to Sacciyā after marriage to give *jāt*. They come here primarily to receive the blessings of the goddess.

The Śvetāmbar Terāpanth is the smallest of the four main Jain sects, and is made up almost entirely of Rajasthani Osvāls. The sect rejects the worship of Jina images in temples and many other aspects of the ritual cultures of the image-worshiping Śvetāmbar Mūrtipūjak Jains. Under the leadership of the late Ācārya Tulsī, the sect has both grown significantly and also been quite successful in adapting its ethics and metaphysics to the demands of modernity.[34]

Knowing the firmness with which Terāpanthīs reject the Mūrtipūjak temple culture, we were surprised to find that Terāpanthīs are the single most prominent group of pilgrims to the Sacciyā temple. The temple complex has seen an extensive construction program over the past several decades, and the prominent inscriptions indicate that this has largely been financed by Terāpanthīs from Shekhawati. The Executive President of the temple trust, himself a Terāpanthī Osvāl with business interests in Jaipur and Kolkata, and son of one of the founders of the trust, said, with little evident hyperbole, that the financial patronage of Sacciyā nowadays is almost exclusively Terāpanthī Osvāl. Many businessmen from this community have made Sacciyā a partner in their firms, so that she receives two, five or even ten percent of the firms' profits.

This same man said that this Terāpanthī Osvāl devotion to Sacciyā dates from only about 1970. While most Osvāls have other goddesses as their lineage goddesses, two patriclans of Shekhawati Osvāls, the Baid-Mehtās and the Copṛās, have Sacciyā as their lineage goddess. A series of miraculous cures, many of cancer, occurred within these patriclans around 1970, all of which were credited to Sacciyā. Devotion to Sacciyā spread first among these patriclans, then among other Osvāl patriclans into which Baid-Mehtā and Copṛā women had married, and finally to other Osvāl patriclans. While Osvāl patriclans are not exclusively Terāpanthī, but include other Śvetāmbar Jains, this particular cult of Sacciyā seems to have been limited to Terāpanthīs.

Due to the charismatic leadership of Ācārya Tulsī and his successor and long-time heir-designate Ācārya Mahāprajña, many Terāpanthī laity have imbibed the basic Terāpanthī ideology that engagement in Jain ritual activities is fruitless unless it is solely dedicated to liberation (*moksa*).[35] Unlike other Jain sects, in which religious activities can have spiritual benefits both in advancing one toward liberation and increasing one's worldly wellbeing (Cort 2001), the Terāpanthī ideology holds that any ritual action done with even the slightest intention of improving one's worldly condition is entirely fruitless, and quite likely even detrimental, in the pursuit of liberation. But the sect has come to define ritual in such a way that it still allows for devotion to non-Jain deities such as

Sacciyā. Several Terāpanthīs whom we interviewed about their devotion to Sacciyā quickly advanced a distinction between religion (*dharma*)—which is focused solely on liberation and involves rituals of meditation, asceticism, and veneration, all done in imitation of the Jinas—and worldly rituals that are not *dharma* and are focused upon "powers" such as Sacciyā. Other deities mentioned in this context included Bherū, Rāmdevṛā, Sālāsar Bālājī, and Kārṇī Mātā. (Sālāsar Bālājī is a popular local deity whose shrine is in Shekhawati [Babb 2004:37-40]. Kārṇī Mātā is a goddess whose shrine is near Bikaner.) They also mentioned many local goddesses, some of them Osvāl lineage goddesses.[36] One informant expressed this distinction in English, "Mahāvīra is our religious deity, Sacciyā Mātā is our family deity."[37] The sect's rejection of worship of Jina images, and the exiling of all rituals aimed at worldly wellbeing from a strictly-defined Jain context, may have even helped focus Terāpanthī attention upon this goddess.

Another informant said that the Terāpanthī monks used to preach against lay worship of goddesses and similar deities, but were losing devotees. Faced with the choice of worshiping a deity who can ensure wealth and health in return, or abandoning that deity to follow a path ostensibly directed only at liberation, many Terāpanthī laity were choosing to pursue tangible pragmatic goals in this life rather than intangible goals in a future life. As a result, the mendicants have down-played their anti-goddess rhetoric, and Terāpanthīs can now participate in the worship of Sacciyā wholeheartedly. For example, Ācārya Tulsī himself wrote, "There is no faith in image worship in the Sthānakvāsī and Terāpanth traditions. But they still worship goddesses, Bālājī, their own lineage deities, and other deities, and make vows to them. This is not done in error. But it is true that these are worldly deities worshiped from a worldly perspective. They have nothing to do with liberation (*mokṣa*), religion (*dharma*), or spirituality (*adhyātma*)" (Tulsī 1995:19).

While Terāpanthī Osvāls are a fairly constant presence at Sacciyā, they are especially conspicuous during the two annual Navrātrīs, the nine-night celebrations of the goddess. At each Navrātrī a different extended family arranges to pay for the observances, in particular the lengthy fire-sacrifice on the eighth night. For many years these families have been exclusively Terāpanthī Osvāls, and there are so many families clamoring for the right to sponsor the observation that the temple trust is being forced to consider how to deal with this demand in an equitable manner. Members of the sponsoring family gather in Osian from their dispersed residences in Jaipur, Delhi, and elsewhere throughout India for the entire nine nights. They reserve for their use most of the block of rooms in the pilgrim guest house on the hill. Every morning and evening they attend the offering of light (*āratī*) to the goddess. When I observed Navrātrī in April 1998, a group of Osvāl young men followed the daily *āratī*s with half-an-hour of vigorous singing of devotional hymns to the goddess. In these songs they asked for help and succor in their lives. There is much here that is generic to temple experience and the worship of the goddess throughout India, albeit manifested with a distinctly mercantile flavor. The songs describe Sacciyā as "Mother of the World" and "Queen of the Three Worlds," who grants her devotees mercy and good fortune.

Give me *darśan* Mother of the World
in your skirt and red scarf,
give me *darśan* Mother of the World.
You are Śiva's queen, the incarnation of Pārvatī,
queen of the three worlds—
good fortune stays forever where you shine.
You are worshiped first of the five deities
both day and night,
give me *darśan* Mother of the World.[38]

Hear my petition
dear Mother of Osian.
Come, sit in my courtyard
in my courtyard
dear Mother of Osian.
Bring hope and faith—
I seek the path.
I have hope, dear Mother,
I have hope every day
but I lose my hope.
Mother, we pass the night in vigil,
Dear Mother of Osian.
Days pass, nights pass, years pass.
Mother, I hang like a garland you have strung.
Mother, I hold out my hands, my fingers of sorrow,
Dear Mother of Osian.
Hear my cry of love dear Mother and come.
Give *darśan* to your devotee, give great joy.
Mother, this devotee clings to your feet.
Dear Mother of Osian.
Dear Mother of Osian, show your mercy.
I give two crores, the rest I deposit.
Hear my song Mother,
Dear Mother of Osian.[39]

Sometimes the assembled Osvāl women, who were quite distinct from the local peasant women due to their expensive silk saris and heavy gold jewelry, joined in the singing. There were also occasional instances of Osvāl women becoming possessed, but these were few, and rather restrained in comparison to possession in other settings in India.[40]

On the eighth night of Navrātrī there was a grand fire sacrifice (*havan*) in the middle of the temple's main pavilion. The couple who performed the sacrifice, aided by a number of local priests, were the husband who had paid for the nine days' observance and his wife. While there is no clear evidence on the matter, we assume that fifty and more years ago the sacrifice on the eighth night was presided over by the local Bhāṭī Rājpūt *jāgīrdārs* who controlled Osian. It is clear that the observance on this night formerly involved the sacrifice of goats, and on occasion also of a buffalo. All this has changed with the rise of the vegetarian Jain Osvāls to prominence at the Sacciyā temple, although there had earlier also been pressure from the local Hindu Māheśvarī merchants against public performance of animal sacrifice, which was declared illegal in Rajasthan in 1975. The Osvāls' moral emphasis on nonviolence, and the explicit Jain rejection of the offering of animals in sacrifice, have resulted in the main sacrifice now being a strictly vegetarian one, although everyone admitted that there may well be privately conducted animal sacrifices to Sacciyā outside the temple complex, and so outside the control of the temple trustees. This was underscored at the conclusion of the sacrifice, when the priests and patrons made sure that all the ingredients were offered into the fire in a final inferno, all the while loudly proclaiming "*pūrṇ āhuti, pūrṇ āhuti.*" While this phrase, which literally means "the sacrifice is complete," is the standard concluding utterance in most fire sacrifices, in this case it also underscored that there was no additional secret offering (of animals) elsewhere.[41]

Pilgrimage to Mahāvīra

The largest of the Jain sects is that of the Śvetāmbar Mūrtipūjaks ("Image-Worshipers"), also known in Rajasthan as Mandirmārgīs and Derāvāsīs ("Temple-Goers").[42] As the name indicates, their religious culture centers on the institution of the temple and the images of the Jinas enshrined therein. Many Mūrtipūjak Jains throughout western India know of the Mahāvīra temple in Osian. This temple is not itself a major pilgrimage goal, but it is an important stopping point for Jains on pilgrimage tours of Rajasthan. This is in part due to the acknowledged beauty of the temple and the image, and the well-known antiquity of both, but also due to the lodging and dining facilities in an area otherwise largely devoid of Jain temples and pilgrim facilities.

A comparison of Osian with other Jain pilgrimage shrines in Rajasthan helps us understand the range of reasons why people go on pilgrimage to an adored deity. Abu and Ranakpur are famous as masterworks of Indian temple architecture. Many Jains echo the opinion of art historians that one goes to Abu to admire the details of the stone carving, and to Ranakpur to admire the total effect of the architecturally complex temple. In a similar fashion Jains go to Jaisalmer to admire the carvings on the five Jain temples in the fort, and then to compare these with the carvings on the nineteenth-century stone *havelīs* (mansions) built by Jain millionaires in the city. Jaisalmer has also played a central role in the religious geographic imagination of western Indian Śvetāmbar Jains, as a bastion of Jain culture and site of some of its most important manuscript libraries, for hundreds of years. Abu, Ranakpur, and Jaisalmer are sites in which one can combine the earning of religious merit with aesthetic enjoyment.

But far more Jain pilgrims in Rajasthan go to Kesariyaji and in particular Nakora. Kesariyaji, in southern Rajasthan near Udaipur, is the site of an image of the Jina Ādinātha, first Jina of this era, that is described by one pilgrim guidebook as "beautiful, wonder-working, and fulfilling of devotees' desires." The guidebook goes on to say, "Here many new miraculous experiences are related by devotees. Devotees who have the aspiration to come here find their desires fulfilled" (*Tīrth Darśan* 1980:186). Nakora is even more popular. The devotional focus is not a Jina image, but the wonder-working protector deity Nākoṛā Bherū. So famous is this deity that Nakora is now one of the best-known, most-visited, and wealthiest Jain temples in Rajasthan, even though the temple's location in the desert outside of Balotra makes it less easily accessible than many other temples.

Temples and deities are significant magnets for pilgrims to the extent that they are famous for miracles, usually related either to health or obtaining wealth. The Jain temple at Osian lacks any such renown and so does not attract many pilgrims. Sacciyā Mātā is the deity in Osian with healing powers, and so draws far larger crowds of worshipers. Most Jains who visit the Mahāvīra temple do so while en route to more popular shrines. The Jain temple at Osian does have several features that could lean toward the wonder-working and desire-fulfilling features of more popular temples. The main image of Mahāvīra is said to have been made from clay and cow's milk by Sacciyā herself (or, in some accounts, the Jain goddess Cakreśvarī). In a side shrine is an image of the snake-deity Puniyā Bābā, the protector deity of the shrine. Neither Mahāvīra nor Puniyā Bābā, nor their images, however, currently exhibits any of the extraordinary powers of those at Nakora and Kesariyaji, and as a result few pilgrims come any significant distance specifically to this temple.

Some Gujarati Jains with whom I spoke about Osian, especially those who were not Osvāls, were ignorant of the existence of the temple of Sacciyā. They had visited Osian as part of group pilgrimages by bus, stopping only to worship at the Mahāvīra temple and perhaps spend the night at the pilgrim resthouse. Gujarati Osvāls might be aware of the role Sacciyā played in the creation of the caste, but here also I encountered a range of attitudes toward the goddess's temple, from a willingness to visit it, to the insistence of one knowledgeable man (who was a Gujarati Osvāl), who had visited the Jain temple on many occasions, that no Jain should go near the goddess temple due to the practice of animal sacrifices. In addition, as mentioned above, Sacciyā is *kul devī* for only a small number of Osvāl patriclans; in the case of those Osvāls who have another goddess as their *kul devī*, such as Āśāpurā, Susvāṇī, or Sindu-Morkhāṇā, it is quite likely that they have never heard of Sacciyā.[43]

Over the course of the past century, many of the Śvetāmbar Mūrtipūjak pilgrims to the Mahāvīra temple have been from the relatively small Mūrtipūjak congregations of Marwar. For several years in the late nineteenth century, the trust was under the guidance of Jodhpur Mūrtipūjak Jains, and many of them come here on the occasion of the annual festival of the temple in the spring. For most of the past century the temple has been under the guidance of Jains from Phalodi, and pilgrims from Phalodi (even if they now are resident in Mumbai or Chennai) are also conspicuous in the annual festival. Another "catchment area" consists of alumni of the school attached to the temple. This school was established in the early years of the twentieth century by several monks to insure a resident Jain presence at the temple. Most of the students now are not Jain, but for many years Jains from surrounding villages made up a significant proportion of the student body. While many, and perhaps even a majority, of these Jain boys came from Sthānakvāsī households, they had to perform daily *pūjā* in the temple as a requirement for attending the school.[44] Many of these alumni are still involved in the affairs of the temple, and attend the annual festival, which coincides with a major school function.

Whereas Sacciyā and other non-liberated deities are understood by Jains to be active deities, who respond directly to the petitions of the devotee, the Jina is understood to be inactive and unresponsive. Instead, the devotee's spiritual condition is improved as a result of a reflexive meditation upon the spiritual values embodied in the image of the Jina.[45] The many hymns Jains sing before images in temples express the goal of awakening in the devotee right faith in the Jain teachings. These teachings are symbolized by the image of the Jina, who for Jains is the only deity to be worshiped (*ārādhnā*) for progress along the path to liberation. A hymn dedicated to the Mahāvīra of Osian says that bowing to Mahāvīra "will always purify your soul" and "removes lust, anger, and ignorance from everyone."[46] One does not receive anything from the Jina in response to worship, for the Jina has nothing to give. Instead, through the act of worship the Jain awakens to right knowledge concerning how to act in the world, and as a result acts in a virtuous manner.

Fluid Theologies

I started this chapter by asking why Hindus and Jains in Rajasthan go on pilgrimage. As we have seen, the answer to this question quickly takes us into the complexities of Hindu and Jain theology, for the answer varies according to the contextualizing factors of kinship, geography, and spiritual orientation. The analysis of deities, images, temples, and pilgrimage shrines involves fluid categories. There are almost as many reasons why people go on pilgrimage as there are pilgrims. The framework of lineage, place, and adoration that I have used is a provisional one, and we found in conversations with informants that these categories easily slid into each other. Attempts on our part to reify and fix these categories in the interest of conceptual clarity were regularly frustrated by our informants. We started our research with the idea that these categories, and especially those of lineage deity and place deity, are fairly fixed. In the course of research, we had to accept that they are fluid, although not in a totally unbounded fashion.

In part this is because the categories of kinship and place themselves are fluid categories in western India, as our efforts to understand better the intricacies of caste organization proved.[47] For some people, kinship and residence are almost synonymous. This is not surprising, since many caste and patriclan names are place names, indicating that a kinship group is frequently defined as those blood relatives who come from a common place. In this case, lineage deities and place deities are largely the same. But the history of western India is a history of nearly incessant migration. Most people are "really" from somewhere else, and so one usually finds a discontinuity between lineage deities and place deities. As one moves, one's family may retain a connection with one or more deities of one's "original" place that is activated on the occasion of crucial lifecycle rituals.[48] How extensive this connection is will depend on a variety of factors, including proximity, wonder-working powers of the deity, and the simple fact that some people are more interested than others in genealogical matters. People establish connections with the deities where they reside, and these local connections can also be activated in lifecycle rituals.

One day we were discussing with an officiant at the Sacciyā temple the circles of deities to whom Osian residents give *jāt*. He turned to a local man who was listening to our conversation, and for a moment became an ethnographer himself. He asked the man where his family gave *jāt*. The man explained that he was by origin a Sīkhvāl Brahman from Merta, and his lineage goddess (*kul devī*) was Brahmāṇī. But since he now was settled in Osian, his family gave *jāt* according to the local traditions, and so gave to Sacciyā, Kesariyā Kaṅvar, and Roivāle Bherū. We see in this example how familial and geographical identities are intertwined.

There is also a connection between the categories of place deity and adored deity. As we saw, deities are frequently known by the name of their place, and so in Osian there are Osiyā Mātā, Osiyā kā Bherū, and Osiyā-Maṇḍan Mahāvīra. People from afar for whom Sacciyā occupies a special place in their devotional universe will refer to her by her place-specific name. This specificity can even be transferred, and so one finds, for example, an image of Osiyā Mātā in the Hathising Jain temple in Ahmedabad. There are also at least six other Sacciyā temples: in Barmer, Juna, Rajaldesar, Churu, and Sirohi in Rajasthan, and Gundala in Kacch. If the Osian Mahāvīra was a wonder-working image, one would find images and temples of Osiyā Mahāvīra elsewhere, as one finds, for example, temples of the wonder-working Kesariyā Ādinātha and Śaṅkheśvar Pārśvanātha throughout western India.[49]

We have also seen how for some people the categories of lineage deity and adored deity overlap. For some Osvāl patriclans Sacciyā is both their lineage goddess and their adored goddess.

But not all deities can occupy these categories in the same way. Sacciyā easily is seen by differing people as a lineage, place, and adored goddess, and for some people she is at once all three. Other deities, however, are more restricted in their identities. Roivāle Bherū is primarily a place deity; his role in lifecycle rites is not as a lineage deity, but as a place deity. No one characterized him as an adored deity. Mahāvīra is primarily an adored deity. He is definitely not a lineage deity. Even the specificity of his location in Osian is rather tenuous: most of the songs sung to him are generic Jain devotional songs to Mahāvīra or the Jina in the abstract, and there is no repertoire of songs specifically to Osiyā Mahāvīra. In this Mahāvīra shares features with Jain temples and images throughout western India, for they rarely function purely as place deities, and even less often as lineage deities.[50]

Why a person goes on pilgrimage depends on who that person is—and a person in India is defined as much by kinship and geography as by personal or even shared spiritual orientation.[51] Hindus and Jains understand themselves in multiple ways. Which aspect of their "personality" is foregrounded on any occasion depends on context. That context is both shaped by and itself helps to shape relationships with deities. Hindus and Jains in Rajasthan, therefore, go on pilgrimage because they are born into kin groups that have long-standing relationships with specific lineage goddesses. They go on pilgrimage because they reside in a place, and that residence entails relationships with specific geographically defined deities. Finally, they go on pilgrimage because of adoration for a deity who is a sacred focus of meaning and value.

Notes

1. On pilgrimage in general, see Turner 1973, Turner and Turner 1978, Stoddard and Morinis 1997, and Barnes and Branfoot 2006. Llewellyn 1998 provides an overview of recent literature on Hindu pilgrimage. Gold 1988 remains the best single study of pilgrimage in Rajasthan.
2. This chapter does not deal with pilgrimage to living holy persons, on which see, among others, McCormick 1997.
3. On the concept of the "sacred complex" see Vidyarthi 1978, Vidyarthi, Saraswati, and Jha 1979, and Vidyarthi and Jha 1974.
4. See Huyler 1999:64–113 for a lengthy analysis of Hindu polytheism using this typology.
5. See Babb 1996:137–73 and 2004:141–84, and Cort 2004 on the Osvāls. The differences among castes that call themselves Osvāl are such that it would be inaccurate to label all Osvāls as members of a single caste; nor does historical evidence allow for a definitive answer as to whether there was ever a single coherent Osvāl social unit.
6. This is the rite known in Sanskrit as *muṇḍana*.
7. "Giving *jāt*" is a generic term in Marwar for this ritual as performed by all castes, and etymologically has nothing to do with the caste name. In Devanagari script, the ritual is spelled *jāt* and the caste is spelled *jāṭ*.
8. See Eck 1998 on this ritual.
9. A well or other body of water is a safe place to dispose of any object that is either very sacred or potentially dangerous. John D. Smith (1991:52) describes how the *bhopo* (also spelled *bhopā*) bards of Rajasthan who sing the epic of Pābūjī take old *paṛ*s (more often spelled *phaṛ*), the narrative scrolls understood to be inhabited by the deity Pābūjī himself, to Pushkar, where they deposit them in the lake. Old images and temple flags are similarly deposited in bodies of water. He adds, "If Pushkar is too far away, a good well may be used instead" (ibid.). Detached parts of the body, such as hair and nails, which are impure and inauspicious and which might be used for black magic should they fall into someone else's hands, are disposed of in a similar fashion. In both cases, of pure but now old holy images, and of impure bodily ejecta, immersion in sacred water serves to make the object "cool" (*ṭhaṇḍā*), and thereby removes its power.
10. See Bharucha 2003:185–97, Binford and Camerini 1974, Khan 1997, and Kothari 1982:17–18.
11. There were in fact two *jāgīr*s in Osian, held by different branches of the same extended family.
12. See Harlan 2003:158–63 for more on this deified heroic ancestor.

13. See Bharucha 2003:105–08, Harlan 2003, and Kothari 1982:4–15.
14. See Gold 1988:64–79, Harlan 1992:197–99 and 2003, and Kothari 1982:13. As Harlan (2003:4–16) notes, there is significant overlap between the categories of *bhomiyā* and *jhunjhār*.
15. Bherū is also oftentimes called Khetarpāl (Sanskrit Kṣetrapāla) or Khetlāu, "Guardian of the Site," and the iconography of the two is largely the same. See Harlan 2003:16 and 135. The local role played by Bherū in Marwar falls to Bālājī in Shekawati in northern Rajasthan, and to either Ghoghā Bāpjī (Cort 2001:33) or various Vīrs in northern Gujarat.
16. While classically oriented text-based scholarship oftentimes stresses the mythic connections between Bherū (Sanskrit Bhairava), also called Bhairon, and Śiva, this relationship is fairly negligible on the local cultic level. On Bherū in Rajasthan see Gold 1988, Harlan 2003:135–48 and 197–204, Kothari 1982:2–24.
17. The Bherū directly associated with the Sacciyā temple is also bilocational. There is an iconic image in a niche next to the main sanctum, and an aniconic image in a small shrine on the plateau behind the temple (along with an image of Bālājī in an adjoining shrine). To add further complexity to these issues, one informant firmly denied that Roivāle Bherū is Sacciyā's Bherū; he said that her Bherū is the Bherū at Mandor just to the north of Jodhpur, which he said is visited by Osvāls from Godwar.
18. The Jains who manage the Mahāvīra temple are clearly ambivalent about the presence of this Bherū. One day we were shown around the temple by the Secretary of the temple trust; he made no mention of the Bherū until we called his attention to it, whereupon he dismissed it as an image that belonged to "other people." The small altar for the Bherū is in a rather dilapidated condition, and receives no mention in any of the literature on the temple. But clearly the Jains are unwilling to remove the image, for to do so would alienate many local Osian residents. While no one expressed it in this way, I suspect that there is a perception that to remove the image might also endanger the temple. Bherūs are commonly found in Jain temples as protectors of the temple and the surrounding neighborhood. This role is clearly expressed in an alternate name by which some call Bherū: Khetarpāl or Khetlāu (Sanskrit Kṣetrapāla), the protector of the vicinity. This identity between the two is also expressed iconographically. Whereas most images of Bherū consist of aniconic rocks covered with vermillion paste, when Bherū is given iconic form in a carved image the iconography is indistinguishable from that of the deity frequently labeled as Khetarpāl.

    When we asked the Secretary of the Jain temple trust about the Bherū, he deflected the question by turning to the nearby image of Puniyā Bābā. He claimed this was the snake that bit Prince Uhaṛ; Ratnaprabhasūri's revival of the seemingly dead boy was instrumental in the conversion of the Osvāls from meat-eating Rājpūts to vegetarian Jains. But we never saw anyone make a special offering to this deity. There is a rule, similar to that found at shrines of other Jain unliberated deities such as Ghaṇṭākarṇ Mahāvīr at Mahudi in north Gujarat (Cort 1997 and 2000), and Nākoṛā Bherū at Nakora in southwest Rajasthan, that no *prasād* offered to Puniyā Bābā can be taken outside the confines of the temple compound, but this would appear to be largely a theoretical matter.
19. See Cort 2001:58–59.
20. There is extensive literature on the Bhojaks, although a focused ethnography on them remains to be written. See, among other sources, Cort 2001:58–60, Singh 1895:320–26, and von Stietencron 1966.
21. See Fuller 1984:49–71, Heesterman 1985:26–44, Quigley 1993:54–86.
22. Here we see one of the functions of ornamentation: to distinguish one image from another, and to guide the eye of the pilgrim, for whom all the visual data are largely homogenous and therefore indistinct and confusing, to that which is centrally important. See the comments of David Freedberg (1989:119), that an aim of elaborate ornamentation "is to reinforce the implicit claim that it is this particular image and not another that works in such and such a miraculous or beneficent way."

23. See Harlan 1992:82–83 and Kothari 1982:26–27.
24. There is extensive literature on Kesariyā Kaṅvar. See, among others, Blackburn et al. 1989:224–27, Khan 1997:232–33, Kothari 1982:18, Lapoint 1978, Pemārām 1977:31–36, and Temple 1884–1900:I:121–209.
25. Rajasthani Nāyaks are different from the middle-caste Nāyaks of Gujarat, who are a caste of musicians and actors, and who intermarry with Bhojaks (Cort 2001:59–60).
26. Further evidence of the gradual change in patterns of untouchable entry into Sacciyā is that an untouchable Meghvāl is on the board of trustees, and a local Meghvāl erected a large image of Bherū on the steps leading up the hill. But in discussion with a Bhojak employee of the trust about images of Bherū on the hill, he completely overlooked this one until I reminded him of it. Installing an image at a shrine does not automatically change everyone else's perceptions of the sacred geography of the site.
27. On Śītalā, see Gold 1994:46 and 62–63, and the sources she cites.
28. On Gaṅgaur see Erdman 1985:165–81.
29. Invoking the category of the Nine Durgās is a strategy for integrating a local goddess temple into a pan-Indian understanding of the goddess. We also saw this at the Dadhimatī temple. The classical reference to the Nine Durgās is in the *Kavaca* (or *Durgā Kavaca*), an appendix to the *Devī Māhātmya* (or *Durgā Saptaśati*) (Coburn 1991:175). There are variant lists of the names of the nine goddesses; see also Slusser 1999.
30. While Bālājī is identified with Hanumān, at the local cultic level he is more of a protector deity than an associate of the Purāṇic deity Rāma, and an undue focus on the textual understandings of Hanumān obscures the many ways that Bālājī overlaps with Bherū and various Vīrs ("heroes"). On Hanumān and Bālājī, see Lutgendorf 2007. See also Kakar (1982:53–88) on a Bālājī shrine in eastern Rajasthan.
31. The inscription is given by Handa (1984:224). It briefly relates the death in meditation in VS 1246 (1189 CE) of Kanakaprabha Mahattara, the disciple of Jinabhadra Upādhyāya. While both of these are fairly common names for medieval Śvetāmbar monks, I have been unable to find any reference to a teacher-disciple pair with these names who lived in the late twelfth century.
32. The footprints of Ratnaprabhasūri were installed on a platform above the earlier set in 1909 by Yati Premsundar of the Upkeś Gacch at the instruction of Muni Jñānsundar (Plate 3). The shrine was later renovated (*jīrṇoddhār*) in 1952 by one Manaklāl, a resident of Phalodi. Handa 1984:232.
33. See Cort 2000:112 and Daniel 1984.
34. See Flügel 1995-96 and Vallely 2002 on the Terāpanth.
35. For statements of the basic Terāpanthī position, which was in large part the basis for the formation of the sect by Ācārya Bhikṣu (Bhikhaṇ) in the eighteenth century, see Mahāprajñā 1993:90–115; Mahāprajñā 1994:18–32; and Mahendra Kumar 1994:4–6, 20–28.
36. The devotion evident from Terāpanthī laity to their *ācārya*s, both living and deceased, expressed both in pilgrimage and monetary donation, indicates that in spite of this ideology there is most likely a strong sense that devotion to the *ācārya*s insures worldly wellbeing also. Some Terāpanthīs on pilgrimage tours around Rajasthan mentioned Sacciyā and the "non-Jain" deities in the same tone as their visits to the *samādhi sthal*s (cremation sites) of the late Ācārya Tulsi and Ācārya Bhikhaṇ (the eighteenth-century founder of the Terāpanth), and the living presence of the current Ācārya Mahāprajñā. This is an area of Terāpanthī culture that needs to be researched, as recent research on Terāpanthīs has focused almost exclusively upon the mendicants and the normative Terāpanthī ideology.
37. But due to the anti-temple position of the Terāpanth, this man did not visit the temple of Mahāvīra in Osian.

38. *Bhajan Mālā* (n.d.), p. 12.
39. *Bhajan Mālā* (n.d.), p. 56.
40. Here we see Jain, merchant caste, and urban middle class emphases on decorum and control expressed even in so seemingly "personal" an experience as possession by the goddess.
41. This is just one example of a broader pattern of the gradual "Baniyaization" of religion in Rajasthan in the decades since Indian Independence, as vegetarian Baniyās (merchant castes) increasingly are coming to prominence over meat-eating Rājpūts. See Babb 2004:231–33.
42. The majority of Jains in Marwar, however, are not Mūrtipūjaks, as the iconoclastic Sthānakvāsīs have been in the majority here for at least the past century.
43. We also encountered several instances of Jains now resident far from Rajasthan who had lost all knowledge of their *kul devī*s, and having heard of Sacciyā had come in a search for their socio-religious roots. After we witnessed one such family inquire from a temple *pujārī* as to whether or not Sacciyā was their *kul devī*, the *pujārī* informed us that he regularly gets such inquiries (and also inquiries as to the residence of patriclan genealogists or Rāvs), and has gained enough knowledge of these details of Osvāl identity that he is frequently able to direct such pilgrims elsewhere.
44. The majority of the Śvetāmbar Jains in this part of Rajasthan are Sthānakvāsī, but many of these Sthānakvāsī congregations for much of this century have not been absolutely strict in their rejection of the temple cult (Guṇsundar 1939:I,248; I,718), perhaps reflecting the earlier influence in Rajasthan of the image-worshiping branch of the Loṅkā Gacch based in Bikaner.
45. See Babb 1996:174–95 and Cort 2001:93–99 on the theology that underlies Jain worship of images of the Jina.
46. "Hymn to Mahāvīra Who Adorns Osian" (*Osiyāṃ Maṇḍan Mahāvīr kā Stavan*). This hymn is from book 687 in the collection of the Jñānsundar Pustak Bhaṇḍār in Jodhpur. It has no cover or title page. It contains hymns for use in the Varddhmān Jain Vidyālay, the Jain boarding school in Osian, and was published in the twenty-third year of the school, circa 1938 CE. They are in standard Hindi, not the local Marwari, and so I surmise that they were composed in the 1930s by a schoolmaster.
47. Some informants attributed this fluidity of understandings of *jāti*, *kul*, *gotra*, and related categories to the effects of modernity, in particular education and migration. A careful reading of the available historical evidence, however, indicates that they have always been highly fluid, and in many ways have become more reified over the past century due to the efforts of "reformers." See Babb 2004 and chapter nine in this volume.
48. This sense of "origin" is expressed in an especially clear manner in Gujarati, where one speaks of one's ancestral place as one's *mūḷ vatan*, "root residence." The metaphor of a tree with its roots, trunk, and branches, is common to genealogies in India, Europe, and North America. This arboreal metaphor is vividly expressed at the temple of Dadhimatī Mātā. On a wall of the compound surrounding the temple is a painting of a tree depicting the 144 branches of the Dāhimā Brahman caste, descended from their root ancestor.
49. On the latter, see Cort 1988.
50. There are, however, some exceptions to this generalization. In Jaipur five Jain temples are characterized as *pañcāyatī* temples. There is at least one for each Jain image-worshiping sect (both Śvetāmbar and Digambar), and several informants said that in earlier times every Jain belonged to a particular *pañcāyatī* temple where the family would record births, marriages, and deaths. I also know of one case of Jains performing *muṇḍan* at a Jain temple: many Digambar Jains perform this rite at the temple of Mahāvīrjī in Karauli district. Formerly this rite was performed on the main steps of the temple. In recent years the temple trust has erected a platform a little distance away from the temple,

next to a shrine containing only the image of the Jina's footprints (not a fully iconic image); but it has not attempted to forbid the practice.

There is one other way in which a Jain image can function as a *kul* and *sthānīya* deity. I know of at least three cases—Mahāvīrjī, the Digambar temple at Padampura in Jaipur district (Nyāytīrth 1997:91-95), and Kesariyā Ādināthā (Humphrey 1991)—where the Jina image is simultaneously identified by local non-Jains as a different deity (respectively Cāndanpurvāle Bābā, Bāṛāvāle Bābā, and Kariā Bābā), and worshiped by them for removing troubles and bringing worldly well-being, and on lifecycle occasions.

51. Ramanujan 1999a is an excellent discussion of the Indian context-sensitive conception of the person.

7

Patronage, Authority, Proprietary Rights, and History

Communities and Pilgrimage Temples in Western India

JOHN E. CORT

The study of medieval Indian temples has focused largely on structures created, endowed, and sustained through royal patronage, as signs of royal prestige, political aspirations, and devotion. The western Indian temples of Sacciyā Mātā and Mahāvīra in Osian, Dadhimatī Mātā in Goth-Manglod, and Raṇchoḍjī in Khed all exhibit an importantly different pattern. Whatever may have been the nature of their original construction and endowment, they have survived for a thousand years due not to exclusively royal support, but largely due to the support and devotion of specific caste communities. In our research we were interested in exploring ways in which the connections between these temples and the caste communities that worship at them could provide insights into institutional continuities in Indian society and culture. Our assumption was that the specific connections between castes and the deities enthroned in these temples could explain both the continuing importance of these temples, and perhaps even their very survival—a rather remarkable fact when one considers how few temples of such antiquity have survived as active religious centers in India.

Our research uncovered much information that challenges a too ready attribution of continuities of caste or community patronage. The currently prevalent origin narrative of the Osian Mahāvīra temple focuses in part on its abandonment in medieval times and then its rediscovery and renovation in the late-nineteenth century. According to the version published by the temple trust, which therefore functions as something of an "official history," what had been a royal capital gradually declined into a small market town, and the Osvāl Jains who had originally lived there emigrated (Vārṣṇey 1988). Due to the total lack of Osvāl inhabitants, the very existence of the temple was eventually forgotten by the Jains. Not until the Jain monk Muni Mohanlāl came to Osian in 1878 was the existence of the temple rediscovered by Jains. One imaginative written version of Mohanlāl's rediscovery relates that the temple was completely covered in sand and lost. One morning Mohanlāl went to perform his morning ablutions in the uninhabited scrub outside the village. As he squatted in the desert, he looked up. Only then did he see the golden finial of the spire, and realized there was still a Jain temple in Osian (Mṛgendramuni 1964).[1] According to the official history, Mohanlāl arranged for the temple to be renovated by Jodhpur and later Phalodi Jains, and the site was thus restored to the Jain pilgrimage geography of western India.

Similarly, one narrative—albeit not the best known one—of the Dadhimatī temple also tells of its near abandonment and then its renovation in the mid-nineteenth century. According to this story, which I have seen in only one source (Vaidya 1988), the Dāhimā Brahman renouncer Viṣṇudās came to the site, and in his presence the ground broke open and the spire of an ancient temple emerged.[2] After various other events, Viṣṇudās got the king of Udaipur to clear the jungle and renovate the temple between 1849 and 1851. This would seem to indicate that according to this one source the temple was in a decrepit and at least semi-deserted state in the early nineteenth century, although the simple fact that Viṣṇudās came to the site indicates that it was still alive in Dāhimā sacred geography.[3]

Several of the temples give other evidence of discontinuities in terms of caste worship and patronage. Sacciyā in Osian has long been described as the *kul devī* of the Osvāls, and so her temple has been tied to the origin narrative of the Osvāls. But our research indicated that while Sacciyā has been important for some Osvāl *gotra*s (patriclans) for many centuries, the Osian temple was largely in the hands of its Bhojak priests, and patronage may have been more from local Bhāṭī Rājpūts, Māheśvarīs, and other castes than from non-local Osvāls. Dadhimatī has presumably always been worshiped by Dāhimā Brahmans who lived in the region around the villages of Goth and Manglod, between which the temple is located. But again, research indicated that it was also important in ritual terms to local non-Dāhimā Brahman castes, especially Biḍyāsar Jāṭs, and control may have been in the hands of non-Dāhimā *pujārī*s (or else one specific group of Dāhimā *pujārī*s) up until the early twentieth century. Similarly, the construction of *dharmśālā*s (pilgrim resthouses) and other facilities at the site in this century by Māheśvarīs, Khātīs, Svarṇkārs, and other castes indicates that members of these castes also attach importance to Dadhimatī.

In other words, it quickly emerged in our research that "continuity" was a very problematic term. The histories of these temples evince not clear-cut continuities of patronage, but rather on-going contestations of patronage, worship, and control—all revolving around basic understandings of authority (*adhikār*) over the temple itself, over worship at the temple, and over the material and spiritual resources embodied in and attached to the temple. These contested claims involve differing understandings of the relationships between the deity and castes, between worshipers and worshiped, and between donor and donated. All of the claims also employ two types of evidence: (1) on-the-ground social realities of who lives around the temple, who worships at the temple, who conducts the rites at the temple, and who pays for the upkeep and renovation of the temple; and (2) narratives detailing historical connections among the temple, the deity, and the community in question.

Authority, proprietary rights, and history thus emerged as a set of interwoven themes that appeared and re-appeared throughout the course of our research. In part they would emerge in the study of any temple and its relationships with various communities; but these themes emerged in specific ways in our research in part because the four temples that were the foci for our research were chosen due to their historical importance for art historians, archaeologists, and historians of religion in South Asia. That these temples are important in the religious and architectural history of western India means that "history" inevitably was going to be an important category in our research. The academic conceptions of history used by scholars only partially overlap with conceptions of history used by communities staking claims to rights of worship and management of these temples, and understanding the differing uses and definitions of "history" as a category of analysis was important in our research.[4]

To state this point in another way, a basic question that has arisen in our research can be put as follows: Who has proprietary rights (*svatva, svāmitva*) at a temple? This is not necessarily a matter of ownership in an exclusive sense; proprietary rights at a temple or other sacred site in India can be multiple and overlapping, although one does on occasion find exclusivist claims.[5] Who has rights can be a disputed question in temples as old as the four which we have studied, and clearly during the more than ten centuries these temples have been in existence different groups have had various kinds of control and proprietary rights. In the twentieth century all of these temples have seen different groups successfully (and unsuccessfully) claiming rights at the temples. In this typological chapter, I explore some of the different claims we have seen advanced in the cases of these four temples, as well as claims not advanced in these cases but evidenced from other temples in India. Attention to the details of such claims will allow us better to understand the social histories of temples in South Asia.

Temple Priests

These claims can take several forms. At their simplest, they are based on the continuity of the priests' service (*sevā*) to the temple, service long preceding the establishment of any of the organizations now legally running the temples. At the Sacciyā temple, for example, the Bhojak *pujārī*s claim special rights at the temple, saying that they were originally brought to Osian from Mundiyar (near Nagaur) to be the servants of the goddess when the Rājpūts were converted into Osvāls. This claim is reinforced by the presence in the central shrine, to the left of the main image of Sacciyā, of an image of Mundiyāṛ Mātā, the *kul devī* of the Mundiyāṛ lineage of Bhojaks serving the temple. They claim to have brought this image with them from Mundiyar. According to another Bhojak source (Śarmā n.d.), the *pujārīs* are descendants of the Brahmans who were appointed to worship the goddess at the time of the creation of the Osvāls. This source, who was the chief priest of the temple for several decades, and one of the founders of the current temple trust, also said that the second goddess in the sanctum is Vaiṣṇāvī, not Mundiyāṛ. There are obviously multiple accounts of the connection between the Bhojaks and Sacciyā.

In some cases these are exclusivist claims, that the *pujārīs* are in total control over the temple. In other cases they are partial claims, that the *pujārīs* have hereditary rights at the temple that cannot be alienated by twentieth-century trustees.[6] We see the latter at the Jain temple of Ranakpur, where the *pujārīs* have successfully claimed that they have rights of service granted to their direct ancestors by the temple's builder Dharaṇā Śāha in the fifteenth century. Many Jain temples in western India have seen protracted struggles between Jain trusts and non-Jain *pujārīs* over the nature of such hereditary rights, with the trusts trying to minimize and even eliminate such rights in order to exert more control over the temples.

In some cases priests try to claim that their position as servants (*sevak*) puts them in a special relationship with the deity. These claims are often rendered less persuasive by the low status accorded to temple priests throughout India.[7] While claims by the priests to exclusive proprietary rights have been advanced in relation to many temples in India, they have seldom if ever been successful, in part because other claims are considered more pertinent, and partly because priests are rarely able to mobilize sufficient resources to press their claims successfully. One prominent exception to this which we studied is the temple of Sālāsar Bālājī in Shekhawati: the Dāhimā Brahman *pujārīs* of this temple have successfully established that it is private property.[8] Similarly, the Dīkṣitar *pujārīs* of the Naṭarāja temple at Cidambaram in Tamil Nadu have successfully established in the courts their rights to manage that temple (Younger 1995:16–17). Thus we see that the category of claims of temple priests to special proprietary rights slides into the category of the claim that a temple is private property, which I discuss below.

At Dadhimatī the priests claimed exclusive rights over the temple early in the twentieth century, but lost a court case on the issue in 1918. The evidence is sketchy, as we only have a few Dāhimā sources, but it appears that the Parāsar *pujārīs* claimed that they had organized the temple, a claim which the Dāhimā Mahāsabhā successfully defeated.[9] A recently published seventh-century inscription, interpreted by its Dāhimā editor to refer to Dāhimā contributions to the original building of the temple, was key evidence against the *pujārīs*.[10] That the Dāhimā Mahāsabhā was represented by prominent officials of several royal courts of Rajasthan, while the *pujārīs* were represented by four of their number from the village of Dugastau which is nearby the temple, and who were undoubtedly less-well educated and less-well connected, was probably also significant in determining the outcome of the court proceedings.

At Sacciyā the Bhojak priests were largely in control of the temple until the early 1970s, although it is unclear whether or not this control was to some extent shared with the local Bhāṭī Rājpūt *jāgīrdār*s and the locally dominant Māheśvarīs. Whatever control the Bhojaks exercised was a matter of customary practice, without the benefit of a legally constituted temple trust. Without such a trust there was the risk of the state government taking over the temple, and so a trust was formed with representation from a broad social base. The priests have gradually lost power in the trust to factions representing other local castes and non-local donors. The extent of the Bhojaks' proprietary rights at the temple has been a source of friction in recent years. The *pujārī*s have formed a union, and briefly went on strike during the spring 1998 Navrātrī to press their demand for the reopening of a stairway leading directly off the back of the hill to their residential neighborhood, which had been closed several years earlier to prevent robberies. The gradual decrease in the number of Bhojaks on the trust, and the forming of a union, both indicate a shift in control over the temple from the *pujārī*s to wealthier patrons, and a restriction of the sphere of the Bhojaks' proprietary rights. These rights used to involve control over matters such as renovations and construction, but now involve only more narrowly circumscribed ritual matters.

All four of these temples evidently were largely in the hands of local priests throughout much of the nineteenth century. At all four, other groups, with either regional or national support, successfully challenged this control, with the result that the rights of the priests have been reduced largely to control over the liturgy and rituals.

Local Dominant Caste

This claim can be stated as follows: "Our caste is socially dominant in the area surrounding the temple, and controls (or is dominant in) many local institutions; therefore we should control (or be dominant over) the temple as well."[11] There is no clear example of this claim in connection with any of the four temples we studied. Some Dāhimā informants said that the Jāṭ agriculturalists around Dadhimatī had tried to make such a claim early in the twentieth century, but further investigation would seem to indicate this wasn't fully the case. After Independence, and the rise to political prominence in the area of the formerly disempowered agricultural Jāṭs, it appears that an important Jāṭ politician tried unsuccessfully to have a Jāṭ boarding school established within the temple precincts. What also appears to have occurred is that the Jāṭs claimed that as the dominant community of the area they had the rights to the land surrounding the temple, both agricultural and mining land, from which the temple derived income.

To a certain extent this does appear to be a relevant model for understanding the Raṇchodjī temple at Khed. There it is not the locally dominant agricultural caste that has claimed rights at the temple, but rather the regionally dominant merchant caste, the Agravāls, who have successfully attained a position of predominance in patronizing the temple due to the financial resources they could bring to bear. To a slight extent the Māheśvarīs of Osian, who are the dominant merchant caste in both the village and the immediate area, appear to have exerted some influence on the temple of Sacciyā in terms of the gradual vegetarianizing of the temple in the twentieth century, in contrast to the preferences of the local Rājpūts and lower castes for animal offerings. But in recent decades the Māheśvarī influence has been largely overshadowed by that of wealthy non-local Osvāl donors.

In the twentieth century the development of modern means of transport has made these temples much more accessible to people from a vastly wider catchment area. As a result, the ways in which these temples function as socio-economic institutions has changed dramatically. Dispersed groups such as the Dāhimās or Osvāls can often mobilize much greater economic and political resources than the local elite, and thus the claims to proprietary rights of a locally dominant caste, which is still based in a rural or small town economy, may be outweighed (and out-bought) by those of a wealthier dispersed community based in the urban, national, and even international economy.

Traditional Patron/s (*Jajmān*)

The classic model for the patron is the king or other royal person who donates money and/or land for the building, maintenance, and/or renovation of a temple. The role of patron might also on occasion be adopted by a local lord (*jāgīrdār*) acting in a royal manner. It is quite likely that the current physical structures of all four of these temples were constructed with some form of royal patronage.

The model of the royal patron has also been adopted by wealthy Jain merchants acting as "merchant princes." The most famous examples of this are the thirteenth-century brothers Vastupāla and Tejaḥpāla, who were responsible for the construction of a number of temples throughout present-day Gujarat and southern Rajasthan. Other examples are Vimala Śāha, who in the eleventh century was responsible for constructing the Vimala Vasahī at Abu, and Dharaṇā Śāha who was responsible for constructing the temple at Ranakpur in the fifteenth century. Near Jodhpur, the temple of Svayambhū Pārśvanātha at Kaparda was built between 1617 and 1621 by Bhānā Bhaṇḍārī, the governor (*hākim*) of Jetaran under King Gaj Singh of Jodhpur (*Tīrth Darśan* 1980:151–53).

We lack any origin myth for the Raṇchoḍjī temple, but the origin myths of Sacciyā, Mahāvīrā, and Dadhimatī all tell of their construction by royal patrons. In the case of the first two, the construction is part of the same larger narrative that also relates the establishment of the Osvāl caste. In brief (Vārṣṇey 1988), Upaldev, the Śaiva king of Upkeshpur (Osian), and all the other meat-eating resident Rājpūts were converted into vegetarian Jain Osvāls by the Jain monk Ācārya Ratnaprabhsūri. Uhaṛ, one of the king's ministers, built the Jain temple. The construction of the temple of Sacciyā (originally Cāmuṇḍā) is not mentioned in the standard account; since she was the patron goddess of the city, her temple was presumably built by Upaldev as part of his establishing the city. Another source (Jñānsundar 1929:91, 1943:111–12) says that the Sacciyā temple was originally also a Jain temple, to Pārśvanātha, built by Upaldev.

The myths of Dadhimatī in several ways recount royal constructions. One story says that a King Māndhātā built the first temple here at the instruction of the goddess herself in the Treta Yuga (Jośī 1994:8).[12] This temple disappeared after many years. A song well-known among Dāhimā Brahman devotees of Dadhimatī, composed in 1853 by one Jeṭhmal of Khimsar, credits the building of the Dadhimatī temple to the king of Udaipur.[13]

While these narratives tell of royal foundings, these temples have been without exclusive royal patronage for much if not most of their existence. Evidence of such later patronage is certainly absent from Mahāvīra, although here the royal patron is replaced by the congregation or *saṅgh* (see below) as patron, and it is in part on the basis of the *saṅgh*'s financing and managing later renovations of the temple that the *saṅgh* has clear proprietary rights over the temple. We did not discover any evidence for the local Bhāṭī Rajpūt *jāgīrdār*s of Osian extending such patronage to Sacciyā, although they clearly had an important role in the ritual life of the temple, and so conceivably might have contributed occasionally toward its maintenance. Nor is there evidence of such support at Raṇchoḍjī, although some informants thought there might have been some patronage in earlier times from the local Rājpūt *jāgīrdār* of Jasol.

Only at Dadhimatī is there clear evidence of recent royal patronage. This is seen most clearly in an inscription of 1851 CE. The text of the inscription details the extensive re-configuration of the temple's surrounding structures funded by the King of Udaipur, and all done at the instruction of Viṣṇudās, a charismatic Dāhimā Brahman renouncer (Śarmā 1915). This did not, however, lead to a claim of any proprietary rights on the part of the Udaipur royal family or state, and the Dāhimās have interpreted this evidence to indicate that while the king financed the constructions, he did not act as patron, and so had no special rights. Two informants said that while the king paid for the renovation, the temple nonetheless belonged to the Dāhimās, because the king acted at the request (*prernā*) of Viṣṇudās. There are also references to donations for renovations of the temple from King Sardār Singh of Jodhpur in 1924 in thanks for the miraculous cure of the queen, but again these have not led to claims of proprietary rights, and have certainly been very much downplayed by the Dāhimā beneficiaries of such donations (Vaidya 1988:28, Jośī n.d.:6). Nor did a donation by King Śer Singh of Jaiṣalmer result in any such claims (Jośī n.d.:6).[14]

Human Descent from the Deity, or Some Other Special Connection to the Deity

The basis of this claim is a genealogical, almost biological one, that a particular community due to the nature of its origin has a special relationship with the deity in the temple, and therefore has special proprietary rights. This is most clearly seen at Dadhimatī, where the Dāhimā Brahmans' origin story involves Dadhimatī's pledge to be their caste-goddess (*kul devī*). The 144 grandsons of Dādhīci performed a grand vegetarian fire sacrifice at the *kuṇḍ* near the site of the contemporary temple. Dadhimatī manifested in the *kuṇḍ* in response to the sacrifice, and agreed to be their *kul devī*. The Dāhimās in this century have based their successful claims to sole proprietorship of the temple, with the temple management being exercized by the Dāhimā Mahāsabhā, the caste association, upon this special relationship, saying that while Dadhimatī is an important goddess for all people living in the general area of the temple, an area they call Dadhimatī *kṣetra* ("The Site of Dadhimatī"), she is uniquely important for them as their *kul devī*.

This is also at the heart of the Osvāl understanding of their relationship to Sacciyā. One Osvāl origin myth locates that origin in Osian, with Sacciyā as the *kul devī* of all Osvāls. This relationship is certainly one factor in the lavish financial support this temple receives from Osvāls.

In contrast to Dāhimā control over Dadhimatī, the recent dominance of Osvāls in the financial affairs of Sacciyā has not led to claims of sole proprietorship. Osvāls recognize that Sacciyā is the *kul devī* of lineages of many other castes (a claim often denied by Dāhimā Brahmans in the case of Dadhimatī), and is clearly of much greater significance to all other castes in the surrounding area than is Dadhimatī. The current Temple Trust uses the broad appeal of Sacciyā to many castes as support for its claim to observe the modern rules of a public temple trust (chapter three). A further factor is that since Sacciyā is located in a much more populous and prosperous area than is Dadhimatī, non-Osvāl support for Sacciyā is greater than non-Dāhimā support for Dadhimatī, and so no single caste community has successfully claimed control over Sacciyā.

Claims of descent-based proprietorship do not occur in the cases of Mahāvīra or Raṇchoḍjī. In both cases the main deity in the temple is a transcendent male figure, with a universal appeal, rather than one with a specific caste-based origin myth.

Rights to worship a deity may also be based on an alternative identity of the image, and even involve alternative forms of worship. A well-known case of this is at the Jain temple of Kesariyā south of Udaipur. Jains worship the main image as the Jina Ādinātha, known here as Kesariyājī. It is also worshiped by local Bhil tribals as Kālājī or Kariā Bābā,[15] and Caroline Humphrey reports that they "take a pride in visiting the temple without the humble demeanour" that is commonly associated with Jain temple visitation. She further says that in the annual chariot festival (*rath yātrā*), the Bhils "dance wildly in front of the procession," in what sounds like a form of possession cult very alien to Jain worship of Jinas (Humphrey 1991:217). Similarly, according to one source, local Jāṭs, Rabārīs, and other similar castes worship the image of Raṇchoḍjī Viṣṇu as Bhūriyā Bābā, and they worship the Hanumān image in a small side shrine as Khoṛiyā Bābā (Gupta 1957, n.d.). In particular, they come to worship these two Bābās at the time of marriage, when they perform the rite known as *jāt denā*, and at the time of the first tonsure of a child, when they perform the rite known as *muṇḍan* or *jhaḍūl utarvānā*.

This right to perform specific rituals to specific deities (or a caste-specific understanding of the main deity) is found at many temples. At the Mahāvīra temple in Osian, many non-Jains come not to worship the Jina image, but to perform *jāt denā* to an image of Bherū on the side of the temple (Plates 30, 31). Another image of the same Bherū is located just outside the front gateway to the temple, and it is here that untouchables perform *jāt denā*. This right, to worship a specific deity within (or on the boundary of) the temple precincts, is very circumscribed, and does not entail any further rights there.

Charismatic Renouncers

Our research has shown that a charismatic renouncer can have a profound impact upon the origin and subsequent history of a temple. Proprietary claims can be based upon a relationship with a particular charismatic renouncer, or such a renouncer can change the nature of the proprietary patterns of a temple. Such renouncers have been significant players in the nineteenth- and twentieth-century histories of three of the temples; only in the case of Sacciyā have they been absent.

The story of Viṣṇudās and Dadhimatī is of a renouncer who almost single-handedly arranged for the renovation of the temple (Śarmā 1915). That he was also a Dāhimā Brahman, and that his son from his pre-renouncer status also played a major role in the renovation of the temple, helped solidify Dāhimā claims to the temple, and shows how renouncers oftentimes continue to work for the welfare of their natal caste. Viṣṇudās did not formally take *saṅnyās*, but rather was a widower who refused a second marriage under the influence of his *vairāgya* or feelings of renunciation, and was called a *brahmacārī* due to his willed celibacy. First he prayed to the goddess and with her aid removed a stone slab placed over the image of the goddess by one Gaurī Śāh that made *darśan* difficult.[16] Later, he became well-known for his performance of eleven fire sacrifices (*homa*), which brought him to the attention of King Sarūp Singh of Udaipur. Between 1849 and 1851, Sarūp Singh renovated the temple and built the surrounding structures at the instructions of Viṣṇudās and his son Baldev.[17] We did not discover any further connections of renouncers with Dadhimatī, and the Dāhimā community more broadly does not appear to be one that has produced many renouncers.

In the case of the Mahāvīra temple, several Jain renouncers played crucial roles in the temple's history. The first of these is the quasi-mythical Ācārya Ratnaprabhsūri, who is credited with first consecrating the image almost 2,500 years ago, after he had converted the local population to Jainism. In more recent times, the "rediscovery" of the temple is credited to the monk Mohanlāl, who is also credited with instructing the Jodhpur Jain community to arrange for the renovation and restoration of what was previously a largely abandoned temple.[18] What is unknown is whether or not this Jain reclamation of the temple was resisted by any local non-Jain communities. After Mohanlāl, in the 1910s the monks Ratnavijay and Jñānsundar were instrumental in putting the management of the temple on a sound footing by instructing the laity overseeing the temple to establish a formal organization to run the temple, and to start efficient financial record keeping. Since there is no resident Jain population in Osian, Ratnavijay also was instrumental in getting the Jains of Marwar to establish a boarding school there, so that the school boys could act as a de facto resident Jain population, and Jñānsundar played a significant role in enabling the school to overcome several near failures in its early years. This has not led to an ongoing relationship between renouncers and the temple, however. This is in part because

Ratnavijay had only one important disciple, who was Jñānsundar, and the latter had only a few disciples, none of whom are alive. As a result there was no disciplic lineage to express any special connection with the temple. This is different from some other Jain temples, such as Mahudi in Gujarat, where the successors of Ācārya Buddhisāgarsūri retain a special connection with the temple (Cort 1997), or Nakora, where successors of Ācārya Himācalsūri retain a special connection. Further, due to the relative paucity of Mūrtipūjak Jains in this area of Marwar, few Mūrtipūjak monks come to Osian.

A charismatic renouncer also seems to have played an important role in the recent rise of the Agarvāls to a position of dominance in the oversight of the Raṇchoḍjī temple. Haridās was a renouncer who had been born an Agravāl, and stayed for some time at the temple.[19] He was instrumental in the formal establishment twenty years ago of a trust to oversee the temple, and it appears that it was in part his charismatic teaching that got many Agravāls involved in temple affairs. Here again, however, there has not been an ongoing influence of renouncers over temple affairs; Haridās's disciple Rāmśaraṇācārya resides in the area, but plays no special role in temple affairs.

Several other temples which we have studied for comparative purposes also reveal the central role played by renouncers. The early twentieth-century renovation of the Jain complex at Nakora was inspired by Sādhvī Sundarśrī and Muni Himmatvijay (later Ācārya Vijay Himācalsūri) of the Tapā Gacch (Sālecā 1991). The early twentieth-century renovation of the Jain temple at Kaparda was inspired by Ācārya Nemisūri of the Tapā Gacch (*Kāparṛā* n.d.). The Jain temple at Gangani, another old site outside of Jodhpur, was renovated under the inspiration of Jñānsundar's last disciple, Muni Premsundar (*Gāṅgāṇī* 1969). Finally, the story behind the origin of the temple of Sālāsar Bālājī in Shekawati revolves around Mohandās, another Dāhimā Brahman renouncer, who lived in the mid-eighteenth century (Rāmdatt 1984, Bedhṛak 1997). Mohandās had a number of direct experiences of the heroic Vīr Hanumān. Eventually a *svayambhū* ("self-born") image of Hanumān was established in Salasar, and the descendants of Mohandās's sister's son Udayrām became the hereditary *pujārīs*.

The Temple as Private Property

In none of the cases we have studied is the temple seen as private property. But there are examples of such. Perhaps the best known in western India are temples of the important Vaiṣṇava Puṣṭimārg (or Vallabh) congregation. In this tradition temples are known as *havelīs*, "palaces" (see Pramar 1989). Many of them are legally considered to be not public temples but rather the private residences of the priests, into which the public is allowed to view the images.

There are two other important examples of privately-held temples that we encountered. One is the Gaṇeśa temple at Moti Doongri in Jaipur, which is the private property of an extended family of Dāhimās, who serve as priests. The other example is that of Sālāsar Bālājī, which is also the private property of an extended family of Dāhimās.

The cases of the Jaipur Gaṇeśa temple and Sālāsar Bālājī temple indicate that some quite important, wealthy temples can be retained as private property. One of the best-known temples in India which retains this status is the temple of Naṭarāja at Cidambaram in Tamil Nadu. Paul Younger (1995:19–20) reports that in both 1954 and 1981 the courts found that the special practices of the Dīkṣitar *pujārīs* were sufficently unique that the community formed a "special denomination," and so it was allowed to continue management of the temple. This is a slightly different sense of "private property" from that found in Jaipur and Salasar, and indicates that this category covers a spectrum of temple-management customs.

The Temple as State Property

"State" can be understood in two ways. In pre-Independence India, all four of the temples we studied were within the boundaries of the State of Marwar. Here, the king himself as the embodiment of the state was seen as the ultimate owner of all property (albeit not with unlimited rights to that land), and land was understood to be "private property" in only a very limited sense. However, in none of the four cases did the royal court actively intervene or oversee the running of these temples. We have uncovered only one instance in which this was even an issue. In the early years of the twentieth century the All-India Dāhimā Mahāsabhā, acting as the umbrella organization of all Dāhimās, worked to establish its proprietary rights to the Dadhimatī temple. On the one hand it established its rights against the priests who claimed proprietary rights as temple servants of long standing. There was also a claim advanced by the owners of one or more local gypsum strip-mining companies that the temple was state property.[20] At issue here was whether or not the companies could use rooms in the temple compound as offices. If the temple were state property, then the companies could use the rooms with permission of the local government representatives. But if the temple were not state property, as eventually the Mahāsabhā established, then the companies would have to seek the Mahāsabhā's permission and pay rent to it.

There are several instances in India in which the temple is not so much state property, as the state as a whole is temple property—or, more properly, god's property, since the state as a whole is ceded to the deity and the king reigns as regent. One example of such a state temple is that of Eklingjī outside of Udaipur. This temple has been under the direct control of the royal family since it was constructed in 1467. Eklingjī (Śiva) himself is recognized as the official ruler of Mewar, and the King serves as his prime minister (Gaston 1997:52, citing Tod 1829:411–12). This was a fairly common practice in medieval India, as we find similar examples from eastern and southern India, in the contexts of the temple of Jagannātha in Puri, Orissa, and the temple of Virūpākṣa in Vijayanagara. In 1230, the Gaṅga king Anaṅgabhīma dedicated the whole of his empire to Jagannātha-Puruṣottama, and declared himself the lord's son and deputy (Kulke 1978a:151–2). This practice was continued by the fifteenth-century Sūryavaṃśi king Kapilendra, who in 1464 described himself as the servant (*sevaka*) of Jagannātha (Kulke

1978b:205). In the mid-fourteenth century the Sangamas, the first dynasty of Vijayanagara, settled in Hampi, their new capital city. They adopted Virūpākṣa, an important local deity, as their family deity, and from then issued official decrees in the name of Virūpākṣa, "suggesting that he was the true lord of the realm" (Asher and Talbot 2006:65; see also Verghese 2000:97-8). Subsequent kings of Vijayanagara continued this practice for the next several centuries. Finally, and closer in time to the present, in the early eighteenth century Sawai Jai Singh, the Kachhwaha ruler who founded Jaipur as his new capital, "considered the god [Govinda Deva, a form of Kṛṣṇa] to be the true ruler of Jaipur and himself, the king, only the god's human agent (Asher and Talbot 2006:254).

There is another way in which a temple can be seen as a vital interest of the state, with the state both claiming some rights for its own and intervening in the process of determining who else has what rights. Every state in India now has a government Temple Management Board (Devsthān), which has the legislated responsibility of overseeing the finances and management of every temple in the state. In some cases these boards have taken over the actual management of the temples themselves. The most famous example in India is that of the Veṅkateśvar Bālājī temple in Tirupati, near Madras, which is by all accounts the wealthiest temple in India. Other well-known examples are closer at hand in north Gujarat, where the goddess temples of Ambājī and Bahucarājī are managed by the state Devsthān. None of the temples we studied is so managed, although several informants indicated that it was the possibility of the Rajasthan Devsthān taking over the Sacciyā temple, which at the time was operating without a legal trust, that helped persuade the priests managing the temple to agree to form a more broadly representative trust in the early 1970s.

The ways in which state Devsthāns oversee temples differ from state to state, and this is far too complex a subject to cover in any depth here. Further, these patterns have changed over the past two centuries of first colonial and then independent Indian rule.[21] But a few examples will help us see in part how Devsthāns function. In the case of the Puṣṭīmārg temple at Nathdwara, the current temple board was established in 1959 by an official Nathdwara Temple Act of the Rajasthan state government. The board consists of the traditional head of the temple (the Tilkayat), the district collector, and nine other members appointed by the State government, all of whom have to be members of the Puṣṭimārg Sampradāy (Jindel 1976:101–05, Verdia 1982:68–72). In Bhubhaneswar, Orissa, the famous Liṅgarāj temple operates under the direction of a Board of Trustees, which itself is appointed by the statewide Commissioner of Endowments, in accordance with the Orissa Hindu Religious Endowment Act of 1939 (Mahapatra 1981:32–38). The Orissa act was based on the earlier Madras act, first passed in 1925 and subsequently amended several times. The Tamil Nadu state government, with its schemes to ensure the proper Āgamic ritual education of the *pujārīs*, would appear to be the most actively interventionist of all the state Devsthāns (Fuller 1984:112–61). In part this may reflect the implementation in Tamil Nadu in the twentieth century of the medieval liturgical Āgama tradition in a modernized educational form (Fuller 1984:135–61, 2003:80–113, and the sources he cites). Our research indicated that there is no such formal liturgical tradition at any of the temples we studied in Rajasthan, and concerns for ritual orthopraxy were noticeably absent.

The state intervenes in another way in all these temples. Each one is officially registered as a protected archaeological monument by the government of the state of Rajasthan, and so the management of each temple has to be careful in its renovation and repairing work not to violate the "originality" of the temple. The national and state archaeological authorities understand this to mean a perceived "original" form and intention of the temple. This does not mean that the temples cannot be extensively renovated and even reconfigured, but we know that state archaeological authorities intervened to block a proposed renovation at Mahāvīra, and also to prevent further painting and installation of decorative mirror-work at Raṇchoḍjī. None of the temples exhibited the degree of control by archaeological control as exhibited at the Liṅgarāj temple, where the Board of Trustees and the Commissioner of Endowments are responsible for the management of the temple, but the Archaeological Survey of India is responsible for the protection of the physical structure (Mahapatra 1981:39, 169–73).

The state further intervenes in the running of temples through the legal provisions of trust and tax laws (see chapter three). While a very small temple may easily be private property, almost any temple that is visited by more than immediate family members falls into the legal definition of a public temple, and if the finances involved are sufficient the temple must be registered as a public trust with the state Register of Trusts. Every trust is required to submit an audited expense report on an annual basis. All four of the temples we studied now fall under this category as registered public trusts with boards of trustees and annual financial reports, which were published documents in the cases of the Sacciyā and Mahāvīra temples. We did encounter one temple that was not registered as a public trust, but was instead considered to be a private business run for the benefit of the *pujārī*s who owned it and who made their livelihood by serving the larger public. This was the Jaipur Gaṇeśa temple. A disadvantage of running the temple as a business rather than a public trust is that income derived by the latter is tax-free, whereas income from a business is highly taxed, with the result that the income tax authorities frequently intervened in the affairs of the Gaṇeśa temple.[22]

The Congregation (*Saṅgh*)

The congregational form of internal organization is much stronger in Jainism than in the various social and religious strands that together constitute "Hinduism." The *saṅgh* is defined in Jainism as the totality of the four sub-communities of monks, nuns, laymen, and laywomen, and in theory it is the final authority on any substantial matter. The *saṅgh* is larger than any individual caste or local community, and in its largest form constitutes the totality of all Śvetāmbar Mūrtipūjak Jains. Thus proprietary rights at a public pilgrimage temple such as Mahāvīra rest not with an individual but with the *saṅgh*. The trust that actually manages the temple is understood to represent the *saṅgh*, and as such is accountable to the larger Jain community, although in actual practice it is largely autonomous. This form of community organization is lacking in any of the other three temples, although it is found in differing forms in certain "sects" of Hinduism, usually those centered around devotion to a particular deity such as Kṛṣṇa and/or the teachings of a particular lineage of gurus.

There is no Jain population in Osian itself, and the Jain population of the surrounding villages is largely Sthānakvāsī. As a result, control of the Mahāvīra temple passed out of Jain hands at an undetermined time in the past. After Mohanlāl came to Osian in 1878, he instructed an important member of the Jodhpur Mūrtipūjak *saṅgh* to take responsibility for the renovation and oversight of the temple.[23] This continued until 1894, when control was transferred to a leading member of the Phalodi *saṅgh*, and control over the temple has been in the hands of Jains whose native place is Phalodi ever since, even though the current manager is a Jodhpur Jain. Up until 1961 the temple was under the control of the same board that ran the Jain boarding school; this board had been legally established in 1915. In 1961 the school was officially registered under the state Charitable Institutions Law of 1958. In 1981 the managements of the school and the temple were separated, and the Seṭh Śrī Maṅgalsiṃhjī Ratansiṃhjī Dev kī Peḍhī Trust was legally registered with the Devsthān. While most of the principal trustees live in Chennai and Mumbai, in almost all cases their families originally came from Phalodi, and they maintain close connections with the town.

History

History enters in various ways into all of these different strategies for claiming proprietary rights. Lawrence Babb discusses differing conceptions of history in greater depth in chapter two, but let me conclude this chapter with a few remarks.

*Pujārī*s claim that the history of their continuous service of the deity gives them proprietary rights. Indian law has recognized the limited validity of such claims, although it has rarely seen them as valid claims to exclusive proprietary rights. We have seen such claims advanced at both Dadhimatī and Sacciyā.

Claims to patronage as *jajmān* are frequently inscribed on stone or copper plates and placed in a visible and permanent location in the temple. These stone or copper-plate inscriptions are major historical sources for our knowledge not only of Indian religious history but of Indian royal and social history as well. Here again this is not a dominant pattern at any of the four temples, and Dāhimās were very explicit in their understanding that the 1851 inscription concerning the donations by the King of Udaipur to the Dadhimatī temple did not in any way weaken the Dāhimās' own claims to proprietary rights, since it was a Dāhimā who organized the donation and supervised the actual work. The Dāhimās have successfully used a seventh-century inscription to bolster their claims to exclusive control over the temple.

Claims to proprietary rights based upon descent or some other special relationship with the deity are based upon the origin myths of the community in question. Calling them "myths" is, of course, to employ the intellectual categories of the European-American academy. They are seen by the communities in question as narratives that profoundly validate their self-identity; I term them myths to indicate that these narratives tend to be community-specific, and are shared only in part with other communities involved with the temple.

Thus history is a multivalent category involved in all of these temples. There is the history of oral and written mythic and origin texts. There is the history of stone and copper-plate inscriptions. There is the history embedded in residence at a place, or (as in the case of Dāhimās at Dadhimatī and Osvāls at Osian) long-term non-residence. There is the history embedded in the very temples themselves. Each of these histories employs different standards of proof (*pramāṇ*), is expressed in different genres of communication, and is fitted into different contexts of meaning. All of them are used to advance claims of proprietary rights at temples.

We thus see that temples can be studied as sites of contestation over financial assets, political assets, spiritual assets, and cultural assets. To the one-time visitor, a temple may appear to be a fixed entity with a clearly-defined identity. We see, however, that when viewed over time, the identities of a temple and the deity enthroned in the temple are tied to the identities of an array of people who are connected to the temple as patrons, builders, renovators, owners, trustees, ritual specialists, devotees, descendants, neighboring inhabitants, government representatives, and pilgrims. The relationships among these people, the temple, and the deity will fluctuate as different people advance various claims to proprietary rights in relation to the temple and/or the deity. The one-time visitor comes away with the impression that the temple is a solid, continuing presence. To an architectural historian, the temple appears to be far more fluid, as the physical structure is renovated, rebuilt, and reconfigured repeatedly over the centuries. In a similar manner, to a social historian the temple also appears to be fluid over time, as it is one node in an ever-shifting array of social groupings and identities.

Notes

1. Unless the temple was buried in rather short order, this story, which is not found in any other account of Mohanlāl's coming to Osian, is improbable. Inscriptions from 1677 and 1732 record repairs made to the temple under the supervision of craftsmen (*sutradhāra*, *sompurā*) (Handa 1984:229–30), indicating that it was in active use within a century-and-a-half before Mohanlāl's coming to Osian. Similarly, the *Osiyā Vīr Stavan* composed by the Jain monk Nayapramod in 1655 describes the temple as in active worship (Śāh 1953:173–74). More recently, an image of Gautam Svāmī was installed in the temple in 1872 CE (VS 1929), just six years before Mohanlāl's visit. (This image is not mentioned by Handa [1984], but has been situated in a prominent location since before the reconfiguration of the temple in the 1960s and 1970s.) Narratives of the "rediscovery" of temples frequently exaggerate the preceding desuetude in order to glorify the hero of the narrative. This observation applies equally to the narrative of Viṣṇudās and Dadhimatī (see below).

The Jain manager of the temple told us a different—and more believable—story concerning Mohanlāl's "re-discovery" of the temple. As he showed us around the temple, he stopped in front of the image of Mohanlāl. Mohanlāl was a great scholar, he said, and so had read about the temple of Osian. He came to see it, but it was covered in sand, with only the temple spire visible. Mohanlāl arranged for a lay patron from Jodhpur to clear away the sand. When he finally entered the temple, Mohanlāl found the sanctum covered by a stone wall. He had one of the workers make a small hole in the wall. When he peered through the wall he saw that the image was still enshrined there, so he had the rest of the wall removed. Similar stone slabs preserved the two large images of Ādinātha on side altars in the main temple.

2. The structural similarities between the Mohanlāl and Viṣṇudās stories, of a temple buried up to the top of the spire which is rediscovered when a charismatic renouncer sees the finial, indicates that we are dealing with a cultural trope. Further, the similarity between this trope of the rediscovery of a buried temple and the many stories in South Asia of the discovery or rediscovery of a buried image (Eichinger Ferro-Luzzi 1987) is quite striking.
3. Again, there is counter-evidence of continuity: according to one source, Paṇḍit Kamalāpati Dādhīc Iṣṭī of Merta arranged for a renovation of the temple in 1780 (*Dādhīc* 3:3–4 [Dec. 1941–Jan. 1942], 95).
4. See Lawrence Babb, chapter two above.
5. The extent to which exclusivist claims are a phenomenon of the gradual penetration throughout India of ideas of exclusive personal property rights that are embedded in English law is a matter that would bear further research.
6. See Fuller 1984 and 1993, and Good 1989, for thorough discussions of these issues in the rather different settings of the large temples in Tamil Nadu.
7. The low status of temple *pujārī*s throughout India has been much discussed; see Fuller 1984:49–71, Heesterman 1985:26–44, Quigley 1993:54–86. Appadurai 1983 also addresses the issue, but from a rather different approach, that priests are of low status due to being Tantric. I think this is an untenable argument.
8. See chapter three on the legal distinctions between public and private temples.
9. This information is from an undated loose page from an issue of *Dadhimatī* magazine, lent to us by a Dāhimā informant, which reports the findings of a Civil Court decision dated 14 January 1918. The same informant also loaned us loose pages from issues of *Dadhimatī* magazine reporting various stages of the quarrel between the Dāhimā Mahāsabhā and the *pujārī*s, dating from 1912, 1917, and 1918.
10. This inscription was published by Pandit Ram Karna Asopa, a Dāhimā and court *paṇḍit* to the King of Marwar. His brother Govind Narayan Asopa almost single-handedly ran the All-India Dāhimā Mahāsabhā for its first several decades. See Ram Karna 1911–12.
11. The concept of the "dominant caste" is from Srinivas 1987:60–115.
12. Other accounts place this event in the Satya Yuga.
13. I have two versions of this song, which differ only in matters of orthography. The song begins with the line "*chand guṇ dadhimathī kā gātā sakal kī sahāy karo mātā.*" *Bhajan Mālā* 1996:12–14, and *Āratī Saṅgrah* 13–14.
14. One informant also claimed that Queen Ahalyābāī Holkar of Indore had contributed to a renovation of the temple; this may well reflect Ahalyābāī's fame as a rebuilder of temples at many important Hindu pilgrimage sites throughout north India. On Ahalyābāī, see Davis 1997:197.

15. Humphrey (1991:218–19) hypothesizes that this tribal deity might be a version of the popular western Indian snake deity Kesariyā Kaṅvar.
16. Again, the similarity to one of the stories of Mohanlāl and the Mahāvīra temple is striking. It is quite possible that the sanctum of each temple was walled shut when the community in control of it could no longer guarantee regular worship and protection of the temple and its main image.
17. This version is based on the lengthy Marwari and Sanskrit inscription carved to commemorate the renovation. Another version has this event occurring 2000 years ago (Dādhīc 1996).
18. Mohanlāl's importance to the Mahāvīra temple was later memorialized in the form of a marble image (*guru mūrti*), installed in a sub-shrine in 1897 CE. The brief inscription on the image gives information about neither the layperson who arranged for its installation nor the mendicant who consecrated it.
19. According to one informant, Haridās was in the Vaiṣṇava Bindugaddī lineage. This would appear to be a local seat of the Nimbarkī tradition. There is a small shrine to Haridās at a nearby temple of Nāḍīvāle Hanumān; this temple is maintained by two Nimbarkī renouncers.
20. *Dadhimatī* 4 (1912). Information on this is also included on several undated loose pages from issues of *Dadhimatī* magazine from the 1910s, loaned us by a Dāhimā informant.
21. See Appadurai 1981, Mukherjee 1977, and Presler 1987 for studies of ways in which the state dealt with temples under colonial rule and since Independence in Tamil Nadu and Orissa.
22. This summarizes what is in fact a rather complex web of legal and financial matters. The relevant laws for Rajasthan are found in Shah 1997 and *Rajasthan Local Laws*.
23. It is not clear from any of our records who controlled the temple prior to 1878, and whether or not there was any resistance to the Jain resumption of control. Osian was only one of a number of places in western India where in the late-nineteenth and early-twentieth centuries the Jains re-asserted control over temples that had come under the control of local Hindu populations after the local Jains all emigrated. In some cases this control was successful only after taking the cases to court, where the Jains' combination of wealth, legal expertise, social standing, and government connections usually allowed them to prevail. Such was the case, for example, at Charup in north Gujarat, a small village just north of Patan, where there was a quarrel between the Jain *saṅgh* of Patan and the Smārta Brahmans of Charup over the Jain temple (Śāh and Śāh 1919). In one case we encountered, after all the Mūrtipūjak Jains had emigrated from the town of Borunda to the east of Jodhpur, the local Sthānakvāsī *saṅgh* took control of the temple. While it may seem odd for the anti-temple Sthānakvāsīs to control a temple, two factors must be taken into account: traditional Marwari (*deśī*) Sthānakvāsīs appear to have been less virulently opposed to the cult of temples than "foreign" (*pardeśī*) Sthānakvāsīs (Guṇsundar 1939:I,248; I,718); and the control of the temple in Borunda also gave the *saṅgh* control over the land endowed to the temple, which consisted of an *upāśray* (monastery-like building) near the temple, and twenty-four bighas of agricultural land.

Part IV

Social Identities

8

Constructing a Jain Mendicant Lineage

Jñānsundar and the Upkeś Gacch

JOHN E. CORT

As we have seen in other chapters in this volume, a key player in the restoration of the Mahāvīra temple at Osian was the Śvetāmbar mendicant Muni Jñānsundar (1880–1955). He encouraged Śvetāmbar Mūrtipūjak Jains of Marwar to support the renovation and maintenance of the temple, and helped establish a Jain boarding school to give a permanent Jain presence in town. Jñānsundar's work at Osian was only one part of a larger life-long project to rewrite Jain history and restructure Jain society, a project that was grand in its ambitions and in the end a notable failure. Looking at Jñānsundar's project allows us, however, valuable insight into what, in the eyes of one mendicant from the first half of the twentieth century, the structures of Jain society should be. His failure to realize this project also allows us insight into some of the practical—as opposed to ideological—organizing features of Jain society.

Jñānsundar is undoubtedly one of the more unique figures in the long history of the Jain tradition. Paul Dundas's succinct description of Jñānsundar as "a pugnacious contro-versialist and something of an eccentric" is, if anything, an understatement (2002:247). Jñānsundar was a prolific author of texts on Jain devotion, ritual, and spirituality. He defended the practice of image-worship (*mūrtipūjā*) against the critiques of the majority Śvetāmbar sect in Marwar, the Sthānakvāsī. He authored far-ranging historical studies in which he attempted to rechart the Jains' understanding of their own history in terms of caste and lineage, and the connections between them. He attempted to fuse the history of the Osvāl castes of western India with, on the one hand, the town of Osian and its temples of Mahāvīra and Sacciyā Mātā, and, on the other hand, the Mūrtipūjak mendicant lineage known as the Upkeś Gacch. This lineage itself is an anomaly in the Jain tradition, for it claims disciplic descent not in common with all other Jain mendicant lineages from Mahāvīra, but instead from Mahāvīra's predecessor, the twenty-third Jina Pārśvanātha. As I have indicated, and we will see in detail, Jñānsundar's attempt to rewrite Jain history, and thereby reorganize the structure of Jain mendicant and lay society in Marwar, was unsuccessful. The years he devoted to this task, despite the clear evidence that almost no other Jains were following him in the details of his project, give evidence to the accuracy of Dundas's characterization of him as eccentric. At the same time, the extensive financial support he was able to garner for his endeavors—hundreds of books published, a boarding school established at Osian, renovation of temples at Osian and Kaparda, a major Jain ritual building constructed in Jodhpur, and much else—indicates that his forceful personality was also a very charismatic and persuasive one.

Muni Jñānsundar

Most of Jñānsundar's life is better documented than that of almost any other Jain mendicant, in large part because of the massive two-volume, 1,350-page biography by his disciple Guṇsundar entitled *Ādarś-Jñān*, "Ideal Knowledge."[1] The wealth of details in the book indicates that most likely it was dictated by Jñānsundar himself, and so is as much autobiography as biography. My discussion of his life is based on Guṇsundar's book, unless indicated otherwise.

Jñānsundar was born as Gayvarcand (also Ghevarmal) in the village of Bisalpur, east of Jodhpur, in Marwar in VS 1937 (1880 CE). The family in earlier generations had been Mūrtipūjak, with *yati*s of the Kaṅvlā Gacch (another name for the Upkeś Gacch) as their family preceptors. Since the mendicants who came to Bisalpur in the late nineteenth century were Sthānakvāsī (before the late nineteenth century full-fledged Mūrtipūjak mendicants had been a rarity in Marwar for many decades, perhaps more than a century), for several generations the family's religious affiliation had been more Sthānakvāsī. In Marwar at this time the divide between the image-worshiping Mūrtipūjaks and the non-image-worshiping Sthānakvāsīs was not as sharp as it became later. The Sthānakvāsīs in Marwar disapproved of the worship of Jina images with material offerings (*dravya pūjā*), but were not ideologically opposed to the non-material veneration (*bhāv pūjā*) of images, and on occasions even the material worship. When Gayvarcand was born, for example, his family performed a ritual lustration (*snātra pūjā*) of a Jina image in a local temple, although this was one of the few times they ever went to the temple. This easy accommodation of both Mūrtipūjak and Sthānakvāsī identities was typical of much of Marwar in the late nineteenth century, before more ideologically iconoclastic mendicants from outside of Marwar started preaching there.

Gayvarcand was given a store to manage by his father in 1894, and married in 1897. Two years later a son died in infancy, and in 1901 he himself nearly died from illness. From this near escape he developed a sense of revulsion (*vairāgya*) for the world. His family resisted his desire to renounce the world and become a Jain mendicant. As a compromise he took four ascetic vows—not to consume unboiled water, not to consume green vegetables, not to eat after sunset, and to avoid sexual intercourse—from Ratnacand, a Sthānakvāsī mendicant in the lineage of his father's guru Rugnāth (Raghunāth). But his ability to maintain these vows was obviously limited. For several years his life was a mixture of associating with Sthānakvāsī mendicants and trying to maintain a family life. During the first nine years of marriage four children were born to him and his wife, but all of them died. In 1906, after hearing in a mendicant's sermon that broken vows are the surest means to a rebirth in a hellish existence, he renewed his vows under Śrīlāl, a Sthānakvāsī mendicant in the Bāīs Ṭolā (Twenty-two Groups), the dominant Sthānakvāsī cluster of lineages in Marwar. Gayvarcand began to associate with mendicants more intensively. He adopted the clothing and conduct of a Sthānakvāsī mendicant, and practiced severe forms of asceticism. For example, in common with many Sthānakvāsī mendicants in Marwar, he used his own urine to clean himself after defecation. He wore only a single loincloth and a single shawl. Because he stopped washing, his body became home to countless lice. This extreme asceticism brought him to the attention of Sthānakvāsī mendicants, several of whom competed to gain him as a disciple. But the competition for his initiation only disappointed him, and in 1906 he performed a self-initiation (*svayam dīkṣā*) and declared himself to be a disciple of Śrīlāl. His relations with the latter, however, were far from amicable, and in 1915 Gayvarcand broke with Śrīlāl.

One of the main issues that precipitated the split was Gayvarcand's public declaration that there is no fault in the worship of images (*mūrtipūjā*). There were widespread debates and discussions on this issue throughout the Śvetāmbar communities of western India in the late nineteenth and early twentieth centuries, and Gayvarcand obviously was well aware of the arguments on both sides. A key point in Gayvarcand's acceptance of the worship of Jina images came during his rainy season retreat in Gangapur in 1913. Near the building in which he was staying was a Mūrtipūjak Jain temple and ritual building (*upāśray*). In the *upāśray* was a small collection of manuscripts, which Gayvarcand studied. In the colophon of a manuscript of the *Niryukti* on the *Ācārāṅga Sūtra*, written in 1351 by the copiest Paṇḍit Bhāvharṣ, he read a description of the stainless fruits of pilgrimage to shrines and *darśan* (ritual viewing) of images. He also read the account in the *Upāsakadaśāṅga Sūtra* of the Jain layman Ānand venerating Jina images, and the account in the *Jñātṛdharmakathā Sūtra* of the Jain laywoman Draupadī worshiping Jina images in a Jina temple. In the *Bhagavatī Sūtra* he read the description of the monks with magical powers (*vidyācara*) who worshiped images, on the basis of which it was clear that the word *caitya* found in many scriptures referred to Jina images.[2] He engaged in discussions on the subject with local Jains. There were also some Terāpanthī *sādhus* in Gangapur for the rainy season retreat. Gayvarcand engaged them in debate on the subject of image-worship, and successfully convinced several Terāpanthī laity that it was an acceptable ritual practice.

From then on Gayvarcand regularly preached that image worship was a proper Jain ritual practice that led to liberation. This led to his break with Śrīlāl. At this time Gayvarcand's conviction was based solely on his independent reading of texts, and conversations with Mūrtipūjak laymen. He had never met a Mūrtipūjak mendicant. In 1915 he inquired from several Jodhpur laymen as to where he might meet such a mendicant, and was told that the Tapā Gacch mendicant Muni Ratnavijay was in Osian. He therefore travelled to Osian. Before meeting Ratnavijay he went to the Mahāvīra temple, and this experience clearly served as a spiritual and aesthetic confirmation of the new direction in his religious life. According to Guṇsundar (1939:I:272), upon entering the temple Jñānsundar was so happy that he took the temple fly-whisk in hand and performed a dance (a common ritual act among Mūrtipūjaks in western India), and said, "O Lord! In what previous life did I acquire the obstructing karma that cheated me of your *darśan*?" (An informant added that Gayvarcand removed his facecloth [*muhpatti*], a defining sign of a Sthānakvāsī mendicant, in front of a side image of Ādinātha in the temple, thus visually signifying his break with his Sthānakvāsī past.) Gayvarcand then went to meet Ratnavijay. He spent a little over a month with Ratnavijay, composing devotional hymns in the temple and studying the different codes of mendicant conduct (*samācārī*) of the Mūrtipūjak *gacch*s. Ratnavijay told him the history of the shrine, and of the conversion to Jainism of Gayvarcand's Osvāl ancestors by Ācārya Ratnaprabhsūri of the Upkeś Gacch. This was a history that Jñānsundar would later retell many times. Ratnavijay urged Gayvarcand, as someone who was local, to take in hand the renovation (*uddhār*) of the shrine. The two of them helped the Phalodi layman who was looking after the temple to establish a formal organization (*peḍhi*) to look after the management of the shrine, and formally inaugurated the new organization as the Maṅgalsiṃh Ratnasiṃh Peḍhi. They chose the name to echo the first initials of Mahāvīra (whose image was the main image in the temple) and Ratnaprabhsūri. Some months later, after the end of the four-month rainy season retreat in 1915, Ratnavijay gave Gayvarcand a new initiation as a full-fledged Mūrtipūjak mendicant (*saṃvegī sādhu*).

Ratnavijay was born in 1872 in Kacch.[3] In 1884 at the age of twelve he was initiated as a mendicant, with the name Ratnacandra, in the Āṭh Koṭī lineage of the Sthānakvāsīs.[4] As was the practice for Sthānakvāsī mendicants, he memorized the Prakrit root texts of the Śvetāmbar *āgama*s, and studied them through Gujarati translations. But he was not satisfied with only this degree of access to the texts, so he studied Sanskrit with a Brahman *paṇḍit* in Bhuj in order to be able to read the Sanskrit commentaries. This was a radical step, for while Mūrtipūjaks insisted that the Sanskrit commentaries were necessary for a full understanding of the root texts, and in essence were inseparably part of the scriptures, Sthānakvāsīs largely rejected the commentaries as later, false interpolations (Dundas 1996). Further, in order to distance them from the corrosive potential of the Sanskrit commentaries, Sthānakvāsī mendicants were forbidden to study Sanskrit. Gayvarcand's disaffection with Sthānakvāsī ideology was also precipitated by an interest in Sanskrit, which began during the rainy season retreat in Gangapur. He realized that he was unable to understand the scriptures adequately because of his lack of knowledge of Sanskrit grammar, and so the local laity arranged for him to study with a *paṇḍit*. When Śrīlāl learned of this, he told the Gangapur laity that they were ruining a good mendicant, and ordered them to stop the instruction.

As a result of Ratnacand's reading the Sanskrit commentaries on the scriptures, in which there are many references to image worship, he came to believe that the worship of Jina images was proper, and so he left the Sthānakvāsī fold. In search of a new guru he went to Radhanpur, where in 1902 he took a new initiation under the Tapā Gacch Muni Dharmvijay (later Ācārya Vijay Dharmsūri), with the new name Muni Ratnavijay.[5] For much of the time before his death in Vapi in southern Gujarat in 1921 he engaged in extensive fasting and meditation, and often travelled alone.

For reasons that are not at all clear, Ratnavijay gave several instructions to Gayvarcand that shaped much of his subsequent career. First, he told Gayvarcand that he was to engage in the renovation (*uddhār*) of his own mendicant lineage (*gacch*). Gayvarcand asked what this lineage was. Ratnavijay explained that Gayvarcand's Osvāl ancestors of the Vaidya Mehtā patriclan had been converted to Jainism by Ratnaprabhsūri of the Upkeś Gacch. This was to be Gayvarcand's lineage, even though at the time there were only domesticated mendicants (*yati*) in the lineage, and no full-fledged mendicants (*saṃvegī sādhu*). (It is not clear to me that there were ever full-fledged mendicants in this lineage in the nine centuries for which we have historical evidence of its existence.) A further explanation for the logic of this unique initiation was that the *yati*s who were Gayvarcand's family preceptors (*kul guru*s) belonged to the Kaṅvlā Gacch, which Ratnavijay explained was another name of the Upkeś Gacch. He also instructed Gayvarcand that he was not to engage in the sectarian (*gacch-mat*) disputes which were widespread in Jain society at the time. Finally, he instructed Gayvarcand not to initiate any laity as mendicant disciples; he could accept as disciples only those who formerly had been Sthānakvāsī mendicants. This last requirement, one I have never heard of elsewhere in Jain history, to a significant extent undermined the instruction to renovate the lineage, for without the ability to initiate laymen as mendicants it proved impossible for the lineage to reproduce itself.

After the end of the rainy season retreat in 1915, Ratnavijay initiated Gayvarcand into the Upkeś Gacch as Muni Jñānsundar, and taught him the rules of the mendicant practice of the Upkeś Gacch. This was largely identical to the Tapā Gacch practice, with the addition of the recitation in the rite of *pratikramaṇ* of some extra verses to the Jain goddess Vairūṭyā Devī and to Ratnaprabhsūri, the great leader of the *gacch* who was credited with converting the Osvāls and Sacciyā Mātā to Jainism seventy years after the decease of Mahāvīra.

Ratnavijay was also responsible for awakening in Jñānsundar his interest in history. One day in Osian, Ratnavijay, Gayvarcand, the manager (*munim*) of the Jain temple, and some students of the newly established Jain Boarding School toured the ruined temples of Osian. Ratnavijay identified one of them as a Jain temple, for in the ruins was a headless and limbless image of the Jina Candraprabha. Ratnavijay showed Gayvarcand the partial inscription on the image,[6] and explained to him the historical importance of this and other inscriptions. From this event Gayvarcand credited his keen interest in history, as recognized by the sobriquet he was later given, "Lover of History" (*itihās premī*).

Despite Ratnavijay's explicit instructions to Jñānsundar not to engage in sectarian arguments, it is obvious that this was precisely what he did. While the determination with which Jñānsundar pursued some of these sectarian disputes is a mark of his personality, a certain amount of criticism of other Jain lineages was unavoidable for one engaged in the process of reforming (or forming) his own lineage, for this process inevitably involves explicitly rejecting practices and doctrines of other lineages.[7] During the period when he was still a Sthānakvāsī but had come to accept the legitimacy of image worship, at the casual request of a layman in Byavar, Gayvarcand had begun to write a book in Hindi verse laying out the arguments in favor of image worship, entitled *Siddh Pratimā Muktāvalī* ("The Pearl Necklace of the Image of the Perfected Being") (Gayvarcand 1918). When he first stayed with Ratnavijay, before his second initiation, he showed the manuscript to Ratnavijay. Ratnavijay urged him to have it published, although not until after he had it proofread by a schooled writer, as it was obviously written by someone who was ignorant of Hindi grammar. In 1915 some local Marwari laymen arranged for both this book and the related *Pratimā Chattīsī* ("Thirty-Six Verses on Images") (Jñānsundar 1916) to be printed in Bombay. Sthānakvāsīs reacted angrily with articles in Jain periodicals criticizing Gayvarcand. Gayvarcand replied with a lengthier defense of images entitled *Gayvar Vilās* ("The Sport of Gayvar") (Jñānsundar 1917). It was in part in response to this negative publicity that Ratnavijay told Gayvarcand that he could not remain a Sthānakvāsī mendicant, but would formally have to become a Mūrtipūjak.

In addition to arguing with the Sthānakvāsīs, Jñānsundar also found himself in quarrels with local mendicants and laity of the Khartar Gacch. In 1916 he spent the first rainy season retreat (*cāturmās*) after his new initiation in Phalodi, where his presence engendered unspecified Mūrtipūjak-Sthānakvāsī and Khartar-Kaṅvlā quarrels. In Phalodi he undertook the beginnings of his study of the history of his new Upkeś Gacch. He studied and copied manuscripts of lineage chronicles (*paṭṭāvalī*) and other historical texts in the local monasteries.

In the late 1910s Jñānsundar spent two years in the Tapā Gacch stronghold of Gujarat. There he met and observed many of the leading Tapā Gacch mendicants. What he saw disappointed him. Even though he had "converted" from Sthānakvāsī to Mūrtipūjak, he was still a mendicant with a strongly ascetic disposition. In contrast to the few material items he retained for his own use, he was alarmed at the amount of material goods that surrounded the mendicants in Gujarat. He began to compose his *Mejhar Nāmā* ("Petition History"), a Gujarati poem that outlined his criticisms. The poem was designed as a letter from this continent addressed to the current Jina Sīmandhara Svāmī in Mahāvideha, telling him all the news about the Jain mendicants in India.[8] Jñānsundar modelled the poem on the *Sīmandhar Jin 125 Gāthānuṃ Stavan* ("125 Verse Hymn to Sīmandhara Jina"), a Gujarati text by the great Tapā Gacch intellectual and reformer Mahopādhyay Yaśovijay (1624–1688) that criticized both the lax conduct of the *yati*s and the anti-image propaganda of the followers of Loṅkā Śāh.

Jñānsundar described the origin of the *Mejhar Nāmā* as follows (Jñānsundar 1935a:46–47):

> I was originally initiated in the Sthānakvāsī order. I took a great interest in studying the rituals (*kriyā*) in the scriptures. When I came into the Mūrtipūjak order I travelled to Gujarat to make a pilgrimage to Siddhācal (Mount Śatruñjay in Saurashtra), that supremely pure place which is the abode of perfection. Along the way I saw the laxity (*śithiltā*) in the conduct (*cāritra*) and rituals (*kriyā*) of the *ācārya*s, *upādhyāya*s, *paṅnyās*s, *sādhu*s and *sādhvī*s (male and female mendicants). My heart could not rest content. During the rainy season retreat in Surat I decided to send a report to Sīmandhara Svāmī, the great soul. I was unable to finish it due to the responsibilities of giving sermons and other tasks. While on pilgrimage to Siddhgiri (Śatruñjay), the text kept growing as I observed the childish play (*bāl līlā*) of the *sādhu*s.

Jñānsundar's last comment is an explicit comparison of the conduct of the Jain mendicants with that of Kṛṣṇa devotees, for whom *līlā* or "play" in imitation of the youthful (*bāl*) Kṛṣṇa is a highly valorized religious practice. The devotional enjoyment of Kṛṣṇa's *līlā* involves the maximum use of all of a person's senses. This is in direct contrast to the Jain religious ideal of ascetic equanimity. Jñānsundar's charge that Tapā Gacch mendicants engaged in *līlā* was therefore a very serious accusation of improper conduct and intention in the Gujarati Jain context.

In the *Mejhar Nāmā* Jñānsundar stressed that the ultimate authority in the Jain community remained with the fourfold *saṅgh* (male and female mendicants, laymen, laywomen) as a whole, not with the *ācārya*s. While this is in line with orthodox Jain understanding of its own internal hierarchy (Cort 2000b), in practice *ācārya*s have often exercised nearly unquestioned authority. According to Jñānsundar, the *ācārya*s were responsible for the propagation of proper knowledge, conduct, happiness, and peace (*jñān*, *ācār*, *sukh*, *śānti*) among the entire Jain *saṅgh*, and in this the *saṅgh* was under the *ācārya*s' authority. But the authority to invest a mendicant with the formal post (*padvī*) of *ācārya* remained only with the *saṅgh* as a whole. When the conduct of the *ācārya*s becomes marked by laxity (*śithiltā*), selfishness (*svārthtā*), concern with pleasure (*sukhśoliyāpan*), and egoism (*ahaṃbhāv*), argued Jñānsundar, then the community as a whole suffered a great loss (Jñānsundar 1935a:3–9).[9]

Jñānsundar then outlined the history of Jainism on this continent in terms of a continual struggle between Jains who have striven to maintain proper conduct and the various forces of laxity. In this his poem was by no means unusual, for there were many similar texts authored in the late nineteenth and early twentieth century in which Digambar and Śvetāmbar, Mūrtipūjak and Sthānakvāsī, and Tapā Gacch and Khartar Gacch polemicists argued that their own position was the true and original Jain path, and all others were later lax deviations. This modern discourse rested upon a late medieval critique of laxity within the Jain tradition. One of the very first Mūrtipūjak texts Jñānsundar had read, the *Kumatikuddālā* ("Digging Out Wrong Doctrines"), in no uncertain terms advanced the superiority of the Tapā Gacch over all other Jain lineages.[10]

Within the Tapā Gacch, this modern discourse was also aimed (on the whole very successfully) at eliminating the institution of the *yati* or semi-domesticated resident monk. Jñānsundar in the *Mejhar Nāmā* discussed the proper conduct of a Jain mendicant, and contrasted it with what he observed in Gujarat. He accused the Tapā Gacch mendicants in Gujarat of being lax in their ritual observances, insufficiently attentive to study, inadequately grounded in meditative equanimity, unduly concerned with physical possessions, desirous of various elevated posts within the mendicant hierarchy, and in other ways exhibiting all the behavior criticized by Mūrtipūjak Jains as being typical of the *caityavāsī*s (temple dwellers), the medieval landed monks who were the forerunners of the *yati*s.[11] Since the criticism of the lax *yati*s in favor of the more orthoprax *saṃvegī* (liberation seeking) mendicants was a cornerstone of the reform and renaissance of the Mūrtipūjak mendicant lineages in the late nineteenth and early twentieth centuries, Jñānsundar's charge, that the *saṃvegī* mendicants were engaging in the very laxity they were supposed to be replacing, hit at the heart of contemporary Tapā Gacch mendicant self-identity. To underscore his criticism of all that he observed, Jñānsundar contrasted his own text, in the form of a letter to Sīmandhara Svāmī giving a spiritual account of the times, to the various documents, contracts, book entries, and duplicate bills of exchange (*kāgad*, *huṇḍī*, *paiṭh*, *parpaiṭh*) that are essential to the life of a shopkeeper or financial accountant. The implication that the Gujarati mendicants were not really mendicants, but only shopkeepers in spiritual guise, would have been lost on none of his audience, since most Jain mendicants are born into merchant communities.

Jñānsundar finished the *Mejhar Nāmā* during the rainy season retreat of 1920, which he spent in Jaghriya in north Gujarat, near his guru Ratnavijay.[12] He showed the poem to Ratnavijay, who urged him to publish it. It was accordingly published in Bhavnagar in 1920, at first serially in a Jain magazine, and then as a separate book. After the retreat Jñānsundar travelled to Ahmedabad, where he met with Ācārya Vijay Nemisūri, one of the leading Tapā Gacch mendicants.[13] The two had already met several years earlier, when Nemisūri made a tour through Marwar, spending one rainy season in the town of Phalodi, a town central to Jñānsundar's own travels, and where he had many patrons and devotees. There Jñānsundar had accused Nemisūri of stealing his own first disciple, one Rūpsundar, whom Nemisūri reiniated as Rūpvijay, so there was already no love lost between the two. Guṇsundar in his biography of Jñānsundar described the latter as reacting to Nemisūri as living not like a mendicant, but in a royal palace: "When [Jñānsundar] saw the ritual building (*upāśray*) of the respected *ācārya*, with all of the books and other items, he became alarmed and thought, 'O! O! Over this mendicancy there is stretched a framework of royal splendor'" (Guṇsundar 1939:I:605). While Jñānsundar was in Ahmedabad the first installment of the *Mejhar Nāmā* was published in a Jain periodical. Nemisūri was furious.

Jñānsundar left Ahmedabad to begin his travel back to Marwar, but Nemisūri sent a lay follower to remonstrate with Jñānsundar. Jñānsundar replied to the layman (Guṇsundar 1939:I:606-07),

> I spent two years in Gujarat. Not only did I hear about, but I saw with my own eyes the childish play of those mendicants. How could I stay where those mendicants were treating Mahāvīra's teachings in such a fashion? The householders there are fine. They stainlessly maintain the vows they have taken. Their conduct is within the bounds of propriety, and they fear harmful karma (*pāp*). But those mendicants have become so enmeshed in consequential action [that generates karmic bondage, as opposed to equanimity], so lax and possessive, that in just a short time they'll become *yatis*. How can one just sit there quietly and not raise a complaint in such a situation? When I was able to sit there quietly, I understood that the teachings were bleeding.
>
> Have you seen Vijay Nemisūri's monastery? There are so many books, clothes, blankets, vessels and the like collected there that it looks like the dwelling of a common householder. On one side you have poor householders who can't find enough food to feed themselves twice daily, nor clothes to cover their bodies, while on the other side are these wealthy Jain mendicants who thrice daily have tea, milk, fruit, sweets, and sherbet, and have muslin and other expensive things to use.

When Jñānsundar told the layman that he planned to go on publicizing his criticisms of the contemporary Mūrtipūjak mendicants, Nemisūri became even angrier and sent some other laymen after Jñānsundar. They threatened Jñānsundar with unspecified dire consequences if he did not desist from publishing further installments of *Mejhar Nāmā*. He replied, "I will not take a single step backward in speaking the truth. I abandoned my home in search of the truth, and I abandoned the Sthānakvāsī community in search of the truth, so why should I now fear these apostates (*pāsattha*) whose conduct is inferior (*hīnācārī*)?" The term Jñānsundar used for Nemisūri and the other lax monks, *pāsattha*, is one that Jains have long used to characterize apostates who fail to live up to the standards of Jain mendicant practice and asceticism (Dundas 1993), and so was obviously used by Jñānsundar to indicate his scorn for those mendicants he was leaving behind in Gujarat. Jñānsundar did agree to one conciliatory act: he wrote to Ratnavijay to ask his advice as to whether or not he should continue to publish the installments of *Mejhar Nāmā*. Ratnavijay simply cabled the publisher to continue the work. This still further increased Nemisūri's anger, and he asked one of his lay followers to pay the publisher whatever it would take to cease publication. In this the layman was unsuccessful.[14]

Nemisūri was not the only person in Gujarat to take exception to Jñānsundar's book. In 1920 a Jain layman named Keśavlāl Ḍ. Śāh published an anti-Jñānsundar pamphlet with the aggressive title, "A Slap on the Face of Jñānsundar" (*Jñānsundar Mukhcapeṭikā*).[15] In it the author, who would appear to be a layman named Devcand,[16] accused Jñānsundar of propagating his own spiteful opinions that were based only on useless and downright lies and insults. Such writings, averred the author, only brought harm to the Jain teachings

(K.Ḍ. Śāh 1920:3–4). In his long poem denouncing Jñānsundar, the author called on the ignorant Jñānsundar to listen to the true Jain teachings, said that he took Mūrtipūjak initiation on his own without a proper guru,[17] that his travelling alone was wrong and capricious (by which he implicitly criticized Jñānsundar's guru Ratnavijay as well), and that he was a master of untruth. Devcand's negative opinion of Jñānsundar is best summarized in the following verse: "The ornamental marks of a mendicant do not shine in him; what shines is the sovereignty of hell."

A final episode that occurred as Jñānsundar was departing from Gujarat, at the pilgrimage shrine of Taranga in northern Gujarat, again indicates Jñānsundar's revulsion at what he had encountered in the name of reformed Tapā Gacch mendicant observance. There he went to gather food at the local kitchen for those undertaking a special fast, known as *updhān*, at the shrine. He was amazed to find that the food, which he expected to be the usual bland, unappealing Jain ascetic food, included such savory and expensive items as almonds and pistachios. When Jñānsundar inquired for whom this rich food was intended, another mendicant said that there was no fault in the mendicants consuming such food, as it had not been prepared especially for them.[18] Jñānsundar was further horrified that evening when the two male mendicants after their evening rite of confession joined with the sixty or so participants in the fast. They were all women, most of them young widows. Jñānsundar described the situation as a *pāp līlā* or play of harmful karma, and bemoaned that irreligion (*adharm*) was being carried on in the name of religion (*dharm*), with the result that a mendicant who was supposed to guard his teachings, great vows, and strict celibacy had become a lord of Kṛṣṇa's cowgirls (*gopiyoṃ ke nāth*). Again, to say that the Jain emphasis on equanimity and asceticism had been displaced by a Vaiṣṇava emphasis on the employment of the senses in devotion to Kṛṣṇa, and to imply that the Jain emphasis on total celibacy in thought, action, and speech had been replaced with the Vaiṣṇava valorization of the sexual union between Kṛṣṇa and the cowgirls, was about as strong a criticism of mendicant behavior as one could make in a Gujarati Jain context. The contrast between the Jina as one who has conquered all passion (*vītrāg*), and Kṛṣṇa as a pseudo-deity who is in the thralls of passion, is of long-standing in western Indian Śvetāmbar Jainism (see the twelfth century *Yogaśāstra* of Hemacandra, II.4–7). Jñānsundar decided to add all that he saw and heard to the *Mejhar Nāmā*.

It should come as no surprise that Jñānsundar never returned to Gujarat. He spent the remaining three-and-a-half decades of his life in Marwar, among other things working to make a success of the Jain boarding school at Osian; it had been a letter from the manager to Ratnavijay and Jñānsundar that there were only ten students left in the school, and no funds, that precipitated Jñānsundar's return to Marwar. He devoted as much time and energy to a Jain boarding school at Kaparda, in an effort to ensure a Jain presence at this otherwise isolated Mūrtipūjak shrine as well. Whereas the Osian school flourished, and today has hundreds of students, the Kaparda school failed. Jñānsundar lived a life of strict asceticism. He wrote prolifically on a wide array of topics. Different sources posthumously credit him with writing 325 or 245 books and pamphlets.[19]

While formally he was in the Upkeś Gacch, in practice Jñānsundar was a leader in the local Tapā Gacch in Jodhpur and Marwar. Throughout the twentieth century this *gacch* has spread from its traditional base in Gujarat and the areas of Godwar in what is now southern Rajasthan that have long been very Gujarati in culture, especially among the merchant castes. It is now found in areas like Marwar, Jaipur, and North India where it was not to be found a century ago. The "Tapā-izing" of Jñānsundar can be seen concretely in two ways. A short 1992 biography of Jñānsundar (Rāṅkā 1992) incorrectly gives his mendicant name as Jñānsundarvijay, appending to his typical Upkeś Gacch name (most Upkeś Gacch *yatis* in Marwar received the lineage name of *sundar*) the most common Tapā Gacch lineage name of *vijay*. A similar hybridization of names occurred for his last disciple, Muni Premsundar, who is listed on the title page of a pamphlet he published in 1967 as Premsundarvijay.[20]

Since the Tapā Gacch did not have its own ritual building (*upāśray*) in Jodhpur, at Jñānsundar's urging the local Tapā Gacch *saṅgh* constructed a large *upāśray* which was opened on 8 August 1942. The very name of this building indicates the extent to which Jñānsundar was part of the Tapā Gacch establishment in Marwar, while at the same time advocating his distinctive Upkeś Gacch version of Tapā Gacch Jainism: Śrī Jain Śvetāmbar Bṛhat Tapāgacchīya Śrī Ratnaprabh Dharm Kriyā Bhavan, or the Ratnaprabh Religious Ritual Building of the Jain Śvetāmbar Great Tapā Gacch. (It is generally known simply as Kriyā Bhavan.) As we have seen, Ācārya Ratnaprabhsūri occupied a foundational place in the Upkeś Gacch self-identity. In 1943, presumably in recognition of his work for the Mūrtipūjaks of the area, the *saṅgh* of Jodhpur elevated him to the position of *ācārya* within the Upkeś Gacch with the new name of Devguptsūri. This was the appropriate title for the head of the *gacch*, which for several centuries had rotated among the three names Siddhsūri, Kakksūri, and Devguptsūri;[21] the last domesticated head of the *gacch*, Kakksūri, had been established on the seat in Bikaner in 1908, but sometime later the Bikaner *saṅgh* decided that he was not fit for the position, and so took away the insignia of office (Jñānsundar 1939b).[22] The post had remained vacant until Jñānsundar's elevation. Jñānsundar died in Pali in 1955 at the age of seventy-five. A memorial image of Jñānsundar was established on the upper floor of Kriyā Bhavan in Jodhpur on 14 May 1974 at the urging of two of his remaining disciples, the nuns Sampatśrī and Maṅglāśrī (Plate 28).

During his life Jñānsundar initiated very few disciples as mendicants, nor did he explicitly insist that his lay followers identify themselves as belonging to the Upkeś Gacch. As I noted above, his own guru Ratnavijay had instructed that he initiate only mendicants who had left the Sthānakvāsī fold. Guṇsundar (1939:II:437–38) listed nine disciples who were initiated up to 1939: six *sādhus* (five former Sthānakvāsīs and one former Terāpanthī) and three *sādhvīs*. Several of these stayed with Jñānsundar for only a short time, then either joined other Mūrtipūjak lineages or else proved unfit for mendicant life according to Jñānsundar's strict standards. The one who stayed with Jñānsundar the longest was his biographer, Muni Guṇsundar. He was born near Nagaur in 1889, initiated as the Sthānakvāsī mendicant Gambhīrmal in 1904, and then initiated into the Upkeś Gacch by Jñānsundar in 1926. According to the label of a portrait of him in Kriyā Bhavan in Jodhpur, he died in 1947.[23] Jñānsundar's last disciple, who was initiated after Guṇsundar wrote his biography and so is not on his list, was Muni Premsundar, a former Terāpanthī mendicant who took a second initiation from Jñānsundar in the 1940s or 1950s. He was active in the renovation of the Mūrtipūjak shrine of Gangani, outside of Jodhpur, in the mid-1950s, and died in Jodhpur in January 1968 (*Gāṅgāṇī* 1969). With him the short-lived tradition of modern full-fledged male mendicants in the Upkeś Gacch came to an end. As of 1998 there was still at least one domesticated *yati* in the Upkeś or Kaṅvlā Gacch, and possibly two. In March 1998 we met Yati Padamsundar, who owned and lived in what had formerly been the Kaṅvlā Gacch *upāśray* in Bikaner, and also spent several months of the year tending to a group of followers in Bombay. He said that he thought there was also a *yati* of the Upkeś Gacch living in Khimsar, near Nagaur, but we were unable to confirm this.[24] The *sādhvī*s initiated by Jñānsundar travelled with *sādhvī*s of the Vallabhsūri sub-lineage (*samuday*) of the Tapā Gacch, a sub-lineage that has been very active and popular throughout Rajasthan for many decades. As of 1998 Maṅglāśrī, one of the two *sādhvī*s who had arranged for the image in Jodhpur, was still alive, an elderly *sādhvī* staying in Jaipur.

Constructing a Jain Social and Ritual Culture

Much of Jñānsundar's work in the last three decades of his life can be characterized as a multi-faceted attempt to define what an ideal Jain mendicant lineage (*gacch*) should look like.[25] This involved establishing the proper history of Jainism, both in India in general and in Marwar in particular. History has long been a fiercely contested subject within the Jain tradition, as alternate histories are directly tied to alternate formulations of both Jain orthopraxy and orthodoxy.[26] There were three intertwined levels to this history.

First, disputes between Digambars and Śvetāmbars over scripture and proper mendicant practice are simultaneously arguments over the "true" history of what happened in the life of Mahāvīra and during the early centuries of the Jain community. Second, disputes between Mūrtipūjaks on the one hand, and Sthānakvāsīs and Terāpanthīs on the other, concerning whether or not the worship of images is an acceptable practice, are also disputes concerning the history of the propagation of the true teachings of Jainism in medieval times. Third, disputes between the two Mūrtipūjak *gacch*s that have been dominant in western India for the past several centuries, the Tapā and Khartar Gacchs, have been as much disputes concerning the authentic history of disciplic succession as they have been over matters of conduct and doctrine.

Jñānsundar wrote on all of these subjects. His presentation of the Śvetāmbar version of ancient and early medieval Jain history in contrast to the Digambar version was unremarkable, differing little if at all from many similar contemporary presentations. His presentation of the historical veracity of image worship, and the concomitant fabricated history of the "Loṅkā Mat" as represented in contemporary Jain society by the

Sthānakvāsīs and Terāpanthīs, was more sustained, and is the part of his historical research best known to the broader Jain and scholarly worlds. It also occasioned the most sustained intellectual and social resistance. Third, he entered into a detailed critique of the Khartar Gacch's historical self-image. At the heart of this part of his project was his argument for the Upkeś Gacch version of how the various Jain castes of western India were "converted" to Jainism, and a refutation of the Khartar Gacch versions of that history.[27]

The Ancient History of Image Worship, and the Spurious History of the Followers of Loṅkā Śāh

Jñānsundar wrote several lengthy books defending the worship of images and refuting the Sthānakvāsīs' versions of their own history. This was a defining issue in Jñānsundar's own redefinition of himself as a Mūrtipūjak mendicant, as we saw above. His earliest publications, *Siddh Pratimā Muktāvalī*, *Pratimā Chattīsī* and *Gayvar Vilās*, laid out the basic Mūrtipūjak defense of image-worship in contrast to the Sthānakvāsī critiques. Jñānsundar preached and in other ways agitated on this issue, and all of his disciples were former Sthanakvāsī and Terāpanthī mendicants who were convinced by his arguments. The latter part of the nineteenth century and the first part of the twentieth century was a time when the Śvetāmbar community of western India was riven by disputes over the orthodoxy of image worship, and so Jñānsundar's efforts were simply one chapter—albeit a very important one—in a much larger story.

Jñānsundar summarized his decades of study and preaching with two books he published in 1936. In *Mūrtipūjā kā Prācīn Itihās* ("The Ancient History of Image Worship") he engaged in a comprehensive survey of the historical evidence in support of image-worship, both within and outside the Jain tradition. He marshalled the textual evidence from early Śvetāmbar scriptures, and the more extensive evidence from the commentaries on those scriptures. He brought in evidence from later Jain texts, as well as archaeological and inscriptional evidence. Perhaps the most creative aspect of his attack on the Sthānakvāsīs was his global history of image worship, designed to show that the worship of images is a universal and therefore "natural" human religious phenomenon. Christians, Jews, Muslims, Parsis, Mongolians, and Native Americans all found a place in Jñānsundar's presentation as image worshipers.

The other aspect of Jñānsundar's defense of Jain image worship involved his historical investigation into the life and teachings of Loṅkā (or Lauṅkā) Śāh, the fifteenth-century initiator of the Śvetāmbar critique of images, and ancestor of the various Śvetāmbar iconoclastic mendicant lineages. In his 1936 *Śrīmān Lauṅkāśāh*, Jñānsundar combined a keen eye for issues of historical consistency with an equally keen proclivity to put his opponents in the worst possible light whenever possible. He showed that the extant Sthānakvāsī stories of the life of Loṅkā, and therefore of the origins of the opposition to image worship, were so internally inconsistent as to be of dubious historical value. Sthānakvāsī authors portrayed Loṅkā as an intellectually gifted layman who through his skills in copying manuscripts of the scriptures came to realize that the contemporary

Śvetāmbar mendicant ritual culture contravened the original teachings of Mahāvīra. Loṅkā therefore broke with the mendicants, bravely taught an inner spiritual path, and eventually took a mendicant initiation that restored the true practices of Jainism. Loṅkā's teachings, according to this history, convinced many Śvetāmbars also to break with the lax and idolatrous mendicants, and led to a far-reaching reform of Jain ritual culture.

Jñānsundar came to the conclusion that all of this was a later fabrication. As Paul Dundas has summarized Jñānsundar's conclusions, they were

> that Loṅkā was driven by necessity to Ahmedabad after the death of his parents and was compelled through poverty to earn his living in an *upāśray* as an undistinguished scribe of whose work nothing has survived and whose lack of learning precluded any ability to understand the Ardhamāgadhi language of the Śvetāmbara scriptures he was copying. Through the contempt in which he was held by his monastic employers and as a result of contact with Muslims, he subsequently formulated his doctrine of rejection of image worship . . . he falsely assumed the role of *ācārya* to teach what he claimed was the true religion of the fordmakers [Jinas] and gathered only a minuscule band of followers . . . (Dundas 2002: 247–48)

In his defense of image worship, Jñānsundar point by point addressed the writings of several leading Sthānakvāsī apologists. He wrote in an intellectual environment in which *ad hominem* attacks on one's intellectual opponents were the norm. At stake, as far as he and the others were concerned, were not mere antiquarian and intellectual minutiae, but the very historical bases of contemporary Jain practice and dogma. Comparison with the fervor of public discourse in the contemporary United States on issues such as abortion, capital punishment, and the role of the American military in global politics gives one a fair sense of the intensity with which the two sides argued.

Not surprisingly, the Sthānakvāsīs replied in a number of ways. Lay and mendicant authors issued pointed rebuttals. The Sthānakvāsīs in Jodhpur, who formed the majority of Śvetāmbars in the area, objected to the sectarian tone of Jñānsundar's writings, a tone that could create sectarian divisions in what was otherwise a more or less single Osvāl Jain community in terms of marriage and commensality. They acted to silence Jñānsundar. In particular, his writings came to the attention of the important Sthānakvāsī mendicant Ācārya Hastīmal, who asked several of Jñānsundar's lay disciples why they allowed such incendiary books to be published.[28] In response, the laity stopped distribution of his books. When we were researching in Jodhpur in 1998, we came across many locked cabinets in the Jñānsundar Pustak Bhaṇḍār ("Library") in Jodhpur containing hundreds of copies of his books.

The Spurious History of the Khartar Gacch

In his project to tie the history of the various Osvāl patriclans as Jain to the Upkeś Gacch Jñānsundar had to contend with a rival history of the "conversion" of the Osvāls, a history that was both better known and more ritually incorporated into the lives of the Osvāls. This was the history put forward by the Khartar Gacch. Jñānsundar's historical project here had two parts. First, he borrowed from a long-standing Tapā Gacch polemic against the Khartar Gacch that questioned the legitimacy of the Khartar Gacch as a lineage of authentic *saṃvegī* or renouncing mendicants, and portrayed them instead as illegitimate *caityavāsī* or lax inhabitants of temples. The second involved publicizing a long-standing but largely ignored alternative Upkeś Gacch history of the conversion of the Osvāls.

For the past half-millennium the two dominant Mūrtipūjak mendicant lineages in western India have been the Tapā Gacch and the Khartar Gacch. In the past century, the Tapā Gacch appears decisively to have won the contest; this outcome was not so clear when Jñānsundar was active, especially not in Marwar, since in his time Tapā Gacch mendicants were seen only rarely in Marwar as they passed through on pilgrimage to Jaisalmer, and there were few Tapā Gacch laity.[29] Both *gacch*s emerged in the early centuries of the second millennium CE out of the less sectarian Śvetāmbar mendicant milieu of four *kul*s.[30] For the first several centuries of their existence each one slowly grew in influence, but they remained just two among the many Śvetāmbar lineages. It appears that rivalry for the support of the Mughal emperors Akbar and Jahangir may have played a decisive role in both their rise to dominance and the development of their inter-sectarian rivalry.[31]

The Tapā Gacch traces its history back to Jagaccandrasūri, who in 1228 in Chittor broke with his former lineage in response to what he perceived as the laxity of the prevailing mendicant practice. He and his followers were given the title Tapā, "ascetic," in recognition of their strict observance of ascetic and in particular dietary restrictions.

The Khartar Gacch claims a slightly earlier origin. The histories of the origin of the *gacch* evince a gradual period of crystallization of the *gacch* out of the setting of the four *kul*s. Khartar Gacch historians credit the origin of the *gacch* to Vardhmānsūri, who in the early eleventh century broke with his domesticated *caityavāsī* teacher Jincandrasūri. He became the disciple of Uddyotansūri and adopted the proper mendicant practice. His disciple was Jineśvarsūri, who in 1024 defeated the *caityavāsī*s in a debate in the royal court of King Durlabh at Anhilvad Patan, and was given the sobriquet Khartar, "Fierce," by the king. Jineśvarsūri's disciple was Jincandrasūri, and his disciple in turn was Abhaydevsūri, the famous eleventh century commentator on nine of the canonical *Aṅga*s. His disciple was Jinvallabhsūri, who is also credited with playing a formative role in the *gacch*. He also was originally a *caityavāsī*, but then became a disciple of Abhaydevsūri and a staunch proponent of proper practice. After him came Jindattsūri (1075–1154) and Jincandrasūri (1140–1166; known as Maṇidhārī because he had a magical jewel [*maṇi*] in his forehead). These last two were the first of the four Dādāgurus or semi-divine charismatic leaders of the *gacch*, and with them the *gacch* began to rise significantly in prominence (Babb 1996).

Jñānsundar read a more sectarian understanding of Jain society onto the earlier materials, but also used the ambiguities in the stories of the Khartar Gacch's early decades to his polemical advantage. His goal in his critique was to sever the connection between

Osvāls and the Khartar Gacch, and instead connect the Osvāl patriclans to the Upkeś Gacch. To do this, he argued that the Khartar Gacch was not an authentic Śvetāmbar Mūrtipūjak lineage, but rather due to blemishes in its origins was flawed in its very essence. To see this flaw, one needed to have a true understanding of the origin of the *gacch*.

Jñānsundar's attacks on the Khartar Gacch version of its own history arose out of his writings on the history of the Osvāl castes, to which I will turn below. In brief, according to the Upkeś Gacch version of this history, most of the Osvāl patriclans (*gotra*) converted to Jainism seventy years after the *nirvāṇ* of Mahāvīra, and the rest of them in the next few centuries.[32] This flew in the face of the history of the Osvāls as presented by the Khartar Gacch. The Khartar Gacch version has been analyzed by L. A. Babb (1996:160–67). According to this history, Jindattsūri during his career converted fifty-seven Osvāl patriclans to Jainism, usually by effecting some sort of miraculous cure. Babb (ibid.:162) reproduces a wall painting from a Khartar Gacch temple in Ajmer, and found in many other Khartar Gacch temples throughout Rajasthan, in which Jindattsūri points to a list of the names of the fifty-seven patriclans he converted.[33] Other Osvāl patriclans claim conversion due to the wonder-working grace of later heads of the Khartar Gacch.

Jñānsundar dismissed the Khartar Gacch history on several accounts. First, since he privileged his own Upkeś Gacch history as true, the conversions had to have occurred over a millennium earlier than according to the Khartar Gacch. He also took issue with the theme found in most of the Khartar Gacch conversion stories of a miraculous cure being the cause of the conversion. (Never mind that Ratnaprabhsūri, a key figure in the Upkeś Gacch history, is described as a wizard [*vidyādhar*] who entered into one story while flying overhead, that he was able miraculously to duplicate himself in order to preside over image installation rituals in two cities simultaneously, and that his miraculous cure of a fatal snake bite was central to the Upkeś story of the Osvāl conversion. Jñānsundar seems not to have been bothered by the questionable historicity of these events.) He said that the Osvāls in these stories seem to have been particularly prone to poisonous snake bites, and Osvāl patriclans seem to have been ready to effect major changes in the ritual life of the entire patriclan simply on the basis of a single person being cured of a snake bite. Further, he argued, if this was the case, then the Khartar *ācārya*s should have gone to Nepal; since that country is infested with snakes, they could have converted far more people to Jainism (Jñānsundar 1926:5).

Jñānsundar also attacked the sources of the Khartar Gacch histories. The Upkeś Gacch histories were maintained by the *mahātmā*s (*yati* genealogists) of the lineage, who had travelled from village to village in Marwar maintaining close ties with their lay followers. As a result, these were reliably old documents. In imitation of the Upkeś Gacch *mahātmā*s, non-Jain genealogists had started writing Osvāl genealogies; but these, insisted Jñānsundar, were not very old (ibid.:82). His estimation of the historical value of the genealogies was quite negative. The traditional non-Jain genealogists, he averred, were unreliable fabulists:

> It isn't necessary to explain that due to ignorance of history our pure India has fallen into a time when the imaginary narratives (*kathā*), stories (*kahānī*), dramas (*rās*) and chronicles (*khyāt*) of ignorant Cāraṇs, Bhāṭs and Bhojaks now occupy the lofty heights in place of history. They have received gold coins for their imaginary chronicles of big kings, and people place full faith in them as if they were divine utterances. Not only that, but inquiring historians such as Mr. Tod have swallowed these tales and filled their own history books with these imaginings. (Ibid.:6)

If the fantastic creations of the traditional genealogists had affected only the history of the kings, it would have been bad enough. But, Jñānsundar continued, "This is also the state of our Osvāl caste. Bhāṭs and Bhojaks have fabricated imaginary chronicles and genealogies to fool the ignorant Osvāls" (ibid.). Khartar Gacch authors who relied on such sources, by extension, were equally foolish.[34]

In the Khartar Gacch, according to Jñānsundar, there wasn't a single genuinely old Osvāl genealogy. The Khartar Gacch *mahātmās* admitted as much, and explained that in the sixteenth century Karamcand Bacchāvat of Bikaner gathered all the Khartar Gacch genealogies together and threw them in a well. Jñānsundar dismissed this story, asking how one man could gather his enemies' genealogies from all over Marwar in one place. In truth, concluded Jñānsundar, "no Khartar *ācārya* has converted any non-Jain to being Jain" (Jñānsundar 1937a:35).

Finally, Jñānsundar criticized the Khartar Gacch authors for employing an inadequate historical methodology. They took texts such as those written by the genealogists at face value, and did not correlate their findings with other sources. This monk known as the "Lover of History" wrote that real history, as practiced by both Western and Eastern scholars, uses a wide array of sources: stone inscriptions, copper plate donations, coins, texts from a wide range of sources, archaeological findings, study of images and other material objects, and the writings of other contemporary historians (Jñānsundar 1926:7; 1929:*prastāvnā* 6).

Jñānsundar's rewriting of the history of the Osvāls, their conversion to Jainism, and their relationships with mendicant lineages, did not go uncontested. For example, in 1930 a Khartar Gacch mendicant named Magnasāgar published *Jain Jāti Nirṇay Samīkṣā*, a point by point rebuttal of one of Jñānsundar's earlier books.[35] Jñānsundar published his final and conclusive study of the Khartar Gacch in 1939 with his *Khartarmatotpatti*, "The Origin of the Khartar Sect." In his introduction to the book, he explained that he had been studying and writing on the history of the Jains of western India for the previous fifteen years. Khartar authors had written some negative things about him and his writings, such as "What gutter did your Ratnaprabhsūri crawl into? What have the eighteen *gotra*s Ratnaprabhsūri established ever done? There was no Ratnaprabhsūri, nor did any Ratnaprabh establish the Osvāls. The 125,000 laity in Osian were converted by Jindattsūri. The lax Kaṅvlā Gacch was established by people of fallen conduct" (Jñānsundar 1939:inside front cover). This book was his response. The tone of this introduction was intended to indicate that Jñānsundar had not willfully or capriciously written such a forcefully contentious book, but rather he had been forced to do so to defend the honor of himself and his lineage from the base attacks of his opponents. The frontispiece of the book was a drawing based on a passage in the *Upakeśa Gaccha Prabandha* of 1327, according to which Ācārya Padmaprabhsūri of the Upkeś Gacch had defeated the Khartar Gacch Ācārya Jinpatisūri (1153–1220) in a debate in the court of King Vīsaldev of Ajmer. The picture showed both Jinpatisūri and Vīsaldeva bowing to Padmaprabhsūri and asking forgiveness for doubting him. Clearly Jñānsundar expected no less a result from his book.

In his analysis of Khartar Gacch history he in part relied upon a Khartar Gacch text authored not too long after the events it described. This was the *Bṛhadvṛtti* ("Large Commentary") of Sumatigaṇi on Jindattsūri's *Gaṇadharasārdhaśataka* ("150 Verses on the Disciples"). Sumatigaṇi was a disciple of Jinpatisūri. While Jinpatisūri was born only one year before Jindattsūri's death in 1154, he was the successor as head of the *gacch* to Jindattsūri's successor Jincandrasūri, and so presumably Sumatigaṇi wrote on events which were still relatively fresh in peoples' memories. The other text on which Jñānsundar relied was the *Pravacana Parīkṣā* ("Examination of the Doctrine") of the sixteenth-century Tapā Gacch controversialist Dharmsāgar, a pungent attack upon the authenticity of the Khartar Gacch (Dundas 1993).

Jñānsundar followed Dharmsāgar in levelling much of his criticism at Jinvallabhsūri. Khartar sources were clear that Jinvallabh was the disciple of the *caityavāsī* Jineśvarsūri of the Kurcapurā Gacch. Jñānsundar repeated the allegation that he had been an orphan who was sold to Jineśvarsūri by his mother. To Jñānsundar this indicated that the initiation was not motivated by any authentic seeking for liberation, but solely by monetary concerns. It was not surprising, therefore, that Jinvallabh abandoned his teacher and commenced studying with Abhaydevsūri, but without taking a second initiation as an authentic mendicant. Jinvallabh was therefore not properly a disciple of Abhaydevsūri, but remained a *caityavāsī*. Jñānsundar said of this new relationship, "Abhaydevsūri was a generous person, and so he taught the scriptures to Vallabh. But at that time Abhaydevsūri couldn't have dreamed that, as it says in the maxim that 'feeding a snake milk only increases its poison,' this *caityavāsī* he was teaching would later start a new sect that propagated deviant teachings (*utsūtra*)" (Jñānsundar 1939:III:3–4). Abhaydevsūri died in 1078. Twenty-nine years later, in Chittor, Jinvallabh started preaching his deviant doctrine that there were really six beneficial moments (*kalyāṇak*) in the life of Mahāvīra. Jinvallabh said that the miraculous event of the transfer of Mahāvīra's embryo from a Brahman to a Kṣatriya mother should be added to the standard list of five. This became the basis of a new sect, known as the Vidhimārg ("Path of Rites"). But, according to Jñānsundar, it was not very successful. For many years Jinvallabh had tried in vain to find someone to initiate him as an *ācārya*, but no one would. Jñānsundar said that this was due to four factors: there was widespread rejection of his new doctrine; he had neither a teacher nor any disciples; what following he had was not a full-fledged four-fold congregation (*caturvidh saṅgh*) of monks, nuns, laymen and laywomen, but instead consisted of a single monk and a handful of laymen; and the Jains had already expelled him from the fold. For reasons that are not clear, one of Abhaydevsūri's successors, Devbhadrācārya, made Jinvallabh an *ācārya* shortly before the latter's death in 1110. But no one accepted that this made Jinvallabhsūri the rightful successor to Abhaydevsūri: "People called Jinvallabh an illegitimate *ācārya*. This was quite appropriate. Who wouldn't call a child illegitimate who was actually born thirty-two years after his father's death?" (ibid.:III:19).[36] Recall here also Jñānsundar's assertion in the *Mejhar Nāmā* that only the fourfold congregation had the right to install a mendicant as *ācārya*; a single mendicant did not have that right, so Devbhadrācārya's promotion of Jinvallabh to *ācārya* was improper.

Two years later Devbhadrācārya installed Jindattsūri as successor to Jinvallabhsūri in the new sect, in another improper promotion. In order to make the new sect successful, Jindattsūri started to propitiate the fierce goddess Cāmuṇḍā. This worship of an unreformed meat-eating goddess by Jindattsūri stands in obvious contrast to the Upkeś Gacch Ratnaprabhsūri's conversion of the meat-eating Cāmuṇḍā of Osian into the vegetarian, and therefore properly Jain, Sacciyā.

Jindattsūri added another deviant teaching to the doctrines of the new sect. In 1147 he was in the royal capital of Anhilvad Patan, where one day he happened to see a single drop of blood on the floor of a temple. This was the cause of the arising in Jindattsūri of powerfully wrong faith (*mithyātva*), and he started preaching that women of menstruating age should not be allowed to worship Jina images. But Patan at that time was a stronghold of Jainism: Kumārpāl was king, there were 1,800 Jain households including those of many millionaires, and the monks Hemcandrasūri and Kakksūri were royal preceptors.[37] Jindattsūri realized that his new doctrine was both illogical and flew in the face of the many stories of Jain heroines worshiping Jina images. But he was a stubborn person, and persisted in his teachings. Eventually realizing that he had no chance of success in Patan, and that he would be expelled from the congregation if he stayed there, one night he sneaked out of town on a fast-moving camel, "just as a thief flees in fear of the police" (ibid.:26).

People abused this new sect with three names. It was called the Cāmuṇḍā Gacch due to Jindattsūri's worship of the goddess; the Auṣṭrīk (Camel) Gacch due to Jindattsūri's ignominious flight from Patan; and the Khartar Gacch in response to Jindattsūri's stubborn insistence on preaching deviant doctrines. His followers adopted the third title as the least objectionable, and changed the meaning of Khartar from "stubborn" to "fierce."

Jñānsundar also had to account for the evident popularity of the Khartar Gacch. This he had done several years earlier in his 1937 *Jain Jātiyoṃ ke Gacchoṃ kā Itihās* ("History of the Gacchs of the Jain Castes"). In the context of his discussion of the conversion of various Osvāl patriclans, he rejected the Khartar claims that many of them were converted by Jindattsūri. Instead, he argued, these patriclans had been converted centuries earlier by Ratnaprabhsūri and other Upkeś Gacch *ācārya*s. Those patriclans that were "converted" to Jainism by Jindattsūri and other Khartar Gacch *ācārya*s had already been Jain. What happened was simply a number of chance events in which laity called upon Khartar Gacch mendicants to perform various rituals when no Upkeś Gacch mendicant was available.

These then led to ongoing ritual relationships between Osvāl patriclans and Khartar Gacch mendicants.

Jñānsundar concluded his hatchet job on Jindattsūri's claims to orthodoxy by allying him to what in the eyes of Mūrtipūjak Jains of western India has been the most egregious and dangerous heretical teaching, the criticism of image worship. He wrote, "The first person to oppose image-worship in Jainism was Jindattsūri. Those who came later such as Lauṅkā Śāh merely imitated Jindattsūri. Granted, Jindattsūri was opposed only to women performing image-worship, and Lauṅkā Śāh opposed both men and women doing it. But the main factor behind [Lauṅkā's] opposition was Jindattsūri" (ibid.:III:28). In sum, Jñānsundar said of the Khartar Gacch, "The people of this sect created various kinds of plots that caused great harm to Jain society, and continue to do so today. This harm has been greater than any caused by [Muslim] kings" (ibid.:III:40).

Jñānsundar also marshalled a number of inscriptions, lineage texts, and other texts to argue that the origin of the Khartar Gacch was not with Jineśvarsūri in 1024, and that the Khartar Gacch texts were filled with other historical inaccuracies. For example, the defining moment in the early Khartar Gacch according to its historians was the debate in 1024 in the royal court of Patan before King Durlabh, in which Jineśvarsūri defeated the *caityavāsīs* and was awarded the sobriquet "Khartar." Jñānsundar pointed out that Durlabh died in 1022. He argued that both Jineśvarsūri and Abhaydevsūri were still in the Candra Kul. The origins of the Khartar Gacch therefore, according to Jñānsundar, should be traced to Jindattsūri, and dated to 1147, and mendicants in this lineage didn't start to use the name Khartar to refer to themselves until the fourteenth century.

Jñānsundar's criticisms of the Khartar Gacch as originating with two mendicants of dubious pedigree served to cast aspersions upon the authenticity of all subsequent mendicants, and therefore the contemporary Khartar Gacch in Marwar. These criticisms, that the Khartar Gacch in some essential way was really just a lineage of bastard *caityavāsīs*, also followed from his earlier criticisms of contemporary Tapā Gacch laxity in Gujarat, and served to highlight his own ascetic rigor. He concluded his lengthy study of the Khartar Gacch with a discussion of nearly two dozen details in which the Khartar Gacch ritual practice of mendicants and laity disagreed with the consensus practice of other *gacchs*. We will return to the issue of proper practice below.

The True History of the Osvāls and the Upkeś Gacch

Jñānsundar's deconstruction of the histories of the Sthānakvāsīs and Khartar Gacch was only part of his larger project. Clearing the underbrush of these rival histories of the Jains of western India went side by side with his writings on what he understood to be the true history, as found in the sources of his own Upkeś Gacch. Guṇsundar in his biography told how soon after his new initiation as an Upkeś Gacch mendicant, Jñānsundar began his study of the history of the Upkeś Gacch as found in various texts in the Upkeś Gacch monasteries of Marwar. There are a number of sources for compiling this history.

Central among these were two Sanskrit texts authored by Kakksūri. The *Nābhinandanajinoddhāra* ("The Renovation of [the Temple of] Ādinātha") told the story of the pilgrimage led by Kakksūri's guru Siddhsūri, and the laymen Deśal Śāh and his son Samarsiṃh, to restore the recently destroyed temple of Ādinātha at Śatruñjay in 1315. In this context he also told the story of the Upkeś Gacch. The closely related *Upakeśa Gaccha Prabandha* (also *Upakeśa Gaccha Cāritra*; "History of the Upkeś Gacch") gave only the history of the *gacch*, and would appear to overlap significantly with the first text. Kakksūri authored both of these texts in Korantapura in 1336 (VS 1393).[38] The material from Kakksūri's texts found its way into a series of subsequent lineage chronicles (*paṭṭāvalī*s).[39] Jñānsundar said he used several of these, and three of them have been published.[40]

The Upkeś Gacch was one of the major *caityavāsī* (domesticated) Śvetāmbar monastic lineages of medieval western India. The earliest inscriptional reference to it dates from 954, and the earliest textual reference from 1016 (Śiv Prasād 1991:62, 69). There were several branches of the lineage, most notably the Koraṇṭ Gacch (Śiv Prasād 1989).[41] By the early twentieth century the Upkeś Gacch was reduced to a handful of *yati*s in various towns and villages of Marwar, and, as I indicated above, by 1998 it was clearly on its last legs.

Perhaps the most noteworthy aspect of the Upkeś Gacch was its idiosyncratic insistence that it was the sole mendicant lineage that traced its disciplic descent, not to the congregation established by Mahāvīra, but instead to the one established by Pārśvanātha. This story appeared full blown in the writings of Kakksūri; in the absence of earlier historical texts or other references, it is impossible to say if he invented this history on his own, or if he repeated an older Upkeś Gacch self-understanding. In either event, it is not clear why the *gacch* promoted this history, although it quite possibly stemmed from an earlier—and now unknown—sectarian rivalry between lineages in western India, in which antiquity was a major factor in claiming authenticity, authority, and prestige. This lineage and its branches also employed the practice, common among Digambar lineages but otherwise unheard of among Śvetāmbars, of rotating a limited number of names among the lineage-heads.

Jñānsundar repeated this history of the *gacch* as starting with Pārśvanātha on many occasions. He related it in the context of his histories of the Osvāls and other castes (1926, 1928, 1929, 1937a), and in separate histories of the Upkeś Gacch (1940, 1943, Devguptsūri 1944). Central to this history was the story of the conversion of the Osvāl caste to Jainism, and the establishment of an authentic Jain congregation, a story he first heard from his guru Ratnavijay. This story has been analyzed in lucid detail by L. A. Babb,[42] and so I will summarize it only briefly here.

According to the Upkeś Gacch history, the sixth successor of the Jina Pārśvanātha was Ratnaprabhsūri. Seventy years after the *nirvāṇ* of Mahāvīra, in the course of Ratnaprabhsūri's travels he and his mendicant followers came to Osian, where they stayed on Luṇādrī hill just outside the city. This was a new frontier town, settled just a few years previously by Rājpūts who had left the nearby city of Bhinmal or Shrimal. Since the residents were all non-Jain, meat-eating Rājpūts, the mendicants could find no suitable alms. They were prepared to leave, but the goddess Cāmuṇḍā encouraged Ratnaprabhsūri to stay on with a small group of mendicants. A short while later the son of the royal minister Uhaṛ was bitten, seemingly fatally, by a snake. The family took the corpse to be burnt, and were stopped by a disciple of Ratnaprabhsūri (in some variants Cāmuṇḍā, dressed as a mendicant), who asked why they were going to burn a living person. They took the body to Ratnaprabhsūri, who sprinkled some water that had been used to wash his feet over the boy and thereby revived him. Out of gratitude, 125,000 inhabitants of Osian accepted Ratnaprabhsūri as their teacher, and so became Jains (Plate 31).[43]

Ratnaprabhsūri instructed them in the ritual and ethical practices of Jainism. In Jñānsundar's definition of Jain ritual and social culture, to be properly Jain meant to be Mūrtipūjak Jain, and so at the heart of this identity there must be a Jina image and temple. At the time of his conversion Uhaṛ was engaged in constructing a temple to Viṣṇu. The construction kept falling down, so Uhaṛ asked Ratnaprabhsūri for help. The *ācārya* instructed him to convert the temple from one for Viṣṇu to one for Mahāvīra. But Uhaṛ needed an image. This problem was solved by Cāmuṇḍā, the goddess of the place, who created a wonderous image of sand and milk. This "self-born" (*svayambhū*) image was not humanly made, but literally of the very earth of Osian itself (Plate 31).[44]

The time came to install the image. By chance, Ratnaprabhsūri was requested by lay followers from the town of Korant to preside over the installation rituals of a Jina image there as well. Since the astrologically proper times for both installations were the same, Ratnaprabhsūri magically duplicated himself, and sent the doppelganger to Korant. When the laity of Korant discovered that they had been duped with a look alike rather than the real *ācārya*, they split off to form the Koranṭ Gacch.

It came time for the annual ritual celebration of Cāmuṇḍā, who was simultaneously the tutelary deity of Osian and the caste deity of the Osvāls—identities easily fused at the time, since the Osvāls had only founded Osian a generation earlier, and were all still residing at what was now their natal place. Since this ritual of necessity involved animal sacrifice, the newly converted Jains were in a quandary. Sacrificing animals violated the prime Jain ethical imperative of *ahiṃsā* (non-harm), but not to offer the animals would insult the goddess and incur her wrath. Ratnaprabhsūri intervened, and after a spiritual contest he overcame the goddess and converted her to vegetarian Jain offerings as well. In recognition that she also now followed the true spiritual path, she was renamed Sacciyā (or Saccikā), "The Truthful Goddess."

The history continued on to relate the deeds of subsequent *ācārya*s of the Upkeś Gacch. The seventh *ācārya*, Yakṣdevsūri, defeated a troublesome male deity (*yakṣ*) and converted him to Jainism, and converted many people in Sindh to Jainism as well. The eighth *ācārya*, Kakksūri, converted many people in Kacch to Jainism. The ninth *ācārya*, Devguptsūri, preached in the Panjab, and the tenth, Siddhsūri, preached in Bengal. In the words of one *paṭṭāvalī*, "In this manner there arose many *Sūri*s in the Upakeśa Gaccha, who were distinguished through their power, their writings, and their unwordliness" (Hoernle 1890:241; *Upakeśa Gaccha Paṭṭāvalī*, p. 192).

The Proper Code of Ritual Conduct of the Upkeś Gacch

As noted above, in the months before his initiation as a Mūrtipūjak mendicant at the hands of Ratnavijay, Jñānsundar engaged in a comparative study of the codes of ritual conduct (*samācārī*) of the different Mūrtipūjak *gacch*s. Ratnavijay explained to him that the code of the Upkeś Gacch was largely the same as that of the Tapā Gacch. The only significant differences are in the performance of *pratikramaṇ*, the twice daily (as well as fortnightly, quarterly, and annual) rite of confession. The Upkeś Gacch liturgy included a verse to Vairūṭyā Devī, a Jain goddess, in addition to the verses in praise of Sarasvatī and Kṣetrapāl found in the standard Tapā Gacch liturgy.[45] This was added by a previous head of the *gacch*, one of the many Siddhsūris, who had been a devotee of this goddess. The other difference was in the performance of the form of meditation known as *kāüssagg*; the Upkeś Gacch code included the recitation of four verses dedicated to Ratnaprabhsūri. These had been added, according to Ratnavijay, in response to the extensive interaction over the years with the Khartar Gacch and its veneration of the four deceased *ācārya*s known as *dādāgurus* (Babb 1996, Laidlaw 1995). Both of these, said Ratnavijay, were recent additions and so could be omitted by Jñānsundar (Guṇsundar 1939:I:320–21).

In 1948 Jñānsundar (by then Ācārya Devguptsūri) published a lengthy discussion of the code of ritual conduct of the Upkeś Gacch. He explained that he had refrained from publishing the Upkeś Gacch code previously. There were no full-fledged mendicants in the *gacch* other than Jñānsundar and his immediate disciples, the laity had adopted the practices of other *gacch*s (for the most part Tapā Gacch), and he didn't want to add to the many conflicts over details of practice in the Jain community. He wrote with a tone of weariness at the intellectual battles he had fought throughout his career. But in an article in the January 1945 issue of the Jain magazine *Jain Dhvaj* ("The Jain Flag"), the Khartar Gacch lay intellectual Agarcand Nāhṭā had published what he claimed to be the Upkeś Gacch code as established by Ratnaprabhsūri. Nāhṭā cited as his source a 1917 article in *Jain Śāsan* ("The Jain Teachings") by Ratnavijay.[46] Jñānsundar said that he had never seen this article, and doubted it had actually been written by his guru, since the code as described was that of the Khartar Gacch, not the Upkeś Gacch. Instead, he surmised that someone in the Khartar Gacch had given a recent Khartar Gacch text to Ratnavijay, who then published it in *Jain Śāsan*. In response to Nāhṭā's article Jñānsundar felt impelled to publish the true and pure code of the Upkeś Gacch, and to clear up any misconceptions.

Jñānsundar said that the code of ritual conduct for all Jain mendicants was derived from the ten rules laid down by Mahāvīra in the *Uttarādhyayana Sūtra*, the Śvetāmbar canonical text understood to consist of Mahāvīra's final sermons. The first three verses of chapter 26 of this text lay out ten rules of deportment and speech that should guide a mendicant's behavior. This posed a problem for Jñānsundar, as he had to explain how the mendicant followers of Pārśvanātha came to observe the rules laid down by Mahāvīra. The

Uttarādhyayana itself provided part of the answer to this. Chapter 23 of this text describes the well-known dialogue between Mahāvīra's follower Gautama and Pārśvanātha's follower Keśi. In particular the two debated whether there was any substantial difference between the five great vows (*mahāvrat*) enjoined by Mahāvīra and the four restraints (*yam*) enjoined by Pārśvanātha. Whereas the former prohibited harm, untruthfulness, taking what is not freely given, sexual activity, and possession, the latter did not explicitly refer to sexual abstinence. In the end, Gautama and Keśi agreed that the two sets were the same in intention, and Keśi and his followers adopted the five great vows of Mahāvīra (Jaini 1979:14–21 and 2003; Dundas 2002:30–33).

Jñānsundar explained that a further ten rules of mendicant deportment found in the *Uttarādhyayana* (26.2–4) also applied to Upkeś Gacch mendicants. He also expanded upon the Gautama-Keśi dialogue to describe other ways in which Ratnaprabhsūri later brought the two codes further into agreement. These changes involved details of context not mentioned in the *Uttarādhyayana*, nor elsewhere in the earliest Jain texts on mendicant conduct; rather, they were specific to the codes of the Śvetāmbar *gacch*s, and so dated from medieval times. Ratnaprabhsūri replaced the single initiation (*dīkṣā*) by a two-stage initiation; mandated wearing a single-colored cloth rather than five-colored cloth; said that mendicants must wear clothes, whereas before this had been optional; mandated that mendicants could no longer stay in one place for the duration of the cold season, insisting instead that monks must change residence every month and nuns every two months; mandated the regular performance of the rite of confession (*pratikramaṇ*) instead of only after a violation; mandated the performance of five forms of confession (morning, evening, fortnightly, four-monthly, and annual) instead of just morning and evening; and forbad the practices of accepting alms from a royal palace and requesting that laity prepare specific dishes (Devguptsūri 1948:*prastāvnā*, 5).

Later, in the body of his book, Jñānsundar slightly elaborated on these changes in a list of ten rules that further spelled out the details of mendicant conduct. In theory, the five great vows were sufficient for any mendicant. However, over time Jains had required clarification and amplification of some of the rules, and so the *ācārya*s of the various *gacch*s had added further rules. This led into the bulk of the book, in which Jñānsundar in a lengthy question-and-answer format addressed a wide array of specifics in Śvetāmbar mendicant and lay practice.

Jñānsundar's list is impressive for the range of rituals it covers. It includes mendicant practices, lay fasts, the performance of the confessional rite of *pratikramaṇ*, image worship, and annual observances. In its breadth it provides us with a fairly comprehensive list of what it is that Śvetāmbar Mūrtipūjak Jains, in particular mendicants, but in the ideal laity as well, actually *do*.

At the same time, the list of ritual practices is almost mind-numbing in its detail. But they indicate how rituals serve in their detailed precision to create and sustain a social identity. To an outside observer, it might not seem to make much difference whether the last line of the *Namaskāra Mantra* is pronounced "*paḍhamaṃ havaï maṅgalaṃ*" or "*paḍhamaṃ hoi maṅgalaṃ*." But this is what serves to distinguish one ritual micro-culture, and therefore a ritually defined social group, from another. Since ritual—action that is done on a repeated basis to create and recreate meaning in the cosmos—is central to human society, ritual differences are central to the delineation of social differences.

An Upkeś Gacch Liturgy for Image Worship

We have seen above how image worship (or its rejection) has been central to Śvetāmbar Jain identities in western India for the past five centuries. Either one does or does not worship images of the Jinas; this is a dividing line with far-reaching consequences. Accordingly, an important part of Jñānsundar's project was to create a distinctively Upkeś Gacch liturgy, so that Upkeś Gacch laity when performing image worship would sing hymns that reinforced the history and practices of their *gacch*. Between 1936 and 1938 he composed the liturgies for three *pūjā*s: a *Snātra Pūjā* or bathing ritual, performed first thing every morning in every temple; an *Aṣṭaprakārī Pūjā*, the basic eightfold ritual done by most observant laity on a daily basis; and a *Baṛī Pūjā*, a larger ritual for use on special festive occasions (Jñānsundar 1937b; Devguptsūri 1946). As Lawrence Babb (2004:171; chapter two above) has pointed out, the performance of the first major public ritual to the image of Mahāvīra in Osian had served as a quasi-sacrifice to establish the eighteen patriclans of the Osvāl caste. Large public rituals define a community, in this case both a *saṅgh* and a *gacch*. Jñānsundar instructed that the basic ritual was to be performed in accordance with the ritual manuals of the Tapā Gacch.

The lengthy text of the *Baṛī Pūjā* ("Great Worship") summarizes the history of the Upkeś Gacch, from Pārśvanātha's first disciple through Ratnaprabhsūri and the rest of the first ten *ācārya*s. The text then leaps to the thirteenth century Siddhsūri (guru of Kakksūri, author of the *Nabhinandanajinoddhāra Prabandha*) who preached for the renovation of Śatruñjay, and then again leaps to the twentieth century. The final verses of the liturgy conclude that the Upkeś Gacch *ācārya*s made the three castes of Osvāls, Śrīmālīs, and Porvāls into Jains (Babb 2004:166; chapter two above), and these are the three pillars of Jain society. There were many renouncing (*tyāgī*) mendicants in the lineage, but over time there came to be only lax *yati*s. Then came Ratnavijay, who restored renunciatory practice to the *gacch*.[47]

History, Ritual, and Identity

Disagreements about history are rarely just disinterested intellectual exercises. Disagreement about the past is usually tied to concerns of the present, as what "really" happened is understood by all the parties to have some sort of connection—perhaps ontological, perhaps paradigmatic—to who those parties are in the present. In the Jain context, this translates into the second element in Jñānsundar's project, the creation of a distinctive, proper, and pure Upkeś Gacch ritual culture. His historical interventions were essential to demonstrate the validity of the practices within this ritual culture. At the same time, given the somewhat attenuated condition of the Upkeś Gacch—mendicants comprising, with the exception of Jñānsundar himself and his tiny handful of disciples, only a few semi-domesticated *yati*s, and laity who were increasingly coming under the growing influence of the Tapā Gacch—this required the creation of that ritual culture. These two features were related, as a major reason that lay people shifted their allegiance to the Tapā Gacch was the sharply increasing number of full-fledged (and therefore institutionally legitimized) *saṃvegī sādhu*s in the *gacch*. If Jñānsundar had been able to initiate a significant number of mendicant disciples, he may very well have also succeeded in retaining an Upkeś Gacch identity among the laity. This part of his project involved the composition of a distinctively Upkeś Gacch liturgy for the central lay ritual of image worship.

Jñānsundar's project also involved an articulation of the minute ways in which Upkeś Gacch performance of a wide array of ascetic, meditative, and venerational rituals differed from their performance in other *gacch*s. Social identity in India is usually enacted through ritual activity that simultaneously gives one a sense of who one is—"this is what we do (or eat)"—and a sense of who one is not—"we don't do what they do (or eat what they eat)" or "we do what appear to be similar things, but we do them differently." Rituals create this identity, and then through the repetitiveness that is a defining characteristic of ritual they continually recreate and reinforce that sense of identity.

In both of these aspects of his project—defining "true" Jain history, and "true" Jain practice—Jñānsundar was doing what many other activist Jains, both mendicant and lay, were also doing in the late nineteenth and early twentieth century, a time of extensive "reforms" within the Jain communities. The third part of his project, however, was more distinctive, and perhaps even idiosyncratic. This was his attempt to construct a historical model of Jainism in which the three major social units of Jainism, the mendicant *saṅgh*, the lay *saṅgh*, and the lay caste (at all its levels of articulation: *varṇa*, *jāti*, and *gotra*), were seen as organically intertwined as a single entity. The relationships within Jain society among these three kinds of social units have always been complex, to say the least, and rarely have been reducible to a simple chart. But this is precisely what Jñānsundar tried to do—in his historical reconstruction at least, for the model of an ideal Jain social structure that he articulated was sufficiently discordant with the on-the-ground realities of Jainism in Marwar that he seems not to have tried to actualize his ideal. Jñānsundar in his presentation of the Upkeś Gacch version of the history of Jains in western India focused on the narratives of how several important merchant caste-clusters—the Porvāls, the Śrīmālīs, and especially his own Osvāls—had become Jain. In his history he fused a mendicant lineage (the Upkeś Gacch), a lay *saṅgh* (those laity whose traditional preceptors were the *yati*s of the Kaṅvlā or Upkeś Gacch), a caste (the Osvāls), two related pilgrimage shrines and their images (Mahāvīra and Sacciyā Mātā in Osian), and even a city (Osian, formerly Upkeshpur), into a single organic unit.

Jñānsundar may not have been alone in such an effort. There are many ways that his project resembles the successful one of the Śvetāmbar Terāpanth, with its fairly close relationship between mendicant and lay *saṅghs*, and its location largely within Vīsā Osvāl patriclans of Rajasthan. The Terāpanth insistence on a single clearly defined hierarchy, with a single *ācārya* on top who is viewed almost as a living twenty-fifth Jina, probably has much to do with the success of the Terāpanth organic model of an ideal Jainism. Jñānsundar's affirmation of the dominant understanding of Jain social hierarchy, with the more diffuse entirety of the fourfold *saṅgh* outranking the centralized authority of an *ācārya*, indicates both how the Terāpanth has diverged from orthodox Jain social order, and what it would have required for Jñānsundar to have been successful in his social project.[48]

What is a full Jain social and ritual culture according to Jñānsundar? At its core is a lineage of mendicants tracing their initiations back to the founder of Jainism, albeit in this case to Pārśvanātha, not Mahāvīra. This lineage is a *saṅgh* of monks and nuns. These mendicants perform their regular ascetic, meditative, and venerational rituals in a proper and pure manner as laid out in the code of ritual conduct (*samācārī*).

These mendicants are supported by a lay community that also performs its regular ascetic, venerational, and devotional rituals in the proper and pure manner according to the rules of the *gacch*. This lay community is simultaneously a *saṅgh* of laymen and laywomen, and a caste (*jāti*) made up of exogamous but commensal patriclans (*gotra*). This caste has a nearly biological connection with the lineage due to a history of conversion—or, more properly, awakening to the truth. This is a history of spiritual parenthood. As Lawrence Babb (2004:183n38; chapter two above) has observed, Jñānsundar's intent was "to stress the complete elimination of the *varṇa* system and the Brahmanical/sacrificial order with which it is associated," and to emphasize that human society is properly based on a shared awakening to the Jain truth. In other words, for Jñānsundar *varṇa* and *jāti* are replaced by *saṅgh* and *gacch* as the important, legitimate units of society.

The intertwined nature of caste and lineage is indicated in a shared name (Upkeś) that signifies the near biological connection of both with a place of origin, Upkeshpur, modern Osian. Neither the caste nor the lineage emerge "naturally" from this place, as both come from elsewhere—Bhinmal in the case of the caste, Pārśvanātha in the case of the lineage. But it is here in Osian that their histories become intertwined, and they find their mutual identities as parts of a fourfold *saṅgh*. Only if there is a fourfold *saṅgh* do we have an authentic Jain community.

Further tying the caste and the lineage together is a shared goddess. Sacciyā is both the *kul devī* (lineage goddess) of the caste and the *adhiṣṭhāyak devī* (foundation goddess) of the lineage, and in both of these roles is responsible for the protection and perpetuation of the community. She is the goddess of the place where the destinies of the caste and the lineage merged.

Since this is a Jain mendicant-caste organic whole, and to be properly Jain means to be Mūrtipūjak, this identity is further cemented by a Jina image. That is the self-born (*svayambhū*) image of Mahāvīra and its temple in Osian.

The early twentieth century was a period of great social flux for Jainism—and here I have to use the socially unspecific "Jainism" rather than "Jains," because what constituted a Jain community, society, or even culture was precisely what was under debate. There were sectarian debates between Śvetāmbar and Digambar, between Mūrtipūjak and Sthānakvāsī, and among and within the different *gacch*s. The regular travels of the mendicants increasingly involved both shoring up a mendicant's (and his lineage's) support among lay congregations, and trying to enlarge those congregations (and hence his lay following) by convincing followers of other sects and lineages of the truth of one's own teachings. Within several branches of Jain society—the Mūrtipūjak Śvetāmbar community, but also the Digambars—there was a widespread movement to redefine what it meant to be an authentic mendicant. This involved argumentation in print and live debate against perceived laxity, and withdrawal of material support from lax pseudo-mendicants. There were also widespread movements for the social "reform" and "uplift" of both castes and lay congregations, in which Jains participated in the larger discourse of modernity in both its Indian and global guises.

Jñānsundar inserted himself in all of this. What was distinctive about this insertion, however, was that he attempted to integrate his activity on castes, lineages, temples, and social reform[49] into a single grand project, to create a single holistic Jain society. His project allows us to see what one modern Jain intellectual thought that a complete Jain society should be. It needed to have an encompassing ritual culture that is based on a proper code of conduct for both mendicants and laity. It needed to be grounded in a proper understanding of the true history of the community. That history was one that integrated mendicant lineage with lay patriclan into a single community.

Jñānsundar's project really never had a chance, for it involved too drastic a rewriting of both history and the on-the-ground social realities. While patriclans and disciplic lineages have been intertwined in complex ways throughout the history of Jainism, the lay patriclan and the mendicant lineage are significantly different social structures in their underlying logics. The patriclan is an ascriptive unit, into which one is born and which irreversibly defines who one is as a human being for the rest of one's life. The patriclan defines marriage and occupation. The lineage is a voluntary unit based upon the spiritual and intellectual conversion or awakening of each individual, who then joins the group of his or her own accord. Joining the lineage involves the individual renouncing those very bonds of marriage and occupation that define a patriclan. To try to fuse these two social units into a single organic whole was in the end a futile enterprise. This was illustrated graphically in Jñānsundar's own early adulthood, when he found his urge toward renunciation, toward the life of a mendicant in a *gacch*, incompatible with his life as a layman, as a married householder who was sexually active and siring children.

Caste and patriclan on the one hand, and *saṅgh* and *gacch* on the other, have never neatly overlapped in Jain history. Any given lay *saṅgh* will include members of several castes, such as Osvāl, Porvāl, and Śrīmālī. The lay membership in the *saṅgh* is shaped by residence, occupation, and familial allegiance. At the same time, members of a caste, such as the Osvāl, will include Jains who are by religious affiliation Mūrtipūjak, Sthānakvāsī, and Terāpanthī. Many castes further include both Jains and Hindus as well. Rarely if ever have these two social units come even close to being coterminous. Whereas Jñānsundar saw ideal Jain society as unified and holistic, in reality it has always been fractured and hybrid.

Notes

1. For previous references to Jñānsundar in English, see Babb 2004:164–78, Dundas 2002:247, and Wiley 2004:113–14.
2. Sthānakvāsīs have claimed for centuries that *caitya* here refers either to wise monks (*jñānī*) or that wisdom (*jñān*) itself, not to Jina images.
3. Information on Ratnavijay comes from Devguptsūri 1949.
4. See Jain and Kumār 2003:334–45 on this lineage.
5. See Wiley 2004:230 on Ācārya Vijay Dharmsūri (1868-1922). He was a major figure in the early twentieth-century reform and renaissance of the Tapā Gacch. He is best known to scholars of Jainism for the extensive help he gave to an entire generation of early European scholars.
6. The inscription read, "*saṃ. 602 vaiśākha māse śukla pakṣe tṛtayā upakeśa vaṃśe adityanāga gautre śāha* . . ." (Guṇsundar 1939:I:325). There is no reference to such an inscription from Osian in either Handa 1984 or Nahar 1918. According to Guṇsundar, Ratnavijay instructed the manager of the temple to place the image in the resthouse (*dharmśālā*) attached to the temple. We have no means of verifying this inscription, which would be by centuries the earliest reference to the Osvāl caste. Nor can we know which of the ruined temples Ratnavijay identified as Jain.
7. Paul Dundas has discussed the Jain hermeneutic principal of *madhyastha* (literally "standing in the middle," or what he translates as "principled neutrality" [2006:269]) and its role in Jain sectarian debates as practiced by medieval Tapā Gacch intellectuals such as Nayaprabhagaṇi, Mahopādhyāya Dharmasāgara, and Mahopādhyāya Yaśovijaya. The writings of the latter two were clearly known to Jñānsundar. Inquiry in the spirit of *madhyastha* requires the author to remain "between the two extremes of strong attachment (*rāga*) and aversion (*dveṣa*)" (Dundas 2004:128; see also 2006:106–07). When properly employed, however, this approach does not result in a *laissez-faire* sort of moral or intellectual relativism. Rather, being *madhyastha* leads the inquirer to correct faith (*samyagdṛṣṭi* or *samyaktva*) in the basic teachings of Jainism and the Jain path to liberation. Being *madhyastha*, therefore, requires one to reject improper views, just as a professional jeweler will reject a glass fake in favor of a real gem (ibid.:129).
8. See Dundas 2002:305–06 on Sīmandhara Svāmī.
9. My copy of *Mejhar Nāmā* is the 1935 fourth printing. I have a photocopy of only Jñānsundar's lengthy 66-page introduction to the poem, not the poem itself. As a result my discussion is based on his detailed summary of the contents.

10. According to Guṇsundar, Jñānsundar thought that this text was by the sixteenth century Tapā Gacch polemicist Upādhyāya Dharmsāgar. Many Jain sources have made the same attribution. However, it was actually authored by the earlier, late thirteenth-century Tapā Gacch polemicist Nayaprabhgaṇi, and the proper title was *Gurutattvapradīpa*, "Light on the Nature of a Spiritual Teacher." It is also known as the *Utsūtrakandakuddāla*, "The Spade to Dig Up the Roots of Heresy." Dharmsāgar obtained a copy and wrote a commentary on it. His attack on all other Jain lineages than the Tapā Gacch was so harsh that the leader of the Tapā Gacch, Ācārya Vijay Dānsūri, threw Dharmsāgar's text into a body of water, and ordered Dharmsāgar to publish a formal apology to the Jain community, in which he rejected what he had written. See Balbir 1999:16n23, Dundas 2004:127–30 and 2006, Darśanvijay 1950:257 (and following him Ratna Prabha Vijaya 1941–50:V.2:133–34).
11. On *yati*s and *caityavāsī*s see Cort 2001:43–46.
12. In addition to his normal activities, Ratnavijay arranged for Jñānsundar to study Sanskrit with Brahman *paṇḍit*s during both of his rainy-season retreats in Gujarat. As we have seen, Sthānakvāsī mendicants traditionally learned only the Prakrit root texts of the Jain scriptures, and to underscore the opinion that the Sanskrit commentaries were inauthentic they were forbidden even to learn Sanskrit. Thus mendicants who shifted from Sthānakvāsī to Mūrtipūjak had to undergo additional training to become full-fledged participants in the Mūrtipūjak intellectual culture.
13. Ācārya Nemisūri (1873–1949) was born in Mahuva in Saurashtra, and took initiation in 1889 from Muni Vṛddhivijay (1834–1893), a former Sthānakvāsī mendicant who was one of the leaders of the reform and renaissance of the Tapā Gacch in the late nineteenth century (and who also initiated Dharmvijay [Dharmsūri], Ratnavijay's guru) (anon. 1992). Nemisūri established a number of religious educational institutions, arranged for the renovation of several Jain shrines (including Kaparda, near Jodhpur, a shrine also important to Jñānsundar), preached to many Terāpanthī families in Mewar and claimed to have converted them to the Mūrtipūjak position, and initiated many mendicants. The sub-lineage (*samuday*) of his mendicant followers is among the largest in the Tapā Gacch today. See Śīlcandravijay 1973.
14. The one book-length biography of Nemisūri I have been able to consult (Śīlcandravijay 1973) contains no reference to this quarrel. The only reference to Jñānsundar comes in the context of the rainy season retreat Nemisūri spent in Phalodi in 1917. Jñānsundar was also there for his retreat. Śīlcandravijay simply mentions that the Mūrtipūjak *saṅgh* was divided into two parties, and that many mendicants, including Jñānsundar, had tried unsuccessfully to bring the two camps together. The lack of discussion of the quarrel between Jñānsundar and Nemisūri may well be because the author of this biography, Muni Śīlcandravijay (since 1996 Ācārya Vijay Śīlcandrasūri), who is one of the leading intellectuals among contemporary Jain mendicants, has a notably irenic personality, and so may have been reluctant to narrate an episode in which neither side comes across in a very good light for a Jain mendicant.
15. The Mūrtipūjak Jains of Ahmedabad in the early 1920s seem to have been keen on slapping their opponents in the face. See Albrecht Wezler's 1993 study of a medieval anti-Brahman text, with the equally pugnacious title, "A Slap on the Face of the Brahmans" (*Dvijavadanacapeṭā*), which was published by two Jain laymen in Ahmedabad in 1923.
16. The title page gives no name for the author; my supposition is based on the colophon verse, in which the author of the long polemical poem that takes up most of the pamphlet refers to himself as Devcandbhāī.
17. Nemisūri also cast aspersions on Jñānsundar's Mūrtipūjak initiation, in part because he argued that the initiations of both Ratnavijay and the latter's guru Dharmsūri were suspect (Guṇsundar 1939:I:429). The issue of the authenticity of Jñānsundar's initiation also surfaced in Surat in 1919, when Dharmsūri himself questioned Ratnavijay's authority to give Jñānsundar his second

confirming initiation (*baṛī dīkṣā*), and so refused to stay in the same *upāśray* with Jñānsundar (Guṇsundar 1939:I:569–71).

18. On the logic of intention, asceticism, and non-harm involved in the Mūrtipūjak mendicant food-gathering rounds, see Cort 1999 and Laidlaw 1995:289-344.
19. The discrepancy here probably stems from the fact that he recycled much material through many differently titled books, and issued multiple editions of many of his books—but he wrote a prodigious number of books however one counts the final total.
20. The use of the alternate, but in the nineteenth century more widespread, name of Kaṅvlā for the *gacch* caused some confusion over the ritual identity of the *gacch*, and led to some people identifying it as a branch of the Tapā Gacch. As an alternate near-homonym, some authors such as Jñānsundar and Śubhkarṇ also used Kamlā. From the early sixteenth through the early twentieth centuries there was a domesticated branch of the Tapā Gacch in southern Rajasthan known as the Kamalkalaś Śākhā or Gacch (on which see Śiv Prasād 2000:259–65 and Darśanvijay 1950:149–51); as of 1917, its head was Mahendrasūri, who resided in Rohida village near Abu (Buddhisāgarsūri 1917:115). The Gujarati Tapā Gacch Buddhisāgarsūri in his account conflated the two *gacch*s, and Guṇsundar reported that when Jñānsundar was in Gujarat many Tapā Gacch mendicants said they thought that the Upkeś or Kaṅvlā Gacch was merely a branch of the Tapā Gacch. Darśanvijay in a list of the thirteen seats (*besṇā*) of the domesticated Tapā Gacch includes the Koraṇṭ Gacch, which was actually a branch of the Upkeś Gacch (1950:256); he expressly says that all thirteen seats followed the same rules of conduct.

    Further complicating the overlap between the two *gacch*s is the Dvivandanak Gacch (whose followers followed or venerated [*vandan*] the teachings of two [*dvi*] Jinas, both Pārśvanātha and Mahāvīra). This splinter group claimed to have split off from the Upkeś Gacch in the later centuries of the first millennium CE under the leadership of Udayvardhan (Tripuṭī Mahārāj 1952–64:I:36-38; Deśāī 1986–97:9:214-15). Another source dates the split to 1210 CE (*Upakeśa Gaccha Gurvāvalī*, p. 83). This lineage eventually merged into the Tapā Gacch as the Tapāratna Śākhā in the mid-sixteenth century. Tripuṭī Mahārāj hypothesize that the alternate name for the Upkeś Gacch of Kaṅvlā Gacch arose from an event in the history of the Dvivandanak Gacch. In the early sixteenth century the head of this lineage was one Ācārya Devguptsūri. He uttered a powerful mantra to hurl into the air the palanquin of Bahādur Śāh, the sultan of Gujarat. The sultan accepted the monk as his guru, and tried to gift him a village. The monk refused, so instead the sultan gave him a special shawl (*kambal* or *kaṅvlā*), from which the alternate name of the Upkeś Gacch derived.

    This multifaceted confusion of identity, coupled with the similarity in conduct, may well have allowed for the ease with which Jñānsundar's Upkeś Gacch mendicants and his lay Tapā Gacch followers in Marwar formed a single ritual culture.
21. The rotation earlier included Ratnaprabhsūri and Yakṣadevsūri; according to Upkeś Gacch history, these two were closed at the order of Sacciyā, the tutelary deity of the lineage, in the late fifth century (Devguptsūri 1943a; *Upakeśa Gaccha Paṭṭāvalī*, p. 190).
22. Yati Padamsundar of Bikaner told the following story. Kakksūri was overly involved in magical practices (*mantra-tantra*) according to the local laity. In particular, he accepted money for performing rituals for laity. He also sold the manuscript collection of the *upāśray* to a scrap paper dealer. In response, two *yati*s in the *gacch*, Premsundar (not the same as Muni Premsundar; Yati Premsundar occupied the seat in Phalodi, and often aided Jñānsundar in performing public rituals) and Mukansundar together with some local laity removed Kakksūri. Kakksūri left Bikaner and retired to the shrine of Kesariyājī in southern Rajasthan about 1930. There were further quarrels between the *yati*s and the local Upkeś Gacch laity, in large part over possession of the house, that resulted in several court cases. In the end Yati Mukansundar purchased the house from the laity.

Padamsundar was Mukansundar's disciple. According to another informant, the Phalodi seat came to an end when Premsundar died sometime in the 1950s or 1960s, and the Kaṅvlā Gacch laity of Phalodi all became Tapā Gacch.

23. Information on Guṇsundar comes from Tansukhdās 1939; I have been unable to ascertain where Guṇsundar died.
24. There was a *yati* living in Khimsar as late as 1980 according to *Tīrth Darśan* 1980:145.
25. Jñānsundar's efforts need to be seen as part of the larger social movements within the Jain communities in the early twentieth century of reform and definition (Cort 2000b).
26. See Cort 1995 for a preliminary discussion of Jain historiography.
27. For a modern presentation of the Khartar vision of Jain history, see Vinaysāgar 2004–06. For a modern Sthānakvāsī history, see Hastīmal 1971–83. See Tripuṭī Mahārāj 1952–64 for the most far-reaching presentation of the Tapā Gacch version of Jain history; a shorter English version of this history, largely derivative of Tripuṭī Mahārāj, is found in Ratna Prabha Vijaya 1941–50.
28. On Hastīmal (1910–1991), see Wiley 2004:94–95.
29. On the non-presence of the main Gujarati Tapā Gacch lineages in Marwar, see also Cort 2001:44–45.
30. These four were the Candra, Nivṛta, Nāgendra, and Vidyādhara. See Dundas 2006:12–13.
31. Information in English on these two *gacchs* is most readily available in Dundas 2006, Klatt 1882, and Wiley 2004:123–24 and 209–10.
32. "Conversion" is a misleading term here, as it is redolent with Christian missionary overtones. The relevant Indic term is *pratibodh*, "awakening [to the truth]."
33. Babb (2006:32) also reproduces a wall painting of the same theme from a Khartar Gacch temple in Jaipur.
34. In particular, in his 1926 *Jain Jāti Nirṇay* ("Judgment on Jain Castes") he criticized the 1910 *Mahājan Vaṃś Muktāvalī* by the Khartar Gacch Yati Rāmlāl on these grounds. See Babb 2004:154–58 on this text.
35. Magnasāgar was evidently a rather controversial person, of whom both Jñānsundar and Guṇsundar had a low opinion. By birth a poor Maiṇā tribal named Māṅgīlāl, his father gave him to the Sthānakvāsī mendicant Svāmī Karmcand in hopes this would increase his own wealth. When other Sthānakvāsī mendicants refused to eat or drink water with him due to his low caste status, Māṅgīlāl left the order and went to Ācārya Kṛpācandrasūri of the Khartar Gacch in Bombay. Kṛpācandrasūri enlisted him to try to bring Gayvarcand into the Khartar fold, and so Māṅgīlāl—by then going by the name Magnasāgar, and dressed as a Khartar Gacch *sādhu*, although the tone of Guṇsundar's description casts doubt on whether or not he had formally taken a new initiation—came to Osian in 1915. He failed in his errand, and asked the manager of the Osian temple for money for the railway fare to return to Bombay. In later years Magnasāgar convinced people to donate money for a rest house in his home village, but then simply passed the money on to his natal father. Guṇsundar also said that Magnasāgar was caught stealing manuscripts and an image from the library at Jaisalmer. Guṇsundar's presentation of Magnasāgar's conduct clearly was intended to show the staunch Jñānsundar in a good light.
36. Here Jñānsundar echoed Dharmsāgar's earlier derisive criticism; see Dundas 2002:246.
37. The relationship between the Jain king Kumārpāl and his royal preceptor Hemcandrasūri is well-known in the annals of western India Jainism (Cort 1998b). Jñānsundar interjected into this setting the head of the Upkeś Gacch as another royal preceptor, expanding upon a reference in Upkeś Gacch history (Hoernle 1890:241; *Upakeśa Gaccha Paṭṭavali*, p. 191).

38. The basis for my dating is the colophons of the handwritten manuscript of the *Ūkeśa Gaccha Caritra* and the published edition of the *Nābhinandanajinoddhāra*. H. D. Velankar (1944:372) gives VS 1392 (1335 CE) as the date of composition. K. C. Jain (1972:180, 285) gives different dates for the two. He gives both 1326 CE and VS 1371 (= 1314 CE) as dates for the former text. He names the text *Upakeśa Gaccha Prabandha* in the first citation, and *Upakeśa Gaccha Caritra* in the second, and nowhere indicates what editions or manuscripts he used; in several places he simply cites Jñānsundar 1943a. He gives 1338 CE as the date for the latter text (ibid.:184, 437, 468). In addition to these two texts being credited to the same author, and the colophons giving the same year of composition, the two manuscripts—the original from which Jñānsundar made his copy of the *Ūkeśa Gaccha Caritra* that is now in Jodhpur, and the single manuscript (he was unable to locate any other manuscripts) in the Ḍahelānā Upāśray in Ahmedabad that Paṇḍit Bhagvāndās Harakhcand used for his 1929 edition—were both copied by the same otherwise unknown monk, Muni Kalaśa (he copied the *Nābhinandanajinoddhāra* alone, and the *Ūkeśa Gaccha Caritra* together with Muni Bhāvacandra), so the overlap may be scribal as much as authorial.
39. For example, while the *Upakeśa Gaccha Paṭṭāvali*, of which Hoernle (1890) gives an abbreviated translation, lists the heads of the *gacch* through the 84th, Siddhsūri, who was installed in Bikaner in 1878, the manuscript Hoernle used went only as far as the 75th head, Siddhsūri, who was installed in Bikaner in 1598. There is a clear break after Kakksūri, author of the *Upakeśa Gaccha Prabandha*, indicating that the chronicler who first compiled the *paṭṭāvali* relied heavily upon Kakksūri's work.
40. In Jodhpur we also found in a library of books that had belonged to Jñānsundar an exercise book with a hand-written copy of both the Sanskrit original and a Hindi translation of the *Upakeśa Gaccha Prabandha*, entitled in this case *Ūkeśa Gaccha Caritra*. We assume that this was Jñānsundar's personal copy, and one he had perhaps prepared for publication. If so, why it was not published remains a mystery.
41. The last reference to the Koraṇṭ Gacch in Śiv Prasād's history of it comes from 1555 (1989:16). Jñānsundar recorded that in 1843 the *śrīpūjya* (domesticated head) of the Koraṇṭ Gacch, Ajitsiṃhsūri, visited Bikaner, where he gave an Osvāl genealogical text to the then head of the Upkeś Gacch, Siddhsūri. Jñānsundar said that as of the time he was writing, there was no longer any Koraṇṭ Gacch *ācārya*, but that the buildings (*posālā*) of the Koraṇṭ Gacch *mahātmā*s were still extant in some towns of Marwar (Jñānsundar 1937a:28–29).
42. Babb 1996:137–73, 2004:162–78, and chapter two in this volume; see also Meister, chapter one in this volume.
43. This Upkeś Gacch account of the conversion of the Osvāls in Osian did not go unchallenged in the contentious context of sectarian rivalry in western India. Ṛṣimohanlāl Yati, in a book published in Bhagalpur, an important trading city on the Ganga in Bihar, wrote that Ratnaprabhsūri awoke the king of Osian to the truth of Jainism in 155 CE (212 VS) and made him a Jain. The residents of the city converted to Jainism at the same time. Ratnaprabhsūri made the king a Śrīśrīmāl, the rest of the royal family Śrīmāl, and the residents of the city Osvāl (Ṛṣimohanlāl 1907:29–30). With reference to what he calls the "eastern Śrīmāls," Lawrence Babb (2004:152) has written, "the link between Śrīmāls and the Khartar Gacch is especially strong," so I surmise that Ṛṣimohanlāl was a Khartar Gacch *yati*. This account was known to Jñānsundar, as we found the book in the small library attached to the Mahāvīra temple in Osian, in which most of the books are from Jñānsundar's personal collection.

    A second alternative account of the events at Osian more clearly fits them within a Khartar Gacch frame. Kṣemsiṃh M. Rāṭhoḍ was a Bīsā Osvāl from Kacch. In his 1948 history of the Osvāls—a book with an obvious emphasis on Osvāls in Gujarat—he said scholarly opinion was that all accounts of the conversion of the Osvāls to Jainism twenty-four hundred years ago are just folk sayings (*dānt kathā*). Rāṭhoḍ insisted that according to historically reliable sources, the Osvāls arose as a Jain community only in the twelfth century. At that time all the inhabitants of the area around Osian were Śaiva. Many of them were left-handed Tantrics, descended from Vajrayāna Buddhists, who worshiped meat-eating goddesses such as Cāmuṇḍā, Mahāmāyā, Jogmāyā, and Osiyā.

The story of the conversion of the Osvāls told by Rāṭhoḍ bears strong similarity to the Upkeś Gacch version. According to Rāṭhoḍ, Jindattsūri (1075–1154), the charismatic leader of the Khartar Gacch, was responsible for the conversion of 130,000 Rājpūts to Jainism in the early twelfth century (see also Babb 1994:115–19, 160–67). He came to Osian with a small group of monks, and stayed on Luṇādrī Hill. Because the inhabitants of the town were all Śaiva, the monks could find nothing to eat. As they were preparing to leave town, a local man asked Jindattsūri to create a miracle (*camatkār*, *labdhi*) to convert the inhabitants. He agreed, and created an illusionary snake out of a ball of cotton. The snake bit Mahipāl, the son of the local king, the Parmār Utpāldev II. As the people were taking the body of the prince to be cremated, they met one of Jindattsūri's disciples, who led them to his guru. Jindattsūri revived the boy, and the king and most of the people accepted Jainism. The rest accepted Jainism after Jindattsūri defeated the rival religious teachers in a series of debates. He arranged for the new Jains to build temples to Pārśvanātha and other Jinas.

The local goddess, Osiyā Devī, became furious at Jindattsūri, blaming him for the people no longer offering her buffaloes and goats. She threatened him with her trident, and tried to sweep him away with a typhoon. But the power of his *mantra*s was much stronger, so he was able to convert her to eating only sweets (Rāṭhoḍ 1948:82–98).

The Khartar association with Osian is also seen in a small shrine attached to the Mahāvīra temple, in which is a three-dimensional image of Jindattsūri consecrated in 1897 CE (VS 1954), and a footprint image of another miracle-working Khartar Gacch leader, Jinkuśalsūri, consecrated in 1903 CE (VS 1960). Handa did not notice either of these in his otherwise comprehensive 1984 survey of the inscriptions from Osian. But informants assured us that the Jindattsūri image had been located in a prominent location before the reconfiguration of the temple compound in the 1960s and 1970s, so it is likely that the image has been in the temple premises since its consecration in 1903.

44. More significantly, she formed the image on Luṇādrī hill, where Ratnaprabhsūri and his followers had been staying, thus further emphasizing the near biological connections among Osian, the Osvāls, Jainism as embodied in a self-born autochthonous Jina image, and the Upkeś Gacch. As part of the rite of consecration of a Jina image, the officiating *ācārya* transmits some of his spiritual virtue, acquired through his asceticism and equanimity, into the image (Cort 2006). In this case Ratnaprabhsūri's ascetic powers on Luṇādrī hill helped shape the very image itself.

45. Vairūṭyā (also Vairoṭyā and Vairoṭī) is one of the sixteen Jain Mahāvidyās, a group of Tantric goddesses (Shah 1947:156–61). She appears originally to have been a goddess who protected against snakebite—a theme we have already encountered several times in this chapter—who was then incorporated into Jain Tantra. U. P. Shah (1987:278) has written that many images of Vairoṭyā are found at the medieval Jain temples at Abu and Kumbhariya, indicating that she was popular until at least the eleventh century CE. She was gradually eclipsed by Padmāvatī, another goddess associated with snakes and serpent deities, who is now by far the most popular Jain goddess among Jains of western India.

46. Agarcand Nāhṭā (1911–1983), a Khartar Gacch layman from Bikaner, was a prolific scholar of late medieval Jain texts from western India (Wiley 2004:152). I have seen neither of the articles by Nāhṭā and Ratnavijay. A similar list of details of practice in the Kavlā (Kaṅvlā) Gacch was published by Ācārya Buddhisāgarsūri (1917:117) around the same time as Ratnavijay's article, and either may be the original source for this information, or may derive from a third common source.

47. We found in the small library attached to the Mahāvīra temple in Osian a number of copies of a second Upkeś Gacch *Baṛī Pūjā*, written in 1915 by Śubhkarṇ Yati of Gwalior. He represented a branch of the

gacch—he terms it the Kamlā Gacch—that is otherwise unknown to me, but which indicates that the Upkeś Gacch was probably more widespread than just Marwar into the early decades of the twentieth century. He gave his lineage as follows:

Devguptsūri
↓
Pāṭhak Bhāmsundar
↓
Pāṭhak Kalyānsundar Muni
↓
Labdhisundar
↓
Pāṭhak Khuśyālsundar
↓
Vakhatsundar Gaṇi
↓
Lakṣmīsundar Kavirāj (his younger brother was Bhavānīsundar)
↓
Nyālsundar (younger brother of Nemsundar)
↓
Nāyaksundar
↓
Paṇḍit Viveksundar Gaṇi
↓
Sumatisundar (head of the *gacch* as of 1915).

48. On the Terāpanth and its social project, see Dundas 2002:254–62 and Flügel 1995–96.
49. He concluded his major study of the Jain castes, the 1929 *Jain Jāti Mahoday*, with a lengthy discussion of the causes for the fallen condition of Jain society. He recommended changing practices relating to child marriage, marriage of old men to young women, bride price, maltreatment of widows, conspicuous consumption, poverty, and other social customs. This was a litany common to many social reformers in India throughout the nineteenth and twentieth centuries.

9

Cleaving to the Goddess

LAWRENCE A. BABB

This final chapter traces the career of Dadhimatī and her temple as it evolved in the midst of accelerating social changes occurring during the late nineteenth and early twentieth centuries. The issue is caste and the kind of social identity it represents. During this period, elite members of many castes, in particular those most affected by urbanization and related social and economic changes, were beginning to develop new understandings of the nature of caste itself in parallel with new ways of managing their affairs as communities. These trends were very much part of the Dāhimā Brahman picture, and revolved, as we shall see, around changing conceptions of the relationship between the goddess and the Dāhimā Brahmans as a social entity. Although the caste is generally known as the Dāhimā or Dāymā Brahmans, many members prefer the designation "Dādhīc Brahman," a preference we shall respect in this chapter. As will be seen, this preference itself is part of our story.

The *Purāṇa*

In order to understand how the Dādhīc Brahmans rethought their caste identity, we must look closely at a book that expresses some of the key ideas in literary form. The book is the *Dadhimathī Purāṇa*, which is an account, in Sanskrit verse (966 verses in 23 chapters), of the origin of the Dādhīc Brahman caste and of the birth and activities of the goddess Dadhimatī.[1] It is impossible to say when or by whom the *Purāṇa* was actually composed, but much of its text appears to have been adopted from preexisting Sanskrit works. Its creator or creators were clearly well-versed in Sanskrit scripture, and just as clearly they had—as we shall see—an agenda involving the identity of their caste. It was most recently published in Jaipur in 1981. The Introduction to that edition refers to an earlier edition published "fifty or sixty years ago" in Ratlam (in present-day Madhya Pradesh) by someone named Kanhaiyālāl Śarmā Mālodyā Pañcolī Dādhīc, about whom we are told nothing more. That would place the first publication in the 1920s (if, indeed, that was its first publication). Perhaps it was composed at that time, or perhaps earlier, or perhaps it was not composed at any single time. I believe that the best we can do is place its composition in the late nineteenth or early twentieth century.

The published *Purāṇa* represented a new way of presenting the caste's account of its own beginning. Before the *Purāṇa* existed, and to a limited extent even today, traditional genealogists—in Rajasthan, known variously as Rāvs, Jāgās, or Bhāṭs—were the recorders and transmitters of the origin myths of many Rajasthani castes, including the Dādhīc Brahmans. At the time the *Purāṇa*'s publication, the origin myths of many castes were appearing in printed form for the first time, usually under the sponsorship of newly-emerging caste associations. By publishing their own versions of their castes' origin myths, caste elites were able to promote reconstituted versions of their castes' histories and social personalities. It must be borne in mind that this was a time of vast social and economic changes taking place all over India, including princely India, which created extraordinary opportunities—in trade, in the professions, in service occupations—for those castes whose members were well positioned to take advantage of them. These new circumstances created both the occasion and the need for updated, or modified, or in various ways sanitized or expurgated versions of caste origin myths, and the publication of such material became one of the most characteristic activities of caste associations.

While we lack detailed information about how these general developments affected the Dādhīc Brahmans, we do know that during this period significant numbers of this relatively well-educated community had already left, or were in the process of leaving, their region of origin to enter service occupations and the professions in towns and cities. This would continue, with the result that there are very few Dādhīc Brahmans living in Dadhimatī's hinterland today. The emigration of the Dādhīc Brahman caste is a crucial factor in our analysis, for the refurbished version of their caste identity, as embodied in the *Purāṇa*, originated in the Dādhīc diaspora. This was also the era of the formation of the Dādhīc Brahmans' caste association, which met for the first time in 1919.

The *Purāṇa* can be regarded as a window into the mindset of the caste's identity theorists as they found themselves confronting certain problems. One such problem was clearly caste unity, which was being tested in a new way by physical dispersal. As we shall see, producing a strong symbolism of caste solidarity was a key item on the *Purāṇa*'s agenda. I strongly suspect that another problem was sensitivity about the quality of their Brahmanical credentials, possibly a consequence of a movement into more cosmopolitan settings in which their status as Brahmans was potentially open to new kinds of scrutiny and challenge. They would have been coming into contact with other regionally prominent

Brahman castes, and also with members of higher status Brahman castes from other regions.[2] On the basis of informants' accounts, we know of at least one incident in the early twentieth century in which a member of the Gauṛ Brahman caste, alleging that he had seen a Dādhīc Brahman pouring water on a Śiva *linga* from a bag made of hide, declared the Dādhīc Brahmans to be Śūdras (or *"halkā Brahmans,"* as one Dādhīc informant said).[3] Reinforcing an unassailable Brahmanical pedigree was, as we shall see, another important agenda of the Purāṇa.

The *Purāṇa* has a long story to tell, set within a series of framing stories, and is far too complex a work to be summarized even in the sketchiest way here. But for our purposes it is enough to focus on the document's basic theme, which is that of constructing a version of Dādhīc Brahman identity. In order to accomplish this, the *Purāṇa* tells two ostensibly separate stories. One is an account of the creation of the Dādhīc Brahman caste, a story taking the form of a genealogy. The other is a narrative of Dadhimatī's origin and deeds. As will be seen, the text's true crux is the fusing of these two stories. We begin with the caste's origin story.

Origin

The Pedigree

The origin story (from which I have stripped a number of embellishments) begins at the beginning of the world when creator-god Brahmā appeared on a lotus growing from Viṣṇu's navel. Brahmā created the sage Atharvā (Skt. Atharvan), whose son was Dadhīci. (We shall return to further details about Dadhīci's birth later.) Pleased by Dadhīci's birth, Brahmā put special power in his body, and predicted that he would destroy demons and that he would be called "Dadhyaṅ" because he was the one who would sprinkle curds (17.16).[4] At a later point, Lord Śiva himself ordered Dadhīci to marry and create progeny, so Dadhīci brought a bride to his house, and then did 1,000 years (*divya*, or "divine" years) of asceticism. Śiva was pleased by this, and ordered him to perform "the asceticism (*tap*) of Dadhimathī [the spelling used in the *Purāṇa*]," saying that she would become "boon-giver" and would become *kul devī* for the protection of his lineage (18.1–4). When Dadhīci began his asceticism, the goddess herself appeared and gave boons and blessings.

Of all of the events of Dadhīci's life, however, the *Purāṇa* assigns greatest importance to his role in Indra's famous conflict with the demon, Vṛtrāsur.[5] In order to make a weapon for Indra to use in the fight, the gods went to Dadhīci to ask for his "body" (meaning his bones), which was filled with the influence of his *vidyā*, *vrat* and *tap*.[6] Knowing they were coming, Dadhīci put some of his semen in a dhoti that he gave to his wife for washing, and she became pregnant merely from standing in the water with it. This detail makes the related points that Dadhīci was a celibate ascetic and that his semen was especially powerful because of his asceticism. When his wife later made her *satī* vow after discovering that Dadhīci had given his life, she cut out her womb and gave it for safekeeping to Brahmā. Brahmā, in turn, entrusted the infant's care to some pipal trees, and from eating their fruit the infant acquired the name Pipplād.[7]

Pipplād was himself a sage of great ascetic power. He and his wife spent eighty-eight years practicing austerities, after which he divided his semen into twelve parts, put them into her womb, and became passionless. She then gave birth to twelve sons: Vṛhadvats, Gautam, Bhārgav, Bhāradvāj, Kaucchas, Kaśyap, Śāṇḍilya, Mahābhāg Atri, Parāśar, Kapil, Garg, and Laghuvats (elsewhere also known as Mam). They, in turn, became renowned sages, and each married and produced twelve sons of his own, who were also great sages.

In those days there was a mighty king named Māndhātā who wanted to conquer the three worlds. To this end, he asked the sage Vaśiṣṭh to perform a sacrifice. Vaśiṣṭh demurred and recommended Pipplād's 144 grandsons instead. On behalf of the king, the 144 sages performed a great vegetarian sacrifice for Dadhimatī, and the *kuṇḍ*—the sacrificial firepit—was what is now the circular bathing tank adjacent to the Dadhimatī temple (Plate 34). She manifested on the spot. They sang her praises. Noting that Dadhīci had given his bones to Indra, they asked that she become their clan goddess (*kul devī*) and fulfill the king's wishes. In response, she promised to be their clan "deity" (*kul devtā*), and added that anyone among them who worshiped a different deity would suffer sorrows and unrealized hopes. She also promised that the king's progeny would all be kings, and that, served by sages of purity (by implication the progeny of the 144), they would worship her emanations in that *kapālpīṭh*.[8] She insisted, however, that sacrifices to her should never involve killing animals. She said that bathing in the *kuṇḍ* would destroy sins, cure illnesses, and much else. She then stepped into the *kuṇḍ* and vanished. Then the king gave *dakṣiṇā* (payment for performing a ritual) to the "non-*dakṣiṇā*-desiring" 144 Brahmans; it consisted of a village and a virgin for each of them, "with pipal leaves" (26.61–2).

The genealogical myth ends here. It is, one can say, precisely at this point that the Dādhīc Brahman caste comes into existence. Now equipped with wives and land, the 144 sages become ex-sages and the apical ancestors of the 144 exogamous patriclans supposedly making up the Dādhīc Brahman caste.

Analysis

The genealogy is clearly a blend of disparate elements. Some of it comes from well-known texts, some from local traditions. Dadhīci was indeed the son of Atharvā, and a famous figure in his own right. The portrayal of Pipplād as Dadhīci's son has a somewhat more obscure textual basis.[9] Eleven of Pipplād's twelve sons are well-known sages and fixtures of Brahmanical genealogies, but Mam seems to be a less well-known addition. The detail of Dadhīci's 144 grandsons is probably a local tradition. Māndhātā is indeed a figure in the *Mahābhārata* (Vana Parva 126.1–40), but the tradition of Dadhīci's sons or grandsons officiating at a sacrifice sponsored by him at Goth-Manglod is obviously local.

Exactly how these materials came to be blended, and by whom, is hard to say. The blend, however, appears to predate the *Purāṇa*, and was probably acquired from the caste's traditional genealogists. This is suggested by the fact that in a version given in an article in the 1891 *Marwar Census Report* (Singh 1997:189–91), which makes no mention of a *Purāṇa*, the line of descent is the same as given in the *Purāṇa* version, as is the role of Māndhātā's sacrifice. The continuity of the sacrificial motif through both versions of the genealogy is unsurprising, because the idea of the sacrifice as the catalyst for the creation or transformation of social groups is deeply embedded in the region's mythic syntax and a common feature of caste origin myths (Babb 2004).

Clearly, however, the *Purāṇa* authors put their own spin on the materials they had at hand. One example involves Pipplād's twelfth son, Mam. In the Census version, in a version reported in Jvālāprasād Miśra's *Jāti Bhāskar* (1996:177–79),[10] and in a version we heard from a traditional genealogist, Mam's descendants "fell away from *dharma*" (in the *Census*'s words), which is usually interpreted as their becoming Muslims. For this reason, they drop out of the caste's line of descent. The presence of this twelfth oddball sage in the group of sages is something of a mystery. It is possible that the original purpose of this part of the myth was to explain the presence of Dadhimatī-venerating Muslims in the region. We never encountered any of these, but many interviewees claimed that they once existed.[11] In any case, nothing is said of this apostasy in the *Purāṇa*. It is hard to imagine that the omission is inadvertent, and it might reflect a desire to suppress the notion that the Dādhīc Brahmans could possibly be agnatically related to a community of Muslims.

There is another alteration that strikes me as particularly significant, because it suggests a degree of alienation of the *Purāṇa* authors from the cultural world in which the genealogical myth originated. It has to do with the moment at which the 144 sages become "domesticated," which is the point at which they accept payment (the *dakṣiṇā*) for their performance of the sacrifice. To understand this incident, it is necessary to know two things. First, a sacrifice cannot be fruitful unless the priests are paid. Second, sages (and, at some ideal level, Brahmans generically) do not—or should not—wish to accept such payment, because doing so is inconsonant with world renunciation, which is held to be a defining Brahmanical virtue. Thus, the dilemma of *dakṣiṇā*.

I believe that the original Dādhīc origin myth resolved this dilemma by means of a myth-image of "subterfuge-by-leaf." James Tod mentions this concept in his *Annals* (1990:III:1629–30) in connection with the origin myth of a Brahman group, *jāti* unspecified, living in Mainar (near Udaipur). According to local legend, King Māndhātā sponsored a sacrifice there that was performed for him by two sages. At the rite's conclusion, the king managed to give them a grant of the lands of Mainar, which they did not want, by concealing it, presumably in the form of a written pledge, in folded betel leaves. In gaining the land, they lost their powers. Previously they had possessed the ability to throw their dhotis into the air after bathing where they would remain aloft, sheltering them from the sun. When the sages lost this power, they became farmers, and their descendants are the Brahmans of Mainar.

We came across the same myth-image when we interviewed a Rāv of the Dādhīc Brahmans in Borunda village in March 1998. His version of the Dādhīc origin myth ended with twelve sages (not 144), who were reluctant to take payment for the sacrifice they had performed for "King Mān." However, they finally accepted payment, which was pledged in writing on betel leaves. Previously, they had possessed the ability to clean their dhotis by tossing them into the air after bathing; the freshly laundered dhotis would then fall back into their outstretched hands. But when they attempted this after performing the sacrifice, they discovered they had lost the power. Very upset, they went to Dadhimatī and confessed to taking payment (which in this version she had instructed them not to do). They then decided to curse King Mān, but when they got to the palace they found twelve women, twelve coins of gold, twelve cows, and twelve parcels of land waiting for each of them. When they asked for King Mān, the women informed the sages that they belonged to them, and would curse them if they were not accepted. So the sages returned to Dadhimatī accompanied by the women; she ordered them to accept the women, and added they would henceforth marry among themselves (that is, the sages' descendants would form an endogamous *jāti*).[12] They had twelve sons each, who were the 144 patriclan ancestors.

The basic theme underlying these variations, including the *Purāṇa* version, is the same: the domestication of sages in a genealogical frame of reference. The myth insists on the caste's descent from distinguished ascetic sages. This, however, presents a problem, which is that of accounting for the transition from ascetic sagedom to the ordinary householdership of patriclan ancestors. Matters come to a head when the time comes to pay the sages for priestly services. In the Tod and Rāv versions, the reluctance to accept payment is overcome by subterfuge. Even so, acceptance of payment results in a severe comedown, symbolized by the loss of magical power. The focus on these events is softened in the *Purāṇa* version. Here there is no subterfuge, although the appropriate reluctance to take payment is mentioned. Nothing is said of lost powers. The *Purāṇa*, I believe, attempts to minimize the sense of comedown that seems quite explicit in the less fastidious Tod and Rāv versions of the tale. That the *Purāṇa* version must have been built on a preexisting and more "folkish" foundation is suggested by the fact that *Purāṇa* mentions that the payment was given "with pipal leaves." But the *Purāṇa* provides no indication of why leaves are mentioned and gets the type of leaf wrong. I think the *Purāṇa* authors might not have understood the point of the episode, suggesting that they were operating at a significant social distance from the cultural milieu that produced the original versions of the Dādhīc origin myth.

Considered as a totality, the genealogy accomplishes two basic things. First, it provides a conceptual basis for a common *jāti* identity uniting a number of exogamous descent groups. The only numerical requirement is that the scheme be capacious enough to accommodate some plausible number of patriclan claimants to Dādhīc identity. The number 144 is a created but necessary convention. There has to be some number, and if you start with twelve, itself a recurrent number in the origin mythology of the region, 144 makes good sense. However, there were certainly never exactly 144 actual exogamous patriclans of the Dādhīc Brahman caste, a point to which we shall return. Second, the genealogy burnishes the Brahmanical ancestry of these patriclans, a feature present in all versions but emphasized by the *Purāṇa*, a document written in Sanskrit along Puranic lines. A Brahman caste must bear a distinguished Brahman pedigree. This the myth supplies, originating from Brahmā and continuing through Dadhīci and his twelve grandsons. As we shall see later, however, the descent-group structure of the scheme cannot be fully Brahmanized.

But before returning to that issue, let us turn to the other principal story the *Purāṇa* tells, that of the goddess Dadhimatī.

The Goddess

Dadhimatī is very much a milky goddess. Dadhi means *dahī*, or curds, and in Sanskrit Dadhimatī means "she who possesses curds." This has apparently been her name for centuries, as evidenced by the fact she is so named in the seventh-century inscription found at the temple (Ram Karna 1911–12). The *Purāṇa*, however, calls her Dadhimathī, as does the Marwar *Census*. The word *mathi* means "churn," and I believe the *Purāṇa* uses it instead of *–matī* in order to render more plausible its own derivation of her name. According to the *Purāṇa*, she is so named because she assisted the gods in churning the milky-rice ocean (*khīrsāgar*), which she had magically turned into a curd ocean (*dadhisāgar*), in order to provide them with *amṛt*, the nectar of immortality (4.3–7).[13] Of course it is always possible that her original name was Dadhimathī, which was then Sankritized to Dadhimatī, in which case we can imagine that her name and persona emerged from a context of domestic worship in the region that focused in some way on milk and churning. In any case, and however you cut it, this is a goddess whose image is deeply connected with milk.

In consistency with Dadhimati's milkiness, her temple's origin myth connects her in a special way with local cowherds. This myth appears to be nearly universally known among her devotees, and is represented pictorially in the temple (Plate 28). According to the myth, the temple's site was at one time nothing but wilderness. The goddess appeared in a vision to a cowherd who happened to be at the spot, and told him that she was going to emerge from the ground, and that he should not be afraid (Plate 28). Some say that the cowherd was actually a Jāṭ, and the ancestor of the numerous Jāṭs of the area. When she began to come forth, there was a tremendous noise and shaking of the ground. Just at the point when her knee (or head, depending on the version) had emerged, the cowherd shouted "Stop, mother!" He was actually trying to call back his fleeing cows, but his cry had the effect of causing the goddess to stop emerging, which is why she takes the form of a low, aniconic stone.

It is important to note that the myth is about the emergence of the stone, not the building of the temple, which local tradition seems to regard as a separate matter. We heard various accounts of how the temple came to be built. According to one,[14] after the goddess emerged, the cowherd met a Dādhīc Brahman by the name of Viṣṇudās. He predicted that the cowherd would become the King of Udaipur. When the prediction came true, the cowherd, now turned king, built the temple. As it happens, Viṣṇudās was a genuine historical figure who persuaded the King of Udaipur to fund a major renovation of the temple. This occurred, however, not in the primordial past but around 1850, which is an indication of the malleability of both narrative and time in the realm of myth.[15]

From all that we know of Dadhimatī, her relationship with her devotees was traditionally *territorial* in character. That is, she was, and perhaps for most of her local worshipers still is, a goddess linked with a particular *place*. (On the differences between deities of place, social groups, and devotional adoration, see chapter six of this volume.) This is indeed the point of the temple's origin myth, which is about how the goddess came to be manifested at a particular point on the earth's surface. She is the goddess of those who live in her vicinity, in her *kṣetra*. From this perspective, she is not the goddess of any particular caste or castes. Her point of connection with social structure is agnatic descent, which is the material out of which patriclans and their lineage segments are made. She is the goddess, that is, of descent groups that live or originate in the hinterland of her temple, and her connection with caste is an indirect byproduct of this. From a wider perspective, Dadhimatī's relationship with her devotees is an expression of regional identity, and not caste identity. We were told repeatedly that members of all the region's castes honor her as patriclan goddess.

This is not, however, the *Purāṇa*'s concept of her relationship with caste, as we now see.

Cleaving to the Goddess

Among the *Purāṇa's* most important assertions is the claim that Dadhimatī and Dadhīci are brother and sister. Indeed, this assertion is arguably the *Purāṇa*'s crux, for it is here that the text's two main narratives—one genealogical, the other the story of the goddess—become one. It is made fairly early in the text, and takes the form of a rather clumsy stitching of the one story to the other. The overall framing narrative is that of a conversation between Vaśiṣṭh and Himālaya, itself set within a conversation between Śiva and Pārvatī. Atharvā's marriage, Vaśiṣṭh says, was without issue. But then, on the advice of the sage Nārad, Atharvā and his wife performed a *vrat* (a votive fast) for the goddess Dadhimatī. She manifested, and granted the boon of a son. Atharvā's wife, however, pleaded for a daughter as well, and, in response, the goddess promised to take birth in their house and entered her womb (3.16–27). Dadhīci's birth took place at an unspecified later time, and is described at a later point in the text.

In the course of relating these details, the text takes a significant detour. Vaśiṣṭh tells Himālaya of how Nārad, in the course of telling Atharvā about the Dadhimatī vrat, also told of how he was told by Brahmā of a *mahākṣetra* of the goddess Mahāmāyā located 32 *kos* north of Pushkar[16] where the goddess's scull (*kapāl*) had fallen from Śiva's hand (3.32–5). Brahmā praises this place in the most extravagant terms. This is a reference to the Dadhimatī temple (or Dadhimatī, the goddess herself), and connects it to the famous incident in which portions of Satī's corpse, shed by grief-maddened Śiva as he rampaged around India, fell at fifty-one points on the earth that became sites of the goddess's power (*śakti pīṭhs*). This is a significant assertion to which we return below.

Dadhimatī's most illustrious deed, as recounted by the *Purāṇa* (7–16), was her defeat of a demon by the name of Vikaṭāsur, an event occurring in the *satyug*. It seems that, as a result of his austerities, Vikaṭāsur had won the boon from Brahmā that he could be killed only by a woman. Apparently invincible, he then attacked and defeated the gods, and built a magnificent city in the Curd Ocean. The desperate gods went to Viṣṇu for advice. He directed them to the goddess Ambikā (i.e., Dadhimatī), who had taken birth in Atharvā's house. They went there, praised the goddess, and begged for her help, which she agreed to give. A great battle ensued, to which the *Purāṇa* devotes much boilerplate descriptive text. The battle's details are not essential to the narrative, but it is worth noting that, in the course of the battle, the goddess generated various *śakti*s from her body—emanations taking the form of goddesses—who created huge havoc in the demon army. The goddess then made the pronouncement that people would worship these goddesses in their houses in the *kaliyug*, and that they would be *kul devī*s under various names. She then reabsorbed them.

The battle ended when the goddess and Vikaṭāsur engaged in personal combat in the Curd Ocean, culminating in the demon-king's death. According to the *Purāṇa*, Vikaṭāsur's bowels had contained *vastusār* (apparently an essence or force that gives the things of the world their qualities[17]) from before the *pralaya*. She removed the *vastusār*-impregnated bowels from his body and gave them to the gods. Viśvakarmā ground them up, mixed the *vastusār* into all *vastus* (i.e., all the things of the world), and in this way, the cosmos and the gods were re-empowered.

At the moment of her victory, the gods praised Dadhimatī in an extremely lengthy *stuti*. They invoked her as, among many other things, Dadhīci's boon-giver and chosen (*iṣṭ*) deity (16.35), as his clan goddess (16.37), and as having been "created" in Dadhīci's lineage (*kul*) (16.39).[18] This is the first a reader or auditor of the text will have heard of Dadhīci in quite some time. In response to the gods' praises, she proclaimed that the day she killed Vikaṭāsur, the bright eighth of the month of Māgh, would thenceforth be known as *jayāṣṭmī*, and that those who celebrate it would have obstacles removed. She then (after giving the *vastusār* to the gods) returned to Atharvā's *āśram*. At this point, the text turns to Dadhīci's birth and the development of the Dādhīc genealogy.

The two narratives converge again at the point of Māndhātā's sacrifice, where, as noted earlier, she pledges to be the Dādhīc Brahmans' patriclan deity and to fulfill Māndhātā's wishes, and then vanishes in the *kuṇḍ*. It is at this point that King Māndhātā gives payment to the 144 priests.

The *Purāṇa* now moves to its conclusion (chapter 23). By the grace of the goddess, Māndhātā became ruler of the earth, honored by the gods. By worshiping the goddess he became the father of three glorious sons and fifty daughters, and prospered greatly. Therefore, the text asserts, doing her *pūjā* can bring every kind of abundance. The text then launches into a lengthy description of the kinds of offerings and observances with which one can honor the goddess, and the benefits of each. The text sternly admonishes Dādhīc Brahmans to worship Dadhimatī, a point to which we return below. The final lines wrap up the framing story and end by affirming the benefits realized by those who hear the *Purāṇa* and stressing the need to give gifts and respect to those who recite it.

Analysis

The *Purāṇa*'s portrayal of the goddess quite obviously borrows heavily from preexisting mythic motifs (and text), which it has recast to suit its own agenda. What we have is the image of a demon-destroying, martial goddess, well known to Puranic and Epic tradition. The *Purāṇa* reworks this image in two ways. First, the generic goddess is recast as a Sanskritized version of a local goddess. Given the milkiness of her local persona, the *Purāṇa*'s emphasis on the Curd Ocean as the venue of the great battle with the demons makes good sense as a Sanskritizing context. Second, having been Sankritized, the goddess is brought into a very special relation with the Dādhīc Brahmans.

In expanding on these points, let us begin by noting that the *Purāṇa*'s representation of Dadhimatī can be seen as an inversion of her traditional image in the region. That image, as we know, is territorial—she is a goddess who belongs to a place, and the place, in a sense, belongs to her. The emphasis is on autochthony, for it is *here* at *this place* that she came from the earth itself. Very different is the *Purāṇa*'s viewpoint. The text says nothing whatsoever about the goddess emerging from the ground. Instead, it refers to the location of the temple in the context of the Satī myth. The Satī myth, of course, is also "positional," but its directionality different. The cowherd myth pulls the goddess up from the ground. The Satī myth, in the *Purāṇa* version as in all versions, pulls the goddess down from the sky. In doing so, it metaphorically shifts the focus away from autochthony and toward the subcontinental universalism of pan-Indian traditions carried by texts.

In consistency with this, the *Purāṇa*'s main focus is not on the temple (of which it says nothing) or the goddess's image (the skull, not dwelt upon) but on the *kuṇḍ*. In the *Purāṇa*'s view, the *kuṇḍ* was the place where the goddess's most significant local manifestation occurred, not the temple. The context of this appearance was a Brahmanical sacrifice to her. And crucially, the *Purāṇa* states that it was this sacrifice that connected the Dādhīc Brahmans into the local social framework, and not prior residency in her territory. Indeed, they settle on the territory only because of the gifts of land, a product of their sacrificial relationship with the king. One implication of this is that apart from Māndhātā and his descendants (who, as far as I know, are not in any way identified with any part of the current regional social scene), this connection—unlike a purely territorial one—is of a sort that cannot be shared with others.[19]

Having uprooted her from the soil, the text configures Dadhimatī as the *caste* deity of the Dādhīc Brahmans. The difference between a caste deity and what she was before is subtle but, in my opinion, significant. Clearly there had always been a special relationship between Dadhimatī and the Dādhīc Brahmans, as the designation Dāhimā shows (a point to be addressed below). But this was a relationship conceptualized on the pattern of clan or lineage goddesshood (i.e., *kul*-goddesshood), which was the same basic pattern as her relationship with the region's other communities. That is, she was the clan goddess of those who lived in her territory, which included Brahmans and many others. From this perspective, she did indeed have a special relationship with *all* the Dādhīc Brahmans, but the relationship was conceived in terms of *kul*, not caste. Even today, Dādhīc informants sometimes say that they have a special relationship with her as a caste precisely because she is the clan goddess of *all* the Dādhīc clans, whereas she is only the goddess of *some* of the clans of other castes. I believe, however, that the *Purāṇa* escalates matters. Now Brahmanized and conceptually uprooted from her native soil, Dadhimatī becomes the goddess of a caste as a caste. As the *Purāṇa* comes to its end, it therefore admonishes Dādhīc Brahmans to worship Dadhimatī, and devotes six stanzas (23.25–30) to making the point that any "Dādhīc" who fails to worship her is "no Dādhīc." This is an expression of a ritual obligation of caste membership, now drifting free of patriclan anchoring.[20]

All of this is reinforced by the manner in which the *Purāṇa* fuses the genealogy to Dadhimatī's story. It does so by portraying her as the sister of Dadhīci. Dadhīci is the apical ancestor of the entire caste and the figure whose own attributes are definitive of the caste's concept of itself as a Brahman caste. As Dadhīci's sister, Dadhimatī enters an agnatic relationship with the caste as a whole, becoming something like a perpetual father's sister, and the relationship partakes of the caste's Brahman status. For a *kul devī* to be seen as an agnate is, I believe, unusual. If anything, the in-marrying bride is a more likely kinship paradigm, for this is the usual relationship between *satī*s—who to some extent occupy the same conceptual and ritual niche as *kul devī*s generically—and the descent groups that venerate them (see Harlan 1992, esp. 133–38). For the Dādhīc Brahmans to claim Dadhimatī as an agnate differentiates them with special clarity from the wider regional congeries of Dadhimatī-worshiping castes. As in the case of the ritual relationship with King Māndhātā, this is a relationship that cannot be shared with other groups.

A notable feature of the *Purāṇa* is its insistent use of the term "Dādhīc" Brahman. It is almost as if the Dādhīc Brahmans have deracinated themselves in parallel with their deracination of their goddess. I say this because the alternative terms—still in general use today—closely link the community to the territory that forms Dadhimatī's hinterland. These terms are "Dāhimā" or "Dāymā" Brahman, and they are clearly references to Dadhimatī as a milky local goddess. It is likely that both terms connect *dahī* (curds) and *mā* (mother)—i.e., as "Curd Mother." Brahmans who came from her territory, her *kṣetra*, were therefore "*Dāhimā*" Brahmans.[21] The Dādhīc Brahmans obviously do not wish to suppress their relationship with Dadhimatī, for she is at the heart of their identity as a caste, especially the kind of caste identity we have seen exemplified in the *Purāṇa*. The caste's magazine, after all, is called *Dadhimatī*. But the designation "Dādhīc" Brahman preserves the relationship with her (as Dadhīci's sister) while shedding the regional association in favor of a more universalistic and high-culture Brahmanical identification with the sage Dadhīci.[22] This clearly why the *Purāṇa* favors "Dādhīc," and never uses the term "Dāhimā." However, although many members of the caste prefer "Dādhīc" nowadays, "Dāhimā" continues to dominate ordinary discourse.

Fallout

The *Purāṇa* is a manifestation of an effort on the part of an educated and activist element among the Dādhīc Brahmans to reconfigure their identity as a community in a way that diverged significantly from older traditions. It is difficult to imagine such surgery on tradition not generating unintended problems, and this has indeed happened. In the remainder of this chapter, I would like to discuss briefly two such difficulties, one internal to the caste, the other in its external relations with other groups. Internally, the reconstructed image of the caste brought certain contradictions in the genealogy into awkward visibility. Externally, the caste's new self-concept generated tension in its relations with other groups in its region of origin.

Brahmanical Kinship

The genealogical problem stems from the fact that Dādhīc Brahmans have committed themselves to a genealogy that, while highly Brahmanical in the ancestry claimed, is fundamentally un-Brahmanical in structure. Ironically, the semi-canonicity of the *Purāṇa*, a document that itself expresses a strong Brahmanizing impulse, has probably locked them into this awkward commitment once and for all.

There is nothing in the least problematic about the genealogy's basic structure, which is that a segmentary system of patrilineages united by common descent from an eponymous ancestor (eponymous, that is, if one insists on "Dādhīc" as the caste's name). Its underlying function is threefold: to provide a Brahmanical pedigree for the Dādhīc Brahmans, to distinguish them from other Brahmans, and to account for the existence of a large number of exogamous patriclans. The pedigree establishing Brahman credentials is the line of descent from Brahmā through Atharvā to Dadhīci.[23] In turn, the claim of descent from *Dadhīci* distinguishes the Dādhīc Brahmans as a separate Brahman *jāti*. And the inflationary burst of Pipplād's descendants creates a sufficient number of empty lineage slots to provide a reasonable if loose fit between the top-down pedigree and the bottom-up social reality of patriclans claiming Dādhīc identity.

The true heart of the genealogy is the claim of descent from Dadhīci, for this is the core of Dādhīc caste identity as constructed by the *Purāṇa*. We cannot know exactly when or how Dadhīci came to be seen as the caste's apical ancestor. On the assumption that the community described in the seventh-century inscription really is ancestral to contemporary Dādhīc Brahmans (a very big assumption, in my view), and assuming also that "Dadhya" has something to do with "Dadhīci," it is possibly very ancient. Ram Karna and Asopa, however, believe that the appellation "Dadhya" Brahman, as found in the inscription, refers to the goddess Dadhimatī rather than the sage Dadhīci (Ram Karna 1911–12:299; Asopa 1988:34). I think it is a reasonable hypothesis that this claim of Dadhīci as caste ancestor has been laid over a primordial caste identity based on the caste's territorial or residential connection with milky Dadhimatī. Even today, the appellation "Dāhimā Brahman" remains entrenched in ordinary speech, despite efforts (of which the

Purāṇa represents an example) to supplant it with "Dādhīc Brahman." As for how Dadhīci was chosen, there is at least a nominal milk connection, for Dadhīci/Dadhyaṅ/Dadhyañc mean "sprinkling curds."

But whatever the antiquity of the connection, and however it might have first been conceived, it is given special emphasis in the *Purāṇa*, which is of a piece with a broader emphasis on polishing up the caste's Brahmanical image. It is, of course, a distinguished Brahman pedigree. But perhaps even more important, by shifting the focus from a regionally-defined identity (Dāhimā) to an identity anchored in Brahmanical descent (Dādhīc), the *Purāṇa* constructs an identity that is both less parochial and more suited to a community increasingly living in diaspora.

There are, however, two problems with the genealogy, one minor and one not so minor. Both have to do with the fact that the scheme is supposed to support a claim of *Brahman* identity. The lesser problem arises from the seemingly inherent contradiction in establishing Brahmanical qualities (as opposed to other qualities a group might have) on the basis of physical descent. How can Brahmans be Brahmans because of descent from ascetic sages if the sages in question are truly ascetic? This is the point of the unusual manner in which of Dadhīci and Pipplād produce their sons.[24] The more difficult issue is that a Brahmanical system of descent, as idealized in the classical genealogical texts, requires *gotra*s. The term *gotra* is, of course, quite commonly used by Rajasthanis to refer to patriclans or patrilineages. This is fine, so long as the context is not Brahmanical. For a caste to claim Brahmanical descent, however, carries the implication that its *gotra*s are of the proper Brahmanical kind, and the Brahmanical system bears little resemblance to the normal descent structure of Rajasthani castes, and this includes the Dādhīc Brahmans.

To explain the nature of the classical Brahman *gotra* system fully is far beyond the scope of this chapter. In essence, however, it is a system of exogamous patriclans, each of which traces descent to a particular founding sage (*ṛṣi*).[25] The founding sages are presented in standard lists, usually of seven or eight. As given by Baudhāyana, for example, the list consists of a group known as the "seven sages"—Jamadagni, Gautama, Bharadvāja, Atri, Viśvāmitra, Kaśyapa, and Vasiṣṭha (our Vaśiṣṭh)—with Agastya added as the eighth. The basic list, usually said to be Brahmā's "mind-born" sons, changed over time, but the principle of exogamy on the basis of descent from eponymous sage-ancestors remained stable.[26] An additional complication was a supplementary rule of exogamy based on *pravara*. The term *pravara* refers to a list of sage-ancestors, usually three, in a given family's line of descent, one of which will be that of the founding sage of the family's *gotra*. Different *pravara* lists form the basis of subdivisions of each *gotra* known as *gaṇa*s. The normal rule is that persons whose *pravara* lists have one name in common may not marry, so the principles of *gotra* and *pravara* exogamy coincide.

At some point in time (we cannot know exactly when, except that it predates the *Purāṇa*) the Dādhīc Brahmans duly supplied their descent system with Brahmanical, or Brahmanical-seeming, *gotra*s. This is the reason for the presence of the twelve named sage-sons of Pipplād in the genealogy; they are there in order to supply the apical sage-ancestors of twelve (or, given the apostasy of Mam's progeny, eleven) *gotras*, which are then further subdivided into branches (the actual exogamous patriclans), in theory numbering 144 (or 132, if Mam's descendants are out of the picture). Obviously, however, the *gotras* were simply imposed upon an already existing system of exogamous patriclans. This scheme was already in place by the late nineteenth century, as we see from the fact that the *Marwar Census Report* lists eleven "*gotras*" with 88 "*khāmps*" distributed among them. There are, however, two big problems with this scheme: a lack of fit with the idealized Brahmanical *gotra* system, and a lack of fit with the on-the-ground realities of Dādhīc Brahman marriage patterns.

On the issue of fit with the idealized Brahmanical system, the essential difficulty, and it is truly basic, is the impossibility of reconciling the Dādhīc Brahman claim of a single apical sage-ancestor for the caste as a whole with the classical Brahmanical system. As we have said, Dadhīci's ancestral role is central to the caste's claim of a Brahman pedigree and to its social identity vis-à-vis other Brahmans. But that claim turns the entire caste into a quasi *gotra*. One potential problem created by this is that of incest, because persons related by agnatic descent should not marry. When presented with this problem, some informants attempted to solve it by suggesting that descent from Dadhīci was disciplic in nature, not biological. This, however, does not fit very well with the *Purāṇa*'s emphasis on semen. Nevertheless, the incest issue is not generally perceived as a problem, most people apparently feeling that the connection is simply too distant to matter. But we should also note that it is structurally impossible for the problem to be acknowledged. If you wish to define *jāti* identity in terms of common agnatic descent from a single ancestor, you have to ignore the issue of incest.

Another problem is that of differentiating *gotras* when you have already established a single sage-ancestor for the caste as a whole. The genealogy differentiates the *gotras* by tracing their descent to Pipplād's twelve (or eleven) sons. This, however, requires that the *gotras*' sage-ancestors be Dadhīci's descendants, which means that they cannot be Brahmā's mind-born sons. Of course, even Dadhīci cannot have this status, because the *Rg Veda* already supplies him with a father, namely Atharvā. Myth (or some myth), however, represents Atharvā himself as Brahmā's eldest son (Dowson 1972:31; his source not named). In any case, the *Purāṇa* deals with Atharvā's birth in a somewhat odd manner. The relevant lines (1.18–19) state that having "seen" Marīci (a famous sage) "and the other sages," Brahmā got them married. Then, in the very next couplet, we learn that "after this" Brahmā created Atharvā and arranged for his marriage. I suspect that the purpose of mentioning only Marīci is both to detract attention from the idea of a fixed and canonical list of seven (or more) famous sages, and to avoid a glaring contradiction by naming sages as Brahmā's mind-born sons who appear later in the *Purāṇa* as Dadhīci's grandsons. I also suspect that placing Atharvā's creation "later" is to avoid the appearance of trying to shoehorn Atharvā into otherwise well-known lists of sages that (judging from Mitchiner's account) do not traditionally include Atharvā. These maneuverings reflect the efforts of the *Purāṇa* authors to stitch together, in a plausible manner, textual materials drawn from different sources and different contexts.

An even more basic difficulty with the scheme, however, is that it has no relationship with the social reality of exogamy. Exogamy belongs to that part of the Dādhīc lineage system that came from the bottom up. From the start, that is, it was a property of already existing exogamous clans, and this has remained true to the present day. In this respect, the system is identical in its essentials to the clan and lineage systems of many other Rajasthani castes.[27] An instructive glimpse into the actual working system is provided by a list of registrants for a marriage fair held in Indore in 1994 (*Dadhimatī* 1994:10–24). There were 183 registrants, boys and girls, and almost every registrant listed two *śākhā*s (i.e., exogamous patriclans), the father's and mother's. None mentioned *gotra*s. As best I can determine, only 69 *śākhā* names occur in this list. Of these, a significant proportion (about 18) is not to be found in a published list of 90 more or less canonical Dādhīc Brahman *śākhā*s (Jośī, n.d.).[28] Also, about a dozen of the names on the list of registrants occur far more frequently than others. These points suggest that *gotra* is simply not a consideration in calculations of exogamy, that most Dādhīc Brahmans belong to a relatively few large patriclans, and that the notion of 144 patriclans is (as we have already said) a convention, an arithmetic contrivance, based on the number twelve. In any case, Dādhīc respondents repeatedly told us that few Dādhīc Brahmans actually know their *gotra*s, and that the actual units of exogamy are the patriclans.

As far as one can tell, this disjunction between theory and practice was never a problem before the twentieth century. And let us be clear on one other point: the problem was never that Dādhīc Brahmans needed to know their *gotra*s in order to contract marriages. Since *gotra*s never regulated marriage among the Dādhīc Brahmans, there was no way *gotra* membership could present difficulties in marriage negotiations. The difficulty, rather, appears to have been a growing sensitivity about the pure functionlessness of the *gotra* system in the context of the Brahmanization impulse so well embodied by the *Purāṇa*. As caste self-conceptualization became more systematized and comprehensive under the aegis of the Dādhīcs' caste association, the *gotra* situation came to be perceived as a kind of scandal. Thus it was that at its fifteenth annual meeting (in 1924) in Calcutta, the Akhil Bhāratvarṣīya Dāymā Mahāsabhā unanimously passed the following motion (Vaidya 1924:unnumbered page):

> The Mahāsabhā regards *sagotra* [intra-*gotra*] marriages as inappropriate by *śāstrīya* [orthodox] standards, but because by custom such marriages are seen here and there, we urge gentlemen of the caste to try to bring this practice gradually to a halt.

This resolution became the inspiration for a very interesting booklet entitled *Dādhīc Vaṃśotpatti va Gotrāvalī* (Vaidya 1924) that was written with the express purpose of making it possible for caste members to adhere to rules of *gotra* exogamy. The problem was that most Dādhīc Brahmans, then as now, did not know their *gotra*s. In the author's words (ibid.: "*Samarpaṇ*," unnumbered page), "in each *gotra* are several *śākhā*s or *nakhs*," and if caste members do not have a full understanding of this they will certainly "eat falsity [be deceived]" and marry within the *gotra*. He goes on to point out that all Hindus know that those belonging to the same *gotra* are *gotraj bhāī* (i.e., *gotra* siblings), and that marriage between them is equivalent to brother-sister marriage and will without doubt take them to hell. *Every Brahman community in India*, he says, observes this rule. He then adds that *Dharmaśāstra* forgives those who act wrongly in ignorance, but in the future, marriages within the *gotras* must stop. The body of the book consists of a reiteration of the caste's genealogy—in essence the same as the version given earlier—followed by a list of *gotras* and their constituent *śākhās*, based, he says, on the records of Rāvs, and various books such as Paṇḍit Jvālāprasād Miśra's *Jātibhāskar* and Paṇḍit Harikṛṣna Śāstrī's *Brāhmaṇotpatti Mārttāṇḍ*.[29]

But all of this was for naught, because it is clear that while the Dādhīc Brahmans' patriclan and lineage system can certainly coexist with nominal or non-functional Brahmanical *gotras*, it *cannot actually be made into a top-down system* of Brahmanical *gotras*. This is because it is a completely different system, built (as we have said) from the bottom up on the foundation of forms of kinship and descent typical of the Rajasthani countryside. These same forms persist today, and most Dādhīc Brahmans remain ignorant of their *gotras*. This circumstance poses an absolute limit to the Brahmanization of the Dādhīc Brahman caste, and I think this must be true of other Brahman castes as well. It would be of great interest to see how other Brahman castes, faced with similar problems of Brahmanization and rationalization of their descent systems, engage these issues. This is, however, a comparative Brahmanology yet to be researched and written.

Temple Disputes

In the matter of the caste's external relations, we find that that the Dādhīc Brahmans' shifting relationship with the goddess has led to disequilibrium in the web of their relationships with other groups. Because my colleagues have already covered this ground in other chapters of this volume, I won't linger over the matter here. I only want to make the point that, to the extent that Dādhīc Brahman identity came to be focused on a notion of exclusive ties with Dadhimatī, there was bound to be conflict with others, because the goddess was and remains ritually important to the other communities living in her vicinity. She is, that is to say, their goddess, too.

One conflict that arose early in the twentieth century (apparently beginning in 1912) was between the Dādhīc Brahmans, then newly-organized under the umbrella of their caste association (founded in 1910), and the Dadhimatī temple's priests (*pujārīs*) (on these matters, see esp. Cort's chapter seven of this volume). The priests were Parāsars, not Dādhīc Brahmans, and it is likely that they had more or less run the temple during the nineteenth century. It appears that they attempted to obtain legal sanction for their control in court by claiming some kind of ancient connection with the temple. They lost the case in 1918, and the seventh-century inscription, with its reference to ancient "Dadhya"

Brahmans, was produced in evidence against them. As Cort points out, they had little chance of success, given their relative weakness compared to the cosmopolitan Dādhīc Brahmans, many of whom were politically well placed in the region's indigenous states.

It is probable that this conflict broke out when it did as a result of changes then taking place on the Dādhīc side. This was the period in which the reconfiguration of Dādhīc identity was fully in process and in which its institutional embodiment, the national association, had recently come into existence. The fact that the association's first and subsequent meetings took place on the temple premises must have been a major provocation. We can imagine that the priests, sensing the wind's direction, decided that it was now or never to make their move.

More significant than the conflict with the priests, however, has been a struggle for control of the temple between the Dādhīc Brahmans and the Jāṭs living in the temple's vicinity (chapter seven). The Jāṭs are extremely numerous in the region, and may said to be the locally dominant caste. As best we can determine, the Jāṭs opposing the Brahmans mostly belong to a subgroup known as Biḍyāsar, an exogamous patriclan of the Jāṭ caste. Their own origin mythology connects them with Dadhimatī, whom they regard as clan goddess. The issues involved in the dispute are both material and ritual-symbolic. Material interests arise because those who control the temple have control of income-producing land adjacent to the temple and access to revenues from the shops set up during the twice-yearly fairs. The ritual symbolic issues have to do with control of the temple as an expression of group identity.

The history of the conflict is tangled and contested. Our knowledge of it is largely based on the somewhat inconsistent testimony of three Dādhīc informants who were, in different ways, involved in the events in question.[30] Judging from what we were told, the conflict's first stirrings occurred in the early twentieth century when the Brahmans began to hold their association meetings at the temple premises. We do not know exactly what happened at that point, but no legal case was involved, and the Brahmans appear to have prevailed. As in their dispute with the temple priests, the Brahmans had cultural and social capital at their disposal that was largely unavailable to their rustic Jāṭ rivals in those days. So matters remained until the post-Independence period when the Jāṭs emerged as a political power to be reckoned with. In the early 1950s, a prominent Jāṭ politician from Nagaur tried to establish a boarding school for Jāṭs on the temple premises, but was unsuccessful. After a hiatus, matters escalated in 1971 or 1972, when the Brahmans created a Trust to run the temple.[31] This resulted in conflict with the Jāṭs that culminated in a court case, filed by the Brahmans, claiming (as we understand it) exclusive rights to the management of the temple. Our respondents give different dates for these events, but in either 1983 or 1990 the Brahmans won the case and control of the temple. The role of Viṣṇudās in the mid-nineteenth century renovation of the temple apparently played a role in buttressing the Brahmans' case, with documents from Udaipur submitted in evidence.

And so the matter stands today—at least for now. Although the Jāṭs continue to agitate at the fairs (according to the Brahmans), the Brahmans do indeed control the temple today and dominate the fairs. A ritual-symbolic affirmation of this state of affairs is the existence of a shrine containing an image of Dadhīci as part of the temple complex. Although the image is older, it was installed in the shrine in 1976 (chapter five), which would have been at the height of the conflict with the Jāṭs. A prominent Dādhīc Brahman activist built this shrine, and in his interview with us he declared his intention to us to build a shrine to Pipplād as well. The Dādhīc shrine completes in architecture what was begun in Sanskrit verse in the *Purāṇa*, which is the fusion of the story of the goddess with the genealogy. At last sister and brother (as the Dādhīc Brahmans maintain) sit side-by-side as a joint embodiment of the social identity of the Dādhīc Brahman caste.

As we have seen, this state of affairs culminates a process that started early in the twentieth century when the caste was becoming physically more scattered than previously, and was—I believe in response—developing a new kind of self-awareness as a caste. Ironically, as the Dādhīc Brahmans left Dadhimatī's presence, they needed her all the more as a symbol of the moral force of the ties that bound and still bind them together as a community. This need has brought them into conflict with others in a way that Brahmanizing their genealogy never could. If the Dādhīc Brahmans want to refine their rules of exogamy, that is nobody's business but their own. But when they claim as their own a goddess who previously belonged to everybody, this is likely to have broader consequences. Having found, in Dadhimatī, a powerful symbolic focus for their own modern identity as a caste, the Dādhīc Brahmans reversed the process: they imposed their identity, as a caste, on her. The resulting disturbances of the social order in her hinterland have probably yet to play out fully.

Notes

1. My analysis is based on the Hindi translation published with the Sanskrit original. Steve Heim assisted in checking key passages against the Sanskrit, for which I extend to him my warm thanks.
2. I thank Catherine Clémentin-Ojha for the perceptive suggestion that extra-regional Brahmans probably also served as relevant cultural models, and quite possibly as the most important models.
3. One of our informants seemed to suggest that this insult was directly responsible for the creation of the *Purāṇa*. The *Purāṇa*'s publication was instigated, he added, by Shiv Shakti Rai, a Dādhīc Brahman who was then prime minister of Ratlam State. This name, however, does not appear in the Introduction to the 1981 edition, which does mention other supporters of the Ratlam publication.
4. For some reason the Hindi translator renders this as perform "*pūjā* of *dadhi*" and glosses *dadhi* (in parentheses) as "*Brahm*." I do not understand what the translator was trying to do.
5. The *Purāṇa* also retells the story (told originally in the *Śatapatha Brāhmaṇa*) of Indra's beheading of Dadhīci because he had accepted the Aśvinkumārs as pupils. See O'Flaherty 1975:56–60.
6. The *Purāṇa* does not include a detail found in other versions of the story, including the version on the Dadhimatī temple's website (http://dadhich.com/index.htm), which is that the gods had given

Dadhīci their weapons for safekeeping, and that he had dissolved them in water that he then drank. We heard a variant of this in Borunda village from a Rāv of the Dādhīc Brahmans. According to the Rāv's story, Dadhīci used Indra's *vajra* to grind his *bhāṅg*; as the *vajra* wore down, Dadhīci gradually absorbed all the particles in his bones.

7. This story obviously has some link with episodes in the *Śiva Purāṇa*. In O'Flaherty's retelling, "Pipplāda was born when a pregnant woman mounted her husband's funeral pyre; another version states that he was born when a woman wearing the loincloth of her brother, stained with his seed, bathed and became pregnant, whereupon in fear of her husband, she deposited the child at the foot of a fig tree (*pippala*), whence his name" (O'Flaherty 1973:62 [taken from *Śiva Purāṇa* 3.25.2, 3.24.5, 3.24.34–64]). Also, the *Purāṇa* (21.1–43) retells a variant of the *Śiva Purāṇa*'s story of Dharma's attempted seduction of Pipplād's wife, Padmā (ibid.: 63).
8. The temple site, which the *Purāṇa* characterizes as the place where Satī's skull fell, as we shall see later.
9. In support of this connection, Vaidya (1924) quotes verses from the *Brahmāṇḍa Purāṇa* (edition unspecified). This source mentions a twelfth son named Alpvats, whom Vaidya identifies as Mamra (i.e., Mam).
10. This book is a product of the early twentieth century, but its exact date of publication is uncertain. The colophon indicates that the text was completed in VS 1971 (1914 CE). My thanks to John Cort for deciphering the colophon.
11. It turns out that there is a Muslim group in Rajasthan known as Nāgauriya Musalmān with some sort of link to Dadhimatī's region. They appear to be a Muslim *jāti* divided into exogamous *gotras*. In April 1998, Rajendra Joshi, Varsha Joshi, and I interviewed members of a Nāgauriya Musalmān community located in the outskirts of Malpura. It emerged that one of their *gotras* is known as Dāymā. However, our informants, one of whom was Dāymā himself, knew nothing of any connection with Dadhimatī.
12. The fact that Dadhimatī ordered them to marry among themselves may be a significant detail. Her divine sanction would circumvent the obvious issue of incest. On this point, however, the *Purāṇa* is silent. As noted later, Dādhīc informants do not regard the incest issue as significant, but professional genealogists might have taken a stricter view.
13. Elsewhere in the text she is said to be so named because she was produced from "churning" curds (1.23).
14. There are other variations of this tale.
15. Many Dādhīc Brahmans believe that the temple was built by the King of Udaipur. One interviewee expressed the belief that Māndhātā was himself the king of Udaipur. A professional Pandit told me that Māndhātā belonged to the *satyug*, whereas the temple was built in the *kaliyug* by the king of Udaipur.
16. This would be about sixty-four miles, which is about the right distance between Pushkar and Goth-Manglod.
17. The Hindi translator glosses this as *carbī* (fat). A learned Dādhīc Brahman Pandit whom I queried about this episode told me that it was, in his words, *aslī tattva*, the essential or original principle or substance of things. He added that, in its absence, there were many troubles in the world and people began to starve and die.
18. Here the text blends two of the three categories of deity outlined in chapter six of this volume: *kul* or *jāti* deities (deities of lineage and caste) and *ārādhya* deities (*iṣṭ*, or favored deities of personal devotion). As we shall see, this comes at the expense of her status as *sthānīya* deity (a deity of place).

19. As we have seen in chapters five and seven, there has been recent royal patronage at Dadhimatī, namely the king of Udaipur's funding of the temple's mid-nineteenth-century renovation and an early twentieth century donation from the king of Jodhpur. These have been downplayed by the Dādhīc Brahmans, and apparently never gave rise to any claim of proprietary rights on the part of the donors. Although there is a passage in the *Purāṇa* (22.51–2) that seems to say that the descendants of Māndhātā will continue a ritual relationship with the Dādhīc Brahmans, the matter is not pursued. The *Purāṇa* projects a vision in which royal patronage plays only a cameo role in the Dādhīc story, on stage long enough to effect the sacrificial transformation of sages into priests, but then dropping out of sight.
20. To put the matter in terms of the concepts developed in chapter six of this volume, the *Purāṇa* is attempting to foreground Dadhimatī's role as *jāti* (caste) deity at the expense of her role as *sthānīya* (place) deity.
21. As noted earlier, the ancient temple inscription refers to a community of Brahmans called "Dadhya" Brahmans. If these people are indeed ancestral to the present-day Dādhīc Brahmans, a claim that should not be accepted uncritically in my view, it would seem that the terminological link between goddess and this Brahman community is very old indeed.
22. The question of whether other castes bear or bore the "Dāhimā" appellation is a puzzling aspect of our tale. Dādhīc Brahmans repeatedly told us that the term "Dāhimā" (or "Dāymā") applies to all the castes of the region—i.e., that its signification is territorial. In a particularly revealing remark, one Dādhīc Brahman went even further, maintaining that the Brahmans are "Dādhīc," while the region's other castes are "Dāhimā." But in fact, the Jāṭs we spoke to (admittedly a small sample) denied that they are known as "Dāhimā," and some members of non-Brahman castes insisted that the term applies *only* to Brahmans. As noted, most Dādhīc Brahmans continue to refer to themselves as "Dāhimā" (or "Dāymā") to this very day, despite the elite preference for "Dādhīc." It is difficult to know exactly what to make of all this. It can at least be said that the term "Dādhīc" is probably recent, a product of the same mindset that generated the *Purāṇa*. An interesting wrinkle on this issue is the fact that "Dāymā" Muslims exist, as noted earlier.
23. There exists an alternative genealogy representing Dadhīci as the son of a different Brahman sage, Cyavana, and a Kṣatriya princess. This version an parently originates in the *Talavakāra Brāhmaṇa*. See Pathak 1966:32–4; also Asopa 1988:17. Pathak also reports an episode from the *Mahābhārata* in which Dadhīci, having been roused from his asceticism by a nymph sent by Indra, ejaculated into the river Sarasvatī who then gave birth to a child, Sārasvata (ibid.:38–9). The *Purāṇa*'s account of Pipplād's unusual conception seems thematically related.
24. Such manipulations of semen are probably common in Brahman origin mythology. As an example, in his *Jātibhāskar* (1996:177) Paṇḍit Jvālāprasād Miśra links the Dādhīc origin myth with that of the Sārasvat Brahmans. Before siring Pipplād, Dadhīci was interrupted in his *tapasya* by an *apsarā* and spilled his seed. Then Brahmā sent Sarasvatī to get the seed, lest it set the earth afire. By means of her yogic power, Sarasvatī placed the semen in her throat, ear, navel, and heart. The four sons that were then born became the apical ancestors of four branches of the Sārasvat Brahmans.
25. By far the most lucid explanation of the system is to be found in Brough 1953. What follows is based on his account.
26. A complete discussion of the evolution of this list is to be found in Mitchiner 1982.
27. Glimpses into the lineage structure of the region's trading castes can be found in Babb 2004.
28. The reason for the inexactness is that judgments had to be made about variant spellings. I have ignored *padvī* names. See Asopa 1988:41–42 on *padvī* names.

29. These two works (Miśra 1996 and Harikṛṣṇa Śāstrī 1996) belong to the early twentieth century. Vaidya does not attempt to attach *pravara* lists to the *gotras*. However, Mukhiyā Rūp Nārāyaṇ did supply such lists in a book called *Dadhīc Jāti Bhāskaraḥ* published in Jaipur in VS 1996. We were unable to obtain a copy of this book, but the *pravara* lists are reproduced in Asopa 1988:23–36. How these lists were derived is totally unclear. Vaidya's list of *gotras* seems more or less identical to the one in Miśra 1996. He also includes the occupational or *padvī* names of some of these, which never had—as far as I know—any significance other than honorific.
30. We did not undertake a systematic inquiry into the Jāṭ side of this story. A Jāṭ politician from Jodhpur told us that the temple was actually built by Jāṭs, but that the *pujārīs* (a belittling reference to the Dādhīc Brahmans) must have taken it over. This was a common sequence of events, he added.
31. One informant told us that the Trust was registered in 1978. Later, a serious dispute broke out between the leadership of the Mahāsabhā and the Trust, but is not relevant to this chapter.

Bibliography

Dates from Indian calendars are roughly translated as follows: the difference between the Gregorian (CE) and the Rajasthani and Marwari versions of the Vikram Saṃvat (VS) calendars has been calculated as 57 years, the difference between the Gregorian and the Gujarati version of the Vikram Saṃvat calendars has been calculated as 56 years (Johnson 1938), and the difference between the Gregorian and the Vīr Nirvāṇ Saṃvat calendars has been calculated as 526 years.

Pre-Modern Sources

Bhāgavata Purāṇa. Tr. Ganesh Vasudeo Tagare. Five volumes. Varanasi: Motilal Banarsidass, 1976–8. Ancient Indian Tradition and Mythology Series 7–11.

Dadhimathī Purāṇa. Jaipur: Śrī Dadhimatī Sāhitya Śodh evaṃ Prakāśan Samiti, n.d. (c. 1981).

Nābhinandanajinoddhāra Prabandha of Kakkasūri. Ed. and Gujarati tr. Pt. Bhagvāndās Harakhcand. Limbdi: Śrī Hemcandrācārya Jain Granthmālā, 1929.

Ūkeśa Gaccha Caritra of Kakkasūri. Handwritten manuscript with Hindi translation in the library of Kriyā Bhavan, Jodhpur.

Upakeśa Gaccha Gurvāvalī. Jinavijaya (ed.), *Vividha Gacchīya Paṭṭāvalī Saṅgraha*, Vol. 1, 7–9. Bombay: Siṅghī Jain Śāstra Śikṣāpīṭh and Bhāratīya Vidyābhavan, 1961. Singhi Jain Series 53.

Upakeśa Gaccha Paṭṭāvalī.

—. Sanskrit text ed. by Muni Darśanvijay. *Paṭṭāvalī Samuccay*, Vol. 1, 177–94. Viramgam: Cāritra Smārak Granthmālā 22, 1933.

—. Abbreviated English translation in Hoernle 1890.

—. Gujarati paraphrase in Tripuṭī Mahārāj 1952–64, Vol. 1, 16–36.

—. Gujarati paraphrase in Deśāī 1986–97, Vol. 9, 193–214.

Upakeśa-Kavalāṃ Gacch Paṭṭāvalī by disciple of Bhaṭṭārak Siddhsūri. Muni Jñānvijay (ed.), *Paṭṭāvalī Samuccay*, Vol. 2, 193–97. Ahmedabad: Cāritra Smārak Granthmālā 44, 1950.

Uttarādhyayana Sūtra. English translation by Hermann Jacobi in *Jaina Sūtras*, Vol. 2, 1–232. Oxford: Clarendon Press, 1895. Sacred Books of the East, Volume 45.

Yogaśāstra of Hemacandra. Tr. Olle Qvarnström. Cambridge: Department of Sanskrit and Indian Studies, Harvard University, 2002. Harvard Oriental Series 61.

Modern Sources

Agarwal, Anil, and Sunita Narain (eds). 1997. *Dying Wisdom: Rise, Fall and Potential of India's Traditional Water Harvesting Systems.* New Delhi: Centre for Science and Environment. State of India's Environment 4.

Agrawala, R. C. 1954a. A Unique Sculpture of the Jaina Goddess Saccika. *Artibus Asiae* 17, 232–34.

—. 1954b. Rājasthān meṃ Jain Devī Saccikā Pūjan. *Jain Siddhānt Bhāskar* 21:1, 1–5.

Anon. 1992. Pū. Munirājśrī Vṛddhivijayjī (Vṛddhicandjī) Mahārāj. Nandlāl Devluk (ed.), *Śāsanprabhāvak Śramaṇbhagavanto*, Vol. 1, 372–73. Bhavnagar: Śrī Arihant Prakāśan.

Appadurai, Arjun. 1978. Kings, Sects and Temples in South India, 1350–1700 A.D. Burton Stein (ed.), *South Indian Temples*, 47–72. New Delhi: Vikas Publishing House.

—. 1981. *Worship and Conflict under Colonial Rule: A South Indian Case.* Cambridge: Cambridge University Press.

—. 1983. The Puzzling Status of Brahman Temple Priests in Hindu India. *South Asian Anthropologist* 4, 43–52.

Archaeological Survey of India (ASI). 1924. *Annual Report, 1921-22, of the Epigraphic Section.*

Archaeological Survey of India, Western Circle (ASIWC). 1891–1921. *Progress Reports.*

Āratī Saṅgrah. N.d. *Śrī Dadhimathī Mātājī Goṭh Māṅglod Āratī Saṅgrah.* Dugastau: Śrī Sva. Nandlāl Pujārī.

Asher, Catherine B., and Cynthia Talbot. 2006. *India Before Europe.* Cambridge: Cambridge University Press.

Asopa, Govindanarayana Sharma (ed.). 1940. *Pandit Ram Karna Asopa Commemoration Volume.* Jodhpur: Abhinandana Grantha Samiti.

Āsopā, Indu. 1993. Aitihāsik Paripreksya meṃ Paṇḍit Rāmkarṇ Āsopā kā Jīvan evaṃ Kṛtitva. Ph.D. thesis, University of Rajasthan.

Asopa, Jai Narayan. 1988. *The Brahmanas, Dadhichi and Dahimas.* Jaipur: Shri Dadhimati Sahitya Shodha evam Prakashan Samiti.

Babb, Lawrence A. 1986. *Redemptive Encounters: Three Modern Styles in the Hindu Tradition.* Berkeley: University of California Press.

—. 1993. Monks and Miracles: Religious Symbols and Images of Origin Among Osvāl Jains. *Journal of Asian Studies* 52, 3–21.

—. 1996. *Absent Lord: Ascetics and Kings in a Jain Ritual Culture.* Berkeley: University of California Press.

—. 1998a. Rejecting Violence: Sacrifice and the Social Identity of Trading Communities. *Contributions to Indian Sociology* (N.S.) 32, 387–407.

—. 1998b. Ritual Culture and the Distinctiveness of Jainism. Cort 1998a, 139–62.

—. 2004. *Alchemies of Violence: Myths of Identity and the Life of Trade in Western India*. New Delhi: Sage.

—. 2006. From Hinduism to Jainism (and Back Again). *Jinamañjari* 34:2, 25–33.

Babb, Lawrence A., Varsha Joshi, and Michael W. Meister (eds.). 2002. *Multiple Histories: Culture and Society in the Study of Rajasthan*. Jaipur: Rawat Publications.

Balbir, Nalini. 1999. About a Jain Polemical Work of the 17th Century. N. K. Wagle and Olle Qvarnström (eds.), *Approaches to Jain Studies: Philosophy, Logic, Rituals and Symbols*, 1–18. Toronto: University of Toronto, Centre for South Asian Studies.

Barnes, Ruth, and Crispin Branfoot. 2006. *Pilgrimage: The Sacred Journey*. Oxford: Ashmolean Museum.

"Bedhṛak," Subhāṣ. 1997. *Sālāsar Bālājī Itihās, Bhajan-Stuti, Añjanimātājī Prākaṭya Sahit*. Chomu: Ruṛmal Bukselar.

Bhajan Mālā. N.d. *Śrī Sacciyāy Bhajan Mālā*. Osian: Śrī Sacciyāy Maṇḍal.

Bhajan Mālā. 1996. *Śrī Dadhimathī Bhajan Mālā*. Goth-Manglod: Śrī Dadhimathī Mātājī.

Bhandarkar, D.R. 1907. Osia. *Archaeological Survey of India, Western Circle, Progress Report, 1906–07*, 36–38.

—. 1910. Meḍtā. *Archaeological Survey of India, Western Circle, Progress Report, 1909–10*, 61–63. Calcutta: Government Press.

—. 1912. The Temples of Osia. *Archaeological Survey of India, Annual Report, 1908–1909*, 100–15. Calcutta: Government Press.

—. 1983. A List of the Inscriptions of Northern India in Brahmi and its Derivative Scripts, from about 200 A.C. *Appendix to Epigraphia Indica*, Vols. XIX-XXIII. New Delhi: Archaeological Survey of India.

Bharucha, Rustom. 2003. *Rajasthan, An Oral History: Conversations with Komal Kothari*. New Delhi: Penguin.

Bhattacharya, Gouriśwar. 1992. Two Inscribed Images of the Jaina Mahiṣamardinī. *East and West* 42, 501–08.

Bhūtoṛiyā, Māṅgīlāl. 1988. *Osvāl Itihās kī Amar Bel*. Calcutta: Priyadarśī Prakāśan.

Biardieu, Madeleine. 1994. *Hinduism: The Anthropology of a Civilization*. Delhi: Oxford University Press.

Binford, Mira Reym, and Michael Camerini (directors). 1974. *An Indian Pilgrimage, Ramdevra*. Madison: Center for South Asian Studies, University of Wisconsin.

Blackburn, Stuart H., Peter J. Claus, Joyce B. Flueckiger, and Susan S. Wadley (eds.). 1989. *Oral Epics in India*. Berkeley: University of California Press.

Bourdieu, Pierre. 1977. *Outline of a Theory of Practice*. Tr. Richard Nice. Cambridge: Cambridge University Press.

Brough, John. 1953. *The Early Brahmanical System of Gotra and Pravara*. Cambridge: Cambridge University Press.

Buddhisāgarsūri, Ācārya. 1917. *Gacchmat Prabandh, Saṅgh Pragati, tathā Jain Gitā*. Bombay: Śrī Adhyātma Jñān Prasārak Maṇḍal.

Coburn, Thomas B. 1991. *Encountering the Goddess: A Translation of the Devī-Māhātmya and a Study of Its Interpretation*. Albany: State University of New York Press.

Coomaraswamy, Ananda K. 1993. *Yakṣas: Essays in the Water Cosmology*. New ed., rev. and enl. Ed. Paul Schroeder. Delhi: Oxford University Press.

—. 1995. Ornament. Michael W. Meister (ed.), *Ananda K. Coomaraswamy: Essays in Architectural Theory*, 55–62. New Delhi: Oxford University Press.

Cort, John E. 1987. Medieval Jaina Goddess Traditions. *Numen* 34, 235–55.

—. 1988. Pilgrimage to Shankheshvar Pārshvanāth. *Center for the Study of World Religions Bulletin* 14:1, 63–72.

—. 1991. Mūrtipūjā in Śvetāmbar Jain Temples. T. N. Madan (ed.), *Religion in India*, 212–23. Delhi: Oxford University Press.

—. 1995. Genres of Jain History. *Journal of Indian Philosophy* 23, 469–506.

—. 1997. Tantra in Jainism: The Cult of Ghaṇṭākarṇ Mahāvīr, the Great Hero Bell-Ears. *Bulletin d'Études Indiennes* 15, 115–33.

—. (ed.). 1998a. *Open Boundaries: Jain Communities and Cultures in History*. Albany: State University of New York Press.

—. 1998b. Who Is a King? Jain Narratives of Kingship in Medieval Western India. Cort 1998a, 85–110.

—. 1999. The Gift of Food to a Wandering Cow: Lay-Mendicant Interactions among the Śvetāmbar Mūrtipūjak Jains. K. Ishwaran (ed.), *Ascetic Culture: Renunciation and Worldly Engagement*, 89–110. Leiden: E. J. Brill.

—. 2000a. Communities, Temples, Identities: Art Histories and Social Histories in Western India. Meister 2000a, 101–28.

—. 2000b. Defining Jainism: Reform in the Jain Tradition. Joseph T. O'Connell (ed.), *Jain Doctrine and Practice: Academic Perspectives*, 165–91. Toronto: University of Toronto, Centre for South Asian Studies.

—. 2000c. Worship of Bell-Ears the Great Hero, a Jain Tantric Deity. David Gordon White (ed.), *Tantra in Practice*, 417–33. Princeton: Princeton University Press.

—. 2001. *Jains in the World: Religious Values and Ideology in India*. New York: Oxford University Press.

—. 2004. Jains, Caste and Hierarchy in North Gujarat. Dipankar Gupta (ed.), *Caste in Question: Identity or Hierarchy?*, 73–112. New Delhi: Sage Publications.

—. 2006. Installing Absence? The Consecration of a Jina Image. Robert Maniura and Rupert Shepherd (eds.), *Presence: The Inherence of the Prototype within Images and Other Objects*, 71–86. London: Ashgate.

Dādhīc, Omnārāyaṇ (ed.). 1996. *Dadhimathī Bhajan Mālā*. Jodhpur: the author.

Dādhīc, S. R. N.d. *Bhagavatī Dadhimatī Māteśvarī kā Saṅkṣipt Itihās evam Dadhīci Ṛṣi kā Jīvan Paricay*. Kucera: author.

Dadhimatī. 1994. *Dadhimatī Māsik* 68:6–7 (June-July), 10–24.

Daniel, E. Valentine. 1984. *Fluid Signs: Being a Person the Tamil Way*. Berkeley: University of California Press.

Darśanvijay, Muni. 1950. Purvaṇī. Muni Jñānvijay (ed.), *Paṭṭāvalī Samuccay*, Vol. 2, 200–75. Ahmedabad: Cāritra Smārak Granthmālā 44.

Davis, Richard H. 1991. *Ritual in an Oscillating Universe: Worshiping Śiva in Medieval India*. Princeton: Princeton University Press.

—. 1997. *Lives of Indian Images*. Princeton: Princeton University Press.

—. 2000. Writing as if Icons are Really Alive. Meister 2000a, 87–100.

Deśāī, Mohanlāl Dalīcand. 1986–97. *Jain Gūrjar Kavio*. Ten volumes. Rev. ed. Jayant Koṭhārī. Bombay: Śrī Mahāvīr Jain Vidyālay.

Devguptsūri, Ācārya [= Muni Jñānsundar]. 1944. *Śrī Pārśvanāthaparamparāyā Itihāsaḥ*. Sanskrit translation of Jñānsundarjī 1943 by Śāstrī Gaurīnātha Śukla. Phalodi: Śrī Ratnaprabhākar Jñān Puṣpamālā 41.

—. 1946. *Śrī Tīrthaṅkardev kī Snātra va Aṣṭaprakārī Pūjā*; and *Paramopkārī Upkeś Gacchācāryoṃ (Ratnaprabhsūri vagairah) kī Baṛī Pūjā*. Phalodi: Śrī Ratnaprabhākar Jñān Puṣpamālā.

—. 1948. *Śrīmad Upakeśagacchīya Śuddhasamācārī*. Phalodi: Śrī Ratnaprabhākar Jñān Puṣpamālā 48.

—. 1949. *Ādarś Ratna: Param Yogirāj Muni Śrī Ratnavijayjī Mahārāj kā Saṅkṣipt Jīvan Jyoti*. Jodhpur: Śrī Ratnaprabhākar Jñān Pustak Mālā. Śrī Jñān Guṇ Puṣpamālā 29.

Devīprasād, Muṅśī. 1896. *Mārwāḍ ke Prācīn Lekh*. Jodhpur: the author.

Dhaky, M. A. 1965–66. Renaissance and the Late Māru-Gurjara Temple Architecture. U. P. Shah (ed.), *Western Indian Art*, 4–22. *Journal of the Indian Society of Oriental Art*, special number.

—. 1967. The Iconography of Sacciya Devi. *Babu Chhotelal Jain Commemoration Volume*, 63–9. Calcutta: Babu Chhotelal Jain Abhinandan Samiti.

—. 1968. Some Early Jaina Temples in Western India. *Śrī Mahāvīr Jain Vidyālay Suvarṇmahotsav Granth*, English section, 290–347. Bombay: Shri Mahavira Jaina Vidyalaya.

—. 1975. The Western Indian Jain Temple. U. P. Shah and M. A. Dhaky (eds.), *Aspects of Jaina Art and Architecture*, 319–84. Ahmedabad: Gujarat State Committee for the Celebration of 2500th Anniversary of Bhagavān Mahāvīra Nirvāṇa.

Dowson, John. 1972. *A Classical Dictionary of Hindu Mythology and Religion, Geography, History, and Literature*. Twelfth ed. London: Routledge & Kegan Paul.

Dundas, Paul. 1993. The Marginal Monk and the True *Tīrtha*. Rudy Smet and Kenji Watanabe (eds.), *Jain Studies in Honour of Jozef Deleu*, 237–59. Tokyo: Hon-no-Tomosha.

—. 1996. Somnolent Sūtras: Scriptural Commentary in Śvetāmbara Jainism. *Journal of Indian Philosophy* 24, 73–101.

—. 2002. *The Jains*. Second ed. London: Routledge.

—. 2004. Beyond Anekāntavāda: A Jain Approach to Religious Tolerance. Tara Sethia (ed.), *Ahiṃsā, Anekānta and Jainism*, 123–36. Delhi: Motilal Banarsidass.

—. 2006. *History, Scripture and Controversy in a Medieval Jain Sect*. London: Routledge.

Eck, Diana L. 1998. *Darśan: Seeing the Divine Image in India*. Third ed. New York: Columbia University Press.

Eichinger Ferro-Luzzi, Gabriella. 1987. *The Self-Milking Cow and the Bleeding Lingam: Criss-cross of Motifs in Indian Temple Legends*. Wiesbaden: Otto Harrassowitz.

Eliade, Mircea. 1971. *The Myth of the Eternal Return, or, Cosmos and History*. Princeton: Princeton University Press.

Erdman, Joan L. 1985. *Patrons and Performers in Rajasthan: The Subtle Tradition*. Delhi: Chanakya.

Evans-Pritchard, E. E. 1940. *The Nuer: A Description of Livelihood and Political Institutions of a Nilotic People*. Oxford: Oxford University Press.

Flügel, Peter. 1995–96. The Ritual Circle of the Terāpanth Śvetāmbara Jains. *Bulletin d'Études Indiennes* 13, 117–76.

Freedberg, David. 1989. *The Power of Images: Studies in the History and Theory of Response*. Chicago: University of Chicago Press.

Fuller, C. J. 1984. *Servants of the Goddess: The Priests of a South Indian Temple*. Cambridge: Cambridge University Press.

—. 2003. *The Renewal of the Priesthood: Modernity and Traditionalism in a South Indian Temple*. Princeton: Princeton University Press.

Gāṅgāṇī. 1969. *Gāṅgāṇī kā Saṅkṣipt Itihās*. Jodhpur: Vyavasthāpak Kameṭī.

Gaston, Anne-Marie. 1997. *Krishna's Musicians: Musicians and Music Making in the Temples of Nathdvara Rajasthan*. New Delhi: Manohar.

Gayvarcand, Muni [= Muni Jñānsundar]. 1918. *Siddh Pratimā Muktāvalī*. Tivari: Jain Saṅgh. Ratnaprabhākar Jñān Puṣpamālā 14.

Gehlot, Sukhvīrsiṅgh, Sohan Kṛṣṇa Purohit, and Nīl Kamal Śarmā (eds.). 1988. *Rājasthān ke Pramukh Abhilekh*. Jodhpur: Hindī Sāhitya Mandir.

Giri, Kamal, and Maruti Nandan Prasad Tiwari. 1989. Rāmakathā Scenes in the Dadhimatī Temple at Goṭh Māngloḍ (Rajasthan). B. P. Sinha (ed.), *Śri Rāma in Art, Archaeology and Literature*, 161–74. Patna: Bihar Puravid Parishad.

Gold, Ann Grodzins. 1988. *Fruitful Journeys: The Ways of Rajasthani Pilgrims*. Berkeley: University of California Press.

—. 1994. Sexuality, Fertility, and Erotic Imagination in Rajasthani Women's Songs. Gloria Goodwin Raheja and Ann Grodzins Gold, *Listen to the Heron's Words: Reimagining Gender and Kinship in North India*, 30–72. Berkeley: University of California Press.

Good, Anthony. 1989. Law, Legitimacy and the Hereditary Rights of Tamil Temple Priests. *Modern Asian Studies* 23, 233–57.

Granoff, Phyllis (ed.). 1990. *The Clever Adulteress and Other Stories: A Treasury of Jaina Literature*. Oakville, Ontario: Mosaic Press.

—. 1993. Halāyudha's Prism: The Experience of Religion in Medieval Hymns and Stories. Vishakha N. Desai and Darielle Mason (eds.), *Gods, Guardians, and Lovers: Temple Sculptures from North India, A.D. 700–1200*, 66–93. New York: The Asia Society.

Guṇsundar, Muni. 1939. *Ādarś-Jñān*. Two volumes. Phalodi: Śrī Ratnaprabhākar Jñān Puṣpamālā. Śrī Jñān Guṇ Puṣpamālā 14–15.

Gupta, Rāmkaraṇ. 1957. Kheṛ (Kṣīrpur). *Kalyāṇ* 31:1 (*Tīrthāṅk*), 292–93.

—. N.d. Kheṛ ke Prācīn Mandir. *Rājasthān Bhāratī* (Vol. ?), 27–34.

Gupta, S. L. 1990. *Gupta's Rajasthan Local Laws*, 2nd ed., Vol. 23. Jodhpur: India Publishing House.

Hall, Kenneth R., and George W. Spencer. 1980. The Economy of Kāñcīpuram: A Sacred Center in Early South India. *Journal of Urban History* 6, 127–51.

Handa, Devendra. 1984. *Osian: History, Archaeology, Art and Architecture*. Delhi: Sundeep Prakashan.

Harikṛṣṇa Śāstrī, Paṇḍit. 1996. *Brāhmaṇotpatti Mārttāṇḍ*. Reprint Bombay: Hemrāy Śrīkṛṣṇadās.

Harlan, Lindsey. 1992. *Religion and Rajput Women: The Ethic of Protection in Contemporary Narratives*. Berkeley: University of California Press.

—. 2003. *The Goddesses' Henchmen: Gender in Indian Hero Worship*. New York: Oxford University Press.

Hastīmal, Ācārya. 1971–87. *Jain Dharm kā Maulik Itihās*. Four volumes. Jaipur: Jain Itihās Samiti.

Heesterman, J. C. 1985. *The Inner Conflict of Tradition: Essays in Indian Ritual, Kingship, and Society*. Chicago: University of Chicago Press.

Hegewald, Julia. 2002. *Water Architecture in South Asia: A Study of Types, Developments and Meanings*. Leiden: Brill. Studies in Asian Art and Archaeology 24.

Herdeg, Klaus. 1967. *Formal Structure in Indian Architecture*. Ithaca, NY: Center for Housing and Environmental Studies, Cornell University.

Hoernle, A. F. Rudolf. 1890. The Pattavali or List of Pontiffs of the Upakesa-Gachchha. *Indian Antiquary* 19, 233–42.

HREC (Republic of India, Hindu Religious Endowments Commission). 1962. *Report, 1960–1962*. Delhi: Govt. of India, Ministry of Law.

Humphrey, Caroline. 1991. Fairs and Miracles: At the Boundaries of the Jain Community in Rajasthan. Michael Carrithers and Caroline Humphrey (eds.), *The Assembly of Listeners: Jains in Society*, 201–25. Cambridge: Cambridge University Press.

Huyler, Stephen. 1999. *Meeting God: Elements of Hindu Devotion*. New Haven: Yale University Press.

Inden, Ronald. 2000. Imperial Purāṇas: Kashmir as Vaiṣṇava Center of the World. Ronald Inden, Jonathan Walters, Daud Ali, *Querying the Medieval, Texts and the History of Practices in South Asia*, 29–98. New York: Oxford University Press.

Iser, Wolfgang. 1978. *The Act of Reading: A Theory of Asthetic Response*. Baltimore: Johns Hopkins University Press.

Jain, Kailash Chand. 1972. *Ancient Cities and Towns of Rajasthan*. Delhi: Motilal Banarsidass.

Jain, Sāgarmal, and Vijay Kumār. 2003. *Sthānakvāsī Jain Paramparā kā Itihās*. Varanasi: Pārśvanāth Vidyāpīṭh.

Jaini, Padmanabh S. 1979. *The Jaina Path of Purification*. Berkeley: University of California Press.

—. 2003. *Cātuyāma-saṃvara* in the Pāli Canon. Piotr Balcerowicz (ed.), *Essays in Jaina Philosophy and Religion*, 119–35. Delhi: Motilal Banarsidass.

Jindel, Rajendra. 1976. *Culture of a Sacred Town: A Sociological Study of Nathdwara*. Bombay: Popular Prakashan.

Jñānsundar, Muni. N.d. *Osvāl Vaṃś Sthāpak Ādyācārya Śrī Ratnaprabhsurīśvarjī kā Jayantī Mahotsav*. Ajmer.

—. 1916. *Pratimā Chatrīsī*. Bhavnagar: Vidyā Vijay Chāpkhāna, Śrī Ośīyā Tīrth (third printing).

—. 1917. *Gayvarvilās, arthāt Battīs Sūtroṃ meṃ Murtīsiddh*. Phalodī: Śrī Ratnaprabhākar Jñān Puṣpamālā.

—. 1926. *Jain Jāti Nirṇay*, Vols. 1–2. Phalodi: Śrī Ratnaprabhākar Jñān Puṣpamālā 81–82.

—. 1928. *Osvāl Porvāl aur Śrīmāl Jātiyāṃ kā Sacitra Prācīn Itihās* (*Jain Jāti Mahoday*). Phalodi: Śrī Ratnaprabhākar Jñān Puṣpamālā 86.

—. 1929. *Śrī Jain Jāti Mahoday*, Vol. 1, sections 1–6. Phalodi: Śrī Ratnaprabhākar Jñān Puṣpamālā 103–108.

—. 1935a. *Mejharnāmo*. Fourth printing. Phalodi: Śrī Ratnaprabhākar Jñān Puṣpamālā 35.

—. 1935b. *Osvālotpatti Viṣayak Śankāoṃ kā Samādhān*. Phalodi: Śrī Ratnaprabhākar Jñān Puṣpamālā 152.

—. 1936a. *Mūrtipūjā kā Prācīn Itihās*. Phalodi: Śrī Ratnaprabhākar Jñān Puṣpamālā 164.

—. 1936b. *Śrīmān Lauṅkāśāh*. Phalodi: Śrī Ratnaprabhākar Jñān Puṣpamālā 167.

—. 1937a. *Jain Jātiyoṃ ke Gacchoṃ kā Itihās*, Vol. 1. Phalodi: Śrī Ratnaprabhākar Jñān Puṣpamālā. Jain Itihās Jñān Bhānu Kiraṇ 12.

—. 1937b. *Śrī Upkeś Gacchācāryoṃ kī Sacitra Baṛī Pūjā*. Phalodi: Śrī Ratnaprabhākar Jñān Puṣpamālā 201.

—. 1939a. *Bhagvān Pārśvanāth kī Paramparā kā Itihās antargat Osvāl Jāti kī Aitihāsiktā*. Phalodi: Śrī Ratnaprabhākar Jñān Puṣpamālā. Śrī Jñān Guṇ Puṣpamālā 13.

—. 1939b. *Kharataramatotpatti*, Vols. 1–4. Phalodi: Śrī Ratnaprabhākar Jñān Puṣpamālā. Jain Itihās Jñān Bhānu Kiraṇ 22–25.

—. 1939c. *Pārśva-Paṭṭāvalī*. Phalodi: Śrī Ratnaprabhākar Jñān Puṣpamālā. Jain Itihās Jñān Bhānu Kiran 21.

—. 1943. *Bhagvān Pārśvanāth kī Paramparā kā Prācīn Itihās*. Two volumes. Phalodi: Śrī Ratnaprabhākar Jñān Puṣpamālā. Śrī Jñān Guṇ Puṣpamālā 34–35.

Johnson, Helen M. 1938. Conversion of Vikrama Samvat Dates. *Journal of the American Oriental Society* 58, 668–69.

Joshi, M. C. 1994. Goddess Cybele in Hindu Śākta Tradition. B. N. Saraswati et al. (eds.), *Art: The Integral Vision*, 203–09. New Delhi: D. K. Printworld.

Jośī, Jagatnārāyaṇ. N.d. *Kuldevī Dadhimathī, Prākaṭya evaṃ Camatkār/Maharṣi Dadhīci*. Indore: the author.

—. 1994. *Bhagavatī Dadhimathī kā Avataraṇ evaṃ Kapālpīṭh kī Aitihāsiktā*. Indore: the author.

Kakar, Sudhir. 1982. *Shamans, Mystics, and Doctors: A Psychological Inquiry into India and its Healing Traditions*. New York: Alfred A. Knopf.

Kalia, Asha. 1982. *Art of Osian Temples*. New Delhi: Abhinav.

Kāparṛā. N.d. *Prācīn Jain Tīrth Śrī Kāparṛājī Svarṇ Jayantī Mahotsav Granth*. Svarṇ Jayantī Mahotsav Samiti.

Kathābhaṭṭ, Jagdīścandra Śarmā. 1990. Akhil Bhāratvarṣīya Dāhimā (Dādhīc) Brāhmaṇ Mahāsabhā kā Saṅkṣipt Paricay. *Dadhimatī* 64:1 (Jan.–Feb.), 5–13.

Khan, Dominique-Sila. 1997. *Conversions and Shifting Identities: Ramdev Pir and the Ismailis in Rajasthan*. New Delhi: Manohar.

Klatt, Johannes. 1882. Extracts from the Historical Records of the Jainas. *Indian Antiquary* 11, 245–56.

Kothari, Komal. 1982. The Shrine: An Expression of Social Needs. Tr. Uma Anand. *Gods of the Byways: Wayside Shrines of Rajasthan, Madhya Pradesh and Gujarat*, 5–31. Oxford: Museum of Modern Art.

Kramrisch, Stella. 1946. *The Hindu Temple*. Two volumes. Calcutta: Calcutta University Press.

Kulke, Hermann. 1978a. Early Royal Patronage of the Jagannātha Cult. Anncharlotte Eschmann, Hermann Kulke, and Gaya Charan Tripathi (eds.), *The Cult of Jagannath and the Regional Tradition of India*, 139–55. New Delhi: Manohar.

—. 1978b. Jagannātha as the State Deity under the Gajapatis of Orissa. Anncharlotte Eschmann, Hermann Kulke, and Gaya Charan Tripathi (eds.), *The Cult of Jagannath and the Regional Tradition of India*, 199–208. New Delhi: Manohar.

Laidlaw, James. 1995. *Riches and Renunciation: Religion, Economy, and Society among the Jains*. Oxford: Oxford University Press.

Lapoint, Elwyn C. 1978. The Epic of Guga: A North Indian Oral Tradition. Sylvia Vatuk (ed.), *American Studies in the Anthropology of India*, 281–308. New Delhi: Manohar.

Llewellyn, J. E. 1998. The Center Out There: A Review Article of Recent Books on Hindu Pilgrimage. *International Journal of Hindu Studies* 2, 249–65.

Lobo, Wibke. 1982. *The Sun-Temple of Modhera: A Monograph on Architecture and Iconography*. München: C. H. Beck. Forschungen zur Allegemeinen und Vergleichenden Archäologie 2.

Lutgendorf, Philip. 2007. *Hanuman's Tale: The Messages of a Divine Monkey*. New York: Oxford University Press.

Magnasāgar, Muni. 1930. *Jain Jāti Nirṇay Samīkṣā*. Ajmer: Śrī Khartargacchīya Jain Saṅgh.

Mahapatra, Manamohan. 1981. *Traditional Structure and Change in an Orissan Temple*. Calcutta: Punthi Pustak.

Mahāprajñā, Yuvācārya. 1993. *Bhikṣu Vicār Darśan*. Ed. Muni Dulahrāj. Ladnun: Jain Viśva Bhāratī. Eleventh printing.

—. 1994. *Acharya Bhikshu: A Revolutionary Visionary (Doctrine and Philosophy)*. Tr. A. B. Shah. Ladnun: Jai Tulsi Foundation.

Mahendra Kumar, Muni. 1994. *Relevance of Acharya Bhikshu's Thoughts in Modern Perspective*. Ladnun: Jai Tulsi Foundation.

Mallison, Françoise. 1983. Development of Early Krishnaism in Gujarāt: Viṣṇu – Raṇchoḍ – Kṛṣṇa. Monika Thiel-Horstmann (ed.), *Bhakti in Current Research, 1979–1982*, 245–55. Berlin: Dietrich Reimer.

Mankodi, Kirit. 1991. *The Queen's Stepwell at Patan*. Bombay: Franco-Indian Research Pvt. Ltd. Project for Indian Cultural Studies 3.

Marriott, McKim. 1976. Hindu Transactions: Diversity without Dualism. B. Kapferer (ed.), *Transaction and Meaning: Directions in the Anthropology of Exchange and Symbolic Behavior*, 109–42. Philadelphia: Ishi.

Maxwell, Thomas S. 1982. The Five Aspects of Śiva (In Theory, Iconography and Architecture). *Art International* 25:3–4, 41–57.

McCormick, Thomas. 1997. The Jaina Ascetic as Manifestation of the Sacred. Robert H. Stoddard and Alan Morinis (eds.), *Sacred Places, Sacred Spaces: The Geography of Pilgrimages*, 235–56. Baton Rouge: Geoscience Publications, Department of Geography and Anthropology, Louisiana State University.

Meister, Michael W. 1972. A Plea for the Restoration of Aesthetics to the Consideration of Jaina Art. *Bulletin of Museums and Archaeology in U.P.* 9, 19–22.

—. 1973. Kṛṣṇa Līlā at Wadhwān and Osiāñ. *Journal of the Indian Society of Oriental Art* (N.S.) 5, 28–35.

—. 1976. Jain Temples in Central India. U. P. Shah and M. A. Dhaky (eds.), *Aspects of Jaina Art and Architecture*, 223–41. Ahmedabad: Gujarat State Committee for the Celebration of 2500th Anniversary of Bhagavān Mahāvīra Nirvāṇa.

—. 1983. Geometry and Measure in Indian Temple Plans: Rectangular Temples. *Artibus Asiae* 44, 266–96.

—. 1985. Temple Building in South Asia: Science as Technology's Constraint. Peter Gaeffke and David A. Utz (eds.), *Science and Technology in India*, 31–36. Philadelphia: Department of South Asia Regional Studies, University of Pennsylvania.

—. 1986a. On the Development of a Morphology for a Symbolic Architecture: India. *Res: Anthropology and Aesthetics* 12, 33–50.

—. 1986b. Regional Variations in Mātṛkā Conventions. *Artibus Asiae* 47, 233–62.

—. 1989. Temples, Tirthas, and Pilgrimage: The Case of Osian. D. Handa and A. Agrawal (eds.), *Ratna-Chandrika*, 275–82. New Delhi: Harman Publishing House.

—. 1990. De- and Re-constructing the Indian Temple. *Art Journal* 49, 395–400.

—. 1991a. The Hindu Temple: Axis and Access. Kapila Vatsyayan (ed.), *Concepts of Space, Ancient and Modern*, 269–80. New Delhi: Indira Gandhi National Centre for the Arts and Abhinav Publications.

—. 1991b. Mauryas of Uparamāla and Medapāṭa. Meister and Dhaky 1991, 273–98.

—. 1991c. Pratīhāras of Jābālipura and Kānyakubja: Phase I. Meister and Dhaky 1991, 153–215.

—. 1991d. Pratīhāras of Kānyakubja and Their Feudatories: Phase II. Meister and Dhaky 1991, 247–70.

—. 1991e. Pratīhāras of Māṇḍavyapura. Meister and Dhaky 1991, 119–52.

—. 1993. Fragments From a Divine Cosmology: Unfolding Forms on India's Temple Walls. Vishakha N. Desai and Darielle Mason (eds.), *Gods, Guardians, and Lovers, Temple Sculptures from North India A.D. 700-1200*, 94–115. New York: The Asia Society.

—. 1995a. Architecture as Ornament, Essential Form. Michael W. Meister (ed.), *Ananda K. Coomaraswamy: Essays in Architectural Theory*, xiii–xx. New Delhi: Oxford University Press.

—. 1995b. Seeing and Knowing: Semiology, Semiotics and the Art of India. *Los Discursos Sobre el Arte*, 193–207. Mexico: Universidad Nacional Autonoma de Mexico, Instituto de Investigaciones Esteticas.

—. 1995c. Sweetmeats or Corpses? Art History and Ethnohistory. *Res: Anthropology and Aesthetics* 27, 118–32.

—. 1995d. Temples, Tirthas, and Pilgrimage: The Case of Osian. N. K. Singhi and Rajendra Joshi (eds.), *Folk, Faith & Feudalism: Rajasthan Studies*, 67–75. Jaipur: Rawat. Original version of Meister 1989.

—. 1995e. The Unity and Gravity of an Elemental Architecture. Bettina Baumer (ed.), *The Agamic Tradition and the Arts*, 125–28. Kapila Vatsyayan (ed.), *Prakrti: The Integral Vision*, Volume 3. New Delhi: D.K. Printworld.

—. 1996. Ritual and Real Time: De- and Re-constructing the Indian Temple. Kapila Vatsyanan (ed.), *Concepts of Time, Ancient and Modern*, 373–87. New Delhi: Indira Gandhi National Centre for the Arts.

—. 1998. Sweetmeats or Corpses? Community, Conversion, and Sacred Places. Cort 1998a, 111–38.

—. (ed.). 2000a. *Ethnography and Personhood: Notes From the Field*. Jaipur: Rawat Publications.

—. 2000b. Ethnography, Art History, and the Life of Temples. Meister 2000a, 7–45.

—. 2003a. Osian. Frederick M. Asher (ed.), *Art of India, Prehistory to the Present*, 441–42. Hong Kong: Encyclopaedia Britannica.

—. 2003b. Vāstupuruṣamaṇḍalas, Planning in the Image of Man. Gudrun Bühnemann (ed.), *Maṇḍalas and Yantras in the Hindu Traditions*, 251–70. Leiden: Brill.

—. 2006. Obscure Objects of Desire. Gerd J.R. Mevisson and Klaus Bruhn (eds.), *Varamātā 1: Festschrift A.J. Gail*. Berlin: Weidler.

Meister, Michael W., and M.A. Dhaky (eds.), 1991. *Encyclopaedia of Indian Temple Architecture*, Vol. II, pt. 2, *North India: Period of Early Maturity*. Princeton: Princeton University Press.

Mirashi, V.V. 1961. The Date of the Dadhimatī-Mātā Inscription. *Studies in Indology,* Vol. 2, 200-06. Nagpur: Vidarbha Samshodhan Mandal.

—. 1964. A Lower Limit of the Date of the *Devī-Māhātmya. Purāṇa* 6, 181-86.

Miśra, Paṇḍit Jvālāprasād. 1996. *Jātibhāskar*. Reprint Bombay: Hemrāj Śrīkṛṣṇadās.

Mitchiner, John E. 1982. *Traditions of the Seven Ṛṣis*. Delhi: Motilal Banarsidass.

Mṛgendramuni, Muni. 1986. Jīvancaritra. Muni Mṛgendramuni (ed.), *Śrī Mohanlāljī Ardhaśatābdī Smārak-granthaḥ*, 1–86. Bombay: Śrī Mohanlāljī Ardhaśatābdī Smārakgranth Prakāśan Samiti.

Mughal, M.R. 1997. *Ancient Cholistan: Archaeology and Architecture*. Rawalpindi: Ferozsons.

Mukherjee, Prabhat. 1977. *History of the Jagannath Temple in the 19th Century*. Calcutta: Firma KLM.

Nahar, Puran Chand. 1918. *Jaina Inscriptions*. Calcutta, 1918. Jaina Vividha Sāhitya Shāstra Mālā No. 8. Reprint Delhi: Indian Book Gallery, 1983.

Nārāyaṇ, Pītambar, and Es. Bhāskaran Nāyar (eds.). 1971–74. *Hindī Sāhitya Sāriṇī*. Two volumes. Hoshiarpur: Viśveśvarānand Saṅsthān. VI Series 50 and 65.

Nyāytīrth, Anūpcand (ed.). 1997. *Digambar Jain Mandir Paricay Jilā Jaypur*. Jaipur: Śrī Digambar Jain Mandir Mahāsaṅgh.

O'Flaherty, Wendy Doniger. 1973. *Eroticism and Asceticism in the Mythology of Śiva*. London: Oxford University Press.

— (tr.). 1975. *Hindu Myths*. Harmondsworth: Penguin.

— (tr.). 1981. *The Rig Veda: An Anthology*. New York: Penguin.

Pathak, Vishwambhar Sharan. 1966. *Ancient Historians of India: A Study in Historical Biographies*. Bombay: Asia Publishing House.

Pemārām. 1977. *Madhyakālin Rājasthān meṃ Dhārmik Āndolan*. Ajmer: the author.

Pramar, V. S. 1989. *Haveli: Wooden Houses and Mansions of Gujarat*. Ahmedabad: Mapin Publishing Pvt. Ltd.

Premsundarvijayjī [sic], Muni. 1967. *Śubh Muhurtādi*. Jodhpur: the author.

Presler, Franklin A. 1987. *Religion under Bureaucracy: Policy and Administration for Hindu Temples in South India*. Cambridge: Cambridge University Press.

Quigley, Declan. 1993. *The Interpretation of Caste*. Oxford: Clarendon Press.

Raheja, Gloria. 1988. *The Poison in the Gift: Ritual, Prestation, and the Dominant Caste in a North Indian Village*. Chicago: University of Chicago Press.

Rajasthan Local Laws, Vol. 23, 2nd ed. 1990. Jodhpur: India Publishing House.

Ramanujan, A.K. 1999a. Is There an Indian Way of Thinking? An Informal Essay. Vinay Dharwadker (ed.), *The Collected Essays of A. K. Ramanujan*, 34–51. Delhi: Oxford University Press.

—. 1999b. Two Realms of Kannada Folklore. *The Collected Essays*, 485–512.

—. 1999c. Who Needs Folklore? *The Collected Essays*, 532–52.

Rāmdatt, Dr. 1984. Sālāsar ke Vīr Hanumān. *Dadhimatī* 58:7, 10–11.

Ram Karna, Pandit. 1911–12. Dadhimatī-Mātā Inscription of the Time of Dhrūhlāna; [Gupta]-Samvat 289. *Epigraphia Indica* 11, 299–304.

Rāmlāl, Yati. 1910. *Mahājan Vaṃś Muktāvalī*. Bombay: Nirṇaysāgar Press.

Rāṅkā, Jhaverīlāl. 1992. Pūjya Muni Jñānsundarvijayjī [sic] Mahārāj. Nandlāl Devluk (ed.), *Śāsanprabhāvak Śramaṇbhagavanto*, Vol. 2, 608–09. Bhavnagar: Śrī Arihant Prakāśan.

Rāṭhoḍ, Kṣemsiṃh M. 1948. *Osvāl Kṣatriya Vṛttānt arthāt Osvāl Komno Itihās*. Bhorara: Śā Rāysī Murjī Bhorarāvālā.

Ratna Prabha Vijaya, Muni. 1941–50. *Śramaṇa Bhagavān Mahāvīra*. Five volumes. Ahmedabad: Śri Grantha Prakāsaka Sabhā.

Reu, Pt. Bisheshwar Nath. 1948. *Report on the Administration of the Archaeological Department and the Sumer Public Library*, Vol. 21. Jodhpur: Government of Jodhpur.

Ṛṣimohanlāl Yati. 1907. *Jain Śvetāmbar Tīrth Prakāś arthāt Jain Tīrth Gāīḍ*. Bhagalpur: author.

Śāh, Ambālāl Premcand. 1953. *Jain Tīrth Sarvasaṅgrah*. Ahmedabad: Śeṭh Āṇandjī Kalyāṇjī.

Śāh, Keśavlāl Ḍ. 1920. *Jñānsundar Mukh Capeṭikā ane Unmārg Poṣak Jain Tantrīne Hit Śikṣā*. Ahmedabad: author.

Śah, Maṅgaḷcand Lallucand, and Cunīlāl Maganlāl Jhaverī Śāh. 1919. *Cārūpnuṃ Avalokan*. Bombay: Śrīkṛṣṇa Prīnṭīng Press.

Sālecā, Campālāl. 1991. Śrī Nākoḍā Pārśvanāth Tīrth kā Itihās. Prem Bhaṇḍārī (editor-in-chief), *Jain Tīrth Śrī Nākoḍā*, 1–16. Jodhpur: Jñān Prakāśan.

Śarmā, Govind Nārāyaṇ. 1915. *Brahmacārījī kā Lekh*. Jodhpur: Pt. Rāmkarṇ Śyāmkarṇ Āsopā. Dadhimatī Granthmālā 23.

Śarmā, Jugrāj. N.d. *Śrī Sacciyāyamātā Mandir kī Pāvan Tīrthsthalī kā Saṅkṣipt Paricay*. Osian: Sva. Jugrāj Śarmā.

Schiefner, F. Anton von. 1906. *Tibetan Tales Derived from Indian Sources*. Tr. W. R. S. Ralston. London: Kegan, Paul, Trench, Trübner & Co.

Schubring, Walter. 1962. *The Doctrine of the Jainas*. Tr. Wolfgang Beurlen. Delhi: Motilal Banarsidass.

Shah, Kesaricand Nemchand. 1997. *The Bombay Public Trusts Act, 1950*, ninth ed., rev. G. M. Divekar. Pune: Hind Law House.

Shah, U. P. 1947. Iconography of the Sixteen Jaina Mahāvidyās. *Journal of the Indian Society of Oriental Art* 15, 114–75.

—. 1987. *Jaina-Rūpa-Maṇḍana*, Vol. 1. New Delhi: Abhinav.

Śīlcandravijay, Muni. 1973. *Śāsan Samrāṭ*. Ahmedabad: Tapāgacchīya Śeṭhśrī Jindās Dharmdās Dhārmik Ṭrasṭ–Kadambagiri Vaṭī.

Singh, Muṅśī Hardayāl. 1895. *Riporṭ Mardumśumārī Rājmārvāṛ vābat San 1891 Īsvī Tīsrāhissā*, Volume 1. Jodhpur: Vidyāsāl. Reprint Jodhpur: Śrī Jagdīś Siṃh Gahlot Śodh Saṅsthān, 1997.

Śiv Prasād. 1989. Koranṭ Gacch. *Śramaṇ* 40:5, 15-43.

—. 1991. Upkeśgacch kā Saṅkṣipt Itihās. *Śramaṇ* 42:7-12, 61-184.

—. 2000. *Tapāgacch kā Itihas*, Vol. 1, Part 1. Varanasi: Pārśvanāth Vidyāpīṭh; and Jaipur: Prākṛt Bhāratī.

Slusser, Mary. 1999. Illustrated Folios from a *Devi Mahatmya* Manuscript. Vidya Dehejia (ed.), *Devi: The Great Goddess: Female Divinity in South Asian Art*, 226–29. Washington: Arthur M. Sackler Gallery, Smithsonian Institution, in association with Mapin Publishing, Ahmedabad, and Prestel Verlag, Munich.

Smith, John D. 1991. *The Epic of Pābūjī: A Study, Transcription and Translation*. Cambridge: Cambridge University Press.

Somani, Ram Vallabh. 1981. *Prithviraj Chauhan and His Times*. Jaipur: Publication Scheme.

—. 1982. *Jain Inscriptions of Rajasthan*. Jaipur: Rajasthan Prakrit Bharati Sansthan.

Spencer, George W. 1969. Religious Networks and Royal Influence in Eleventh Century South India. *Journal of the Economic and Social History of the Orient* 12, 42–56.

Srinivas, M. N. 1987. *The Dominant Caste and Other Essays*. Delhi: Oxford University Press.

Stein, Burton. 1960. The Economic Function of a Medieval South Indian Temple. *Journal of Asian Studies* 19, 163–76.

—. 1961. The State, the Temple and Agricultural Development: A Study in Medieval South India. *The Economic Weekly* 12:4–6 (Feb. 4), 179–87.

—. (ed.). 1978. *South Indian Temples*. New Delhi: Vikas Publishing House.

Stietencron, Heinrich von. 1966. *Indische Sonnenpriester: Sāmba und die Śākadvīpīya-Brāhmaṇa*. Wiesbaden: Otto Harrassowitz.

Stoddard, Robert H., and Alan Morinis (eds.). 1997. *Sacred Places, Sacred Spaces: The Geography of Pilgrimages*. Baton Rouge: Geoscience Publications, Department of Geography and Anthropology, Louisiana State University.

Śubhkarṇ Yati. 1916. *Dādājī Śrī 1008 Śrī Ratnaprabhasūri ādi Guruvaroṃ kī Bṛhatpūjā aur Laghupūjā*. Ed. Paṇḍit Tribhuvandās Amarcand Salot. Palitana: Śeṭh Jogrājjī Bed.

Tansukhdās, Mahātmā. 1939. Munivaryya Śrī Guṇsundarjī Mahārāj kā Saṅkṣipt Paricay. Guṇsundar, Vol. II, 709–27.

Temple, R.C. 1884–1900. *The Legends of the Panjab*. Bombay: Education Society; and London: Trübner. Reprint New York: Arno Press, 1977.

Thapar, Romila. 1986. Society and Historical Consciousness: The Itihāsa-Purāṇa Tradition. Sabyasaschi Bhattacharya and Romila Thapar (eds.), *Situating Indian History*, 353–83. Delhi: Oxford University Press.

Tīrth Darśan. 1980. Madras: Śrī Mahāvīr Jain Kalyāṇ Saṅgh.

Tivārī, Rāmkumār. 1997. *Dadhimathī Mātājī*. Salasar: Mahāvīr Prasād Pujārī.

Tod, James. 1990. *Annals and Antiquities of Rajasthan*. Three volumes. Introduction and notes by William Crooke. Reprint Delhi: Low Price Editions. Original London: George Routledge and Sons, 1829.

Tripuṭī Mahārāj (Munis Darśan, Jñān, and Nyāy Vijay). 1952–1964. *Jain Paramparāno Itihās*. Three volumes. Ahmedabad: Śrī Cāritrasmārak Granthmālā.

Tulsī, Ācārya. 1995. *Terāpanth aur Mūrtipūjā*. Churu: Ādarś Sāhitya Saṅgh Prakāśan. Eighth printing.

Turner, Victor. 1973. The Center Out There: Pilgrims' Goal. *History of Religion* 12:191–230.

Turner, Victor, and Edith Turner. 1978. *Image and Pilgrimage in Christian Culture: Anthropological Perspectives*. New York: Columbia University Press.

Vaidya, Durgāprasād. 1988. Kapāl Pīṭh Tīrth kā Māhātmya. *Dadhimathī Mandir Pranyās Patrikā* 2, 27–8.

Vaidya, Paṇḍit Śrīnārāyaṇ. 1924. *Dādhīc Vaṃśotpatti va Gotrāvalī*. Viśva Vilās Yantrālay Kāmṭhī.

Vaiṣṇav, Bhaṅvarlāl. 1973. *Kheṛ Mandir*. Balotra: Vaiṣṇav Prakāśan.

Vallely, Anne. 2002. *Guardians of the Transcendent: An Ethnography of a Jain Ascetic Community*. Toronto: University of Toronto Press.

Van Gennep, Arnold. 1960. *The Rites of Passage*. Tr. M. B. Vizedom and G. L. Caffee. Chicago: University of Chicago Press.

Vārṣṇey, Makkhanlāl. 1988. Jain-Tīrth Osiyāṃ. Makkhanlāl Vārṣṇey, (ed.), *Śrī Vardhmān Jain Śikṣaṇ Saṅgh Osiyāṃ (Jodhpur) Hīrak Jayantī Smārikā*, 61–5. Osian: Śrī Vardhmān Jain Śikṣaṇ Saṅgh.

Vasavada, Rabindra J. 2001. *Temple of Mahavira Osiaji*. Ahmedabad: Lalbhai Dalpatbhai Institute of Indology.

Vaśiṣṭh, Nīlimā. 1988. *Osiyāṃ kā Jain Mandir*. Osian: Śrī Varddhamān Śikṣaṇ Saṅgh.

Velankar, Hari Damodar. 1944. *Jinaratnakośa: An Alphabetical Register of Jain Works and Authors, Vol. 1, Works*. Poona: Bhandarkar Oriental Research Institute.

Verdia, H. S. 1982. *Religion and Social Structure in a Sacred Town: Nathdwara*. Delhi: Researchco.

Verghese, Anila. 2000. *Archaeology, Art and Religion: New Perspectives on Vijayanagara*. New Delhi: Oxford University Press.

Vidyālaṅkar, Dharmcandra. 1992. *Jāṭoṃ kā Nayā Itihās*. New Delhi: Akhil Bhāratvarṣīya Jāṭ Mahāsabhā.

Vidyarthi, L. P. 1978. *The Sacred Complex in Hindu Gaya*. Second ed. Delhi: Concept.

Vidyarthi, L. P., and Makhan Jha (eds.). 1974. *Symposium on the Sacred Complex in India*. Ranchi: Council on Social and Cultural Research, Bihar.

Vidyarthi, L. P., B. N. Saraswati, and Makhan Jha. 1979. *The Sacred Complex of Kashi: A Microcosm of Indian Civilization*. Delhi: Concept.

Viennot, Odette. 1976. *Temples de l'Inde centrale et occidentale: Étude stylistique et essai de chronologie relative du Vie au milieu du Xe siècle*. Two vols. Paris: Adrien Maisonneuve. Publications de l'École Française d'Extrème-Orient, Mémoires Archéologiques, Vol. 11.

Vinaysāgar, Mahopādhyāy. 1988. *Nākorā Pārśvanāth Tīrth*. Jaipur: Kuśal Saṅsthān.

—. 2004-06. *Khartar Gacch kā Bṛhad Itihās*. Two volumes. Jaipur: Prākṛt Bhāratī Akādamī.

Waghorne, Joanne Punzo, and Norman Cutler (eds.). 1985. *Gods of Flesh, Gods of Stone*. Chambersburg, PA: Anima Publications.

Wezler, Albrecht. 1993. "A Slap on the Face of the Brahmins": Introducing a Little-Known Jain Text of Polemical Objectives. Rudy Smet and Kenji Watanabe (eds.), *Jain Studies in Honour of Jozef Deleu*, 485–501. Tokyo: Hon-no-Tomosha.

White, Leslie A. 1959. *The Evolution of Culture: The Development of Civilization to the Fall of Rome*. New York: McGraw-Hill.

Wiley, Kristi L. 2004. *Historical Dictionary of Jainism*. Lanham, MD: Scarecrow Press.

Yokochi, Yuko. 2004. The Rise of the Warrior Goddess in Ancient India: A Study of the Myth Cycle of Kauśikī in the *Skandapurāṇa*. Ph. D. thesis, Rijksuniversiteit Groningen.

Younger, Paul. 1995. *The Home of Dancing Śivan: The Traditions of the Hindu Temple in Citamparam*. New York: Oxford University Press.

Index

PLATES

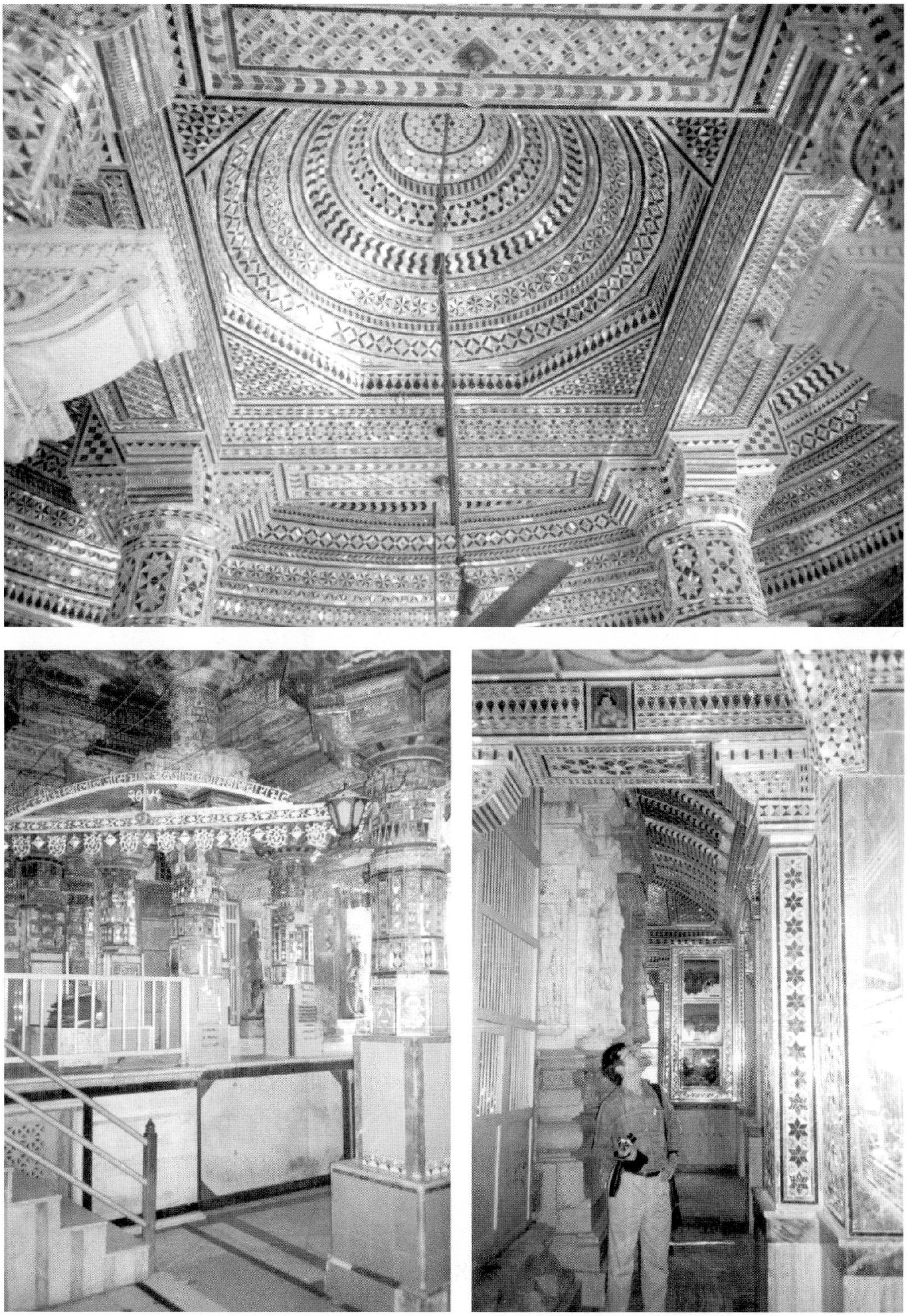

Plate 1. Khed, Raṇchoḍjī temple: mirrored ceiling in *gūḍha-maṇḍapa* (top); view into north ambulatory corridor (bottom right); Osian, Sacciyā Mātā temple, view of *gūḍha-maṇḍapa* looking toward the eighth-century Sūrya shrine (bottom left).

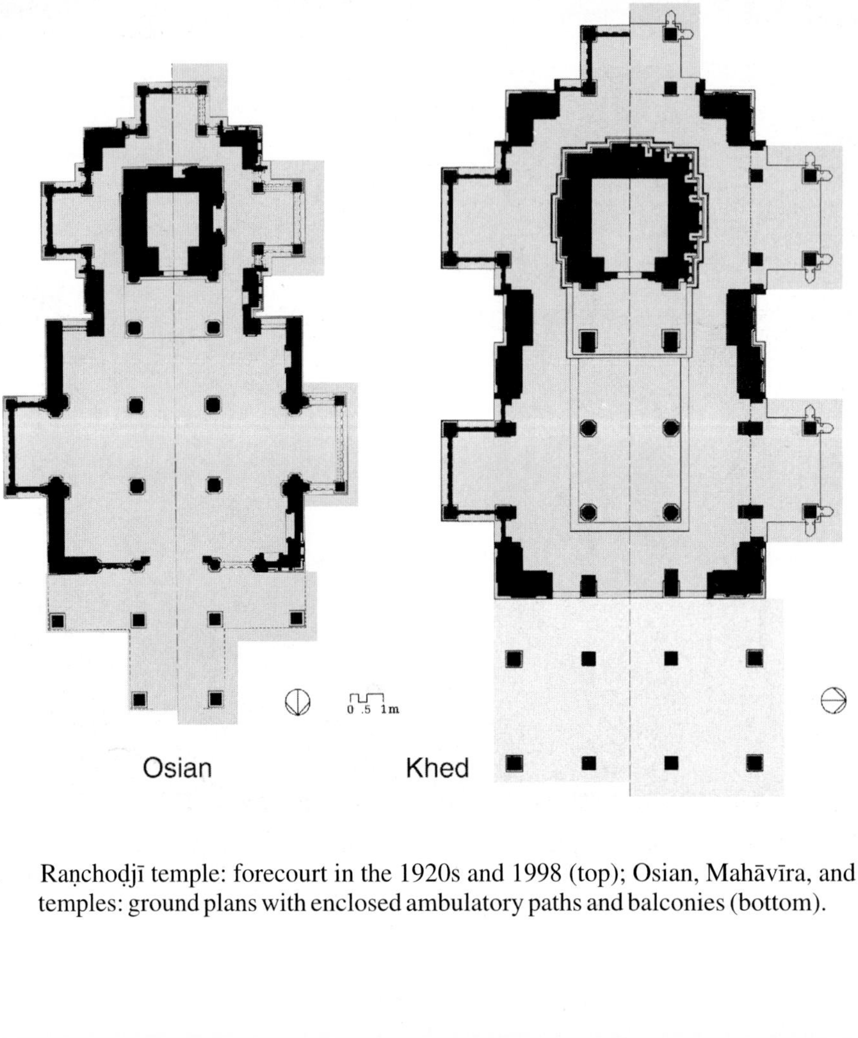

Plate 2. Raṇchoḍjī temple: forecourt in the 1920s and 1998 (top); Osian, Mahāvīra, and Khed temples: ground plans with enclosed ambulatory paths and balconies (bottom).

Plate 3. Raṇchoḍjī (top) and Dadhimatī Mātā (bottom): temple compounds extended in the nineteenth and twentieth centuries.

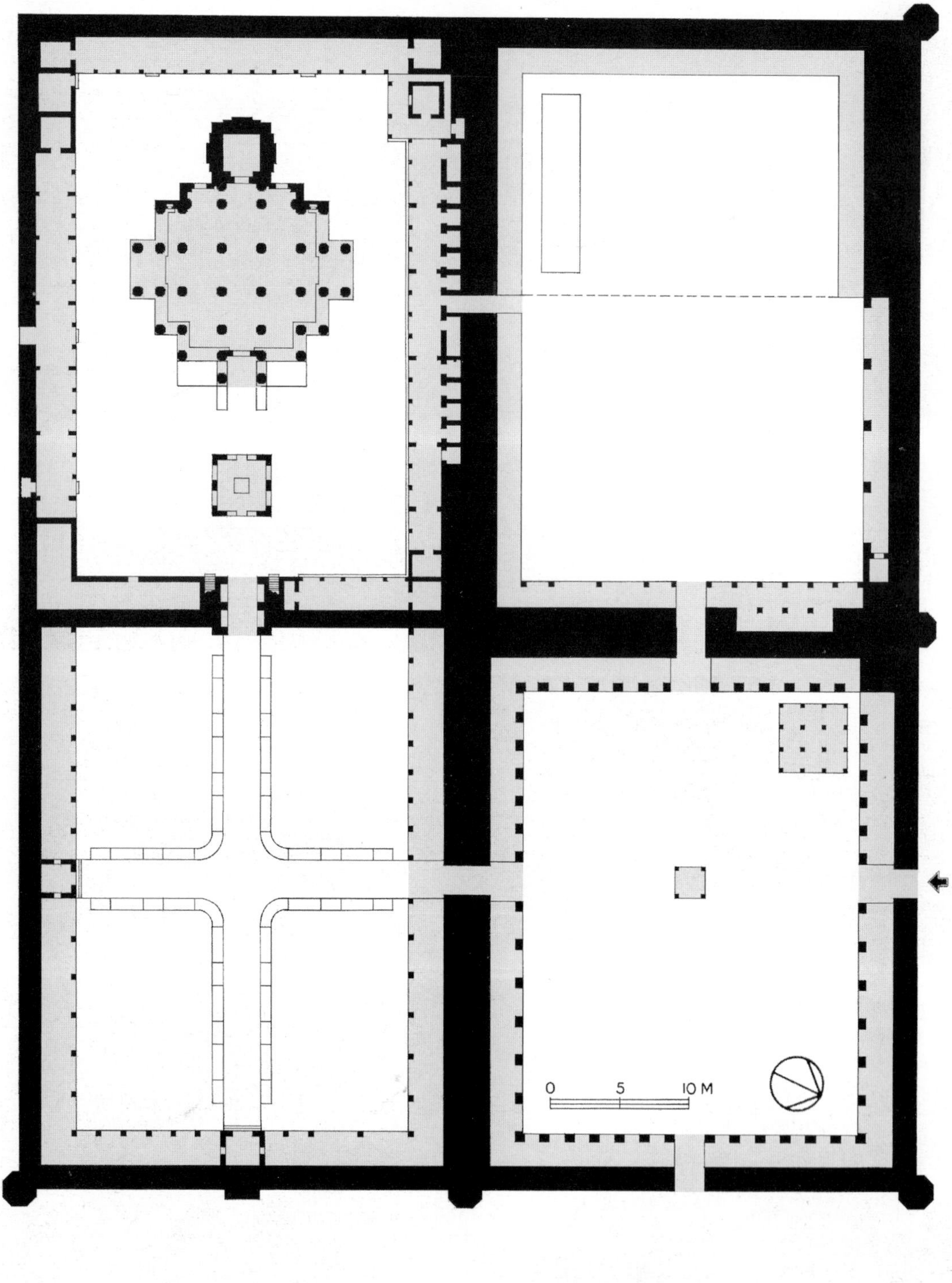

Plate 4. Dadhimatī Mātā temple: ground plan, ninth-century shrine, and the four nineteenth century *cauks*.

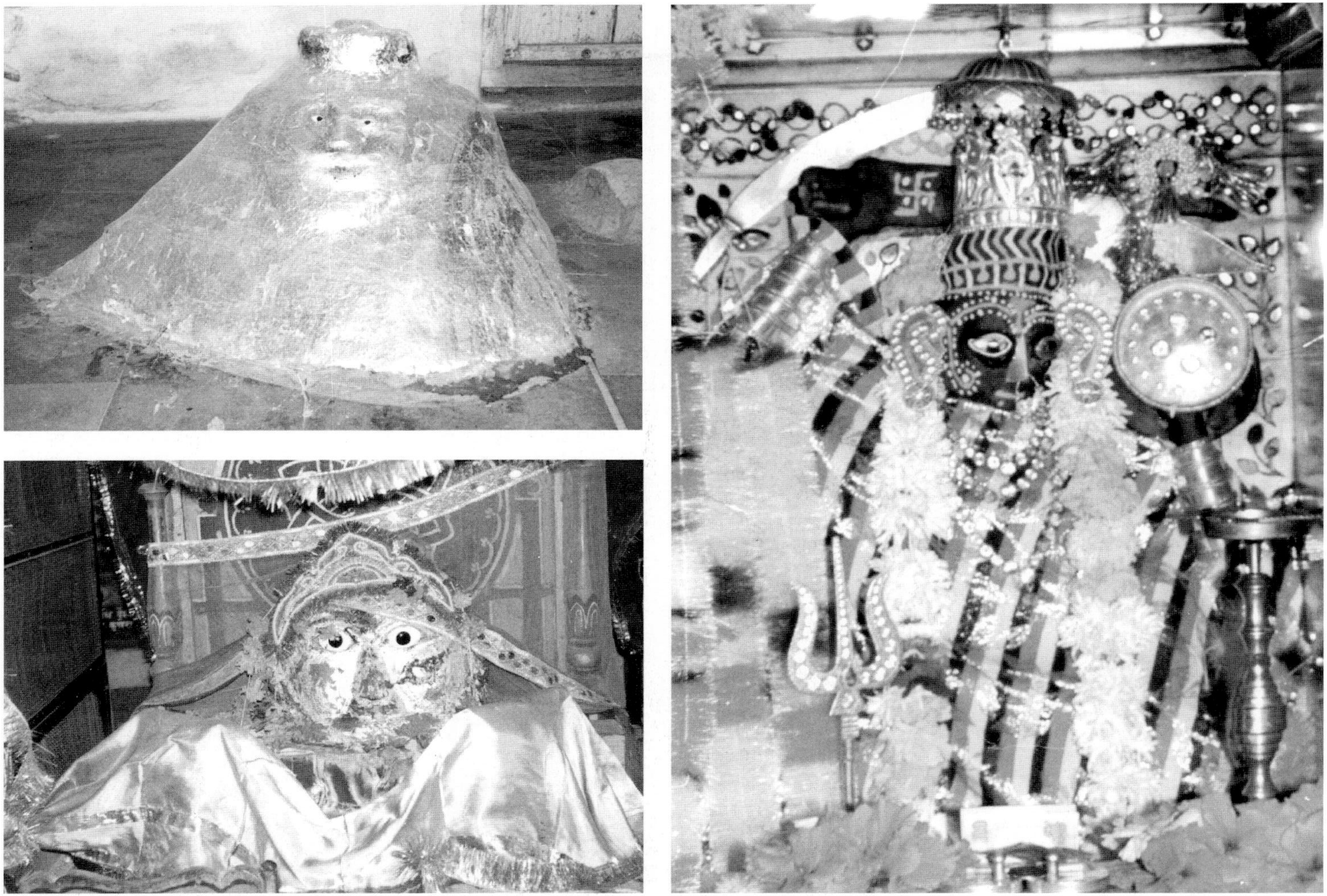

Plate 5. Autochthonous goddesses in Rajasthan: Udaipur, roadside *sthāna* (top left); Goth-Manglod, Dadhimatī Mātā (bottom left); Osian, Sacciyā Mātā (right).

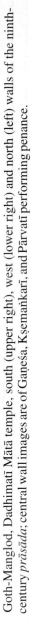

Plate 6. Goth-Manglod, Dadhimatī Mātā temple, south (upper right), west (lower right) and north (left) walls of the ninth-century *prāsāda*; central wall images are of Gaṇeśa, Kṣemaṅkarī, and Pārvatī performing penance.

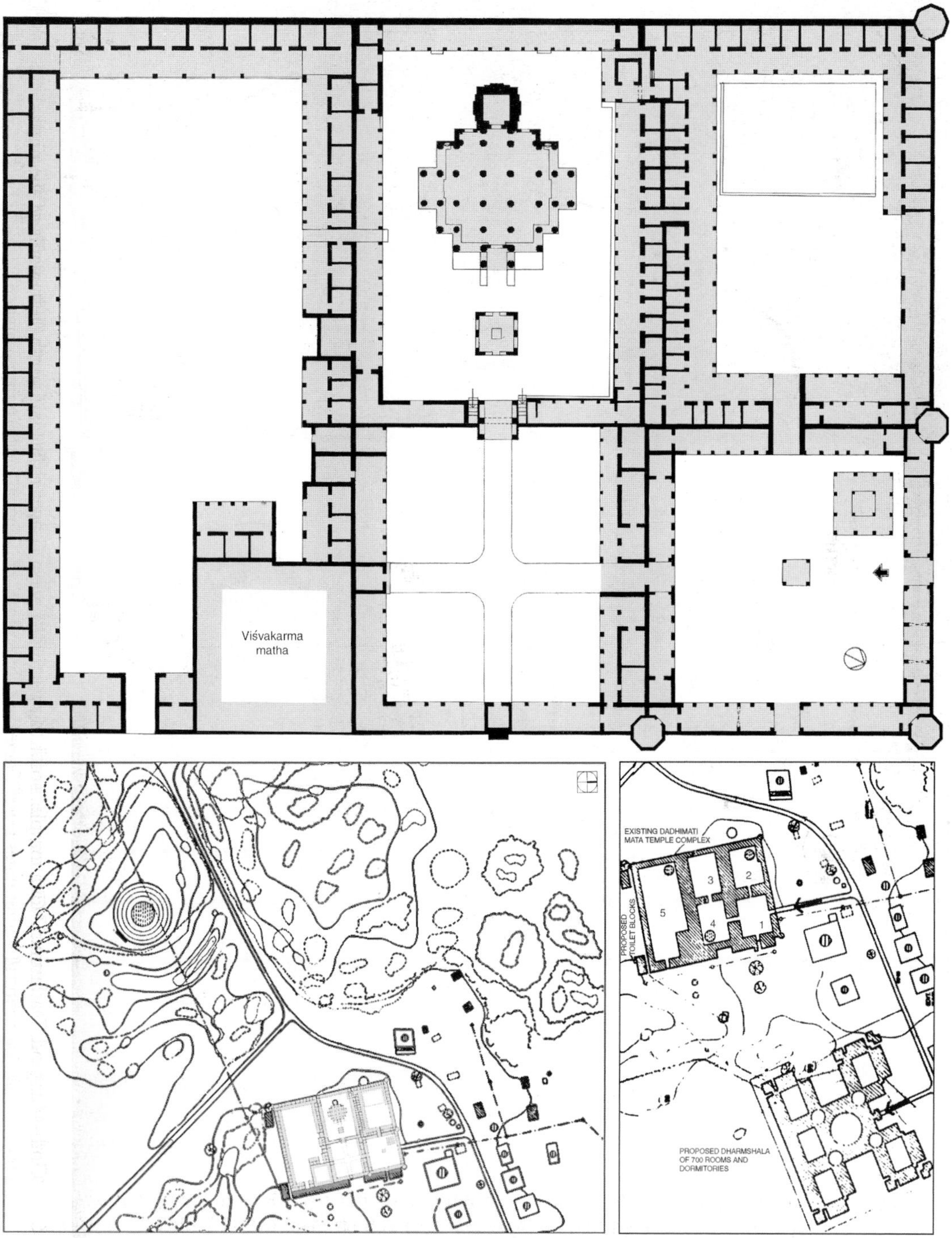

Plate 7. Dadhimatī Mātā temple: expansions in the twentieth century (top); site plan (bottom left), and location of the proposed new "Dharmshala of 700 rooms and dormitories" (bottom right).

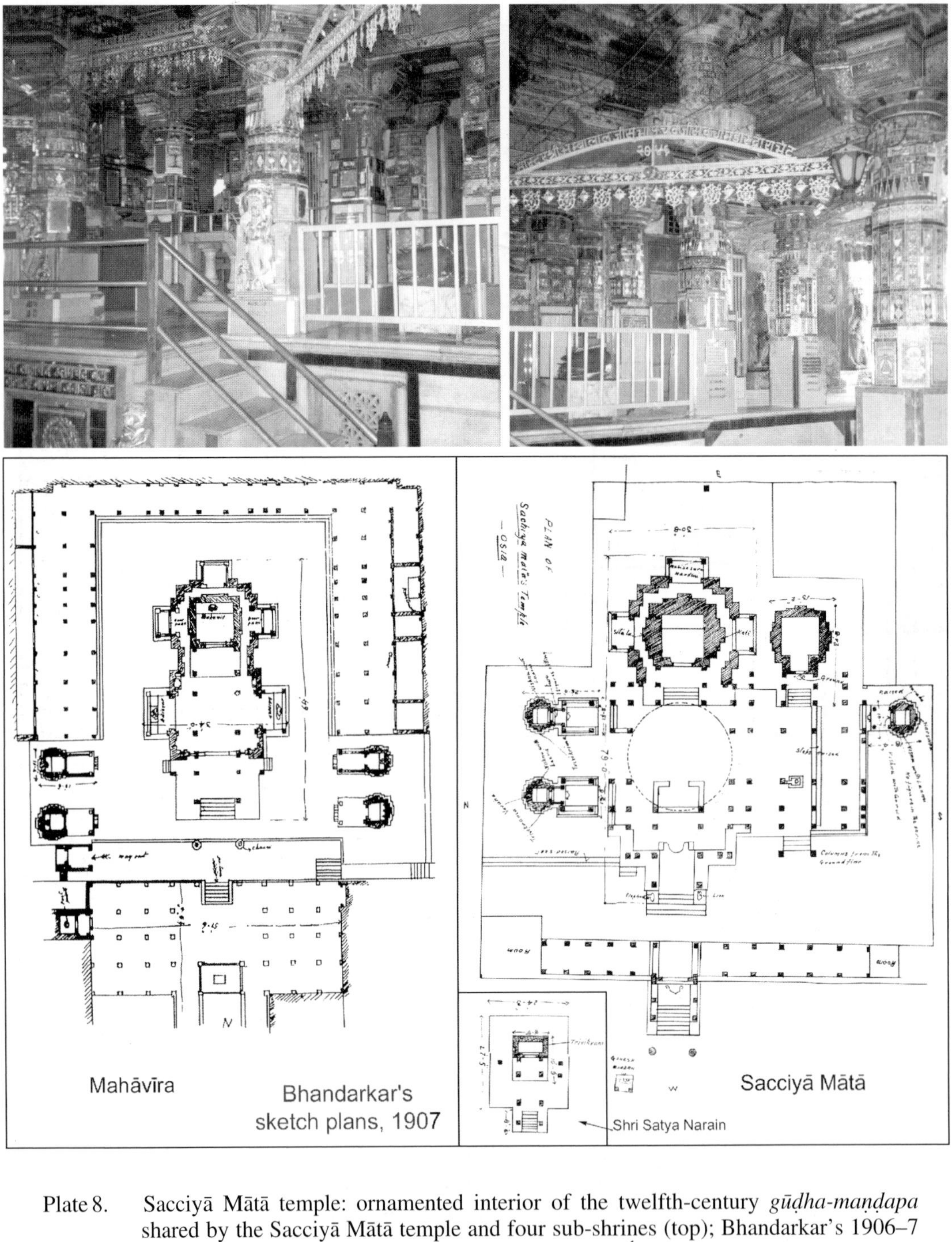

Plate 8. Sacciyā Mātā temple: ornamented interior of the twelfth-century *gūḍha-maṇḍapa* shared by the Sacciyā Mātā temple and four sub-shrines (top); Bhandarkar's 1906–7 rough sketches of the Mahāvīra, Sacciyā Mātā, and Śri Satyanārāyaṇa ground plans (bottom).

Plate 9. Sacciyā Mātā and Mahāvīra temples, 1972.

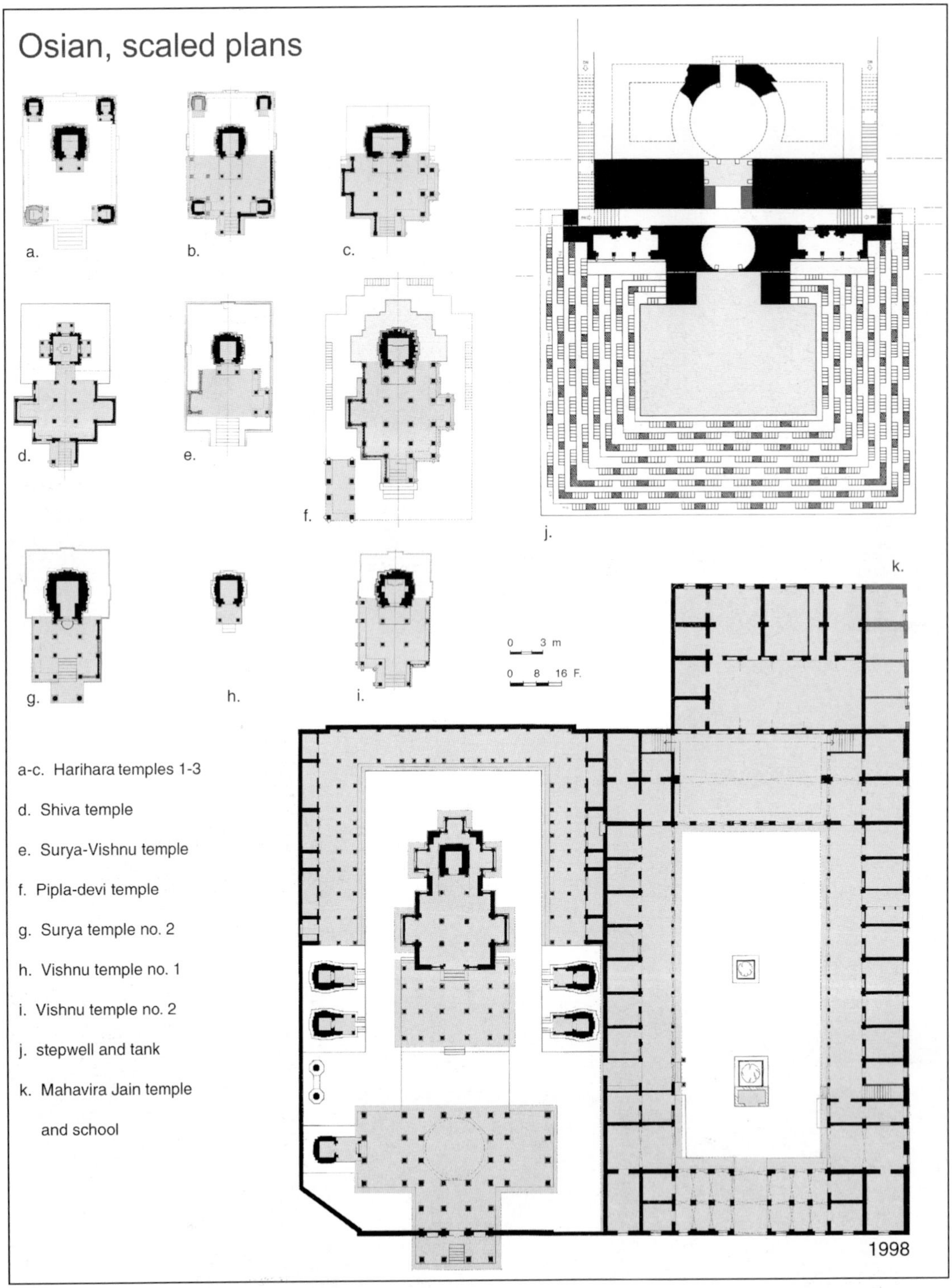

Plate 10. Osian: scaled ground plans. The Mahāvīra temple plan shows the compound with revisions and additions, ca. 1998.

Plate 11. Osian, eighth-century temples: Sūrya temple no. 2 (with a replacement tenth-century *śikhara*) (top left); Harihara temple no. 1 (upper right); Sūrya temple no. 1, with the tower of the twelfth-century replacement of the Sacciyā Mātā temple behind (lower right); and Harihara temple 2 (lower left).

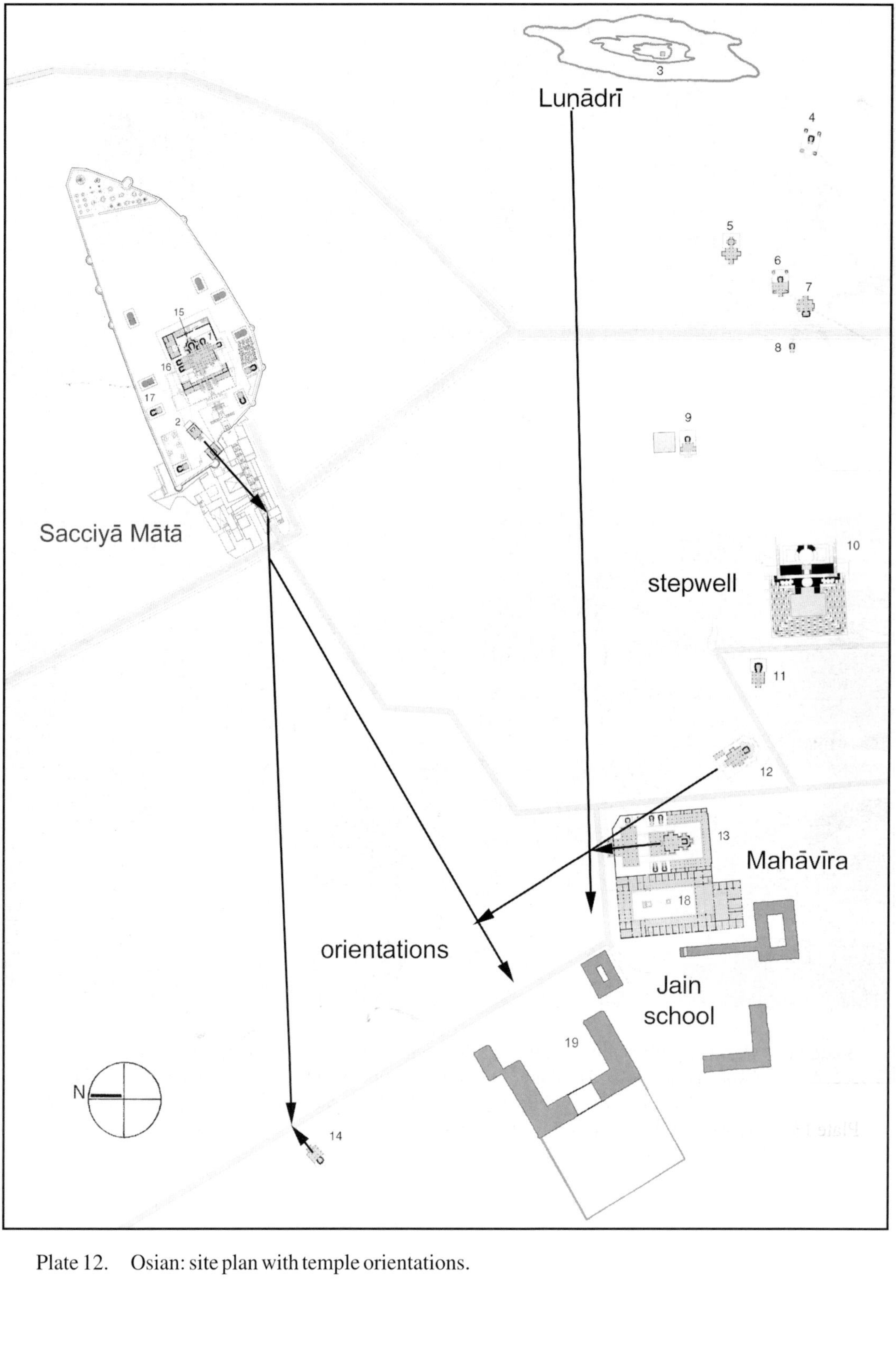

Plate 12. Osian: site plan with temple orientations.

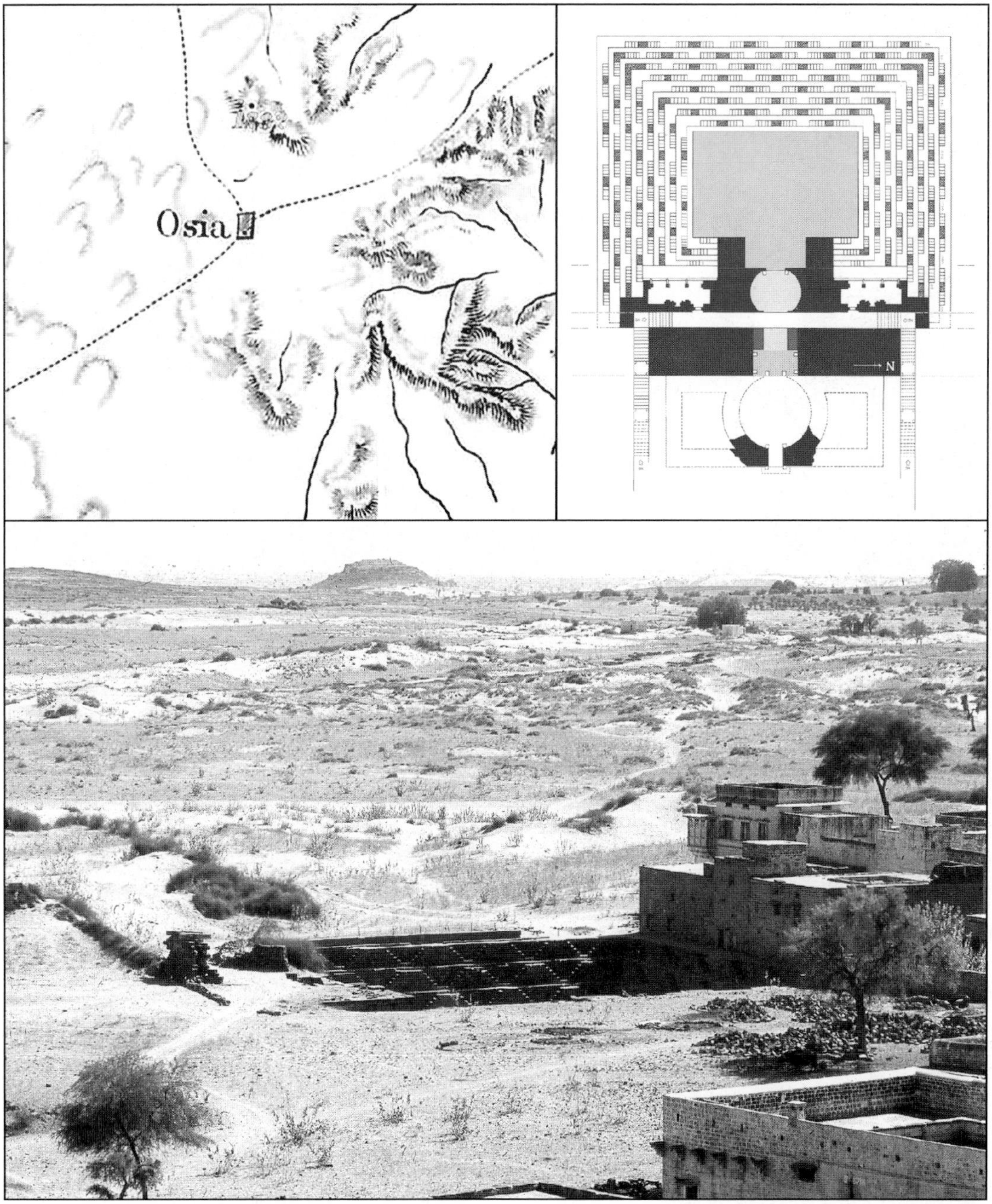

Plate 13. Osian, step-well: catchment area (upper left); plan (upper right); and view from Sacciyā Mātā temple (bottom).

Plate 14. Osian, step-well: recent excavation of lower levels (top); illustrations of Ratnaprabhasūri and Svayamprabhasūri at Osian from Jñānsundar, *Jain Jāti Mahoday*, 1929 (lower left); Mandor (Jodhpur), rock-cut step-well, inscribed VS 742/685 CE, and an image of Mahādeva carved on the rock-face above (lower right).

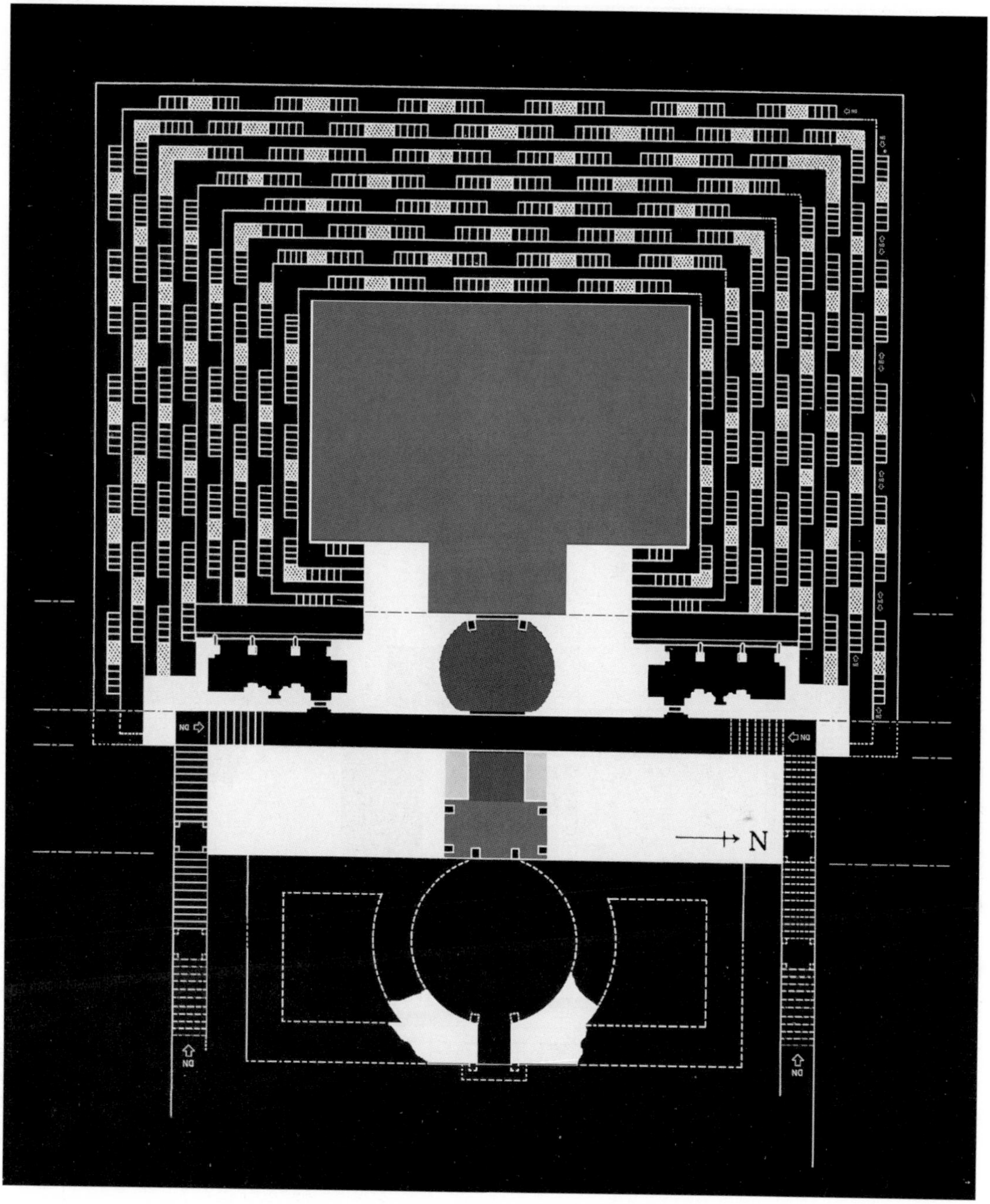

Plate 15. Osian: plan, drop-well, step-well, and tank.

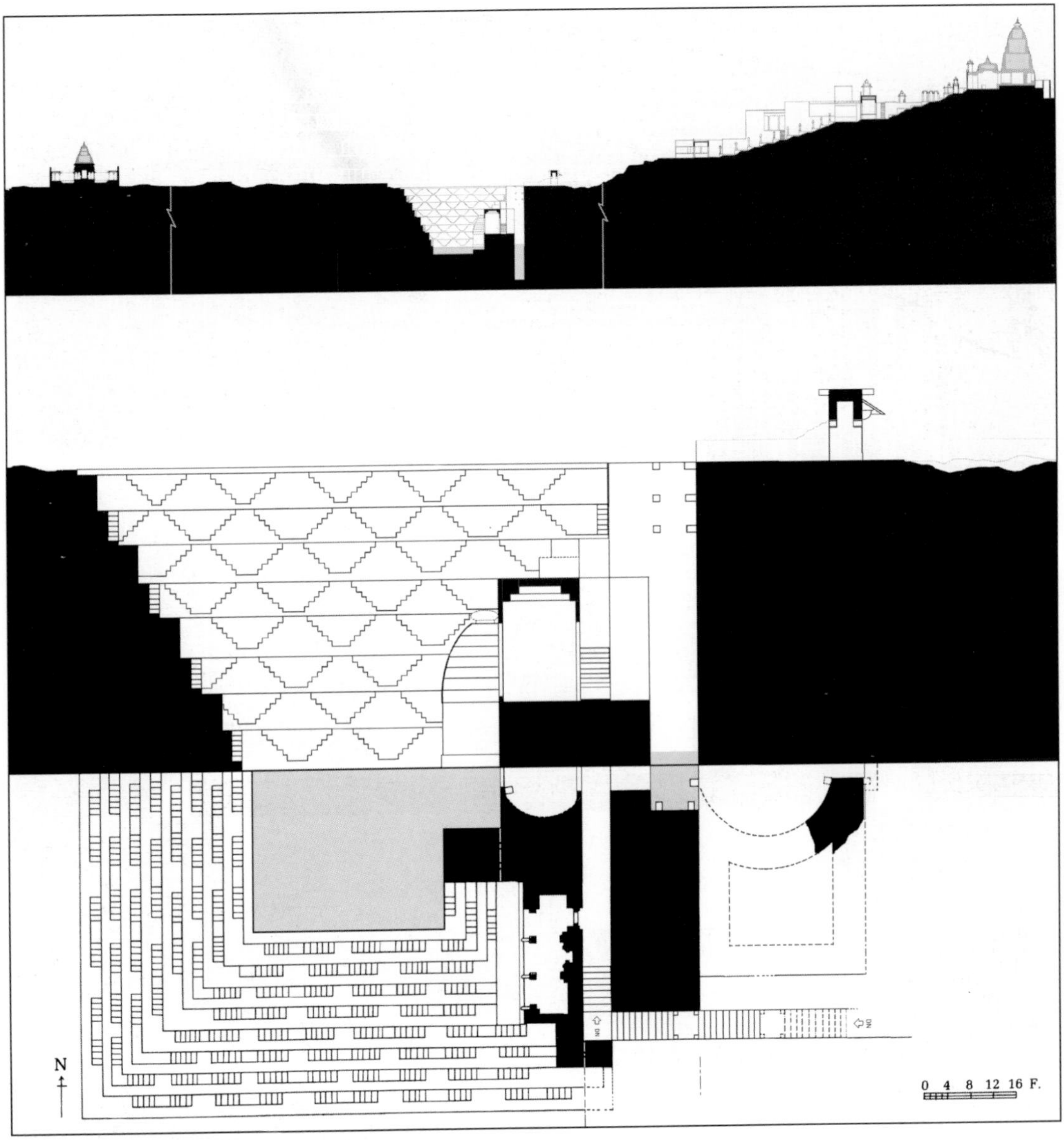

Plate 16. Osian: section of site (top); step-well, elevation, and plan (bottom).

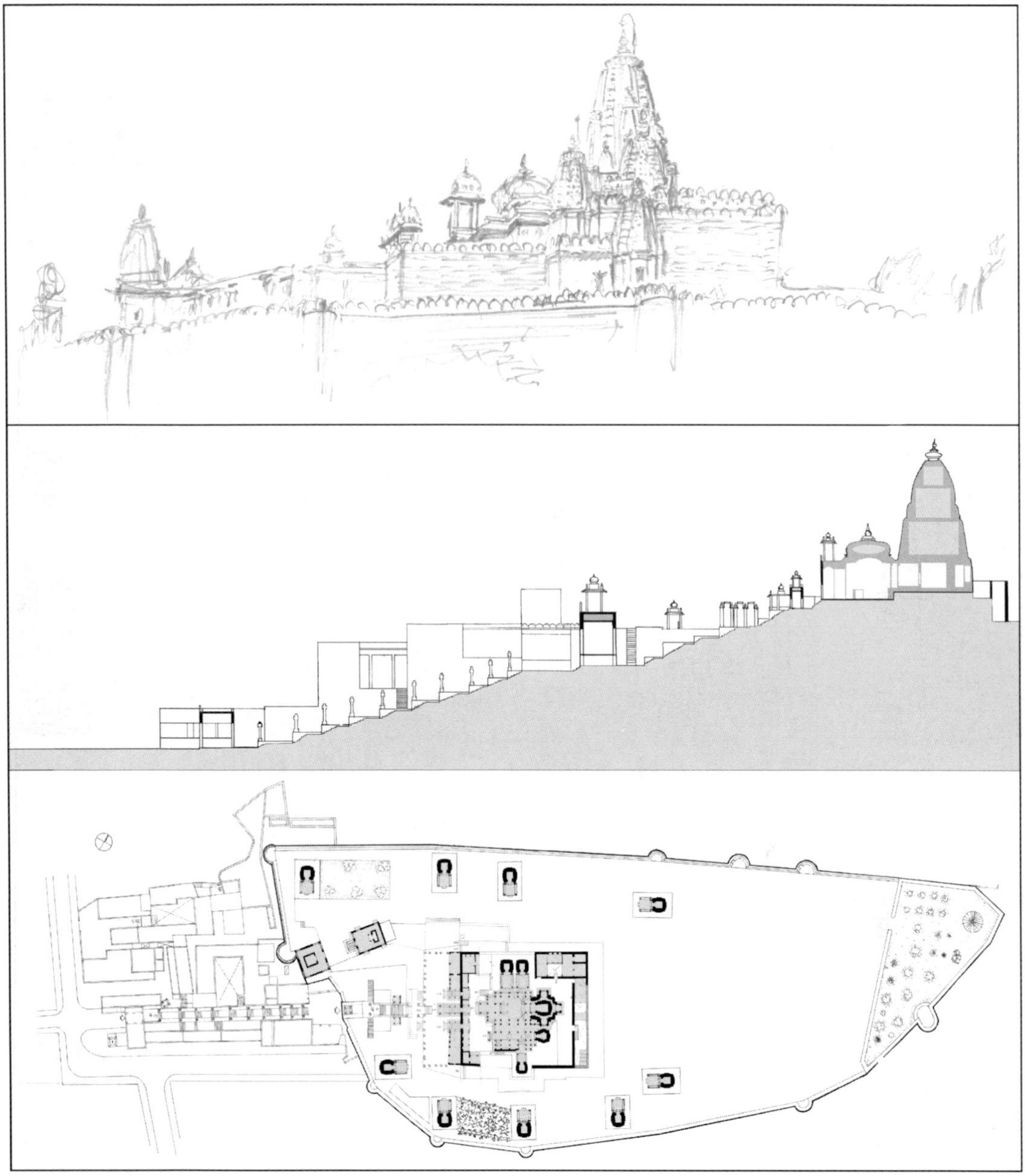

Plate 17. Sacciyā Mātā hill: sketch by Ajit Parikh (top), section (center), and site plan (bottom).

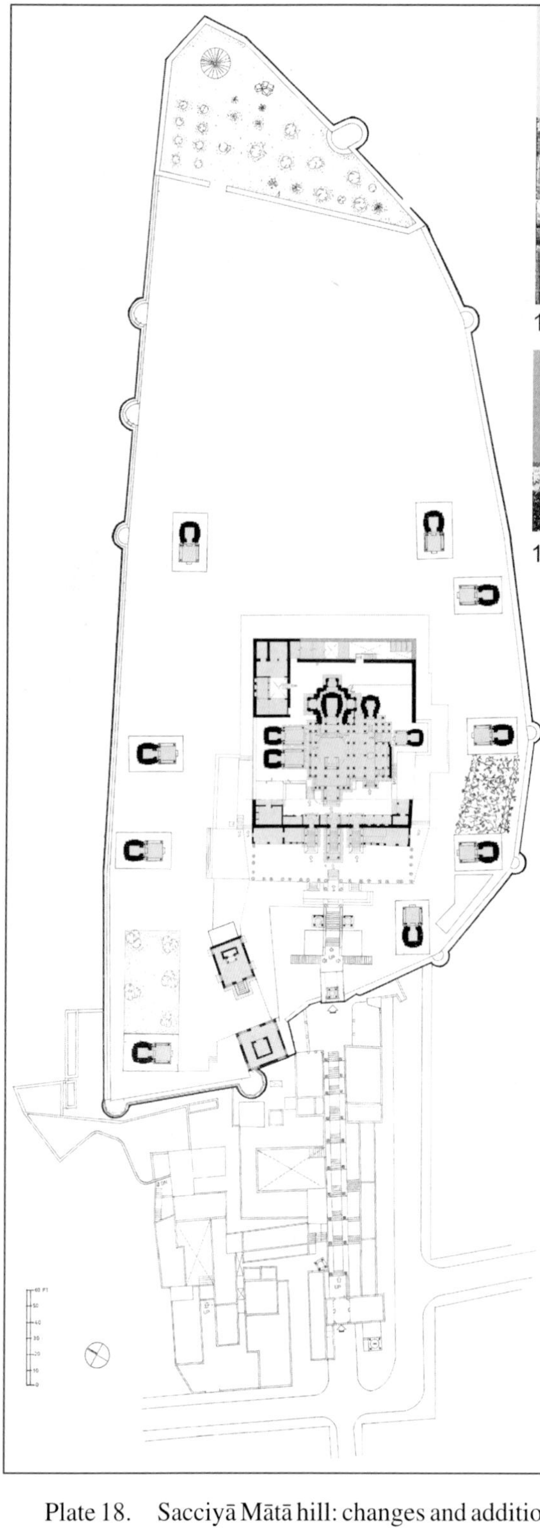

1972

1998

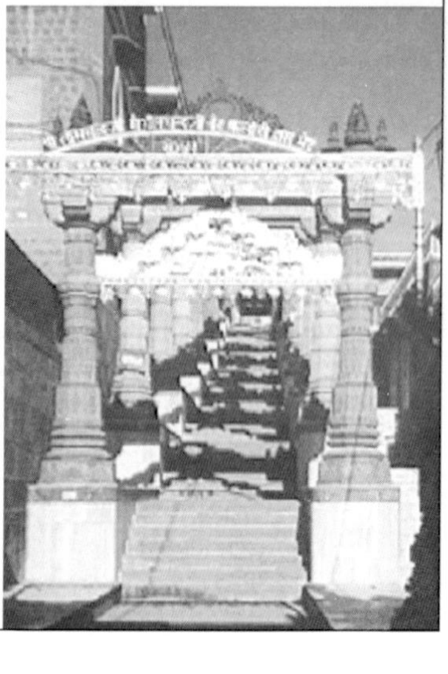

Plate 18. Sacciyā Mātā hill: changes and additions, 1972–98.

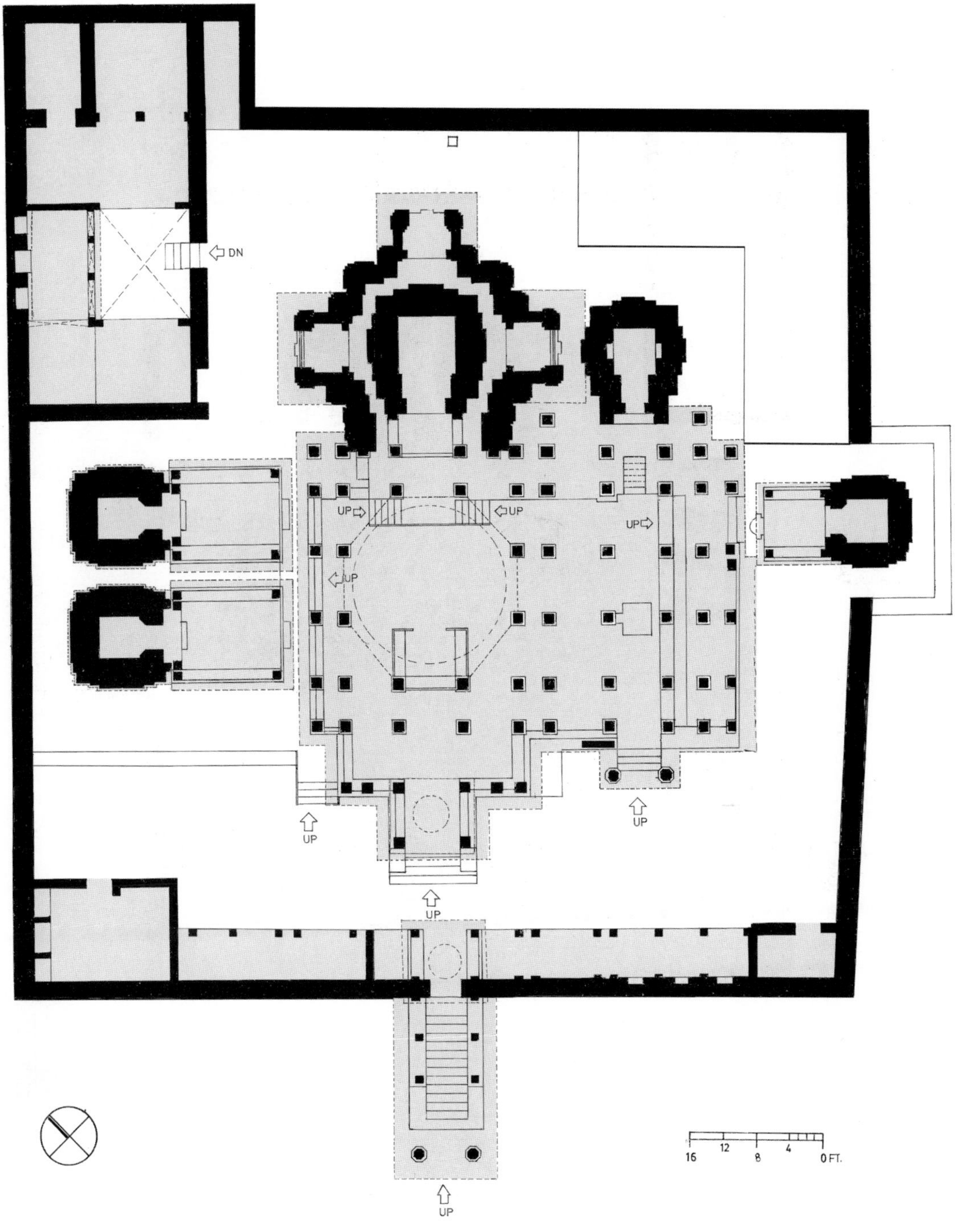

Plate 19. Sacciyā Mātā temple compound: ground plan, 1972.

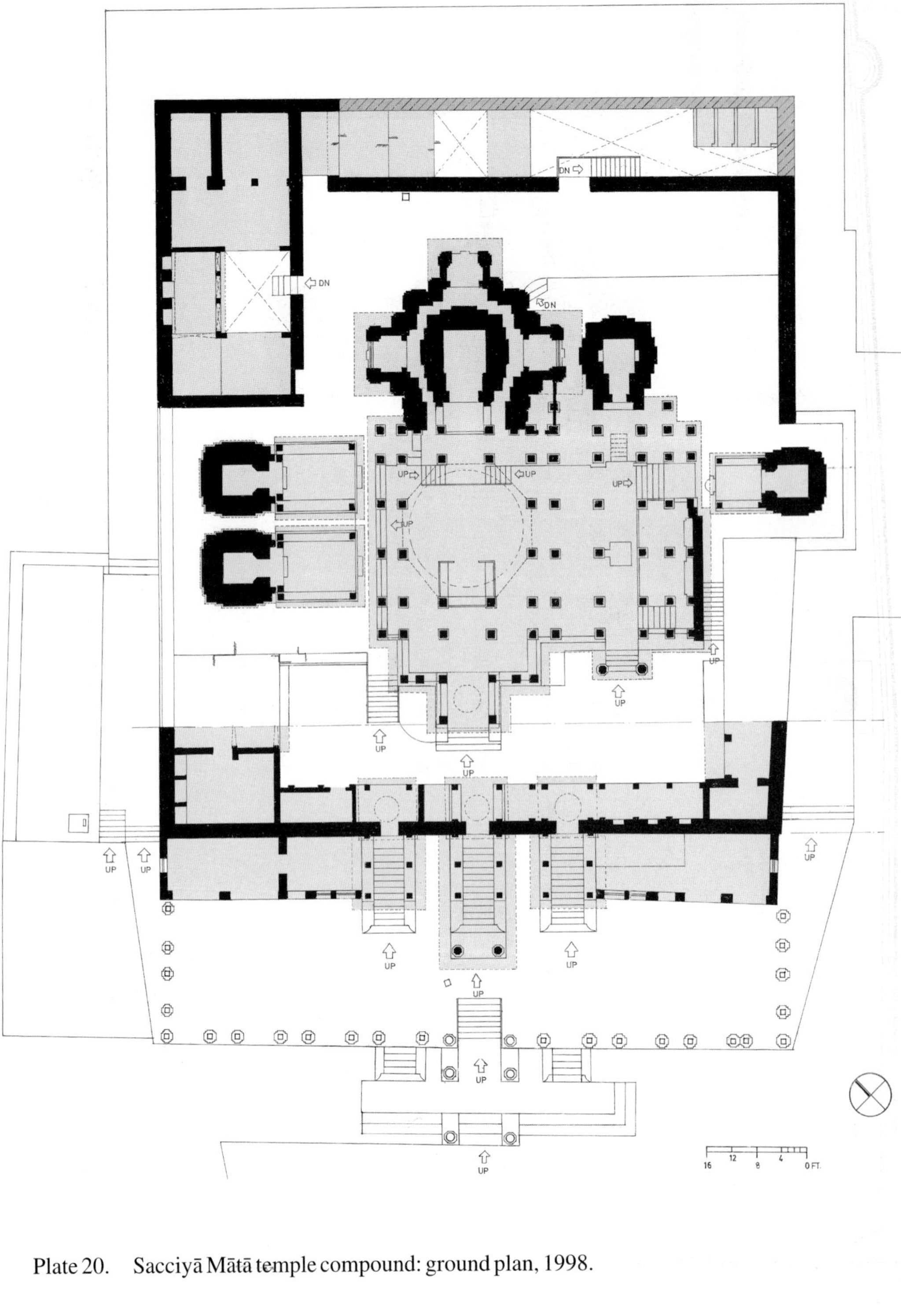

Plate 20. Sacciyā Mātā temple compound: ground plan, 1998.

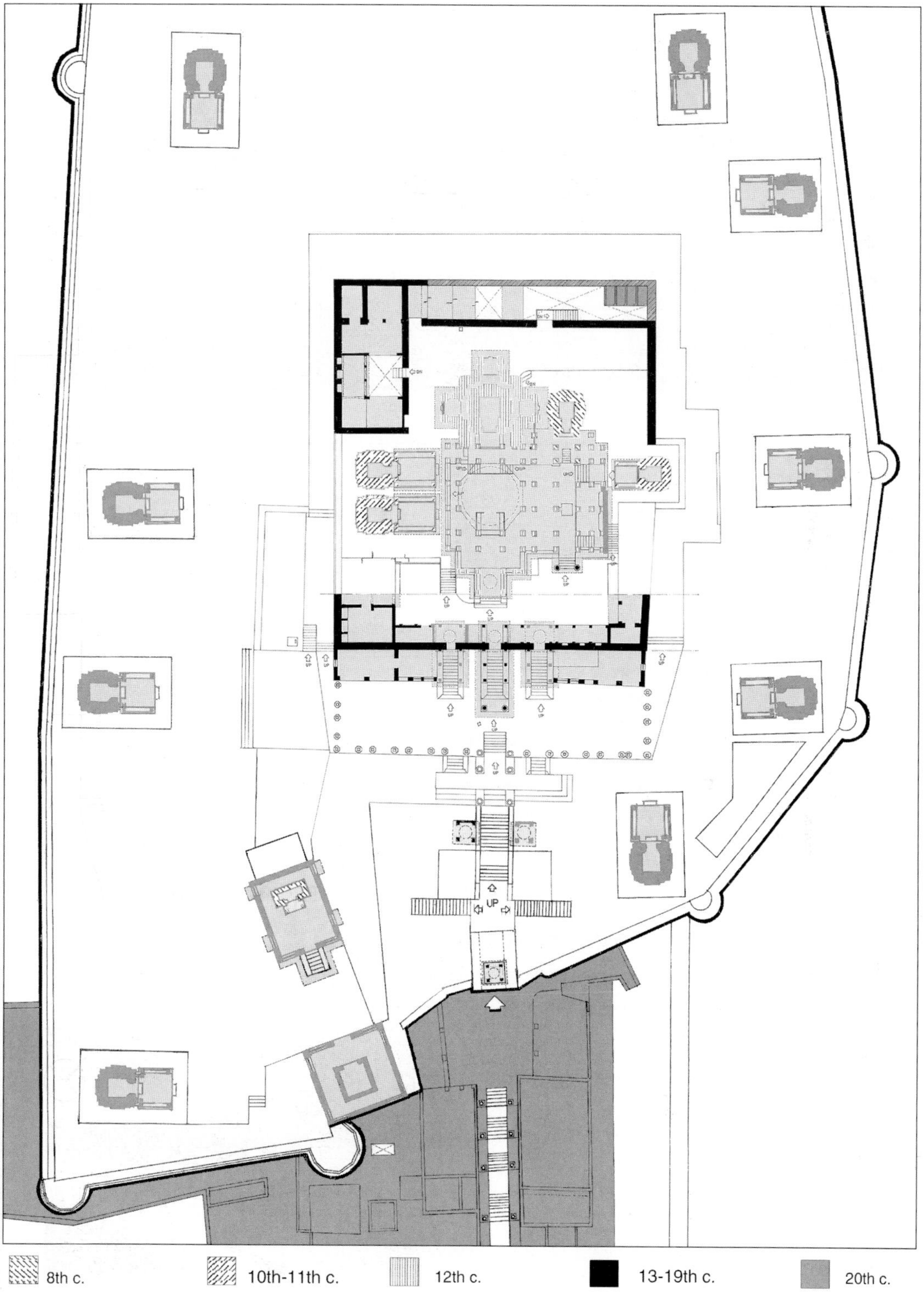

Plate 21. Sacciyā Mātā hill: phases of development.

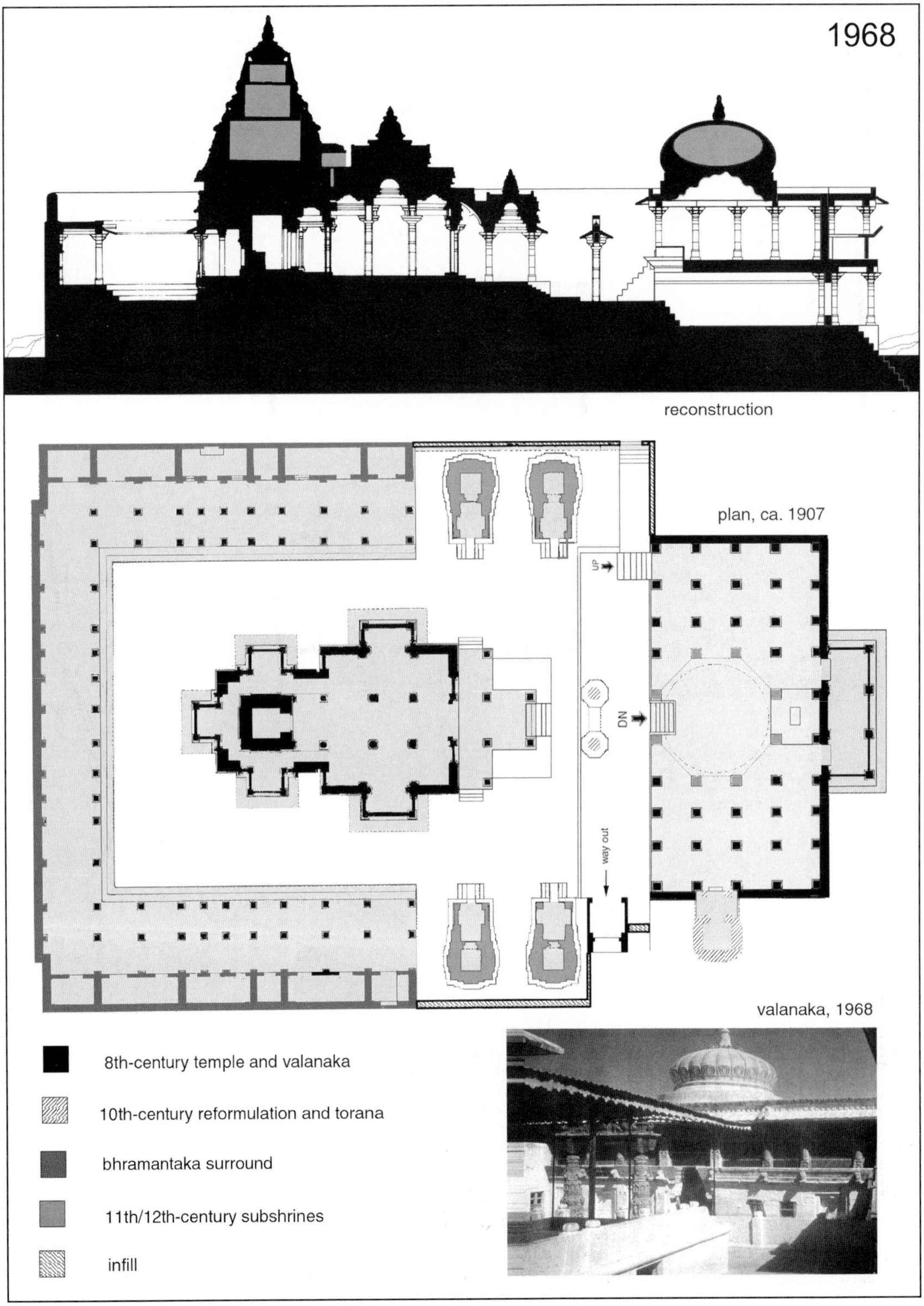

Plate 22. Mahāvīra temple, phases of development: section and ground plan (top) with reconstruction of the two-story entry hall (lower right).

Plate 23. Mahāvīra temple: demolished two-story entry hall (*valānaka*), court with *toraṇa*, and NE side entry, documented in 1968.

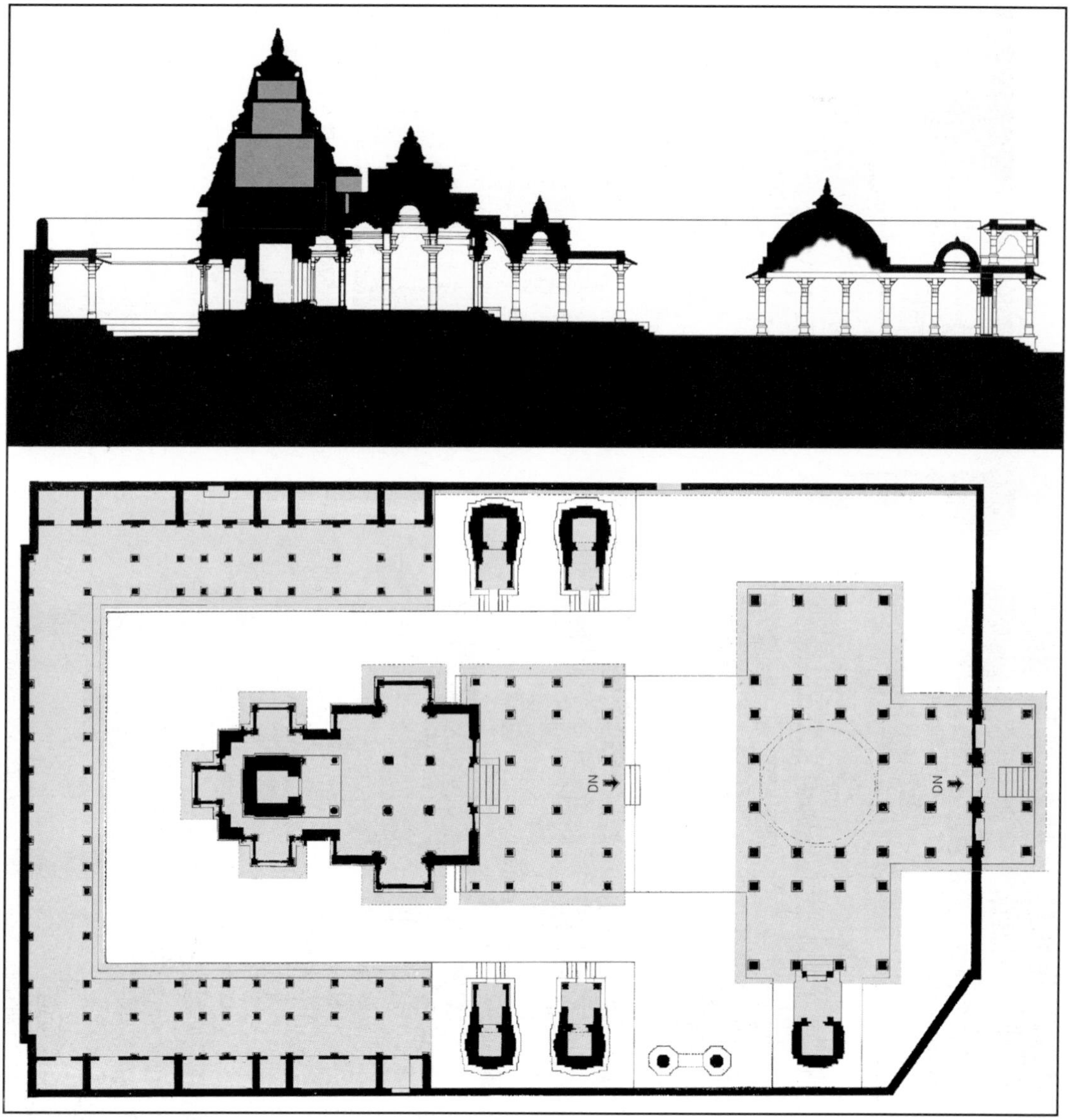

Plate 24. Mahāvīra temple: section and ground plan with single-story entry hall, ca. 1998.

Plate 25. People as agents of change: Chuna Ram Prajapat, sculptor and mason (top); Chuna Ram with Gepu Khan, mason and architect (lower right); Bhanu Prakash, *pujārī*, Mahāvīra temple (lower left).

Plate 26. Sacciyā Mātā temple *gūḍha-maṇḍapa*, Kṣemaṅkarī sculpture, possibly the original eighth-century cult-image (left); Sūrya temple no. 2, north *bhadra*, sculpture of Durgā slaying the buffalo demon Mahiṣa, eighth century (upper right); Sacciyā Mātā temple, sanctum, image of Sacciyā Mātā in the form of Mahiṣāsuramardinī (lower right).

Plate 27. Dadhimatī Mātā temple: portable image in procession on the eighth day of Navrātrī (top). Didwana, Pādāmātā temple, north wall, ca. ninth century (bottom): Mahiṣāsuramardinī on the *bhadra*, with a small scene showing Durgā emerging from the earth in front of cowherds and cattle (bottom, upper left).

Plate 28. Jodhpur, Kriyā Bhavan: painting of Jñānsundar and marble *guru mūrti* of Jñānsundar (top left and center right) (photographs Babb). Osian, Luṇādrī hill, *dādābāṛī*, installed by Yati Premsundar 1909, renovated 1952 (top right). Goth-Manglod, Dadhimatī Mātā temple: marble sculpture of Dadhīci enshrined in the northwest corner of the temple's colonnade (bottom left); framed in *gūḍha-maṇḍapa*: a painting of Dadhimatī's emergence witnessed by a cowherd and a colored print of Dadhīci giving up his flesh (bottom, center and right).

Plate 29. Osian *sthānas* in community worship: Pīpalā Devī temple, sanctum, eighth-century icons of Kubera, Durgā-Mahiṣāsuramardinī, and Gaṇeśa (top); Luṇādrī hill, *dādābāṛī*: lower footprints, Kanakaprabha, 1189 CE, upper footprints, Ratnaprabhasūri, installed by Yati Premsundar, 1909 CE (bottom left). Kesarīya Kaṅvar installed in Viṣṇu temple no. 1; Bhojak Bhomiyā, 1823 CE; Bhāti *jhunjhār* (bottom, center to right).

Plate 30. Osian, Mahāvīra temple, reconfigured courtyard, *jāt denā* ceremony in front of Bherū shrine (top); dressed images of Sacciyā Mātā during Navrātrī and Mahāvīra during annual temple festival (bottom).

Plate 31. Osian, Jain school collection, photograph of a nineteenth-century *paṭṭāvalī* miniature painting showing Ratnaprabhasūri converting Sacciyā Mātā and a cow locating the image of Mahāvīra (top left and right); *jāt denā* ceremony in front of renovated Bherū altar mounted on the west *bhadra*-balcony of the Mahāvīra temple (bottom).

Plate 32. Osian, Sacciyā Mātā complex: pilgrims ascending the hill on the eighth day of Navrātrī (upper left); *jāt denā* procession placing coconuts on each step (top right; bottom left) and making offerings (lower right).

Plate 33. Osian, interviews and interactions: Meister and Babb on roof of the old Jain school; Babb interviewing Om Prakash Sharma (top); Cort and Vimal Sharma, in front of a memorial photograph of his father, Jugrāj, at the entry gate to Sacciyā Mātā hill (bottom).

Plate 34. Osian, Mahāvīra temple, *valānaka* entry hall, renovated and reinstalled eleventh-century ceiling; Goth-Manglod, Dadhimatī temple complex, *kapāl kuṇḍ*.

Mambo

Your visual blueprint™ for building and maintaining Web sites with the Mambo Open Source CMS

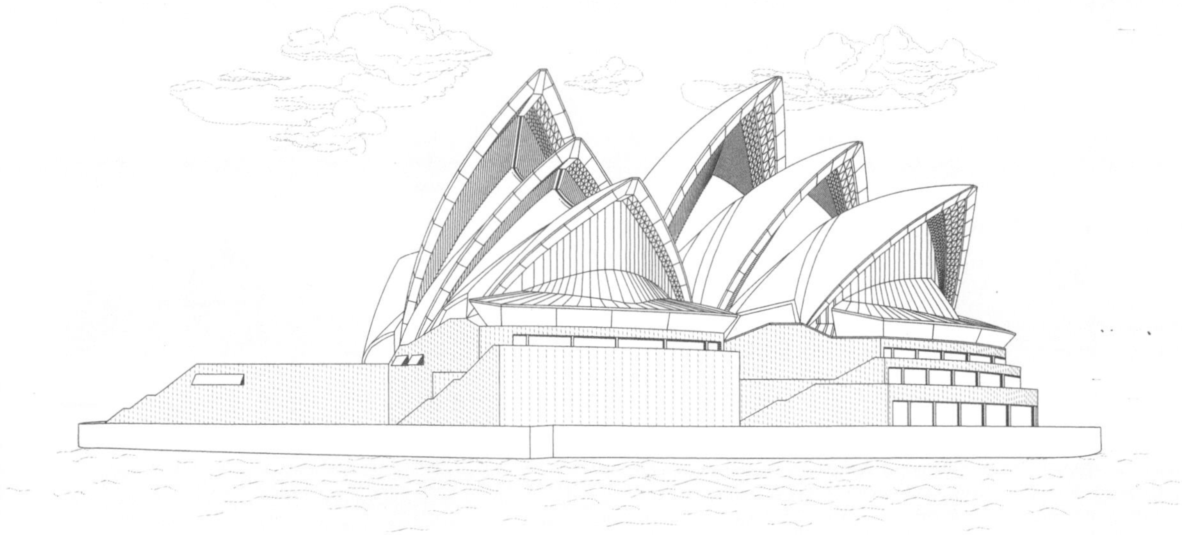

by Ric Shreves

WILEY

Wiley Publishing, Inc.

Mambo: Your visual blueprint™ for building and maintaining Web sites with the Mambo Open Source CMS

Published by
Wiley Publishing, Inc.
111 River Street
Hoboken, NJ 07030-5774

Published simultaneously in Canada

Library of Congress Control Number: 2006923795

ISBN-13: 978-0-470-04056-0

ISBN-10: 0-470-04056-4

Manufactured in the United States of America

10 9 8 7 6 5 4 3 2 1

1D/SR/QW/QW/IN

Trademark Acknowledgments

Contact Us

For general information on our other products and services please contact our Customer Care Department within the U.S. at 800-762-2974, outside the U.S. at 317-572-3993 or fax 317-572-4002.

For technical support please visit www.wiley.com/techsupport.

Sydney Opera House

A masterpiece of twentieth century architechture, Australia's Sydney Opera House is among the most recognizable structures in the world. It appears like a stately vessel sailing into Sydney Harbor, where its freestanding, sculptural tripartite form bears tribute to the vision of architect Jorn Utzon, who withdrew from the project amid political scandal in its eleventh year. Five years later, in 1973, the Opera House was completed under the direction of Peter Hall and opened to worldwide acclaim. Learn more about Australia's wonders, both constructed and natural, in *Frommer's Australia*, available wherever books are sold or at www.Frommers.com.

WILEY

Sales

Contact Wiley at (800) 762-2974 or (317) 572-4002.

PRAISE FOR VISUAL BOOKS...

"This is absolutely the best computer-related book I have ever bought. Thank you so much for this fantastic text. Simply the best computer book series I have ever seen. I will look for, recommend, and purchase more of the same."

—David E. Prince (NeoNome.com)

"I have several of your Visual books and they are the best I have ever used."

—Stanley Clark (Crawfordville, FL)

"I just want to let you know that I really enjoy all your books. I'm a strong visual learner. You really know how to get people addicted to learning! I'm a very satisfied Visual customer. Keep up the excellent work!"

—Helen Lee (Calgary, Alberta, Canada)

"I have several books from the Visual series and have always found them to be valuable resources."

—Stephen P. Miller (Ballston Spa, NY)

"This book is PERFECT for me — it's highly visual and gets right to the point. What I like most about it is that each page presents a new task that you can try verbatim or, alternatively, take the ideas and build your own examples. Also, this book isn't bogged down with trying to 'tell all' – it gets right to the point. This is an EXCELLENT, EXCELLENT, EXCELLENT book and I look forward to purchasing other books in the series."

—Tom Dierickx (Malta, IL)

"I have quite a few of your Visual books and have been very pleased with all of them. I love the way the lessons are presented!"

—Mary Jane Newman (Yorba Linda, CA)

"I am an avid fan of your Visual books. If I need to learn anything, I just buy one of your books and learn the topic in no time. Wonders! I have even trained my friends to give me Visual books as gifts."

—Illona Bergstrom (Aventura, FL)

"I just had to let you and your company know how great I think your books are. I just purchased my third Visual book (my first two are dog-eared now!) and, once again, your product has surpassed my expectations. The expertise, thought, and effort that go into each book are obvious, and I sincerely appreciate your efforts."

—Tracey Moore (Memphis, TN)

"Compliments to the chef!! Your books are extraordinary! Or, simply put, extra-ordinary, meaning way above the rest! THANK YOU THANK YOU THANK YOU! I buy them for friends, family, and colleagues."

—Christine J. Manfrin (Castle Rock, CO)

"I write to extend my thanks and appreciation for your books. They are clear, easy to follow, and straight to the point. Keep up the good work! I bought several of your books and they are just right! No regrets! I will always buy your books because they are the best."

—Seward Kollie (Dakar, Senegal)

"I am an avid purchaser and reader of the Visual series, and they are the greatest computer books I've seen. Thank you very much for the hard work, effort, and dedication that you put into this series."

—Alex Diaz (Las Vegas, NV)

Credits

Project Editor
Maureen Spears

Acquisitions Editor
Jody Lefevere

Product Development Supervisor
Courtney Allen

Copy Editor
Scott Tullis

Technical Editor
Chad Auld

Editorial Manager
Robyn Siesky

Business Manager
Amy Knies

Permissions Editor
Laura Moss

Media Development Specialist
Laura Atkinson

Manufacturing
Allan Conley
Linda Cook
Paul Gilchrist
Jennifer Guynn

Book Design
Kathryn Rickard

Production Coordinator
Jennifer Theriot

Layout and Graphics
Jennifer Click
Joyce Haughey
Melanee Prendergast
Heather Ryan
Amanda Spagnuolo

Screen Artists
Ronda David-Burroughs
Jill A. Proll

Cover Illustration
Joni Burnes

Proofreader
John Greenough

Indexer
Ty Koontz

Vice President and Executive Group Publisher
Richard Swadley

Vice President and Publisher
Barry Pruett

Composition Director
Debbie Stailey

About the Author

Ric Shreves is a partner in Water & Stone (www.waterandstone.com), a Web development company that specialises in Open Source Content Management Systems. Since 1996, Ric has been building Web sites and has extensive experience with content management systems. Over the years he has worked on CMS-powered Web sites for BASF, Colgate-Palmolive, Tesco, FPDSavills, Sino Group, CBRichard Ellis, Mercy Corps, University of North Carolina, and many, many others. He is an active member of CM Professionals and of the Mambo Foundation.

Ric currently resides in Bali where he is testing his theory that an IT professional should be able to make a living anywhere with a notebook computer and an Internet connection. He says so far all he has been able to prove is that is a beautiful theory...

Author's Acknowledgments

I would like to thank Jody Lefevere, the Acquisitions Editor who had the vision to see that the Mambo project needed a text of this nature, Maureen Spears whose patience and measured work brought the text to fruition, despite my efforts, and Scott Tullis, who meticulously copy edited the book. Chad Auld, my Technical Editor, gets a big "Thank You!" because he no doubt saved me from embarrasment many times over. Finally, a big heartfelt thank you goes to my wife Nalisa who patiently allowed me to prioritize this text over a number of matters that I could have, and should have, been helping her complete. (She also gets credit for more than a few of the good ideas you will find in these pages.)

TABLE OF CONTENTS

3 MANAGE THE MAMBO TEMPLATES 36

4 MANAGE SITE USERS 50

5 CREATE AND MANAGE SECTIONS AND CATEGORIES 64

TABLE OF CONTENTS

12 ADVANCED TECHNIQUES WITH MODULES 230

TABLE OF CONTENTS

HOW TO USE THIS BOOK

Your visual blueprint™ for building and maintaining Web sites with the Mambo Open Source CMS uses clear, descriptive examples to show you how to create Web sites with Mambo. If you are already familiar with Mambo, you can use this book as a quick reference for many Mambo tasks.

Who Needs This Book

This book is for the experienced computer user who wants to find out more about Mambo. It is also for more experienced Mambo users who want to expand their knowledge of the different features that Mambo has to offer.

Book Organization

Your visual blueprint™ for building and maintaining Web sites with the Mambo Open Source CMS has 15 chapters and 3 appendixes.

Chapter 1, Introducing Mambo, shows you the basics of the Mambo system and introduces fundamental concepts.

Chapter 2, Configure Mambo, demonstrates how to use the global configuration settings of Mambo to customize your site to match your needs.

Chapter 3, Manage The Mambo Templates, provides you with the information you need to install and manage the site's templates and CSS files.

Chapter 4, Manage Site Users, gives a detailed explanation of the different user groups available in Mambo and explains how they can be used to best effect.

Chapter 5, Create And Manage Sections and Categories, explains how to set up the content hierarchies and organizational schema for your site.

Chapter 6, Create And Manage Content, illustrates the basics of content management, page creation and editing.

Chapter 7, Add Images and Media to Mambo, demonstrates how you can add and manage media content within your content pages.

Chapter 8, Advanced Content Techniques, explains how you can achieve more complex hierarchies and demonstrates content management techniques.

Chapter 9, How To Work with Menus, shows you the Mambo menu system and how you can create and manage your menus.

Chapter 10, How to Work with Components, gives you the information you need to employ the components that are bundled with your Mambo site.

Chapter 11, Site Module Basics, enables you to work with the various modules bundled with your Mambo site and includes an explanation of all their functions and options.

Chapter 12, Advanced Techniques with Modules, demonstrates how you can achieve a variety of advanced effects with the modules and how to create new modules.

Chapter 13, How to Work with Mambots, illustrates how you can manage the Mambots included with the system and explains the functions and options associated with each one.

Chapter 14, Administering a Mambo Site, covers the skills you will need to manage and maintain your Mambo site, including site backups.

Chapter 15, Extend Your Mambo Site, discusses how you can extend your Mambo site with third party plug-ins.

The Appendixes cover Mambo installation, the licensing of the Mambo code, and how to configure the MOStlyCE WYSIWYG Editor.

What You Need to Use This Book

The Mambo core files require:

- A computer running the Apache Web server
- The MySQL database and PHP.

Administering a Mambo site requires only the use of a browser; Internet Explorer and Firefox tend to work best with the Mambo system.

The Conventions in This Book

A number of styles have been used throughout *Your visual blueprint™ for building and maintaining Web sites with the Mambo Open Source CMS* to designate different types of information.

`Courier Font`

Indicates the use of code such as tags or attributes, scripting language code such as statements, operators, or functions, and code such as objects, methods, or properties.

Bold

Indicates information that you must type.

Italics

Indicates a new term.

Apply It

An Apply It section takes the feature from the preceding section one step further. Apply It tips allow you to take full advantage of Mambo's features by applying what you have learned to a practical example.

Extra

An Extra section provides additional information about the preceding section. Extra tips contain the inside information to make working with Mambo easier and more efficient.

Why Use Mambo?

The Mambo Open Source Content Management System is a server-based tool that enables you to easily create and maintain highly functional Web sites. Mambo is very powerful and easy to use, making it equally suitable for developers skilled in IT or for hobbyists and do-it-yourselfers. Mambo is not the only Open Source Content Management System in existence today. Nonetheless, despite the presence of a number of competing programs, Mambo has been downloaded over 5 million times and powers hundreds of thousands of Web sites.

Mambo comes as a single archive of files that you install on a Web server. Mambo's technical requirements for the hosting environment are not demanding; as a result, you can install the system on most Web hosts without difficulty.

Once you extract the Mambo file archive on the server, installation is a simple matter that you handle via a wizard interface. Total installation time varies, but generally speaking you can start with the file archive and less than 20 minutes later have a fully functional Web site, complete with an administration system. The full technical requirements and the installation process are detailed in Appendix A. Five factors, each discussed in detail in this section, combine to make Mambo so popular.

Content Management

Mambo's strength is content management. The system gives you the ability to create, edit, and organize content in a variety of formats, using only a Web browser. The administration system includes tools to ease the burden of content management, including an easy-to-use WYSIWYG (What You See Is What You Get) editor. The WYSIWYG editor makes it possible to format text without having to understand or use HTML code. Basically, if you can use Microsoft Word to format text, then you can use the Mambo WYSIWYG editor because the interface and the tools are visually and functionally similar.

The Mambo content management system also supplies the tools you need to organize content pages into sections and categories and create navigation structures. The navigation can reflect the content hierarchy or you can make it separate from the organizational schema applied to the content. The flexibility to create various navigational structures is a key to working with sites that contain large amounts of content. Menus and submenus can present the content to users in various fashions, and you can organize content inside the administration system in a schema that promotes ease of use for the site administrators.

Mambo also enables you to establish workflow hierarchies, where one class of user can contribute text, another can edit it, and yet another can publish it. Workflow controls are a necessity for large or corporate sites and sites that require some degree of review and accountability in the content creation process.

In Mambo, you can manage multilingual text content as well as content like images or files. The range of options the system presents makes it possible to employ Mambo for public and commercial Web sites, for private intranets, for personal sites, or for virtually anything in between. To learn more about the content management capabilities of Mambo, read Chapters 5 to 8.

User Management

The admin interface of the Mambo system includes all the tools you need to manage users and access privileges. While the Mambo user group hierarchies are limited in number, they do provide sufficient variety for content workflow for a variety of classes of administrators. The system includes enough flexibility to manage anything from a small site to a full online community. For more information about managing users with Mambo, read Chapter 4.

Flexibility

You control the look and feel of a Mambo site through the use of template files. You do not need to understand an arcane or proprietary syntax to build your own templates or to modify the templates. Mambo templates are standard PHP files where HTML and CSS do the formatting. The flexibility and ease of use of the template system is one of the keys to Mambo's success because it allows developers to create highly customized sites.

The Mambo code base is also very tolerant of users making modifications to the system. Many Mambo developers today started out by downloading and installing Mambo and then exploring what they could do with the files. It is hard to crash a Mambo site and even more difficult to permanently damage one. In the event you do succeed in crashing the site, you can easily restore it from a backup, or by reinstalling the core files.

Extensibility

Mambo was released to the Open Source world in April of 2001. In the following years, the system grew in complexity, ability, and scale. Additionally, a number of people developed a variety of extensions for Mambo. Today, third-party components, modules, and templates exist in significant numbers. Through the use of third-party extensions, you can customize Mambo to a great degree without having to do any programming yourself. You can find catalog management tools, shopping carts, forums, file management systems, multimedia tools, and other extensions across a broad range of categories. Many of the third-party extensions are free of charge while others are proprietary in nature and require the payment of a small fee.

Mambo is designed to accept and integrate third-party extensions automatically. The system includes automated installers that accept a third-party component, Mambot, module, or template easily and allow you thereafter to administer that new functionality inside the Mambo admin interface. The various manners for extending your Mambo site are discussed at length in the chapters that follow.

Free Open Source Software

Mambo is free software released under the GNU GPL (General Public License). The GPL provides protection for the source code and gives assurance that Mambo will remain free and open in the future. The license also means that you can use Mambo on any type of Web site free of charge. Developers can modify and redistribute the Mambo code set, as long as they respect the restrictions that GPL imposes.

Though it is an Open Source project, Mambo is backed by a stable corporate organization known as the Mambo Foundation. The corporate structure that Mambo uses is similar to that employed by other major Open Source projects like Mozilla and Eclipse. The nonprofit Mambo Foundation was created in August of 2005 to hold the rights to the Mambo brand and to shelter and promote Mambo. The existence of the Foundation helps assure users of continuity of development and that the code is backed by a dedicated professional organization. The Mambo license is discussed further in Appendix B.

Understanding Key Mambo Concepts

Like any large system, Mambo does have its own vocabulary — or set of words and phrases that have specific meanings within the context of Mambo. Compared with other large systems, Mambo does not overly burden you with acronyms and specialized terminology; nonetheless you should become familiar with Mambo verbiage. The list assembled here will see you through the vast majority of situations in fine form.

Home Page versus Frontpage

Generally, when people speak of the *front page* of a Web site, they mean the site's entry page, or home page. In Mambo, when someone speaks of the *front page* in Mambo, they are referring to a specialized tool called the *Frontpage Manager*.

The Mambo Frontpage Manager manages the content items on the home page of the Web site. With the Frontpage Manager you can publish or unpublish items on the home page, or you can reorder or even change the format of the items on the home page. A key point to note is that with some Web sites, the Frontpage Manager may not actually control the home page; use of the Frontpage Manager is optional. The default configuration is for the Frontpage Manager to manage the home page. However, developers sometimes bypass the Frontpage Manager and build a different type of home page — one that uses other materials or components instead of the Frontpage Manager.

Sections versus Categories

Sections and Categories are the two key organizational groups for your content. *Sections* are the highest level. *Categories* fit within Sections, and *Content Items* fit within Categories. You must assign all Categories to a Section. Likewise, a Section must have Categories, or it cannot hold Content Items. When you first create a Section it is empty until you create Categories and assign them to a Section. As you create Categories they too are initially empty, until you create Content Items to go into those Categories.

The Section/Category/Content Item hierarchy is the standard hierarchy in Mambo. Users who want to have only a 2-level hierarchy or a flat hierarchy still need to create Sections and then Categories. Most often, you handle this situation by either creating one Section to hold all the Categories, or by creating a redundant Section to hold each Category of the same name.

In Mambo, the only way to bypass the standard hierarchy is to use Static Content Items, which are pages that exist individually, outside of the standard Sections/Categories structure. For more about creating and managing Sections and Categories, see Chapter 5.

Content Items versus Static Content Items

The Web pages you create using the content editor can take one of two forms, either *Content Items* or *Static Content Items*. There is no difference in the way you create the pages nor in the nature of their contents; rather, the difference lies in the way they relate to other content and the content hierarchy.

Content Items are pages that belong to Categories. As noted earlier, Categories, in turn, belong to Sections. Therefore, by definition, a Content Item is a content page that belongs to a Section and a Category. A Content Item is grouped with other pages in the same Category and can be grouped with other items in the same Section. The relationship in the hierarchy is fixed.

By contrast, Static Content Items are individual pages having no formal affiliation with a Category, a Section, or even another page. Static Content Items stand alone, independent from the site's content hierarchy. As a result, Static Content Items tend to be favored for creating individual pages that are somehow different from other pages on the site, or that do not need a Category or a Section to fit within the site. Therefore, a common use for Static Content Items is to create pages which stand alone in the site's hierarchy, like a Privacy Policy page or a Terms and Conditions page. Static Content Items are also popular with small sites with flat information hierarchies.

Newsfeed versus Newsflash

Despite the similarities in their names, these two items are totally unrelated. RSS is commonly used by blog sites and news sites as a convenient tool for distributing their content. A site administrator can set up an RSS feed for the site's contents, and then others can subscribe to the feed to receive the new content automatically by way of an RSS Newsfeed reader. Mambo provides methods for both receiving and viewing Newsfeeds and for turning your site's content into an RSS Newsfeed that other people can see. A component called the Newsfeed Manager handles the management of incoming Newsfeeds. The Newsfeed Manager is discussed in Chapter 10.

In contrast, a *Newsflash* is nothing more than a Mambo module that enables the display of content in a particular format. The Newsflash display format is configurable, but in the default configuration, it displays a short piece of content drawn randomly from one of the content categories. Each time a page containing the Newsflash is loaded, the Newsflash module displays a different content item. The Newsflash module is discussed in Chapter 11.

Components versus Modules versus Mambots

You generally extend functionality in Mambo by installing either a component, a module, or a Mambot and letting them do the work. For a complex feature, the system may use a combination of these functional units. Understanding the differences between these items is more a matter of technical accuracy than necessity for the user. As far as most users are concerned it does not matter whether something is a component or a module or something else entirely. The situation is exacerbated by the fact that the distinction between the items is more a matter of form than function.

Components

A *component* provides a major functionality — for example, a forum or a file management system. A component's output typically appears in the main content area of a page, rather than in the side columns. You manage components via the Components menu. For more on components, see Chapter 10.

Modules

Modules come in three flavors. They are either helper applications that assist components in performing a job, small independent functional units, or simply ways of displaying content in an abbreviated form. Typically modules appear on the page in either of the side columns or at the extreme top or bottom of the page. Modules are discussed further in Chapters 11 and 12.

Mambots

Mambots are completely different in nature. They tend to invisibly integrate into the site and are, therefore, not visible to users and administrators. They provide valuable service by adding a behind-the-scenes functionality to the site as a whole. These items are probably best demonstrated by reference to examples: The WYSIWYG editor is based on a Mambot. A Mambot is also responsible for enabling search-engine-friendly URLs throughout the site. Mambots are discussed further in Chapter 13.

Access the Admin System

You must log in to the Mambo administration system to administer your site. The log in requirement enhances system security and helps prevent unauthorized visitors from making undesired changes or accessing private information.

By default, Mambo comes with a password-protected administration interface. If you have ever worked with other content-management systems, you know that some systems require you to manually set up secure access for the administrators. Mambo gives the protection automatically in the default configuration. During the installation process, Mambo creates the administration section and the first user for the system, who is named *admin*. The last stage of the Mambo installation wizard asks you to select a password for the user named *admin*. The first time you access the administration panel of a fresh installation of Mambo, you use the username *admin* and the password you selected during installation.

If someone else sets up your Mambo system for you, ask him or her for the username and password details.

The URL for the administration system login is always the same with Mambo sites. The standard format is the domain name, followed by /administrator. So, for example, if your site is named www.mysite.com, your administration access through the address is www.mysite.com/administrator.

Note that while Mambo has a password-protected interface for the administration system, users should always take steps to maintain the integrity of their usernames and passwords because the default system provides little real security. The majority of hackers access systems through the admin interface because they have either observed a user login and guessed a username and password, or can take advantage of users who allow the browser to store their username and password. Make sure you protect yourself from these common mistakes.

Access the Admin System

1. Direct your browser to the Admin Access Screen by typing the URL in the browser.

   - If you have installed the sample data you can also click the Administrator button on the Main Navigation.

   The Admin Access Screen loads.

2. Type your username.
3. Type your password.
4. Click Login.

   If you entered the correct username and password, the admin home page loads.

   If you did not enter the correct username and password, the system prompts you to try again.

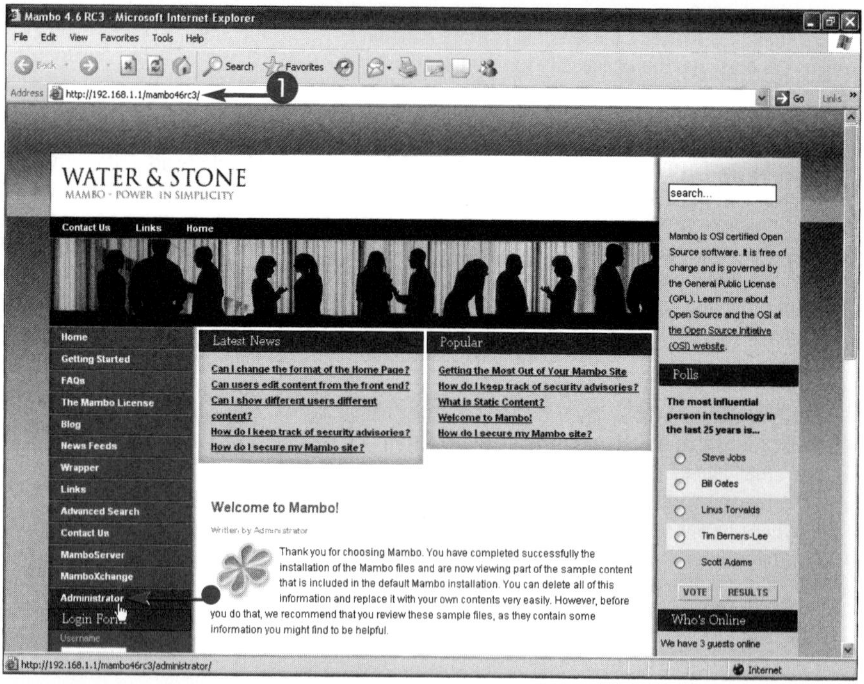

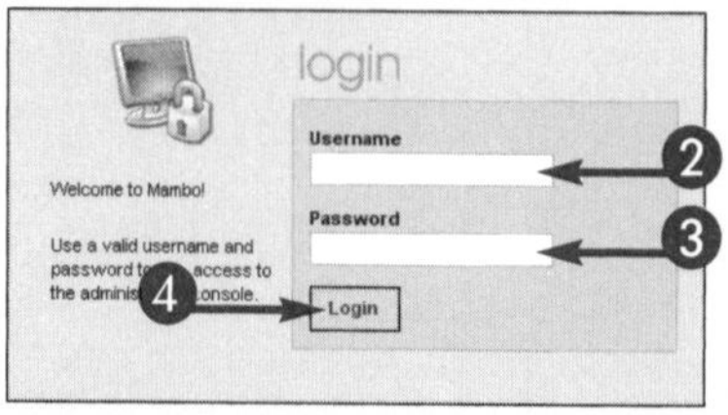

Introducing the Admin Interface

The admin home page, or Control Panel, provides useful information and quick access to a variety of tools. The Control Panel is a workspace and, as such, is a view of the admin system you return to repeatedly. To save time and effort and to enhance your effectiveness in monitoring your site, consider familiarizing yourself with the Panel layout.

Although the Control Panel interface is standardized, the tools and information vary according to a user's access privileges; higher-level users, like Administrators and Super Administrators, can access more tools and information while lower-level users see a limited set of tools and details. The interface reflection of the user's access levels is one of the security features of Mambo. For more on user groups and privileges, see Chapter 4.

The control panel also contains a feature that allows you to switch between a simple and an advanced version of the interface. As an administrator, you may find the amount of information in the admin interface daunting, and if you have a narrow-bandwidth market, you may not want to load all the tools each time a new page loads. If you want a more basic interface, Mambo has a Simple Mode with fewer tools and details. Power users will no doubt keep the interface in Advanced Mode to see all available tools. To switch between the two modes, see the section "Toggle between Simple and Advanced Mode."

Introducing the Admin Interface

A Main Navigation

Gives you access to all the functionality in the Mambo administration system. The choices are arranged thematically and there is some redundancy.

B Location Bar

Shows you where you are and which admin component is active.

C Quick Icons

Handy palette of shortcuts that takes you directly to the most commonly used functions in the admin system. All the choices shown here also exist under the Main Navigation, but the icons provide one-click access.

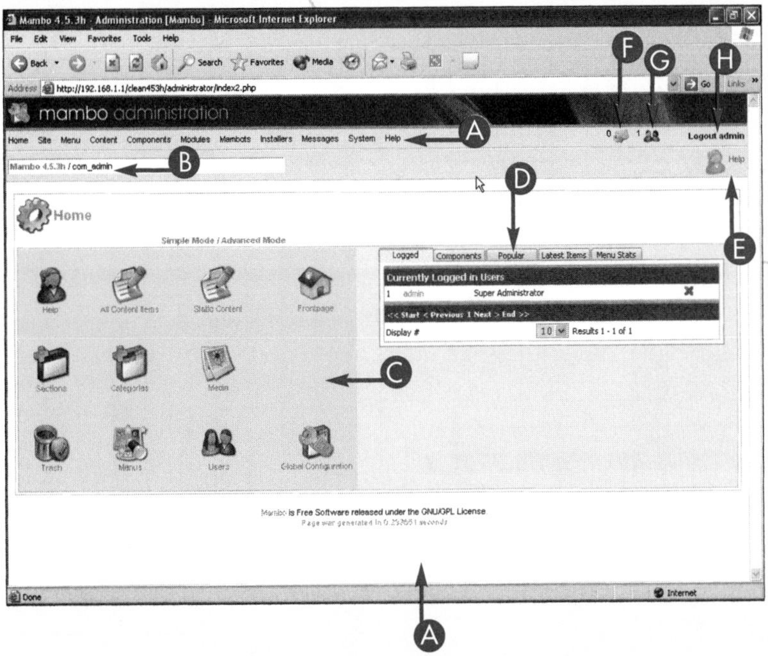

D Tab Bar

Provides different information to the administrator.

E Online Help

Takes you to context-sensitive Help files. Clicking the icon triggers a pop-up window that loads the relevant information.

F Messages

The number of messages waiting for you in the Admin Messaging System.

H Logout

The link to log out of the admin system. Logging out takes you back to the Home Page.

G Users

The number of users on the site. This figure updates every time the page refreshes. There is always some delay between a user exiting the site and the counter subtracting the user, so this is an approximate number.

Change Tab Views

To quickly access different views, which contain various pieces of information and links, you can switch between tabs in the Tab Bar in the admin interface. The Tab Bar gives a prompt look at user activity and access to components and content. It contains five tabs: Logged, Components, Popular, Latest Items, and Menu Stats.

The Logged tab shows a list of the registered users currently logged in to the system. It shows the users' names and user group assignments and gives Administrators and Super Administrators the ability to force a user to log out. For more on forcing a user to log out, see Chapter 4.

The Components tab contains a list of the components installed in the system and a set of links to the primary tasks associated with each. This tab gives quick access to a component's primary functions, and the links it contains echo those you find under the Components menu.

The Popular tab is a list of the most popular content items on the site, along with the dates they were created and the number of times they have been viewed. You can quickly open the item in an editing window via the item's name.

The Latest Items tab is a list of the Content Items most recently added to the site, along with the dates they were created and their authors. Again, you can open the item in an editing window via the item's name. Additionally, you can use the author's name to open the Edit User screen for the author.

The Menu Stats tab shows you the names of all the published menus along with the number of items on that menu. You can use a menu's name to take you to the editing screen for that menu.

Change Tab Views

1. From the Control Panel in the admin interface, click a tab.

Note: For more on the admin interface, see the section "Introducing the Admin Interface."

The tab content opens.

- The Logged tab shows a list of registered users currently logged in to the system.
- The Component tab lists the components installed on the system.
- The Popular tab shows the most popular Content Items.
- The Latest Items tab shows the most recently added item loads.
- The Menu Stats tab shows a list of the menus in the system.

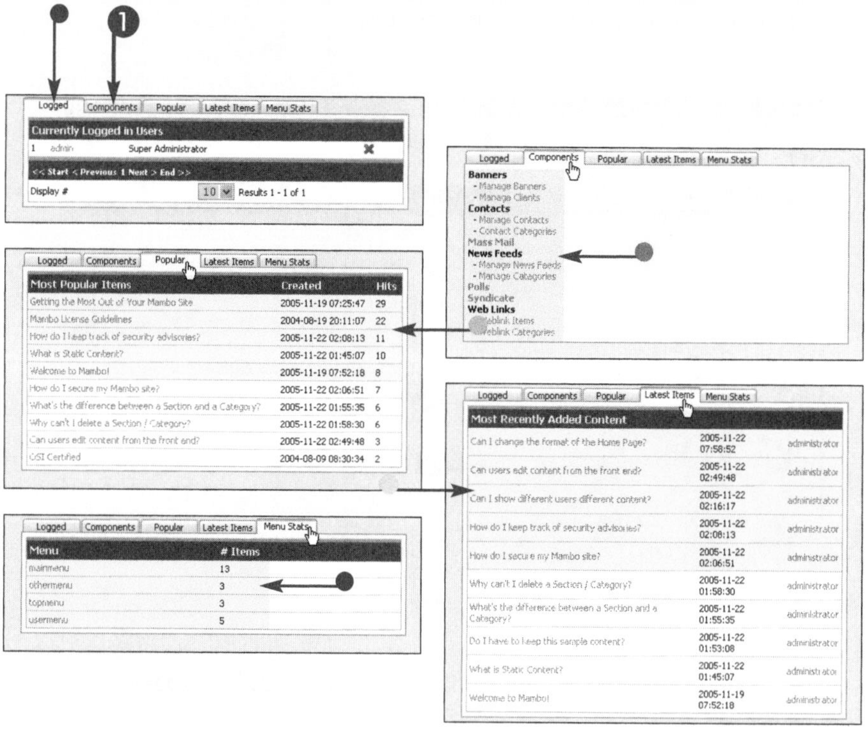

Toggle between Simple and Advanced Mode

You can change your view of the Mambo admin interface by switching between Simple and Advanced (default) Mode. Users who want fewer distractions and a faster-loading interface should use the Simple Mode because it shows only the most common tools. Users who are not concerned about bandwidth and who want to have all the tools available should leave the system in Advanced Mode. You may find it desirable to use Simple Mode while editing the content, due to the expanded viewing and editing area, then switch to Advanced Mode to add the final configuration details before publishing the item.

The difference between the Simple and Advanced Modes lies entirely in presentation. No tools are permanently blocked or restricted in Simple Mode. Simple Mode just removes the less frequently used options from the viewable area. For example, the Control Panel in Advanced Mode shows a wide variety of options. If you switch the view to Simple Mode, the shortcut icons are reduced in number from eleven to four. The four visible choices manage content, while the hidden choices relate to ancillary tasks, like Global Configuration and User Management.

The option to switch between Simple and Advanced Modes exists on the Control Panel page and on the Content Item editing pages. On the Content Item editing screen, turning on Simple Mode hides the parameters and other advanced function tabs on the right side of the page, leaving the content editing area to expand the width of the window.

Toggle between Simple and Advanced Mode

USING THE CONTROL PANEL

1. On the Control Panel, click Simple Mode.

   The simplified interface appears.

   - You can click Advanced Mode to redisplay the advanced options.

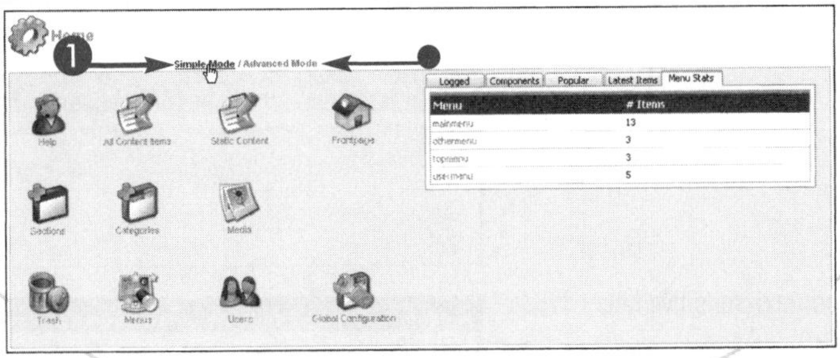

USING THE CONTENT EDITING SCREEN

1. On a content editing screen, click the Hide Advanced Details link.

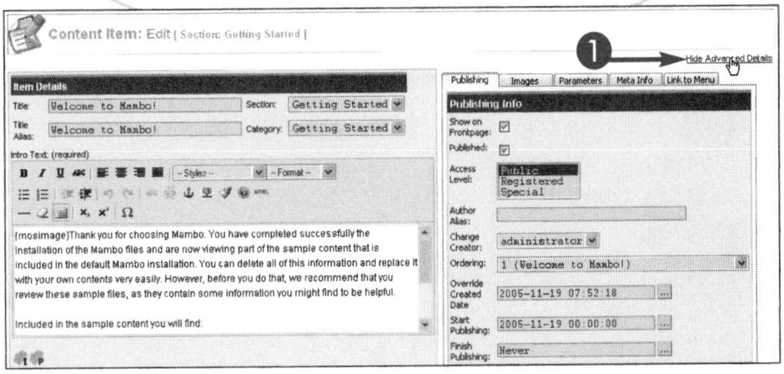

The right-hand tabs disappear and the content area expands.

- You can click the Show Advanced Details link to redisplay the advanced options.

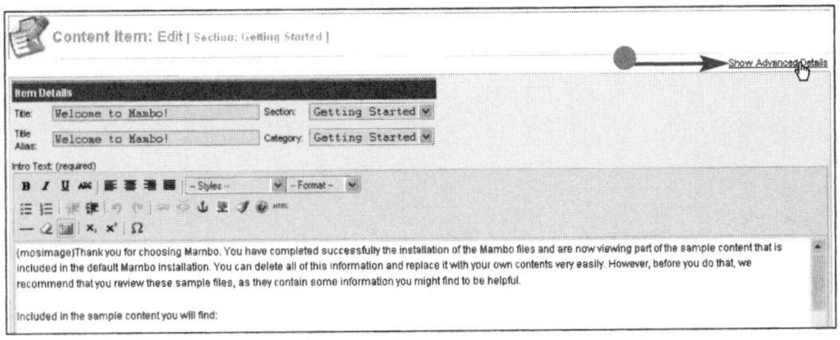

View Help Files

You can access Help files at any time while administering your Mambo system. The Mambo Help files are intended to assist administrators with the common tasks associated with content and user management and can also help with the specifics of the interface. The system even includes a context-sensitive Help option that displays a window containing information about the screen the user is viewing at the time.

A variety of Help files are included in the Mambo distribution, and you can access them at any time from the admin system nav bar. The embedded Help files are arranged topically so that you can either browse or search them. Note that if your site has access to the Internet — that is, it is installed on a server with access to the Internet — you can draw the contents of the Help files from the live Help site maintained by the Mambo team. The default setting of the system uses Help content that is embedded within your local Mambo system. If you prefer instead to draw the Help file contents from the live Help site, you can change the system settings through the Global Configuration Server tab. Be aware, however, that if your Mambo site cannot access the Internet, or if the Help site is not responding, then the Help link will display a 404 error message. For more information on setting Global Configuration options, see Chapter 2.

You can access context-sensitive Help files at any time using the Help icon on the top right side of a page. The context-sensitive files are embedded within the Mambo distribution and provide information specific to the screen that is displayed.

View Help Files

1. On the Control Panel, click the Help icon.

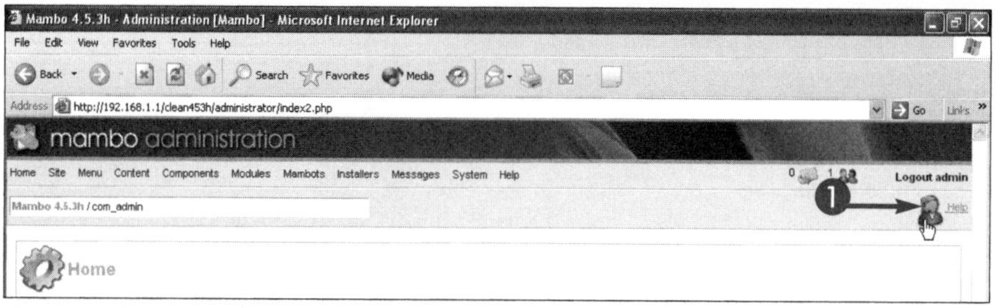

The context-sensitive help appears.

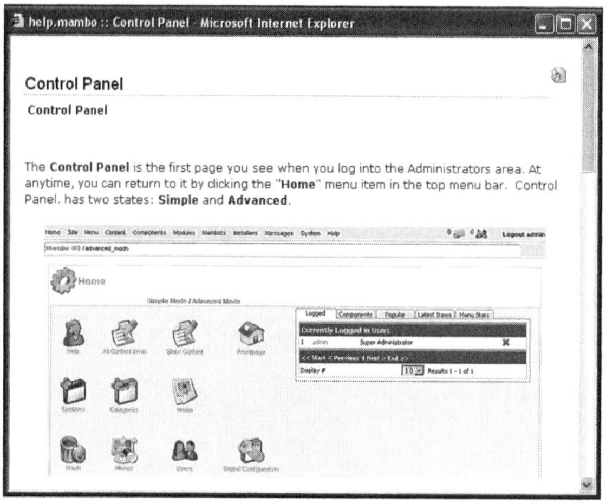

View System Information

You can view a summary of key information about your server's operating system and your Mambo system and files using the System Information option in the Mambo admin interface. The ability to quickly access accurate information about your system and your file permissions is very helpful when you or someone else is troubleshooting a Mambo installation. Mambo presents all of the relevant information together under an admin menu so you do not have to use or remember arcane system-level commands or FTP to learn basic facts about your configuration.

The Mambo system presents the information in two places for ease of use. The most direct path is through the System Information option on the System menu. You can also reach the information by selecting the Help option on the main nav and then selecting the System Information option that appears on the Help screen.

No matter how you access the System Information you have three tabs of information. The first tab is titled System Info and includes details of your operating system and key components, along with an edited view of your configuration.php file. Note that there is some information edited out of the configuration.php file: sensitive information, like passwords that can impair your system security if disclosed to the wrong person. The System Info tab also displays the version number of your Mambo installation, which is essential information for troubleshooting. The second tab, PHP Info, shows detailed information about the version of PHP running on your server. The third tab, Permissions, summarizes the file access permissions of key directories in the Mambo installation.

Note that the System Information screens are purely informational in nature. There are no tasks or functions associated with these pages. The pages are, in other words, simply reference materials.

View System Information

1. Click System.
2. Click System Information

   Alternatively, you can click the Help icon from the main nav and then click System Info to reach the System Information page.

   The System Information page loads.

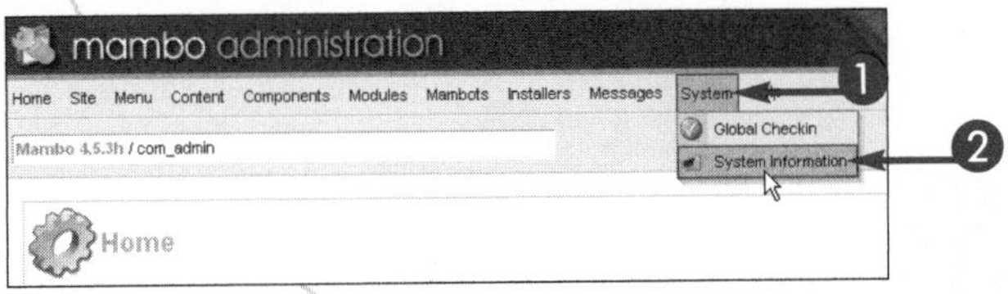

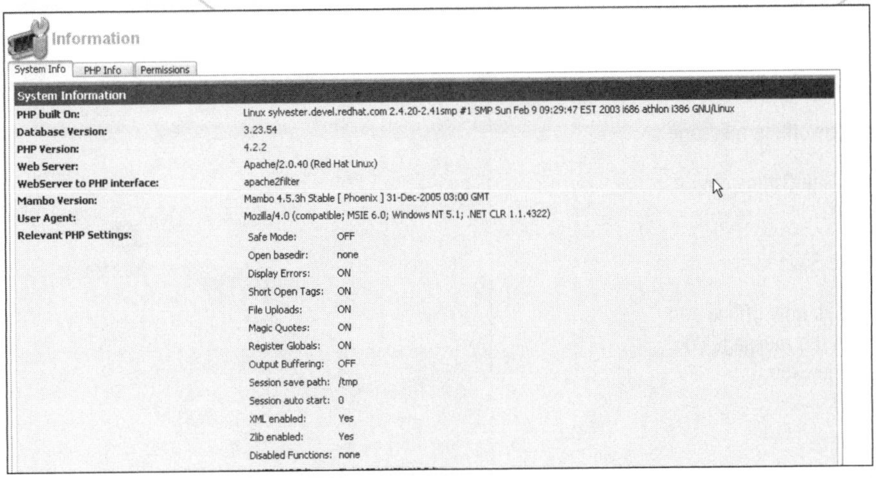

Take Your Site Offline

You can hide your Web site from view by selecting the Site Offline option in the Global Configuration screen. This command is most useful when you are making extensive changes to the site and you do not want to confuse visitors or let them see the work in progress. This feature should also be used while patching the system so that no users are currently using Mambo site resources that are to be updated with the new patch. It is possible that if the site is left online during a patch that some files may not be updated as expected.

When a site is taken offline by means of the Site Offline command, visitors may still come to the site, but instead of being greeted by the standard home page, they see only a single Web page with a message on it. The system provides a default message, or you can create a custom message.

The effect of taking a site offline is immediate. Site visitors browsing the site will see the site content disappear and a temporary page in its place. Even users who are logged in to the system will find only the temporary page. The immediate effects of this command open up the possibility for unintended side effects. Users who are in the middle of a task may not be able to complete their task. Accordingly, you should use this command with due deference to the users in order to keep disruption to a minimum.

When the time comes to restore the site for the public, you only need to change the state of the Site Offline option and your site immediately becomes accessible again.

Take Your Site Offline

1. Click Site.
2. Click Global Configuration.

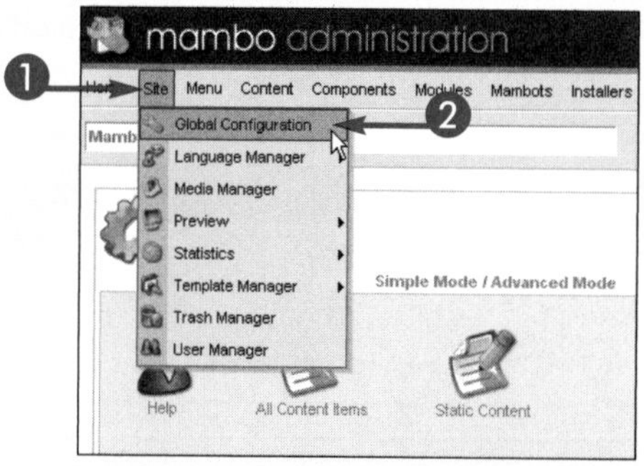

The Global Configuration page loads.

3. Type your offline message.
4. For the Site Offline option, click Yes.
5. Click the Save icon.

The site is now offline and displays the message you entered in Step 3.

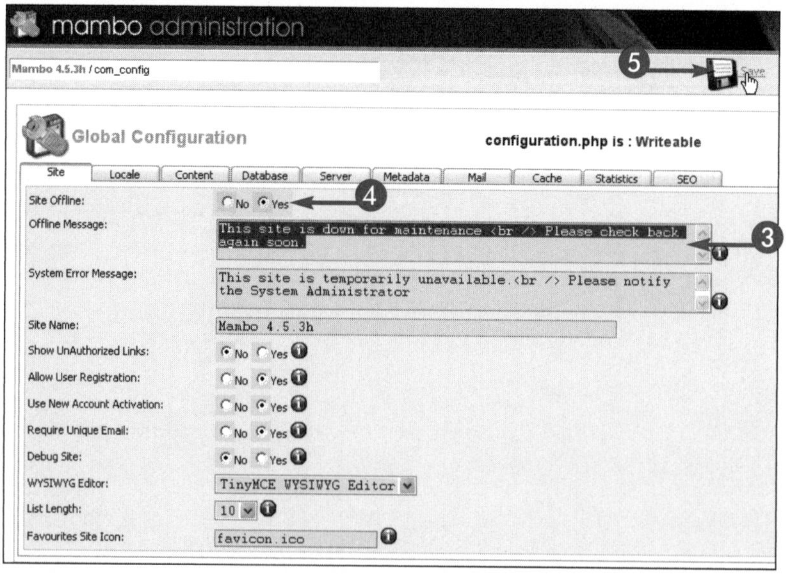

Enable Write Permissions on Files

You must enable write permissions on key files and directories to make certain types of changes to the Mambo system. During the installation process, the Mambo installer requires that the permissions on certain directories be set to allow the installer to write to the directories. Once you install the system, you may still need to enable write permissions on some files in order to make changes to those files. For example, you must make the configuration.php file write-enabled if you want to make changes to your Global Configuration settings. Editing template files similarly requires that you set certain files within the template directories to allow the system to write to the files.

Unfortunately, you cannot change the permissions of files that already exist in the system from inside the Mambo system. You must access the files in another manner to make the required adjustments. You typically change a file's permissions using an FTP program and the CHMOD command. While some users can perform this task via their Web host's control panel and file manager, the CHMOD command is the standard approach to managing file permissions and is explained in this section.

For new files, you can use the Global Configuration Manager to enable Mambo to set file permissions automatically; this process is explained in Chapter 2. As noted in Chapter 2, the use of a blanket approach to setting file permissions is a potential security risk. The best practice is to execute the necessary changes on a case-by-case basis, and when you have finished making your changes to the file, you should remove the write permissions, unless they are necessary for system functions.

Enable Write Permissions on Files

1. Access your site via FTP.
2. Select the file you want to modify.
3. View Properties.

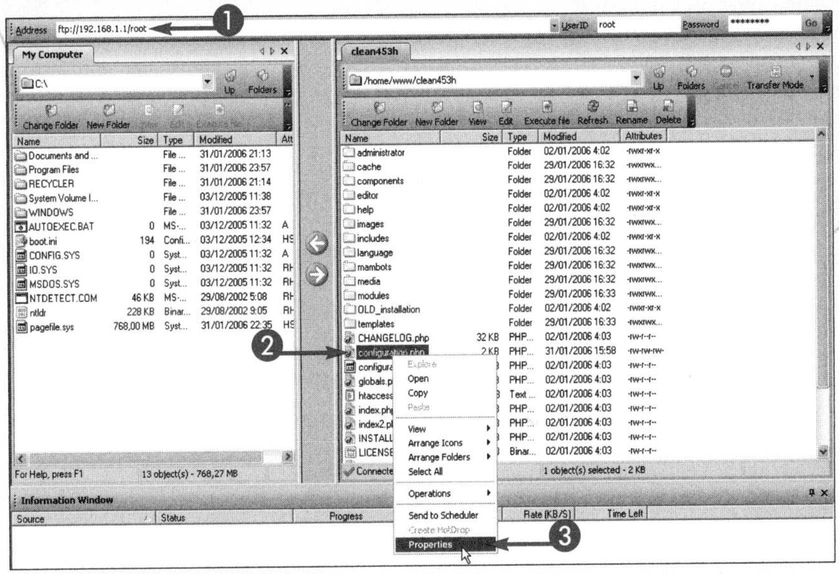

The Properties window displays permissions.

4. Change the numerical value to **777**.
5. Click OK.

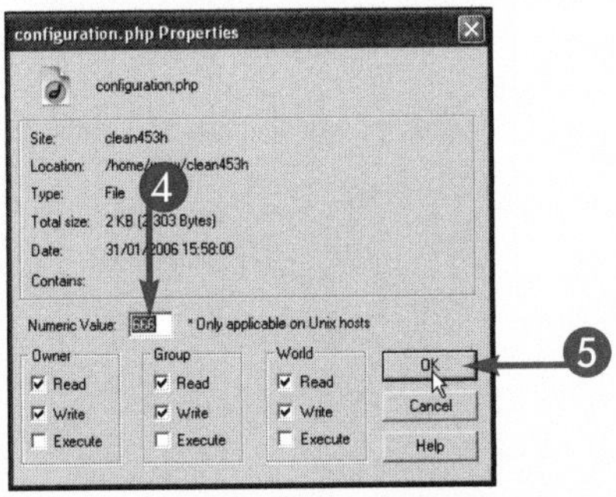

The Right Tools for the Job

Mambo is not dependent on a particular toolset and allows you to work with virtually anything you choose. Still, some tools do work better than others and, perhaps more importantly, some tools make administering the site faster and easier.

Browser

You can view the admin system of a Mambo Web site with any browser. However, certain tools, particularly the WYSIWYG editor, perform best with either the Microsoft Internet Explorer browser or the Mozilla Firefox browser. Accordingly, for admin purposes, only those browsers are recommended. Note that this has nothing to do with the front end of the Web site. Visitors to a Mambo site can still enjoy the site equally well on any browser or system.

Regardless of whether you choose IE or Firefox, you should always try to have a copy of other popular browsers on your machine so that you can check the display of the front end of your site from browser to browser. If you want to serve the broadest sample of viewers, you should always check the site on IE, Firefox, Safari, and Opera.

FTP Client

An FTP client is an optional tool, but one that sometimes comes in handy. FTP is a method of moving files back and forth between your local computer and the server. An FTP client is a program that uses FTP to move files. Some people may need FTP to move the Mambo installation files to their server. Other people will find Mambo already installed by their Web host or the Web developer. Even in the latter situation, having an FTP client at your disposal can make certain tasks simpler or faster. For example, you can move a large number of image files to your server faster with FTP than with the Mambo Media Manager. An FTP client is also useful for managing file permissions, as discussed in the earlier section "Enable Write Permissions on Files."

There is a wide variety of FTP clients available. While this book uses WS FTP Pro for the examples in this book, virtually any client can perform the same tasks.

HTML Editor

You do not need an HTML editor to manage content in Mambo; the WYSIWYG editor handles all of the formatting for you. HTML skills, however, are very useful if you want to work on content offline. With an HTML editor, you can work on a Content Item offline and then move the item, complete with HTML tags, into the content editor window. This approach to content management can save time. If you live in a narrow-bandwidth environment, you will find that working on content offline, rather than editing it on the server, not only saves time, but also much frustration.

Although a new user may find Adobe's Dreamweaver a bit intimidating, it is an excellent HTML editor. One of the nice options available for Dreamweaver users is the Mambo extension, which you can download from http://source.mambo-foundation.org. The extension automates the insertion of module placeholders and generic header materials necessary to build Mambo templates. Although the extension is limited in its capabilities, it can help you create (or convert) Mambo templates and is therefore a timesaver worth investigating.

If you do not know how to use Dreamweaver, you may want to take the time to learn; but if not, stick with your favorite editor.

Before You Get Started

One of the best things about Mambo is that the system is designed to tolerate reasonable amounts of misuse without faltering. Nonetheless, to avoid problems, there are a few basic principles you should keep in mind while operating a Mambo system. Some of the points covered in this section are basic ideas that apply to any server-based system, and others are unique to Mambo. All of the points relate to good work habits, and you cannot go wrong by respecting these simple rules.

Be Secure

To preserve your security, observe the following practices:

- Do not disclose your password to others.
- Always log out when you walk away from the computer — if you do not, others can use your open access to make changes to the system, including creating a new username and password for themselves, or locking you out of the system!
- Do not allow the browser to remember the username and password for you, unless the computer is secure and restricted to only your access.
- When you finish working, always log off.
- Subscribe to the Mambo Security Announcements mailing list to stay updated of security issues. To join the list, send an e-mail to security-notification@mambo-foundation.org.

Stay in Step

Mambo is a dynamic Open Source project, and that means new versions are released periodically. Sometimes new releases are optional. In other cases, a new release may be a patch or a response to a security vulnerability. Best practice is to stay in step with the most current version of the software. Periodically visit the official Mambo sites for new developments.

When in Doubt, Back it Up!

Back up your system periodically. For most users, backing up the database is sufficient. Mambo provides a backup mechanism in the default installation — use it regularly and keep the copies of the backup safe. Users who make extensive modifications to files in the Mambo system may want to maintain a full backup, or at least copies of all files they have modified. Backups of changed files can also make your life easier when the time comes to upgrade your Mambo site to a new version.

Keep it Clean

Cutting and pasting text into Mambo directly from Microsoft Word is not recommended. Word includes a wide range of unnecessary HTML tags. If you cut and paste directly from Word, unnecessary code pastes with it. The bloated Word text can increase page size significantly — sometimes by up to 200 percent! So even though pasted Word text retains most of its formatting, it does so at the cost of page size. Your site will slow down and be harder to maintain in the future.

There are three solutions:

- Cut the text from the Word document, and then paste it into Notepad or another very basic text editor. Doing so strips out all the formatting. Next, cut the text from the Notepad document and paste into Mambo. This cleans the code. You can format the text using the Mambo formatting commands.
- Format your text using an external HTML editor, then move the HTML code as a whole into the editor window.
- Some WYSIWYG editors include a "Clean Up Word HTML" button. If you cut and paste from Word, you can then highlight the text and click the button to execute an automatic clean up. This generally works pretty well.

An Introduction to the Global Configuration Manager

You can use the Global Configuration Manager to make fundamental changes to your site. The choices on the various screens in the Global Configuration Manager enable a wide range of options for content layout, site display, and related functions. Mambo sets many of the items in Global Configuration when you install the site, and you probably will not have to adjust them again for the life of the site. You may, however, periodically change some of the other items depending on the needs of the Site Administrator.

The Global Configuration Manager is a powerful tool, and, accordingly, misuse of its options can take your site offline or even crash it, making it inaccessible to every user. You should, therefore, restrict access to only those users who belong to the Super Administrator group. You should not change settings relating to the server and the database unless you have a clear understanding of the implications and you appreciate how to fix any problems you may create; this is not one of the areas in Mambo where it is safe to make changes at random to learn from the results.

A Site

Take your site offline, set up user registration, name the site, set up a WYSIWYG editor, and control list lengths and the favicon.

B Locale

Sets the language encoding for the site and provides time offset to overcome local server time.

C Content

Contains a variety of options relating to the display of Content Items.

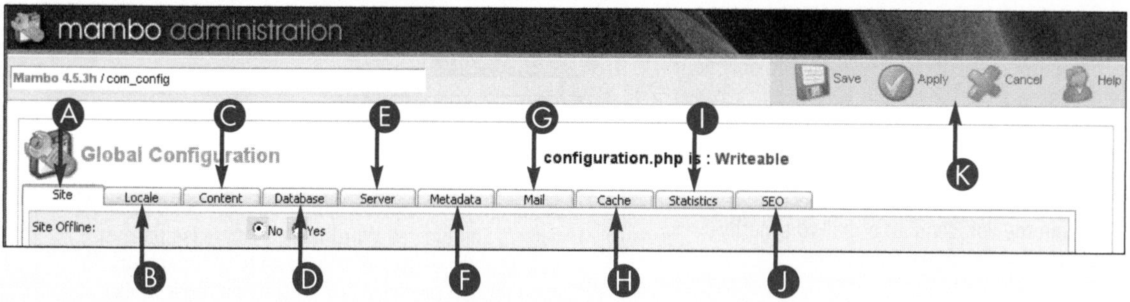

D Database

Provides basic information about the MySQL database that your site uses.

E Server

Has basic server information, such as your absolute path, and options to enable GZip page compression, alter login session length, report errors, register globals, link to the help server, and control file permissions.

F Metadata

Sets the global metadata for your site.

G Mail

Configures how the Mambo system sends mail.

H Cache

Has controls to enable and set caching.

I Statistics

Lists options for recording system statistics, such as page views and search strings.

J SEO

Activates search-engine-friendly URLs and dynamic page titles.

K Main Toolbar

Has icons for saving changes, applying changes without exiting, canceling any action in progress without saving, and exiting the Global Configuration Manager.

Change the Site Name

You can change the name of your site using the Global Configuration Manager. Modifying the site name is desirable to enhance or refocus your branding or to simply make a change for the sake of variety. Some site owners use the feature to add keywords and concepts to the page titles in hopes of enhancing their search engine rankings.

During installation, the Mambo installer prompts you to give a name to your site. You can change the name entered during installation at any time from the Global Configuration Site tab. The site name appears on visitors' browser title bars as they view each page of the site. The name also appears in emails that the system generates. Many search engines index the site name as they index the page titles; therefore the information you put into the Site Name field appears in the search results of search engines, including those of Google.

The system does not put a limit on the length of the site name. However, as a practical matter, remember that 135 characters is the maximum that fits in the title bar of a browser when the viewer's display resolution is set to 1024 x 768. If the visitor's display resolution is set lower, the number of visible characters is considerably less. For search engine purposes, remember that Google only displays the first 66 characters of a page title.

Note also that because the system-generated email uses the site name, an extremely long site name can be inconvenient. Also, remember that the Site Name function is merely a description that the system uses. The Mambo Site Name function has no impact on the domain name, or URL, of your Web site.

Change the Site Name

1. Click Site.
2. Click Global Configuration.

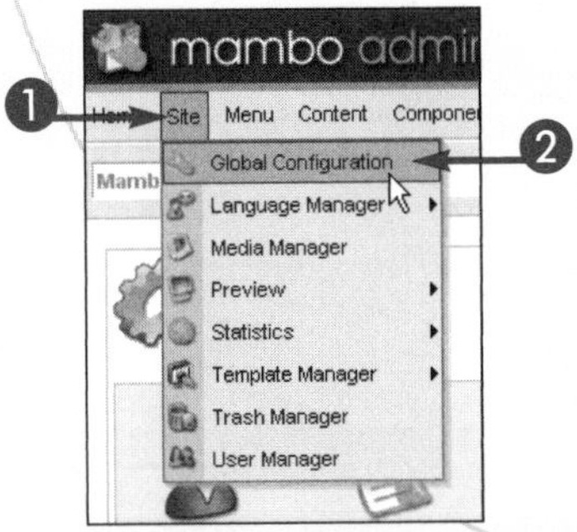

The Global Configuration Manager loads.

3. Click the Site tab.
4. Type a site name.
5. Click the Save icon.

Mambo changes the site name and the system takes you to the Control Panel.

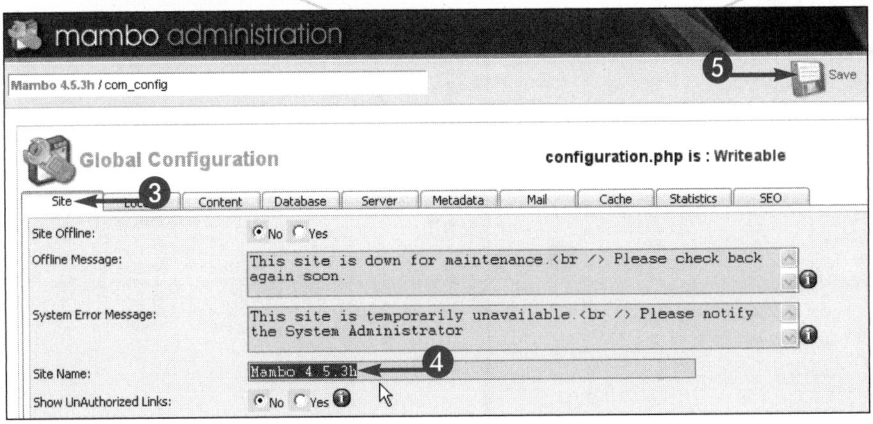

Set a Favicon

You can change a site's favorites icon from the Global Configuration Site tab. The favorites icon, or favicon, appears next to a site's name in the browser bookmarks list. In some browsers the favicon also appears when you view the site, either on a tab or in the address bar. You can change the default favicon to a unique image that reflects your brand or your site's identity.

The Mambo system uses the Mambo flower as the default favicon for all sites. The default installation shows this favicon and continues to do so unless you take steps to replace it. The Site Favorites Icon control on the Global Configuration Site tab allows you to specify a new favicon, but you must first upload one into the system. The best course is to delete the old favicon file first, then upload your new favicon. To hide the Mambo favicon and display no favicon on your site, simply leaving the Site Favorites Icon field blank does not do the job. Mambo is persistent and continues to display the default icon if you leave the Site Favorites Icon field blank. To defeat the default favicon, you must either upload one of your own, or you must delete the default favicon file from the Mambo/images directory. Remember, if you upload a new file, use the same name or some browsers may fail to recognize and display the new favicon file.

Set a Favicon

1. Access your server by FTP.
2. Open the images directory.

   The list of the directory's contents appears.
3. Rename the favicon.ico file.

   Alternatively, you can delete the file if you prefer.

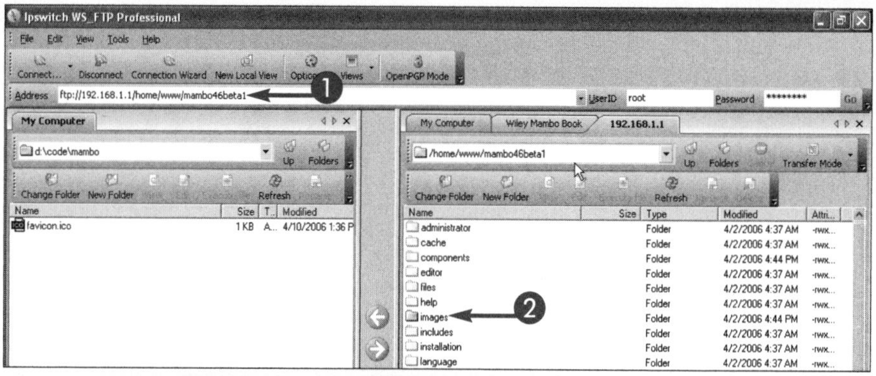

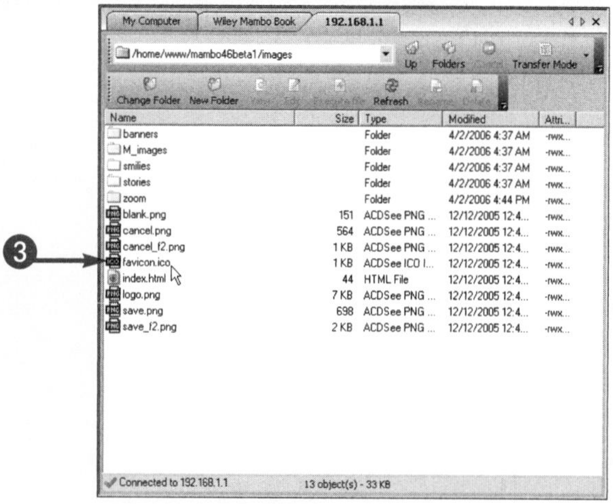

4. Locate the new favicon file on your local machine.

5. Upload a new favicon.ico file to the server.

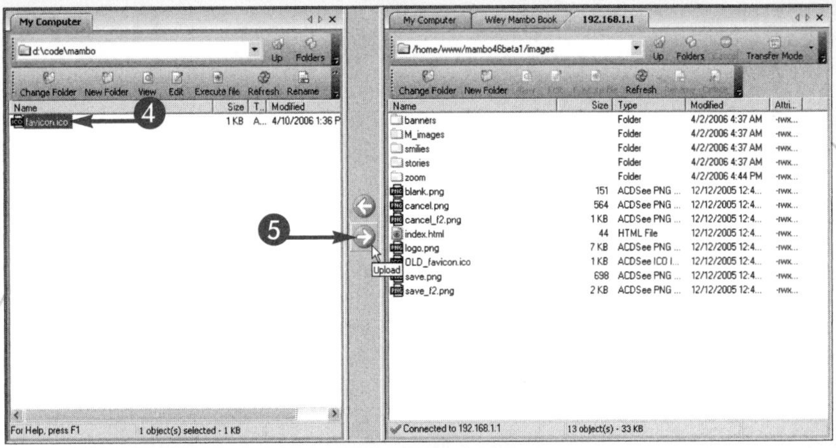

- The new favicon.ico file is now in the system.

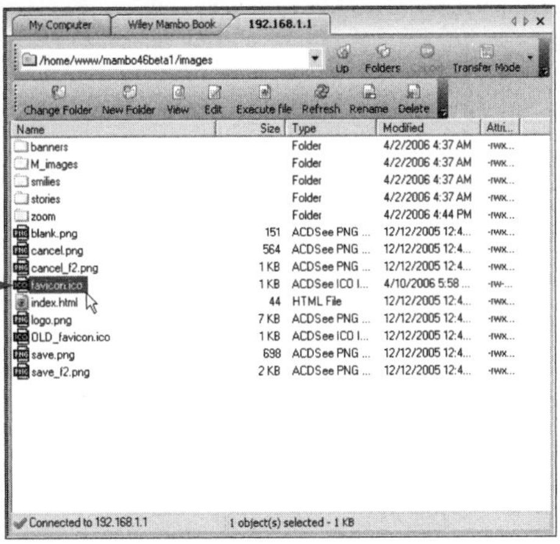

Apply It

Making your own favicon is a relatively straightforward task. To begin, open your favorite image-editing application, and then either open the artwork you want to modify or create a new image. You can start with any size image you like, but the end result must be 16 x 16 pixels. As a result of the size constraint, a square image or canvas often works best. Note also that your favicon can use up to 256 colors, but the maximum file size is 1046 bytes.

When you finish working on your graphic, scale it to 16 x 16 pixels. Save the graphic as a GIF or JPG. For the next step, you need an icon editor or graphics converter. Irfan View is a good free icon editor that can handle the formats you need for this job.

Use Irfan View, or whatever icon editor you choose, to open up the 16-x-16-pixel logo you just created. Click File and then Save As. Make sure you save the file as favicon.ico. Once Irfan converts the file, you are ready to go.

Set Up a WYSIWYG Editor

You can choose between a plain text editor and an easy-to-use WYSIWYG editor for managing your Content Items. Enabling the WYSIWYG editor makes adding and editing content simpler, because the tool is designed to format items without the need to input HTML code. The editor also automates more complex tasks, like adding images, tables, and hyperlinks.

WYSIWYG stands for *What You See Is What You Get*. WYSIWYG editors allow you to select and apply formatting by clicking buttons instead of typing in codes. The editors also make it possible to view the formatting immediately in the same window. The functionality is very similar to what most people are used to from working with applications like Microsoft Word. In fact, most of the task buttons in the WYSIWYG editor use the same icons you would see in Word. The editor, therefore, makes it possible for anyone with basic skills to enter and format text quickly and accurately.

Mambo comes bundled with a powerful WYSIWYG editor called MOStlyCE. You enable the editor from the Global Configuration Site tab, but the configuration options for the editor are located under the Components menu. There are also a number of third-party WYSIWYG editors available for Mambo. You can add additional editors without difficulty, and you can switch between editors using the controls on the Site tab. For more information about the configuration of MOStlyCE, see Chapter 10.

You may also work without a WYSIWYG editor by using the plain text editor that is built into the system. The plain text editor has two advantages: First, it is the fastest-performing option because it does not have to load additional code, buttons, images, and so on. Second, for those who prefer to code by hand, the text editor is your best choice because it gives full control over the HTML formatting of the Content Items.

Set Up a WYSIWYG Editor

1. Load the Global Configuration Manager.

   Note: To open the Manager, see the section "Change the Site Name."

2. Click the Site tab.

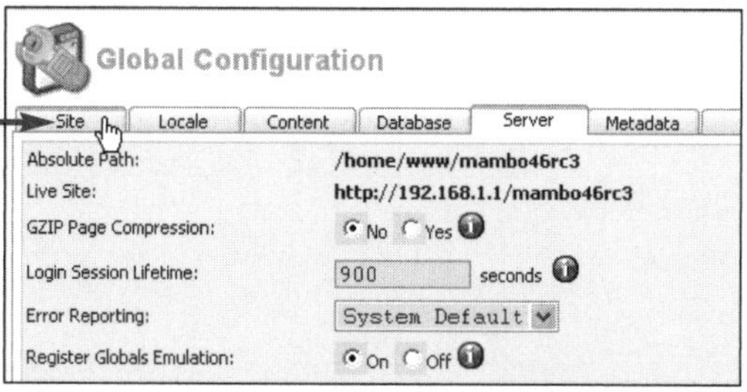

   The Site screen loads.

3. Click here and select WYSIWYG Editor.

4. Click the Save icon.

   Mambo enables the editor and the system takes you to the Control Panel.

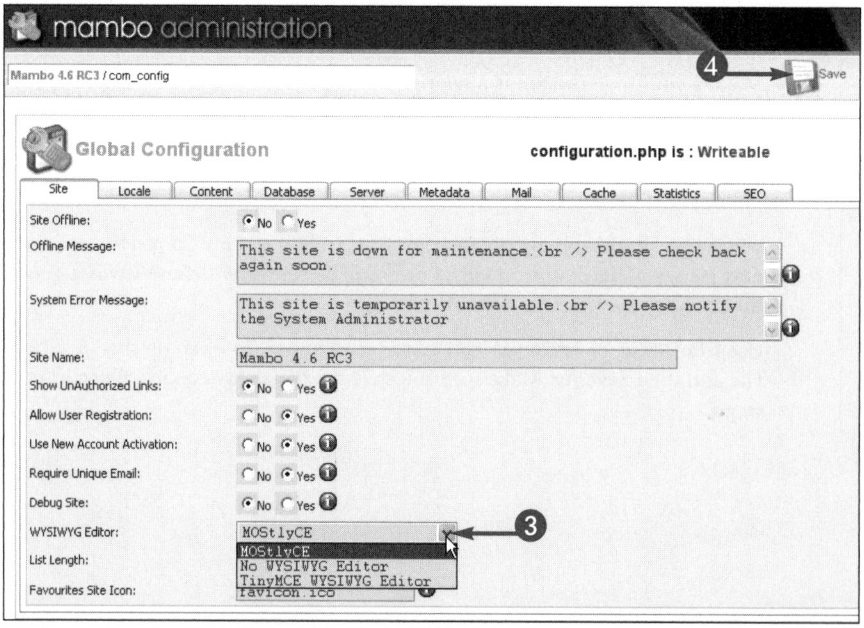

Change Time, Language, or Country Settings

You can localize the time and the language settings for your Mambo site. The ability to change the default language of the site allows you to customize your site for your audience and administrators. You can offset time settings to account for servers and audiences located in a different part of the world.

Mambo has the ability to handle multiple languages through the installation of language packs. The default installation comes bundled with only one language: English. When you install additional language packs, the Super Administrator can activate an alternative default language using the Language control on the Locale tab in the Global Configuration Manager. For more information about installing language packs, see Chapter 15.

When you change the default language of the site, you should also change the Country Locale setting from the default "en_GB." The default setting reflects English as per the conventions of Great Britain. You should change the setting to mirror the default language pack selected. You find the Country Local control on the Locale tab in the Global Configuration Manager.

In many cases, the server on which the site is installed is located in a different time zone than the target audience. Mambo lets you adjust the time used on the site by offsetting the server's time stamp. The time stamp appears on Content Items with the creation date and modified date. Some components and modules also use the time stamp. The time offset control is located on the Locale tab in the Global Configuration Manager. Note that if you mouse over the info icon next to the Time Offset combo box, a popup appears and shows you the current time, as per the current setting of the Time Offset control.

Change Time, Language, or Country Settings

1. Load the Global Configuration Manager.

Note: To open the Manager, see the section "Change the Site Name."

2. Click the Locale tab.

The Locale screen loads.

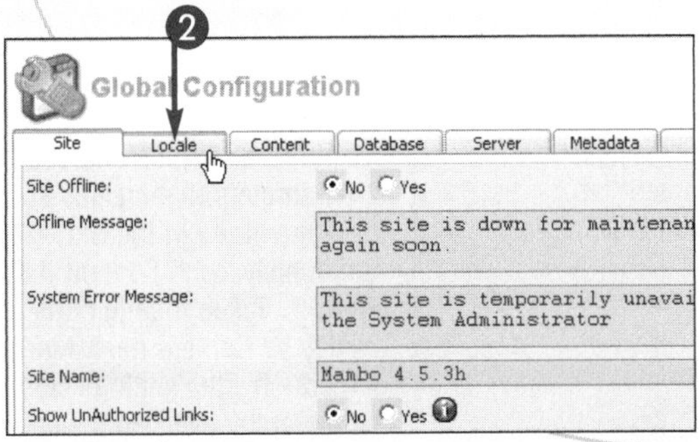

3. Click here and select a language.
4. Click here to set the time offset.
5. Click here to set the country locale.
6. Click the Save icon.

Mambo saves the changes you made and the system takes you back to the Control Panel.

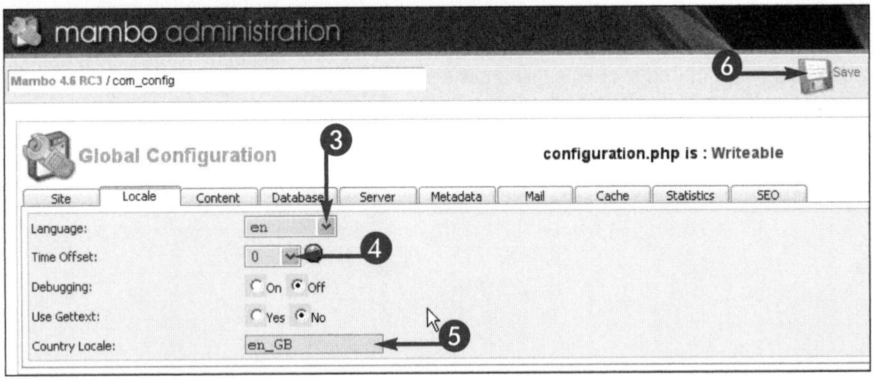

Configure Content Item Display

You can use the Global Configuration Manager to establish the default display of Content Items. The controls on the Content tab provide an assortment of choices affecting the display of author information, publication data, navigation, and related options for Content Items. Setting the options in the Global Configuration Manager creates defaults that automatically apply each time you create a new Content Item.

Understanding Content Tab Options

When you create a new Content Item, the Mambo system applies the default options set in the Global Configuration Manager, unless they have been overridden elsewhere. Therefore, you should use the Content tab controls to set the options in the manner you want to see them displayed in the majority of the cases on the site. Setting up the options properly saves you time and gives the site consistency and improved usability.

The majority of the options available on the Content tab allow you to specify information or functionality that appears on the Content Items themselves. For example, Item Rating Voting enables site visitors to rate Content Items on a scale of one to five. You can add additional functionality to Content Items by displaying PDF icons, Print and Email-to-a-friend icons, or text links. Navigation options for Content Items are set from the Content tab, including the options that control the manner in which multi-page content appears.

Content Tables Formatting

Some of the commands also impact the display of content tables, that is, the lists of Content Items that show a site visitor the contents of a particular category. Specifically, the commands relating to the author name, the creation date, and the number of hits all affect the content tables. For more on creating content tables, see Chapter 9.

The Linked Titles and Read More Link Commands

The Linked Titles and Read More Link commands have a narrower function than the other options on the Content tab. Linked Titles and the Read More Link are only applicable to Content Items that employ both Intro Text and Main Text. If a Content Item uses only the Intro Text field, and not the optional Main Text field, then the Linked Titles and Read More Link commands have no effect on the Content Item.

Overriding the Global Defaults

Once you set the global defaults, you can override them at several levels. The Menu editing screen presents a choice of parameters that include some of the options listed on the Content tab in the Global Configuration Manager. Additionally, each Content Item has a set of Parameter controls. Taken together, the options allow you to vary the display by Content Item, Menu Item, or globally. In terms of hierarchy, the settings closest to the Content Item in the hierarchy override the settings further down the chain. In other words, Content Item parameters are the highest priority, with Menu Items next. The lowest level in the hierarchy is the Global Configuration settings. To learn more about managing Menu Items, see Chapter 9. For more on Content Item parameters, see Chapter 6.

Enable Intro Text Links

You can control the appearance of the links leading from the Intro Text in Content Items. Mambo allows you to create Content Items that have either one or two parts. The first part, and the only required part, is the Intro Text. If your article is short, or you are writing a blog-type site, you may want to use only Intro Text. If you are writing longer Content Items you will probably use both the Intro Text and the Main Text. Main Text is literally an extended version of the article, or a continuation of the Intro Text. If you use both Intro Text and Main Text, you must make a link between the two parts of the Content Items. The Global Configuration Manager Content tab gives you two options for making those links automatically.

One option for linking between Intro Text and Main Text is the use of Linked Titles. If you select the Linked Titles option on the Content tab, the Content Item titles become hyperlinks that take you to the page that contains the Main Text of the Content Item. If you do not select this option, the titles appear as normal titles, with no hyperlink.

The second option for linking between Intro Text and Main Text is the Read More Link option. As the name implies, when you select this option, the phrase Read More appears at the end of the Intro Text. The phrase is hyperlinked, so that when users click Read More they are taken to the page containing the Main Text of the Content Item.

You can elect to use one, both, or neither of the options for Intro Text links.

Enable Intro Text Links

1. Load the Global Configuration Manager.

Note: To open the Manager, see the section "Change the Site Name."

2. Click the Content tab.

   The Content screen loads.

3. Click a preference for the Linked Titles option.

4. Click a preference for the Read More Link option.

5. Click the Save icon.

   Mambo saves the choices and the system takes you back to the Control Panel.

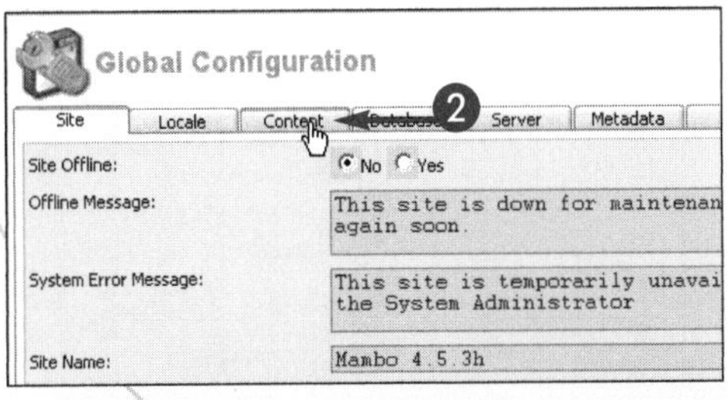

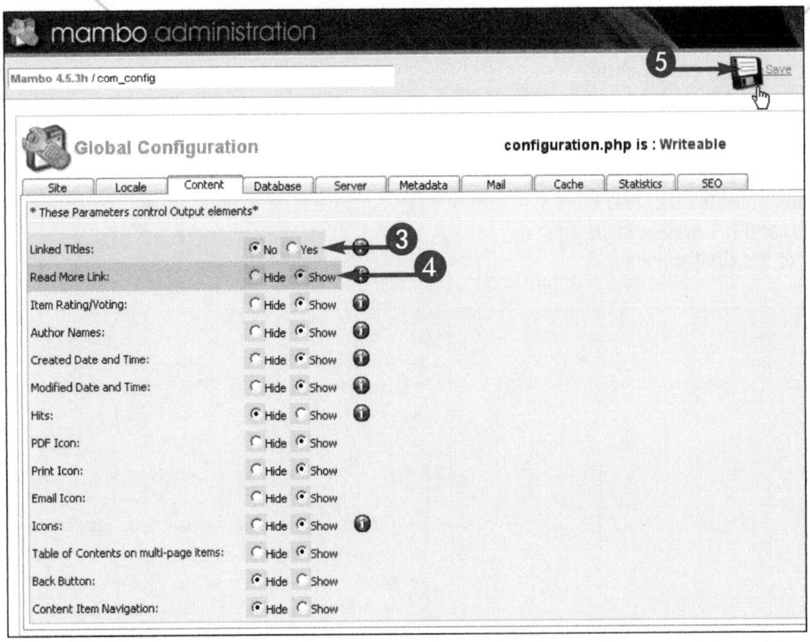

Enable Item Rating

You can allow visitors to rate the Content Items on your site on a scale of one to five. Ratings are a simple and effective way to engage users and add interactivity to a Web site. A Content Item voting mechanism is included in the default Mambo system, and you can turn it on and off at any time.

You enable Content Item voting through the Content tab of the Global Configuration Manager. Once enabled, the Content Item voting feature appears on all Content Items on the site. You can override the control at the Content Item level, meaning that it is possible to turn on rating for some items and turn it off for others by setting the parameters for individual Content Items. For more information about overriding the global settings, see Chapter 6.

When you activate the ratings option, Content Items display the users' ratings underneath the item title. If users have not cast votes, the rating simply shows as blank. The ratings scale ranges from one, for poor, to five for best. Users who want to vote can select the score they want to give the item and then select the Rate button. Mambo instantly averages the vote into the previous votes and displays the results under the title of the Content Item.

Ratings that users give to the Content Items apply for the life of the item. There is no mechanism for editing or resetting the Content Item ratings. If you do not want the rating to show any more, you can use the Content Item parameters and disable the feature for that Content Item.

Enable Item Rating

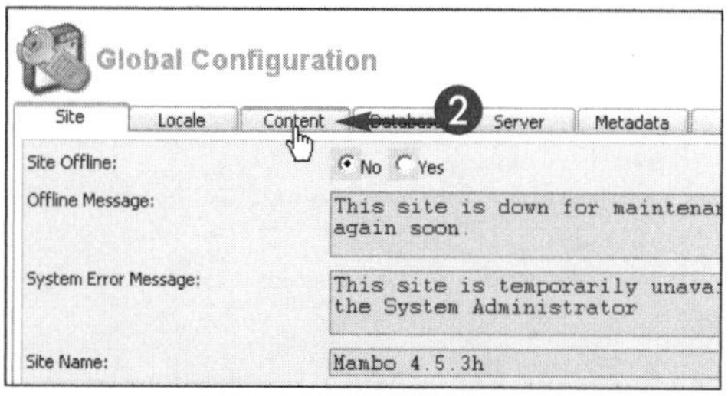

1. Load the Global Configuration Manager.

Note: To open the Manager, see the section "Change the Site Name."

2. Click the Content tab.

   The Content screen loads.

3. Click the Show option of the Item Rating/Voting item.

4. Click the Save icon.

   Mambo activates the Item Rating and the system takes you back to the Control Panel.

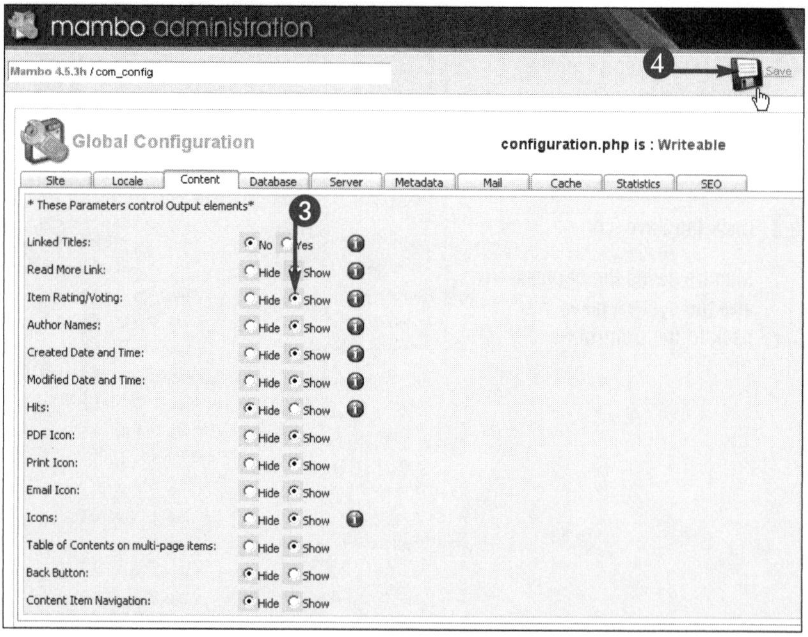

Display Author Information

You can use the Author Name control on the Content tab of the Global Configuration Manager to hide or display the names of the authors of Content Items on your Web site. Displaying the authors' names along with your Content Items is a good way to humanize your site and to improve accountability. Visitors tend to trust content more when there is a person's name associated with it. Nonetheless, in some situations, you may not want to display the authors' names, particularly where the site has only one author or in cases where you want to maintain a cleaner interface with less clutter.

The Author Name option located in the Global Configuration Manager is very limited in functionality; it can only show or hide the name. When you set the Author Name to the Show option, the system automatically displays the name of the person who created the Content Item as the author of the Content Item. The system assumes that the creator is the person who is logged in. If someone else uses your login to create an item, the item shows your name as the author. To escape the system's default assumptions for an individual Content Item, you must override the Global Configuration settings through the controls that are available in the parameters and publishing tabs of individual Content Items. For more information on overriding the global settings for individual Content Items, see Chapter 6.

Note that the placement of the author name is fixed, which means you cannot move it. The name appears under the title of the Content Item. If you want the name to appear elsewhere, you cannot use the automatic Author Name option.

Display Author Information

1. Load the Global Configuration Manager.

Note: To open the Manager, see the section "Change the Site Name."

2. Click the Content tab.

   The Content screen loads.

3. For the Author Name option, click a preference.

4. Click the Save icon.

   Mambo saves the selection and the system takes you back to the Control Panel.

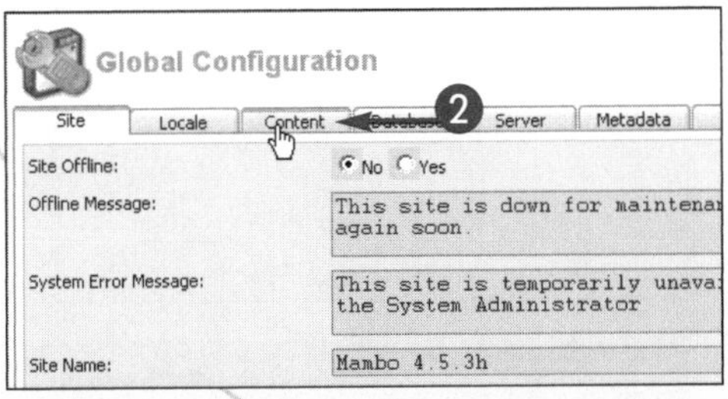

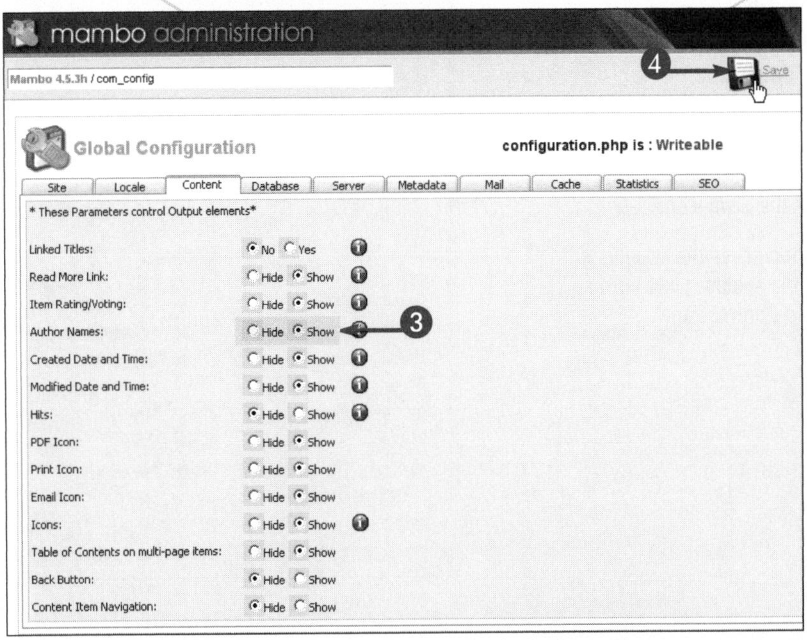

Display Content Publication Information

You can automatically display both the creation date and the date a Content Item was last modified. Displaying content creation and update information gives visitors some context for the content and helps them assess how active the site is and whether the information it contains is up to date. The Content tab in the Global Configuration Manager allows you to set the default state for the publication information options. You can override the global Creation Date controls at the Content Item level.

Two options are presented on the Content tab. One option allows you to show or hide the Created Date and Time. Another option allows you to show or hide the Modified Date and Time. Selection of the values on the Global Configuration Manager sets the default state for all Content Items; but if you want to change created date settings for an individual Content Item, you may do so by way of the Parameters setting on any Content Item.

The time and date the system uses for both Content Creation and Date Modified are automatically generated based on the date and time the creation or modification occurred. In some situations you may want to alter the creation date. You can specify the Creation Date on the Parameters for an individual Content Item by entering the desired date in the Override Created Date field. Note that you cannot alter the time stamp or the Modified Date and Time data. For more on overriding the system's publication information, see Chapter 6.

Typically the Creation Date appears at the top of the article under the Title. The Modified Date and Time appears immediately below the article.

Display Content Publication Information

1. Load the Global Configuration Manager.

Note: To open the Manager, see the section "Change the Site Name."

2. Click the Content tab.

   The Content screen loads.

3. Click either the Hide or Show option for the Created Date and Time item.

4. Click a preference for the Modified Date and Time option.

5. Click the Save icon.

   Mambo saves the selections and the system takes you back to the Control Panel.

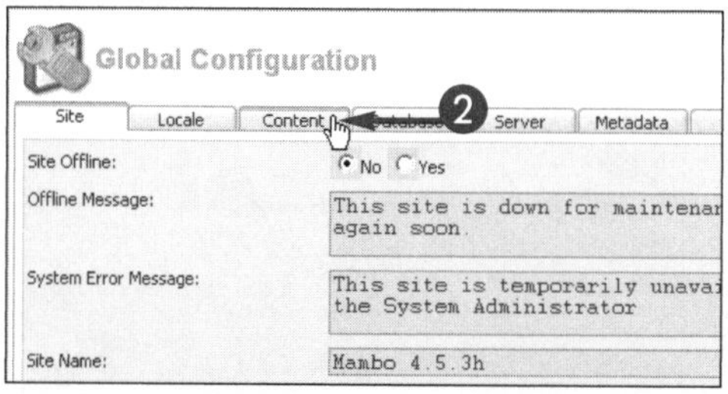

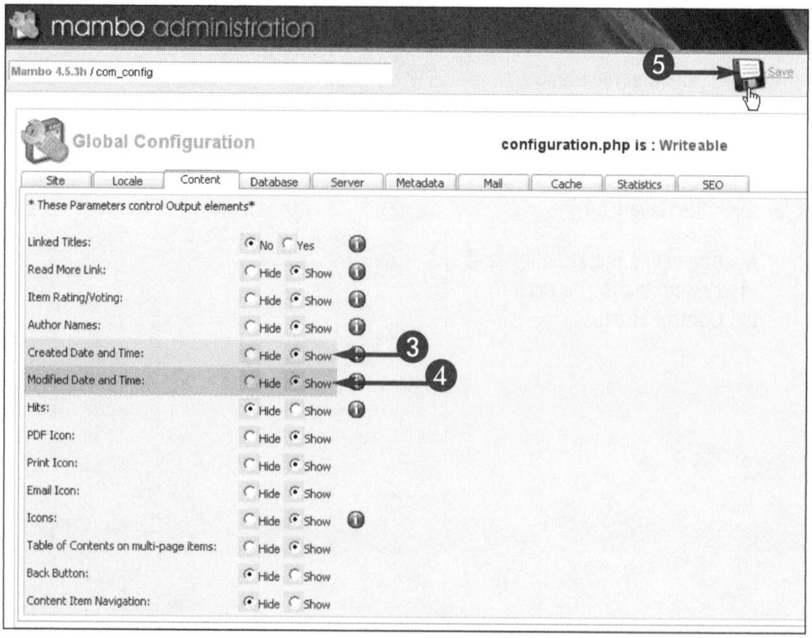

Activate PDF, Print, and Email Features

You can configure your Mambo site to offer users a variety of helpful tools for Content Items. Mambo can automatically turn Content Items into PDFs, print Content Items in a convenient and readable format, and notify other people about the Content Items via email. You can set the options for each function for the entire site via the Content tab in the Global Configuration Manager. You can override the individual options at the item level. For more information about overriding the global settings, see Chapter 6.

The PDF, Print, and Email to a Friend features are automatic features in the default Mambo system. You can switch each feature on or off independently. When switched on, the feature appears on each Content Item. Mambo indicates the feature either by an icon, or by a text link located at the top right of the Content Item near the title. Activating the icon or the text link initiates the action.

While the Content tab sets the default options for all Content Items, you can override the global settings. The Content tab allows you to change the settings for one or more of the features. Changes to the options in the tab apply only to that one Content Item. The system gives you the flexibility to match the features to appropriate items and to add variety and functionality to your site while avoiding unnecessary clutter.

The Icons control on the Content tab specifies whether the system employs icons or text links to indicate the PDF, Print, and Email to a Friend functions. The functionality is the same with either icons or text; only the presentation of the link changes.

Activate PDF, Print, and Email Features

1. Load the Global Configuration Manager.

Note: To open the Manager, see the section "Change the Site Name."

2. Click the Content tab.

   The Content screen loads.

3. Click a preference for the PDF icon, Print icon, Email icon, or Icons option.

4. Click the Save icon.

   Mambo saves the choices and the system takes you back to the Control Panel.

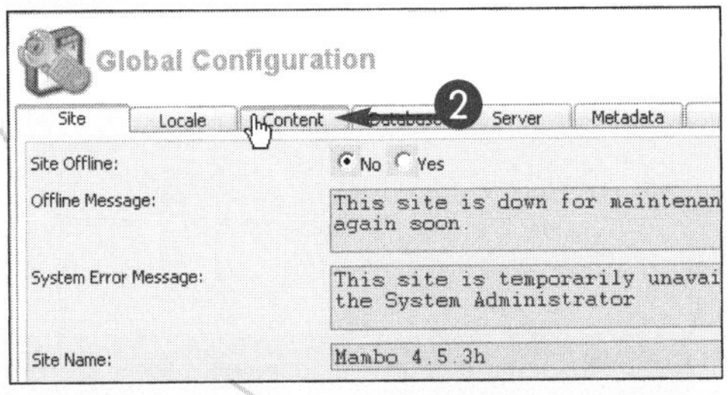

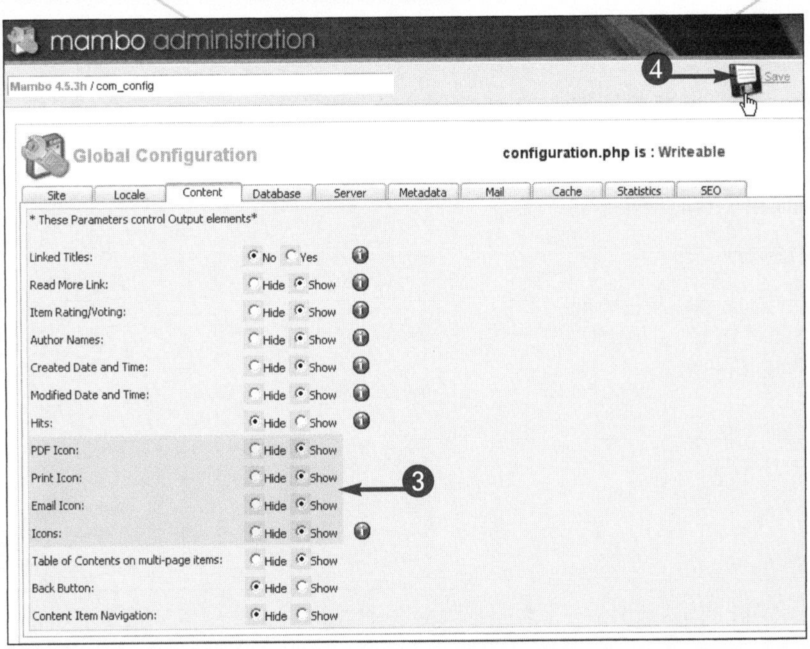

Configure Content Navigation Options

You can use the Global Configuration Manager to set navigation options for the pages on your Web site. The Content tab includes three options that allow you to add navigational controls on Content Items. The use of basic navigational controls allows users to move more easily between Content Items and thereby enhances the usability of your site.

The Content tab includes three options that affect navigation. The first option is Table of Contents on multi-page items. As the name implies, the option is only applicable if you are creating multi-page Content Items. If you enable this choice, multi-page Content Items automatically display a table of contents on each page. Inside the table of contents are links to each page of that particular Content Item. This is a very useful feature and is commonly seen on publication-oriented Web sites.

The second option is a Back Button. The two choices are Show and Hide. The Show option allows you to include a Back button at the bottom of all the pages on the site. When users activate the Back button, they are taken to the page they viewed previously.

The third choice, Content Item Navigation, gives you the option to either show or hide navigation. If you choose Show for the Content Item Navigation option, then each Content Item includes a previous and a next button that allows users to move through the site contents. The feature is particularly useful on sites where the content bears some logical sequential relationship.

You can override some of the controls at either the Menu Item or Content Item levels. Overriding the global choices allows you to turn the feature on for some items, and off for others.

Configure Content Navigation Options

1. Load the Global Configuration Manager.

Note: To open the Manager, see the section "Change the Site Name."

2. Click the Content tab.

   The Content screen loads.

3. Click a preference for the Table of Contents option.
4. Click a preference for the Back Button option.
5. Click a preference for the Content Item Navigation option.
6. Click the Save icon.

   Mambo saves the choices and the system takes you back to the Control Panel.

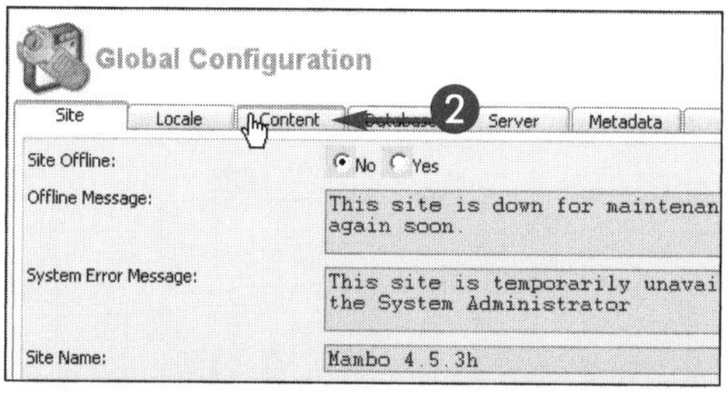

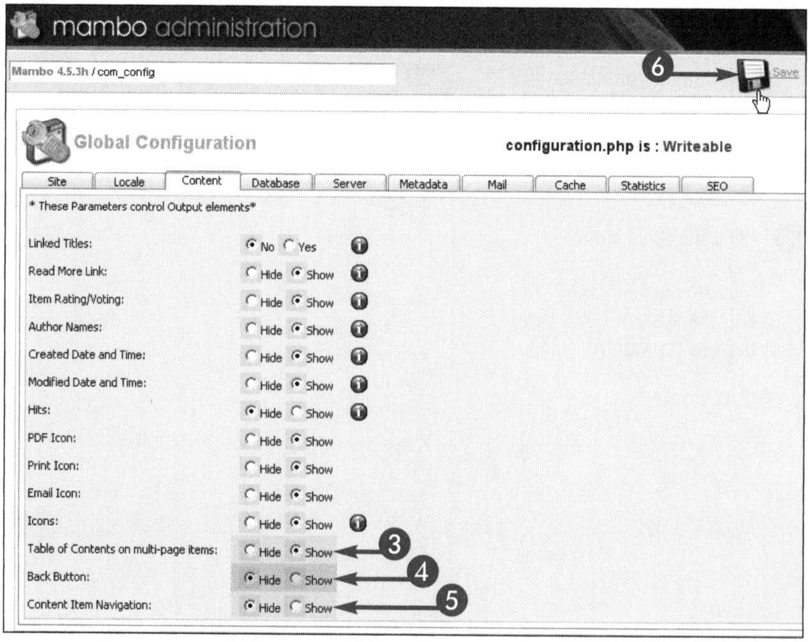

Configure Database Options

You can change the information that the Mambo system uses to connect with the MySQL database. This command is useful in cases where you have set up a second database and want to point your site to the new database. It is also useful in cases where you want to change your database access information for security purposes.

You can gain access to your database connection information via the Database tab in the Global Configuration Manager. On the Database tab, you have options for viewing or changing your Hostname, MySQL username, password, and database name. You can also change the MySQL Database Prefix, which relates to the table names that the Mambo installer creates.

You must use the controls on the Database tab with caution; this is one area of the site where you cannot experiment freely. You should never change the basic information relating to your hostname and MySQL connection details unless you know what you are doing and have made the parallel changes to your database. If you change these details without changing the information at the database itself, your site will crash and prevent you from viewing the site or logging in to the admin system. Similarly, changing the database prefix will crash the site if the new prefix does not point to a valid database.

The controls on the Database tab are invaluable should you need to change your MySQL username or password for security reasons. The database prefix option is useful if you are running more than one Mambo installation on your MySQL system. In the latter situation, you can set up one Mambo system using the default "mos_" prefix and any subsequent installations using a different prefix.

Configure Database Options

1. Load the Global Configuration Manager.

Note: To open the Manager, see the section "Change the Site Name."

2. Click the Database Tab.

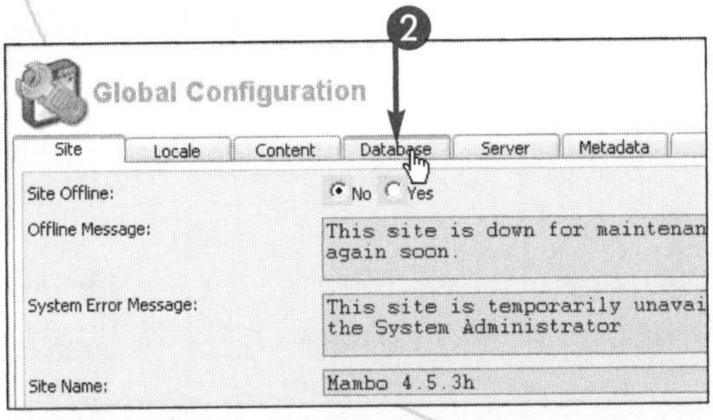

The Database screen appears.

3. Make any necessary changes.

Note: You can cut yourself off from access to your site by improper use of this command. Make sure you have made the changes to the database and the information is correct.

4. Click the Save icon.

The database details change and the system takes you back to the Control Panel.

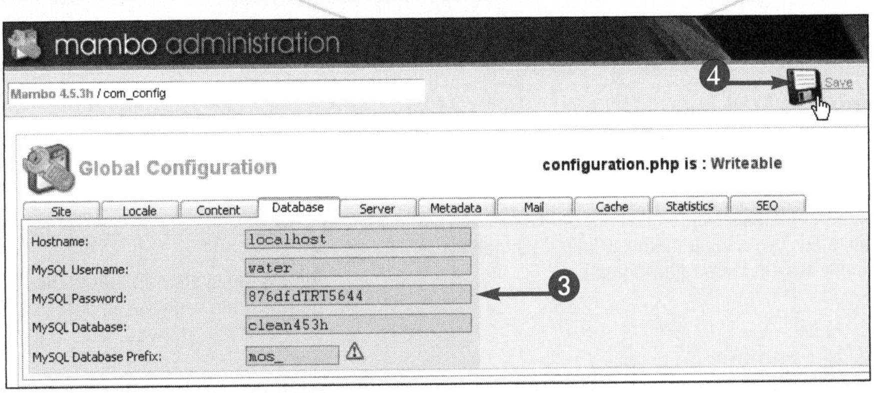

Understanding Server Options

The Server tab in the Global Configuration Manager contains a variety of information and options relating to the server on which your Mambo site is installed. The information on the Server tab is useful for troubleshooting and for configuring some components. The options on the Server tab cover a number of disparate areas, including login times, performance enhancements, Help files, and settings that relate to the installation of new components and modules.

A Absolute, or Full, Path

The location of the Mambo installation on your server.

B Live Site

The URL for the front end of the live site.

C GZIP Page Compression

Employs GZIP Page Compression to enhance site performance. The option applies only if the server supports GZIP.

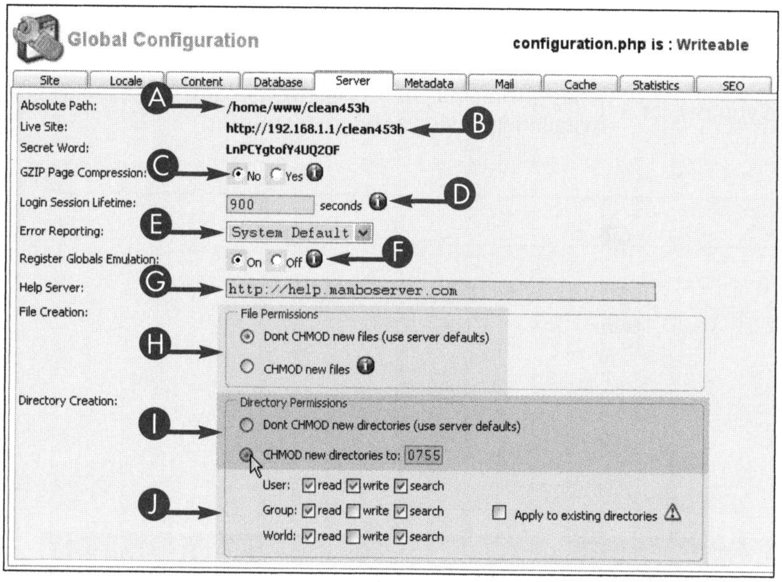

D Login Session Lifetime

Determines how long logged-in users can be inactive before the site automatically logs them out. Because this is a security issue, you should make the number reasonably low.

E Error Reporting

Enables site error reporting, which is a site diagnostic utility for programmers. The control should be set to System Default at all other times.

F Register Globals Emulation

A server setting which, if used improperly, can enable hackers to gain access to a server. By default, the setting is disabled. You should enable it only if you have difficulty running older components.

G Help Server

Establishes the link to the Help server which you can use to get live, updated Help files.

H File Creation

Allows the system to automatically set file permissions. Use this when you cannot access your FTP site and you need to alter some file permissions.

I Directory Creation

Allows the system to automatically set directory permissions. Use this in cases where you cannot access your FTP site and you need to alter some directory.

J Extended CHMOD Settings

Selecting the CHMOD new files option makes these options appear.

Create Site Metadata

You can specify the global metadata that appears with your Web site. Metadata is useful both for search engine indexing purposes and for maintaining concept relationships between Content Items via the use of keywords and phrases. Metadata is a primary tool for advanced document management systems because it enhances search efficiency and allows users to identify quickly main themes and primary relationships between documents.

Mambo provides two separate places for you to create metadata. The Metadata tab of the Global Configuration Manager includes several options that are applied globally to the site. In addition, each Content Item includes a Metadata tab that provides you with a place to enter a description and keywords that are applied specifically to that particular Content Item. Effective use of both tools in the system is the only way to make the best use of metadata in the context of a Mambo site.

The Metadata tab of the Global Configuration Manager presents two text fields for your use: Global Site Meta Description includes a description of the site as a whole. The content of this field appears in the Description metatag, which is used heavily in the display of search engine results; this is the text that appears under the site's name on most search engine result pages. The Global Site Meta Keywords field provides a place to insert words or phrases that are included in the Keywords metatag.

Two additional controls appear on the Metadata tab. Show Title Meta Tag adds the Title metatag to the site's metadata. The content of the Title metatag is your site's name, as entered in the Global Configuration Manager. The second control is to show or hide the Author metatag. The contents of the Author metatag come from the content creator, as specified by the parameters set during Content Item creation or editing.

Create Site Metadata

1. Load the Global Configuration Manager.

Note: To open the Manager, see the section "Change the Site Name."

2. Click the Metadata tab.

   A new screen loads.

3. Type a Global Site Description.
4. Type keywords.
5. Click a Show Title Meta Tag preference.
6. Click a Show Author Meta Tag preference.
7. Click the Save icon.

   Mambo saves the metadata and the system takes you back to the Control Panel.

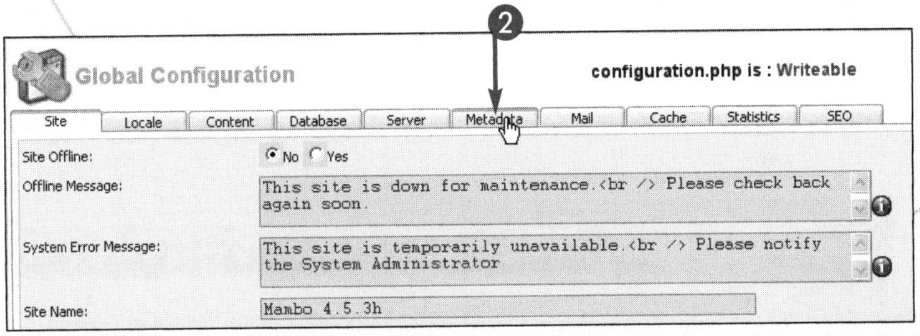

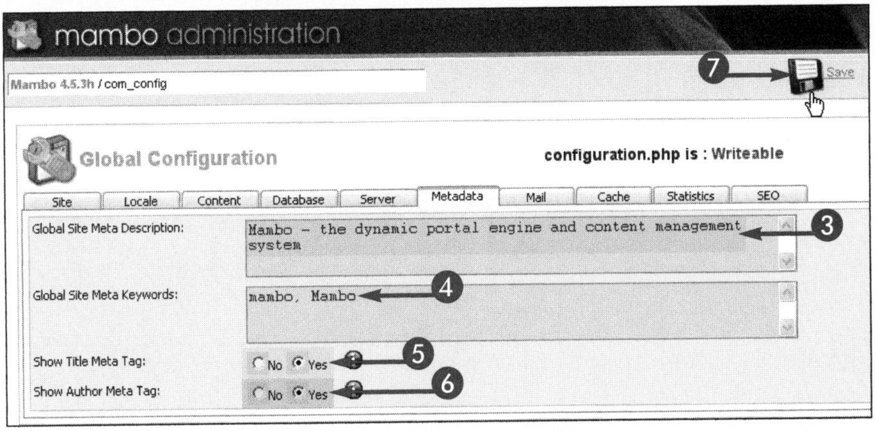

Configure Email Options

You can enable your Mambo site to send out emails. During installation, your Mambo system installs a default configuration for the interface with the mail server on your Web host. Sometimes you may want to modify those settings, or you may want to change the details that appear in the emails sent from the system. To make modifications to the settings or to the basic information in the system emails, you can do so from the Mail tab on the Global Configuration Manager.

Mambo automatically sets your outgoing mail server options to the most common configuration. You may not need to modify the default configuration at all. If you do need to make changes, the system allows you to change the mail protocol, and basic information sent with the email, such as the sender's name and email address.

Mambo supports three mail protocols: either PHP mail, SendMail, or SMTP. You can select from these options on the Mail tab. If you select SendMail for your site's mail function, you need to enter the path to SendMail in the field provided. If you want to use SMTP, you also need to specify whether authentication is required and provide the details of the username, password, and host name. You can input all the information via the Mail tab.

Email sent from your Mambo system includes a sender's email address and the name of the site. The default is to use the Super Administrator's email address and the site name you input during installation. You can modify both the email address and the site name from the Mail tab.

Configure Email Options

1. Load the Global Configuration Manager.

Note: To open the Manager, see the section "Change the Site Name."

2. Click the Mail tab.

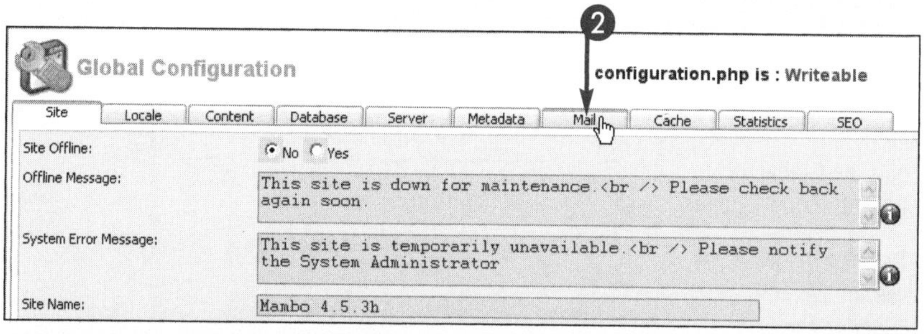

A new screen loads.

3. Set options applicable to your mail server.

4. Click the Save icon.

The Mail settings change and the system takes you back to the Control Panel.

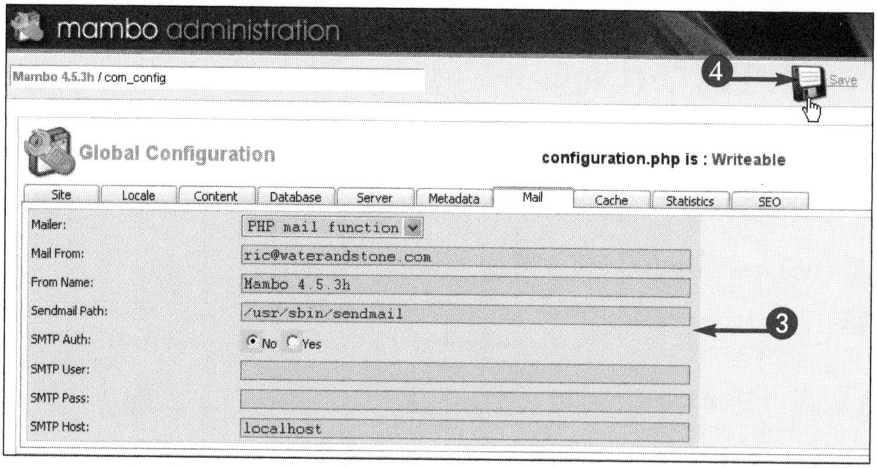

Enable Caching

You can control the caching of your site's contents on the server. Caching allows you to buffer the output of your site and gain improved performance. When caching is active, the server produces the content directly from the cache folder, and the display is much faster for site visitors. If your site is very busy, caching can also decrease the load on your server, which may prevent bottlenecks.

The primary site cache controls are located on the Cache tab in the Global Configuration Manager. The only variables are whether you want to enable or disable caching, where you want to store the cache, and for how long. The system default has caching disabled. The system also uses an existing folder as the default location for the cached contents. Unless you have a compelling reason to change the Cache Folder, use the default. The Cache Time variable tells the system how long to hold the files in the cache. Once the cache time specified expires, Mambo purges the content from the cache folder. The system default is 900 seconds. You may want to make this longer or shorter, depending on how often your site's contents change. If, for example, you run a site where the contents rarely change, you can increase the cache. On the other hand, if you run a site with time-sensitive content, you may want to make the cache shorter.

Note that in addition to the primary site cache controls in the Global Configuration Manager, some components and modules have optional cache parameters you can control. Appropriate application of the Mambo cache can improve the performance of your site. If you are not familiar with this technology, experiment with it. Changing the caching controls creates no risk to the site.

Enable Caching

1. Load the Global Configuration Manager.

Note: To open the Manager, see the section "Change the Site Name."

2. Click the Cache tab.

A new screen loads.

3. Enable the cache.
4. Click here and set the cache folder.
5. Click here and set the cache time.
6. Click the Save icon.

The cache settings change and the system takes you back to the Control Panel.

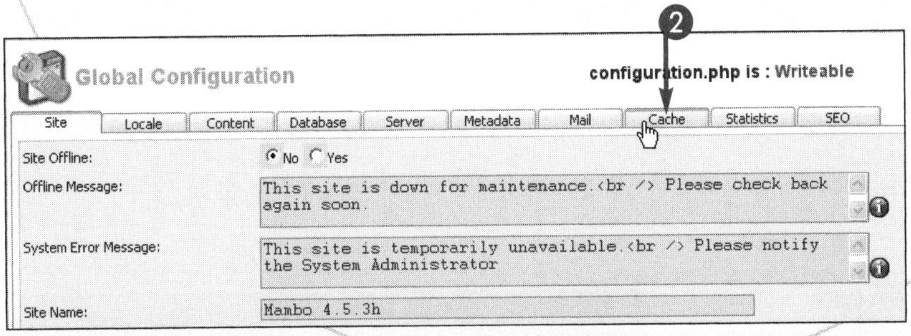

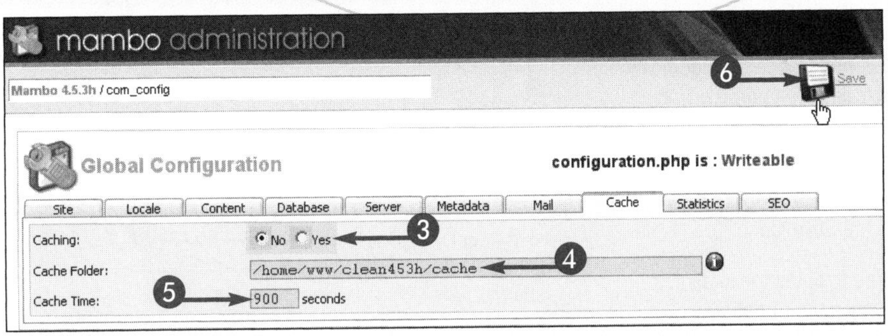

Enable Site Statistics

You can use the Mambo system to keep track of basic visitor activity on your Web site. Mambo can capture information about your visitors and their activities on the site and provide easy-to-read summary reports of the statistical data. While the Mambo Web traffic reporting options are not nearly as rich as those you will find in a dedicated Web traffic analysis program, they are useful as a quick snapshot of activity; and, of course, if your Web host does not provide a Web traffic stats system, the Mambo reports are a welcome substitute.

You enable Site Statistics via the Statistics tab in the Global Configuration Manager. By default, enabling the statistics function allows the Administrators to view site activity reports for four areas of activity: the operating system on the visitors' computers, the browsers that visitors use, the domains that visitors come from, and the pages visitors view on your site. Additionally, there are two other options on the Global Configuration Manager. If you select the Log Search Strings option, the system records the search words and phrases site visitors enter into your site search box. Enabling the Log Content Hits by Date option means the system records not only what pages were visited, but also the dates on which they were visited. Note that if your site is very active, both the Log Search Strings and Log Content Hits by Date options can utilize considerable amounts of disk space, and therefore you should use these with caution.

You can view Site Statistics from the Statistics choice on the Site Menu. The statistics gathered are cumulative and you cannot reset or modify them through the Mambo system.

Enable Site Statistics

1. Load the Global Configuration Manager.

Note: To open the Manager, see the section "Change the Site Name."

2. Click the Statistics tab.

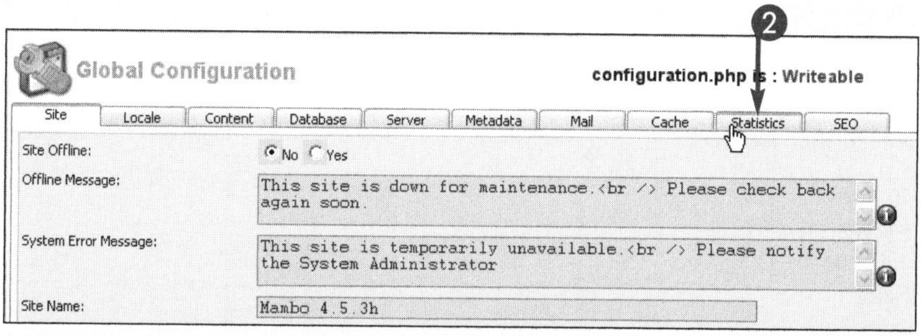

A new screen loads.

3. Enable Statistics.

4. Click a preference for logging hits by date.

5. Click a preference for logging search strings.

6. Click the Save icon.

Mambo enables the statistics and saves the options.

The system takes you back to the Control Panel.

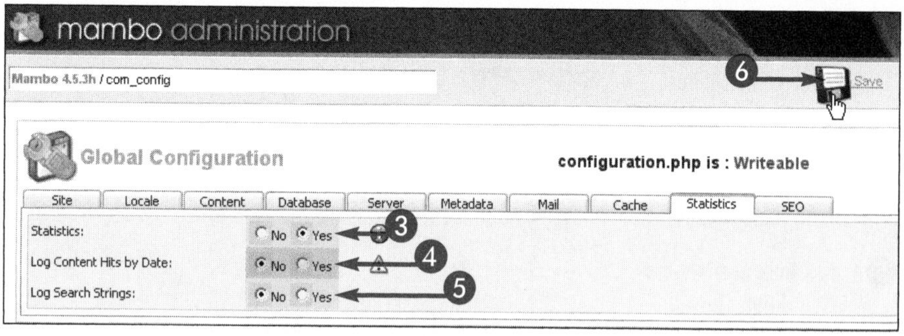

Enhance Search Engine Optimization

You can make your site more search engine friendly by employing the options on the SEO tab in the Global Configuration Manager. A more search engine friendly site means better search engine indexing and potentially higher ranking on the search engine results page. Good search engine optimization (SEO) makes it easier for visitors who employ the search engines to find your site and is a key to an effective online marketing strategy.

Enabling the Search Engine Friendly URLs option on the SEO tab changes the site's URLs. With Search Engine Friendly URLs disabled, a typical Mambo site URL looks like the following example:

```
http://192.168.1.1/mambo46beta1/index.
php?option=com_content&task=category&
sectionid=4&id=16&Itemid=27
```

With Search Engine Friendly URLs enabled, the same URL looks like this:

```
http://192.168.1.1/mambo46beta1/getting_
started
```

The latter example is more accessible to the search engines because it omits the database operators ?, =, and &, which can cause problems for search engine spiders.

Note that enabling the Search Engine Friendly URLs option requires the Apache Web server and that you also rename one file in the root Mambo directory. For the option to work, you must access the root directory and change the htaccess.txt file to .htaccess.

When you enable the Dynamic Page Titles option, Mambo automatically includes the name of the article or component that the user is viewing in the page title. With the option disabled, all the site's page titles become the same — that is, the same as the name of the site. With the option enabled, the page titles become the name of the site plus the name of the page or component that the user is viewing. Dynamic Page Titles make your pages more search engine friendly and helps users who bookmark your pages.

Enhance Search Engine Optimization

1. Load the Global Configuration Manager.

Note: To open the Manager, see the section "Change the Site Name."

2. Click the SEO tab.

   The SEO screen loads.

3. Enable Search Engine Friendly URLs.

4. Select a preference for dynamic page titles.

5. Click the Save icon.

   The system takes you back to the Control Panel.

6. Access the site root via FTP.

7. Rename the file "htaccess.txt" to ".htaccess."

   Search engine friendly URLs are enabled.

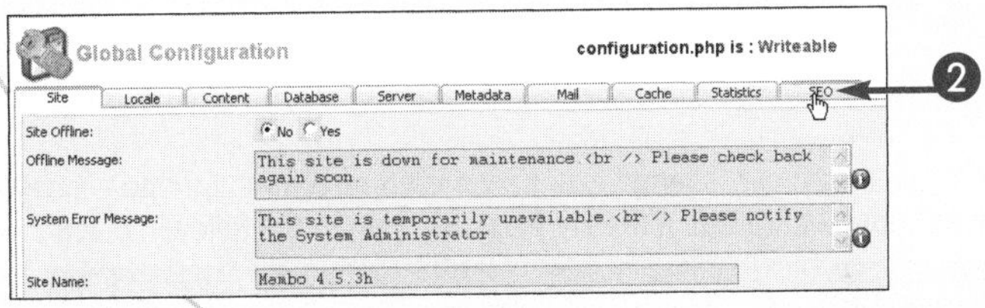

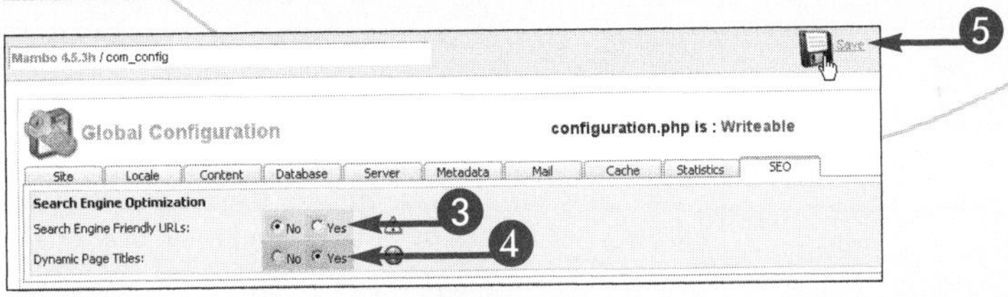

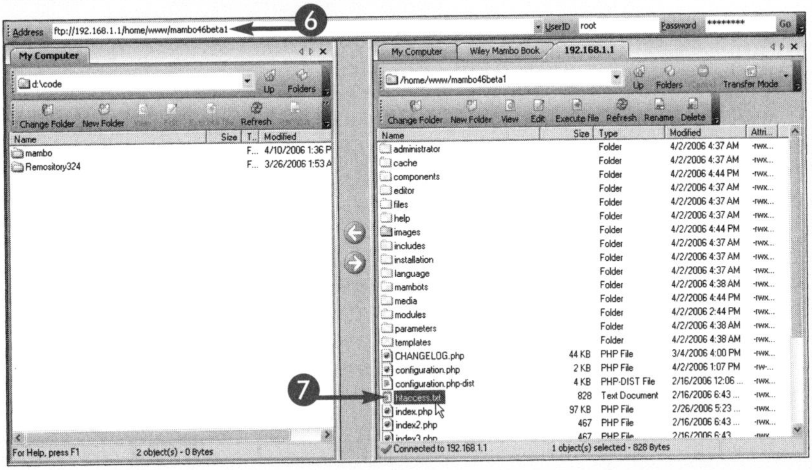

Understanding Mambo Templates

You can control the appearance of your Mambo site using template files. Flexible templating is one of the keys to Mambo's success. Mambo templates are relatively easy to create and modify. Unlike many other CMS systems, Mambo does not require you to learn specialized syntax or a unique programming language. Additionally, a large number of free or low-cost templates are available on the Web. These factors mean that you have a lot of choices for the look and feel of your Mambo site.

Mambo has templates for both the front end of your site and for the admin system. Front end templates, which visitors to your Web site can view, are called Site Templates. The templates that control the appearance of the Administration interface are called Admin Templates. This chapter shows you how to work with Site Templates, and Admin Templates are addressed later in the book in Chapter 14.

The default installation of Mambo includes sample templates for both 1024 x 768 and 800 x 600 screen sizes. The default templates have been tested for optimal compatibility and have a variety of module placeholders and content layouts. While you may use and modify the default templates freely, you can also obtain additional template files to install in the system. There is no limit to the number of templates you can install or use.

A Mambo template can be as simple as a single PHP file, but the default templates included in the system all have several pieces that work together to create the look and feel on your site. If you want, you can view the various parts of the templates by accessing the directories where you installed the Mambo core files. Site Templates are located inside the /templates directory. The Admin Templates are located in the /administrator/templates directory. Admin Templates have the same structure as Site Templates; inside each directory you can find the same elements.

Template Files

There is a separate directory for each of the templates. Inside each directory you find elements that combine to create the templates you see in the system. The various template files are listed in the following table.

ELEMENT	DESCRIPTION
`index.php`	This is the file most people think of as the "template." It contains all the code to place the design elements on the page and the placeholders for the functionality.
`templateDetails.xml`	Contains information about the template. Mambo uses this file to describe, define, and install the template. The file also includes the information on the author's identity, the files to be installed and their locations.
`template_thumbnail.png`	A thumbnail image of the template. This small image file gives you a preview of the template. Note that this file may not always be in the PNG format; some designers may use JPG or GIF file formats.
`/css`	A directory containing the CSS for the index.php file. The CSS file is always named `template_css.css`.
`/images`	A directory containing the images used in the index.php file.

Building Your Own Templates

The best way to begin building your own templates is to examine one of the default templates and experiment with it. Few elements are absolutely required, and you can easily identify them. While you must maintain the required elements for the system to work properly, outside of those restrictions you can do just about anything with your template. The default templates deployed with the system provide you with ready-made examples of best practices in the creation of Mambo templates, and they are an excellent place to start learning how to build or customize Mambo templates.

Live Web sites are not the place to learn how to edit a template file. Working on a live site is slow and can be frustrating because erroneous changes to the template may cause the site to perform abnormally, or to not appear at all. For this reason, consider learning how to create Mambo templates offline.

To get started, copy the template directory to your local machine. Open the template's index.php file locally using your chosen HTML editor. Note that previewing a template as you work on it requires the use of a machine that can execute PHP code. This means you cannot preview the template file locally unless you have it set up as a server in its own right. Therefore, the downside of working locally is that you can see the template properly only when you try to preview it locally. To see the page appear with the content, and with the components and modules in place, you must move the file to a server.

You can work around the need for a server in one of two ways. Either install locally a server, for example the XAMPP mini server which runs on Windows (www.apachefriends.org), or temporarily convert the index.php file into an HTML file, which will work in your local browser. To do this, remove the opening and closing PHP tags from the index.php file and then save the file as index.html. You can now preview the page elements locally, though again, if you want to see the page appear with the content, components, and modules in place, you must move it to a server. Remember before you move it to the server to add back in the PHP tags and to save the file as index.php. Remember also to copy back to the server any dependent files which you may have changed while editing — for example, CSS files.

Template Placeholders

Mambo templates are fundamentally HTML files with PHP elements included. Accordingly, anyone with basic HTML skills can quickly learn how to make his or her own templates or modify an existing template to achieve the desired look and feel. Basic HTML elements are used to create a template's layout. You place the modules and components inside the layout by means of PHP includes. You place modules by way of statements like this:

Example

```
<?php mosLoadModules('left'); ?>
```

You include the main body, which controls where the components will appear, using this statement:

Example

```
<?php mosMainBody(); ?>
```

You can also use PHP statements to assist with the management of images and to set certain requirements at the top and bottom of the index.php document.

Introducing the Template Manager

You can use the Template Manager to assign the templates that you use on your site, and thus control the look and feel of a site. As explained in the section "Understanding Mambo Templates," Mambo uses templates to control the general page layout. With the Template Manager, you can set the default site template, assign different templates to different pages, change template assignments, install new templates, and preview templates. You can also modify the code or the CSS for a template or delete templates completely.

You find the Template Manager inside the admin interface, under the Site menu. Only users that you have assigned to the Super Administrator user group can access this tool. The Template Manager is available for both Site Templates and for Admin Templates. There are separate navigation choices for each one, but the basic functions for each version are identical.

Introducing the Template Manager

A Template Name

Lists all the templates currently installed in your system. To invoke most functions, you must first select the template on which you want to perform the operation.

B Default

Sets the designated template as the default template for the site.

C Assign

Assigns templates to specific pages.

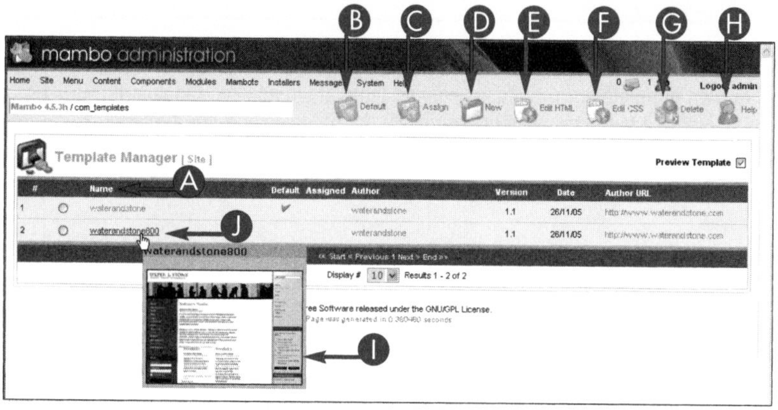

D New

Takes you to the Template Installer.

E Edit HTML

This edits the code of a template in your browser window.

F Edit CSS

Edits the CSS (Cascading Style Sheet) of the template in your browser window.

H Help

Opens the help files.

J Preview Template

Activates the mouse-over preview feature.

G Delete

Deletes a template file.

I Preview

Positioning the cursor over the name of the template causes a thumbnail image of the template, along with its name, to appear automatically.

Change the Default Template

To change the look and feel of your entire site, you can use the Template Manager to change the system's default template assignment. The Mambo system's default installation comes with one template assigned to all the site's pages. This configuration is the most common configuration for Mambo sites and is most appropriate for portal-type sites or for very simple sites where one look and feel is fine throughout. You can also use the Template Manager to assign more than one template to a site. For additional information on assigning more than one template to a site, see the section "Employ Multiple Templates," later in this chapter.

Using only one template gives the site's pages the same basic design. Although you can achieve some variety within pages by varying the assignment of modules and by changing the formatting of the content inside of Content items, the basic elements contained in the template remain the same.

When you assign only one template to the entire site, altering the default template changes the look and feel of the entire site. When you assign more than one template, the default template still serves an important function: any page not specifically assigned to another template displays the default template. Also note that the system automatically assigns the default template to new components and content sections.

On this topic, be aware of one limitation of the system: the default template also displays automatically for the search results page and for the page that shows automatically after a contact form is submitted. At the time of this writing, there is no way to assign another template to those pages, so make sure you plan for this when making your choice for the default template.

Change the Default Template

1. Click Site.
2. Click Template Manager.
3. Click Site Templates.

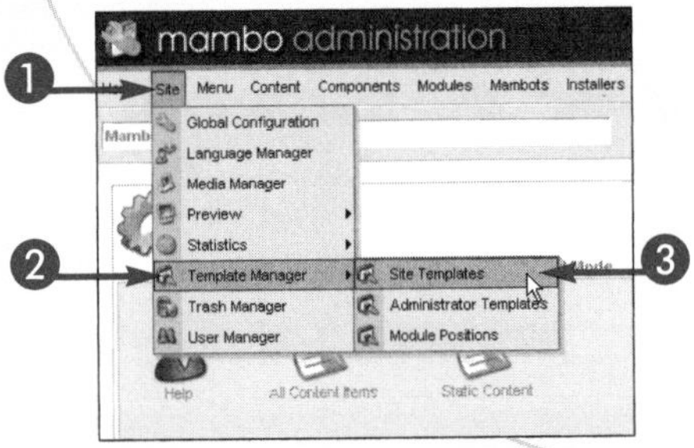

The Template Manager loads.

4. Click the radio button of the template that you want to make the default template.
5. Click the Default icon.

A check mark appears in the Default column of the template you selected, indicating that the template is now the site default.

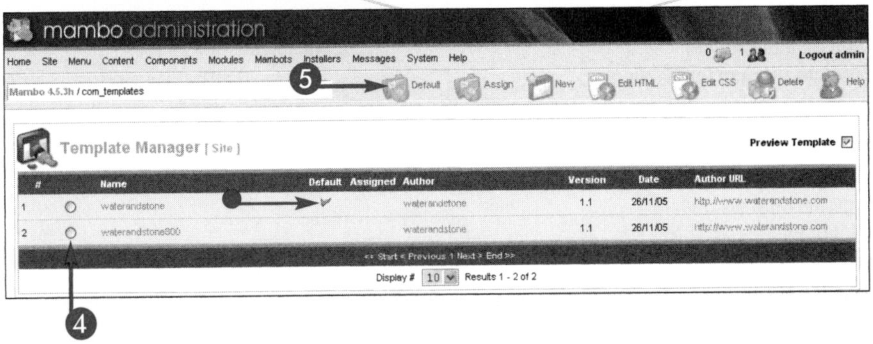

Install a New Template Automatically

You can automatically install templates using the Universal Installer, and in doing so, add functionality to the Mambo core. The Universal Installer allows you to upload preconfigured template packages to your Mambo site. New templates can extend the functionality of your site and provide you alternatives for the front end appearance of your Web site. The Universal Installer is the easiest way to install templates to extend your Mambo site.

When you obtain a preconfigured template for your Mambo site, it is delivered in the form of a zip file archive. The archive should contain all the files necessary to install and use the new template. If the template has been created properly, you should not need to make any additional changes to get it to function properly, although, of course, you may need to configure it to fit your needs after installation.

The Universal Installer presents three options to users: Upload Package File, Install from HTTP URL, and Install From Directory. The first option provides for automatic installation of a zip archived module file; the second allows you to input the URL of the archived file and allows the system to retrieve and install the package; and the third option is a manual installation technique, covered in the next section. Note that the first method functions properly only if your server supports GZip or a similar utility that enables extraction of zip file archives. Similarly, the second option is dependent on server settings. If you do not configure your server to permit the access and installation of an archive from another server, this option does not work for you. Although the first and second options are the easiest to use, if your server does not support either option, you need to use manual installation, as detailed in the next section, "Install a New Template Manually."

Install a New Template Automatically

1. Click Installers.
2. Click Universal.

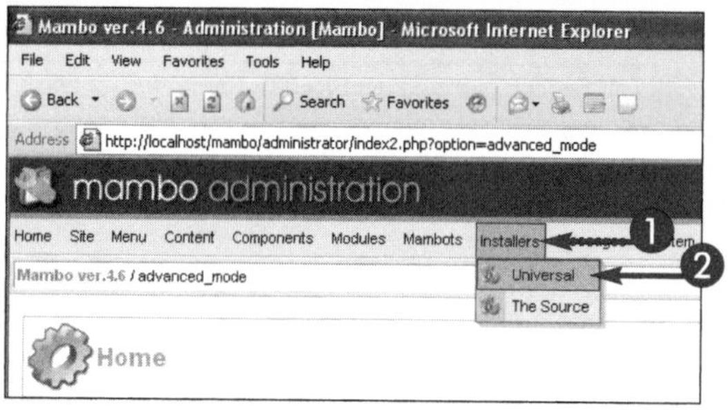

The Universal Installer loads.

- A list of directories, along with an indication of whether they are writeable, appears here.

Note: If any of the directories show as unwriteable you must change the permissions (read/write status) of the directory. For more on how to change file permissions, see Chapter 1.

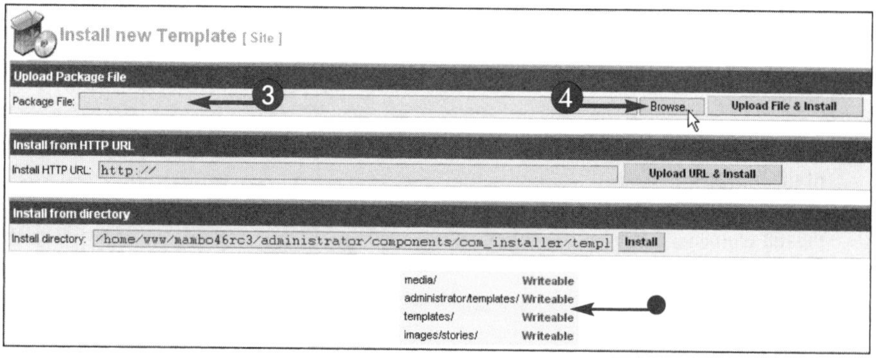

3. Select the Upload Package File option.
4. Click Browse.

The Choose file dialog box appears.

5. Navigate to the location of the archive.
6. Select the file.
7. Click Open.

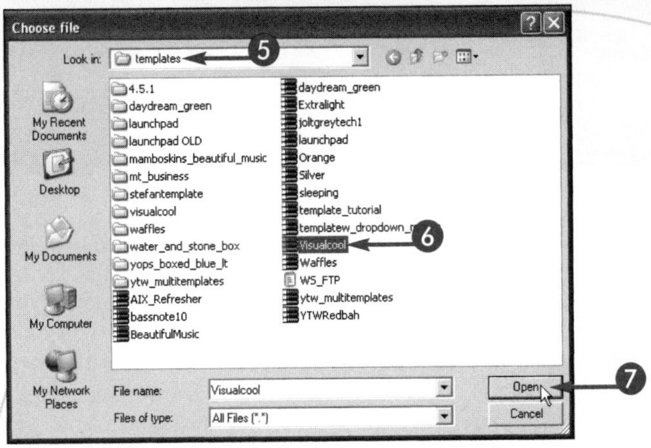

The popup closes and returns you to the Installer.

8. Click Upload File & Install.

If you are successful, you see a confirmation message when the screen reloads.

If you are not successful, you see a message indicating failure.

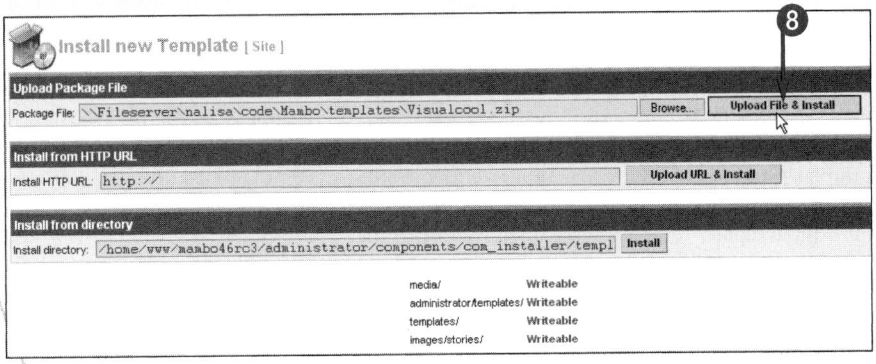

Extra

When you acquire a Mambo template from a third-party developer, make sure to verify that it contains all the elements that are necessary for automatic installation. A proper template package is delivered as a zip archive file and contains all of the elements outlined in the preceding section, "Understanding Mambo Templates." While best practices dictate that a template developer create the template package in a standard format that allows for easy installation, experience indicates that this is not always the case.

If all the elements are in place and properly formed, the installer should work as described in this section and all the template features should work without the need for adjusting the template files. If elements are missing or contain errors, you may need to manually install, as outlined in the next section, "Install a New Template Manually." Note that sometimes even an incorrectly created template installs; but once installed, it may not have all features available. For example, the template preview feature may fail if the thumbnail image is missing.

Install a New Template Manually

You can install templates without using the automatic installer described in the section, "Install a New Template Automatically." You must manually install a new template if your server does not support GZip or another utility for extracting file archives, or if you have some but not all of the various template files.

You manually install using the Install From Directory option in the Template Installer, or you can simply copy the files to the server by FTP. Both methods require moving files up to the server outside of the Mambo system. The method you use depends largely on the nature of the template.

If you have a proper template package, that is, a template with a complete set of properly formed files, you should use the Install From Directory option outlined in this section. If your template files are incomplete, you cannot use this option and instead must transfer your template files to a new directory inside the Mambo template directory on the server. However, installing a template without the Template Installer means that you cannot automatically uninstall the template. To uninstall the incomplete template later, you must again navigate to the Mambo template directory on your server and physically remove the files.

You access the Template Installer either by using the direct links to the installer from the Site and Installers menus, or the New icon in the Template Manager to open the Installer.

Once you install your package, you can preview the new template using the Preview function by setting the new template as the default template and viewing the Web site, or by assigning it to a specific page or function and then viewing the Web site. For more on the Preview function, see the section "Introducing the Template Manager." For more on assigning the template to a specific page, see the section "Employ Multiple Templates."

Install a New Template Manually

1. If they are zipped, extract the template files from the zip archive.

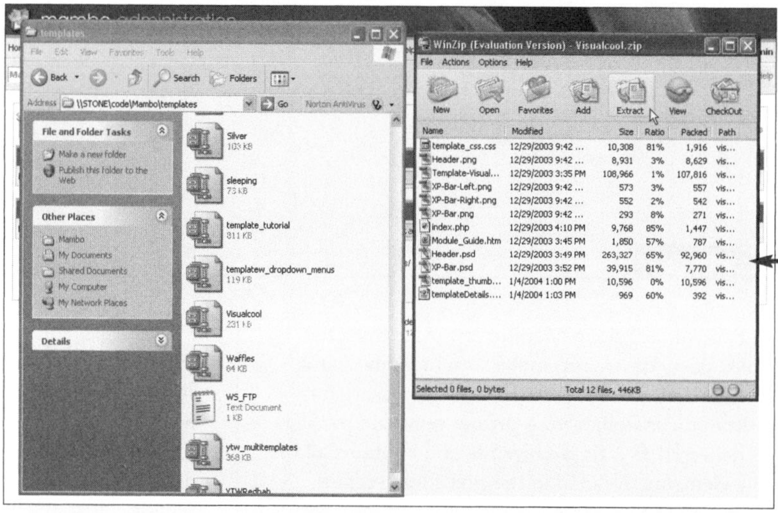

2. Access your server via FTP.
3. Create a directory inside the /templates directory.
4. Move the template files into the new directory and note the location.

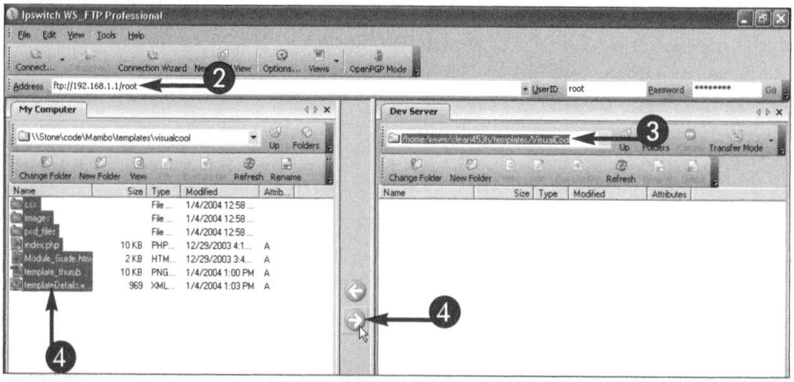

5. Select the Installer option from the menus or click the New icon.

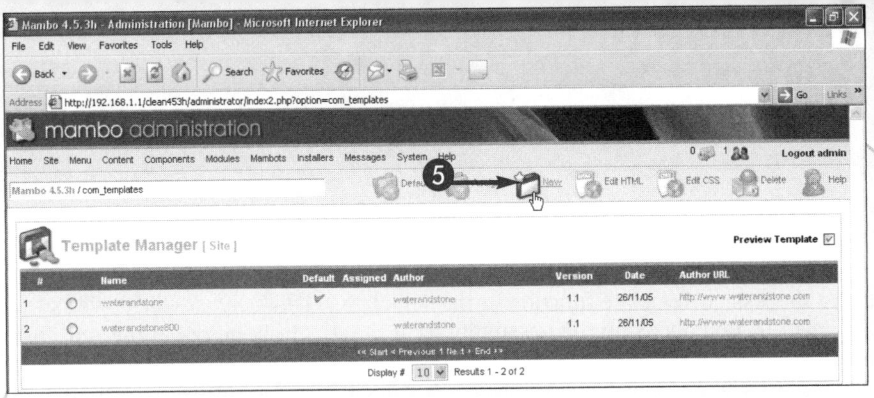

6. Type the full path to the directory containing the files here.

   - You can click the Back to Templates link to abort and return to the main page of the Template Manager.

7. Click Install.

   If you are successful, you see a confirmation message when the screen reloads.

   If you are not successful, you see a message indicating failure.

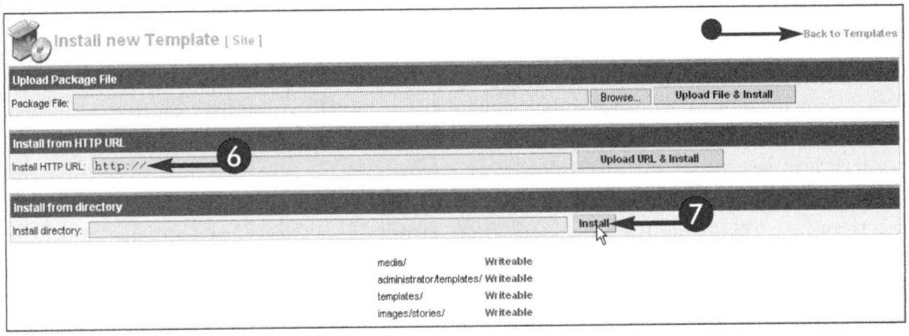

Extra

While it may initially seem that manual installation is inconvenient, this is not always necessarily the case. Manual installation is a useful alternative for developers. For example, if you are working on a template and you want to test it on a system during development, it is not efficient to take the time to create a full installation package. It is much more convenient to simply FTP the files up to the server and then turn the template on using the Template Manager. Manual installation makes it possible to work, preview, and revise without having to spend extra time creating files that are necessary for a proper template package, but are unnecessary for testing purposes.

To preview templates while they are still under development, you need to know what files are absolutely necessary for Mambo. To work without the use of the Installer, the only things you need for a valid template are an index.php file and the CSS file. Indeed, the latter is only required to meet the needs of other elements in the Mambo system; it is not absolutely needed to render the template if you define the styles for the template inside the index.php file. If you want to use the Installer, you must also have the XML file that defines the template, author, and related files information.

Employ Multiple Templates

The Mambo system gives you the flexibility to employ multiple templates with relative ease. You can assign templates to appear on only select pages using the Assign Template function in the Template Manager. This function opens up the possibility for a single site to have multiple templates. You can assign templates to particular pages based on function, the need for a particular layout, or simply for the sake of variety.

Not all pages may be available for template assignment. The question of whether you can assign a page or a component to a specific template is related to a third element: the site menus. You can match a template only to those pages or components that are linked to a menu and published. It is also important to remember that pages inherit template assignments based on their parent page. By way of example, if you assign a template to the News section, then all pages within that section use the same template. To vary from the default inheritance principal, you must publish menu navigation links to the pages you want to change.

Check marks in the Assigned column of the Template Manager indicate templates that are assigned to particular pages. Note that you must select a template and use the Assign button in order to see which pages the template is assigned to; you cannot tell which template is assigned to which page merely by looking at the Template Manager.

There is no limit to how many templates you can assign on one site, nor is there a limit on the number of pages you can assign to a template. You can change assignments at any time by revisiting the Template Manager.

Employ Multiple Templates

1. Click Site.
2. Click Template Manager.
3. Click Site Templates.

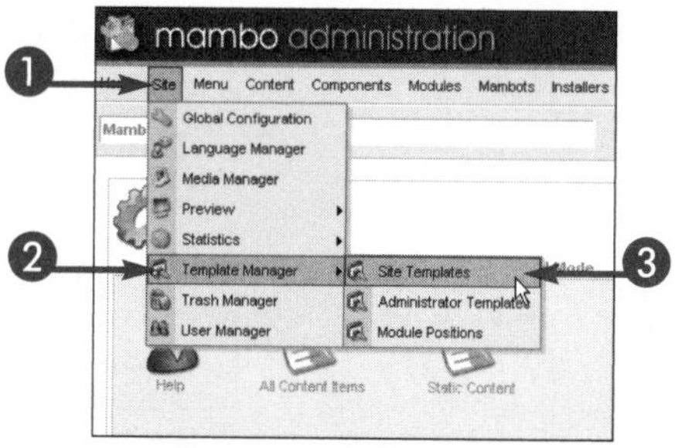

The Template Manager loads.

4. Click the radio button of the template you want to assign.
5. Click the Assign icon.

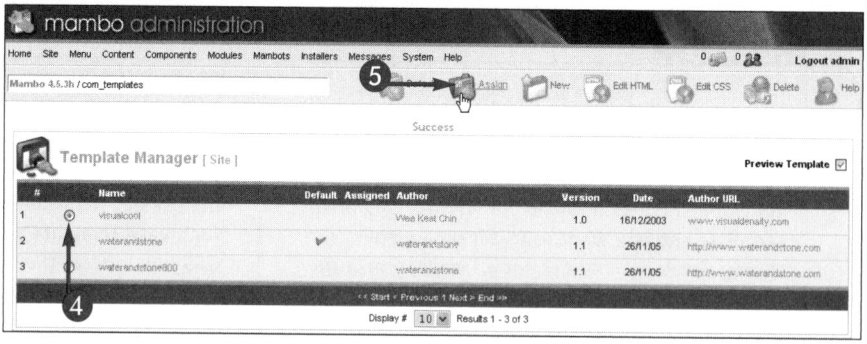

A new page loads, containing a list of all the navigation links in your site.

6 Select one or more pages to which you want to assign the template.

You can make multiple selections by clicking while holding down the Ctrl key.

7 Click the Save icon.

- You can click the Cancel icon to return to the main page without saving your changes.
- A new page loads showing your template with a check mark in the Assigned column.

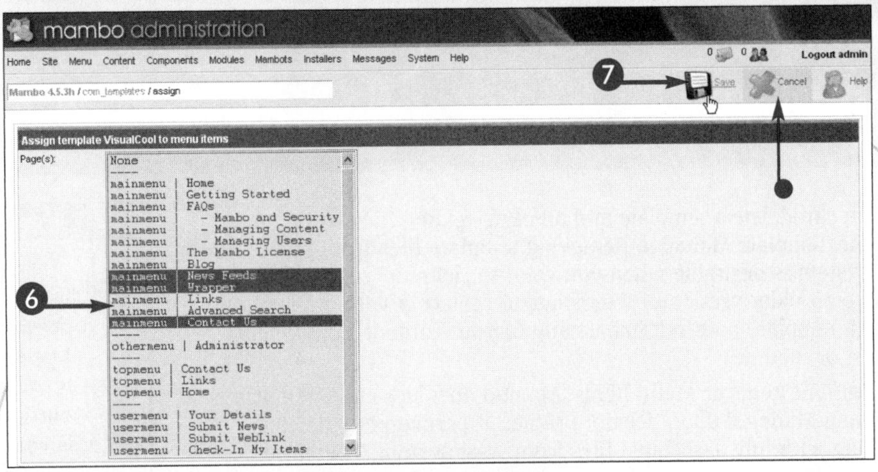

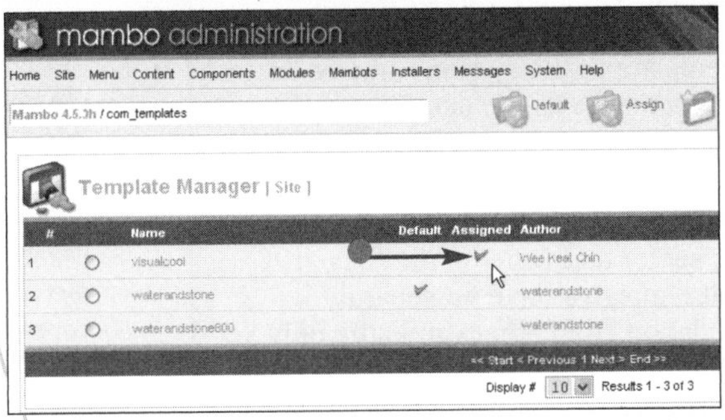

Extra

When do you need more than one template? It is a question with no firm answer other than: Whenever you want one. The most frequent use is creating a home page that has a different content layout than the internal pages. Another common use for a second template is for creating a *splash page,* that is, an entry page to the site that is purely ornamental or is necessary to present users with a critical choice, like a language or location selection. You can also build multiple templates to reflect the content of the page or the functions to which they are assigned. It might be desirable, for example, to use a different template for a contact form, or for a complex component that requires more of the screen.

Note that you do not have to build multiple templates to achieve a professional and interesting look and feel; you can achieve variety in other ways such as by changing module assignments and by working creatively with the layout of the Content Items. If you are fluent with CSS, you can also use your style sheets to bring variety to your pages.

Delete a Template

You can delete a template and all of its related files using the Template Manager. Removing template files from your system is desirable when you want to clean up your installation or remove an older version of a template to replace it with a newer one. Deleting a template does not impact any of your content, components, Mambots, or modules.

Unlike Content Items or Menu Items, Mambo does not move templates to the Trash Manager upon deletion; rather, it permanently deletes them along with any associated files from your system. Therefore, think carefully before you confirm deletion. The only way to get the template back is to reinstall it from scratch. Because you cannot undo a deletion, you may want to leave the template in the system, unused. If you assign a template to a page and do not set it as the default, the files are completely inactive. Because Mambo does not call the template, the presence of the unused files does not impair your site's performance.

Alternatively, you can backup the files prior to deletion by accessing the Mambo templates directory on the server and copying the files to your local machine. Note the default templates have no separate installation package; therefore, reinstallation from a backup is the only way to restore them once you delete them.

Extra

In certain cases, the automatic deletion feature of the Template Manager may not be available. If you have installed a template outside of the system — that is, manually by FTP and without using the Install from directory function in the Template Installer — you must delete the template manually. To do this, you must access the server via FTP or by way of your Web hosting control panel, then navigate to the Mambo templates directory and delete the directory containing your template files.

Delete a Template

1. Inside the Template Manager, select the template you want to delete.
2. Click the Delete icon.

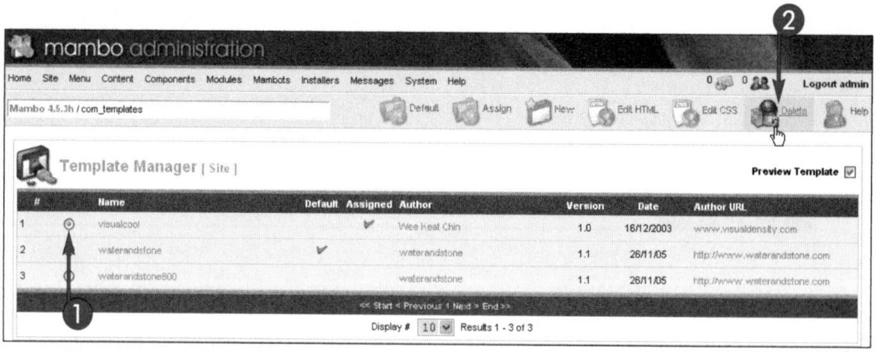

A dialog box asks you to confirm the deletion.

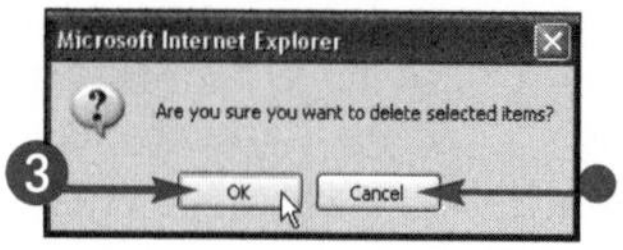

3. Click OK.

- You can click Cancel and return to the Template Manager.

Mambo deletes the template and all related files from the server.

Note: You cannot delete the default template.

Edit a Template

The Edit HTML function in the Template Manager allows you to view the code of an individual template file and to edit it inside your browser window. Because template files are a mix of HTML and PHP code, you can edit them easily. The Edit HTML feature provides a simple plain text editor that is useful for making minor changes or corrections to a template, but the limitations imposed by working on the code on a server via a browser are significant.

If you are skilled in HTML you will most likely make any major changes in a dedicated HTML editor and move your work to and from the server using FTP. The admin interface simply is not the best place to make extensive modifications to the code of a page. The Template Manager gives you access to the file, but you are restricted to editing the raw code with only a text editor. There is no WYSIWYG editor, no undo option, no spell-checker, and no ability to preview your work without publishing it on the front end of the site.

The Edit HTML function also requires some caution because it opens up the possibility for you to wreck your template by entering improper syntax or accidentally deleting something. Be careful here: if you do not know what you are doing, do not try this. Regardless of your experience level, maintain good work habits and back up the template's index.php file before you make any changes. If things go wrong you can always restore the old file. Only the most experienced users should attempt to edit a template that is live on a site, and even then, caution is strongly urged.

Edit a Template

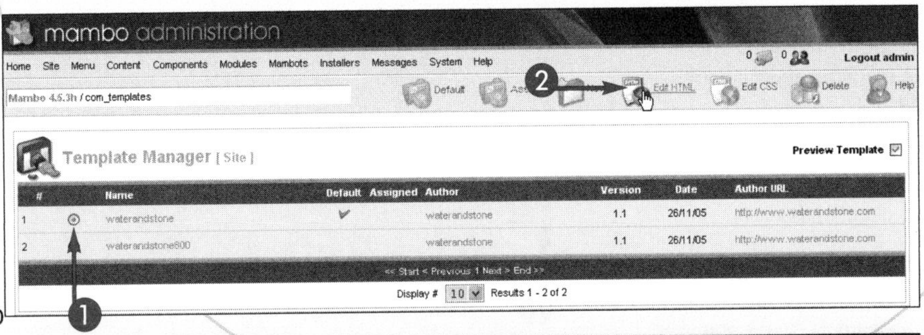

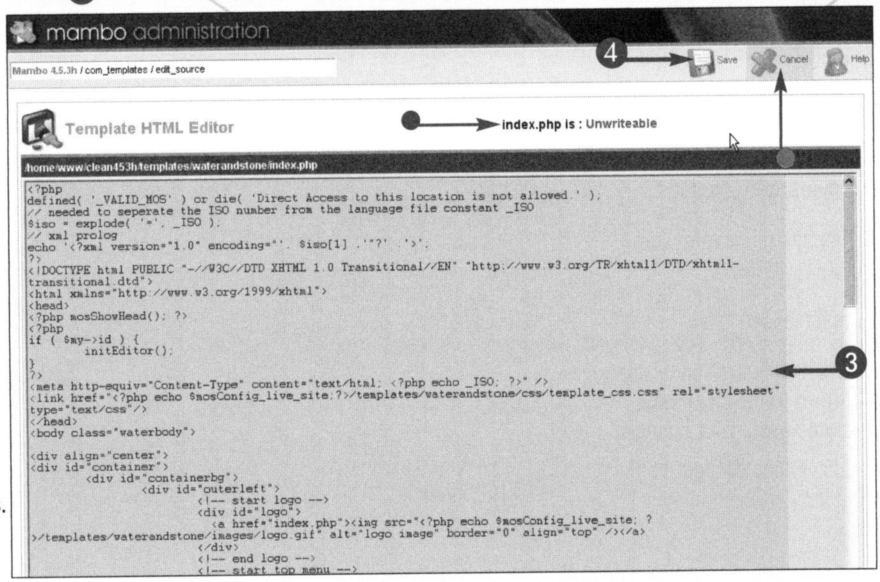

1. Inside the Template Manager, select the template you want to edit.
2. Click the Edit HTML icon.
   - A status line indicates whether the file is writeable. If the message is "index.php is: Writeable," you can edit. If not, you must change the permissions (read/write status) of that file.

Note: For more on how to change file permissions, see Chapter 1.

3. Make changes to the template code.
4. Click the Save icon.
   - Clicking Cancel cancels your changes.

Mambo saves the changes to the template code and they are immediately effective.

Edit the CSS File for a Template

You can edit the style definitions contained in a template's CSS file from within the Template Manager. Cascading Style Sheets (CSS) control the appearance of the text and other items on the template pages. By way of the Edit CSS command, the Template Manager gives you the option to edit the CSS for a template without leaving your browser.

Although the browser interface gives you only a text editor to work with, this is not a problem because CSS files are basically simple text files. In other words, you have all the tools you need to edit the CSS right in your browser window! Moreover, by editing the CSS using the Template Manager, you can preview the changes on your site as you work. Sometimes this is actually preferable to working offline, where you cannot always easily preview the changes.

Increasingly, Mambo templates and the Mambo system rely on the use of CSS for styling pages, in an effort to separate presentation from content. The use of CSS increases a site's efficiency and decreases the download times. Unfortunately, for many people, CSS is still a struggle. As a consequence, many people tend to work by trial and error. If you are one of those still struggling with the use of CSS, please note that the Edit CSS option in the Template Manager opens up the possibility for you to wreck your template's formatting; you can enter improper syntax or accidentally delete something. Be careful here; if you do not know what you are doing, do not try this. Regardless of your experience level, maintain good work habits and back up the template's template_css.css file before you make any changes. If things go wrong you can always restore the file.

Edit the CSS File for a Template

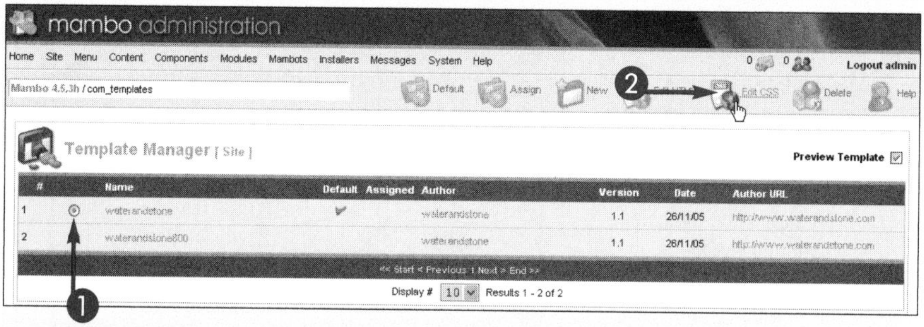

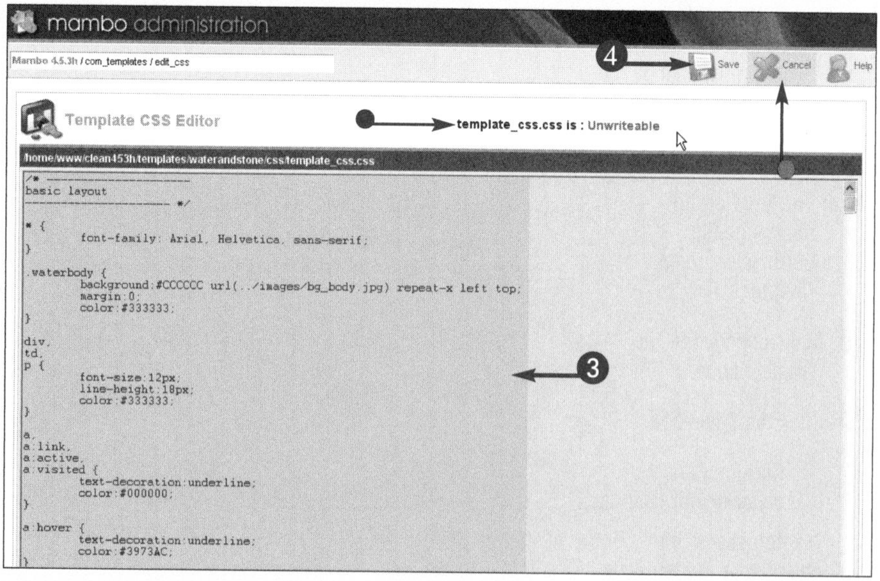

1. Inside the Template Manager, select the template you want to edit.
2. Click the Edit CSS icon.

   A new page loads.

   - A status line indicates whether the file is writeable. If the message is "index.php is: Writeable," you can edit. If not, you must change the permissions (read/write status) of that file.

Note: For more on how to change file permissions, see Chapter 1.

3. Make changes to the template code in this window.
4. Click the Save icon.

   - You can click the Cancel icon to return to the main page without saving your changes.

   Mambo saves the changes to the CSS and they are immediately effective.

Mambo CSS Tips and Tools

The Mambo templating system suffers from several shortcomings relating to CSS. To manage your templates and CSS files more easily, you can adopt some of the tips and tools suggested below.

You should understand that Mambo was originally designed to run only one template per site. Subsequently, the ability to use multiple templates was added to the system, but the feature for editing CSS was never updated to handle multiple templates. As a result, strictly applying the traditional template structures creates redundancies in CSS, because each template is likely to have its own CSS directory containing its own CSS file. This means that if you make a change across multiple templates, you must make the change multiple times — once in each template's CSS file!

To simplify handling multiple templates, consider deviating from the default template structures. Additionally, to simplify identifying classes and styles, consider employing the Firefox browser with the Web Developer Extension installed.

Multiple Templates with One CSS

Ideally, a system should use one CSS file shared across multiple templates. This suggested approach reduces overhead, decreases maintenance time, and eliminates the possibility of errors and inconsistencies that a user may introduce during the course of maintenance and customization. At this time, however, this approach is not in place in the Mambo template management system.

You can force the system to use a more efficient shared-CSS approach by manually creating a master CSS directory and file for all the templates on your site to use. You can take this approach and still maintain the ability to edit the master CSS via the Template Manager. To implement this approach, combine all the styles you need into one CSS file and place that file in the default template's CSS directory. Link all the templates to the master CSS file. If you follow this strategy, you must deal with only one CSS file and you can control the appearance of all the templates assigned on your site through the Edit CSS command in the Template Manager.

Working with the Web Developer Extension

In the context of CSS, there is an invaluable extension for the Firefox browser. If you are using Firefox, visit the Mozilla Web site and search for the Web Developer extension. Download and install it in your Firefox browser. Under the Information tab on the extension toolbar is a link called Display ID and Class Details. This option annotates the pages in your browser window and shows where classes and IDs are being used on the Web page. This is a great way to figure out exactly what class or ID is controlling the output of a particular item in Mambo — not always an easy task with the components and modules. You can find extensions for the Firefox browser at: www.mozilla.com/extensions/.

Second, the Web Developer extension lets you view and edit the live CSS for the site. This is a wonderfully useful tool because you can make changes and view their effects as you work. You have the freedom to experiment and play with the CSS without hurting the site. Only you can see the changes; it does not affect other visitors. Once you have things how you want them, copy the changes and paste them into the CSS editor in the Template Manager and you are done.

An Introduction to the User Manager

You can use the Mambo User Manager to create and manage access privileges for the people who visit and administer your site. The User Manager is one of the simpler and more straightforward interfaces in the admin system. It is located under the Site menu and contains all the controls you need to add, edit, and delete users from the Mambo system. All users, both those registered for the front end and those registered for the admin system, are controlled in one place. Even if the site has only one user, the User Manager comes in handy because you can use this tool to change the password and details for the Super Administrator.

Being able to assign users to various groups is a key function of the User Manager and serves several purposes. It allows the system administrators to ensure system security and privacy by restricting low-level users from viewing private information or performing actions that can negatively affect the site or other users. You can also utilize user groups to establish workflows for content creation, editing, and publication. For more on the various user groups, see the section "Understanding Mambo User Groups."

A Task Icons

Basic tasks related to user management.

B Name

Lists all users individually, by their registered name. To invoke most functions, you must first select the user and then click the appropriate task icon. Alternatively, to edit the user, you can open the item directly by clicking the name.

C Logged In

Indicates whether a user is currently logged in to the system.

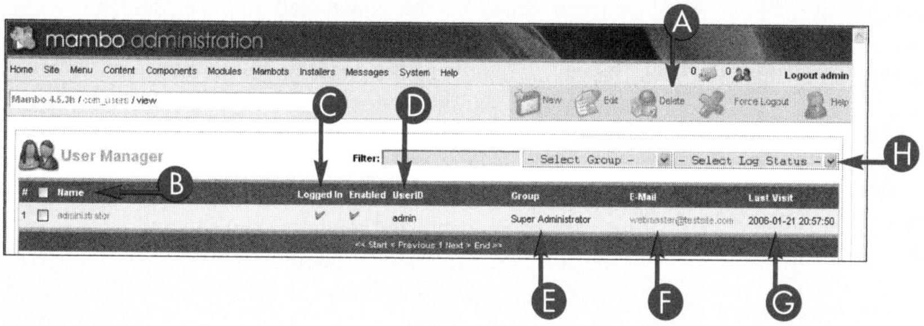

D User ID

The login ID or "username" of each user.

E Group

Indicates the user group to which the user belongs.

G Last Visit

The last date the user visited the site and logged in.

H Filter

Sorting and search controls for the list of users. These are helpful on sites with large numbers of registered users.

F Email

Each user's registered email address.

Understanding Mambo User Groups

The key to managing users in the Mambo system is understanding the user levels and what they can and cannot do. Each user in the system is assigned to a user group. Each group has different rights and privileges. At the most basic, a user can log in only to the front end of the Web site and view content or components that have been restricted to registered users. At the most advanced, a user has full control of the Web site. In between lie the variety of user groups described in the following table.

User Group Limitations

Mambo comes with a limited set of user groups. You cannot create custom user groups in Mambo nor can you assign an individual user to his or her own unique level, or to specific pages of the sites. In Mambo, all users in any particular group share the same privileges. The limited nature of the user management function is one of the primary criticisms of the present Mambo system and one of the priorities for the future of Mambo development. There are some third-party solutions that provide more flexibility for user management.

Mambo User Groups

The table shows you the various user groups in the default Mambo installation and the rights and privileges associated with each user group.

TASKS	SUPER ADMINISTRATOR	ADMINISTRATOR	MANAGER	PUBLISHER	EDITOR	AUTHOR	REGISTERED
Edit Global Configuration	X						
Access Template Manager	X						
Access Language Manager	X						
Create and Delete Users	X	X					
Install/Uninstall Modules, Components, and Mambots	X	X					
Create Sections	X	X	X				
Create Categories	X	X	X				
Access Front Page Manager	X	X	X				
Create/Edit/Delete Menu Items	X	X	X				
Access to Admin System	X	X	X				
Approve (Schedule) Pages	X	X	X	X			
Publish/Unpublish Pages	X	X	X	X			
Edit Work of Others	X	X	X	X	X		
Create Content Items	X	X	X	X	X	X	
View Password Protected Areas on Front End	X	X	X	X	X	X	X

Create a New User

You can add a new user to the Mambo system via the User Manager. Creating additional users with administration privileges helps distribute the burden of site administration and content creation. The default Mambo system contains only one user after the installation routine completes. The default user is a Super Administrator by the name of "admin." The first time you log in to the Mambo admin system, you do so as this user. You may continue to use this account indefinitely, or you can create one or more alternate accounts. You can also edit the Super Administrator account to change the details, including the password. For more information on editing user accounts, see the section "Change an Existing User's Details."

Only Super Administrators and Administrators have access to the User Manager. That means that only a Super Administrator or Administrator group's user can create, modify, or delete user accounts. There is no set limit to the number of users in a Mambo system, nor is there a limit on the number that you can assign to any one group. While the system does not impose a restriction on the number of users, system performance can degrade when very large numbers of users are registered.

You must specify a name, username, email address, and password for each user you create. You must also assign the user to a group. Although the privileges vary from group to group, the process for creating a new user is the same for each group, as outlined in the following steps.

Create a New User

ENTER NEW USER INFORMATION

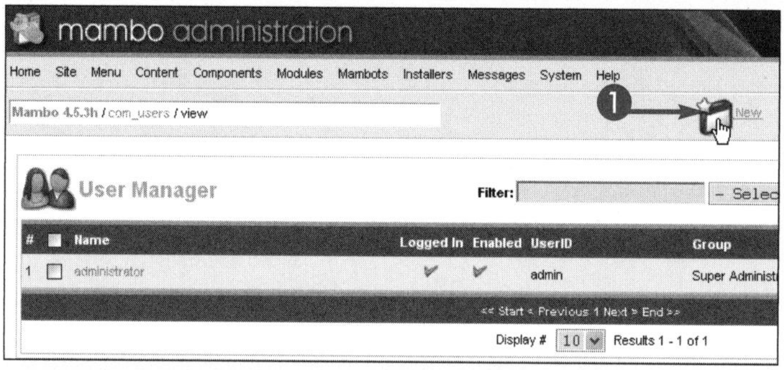

1. From within the User Manager, click the New icon.

   A new page loads.

2. Type the user's real name.
3. Type a username.
4. Type a password.
5. Reconfirm the password by entering it again.

Note: Passwords must match or an error message will appear.

6. Select the user group for this user.
7. Click the Save icon.

   You can click the Cancel icon to exit without saving and return to the main User Manager screen.

   A new user is created.

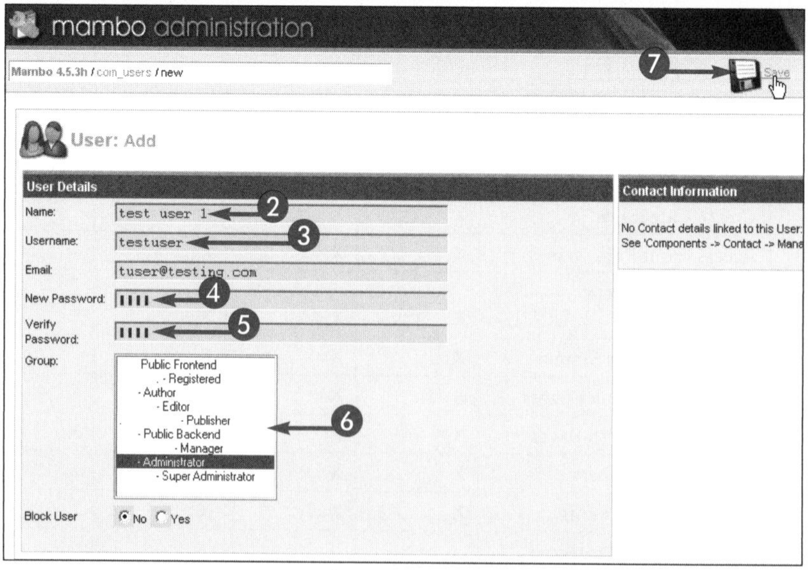

ENABLE USER TO RECEIVE SYSTEM NOTIFICATIONS

1. From the User Manager, click the check box of the user you want to edit.
2. Click the Edit icon.

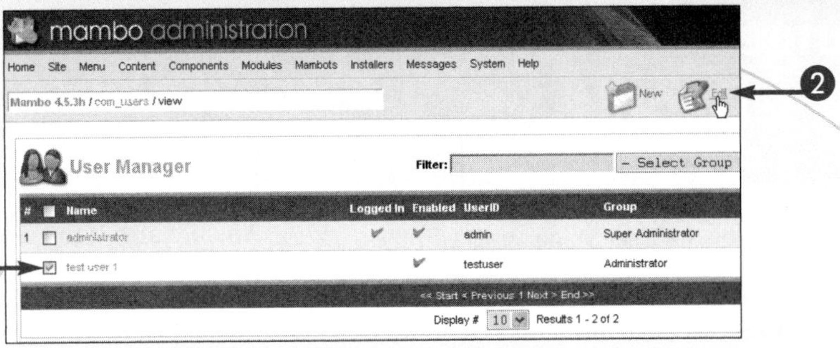

A new page loads.

3. For the Receive Submission Emails option, click Yes.
4. Click the Save icon.

The user can now receive automatic submission emails from the system.

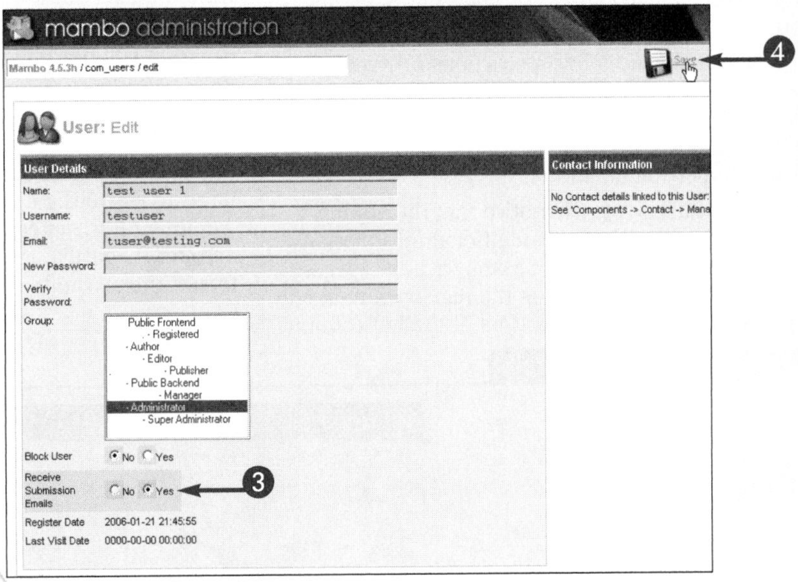

Extra

The Mambo system does not impose significant restrictions on the type or content of the passwords that the Administrator assigns or that the users create. Unfortunately, this opens the possibility that people may choose, at the very least, less-than-optimal passwords, and at the very worst, completely insecure passwords. What is a good password? The convenient answer is "one that you can remember." Sadly, convenience in this case can work against you, because what is easy to remember is often easy to hack.

For the sake of expediency, far too many people make the mistake of using their username as their password, thereby creating the least secure combination of username and password. Other users do only slightly better when they choose easy-to-discover facts for their password, like their birth date or their maiden name. Words that you can find in the dictionary are also terribly insecure passwords; hackers have long employed very efficient programs for cracking passwords by using brute computing power to try every entry in the dictionary.

The best passwords are a combination of numbers and letters, in a mix of upper and lower case. Additionally, a minimum of six to eight characters is preferred.

Change an Existing User's Details

You can employ the User Manager to edit the details associated with any user. You most commonly need the feature to reset a user's password, but it also serves other purposes, for example, changing a user's email address or reassigning the user to a more powerful or a more limited user group.

The Mambo system places few restrictions on how you can modify a user's account. The Super Administrator is the only class that is in some way restricted. You cannot change the user group of a Super Administrator, nor can you delete a Super Administrator.

When you edit a user, you will notice that the editing screen for a user contains some additional information that does not appear on the User Manager home page. One piece of useful information is the registration date of the user, which appears at the bottom of the left column.

Additionally, if the user is linked to a contact form, the right side of the user editing screen will contain the information that appears in that contact item. You can access the information in the linked contact item directly from the user editing screen via the Change Contact Details button. If a user is not linked to a contact item, the right column remains empty.

Super Administrator accounts also have one further option, that is, to receive submission emails from the site. You can also control the setting for this option via the user editing screen. Note that while Administrators have access to the User Manager, only a Super Administrator can edit another Super Administrator's account. Logically, it is possible for Super Administrators to edit the accounts of Administrators.

Change an Existing User's Details

1. From the User Manager, click the check box of the user you want to edit.
2. Click the Edit icon.

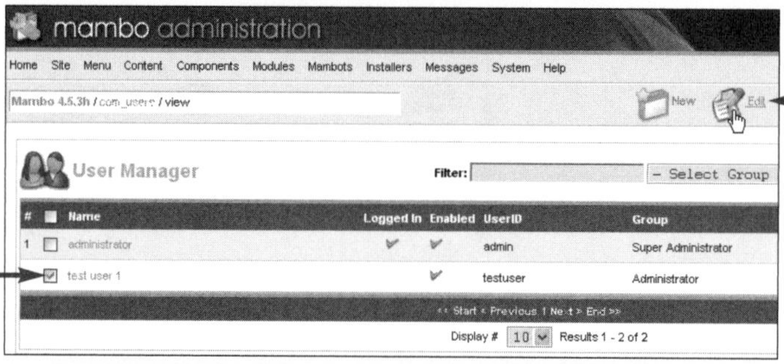

A new page loads.

3. Make any changes to the user's details.
4. Click the Save icon.

You can click the Cancel icon to return to the main screen without saving.

Mambo saves the changed user details.

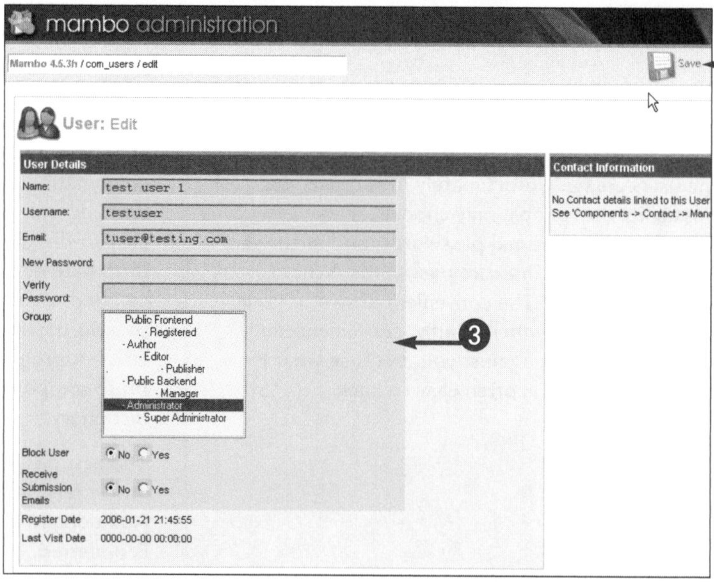

Link a Contact Form to a User

You can create a link between a user and a Mambo-generated contact form. Linking a user to a contact form causes Mambo to send the form submissions directly to that user. The feature is time-saving and useful: If the site has more than one contact form, you can easily set the feature to send all contact form submissions to one person. In the event the user details change in the User Manager, you do not have to update the contact form; the system maintains the link automatically.

You can create links between a user in any user group and any contact item, and you can send multiple contact items to any one user. The system, unfortunately, does not provide a way to send one contact item to multiple users. Note also that this feature is available only for contact forms created with the Mambo Contact component. You cannot link or update hand-coded forms, or forms contained in third-party components automatically.

To create a link between a user and contact form, you must generate the user and the contact form independently, and then join them through the admin system. You can join a user to a contact form at the time that you create the form, or afterwards by editing an existing form. The tool for creating the linkage is located in the Contacts component, under the Components menu. While you can make the link only from within the Contacts component, once the link is created, you can edit it from either the Contacts component or from the user editing screen inside the User Manager. Likewise, you can also edit the user details from the Contact Manager screen under the Components menu.

Link a Contact Form to a User

1. Click Components.
2. Click Contacts.
3. Click Manage Contacts.

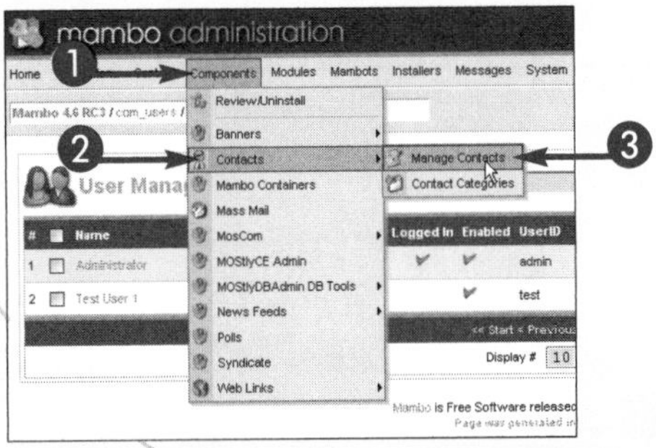

4. Click the check box of the user you want to edit.
5. Click the Edit icon.

The Contact Editing screen loads.

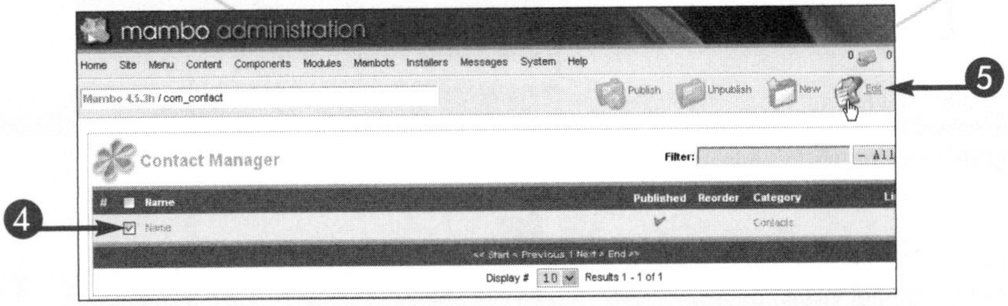

6. Click here and select the name of the user.
7. Click the Save icon.

Form submissions now go to that user and the name of the linked user appears.

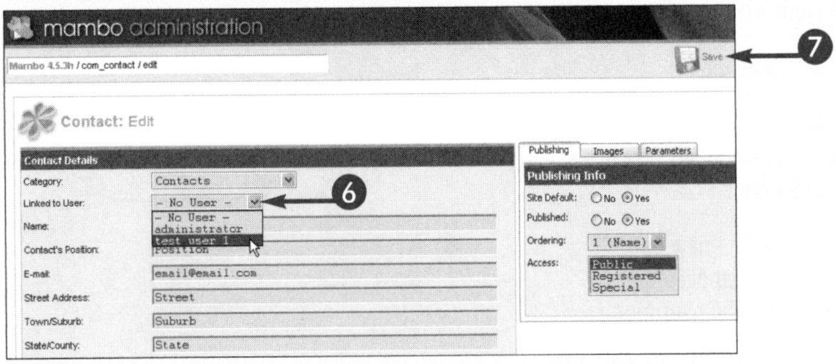

Set User Privileges

You can change a user's privileges in the system by changing the user's group assignment. You generally change group assignments in order to increase or decrease a user's status within the hierarchy of users that exists within the Mambo User Manager. Changing a user's privileges expands or restricts the user's access to certain content or functionalities.

You can apply changes in user privileges to any user except a Super Administrator. In Mambo, once a user is a Super Administrator, the user always remains a Super Administrator. The only way to restrict Super Administrators is to block them from the system using the Block User command, explained in the next section, "Block a User." Granting user privileges carries with it security implications. You should never make user access greater than is necessary. Unnecessary access to components and content creates opportunities for a user to make unauthorized changes to the site.

Higher-level users may also have access to user details and other data, which has privacy implications. This is not a question of whether you trust an individual user. Most frequently unauthorized access occurs without the original user's knowledge, where for example, an unauthorized person deduces or steals a username and password. Every good Webmaster knows that by carefully controlling the rights given to users, you can help avoid the possibility of abuse of the site.

Super Administrator rights are the area of greatest concern. The Super Administrator can change Global Configuration settings that can impair the entire site. Super Administrators can also install or uninstall components, Mambots, and modules, thereby affecting the site functionality. Accordingly, you should keep the number of Super Administrators to an absolute minimum.

Set User Privileges

1. From the User Manager, click the check box of the user you want to edit.
2. Click the Edit icon.

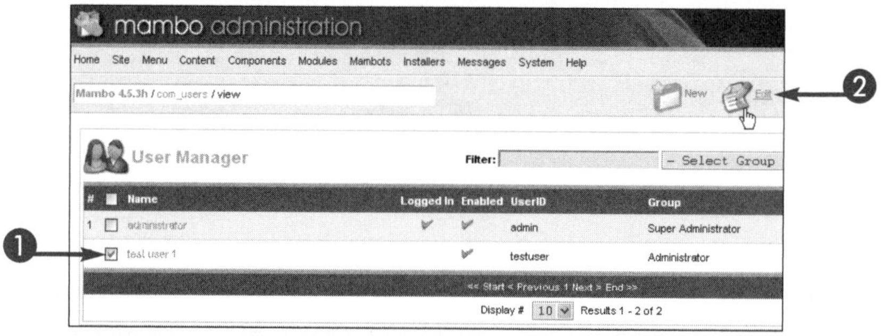

A new page loads.

3. Select the user group to which you want to assign the user.

Note: "Public Frontend" and "Public Backend" are not levels, merely descriptive labels.

4. Click the Save icon.

You can click the Cancel icon to return to the main screen without saving.

Mambo sets the new user privileges and applies them the next time the user logs in.

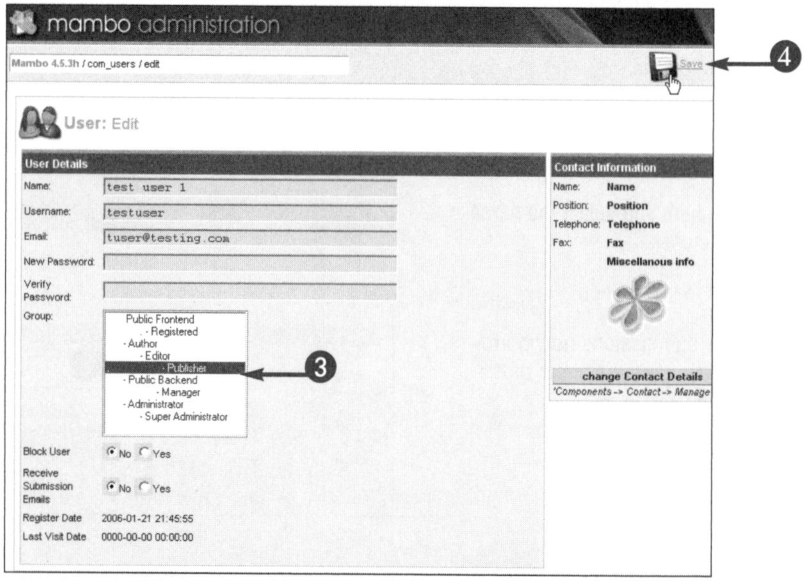

Block a User

The User Manager gives an Administrator or a Super Administrator the ability to block a user from logging in to the system. This feature enhances security and site management and prevents a system's abuse by the blocked user. A System Administrator may block a user as a temporary measure to give the Administrator time to contact the user directly and to investigate whether something is truly amiss. If the Administrator can remedy the problem, he or she can then restore the user's privileges with the click of the mouse. If the problem is serious, the Administrator can block the user permanently.

As an alternative to using the simple Block User functionality contained in the User Manager, a System Administrator can block a user by changing the user's password. You should note, however, that a user can defeat a changed password if he or she can access the Password Reminder function on the site, because the user can simply request a new password. Using the Block User functionality has the additional advantage of suspending a user's ability to receive system notification emails, which may be desirable for security or privacy reasons. Given the range of options and the consequences of each, the Block User option is the easiest and surest path of securing the site in the event of a problem user.

Note that if you block a user, he or she remains blocked until another Administrator or Super Administrator enters the admin system and unblocks the user. If the system has more than one Administrator or Super Administrator, any of them can lift the block and give the user access to the system. A persistent problem user can always reregister on sites that allow user registration. In those cases, there is simply no substitute for diligent site administration.

Block a User

1. Click the check box of the user you want to edit.
2. Click the Edit icon.

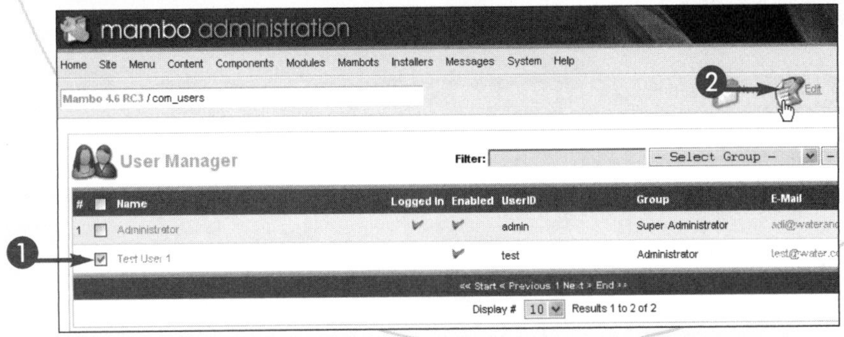

A new page loads.

3. For the Block User option, click Yes.
4. Click the Save icon.

If you want to exit without saving, simply click the Cancel icon.

Now, the user cannot log in.

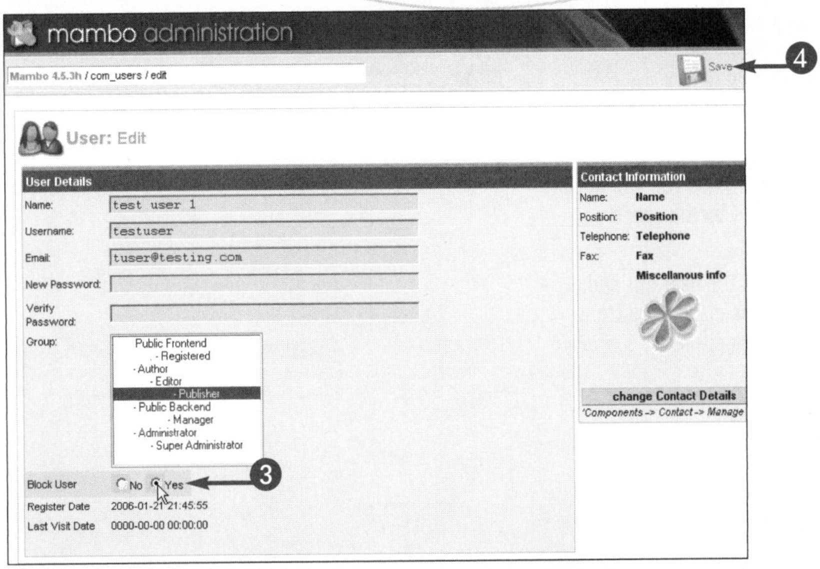

Force a User to Log Out

Another security tool for Mambo site administration is the Force Logout command. Administrators may want to use this option when a problem user is active on the site and is logged in. In that case, the Administrator may need to force the user to log out to prevent them from exercising privileges within the system that may cause disruption or compromise privacy.

You access the Force Logout command from one of two locations: the Logged Tab of the Control Panel, or the User Manager. Both locations are easy to access and results are immediate.

It is important to note that the Force Logout command does not impair a user's ability to log in to the system. The command is a quick solution to an immediate problem; it is not a long-term solution. To be effective as a security tool, you must combine Force Logout with steps to block the user's access to the system. A Super Administrator must simultaneously block the user's access or the user can just log in again immediately after being forced to log out. For more on the Block User command, see the previous section, "Block a User."

Extra

While Mambo gives you the tool to stop the abuse, identifying the abuse early is a different problem altogether. Some cases of abuse are obvious — for example, when a user makes unauthorized changes to the contents of a site. In those cases, the Super Administrator must move quickly to block the user before any further damage can occur. In other cases, the Super Administrator can spot a potential problem in advance by watching the site activity. If the Super Administrator feels that a problem may exist, he or she should consider blocking the user to allow time to investigate.

Force a User to Log Out

1. From the User Manager, select the user's name.
2. Click the Force Logout icon.

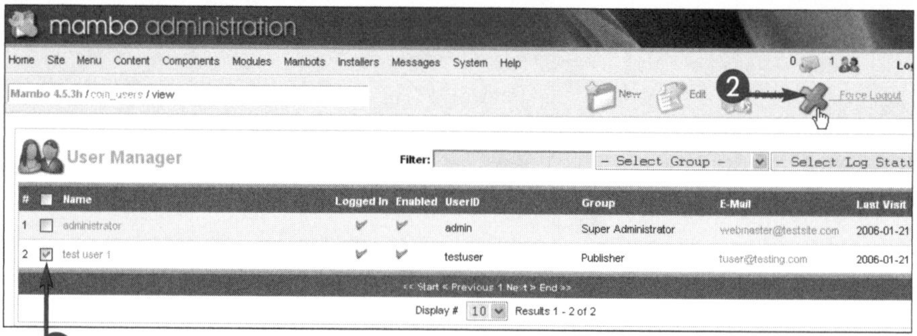

The user status no longer shows that he or she is logged In.

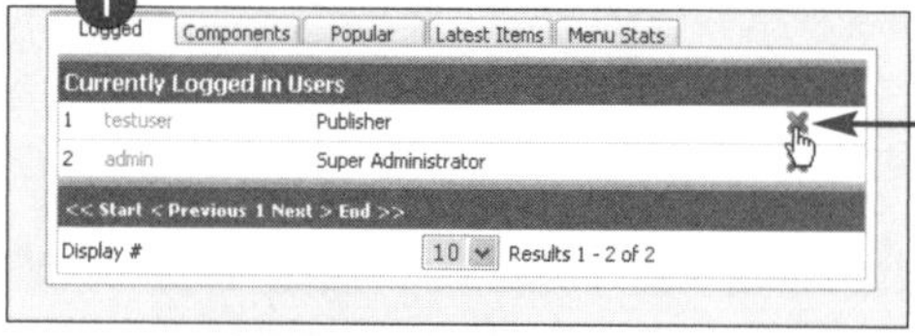

- Alternatively, from the Control Panel, you can click the cross by the user's name.

Mambo logs the user out and the username disappears from the list of logged-in users.

Delete a User

You can delete one or more user accounts via the Delete command in the User Manager. You may find the deletion of users desirable for a variety of reasons — from security to simple housekeeping. For security purposes, although it is not absolutely necessary to delete the accounts of blocked or inactive users, it is a good idea. Unused accounts are a common way for hackers to gain entry into a system. If the Super Administrator has blocked the account, this should not be a problem, but it is better to be on the safe side and eliminate the risk entirely by deleting unneeded accounts.

Some community-oriented sites may have hundreds if not thousands of users. Large lists of user accounts can significantly affect the performance of the admin system. The difference in performance is most noticeable in the User Manager, which begins to slow down while Mambo tries to load the multitude of users into the User Manager interface for the System Administrator's review.

Mambo keeps track of all the users, even those who no longer use the system. While it is desirable for the system to persist the user data, it also means the System Administrator must make an effort to police and maintain the system. There is no automatic way to remove inactive users; the System Administrator must go through the user records and delete each one manually using the Delete command in the User Manager. Identifying the unused accounts can be time consuming, but the Mambo User Manager helps with this task by displaying the date of the last visit of each user. Viewing the Last Visit date is a good way to judge whether a user is still active, or if he or she has ceased to use their privileges.

Delete a User

1. Select the user you want to delete.
2. Click the Delete icon.

A confirmation dialog box appears.

3. To confirm the deletion, click OK.

- You can click Cancel to return to the main screen without saving.

Mambo completely removes the user from the system.

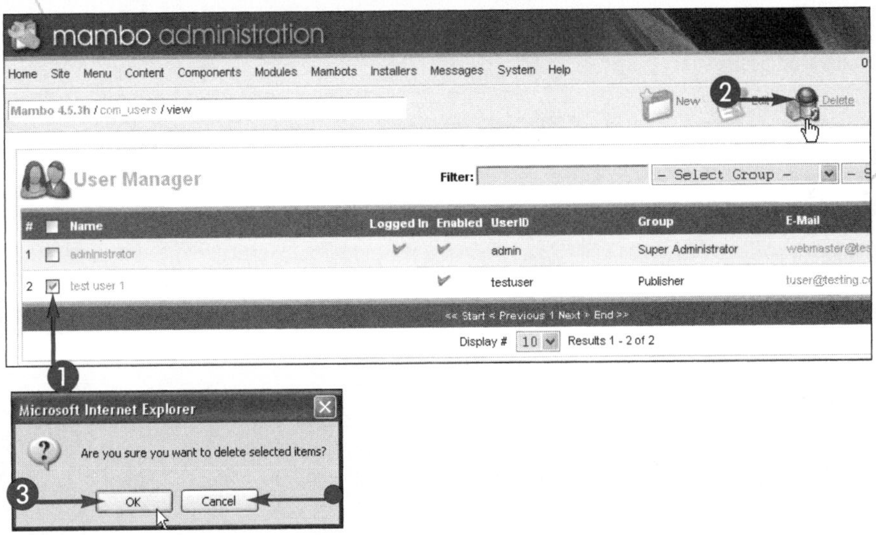

Manage Content from the Front End

Certain classes of users can manage content from the front end of a Mambo Web site. This feature is very useful where you want users to contribute news or other types of articles to the site. Use of this technique also means you do not have to give members of the content creation team access to the admin system, which enhances your site's security and reduces the possibility of unskilled users making undesired changes to other parts of the site.

The user groups contained in the Mambo system can be classified into two categories: those with access to both the front end and the back end, and those who can access only the front end. The user groups that can log in to the front end only are: Registered, Author, Editor, and Publisher. The Author, Editor, and Publisher groups were created specifically to enable content management from the front end of a site. For more information on the privileges attached to each user group, see Chapter 3.

Setting up a site to allow the editing of content from the front end is a combination of making the tools available, making the content sections available, and making sure the users have been assigned to the proper groups. The only tool that is absolutely necessary is a login interface. Without a login box on the front end, the front end users cannot gain access to the system. Additionally, if you want the authors, editors, and publishers to have a WYSIWYG content editor at their disposal, you have to make sure one is installed and enabled; that topic is covered in Chapter 2.

Manage Content from the Front End

ASSIGN AND ENABLE THE LOGIN MODULE

1. Click Modules.
2. Click Site Modules.

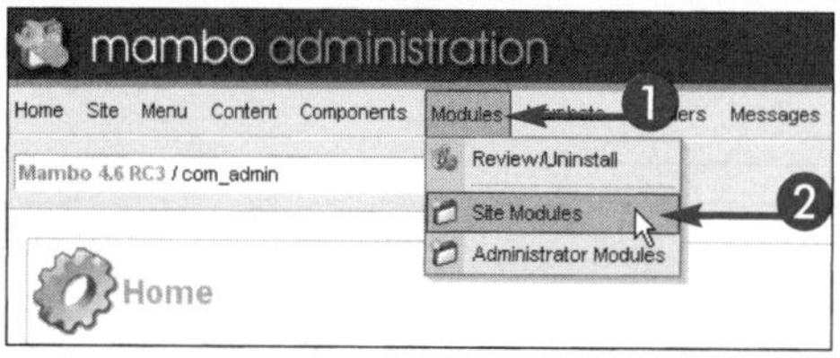

The Site Module Manager loads.

3. Click the Login Form module.
4. Click the Edit icon.

The Module Editing page loads.

5. Assign the module to the position in which you want the login interface to appear.
6. Assign the module to the pages on which you want the login interface to appear.
7. Publish the module.
8. Click the Save icon.

Mambo publishes the Login module and it appears on the selected pages.

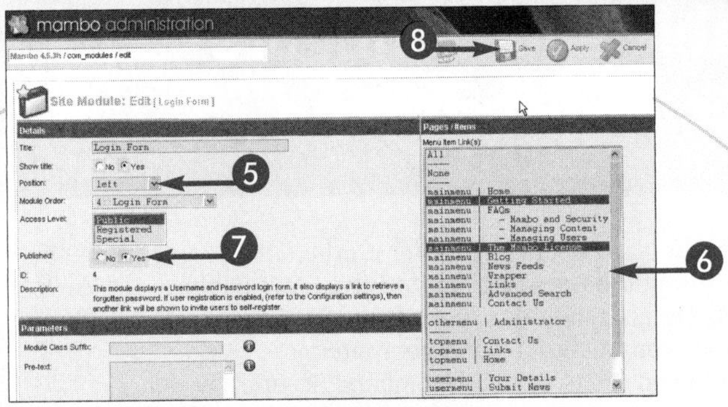

CREATE AN AUTHOR

1. From the User Manager, click the New icon.

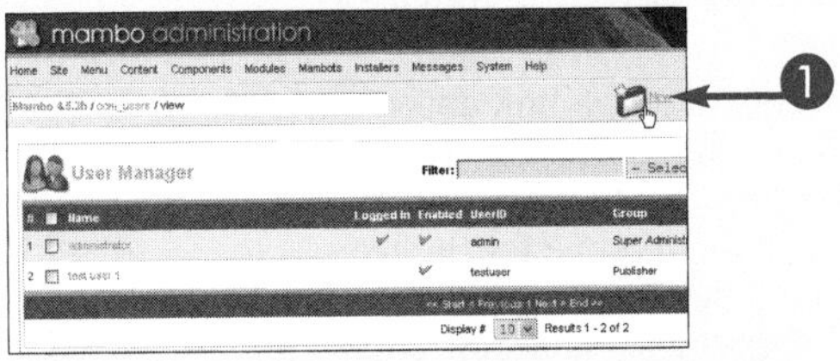

A new page loads.

2. Type the user's details.
3. Select the Author user group.
4. Click the Save icon.

A user with Author privileges now exists.

You can repeat Steps 1 to 4 in this subsection as needed to create users in the Editor or Publisher groups.

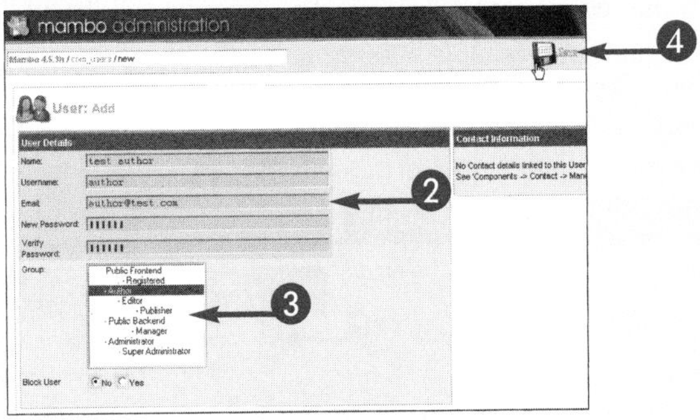

Note: See the section "Set User Privileges" for more information.

Extra

To determine which classes of users are necessary for your site, you must decide how you want the content management workflow to function. Smaller sites logically favor a more streamlined structure. A more complex site with many contributors may use all the various groups. Consider the following examples:

SITUATION	SOLUTION
Users contribute articles	Assign the users to the Author group; let an Administrator or Super Administrator handle editing and publication.
Users contribute and someone else edits contributions into suitable form	Assign users to the Author group and the editors to the Editor group; let an Administrator or Super Administrator handle publication.
Users handle content editing and publication	Use all three of the front-end-only groups, that is, Author, Editor, and Publisher.
Separate the content creation tasks from the general site administration	Assign users to all three of the front-end-only groups. Assign someone to the Manager class to access the admin system for the creation of sections, categories, and Menu Items.

Enable and Configure User Registration

You can allow users to register on the site by enabling the User Registration feature. Enabling User Registration has two advantages. First, it helps build a community around your site by encouraging visitors to become members. Second, by allowing users to register themselves, it decreases administrative burden.

If you enable the user registration, a link appears inside the Login box on the front end of the site. The Site module named "Login Form" produces the Login box and therefore you must enable the module for the feature to work. Once you enable the module, a hyperlink with the label "No account yet? Create one" appears. This link takes the user to the registration form.

The registration form is very simple. Users need only disclose their name and email address and select a username and password. The fields on the user registration form are fixed and cannot be altered. If you want to gather more information during the registration process, you should investigate adding a third-party component to allow for the creation of customized registration forms.

Among the options you can select for user registration are two important security features. The first is the Use New Account Activation option. If you select this option, the system automatically sends an email to a newly registered user's email address. The email contains a link that the user must click to confirm the registration and activate the new account. This feature is designed to filter automated scripts and bots that might try to set up accounts on the site — a technique that spammers and hackers often use. The second feature is the Require Unique Email option, which is intended to keep people from setting up multiple accounts.

Enable and Configure User Registration

1. Click Site.
2. Click Global Configuration.

Note: This option is available only to members of the Super Administrator user group.

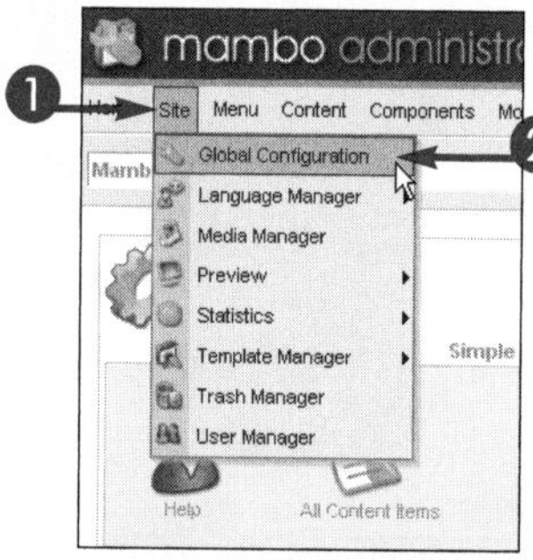

The Global Configuration Manager loads.

3. For Allow User Registration, click the Yes option.
4. Click whether you want to use the confirmation email.
5. Click whether you want to require a unique email address.
6. Click the Save icon.

Mambo enables and configures the User Registration.

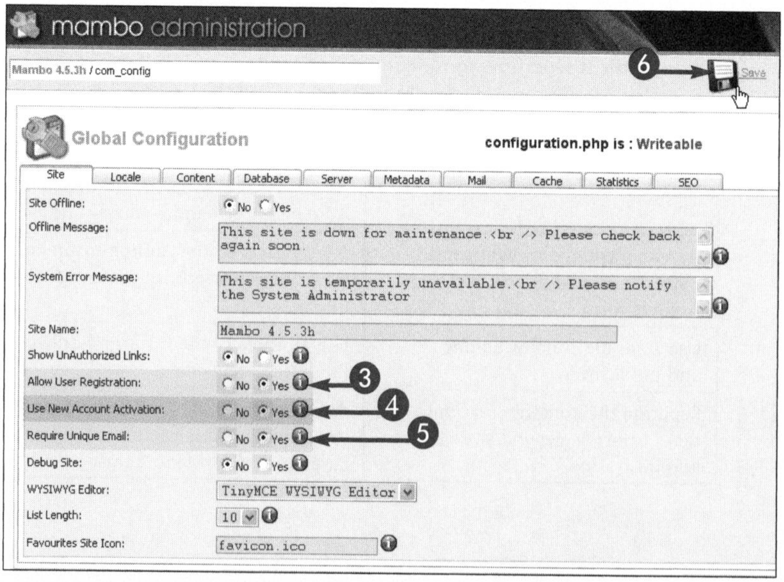

ASSIGN AND ENABLE THE LOGIN MODULE

1. Access the Site Module Manager.

   Note: To access the Site Module Manager, see the section "Manage Content from the Front End."

   The Site Module Manager loads.

2. Select the Login Form module.

3. Click the Edit icon.

   The Module Editing page loads.

4. Assign the module to the position in which you want the login interface to appear.

5. Assign the module to the pages on which you want the login interface to appear.

6. Publish the module.

7. Click the Save icon.

   Mambo publishes the Login module containing the User Registration link, and the link appears on the selected pages.

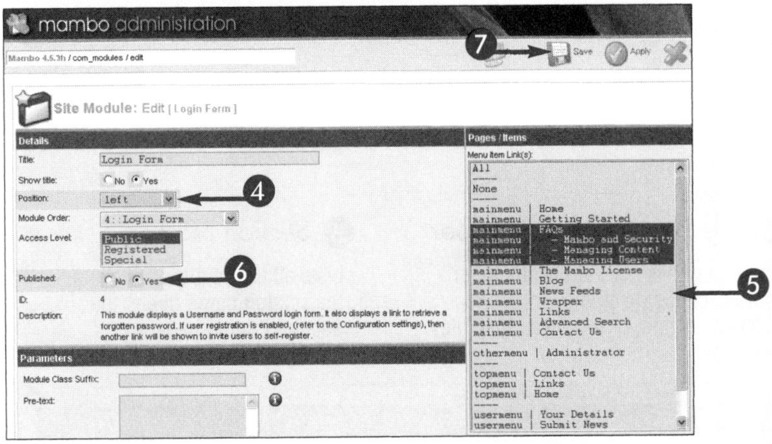

Extra

Users who register by way of the user registration form are automatically assigned to the user group named Registered. The Registered group is the most limited of the user groups and only gives the users access to content, menus, and components that the System Administrator has set to the access level "Registered." For more information on user privileges, refer to the section "Understanding Mambo User Groups." An Administrator or a Super Administrator can change the user's privileges via the User Manager, as explained in the section "Set User Privileges."

By default, Mambo creates a connection between registered users and the default User Menu. If you have not modified the default installation, when registered users log in, they see the User Menu. The contents of that menu in the default configuration include links that allow users to edit their own profile and to submit Web links into the Web Links component. Administrators can edit the menu via the User Menu choice under the menu named, appropriately, Menu. You can also unpublish the menu via the Site Modules Manager. You can find more on the menus topic in Chapter 9. Site modules are discussed at length in Chapter 11.

An Introduction to the Section Manager

The Mambo Section Manager gives you access to all existing Content Sections. With the Manager, you can make changes to, create, or delete sections. On the Content menu, the Content by Section heading has links to all the individual sections, but the only place to create, edit, and delete the sections themselves is the Section Manager. You access the Section Manager either from the quick icons on the Control Panel or from the Section Manager link on the Content menu.

Although simple, the interface holds a number of useful tools. The Section Manager gives an overview of the relationship between the sections and their subsidiary categories. If you publish only the section landing pages, you edit content with the Section Manager. To edit a section landing page's content, see the section "Create Content Sections." To publish section landing pages or create menu links to pages at various levels of the site's content hierarchy, see Chapter 9.

A Selection Manager Toolbar

Icons to publish or unpublish one or more sections, to create, copy, edit, delete a section, or to access Help files.

B Section Name

Lists all the sections. Clicking the section name opens the Section Editing page.

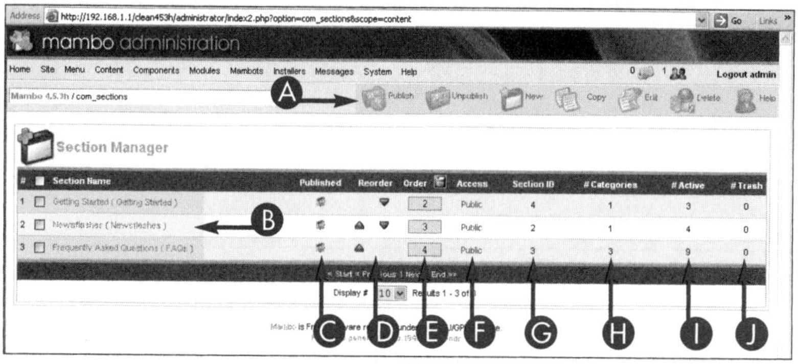

C Published

Shows the publication state. The icon toggles the state.

D Reorder

Reorders sections by moving them up or down relative to the others on the list.

E Order

Reorders the Section list when you change a section's numerical sequence and click the Save icon.

F Access

The current access state of the section. The icon toggles the state.

G Section ID

A system-generated identification number.

H # Categories

The total number of categories assigned to the section.

I # Active

The number of active categories assigned to the section.

J # Trash

Shows how many categories assigned to the section are currently in the Trash Manager.

An Introduction to the Category Manager

With the Mambo Category Manager, you can access all existing Content Categories and change them. You can also create or delete categories. The Content menu under each section name beneath the Content by Section heading has links to the individual categories. You either access the Category Manager from the quick icons on the Control Panel or from the Category Manager link on the Content menu.

Although very simple, the interface holds a number of useful tools. The Category Manager shows an overview of the relationship between the categories and their Content Items and the sections to which they belong. If you publish only the category landing pages, you use the Category Manager to make edits to the landing page content. To edit a category landing page's content, see the section "Create Content Categories." To publish section landing pages or create menu links to pages at various levels of the site's content hierarchy, see Chapter 9.

A Category Manager Toolbar

Icons to publish or unpublish one or more existing categories, to create, move, copy, edit, or delete a category, and to access Help files.

B Filter

Filters the Category list to show the categories belonging to only one section.

C Category Name

Lists all the categories. Clicking the name opens the Category Editing page.

D Published

Shows the publication state. The icon toggles the state.

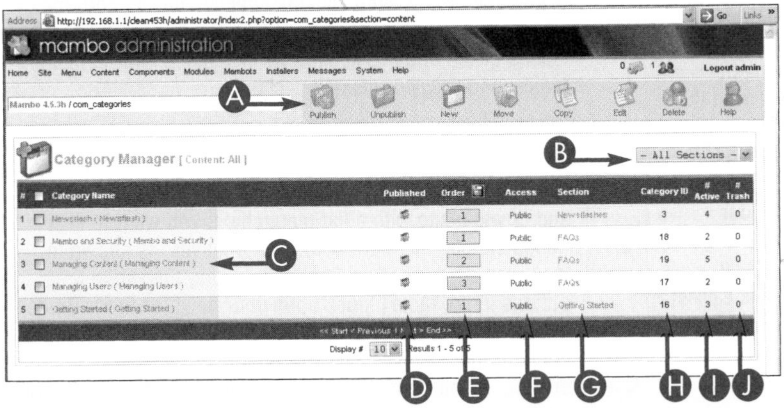

E Order

Reorders the Category list when you change a category's numerical sequence and click the Save icon.

F Access

Shows a category's current access state. Click the icon to toggle the state.

G Section

Shows the section to which the category belongs. Clicking the name opens the Section Editing page.

H Category ID

A system-generated identification number.

I # Active

The number of active Content Items assigned to the category.

J # Trash

Shows how many Content Items assigned to the category are currently in the Trash Manager.

Mambo Content Hierarchies

The Mambo system has a number of alternatives for creating content hierarchies, from flat hierarchies to multi-tier structures. You can find the greatest flexibility by understanding how to employ the combination of sections, categories, Content Items, and Static Content Items. If you do not understand the distinctions between sections and categories, or between Content Items and Static Content Items, review Chapter 1.

The default Mambo installation is intended to handle a multi-tier content hierarchy of no more than three levels. At the top of the hierarchy are the Content Sections. At the middle level are the Content Categories. By definition, categories must belong to sections. At the lowest tier are the Content Items, which belong by definition to categories. You cannot have categories without sections or Content Items without categories.

While no category can belong to more than one section and no Content Item can belong to more than one category, you can overcome that limitation by copying the category or Content Item and moving it to the new section or category. If you create more than one instance of a section, category, or Content Item, you must update each occurrence separately. It is not possible to automatically synchronize Content Items, which are located in different categories or sections.

Linking Site Navigation with Menu Items

You can link your site navigation to any of the levels. When you create a Menu Item, you have a choice of what to link to: a section, a category, a Content Item, or a Static Content Item. The relationship between Menu Items and the Content Hierarchy is the key to how you display to visitors the organizational scheme of the content of your site. Using your Menu Items to impose order on the content in the admin system is one of Mambo's most powerful features because it allows you to create either a consistent organization scheme for both the front end and the back end, or to create one structure for your visitors and another for your administrators. For a large site, you may find that an organizational scheme that allows easy user navigation may not always be the easiest to administer. For more on creating and managing Menu Items, see Chapter 9.

Site Organization Schema

If your site is of medium to large size, you are well-advised to spend some time thinking about the organization of the content within the Mambo hierarchies, because the organization schema directly impacts both the site navigation and the ease of administration. The following sections give some possibilities for managing your content in a logical and easy-to-maintain fashion.

Creating a Flat Hierarchy

A small-site owner may want to avoid all this complexity and create a site with a flat hierarchy. If you want to keep things simple, there are several alternatives, as shown in the following table. Deciding from among the various options in the table hinges upon your need for the features attached to Static Content versus Content Items, the configuration choices available, and your needs for creating Menu Items. Another consideration is the pathway feature that appears on many sites. The pathway is present in the default installation and shows you where you are in the hierarchy and provides links to the levels in the hierarchy above you. If you employ the pathway on your site, you will soon discover that the placement of Content Items within the hierarchy impacts the pathway, and this may in turn impact your decision about which organizational technique to apply.

ORGANIZATION TECHNIQUE	CONSIDERATIONS & APPLICATION
Static Content Only	The simplest approach, this avoids the need to use sections and categories. For more on Static Content Items and whether they are right for your needs, see Chapter 6.
One Section, One Category	Create one section and one category and place all the Content Items in the single category. Link your Menu Items directly to the Content Items.
One Section, Multiple Categories	An option of moderate complexity executed by placing each Content Item in its own category. Give your categories and Content Items the same or similar names for the sake of simplicity of administration. Link your Menu Items directly to the Content Items.
Multiple Sections, Multiple Categories	The most complex option, this creates one section and one category for each Content Item. Give your sections, categories, and Content Items the same or similar names. Link your Menu Items directly to the Content Items.

Creating a Two-Tier Hierarchy

If your site needs only two tiers for the content hierarchy, Mambo offers two clear options for handling the organization, as presented in the following table:

ORGANIZATION TECHNIQUE	CONSIDERATIONS & APPLICATION
One Section, Multiple Categories	The simplest method, the categories become the top level of your hierarchy and the Content Items placed inside the categories become your lowest tier. Do not link your Menu Items to the section so that it remains invisible to site visitors.
Multiple Sections, Multiple Categories	Creates perhaps unneeded redundancy but keeps the administration system in parallel with the front end. Easiest to give the sections and categories the same or similar names for the sake of simplicity of administration. Link your Menu Items to the categories.

Creating a Three-Tier Hierarchy

A three-tier structure is perhaps the easiest to create because it flows naturally from the system. You place sections at the top, categories at the middle level, and Content Items at the lowest level. You link your Menu Items directly to the sections.

Creating a Four-Tier Hierarchy

While the default system's content hierarchy is tailored to three tiers, it is possible to create a fourth tier through the use of Static Content Items. By definition, Static Content Items do not belong to categories or to sections. Static Content Items are completely independent. Because Static Content Items are not part of the hierarchy that is applicable to other Content Items on the site, they effectively create a separate class or tier of Content Items.

Create Content Sections

You can create new Content Sections through the Mambo Section Manager. Sections are the top level of the Mambo content hierarchy; they hold and organize categories. If you add new content to your site, you will probably begin by creating a section, followed by one or more categories, and then your Content Items.

The default installation of Mambo contains a limited number of sections, but you can add as many as you like. As a practical matter, consider restricting the total number of sections. It is more efficient to use the sections to group together sets of categories and use the categories in turn to group together sets of Content Items. Too many sections increases your administration burden and makes it hard to find things in the admin system.

You may or may not link a section into a Menu Item. If you do choose to link to the section directly, when users click the link, they go to the section landing page. That page should contain, at the very least, links to the Categories contained in that section. You can also add images to the landing page for decoration, or you can leave the page blank except for the links. You can also add content to the section landing page. The Create Section function contains a text area, complete with WYSIWYG editor, for you to enter content for the section landing page. You can make the content as long as you want. The landing page can contain anything you want to place in a Content Item. You can even create multiple pages of content, courtesy of the ability of the Mambo system to create multi-page content with the MOSpagebreak function.

Create Content Sections

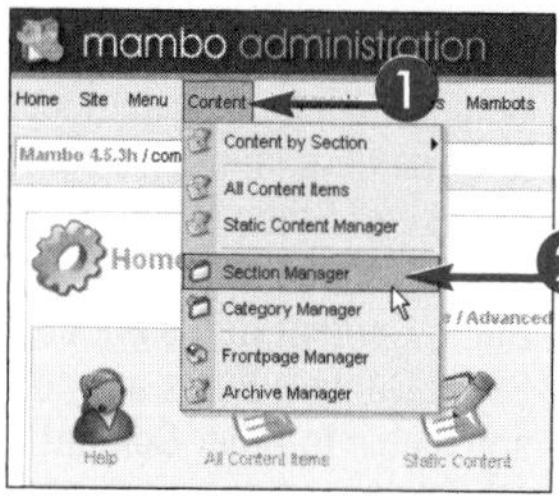

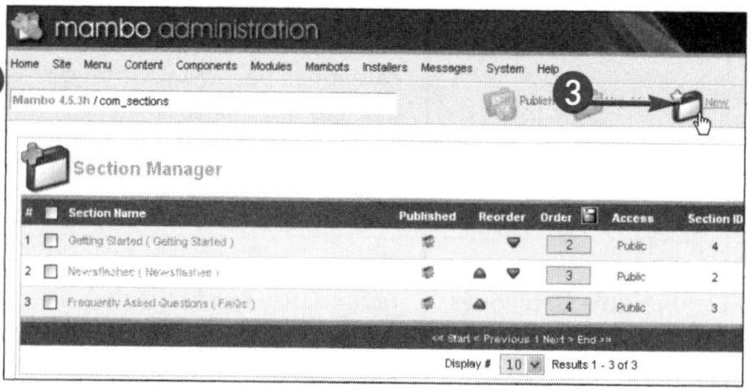

1. Click Content.
2. Click Section Manager.

   The Section Manager loads.
3. Click the New icon.

   The New Section screen loads.

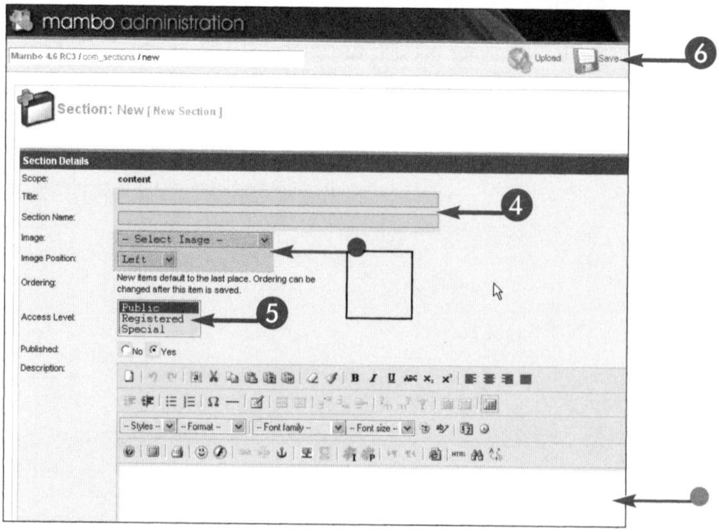

4. Type a title and name for the section.
   - You can click in these areas to select an image and a position for the image.
5. Click an access level.
   - You can add text by typing here.
6. Click the Save icon.

   Mambo adds a new section to the system.

Create Content Categories

You can create new Content Categories with the Category Manager. Categories are the middle level of the Mambo content hierarchy that hold and organize Content Items. Before you can create a category you must create at least one section.

The default installation of Mambo contains a limited number of categories, but you can add as many as you like. As a practical matter, try to group your categories together logically and organize similar categories together within sections. Similarly, you should organize your Content Items in a logical fashion and group them together inside of categories. A methodical approach to the organization of your content makes site administration easier and enables you to create a usable navigation scheme.

You may or may not link a category to a Menu Item. If you do choose to create a Menu Item that links to a category directly, users who click the Menu Item are taken to the category landing page. The category landing page should contain, at the very least, links to the Content Items contained in that category. You can also add images to the landing page for decoration, or you can leave the page blank except for the links. You can also add content to the category landing page. The function for creating new categories contains a text area, complete with WYSIWYG editor, for you to enter content for the category landing page; you can make the content as long as you want. The landing page can contain anything you want to place in a Content Item. You can even create multiple pages of content, courtesy of the ability of the Mambo system to create multi-page content with the MOSpagebreak function.

Create Content Categories

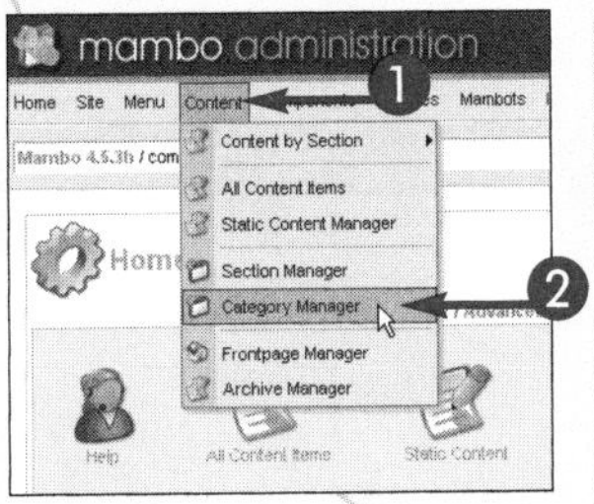

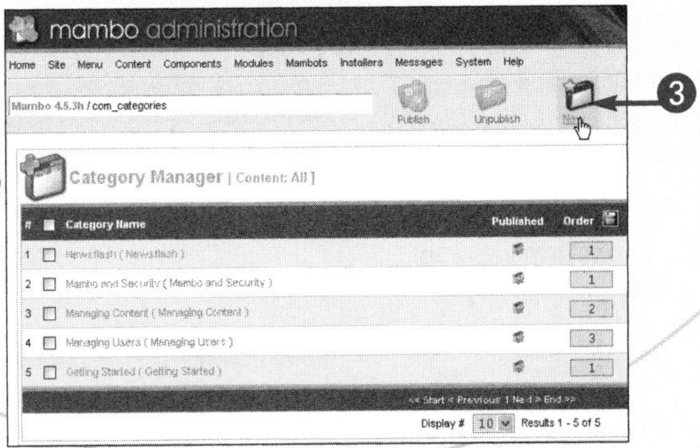

1. Click Content.
2. Click Category Manager.

   The Category Manager loads.
3. Click the New icon.

   The New Category screen loads.
4. Type a title and name for the category.
5. Click here and assign the category to a section.
   - You can click these areas to select an image and a position for the image.
6. Click here to set the access level.
   - You can type text here.
7. Click the Save icon.

   Mambo adds the new category to the system.

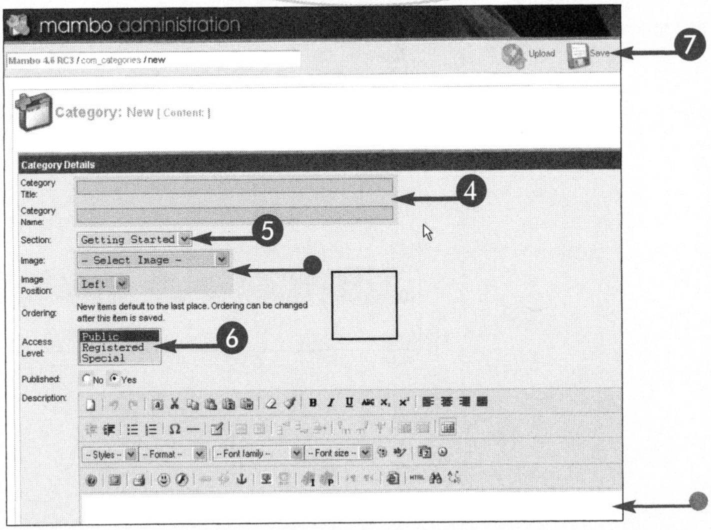

Publish a Section

You must publish a section for the contents to become visible to your site's visitors. While you can view and edit a section within the administration system without publishing it, you must publish the section for visitors to see the section's contents from the front end of the Web site.

During site construction or the creation of new content, it is generally best to leave the section unpublished. If you publish while you are editing, site visitors can see the work in progress. When the item is in final form, display it on the site by publishing the section.

Publication is a requirement for sections, categories, and Content Items. Failure to publish an item affects all items below it in the hierarchy. If you fail to publish a section, the categories and Content Items inside of the section do not appear, even if the categories and Content Items themselves are published. Generally speaking, the publishing hierarchy flows only one way; failing to publish a category or a Content Item does not impact the section to which it is assigned. An exception to the general rule is when you select the Mambo system option Hide Empty Sections, in which case a published section that contains published Content Items, but does not contain any published categories, will not display to site visitors.

There are two ways to publish a section. You can publish a section either with one click directly from the Section Manager, or by opening the section editing screen and selecting Publish from the parameters inside the editing window. Always check the front end of the Web site after invoking the publication command to make sure that the result is what you expected.

Publish a Section

1. Load the Section Manager.

Note: To load the Section Manager, see the section "Create Content Sections."

2. Click the icon in the Published column for the item you want to publish.

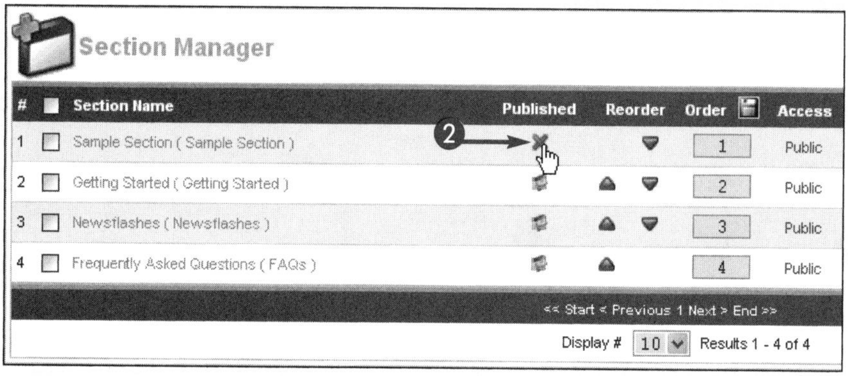

- Mambo publishes the section.

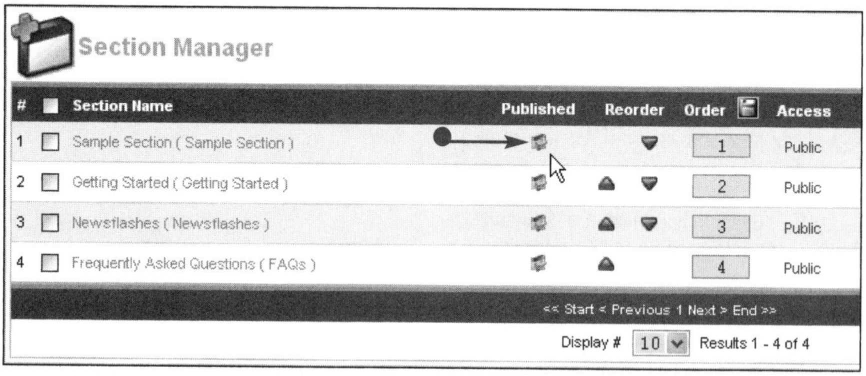

Publish a Category

You must publish a category for the contents to become visible to your site's visitors. While you can view and edit a category within the administration system without publishing it, you must publish the category for the category and the Content Items inside of it to be seen from the front end of the Web site.

During site construction or the creation of new content, you should generally leave the category unpublished. If you publish the category while you are editing, site visitors can see the work in progress. When you have the item in final form, you can display the category on the site by publishing the category.

Publication is a requirement for sections, categories, and Content Items. Failure to publish an item affects all items below it in the hierarchy. If you fail to publish a category, it prevents the visitor from seeing the Content Items within that category, even if you have published the Content Items themselves. Generally speaking, the publishing hierarchy flows only one way; failing to publish a Content Item does not impact the category to which the Content Item is assigned. An exception to the general rule is when you select the Mambo system option Hide Empty Sections, in which case site visitors cannot view a published category that does not contain any published Content Items.

You have two ways to publish a category: you can publish a category with one click directly from the Category Manager, or you can publish a category by opening the category editing screen and selecting Publish from the parameters inside the editing window. Always check the front end of the Web site after invoking the publication command to make sure that the result is what you expected.

Publish a Category

1. Load the Category Manager.

Note: To load the Category Manager, see the section "Create Content Categories."

2. Click the icon under the Published column for the category you want to publish.

- Mambo publishes the category.

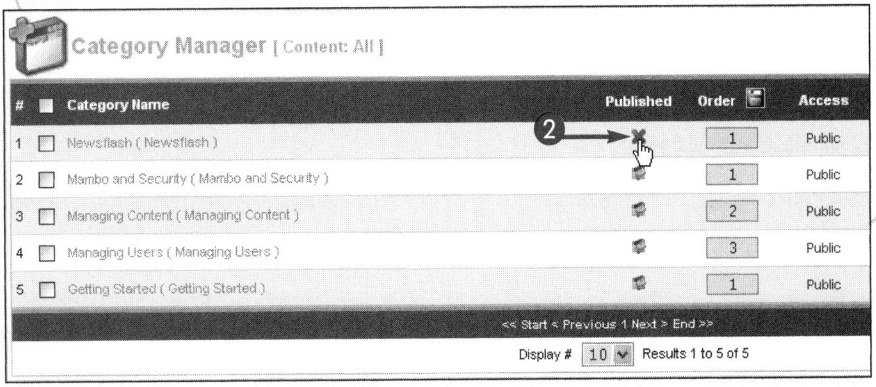

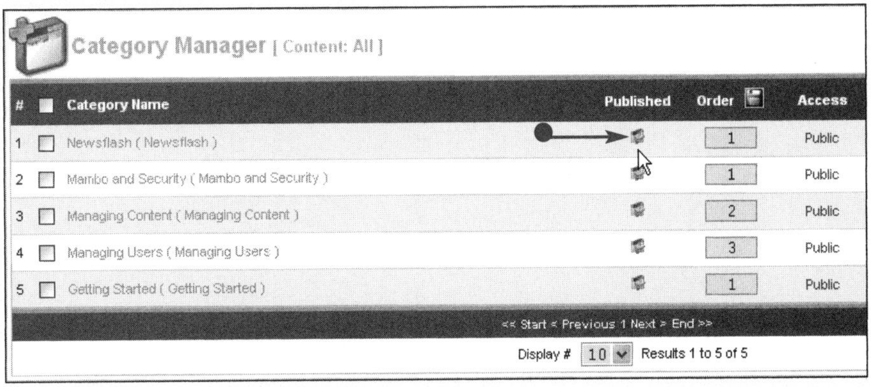

Unpublish a Section

You can remove a section from public view by unpublishing it. While the section remains visible to those who can access the Section Manager inside the administration system, site visitors cannot see it. The ability to control publishing of items on a case-by-case basis is a very useful feature of the Mambo system. You can temporarily unpublish items when you need to perform maintenance on the site, or when you want to update an item. You can permanently unpublish an item when you want to remove it from further display.

Unpublishing a section only removes the item from the front end of the Web site. It does not delete the item or impair your ability to publish the section again if you should choose to do so. Unpublished sections are held in the system like any other section, and there is no difference in the way you manage unpublished items in the administration system. You can still add categories to unpublished sections or edit the section and its landing page, but you cannot see the results on the front end of the Web site until you republish the section.

You can unpublish a section in two ways: with one click directly on the Published icon that is visible on the Section Manager, or by opening the section editing screen and selecting No to the publish parameters inside the editing window.

Note that unpublishing a section results in all categories and Content Items inside that section disappearing from the front end of the Web site. The items remain hidden from view until you republish the section.

Unpublish a Section

1. Load the Section Manager.

Note: To load the Section Manager, see the section "Create Content Sections."

The Section Manager loads.

2. Click the Published icon.

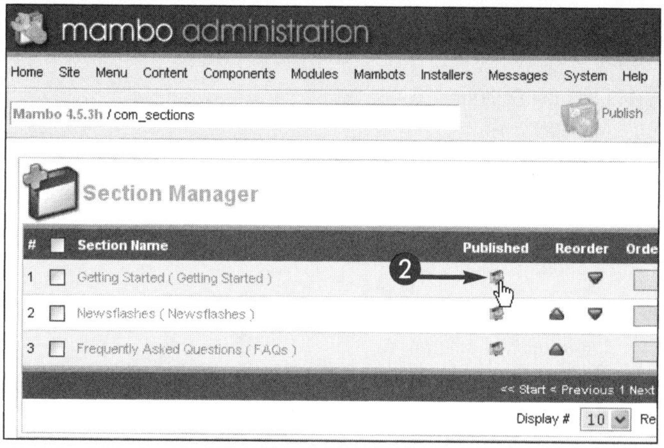

- Mambo unpublishes the section.

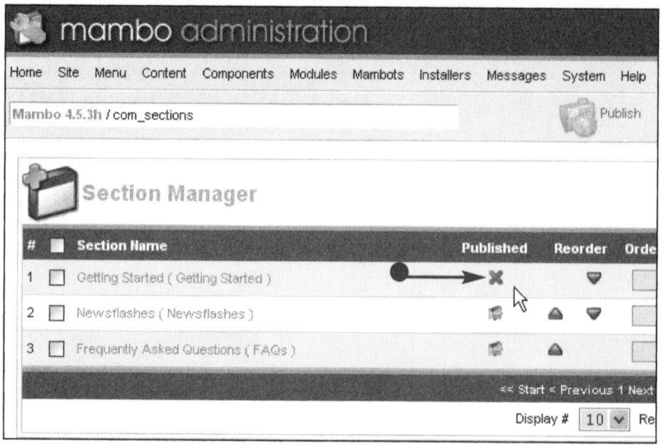

Unpublish a Category

You can remove a category from public view by unpublishing it. While the category remains visible in the administration system, the site visitor sees neither it nor any of its Content Items. The ability to control publishing of items on a case-by-case basis is a very useful feature of the Mambo system. You can temporarily unpublish items when you need to perform maintenance on the site or when you want to update an item. You can permanently unpublish an item to remove it from further display.

Unpublishing a category only removes the item from the front end of the Web site. It does not delete the item or impair your ability to publish it again if you choose to do so. Unpublished categories are held in the system like any other category, and there is no difference in the way unpublished categories are managed in the administration system. You can still add Content Items to unpublished categories or edit the category and its landing page, but you cannot see the results on the front end of the Web site until you republish the category.

You have two ways to unpublish a category: with one click directly on the Published icon that is visible on the Category Manager, or by opening the category editing screen and selecting No to the publish parameters inside the editing window.

Note that unpublishing a category causes all the Content Items assigned to that category to disappear on the front end until you republish the category.

Unpublish a Category

1. Load the Category Manager.

Note: To load the Category Manager, see the section "Create Content Categories."

2. Click the Published icon.

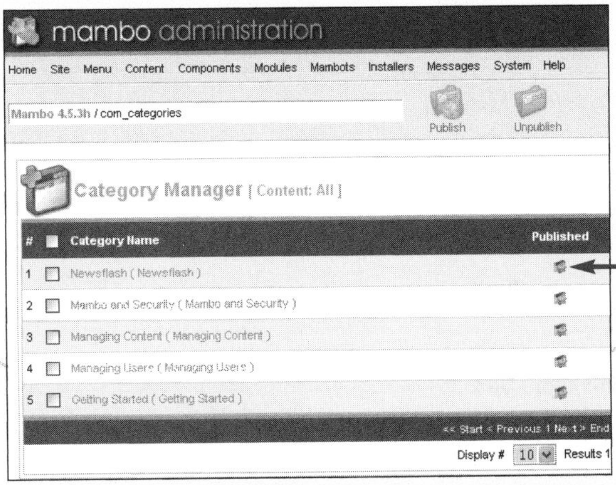

- Mambo unpublishes the category.

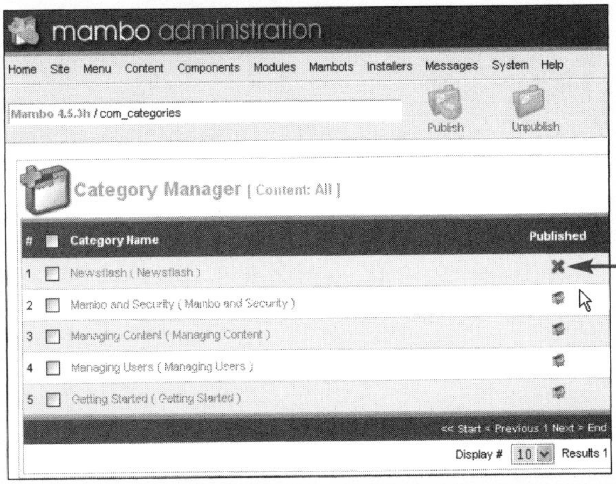

Edit an Existing Section

You can edit an existing section to change the information it contains. The editing screen enables you to change the name or the attributes of the section and to change the content that appears on the landing page. The editing screens also provide a method for creating links to the various menus in the system, allowing you to create menu links to the section quickly, directly from the section editing screen instead of having to use the Menu Manager.

The right column of the section editing screen includes two tools that do not appear when you create a new section. The tools in the right column allow you to view the existing menu links to the section, if any, or to create new links to the various menus in your system. The Existing Menu Links information only appears if you have already linked the item to a menu. Although the displayed data is informational in nature, it provides hyperlink shortcuts to the menus and the Menu Items connected to the section. The Link to Menu function appears on all section editing screens, regardless of whether you have already linked the item to a menu. Using the controls in the Link to Menu section, you can add a new Menu Item to any of the existing menus. The new Menu Item links to the section you are editing. You can choose both the format for the link and the name of the link. If you want to edit an existing Menu Item, simply click the item's name in the Existing Menu Links section.

Edit an Existing Section

1. Load the Section Manager.

Note: To load the Section Manager, see the section "Create Content Sections."

2. Click the section you want to edit.
3. Click the Edit icon.

The Section Editor loads.

4. Make any changes you want.
5. Click the Save icon.

Mambo saves your changes and returns you to the Section Manager.

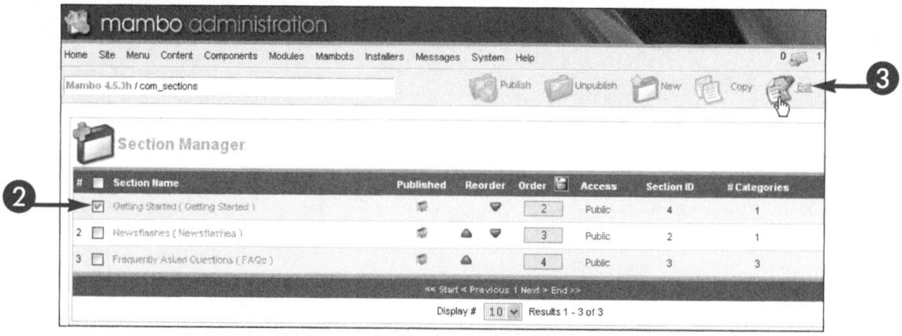

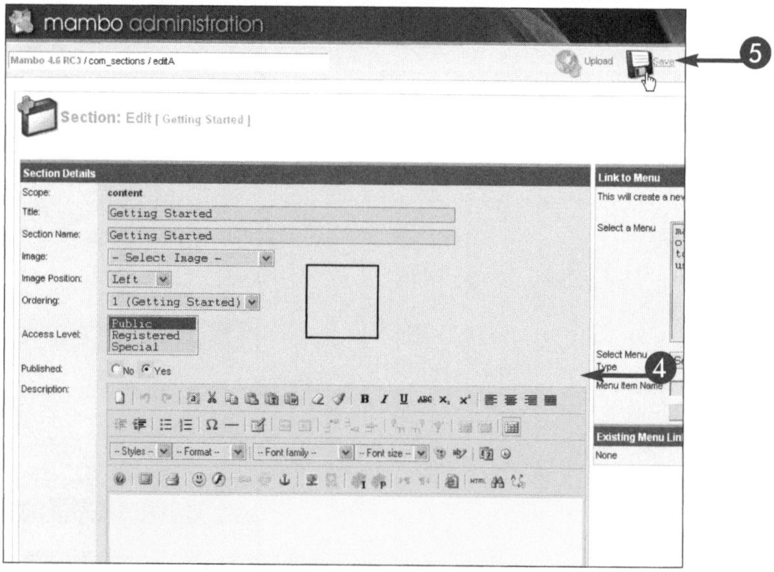

Edit an Existing Category

You can edit an existing category to change the information it contains. The editing screen enables you to change the name or the attributes of the category and to change the content that appears on the landing page. The editing screens also provide a method for creating links to the various menus in the system, allowing you to create menu links to the category quickly, directly from the category editing screen instead of having to use the Menu Manager.

The category editing screen is very similar to the section editing screen, but it does include one extra control in allowing you to reassign the category to a different section.

The right column of the category editing screen includes two tools that do not appear when you create a new category. The tools in the right column allow you to view the existing menu links to the category, if any, or to create new links to the category from the various menus in your system. The Existing Menu Links information appears only if you have already linked the item to a menu. Although the displayed data is informational in nature, it provides hyperlinks to the menus and the menu Items connected to the category. The Link to Menu function appears on all category editing screens, regardless of whether the item is already linked to a menu. Using the controls in the Link to Menu section, you can add a new Menu Item to any of the existing menus. The new Menu Item links to the category you are editing. You can choose both the format for the link and the name of the link. If you want to edit an existing menu item, simply click the item's name in the Existing Menu Links section.

Edit an Existing Category

1. Load the Category Manager.

Note: To load the Category Manager, see the section "Create Content Categories."

2. Click the category you want to edit.
3. Click the Edit icon.

The Category Editor loads.

4. Make any changes you want.
5. Click the Save icon.

Mambo saves your changes to the system and returns you to the Category Manager.

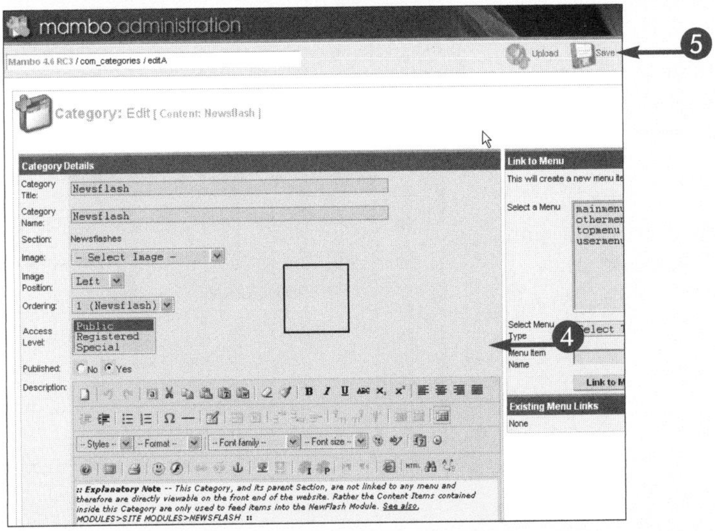

Move a Category

You can move any category in the system from one section to any other section in the system. Located in the Category Manager, the Move function is a useful tool for reordering your content hierarchy. The function is a timesaver because it allows you to move the category together with all of the Content Items that are assigned to it. The power to make changes to the relationships between sections and categories after you create categories adds significant flexibility to the system, because administrators can change content structures without deleting and recreating the information or reworking the navigation links.

When you initiate the Move command, the system displays a list showing both the name of the category and all the Content Items in that category. You need to select a new section for the contents and confirm your intention to move everything. Failure to confirm the move simply leaves the items where they are.

Moving a category does not affect the name, the formatting, or the contents of the category or the Content Items. All items retain their published state. That is, if you published the item before the move, it remains published after the move. Likewise, unpublished items remain unpublished. The Mambo system also automatically updates links between items and Menu Items.

You must create the section you want to move before you activate the Move command. Note that if you did not publish the section that you want to move the items to, the category and the Content Items that you move into that section become invisible on the front end of the Web site until you publish the section.

Move a Category

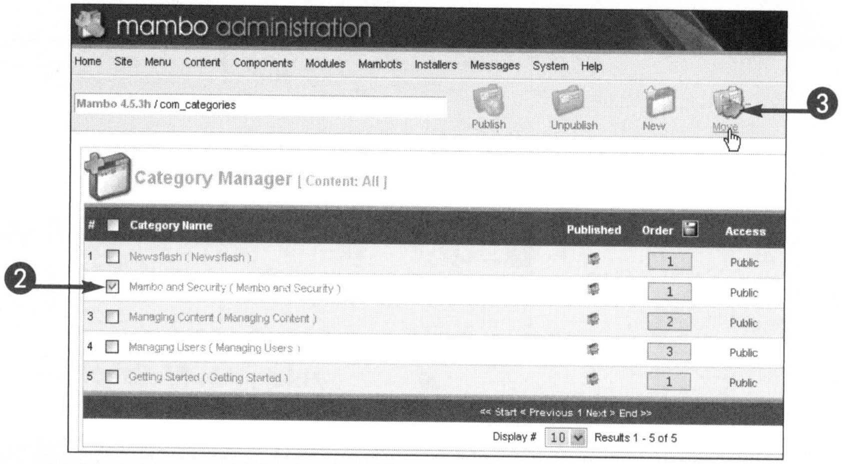

1. Load the Category Manager.

Note: To load the Category Manager, see the section "Create Content Categories."

2. Select the category you want to move.
3. Click the Move icon.

The Move Category page loads.

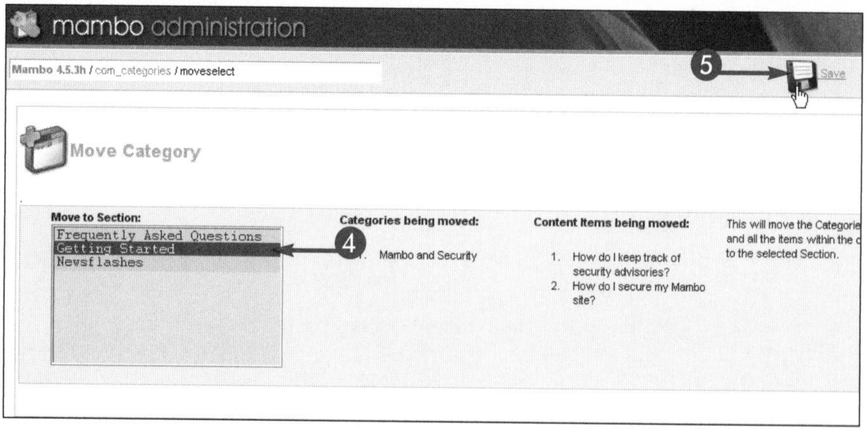

4. Select the section to which you want to move the category.
5. Click the Save icon.

Mambo moves the category to the section and returns you to the Category Manager.

Duplicate a Section

You can copy an entire section with the Section Manager to quickly duplicate an entire group of contents at one time. This is very useful when you are building and want to create a new section with the same properties as an existing section. Using the Copy command to create new sections promotes efficiency and consistency; it is much easier to copy sections than to try to synchronize the attributes of a number of new sections as you create them from scratch one by one via the Section Manager's New command. For more on creating sections using the New command, see the section "Create Content Sections" earlier in the chapter.

The Section Manager's Copy function gives you the power to simultaneously copy a section together with all of its categories and Content Items.

Duplicating a section is fast and easy simply by selecting the section and then using the Copy icon to duplicate it. Mambo prompts you for a new section name, and then immediately copies the section, placing it on the list of sections in the Section Manager. The original section shares all its attributes and contents with the new section. The only differences between the original and the copy is the name and the fact that the new section is not linked to any Menu Items.

After you create a new section with the Copy control, you can edit the contents, if you want, or simply add a menu link to the section or its various items. On the front end of the Web site, the section appears visually in a manner consistent with the original section.

Duplicate a Section

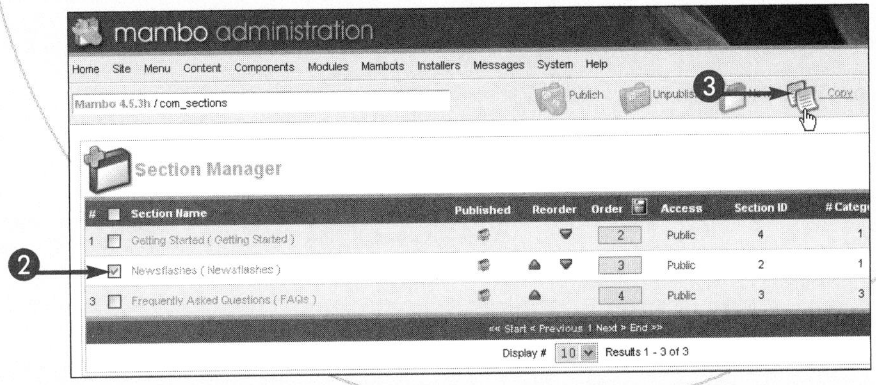

1. Load the Section Manager.

Note: To load the Section Manager, see the section "Create Content Sections."

2. Select the section you want to copy.
3. Click the Copy icon.

   The Copy Section page loads.

4. Type a name for the section.
5. Click the Save icon.

   Mambo copies the section and returns you to the Section Manager.

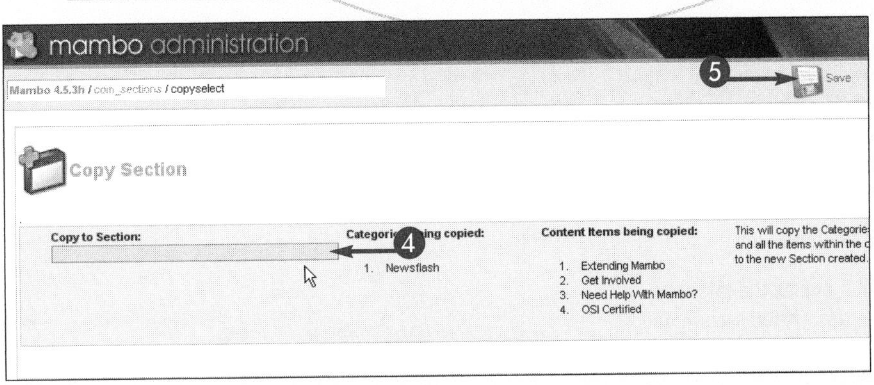

Duplicate a Category

You can copy an entire category with the Category Manager to quickly duplicate an entire group of contents at one time. This is very useful when you are building and want to create a new category with the same properties as an existing category. Using the Copy command to create new categories promotes efficiency and consistency; it is much easier to copy categories than to try to synchronize the attributes of a number of new categories as you create them from scratch one by one via the Category Manager's New command. For more on creating a category using the New command, see the section "Create Content Categories" earlier in the chapter.

The Category Manager's Copy function gives you the power to simultaneously copy a category together with all of its Content Items. Duplicating a category is fast and easy. You simply select the category and then use the Copy icon to duplicate it. Mambo prompts you to select the section you want to assign the category to, and then immediately copies the category, placing it on the list of categories in the Category Manager. The original category shares all attributes and contents with the new category. The only differences between the original and the copy are the name and the fact that the new category is not linked to any menu items.

After you have created a new category with the Copy control, you can edit the contents if you want, or simply add a menu link to the category or its various items. On the front end of the Web site, the category appears visually in a manner consistent with the original category.

Duplicate a Category

1. Load the Category Manager.

Note: To load the Category Manager, see the section "Create Content Categories."

2. Select the category you want to copy.
3. Click the Copy icon.

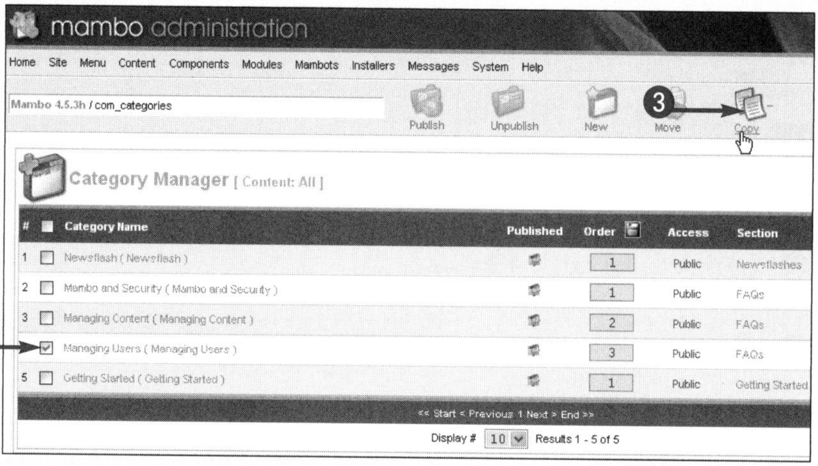

The Copy Category page loads.

4. Select the section to which you want to copy the category.
5. Click the Save icon.

Mambo copies the category to the designated section and returns you to the Category Manager.

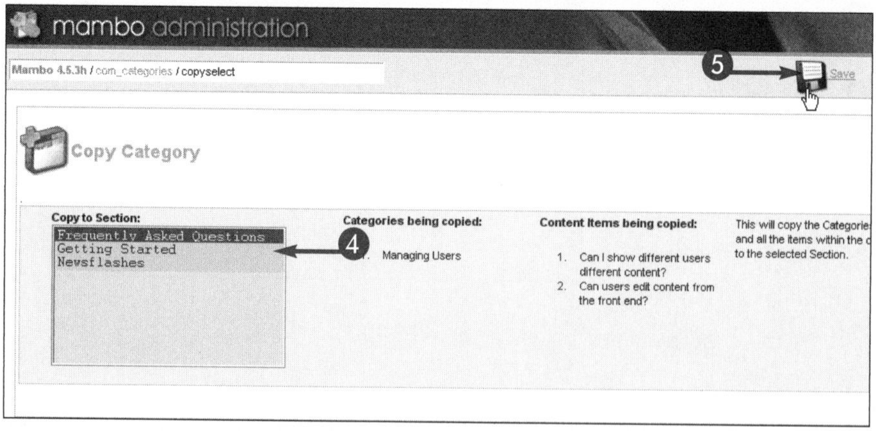

Delete a Section

You can delete and remove a section completely from your Mambo system. Deleting a section allows you to clean up unwanted clutter from your admin interface and helps you keep your content organized without the distraction of unused or unwanted sections. Admin systems with numerous unused sections, categories, or Content Items tend to be harder to work with and present more possibilities for confusion or mistakes.

Before you can delete a section, you must remove all categories from the section. You cannot delete a section that contains categories. If you attempt to do so, the system generates an error message and the deletion fails. To identify whether you can delete a section, view the Section Manager. The Section Manager displays a list of all the sections in the system along with an indication of whether each of those sections contains any categories or Content Items. The Section Manager also tells you how many items are in each section and whether the items are active or are located in the Trash Manager. You must eliminate both the active items and those in the Trash.

To eliminate the categories and Content Items from a section, either delete the categories and Content Items one by one or move them all to another section using the Move command. If you choose to delete the categories and the Content Items, make sure you also delete them from the Trash Manager. For more on deleting categories, see the section "Delete a Category" later in the chapter. The deletion of Content Items is covered in Chapter 6. Moving a category is covered in the previous section "Move a Category." For more on the Trash Manager, see Chapter 6.

Delete a Section

1. Load the Section Manager.

Note: To load the Section Manager, see the section "Create Content Sections."

2. Select the section you want to delete.
3. Click the Delete icon.

   A confirmation popup appears.

4. Click OK.

   Mambo deletes the section.

   - You can click Cancel to cancel the action and return to the Section Manager.

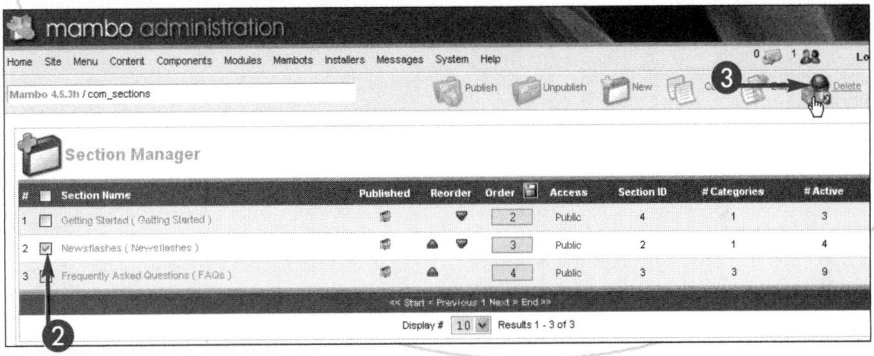

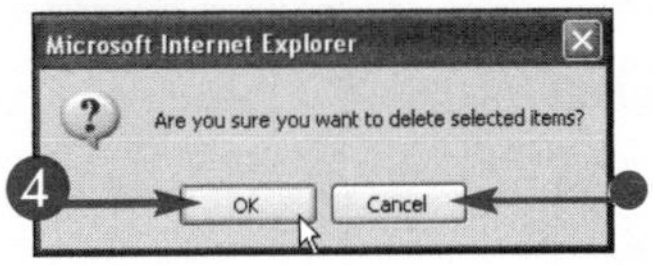

Delete a Category

You can delete and remove a category completely from your Mambo system. Deletion of a category allows you to clean up unwanted clutter from your admin interface and helps you keep your content organized without the distraction of unused or unwanted categories. Admin systems with numerous unused sections, categories, or Content Items tend to be harder to work with and present more possibilities for confusion or mistakes.

Before you can delete a category you must remove all Content Items from the category. You cannot delete a category that contains Content Items. If you attempt to do so, the system generates an error message and the deletion fails. The error message says that the deletion failed because the category "contains records." In this case the term "records" refers to Content Items. To identify whether you can delete a category, view the Category Manager. The Category Manager displays a list of all the categories in the system along with an indication of whether each of those categories contains any Content Items. The Category Manager also tells you how many items are in each category and whether the items are active or are located in the Trash Manager. You must eliminate both the active items and those in the Trash.

To eliminate the Content Items from a category, either delete the Content Items one by one or move them all to another category using the Move command. If you choose to delete the Content Items, make sure you also delete them from the Trash Manager. To delete or move Content Items, see Chapter 6. For more on how to use the Trash Manager, see Chapter 6.

Delete a Category

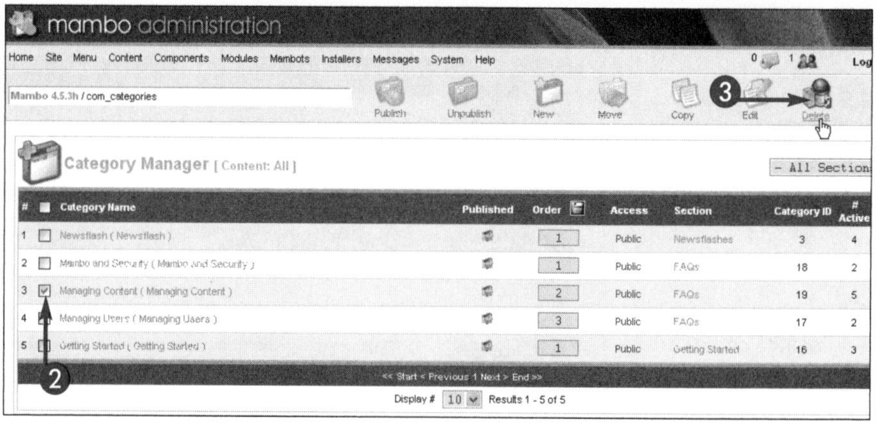

1. Load the Category Manager.

Note: To load the Category Manager, see the section "Create Content Categories."

2. Select the category you want to delete.
3. Click the Delete icon.

A confirmation popup appears.

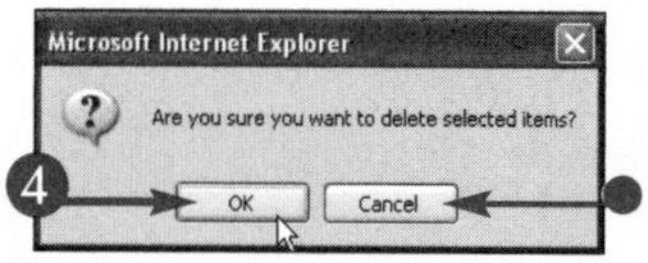

4. Click OK.

Mambo deletes the category.

- You can click Cancel to cancel the action and return to the Category Manager.

Restrict Access to a Section or Category

You can restrict access to a section or a category to make the contents available to only certain classes of users. Access restrictions are an effective way to create premium content areas for your site members, or to provide private and confidential information you do not want to show to general public visitors to your Web site.

The access controls for both sections and categories work in exactly the same fashion. In both cases, there are two options for changing the access settings. The easiest option to use is the Access switch on the Section Manager or Category Manager screens. You can change the state of the Access switch by clicking it. The other alternative is to open an individual section or category for editing and change the Access control that appears on the editing screen. The result of either action is the same.

There are three access levels in the system. The Public access level makes the section or category available to all visitors. Registered restricts access to only site visitors who are registered and logged in to the system. The Special class is for your front-end content managers. The relationship between access level and user groups is discussed in detail in Chapter 4.

Note that the hierarchical relationship between sections, categories, and Content Items is also reflected in the access levels. If you restrict access to a section you will also restrict access to the categories and Content Items within the section. If, however, you use the unrestricted Public access setting for your section, you can restrict the access of the categories and Content Items within that section. Restricting a category likewise restricts the Content Items within that category.

Restrict Access to a Section

1. Load the Section Manager.

Note: To load the Section Manager, see the section "Create Content Sections."

2. Click the Access level next to the section you want to restrict.

- The access level for the item changes, as does the indicator.

Clicking the icon again displays the third access level option.

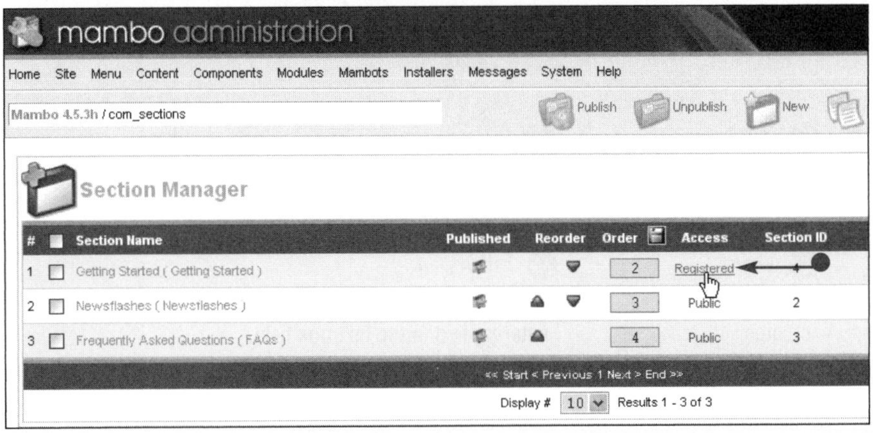

An Introduction to the Content Items Manager

The Content Items Manager is one of the most frequently visited pages in the admin system. Understanding the tools on this page and the options they present makes your work with Mambo easier and more efficient. Although Mambo presents the Content Items Manager interface in a variety of situations, the screen controls and layout are always the same. You see the Content Items Manager when you select the All Content Items choice under the Content menu, or if you choose to view the Content by section. The Content Items Manager also appears every time you save and exit a Content Item.

Ⓐ Toolbar

Contains icons with key functionalities associated with Content Items management. You typically select a Content Item, then click an icon to initiate the action.

Ⓑ Title

Lists all Content Items alphabetically by section.

Ⓒ Published

Shows the item's published state, which you change via the icon.

Ⓓ Front Page

Shows if you have assigned the item to the front page component. You change the state via the icon.

Ⓔ Reorder

Reorders a Content Item relative to others in the same category via the up and down arrows.

Ⓕ Order

You order the Content Item relative to others in the same category by changing the sequence and clicking the save icon.

Ⓖ Access

Shows the access level assigned to this item. Click to cycle through the options.

Ⓗ ID

System-generated ID number

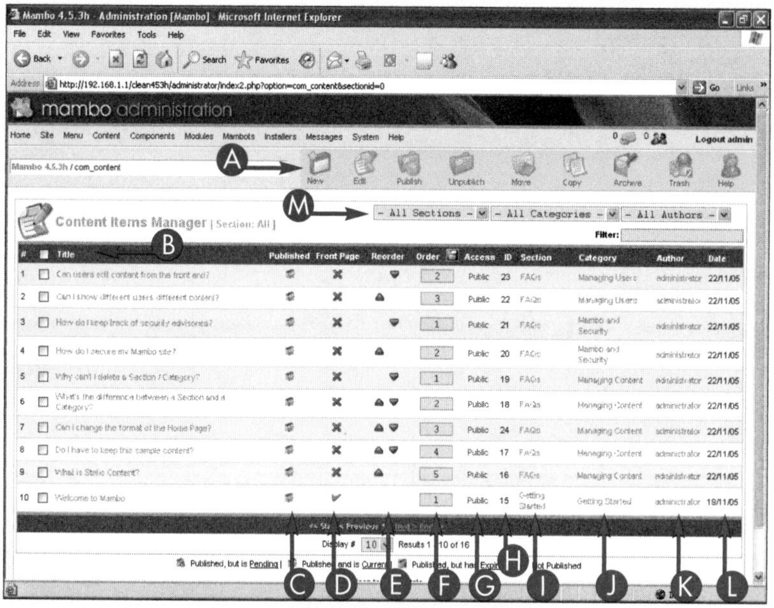

Ⓘ Section

The section to which the item is assigned.

Ⓙ Category

The category to which the item is assigned.

Ⓚ Author

The author associated with the item.

Ⓛ Date

The date the item was created.

Ⓜ Filters

Sort and filter the list of items. You can also search by entering text in the text box field.

An Introduction to the Content Item Editing Screen

The Content Item Editing screen is one of the most important in Mambo because its tools enable you to create and edit new Content Items. Understanding the tools and options is essential to achieving good-looking and coherent Content Items for your Web site.

Many of the options in the Content Items Editing screen interact with other tools in the Mambo system. For example, several options on the Publishing and Parameters tabs relate to the Global Configuration Manager and override the global Content settings on an item-by-item basis. The Meta Info tab lets you append information to the global site metadata. The Images tab works in concert with the Media Manager. Finally, the Link to Menu tab relates to the Menu Manager and the various menus in the system. For more on setting global content configuration options and metadata for the site as a whole, see Chapter 2. For more on adding images and working with media, see Chapter 7. To understand how to work with menus, see Chapter 9.

A Content Item Editing Icons

Contains icons that:preview the item; add media, including images; save changes to the item; apply changes without exiting the page; cancel and return to the Content Item Manager; and access Help files relevant to this page.

B Item Details

These fields help you create or assign:a mandatory title for all Content Items; an optional alias for the convenience of the Administrator; a section or category to your Content Item (mandatory except for Static Content Items); the required intro text field; and the main text field (optional).

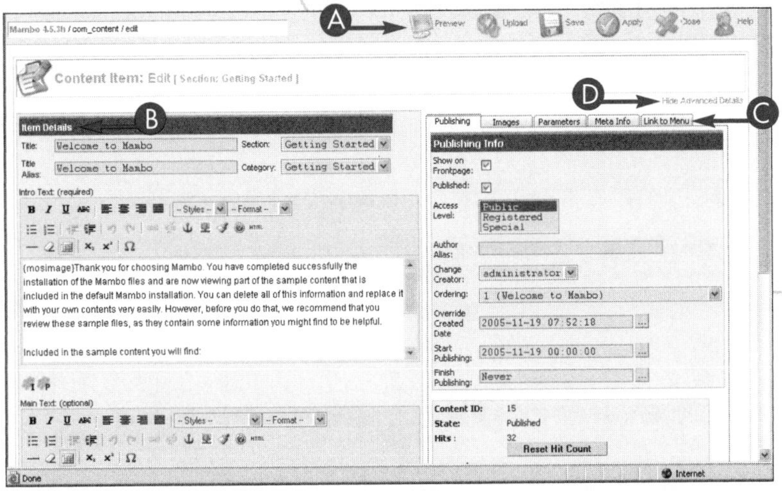

C Content Item Tabs

Include tabs with publishing controls and options, MOS image commands, optional parameters for controlling the format of the Content Item, and Menu Item links.

D Hide Advanced Details

Toggles Simple Mode for the admin interface. The use of this command is discussed in Chapter 1.

Create a Content Item

You can create new Content Items for your Mambo site from the Content Items Manager interface. Adding pages to an existing site is one of the core functions of any Content Management System, and Mambo largely automates this process, enabling the site administrator to concentrate on the content rather than the programming. The administrator needs no programming skill to add Content Items; instead, he or she simply inputs the content and specifies the variables related to the desired page appearance and features.

Basic Content Item creation requires only the addition of content. The new Content Item immediately appears inside of the section and category and on the front end of the Web site. To create a more customized appearance or take advantage of some of the advanced features that Mambo provides, you must familiarize yourself with the wide range of available parameters for Content Items. For an explanation of the various parameters, see the section "Understanding Content Item Parameters."

Before you create a Content Item, you should decide where you want to place it in the content hierarchy. You must assign all Content Items to a category, and, in turn, you assign all categories to sections. Note that the section and category to which you assign a Content Item must exist before you can create the Content Item. You cannot create new sections or categories from within the Content Item Manager.

You can assign existing Content Items to menus, and you can edit or move the items around within the Content hierarchy. The system is very flexible in handling Content Items and very forgiving if you should change your mind after you create an item.

Create a Content Item

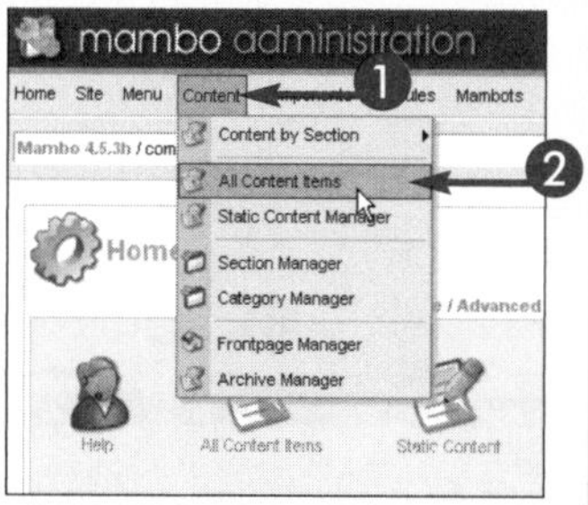

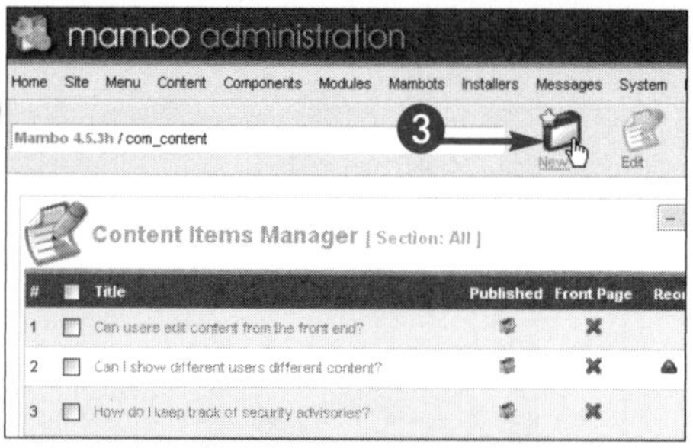

1. Click Content.
2. Click All Content Items.

   The Content Items Manager loads.

3. Click the New icon.

   The Content Item Creation screen loads.

4. Type the contents you want to appear.
5. Click the Save icon.

   Mambo creates a new Content Item and the system returns you to the Content Items Manager.

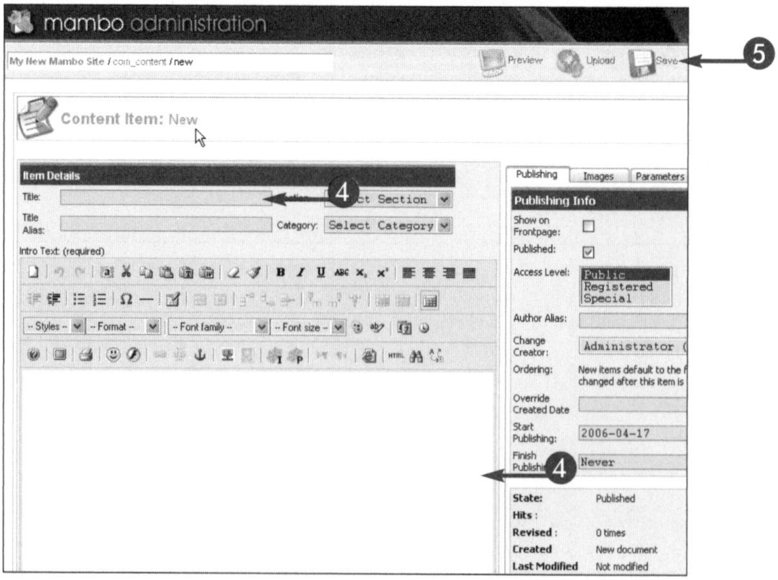

Preview Your Work

You can preview a Content Item from inside the Content Item Editing screen. Because the Preview feature enables you to check how a Content Item will look on the site without having to publish an item, you can avoid disruption to a live site. You also save time because you do not need to publish the item and then go to the front end of the Web site to see it. You can most effectively use preview during the initial creation of the Content Item on a live site, checking your work as you go.

While creating or editing a Content Item, you can stop and preview your work at any time using the Preview icon, which opens a window. This window lets you to check the Content Item, as well as the results of the MOSimage and MOSpagebreak commands. It is also useful for checking text with any applied CSS formatting. Unfortunately, the preview does not show you the template, so you cannot use it to view the Content Item relative to other page elements or modules. If you want to see what the Content Item looks like inside your template, you are forced to publish the Content Item and view it on the front end of the Web site.

Once you are satisfied from the Preview window that your work is ready for public viewing, you can publish the item. Remember to always check your work after you publish to assure that the appearance of the item is consistent with your expectations.

Preview Your Work

1. Load the Content Items Manager.

Note: To Load the Content Items Manager, see the section "Create a Content Item."

2. Click a Content Item.
3. Click the Edit icon.

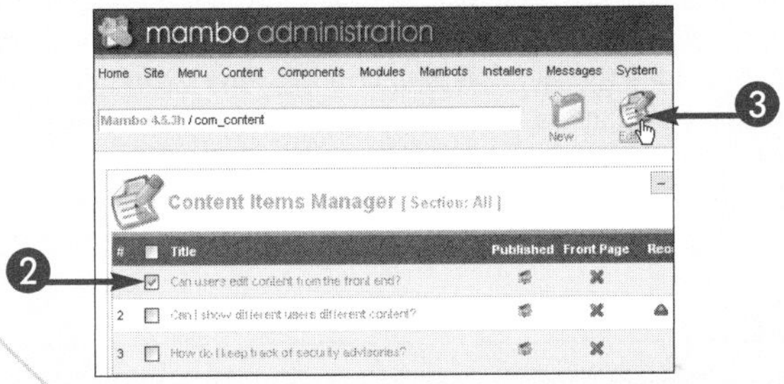

The Content Item Editing screen loads.

4. Click the Preview icon.

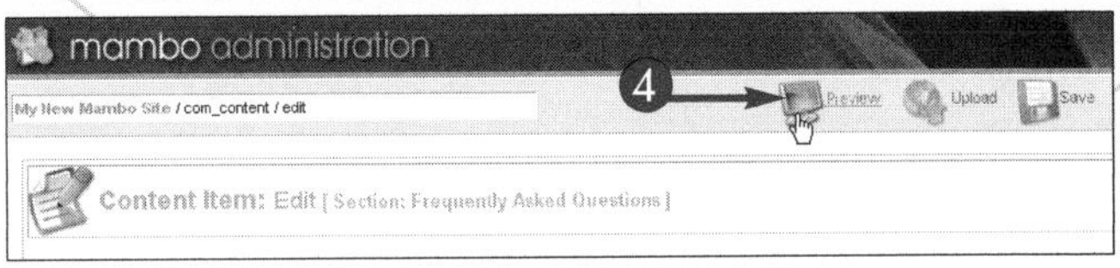

A window appears displaying the Content Item.

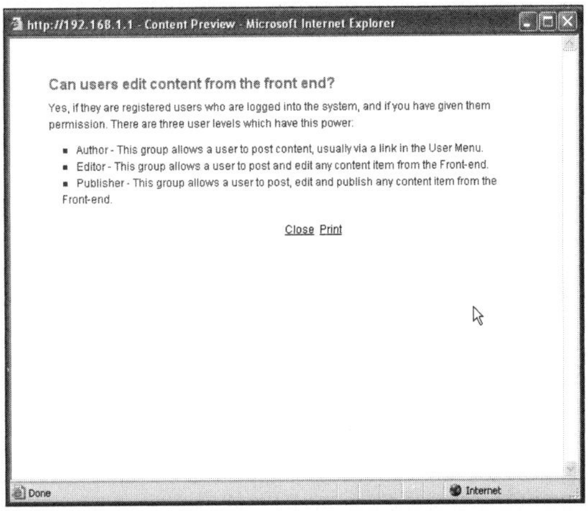

Understanding Content Item Parameters

Each Content Item and Static Content Item includes a number of configurable parameters that control the appearance of the item and the options that a page has available for site visitors. The Parameters tab is located in the right column inside the Content Item Editing window, together with the Publishing, Images, Meta Info, and Link to Menu tabs. Note that if you display the Content Item Editing page in Simple Mode, the right column is hidden; to see the full range of options, you must switch to Advanced Mode. For more on switching between Simple and Advanced Mode, see Chapter 1.

Correct use of the parameters attached to Content Items is one key to customizing and personalizing your Mambo site. Understanding all the available options available allows you to better tailor the contents and the functions for your users and to avoid needless uniformity between different types of content. For example, in certain areas of your site, you may not want to grant users the ability to print a page. In that situation, use the parameters to hide the print icon. Similarly, if you do not want the author name to appear on some Content Items, use the parameters to hide the name on only those items.

Content Items, the Global Configuration Manager, and Menu Items

The parameters attached to each Content Item override the sitewide settings contained in the Global Configuration Manager. Applying parameters to a Content Item affects only that individual Content Item. If you want to make similar changes to other items you must do so to each one. To implement your changes throughout the site, you must establish the settings you want in the Global Configuration Manager. For more information on using the Global Configuration Manager to control Content Item appearance, see Chapter 2. Note that Menu Items also include parameters which you can use to affect the formatting of the Content Items and Static Content Items to which the Menu Items link. Therefore, when you are troubleshooting a layout problem, be certain to check the parameter settings in all three areas: Global Configuration, Menu Item, Content Item. The situation can become even more complicated if you have more than one Menu Item linking to a Content Item, because each Menu Item has its own set of parameters. For more on how Menu Item parameters can influence content, see Chapter 9.

Content Item Parameters

To help you fully understand the Content Item parameters that you have available to you, the illustration shows the interface, and the table explains the various parameters.

View of the Content Item Parameters

The following illustration shows the location of all relevant parameters.

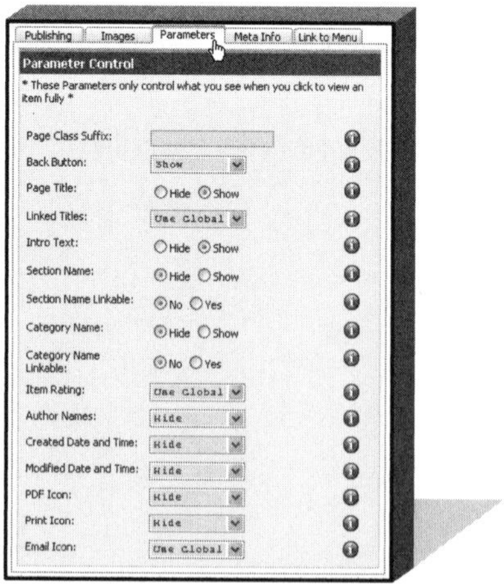

Content Item Parameter Functions

The following table lists each of the choices that appear on the Parameters tab in the Content Item Creation and Editing pages. Note that there is no difference between the parameters that appear on the Content Item Creation and Editing screens; however, there are slightly more options available for normal Content Items than for Static Content Items. The differences between the two types of items are noted in the following table where relevant to each control.

PARAMETER	FUNCTION
Menu Image	Select a small image to appear on the Menu Item link for this Content Item. Note this parameter is only available for Static Content Items. The intention of this option is to provide graphical symbols which make using the navigation easier to see and understand, but often developers use it for purely decorative purposes.
Page Class Suffix	Adds a suffix to the CSS classes applied to this page, allowing you to format a Content Item individually. This command works in conjunction with the Cascading Style Sheets and requires you to create classes of the same name in the CSS to have any effect.
Back Button	Displays or hides a Back button on the Content Item. Clicking the Back button takes users back to the previous page they were viewing.
Page Title	Displays or hides the page title on the Content Item.
Linked Titles	Determines whether the title to the item is a clickable hyperlink. This is applicable only if you display the Page Title. Note this parameter is not available for Static Content Items.
Intro Text	Displays or hides the Intro Text on the same page that shows the Main Text. This is applicable only if you use both the Intro Text and the Main Text. Note this parameter is not available for Static Content Items.
Section Name	Displays or hides the Section Name at the beginning of the Content Item. Note this parameter is not available for Static Content Items.
Section Name Linkable	Determines whether the Section Name is a clickable hyperlink. This is applicable only if you display the Section Name. Note this parameter is not available for Static Content Items.
Category Name	Displays or hides the Section Name at the beginning of the Content Item. Note this parameter is not available for Static Content Items.
Category Name Linkable	Determines whether the Category Name is a clickable hyperlink. This is applicable only if you display the Category Name. Note this parameter is not available for Static Content Items.
Item Rating	Displays or hides the Item Rating option which allows site visitors to vote and rate the Content Items.
Author Names	Displays or hides the Author's Name.
Created Date and Time	Displays or hides the time and date of creation of the Content Item.
Modified Date and Times	Displays or hides the time and date the Content Item was last modified.
PDF Icon	Displays or hides the icon that allows users to create a PDF out of the Content Item.
Print Icon	Displays or hides the icon that allows users to print the Content Item.
Email Icon	Displays or hides the icon that allows users to send a link to the Content Item by email.

Assign a Content Item to the Home Page

Mambo enables you to assign any normal Content Item to the home page of your Web site. The system's flexibility makes it possible for you to have a dynamic home page that attracts repeat visitors, yet remains easy to administer.

The default implementation of Mambo uses the Frontpage Manager to manage all of the Content Items on the Web site's home page. If your site uses the Frontpage Manager to handle the home page, Mambo enables the automatic management of your home page items.

Once you create or edit a Content Item, you can assign this item to the Frontpage Manager via the Show on Front Page option, which is located inside the Content Item Editing screen on the Publishing tab. You can quickly see which of your Content Items are assigned to the Frontpage Manager from the Content Items Manager screen. Items assigned to the Frontpage Manager exhibit a green check mark in the Front Page column. Note that the icons in the Front Page column are active and you can change the icon's state, and thus directly assign or unassign items to the Frontpage Manager.

Be aware that assigning a Content Item to the Frontpage Manager does not always assure that the item will show on the site's home page. The options selected in the Frontpage Manager and in the Menu Item parameters relating to the Frontpage Manager all impact what shows on the site's home page. For more details on the Frontpage Manager, see the next section, "An Introduction to the Frontpage Manager." For more on managing Menu Item parameters, see Chapter 9.

Assign a Content Item to the Home Page

1. Load the Content Items Manager.

Note: To Load the Content Items Manager, see the section "Create a Content Item."

2. Click the red X in the Front Page column.

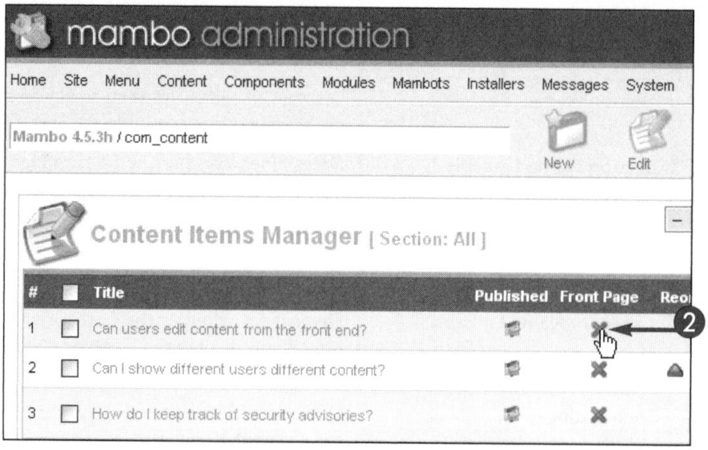

- The icon changes to a green check mark and the item is now assigned to the Frontpage Manager.

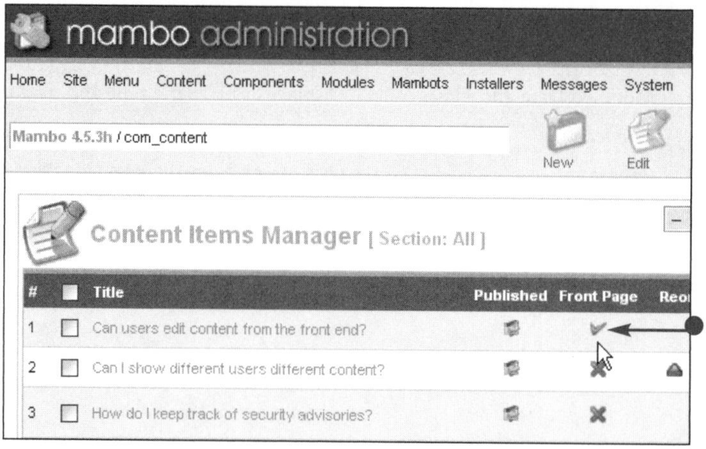

An Introduction to the Frontpage Manager

You can use the Frontpage Manager to ease the burden of your Web site's home page administration. When you assign Content Items to the front page, they are in fact assigned to the Frontpage Manager. The options on the Frontpage Manager make it easy to publish, unpublish, or reorder the home page content. The Manager also includes shortcuts to the Content Items and the sections and categories to which they belong, enabling you to make edits to those items without searching through the admin interface to find things. This makes the Frontpage Manager especially indispensable on a very large, complicated site.

Although the default Mambo implementation utilizes the Frontpage Manager to manage the home page, in some instances the Manager is totally irrelevant, making it necessary for you to bypass the feature so that it becomes meaningless to the site administrator. The Frontpage Manager is not mandatory, and some Web developers do not choose to use the Frontpage component for their home page. If someone else built the site you are administering, you must ask how they manage the items on their home page.

A Toolbar

Contains icons with key functionalities for managing the Content Items on the home page. You select a Content Item and click an icon.

B Title

Lists all the Content Items assigned to the Frontpage Manager.

C Published

Changes the item's published state.

D Reorder

Reorders content relative to others by moving it up or down in the order.

E Order

Orders a Content Item relative to others by renumbering the ordering sequence.

F Access

Shows the assigned access level. Click to cycle through the options.

G Section

Shows the section to which the item is assigned.

H Category

Shows the category to which the item is assigned.

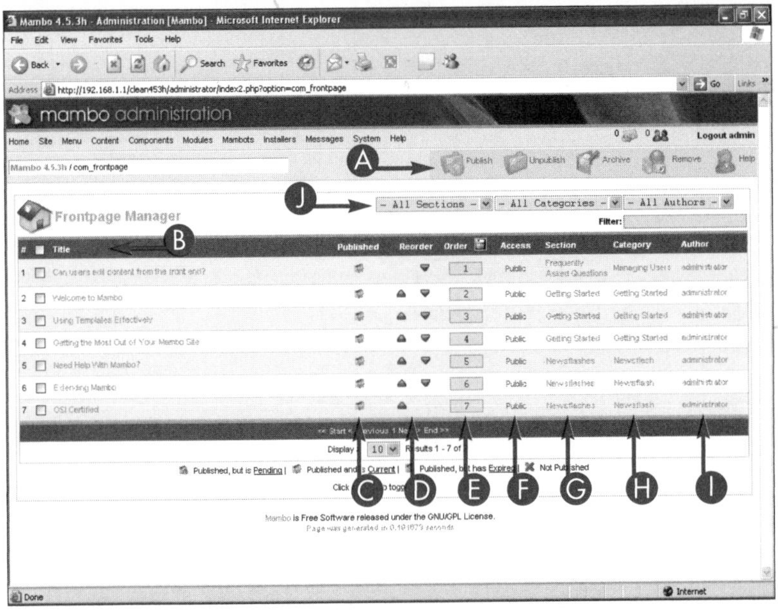

I Author

Shows the author associated with the item.

J Filters

Sorts and filters items. You can also search via the text box field.

Manage the Layout of Your Home Page

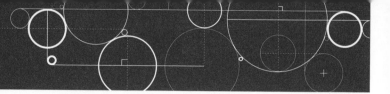

You can control the formatting of the Content Items on your home page and create a variety of different page layout styles. You can use the Frontpage Manager together with the Menu Item parameters to create a portal look, a blog look, or something entirely different.

You should assign the Content Items you want to appear on the home page using the Frontpage Manager. With the Frontpage Manager, you can control the most basic aspects of layout — that is, the number of items published and in what order. In addition, you use the Menu Item parameters related to the Frontpage component to control the layout of the Content Items and the options available for the site visitors. The Menu Item parameters enable you to determine the maximum number of items that you can display, the number of columns that appear, and whether the items are shown with introductory text or simply as hyperlinks.

If your site varies from the default settings and no longer employs the Frontpage Manager to handle the home page, then the layout management techniques discussed in this section are not applicable to your site. You need to speak with the developer who helped create your site to determine how he or she has set up home page management.

Assuming that the Frontpage Manager still plays the default role in managing your home page, you can access the Menu Item parameters for your home page by visiting the Menu Manager and locating the Home link. If you have no published link bearing that name, look for the Menu Item attached to the Type "Component - FrontPage."

Manage the Layout of Your Home Page

OPEN THE FRONTPAGE MANAGER

1. Click Content.
2. Click Frontpage Manager.

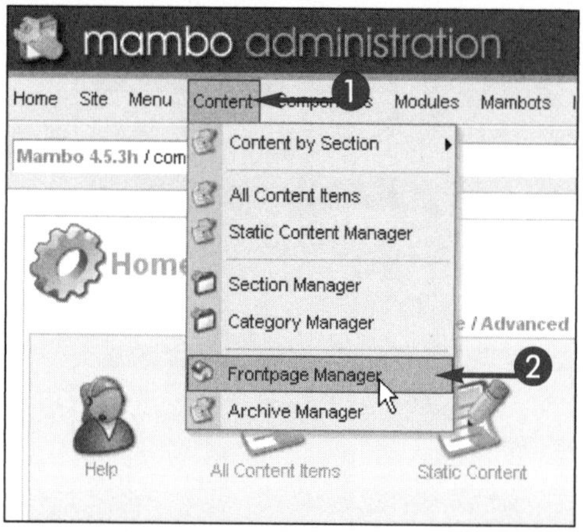

The Frontpage Manager loads.

3. Make any changes in order or publication status.

Mambo applies the changes immediately.

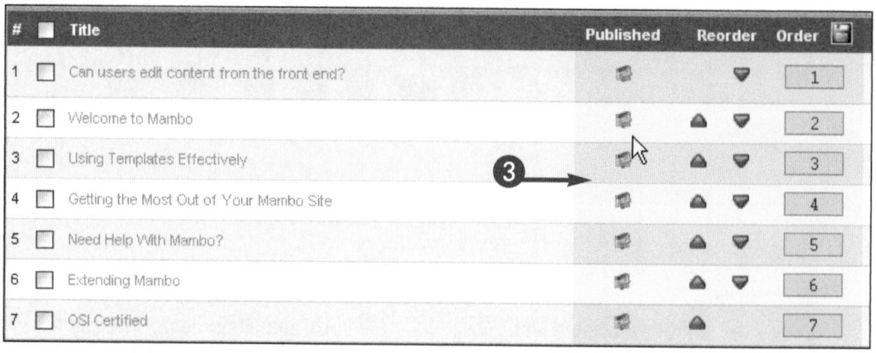

MODIFY MENU ITEM PARAMETERS

1. Click Menu.
2. Click mainmenu.

   The Menu Manager loads.

3. Click the Home option.
4. Click the Edit icon.

   The Edit Menu Item screen loads.

5. Change parameters as desired.
6. Click the Save icon.

   Mambo applies the changes to the home page Items and you are returned to the Menu Manager.

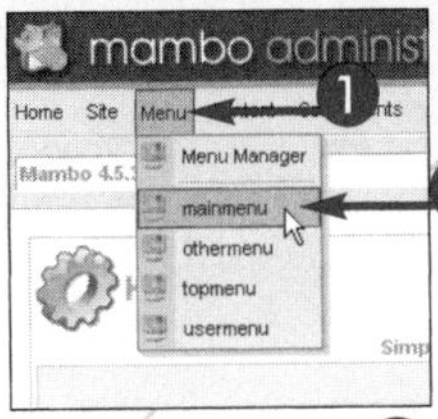

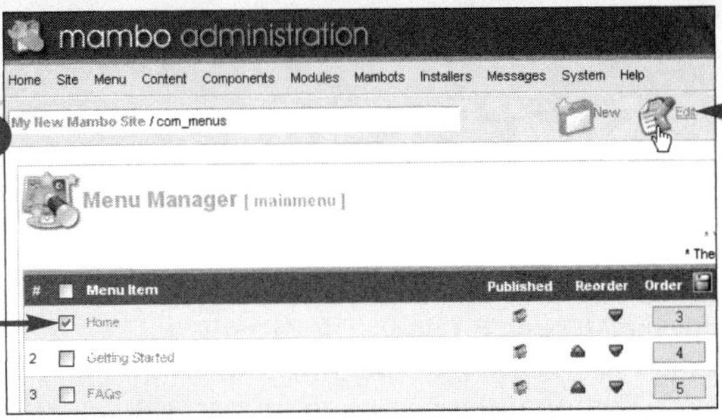

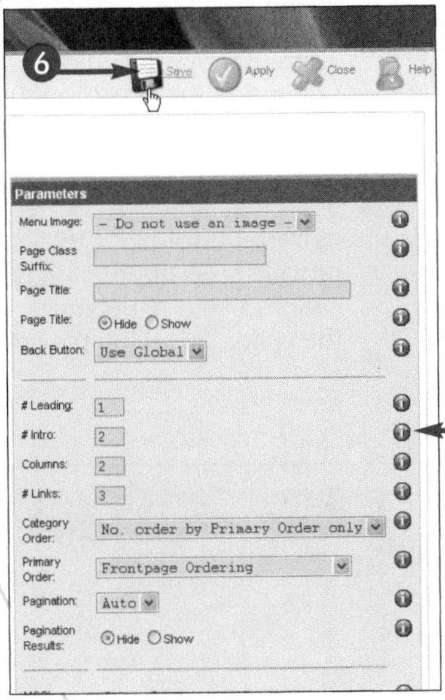

Apply It

The parameters associated with the Menu Item linked to the Frontpage component are the keys to controlling the layout. The default Mambo layout uses one leading article that spans the entire width of the page, followed by two articles side by side – that is, in two columns. Here is how to achieve two common variations.

CREATE A 1-COLUMN LAYOUT

One-column layouts are very common with portals and blog sites. In this layout, the articles appear one after the other and each spans the page. To create a page in this format, open the Menu Item and set the Columns parameter to 1. The default Mambo system shows only 3 articles with introductory text. To display more, change the setting for # Intro.

CREATE A 2-COLUMN LAYOUT

A two-column layout is useful for displaying large amounts of information. To achieve this look, open the Menu Item and set the parameter # Leading to 0. The default Mambo system shows only three articles with introductory text. To display more, change the setting for # Intro.

Add and Edit Text with the MOStlyCE Editor

You can add and format the contents of a page easily with the MOStlyCE Editor. The MOStlyCE content editor is enabled by default in your Mambo installation. With the editor, you can format text and images within a Content Item without having to work with HTML code. For a complete summary of the tools contained in MOStlyCE, see the section "Guide to the MOStlyCE WYSIWYG Editor."

Mambo provides the MOStlyCE editor for both Content Items and Static Content Items, and it is available for both the Intro Text and the Main Text areas. You can configure the editor in a variety of manners. You can find configuration options under the Components menu. For more on configuring your MOStlyCE editor, see Chapter 10 and Appendix C.

In the event you want to view the code, you can always switch to Plain Text Mode by selecting the Plain Text Mode button. Alternatively, if you prefer to work entirely without the WYSIWYG tools, you can disable the MOStlyCE editor for the entire site via the Global Configuration Manager. For more on switching between editor options, see Chapter 2. For more on working without the WYSIWYG Editor, see the section, "Add and Edit Text Without a WYSIWYG Editor."

Additionally, you can extend your Mambo system using other text editing tools. You can download and install other powerful third-party WYSIWYG editors, some of which provide specialized options. To add a different WYSIWYG editor to your Mambo site, you must download and install the editor, following the instructions from the developer.

Add and Edit Text with the MOStlyCE Editor

1. Load the Content Items Manager.

Note: To load the Content Items Manager, see the section "Create a Content Item."

2. Click a Content Item.
3. Click the Edit icon.

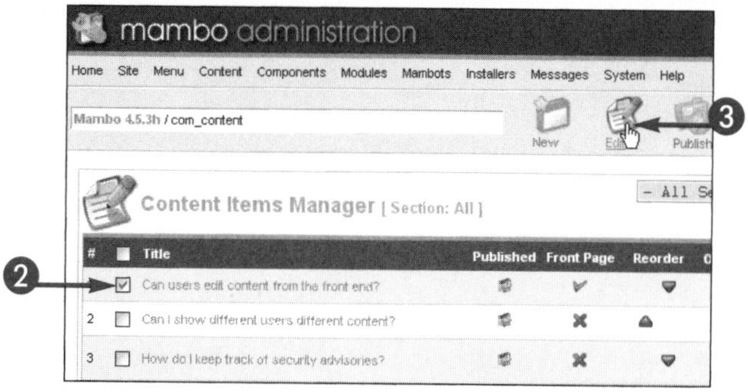

The Content Item Editing screen loads.

4. Click to select the text.
5. Apply formatting by clicking the tool buttons.

Mambo Formatting is applied immediately.

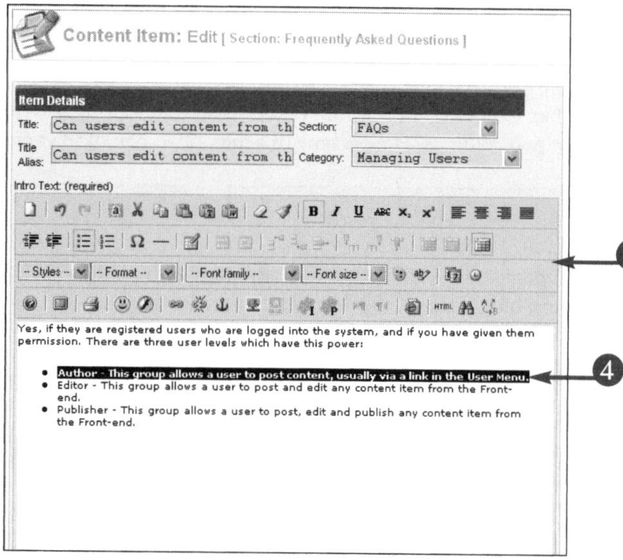

Add and Edit Text Without a WYSIWYG Editor

With Mambo, you have the option of creating and editing Content Items using only a plain text editor. While the system includes a very good WYSIWYG editor, some administrators choose to work without the tool, preferring instead to use the simple plain text editor that Mambo also distributes. The primary reasons for electing not to use the WYSIWYG editor have to do with speed and the ability to see the code as you work on it. Because the plain text editor does not have all the buttons and tools that come with the WYSIWYG editor, it tends to load faster and work faster. Additionally, experienced users often feel they have more control over the pages when they can work directly on the HTML code. For most people, the choice between tools simply comes down to a work habit preference.

If you cannot use HTML with confidence, you probably should stick with the WYSIWYG editor. The Mambo MOStlyCE WYSIWYG Editor is discussed at length in the sections, "Add and Edit Text with the MOStlyCE WYSIWYG Editor" and "Guide to the MOStlyCE WYSIWYG Editor." In all other regards, creating or editing a Content Item with the plain text editor is identical to the process explained in these two sections.

Chapter 2 contains an explanation of how to switch between the plain text editor and the WYSIWYG editor.

The plain text editor presents you with a blank box into which you enter your text. As you type the text, you must also add the HTML codes that format your text. While most of the automated formatting controls are not available in plain text mode, the MOSimage tool and the MOSpagebreak command are available. The MOSimage tool is explained in Chapter 7. The MOSpagebreak command is discussed in the section "Create Multi-Page Content Items," later in the chapter.

Add and Edit Text Without a WYSIWYG Editor

1. Load the Content Items Manager.

Note: To load the Content Items Manager, see the section "Create a Content Item."

2. Click a Content Item.
3. Click the Edit icon.

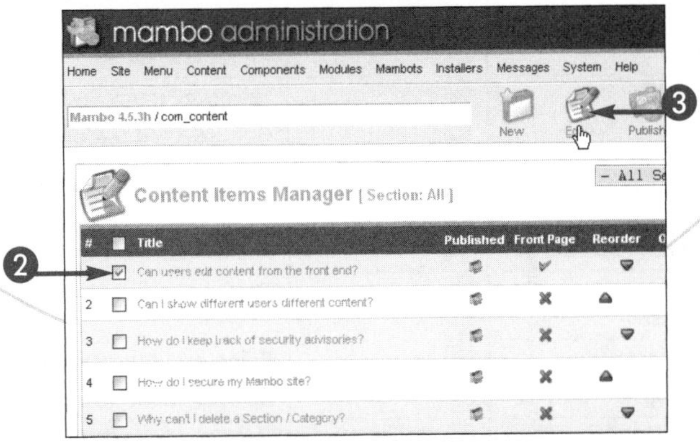

The Content Item Editing screen loads.

4. Type content in the text box.

Content appears as plain text unless you format it manually.

This example shows the system without an active WYSIWYG editor.

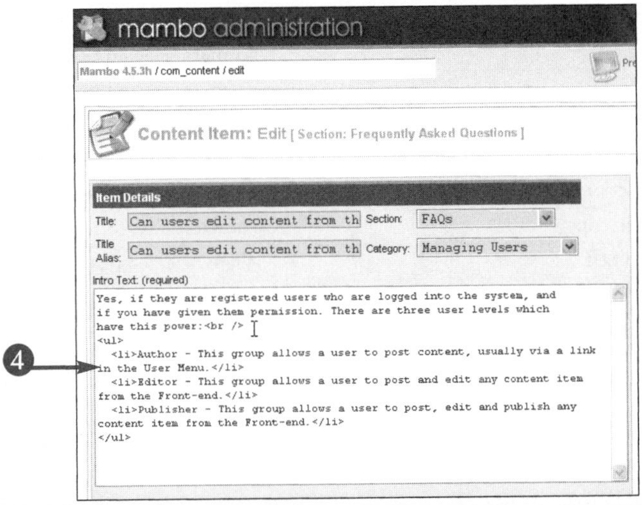

Guide to the MOStlyCE WYSIWYG Editor

You can format your content easily using the MOStlyCE WYSIWYG Editor. WYSIWYG is an acronym that stands for What You See Is What You Get and applies to an entire class of content formatting tools that allow you to format text easily via icons and shortcuts. WYSIWYG editors make content management much easier because they provide a familiar environment not unlike what most users have seen and used in Microsoft Office applications. A WYSIWYG editor allows users not fluent in HTML coding to format text quickly and with a high level of sophistication.

Mambo comes bundled with a powerful WYSIWYG editor called MOStlyCE, which not only enables you to format your text, but also gives you tools for adding images and other files, creating hyperlinks to other Web pages, and creating tables to assist with the layout of complex data. The following illustration and table show the WYSIWYG Editor interface and summarize all its tools.

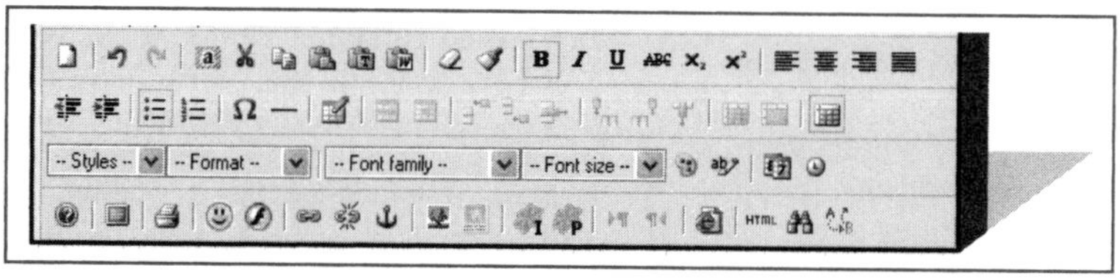

COMMAND	ICON	ACTION
New Document		Clears all content from editing window.
Undo		Undos last action.
Redo		Redos last action.
Select All		Selects all items and text.
Cut		Cuts selected text and holds in Clipboard.
Copy		Copies selected text and holds in Clipboard.
Paste		Pastes text from Clipboard.
Paste as Plain Text		Pastes material from Clipboard as plain text without formatting.
Paste from Word Document		Pastes material from Clipboard with Word formatting.
Clear formatting		Removes all formatting from selected text.
Clean Up Word Code		Removes unnecessary tags from Word formatting.
Search		Searches Content Item for occurrences of a word or phrase.
Replace		Finds and replaces text in the Content Item.
Bold		Formats selected text as Bold.
Italic		Formats selected text as Italic.
Underline		Formats selected text with Underline.
Strikethrough		Formats selected text with Strikethrough.
Subscript		Formats selected text as Subscript.
Superscript		Formats selected text as Superscript.
Align Left		Aligns selected text to the left.
Align Center		Aligns selected text to center.

Align Right		Aligns selected text to the right.
Justify Full		Fully justifies selected text.
Outdent		Outdents selected text.
Indent		Indents selected list.
Bulleted List		Formats selected text as bulleted list.
Numbered List		Formats selected text as numbered list.
Insert Special Character		Views character map to select and insert special character.
Insert Line (HR)		Inserts a line across the Content Item width (this is the HTML <HR> command).
Insert Table		Inserts an empty table in the Content Item.
Table Row Properties		Views and modifies the properties of a table row.
Table Cell Properties		Views and modifies the properties of a table cell.
Insert Row Before		Inserts a new row in the table before the selected row.
Insert Row After		Inserts a new row in the table after the selected row.
Delete Row		Deletes the selected row from the table.
Insert Column Before		Inserts a new column in the table before the selected row.
Insert Column After		Inserts a new column in the table after the selected row.
Delete Column		Deletes the selected column from the table.
Split Table Cells		Divides a cell into two or more cells.
Merge Table Cells		Merges two or more cells into one.
Use Table Visual Aid		Toggles invisible elements to allow for easier population of table.
Styles	-- Styles --	Applies CSS styles to text.
Format	-- Format --	Applies preset HTML formatting to text.
Font Family	-- Font family --	Selects a font from the list to apply.
Font Size	-- Font size --	Sets the size of the selected text.
Font Color		Sets the color of the selected text.
Highlight		Adds a background color to selected text.
Help		Opens Help files for editor.
Toggle Full Screen Mode		Pops up the editing window in full screen mode.
Print		Prints the Content Item.
Insert Emoticons		Inserts a graphical emoticon in the Content Item.
Insert Flash		Inserts a Flash file into the Content Item.
Insert Link		Attaches a hyperlink to the selected text.
Remove Link		Removes a hyperlink from the selected text.
Insert Anchor		Inserts an anchor within the Content Item.
Insert Image		Inserts an image into the Content Item.
Insert Caption		Inserts a caption for the selected image.
MOSimage		Inserts the MOSimage placeholder.
MOSpagebreak		Inserts the MOSpagebreak command.
Left to Right Text		For text that reads left to right.
Right to Left Text		For text that reads right to left.
Insert HTML Template		Inserts a pre-built HTML template for use in the Content Item. Note that this is configurable.
Toggle Plain Text Mode		Changes to Plain Text Mode to enable hand coding HTML.
Date		Inserts the date.
Time		Inserts the time.

Create a Static Content Item

You can create Static Content Items through use of the Static Content Manager. Pages created in the Static Content Manager reside outside of the Mambo content hierarchy and do not use the two part Intro Text/Main Text structure. When you want to add a page that is not part of a section or a category, you do so by adding a Static Content Item.

Creating and editing Static Content Items is almost identical to the process for creating and editing normal Content Items with only two differences: First, you do not have to assign Static Content Items to categories or sections. Second, you do not have to worry about managing the distinction between Intro Text and Main Text.

Static Content Items have only one text box in which to enter all your text and images. If your site employs a WYSIWYG editor, the formatting controls become available for Static Content Items. The MOSimage and MOSpagebreak functionalities are also available in the Static Content Manager, as are all the other tools you need to create, format, and edit a page of content. The Parameters options in the Static Content Item are essentially the same as those for other Content Items, although they are slightly simpler and lack the Section and Category controls. For a complete explanation of the available parameters, see the section "Understanding Content Item Parameters," earlier in the chapter.

Because Static Content Items are not part of a category or section, Mambo does not automatically add them to any of the navigation menus on your site. In order for a Static Content Item to be visible to visitors, you must create a new Menu Item that links to the Static Content Item and publish it for the site visitors.

Create a Static Content Item

1. Click Content.
2. Click Static Content Manager.

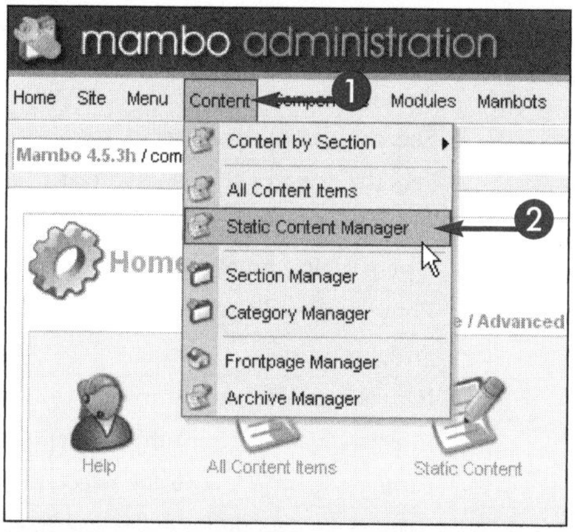

The Static Content Manager loads.

3. Click the New Icon.

The Static Content Item creation screen loads.

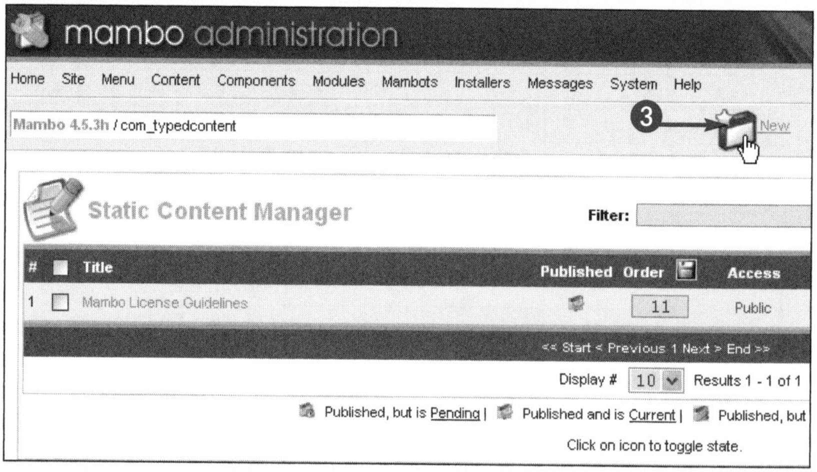

4 Type content in the text box.

5 Click the Save icon.

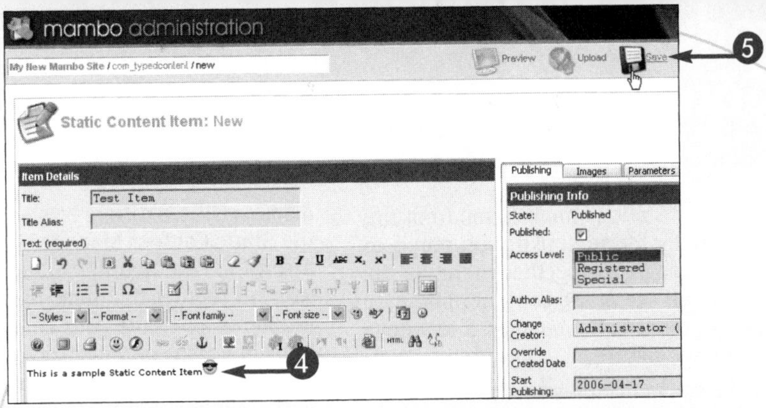

- Mambo creates the new Static Content Item and returns you to the Static Content Manager.

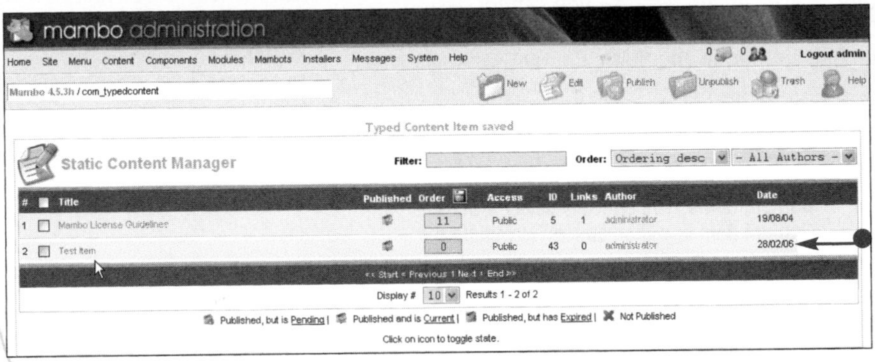

Extra

Static Content Items can play a strategic role within your site's content planning and execution. As discussed in Chapter 5, Static Content Items are very useful when you are working with a flat content hierarchy, but you may also find them useful in a wide variety of other situations. For example, when you want to display a Content Item directly from a menu, but you do not want it as part of a Section or Category list, the best course is to create a Static Content Item and link directly to it. Static Content Items are also particularly well suited for pages that stand alone in the hierarchy, such as for your privacy policy or terms of use page.

Because Static Content Items cannot use Intro Text and because you cannot archive them, you should not use them for certain tasks. For example, you should not use them for reporting news items or other items you may want to archive at some point. You also cannot assign Static Content Items to the home page via the Frontpage Manager, which makes them inappropriate as a tool for presenting content on your site's home page.

An Introduction to the Static Content Manager

Mambo separates Static Content Items from the content hierarchy for administration purposes and groups these items together in the Static Content Manager. Although the Static Content Manager is largely similar to the Content Items Manager, a few key differences give it a unique nature.

Some differences make sense from a structural standpoint. For example, because you cannot assign Static Content Items to the Frontpage Manager, there is no Frontpage column in the Static Content Manager's display. Others differences seem arbitrary. For example, the Static Content Manager does not have easy-to-use arrows for the Reorder column. This means that if you want to reorder the items on the list, you must number the items and save your changes. The Static Content Manager also contains, for no apparent reason, a column that shows how many menu links there are to the various items. For more on the Content Item Manager, see the section "An Introduction to the Content Items Manager."

A Toolbar

Contains icons for the management of Static Content Items. You typically select a Static Content Item and then an icon to initiate the action.

B Title

Lists all the Static Content Items.

C Published

Shows the item's published state, which you change via the icon.

D Order

Orders the item, relative to others when you select the icon and then click the Save icon.

E Access

Shows the item's access level. You can cycle through the access level options.

F ID

System-generated ID number.

G Links

Indicates how many Menu Items link to each Static Content Item.

H Author

The author associated with the item.

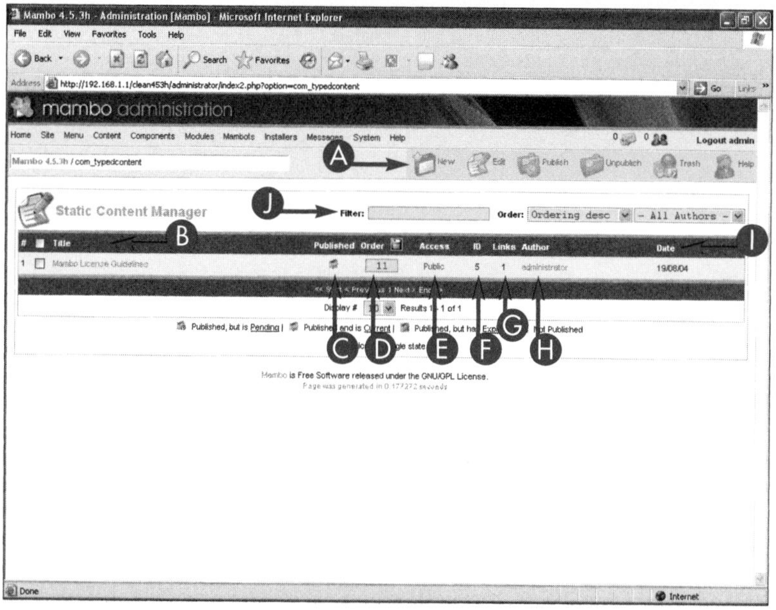

I Date

The date the item was created.

J Filters

Sorts and filters the list of items. You can also search using the text box field.

Publish a Content Item

Although you can view and edit a Content Item within the admin system without publishing it, you must publish the item so that visitors to your Web site can see it. During site construction or new content creation, it is generally best to leave the Content Items unpublished because publishing an item while you edit it results in users viewing your work-in-progress. The better practice is to create and edit Content Items in the unpublished state, and to publish them only when you have them in final form.

Publication is a requirement for sections, categories, and Content Items. Failure to publish a parent item affects the child items below it in the hierarchy. In other words, simply publishing a Content Item may not be sufficient to make it show up on the front end of the Web site; you must ensure that the category and the section to which the item belongs are also published. The only exception to this rule is where you create a Menu Item that links directly to a Content Item; in that case, the publishing state of the category and sections do not impact the visitor's ability to view the Content Item.

There are two ways to publish a Content Item. You can publish with one click directly from the Content Items Manager, or you can publish by opening the Content Item editing screen and selecting Publish from the parameters inside the editing window. Always check the front end of the Web site after invoking the publication command to make sure that the result is what you expected.

Publish a Content Item

1. Load the Content Items Manager.

Note: To Load the Content Items Manager, see the section "Create a Content Item."

2. Click the red X in the Published column.

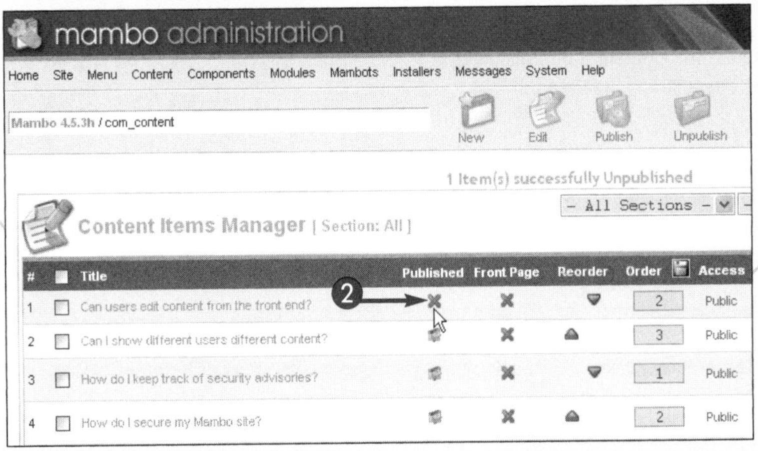

- The red X changes to a blue-and-white icon with a green check mark.

The item is now Published.

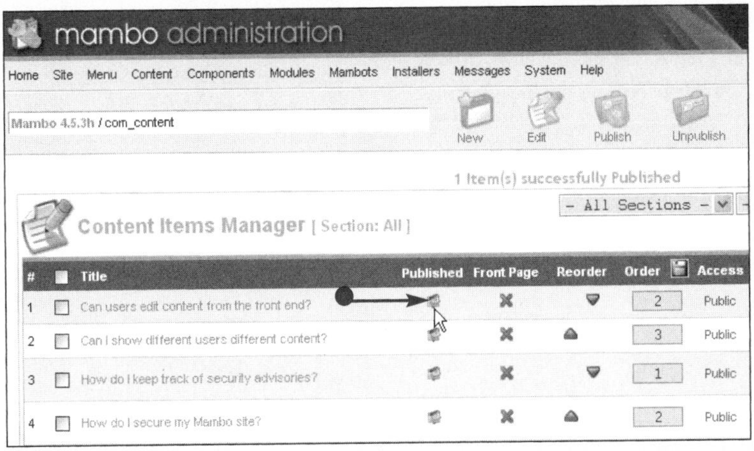

Unpublish a Content Item

You can remove a Content Item from public view by unpublishing it. Although the Content Item remains visible to those who can access the Content Item Manager inside the admin system, site visitors cannot see it. The ability to control publishing of items on a case-by-case basis is very useful because you can temporarily unpublish items to perform necessary maintenance on the site or to update an item. You can also permanently unpublish an item to remove it from further display.

Unpublishing a Content Item only removes it from the front end of the Web site. It does not delete the item or impair your ability to publish the Content Item again if you should choose to do so. Mambo holds unpublished Content Items within its system like any other Content Item. There is no difference in the way unpublished items are managed in the administration system. You can still edit the Content Item, but you cannot see the results on the front end of the Web site until you republish the item. During editing you can use the Preview command to view the Content Item with the CSS and the images in place. Previewing Content Items is discussed earlier in the chapter in the section "Preview Your Work."

There are two ways to unpublish a Content Item. You either unpublish via the Publish icon, which you find on the Content Item Manager, or you can open the Content Item Editing screen and select the No option to the publish parameters inside the editing window.

Unpublish a Content Item

1. Load the Content Items Manager.

Note: To load the Content Items Manager, see the section "Create a Content Item."

2. Click the blue-and-white icon with a green check mark in the Published column.

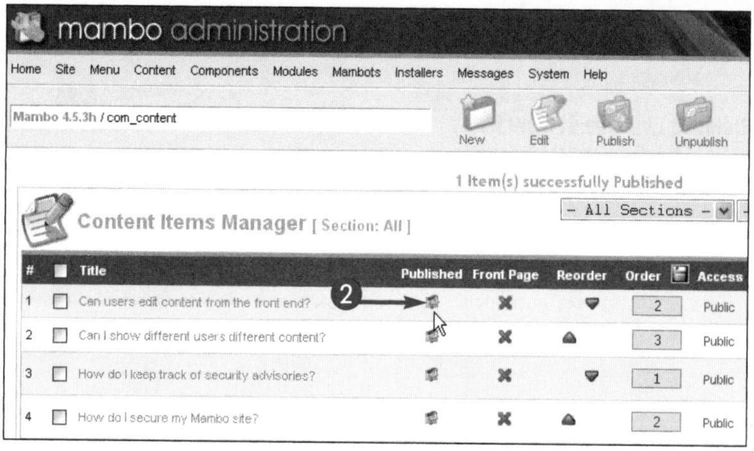

- The blue-and-white icon with a green check mark changes to a red X. The item is now Unpublished.

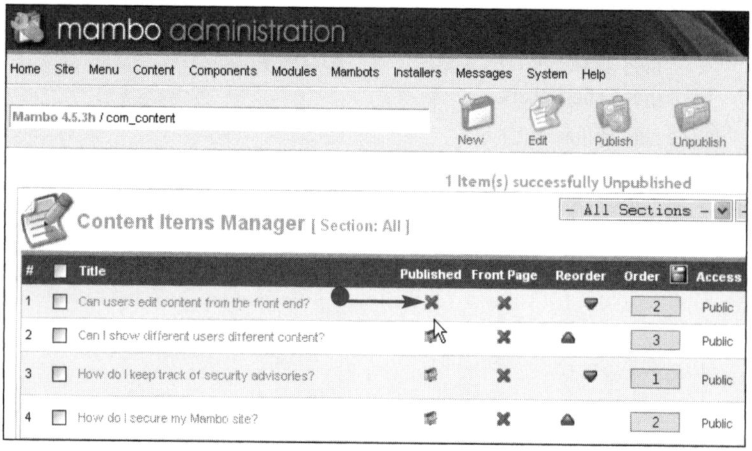

Control Output with Introduction and Main Text

You can divide a Content Item into two parts and thus create a short Introduction together with a Main Text section, which gives you more options to display the items. Splitting an article into two parts, with one part functioning as a brief intro to the longer article, is fundamental to creating news sites, portal sites, and blog sites with lengthy entries. Creative use of the Intro Text feature peaks visitors' curiosity and encourages them to read the rest of the article. The Intro Text also gives you a way to display more items on a page. By keeping the length of the Intro Text within reason, you can display several Content Item Intro Text sections on one page.

The Content Item Creation and Editing screens automatically divide the text input area into two parts, called Intro Text and Main Text. While the Intro Text field is required, the Main Text field is optional. When you split content across both text boxes, Mambo automatically assumes you want to use the Intro Text/Main Text formatting for the Content Item. The system assigns the Intro Text along with a Read More link to the first page where the item is listed. When site visitors click the Read More link, Mambo takes them to a dedicated page containing the Main Text of the Content Item.

If you want to forego the Intro Text functionality, you simply enter the entire content into the Intro Text box; you do not place any text in the Main Text box. Content created in this manner shows the entire Content item on the first page where the item appears.

Control Output with Introduction and Main Text

1. Load the Content Items Manager.

Note: To Load the Content Items Manager, see the section "Create a Content Item."

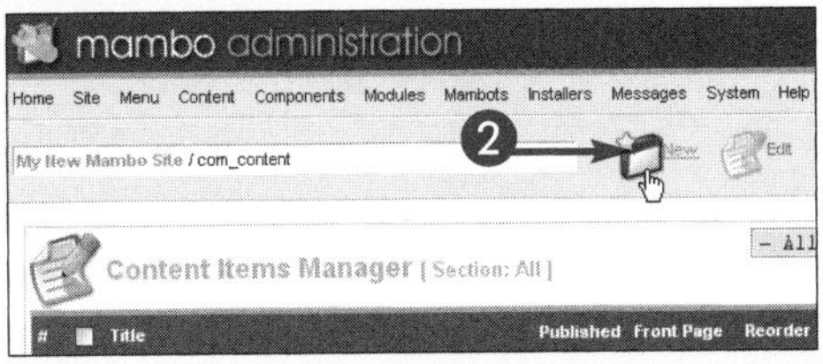

2. Click the New icon.

The New Content Item screen loads.

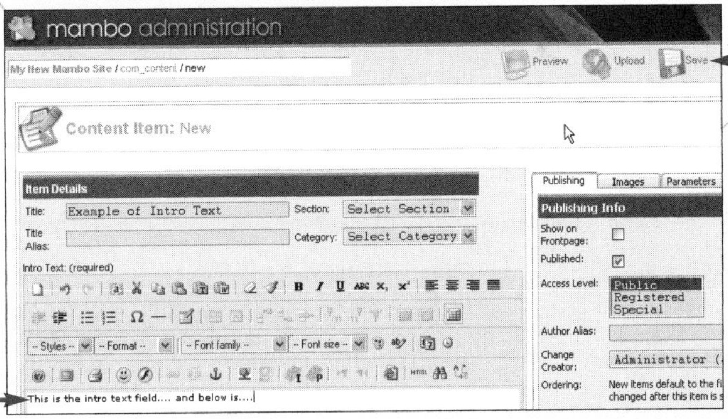

3. Type text in the Intro Text box.

4. Type text in the Main Text box.

5. Click the Save icon.

Mambo creates a Content Item with both Intro Text and Main Text, and then returns you to the Content Items Manager.

Link a Content Item to a Menu

You can link a Content Item to a menu quickly and easily with the Link to Menu command inside the Content Item Editing interface. While there are other methods for linking items to menus, the Link to Menu command has the benefit of immediacy because you can create a Content Item and link it to a menu all without leaving the Content Item Editing window.

The Link to Menu tab displays all the information that you need to know about a link. It displays a list of all the existing menus in the system as well as any current links between Content Items and menus. If a Content Item is already linked directly to a menu, that information also appears on the tab, along with the name of the link and whether the Menu Item is published. If there are no Menu Items linked to the Content Item, the system shows the word *None* under the Existing Menu Link heading.

Creating a new Menu Item to link to a Content Item involves simply selecting the menu where you want the link to appear and then giving the link a name. The Link to Menu button creates a Menu Item on the menu and with the name you have specified. Mambo publishes the newly created Menu Item by default. If you want to unpublish or delete the Menu Item, you must access the Menu Manager and change the published status, or completely delete the Menu Item. You cannot unpublish or delete Menu Items from the Content Item Editing screen. Note that you can also create links to Content Items directly from the Menu Manager. For more on working with the Menu Manager, see Chapter 9.

Link a Content Item to a Menu

1. Load the Content Items Manager.

Note: To load the Content Items Manager, see the section "Create a Content Item."

2. Click a Content Item.
3. Click the Edit icon.

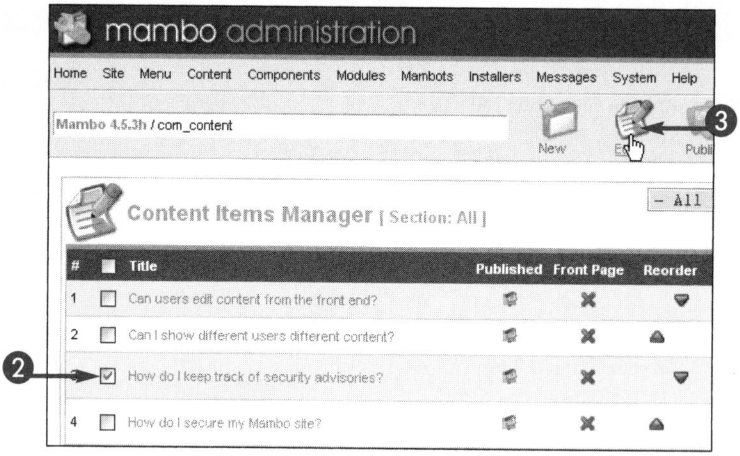

The Content Item Editing screen loads.

4. Click the Link to Menu tab.
5. Click a menu.
6. Type a name for the link.
7. Click Link to Menu.

Mambo creates a new Menu Item and links it to the Content Item.

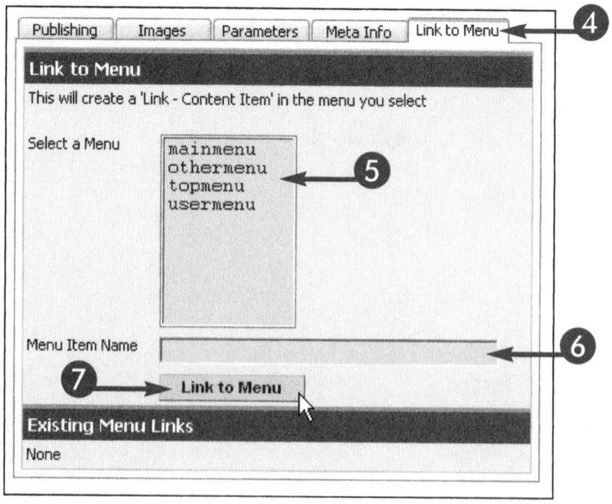

Set a Content Item's MetaData

You can provide metadata specific to individual Content Items. This is useful not only for search engine marketing purposes, but also for enabling tools like the Mambo Related Items module. Although the Global Configuration Manager provides the Metadata tab, which you use to specify metadata for your site as a whole, the Content Items creation and editing screen gives you a place to add additional info that appears only for a particular Content Item. For more on adding metadata to the site as a whole with the Global Configuration Manager, see Chapter 2.

As you create or edit a Content Item in Mambo, you see a set of tabs in the right-hand column. The Meta Info tab has two boxes: Description and Keywords, which correspond to the Description and Keyword metatags.

When you add metadata to a Content Item in the Meta Info tab, the information appends to the site's global metadata for the Content Item. For example, if you enter the keywords "sailing, catamarans, tri-hull, yacht" on the Global Configuration Manager Metadata tab, and the keywords "regatta, Phuket Yacht Club, marina" for a Content Item, at run time the system displays the Keywords metatag field as follows: "sailing, catamarans, tri-hull, yacht, regatta, Phuket Yacht Club, marina." The same logic applies to the Description field.

Note that the right-hand column of tabs is visible only when the admin system is in Advanced Mode. If you have the system set to Simple mode, you do not see the right column. For more on the Simple and Advanced Modes and how to switch between them, see Chapter 1.

Set a Content Item's MetaData

1. Load the Content Items Manager.

Note: To load the Content Items Manager, see the section "Create a Content Item."

2. Click a Content Item.
3. Click the Edit icon.

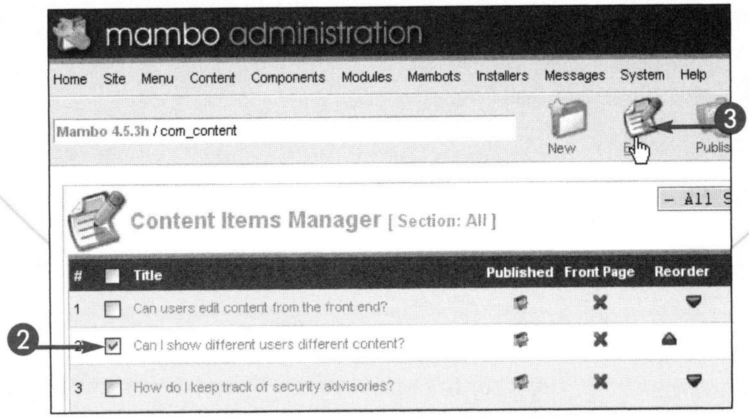

The Content Item Editing screen loads.

4. Click the Meta Info tab.

The Meta Info tab appears.

5. Type a description.
6. Type keywords.
7. Click the Save icon.

Mambo saves the metadata for the Content Item and returns you to the Content Items Manager.

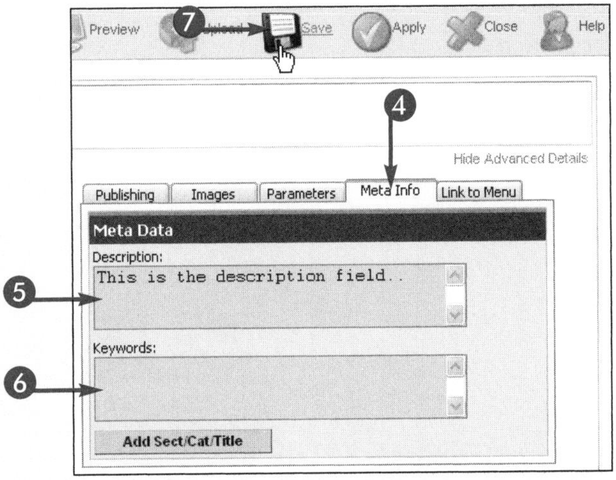

Set Publishing Start and Stop Dates

You can control the start and stop dates for Content Item publication. Mambo gives you complete control over when an item becomes visible to site visitors and for how long. Controlling publication start and stop dates is essential for time-sensitive information. The feature also helps you manage workload by letting you load information in advance of the date you need it to appear on the site.

The default setting, which requires no special action on your part, is for Mambo to publish your material immediately and for it to remain published indefinitely, but you can alter the schedule to suit your needs. With this default setting, as soon as you apply or save your change, site visitors can view the Content Item on the front end of the Web site. While the instant publishing aspect of Mambo is convenient, you should remain wary not to publish something before it is ready for public view, lest the site visitors see incomplete or untimely content.

To publish a Content Item at an indefinite point in the future, simply deselect the Published option on the Publishing tab inside the Content Item Editing screen. When you are ready to publish, follow the instructions in the section "Publish a Content Item," earlier in the chapter.

Alternatively, to begin publishing at a specific date in the future, you can leave the Published option selected, but also set a start date using the Start Publishing date field; when you do so, the system automatically publishes the item on that date.

You can automatically stop publishing by selecting a date in the Finish Publishing date field. Once you set this field, the Mambo system ceases publishing the Content item on the date specified.

Set Publishing Start and Stop Dates

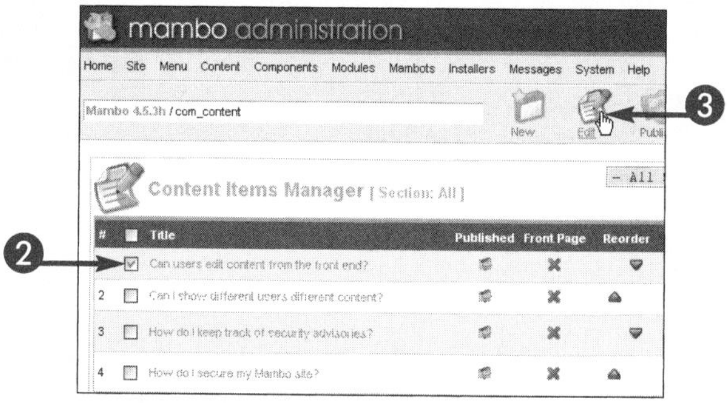

1. Load the Content Items Manager.

Note: To load the Content Items Manager, see the section "Create a Content Item."

2. Click a Content Item.
3. Click the Edit icon.

The Content Item Editing screen loads.

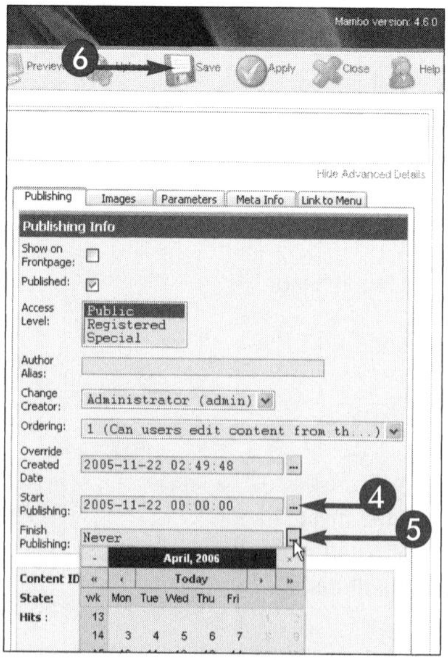

4. On the Publishing tab, click the Start Publishing button and select a date.
5. Click the Finish Publishing button and select a date.
6. Click the Save icon.

Mambo sets the Start and Stop Publishing dates and returns you to the Content Items Manager.

Control Publishing Information

You can control the publishing information associated with any Content Item. The options on the Publishing tab inside the Content Item Editing interface enable you to specify information relating to the creator or author of the Content Item, as well as information relating to the creation date of the item.

The controls are particularly useful to override the automatically generated data relating to the item creation date, owner, and author. You commonly employ this option to show a different author, or to specify a different creation date, for example when you input an article for another author and you want it to appear under the author's name, or when the item was originally published in the past and you want the date on the Web site's Content Item to reflect the original article's publication date.

When you create a new Content Item, Mambo automatically associates certain information with the item. The system sets the creation date and time according to when the Content Item was created. The system also lists the administrator who was logged in at the time as both the creator and the author of the Content Item.

The tools in the Publishing tab in the Content Item Editing screen override the default data, albeit with some limitations. The creator choices are restricted because you must choose a registered user within the system. However, you can enter anything you like in the field labeled Author Alias. If you use the Author Alias field, the system displays that name as the item's author. If you leave the field blank, the system lists the creator as the author. You can override the content creation date by selecting a date from the calendar you find on the Override Created Date field. Note that although you can change the creation date, you cannot override the date the article was last modified.

Control Publishing Information

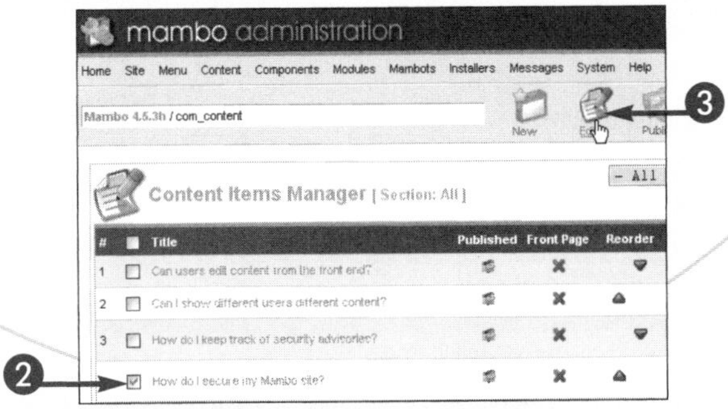

1. Load the Content Items Manager.

Note: To load the Content Items Manager, see the section "Create a Content Item."

2. Click a Content Item.
3. Click the Edit icon.

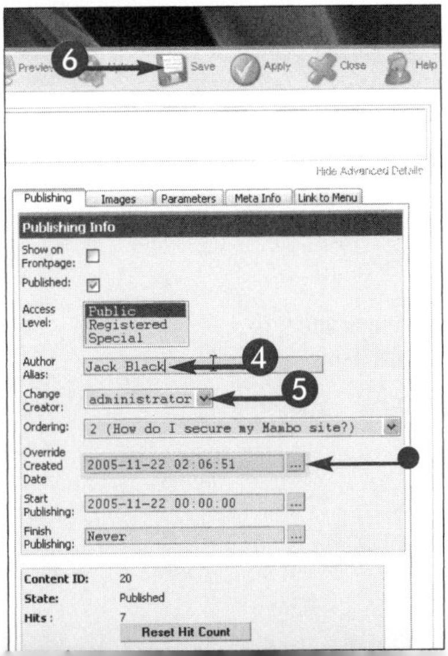

The Content Item Editing screen loads.

4. On the Publishing tab, click the creator.
5. Type an author alias.
   - To override the created date, you can click here and select a new date.
6. Click the Save icon.

Mambo saves the changes to the Content Item and returns you to the Content Items Manager.

Create Multi-Page Content Items

You can use the MOSpagebreak function to create a Content Item with multiple pages. MOSpagebreak makes it easy to split one Content Item into multiple pages while still maintaining the ability to edit all the pages in one editing window. While site visitors see multi-page content, the administrator need only deal with one Content Item. Splitting a long Content Item into multiple pages is often desirable to improve the usability of your Web site, or to allow the administrator to force multiple page views for advertising purposes.

You can use the MOSpagebreak command either with or without the WYSIWYG editor. Using the command requires you to place the cursor where you want the break to occur and then click the MOSpagebreak icon. The split of the Content Item does not appear in the Content Item Editing window. You only see `{mospagebreak}` in the text.

You can place as many MOSpagebreak commands as you like either in the Intro Text, the Main Text, or both. Each instance of MOSpagebreak creates a new page for the site viewer. The use of the command also triggers the automatic creation of a Table of Contents for the Content Item, assuming you have selected this option in the Global Configurations settings. For an explanation of the Global Configuration content settings, see Chapter 2.

The system-generated Table of Contents appears on each page of the Content Item and includes links to each of the pages created by the MOSpagebreak. In the default configuration, the system simply labels the pages with numbers — page 1, page 2, page 3, and so on. If you want to add a custom title to the pages in the Table of Contents, modify the MOSpagebreak to include the title attribute, such as `{mospagebreak title=next page}`.

Create Multi-Page Content Items

1. Load the Content Items Manager.

Note: To load the Content Items Manager, see the section "Create a Content Item."

2. Click a Content Item.
3. Click the Edit icon.

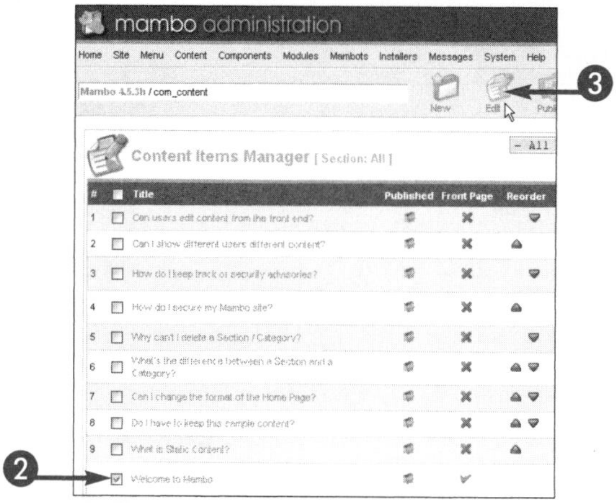

The Content Item Editing screen loads.

4. Position the cursor where you want to place the page break.
5. Click the MOSpagebreak icon.
6. Click the Save icon.

Mambo saves the page break and returns you to the Content Items Manager.

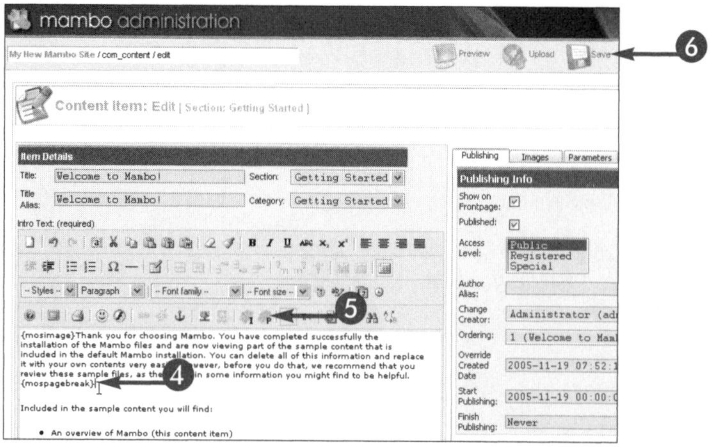

Restrict Access to an Item

You can restrict access to a Content Item to make the contents available to only certain classes of users. Access restrictions are an effective way to make premium content areas for your site members, or to provide private and confidential information you do not want to show to general public visitors to your Web site.

There are two methods for changing the access levels for a Content Item. The easiest method involves activating the Access switch on the Content Item Manager screens to change the switch's state. The other alternative is to open an individual Content Item and change the Access control that appears on the editing screen. The result of either method is identical. The steps in this section demonstrate the latter.

Mambo has three access levels. The Public access level makes the Content Item available to all visitors. Registered restricts access to only site visitors who are registered and logged in to the system. The Special class is typically used for your front-end content managers. Chapter 4 discusses the relationship between access level and user groups in detail.

Note that the hierarchical relationship between sections, categories, and Content Items is also reflected in the access levels. If you restrict access to a section, you also restrict access to the categories and Content Items within the section. If, however, you use the unrestricted Public access setting for your section, you can restrict the access of the categories and Content Items within that section. Restricting a category likewise restricts the Content Items within that category.

Restrict Access to an Item

1. Load the Content Items Manager.

Note: To load the Content Items Manager, see the section "Create a Content Item."

2. Click a Content Item.
3. Click the Edit icon.

   The Content Item Editing screen loads.

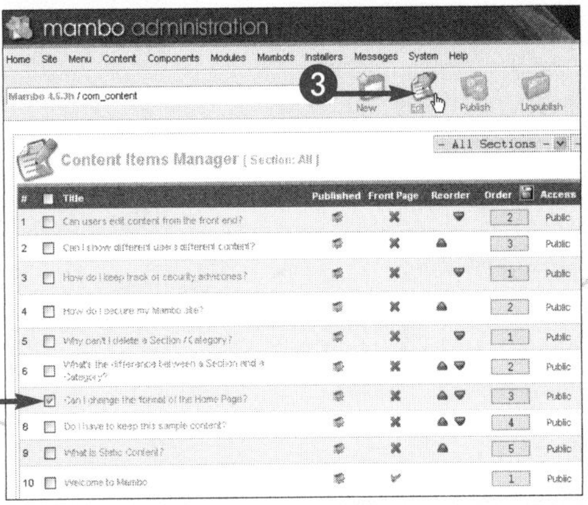

4. Click the desired access level.
5. Click the Save icon.

   Mambo saves your changes to the Access Level and returns you to the Content Items Manager.

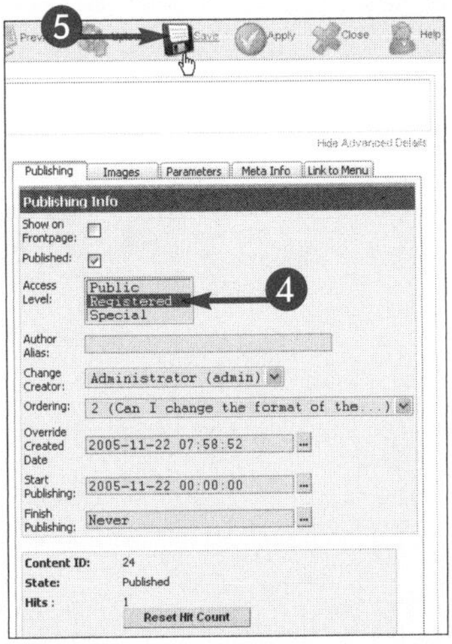

Move a Content Item

You can move any Content Item in the system from one Category to any other category in the system. The Move function, located in the Content Items Manager, is a useful tool for reordering your content hierarchy. The function is also a timesaver because you can move multiple Content Items simultaneously. The ability to change relationships between sections, categories, and Content Items after you create Content Items makes it easy to change content structures without having to delete and re-create the information or rework the navigation links.

When you initiate the Move command, the system displays a list showing both the name of the categories and sections in the system. You must select the category to which you want to move Content Item and then confirm the action. Failure to confirm the move simply leaves the items where they are.

Moving a Content Item does not affect the name, the formatting, or the contents of the item. The Content Item retains its published state; that is, if you published the item before the move, it remains published after the move. Unpublished items remain unpublished. Mambo automatically updates any Menu Items that you link to the items.

You must create the category you want to move the Content Items to before you can use the Move command. Note that if you do not publish the category to which you move the items, the Content Items are not visible on the front end of the Web site until you publish the category.

Move a Content Item

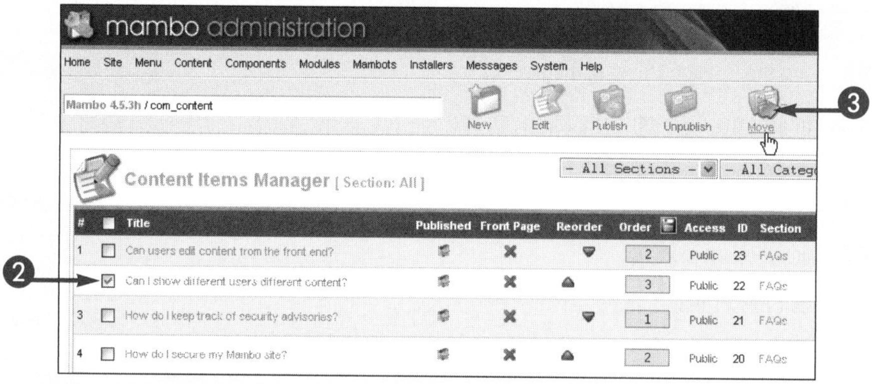

1. Load the Content Items Manager.

Note: To load the Content Items Manager, see the section "Create a Content Item."

2. Click a Content Item.
3. Click the Move icon.

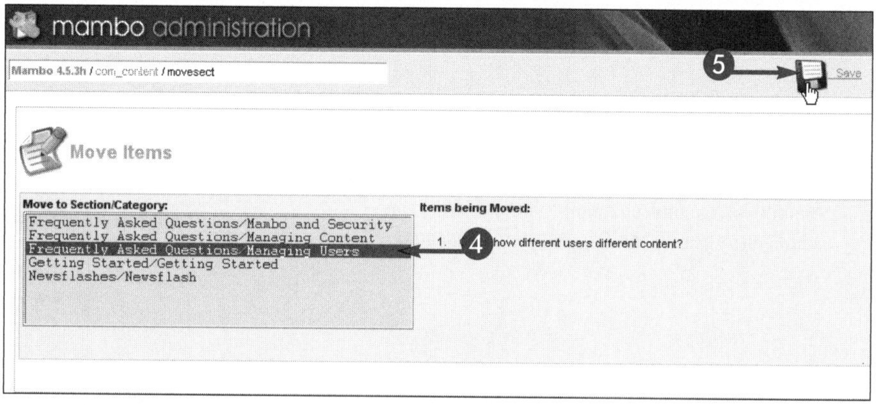

A new screen loads.

4. Click the Section/Category.
5. Click the Save icon.

Mambo moves the item to the new Section/Category and returns you to the Content Items Manager.

Duplicate a Content Item

You can use the Content Items Manager's Copy function to copy one or more Content Items simultaneously. The tool is a quick way to duplicate an entire group of Content Items at one time. This feature is a very useful tool when you want to build a site with new Content Items that have the same properties as an existing Content Item. Using the Copy command to create new Content Items promotes efficiency and consistency; it is much easier to copy Content Items than to try to synchronize the attributes of numerous new Content Items that you create from scratch one-by-one via the Content Items Manager's New command. For more on creating Content Items using the New command, see the section "Create a Content Item."

To duplicate an item, you need only select the Content Item and then activate the Copy icon. Mambo prompts you to select the category to which you want to copy the Content Item. After you have done so, the Content Item immediately appears on the list of Content Items in the Content Item Manager. The new Content Item shares all of the attributes and contents of the original Content Item.

After you create a new Content Item, you can change the name and edit the contents. On the front end of the Web site, the new Content Item appears visually in a manner consistent with the original Content Item.

Note that because the system gives you the chance to elect the section and category assignment of the copied Content Item, you can use the function to copy items either to the original section and category, or to a different location. This flexibility in the Copy function makes it practical for you to create Content Items that you can use as templates for the creation of additional, similar Content Items.

Duplicate a Content Item

1. Load the Content Items Manager.

Note: To load the Content Items Manager, see the section "Create a Content Item."

2. Click a Content Item.
3. Click the Copy icon.

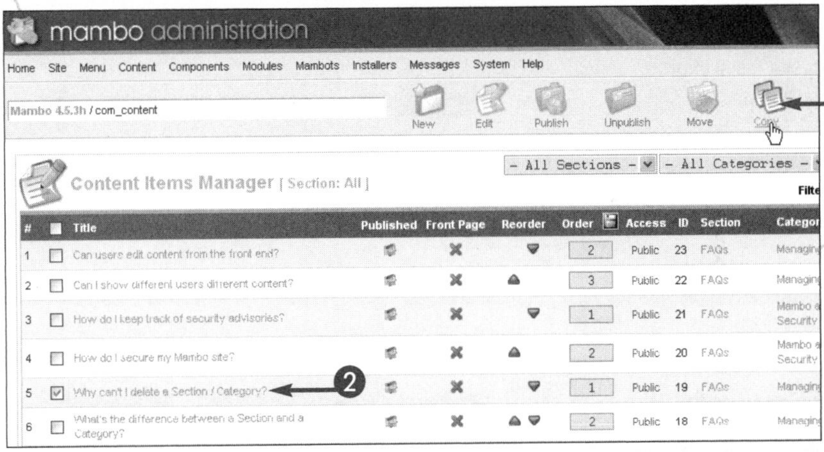

A new screen loads.

4. Click the Section/ Category.
5. Click the Save icon.

Mambo copies the item to the selected Section/ Category and returns you to the Content Items Manager.

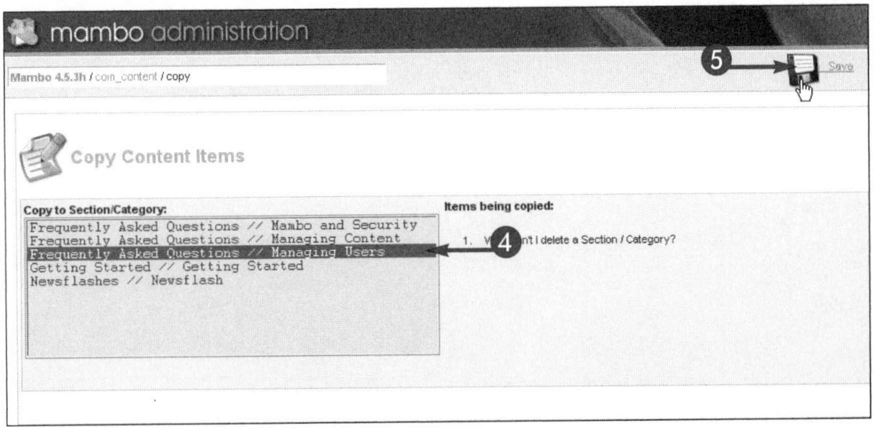

Move a Content Item to the Trash Manager

You can remove a Content Item from the Content Items Manager by sending it to the Trash. This is an easy way to keep your Content Items Manager clear of unwanted files. Mambo does not delete Content Items that you send to the Trash, but it hides these items from public view and removes them from the Content Items Manager. Moving an item to the Trash unpublishes the item and disables all Menu Items linked to the Content Item. Items you move to the Trash stay there indefinitely until you take further action.

All Content Items sent to the Trash are administered through the Trash Manager, which is located under the Site Menu. The Trash Manager provides only two functionalities: deleting an item permanently or restoring the item. For more on deleting an item permanently, see the section "Delete a Content Item Permanently," later in the chapter. For more on restoring items that you have previously moved to the Trash Manager, see the next section, "Restore a Content Item from the Trash Manager."

The Trash Manager permits you to view a list of the Content Items relegated to the Trash. However, if you want to view the contents of the item itself, you must restore the item to the Content Item Manager.

Note that when you elect to move a Content Item to the Trash, Mambo does not ask you to confirm the move, but rather, moves the Content Item immediately. Be careful not to unnecessarily move items to the Trash because Mambo immediately unpublishes them and renders them unavailable to your site visitors. To undo your actions, you must go through the process of restoring the item to make the item visible again on the front end of the Web site.

Move a Content Item to the Trash Manager

1. Load the Content Items Manager.

Note: To load the Content Items Manager, see the section "Create a Content Item."

2. Click a Content Item.

3. Click the Trash icon.

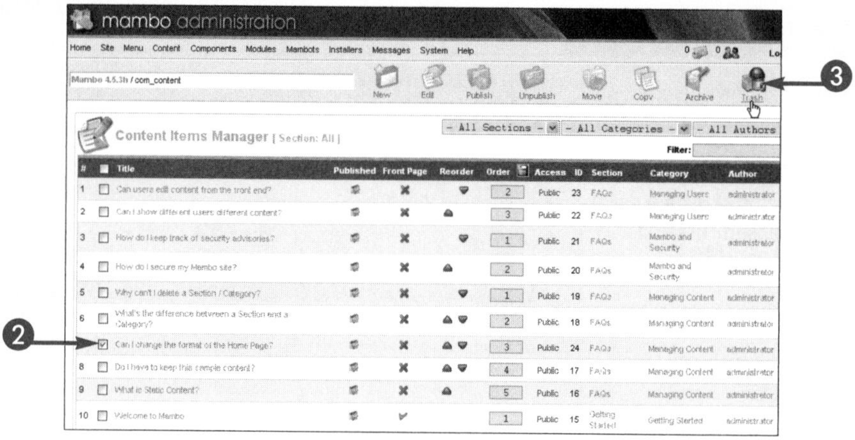

- Mambo removes the item from the Content Items Manager and places it in the Trash Manager.

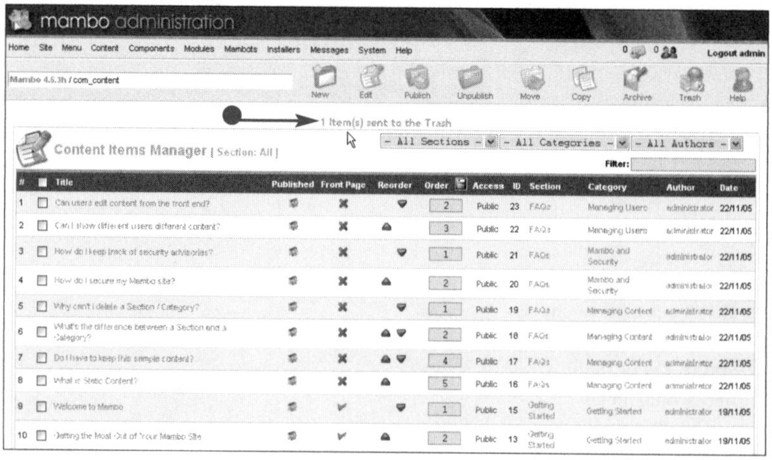

Restore a Content Item from the Trash Manager

You can move a Content Item or a Static Content Item from the Trash back to the live area of your Web site, a process referred to as *restoring* an item. When you execute the Restore command from within the Trash Manager, Mambo moves a normal Content Item back to the Content Items Manager. If you choose to restore a Static Content Item, Mambo moves the item back to the Static Content Item Manager. The Restore command is a blessing when you have unintentionally deleted a Content Item from the Content Items Manager. To review the distinction between Content Items and Static Content Items, see Chapter 1. For more on sending an item to the Trash, see the preceding section "Move a Content Item to the Trash Manager."

When you select a Content Item and activate the Restore command, the system requires that you confirm the action. Once confirmed, the system immediately moves the item back to the section and category where it originally appeared. Newly restored Content Items are unpublished and placed last in the order of items by default. In the case of Static Content Items, Mambo simply restores the item to the Static Content Manager. Once restored, a Content Item is fully functional and you can view, publish, edit, copy, or move it within the system.

To make a restored Content Item, and the Menu Items linked to it, visible to your site visitors, you must publish the Content Item. For more on publishing Content Items, see the section "Publish a Content Item," earlier in the chapter.

Note that Static Content Items are not listed in the Trash Manager as Static Content, but rather as *Typed Content*. This name is a legacy from previous versions of the Mambo system.

Restore a Content Item from the Trash Manager

1. Click Site.
2. Click Trash Manager.

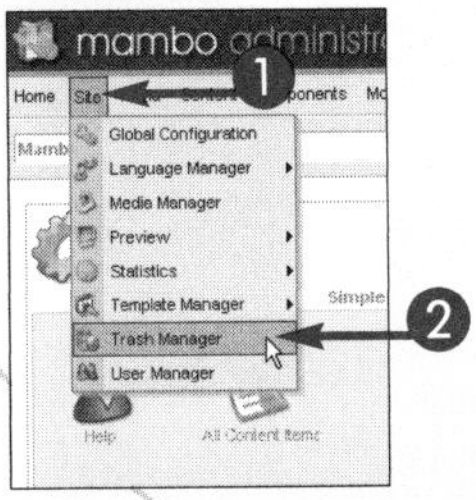

The Trash Manager loads.

3. Click the Content Item.
4. Click the Restore Icon.

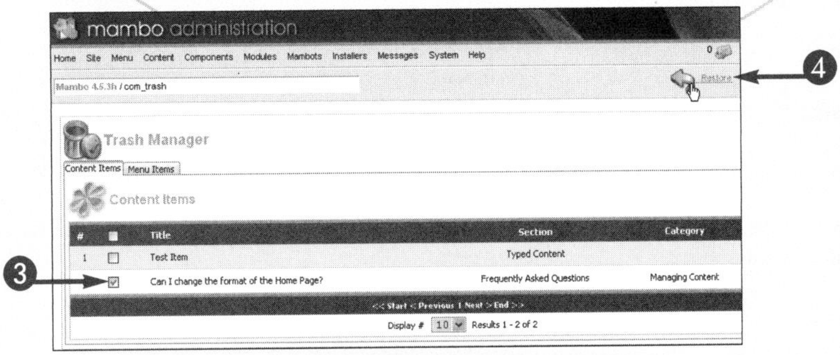

A new screen loads with a summary of the items to be restored.

5. Click the Restore button.

A dialog box asks for confirmation.

6. Click OK.

Mambo restores the item and returns you to the Trash Manager.

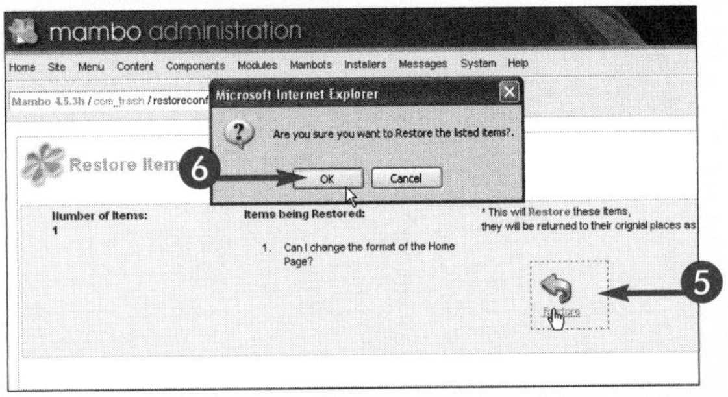

Delete a Content Item Permanently

You can delete a Content Item permanently and remove it from the Trash Manager. Permanent deletion is, as the name implies, final. You cannot restore an item after you have deleted it from the Trash Manager. In line with the finality of the act, Mambo asks you to confirm your action before it performs the final deletion.

Although you may not want to rush into deleting items, there are times when it is necessary or desirable. At the most basic, deleting unnecessary Content Items helps keep the system clean of unnecessary files. For small sites, this may be a matter of little consequence, but for larger sites, this becomes a necessary part of site maintenance and helps your administrators avoid confusion. Additionally, if you want to delete a section or a category you must first empty the section or category completely. The system requires not only the deletion of both published and unpublished Content Items in the live area of the site, but also any related Content Items located in the Trash Manager. If you try to delete the section or category before you eliminate all of the live and trashed items, the system displays an error message. You can identify whether you have trashed items attached to the section or category by viewing the Section or Category Manager. A separate column shows the number of items live and the number of items in the Trash. For more on how to use the Section and Category Managers, see Chapter 5.

Deleting a Content Item does not delete the Menu Items that link to that Content Item, and it does not affect the category and section to which the Content Item belongs. Deleting a Content Item also has no impact on any images the system holds.

Delete a Content Item Permanently

1. Load the Trash Manager.

Note: For more on loading the Trash Manager, see the section "Restore a Content Item from the Trash Manager."

2. Click the Content Item.
3. Click the Delete icon.

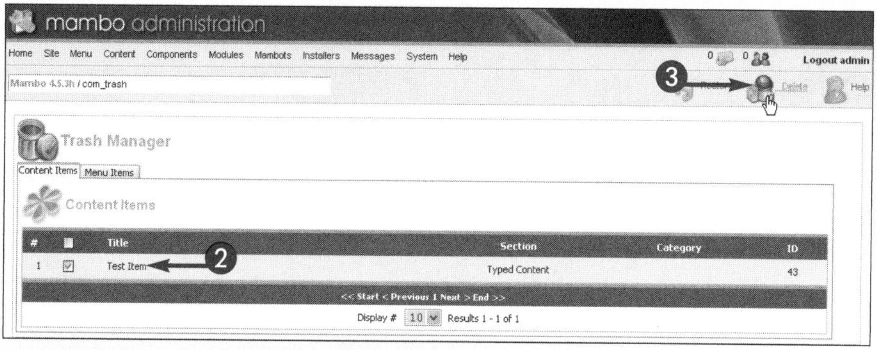

A new screen loads with a summary of the items to be deleted.

4. Click the Delete button.

A dialog box asks for confirmation.

5. Click OK.

Mambo permanently deletes the item and returns you to the Trash Manager.

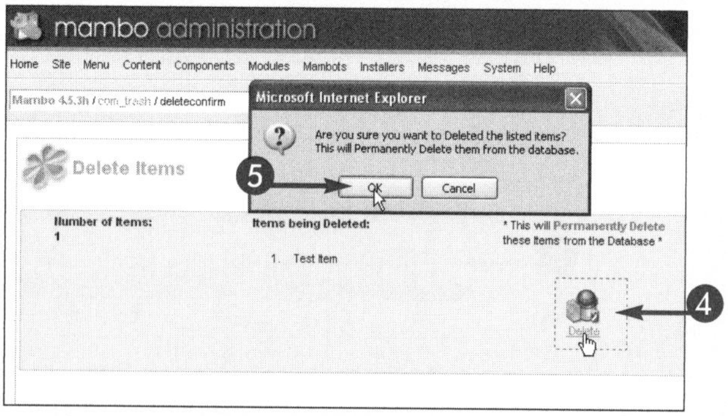

Work with Content Archives

With Mambo, you can store older Content Items chronologically in the Archive Manager. Archiving content helps keep both the front end and the back end of your Web site organized by removing older, less frequently visited content from the main content areas and storing it in a collective archive area that you can search and view by date. Archiving is essentially an organizational tool. Your decision to archive content should be based on how you want visitors to see your Content Items or how much flexibility you need as an administrator.

The Archiving Process

When you archive Content Items within the Content Items Manager, Mambo immediately removes the items from the Content Items Manager and relegates them to the Archive Manager. For more on moving Content Items into the archive, see the next section, "Archive a Content Item."

Moving items to the archive is only part of the process. Because the default Mambo installation has no Archived Content Items, and therefore no Menu Items linked to the archives, you must create one or more Menu Items and link them to the archives if you want site visitors to access the archives. With the Menu Manager, you can display archived items either collectively or grouped by section or category. When you create a Menu Item, you can link either to a list of all the archived items or a list of archived items for a particular section or a specific category. Creating links to discreet sections and categories within the archives means that you can generate multiple Menu Items that link to different groupings of archived items. You can assign various Menu Items to a particular section and category where the Content Items were originally published. Creating and assigning the Menu Items to display archived items in context with current Content Items keeps the content organized in a logical fashion for site visitors. For more on creating the various types of Menu Items, see Chapter 9.

The Archive Structure

Mambo organizes archived items chronologically — by their creation date and not by their publication or archive date — and you cannot override this order. When a visitor clicks an archive, Mambo presents a set of Menu Items containing lists of months and years. The visitor must select a month and a year to display the Content Items for that period.

Although you cannot alter the organizational scheme or the search mechanism for the archive, you can control the archive page layout. You can control layout using the parameters attached to the Menu Item. The options and process are the same as that for any other type of Menu Item. For more on using Menu Item parameters to affect the format of pages, see Chapter 9.

The Unarchiving Process

In the admin system, all archived items are collected together in the Archive Manager. After you archive a Content Item, it no longer appears in the Content Items Manager and you can no longer edit the item, unless you unarchive it. For more on unarchiving Content Items, see the section "Unarchive Content."

The Archive Module

The default Mambo deployment includes an Archive module, which when published, displays a list of the months in which you have archived content. When users click a month's name, they see all the archived items for that particular period. For more on the Archive module, see Chapter 11.

Archive a Content Item

You can move any normal Content Item into an archive. Archiving content is a good way to keep your site focused on fresher Content Items while keeping older content organized and available for your visitors. Note that the Archive option is available only for normal Content Items; you cannot add Static Content Items to an archive.

You archive items from the Content Items Manager screen, where you have the option of selecting only one or multiple items simultaneously. When you activate the Archive command, Mambo immediately removes the items from the Content Items Manager and places them in the Archive Manager. Archived Items remain associated with their assigned categories and sections, but are accessible only via the Archive Manager.

Archived items are essentially "frozen." You cannot edit, duplicate, or move them from one category to another.

The Archive Manager has only three tasks that you can perform on an archived item: You can reorder an item relative to other archived items, you can move the item to the Trash, or you can unarchive the item. If you need to make changes to an archived item or want to duplicate it or move it between categories, you must first unarchive the item before you can make changes to it in the Content Items Manager. For more on unarchiving an item, see the next section, "Unarchive Content."

Archiving is a useful tool when you use it judiciously. With larger sites, it can make your presentation more focused. On sites where chronology is a key organizational issue, like a news site or a blog, archiving Content Items is also a logical way for site visitors to search for older materials.

Archive a Content Item

1. Load the Content Items Manager.

Note: To load the Content Items Manager, see the section "Create a Content Item."

2. Click a Content Item.
3. Click the Archive icon.

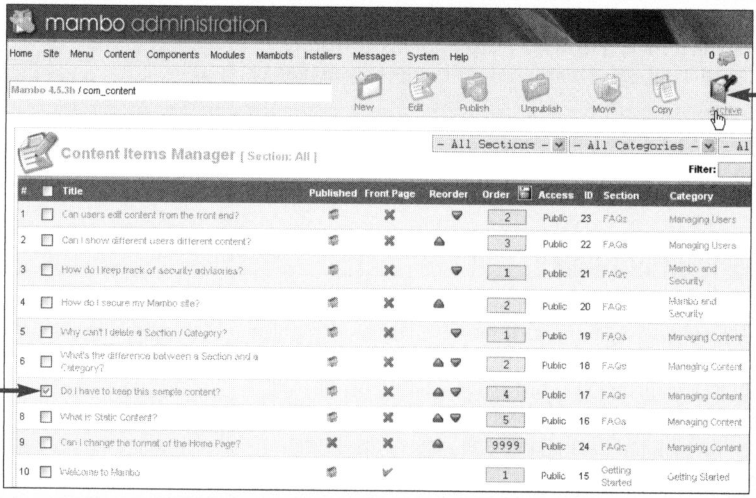

- Mambo removes the item from the Content Items manager and moves it to the Archive Manager.

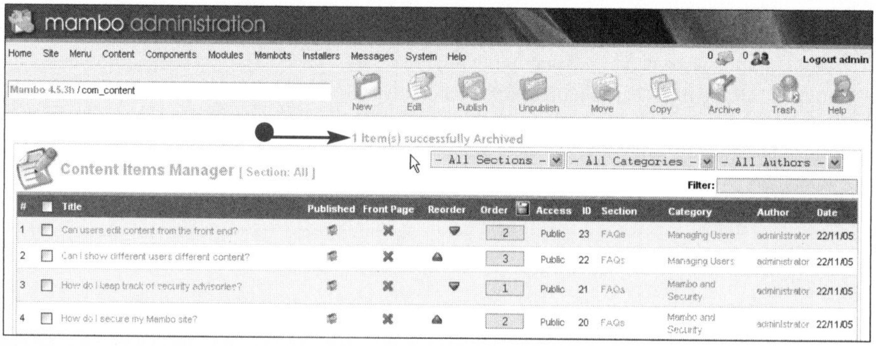

Unarchive Content

You can unarchive a Content Item and move the item back into the Content Items Manager. You must move an item out of the Archive Manager if you want to make changes to the item because you cannot edit, duplicate, or move an archived Content Item from one category to another from within the Archive Manager.

The process of unarchiving a Content Item is initiated from within the Archive Manager. To unarchive one or more items, select the Content Items and activate the Unarchive command on the toolbar. When you click the Unarchive icon, Mambo immediately removes the selected Content Items from the Archive Manager and moves them back to Content Items Manager. To see the items, you must exit the Archive Manager and visit the Content Items Manager.

Mambo restores unarchived items to the Content Items Manager as unpublished Content Items. This means site visitors cannot view them. If you want the site visitors to see the newly unarchived Content Items you must visit the Content Items Manager and publish the Content Items. Publishing Content Items is covered in the earlier section "Publish a Content Item."

Moving Content Items back and forth between the Archive Manager and the Content Items Manager has no impact on the contents of the items, other than the change in the publishing state when you unarchive the Content Item. In contrast, on both the front and back end of the Web site, moving Content Items in and out of the archive does affect the way in which the Content Items are accessed, because the Menu Items that link to the Content Items vary depending on where the items are located.

Unarchive Content

1. Click Content.
2. Click Archive Manager.

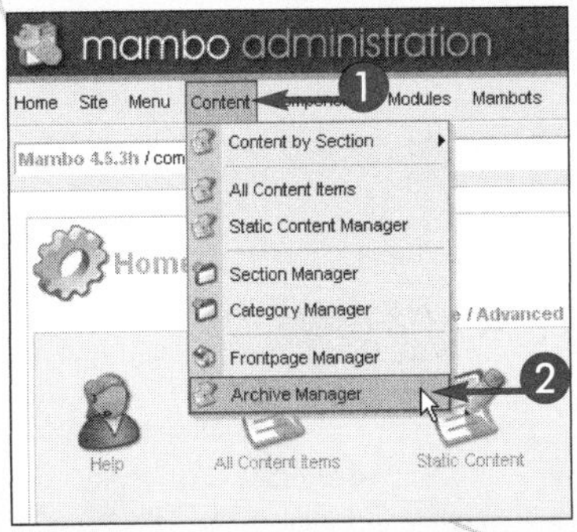

The Archive Manager loads.

3. Click the Content Item.
4. Click the Unarchive icon.

The Content Item is removed from the Archive Manager and returned to the Content Items Manager.

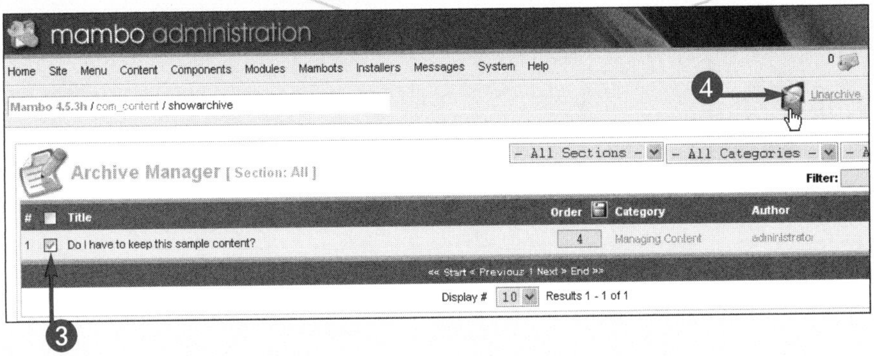

Overview of the Media Manager

The Mambo system includes a tool for managing media files. The site administrators can view thumbnails of the files in the system, upload new files, delete existing files, create directories, and identify the proper URLs for the media in the system. You are likely to use the Media Manager for three primary tasks: To view a list of all the media files and image thumbnails in the system, to add new media without using FTP, and to discover the path to a file, needed to manually add links to media inside your Content Items.

You should understand the connection between the Media Manager and the MOSimage function, as described in the section "Insert an Image with MOSimage," to use both effectively. Images that you upload into the Media Manager appear in the MOSimage dialog box and you can insert them into Content Items via the MOSimage command.

A Toolbar

Icons for uploading files entered in the Upload field, creating new directories based on the name entered into the Directory field, and giving Help for the screen.

B Directory

The name of the currently active directory. The Up Level arrow moves you up one level in the directory tree.

C Files

Thumbnails of the files located in the active directory. Each thumbnail includes the full name and extension of the file, a Pencil icon that displays the path to the file in the Code field, a Trash icon to delete a file, and the dimensions of the image file.

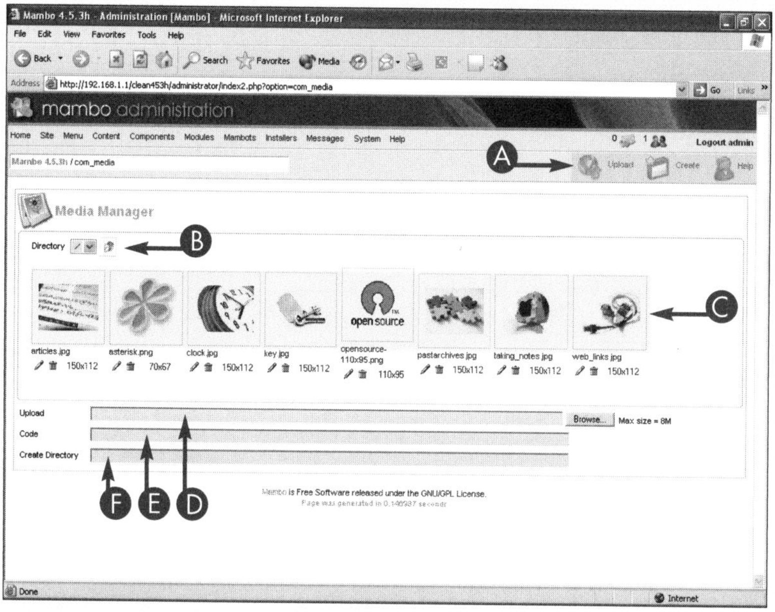

D Upload Field

For locating a new file for uploading. You locate a file via the Browse button, and then click the Upload icon to execute the command.

E Code Field

Displays the path to the file when you click the Path icon.

F Create Directory Field

When you enter the name for a new directory and click the Create icon, Mambo creates the new directory as a subdirectory to the currently active directory.

Upload Media

You can add new media files, such as new images and links to downloadable files, to enhance your Mambo site. With this feature, you can add images to your content as well as helpful PDF files or PowerPoint presentations.

The file upload function in the Media Manager is essentially a substitute for FTP. The Media Manager is well suited for moving individual files or small numbers of files. If, however, you want to add or delete a large number of files at one time, you are probably better off using FTP because the Media Manager does not support batch processes; in other words, you must move the files one at a time with the Media Manager.

When you upload a new file successfully, it immediately appears on the list of files. If the new file is an image file, you see a thumbnail of the image. Non-image files display icons that represent their file type. Note that when you upload a file, it goes in the directory that you have active at that time.

The system supports a variety of file types. The default installation accepts files of the following types: GIF, PNG, JPG, BMP, PDF, SWF, DOC, XLS, or PPT. If you attempt to load another type of file, the upload may fail and display an error message.

Note that the Media Manager is not intended for editing or modifying media files and contains no tools for resizing, optimizing, or otherwise changing image files. Therefore, you should edit, size, and optimize images before you move them into the system.

Upload Media

1. Click Site.
2. Click Media Manager.

The Media Manager loads.

3. Click Browse.

The Choose file dialog box appears.

4. Select the file to upload.
5. Click Open.

The system returns you to the Media Manager.

6. Click the Upload icon.

Mambo uploads the image and displays a confirmation message.

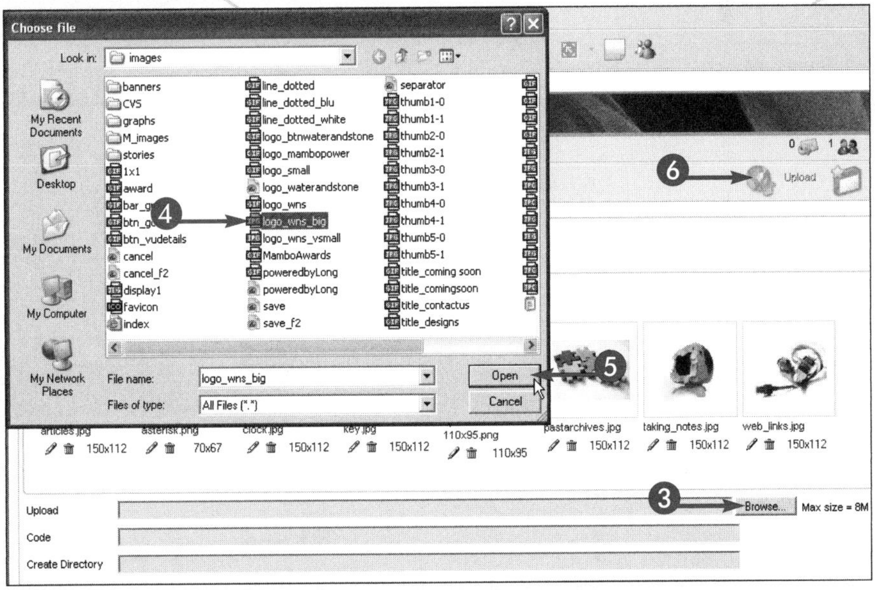

Delete Media

You can delete existing media from the Mambo system through use of the Media Manager. You can use this function to either clean up directories by removing old or unwanted files, or you can delete a file as part of the process of replacing the file with a new one or moving the file to a new directory.

File deletion from the Media Manager is permanent. Unlike Content Items or Menu Items, media files do not get sent to the Trash Manager and you cannot automatically restore them. The only way to recover a deleted media file is to upload the file again. It is a good idea to keep backups of all your media files in a safe place offline in case you need to restore a file deleted erroneously or lost due to a technical problem with the server. To edit an existing media file, you must remove the current file from the system before you upload the revised file. Mambo does not allow you to overwrite an existing file; that is, you cannot upload a new file with the same name as an existing file.

The Media Manager does not support moving or copying files. To move a file to a different directory, you must upload it again to the new directory. You should delete the old file to avoid confusion.

Do not confuse deletion with downloading. The Media Manager does not give you the ability to download or export the files contained in the system. Deletion is simply removal. If you want to back up your media files, you need to use FTP to access the directories on the server and copy the files to your local computer.

Delete Media

1. Load the Media Mananger.

Note: To load the Media Manager, see the section "Upload Media."

2. Click the Trash icon.

A confirmation dialog box appears.

3. Click OK.

- You can click Cancel to cancel the deletion.

Mambo deletes the file.

Find a File Link

You can find the path to a media file using the Media Manager path function. A file's exact address is required if you want to add the file to a Content Item manually. The Media Manager helps you acquire the information you need quickly and easily and formats it automatically for quick cutting and pasting.

The path function works differently for image and non-image files. For image files, the Path icon provides all the HTML tag information in the Code field. You can simply cut and paste this information directly into a Content Item. The code for a typical image file looks like this:

```
<img src="http://www.mysite.com/images/
stories/articles.jpg" align="left"
hspace="6" alt="Code" />
```

The code includes several attributes that you may or may not want, including `align=left`, `hspace="6"`, and `alt="Code"`. If you are not happy with those values, you need to change them before or after you paste the code into the Content Item. You can manually add other attributes if you want.

For non-image files, the code that Mambo produces is slightly different, though still ready for you to cut and paste directly into a Content Item. The code for a typical non-image file looks like this:

```
<a href="http://www.mysite.com/images/
stories/catalog.pdf">Insert your text
here</a>
```

Note that the code includes a place for you to enter text for the link to the file. You must replace `Insert your text here` with the message of your choice. Once in the Content Item, the message text becomes a hyperlink to the media file. You can manually add other attributes if you so desire.

Find a File Link

1. Load the Media Manager.

Note: To load the Media Manager, see the section "Upload Media."

2. Click the Path icon of the file you want to find.

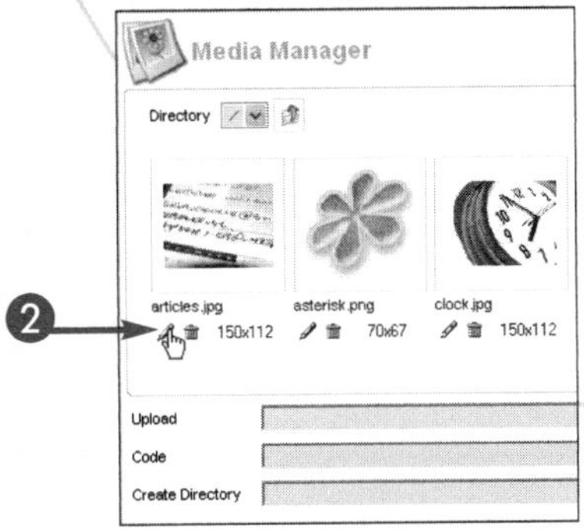

- Code with the path appears in the Code window.

You can cut and paste this code directly into a Content Item.

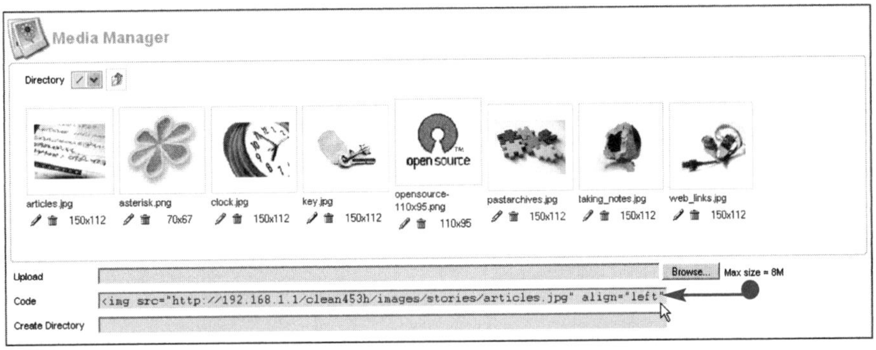

Insert an Image with MOSimage

You can insert images easily through the use of the MOSimage function. MOSimage was designed to allow people who are not fluent with HTML code to enter and format images inside of Content Items. The system is simple to use, but does require an understanding of both the Media Manager and the MOSimage controls located in the Content Item creation and editing screens.

The MOSimage function only provides a way to add and order images to a Content Item. You cannot use MOSimage to upload or add new images to the system; instead, you must use the Media Manager. For more information on how to add new image files to your Mambo system, see the section "Upload Media" earlier in the chapter.

When creating or editing a Content Item, the right-hand column of the screen includes a tab called Images, which displays the MOSimage Control. Note also the MOSimage placeholder icons located under the Intro Text and Main Text boxes. The process of adding an image involves selecting a position for the image inside the Content Item, and then selecting the image and applying the attributes to the image. You can perform all the steps using the MOSimage placeholder and the MOSimage Controls. Be aware that you can assign only one image to an MOSimage placeholder. To place multiple images, you must use multiple MOSimage placeholders. There is no limit to the number of MOSimage placeholders you can place in a single Content Item.

The MOSimage function has two significant limitations. First, you can use it only with image files. You must add all other file types manually. Second, you cannot see images you add via the MOSimage tag in the Content Item Editing window; you see only the MOSimage tag. To overcome these limitations, you can insert images manually per the section "Insert an Image Manually."

Insert an Image with MOSimage

1 Open the Content Item to which you want to add the image.

2 Click the Images tab.

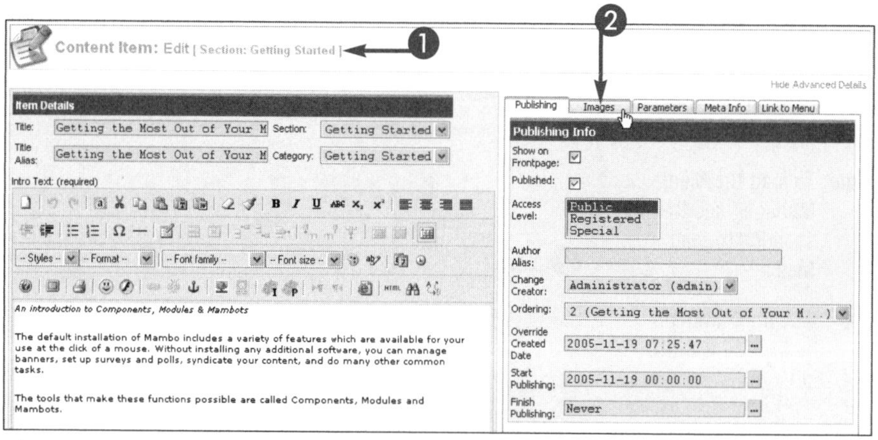

The MOSimage Control appears.

3 Place the cursor where you want the image to appear.

4 Click the MOSimage placeholder icon.

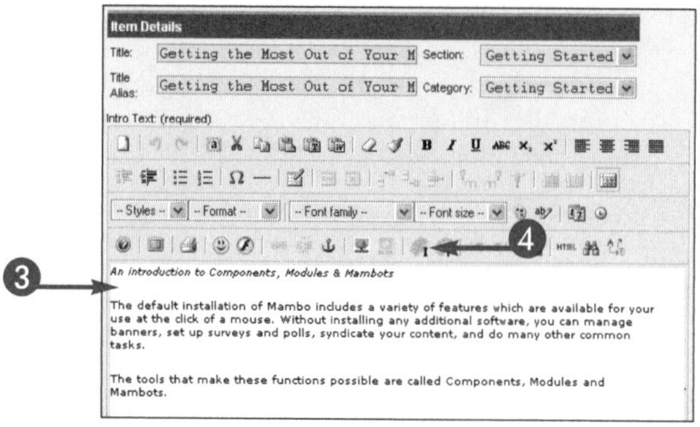

- The MOSimage link appears in the Content Item.

5 Select the image you want to appear.

6 Click Add.

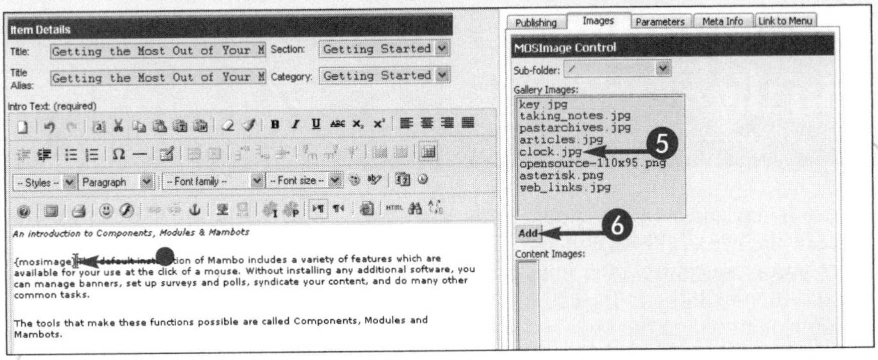

The Content Images box updates.

7 Click the image.

8 Click in these areas to type or to set attributes.

9 Click Apply.

Note: You may need to scroll down to perform Steps 8 and 9.

Although you do not see it in the Content Item editing window, the image appears in the Content Item on the front end of the Web site.

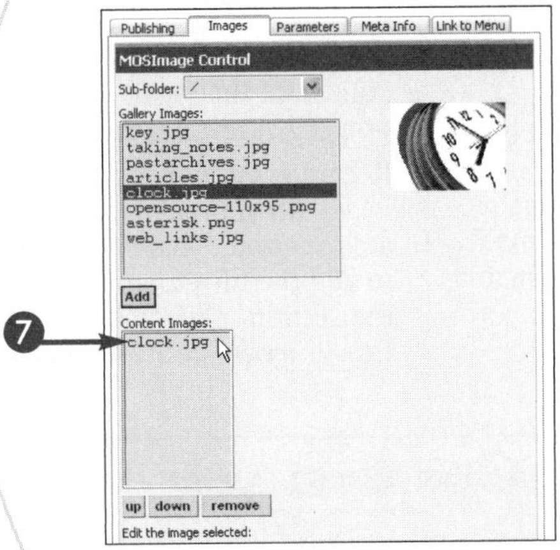

Extra

If you want to have more than one image in a Content Item, you need to use multiple MOSimage placeholders. Each time you add a placeholder, you must add a new image file. Note also that you cannot select an image for use more than once in the same Content Item unless you create two incidents of the image file with different names. You can keep track of the images via the MOSimage Control field labeled Content Images. There is one image per placeholder, and the order of the images in the Content Images field determines the order the images appear in the Content Item. You can reorder images by clicking the Up and Down buttons below the Content Images field.

You can delete an image that you have assigned to a Content Item by selecting the image's name on the Content Images list and then clicking the remove button located below the Content Images field. Deleting an item from the MOSimage Control does not remove the item from the Mambo system; it removes the image only from the Content Item.

Insert an Image Manually

You can insert images into Content Items manually, without the use of the MOSimage function. This gives you more control over image placement and attributes, and the flexibility to include images from directories outside of where the Mambo Media Manager stores images. In addition, you can see the image rather than just an MOSimage tag in the Content Item Editing window. For more on the MOSimage function, see the section "Insert an Image with MOSimage."

You can insert images manually in one of two methods. For the first method, if you have some fluency with HTML, you can type the image code directly into the Content Item with the editor in HTML (plain text) mode. In the second method, you use the Insert Image function included in the WYSIWYG editor. This requires no knowledge of HTML because the technique is very similar to the manner in which you add an image in a Microsoft Office application.

When you manually insert an image into a Content Item, you must know the exact location of the image file. If you use the Media Manager to handle your images, you can use the Path function to find the file's location. For more on identifying the proper link for a file, see the section "Find a File Link." If you manage your images outside of the Media Manager, you must note down the proper address for the file in order to make the link.

Regardless of which approach you choose, if you link to an image on your server, you need to get the image files into a directory on your server. You can use the Media Manager to add the files to your Mambo system, as described in the section "Upload Media." Alternatively, you can use FTP to move the files up and place them in directories.

Insert an Image Manually

USING HTML

1. Open the Content Item to which you want to add the image.
2. If you are using a WYSIWYG editor, click HTML (plain text) mode.

   An HTML window appears.
3. Type the code where you want the image to appear.
4. Click Update.

   You are returned to the Content Item and the image becomes visible.
5. Click the Save icon.

   Mambo places the image and it becomes visible if the item is published and current.

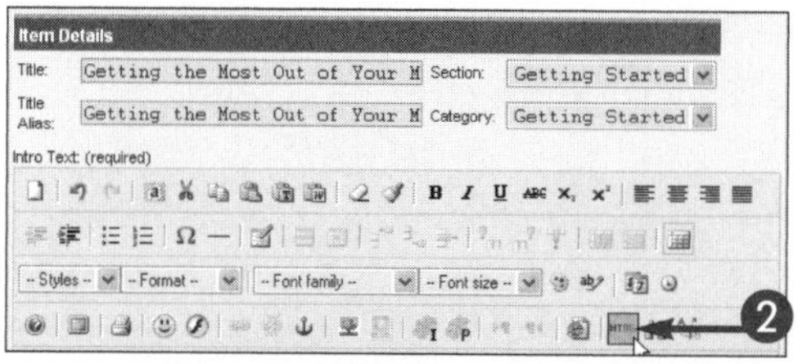

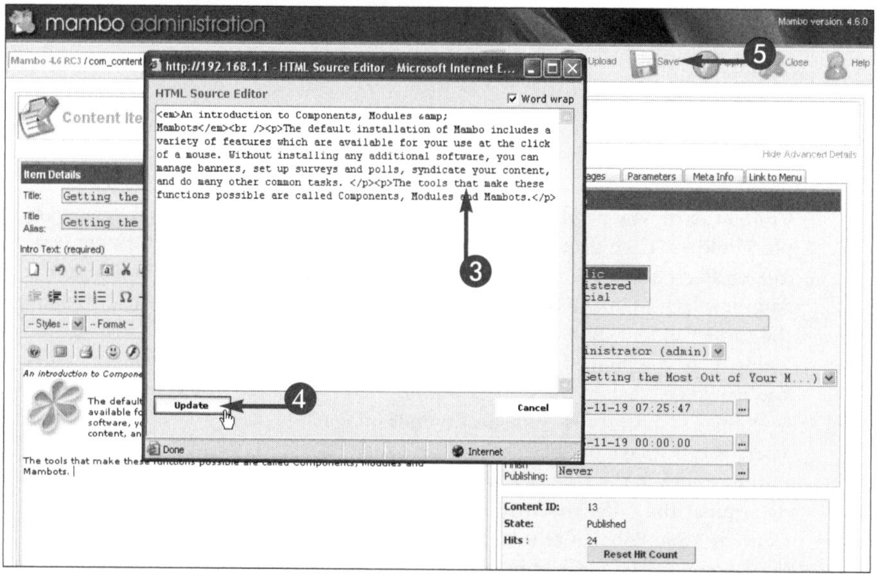

USING THE WYSIWYG EDITOR

1. Open the Content Item to which you want to add the image.
2. Click the Insert Image button.

   The Insert/edit image dialog box appears.
3. Type the location of image file.
   - You can view the image in this area.
4. Click Insert.
   - You are returned to the Content Item and the image is visible.
5. Click the Save icon.

   Mambo places the image and it becomes visible if the item is published and current.

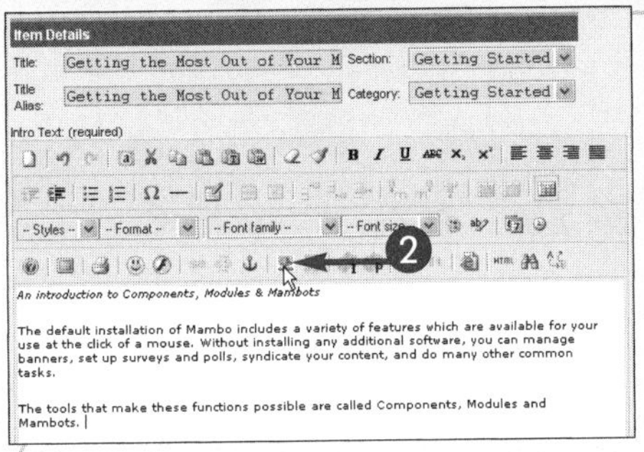

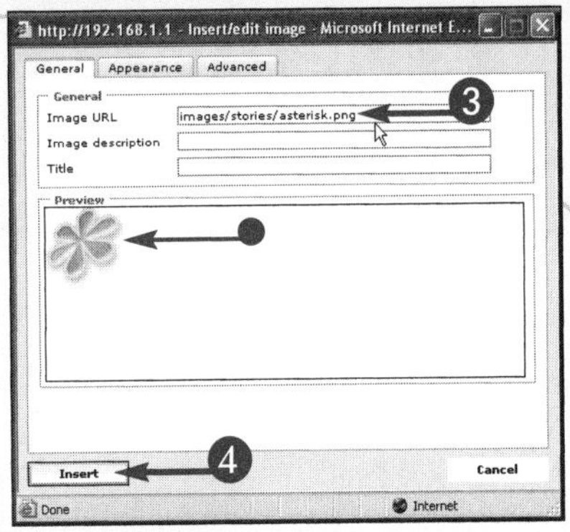

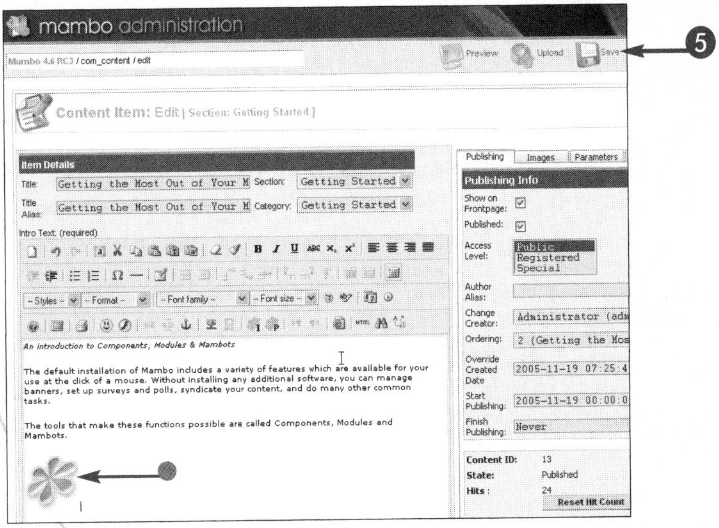

Apply It

The HTML code to insert an image into a Content Item is very simple. All you need is the `<img>` tag and the location of the image file. If your image file is located at www.mysite.com/images/sample.jpg, the code to insert the image appears as follows:

Example

```
<img src="http://www.mysite.com/images/sample.jpg" />
```

You can use the `align` attribute to position the image relative to the text. If you want the image to appear on the right with the text on the left side, you simply modify the image tag as follows:

Example

```
<img src="http://www.mysite.com/images/sample.jpg" align="right" />
```

You can add space around an image to enhance your layout by using the `vspace` (vertical space) and `hspace` (horizontal space) attributes. The following puts 10 pixels of space on each side of the image and 8 pixels of space above and below the image.

Example

```
<img src="http://www.mysite.com/images/sample.jpg" align="right" vspace="8" hspace="10" />
```

Add a File to a Content Item

In addition to images, you can link other types of files to your Mambo Content Items. You can add files for download by visitors and files that will appear when visitors click on them. The system allows you to hyperlink to any type of file, though the Media Manager limits the range of files you can manage with that tool. To learn more about what types of files you can manage with the Media Manager, see the section "Upload Media."

If you are using the Media Manager to handle your files, then the addition of a file to a Content Item is a simple matter of cut and paste. The Media Manager gives you the code to insert into the Content Item. For more information on how to get the code, see the section "Find a File Link." Once you have the code, you only need to put the WYSIWYG editor in HTML (plain text) mode and then paste the code into the Content Item.

If you are not using the Media Manager to handle your file, you must note the location of the file, then hand code the HTML tags into the Content Item using the WYSIWYG editor in HTML (plain text) mode.

Alternatively, if you are using the WYSIWYG editor, you can add a link to a file within the Content Item by first adding an image or a word or phrase, then using the link command to hyperlink the image, word, or phrase to the file. Using the WYSIWYG editor to create the hyperlink allows you to avoid hand coding or cutting and pasting in HTML. The WYSIWYG editor uses a Windows-type browse dialog to help you with the creation of the link.

Add a File to a Content Item

USING HTML

1. Open the Content Item to which you want to add the file.
2. If you are using a WYSIWYG editor, click HTML (plain text) mode.

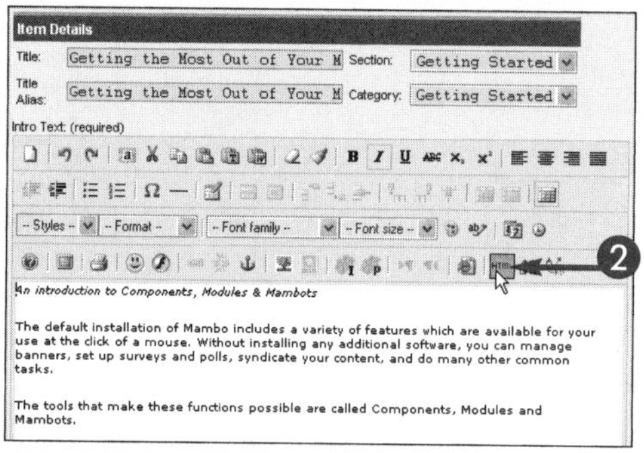

An HTML window appears.

3. Type the HTML code where you want the link to the file to appear.
4. Click Update.

   Mambo returns you to the Content Item and the link is now active.

5. Click the Save icon.

   Mambo places the link and it becomes visible if the item is published and current.

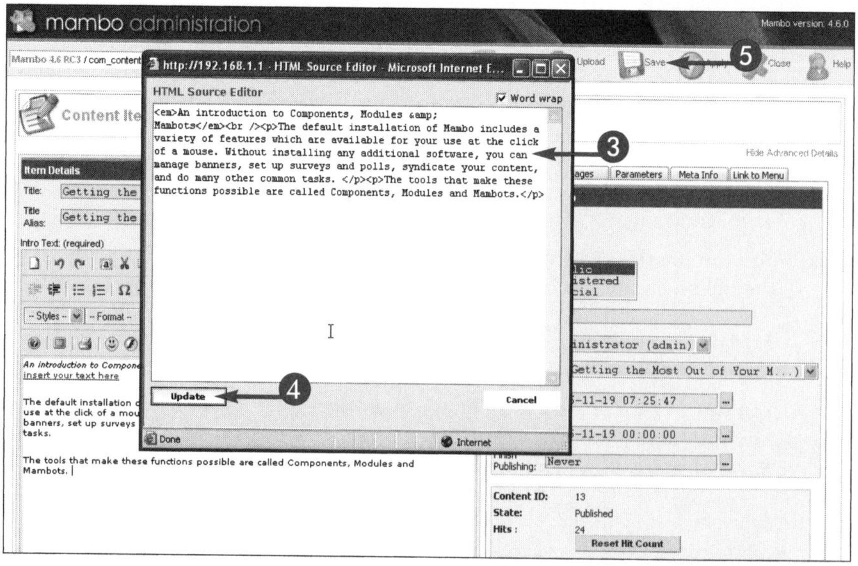

USING THE WYSIWYG EDITOR

1. Open the Content Item to which you want to add the link to the file.
2. Highlight the text or the image where you want to place the link.
3. Click the Create Hyperlink icon.

   The Insert/edit link dialog box appears.
4. Type the location of the file.
5. Click in these areas to type or set attributes.
6. Click Insert.

   Mambo returns you to the Content Item editing screen.
7. Click the Save icon.

   Mambo places the link and the link becomes visible if the item is published and current.

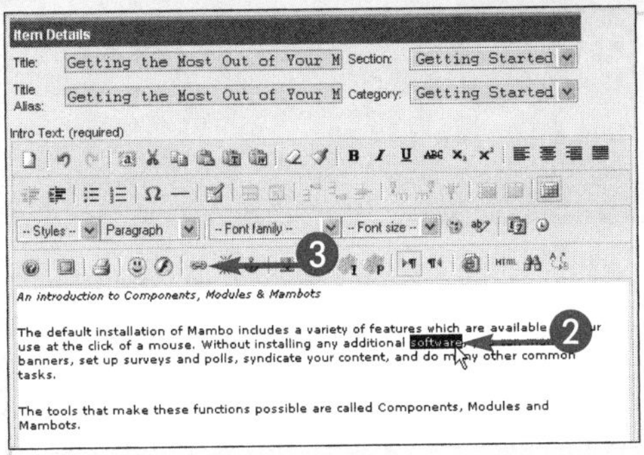

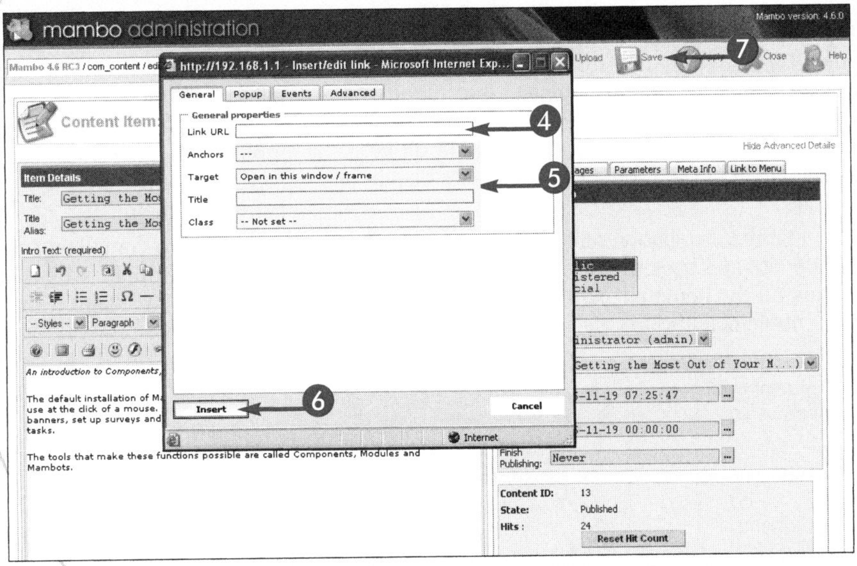

Apply It

The HTML code you need to insert a hyperlink to a file inside a Content Item is very simple. All you need is the <a> tag and the location of the file. For example, if the file is located at www.mysite.com/images/catalog.pdf, the code to insert the image appears as follows:

Example

```
<a href="http://www.mysite.com/images/catalog.pdf">View our catalog</a>
```

You can use the `target` attribute to open the file in a new window.

Example

```
<a href="http://www.mysite.com/images/catalog.pdf" target="_blank">View our catalog in new
window</a>
```

If you add the link to an image file, it creates a border around the image. If you do not want the border to appear, you must add the `border` attribute to the image file and specify `0`.

Example

```
<a href="http://www.mysite.com/images/catalog.pdf" target="_blank"><img src="
http://www.mysite.com/images/catalog.jpg" border="0" /></a>
```

Create a Home Page Without the Frontpage Manager

You can build a custom home page for your site without using the Mambo Frontpage Manager. You may want to use an entry page for your site that does not depend upon the Frontpage Manager's functionality, such as a *splash page*, which creates an initial impression or mood. Another situation for bypassing the Manager is to create a simple home page that requests user information for determining what content to display, such as an entry page that requires a user to select a location or preferred language. Or you may want to display the output of a component on your home page instead of the Frontpage Manager's display of Content Items.

The default Mambo installation relies on only one template for the entire site and uses the Frontpage Manager to display items on the home page and control their layout. The default implementation is well suited for portal-type sites and information-heavy sites. If, however, you want your site to make a different sort of impression on visitors, you may want to explore other options.

To publish another page or a component from your site, you simply unpublish the Frontpage Manager. This causes neither the site to fail nor a blank page to appear; instead, Mambo displays the first item on the menu entitled "mainmenu." Because the system consistently defaults to the same alternative — the first choice on the mainmenu — you can use this to your advantage to publish any page or component you want on the home page, simply by making it the first Menu Item on the mainmenu menu.

If you want a completely unique page for your home page, you should create a purpose-built template for the page and then assign it to your home page Menu Item link. For more on working with menus, see Chapter 9.

Create a Home Page Without the Frontpage Manager

1 Click Menu.

2 Click mainmenu.

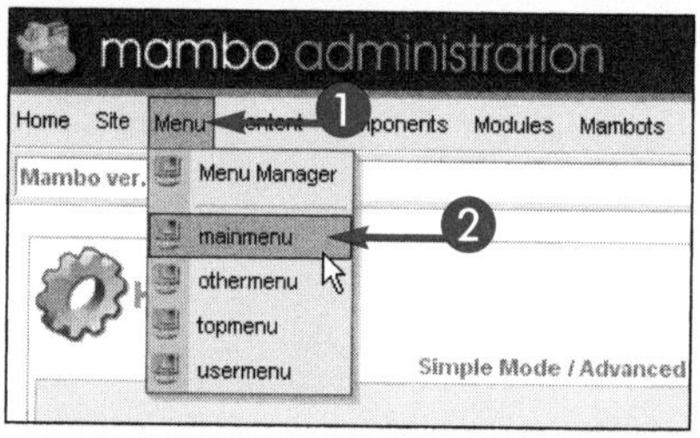

The mainmenu editing screen loads.

3 Click Home.

4 Click the Unpublish icon.

Mambo unpublishes the Frontpage Manager.

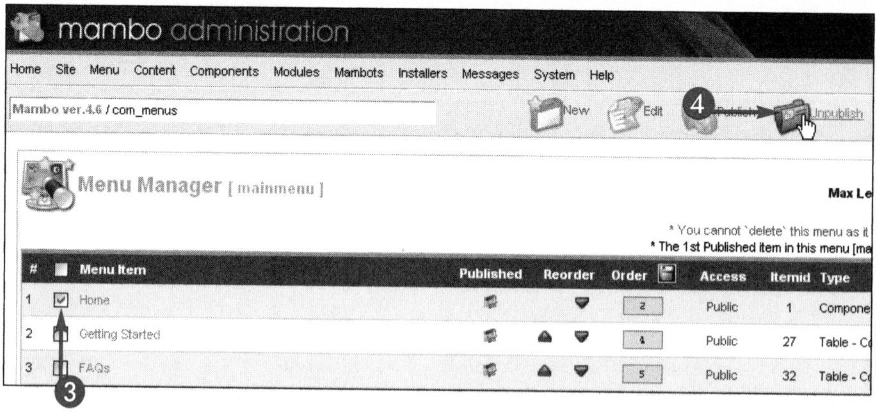

On the front end of the Web site, the home page now displays the first item on the mainmenu.

5. Reorder the mainmenu items.

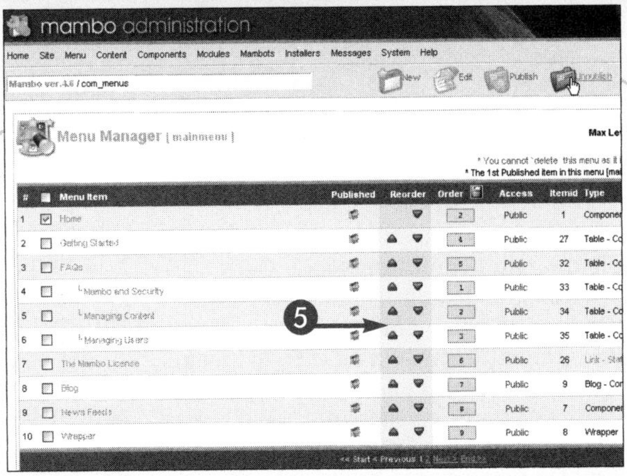

- On the front end of the Web site, the home page changes to reflect the new ordering.

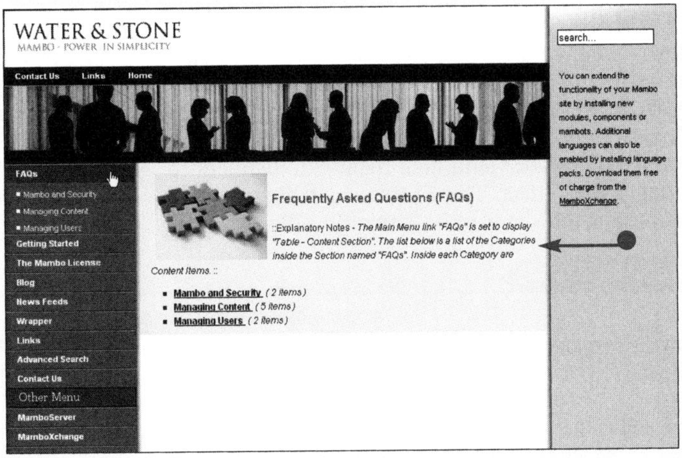

Apply It

When you unpublish the Frontpage Manager on a site, the link named "Home" disappears with it. If you want to have a link to the home page on the navigation you must create a new one. Start by going to the Menu Manager and opening the menu where you want the new link to appear. Create a new link, and for the menu type select "URL." In the blank provided, type the URL ***www.yoursite.com/*index.php**, substituting for *www.yoursite.com* your domain and the directory where your Mambo site is located (if necessary).

In rare situations, you may want to create a home page that exists entirely outside of the Mambo system. Should you need to create a totally independent home page, your best bet is to set up the page at the same root directory as your Mambo site and give the page a name other than index.php, which is reserved by Mambo; in Apache you can use the .htaccess file to direct site visitors to the proper file. Should it become necessary to name your independent home page "index.php," you must place your Mambo installation in a separate directory and link to it from your home page.

Create a Blog Layout

You can create a blog-style layout by using a combination of Menu Item settings and parameters. While the default Mambo system is not designed for use as a Blogging CMS, you can organize and display Content Items in a blog-style layout. Blog layouts organize the Content Items chronologically, typically as a series of short articles similar to a daily journal. Not only is the layout style very popular for personal sites, but it also represents a logical way to organize and display time-sensitive content.

To achieve a blog-style layout, create a new Menu Item and configure it to the Blog menu type. The traditional blog layout features complete articles ordered in chronological order, with the most recent entries first. The parameters for the Menu Item require adjustment to achieve the proper effect. The # Intro, # Leading, and Columns parameters control the formatting. You achieve a traditional blog layout by setting the # Intro and # Leading parameters to however many Content Items you want to display at one time, and setting the Columns parameter to 1. To achieve the chronological ordering, set the Primary Order parameter to Most recent first. Other controls in the Parameters screen that set various options for the information appear with each Content Item. You can find a full discussion about creating Menu Items and the various parameters associated with them in Chapter 9.

By experimenting with the Menu Item parameters, you can come up with a number of variations on the traditional blog format. Experiment a bit with the settings because the best result often depends on a number of variables, including the width of your template, the length of your articles, and the use of images.

Create a Blog Layout

1. Load the mainmenu editing screen.

Note: To load the mainmenu editing screen, see the section "Create a Home Page Without the Frontpage Manager."

2. Click the New icon.

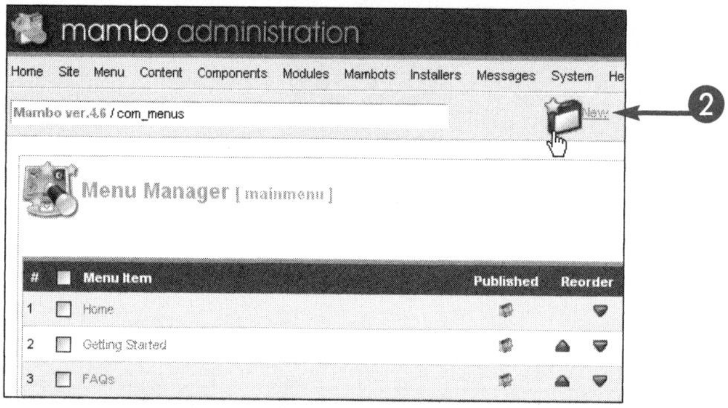

The New Menu Item screen loads.

3. Click Blog – Content Category.
4. Click the Next icon.

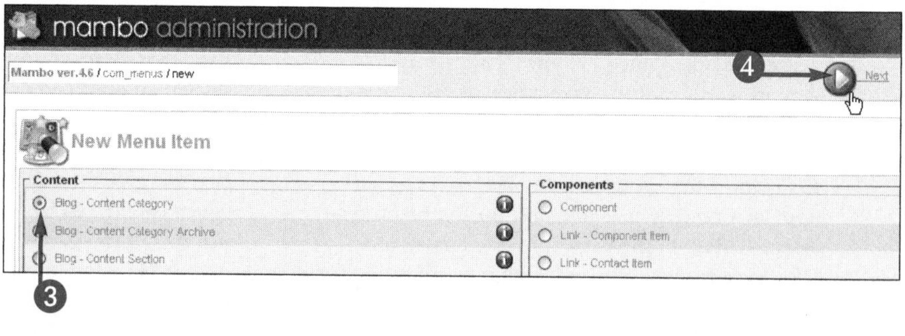

The Edit Menu Item screen loads.

5. Type a name for the link.
6. Select the content category that you want to display.
7. Type a setting for the # Leading, # Intro, and Columns parameters.

   This example sets the # Leading to 0, the # Intro to 5, and the Columns to 1, which are the settings for a traditional blog layout.

8. Click here and set the Primary Order to Most recent first.
9. Click the Save icon.

   On the front end of the Web site, Mambo shows the category content with a blog-type layout.

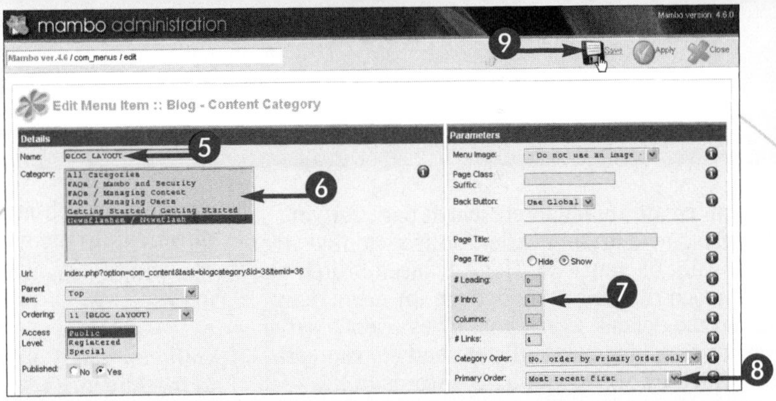

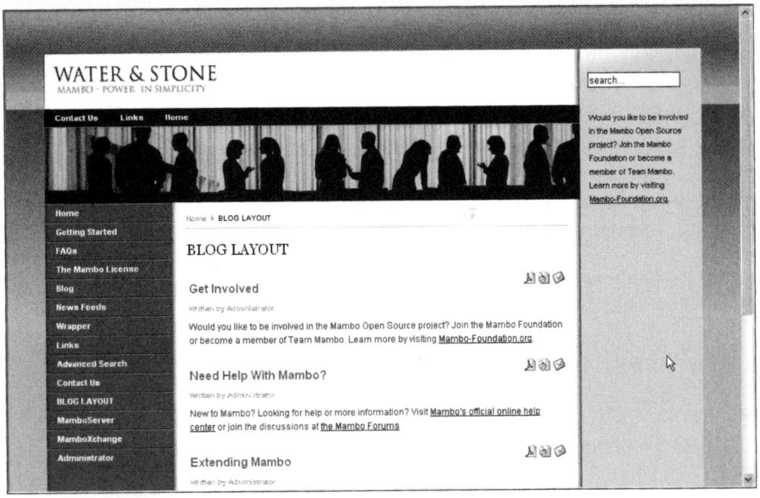

Apply It

In the traditional blog format, entire articles appear one after the other. If you want to maintain the traditional layout, do not use the Main Text content box when you create your Content Items. Instead, place the entire article in the Intro Text box. For more on creating Content Items and working with Intro Text and Main Text, see Chapter 6.

Because blog sites are organized chronologically, you might find it useful to have access to older Content Items by date. The Archives module is very useful for setting up a chronological navigation system for your historical blog entries. Simply publish the Archives module where you want it to appear, and then, each month, archive the previous month's Content Items. For each month in which you have archived Content Items, a navigation choice appears in the module; clicking the link displays that month's Content Items. Archiving the Content Items monthly also has the added advantage of keeping the site clean and current. For more on archiving Content Items, see Chapter 6. For more on the Archive module, see Chapter 11.

Create an Advanced Search Page

You can create an advanced search page for your Mambo site to make it easier for users to find what they want on your site. The Advanced Search tool in Mambo, which contains more options for users than are shown in the default search box, gives users a set of tools to make searching more efficient and convenient. Users can search by phrase, for all the words in the query, or for individual words. Users can also control the ordering of the result set. For larger sites, the Advanced Search option is really indispensable because the basic search box frequently returns very large result sets.

In the default configuration of Mambo, the Advanced Search options appear either when you click the Advanced Search link on the mainmenu, or as part of the results set when you search using the search box. If the Advanced Search link is removed or deleted from your installation, you must set it up again manually to enjoy a direct link to the functionality.

The URL for the Advanced Search function is `http://www.yoursite.com/index.php?option=com_search`, where you replace *www.yoursite.com* with your site's domain name. You can create the link to the Advanced Search page by either inserting the URL into a Content Item, or by creating a new Menu Item, selecting Component as the menu type, and then selecting Search on the Item Creation screen. For more on creating and configuring new Menu Items, see Chapter 9. You can find more search box options from various third-party developers. You can plug in a variety of different tools, from an advanced site search with more options, to search boxes that search the Web rather than just your site. For more on extending your Mambo site with third-party plug-ins, see Chapter 15.

Create an Advanced Search Page

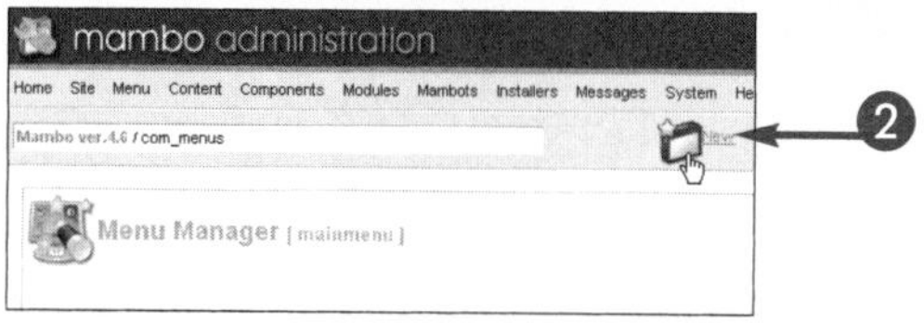

1. Load the mainmenu editing screen.

Note: To load the mainmenu editing screen, see the section "Create a Home Page Without the Frontpage Manager."

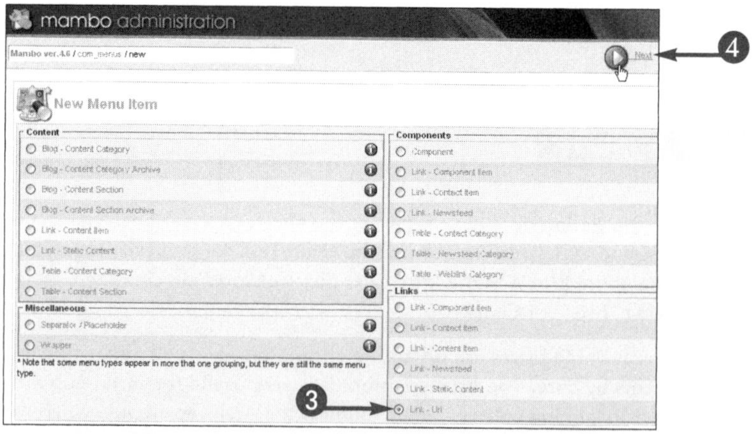

2. Click the New Icon.

   The New Menu Item screen loads.

3. Click Link – Url.
4. Click the Next icon.

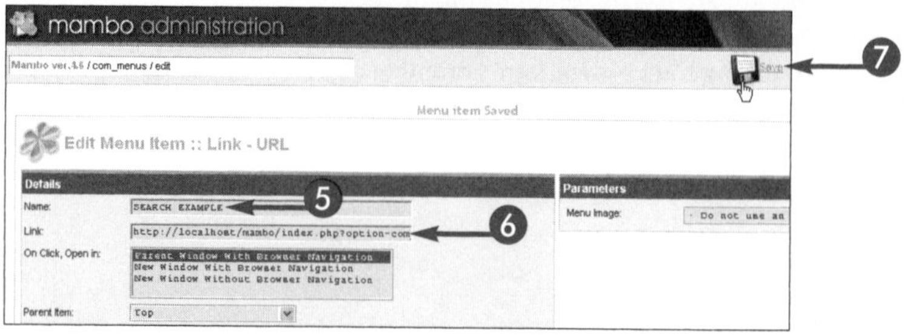

   The Add Menu Item screen loads.

5. Click here and select Search.
6. Type a name for the link.
7. Click the Save Icon.

   Mambo saves the new Menu Item and it appears on the site in the mainmenu.

Display the Current Date

With a single line of PHP code, you can customize your site to display the current date and time. Mambo and PHP combine to provide the date and time feature. A single, simple line of code calls the PHP function, and you can easily add this code to your templates. The Mambo language file controls the contents and the format of the display.

To insert the code, you need to edit your template to include the following line:

```
<?php echo (strftime (_DATE_FORMAT_LC)); ?>
```

Place the code wherever you want the date and time to appear in the template, then save the template. The date and time appear automatically once you publish the template. For more on editing your template, see Chapter 3.

The Date Format string inside the language file allows you to control how the date and time appear and to what level of detail. You can access the language file through the Language Manager, and you can edit the language file directly from within your browser. Basic instructions for formatting the date and time are explained inside the language file comments. Look in the language file for the string `_DATE_FORMAT_LC` to find the comments and the options available. For more on how to edit your language file, see Chapter 14.

Note that you cannot place this command inside of Content Items. Because the command requires PHP to execute the function, you must place the command in the template file where the system can read it when executing the template.

Display the Current Date

1. Click Site.
2. Click Template Manager.
3. Click Site Templates.

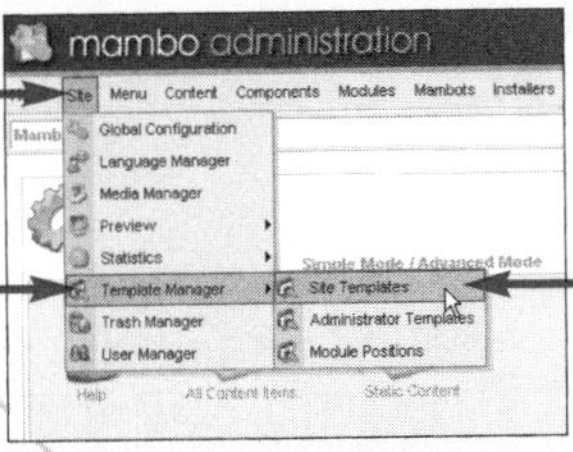

The Template Manager loads.

4. Click the active template.
5. Click the Edit HTML icon.

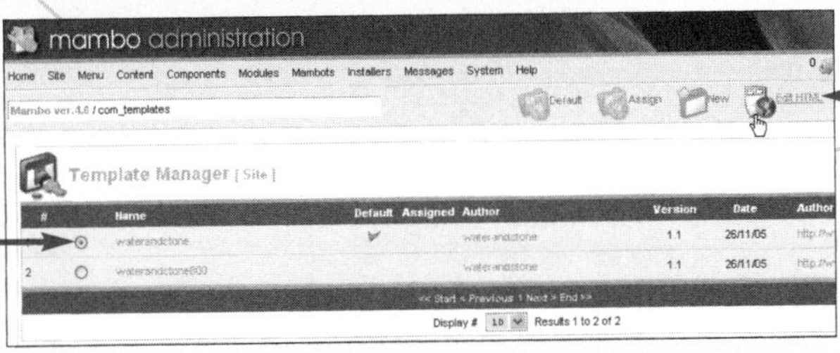

The Template HTML Editor window loads.

6. Position the cursor where you want the date to appear and type **<?php echo (strftime (_DATE_FORMAT_LC)); ?>**.
7. Click the Save icon.

Mambo saves the changes and the site now displays the date and time.

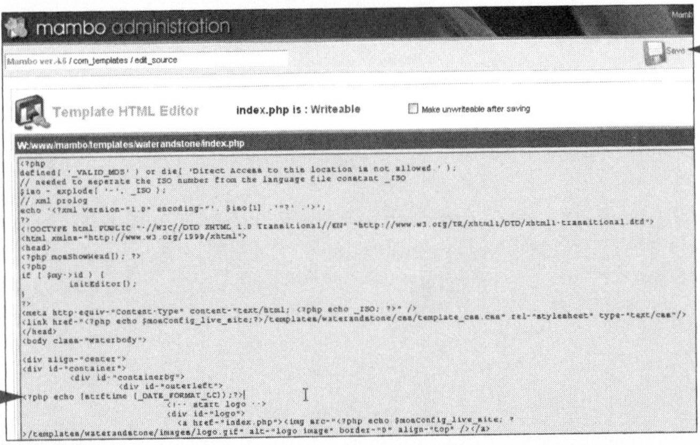

Display Content Using a Wrapper

You can display external content within your Mambo site templates by using the Wrapper option. The term *wrapper* is the name Mambo gives to the iFrame functionality. Mambo uses an iFrame to wrap content from outside the Mambo system and display it within your site template without you having to do any special coding. You can use this option to display pages you have created outside of Mambo and saved on your server, or to display pages from another site.

The creation of a Wrapper is simple, and the system provides configuration parameters that control the Wrapper's basic formatting. You can use the Wrapper option to display the pages inside your main content area, or you can insert wrapped content within a module, using the Wrapper module.

To create a wrapped page, you need to first create a new Menu Item, choosing for it the Wrapper menu type. The Add Menu Item screen provides a space for you to enter the URL of the target page and presents several parameters that affect the Wrapper's formatting. For more on how to create new Menu Items, see Chapter 9.

The Wrapper Module lets you wrap a page and position it via a site module. The Wrapper Module options are very similar to those for creating a wrapped page, with spaces for you to specify the URL and to do some very basic formatting. The default Mambo installation includes a Wrapper module, but it is unused in the default site configuration. You can use the module by editing the contents, assigning the module to a position, and publishing it. You create subsequent Wrapper modules by duplicating the default Wrapper module. For more on how to use the Wrapper module, see Chapter 11.

Display Content Using a Wrapper

1 Load the mainmenu editing screen.

Note: To load the mainmenu editing screen, see the section "Create a Home Page Without the Frontpage Manager."

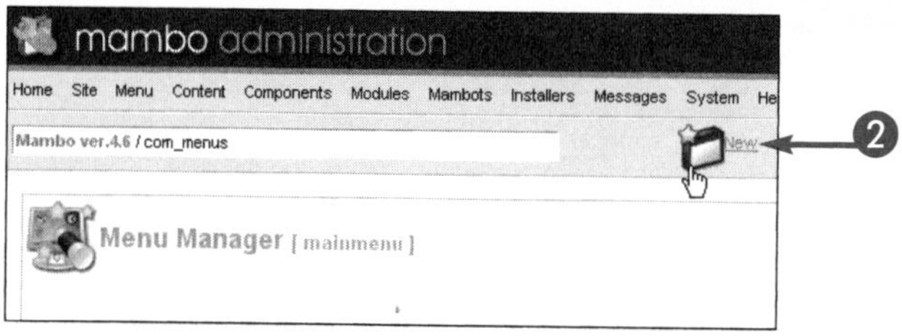

2 Click the New icon.

The New Menu Item screen loads.

3 Click the Wrapper option.

4 Click the Next icon.

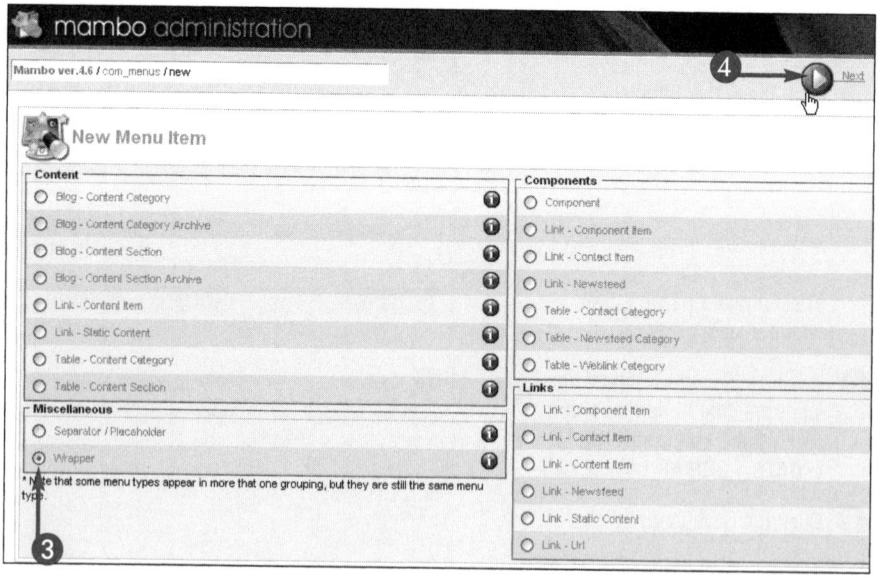

The Edit Menu Item screen loads.

5. Type a Name for the link.

6. Type the URL for the page you want to wrap.

7. Click the Save Icon.

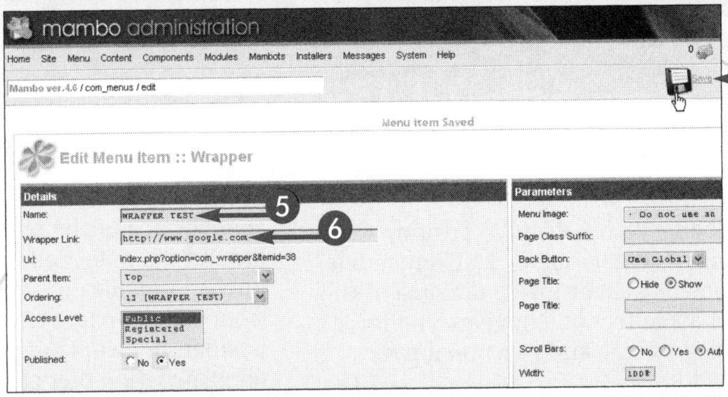

- Mambo wraps the URL with an iFrame and adds a link to the wrapped page to the Main Nav.

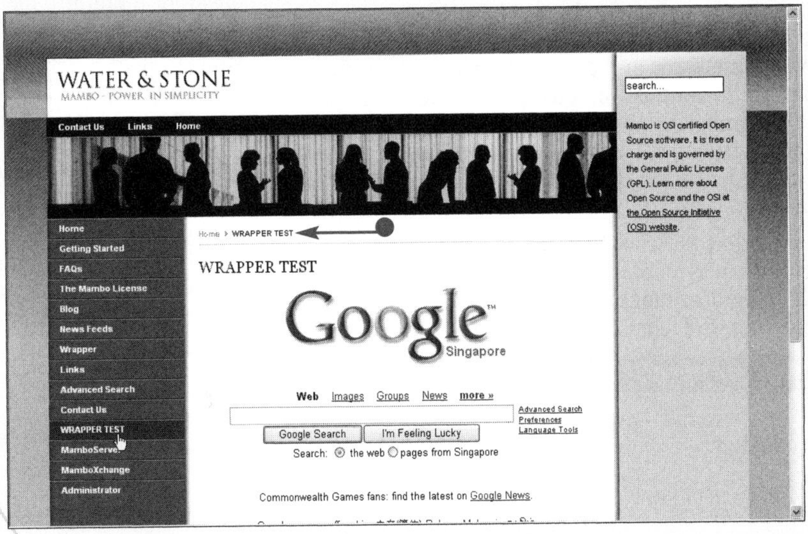

Extra

Obtaining good appearance from wrapped content is somewhat of an art. The principle problem relates to the size of your content area relative to the size of the page you want to wrap. When your site's content area is smaller than the page you wrap, the wrapped content appears inside your template with scroll bars. To get the content to fit neatly without scroll bars, you must make sure the item you want to wrap is smaller than the content area in your template. Parameters within the Wrapper option allow you to force scroll bars to show or hide. Ideally, when the item is smaller than your content area, the scroll bars do not show; but to make sure, set the Scroll Bars parameter to No.

If you want to wrap content from another site inside your site, be sensitive to the copyright and usage issues. You should not wrap other people's content without their permission. The situation is compounded by the fact that you are displaying the content inside your site design. Site visitors may assume that because the content appears on your site inside your template, that you created it. While best practice is to seek the authors' permissions before publishing their content, at the very least you should include a clear statement as to the source and ownership of the wrapped content.

Using Modules to Embed Content and Links

You can use module placeholders to position modules inside of content areas. Placing modules inside of a Content Item or inside the area of the template normally set aside for content gives you more possibilities for creating unique and functional page layouts.

You normally place modules by way of module placeholders coded into the template. The template placeholders are static and do not change position from page to page. In contrast, module placeholders that you insert into Content Items are dynamic and you can change them from page to page; they are not, in other words, dependent upon the placeholders being coded into the template.

Inserting module placeholders into the template is the most common way of placing modules. Besides the far left and far right columns, you can insert module placeholders in the template above or below the main content area of the template. By inserting placeholders around the main content area, you can assign and publish modules inside those areas to achieve variety from page to page, or from section to section. Module position holders take up very little space inside the template when there are no modules published in that position; therefore, modules can be assigned to some pages and not to others without disrupting the layout.

You can insert module placeholders directly into Content Items using the `{mosloadpositions}` command and the Load Positions Mambot. To use the command, simply insert the code `{mosloadpositions` *`handle`*`}` inside the Content Item, where *handle* is the name of the module position. Once you save and publish the item, any modules that you assign to that position appear inside the Content Item. Note that you must publish the Load Positions Mambot to enable the `{mosloadpositions}` command. For more on the Load Positions Mambot, see Chapter 13.

Using Modules to Embed Content and Links

1. Click Content.
2. Click All Content Items.

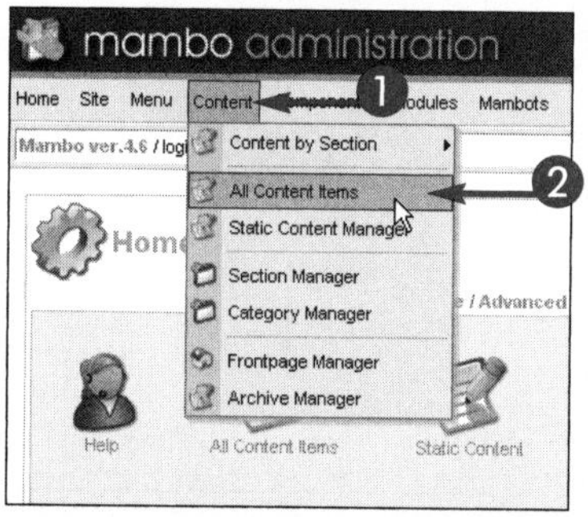

The Content Items Manager loads.

3. Click the Content Item to which you want to add the module position.
4. Click the Edit icon.

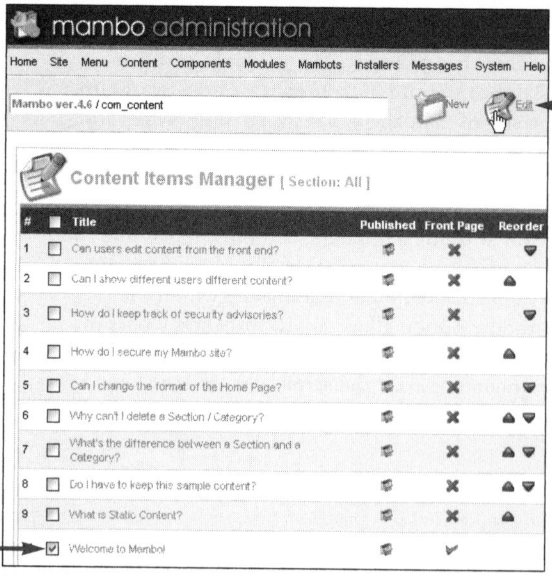

The Content Item editing screen loads.

5. Place the cursor where you want to add the module position holder.

6. Type **{mosloadpositions user1}**.

7. Click the Save Icon.

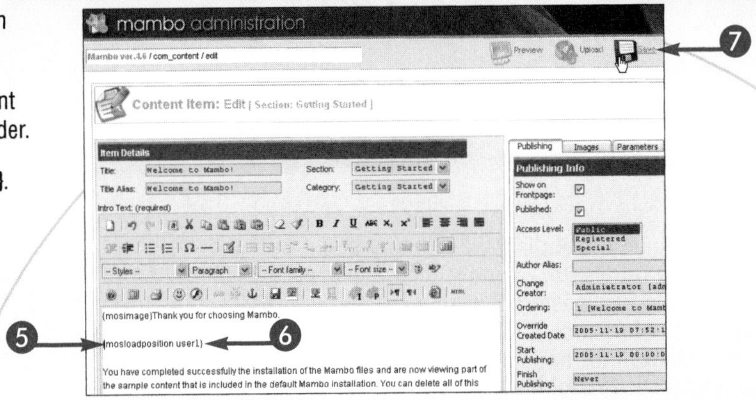

- The module position holder is now active inside the Content Item.

Mambo displays modules that you publish and assign to the user1 position and to the page.

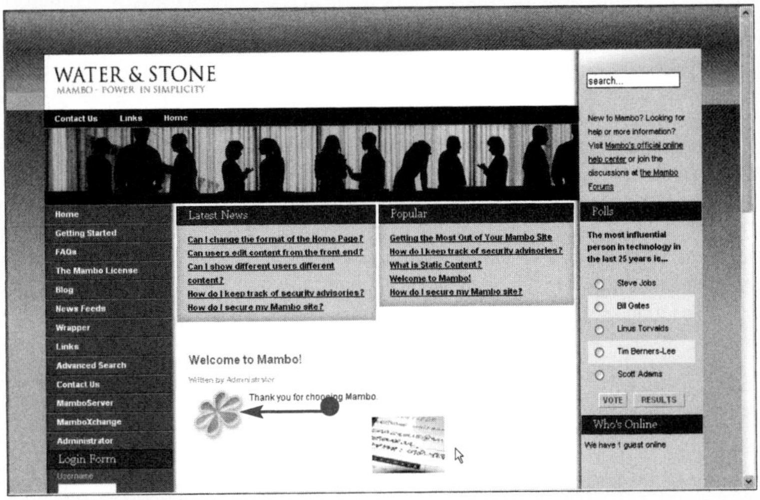

Apply It

The {mosloadpositions} command opens up some interesting possibilities for creating richer Content Items. Here are just a few ideas of what you can do with the command:

Insert a Random Image	Create a Content Item with a randomly rotating image by inserting the `{mosloadpositions}`command in the Content Item, and then assign the Random Image module to the position and the page.
Insert an Ad	Insert an advertisement inside a Content Item by placing the `{mosloadpositions}` command where you want the ad to appear. Next, assign Banner modules to the position and the page.
Insert Related Content	Insert links to related items by placing the `{mosloadpositions}` command in the Content Item and then assigning the Related Items module to the position and the page.
Insert a Wrapper	Insert Wrapped content inside a Content Item by using the `{mosloadpositions}`command and then assigning the Wrapper module to the position and the page.

Manage Complex Content Hierarchies

Although the Mambo system is flexible and gives administrators a number of options, even the most experienced Webmasters find themselves uniquely challenged by complex content hierarchies. By default, Mambo is optimized for handling sites with a three tier hierarchy that the Section/Category/Content Item structure presents. But to create a site with more than three levels, or to implement a complicated or inconsistent structure, is a struggle. Organizing your site well can help you avoid problems resulting from complex content. There are trade-offs in coaxing your Mambo system into handling advanced content structures, but with good planning and the creative use of Menu Items, you can achieve the results you desire.

The Challenge

Two practical challenges frame a complex content hierarchy. You must create a usable site navigation structure for site visitors. However, you need to create an administration structure that promotes efficient site management. While invariably there is some trade-off between the two competing concerns, you can avoid completely sacrificing one for the sake of the other.

Escaping the Default Three-Tier Structure

You can escape the default hierarchical structure using Static Content Items, which are independent of the structure, belonging to neither sections nor categories. Moreover, Mambo's menu management system gives a great deal of flexibility for creating navigational structures independent of the content structures. As an administrator, you can create Menu Items that link to either sections, categories, Content Items, or Static Content Items. The system, in other words, links directly to any level of the hierarchy or to the Static Content Items. Ideally, your sites will have a front end navigation structure and a back end content organization scheme that are parallel and consistent. However, with complex hierarchies, sometimes slavish devotion to maintaining parallel structure produces less than optimal results.

Creating Variance between Menus and Structure

Mambo's default structure creates a nested hierarchy, with sections at the top of the pyramid, categories nested inside sections, and Content Items nested inside categories. This default structure imposes greater limits for the administrator than for the site visitor because the administrator is locked into the nested structure. However, on the front end of the Web site, you can completely avoid this hierarchy, courtesy of the options that Mambo menus present. To review the relationships between the various items in the hierarchy, see Chapter 5.

A Four-Tier Hierarchy Example

This topic is perhaps best served by way of an example: Assume you want to create a Web site featuring your favorite recipes for two broad divisions: Food and Drinks. You might, come up with the following structure:

TIER 1	TIER 2	TIER 3	TIER 4
Food	Entrees	Salads	Recipe Items
		Soups	Recipe Items
	Main Courses	Fish	Recipe Items
		Fowl	Recipe Items
		Meat	Recipe Items
		Vegetarian	Recipe Items
	Desserts	Recipe Items	
Drinks	Cocktails	Recipe Items	
	Highballs	Recipe Items	
	Cordials	Recipe Items	

Although not terribly complex, this example actually exceeds the capabilities of Mambo's three-tier hierarchy and shows the need for four levels.

Setting Up the Four-Tier Example

For the previous example, the administration side of the Web site is best served by simply creating sections for the topics Entrees, Main Courses, Desserts, Cocktails, Highballs, Cordials, and so on. Within the section Entrees, you can create the categories Salads and Soups. Inside the categories Salads and Soups you can create the individual recipes as Content Items. Now, although the administrators do not have the distinction Food and Drinks to assist them in locating the proper Content Items within the administration system, the sections should be descriptive enough to promote efficient management.

On the front end of the Web site you cannot so easily escape confusion because you must give the top tier, Food and Drinks, some significance in the organizational scheme. The best solution is to create Static Content Items for both Food and Drinks and place introductory text in those items. In the course of creating your Menu Items, you can directly link to the Static Content Items for Food and Drinks, and then create separate Menu Items for each section and each category. For more on how to create Static Content Items, see Chapter 6. For more about Menu Items, see Chapter 9.

A Five-Tier Example

To complicate matters, assume that post creation of the previous structures, you decide to further subdivide the Fish Category. The example now shows five tiers. Moreover, assume you must retrofit the new tier into the existing site.

TIER 1	TIER 2	TIER 3	TIER 4	TIER 5
Food	Main Courses	Fish	Freshwater	Recipe Items
			Ocean Fish	Recipe Items
			Shellfish	Recipe Items

Setting Up the Five-Tier Example

To solve this problem without reworking the entire site's content structure, you must fit a new tier below the Category level, and in that tier you must place links to the recipes. The fastest solution, though not elegant for administration purposes, is to create Static Content Items for each of the recipes, and then create Content Items to act as entry pages for each of the new subcategories. In other words, create one Content Item for Freshwater Fish, one for Ocean Fish, and one for Shellfish. You assign each of the new Content Items to the category Fish. When you create each Content Item, you add to it via the content editing window links to the Recipes (Static Content Items) that belong to the subcategory. To complete the task, you create three new Menu Items, one each for the subcategories, and link the Menu Items directly to the new Content Items. On the front end of the site, you have created rather neatly and easily a new tier with consistent navigation and organization. Unfortunately, on the back end, you must spread your recipes between the standard Sections/Categories structure and the Static Content Items. Moreover, you must manually update the subcategory pages each time you add a new recipe to Freshwater Fish, Ocean Fish, or Shellfish.

Content Management from the Front End

Mambo gives you flexibility by providing options for managing your content from either within the administration system or from the front end of the Web site. Although most administrators focus on using the admin system for their content management needs, you can accomplish many things from the front end of your site. Front end content management is a convenient timesaver and a good way to build community because it enables others to contribute materials to your site. For a basic site, front end content management is a quick way to log in and create Content Items. For a larger site, front end editing options give administrators a way to share the workload; site authors can create and submit items independently without having access to the administration system.

User Groups for Front End Management

The Mambo user hierarchy anticipates front end content management by providing user groups tailored to create a workflow for content creation, editing, and publication. Users who belong to the Author, Editor, or Publisher group can log in to the front end of the site and work with Content Items, but cannot access the back end administration system. Additionally, the Manager class exists to supplement the front end user groups. Users assigned to the Manager group have access to the administration system but their privileges are limited to creating sections and categories — tasks that cannot be performed from the front end of the Web site. For more on the various classes of users and their privileges, see Chapter 4.

Front End Content Management Workflow

Typically, front end content management has a specific workflow. Mambo presents *Author* class users with a limited set of sections and categories in which they can create new Content Items. Authors cannot schedule or publish the Content Items they create, and can view only the items they have created. A second class of users, *Editors*, review and edit submissions from all the various Authors, but do not actually publish the content. A third user group, *Publisher*, can review, edit, and publish the Content Items. Not all sites need or want to use all three categories, but the options are there if you want to create a formal content creation, review, and publication workflow.

Front End Tools

You can do everything, from Content Item creation to editing to publishing, from the front end. During the process, the user has a limited but sufficient set of tools and options, including the WYSIWYG editor, MOSimage, MOSpagebreak, and basic Content Item parameters. The tools become visible after the user logs in to the front end of the site. In the default installation of Mambo, once a user logs in, a new menu becomes available. The menu includes the links to the various tools. The Submit link opens the Content Item creation screen. Editors and Publishers can review pending Content Items by browsing the site. Additionally, the User Menu also contains a link to the Check In functionality. For more about Content Item creation, see the next section, "Create Content Items from the Front End." For more about the Check In functionality, see Chapter 14.

Create Content Items from the Front End

Users with proper access privileges can log in to your Web site and add new Content Items. The functionality is enabled in the default implementation of Mambo, and you access it simply by logging in to the front end of the Web site.

The ability to create new Content Items is not available to all users. Only users who belong to the user group Author and above can create new Content Items. Authorized users have the WYSIWYG editor, the MOSimage and MOSpagebreak commands, and basic Content Item parameters available to them. One limitation of working from the front end is that all the tools must fit within the Content area of the site; this can lead to a rather small workspace. If users find the workspace too limiting, the only choice is to grant them access to the admin system.

If a user from the Author or Editor user group creates a Content Item, the item remains unpublished until a higher-level user reviews and approves the content. If a user from the Publisher group, or a higher-level access group, creates a Content Item, the user can publish the Item, as per the options selected on the Publishing tab in the Content Editor. As a point of convenience, users with admin system access can always log in to the admin system to review, edit, and publish Content Items submitted from the front end of the Web site.

Note that while the functionality is native to the default Mambo system, the Content Section and the navigation link necessary to access the front end content management tools are only installed if you install the sample data.

Create Content Items from the Front End

1. Log in.

   The User Menu appears.

2. Click Submit FAQ.

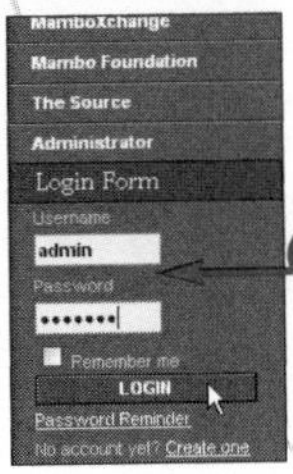

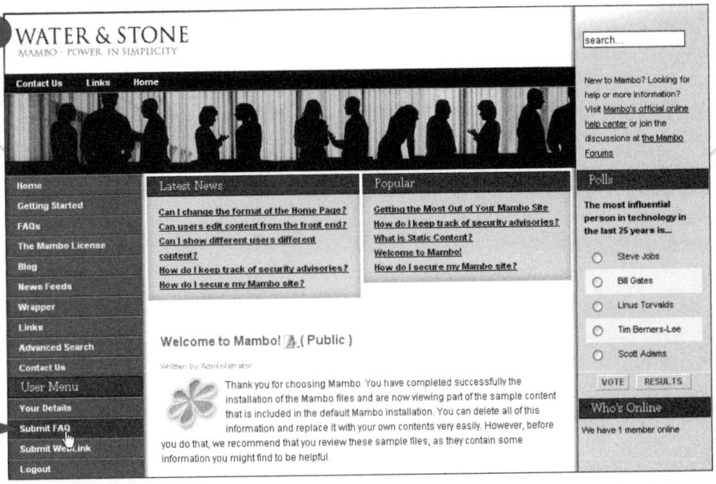

The Add Content screen loads.

3. Type a title.
4. Click here and select a category.
5. Type text for the item.
6. Click the Save icon.

   Mambo creates the Content Item, but does not publish it.

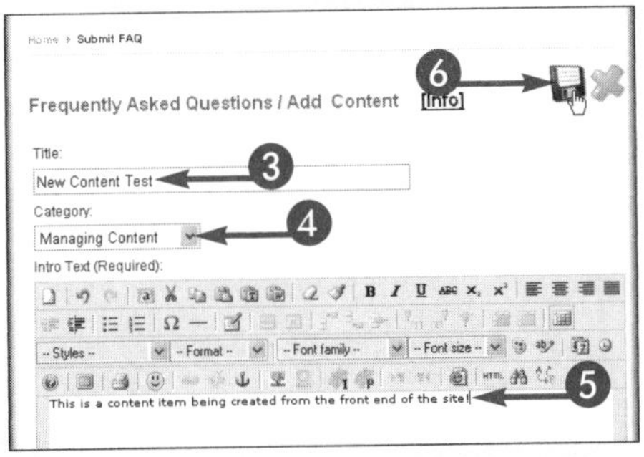

Edit Content Items from the Front End

You can edit Content Items from the front end of your Web site, without the need for logging in to the admin system. If you are assigned to the user group Editor or above, Mambo gives you access to all the Content Items from the front end. Editing from the front end is fast and easy and can save you the time and trouble of opening the administration interface to perform the task.

To edit a Content Item, all a user needs to do is log in to the front end of the site. If a user belongs to the Editor group or a higher-level user group, an editing icon appears beside the title of each Content Item. This editing icon opens a Content Item editing screen complete with WYSIWYG Editor and access to MOSimage, MOSpagebreak, and basic parameters. The user can make changes and save the item. Users belonging to the Editor group can edit only the various Content Items; they cannot publish the items. Users belonging to the Publisher group or higher can publish pending Content Items.

Administrators sometimes create users in the Editor group to allow a more senior writer or staff member to review the pending submissions from the various Authors for oversight and quality control purposes. Once the Editor approves a reviewed Content Item, the Publisher can then publish the item and make it visible to the site visitors. Administrators who do not require such a formal system may find it necessary to create only a Publisher group that can handle both the editing and the publishing of the Content Items that various Authors submit. For more about the various User Groups and their rights and privileges, see Chapter 4.

Edit Content Items from the Front End

1. Log in.

Note: For more on logging in, see the section "Create Content Items from the Front End."

The User Menu appears.

2. Click the Edit icon of the Content Item you want to edit.

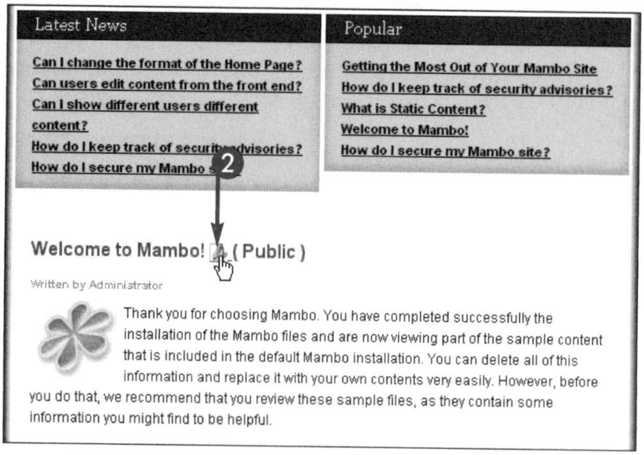

The Edit Content screen appears.

3. Make any changes needed.

4. Click the Save icon.

Mambo saves the changes to the Content Item.

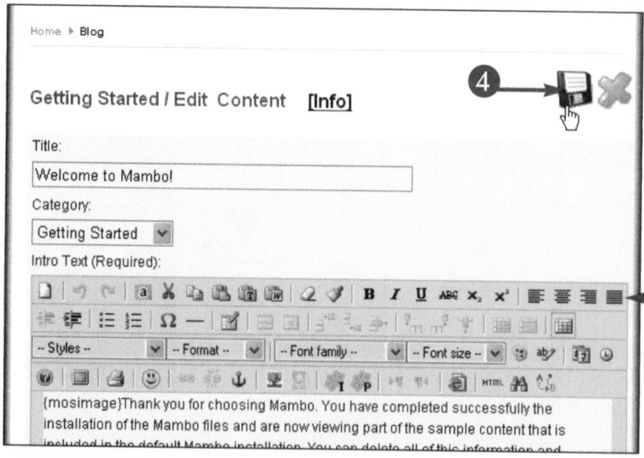

Publish Content Items from the Front End

You can publish new Content Items from the front end of your Mambo Web site without logging in to the admin system. Any user who has access privileges of Publisher or higher can approve and publish Content Items. Publishing from the front end is fast and easy and can save you the time and trouble of opening the administration interface to perform the task.

A user assigned to the Publisher group cannot access the admin system and must log in to the front end of the Web site. Once logged in, the user can create new Content Items via the Submit link. Alternatively, the user can navigate to the various sections and categories and find articles contributed by others. A Publisher can review, edit, or publish the works of others.

Content Items created from the front end include the same parameters as items created through the admin system. The parameters cover the standard options, including publishing. The Publishing tab of the Content Item parameters allows the Publisher to set the start and stop dates for the publication of the Content Item. For more information on managing Content Item publication parameters, see Chapter 6.

Anyone with the proper access privileges can publish pending Content Items. The act of publishing a Content Item from the front end or the back end of your Web site has the same results. Similarly, any user belonging to the group Publisher or above can unpublish any Content Items from the front end.

Note that with larger sites it is often faster to identify pending Content Items from the admin system's Content Item Manager. Front end users have to browse the site to find pending items, whereas the Admin users can review the Content Items at a glance.

Publish Content Items from the Front End

1 Log in.

Note: For more on logging in, see the section "Create Content Items from the Front End."

The User Menu appears.

2 Browse the site for unpublished Content Items.

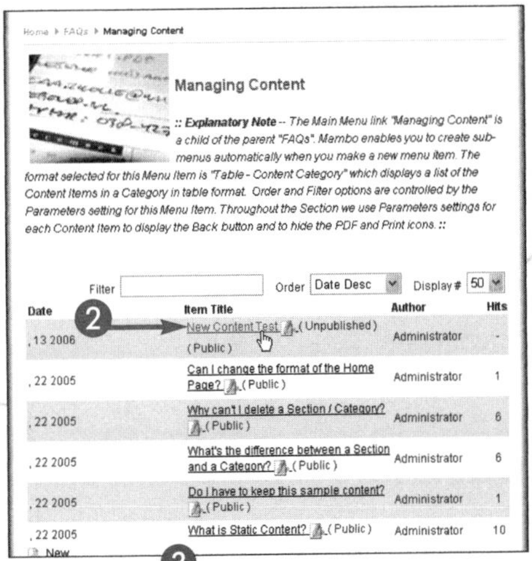

3 Click the Edit icon.

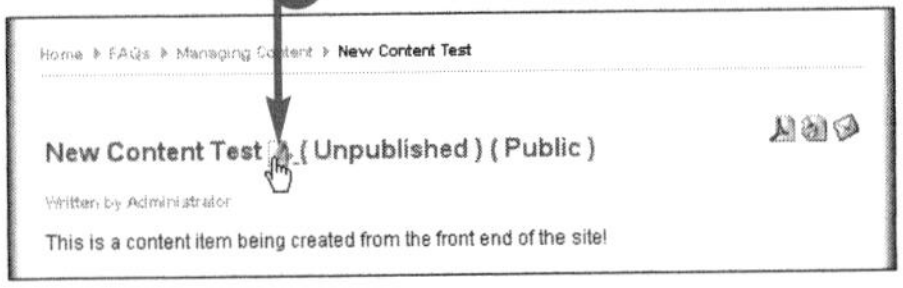

The Content Item editing screen appears.

4 Click here and select Published.

5 Click the Save icon.

Mambo publishes the Content Item.

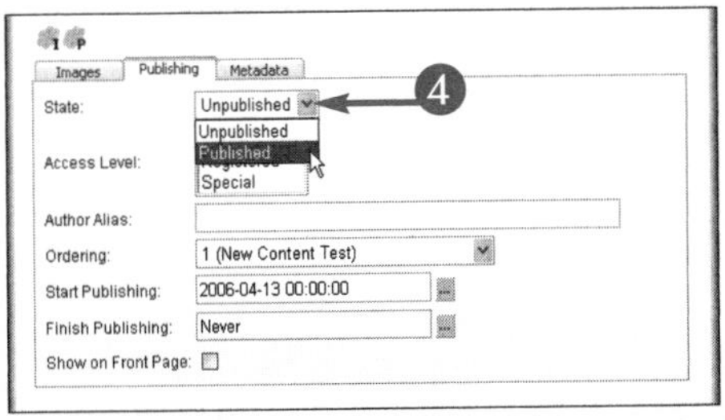

An Introduction to the Menu Managers

The Mambo system includes two types of Menu Managers, which unfortunately bear the same name. The two Menu Managers are different both in terms of the information they display and their function. Learning how to use both Menu Managers is a necessary skill for creating your Web site.

The Master Menu Manager

The first type of Menu Manager can be described as the Master Menu Manager. The label is appropriate because this Menu Manager controls all the individual Menus in the system. There is also only one instance of the Master Menu Manager. As you will see shortly, there can be multiple versions of the other type of Menu Manager.

Ⓐ Master Menu Manager Toolbar

Icons for creating a new menu, editing an existing menu, making a copy of a menu, deleting a menu, or to access help files for this screen.

Ⓑ

An ID number assigned automatically to the menu by the system.

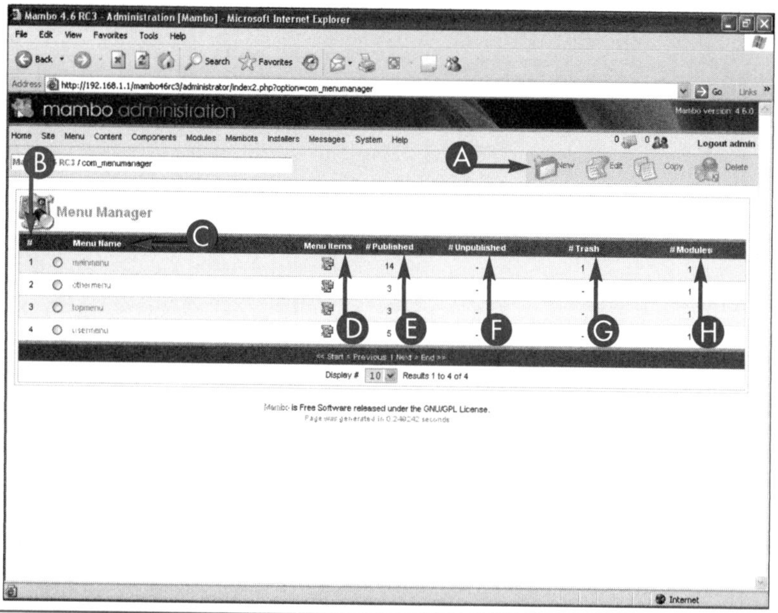

Ⓒ Menu Name

The name for the menu.

Ⓓ Menu Items

Opens the Individual Menu Manager for access to the Menu Items.

Ⓔ # Published

Shows the total number of published Menu items.

Ⓕ # Unpublished

Shows the total number of unpublished Menu items.

Ⓖ # Trash

Shows the total number of Menu items currently in the Trash Manager.

Ⓗ # Modules

Shows the total number of modules associated with the menu.

The second type of Menu Manager can be described as the Individual Menu Manager. There is one Individual Menu Manager for each menu in the system. The Individual Menu Manager actually manages the Menu Items contained in the menus. An Individual Menu Manager interface is described below:

A Individual Menu Manager Toolbar

Icons for creating a new Menu Item, editing an existing Menu Item, publishing or unpublishing one or more existing Menu Items. You also have icons for moving, copying, or trashing Menu Items as well as to access help files.

B Menu Item

The names of all the Menu Items. You can access the item by clicking the name.

C Published

Shows the item's published state, which you change by clicking the icon.

D Reorder

Reorders a Content Item relative to others in the same category via the up and down arrows.

E Order

You order the Content Item relative to others in the same category by changing the numerical sequence and clicking the Save icon.

F Save

Click to save changes after ordering.

G Access

Shows the access level assigned to this item. Click the icon to cycle through the options.

H Item ID

System-generated ID number.

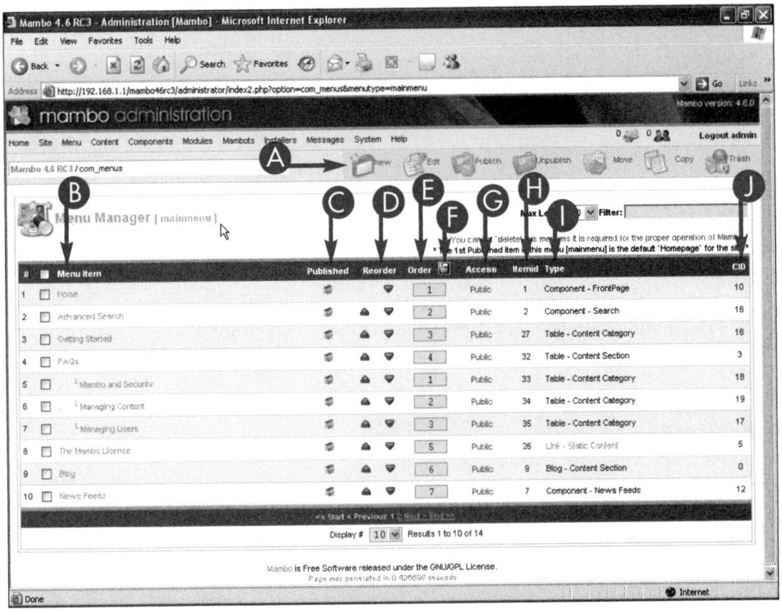

I Type

Indicates Menu Item format.

J CID

System-generated ID number.

Understanding Mambo Default Menus

Installation of Mambo without the sample data creates a system with only one menu. If you install the sample data, the system includes four menus. The default menus include the Main Menu, which is a core file and which you cannot delete, as well as three optional menus, named Other Menu, Top Menu, and User Menu.

In this section, the Mambo default menus are explained in some detail, along with the Menu Items that are included with the sample data from the Mambo installation. The site administrators can modify or delete all the menus and Menu Items with the sole exception of the Main Menu, which they can edit but cannot delete.

Main Menu

The Main Menu holds the primary navigation for the default site installation. The Main Menu and its corresponding module of the same name are core Mambo files and you cannot delete it. You can edit the menu, but it is not advisable to change the menu's name, nor delete the Menu Item named Home. If you do not want to use the Front Page Manager, which is linked to the Menu Item named Home, the best course is to unpublish it. The Content Items included in the sample data are designed to provide Mambo users with information to help them get started.

The Menu Items are similarly didactic in nature, representing examples of the various formatting techniques available in the system. The Menu Items are described as follows:

MAIN MENU ITEM	DESCRIPTION
Home	Links to the Frontpage component. For more on working with the Frontpage component, see Chapter 6.
Getting Started	A Table-Content Category Format Menu Item.
FAQs	A Table-Content Section Format Menu Item. This Menu Item is a parent of the following items.
Mambo and Security	A Table-Content Category Format Menu Item. This Menu Item is a child of the FAQs parent Menu Item.
Managing Content	A Table-Content Category Format Menu Item. This Menu Item is a child of the FAQs parent Menu Item.
Managing Users	A Table-Content Category Format Menu Item. This Menu Item is a child of the FAQs parent Menu Item.
The Mambo License	Links to a Static Content Item.
Blog	A Blog-Content Section link.
Newsfeeds	Links to the Newsfeed component. For more on working with the Newsfeed component, see Chapter 10.
Wrapper	A Wrapper link set to wrap the Open Directory Web site. For more on working with Wrappers, see Chapter 8.

As previously stated, besides the Main Menu, Mambo has three optional menus: Other Menu, Top Menu, and User Menu. These menus serve particular purposes and you can use them in a variety of manners.

The Other Menu

The Other Menu is only present if you installed the sample data with the installation. The menu is a standard public menu designed to provide an example of a generic menu.

OTHER MENU ITEMS	DESCRIPTION
MamboServer.com	A Link-URL format Menu Item that directs users to www.mamboserver.com.
MamboXchange.com	A Link-URL format Menu Item that directs users to www.mamboxchange.com.
Mambo Foundation	A Link-URL format Menu Item that directs users to www.mambo-foundation.org.
The Source	A Link-URL format Menu Item that directs users to source.mambo-foundation.org.
Administrator	A Link-URL format Menu Item that directs users to the login page for the admin system of their site.

The Top Menu

The Top Menu is only present if you installed the sample data. This menu is placed in the Top module position and is located above the header image. The menu is intended to show an example of a horizontal format menu.

TOP MENU ITEMS	DESCRIPTION
Home	A redundant link to the Frontpage component.
Links	A link to the Weblinks component. For more on working with the Weblinks component, see Chapter 10.
Contact Us	A Link-Contact Item Format Menu Item.

The User Menu

The User Menu is only present if you installed the sample data with the installation. The menu is a restricted-access menu designed to show how to configure a menu that will only be visible to registered users who are logged in to the system.

USER MENU ITEMS	DESCRIPTION
Your Details	A Link-URL Format Menu Item that directs users to a page where they can update or edit their personal account details.
Submit FAQs	A Link-URL Format Menu Item that directs users to a page where they can submit new Content Items. This link only functions for users who are members of the Author group or above.
Submit Weblink	A Link-URL Format Menu Item that directs users to a page where they can submit a new Weblink for the Weblinks component.
Check-in My Items	A Link-URL Format Menu Item that checks in the user's Content Items.
Log out	A link to the Login component. Because users can only see this Menu Item when they are logged in, the link initiates a logout routine.

Manage an Existing Menu

You can edit an existing menu and its Menu Items. Mambo has enough flexibility for you to retain the existing default menus and build off of them for your site. You can change the Menu name, characteristics, and placement. You can also customize the items on the menu, within limits. Using the existing menus and their contents is a quick way to build up a new site.

Managing menus invariably requires working with both the Menu Manager and the Module Manager. Parameters that affect the menus and their items are split between the two areas.

You rename menus by way of the Master Menu Manager. Placement and configuration of the menu requires you to open and edit the contents of the Menu module that is related to the menu. Each menu, when created, also creates a parallel module that is located in the Site Module Manager. You must locate the module for your menu in order to make the formatting changes. Menus are fully editable; at editing time, you have the same options available that you do at the time you created the menu. Note that you cannot delete the default Main Menu in your Mambo site as it is a core file required by the system.

Although you can edit Menu Items after creation, you are subjected to several limitations. Upon creation, the creator must select a format for the Menu Item, which you cannot edit. The Menu Item's format dictates the parameters that are available when you edit the Menu Item. For more information on working with the various Menu Item formats, see the section "An Introduction to Menu Item Formats."

Manage an Existing Menu

1. Click Menu.
2. Select the menu you want to manage.

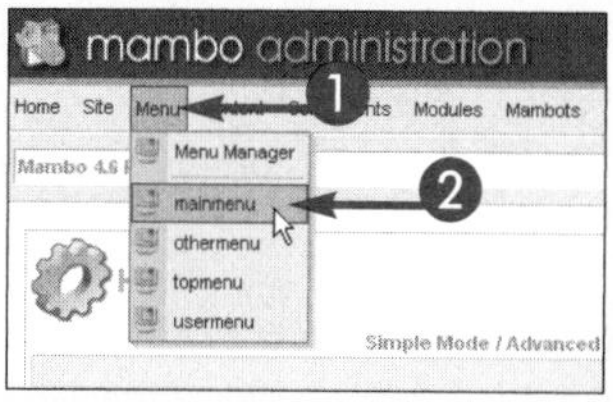

The Individual Menu Manager loads.

3. Click the Menu Item you want to manage.
4. Click the Edit icon.

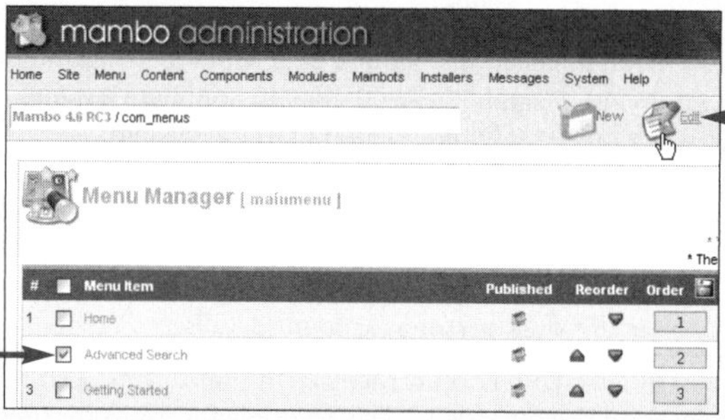

The Menu Item Editing screen loads.

5. Make any changes you want.
6. Click the Save icon.

Mambo saves your changes to the system and returns you to the Individual Menu Manager.

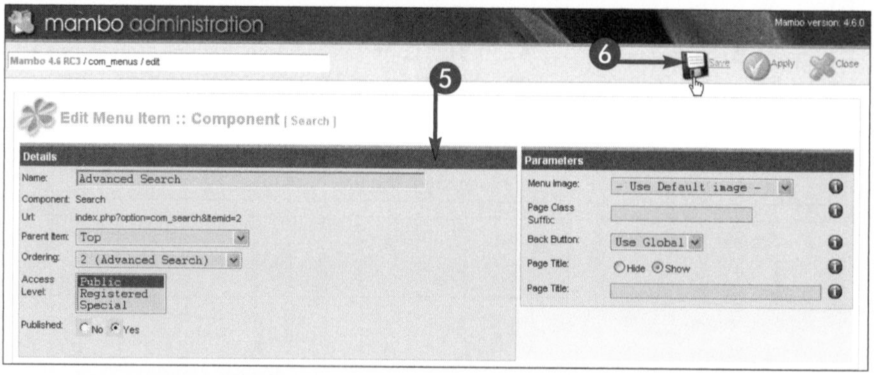

Reorder Menu Items

You can change the order in which the items in a menu appear. By reordering your Menu Items, you can customize the navigation of your Web site and optimize the display in a logical and easy-to-use fashion.

The ability to reorder Menu Items makes it possible to arrange your items in a fashion that best suits your users and your content. Grouping navigation choices based on functionality or upon subject matter divisions are the two most common methods of organization, though you have the freedom to arrange things in any manner that suits your needs.

The system provides multiple ways to affect Menu Item ordering. From the Menu Item Manager you can either reorder items using the up and down arrows in the Reorder column, or you can renumber the Menu Items using the Order column. From inside the Menu Item editing screen, a combo box enables you to order the Menu Item easily. Of these three different techniques, the fastest way to affect multiple Menu Items is to use the Order column in the Menu Item Manager. The arrows are too slow to work with easily, and the Ordering command inside the editing interface only lets you change the order of the one Menu Item you are editing.

Note that the ordering affects the menu sitewide. You cannot create different orders of the same Menu Items on different pages. If you want to create a different order on different pages, you will need to rely on another approach, such as spreading the Menu Items to different menus in different positions and using different templates on different pages. For more information on how to use multiple templates, refer to Chapter 3.

Reorder Menu Items

1. Load the Individual Menu Manager, which contains the Menu Items you want to reorder.

Note: To load the Individual Menu Manager, see the section "Manage an Existing Menu."

2. Click the numbers to reorder the items.

   - Alternatively, you can click the arrow for up or down and the Menu Item moves up or down one position on the list.

3. Click the Save icon.

The Menu Items are reordered consistent with the numbering.

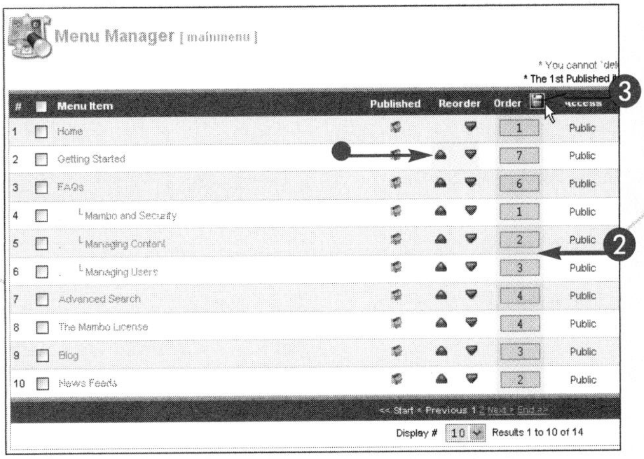

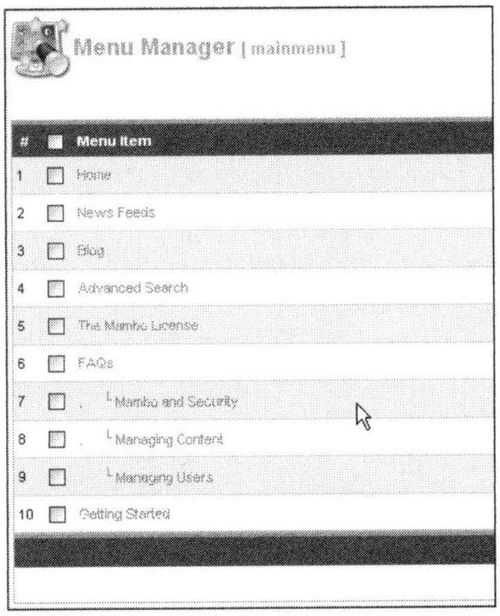

Create a New Menu

Using the Master Menu Manager, site administrators can create new menus for a Mambo Web site in one simple step. Administrators can use the Menu Manager to create both public and private menus and, through the use of the menu's module, place them on the page.

Menu creation in Mambo actually requires the coordination of the Menu Manager and the Module Manager, but Mambo automates this task so all you have to do is go to the Menu Manager and select the New icon; give the new menu a name and you are done. Behind the scenes, the Mambo system creates the menu and a Menu Manager for the new menu, and creates the necessary corresponding module for the new menu. You can also create new menus by making a copy of an existing menu.

You can add new Menu Items through the menu's manager, but you format the menu's layout through the menu's module. The module also dictates the menu placement; the menu appears in the module position to which you assign it. To learn how to add new Menu Items, see the section "Add an Item to a Menu." The Menu module is discussed in Chapter 11.

You can restrict the access of a new menu to only registered users. This technique completely hides the menu from unregistered site visitors and is an effective technique for hiding navigation choices you only want to be available to your registered users. For more information on how to create a restricted-access menu, see the section "Create a User Menu."

Create a New Menu

1. Click Menu.
2. Click Menu Manager.

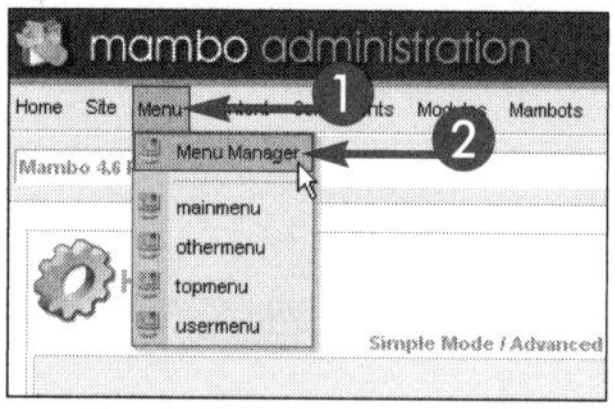

The Master Menu Manager loads.

3. Click the New icon.

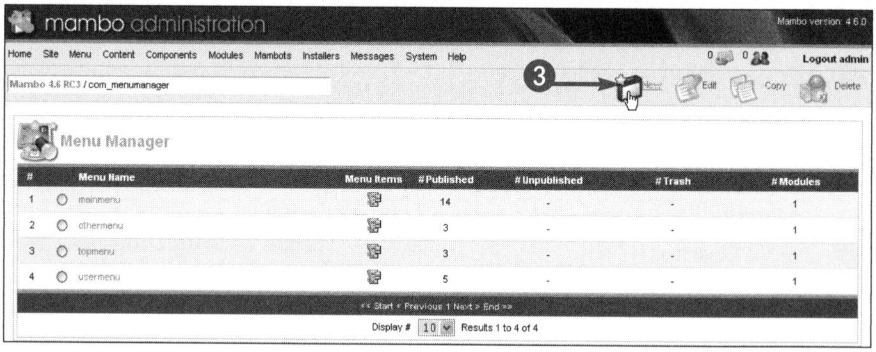

The New Menu screen loads.

4. Type a name for the menu.

Note: You must make the name unique and it cannot contain any spaces.

5. Type a name for the menu's module.

6. Click the Save icon.

- Mambo creates the new menu and returns you to the Master Menu Manager.

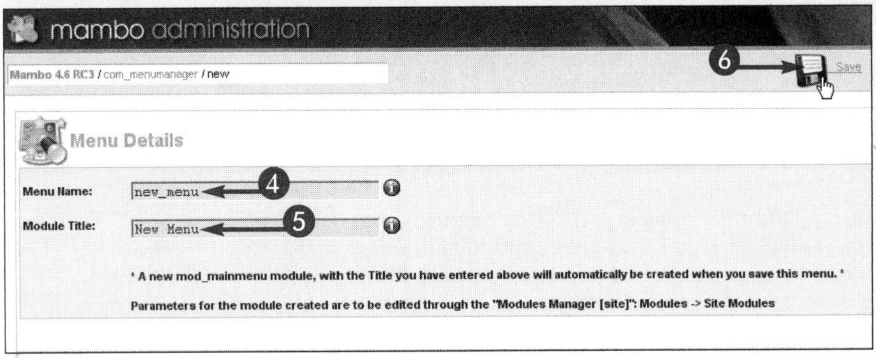

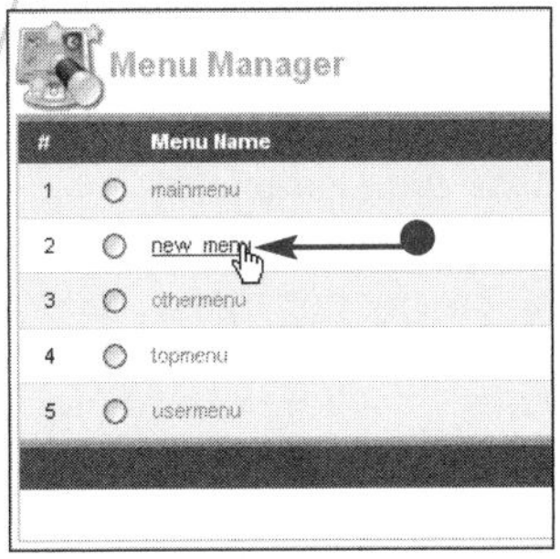

Apply It

It is also possible to create a new menu quickly by using the Copy command in the Master Menu Manager. The Copy command creates a duplicate of the original menu complete with Menu Items. All you need to do is access the Master Menu Manager, select the menu, and then click the Copy icon. The system prompts you to name the menu and the associated module and then you are finished. The new menu has the same Menu Items as the original and the same layout attributes. The Copy command is an easy way to create a redundant navigation menu. After you create a new menu, you need to access the associated menu module to select the layout parameters for the menu. The menu module lets you position the menu and format the look and feel of the menu. You can create vertical, horizontal, or multi-tiered menus. The system supports a great deal of flexibility in menu styling, but if it is not enough for you, there are some excellent third-party tools that specialize in formatting menus.

Add an Item to a Menu

You can add new items to any of the menus using the Individual Menu Managers. An Individual Menu Manager controls each menu, and each Menu Manager automates the creation of new links, which Mambo calls Menu Items. Mambo's ability to link to any type of Content Item or component enables you to create a wide variety of effective navigational schemes for sites.

There are several steps to creating a Menu Item. The steps involve specifying the nature and the format of the page to which the item will link. You also need to select the target for the link and give the item a name. Mambo connects a significant amount of the formatting and control of the target of the link to the Menu Items themselves. As a result, you often have to use the Menu Item's parameters in connection with the target's parameters to achieve the look and feel you want. The Menu Item formats are discussed at length in the section "An Introduction to Menu Item Formats."

The parameters attached to each Menu Item relate primarily to the appearance and options that are available to visitors once they click the link. The parameters vary according to the format selected for the Menu Item and the nature of what the item is linked to. The Menu Item parameters are outlined in the section "Understanding Menu Item Parameters."

There is no limit to the number of Menu Items you can put on any one menu, and you can copy Menu Items between menus, allowing for redundant navigation schemes. For more on how to copy Menu Items, see the section "Duplicate a Menu Item."

Add an Item to a Menu

1. Load the Individual Menu Manager to which you want to add the new Menu Item.

Note: To Load the Individual Menu Manager, see the section "Manage an Existing Menu."

2. Click the New icon.

Page 1 of the New Menu Item dialogue loads.

3. Select the Menu Item format you want.

4. Click the Next icon.

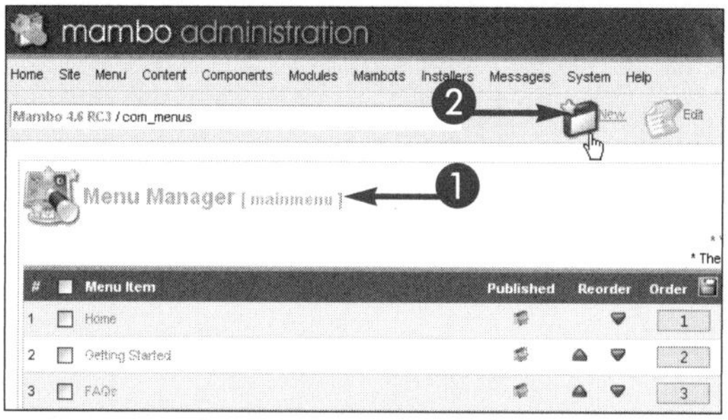

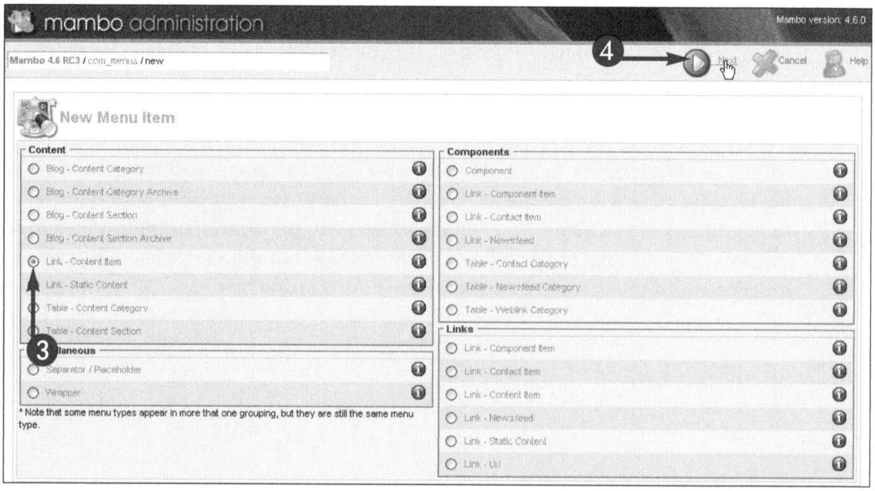

5 Type a name for the Menu Item.

6 Click here and select the content of the link, the parent, if any, and the access level.

7 Set the parameters you want.

8 Click the Save icon.

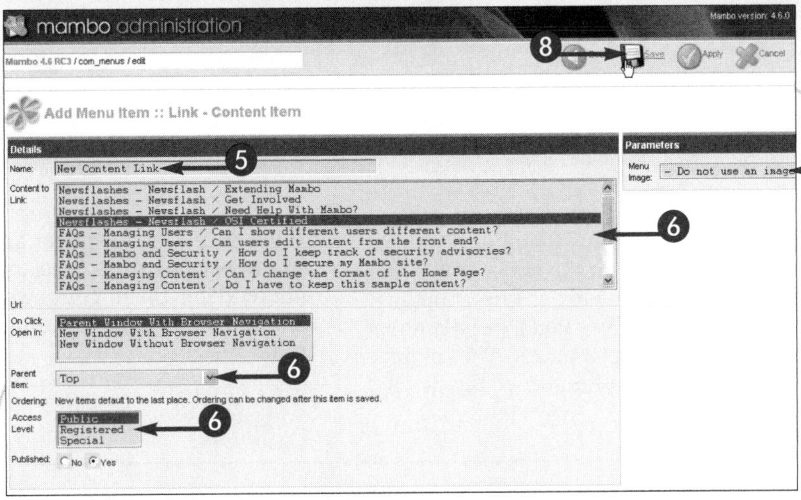

- Mambo creates the new Menu Item and returns you to the Individual Menu Manager.

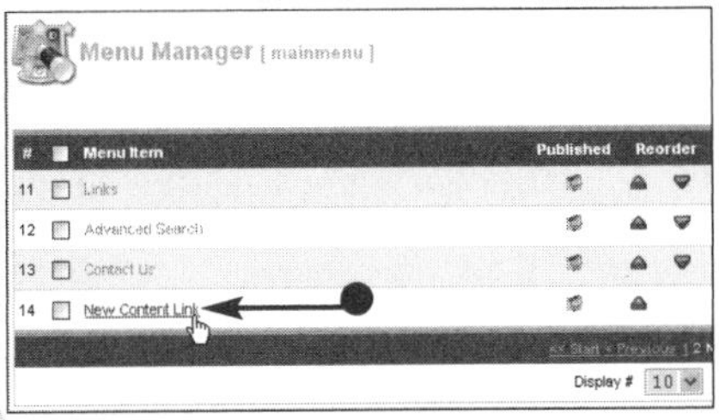

Extra

If you have never used the system before you should install the sample data during the installation process as the sample data contains a number of examples of the various Menu Item formats. Even if you are familiar with the system, you may want to install the sample data. The example menus and Menu Items in the sample data cover a number of common functionalities and give you a head start on building your site. During installation, Mambo prompts you to install the sample data; simply check the box and click Next; the system does the rest.

If you want to edit an existing Menu Item, you may run into one of the limitations of the system: you cannot change a Menu Item's format after you create it. This is one of the few areas in Mambo where you cannot modify something after its creation. If, for example, you want to change a Menu Item from Table-Content Section format to Table-Content Category format, your only option is to delete the old Menu Item and create a new one.

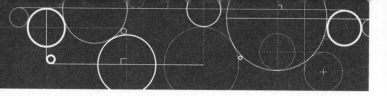

An Introduction to Menu Item Formats

In the process of creating a new Menu Item, Mambo asks you to select a format for the target of the Menu Item. The page containing the list of format options is a bit bewildering because it gives you a large number of items with no examples or explanations. The confusion is compounded by the fact that a number of the items sound suspiciously similar and are in fact repeated in several places with no explanation as to what, if anything, differentiates them. For newcomers to Mambo, the Menu Item format page is probably one of the most confusing in the system.

Page Layout Options

It helps if you understand how Mambo describes the page layout possibilities created by the various formatting options. There are three options: Blog Format, Table View, and Full View.

Blog Format

Blog Format displays the title of an article and all or part of the Content Item. You can control the exact output through the Menu Items' parameters, which you can use to specify the number of items and columns that display.

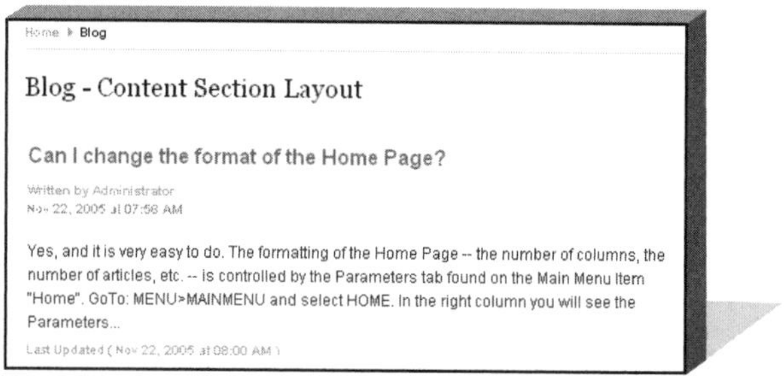

Table View

Table View displays a list of individual Content Items by title. Table View can also display additional information such as the publication date, name of the author, number of hits, and so on. In some cases Table View also gives additional functionality on the page, providing a search option as well as options to control the sort order and the number of items that appear. Each title in the table is hyperlinked to the underlying Content Item.

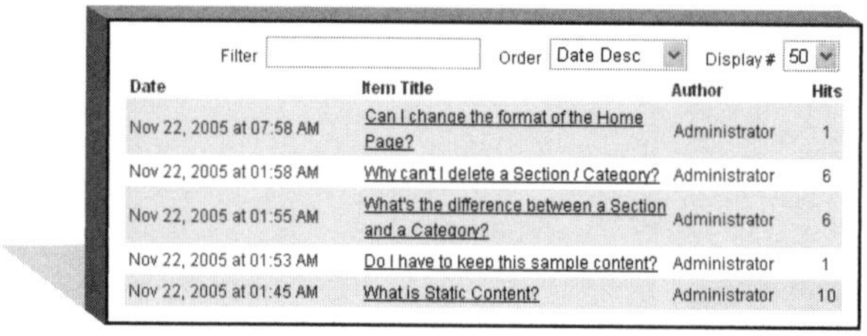

Full View

Full View simply displays a Content Item or component when a user clicks on the Menu Item.

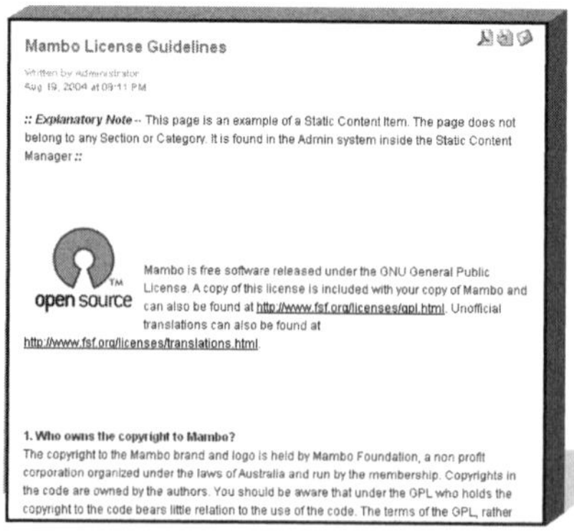

The following table lists the choices that appear on the Menu Item formats page along with a short description of what you will get if you select the option.

LABEL	DISPLAYS
Blog-Content Category	All the pages within an individual category, laid out in blog format.
Blog-Content Category Archive	All the archived pages within an individual category, laid out in blog format.
Blog-Content Section	All the contents of a section, laid out in blog format. Automatically includes all the Content Items from all the categories within the selected section.
Blog-Content Section Archive	All the archived contents of a section, laid out in blog format. Automatically includes all the archived Content Items from all the categories within the selected section.
Link-Content Item	An individual Content Item, displayed in full view. Note this option appears twice on the page.
Link-Static Content	An individual Static Content Item, displayed in full view. Note this option appears twice on the page.
Table-Content Category	The names of all the Content Items within that specific category in table format, with links to those items. The Menu Item includes a space where you can enter text and images on the page above the table.
Table-Content Section	The names of all the categories within a section in table format, with links to pages listing the contents of each category. The Menu Item includes a space where you can enter text and images on the page above the table.
Separator/Placeholder	Displays a break between items in the menu, either a space or separator or placeholder. This is, in other words, a formatting tool; it does not create a link to any content or functionality.
Wrapper	Use this choice to create a Wrapper. For more information on Wrappers, see Chapter 8.
Component	Displays a component in full view.
Link-Component Item	An individual component item in full view. Note that not all components have distinct items that can be linked to individually. Note also that this option appears twice on the page.
Link-Contact Item	An individual contact from the Contacts component in full view. Note this option appears twice on the page.
Link-Newsfeed	Allows you to link directly to a newsfeed from the Newsfeed Manager. Displays in full view. Note that this option appears twice on the page.
Table-Contact Category	All the contacts from a particular Contact category in table format, with links to details pages for each contact.
Table-Newsfeed Category	All the feeds from a particular Newsfeed category, as defined in the Newsfeed component, with links to details pages for each contact. The table may also include name of newsfeed, number of articles, and address.
Table-Weblink Category	All the Weblinks contained in a particular Weblink category in table format.
Link-URL	Usually used to link to either a page not on the site or a page (or function) located on your site, but built outside of Mambo. Displays in full view.

Understanding Menu Item Parameters

Each Menu Item includes a number of parameters that allow you to control the appearance of the item and the options available for viewers.

The parameters attached to each Menu Item let you override the sitewide settings contained in the Global Configuration Manager. Applying the parameters to a Menu Item affects only that individual Menu Item. If you want to make similar changes to other items you must do so to each one; or if you want to implement the changes throughout the site, you should establish the settings you want in the Global Configuration Manager. For more on how to use the Global Configuration Manager to control Menu Item appearance, see Chapter 2.

Understanding the various Menu Item parameters is an important key to gaining full control over site formatting. Note that there is a relationship between the Menu Item parameters, the Global Configuration Settings and the Content Item parameters. If you are troubleshooting a display problem, be certain to check all three areas.

The Parameter Tab

The following figure shows the parameters available to you on the Parameter tab. The Parameter tab is located in the right column inside the Menu Item Editing window.

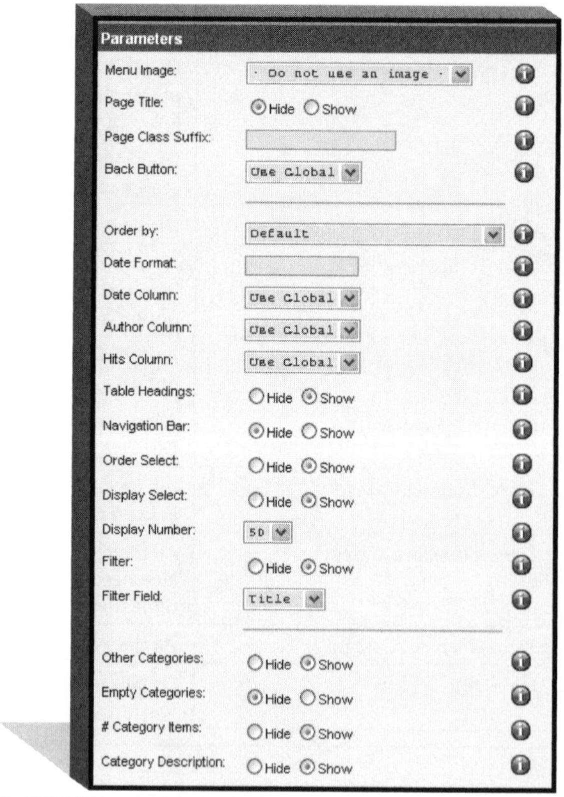

The following table lists the choices that typically appear on the Parameters tab in the Menu Item creation and editing pages. There are slightly more options available for some Menu Item formats than for others, and exactly which parameters are available relates to the nature of the Menu Item format and target selected.

PARAMETER	FUNCTION
Menu Image	Places a small image next to the name of a Menu Item. Contents of the drop-down menu are drawn from the image/stories directory on the server. You can add your own images to the list by placing images files in the image/stories directory.
Page Class Suffix	Adds a unique identifier to the CSS class for this Menu Item to allow individual Menu Item styling. To make this work you must also create the class in the CSS for the template.
Back Button	Displays a Back button on the page. When a site visitor clicks the Back button they are taken to the previous page they were viewing.
Page Title (text field)	Sets a page title other than the default name. Leave it blank to display the default page name.
Page Title (hide/show)	Controls display of page title.
# Leading	Determines how many Content Items are shown as Leading items; that is, items that span the entire available width of the main content area.
# Intro	Determines how many Content Items are shown with Intro Text displayed (rather than just showing the title of the page).
Columns	Determines how many columns appear after the Leading Item.
# Links	Determines the number of links to items to show (beneath any Intro items).
Category Order	Sets the sort order for the categories on the page.
Primary Order	Sets the sort order for the items on the page.
Pagination	Displays pagination support, which allows creation of multi-page Content Items.
Pagination Results	Shows the pagination on the page.
MOSimages	Displays the MOSimages command.
Description	Displays the section/category/item description.
Description Image (sic)	Displays an image to go with the section/category/item description.
Category Name	Displays the name of the category to which the Content Item belongs.
Category Name Linkable	Uses linked category name titles.
Item Titles	Displays the item's title.
Linked Titles	Uses page titles as hyperlinks.
Read More	Uses a "read more" link where needed on Content Items.
Item Rating	Allows visitors to vote on (rate) Content Items.
Author Names	Shows Author names on Content Items.
Created Date and Time	Displays the date and time the Content Item was created.
Modified Date and Time	Displays the date and time the Content Item was last modified.
PDF Icon	Displays the PDF icon, which enables users to turn a Content Item into a PDF document.
Print Icon	Displays the Print icon, which enables users to print a Content Item easily.
Email Icon	Displays the email icon, which enables users to send via email a link to the Content Item.

Publish a Menu Item

You must publish a Menu Item to make it visible to your site's visitors. Although you can view and edit a Menu Item within the administration system without publishing it, you must publish the Menu Item for it to be seen from the front end of the Web site.

During site construction or the creation of new menu it is generally best to leave the Menu Items unpublished. When the item is in final form, display it on the site by publishing it. If you publish while you are editing, site visitors can see the work in progress.

Failure to publish a Menu Item results in the content or component that links to the item being unavailable for site visitors, unless there is a link elsewhere on the site. Failure to publish a parent Menu Item also hides all the child Menu Items from view. Note also that publishing a Menu Item alone may not be sufficient to display a Content Item. You must publish Content Items, categories, and sections themselves to make them visible. For more information on publishing Content Items, see Chapter 6. For more information on sections and categories, see Chapter 5.

There are two ways to publish a Menu Item. You can publish a Menu Item with one click directly from the Menu Items Manager, or you can publish a Menu Item by opening the Menu Item editing screen and selecting the Publish option from the parameters inside the editing window. Always check the front end of the Web site after invoking the publication command to make sure that the result is what you expected. The result of both methods is the same, but publishing an item directly from the Menu Items Manager is the faster method, and is shown in the example below.

Publish a Menu Item

1. Load the Individual Menu Manager containing the Menu Item you want to publish.

Note: To Load the Individual Menu Manager, see the section "Manage an Existing Menu."

2. Click the red X in the Published column.

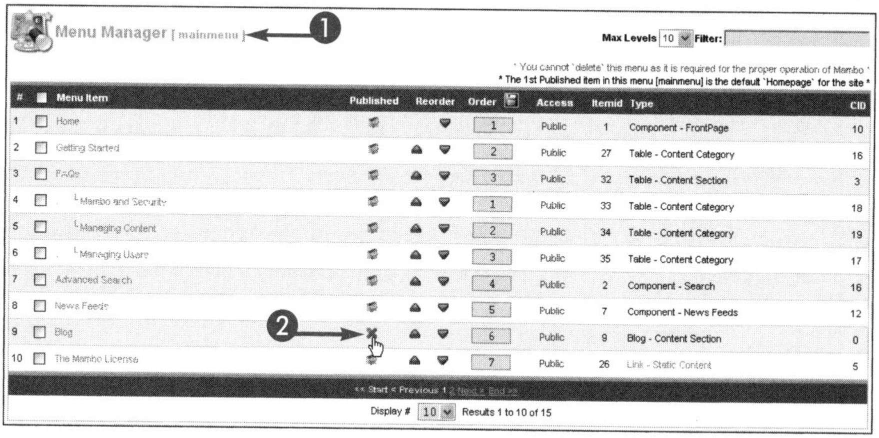

- The red X changes to a blue-and-white icon with a green check mark.

The Item is now published.

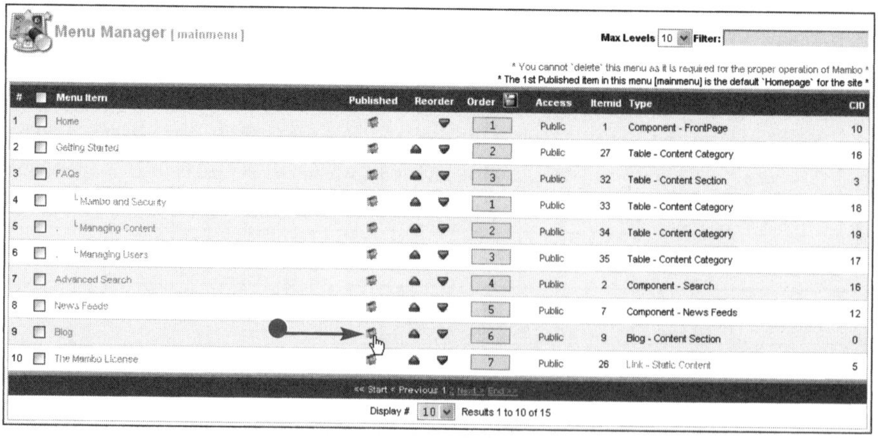

Unpublish a Menu Item

You can remove a Menu Item from public view by unpublishing it. Although the Menu Item remains visible to those who can access the Menu Managers inside the admin system, site visitors cannot see unpublished Menu Items. You can temporarily unpublish items when you need to do maintenance on the site or when you want to update an item. You can permanently unpublish an item when you want to remove it from further display.

Unpublishing a Menu Item only removes the item from the front end of the Web site. It does not delete the item or impair your ability to publish the Menu Item again if you should choose to do so. Unpublished Menu Items are held in the system like any other Menu Item, and there is no difference in the way unpublished items are managed in the administration system. If you want to edit an unpublished Menu Item, you cannot see the results on the front end of the Web site until you republish the Menu Item. Note that unpublishing a Menu Item may disable a link to a Content Item, but it does not itself unpublish the Content Item. Site visitors can still access published Menu Items regardless of the state of the Menu Items, by either clicking other links or through direct access such as bookmarks.

There are two ways to unpublish a Menu Item. You can unpublish a Menu Item with one click directly on the Publish icon that is visible on the Menu Item Manager. You can also unpublish a Menu Item by opening the Menu Item editing screen and disabling the Publish parameters inside the editing window. The result of both techniques is the same, but unpublishing an item directly from the Menu Items Manager is the faster method, and is, therefore shown in the steps in this section.

Unpublish a Menu Item

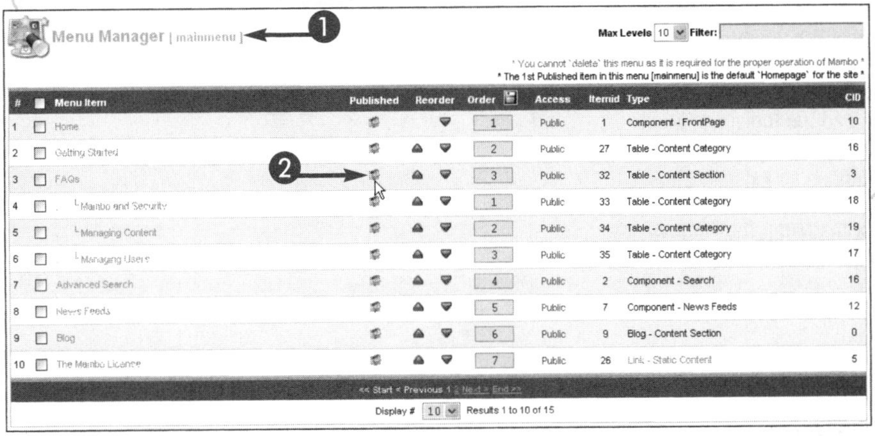

1. Load the Individual Menu Manager, which contains the Menu Item you want to unpublish.

Note: To load the Individual Menu Manager, see the section "Manage an Existing Menu."

2. Click the icon with the green check mark in the Published column.

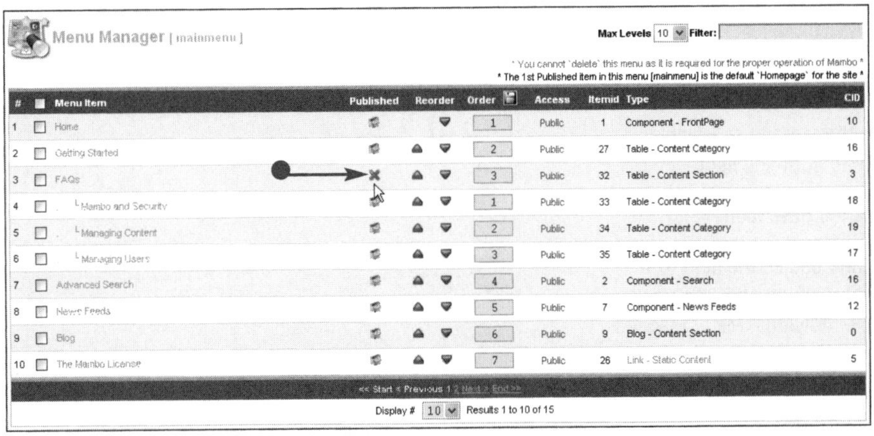

- The blue-and-white icon with a green check mark changes to a red X.

The item is now unpublished.

Duplicate a Menu Item

You can copy a Menu Item with the Individual Menu Managers. The Menu Manager's Copy function duplicates one or more Menu Items simultaneously, which is very useful for building your site by creating new Menu Items with the same attributes as an existing Menu Item, or for creating redundant navigation links on different menus.

You can quickly duplicate a Menu Item by select the Menu Item and then activating the Copy icon. Mambo then prompts you to select the menu you want to copy the Menu Item to, and once you do so, copies it immediately so that it appears on the list of Menu Items in the Menu Item Manager. The new Menu Item shares all the attributes and Menus of the original Menu Item.

After you create a new Menu Item with the Copy command, you can change the name and edit the item. On the front end of the Web site, the Menu Item visually appears in a manner consistent with the original Menu Item. Using the Copy command guarantees that you create new Menu Items efficiently and consistently because copying Menu Items is easier than synchronizing the attributes of a number of new Menu Items if you were to create them from scratch one by one via the Menu Item Manager's New command. For more information on how to create Menu Items using the New command, see the section "Add an Item to a Menu."

Note that the Copy function is very similar to the Move function, discussed in the next section, the difference being that the Move command moves the Menu Item to a new menu, removing them from the original menu whereas the Copy command duplicates, and if instructed, moves the Menu Item, leaving the original Menu Item in place on the original menu.

Duplicate a Menu Item

1. Load the Individual Menu Manager that contains the Menu Item you want to duplicate.

Note: To load the Individual Menu Manager, see the section "Manage an Existing Menu."

2. Click the Menu Item you want to duplicate.
3. Click the Copy icon.

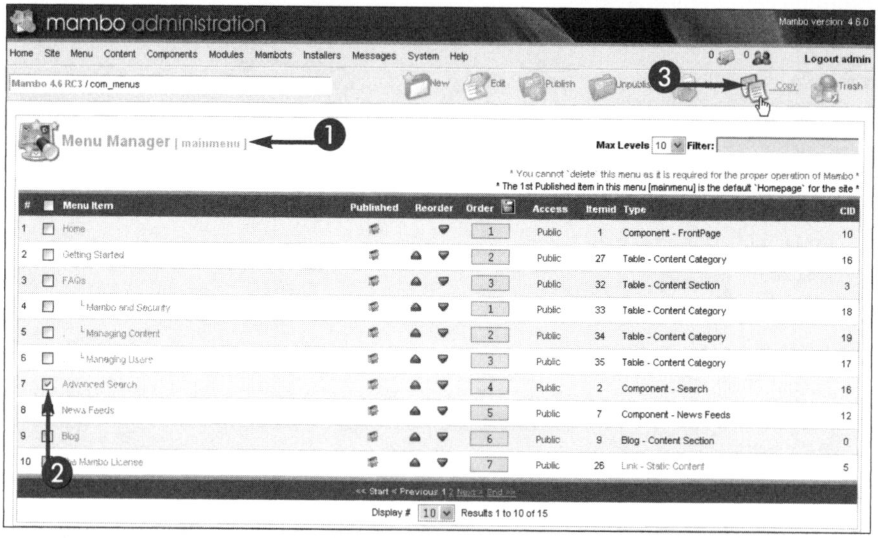

A new screen loads.

4. Select the menu to which you want to copy the item.
5. Click the Save icon.

Mambo copies the item to the selected menu and returns you to the Individual Menu Manager.

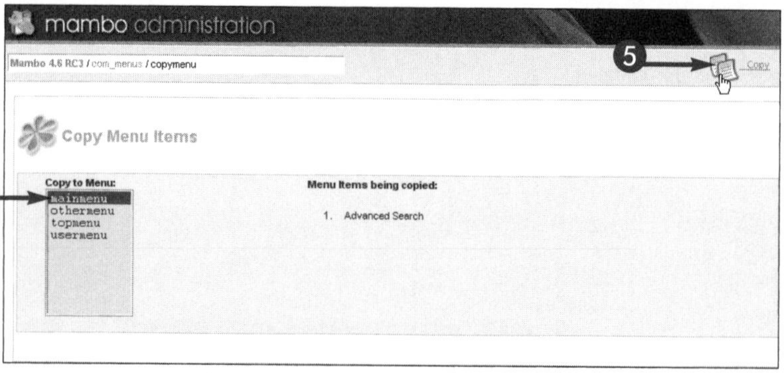

Move a Menu Item

You can move any Menu Item in the system from one menu to any other menu in the system. The Move command is located in the Individual Menu Managers and is very similar to the Copy function, discussed in the preceding section. The key difference between the two commands is that the Move command not only moves the Menu Item to a new menu, but it also removes the Menu Item from the original menu. The Copy command duplicates the Menu Item and then, if so instructed, moves the Menu Item as well, leaving the original Menu Item in place on the original menu. The Move command saves you time and effort by moving a Menu Item where you need it, rather than have you deleting and re-creating the item.

When you initiate the Move command, the system displays a list showing the names of the various menus in the system. You must select a menu where you want to move the Menu Item and then confirm the action. Failure to confirm the move simply leaves the Menu Items where they are.

Moving a Menu Item does not affect the name, the formatting, or the contents of the item. Also, the Menu Item retains its published state; that is, if you published the item before the move, it remains published after the move.

The menu to which you want to move the Menu Items must already exist before you can move Menu Items to the menu. Note also that if the menu to which you move the items is unpublished, then the Menu Items moved into that menu may not be visible on the front end of the Web site until you publish the menu.

Move a Menu Item

1. Load the Individual Menu Manager from which you want to move the Menu Item.

Note: To load the Individual Menu Manager, see the section "Manage an Existing Menu."

2. Select a Menu Item.
3. Click the Move icon.

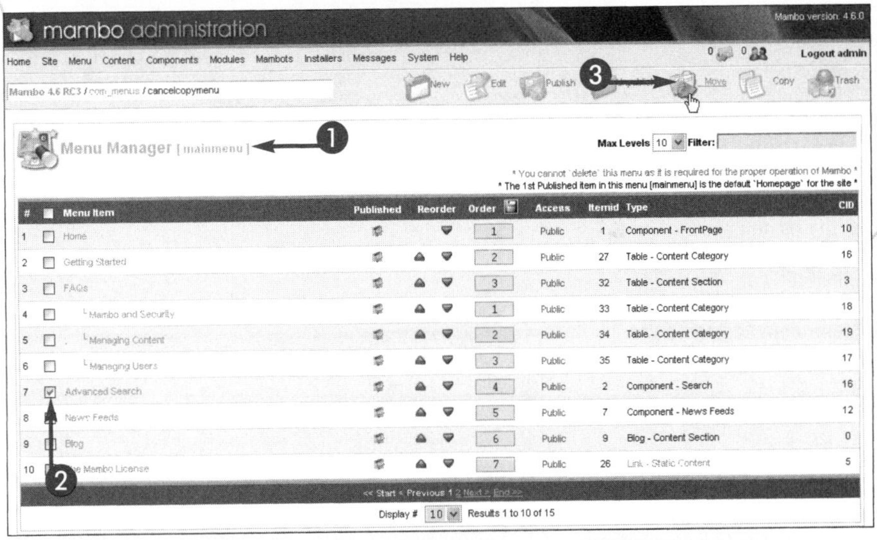

A new screen loads.

4. Select the menu to which you want to move the item.
5. Click the Move icon.

Mambo removes the item from the original menu and moves it to the new Menu, returning you to the original Individual Menu Manager.

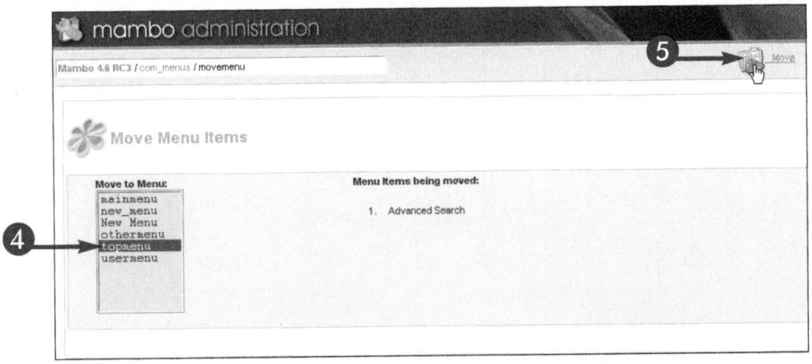

Control Content Table Formats

If your site uses Menu Items employing the Content Table format, you can configure the layout of the table and the options that appear with it. The Content Table format option is a popular and practical choice for displaying Content Items from a section or category. There are a number of table parameters that enable you to customize the table display to fit your site's layout.

The Content Table format parameters are accessed via the Menu Item Editing or Creation screens. The relevant parameters are located on the bottom half of the Parameters column. The Date, Author, and Hits Column parameters enable you to hide or display the various data. The Table Headings parameter determines whether the table appears with data labels in the header. The Navigation Bar parameter the display of a set of links that let the user page through the Content Items using Next/Previous buttons or page numbers. The Order Select and Display Select parameters determine whether the user is given options to control the ordering and number of items displayed. The Display Number parameter determines the number of items that display. The Filter options enable you to provide users with a search tool and to specify what it will search.

If you select the Menu Item format Table–Content category, there are an additional set of options at the very bottom of the Parameters column. The options are all category-related and control whether a hyperlink to the other categories in the section will display and, if so, in what format.

By default, the Mambo system enables all the options relating to the display of the tables. You may not want to display all the options on every site.

Control Content Table Formats

1. Load the Individual Menu Manager that contains the Menu Items you want to format.

Note: To load the Individual Menu Manager, see the section "Manage an Existing Menu."

2. Select the Menu Item.
3. Click the Edit icon.

The Menu Item Editing screen loads.

4. Set the parameters you want.
5. Click the Save icon.

Mambo saves the changes and returns you to the Individual Menu Manager.

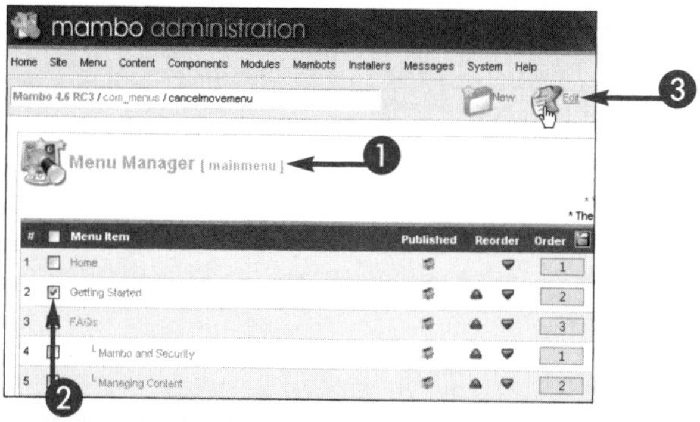

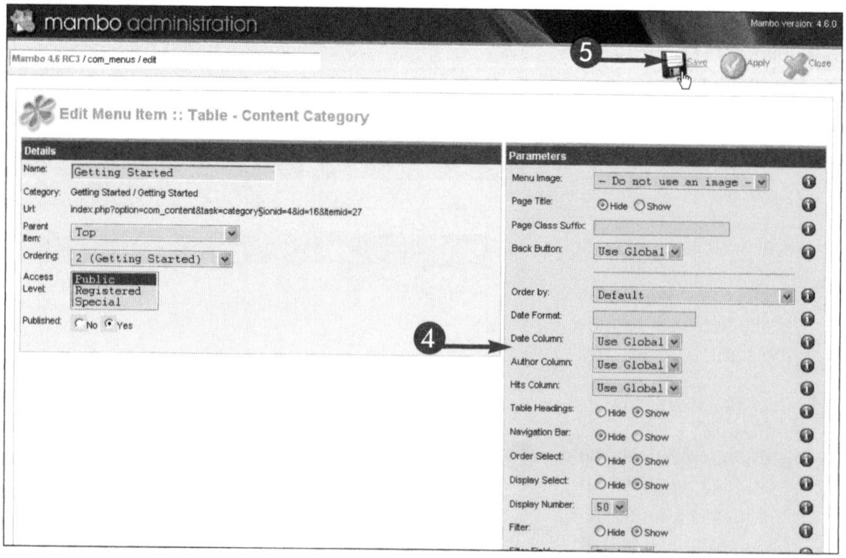

Create a Multi-Level Menu

You can automatically create menus that employ multiple levels of items nested one within the other. Menus with multiple levels are a popular way of creating subnavigation within a convenient, logical, and space-saving format.

Mambo allows administrators to add new Menu Items to menus and to specify the relationship of items to each other. Items at higher levels are called parent items, and those below are called children.

You can establish parent-child relationships between Menu Items at any time. By creating parent-child relationships between Menu Items you can create a hierarchy of Menu Items with two or more nested tiers. For example, if you want to create a site where the highest level is the grouping Food, within the Food group you can have subtopics for Entrees, Mains, and Desserts. Inside each subtopic you have Content Items for the individual recipes. Using the Menu Manager you can create a Menu item named Food, and then create children items named Entrees, Mains, and Desserts. You can create further Menu Items linked to the Content Items, which are children to the parents Entrees, Mains, and Desserts.

You can see another example in action in the default deployment of Mambo. In the Mambo admin system under the Content Menu, you find a child named Content by Section, which in turn has a child named Getting Started, which also has a child named Getting Started Items. As you position your mouse over each item in turn, the next level of subnavigation appears.

Parameters in the module enable you to specify whether the nested levels are hidden by default, as in the Mambo admin system example, or whether the menu is expanded by default.

Create a Multi-Level Menu

1. Load the Individual Menu Manager to which you want to add a multi-level menu.

Note: To load the Individual Menu Manager, see the section "Manage an Existing Menu."

2. Select the Menu Item you want to move to the second level.

3. Click the Edit icon.

The Menu Item Editing screen loads.

4. Click here and select the parent item.

5. Click the Save icon.

Mambo demotes the Menu Item to the second level and returns you to the Individual Menu Manager.

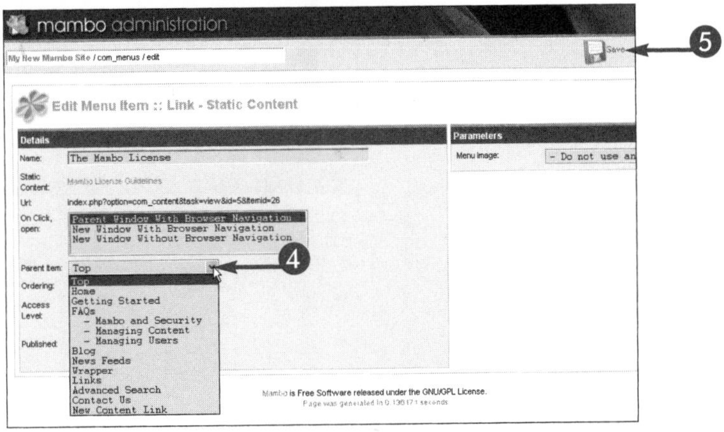

Using Images in Menus

You can configure your system to automatically display small images alongside the subnavigation links in your menus to give your site visitors a visual navigation presentation. Images specified by the Indent Image commands appear immediately to the left of the name of the Menu Item when the menu is expanded, making this option an easy way to customize and improve the appearance of the menus on your site. The Indent Image option is limited to no more than six levels of subnavigation.

Like most other options relating to the formatting of the menu itself, the Indent Images commands are parameters located in the Menu module. The command affects only child items in your menus; that is, subnavigation or Menu Items below the top level in your navigation hierarchy. The Mambo system provides several options, including options for using either the system's default images, a custom selection from images uploaded by the user, or images specified in the template's CSS file.

The system's default images are located inside the /images/M_images directory. The Mambo system offers a number of choices for the Indent Images command. If you find the default images insufficient or inappropriate for your needs, you can upload your own images to the M_images directory and select your images for use in the subnavigation. Moving images to the M_images directory requires you to work outside of the Mambo system because the Mambo Media Manager does not connect with the M_images directory.

If you specify subnavigation images in your template's CSS file, you must select the Template option in the Indent Image parameter, because this overrides the system's insertion of default images and prevents a conflict with the images designated in your style sheet.

Using Images in Menus

1. Click Modules.
2. Click Site Modules.

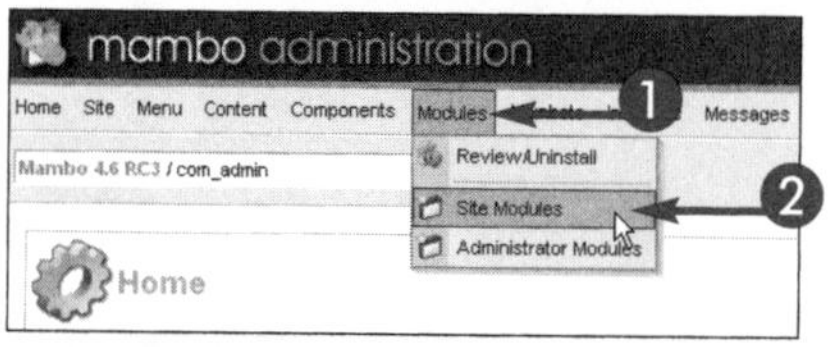

The Module Manager loads.

3. Select the Menu Module for the menu you want to format.
4. Click the Edit icon.

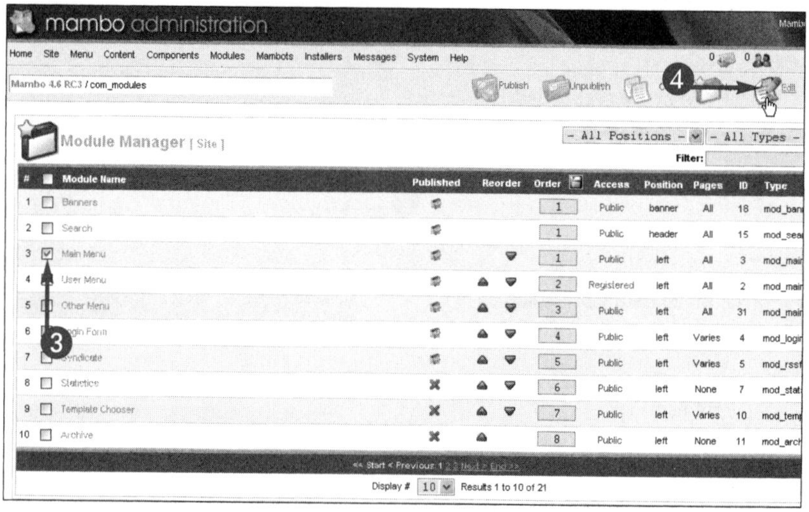

The Module Editing screen loads.

5. Select the source for the Indent Images parameter.

Note: If you select the Use Params Below option, you must also set the specific images for various levels using the combo boxes for each level of child menu Items.

6. Click the Save icon.

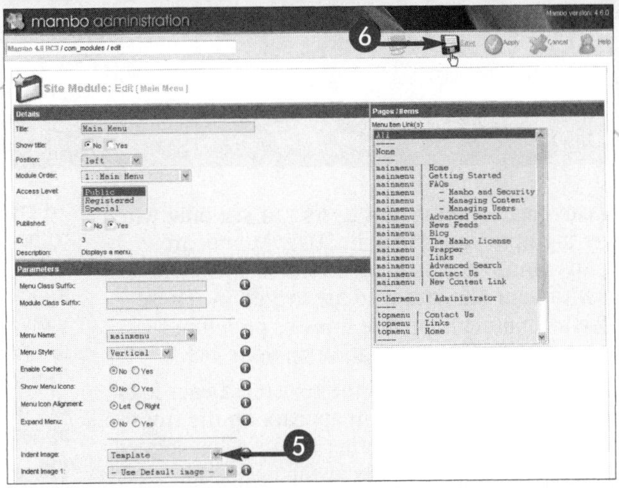

Mambo saves your changes and returns you to the Module Manager.

- On the front end of the Web site, the images are now active on the child Menu Items.

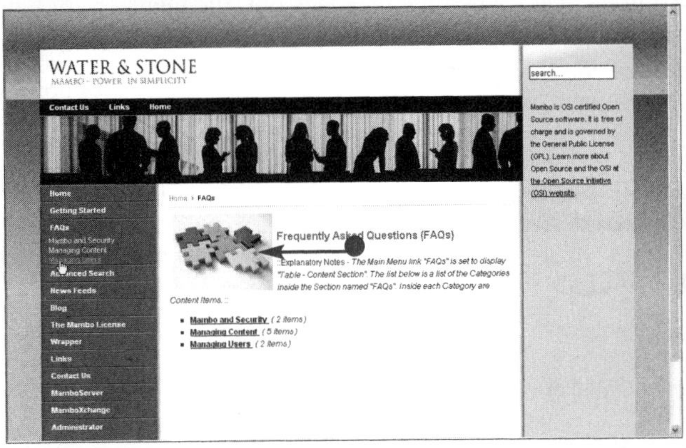

Extra

If you want to upload your own images to use for the subnavigation, keep the image size small. The default images in the system are 9 x 9 pixels. You can use any image format you like for your Indent Images, but the best practice is to use either the GIF or PNG format with the background transparent.

If you want to specify Indent Images in your template's CSS, you should package the images along with the template files. Place your template images inside the /images directory in the template directory. If you include the images with the template, you can install the entire package at one time instead of having to install the template and then move the images up separately. Using the CSS to specify the images is, from a purist's perspective, the best approach to the problem because you can control the spacing alignment and other attributes of the image from within the CSS. If you use the system to handle the Indent Images, you have little control.

Create a User Menu

You can create menus that users can see only when they log in to your Web site. User Menus are menus whose access is restricted to users who are registered with your site and who are logged in. These menus effectively provide private links or premium information to encourage registration on your site.

User Menus remain hidden until the registered user logs in to the Web site. The User Menu appears on the front end of the site regardless of whether the user has logged in via the front end Login Module or the back end Administrator's login. When the user logs out, the menu and the Menu Items hide again.

Mambo gives you the option to create either restricted-access Menu Items or entire restricted-access menus.

To create an effective user menu, you need to limit access to both the menu and the Menu Items it contains. If you restrict access to the menu only, the menu does not appear until users log in; however, it is possible they can view the pages to which the Menu Items link, either as a result of links from other items, or by bookmarking the items or otherwise accessing them directly. If you restrict the Menu Items but not the menu, the menu heading appear, even when the links do not.

The configuration option that enables you to restrict access to a menu is located in the Menu Module. Like other areas of the Mambo system, you can choose between Public, Registered, and Special access. For more information about how access levels relate to user privileges, see Chapter 4.

Create a User Menu

RESTRICT ACCESS TO A MENU

1. Click Modules.
2. Click Site Modules.

The Module Manager loads.

3. Change the access level of the module to Registered by clicking the Access column.

- The label changes to *Registered* and the access is now restricted.

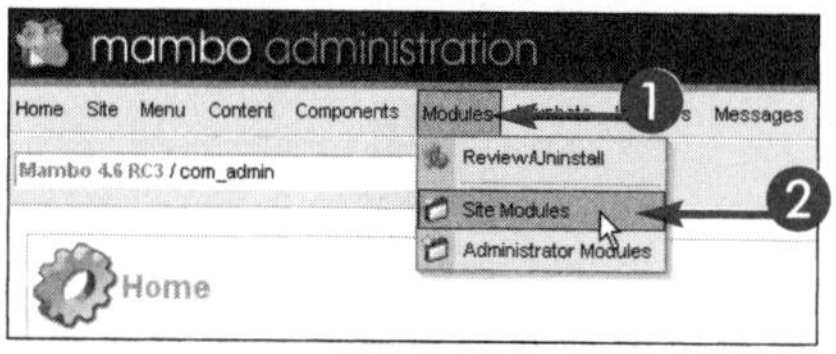

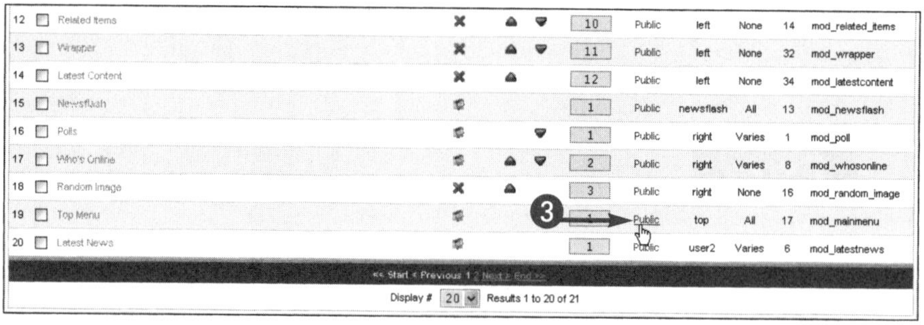

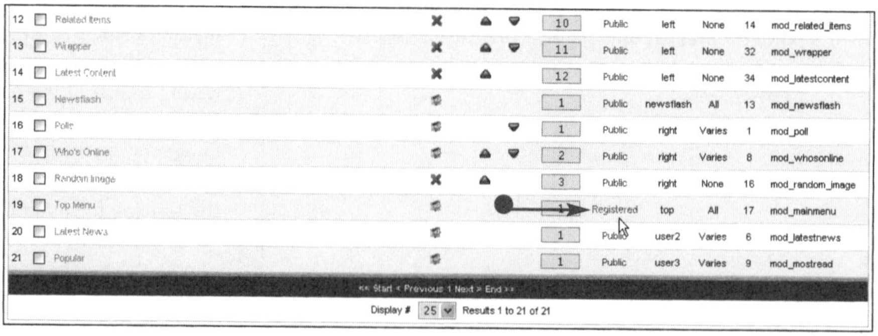

RESTRICT ACCESS TO MENU ITEMS

1. Load the Individual Module Manager for the new restricted-access menu.

Note: To load the Individual Menu Manager, see the section "Manage an Existing Menu."

2. Change the access level of the Menu Items to Registered by clicking the Access column.

   - The label changes to *Registered* and the access is now restricted.

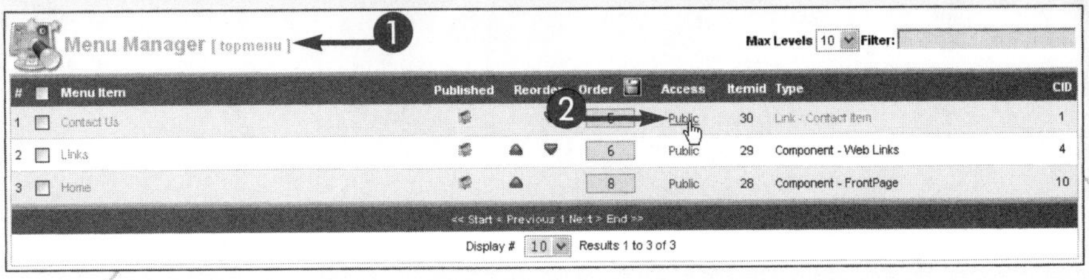

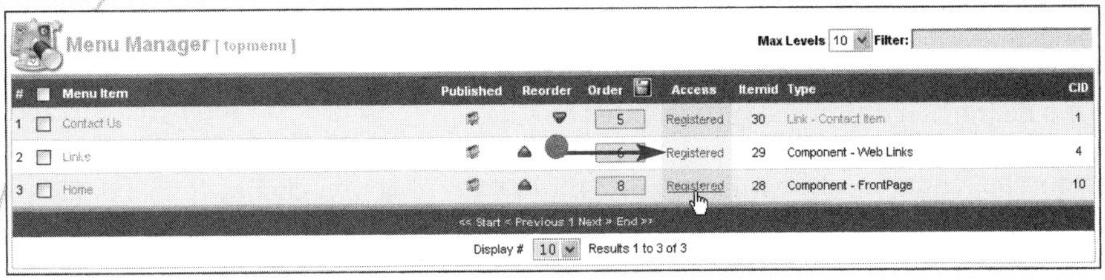

Extra

Although the example in this section deals with the creation of a menu that is restricted to Registered users, you can use the same technique to create a menu that is restricted to Special users. Special users, as discussed in Chapter 4, are those who belong to a user group with a higher level of access than the Registered group. Restricting access to the Special category is typically done when creating a menu containing Menu Items intended for users who are authorized to add, edit, or publish Content Items from the front end of your Web site. In the sample data included with the default Mambo installation, the User Menu is actually a mix of Registered and Special User functionality.

The Global Configuration Manager includes an option that affects the creation of restricted-access Menu Items. The option Show Unauthorized Links overrides the hiding of restricted-access Menu Items. The option, when selected, shows users restricted Menu Items on the menu but does not let them click and view the pages that the Items link to. When the user clicks an item for which they do not have access, they are prompted to log in.

Delete a Menu

You can delete and remove a menu completely from your Mambo system. Deleting a menu cleans unwanted clutter from your admin interface and helps you keep your Master Menu Manager organized without the distraction of unused or unwanted menus. Admin systems with numerous unused menus or Menu Items tend to be harder to work with and present more possibilities for confusion or mistakes.

Before you delete a menu, be warned that this automatically removes all Menu Items attached to that menu, whether published, unpublished, or located in the Trash Manager. Deleting a menu also deletes the associated menu module, so be certain you want to eliminate all those items before you delete the menu. To identify whether your menu contains any items you want to keep, view the Master Menu Manager. The Master Menu Manager displays a list of all the menus in the system along with an indication of whether each of those menus contains any Menu Items. The Menu Manager shows how many items are in each menu, the number of items that are active, and the number located in the Trash Manager.

If you choose to delete the menu, Mambo prompts to you to confirm the deletion and lists all the Menu Items that it will delete along with the menu. Check the list carefully. If you want to preserve any of the Menu Items, move them to another menu, or restore them from the Trash Manager and then move them to another menu. For more on how to move items between menus, see the section "Move a Menu Item." For more on how to restore items sent to the Trash, see the section "Restore a Menu Item from the Trash Manager."

Delete a Menu

1. Click Menu.
2. Click Menu Manager.

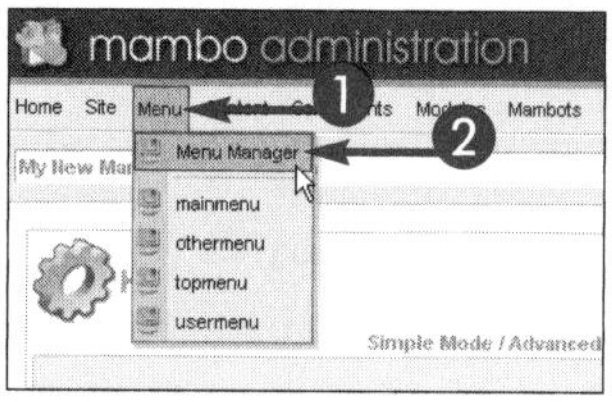

The Master Menu Manager loads.

3. Select the menu you want to delete.
4. Click the Delete icon.

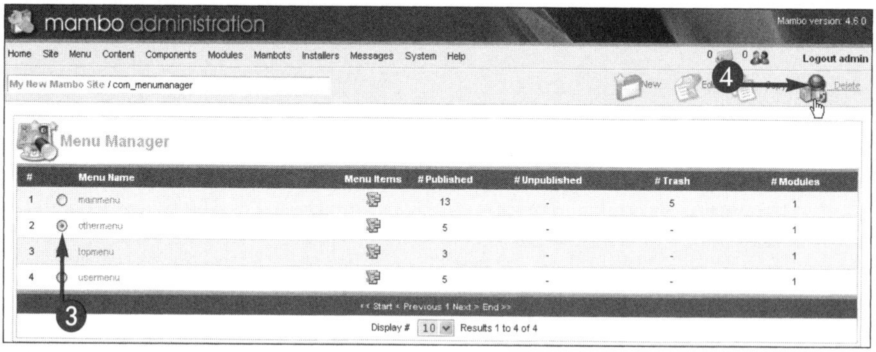

A confirmation window appears.

5. Click the Delete button.

Mambo deletes the menu, its Menu Items, and the associated module.

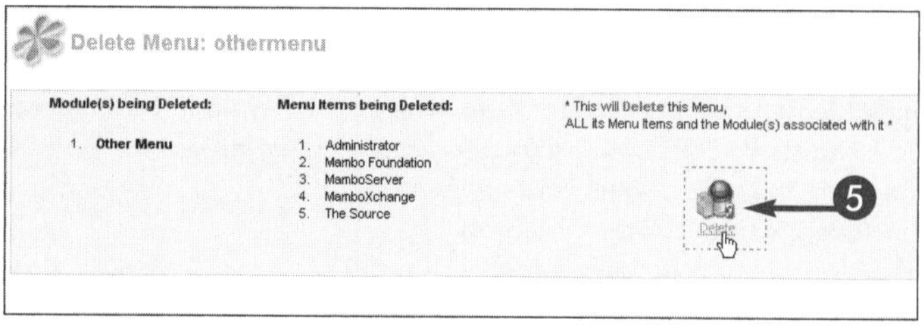

Move a Menu Item to the Trash Manager

You can remove a Menu Item from a menu without deleting it permanently by sending it to the Trash. Sending a Menu Item to the Trash is an easy way to keep your Individual Menu Managers clear of unwanted or unused Menu Items. All Menu Items sent to the Trash are administered through the Trash Manager, which is located under the Site Menu.

Menu Items sent to the Trash are not deleted from the system, but they are unpublished from public view and removed from the menu. The Trash Manager provides only two functionalities: deleting an item permanently or restoring the item. For more information on how to delete an item permanently, see the section "Delete a Menu Item Permanently." For more on how to restore items moved to the Trash Manager, see the section "Restore a Menu Item from the Trash Manager."

You can view a list of the Menu Items relegated to the Trash Manager via the Menu Items tab by visiting the Trash Manager. Viewing the Menu Item itself, however, requires you to restore the item to the Menu Item Manager.

Note that when you elect to move a Menu Item to the Trash, you are not asked for confirmation by the system. Instead, as soon as you click the Trash icon, Mambo immediately moves the Menu Item. Be sure not to unnecessarily move items to the Trash because Mambo unpublishes them immediately and renders them unavailable to your site visitors. To make the Menu Item visible again on the front end of the Web site, you must go through the process of restoring the item. For more information on restoring a Menu Item, see the next section "Restore a Menu Item from the Trash Manager."

Move a Menu Item to the Trash Manager

1. Load the Individual Menu Manager.

Note: To load the Individual Menu Manager, see the section "Manage an Existing Menu."

2. Select the Menu Item you want to move to the Trash.
3. Click the Trash icon.

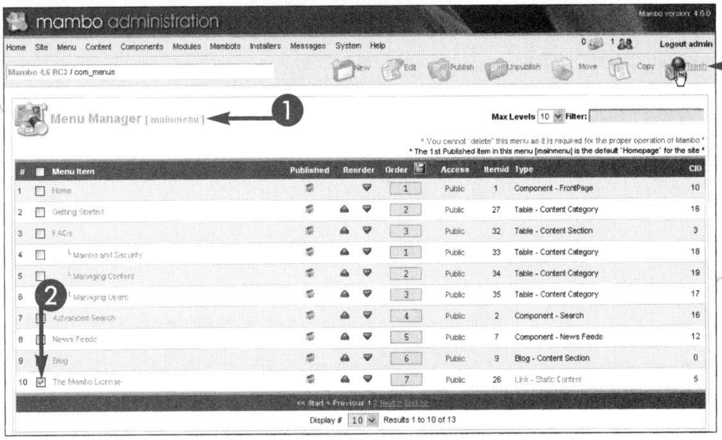

- Mambo removes the item from the Individual Menu Manager and moves it to the Trash Manager.

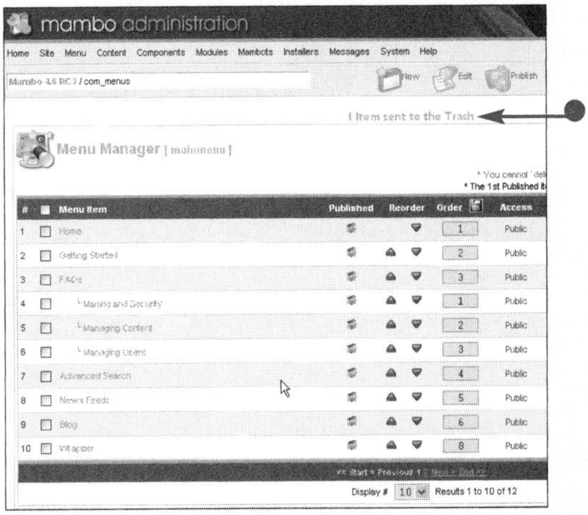

Restore a Menu Item from the Trash Manager

You can move a Menu Item previously sent to the Trash from the Trash Manager and send it back to the live area of your Web site. The process of moving an item from the Trash Manager back to functionality is called *restoring* a Menu Item. You execute the Restore command from within the Trash Manager and as a results, the Menu Item moves back to the specific menu from which it was removed and becomes visible and active in the Individual Menu Manager. The Restore command is particularly a blessing where you have unintentionally deleted a Menu Item from the Individual Menu Manager.

Menu Items are stored apart from Content Items in the Trash Manager. The Menu Items tab lists all the Menu Items held in the Trash Manager. The Menu Items page tells you the item names, as well as the menus they came from and the type of item — that is, the Menu Item Format. When you select a Menu Item and use the Restore command, the system requires confirmation, after which it immediately moves the Menu Item back to the menu where it appeared originally. Newly restored Menu Items are unpublished and default to the last place in the order of items. Once restored, a Menu Item is fully functional, meaning that you can view, publish, edit, copy, or move it within the system. For more information on how to send Menu Items to the Trash, see the section "Move a Menu Item to the Trash Manager."

To make a restored Menu Item visible to your site visitors, you need to publish the Menu Item. For more information on publishing Menu Items, see the section "Publish a Menu Item."

Restore a Menu Item from the Trash Manager

1. Click Site.
2. Click Trash Manager.

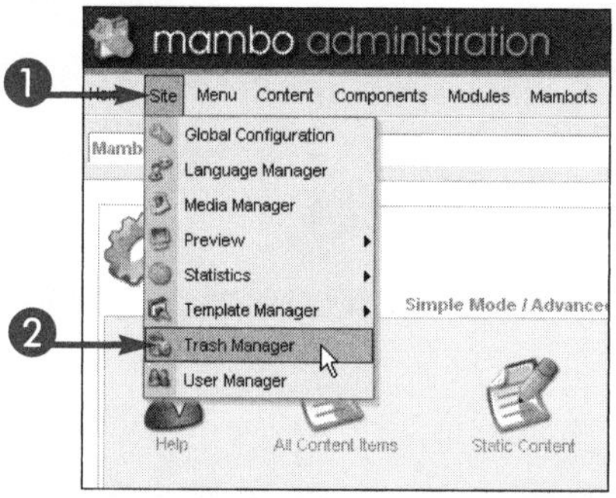

The Trash Manager loads.

3. Click the Menu Items tab.

The Menu Items list loads.

4. Select the Menu Item.
5. Click the Restore icon.

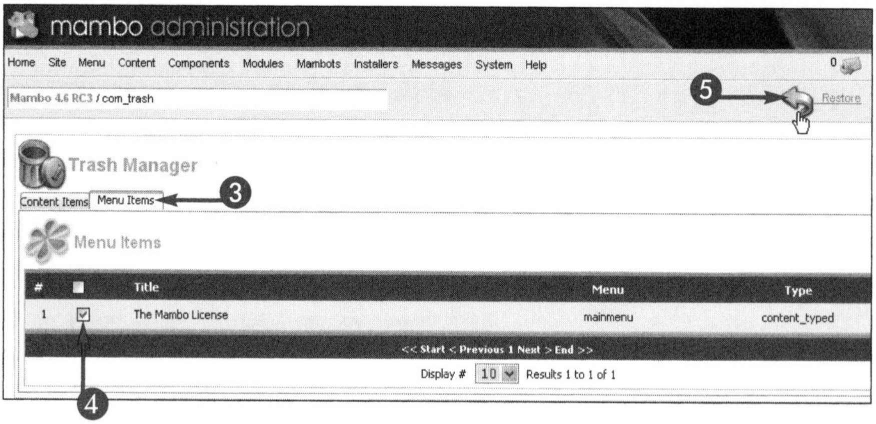

A new screen loads with a summary of the items to be restored.

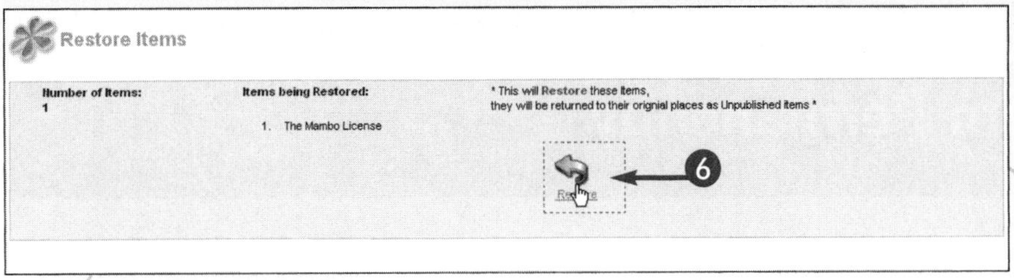

6 Click the Restore icon.

A dialog box asks for confirmation.

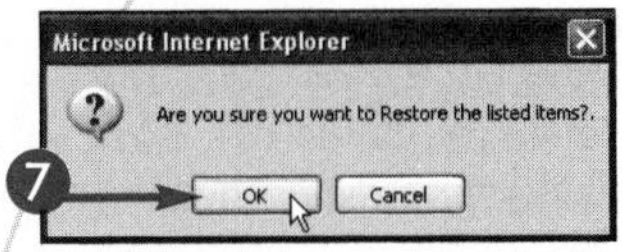

7 Click OK.

Mambo restores the item and returns you to the Trash Manager.

Extra

As clumsy as it may sound, if you want to view a Menu Item to decide whether it is worth restoring, you have no choice but to restore it! There is no preview facility in the Trash Manager, and there is no way to learn more about the link beyond what is presented on the Menu Items tab in the Trash Manager.

An easy way to provide a test bed for new Menu Items and to check Trashed Menu Items is to create a menu that is used only for testing purposes. Set the menu to Unpublished and the access level to Special. Assign the menu to an unobtrusive location and a less-visited page. When you need to test new Menu Items or view old ones you have tossed in the Trash, publish the menu, log in to the admin system, and then visit the front end of the Web site where you placed the menu. As a high-level user, you will be able to see the menu and explore the Menu Items. (With the access set to Special, casual visitors and regular Registered users will not be able to see it.) When you are finished, unpublish the menu.

Delete a Menu Item Permanently

It is possible to delete a Menu Item permanently and remove it from the Trash Manager. Permanent deletion is, as the name implies, final. You cannot restore an item after you have deleted it from the Trash Manager. In line with the finality of the act, Mambo asks you to confirm before final deletion occurs.

Although you may not want to rush into deleting items, there are times when it is necessary or desirable. At the most basic, deleting unneeded Menu Items helps keep the system clean of unnecessary files. For small sites, this is a matter of little consequence, but for larger sites, it is a necessary part of site maintenance because it decreases administrator confusion.

You delete a Menu Item permanently from within the Trash Manager; accordingly, the first step is to move the Menu Item to the Trash. For more on how to send an item to the Trash, see the section "Move a Menu Item to the Trash Manager." Access the Menu Items tab in the Trash Manager to see the list of items, then select and delete the items you want to remove completely from the system. Note that if you delete an entire menu, this automatically clears out all Menu Items that were previously on the menu from the Trash Manager. For more on how to delete menus, see the section "Delete a Menu."

Deleting a Menu Item does not delete the Content Item or component that is linked to that Menu Item, and it does not affect the menu on which the Menu Item was located. Deleting a Menu Item also has no impact on any Indent Images held in the system.

Delete a Menu Item Permanently

1. Click Site.
2. Click Trash Manager.

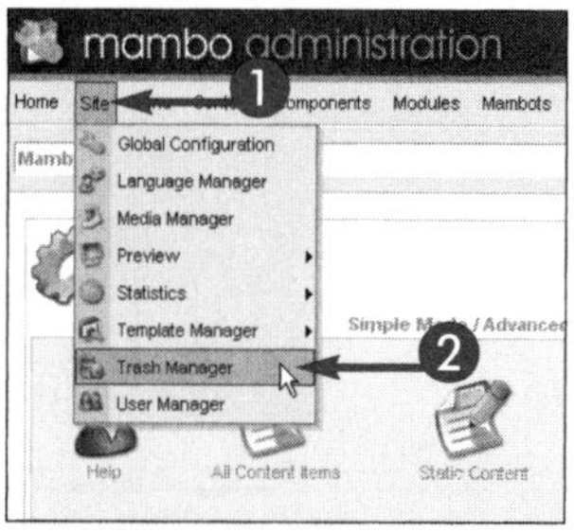

The Trash Manager loads.

3. Click the Menu Items tab.

The Menu Items list loads.

4. Select the Menu Item.
5. Click the Delete icon.

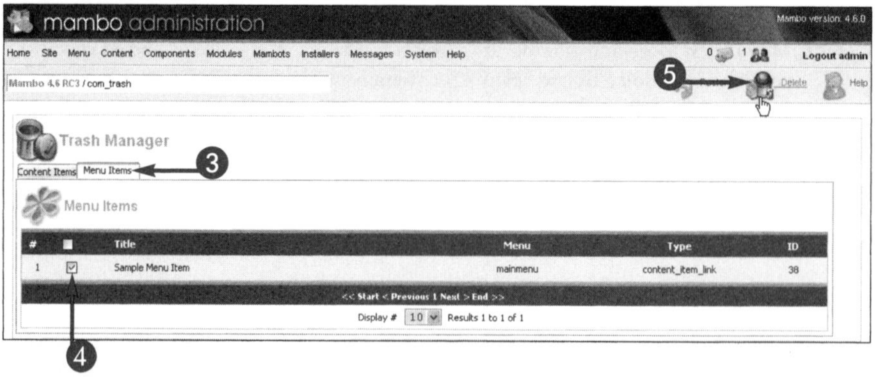

A new screen loads with a summary of the items to be deleted.

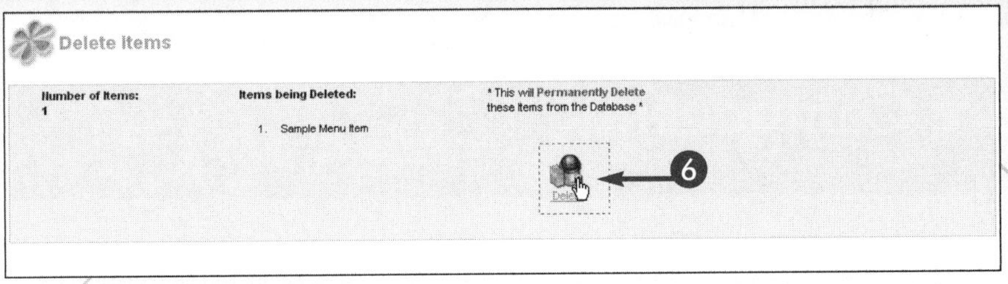

6 Click the Delete button.

A dialog box asks for confirmation.

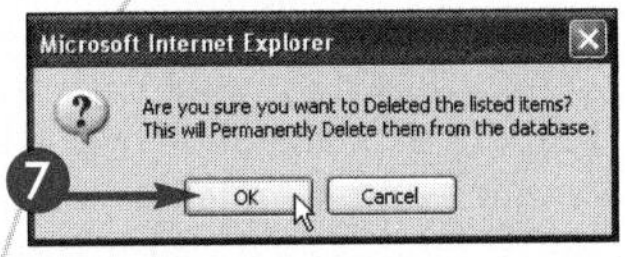

7 Click OK.

Mambo deletes the item permanently and returns you to the Trash Manager.

Extra

Although you are encouraged to keep your site free of unnecessary items, you may find that permanently deleting Menu Items counterproductive, because properly formatted Menu Items represent an investment of energy, and creating new Menu Items with the same configuration is time consuming. Think of your existing Menu Items as templates for future Menu Items. If you have Menu Items that you have configured to your satisfaction and that have usable format in other situations, it is probably worthwhile to keep the items for use in the future. You can keep Items in the Trash Manager indefinitely without harm to your site's performance.

Parent and child Menu Items behave somewhat unusually in the Trash Manager. You can restore a parent item without its child items, but not the other way around. The child items are dependent on the presence of their parent item. If you delete the parent item permanently, the child items still appear in the Trash Manager, but you cannot restore them because their parent item has been deleted.

Understanding Core Components

You can use components to add additional elements of functionality to the Mambo core or to customize the functionality of other features on your site. Typically a component is a self-contained functional unit and most, like the News Feeds component, produce output that appears in the main content area of your templates. Others, like the Mass Mail component, work behind the scenes to power less visible functionality. Still others, like the MOStlyCE Editor component, simply provide configuration options.

You need to configure most components in some manner to enjoy the full benefits of their functionality. Configuration options vary from component to component, consistent with their varied functions. Unlike modules and Mambots, you do not need to publish components. Once you install and configure a component, it is generally ready to go to work. Note also that, unlike modules and Mambots, there is no Components Manager interface. Each component is independent, and you must deal with it separately via the links to the component off the Admin navigation.

Menu Items and Components

If a component's output appears in the main content area of your template, you must create a Menu Item to link to the component for site visitors to see the output. In the default deployment, links are already in place to the Contacts, News Feeds, and Weblinks components. If you create a new Menu Item and select the Component option for the Menu Item type, in the list that appears, you find several components that are not on the Components menu. The Component list on the New Menu Item Creation screen shows all the items on the Components menu as well as Search and Login. While neither Search nor Login have a configuration screen, you can link directly to them if you want them to appear in the main content area. If you install the sample data in the default Mambo site, the menu includes a link to Advanced Search that connects to the Search component. The list of components in the New Menu Item Creation screen also includes links to MOStlyCE and MOStlyDB; however, you should not try to create a menu item linking to those components because no output will appear on the front end of the Web site from either component. For more on creating Menu Items, see Chapter 9.

Components with Modules or Mambots

Some components work in conjunction with modules or Mambots. The Banners and Polls components, for example, show no output if you do not properly configure and publish their related modules. Similarly, the Syndication component sets up the Syndication function, but you must publish the Syndicate Module for site visitors to gain access to RSS feeds that allow them to view the output of the Syndication function. The MOStlyCE Editor component provides access to the configuration options for the MOStlyCE WYSIWYG Editor, but unless you publish it and enable the MOStlyCE Mambot from the Global Configuration Manager, the component has no affect at all. For more on the modules included with the default Mambo deployment, see Chapter 11. For more on Mambots, see Chapter 13. See Chapter 2 for more on the Global Configuration Manager.

In addition to the default components bundled with your Mambo site, a large number of third-party components are designed to work with the Mambo system. You can download and install components easily and thereby extend your site's functionality. For more on where to find additional components, see Chapter 15. The subject of installing components is covered in the sections "Install a Component Automatically" and "Install a Component Manually," later in the chapter.

The components deployed in the default Mambo installation provide a variety of useful functionality. To help you get started, the following table lists all the components included in a default Mambo site, with a short synopsis of each component's function.

COMPONENT NAME	DESCRIPTION
Banners	Works in conjunction with the Banners module. The component controls the set up of the banner clients and the Banners themselves. The module controls the display of the Banners on the site. You must publish the module to make the component's output visible.
Contacts	Manages the site's Contacts and Contact forms. The component is designed to provide one place where you can manage all Contacts and the parameters associated with their related Contact forms. To see output from this component, the site must include menu items that link to the Contacts.
Mass Mail	Allows the Super Administrator to send emails from within the system to all registered site members.
MOStlyCE	This is ancillary to the MOStlyCE Editor Mambot. The Mambot provides functionality while the component gives access to various configuration options that customize the interface of the editor and the tools. The component has no effect if you do not publish the Mambot of the same name.
MOStlyDBAdmin DB Tools	Enables you to backup, restore, or query your MySQL database from within the Mambo Administration system.
News Feeds	Sets up the aggregation of RSS News Feeds from other sites for display on your site. The output of this component appears in the main content area of the template and requires a Menu Item linked to the component.
Polls	Works in conjunction with the module of the same name. You set up and configure the polls with the component. You use the module to position and control the output. You must publish the Polls module for the output of this component to be visible.
Syndicate	Contains the configuration options for your site's RSS syndication. The settings in this component affect the output that the Syndication function generates, and this output appears to others who subscribe to your RSS feed. To enable the output for your site visitors you must publish the Syndicate module.
Weblinks	Provides a way to organize and categorize links to external Web sites. The output of this component appears in the main content area of the template and requires a Menu Item linked to the component.

Install a Component Automatically

You can automatically install components using the Universal Installer, and in doing so, add functionality to the Mambo core. The Universal Installer allows you to upload preconfigured component packages to your Mambo site. If your component comes bundled with any dependent modules or Mambots, the Universal Installer automatically detects the various plug-ins and installs them into the proper directories. The Universal Installer is the easiest way to install components to extend your Mambo site.

When you obtain a preconfigured component for your Mambo site, it is delivered in the form of a zip file archive. The archive should contain all the files necessary to install and use the new component. If the component has been created properly, you should not need to make any additional changes to get it to function properly, although of course you may need to configure it to fit your needs after installation.

The Universal Installer presents three options to users: Upload Package File, Install from HTTP URL, and Install From Directory. The first option provides for automatic installation of a zip archived component file; the second allows you to input the URL of the archived file and allows the system to retrieve and install the package; and the third option is a manual installation technique, covered in the next section. Note that the first method functions properly only if your server supports GZip or a similar utility that enables extraction of zip file archives. Similarly, the second option is dependent on server settings. If you do not configure your server to permit the access and installation of an archive from another server, this option will not work for you. Although the first and second options are the easiest to use, if your server does not support either option, you need to use manual installation, as detailed in the next section, "Install a Component Manually."

Install a Component Automatically

1. Click Installers.
2. Click Universal.

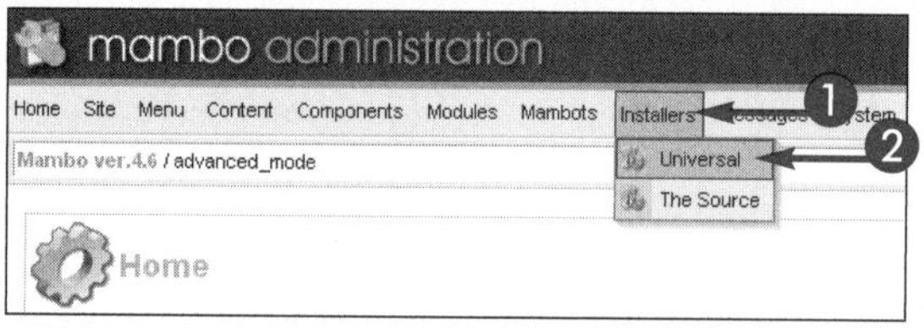

The Universal Installer loads.

- A list of directories, along with an indication of whether they are writeable, appears here.

Note: If any of the directories show as unwriteable you must change the permissions (read/write status) of the directory. For more on how to change file permissions, see Chapter 1.

3. Click Browse.

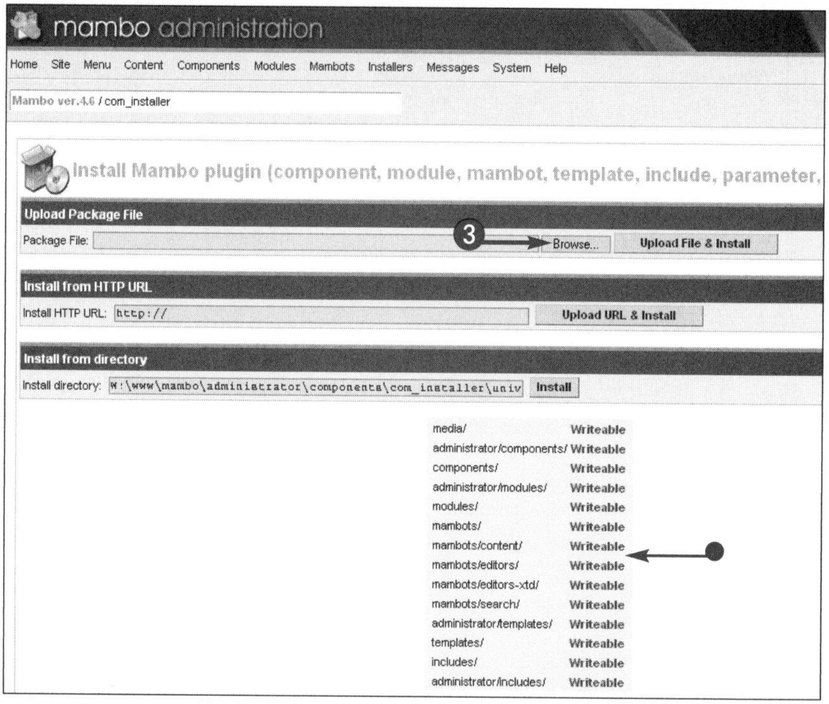

The Choose file dialog box appears.

4 Navigate to the location of the archive.

5 Select the file.

6 Click Open.

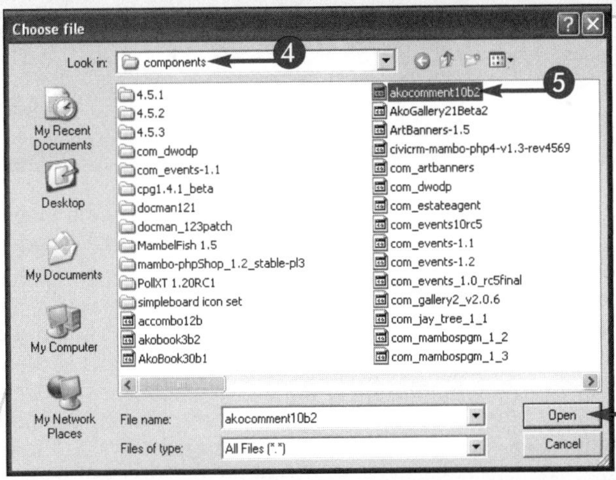

The popup closes and returns you to the Installer.

7 Click Upload File & Install.

If you are successful, you see a confirmation message when the screen reloads.

If you are not successful, you see a message indicating failure.

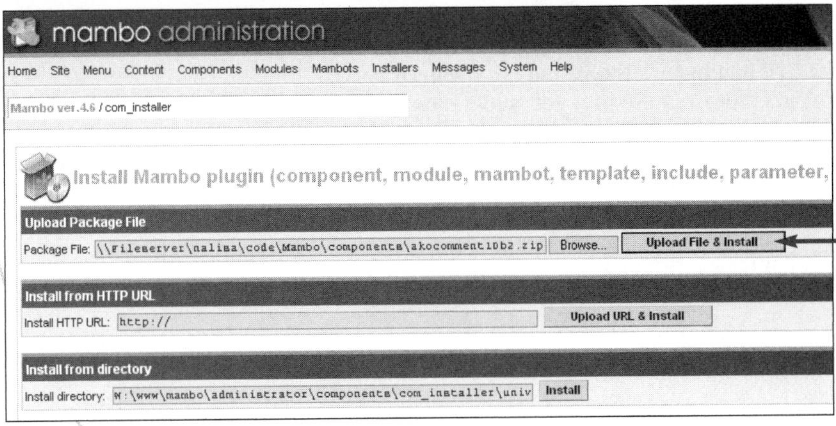

Extra

Components are at the heart of Mambo's functionality. Although the basic system supplies the critical content management and user management functions, the components add the extras. Extending a Mambo site is most often accomplished by adding new components. Unfortunately, users running their sites on servers that are in safe mode sometimes have difficulty installing components. Safe mode restricts your ability to perform certain tasks and some shared Web hosts use the setting as a way to prevent users from harming other Web sites that are installed on the same hardware. Should you encounter problems with the installation of a component, check with your Web host's customer support to verify whether the server is running in safe mode.

Component compatibility is also an issue of concern. Make sure the components you select are compatible with the version of Mambo you are running. Components that work with older versions of Mambo may not work with the newest version. Although it is sometimes tempting to install an old component to see if it works, you are asking for trouble because old components may work, but may leave your site exposed to security problems or create other issues that may not be initially apparent.

Install a Component Manually

You can install components, and thus add functionality to the Mambo core, without the use of the automatic installer described in the previous section, "Install a New Component Automatically." Manual installation is required if your server does not support GZip or another utility for extracting file archives. In certain other circumstances you may want to install a component manually, such as if you have some but not all of the various component files.

You have two options for performing manual installation. You can either use the Install From Directory option in the Universal Installer, or you can simply copy the files to the server by FTP and bypass the Install From Directory function. Both methods require that you move files to the server outside of the Mambo system. The choice of which manual installation method to use depends largely on the nature of the component with which you are working.

You can access the Component Installer through direct links from either the Components or Installers menus.

If you have a proper component package — that is, a component that contains a complete set of properly formed files — you should use the Install From Directory option outlined in this section. If your component files are incomplete, then you cannot use this option; instead, you must transfer the component files to the Mambo Component directory on the server. Note, however, that installing a component without using the Install From Directory function means that you cannot automatically uninstall the component, which forces you to uninstall the files one by one should you decide at some point in the future to delete them from your system. Accordingly, the preferred practice, and the easiest — outside of the upload a package file — is to use the Install From Directory function.

Install a Component Manually

1. If they are zipped, extract the component files from the zip archive.

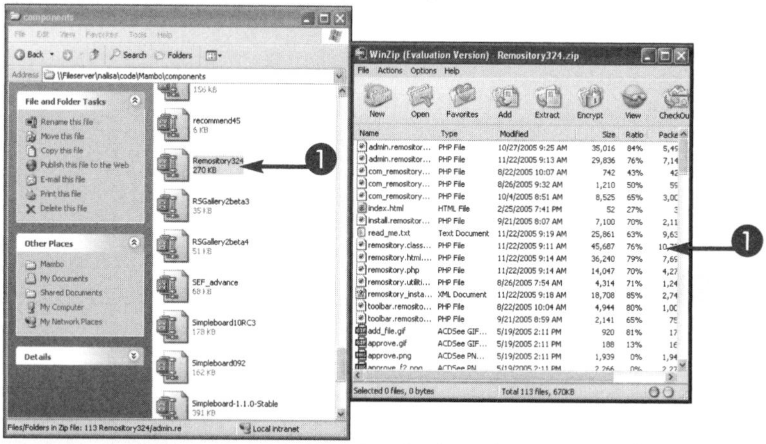

2. Access your server via FTP.
3. Move the component files into the directory and note the location.

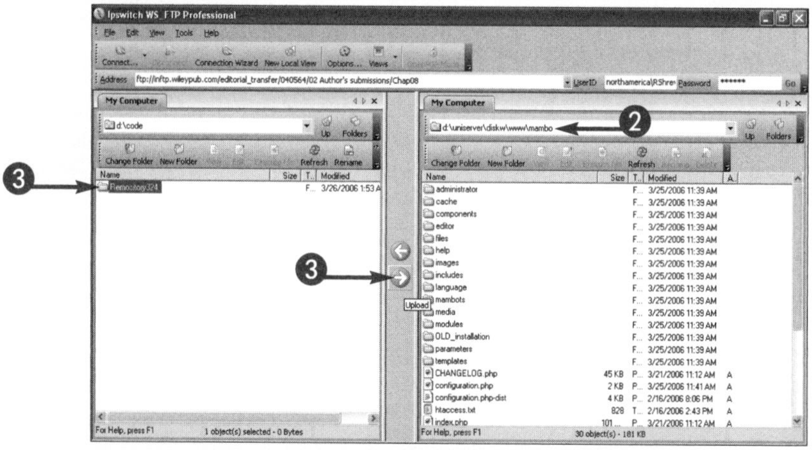

4. Load the Universal Installer.

Note: To Load the Universal Installer, see the section "Install a New Component Automatically."

5. Type the full path to the directory containing the files.

6. Click Install.

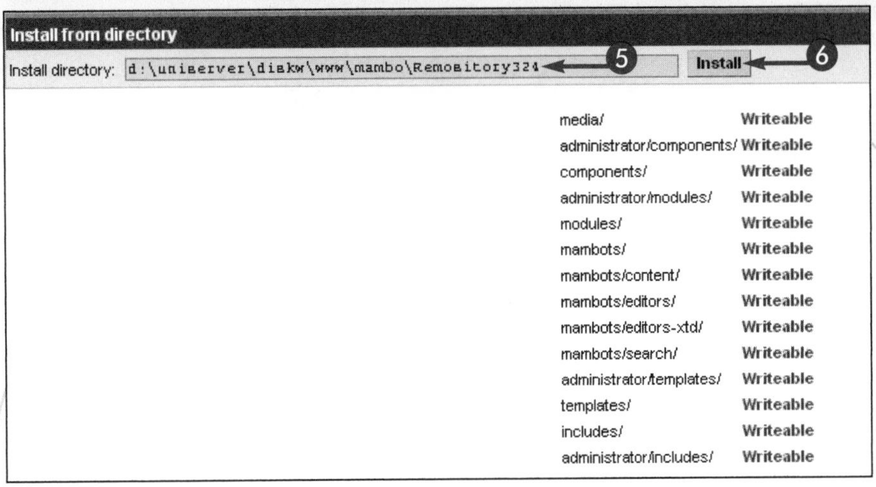

- If you are successful, you see a confirmation message when the screen reloads.

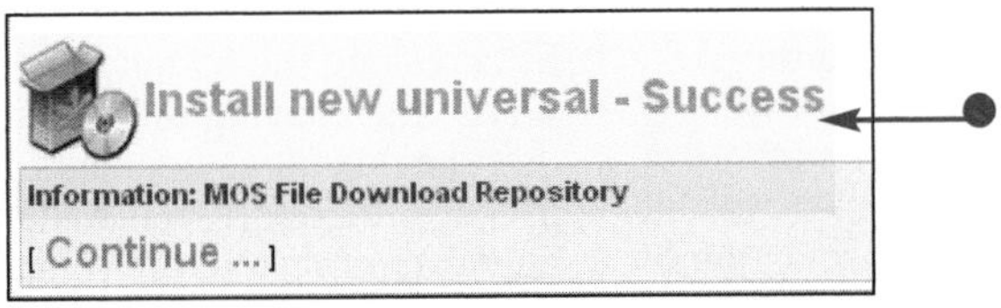

If you are not successful, you see a message indicating failure.

Extra

If you want to build and test your own components, the Install From Directory option is the easiest and fastest installation method. Unlike the Upload Package File and Install from HTTP URL options, the Install From Directory approach does not require a perfectly formed installer package. With the Install From Directory approach, you can transfer the bare minimum of necessary files to your server via FTP and then access the Installer from the Admin system, as discussed earlier.

Unlike templates or Mambots, components often require you to install files in more than one place. Typically a component has files that reside in both the front end and back end of the Web site. Accordingly, you need to make sure you get the right files in the right directories, or else your component will fail. Files for the front end functionality of a component reside in the /components directory. Files for the back end of the Web site reside in the Administrator/components directory. Of course, if you want to delete an installed component manually, you need to check both directories and clean them out.

Uninstall a Component

You can uninstall a component automatically and remove all the files from your server. Removal of a component is desirable when you want to clean up your server and remove unnecessary files, or when you need to install an updated version of the same component.

If you have used the Universal Installer or the Install From Directory functionality, the component removal is easy and automatic. If, on the other hand, you have installed the component manually via FTP without using the Install From Directory functionality, you must uninstall the component manually by accessing the server via FTP and deleting the files you previously moved to the server. A discussion of the Universal Installer is included earlier in the section entitled "Install a New Component Automatically." Manual installation by way of the Install From Directory functionality is covered in the section "Install a New Component Manually."

Unlike Content Items or Menu Items, components are not moved to the Trash Manager upon deletion. Think carefully before you confirm deletion because Mambo completely deletes the component and all of its associated files from your system. The only way to get the component back is to reinstall it from scratch.

Because you cannot undo component deletion, you may want to leave the component in the system, unused. If you do not publish a component, the files are completely inactive and do not impair your site's performance.

Alternatively, you can backup the files prior to deletion by accessing the Mambo Components directories on the server and copying the files to your local machine. Note that the default components have no separate installation package; therefore, reinstallation from a backup is the only way to restore the components once you delete them. For more on backing up your Mambo site, see Chapter 14.

Uninstall a Component

1. Click Components.
2. Click Review/Uninstall.

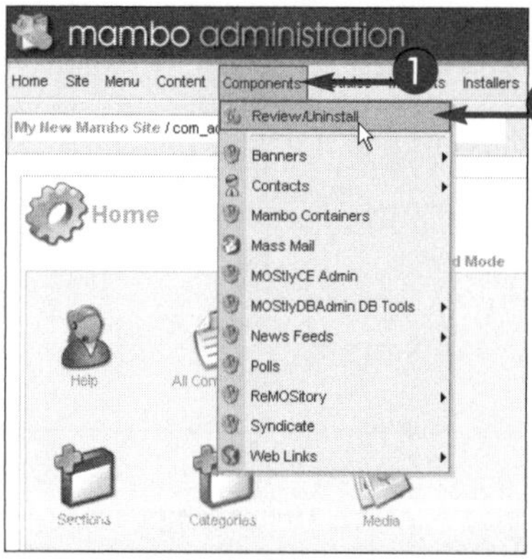

The Installed Components screen loads.

3. Click the component you want to uninstall.
4. Click the Uninstall icon.

Mambo deletes the component and all of its parts from the system.

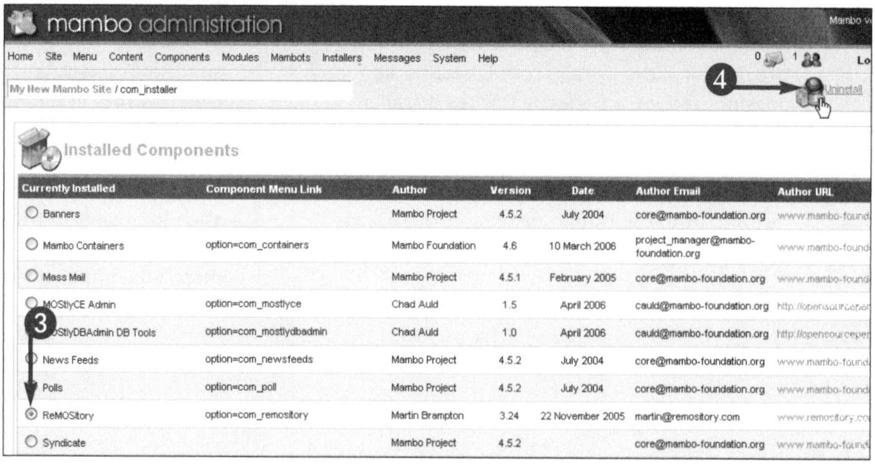

Create and Manage Banner Clients

You can create and manage clients for your banner ads by using the Banner component. The first step in setting up Banner ads on your Mambo site is to create at least one banner client. You create and subsequently edit and modify banner clients by means of the Banner component. Banner ads are tied to banner clients in the Mambo system. Banner ads are useful for displaying marketing messages on your site and may even provide a source of revenue when your site traffic is sufficient to merit sales of banner space.

The Banner Component and its related module are both active by default in the Mambo installation package. If you installed the sample data at setup, you will see them on banners at the bottoms of the pages in the site. If you publish the Banners module, but do not install the sample data because the component has no clients and no banners, nothing appears on the site.

Because you must assign banners to clients, you must create at least one client prior to uploading any banners to set up the new banner. You create new clients from within the Banner component, under the heading Manage Clients. The system requires you to supply only a name for the client, a contact for the client, and an email address for the contact. The New Client Creation screen also includes a field for notes and extra information, but the fields are optional.

The Banner system is very basic and does not, for example, allow you to tie campaigns to clients. Accordingly, you may find it useful to think of clients in terms of campaigns — that is, to create a separate client for each campaign, thereby facilitating individual configuration and tracking of each campaign.

Create and Manage Banner Clients

1. Click Components.
2. Click Banners.
3. Click Manage Clients.

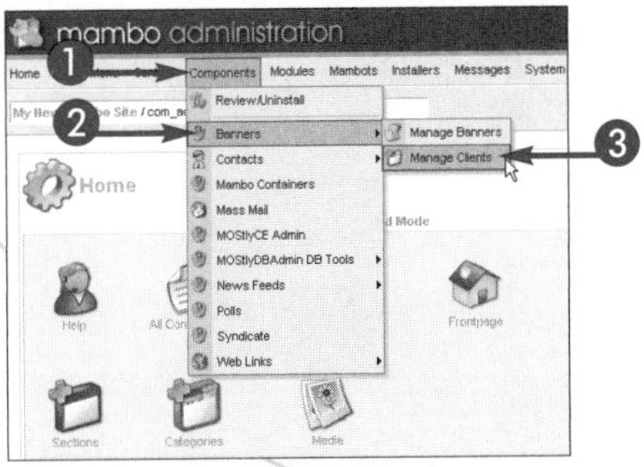

The Banner Client Manager loads.

4. Click the New icon.

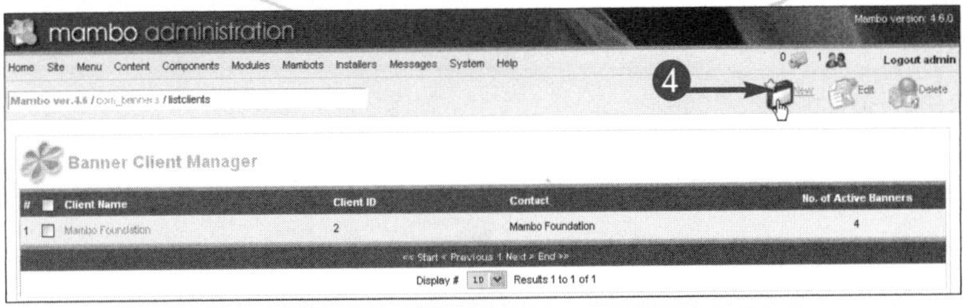

The New Client screen loads.

5. Type a name.
6. Type a contact.
7. Type a contact email.
8. Click the Save icon.

Mambo creates a new Banner Client and returns you to the Banner Client Manager.

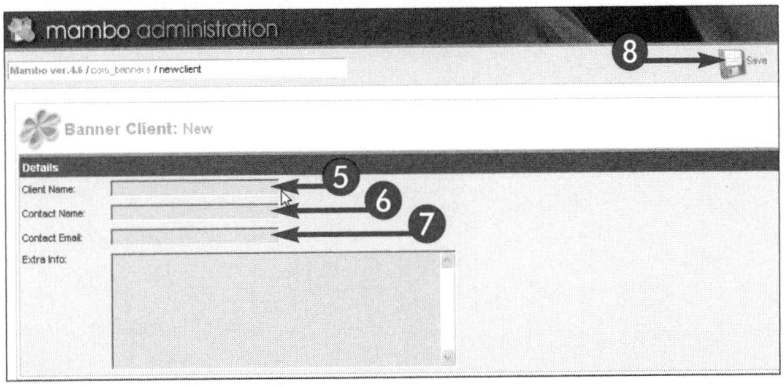

Create and Manage Banners

You can add new banner ads to your Mambo Web site through the Banner component. Although the Banner module displays banners, you use the Banner component to add new banners to the system and to set their configuration options. You also need the Banners component to modify the options associated with existing banners and to hide banners when you want to remove them from display.

The Banner Manager includes all the tools you need to upload new banner ads to the system and to set the parameters that control the banners. You cannot, however, actually create a new graphical file for a banner ad within Mambo. You must perform any necessary graphics work outside the system.

The first step to setting up a new banner campaign is the creation of a client, as discussed in the previous section, "Create and Manage Banner Clients." Assuming a client exists, you need to complete two steps. First, you must upload the banner ad to the system, and second, you must assign the banner to a client and configure the settings for the banner. Upon successful completion of these steps, the banner appears automatically per the Banner module settings. For more on how to work with the Banner module, see Chapter 11.

The Mambo Banner Manager supports only two different types of banner campaigns: Impression campaigns, in which the banner appears a set number of times, and Open Ended campaigns — that is, campaigns with a definite start date but without a set ending date. The configuration settings of the individual banners determine the campaign type. For Impression campaigns, specify the number of impressions in the provided field. For Open Ended campaigns, select the Unlimited option.

Create and Manage Banners

1. Click Components.
2. Click Banners.
3. Click Manage Banners.

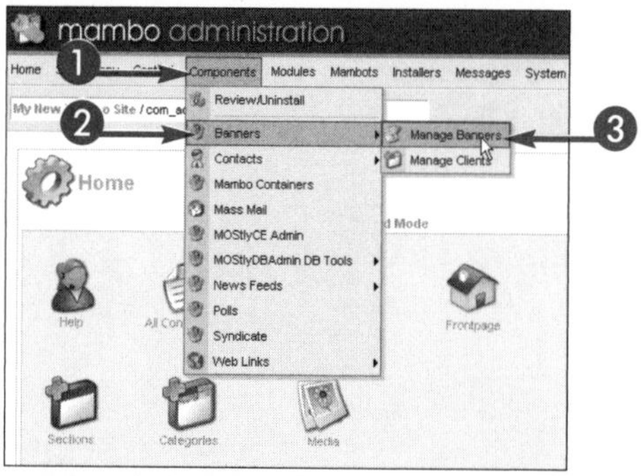

The Banner Manager loads.

4. Click the New icon.

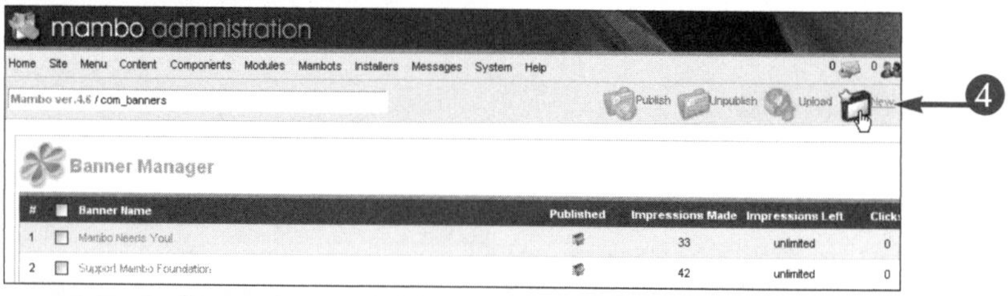

The New Banner screen loads.

5. Click the Upload icon.

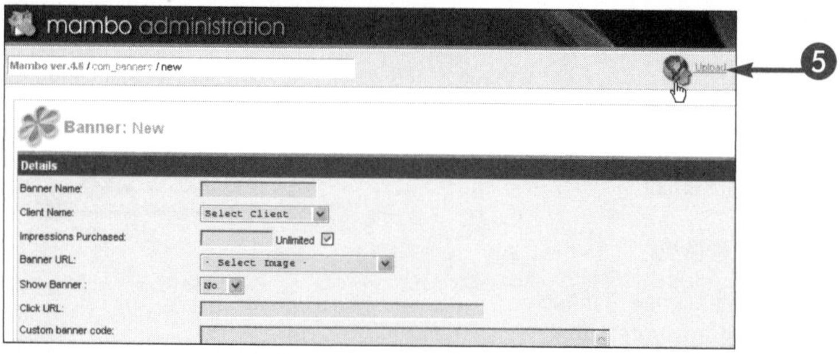

The Upload a file window appears.

6. Click Browse.

   The Choose file window appears.

7. Select the Banner.

8. Click Open.

9. Click Upload in the Banner Upload window.

   Mambo uploads the banner to the system.

   The New Banner screen loads.

10. Type a name.

11. Click in these areas to select a client, a banner ad, and campaign settings, and to set the Show Banner option.

Note: If the banner you just uploaded does not appear in the drop-down box listing the banners, reload the page.

12. Type a destination URL.

13. Click the Save icon.

    Mambo sets the new banner in the system and returns you to the Banner Manager screen.

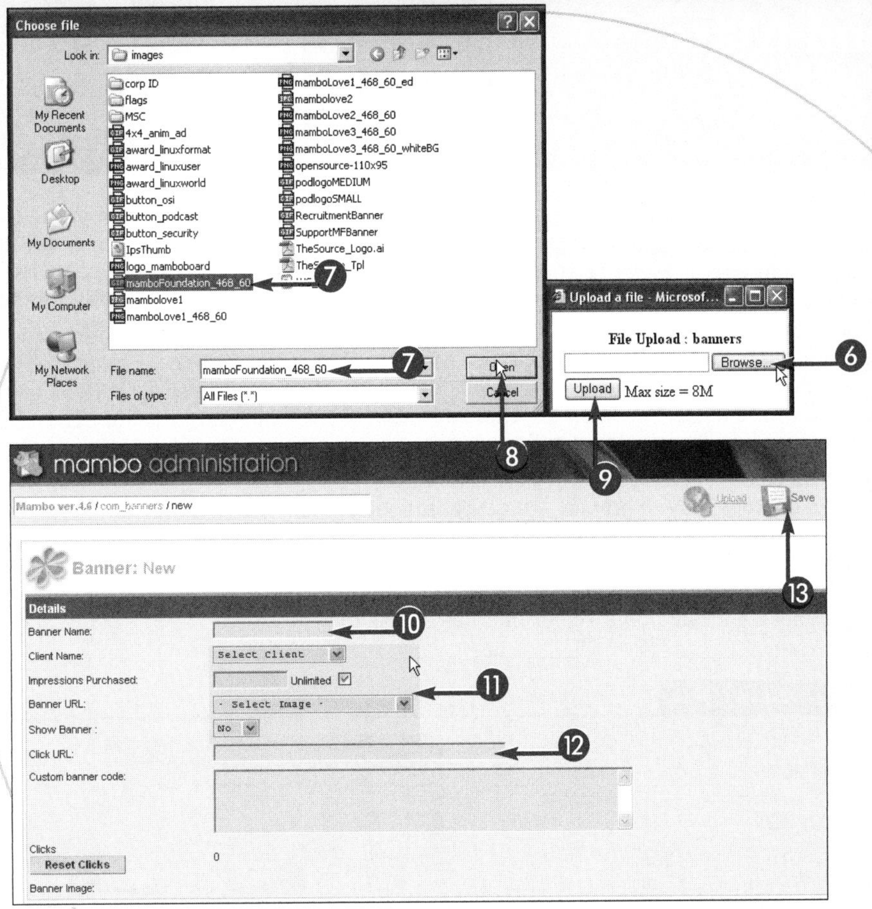

Extra

Banner sizes and formats are standardized. You should take the standards into account when planning your site layout and when creating new banners for yourself or others. The most common banner format is 486 pixels long by 60 pixels in height, a format known as the *full banner*. Increasingly, other formats, including vertical banners, or *skyscrapers*, are becoming quite common. For more about banner formats, sizes, and the generally accepted norms for this changing area of Web advertising, visit the home of the Interactive Advertising Bureau at www.iab.net.

To display more than one banner advertisement at a time on your Web site, you can create copies of the Banners module and publish them on the pages and in the positions where you want the ads to appear. You can run multiple instances of the Banners module, either assigned to the same or different pages. Multiple Banners modules work smoothly and without conflict and, by using the parameters contained in the module, you can even set them to run particular clients' ads in particular places. For more about the Banners module, see Chapter 11.

Send Mass Mail to Users

You can send email to some or all of the registered users of your Web site through use of the Mass Mail component. The Mass Mail function is provided as a convenience to site Administrators. If you need to send announcements or notices to your users, the Mass Mail function is probably the easiest way to do it. The component uses the mail server on your Web host to send email to the users, based on the email address they provided in their registration details.

The Mass Mail component does not display content on the Web site; it exists only to provide a practical function for Super Administrators. The component relies on the mail server settings established in the Global Configuration settings and is, of course, dependent on your Web site being located on a server that has access to both a mail server and the Internet. In other words, if your Web site exists on an Intranet or local machine, this function lacks the access necessary to send emails. For more on Global Configuration options, see Chapter 2.

Sending email to your users is fast and easy. The Mass Mail Component interface is a simple form in which you select the user groups to whom you want to send the email, enter the subject and the message, and then click Send. The component provides only two parameters. The first parameter is Mail to Child Groups. When you select this option, Mambo sends the mail to the selected groups as well as to any subgroups. The second parameter is Send in HTML mode, which enables the use of HTML tags and formatting in the message body.

Send Mass Mail to Users

1. Click Components.
2. Click Mass Mail.

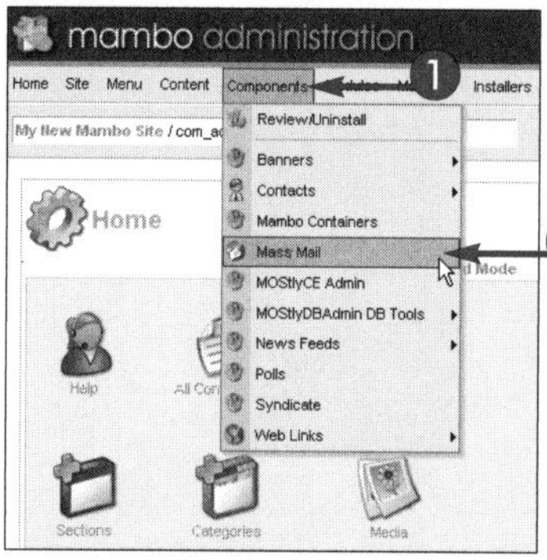

The Mass Mail screen loads.

3. Select User Group(s).
4. Type a subject.
5. Type a message.
6. Click the Send Mail icon.

Mambo sends the message to the users.

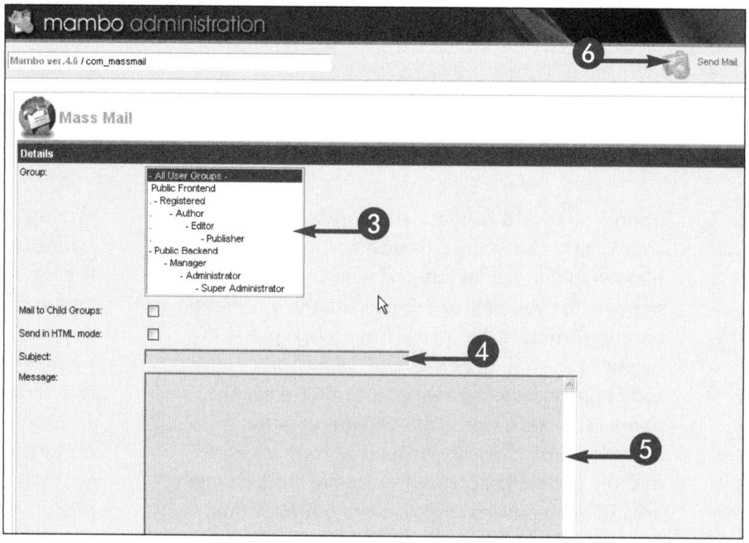

Manage Contact Categories

You can create and manage categories for organizing the contacts on your Mambo site. You most frequently use the contacts for your Mambo site to set up Contact forms which allow Mambo to directly send the output of a form to a particular contact. However, before you can create the contacts you must create categories for them; you cannot have contacts without categories. To create and manage those categories, you use the Contact Category Manager located under the Components menu.

If you installed the sample data with your Mambo site, you will see that the system already includes one category, labeled simply Contacts. You can keep and edit the default category, or you can delete it and create new categories. If you did not install the sample data you need to create at a least one category before you begin loading your Contact Items. For more on creating new Contact Items, see the next section, "Manage Contact Items."

Most small sites probably require only one category to hold all the site's contacts. If you have a larger site, however, you may find creating multiple categories very useful. For example, assume you are building a site for a multinational company with Sales and Administrative offices in a number of countries. You may find it advantageous to create different categories for each country and then assign the contacts accordingly. The use of categories in the example helps decrease the odds of confusing the Sales Office in the UK for the Sales Office in the USA. Thereafter, if you want to create separate Contact Forms for the various countries, you can have the output of the forms sent to the contact for the appropriate country.

Manage Contact Categories

1. Click Components.
2. Click Contacts.
3. Click Contact Categories.

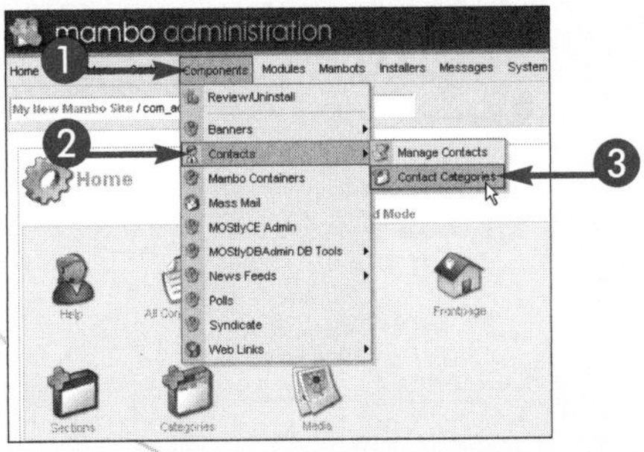

The Category Manager loads.

4. Click the New icon.

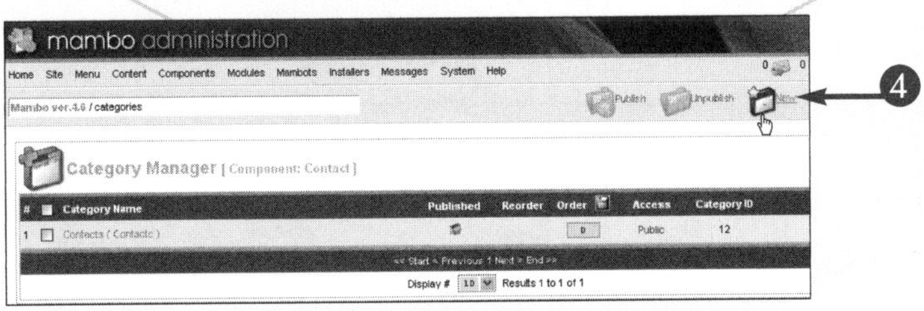

The Category screen loads.

5. Type a title.
6. Type a name.
7. Click the Save icon.

Mambo creates a new Contact Category and returns you to the Category Manager.

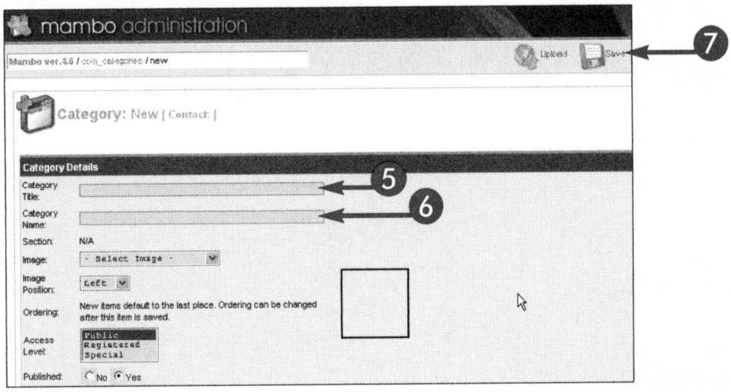

Manage Contact Items

You can create and manage contacts and contact forms for your Web site through the Contacts component. The contact management functionality built into the default Mambo system allows for both the creation and display of contact information as well as creation of forms that site visitors can use to send messages to those contacts.

The Contacts component uses the standard Mambo Category/Item structure in which all items must belong to categories. Accordingly, you must have at least one Contact Category before you can add any Contact Items. If you installed the sample data with your Mambo site, you find only one category, entitled Contacts, in existence, and that within that category there is one generic Contact Item. You can either keep and edit that category and Contact Item, or delete them and create your own categories and items. For more on creating and managing Contact Categories, see the previous section, "Manage Contact Categories."

You can create and manage new Contact Items from the Components menu, under the heading Contacts. The New Contact Item screen offers a number of parameters and gives you the option of inputting a variety of data concerning the contact; however, the only required fields are the Name and Category. The parameters attached to each Content Item include the option to hide or display a wide variety of different items, allowing you to extensively customize the Contact Items' appearance. Among the available options are several relating to the form you can display on the Contact Item page. For example, you can provide visitors a form that they can complete and send to the contact from the front end of your Web site.

Manage Contact Items

1. Click Components.
2. Click Contacts.
3. Click Manage Contacts.

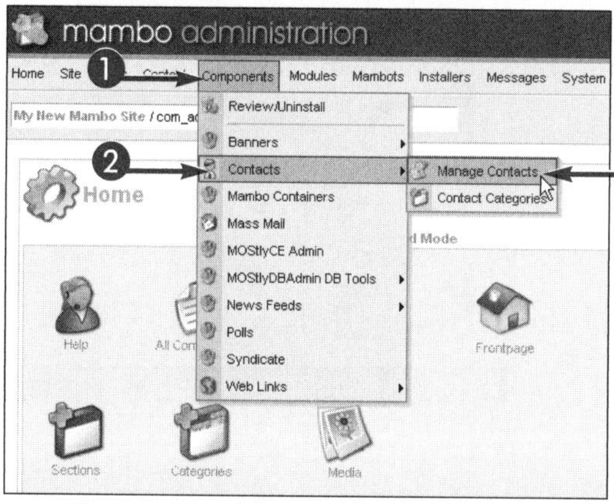

The Contact Manager loads.

4. Click the New icon.

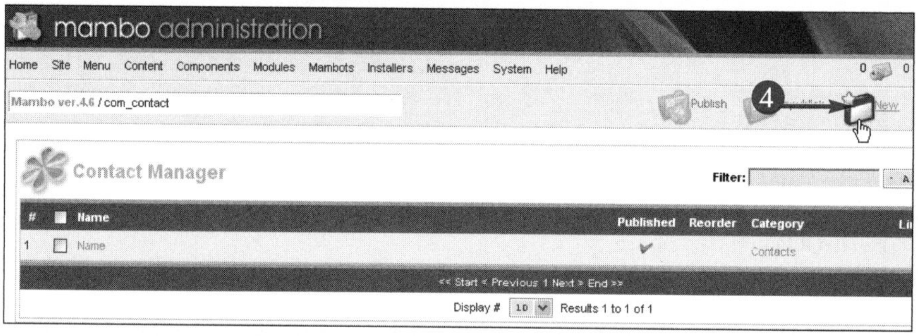

The Contact screen loads.

5. Select a category.
6. Type a name.
7. Type a position.
8. Type an email address.
9. Click the Parameters tab.

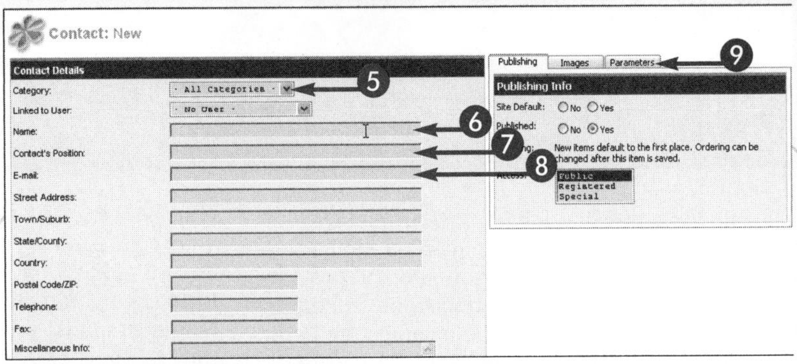

The Contact Parameters tab opens.

10. Set any parameters you want.
11. Click the Save icon.

Mambo creates a new contact and returns you to the Contact Manager.

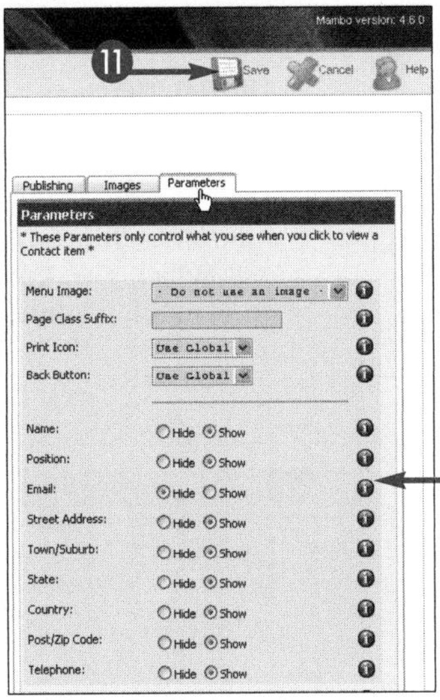

Extra

You can link Contact Items to users who are registered with your site. You generally tie a Contact to a Site Administrator in order to send contact form output directly to the Administrator. Tying users to contact forms makes it easy to assign Site Administrators to keep up with the form. For example, if you are selling products, you can link a Contact Item to your products page and link the output of that Contact Item's form to someone on your sales team. For more on managing this feature in conjunction with your site user privileges, see Chapter 4.

Among the Contact Item parameters is the option to hide or display the contact's email address. Although many people do not like to display email addresses on their Web site due to concerns over SPAMmers "harvesting" their email addresses, the default Mambo system includes a Mambot, called Email Cloaking that protects email addresses. If you display email addresses on your Web site, you should make sure you publish this Mambot. For more on Mambots, see Chapter 13.

Create a Poll

You can add a poll or a survey to your site by using the Poll component and the Poll module. Polls create interactivity on your site and provide a way for the Administrator to pose questions and gather information from site visitors. Mambo includes the Polls function as part of the default deployment of the core.

In the default Mambo installation, the Poll module is published and appears on the home page. You find the poll's question and the answer options in the Poll component, which works together with the module to create the Poll functionality. The component provides the content management aspects of the function, while the module handles the display. For more on the Poll Module, see Chapter 11.

To create a new poll, you use the New icon in the Poll component. You must supply a title and choices for the poll. Note that the title also functions as the question for your poll. You may supply one question and up to twelve answer choices for your poll. The Poll screen also includes a parameter entitled Lag, which determines how long users must wait before they can vote again; setting the Lag function to a large value helps prevent a user from voting again and again and skewing the poll results.

The Poll function is somewhat limited. For example, you can view results only from the front end of the site, and Mambo supports only one poll format. You must also start and stop publication of the poll manually. If you want more functionality, you can add third-party add-ons, which give you more options. For more information on extending your site, see Chapter 15.

Create a Poll

1. Click Components.
2. Click Polls.

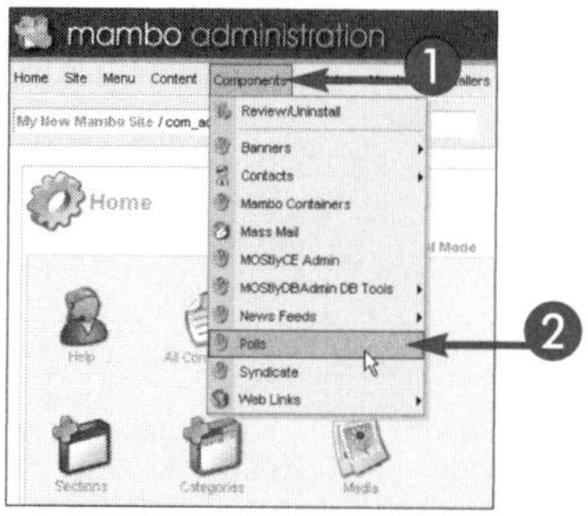

The Poll Manager loads.

3. Click the New icon.

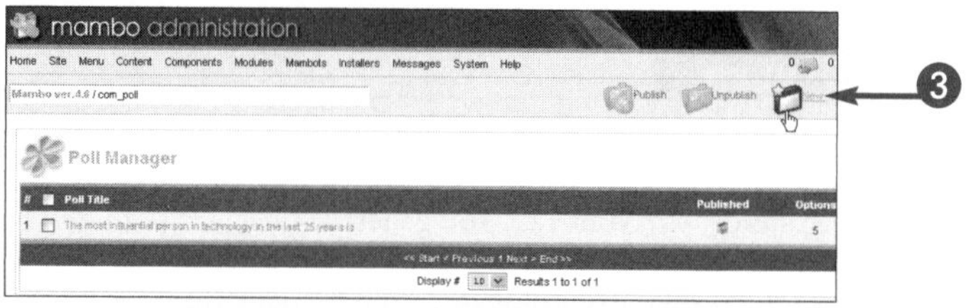

The Poll screen loads.

4. Type your question.
5. Type the answer choices.
6. Select the pages where you want the poll to appear.
7. Click the Save icon.

   Mambo creates the new poll and returns you to the Poll Manager.

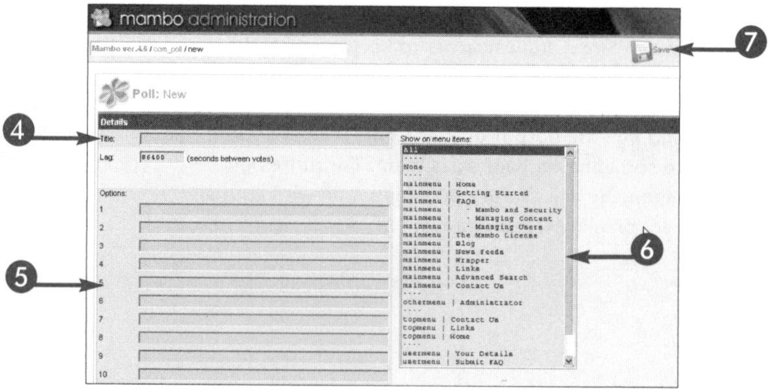

Configure MOStlyCE

You can extensively configure the settings relating to the MOStlyCE WYSIWYG editor, which allows you to get the most out of the tool and customize it to your individual needs. The MOStlyCE editor is a very powerful tool that makes it easy to edit and format your Content Items. The editor includes a wide variety of options and configuration choices. Although a Mambot powers the MOStlyCE editor, the parameters that control the editor are located in the MOStlyCE Admin component.

The MOStlyCE Admin component is similar to the Syndicate component in the sense that it is only a configuration utility. Because the component provides no independent functionality, you must publish the MOStlyCE Mambot for the component to be of use. Similarly, you must set the Global Configuration Settings to enable the MOStlyCE editor. For more on the Mambots, see Chapter 13. For more information on the Global Configuration settings, see Chapter 2.

The MOStlyCE Admin settings are covered at length in the Appendix C, but in broad terms, the options provide ways to change how the system presents the editor's interface and how the tools work. The configuration settings give you an effective way to customize the functions to fit your site's needs.

The default configuration is set to a broad level of functionality that will suffice for the majority of users' needs. Given the range of options available, you may find yourself experimenting to find the configuration that best suits your needs.

Configure MOStlyCE

1. Click Components.
2. Click MOStlyCE Admin.

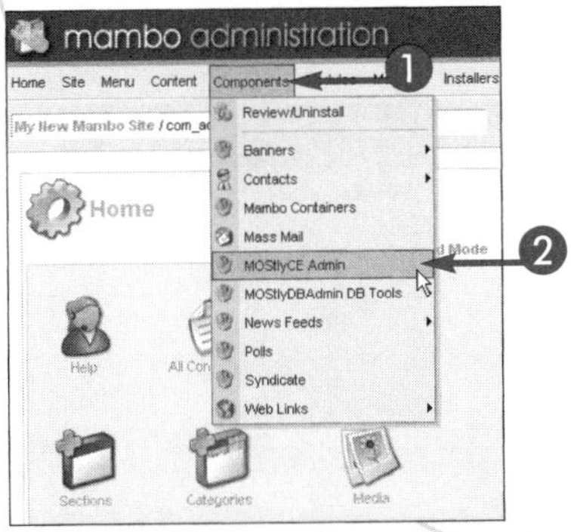

The MOStlyCE Configuration screen loads.

3. Select the options you want.
4. Click the Save icon.

Mambo saves the configuration changes.

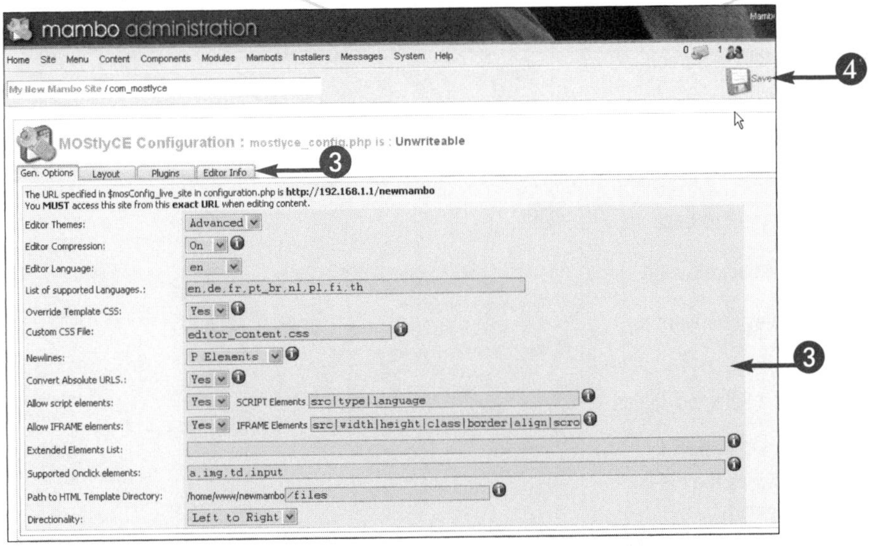

Using MOStlyDBAdmin DB Tools

You can perform basic management tasks on your MySQL database without having to leave the Mambo administration system. The MOStlyDBAdmin tool gives you the ability to backup, restore, or query your MySQL database. The tool is located on the Components menu, and you most frequently use it as an easy way to periodically back up your site.

MOStlyDB makes the management of basic database tasks a simple matter. You can now conduct tasks that required you to exit the system and use another tool, like phpMyAdmin, from within the system. The tool is more limited than dedicated database management utilities, but it does cover the three most common database tasks and leaves you no excuse for not conducting regular database backups!

The primary function the tool provides is database backup. Selecting the Backup Database choice from the menu presents you with various options for backing up the database, including choices relating to the format of the backup file, where you want to store it, and which tables you want to backup.

Selecting the Restore Database option from the menu allows you to select the location of the file to use for the restore and the button to execute the action. Selecting the Query Database option from the menu presents you with a text box into which you can enter your query. You can enter more than one query at a time and execute them if you select the Batch Mode checkbox. The page also includes buttons to execute the command and to clear the text box.

Before you perform either the restore or the query action, consider backing up the database and storing it on your local machine. In the event the restore or query produces an undesirable result, you can restore your database from the backup.

Using MOStlyDBAdmin DB Tools

USING THE BACKUP TOOL

1. Click Components.
2. Click MOStlyDBAdmin DB Tools.
3. Click Backup Database.

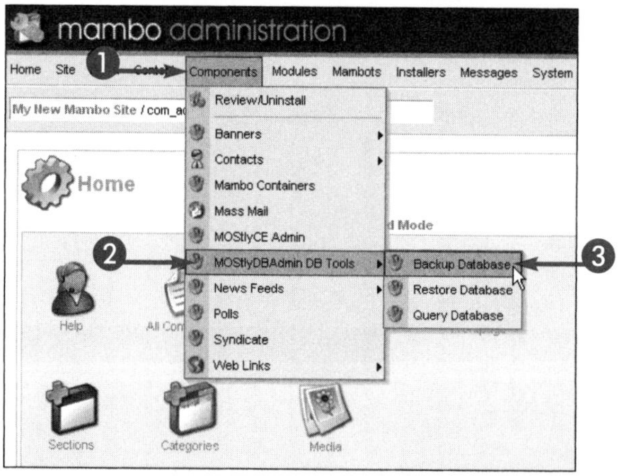

The Backup Database screen loads.

4. Click the backup location you want.
5. Click what you want to back up.
6. Click the file format you want.
7. Click which tables you want to back up.
8. Click Backup the Selected Tables.

The system backs up the database and stores the file where you indicated.

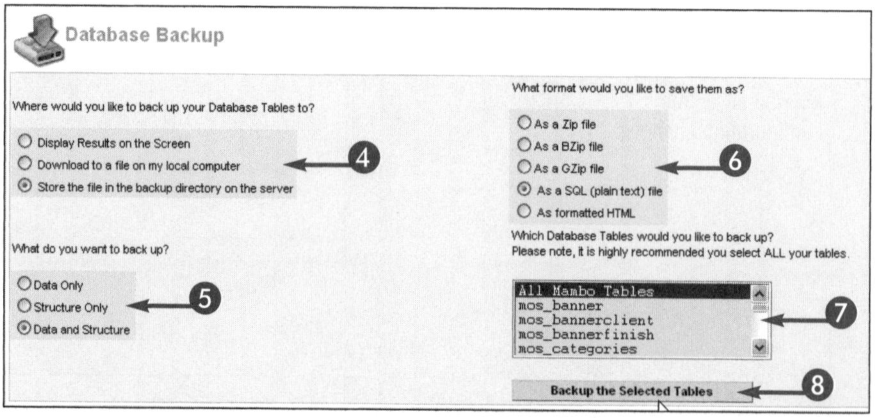

USING THE RESTORE TOOL

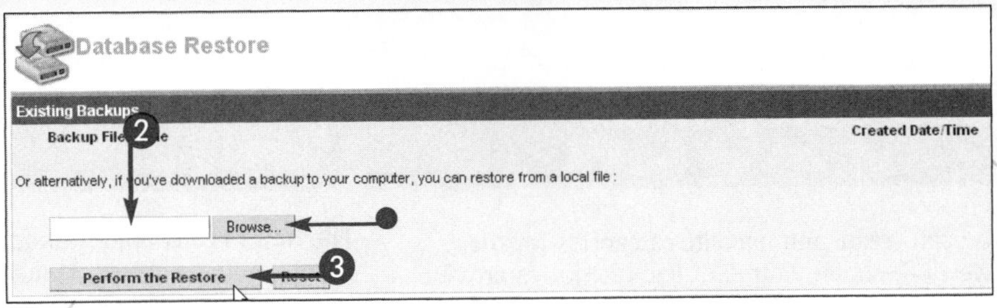

1. Follow steps 1 to 3 in the subsection "Using the Backup Tool" on the previous page, clicking Restore Database for step 3.

   The Restore Database screen loads.

2. Type the location of the file to restore.

   - You can click Browse to browse for the file.

3. Click Perform the Restore.

   The system restores the data from the file.

USING THE QUERY TOOL

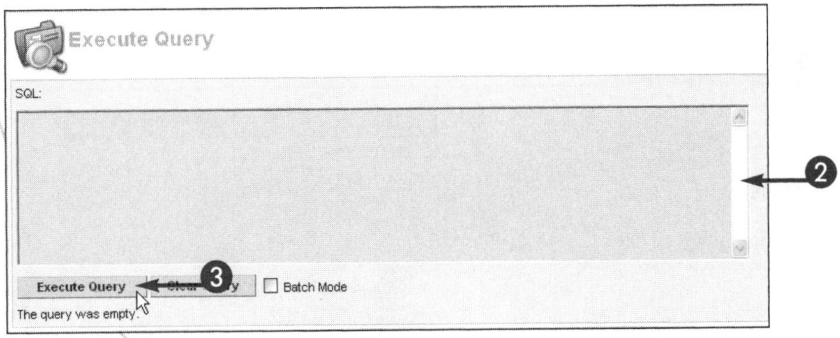

1. Follow steps 1 to 3 in the subsection "Using the Backup Tool" on the previous page, clicking Query Database for step 3.

   The Query Database screen loads.

2. Type your query.

3. Click Execute Query.

   Mambo runs the query on the Database.

Extra

The options presented by the Backup Database screen include a choice of where you want to back up the database tables. One of the options is to display the results on the screen. Another set of options concerns the formatting of the backup file, including an option to format as HTML. Taken together, if you set the system to "Display results on the screen" and "as formatted HTML" and click Backup, the system gives you a look at the content of the database tables, right there inside your Mambo admin interface! This is a great little timesaving shortcut that lets you reference the contents of the tables quickly and without having to exit the system.

In terms of what you should back up and where, the safest course is to back up all tables to your local machine. Backing up both data and structure is the most complete option. In terms of the format of the backup, generally the easiest course is to save as a zip file that you can then restore via the MOStlyDBAdmin component. Note that this component only backs up the contents of your database. It does not back up the site files. For more on backing up your site, see Chapter 14.

Manage News Feeds Categories

You can create and manage categories for the News Feeds on your site. The categories provide a structure you can use to organize the various News Feeds Items. You must assign all News Feeds Items to categories; therefore, you must set up at least one category before you begin to add News Feeds to your site.

If you loaded the sample data when you installed your Mambo site, you will find that the News Feeds component already contains several categories and a number of News Feed Items. You can edit the default categories and modify, delete, or add to the existing News Feeds through the News Feeds Manager. If you did not install the sample data, you must create at least one News Feed category. For more information on adding News Feed Items to your site, see the next section, "Manage News Feeds."

The News Feeds option under the Components menu gives you two choices: Manage News Feeds and Manage categories. The Manage Categories option gives you access to a screen where you can add, delete, or edit the News Feeds Categories. The New News Feeds Category screen gives you the option to add text or images to appear with each category. The MOSimage and MOSpagebreak commands are available as well. When users activate a Menu Item linked to the News Feeds component, Mambo presents them with an introductory page containing a list of categories. Any text or images you enter when you create or edit the News Feeds Category display when a user clicks on the Category link on the main News Feeds Component page.

Manage News Feeds Categories

1. Click Components.
2. Click News Feeds.
3. Click Manage Categories.

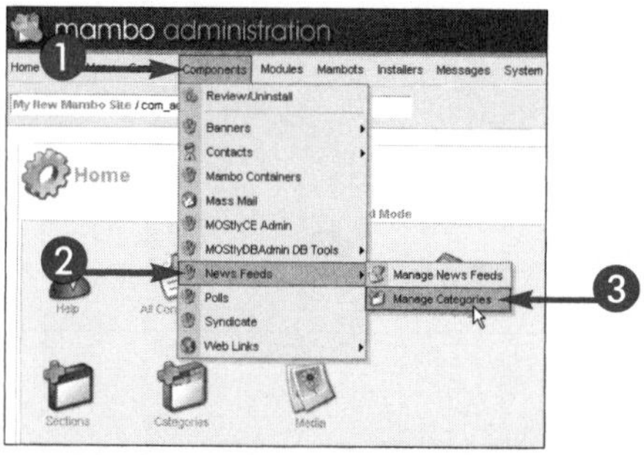

The Category Manager loads.

4. Click the New icon.

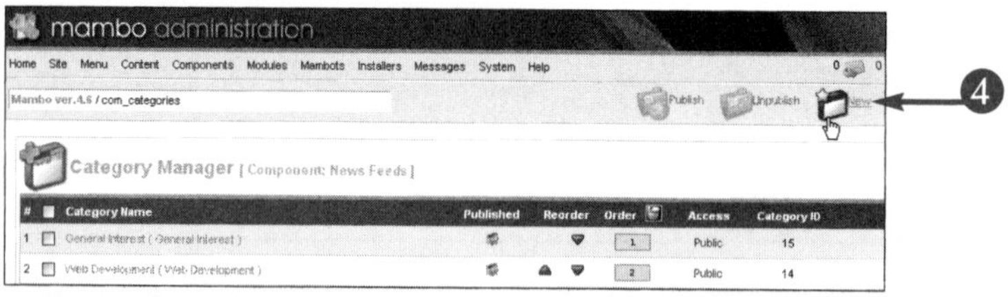

The Category screen loads.

5. Type a title.
6. Type a name.
7. Click the Save icon.

Mambo creates a new News Feeds Category and returns you to the Category Manager.

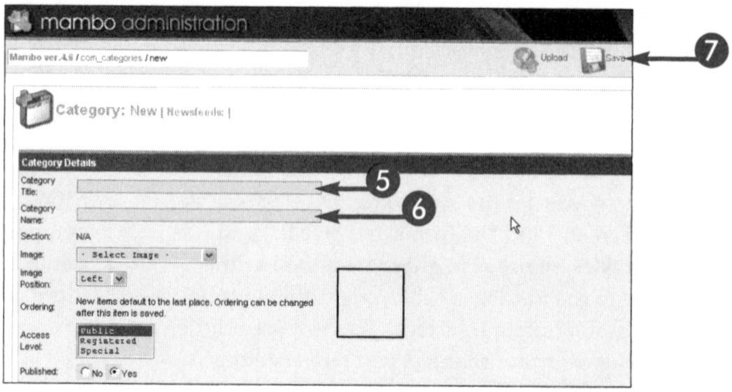

Manage News Feeds

You can add new News Feeds to your site or edit existing ones through the News Feed Manager. *News Feeds*, as Mambo uses the term, are content syndicated using the RSS protocol. The News Feeds component handles the work of gathering, organizing, and displaying the News Feed output from the various RSS feeds you collect. News Feeds are an easy way to enrich the content of your site by tapping into outside content sources.

The default Mambo system's sample content includes a number of News Feeds, organized into various categories. You can keep the default News Feeds or delete them without concern. Adding a new News Feed requires you to know the URL of the RSS feed. Typically, visitors can discover the proper URL by visiting the site that produces the feed and searching for the RSS button or link. Note that Mambo also requires you to assign all News Feed Items to a category; therefore, your must create at least one News Feed category before you can start adding items. For more information on how to create and manage News Feed Categories, see the section "Manage News Feeds Categories."

News Feed Items include several configuration options. One option relates to the number of articles that you want to show on your site. You set the Number of Articles option to whatever value best fits your layout. Another option relates to how often your site checks the syndicating site's RSS feed to see if it has been updated. As a matter of courtesy, make sure that you do not set your configuration options to check the RSS feed too often because this may increase the burden on the Web server hosting the site that supplies the content.

Manage News Feeds

1. Click Components.
2. Click News Feeds.
3. Click Manage News Feeds.

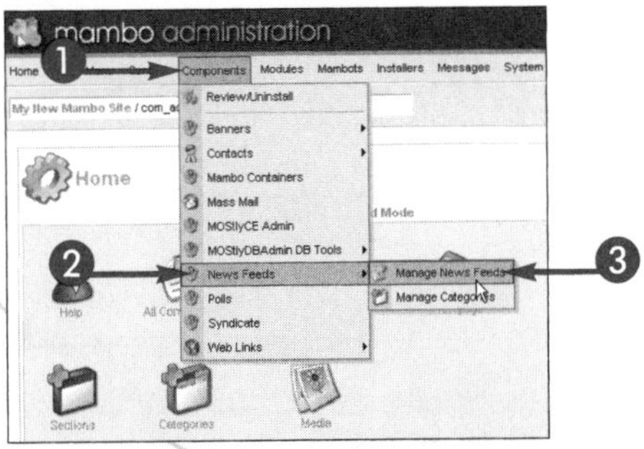

The Manager loads.

4. Click the New icon.

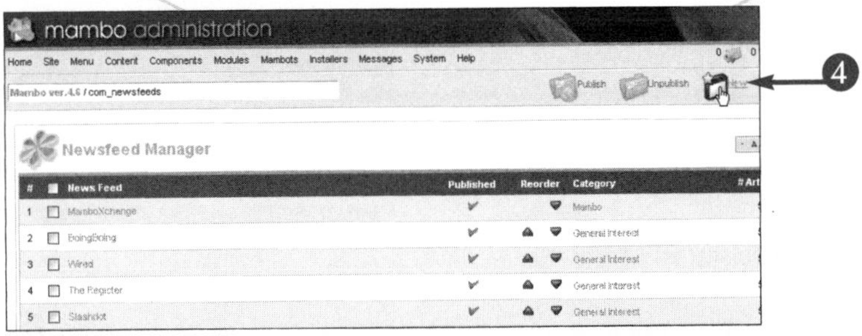

The Newsfeed screen loads.

5. Type a name.
6. Click a category.
7. Type the link (URL).
8. Click the Save icon.

Mambo creates a new News Feed and returns you to the Newsfeeds Manager.

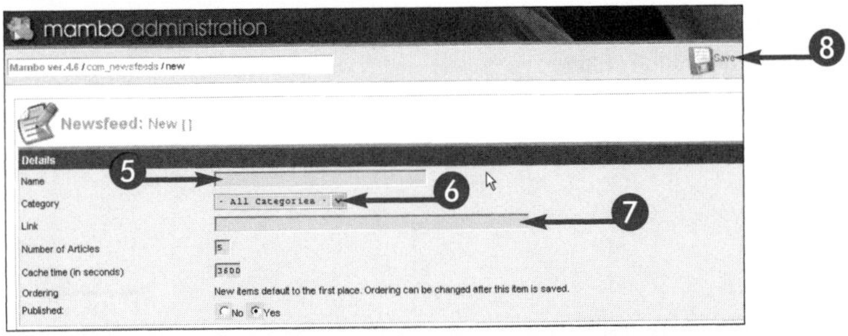

Syndicate Your Content

You can control the syndication of your site's contents by way of the Syndication component. The component works in conjunction with the Syndicate module to create options for visitors to subscribe to the RSS feeds that your Mambo site generates. RSS, which allows people to receive updates of your site's contents without having to visit the site, is a popular tool that can extend the reach of your site and attract new visitors.

The Syndication component, like the MOStlyCE Admin component, is merely a configuration utility. The settings contained on the component are designed to configure the information that the site's RSS generator distributes. RSS feeds are generated automatically by Mambo and are available for anyone who knows the URL. Publication of the Syndicate module is the most common way to publicize the URLs because the module contains links to a variety of RSS formats. For more on Syndicate module, see Chapter 11.

The Syndication Manager has configuration options that customize your site's RSS output by specifying the name, description, and amount of information that is distributed. Note particularly the Caching options. Caching the output decreases the load on your server, and therefore you should utilize it for a heavily used site; however, be careful not to set the length of time too long or your RSS feeds will not update in a timely fashion when your content changes. Also worthy of special note is the Live Bookmarks option. Live Bookmarks are an RSS option that the Firefox Web browser uses. When you enable Live Bookmarks, visitors who have bookmarked your page in the Firefox browser see links directly to the new Content Items on their bookmarks list.

Syndicate Your Content

CONFIGURE SYNDICATION

1. Click Components.
2. Click Syndicate.

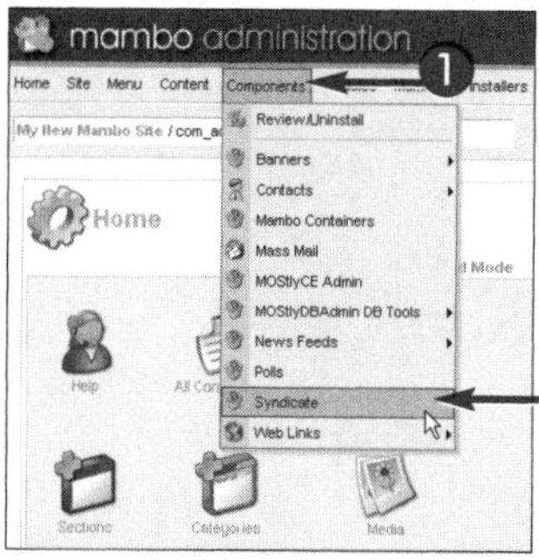

The Syndication Settings screen loads.

3. Type a title.
4. Type a short description.
5. Enable Live Bookmarks.
6. Click the Save icon.

Mambo saves the settings and returns you to the Admin control panel.

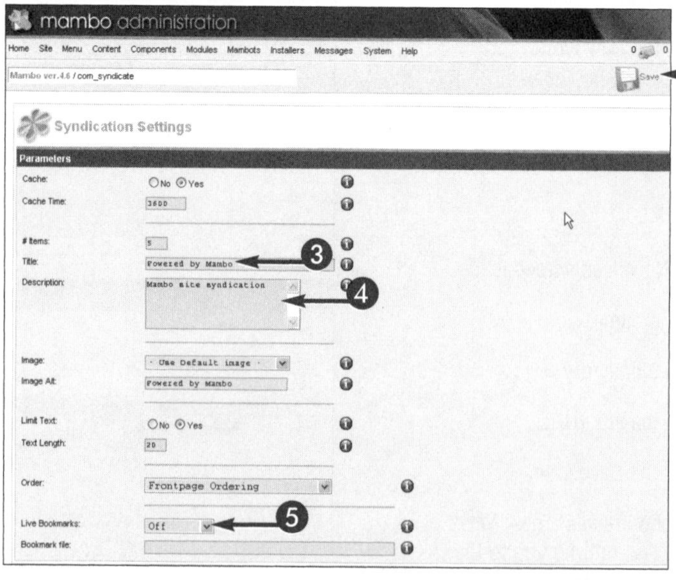

DISPLAY SYNDICATION LINKS

1. Click Modules.
2. Click Site Modules.

   The Module Manager loads.

3. Make sure the Syndicate module is published in a visible position.

   The Syndicate module displays links to the various RSS feeds for your site.

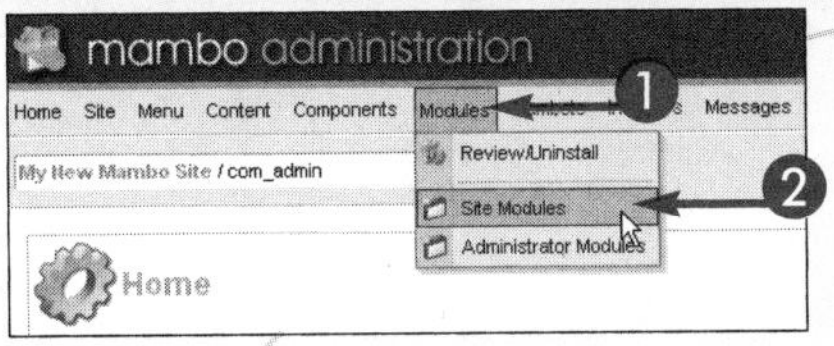

Extra

Mambo supports a variety of RSS formats. The Syndicate module gives site Administrators the option to display any or all of the following formats: RSS 0.91, RSS 1.0, RSS 2.0, Atom 1.0, and OPML. Mambo acknowledges that different users prefer certain feed formats over others. Unless you have a compelling reason not to do so, the best practice is to pass all the choices on to your users by enabling all the formats. The following table compares the formats:

FORMAT	WHICH IS BEST?
RSS 1.0 and RSS 2.0	These are actually forks of the same standard. RSS 2.0 may seem an updated RSS 1.0, but that is not the case; they are competing parallel standards.
RSS and Atom	Very similar in purpose and output. The debate between the RSS and Atom standards is ongoing, but as a general rule, Atom provides a more compliant feed.
OPML	In contrast, this was created as an outlining tool, and the output of an OPML file is rather different than an RSS or Atom feed and is not preferred by most users.

Manage Weblink Categories

The Weblinks function in Mambo allows you to create categories in which to organize your collection of links to external sites. The Weblinks component is located under the Component menu and gives functionality to organize, add, edit, and delete Weblinks. Providing links to other sites not only helps site visitors, but it also enhances and promotes your site through the exchange of links with other Webmasters.

If you installed the sample data when you ran the installation routine for your Mambo site, you see only one Weblink category, named Mambo. Within that category, you find a variety of links to Mambo resources. You can add, edit, or delete the category and the links. If you do not install the sample data, the Weblinks component is initially empty and you need to add a new category before you can begin adding Weblink Items. For more on how to add links to your Weblinks component, see the next section, "Manage Weblink Items."

The Weblinks option under the Components menu gives you two choices: Weblink Items and Weblink Categories. The Weblink Categories option accesses a screen where you can add, delete, or edit the Weblink Categories. Note that you can also add text or images to display with each category. The MOSimage and MOSpagebreak options are available as well. When visitors to your site use a Menu Item linked to the Weblinks component, Mambo presents them with an introductory page that contains a list of categories. Any text or images you enter when you create or edit the Weblink Category display when users click the Category link on the main Weblinks page.

Manage Weblink Categories

1. Click Components.
2. Click Web Links.
3. Click Weblink Categories.

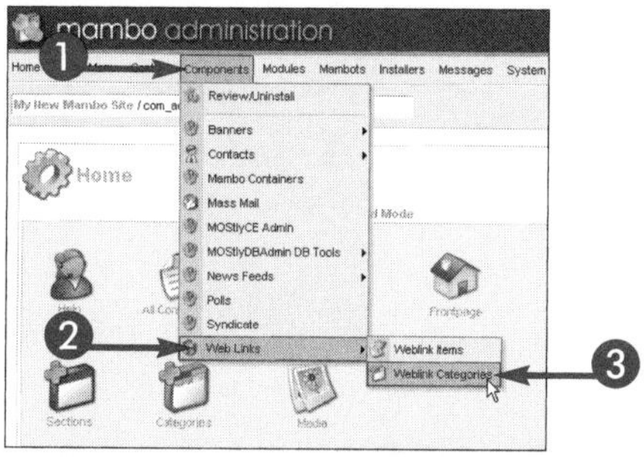

The Category Manager loads.

4. Click the New icon.

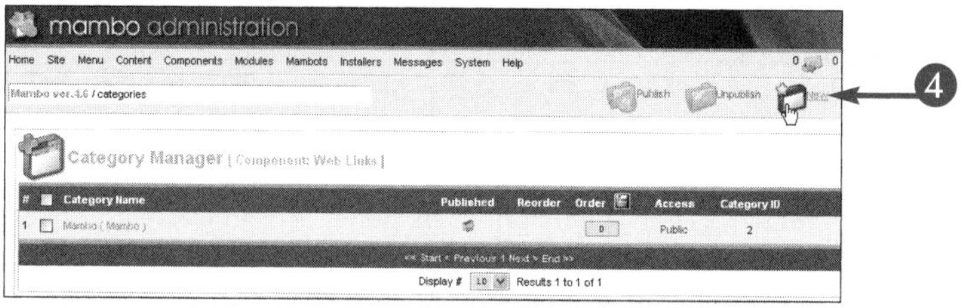

The New Category screen loads.

5. Type a title.
6. Type a name.
7. Click the Save icon.

Mambo creates a new Weblink category and returns you to the Category Manager.

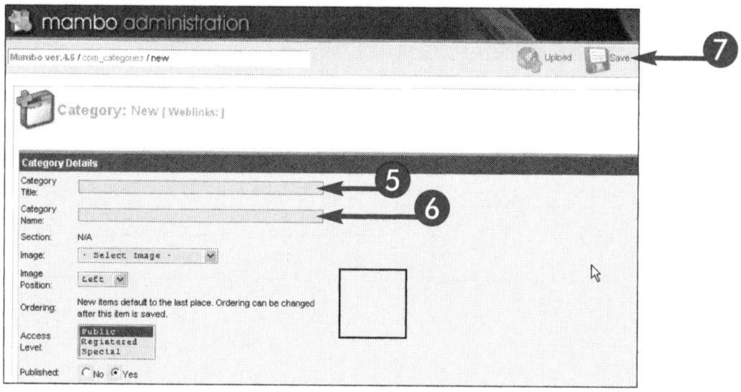

Manage Weblink Items

You can create and display lists of links to external Web sites through the use of the Weblink component. The component provides the ability to create categories and link items and to group the link items inside the categories. The Weblink function enables the creation of links pages, which are a common feature of many Web sites. Links pages are popular because they help users find related information and provide promotional opportunities for Webmasters.

The Weblink component uses the standard Mambo Category/Item structure in which all items must belong to categories. Accordingly, you must have at least one Weblink Category before you can add any Weblink Items. If you installed the sample data with your Mambo site you will find that one category entitled Mambo already exists and that within that category are a number of links related to Mambo.

You can either keep that list, edit it, or delete it and create your own categories and items. For more on creating and managing Weblink categories, see the section "Manage Weblink Categories."

You can create and manage new Weblink Items from the Components menu. To create a new link, you only need to know the URL of the external site. The New Links page also includes fields for giving the link a name and for adding a short description. There is only one parameter associated with Weblink Category: Target. The Target attribute enables you to determine what happens when a visitor clicks a link. If you want the link to appear in the same window as your site, replacing your site in the visitor's browser, select the Parent Window With Browser Navigation option. If you want the link to open in a new window, select either the New Window With Browser Navigation or the New Window Without Browser Navigation option.

Manage Weblink Items

1. Click Components.
2. Click Web Links.
3. Click Weblink Items.

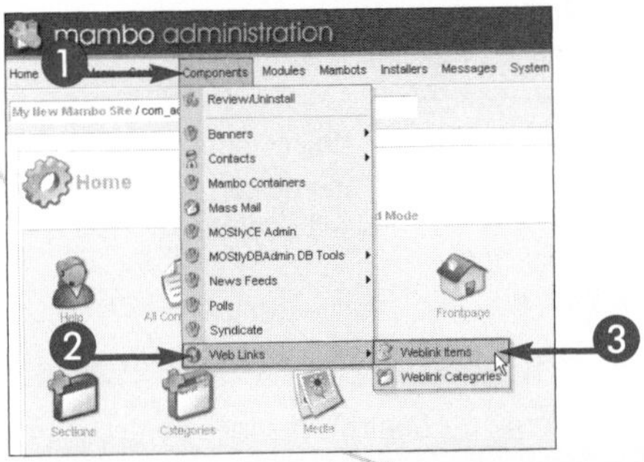

The Weblink Manager loads.

4. Click the New icon.

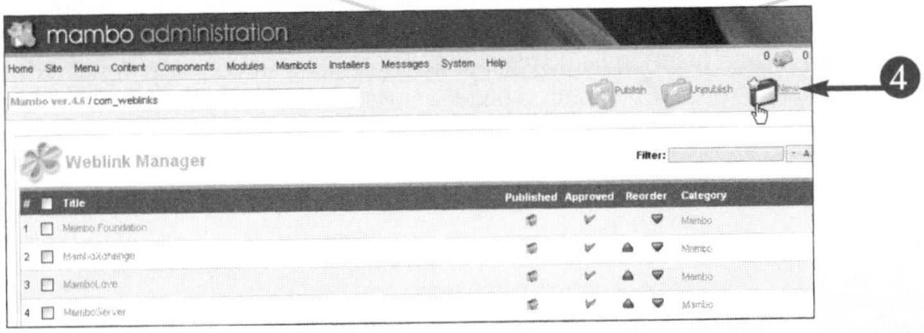

The New Weblink screen loads.

5. Type a name, a link (URL), and a description.
6. Click a category.
7. Click a target.
8. Click the Save icon.

Mambo creates a new Weblink and returns you to the Weblink Manager.

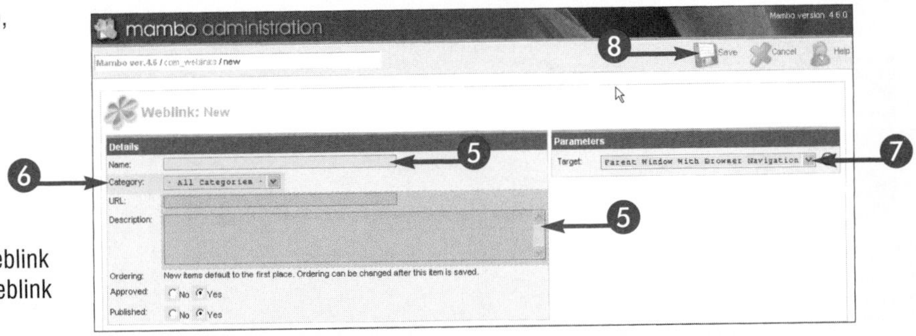

Understanding Core Site Modules

You can use Site Modules, which place small functional or display units on your page, to extend your site's functionality or to control output on the Web page. Wise and creative use of modules allows you to add variety to your Web pages and build a richer Web site. Although completely self-contained, most modules relate in some manner to another part of the site, such as to a component or a Content Item.

The default Mambo installation includes a significant number of Site Modules with a wide range of common functionality. Not all system modules are published on the default site. To explore an unpublished module, you must assign it to a page and publish it.

Module Placeholders and Options

Module *placeholders*, which are coded into the templates, determine the modules' positions. Although module placeholders can appear anywhere in a template, you usually locate them in the side columns or at the top or bottom of the page. You can change module assignments from section to section throughout the site to achieve visual variety and to create relevant relationships between content and functionality. Each module includes a configuration screen with various options that affect the function and/or formatting of the module. Learning what options are available to you is one of the keys to getting the most out of Mambo.

Site Modules

To get you started, this section shows all the Site Modules published in the default Mambo site, with a short synopsis of the module's function.

The Login Form, Other Menu, Polls, and Who's Online Modules

This figure shows the Login Form, Other Menu, Polls, and Who's Online modules and their locations on a Web site.

Unless otherwise indicated, these modules are published in the default installation. For more on the Polls component, see Chapter 10.

A Login Form

Displays a Username and Password login form, which includes links to a Password Reminder function and, if User Registration is activated, the registration form. This module displays the Login Form on the left side of the home page, under the Login Form heading.

B Other Menu

Controls the menu on your site named "Other." This module is located immediately under the primary navigation on the left side of the Web pages.

C Polls

Displays the polls that you set up in the Polls component. This module displays the poll on the home page's right side under the Poll heading.

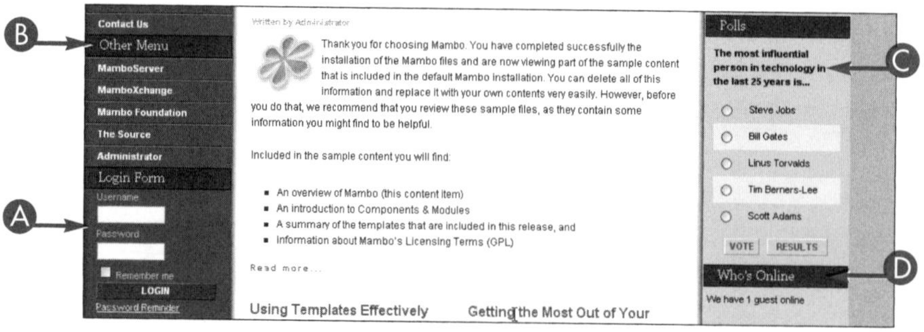

D Who's Online

Displays the number of users currently accessing the Web site. This module appears on the home page's bottom right side under the Who's Online heading.

Latest News, Main Menu, Newsflash, Popular, Search, and Top Menu Modules

The following figure shows the Latest News, Main Menu, Newsflash, Polls, Popular, Search, Top Menu, and Who's Online modules and their locations on a Web site. Unless otherwise indicated, these modules are published in the default installation. For more on menus, see Chapter 9.

A Latest News

Shows the most recently published Content Items. Appears at the top of the content area, under the Latest News heading.

B Main Menu

Controls the menu on your site named "Main." This module is responsible for displaying the primary navigation you see on the left side of the Web pages.

C Newsflash

Relating to the Content Items, this selects and displays one or more published items and can be set to randomly select the item. This module displays the text that appears immediately under the search box on the home page's top right.

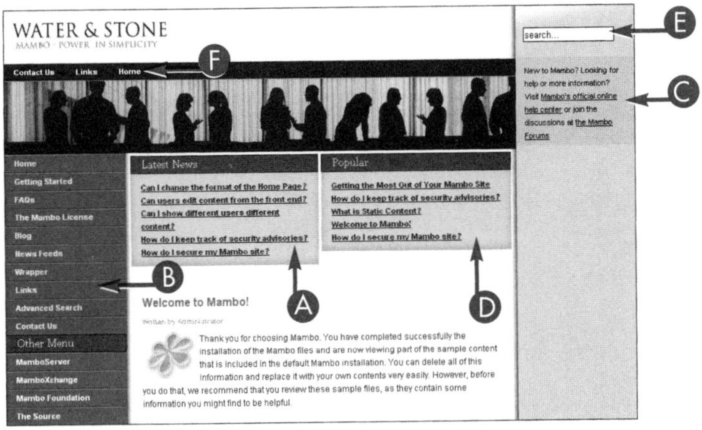

D Popular

Shows the currently published items that users have viewed most often. This appears at the top of the content area, under the Popular heading.

E Search

Functional in nature, this displays a search box for users to search the Web site. This module is responsible for displaying the search box you see at the top right of the Web pages.

F Top Menu

Controls the menu on your site named "Top." In the default installation, this module is active and is responsible for displaying the navigation choices you see above the header image on the Web pages.

continued

Understanding Core Site Modules (continued)

Site Modules *(continued)*

The Banner and Syndicate Modules

The following figure shows the Banner and Syndicate modules and their locations on a Web site. In the default installation, the Banner module is published. Note that the Banner module is assigned to different placeholders in the 1024 x 768 and 800 x 600 templates. In the 1024 x 768 template, the banners appear at the bottom center of the Web page. The 800 x 600 template displays banners at the top of the main content area, under the header image. In the default installation, the Syndicate module is published and displays the five buttons under the Syndicate heading at the home page's bottom left.

For more information on the Banner component, see Chapter 10.

A Banner

The Banners module is a display unit and is related to the Banners component. The module's function is to display the advertising banners that are uploaded and managed from the Banners component.

B Syndicate

This module displays links to the site's RSS feeds, which visitors can use to view your content remotely, via an RSS reader.

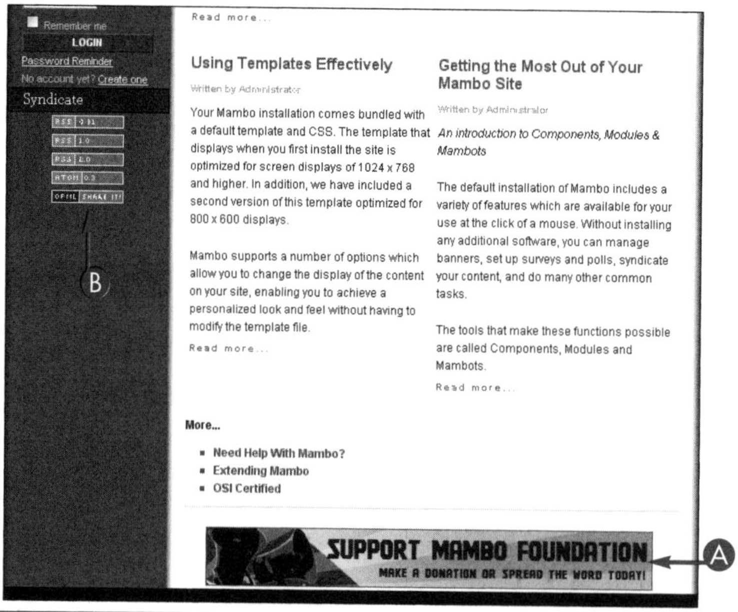

Other Core Site Modules

Because a number of the core site modules are not published by default, it is impossible to show everything in figures. Therefore, the following table gives the remaining core site modules and a description of what they do. For more on archiving content, see Chapter 6. For more on menus, see Chapter 9.

CORE SITE MODULE	DESCRIPTION
Archive	This module relates to the archived Content Items and displays a list of the calendar months which contain archived items. In the default installation, this module is not published.
Random Image	Displays a random image from a directory. In the default installation, this module is not published.
Related Items	You use this on Content Item pages to display links to related Content Items. The determination of whether items are related is made with reference to the metadata of the Content Items. In the default installation, this module is not published.
Sections	Relates to the content structure and shows a list of the content Sections on the site. In the default installation, this module is not published.
Statistics	Displays brief information about your server installation and Web site. In the default installation, this module is not published.
Template Chooser	Functional in nature, this allows visitors to change the site template by selecting the template they want to see from a list of installed site templates. In the default installation, this module is not published.
User Menu	Controls the menu named "User." Typically the User menu is restricted to registered users, meaning that a user must register and log in to see this menu. The choices on this menu relate to information that is not available to the general public, but only to registered users. In the default installation, this module is published and displays a menu below the primary navigation on the Web pages. In the default system, this menu is restricted to registered users, so it appears only if the user is logged in to the front end of the system.
Wrapper	Functional in nature, this creates an iFrame window in which the Web pages appear. In the default installation, this module is not published.

An Introduction to the Module Manager

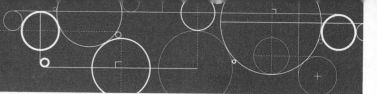

You can use the Module Manager to create, manage, and place modules on the pages throughout your site. The Module Manager interface gives you access to all the modules in the system, along with a quick overview of a module's status and placement. You can reorder, publish, or unpublish modules directly from the main Module Manager screen. Tools on the Module Manager page allow you to create new modules, or delete unwanted ones from the system.

You find the Module Manager inside the admin interface, under the Modules menu. Only users that you assign to either the Super Administrator or the Administrator User Groups can access this tool. The Module Manager is available for both site modules and for admin modules. Each version has separate navigation choices, but identical basic functions. For more on admin modules, see Chapter 12.

A Module Name

Lists all the modules currently installed in your system. You must first select a module here before selecting an operation.

B Published

Toggles the module to a published state.

C Reorder

Affects module order, relative to others in the same module position. Arrows move the module up or down in the order.

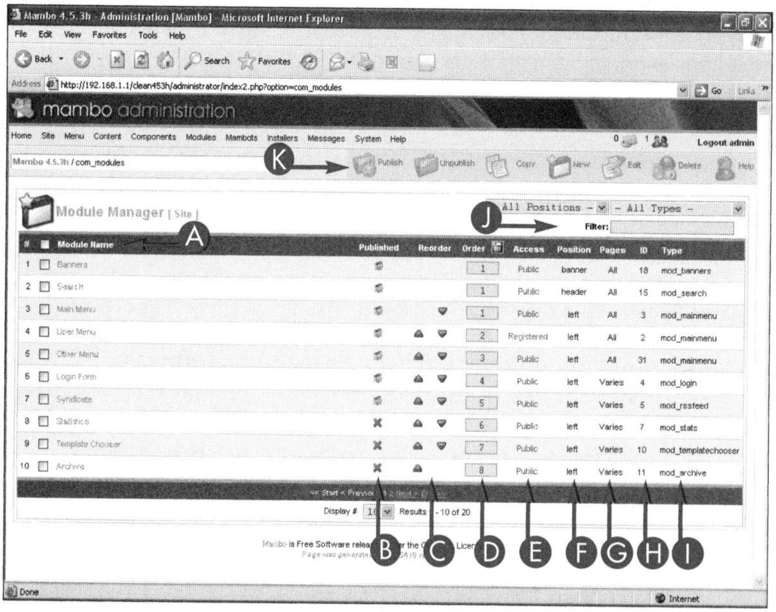

D Order

Affects module order, relative to others in the same module position, by renumbering the order sequence.

E Access

Cycles through the access level options.

F Position

The position to which the module is assigned.

G Pages

The pages on which the module appears. Includes the All, None, and Varies options.

I Type

The name of the module component. Useful for locating the module in the code.

J Filter

Searches and sorts the list of modules.

K Toolbar

Includes icons to publish, unpublish, copy, or delete selected modules. Also has icons that take you to the New Module Creation page, the Module Editing page, or to Help files.

H ID

System-generated ID number.

Publish a Module

You must publish a site module before a site visitor can view it. Once published, a module immediately appears on the pages and in the position to which you have assigned it.

Several processes combine to produce a module's appearance on a Web page. Publishing is the key factor — if it is not published it will not appear, even if all the other parts of the process have been completed. The other required elements for module publication are page assignment and module placement. Additionally, in cases where the module is related to a component or a Mambot, there may be other prerequisites that must be fulfilled before the module will appear or is fully functional. Assigning a module to a page is dealt with in the section "Assign a Module to a Page." Module position assignments are covered in the next section, "Change a Module Position."

You can either publish a module directly from the Module Manager, or by opening the editing screen for a module and enabling the Published option. Be certain that the module you are publishing has been assigned to the proper pages, and that the module position to which it is assigned is a valid position on the template being used for the page or pages where you have assigned the module. The way the system handles modules is quite flexible and forgiving. If you make a mistake regarding page placement or module position, you can easily fix it by editing the module after publication.

Note that unpublishing a module cancels the module's display immediately, though it does not affect the module in any other way; unpublishing essentially "suspends" a module's performance, nothing more.

Publish a Module

1. From the Module Manager, select the module you want to publish.
2. Click the Edit icon.

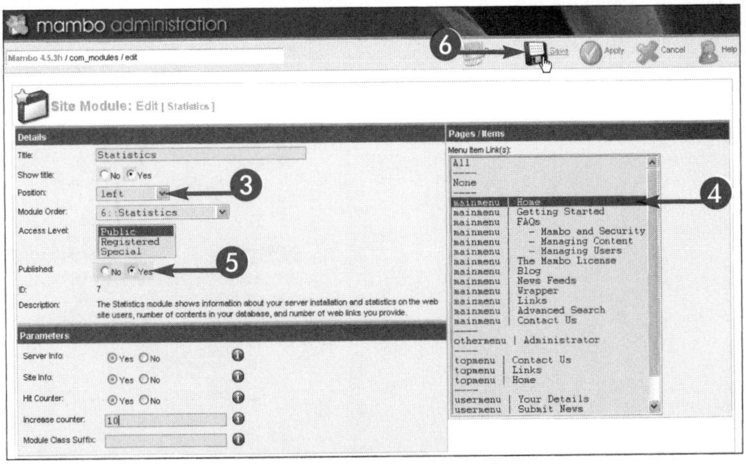

The Module Editing page loads.

3. Click here to assign your module a position.
4. Click here to assign the module a page.
5. In the Published area, click the Yes option.
6. Click the Save icon.

The module now appears on the designated pages.

Change a Module Position

You can change where a module appears on a page by changing the module position selection. This feature is particularly useful if you want to move things around and experiment with your page layout.

Module position assignments are related to the module position holders located in the templates. When you assign a module to a position, the module appears wherever you have placed the module position holder with the same name in the template. The module position selection combo box in the Module Editing page does not automatically detect which module positions are valid in the templates you are using. This means that you have to make sure you assign the module to a valid position or the module will not appear on the site. For more on how to find the module position holders in a template, see the section "Locate Module Position Holders" later in the chapter.

When considering where to place the modules, think in terms of the page content. Effective module placement enriches content and provides users access to relevant tools. Feel free to experiment with module placement. The system is very tolerant and you can change module positions back and forth without fear of causing problems with the site.

Note that while you can assign multiple modules to a single position, you cannot assign a single module to multiple positions. To display a module in more than one position, or in different positions on different pages, you must create multiple instances of the module, or multiple templates with different module position holders in each. For more on how to run multiple instances of a module, see Chapter 12. A discussion of how to use multiple templates is in Chapter 3.

Change a Module Position

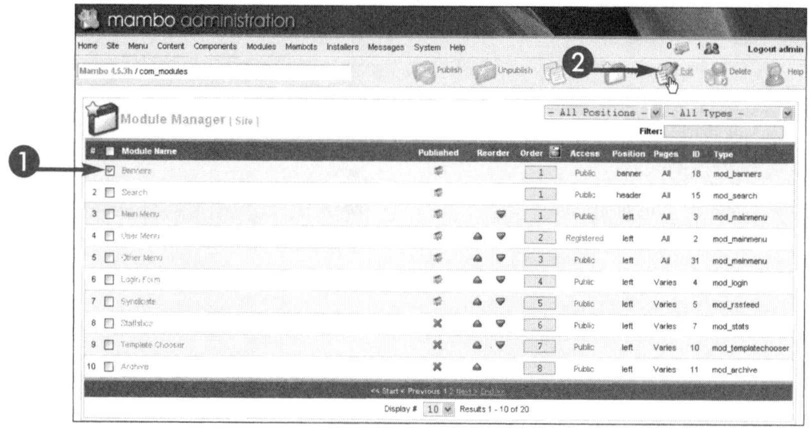

1. From the Module Manager, select the module you want to edit.
2. Click the Edit icon.

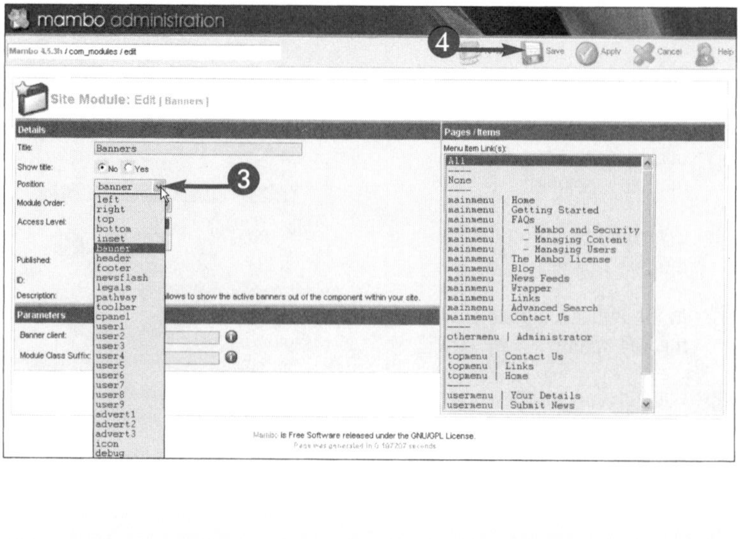

The Module Editing page loads.

3. Click here and select the desired position.
4. Click the Save icon.

The module moves to the new position.

Change a Module's Order

You can change the order in which a module appears on the page. You use this feature when you have more than one module assigned to a single module position and you want to change the modules' order relative to each other. Assigning more than one module to a single position is useful when you have a limited number of module positions on a page and you want to run multiple modules. Changing order is then a useful tool for keeping track of those modules.

The system provides multiple ways to affect module ordering. From the Module Manager you can either reorder items via the up and down arrows in the Reorder column, or you can renumber the modules using the Order column. From inside the Module Editing screen, a combo box lets you order the module easily. Of these three different techniques, the fastest way to affect multiple modules is to use the Order column in the Module Manager. The arrows are too slow to work with easily, and the Ordering command inside the editing interface only lets you change the order of the one module you are editing.

Note that ordering affects the module position sitewide. You cannot create different orders of the same modules in the same positions on different pages. If you want to create a different order on different pages, you need to rely on another approach, such as spreading the modules to different positions and using different templates on different pages. For more information on how to use multiple templates, please refer to Chapter 3.

Change a Module's Order

1. Access the Module Manager.
2. Click arrows to move the module up or down.

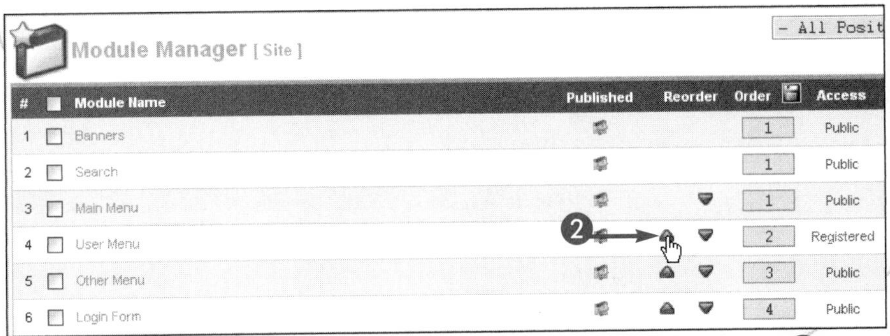

The module moves up or down on the list.

- Alternatively, you can click here to change the numbers in the column and, thus, the order.

3. Click the Save icon to reorder the modules with the numbering.

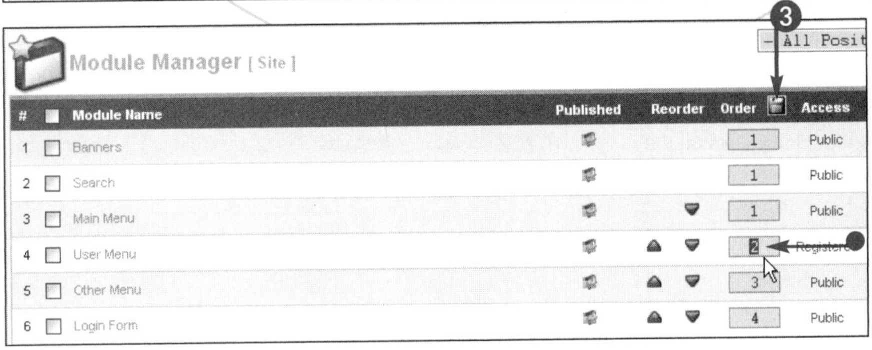

Assign a Module to a Page

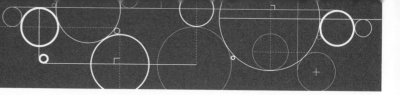

You can assign a module to appear on all pages of your site or only on select pages. Assigning modules where you want them gives you the flexibility to tailor your module placements to relevant content and to vary your site's look and feel from page to page or from section to section.

Assigning a module is easy, but in order to effectively work with this tool, you need to understand the relationship between module assignments and the site navigation so you can effectively plan your menu structure and module placement. Only published pages that you have linked to the site's menus are eligible for module assignment. This does not prevent you from placing modules on pages that do not appear on a menu; it means only that you cannot assign a specific and unique arrangement of modules to that page. A module can appear on a non-menu page if you assign the module to all the pages of the site. Non-menu pages also inherit the module assignments of their parent section and category.

Another factor to keep in mind is how to handle sites that have multiple redundant menu choices. The default Mambo site, for example, contains a main menu and a top menu, and there are some common links that appear on both menus. Where the same link appears in more than one place, you have to assign the module to both instances of the link to maintain consistency. So, again looking at the default site, if you assign a module to the Contact Us link on the main menu, you must assign the same module to the Contact Us link on the top menu.

Assign a Module to a Page

1. From the Module Manager, select the module you want to assign.
2. Click the Edit icon.

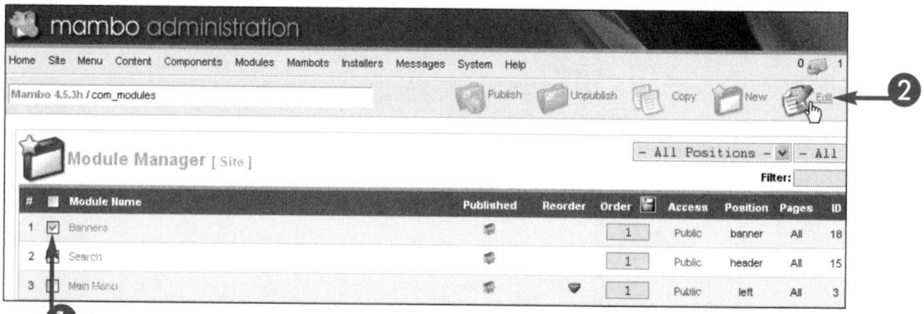

The Module Editing page loads.

3. Select one or more pages.
4. Click the Save icon.

The module appears on the selected pages.

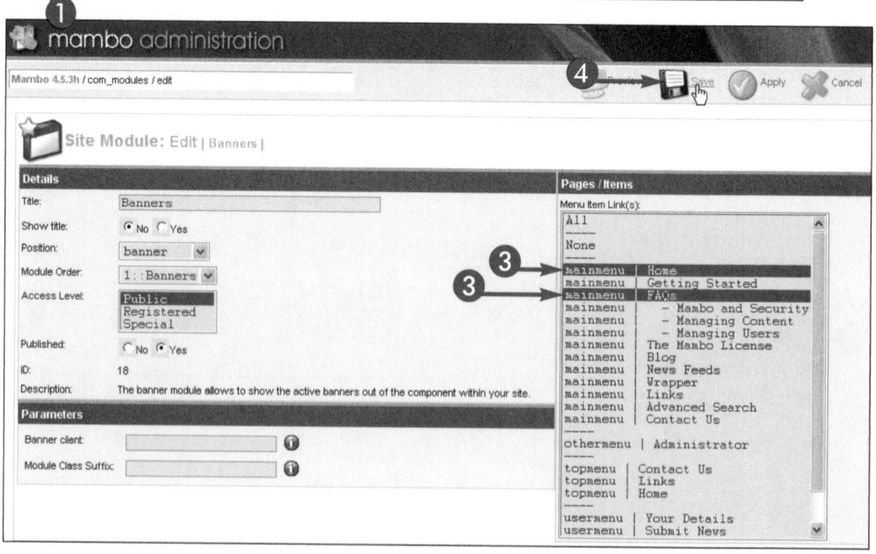

Restrict Access to a Module

You can restrict access to modules so that only members of certain user groups can see the modules. This technique is useful when you want to hide a module from the general public but make it available to registered users. Mambo provides three access levels for front-end modules. The access level you select depends on who you want to see the module.

The Public access level lets anyone see the module, assuming that you have published it in a valid position. This is the most common module setting, and you should use it when you want everyone who visits the site to see the module.

The Registered access level is a restricted access level. Only registered users can see a module whose access level is set to Registered. Note that users must log in to the site in order for the system to recognize them as registered users and allow them to see the module. The system makes no distinction between user groups in determining whether to display this content. It does not matter whether you are a member of the Super Administrator group or simply a member of the Registered group; the system displays only modules that are set to Registered.

The Special access level is very similar to the Registered level but with one crucial difference: in order to see a module marked as Special, the user must log in, and the user must belong to a user group higher than Registered. In other words, the user must be assigned to the Author user group or higher to see a module marked as Special. For more information on the various user groups, see Chapter 4.

Restrict Access to a Module

1. From the Module Manager, select the module you want to edit.
2. Click the Edit icon.

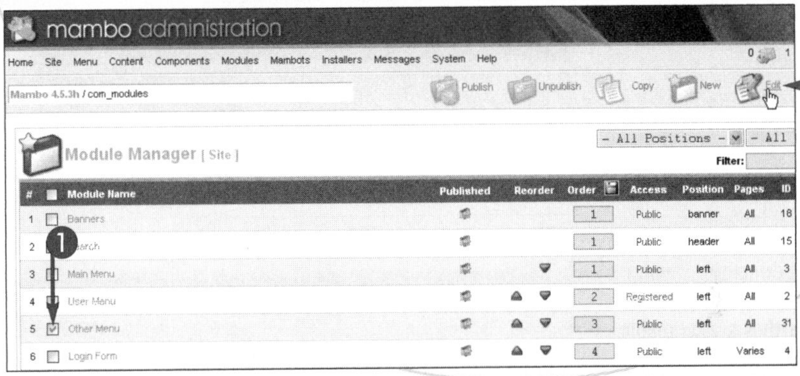

The Module Editing page loads.

3. Select the desired Access Level.
4. Click the Save icon.

Mambo saves the module's access level, which becomes effective.

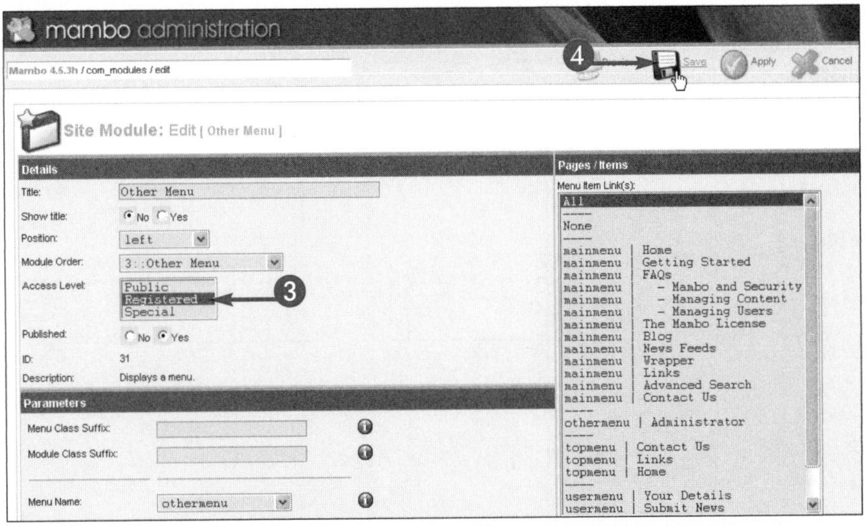

Install a Module Automatically

You can automatically install modules using the Universal Installer, and in doing so, add functionality to the Mambo core. The Universal Installer allows you to upload preconfigured module packages to your Mambo site. New modules can extend the functionality of your site or provide you alternative ways of displaying content. The Universal Installer is the easiest way to install modules to extend your Mambo site.

When you obtain a preconfigured module for your Mambo site, it is delivered in the form of a zip file archive. The archive should contain all the files necessary to install and use the new module. If the module has been created properly, you should not need to make any additional changes to get it to function properly, although of course you may need to configure it to fit your needs after installation.

The Universal Installer presents three options to users: Upload Package File, Install from HTTP URL, and Install From Directory. The first option provides for automatic installation of a zip archived module file; the second allows you to input the URL of the archived file and allows the system to retrieve and install the package; and the third option is a manual installation technique, covered in the next section. Note that the first method functions properly only if your server supports GZip or a similar utility that enables extraction of zip file archives. Similarly, the second option is dependent on server settings. If you do not configure your server to permit the access and installation of an archive from another server, this option will not work for you. Although the first and second options are the easiest to use, if your server does not support either option, you need to use manual installation, as detailed in Chapter 12.

Install a Module Automatically

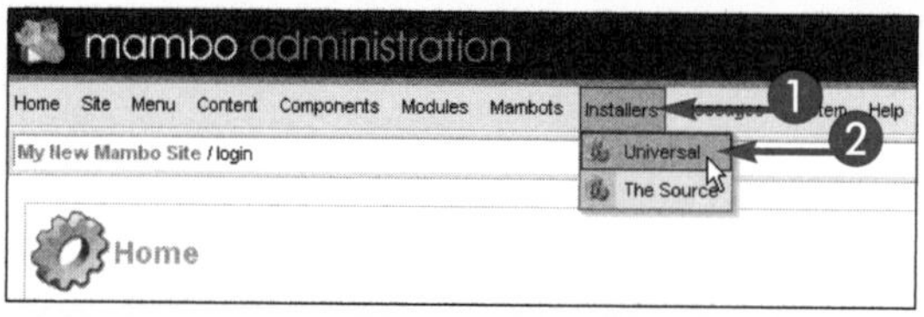

1. Click Installers.
2. Click Universal.

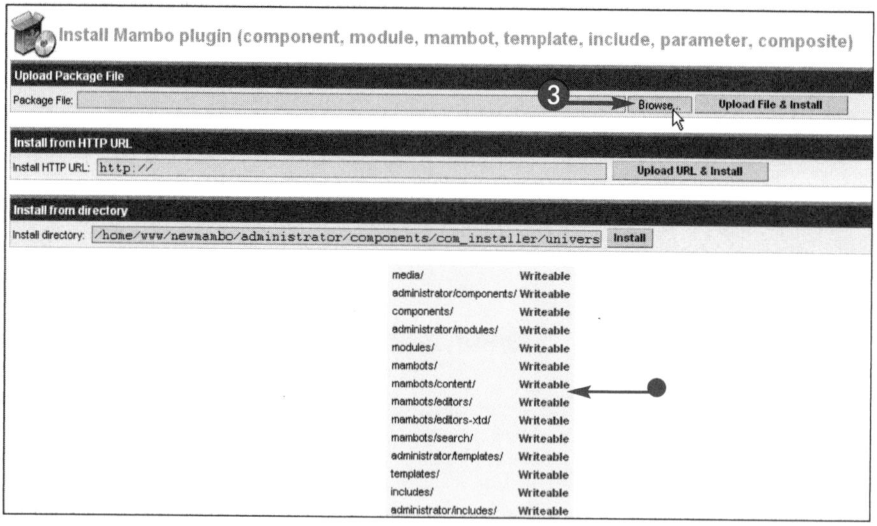

The Universal Installer loads.

- A list of directories, along with an indication of whether they are writeable, appears here.

Note: If any of the directories show as unwriteable you must change the permissions (read/write status) of the directory. For more on how to change file permissions, see Chapter 1.

3. Click Browse.

The Choose file dialog box appears.

4. Navigate to the location of the archive.
5. Select the file.
6. Click Open.

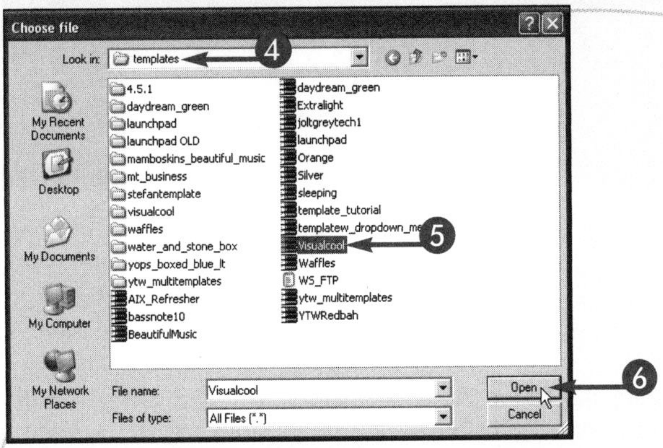

The popup closes and returns you to the Installer.

7. Click Upload File & Install.

If you are successful, you see a confirmation message when the screen reloads.

If you are not successful, you see a message indicating failure.

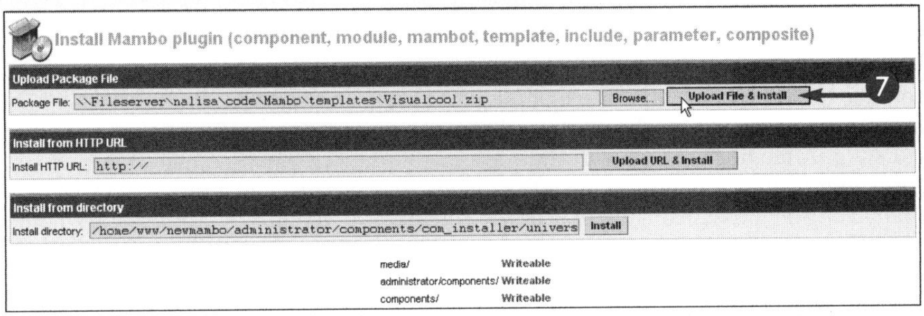

Extra

When you acquire a Mambo module from a third-party developer, make sure to verify that it is compatible with the version of Mambo on which you intend to install the module. Though the Mambo development team and the third-party developers strive to maintain compatibility across versions, there are no guarantees that an older module will work on the newest version of the system, or vice versa. The best practice is to always check compatibility before you install the module.

Occasionally installation of a module may fail for reasons unrelated to incompatibility. If that happens, check the zip archive. Sometimes the developer includes extra files in the zip archive, often for your reference, along with another zip file, which is the actual module package that the Installer needs. Unzip the original package locally, check the contents and see if there is a second zip file inside, and then try installing that inner zip file. While there is no formal naming convention for zipped module packages, many developers follow an informal practice of naming the installer package "mod_name.zip."

Copy an Existing Module

You can make a copy of any module in the system by using the copy function in the Module Manager. Duplicate modules are useful because you can modify them at will, and still keep a "clean" unaltered original version of the module. Additionally, creating multiple instances of a module allows you to place the same module in different positions on different pages, thereby allowing you to vary page layout as well as the site's look and feel. Advanced techniques for using modules are discussed in Chapter 12.

When you use the copy command, the module you copy is duplicated exactly, except for the name and the published state. A module created with the copy command is automatically named "Copy of (original module name)." The published state of a newly copied module is automatically set to No.

After copying the module, you can alter the configuration options of the new modules as you please. Changes that you make to one version of the module do not impact other instances of the module.

The system imposes no limitation on how many times you can copy a module, or on how many instances of a module you can run simultaneously. Thus, while the system allows you to assign one module to multiple positions, the copy module functionality gives you a way to achieve that appearance by creating multiple instances of the same module and assigning them to different positions.

Note that deleting a copied module has no impact on the original module. However, using the uninstall command to uninstall a module automatically deletes all instances of the module — both the original and any copies. Uninstalling modules is discussed in the section "Remove a Module."

Copy an Existing Module

1. Access the Module Manager.
2. Select the module you want to copy.
3. Click the Copy icon.

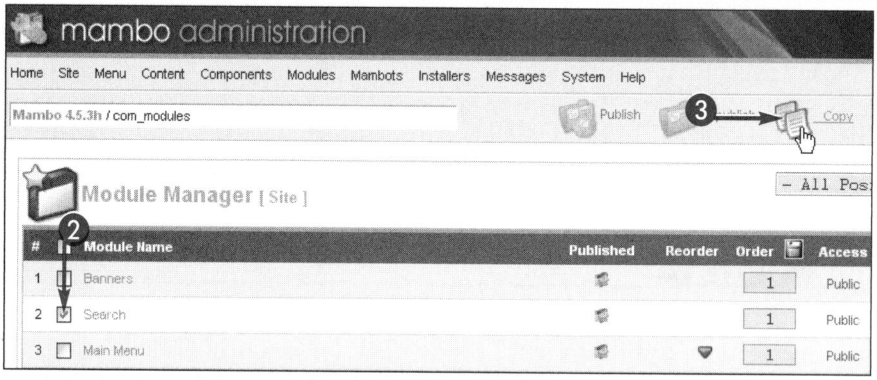

- Mambo copies the module, which appears on the list with the name "Copy of (name of original module)."

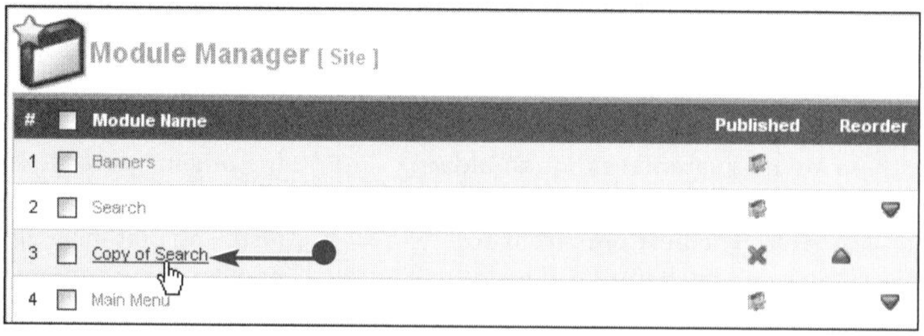

Locate Module Position Holders

You can quickly locate the active module position holders in a template by using the Site Preview function. This handy tool saves you time by allowing you to determine at a glance whether a module position is available in the template you are using and where exactly it is located.

Module position assignments are related to the module position holders located in the code of the templates. When you assign a module to a position, the module appears wherever the module placeholder with the same name is placed in the template. This opens the door for some illogical placements, depending on the way the template was built. Ideally, templates should use a very consistent and logical structure — the left, right, top, and bottom module placeholders all appear where you might expect — but in reality, variations in template designs and coding practices mean that often things are not where you expect them to be. To help avoid surprises, you can use the preview feature to see the module placements in the default template.

You find the function, called Preview Inline with Positions, under the Site menu. The limitation with this command is that it shows only the module positions in the default template. In other words, if you are using multiple templates, you cannot use this function to locate module position holders for any template other than the default template.

The preview output shows you both where the position holders are located and the names of the positions. This allows you to make your module assignments accurately, regardless of how the template designer may have designated the various positions.

Locate Module Position Holders

1. Click Site.
2. Click Preview.
3. Click Inline with Positions.

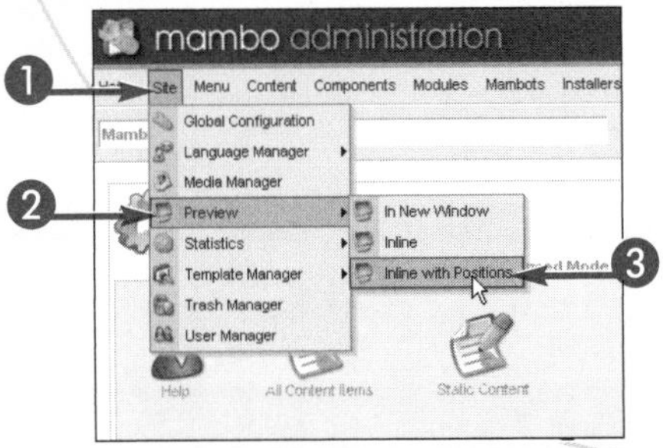

The Preview Inline with Positions page loads.

Mambo marks the available positions with gray boxes.

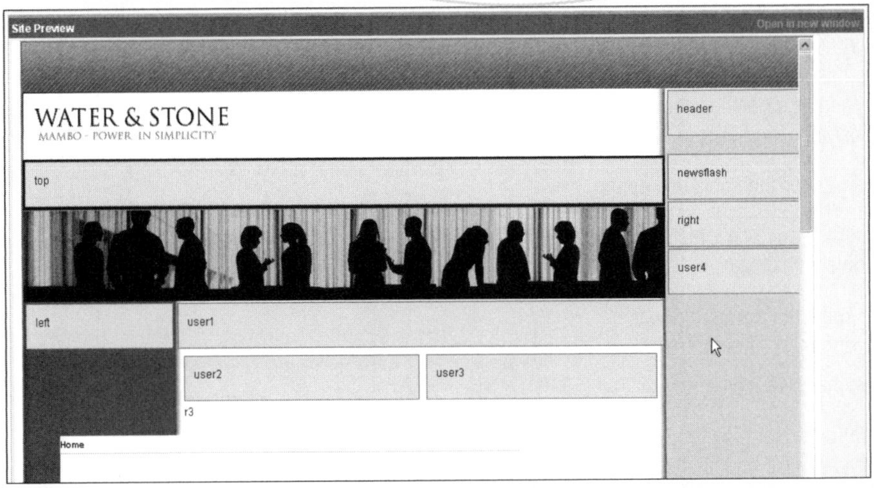

Configure the Banner Module

You can use the banner module to place banner advertisements or other graphical announcements on your Web site. You use the module to specify the placement and position of the banners on the page. The banner module works in conjunction with the Banner component, which has tools for managing banners and clients.

The module is well suited for positioning banner ads because it links directly into the Banner component. The Banner component tracks the number of appearances of a particular ad and the number of times someone clicks the ad. Via the Banner component, you can also assign a URL, which appears when someone clicks the ad. Note that you must set up and configure the Banner component properly or the Banner module will have nothing to display. For more on working with the Banner component, see Chapter 10.

The options available on the Banner module configuration screen are quite limited and relate primarily to the positioning of the module and the assignment of the module to particular pages.

Only two parameters are available for this module. The Banner Client parameter allows you to tie a Banner module to the banner ads of one or more specific clients. If you are running only one instance of the Banner module, this parameter is probably of no use to you. However, if you want to run multiple instances of the Banner module, you can use this parameter to tie the banners of particular advertisers to particular pages on the site. The Module Class Suffix parameter enables you to tie the module to a specific CSS class. This is useful if you want the module to have a particular appearance, such as a colored background.

Configure the Banner Module

1. From the Module Manager, select the Banner Module.
2. Click the Edit icon.

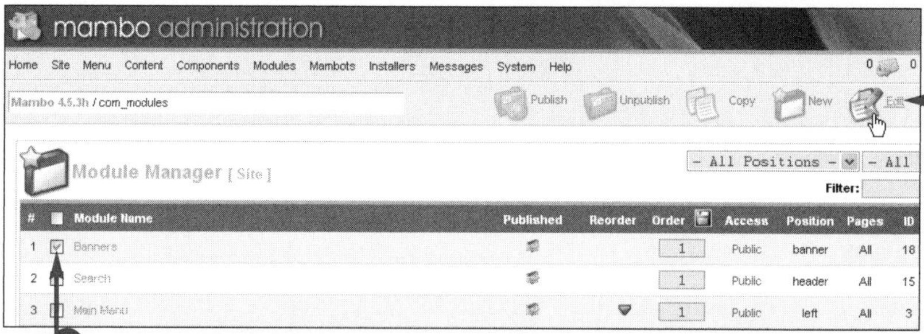

The Banner Module Editing page loads.

3. Click these areas for the Show Title option as well as to select the module's position, order of appearance, and access level.
4. Click Yes for the Published option.
5. Click the pages on which the module will appear.
   - You can click here to set optional parameters.
6. Click the Save icon.

Mambo configures the module and it appears on the site.

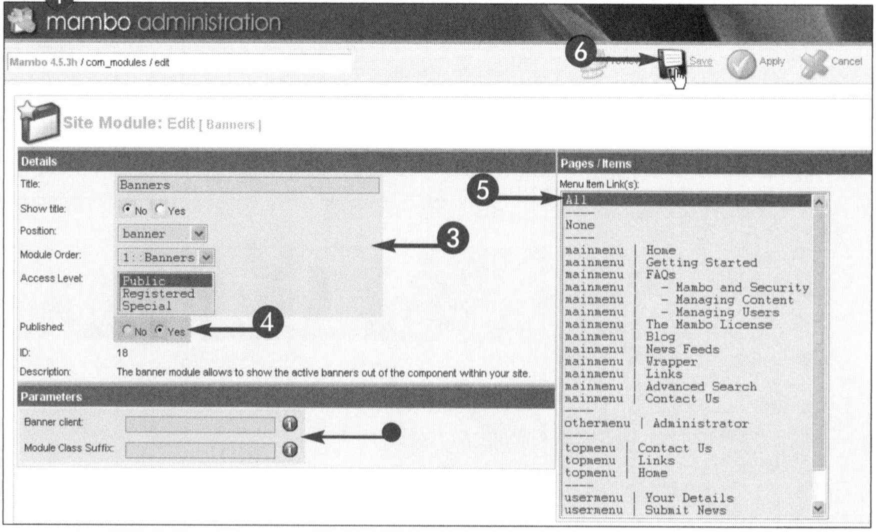

Configure the Search Module

You can use the Search module to place a search box on the pages of your site. The search box that the Search module produces allows site visitors to search through your Web pages for specific words or phrases. The results of the search display on a page, which lists results in order of relevance complete with search terms highlighted and clickable links. There are several parameters associated with this module.

The Module Class Suffix parameter enables you to tie the module to a specific CSS class. This is useful if you want the module to have a particular appearance, such as a colored background or a different font.

The Enable Cache parameter allows you to set caching for this module. Caching the output of a module is a way to improve the performance of a Web site because it decreases the load on the server. Caching is recommended for most sites; however, be aware that if the contents of your site change very frequently, caching may sometimes result in inaccurate or incomplete search results.

Box Width sets the width of the search box. The Box Width does not limit the actual length of the query, only how much of it shows in the search box.

The Text parameter allows you to control the text that appears in the search box by default.

The Search Button, Button Position, and Button Text parameters all determine whether, where, and how a Search button appears. Users click the button to start the search. If you do not elect to display a Search button, the search starts when the user hits Return.

Configure the Search Module

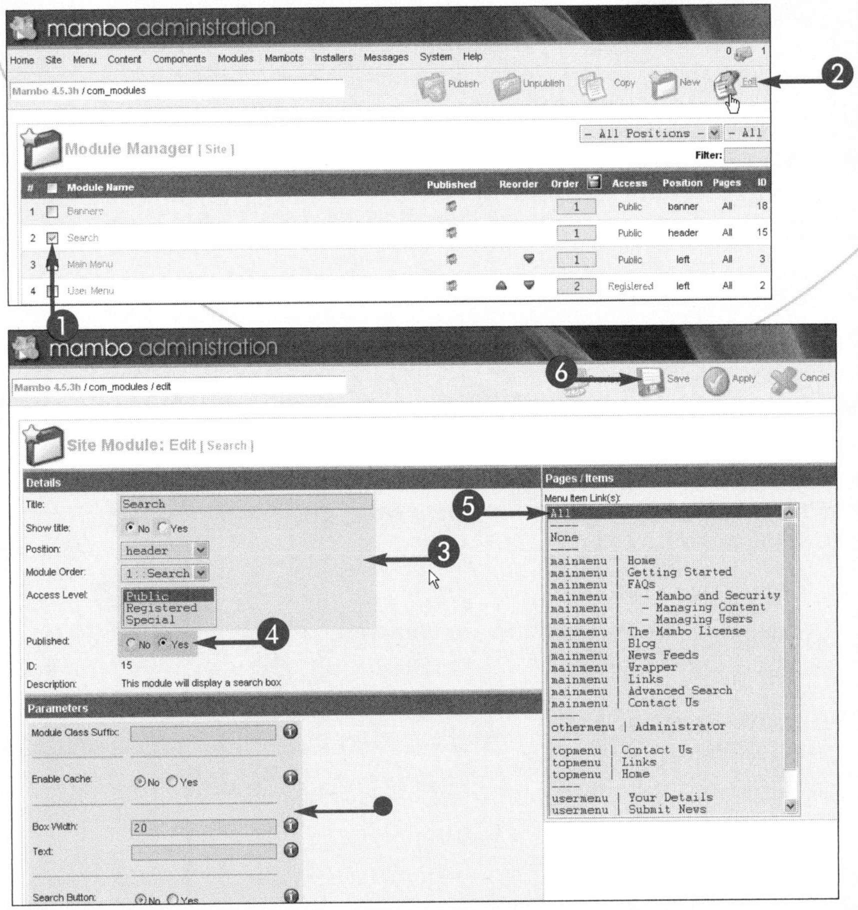

1. From the Module Manager, select the Search Module.
2. Click the Edit icon.

The Search Module Editing page loads.

3. Click these areas to select Show Title options, and the module's position, order of appearance, and access level.
4. For the Published option, click Yes.
5. Click the pages on which the module will appear.
   - You can click these areas to set optional parameters.
6. Click the Save icon.

Mambo configures the module and the module appears on the site.

Configure a Menu Module

You can configure the output of the various menus via the Module Manager. You can change the appearance and access levels of any of the menus by finding the related module and changing the configuration and parameters contained in the Menu module.

The default Mambo installation includes the Main, Top, User, and Other menus. There are multiple instances of the Menu module, one for each menu in the system. In Mambo, Menus and Menu modules are necessarily related. Whenever you create a new menu using the Menu Manager, the system automatically creates a new Menu module. You cannot display a menu without a Menu module. The menu is used for managing the Menu Items, and the Menu module for managing the Menu as a whole. The Menu module therefore controls where the menu appears on the page and what format it takes. For more on managing menus, see Chapter 9.

The parameters associated with the Menu modules give a great deal of control over menu layout and appearance. Fluency with the Menu module parameters is a key to creating effective menu and navigation structures. There are many third-party components available which are designed to extend the Mambo menu system, but it is possible to do quite a lot with the default system.

In addition to the unique menu parameters, outlined in the next section, "Understanding Menu Module Parameters," the access level option is often used to create menus that appear only to Registered or Special users. To create a site with multiple levels of front-end site users, you should take the time to understand the relationship between access levels and User Groups. The User Menu, for example, is by default assigned to an access level of Registered. You can set other menus to Public or Special depending on whom you want to have access to the choices on that particular menu. See Chapter 4 for more information on managing users. The section "Restrict Access to a Module" earlier in this chapter also contains useful information on this point.

Configure a Menu Module

1. From the Module Manager, select the Menu module you want to edit.
2. Click the Edit icon.

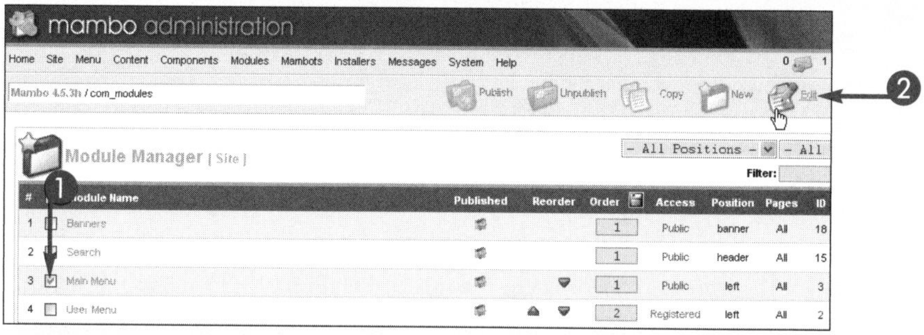

The Menu Module Editing page loads.

3. Click these areas to select the appropriate Show Title options as well as the module's position, order of appearance, and access level.
4. For the Published option, click Yes.
5. Click the pages on which you want the module to appear.
   - You can click these areas to set optional parameters.
6. Click the Save icon.

Mambo configures the module and it appears on the site.

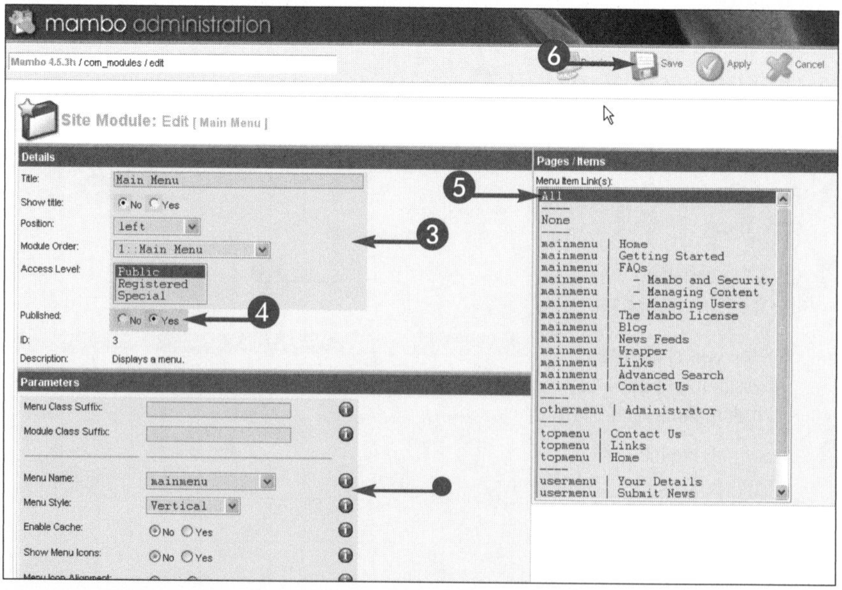

Understanding Menu Module Parameters

You can use parameters to create menus of different styles and formats. While some parameters, such as Enable Cache, are common to other types of modules, most are unique to Menu modules. Combining parameters with a creative use of CSS gives you a wide range of formatting and display options. Several options relate to using images with menus. Although the default Mambo system has basic images suitable for menus, you can always upload more to your site via FTP. You must place images in the /images/M_images directory. The following table lists Menu modules and their functions.

PARAMETER	DESCRIPTION
Module Class Suffix	Adds a unique identifier to the CSS class for this module to allow individual module styling. Useful for giving menus a particular appearance, such as a colored border.
Menu Class Suffix	Adds a unique identifier to the CSS class for this menu to allow individual menu styling. Useful for giving menus a particular appearance, such as a colored border or a particular font and font size.
Menu Name	Changes the menu with which the module is associated.
Menu Style	Controls the menu layout. Horizontal produces a menu with the items arranged in a single row. Vertical produces a menu where the items are lined up in a column. Flat List uses the HTML List Item (unordered list) syntax.
Enable Cache	Sets caching for this module. Caching the output of a module can improve a Web site's performance because it decreases the load on the server.
Show Menu Icons	Enables the use of icons beside the menu item names. This allows you to add a graphic to your Menu Items.
Menu Icon Alignment	Determines the alignment of the icon relative to the name of the Menu Item.
Expand Menu	For multi-tier menus only. This controls whether the default state of the menu expands, showing all levels, or collapses, showing only the top-level items.
Indent Image	To place images next to the text on indented Menu Items, you can choose the source of the image with this parameter. Choices include Template, the template's CSS for the image; Mambo Default Images, the Mambo default image collection; None; and Use Params Below, which activates the boxes below this parameter so you can select whatever image you want for each of the tiers in the menu. The last parameter is only relevant if you have a multi-tiered menu.
Indent Image 1-6	Relates to the Indent Image parameter, and is active only when you set the Indent Image Parameter to Use Params Below. There are six choices, enabling you to create menus up to six tiers deep, each with a unique image besides the text for the Menu Items in each tier.
Spacer	Sets a spacer between each Menu Item, which is useful only if you have the Menu Style set to Horizontal and if you use a character for your spacer. The character can either appear on the keyboard or as an ASCII equivalent that you type into the box.
End Spacer	Allows you to use a unique end spacer for a horizontal menu.

Configure the Login Form

You can place a login form on your Web site with the Login Form module. The form allows visitors to the site to log in and thereby gain access to areas of the site not available to other users. For more on how to restrict access to content, see Chapter 6.

The Form includes a link to the Password Reminder function, which allows registered users who have forgotten their password to have a new one automatically generated and sent to their email address. Additionally, if the System Administrator enables user registration, the Login Form can contain a link to the registration form. For more on enabling user registration, see Chapter 4.

The parameters associated with this module are very simple. The Module Class Suffix parameter enables you to tie the module to a specific CSS class so you can give your login box a particular appearance, such as a colored background or a border. The Pre-Text and Post-Text parameters allow you to specify text to appear before or after the form, respectively. The Login and Logout Redirection URL parameters define the URL to which users are taken when they log in and log out, respectively. If you do not specify a URL, users are taken to the home page. The Login and Logout Message Parameters establish greeting and goodbye messages for users as they log in and log out.

The Greeting parameter and the Name/Username parameters work together. Greeting sets the text shown on the screen, along with the user's name, while the user is logged in. Name/Username determines whether the Greeting utilizes the user's name or username. Taken together, the two parameters allow you to set up a personalized message for a logged-in user, such as "Welcome back, John."

Configure the Login Form

1. From the Module Manager, select the Login Form module.
2. Click the Edit icon.

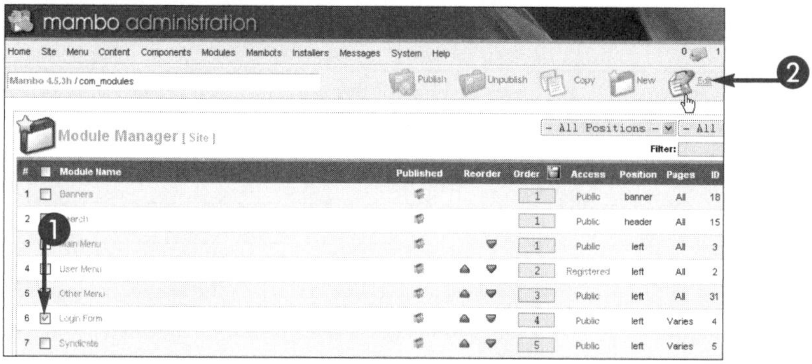

3. Click these areas to set the Show Title options as well as to select a module position, an order of appearance, and an access level for the module.
4. Click Yes for the Published option.
5. Click the pages on which you want the module to appear.
   - You can click here to set optional parameters.
6. Click the Save icon.

Mambo configures the module and the module appears on the site.

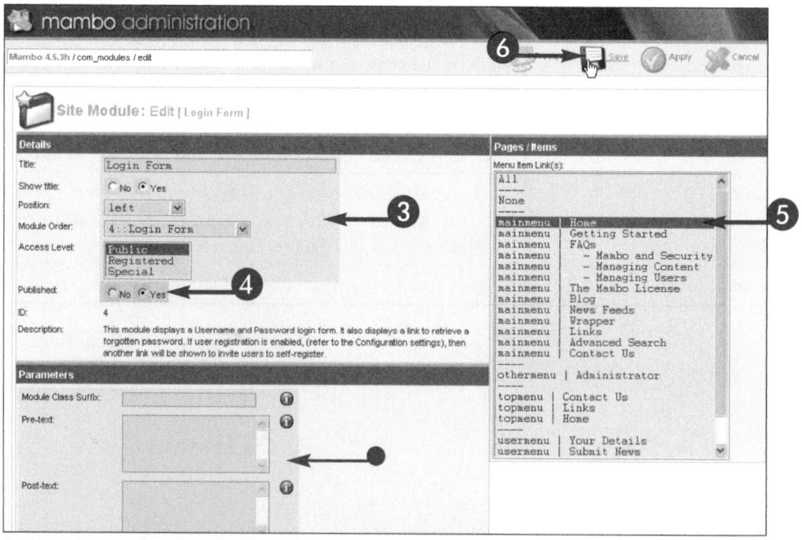

Configure the Syndicate Module

You can syndicate the contents of your site via RSS by using the Syndicate module. RSS syndication provides an easy way for people to access the content of your Web site remotely through RSS readers. Readers automatically check sites periodically for changes, then grab the contents and display them for the viewer. This feature is highly desirable if you are trying to build awareness of your site's contents and want others to access the information remotely, or where you want to publish your content on RSS-enabled news aggregators.

Mambo automatically creates the XML formats to syndicate your content via the RSS protocol. To use this function, you need only publish the RSS module, which then displays a set of standard RSS icons. The standard icons notify users that RSS is available on your site and also provides them with the links for their RSS reader or aggregator.

The parameters associated with this module reflect the various options available for RSS syndication. The Text parameter sets intro text for the module. The Enable Cache parameter sets caching for the module. Caching the output of a module is a way to improve the performance of a Web site because it decreases the load on the server. Caching is recommended for most sites; however, be aware that if the contents of your site change very frequently, you may not find caching very desirable. Module Class Suffix ties the module to a specific CSS class. This is useful if you want the module to have a particular appearance, such as a colored background or a different font. The RSS, Atom, and OPML parameters allow you to decide which formats of feeds your site offers. The RSS, Atom, and OPML Images parameters set the icons associated with each feed type.

Configure the Syndicate Module

1. From the Module Manager, select the Syndicate module.
2. Click the Edit icon.

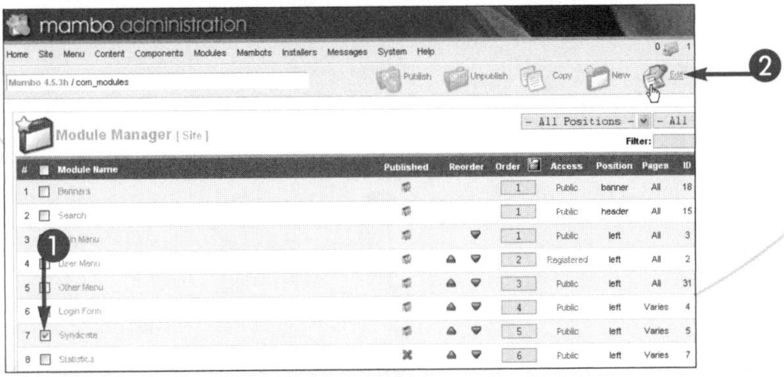

The Syndicate Module Editing page loads.

3. Click these areas to set the Show title option as well as to set a position, an order of appearance, and an access level for the module.
4. Set Published to Yes.
5. Click the pages on which you want the module to appear.
   - You can click these areas to set optional parameters.
6. Click the Save icon.

Mambo configures the module and it appears on the site.

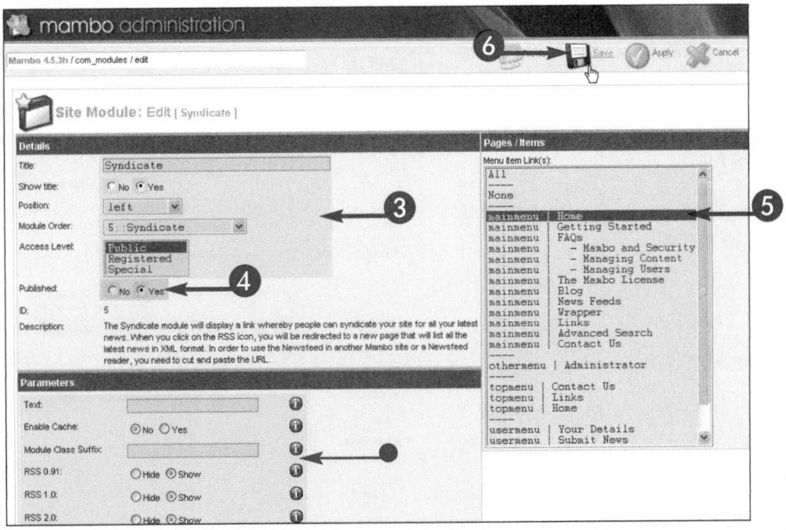

Configure the Statistics Module

You can display basic information about your server and your site for users by publishing the Statistics module. The module output shows the number of users, the number of visits, and some simple details of your server installation. The display of the statistics is a basic function you often find on community-oriented portal sites. Note that display of information about your server may not always be desirable because it does provide facts that could be useful to someone intent on hacking or compromising your site.

Mambo gives you several parameters for your Statistics module. The Server Info option displays essential information about the server where your Mambo site is installed, including the operating system of your server, the version of PHP running on the server, the version of MySQL, the current time at the server, whether caching is enabled, and whether GZip is enabled. The Site Info option displays essential information about your site, including the number of registered members, the number of news items, and the number of weblinks in the Web Links component. The Hit Counter option shows the historical number of visits to the site. The parameters associated with this module control the display of the information items outlined earlier. Server Info enables or disables the display of the server information. Site Info enables or disables the display of the site information. Hit Counter enables or disables the display of the historical visitor traffic. The Increase Counter parameter allows you to increase the number of visits shown on the Hit Counter. Module Class Suffix ties the module to a specific CSS class. This is useful if you want the module to have a particular appearance, such as a colored background or a different font.

Configure the Statistics Module

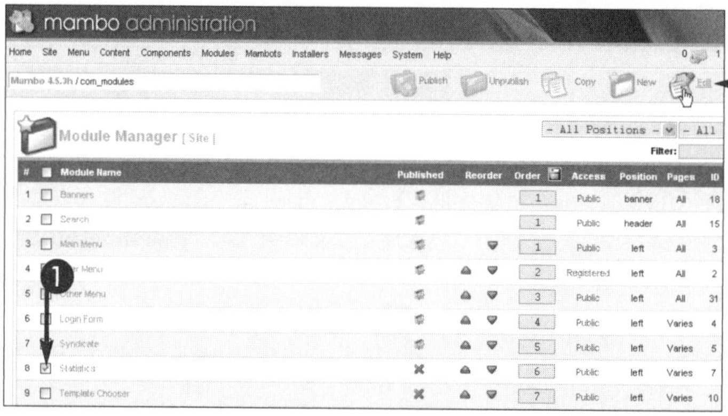

1. From the Module Manager, select the Statistics module.
2. Click the Edit icon.

The Statistics Module Editing page loads.

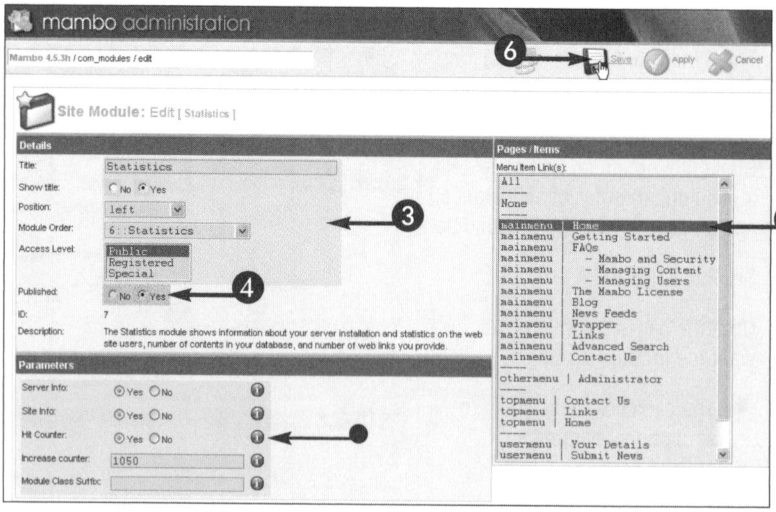

3. Click these areas to set the Show Title option as well as to select the module's position, order of appearance, and access level.
4. Click Yes for the Published option.
5. Click the pages on which you want the module to appear.
   - You can click these areas to set optional parameters.
6. Click the Save icon.

Mambo configures the module and it appears on the site.

Configure the Template Chooser

You can let site visitors pick the template they want to see on the site by enabling the Template Chooser module. This is a fun feature that lets users alter the appearance of your site by changing the template they see. The change appears only to the individual user; it does not affect the site for other users. Aside from the fun factor, this feature is also useful during site development because you can experiment with different templates from the front end, rather than having to go back and forth as you change templates through the admin system's Template Manager and then view them on the front end. For more information about how to change templates using the Template Manager, see Chapter 3.

The Template Chooser displays all templates installed on the site. If you want to use this feature, make sure that all the templates installed are appropriate and function properly with your selection of components, modules, and content layout.

There is a limited number of parameters connected to this module. The Max. Name Length parameter sets a limit on the length of the template name displayed inside the module. This is useful to prevent a long name from breaking the module layout. Show Preview shows a thumbnail image for previewing the templates. If you enable this, the Width and Height parameters also become active. The Width and Height parameters define the size of the thumbnail preview of the templates. You must enable the Show Preview parameter for these parameters to be meaningful. Module Class Suffix ties the module to a specific CSS class. This is useful if you want the module to have a particular appearance, such as a colored background or a different font.

Configure the Template Chooser

1. From the Module Manager, select the Template Chooser module.
2. Click the Edit icon.

   The Template Chooser Module Editing page loads.

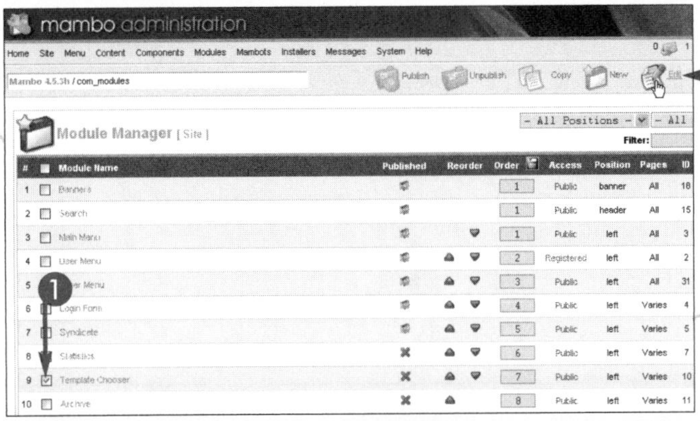

3. Click these areas to set the Show Title option, as well as to select the module's position, order of appearance, and access level.
4. Click Yes for the Published option.
5. Click the pages on which you want the module to appear.
   - You can click these areas to set optional parameters.
6. Click the Save icon.

   Mambo configures the module and it appears on the site.

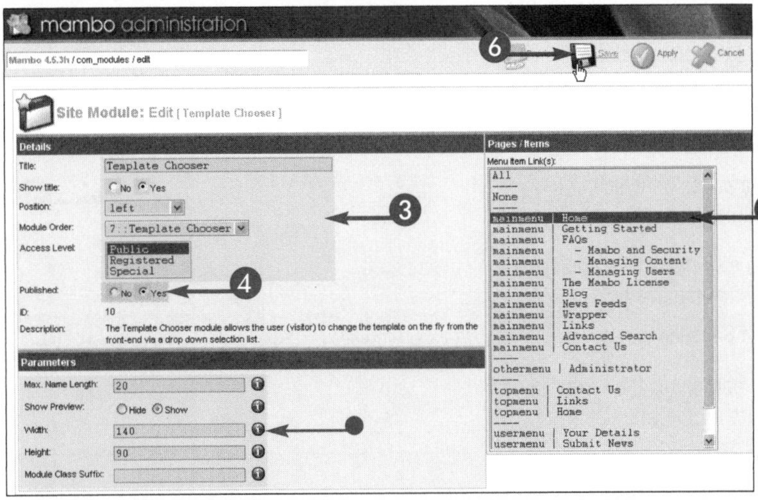

Configure the Archive Module

You can show users a list of months with links to archived Content Items. This feature is useful for content sites where the Administrator wants to archive old Content Items. Publishing the Archive module allows site visitors to access the archived items by the month in which they were archived. The module shows the most recently archived items first. You commonly employ this feature on blog-type sites where contents are organized chronologically. It is also useful on news sites or other sites containing time-sensitive information.

The Archive module relates only to archived Content Items; therefore, links appear only for the months with archived content. If no content was archived, the module appears as blank. If all the information for a particular month is unarchived, the month no longer appears in the Archive module. For more information on archiving Content Items, see Chapter 6.

One of the limitations of this module is that you cannot use it in relation to specific sections or categories. It relates only to the contents of the Archive Manager as a whole.

There is a limited number of parameters associated with the Archive module. Count sets a limit on the number of links that appear in the module. Enable Cache sets caching for the module. Caching the output of a module is a way to improve the performance of a Web site because it decreases the load on the server. Caching is recommended for most sites; however, be aware that if the contents of your site change very frequently, caching may not be desirable. Module Class Suffix ties the module to a specific CSS class. This is useful if you want the module to have a particular appearance, such as a colored background or a different font.

Configure the Archive Module

1. From the Module Manager, select the Archive module.
2. Click the Edit icon.

   The Archive Module Editing page loads.

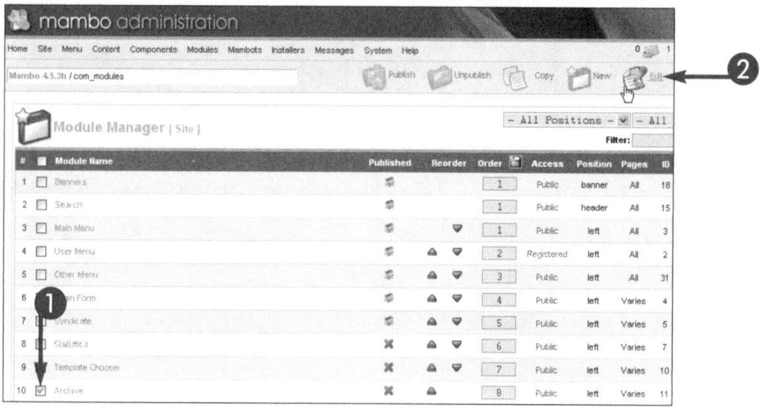

3. Click these areas to set the Show Title option, as well as to select the module's position, order of appearance, and access level.
4. Click Yes for the Published option.
5. Click the pages on which you want the module to appear.
   - You can click these areas to set optional parameters.
6. Click the Save icon.

   Mambo configures the module and it appears on the site.

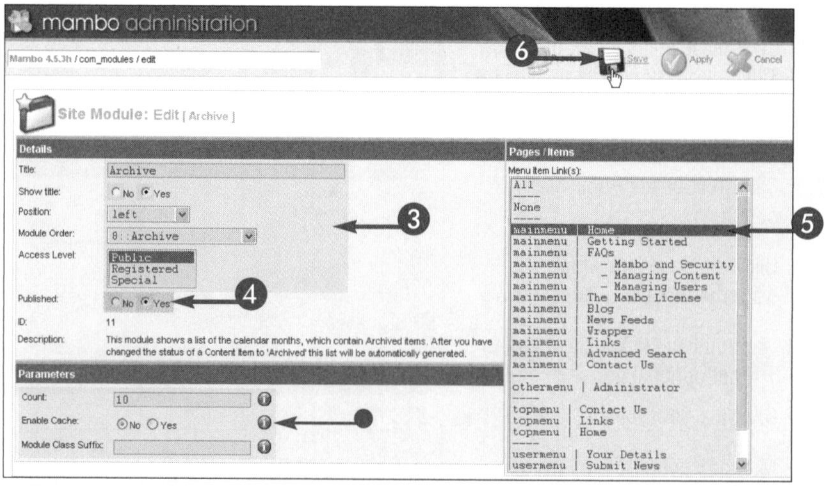

Configure the Sections Module

You can use the Sections module to provide easy access to the content structure and to help drive traffic into your Content Items. With this module, visitors to your site see a list of all the sections on the site with links to each section. You can set up a navigation shortcut and position it where you want using the module assignment options.

The module is also related to the site's Global Configuration settings. On the Global Configuration Site tab, when you disable the Show Unauthorized Links option, the site shows only the links to content that is open to the public. Once a user logs in, registered and special-access-level content links appear to users of the appropriate user group. If you enable this option, site visitors see only a list of all content sections, even those sections to which you have restricted access. If users click one of the restricted sections, they are prompted to log in. The feature essentially provides a "teaser" to help motivate unregistered users to become members of your site using the promise of more content as an incentive. For more information about restricting access to content, see Chapter 6. For more information setting the site's Global Configuration, see Chapter 2.

There are only two parameters for this module. The Count parameter sets the maximum number of sections that appear in the module. Module Class Suffix ties the module to a specific CSS class. This is useful if you want the module to have a particular appearance, such as a colored background or a different font.

Configure the Sections Module

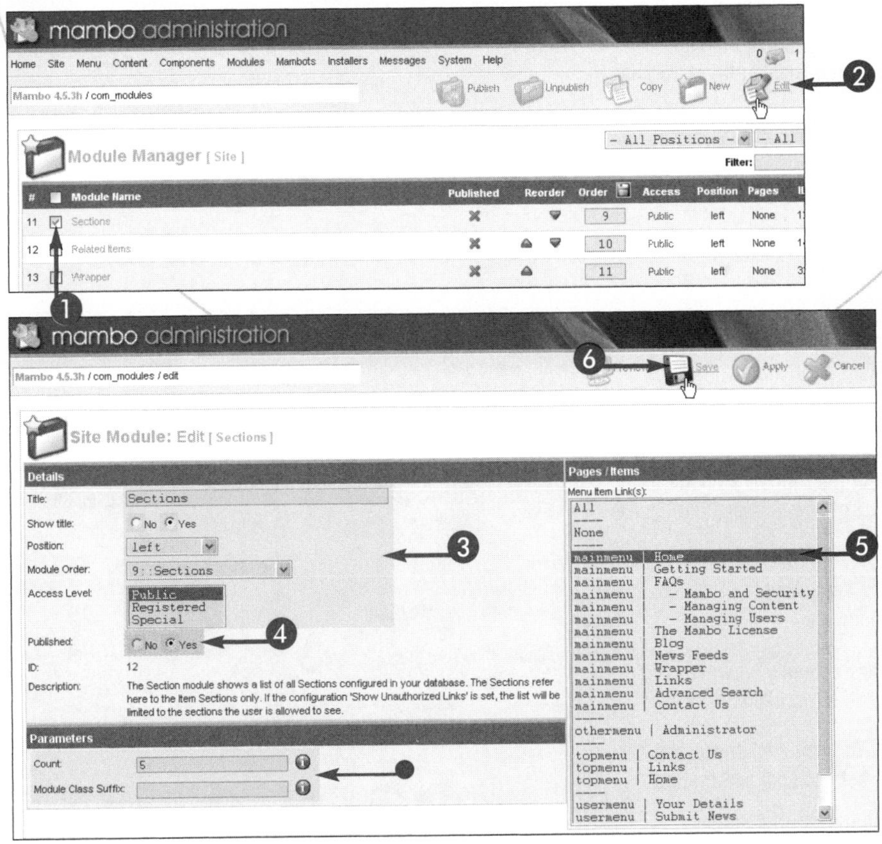

1. From the Module Manager, select the Sections module.
2. Click the Edit icon.

   The Sections Module Editing page loads.
3. Click these areas to set the Show Title option, as well as to select the module's position, order of appearance, and access level.
4. Click Yes for the Published option.
5. Click the pages on which you want the module to appear.
   - You can click these areas to set optional parameters.
6. Click the Save icon.

   Mambo configures the module and it appears on the site.

Configure the Related Items Module

You can use the Related Items module to display a list of links to related Content Items for your visitors. This feature is very useful on content pages because it creates connections between Content Items on your site. Visitors tend to appreciate this feature because it helps them find related information and, thus, makes your site more useful.

The Related Items functionality works by looking at the keywords entered in each of the Content Item's metadata. When a Content Item appears, the Related Items module looks at the keywords for that Content Item, compares them to other Content Items on the site, and then displays a list of links to items with the same keywords. You must input the keywords for each Content Item manually into the provided metadata fields. The function is, therefore, dependent upon the content creators inserting relevant keywords into the various Content Items, and it is dependent on them doing it in a consistent fashion. For more on how to set metadata for a Content Item, see Chapter 6.

There are only two parameters for the Related Items module. The Enable Cache parameter sets caching for the module. Caching the output of a module is a way to improve the performance of a Web site because it decreases the load on the server. Caching is recommended for most sites; however, be aware that if the contents of your site change very frequently, caching may not be desirable. Module Class Suffix ties the module to a specific CSS class. This is useful if you want the module to have a particular appearance, such as a colored background or a different font.

Configure the Related Items Module

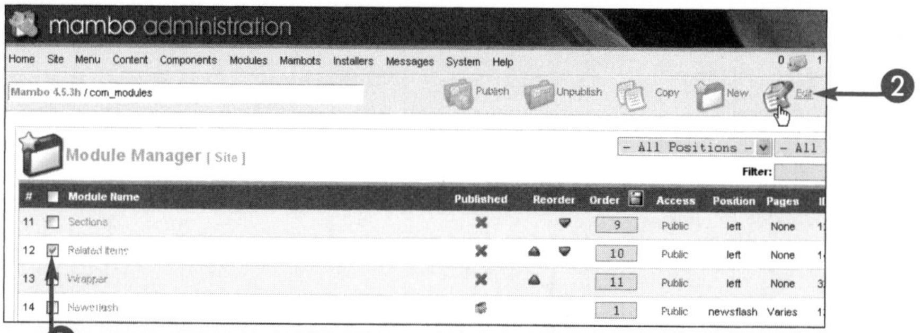

1. From the Module Manager, select the Related Items module.

2. Click the Edit icon.

The Related Items Module Editing page loads.

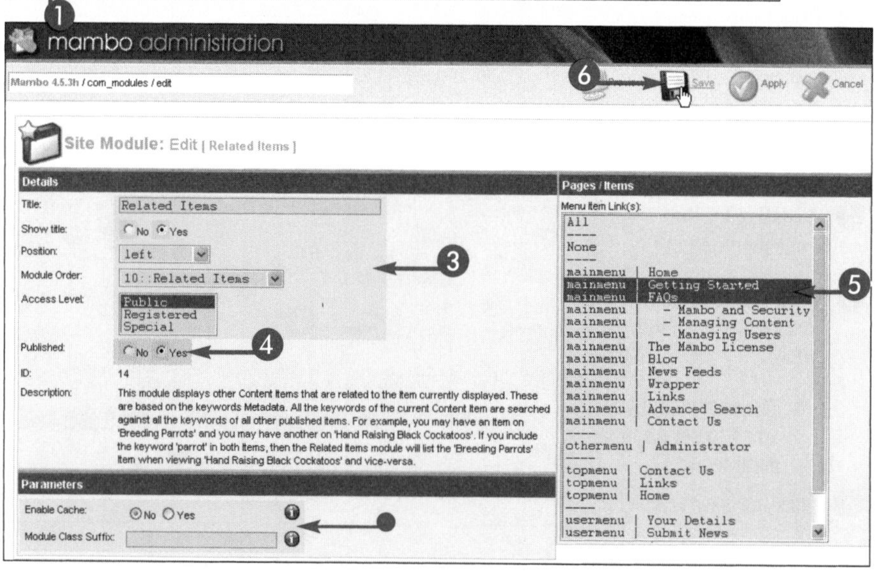

3. Click these areas to set the Show Title option, as well as to select the module's position, order of appearance, and access level.

4. Click Yes to set the Published option.

5. Click the pages on which you want the module to appear.

   - You can click these areas to set optional parameters.

6. Click the Save icon.

Mambo configures the module and it appears on the site.

Configure the Wrapper Module

You can display the contents of another Web page on your Web site using the Wrapper module. This feature is useful for displaying content located on another server, or for displaying content created outside your Mambo system but located on your server.

Wrapper modules work in the same manner as a wrapper page. The module creates an iFrame and then within that iFrame automatically calls and displays another Web page. Note that if you use a Wrapper to display content from another location, there may be a delay before the content appears. To learn more about the Wrapper option for page creation, see Chapter 8.

The Wrapper module parameters allow you to specify the address of the Web page you want to display and to control the appearance of the iFrame window.

Module Class Suffix ties the module to a specific CSS class. This is useful if you want the module to have a particular appearance, such as a colored background or a different font.

The URL parameter is for specifying the address of the page you want to display inside the iFrame. Note that you must type in the full URL, including the "http://" prefix, unless the page is on your local domain and you have enabled the Auto Add parameter in this section. The Scroll Bars parameter controls whether the iFrame includes left/right and up/down scroll bars. Width and Height dictate the size of the iFrame. Auto Height automatically sets the height of the iFrame to match the wrapped page. Note that you can use this option only when the page you want to wrap is located on your domain. Auto Add automatically adds the necessary prefix to the address you enter in URL parameter. Note that you can use this option only where the page you want to wrap is located on your domain.

Configure the Wrapper Module

1. From the Module Manager, select the Wrapper module.
2. Click the Edit icon.

   The Wrapper Module Editing page loads.
3. Click these areas to set the Show Title option, as well as to select the module's position, order of appearance, and access level.
4. Click Yes to set the Published option.
5. Click the pages on which you want the module to appear.

   - You can click these areas to set optional parameters.
6. Click the Save icon.

   Mambo configures the module and it appears on the site.

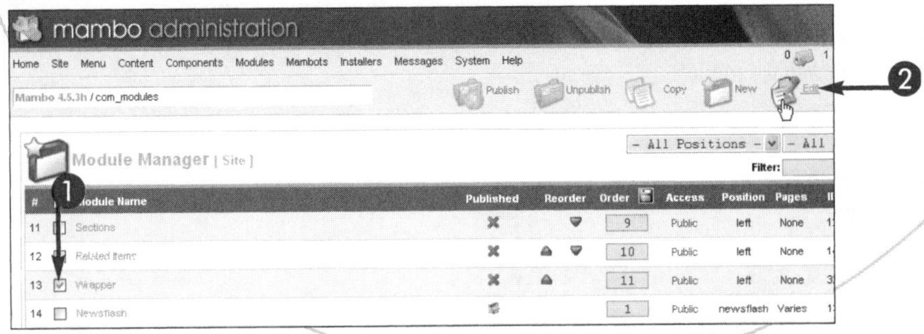

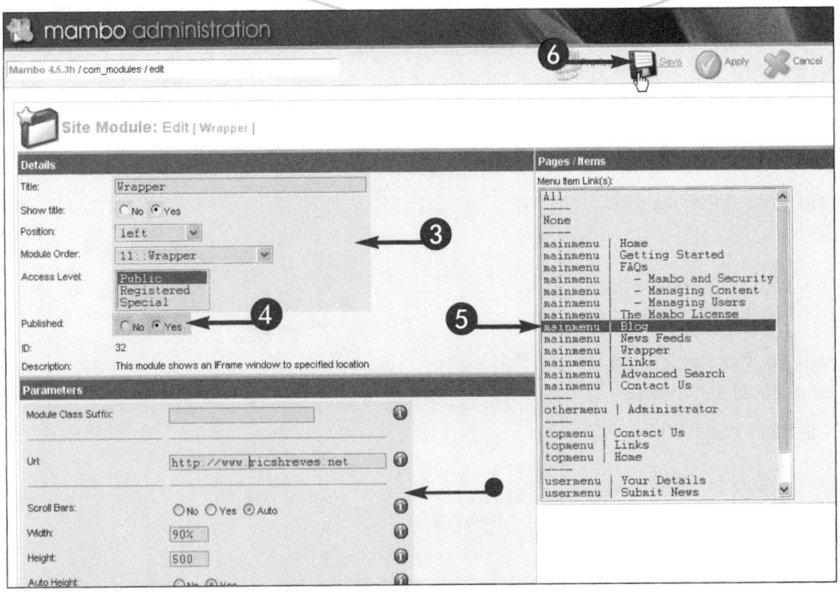

Configure the Newsflash Module

You can use the Newsflash module to pull Content Items from a content category and display them in a module. The module is an effective tool for displaying short messages on the site. The default site installation uses this technique to display text at the top right of the home page. The text changes each time the page is refreshed.

You can specify the source of the content displayed. All content categories are eligible for display by the Newsflash module. You can run multiple instances of this module to display more than one category. For more information on using multiple instances of a single module, see Chapter 12.

There are a number of parameters attached to this module. Category allows you to select the source of the Content Items displayed. Style sets the manner of the display; Content Items can be randomized or shown in either horizontal or vertical format. The Show images option enables the display of Content Item images. Linked Titles and Read More determine whether the user can click the item to go to the full version of the item. No. of Items determines how many items are displayed in the module. You only use it when the Style parameter is set to Horizontal or Vertical.

Enable Cache sets caching for the module. Caching the output of a module is a way to improve the performance of a Web site because it decreases the load on the server. Caching is recommended for most sites; however, be aware that if the contents of your site change very frequently, caching may not be desirable.

Module Class Suffix ties the module to a specific CSS class. This is useful if you want the module to have a particular appearance, such as a colored background or a different font.

Configure the Newsflash Module

1. From the Module Manager, select the Newsflash module.
2. Click the Edit icon.

   The Newsflash Module Editing page loads.

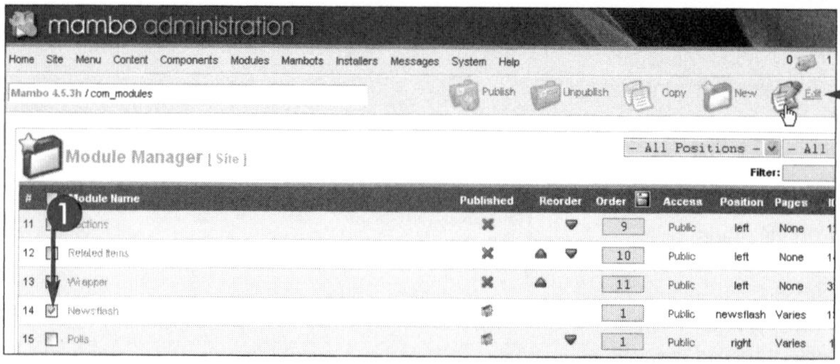

3. Click these areas to set the Show Title option, as well as to select the module's position, order of appearance, and access level.
4. Click Yes to set the Published option.
5. Click the pages on which you want the module to appear.
   - You can click these areas to set optional parameters.
6. Click the Save icon.

   Mambo configures the module and it appears on the site.

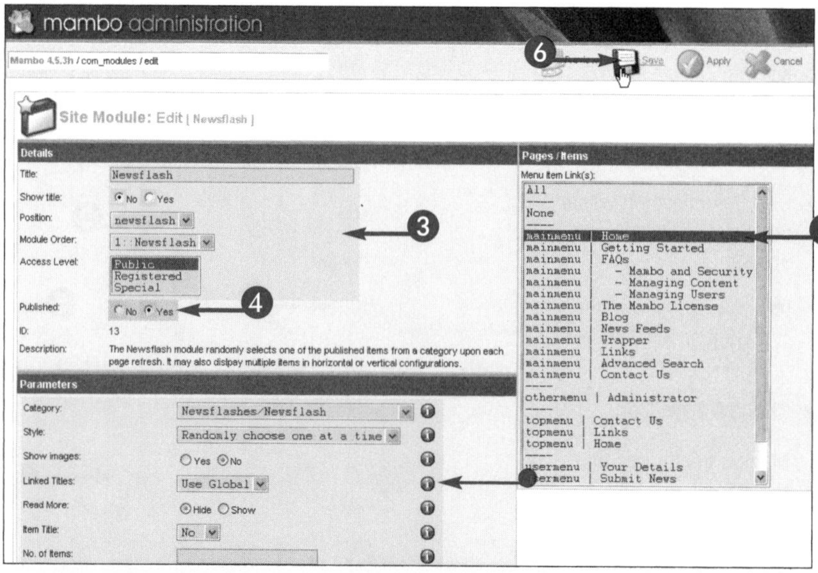

Configure the Polls Module

You can set up and display a poll for site visitors using the Polls module and the Polls component. Polls, or surveys, are a popular feature for Web sites because they create interactivity and provide a mechanism for gathering user feedback and information.

The Polls module is connected to the Polls component. The module controls the display of all poll items created with the component. Note that the Polls module is different from other modules in that multiple polls are run from one instance of the module. When you create a new poll in the Polls component, you must assign the poll to one or more Menu Items. Thereafter, you must assign the polls to the same pages if you want the polls to appear. If you use the default structure for poll management, Mambo assigns all the polls throughout the site to the same module position. If you want to vary the module positions between polls, you must create a copy of the Polls module and use separate instances to control individual polls. For more information on the Polls component, see Chapter 10. For more on working with multiple instances of a module, see Chapter 12.

The Polls module contains only two parameters. Enable Cache sets caching for the module. Caching the output of a module is a way to improve the performance of a Web site because it decreases the load on the server. Caching is recommended for most sites; however, be aware that if the contents of your site change very frequently, caching may not be desirable. Module Class Suffix ties the module to a specific CSS class. This is useful if you want the module to have a particular appearance, such as a colored background or a different font.

Configure the Polls Module

1. From the Polls Manager, select the Polls module.
2. Click the Edit icon.

   The Polls Module Editing page loads.
3. Click these areas to set the Show Title option, as well as to select the module's position, order of appearance, and access level.
4. Click Yes to set the Published option.
5. Click the pages on which you want the module to appear.
   - You can click these areas to set optional parameters.
6. Click the Save icon.

   Mambo configures the module and it appears on the site.

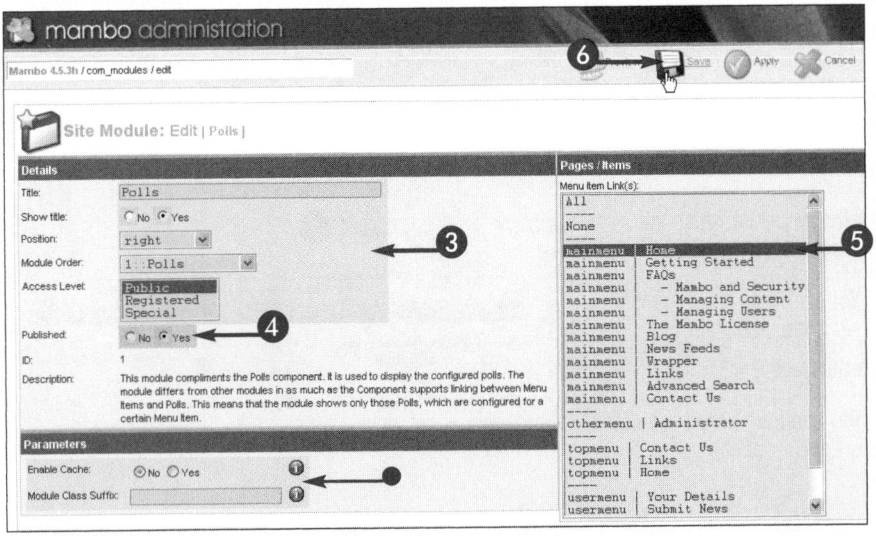

Configure the Who's Online Module

The Who's Online module allows you to display a list of the number of users that are active on the site and the actual names of the users. The module is useful for community sites where people are curious about levels of site activity or where they want to know if certain users are active. Features like Who's Online are one way of demonstrating that a site is vital and can help people feel more like they are members of a community.

The module gives you the choice of displaying the information anonymously or by username. For a user's name to appear on the site, the user must have both registered with the site and logged in to the system. Until a user logs in, they appear only in the anonymous Guest count. Once the user logs in, their username appears below the Guest count. If the user logs out, their name disappears and they are again counted as an anonymous Guest.

There are only two parameters associated with the Who's Online module. The Display parameter determines what information Mambo shows. The three choices are # of Guests/Members, which shows only the number of guests and users that are online at the time; Member Names, which displays the names of all the registered and logged-in users; and Both, which displays both a count of all the guest users and the names of all the registered and logged-in users. The Module Class Suffix parameter ties the module to a specific CSS class. This is useful if you want the module to have a particular appearance, such as a colored background or a different font.

Configure the Who's Online Module

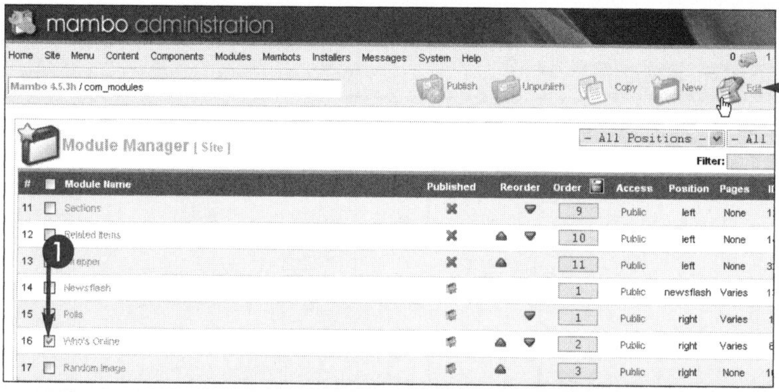

1. From the Module Manager, select the Who's Online module.
2. Click the Edit icon.

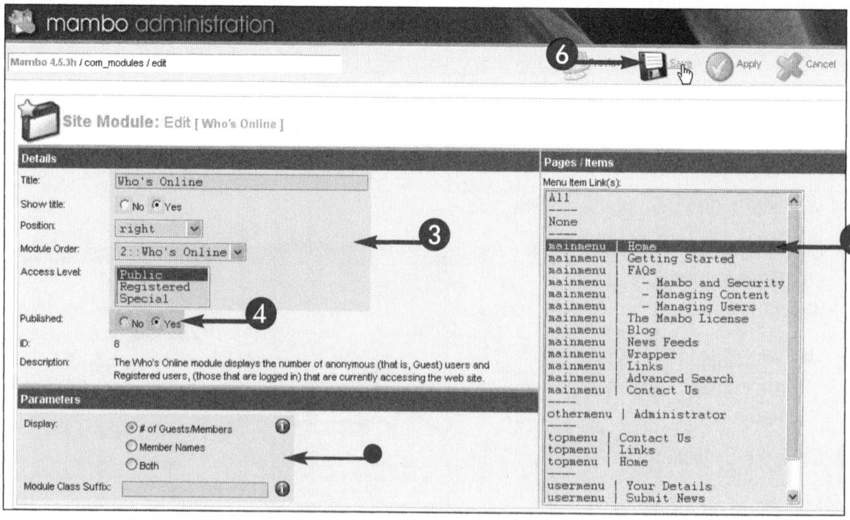

The Who's Online Module Editing page loads.

3. Click these areas to set the Show Title option, as well as to select the module's position, order of appearance, and access level.
4. Click Yes to set the Published option.
5. Click the pages on which you want the module to appear.
   - You can click these areas to set optional parameters.
6. Click the Save icon.

Mambo configures the module and it appears on the site.

Configure the Random Image Module

You can display an image selected randomly from a local directory using the Random Image module. The module produces a dynamic image area on a page, and can even rotate the header image on a Web page or display advertising banners. Because the image changes each time the page is reloaded, the module is an effective way to add variety and interest to a site.

You must place all the images that this module uses in the same directory on the server where your Mambo site is located. You must make all images the same file type. Although the system allows you to force images to resize, it is generally better practice to size the images in advance and to add them to the system in a uniform format. Consider optimizing the images before you upload them to decrease their size and loading time.

The Random Image module includes several parameters that allow you to control the appearance and formatting of the images. The Image Type parameter specifies the format of the images to be displayed. Note that you must select only one format. The Image Folder parameter tells the system where to find the image files. The Link parameter allows you the option to attach a URL to an image, making the image clickable. This feature lets you use the Random Image module to display advertisements, like a banner management tool. Width and Height are optional parameters and, if set, force the image to resize to the dimensions given. Module Class Suffix ties the module to a specific CSS class. This is useful if you want the module to have a particular appearance, such as a colored background or a different font.

Configure the Random Image Module

1. From the Module Manager, select the Random Image module.

Note: To access the Module Manager, see the section "An Introduction to the Module Manager."

2. Click the Edit icon.

The Random Image Module Editing page loads.

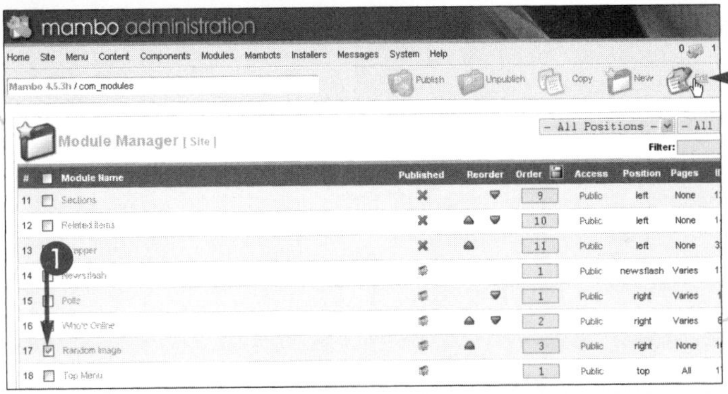

3. Click these areas to set the Show Title option, as well as to select the module's position, order of appearance, and access level.

4. Click Yes to set the Published option.

5. Click the pages on which you want the module to appear.

   - You can click these areas to set optional parameters.

6. Click the Save icon.

Mambo configures the module and it appears on the site.

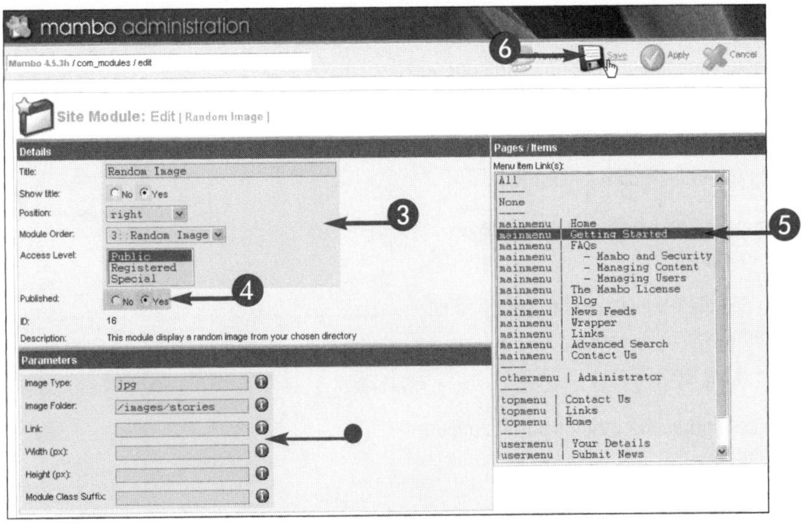

Configure the Latest News Module

You can display a list of the most recently published Content Items with the Latest News module. This module is a useful way to draw visitors' attention to the most recent additions to your site. The Latest News module is very flexible and opens up a variety of possibilities for you to display information. You can make it section- or category-specific, and you do not have to limit yourself to a particular type of Content Item.

The module provides several important parameters. Module Class Suffix ties the module to a specific CSS class. This is useful if you want the module to have a particular appearance, such as a colored background or a different font. Enable Cache sets caching for the module. Caching the output of a module is a way to improve the performance of a Web site because it decreases the load on the server. Caching is recommended for most sites; however, be aware that if the contents of your site change very frequently, caching may not be desirable.

Module Mode presents a choice between displaying only content from the sections and category, displaying only static content, or both. This parameter has implications for the rest of the parameters discussed in this section. Frontpage Items is a filter that gives you the option to show or exclude items that appear on the front page. You use this parameter only if the Module Mode is set to the Content Items option.

Count sets the maximum number of items that appear in the module. Category ID and Section ID provide the mechanism for specifying which contents are shown. These parameters use the numeric ID numbers that appear in the Section Manager and the Category Manager. You use these parameters only if the Module Mode is set to the Content Items option.

Configure the Latest News Module

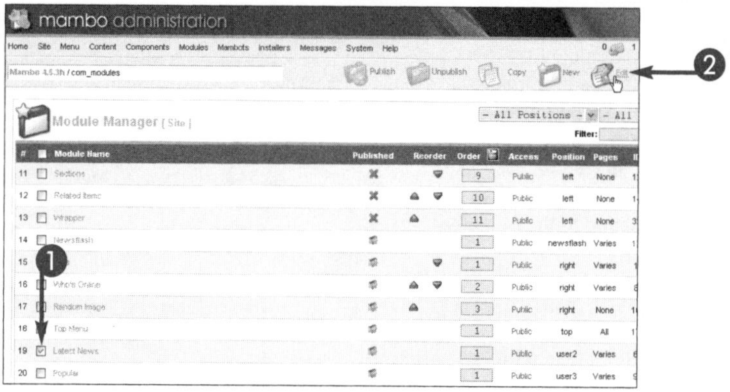

1. From the Module Manager, select the Latest News module.
2. Click the Edit icon.

The Latest News Module Editing page loads.

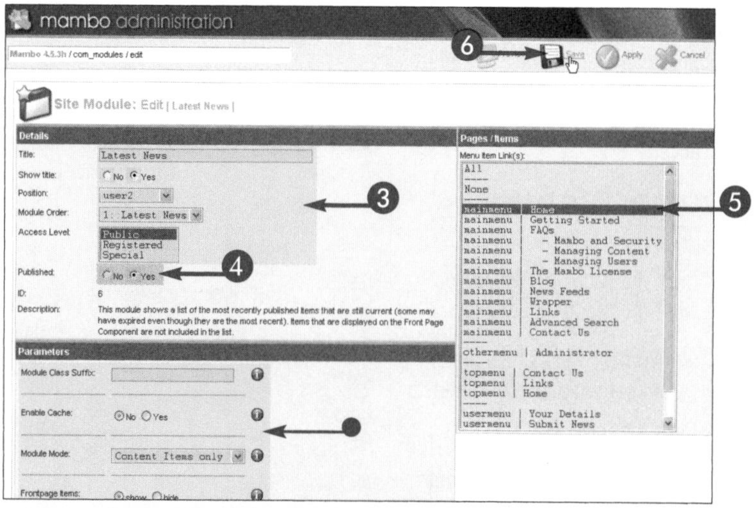

3. Click these areas to set the Show Title option, as well as to select the module's position, order of appearance, and access level.
4. Click Yes to set the Published option.
5. Click the pages on which you want the module to appear.
   - You can click these areas to set optional parameters.
6. Click the Save icon.

Mambo configures the module and it appears on the site.

Configure the Latest Content Module

You can display one or more of the most recently published Content Items with the Latest Content module. This module is similar to the Latest News module, discussed in the last section, but whereas the Latest News module only displays links to the Content Items, the Latest Content module shows not only the Content Items' titles, but also the Intro Text for the Content Item. The Latest Content module is a useful alternative for displaying a Content Item or Items in various places on your page.

The module provides several parameters. Module Class Suffix ties the module to a specific CSS class. This is useful if you want the module to have a particular appearance, such as a colored background or a different font. Enable Cache sets caching for the module. Caching the output of a module is a way to improve the performance of a Web site because it decreases the load on the server.

Module Mode presents a choice between displaying only content from the sections and category, displaying only static content, or both. Frontpage Items is a filter that gives you the option to show items that appear on the front page. Read More determines whether the Read More link is included for Content Items, which have both Intro Text and Main Text. You use these two parameters only if the Module Mode is set to the Content Items option.

Item Title determines whether the title is included with the Intro Text. Show Images displays or hides the images included in the Content Item.

Count sets the maximum number of items that appear in the module. Category ID and Section ID provide the mechanism for specifying which contents are shown. These parameters use the numeric ID numbers that appear in the Section Manager and the Category Manager.

Configure the Latest Content Module

1. From the Module Manager, select the Latest Content module.
2. Click the Edit icon.

   The Latest Content Module Editing page loads.
3. Click these areas to set the Show Title option, as well as to select the module's position, order of appearance, and access level.
4. Click Yes to set the Published option.
5. Click the pages on which you want the module to appear.
   - You can click these areas to set optional parameters.
6. Click the Save icon.

   Mambo configures the module and it appears on the site.

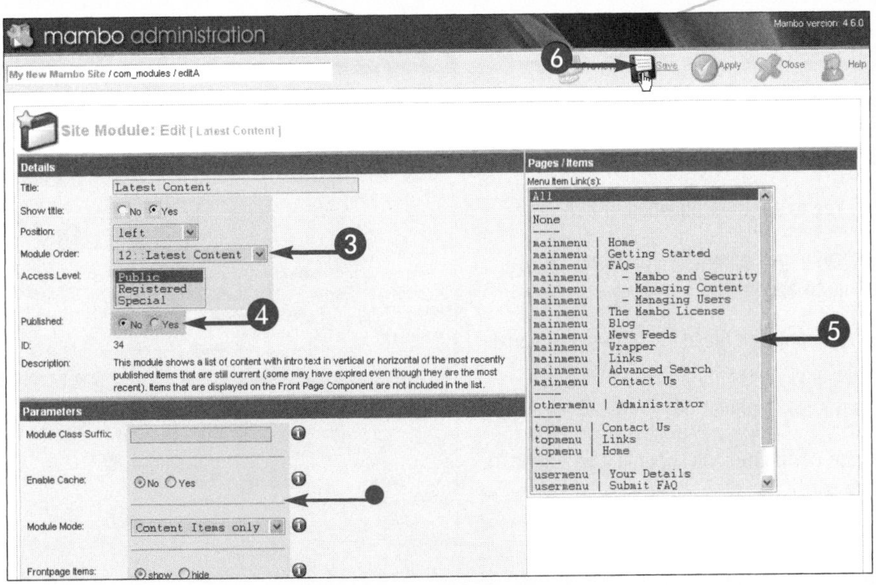

Configure the Popular Module

You can display a list of the most popular published Content Items with the Popular module. This module is a useful way to draw visitors' attention to the most popular Content Items on your site. The Popular module is very flexible and opens up a variety of possibilities. You can make it section- or category-specific, and you do not have to limit yourself to a particular type of Content Item.

The module provides several important parameters. Module Class Suffix ties the module to a specific CSS class. This is useful if you want the module to have a particular appearance, such as a colored background or a different font. Enable Cache sets caching for the module. Caching the output of a module is a way to improve the performance of a Web site because it decreases the load on the server. Caching is recommended for most sites; however, be aware that if the contents of your site change very frequently, caching may not be desirable. Module Mode presents a choice between displaying only content from the sections and category, displaying only static content, or both. This parameter has implications for the rest of the parameters that are discussed in this section. Frontpage Items is a filter that gives you the option to show or exclude items that are displayed on the front page. You use this parameter only if the Module Mode is set to the Content Items option. Count sets the maximum number of items that appear in the module. Category ID and Section ID provide the mechanism for specifying which contents are shown. These parameters use the numeric ID numbers that appear in the Section Manager and the Category Manager. You use these parameters only if the Module Mode is set to the Content Items option.

Configure the Popular Module

1. From the Module Manager, select the Popular module.
2. Click the Edit icon.

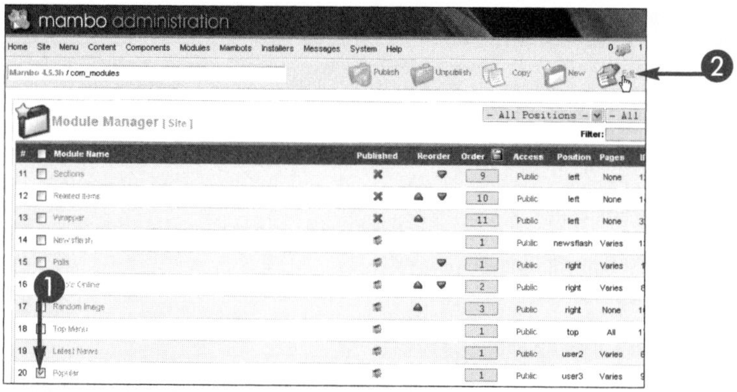

The Popular Module Editing page loads.

3. Click these areas to set the Show Title option, as well as to select the module's position, order of appearance, and access level.
4. Click Yes to set the Published option.
5. Click the pages on which you want the module to appear.
   - You can click these areas to set optional parameters.
6. Click the Save icon.

Mambo configures the module and it appears on the site.

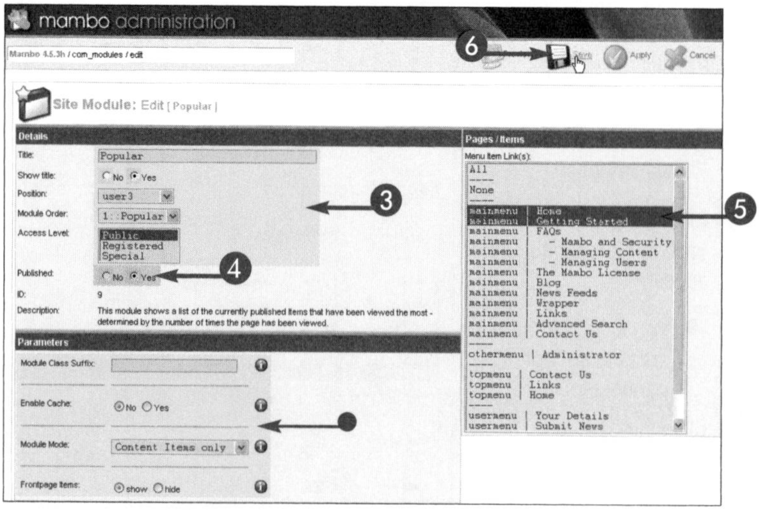

Remove a Module

You can uninstall an entire module or simply delete an instance of a module using the tools in the Module Manager and the Module Installer. Uninstalling a module removes all of the related files, but it does not impact any of your content, your components, or Mambots. Deleting an instance simply removes that one occurrence of the module while leaving the underlying module files on the server.

To properly eliminate a module completely, you use the uninstaller function in the Module Installer, which removes all instances of the module and the underlying code from the server. You can, in contrast, delete one or more instances of a module without uninstalling the entire module using the Delete command in the Module Manager interface. To complicate things slightly, you cannot uninstall certain modules at all because they are part of Mambo's core.

Note that unlike Content Items or Menu Items, Mambo does not move modules, but rather, permanently deletes them. Think carefully before you confirm deletion because the module and all of its associated files are completely eliminated from your system. The only way to get the module back is to reinstall it from scratch.

Given these facts, consider simply leaving the module in the system, unused. If you have not published a module, the files are completely inactive. Because Mambo does not call the module, the presence of the unused files does not impair your site's performance. Alternatively, you can backup the files prior to deleting them by accessing the Mambo module directory on the server and copying the files to your local machine.

Extra

To modify existing core modules, copy the module and make the changes on the copy. Then, unpublish the original module and publish the copy in its place. Subsequently, if you delete an instance accidentally, you still have the original module to work from.

Remove a Module

UNINSTALL A MODULE

1. Click Modules.
2. Click Review/Uninstall.
3. In the Review/Uninstall page, click the module you want to uninstall.
4. Click the Uninstall icon.

   Mambo deletes the module and all its parts from the system.

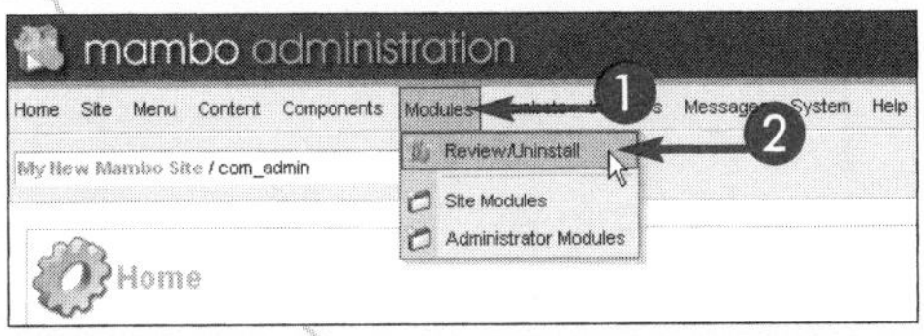

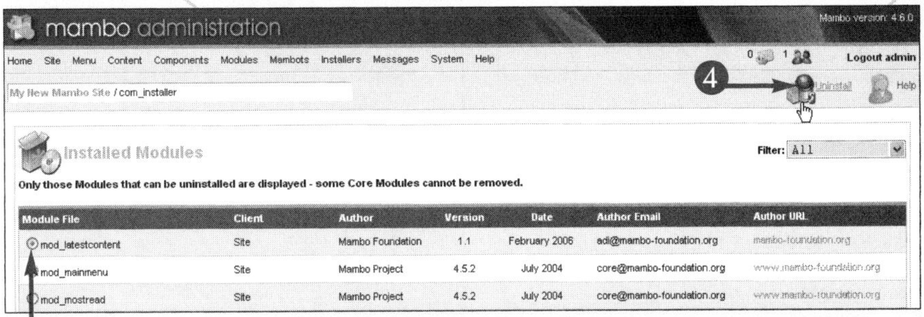

DELETE AN INSTANCE OF A MODULE

1. From the Module Manager, select the module you want to delete.
2. Click the Delete icon.
3. Click OK to confirm the deletion.

   Mambo deletes the instance of the module.

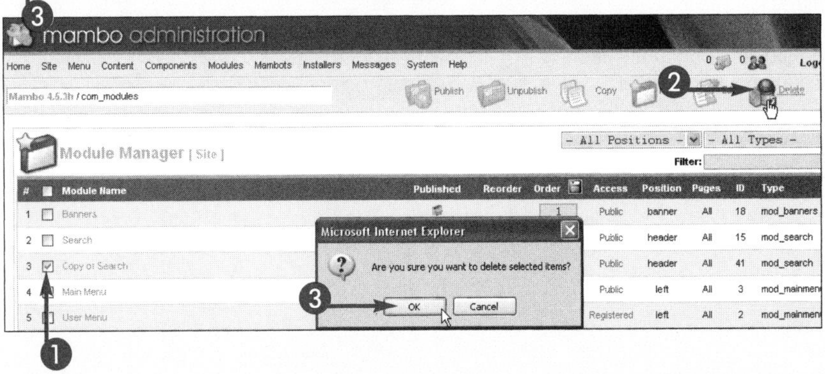

Install a Module Manually

You can install modules without the use of the automatic installer described in Chapter 11. Manual installation is required if your server does not support GZip or another utility for extracting file archives. In certain circumstances you may need to install a module manually, such as if you have some, but not all, of the various module files.

You perform manual installation using the Install From Directory option in the Universal Installer, or you can simply copy the files to the server by FTP. Both methods require you to move files to the server outside of the Mambo system. The method you use depends largely on the nature of the module you are working with.

If you have a proper module package — that is, a module that contains a complete set of properly formed files — you should use the Install From Directory option outlined in this section. If your module files are incomplete, you cannot use this option; instead, you must transfer your module files to the proper directory inside the Mambo installation on the server.

Be aware that installing modules without the Install From Directory tool brings two complications with it. First, you must make sure you have the right files into the right locations. Modules intended for use on the front end of the Web site go into the /modules directory. Administrator modules go into administrator/modules directory. Second, installing a module without the Install From Directory option means that you cannot automatically uninstall the module. You must manually delete all the files you installed previously if you want to remove the module completely in the future. For more on uninstalling modules manually, see Chapter 11 and the later section "Remove an Administrator Module."

Install a Module Manually

1. If they are zipped, extract the module files from the zip archive.

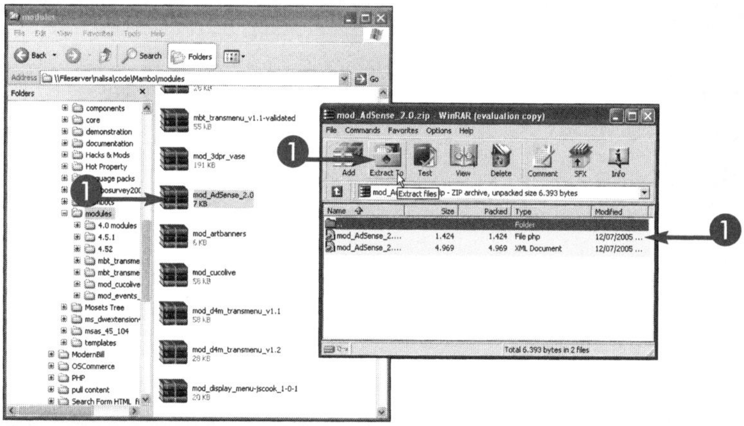

2. Access your server via FTP.
3. Create a directory inside the Mambo root directory.
4. Move the module files into the new directory and note the location.

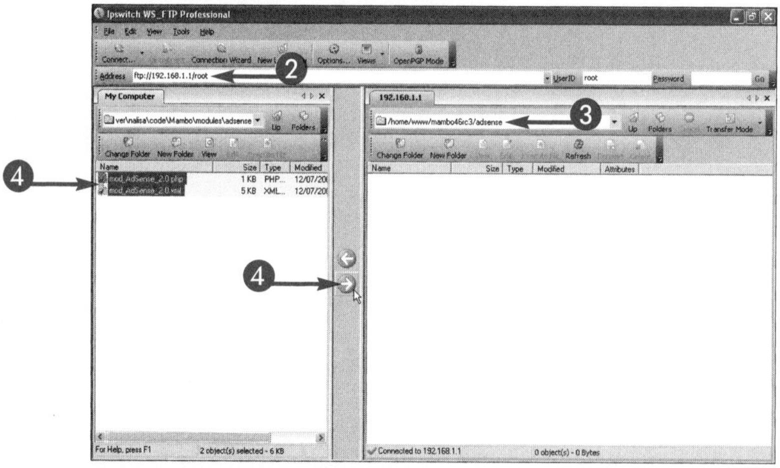

5 Click Installers.

6 Click Universal.

The Universal Installer loads.

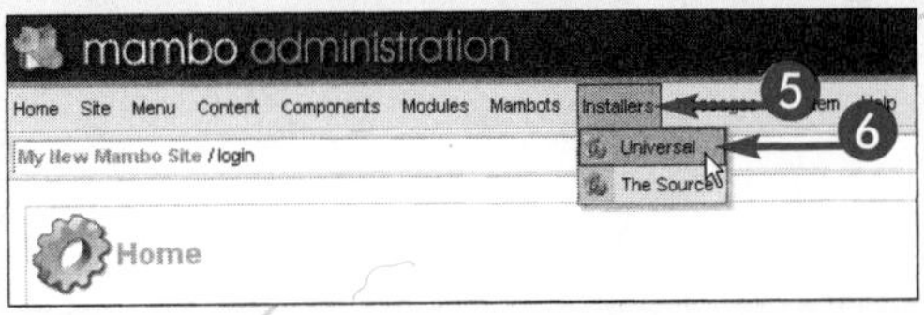

7 Type the full path to the directory containing the files here.

8 Click Install.

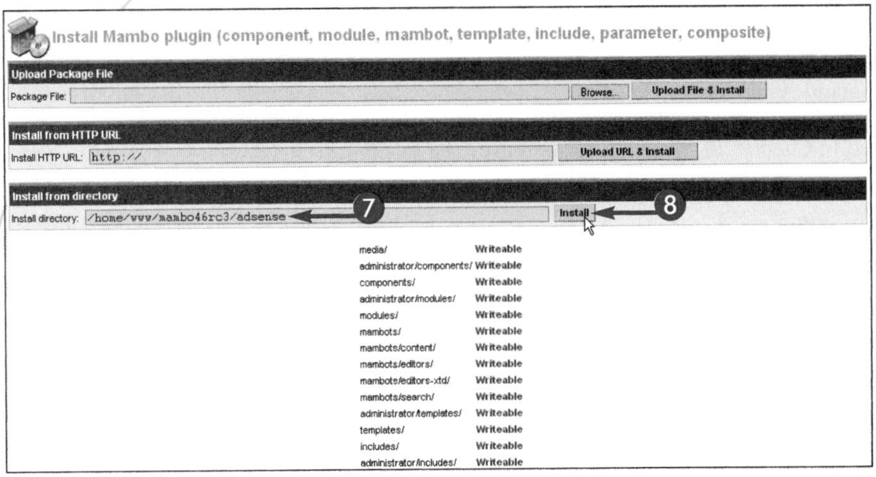

- If you are successful, you see a confirmation message when the screen reloads

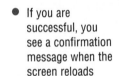

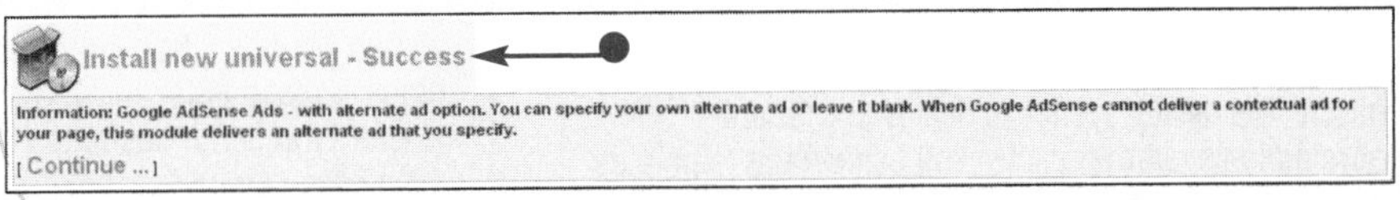

If you are not successful, you see a message indicating failure.

Extra

If you install your new module manually and without the aid of the Install From Directory option described in this section, you must take an additional step for it to fully work. Mambo modules do not work properly unless you add them to the database, so you must manually update the database tables by accessing your database with phpMyAdmin (or a similar tool) and opening the table named mos_modules. You can then create a new entry for your new module in the mos_modules table. You can model your entry on the database entries already in the table. Note that parameter values, placement, and other configuration options are specified in the table. You must enter the values you want to apply to your module.

You must store images for a module in a separate folder in the /modules directory. You should name the folder after the module and link it to the module file by a statement in the XML file. The XML file itself should follow proper XML format and syntax or else the system may have trouble processing the file and may present less than helpful error messages during the installation process.

Understanding Core Administrator Modules

The default deployment of your Mambo site includes an assortment of both site modules and administrator modules. The site modules, discussed in Chapter 11, give functionality for the front end of the Mambo Web site. The administrator modules provide functionality for the back-end administration system of your Mambo site.

Default Deployment

The default deployment includes twelve administrator modules, which are outlined below. All the administrator modules are assigned to visible positions and are published by default. You should not unpublish any of these modules without good reason because decreased functionality will result for the site administrators. Administrator modules appear in the Administrator Module Manager, which is explained further in this section.

The Mambo admin system uses only one template throughout. The default system is deployed with one alternative administrator template. You can switch templates but both of the alternatives in the core are essentially identical in module placement.

Site Modules Versus Administrator Modules

Compared to the site modules in your Mambo site, the administrator modules offer fewer choices and contain little fat or extraneous functionality. While the default Mambo installation comes bundled with a wide variety of site modules, the number of administrator modules is quite limited and all are engaged at deployment — none are consider to be optional. Similarly, the site modules often contain a number of parameters, which you can edit to tailor the presentation and functionality of the module, in contrast, the admin modules offer few parameters and are generally deployed to their utmost by default.

While you may decide that you do not want all the administrator modules active on your site, the vast majority of Mambo users never make any changes to these modules, simply leaving the admin modules untouched in the default site. However, should you want to make a customized admin interface, the option to modify the usage of the admin modules is always there.

Customizing the Admin Interface

If you want to gain more alternatives for module placement within your admin interface, you must either create a new admin template or edit the existing ones. Working with the admin templates is covered in Chapter 14. To explore how to further customize your admin interface, you may want to edit the existing modules to make changes to their presentation or their display of information. For more information on this topic, see the section "Modify an Existing Module," later in this chapter. There are two common reasons for making changes to the administration system: First is the desire to present a branded interface, in which case you will probably simply want to change the appearance of the default template and leave the modules alone. Second, some administrators edit the interface to restrict access to certain tools, in this situation you need to manage the admin modules effectively because you may want to unpublish some modules. For more information, see the section "Publish or Unpublish an Administrator Module," later in this chapter.

Administrator Modules

To help you get started, the following table gives a list of all the administrator modules included in the default Mambo installation, with a short synopsis of each module's function.

MODULE NAME	DESCRIPTION
Logged	Displays a list of users who are logged in to the system. The output of this module appears on the Logged tab on the admin control panel.
Components	Displays of all the installed components. The list appears in the Components tab on the admin control panel, along with hyperlinks to the components.
Popular	Calculates and displays the list of most commonly viewed Content Items. The output of this module appears on the Popular tab on the admin control panel. Note that it does not include archived items in its display items.
Latest Items	Calculates and displays the list of the most recent Content Items. The output appears in the Latest Items tab on the admin control panel and only applies if the Content Item is current and published.
Menu Stats	Displays a list of all the menus in the system along with counts of the Menu Items that appear on each of the menus. The output appears in the Menu Stats tab on the admin control panel, along with a hyperlink to the individual menu manager of each menu.
Unread Messages	Displays the count of unread system messages. The output appears next to the Mail icon at the top right of the admin control panel. The messages count includes both messages that other administrators send to you as well as automatic notifications that the Mambo system generates.
Online Users	Displays the count of users currently visiting the site. The output appears next to the Users icon at the top right of the admin control panel. The information is only approximate; you should not rely on it for complete accuracy.
Quick Icons	Displays the list of icons on the admin control panel that link to the various functionalities in the Mambo admin system.
System Messages	Interfaces with the administrator's messaging functionality to provide internal messaging for admin users and for automatic notifications that the Mambo system generates.
Pathway	Displays the pathway in the box underneath the navigation bar at the top left of the admin system pages.

Third Party Admin Modules

There exist few options to extend your Mambo site through the addition of third party admin modules. The lack of options is generally a reflection of the mature state of the Mambo admin system — the default deployment covers the needs of the vast majority of the system's users and as a result the users find little desire to code their own solutions. That said, should you want different or additional functionality for your admin system you probably must modify an existing module or code a new module yourself. For more information on modifying an existing module, please see the section "Modify an Existing Module." To learn more about creating new modules, see the section "Understanding How to Create Your Own Module."

Remove an Administrator Module

You can uninstall an entire administrator module or simply delete an instance of a module using the tools in the Administrator Module Manager and the Module Installer. Although you may never have a reason to remove an administrator module, in the event you decide to customize the appearance of your admin system, you will want to know how to accomplish this task. Uninstalling a module removes all of the related files but does not impact any of your content, components, or Mambots. Deleting an instance simply removes that one occurrence of the module while leaving the underlying module files on the server.

The proper way to completely eliminate a module is to use the uninstaller function in the Module Installer, which eliminates all instances of the module and the underlying code from the server. You can, in contrast, delete one or more instances of a module without uninstalling the entire module by using the Delete command in the Module Manager interface. To complicate things slightly, you cannot uninstall some modules at all because they are part of the core.

Note that unlike Content Items or Menu Items, Mambo does not move modules to the Trash Manager upon uninstall; instead, it permanently deletes them. Therefore, think carefully before you confirm uninstall because Mambo will remove the module and all of its associated files completely from your system. The only way to get the module back is to reinstall it from scratch.

Given these facts, you may consider simply leaving the module in the system, unused. If you do not publish a module, the files are completely inactive. Because Mambo does not call an unpublished module, the presence of the unused files does not impair your site's performance.

Remove an Administrator Module

UNINSTALL A MODULE

1. Click Modules.
2. Click Review/Uninstall.

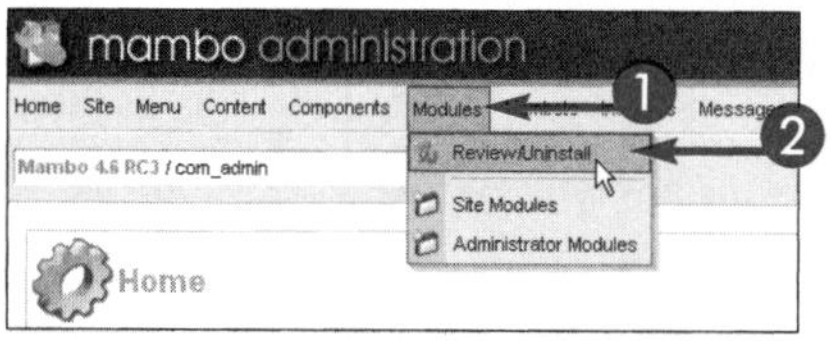

The Installed Modules page loads.

3. Click the Module you want to uninstall.
4. Click Uninstall.

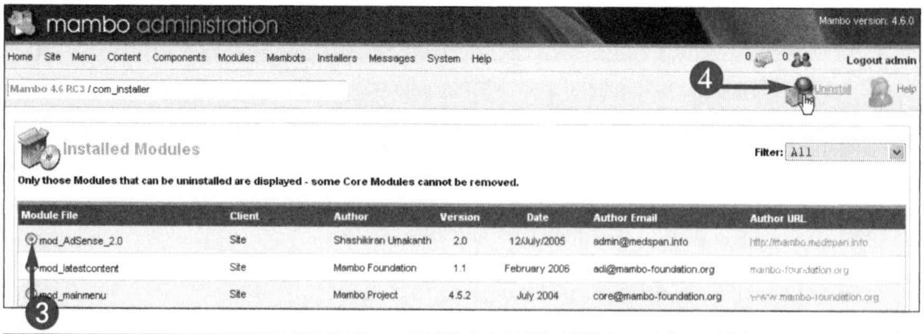

- Mambo deletes the module and all of its parts from the system.

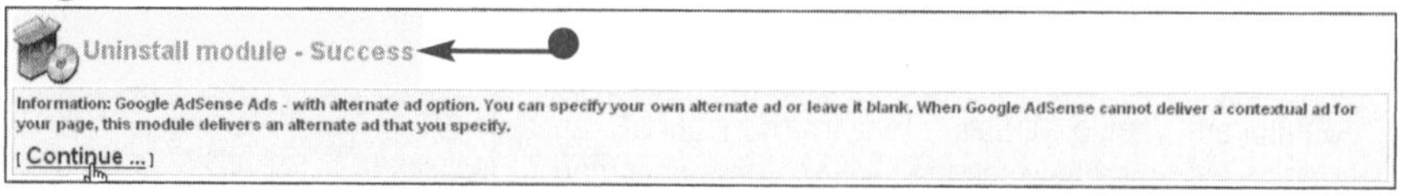

DELETE AN INSTANCE OF A MODULE

1. Click Modules.
2. Click Administrator Modules.

   The Administrator Module Manager loads.

3. Click the module instance you want to uninstall.
4. Click the Delete icon.

   Mambo deletes the instance of the module from the system.

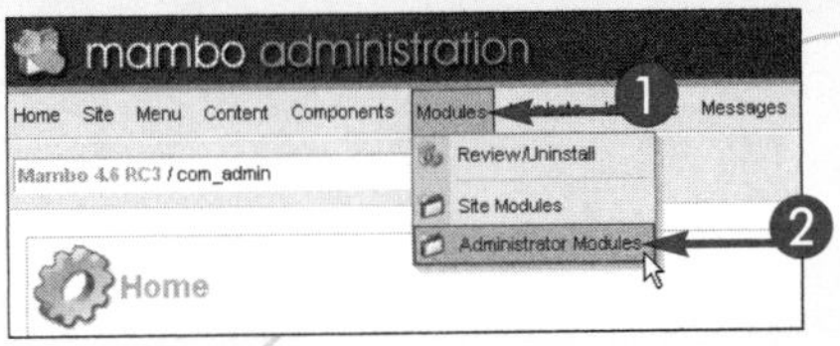

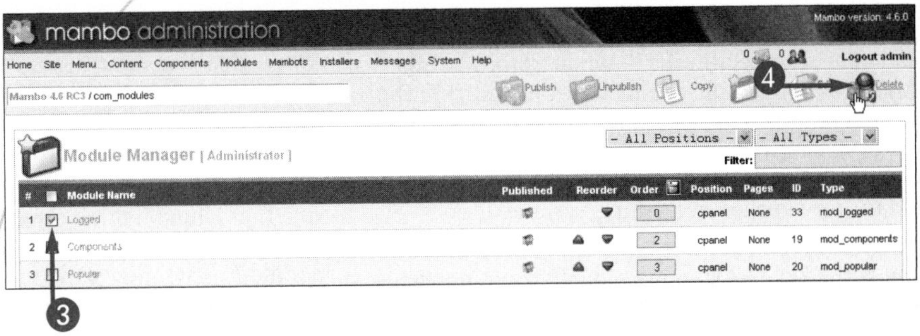

Extra

You should not delete the core administrator modules from the system unless you have an exceptional circumstance. You cannot remove a number of the modules from the system at all and therefore they do not appear on the Review/ Uninstall screen's list of modules. Of the twelve administrator modules contained in the default system, only four are listed on the uninstall screen. The following administrator modules are necessary for the proper operation of the system and you should not remove them from the server:

DO NOT DELETE!

```
Components (mod_components)
Unread Messages (mod_unread)
Online Users (mod_online)
Quick Icons (mod_quickicon)
System Messages (mod_mosmsg)
Pathway (mod_pathway)
Toolbar (mod_toolbar)
Full Menu (mod_fullmenu)
```

Remember the distinction between instances and the underlying module files: A single module can power many instances. Every time you make a copy of a module, you create a new instance of the module. Deleting instances does not delete the module itself, although deleting the only instance of a module may require you to reinstall the module to gain access to the parameters for that module.

Publish or Unpublish an Administrator Module

You can publish or unpublish administrator modules from within the Administrator Module Manager. By default, the modules included in the core deployment are published. As site administrator, you may want to disable certain modules and you may need to add new modules and publish them. The Administrator Module Manager supplies everything you need.

Several processes combine to enable a module's output. Publishing is the key factor — if a module is not published it does not appear, even if you have completed all the other parts of the process. The other required element for module publication is placement of the module in a visible Module Position Holder. Module position assignments are covered in the next section, "Change an Administrator Module's Position."

You can publish a module either directly from the Administrator Module Manager, or by opening the module's editing screen and publishing the module. Be certain that the module you want to publish is assigned to a valid module position on the administrator template. The way the system handles modules is quite flexible and forgiving. If you make a mistake in module position, you can fix it easily by editing the module after publication.

Note that Unpublishing a module cancels the module's display immediately, although it does not affect the module in any other way; unpublishing is not the same as deleting a module. Unpublishing essentially "suspends" a Module's performance, nothing more.

Generally speaking, most administrators leave all the default modules published, although in some situations, where perhaps you do not want other administrators to have access to all the modules, you may want to hide the modules by unpublishing them.

Publish or Unpublish an Administrator Module

1. Open the Administrator Module.

Note: To open the Administrator Module, see the section "Remove an Administrator Module."

2. Click the module you want to publish or unpublish.
3. Click the Edit icon.

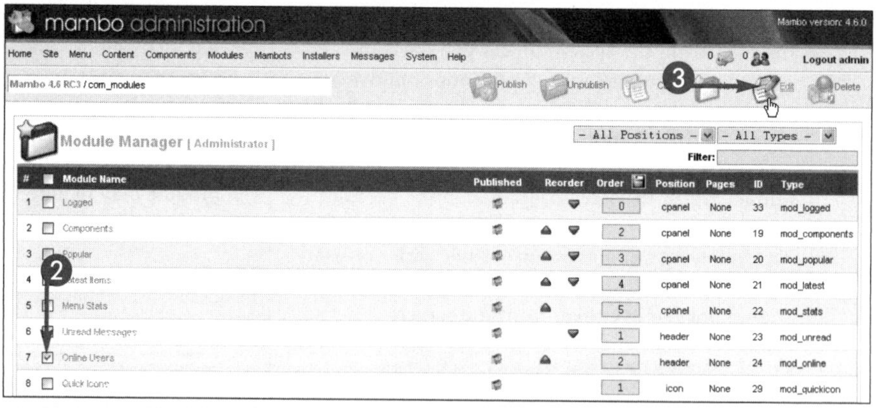

The Module Editing page loads.

4. For the Published option, click the Yes or No to indicate the desired Published state.
5. Click the Save icon.

The Module no longer appears on the Admin interface.

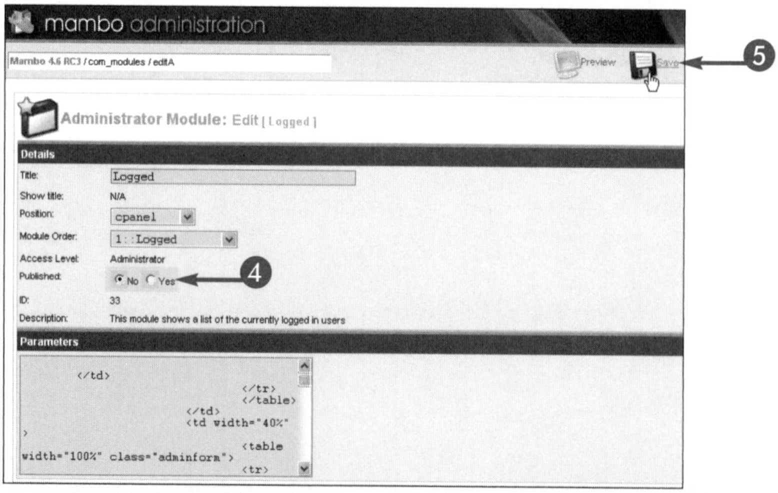

Change an Administrator Module's Position

You can change where a module appears in the admin template by changing the module position selection. This feature is particularly useful if you want to move things around and experiment with your administrator template's page layout. Module position assignments are related to the module position holders located in the templates. When you assign a module to a position, the module appears wherever you place the module position holder of the same name in the template.

The module position selection combo box in the module editing window does not automatically detect which module positions are valid in the templates. This means that you have to make sure you assign the module to a valid position or the module will not appear. There is no simple tool for locating the module position holders in the admin templates. You must open the template files with an external editing program to find the placeholders.

When considering where to place the modules, it is a good practice to think in terms of access to tools. Effective module placement should provide users with all the relevant tools they need to do their job in an accessible location. The default Mambo installation uses a very basic, but very practical, module placement schema. So although you can create new templates and move things around, the admin system should emphasize ease of use over appearances; do not forget that the admin system is a workplace and should be arranged suitably. Note that the system is very tolerant and you can change the module positions back and forth without fear of causing problems with the site.

Change an Administrator Module's Position

1. Open the Administrator Module.

Note: To open the Administrator Module, see the section "Remove an Administrator Module."

2. Click the module whose position you want to change.
3. Click the Edit icon.

   The Module Editing page loads.
4. Click here and select the desired position.
5. Click the Save icon.

   Mambo moves the module.

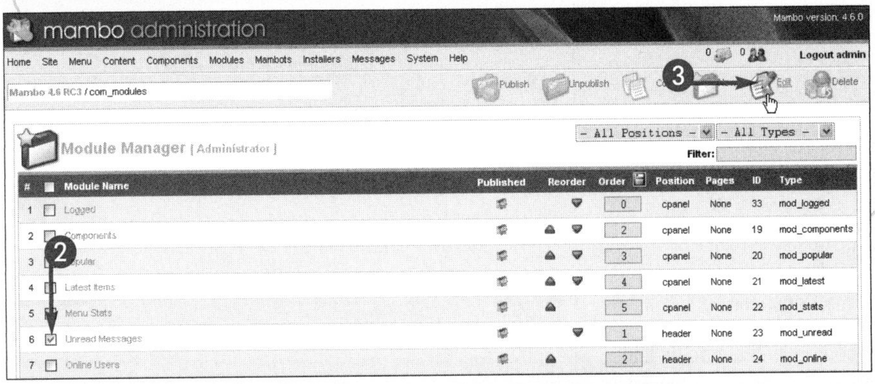

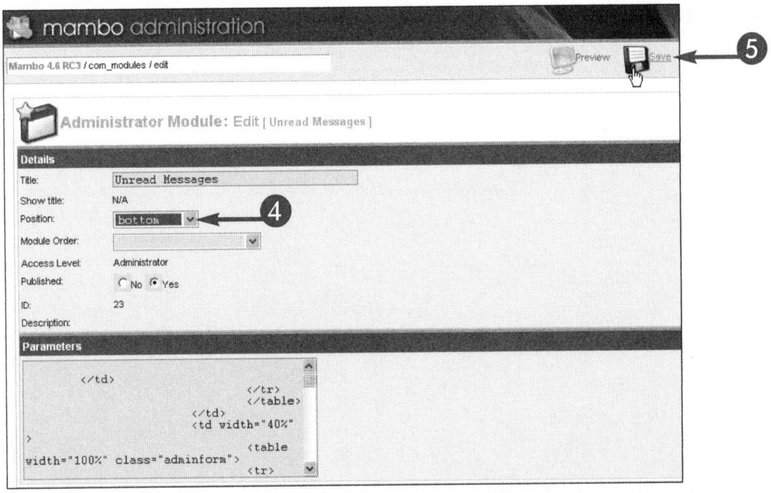

Copy an Administrator Module

You can make a copy of any administrator module in the system by using the copy function in the Administrator Module Manager. Duplicate modules are useful because you can modify them at will; this enables you to keep a "clean" unaltered version of the original module as a backup in case a problem occurs with the duplicate and you want to restore an original version.

When you use the copy command, the module you select to copy is duplicated exactly, except for the name and the published state. Mambo automatically names the duplicated module "Copy of (original module name)." The state of a newly copied module is Unpublished.

After copying the module, you can alter the code of the new modules as you please. Changes that you make to one version of the module do not impact other instances of the module. For more on how you can modify modules, see the section "Modify an Existing Module."

The system imposes no limitation on how many times you can copy a module, or on how many instances of a module you can run simultaneously. However, you should avoid cluttering the admin interface with too many modules because this is likely to impair the usability of the admin system.

Note that deleting a module created with the module copy function has no impact on the original module. However, using the uninstall command to uninstall a module automatically deletes all instances of the module — both the original and any copies. Uninstalling modules is discussed in the section "Remove an Administrator Module."

Copy an Administrator Module

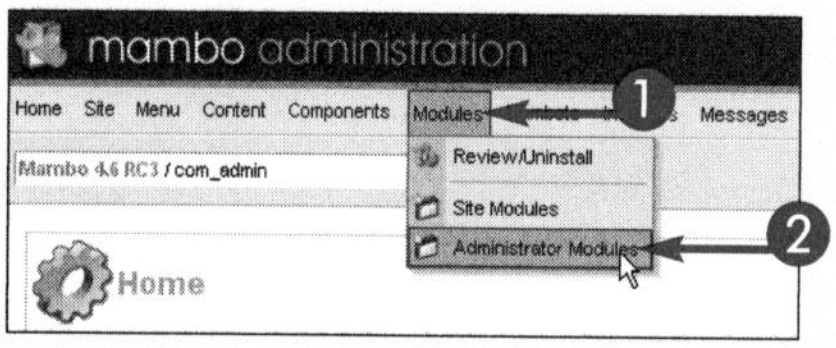

1. Click Modules.
2. Click Administrator Modules.

The Administrator Module Manager loads.

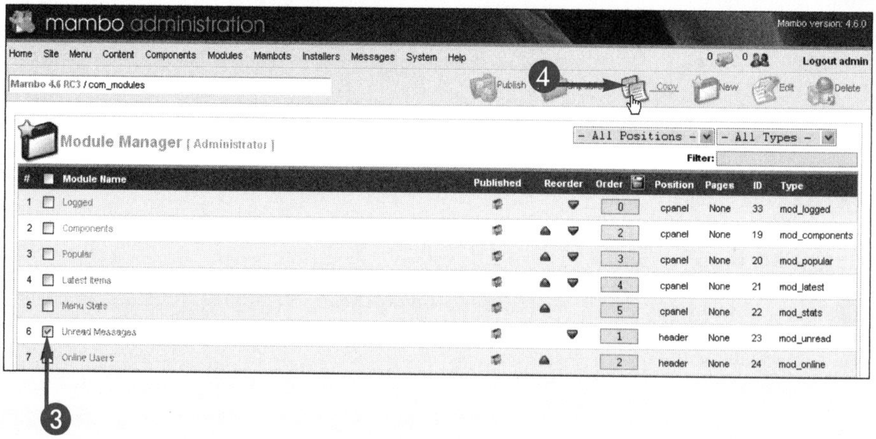

3. Click the module you want to copy.
4. Click the Copy icon.

Mambo copies the module and the module appears on the list with the name "Copy of (name of original module)."

Understanding How To Create Your Own Module

Mambo gives you several options for creating custom modules for your Web site. You can create a new module from scratch, modify an existing module, or use the New command in the Module Manager interface. The technique you choose relates primarily to your skill level and the result you want to achieve.

Mambo modules can be simple or complex affairs. The desired functionality dictates the module's complexity. If, for example, you like the basic manner in which an existing module works, but need to change the presentation or some element of the functionality, you can simply copy the module and make your changes to the code. The skill required to make changes to an existing module depends on the level of customization. Presentation-level adjustments are relatively easy, while modifications to a module's functionality become increasingly complex depending on the task or the desired result. For more on modifying an existing module, see the section, "Modify an Existing Module."

Using the New Module Function

To create a simple module, for example to hold a graphic or a message, the easiest path is to use the New Module functionality in the Module Manager. The New icon opens an empty module container into which you can add content like text, images, or HTML. For more on creating a custom module to display content, see the section "Create a Module to Display Content Items." Additionally, the New Module container includes all the controls you need to acquire and publish an RSS feed. For more on creating a custom module to hold an RSS feed, see the section "Create a Module to Display an RSS Feed."

Creating a new module using the New command in the Module Manager does have some limitations and may not satisfy users who require a module to do more than simply display Content Items or an RSS feed. Modules you create using the New command cannot handle PHP or advanced HTML tags. The limitations imposed by the system restrict the New Module functionality so much that many people find it necessary to either modify an existing module or write their own modules from scratch. A discussion of modifying an existing module is covered in the next section, "Modify an Existing Module."

Creating from Scratch

If you choose to create a new module from scratch, you need to create two essential files: a PHP file holding the module code and an XML file holding information about the module. Use an existing core module to reference the necessary formatting and the contents of the XML file. If you additionally require images for your module, create a dedicated folder for them inside the /modules directory and name it after your module for ease of reference.

Learn More

There is a section on modules included in the Mambo API on the Web site: help.mamboserver.com. Unfortunately, at the time of this writing it was rather limited. As is often the case with Mambo, the best way to learn is to simply try your hand at creating a new module.

Modify an Existing Module

You can modify the presentation or functionality of an existing module by editing the module's files. You cannot modify module files from within the Mambo administration system. You need to copy the files from your server and make your changes offline, then move the files back up to the system and install the newly modified module.

Modifying an existing module is one of the easiest ways to customize your Mambo site. Presentation-level changes are the easiest to make and typically involve only basic HTML or PHP skills. Functionality changes can be trickier and difficult if you are not skilled at PHP.

You begin by using the Module Manager to make a copy of the module you want to modify. Unpublish the original module and then make your changes on the duplicate. Leave the original module untouched so that it remains in the system as a point of reference; this file can serve as a backup in case you have a problem and want to roll back to a clean version of the code.

You can find module files in two different locations on the server. The front-end module files are in the /modules directory, and administrator modules in the administrator/modules directory. Make sure you copy all the files from the server before you begin your work. When you restore the files to the server, you can overwrite the files of your duplicate module, but to avoid mistakes, make sure you have archived a clean version of the original module, as described in the section "Copy an Administrator Module." Do not overwrite the original module's files. Work carefully and methodically because good work habits can save you frustration and lost time.

Modify an Existing Module

1. Access your site by FTP.
2. Access the /modules directory.
3. Copy the files of the module you wish to modify to your local machine.

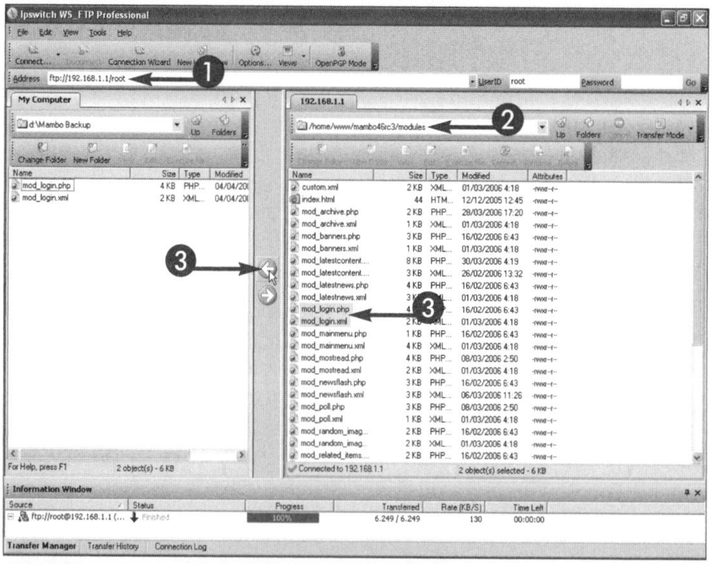

4. Make a copy the original files to create a backup.

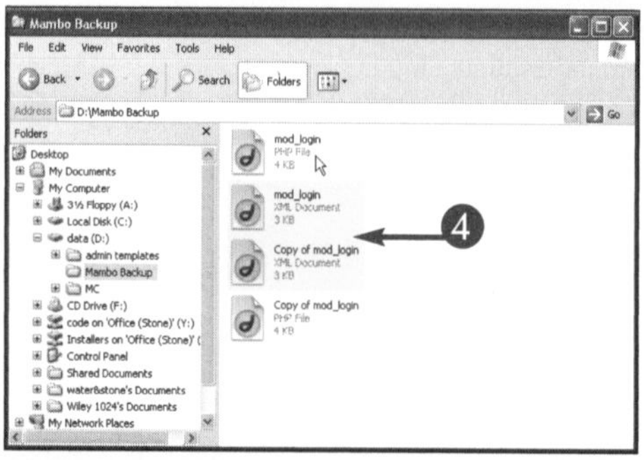

5. Open the module's PHP file with an editor.

6. Make any changes you wish to the file and save the file.

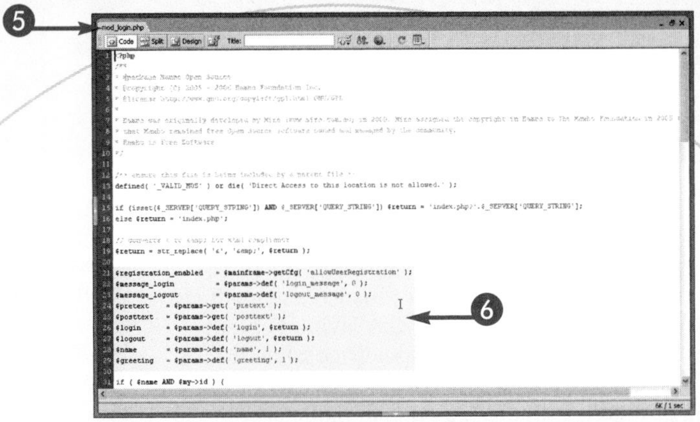

7. Access the site by FTP.

8. Access the /modules directory.

9. Copy the module files to the server.

   The modified files overwrite the original files and are now available for use on the site.

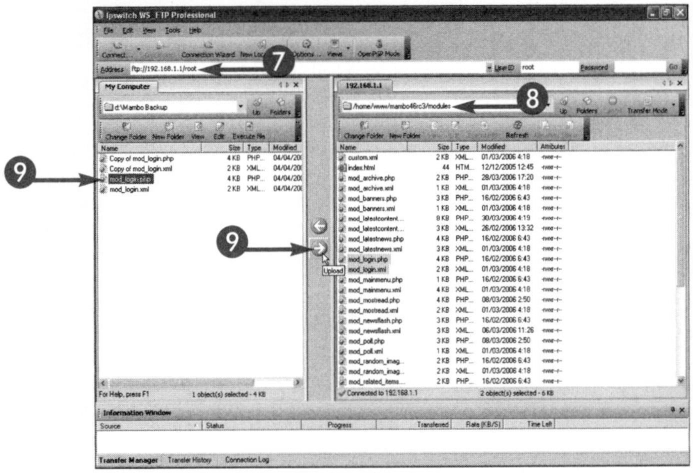

Extra

Testing Modules is problematic. Creating a properly installable module is best, so that you can take advantage of the Mambo installer and avoid having to make manual database entries, as described in the section "Install a Module Manually." Unless your module is complex or has many dependencies, it is probably worth the time it takes to go ahead and create the files needed to use the installer. Be methodical about your work and keep the module's XML file in step with any changes you have made to the PHP file or related files, or the installer will not work properly and you may be forced to clean up the directories or the database manually before you can test further.

If you are interested in learning more about the functioning of the Mambo site and administrator modules, review the Mambo API located on the Mambo Help site at help.mamboserver.com/api/. The API contains information on the various classes and files and their functions within modules. You can find further assistance by visiting the Mambo forums at forum.mamboserver.com and posing questions to the community. You need to register to be able to post questions.

Create a Module to Display Content Items

You can create a custom module to display Content Items on your Mambo site. Although Content Items are normally positioned within the main content area on a Mambo site, you can also use modules to hold and display Content Items. Displaying Content Items in module positions opens up new possibilities for producing a more varied Web site.

The simplest method to display Content Items via modules involves modifying the configuration of two of the existing system modules: the Newest Content Module and the Most Recent Items Module. As its name implies, the Newest Content Module displays the newest Content Item on your site. You can always force this module to display a specific Content Item by overriding the Publication Date settings on a Content Item to show that the Content Item in question is the most recent. For more information about setting the parameters on a Content Item, see Chapter 6. Although the Most Recent Items Module displays the most recently published Content Items on your site, you can configure it to show only a specific category and you can control how many items it shows. For more on both of these modules, see Chapter 11.

If modifying an existing module is not sufficient for your needs, you must use the content editing capabilities of the module itself to publish your content. The New Module Creation screen includes a text field into which you can enter whatever information you want. The text field includes an instance of the WYSIWYG editor and lets you use the MOSimage and MOSpagebreak commands. Simply create a new module and then enter the content you want directly into the interface. At run time, the module displays the content.

Create a Module to Display Content Items

1. Click Modules.
2. Click Site Modules.

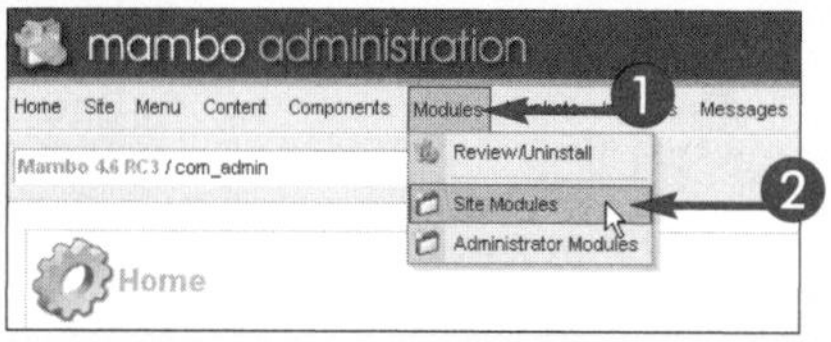

The Module Manager loads.

3. Click the New icon.

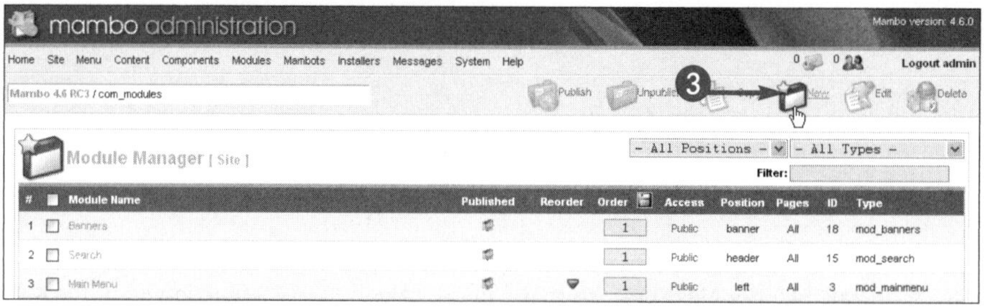

The New Site Module screen loads.

4 Type a title for the module

5 Type your content.

6 Click the Save icon.

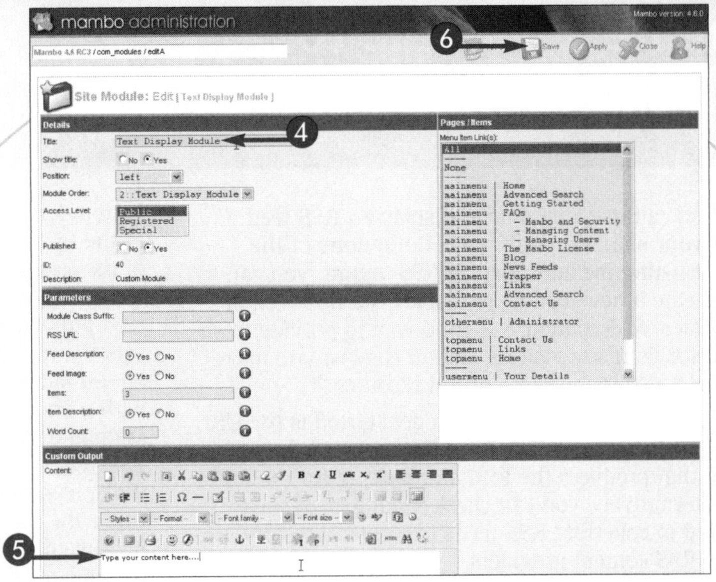

- Mambo saves the module and returns you to the Module Manager.

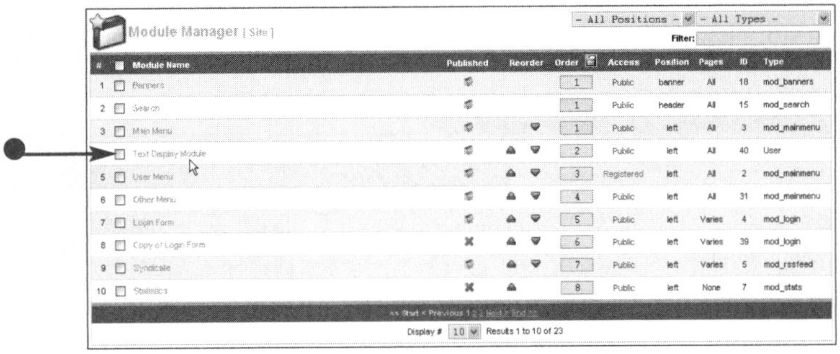

Extra

You can use the WYSIWYG editor in the New Module screen to input and format either text or images. Additionally, you can use custom modules to display virtually anything you can code into HTML. Although you cannot use specialized tags, like form tags, within the New Module text box, you can still do a lot within the bounds of normal HTML. Using HTML formatting within custom modules is an effective way to create callout boxes or other attention grabbing devices to deliver ads, related text information, or images. Selective placement of well-designed custom modules is one of the best ways to get more out of your Mambo system.

Check all newly created modules inside your template because sometimes a module's contents is too big for the template and breaks the template's layout, resulting in an unattractive mess on your Web site. To avoid problems with the module's display, restrict the module's content to a specified width by using either a table of fixed width or a `div` tag.

Create a Module to Display an RSS Feed

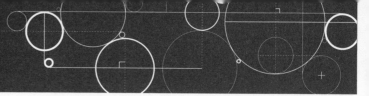

You can use a module to display an RSS feed on your site. Although, by default, none of the existing modules display RSS output, you can easily create a new module to display the RSS feed of your choice. RSS content is a good way to provide fresh content for your site visitors and an easy way to make your site a richer and more useful resource.

The only information you need to get started is the URL of the RSS feed. You can usually find the URL by visiting the site that produces the feed and looking for the RSS icon. Alternatively, you can check a number of sites dedicated to collecting RSS feeds to view a directory of various RSS content providers.

You use the New icon to load the Site Module: New screen, where you can view RSS configuration parameters at the bottom left. The options include a place to paste the URL of the feed and several options that configure the display of the feed on your site. Enabling the Feed Description and Feed Image options displays the text and images the feed publisher has set for his or her feed. The Items field sets the number of items to display. The Item Description option allows you to choose between titles only or titles with a short description. When you disable the option, Mambo only displays the item titles. The Word Count field lets you specify the length of the item; setting it to 0 displays the entire item. Enable Cache allows you to cache the feed output; keeping this option enabled is best because disabling it results in your site checking the feed for updates every time someone accesses your site.

Create a Module to Display an RSS Feed

1. Click Modules.
2. Click Site Modules.

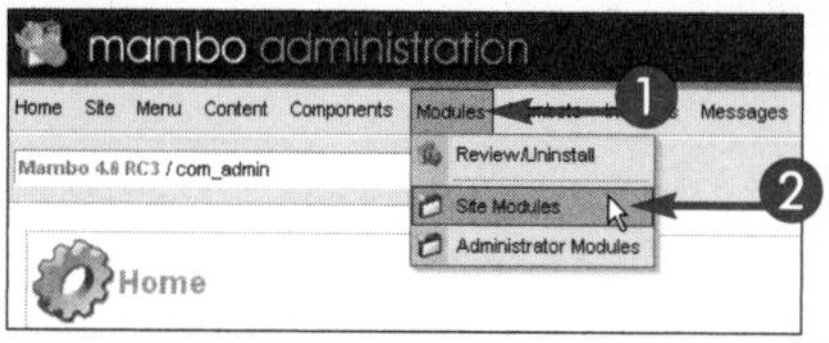

The Module Manager loads.

3. Click the New icon.

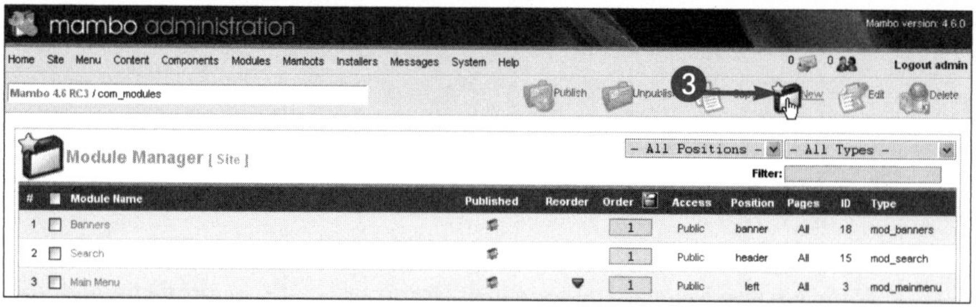

The New Site Module screen loads.

4 Type a title for the module.

5 Type the RSS URL.

6 Select the parameters you want to apply.

7 Click the Save icon.

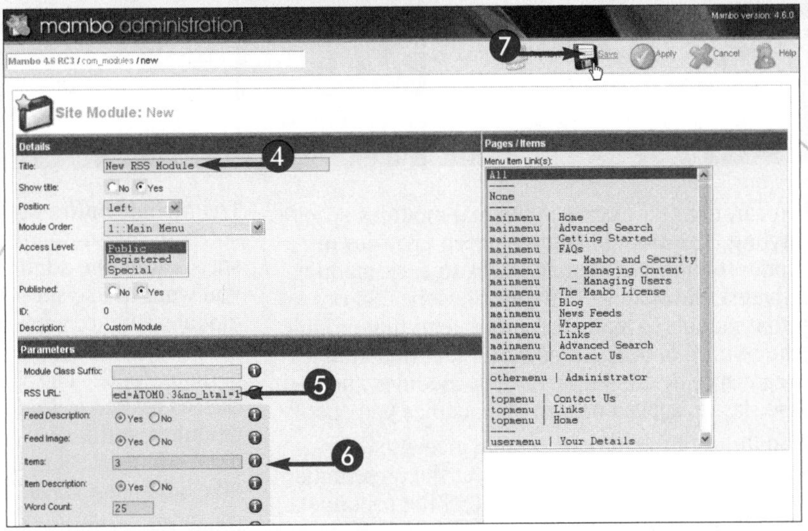

- Mambo saves the module and returns you to the Module Manager.

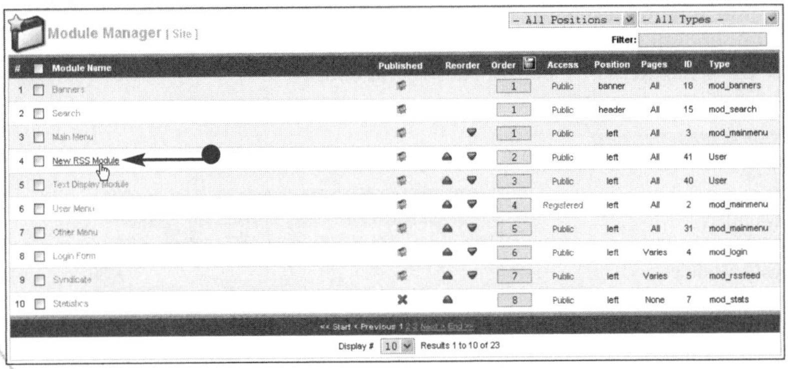

Extra

RSS feeds are available for an incredibly wide range of sites and topics. Not only do bloggers typically use RSS to syndicate their entries, but increasingly so do mainstream publications. Finding new RSS content is time consuming and requires you to shift through the masses of options to find the proper content and quality for your site. While you can always go to a major search engine like Google and search for RSS feeds, it is often easier to visit one of the following specialized RSS directories where you can search or browse by category:

SPECIALIZED RSS DIRECTORIES
www.feedster.com www.syndic8.com www.technorati.com

Caching your RSS module both improves your site's performance and benefits the producer of the feed. If you disable the cache on your RSS module, the Mambo system checks the feed every time someone loads the page on which you have the module. This makes your content current, but it also slows the system down and it can place stress on the user's Web server, which has to respond to the RSS query. As a matter of courtesy, enable the cache.

Style a Module with CSS

You can use CSS to give individual modules specific styling. The Module Editing screen provides an option to attach a Module Suffix to each module. When activated, the Module Suffix modifies the CSS classes used by that module to make them unique to that module. The Module Suffix option is a powerful tool that enables you to create specific classes for specific modules and then have those classes applied only to the modules you specify.

The CSS abilities of the Mambo system give site administrators a great deal of control over the presentation of the site's contents. Each template's CSS file contains a full set of classes, tags, and IDs that control the appearance of the site. Site administrators can add to the CSS either by editing the file offline or by using the CSS editing options for the template. For more on editing the CSS online via a browser, see Chapter 3.

The Module Suffix option works by attaching a unique suffix to the standardized Mambo module class, as specified by the administrator. For example, assume that you want to use specific formatting for one of your Polls modules. To accomplish the unique formatting of one instance of the module you specify a Module Suffix, perhaps "poll." The Mambo system then appends to all classes related to that particular instance of the Polls module a suffix of "_poll." To perfect the change, you must edit the CSS to include a set of classes designed to take advantage of the unique suffix.

Using the technique to fullest effect requires two steps: first you must specify a Module Class Suffix, and second, you must create the classes that the suffix calls.

Style a Module with CSS

1. Click Modules.
2. Click Site Modules.

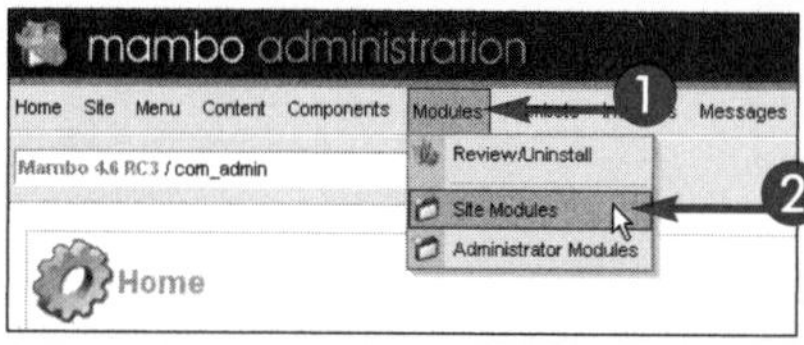

The Module Manager loads.

3. Select the module you want to style.
4. Click the Edit icon.

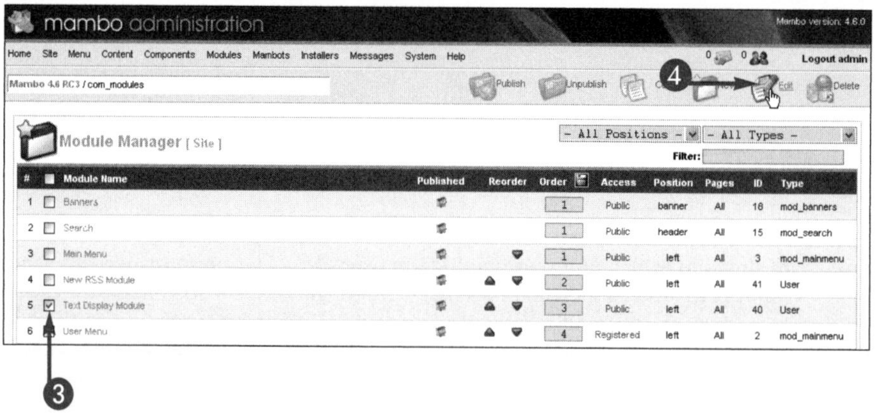

The Module Editing screen loads.

5. Type a Module Class Suffix.
6. Click the Save icon.

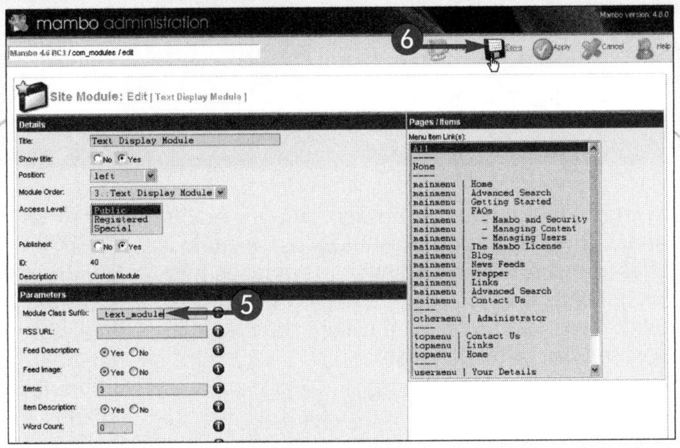

7. Access the active template's CSS editing screen.
8. Add the classes for your module.
9. Click the Save icon.

The style now appears for the module.

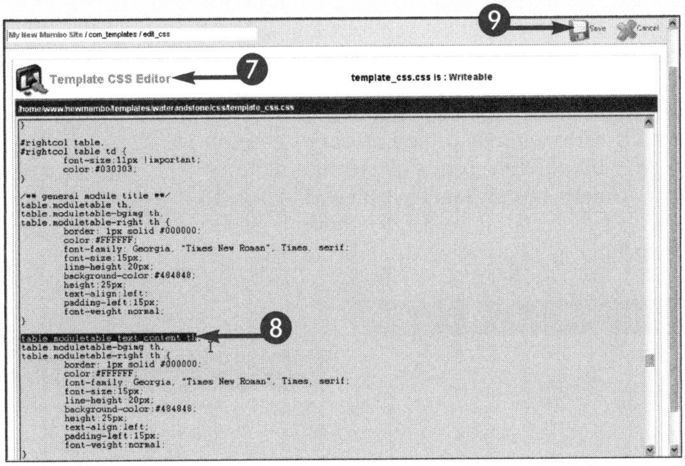

Apply It

Activating the Module Class Suffix command inside a module only works if you create the classes to control it in the CSS. The CSS for the default templates is in the /CSS directory inside the template folder. In the default configuration, you can also edit the CSS via the Edit CSS command in the Template Manager. For more information, see Chapter 3. To create the necessary classes you must first duplicate the following classes.

DUPLICATE THESE CLASSES:

```
table.moduletable
table.moduletable table
table.moduletable td
table.moduletable th
```

Once you duplicate them, add the suffix you specified for the Module Class Suffix to each one. For example, if you specify the suffix "_poll", and your Module Class Suffix is "_poll", you should modify the list of classes above to appear as follows:

CREATE THE FOLLOWING CLASSES:

```
table.moduletable_poll
table.moduletable_poll table
table.moduletable_poll td
table.moduletable_poll th
```

You can now edit the new classes and Mambo reflects your changes to the new classes in the module.

Run Multiple Instances of a Module

You can run more than one instance of a module in Mambo. Running multiple instances of a module is useful in two situations: where you want separate appearances of the module to appear differently on different pages, or where you want to show the same module in different positions on different pages.

Some modules, like the Banners Module or the Polls module, are set up in anticipation of the creation of multiple instances of the module. With the Banners module, you can create multiple versions and tie each one to different Banner clients, which allows you to tie individual Banner clients to particular module positions or Content Items. With the Polls module, you can set up multiple polls with the Polls component and then run the different polls on different pages by creating multiple modules. For more on the Banners and Polls modules, see Chapter 11. You can, however, run multiple instances with any module by duplicating the module and assigning the duplicates to different positions or to different pages.

Mambo treats each instance of a module as unique. Accordingly, there is no conflict between multiple duplicate modules. This gives you a great deal of flexibility to run modules in different positions on different pages. You can achieve the same effect by creating multiple templates and moving the Module Position Holders from template to template, but it is faster and easier to simply create multiple instances of the same module and avoid having to create and manage multiple templates. For more on using multiple templates on your site, see Chapter 3.

To avoid confusion, consider giving duplicate modules distinct names. Naming the modules according to their specialized functions makes site administration easier and less prone to error.

Run Multiple Instances of a Module

1. Access the Module Manager.

Note: You can access the Module Manager, by clicking Modules and then Module Manager."

2. Select the module you want to copy.
3. Click the Copy icon.

   Mambo copies the module and appears on the list with the name "Copy of (name of original module)."

4. Select the duplicate Banner module.
5. Click the Edit icon.

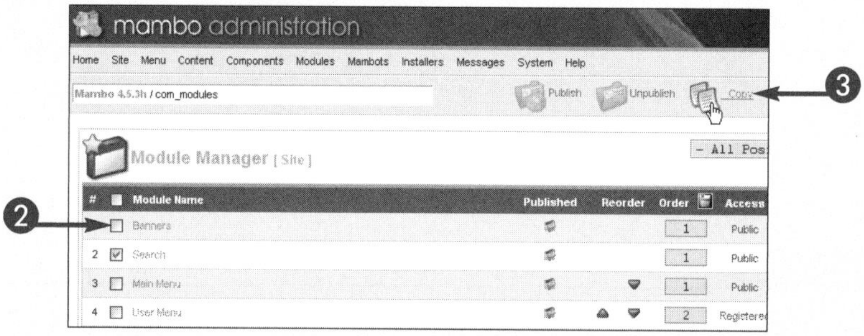

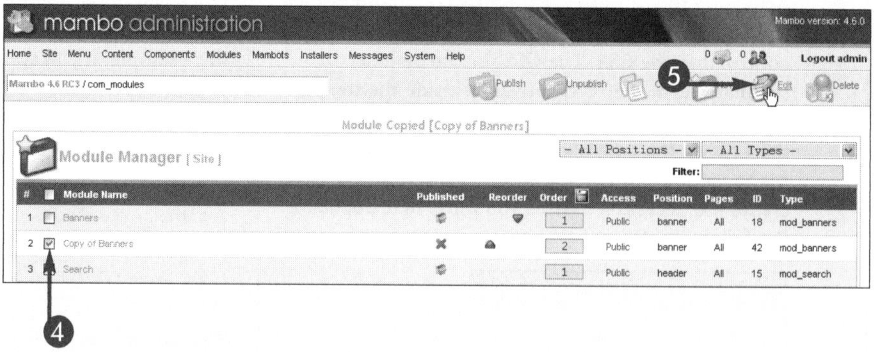

The Module Editing Screen loads.

6 Click here to select a different position for the module.

7 Select the pages where you want it to appear.

8 For the Published option, click Yes.

9 Click the Save icon.

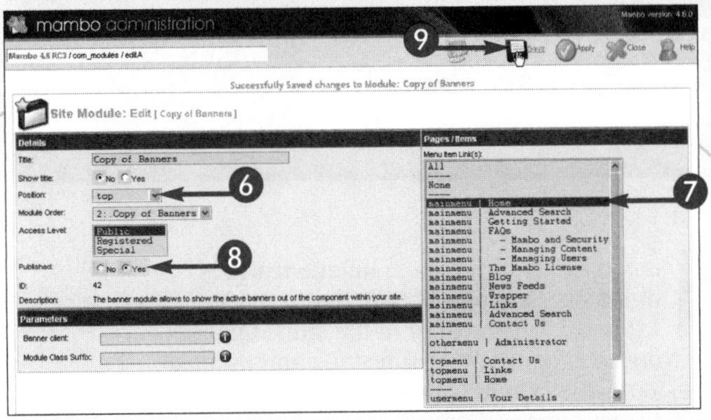

- Mambo publishes the duplicate module to a separate module position and the module appears on the page.

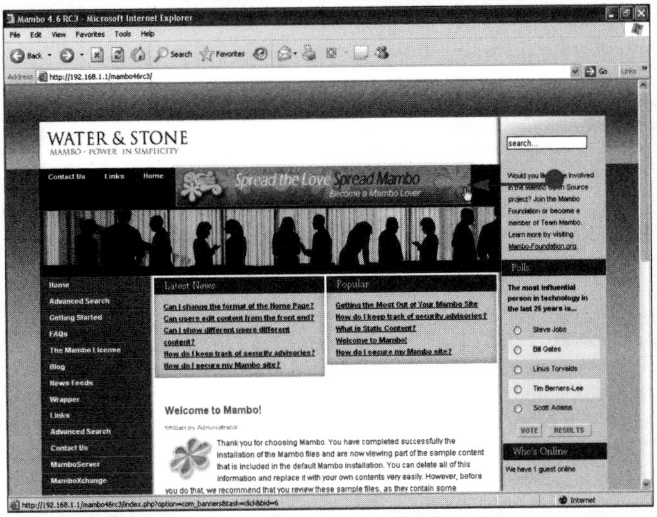

Extra

Every time you copy a module you create a new instance of the module. All instances of the same module are based on the same underlying module files. Each instance carries its own unique parameters and options, which is what makes it unique. You can delete the instances without impacting the underlying module files that enable the instances. However, it is not a good idea to delete the only instance of a module; you need to reinstall the module to access the parameters.

Use of multiple instances of modules is probably one of the most underused techniques in Mambo, but it is ironically one of the best ways to gain extra flexibility with the front end of the system. The flexibility of multiple instances is directly related to the number and placement of the module position holders, because more, well placed position holders open up more possibilities for you to use multiple instances creatively. Accordingly, if you want to choose templates for your site that offer you the most flexibility, choose templates that contain well-conceived and plentiful module position holders.

Understanding Core Mambots

Mambots, one of the most unique features of Mambo, are bits of code that provide extended functionality to the site. Mambots generally work to enhance other functions and to make the site easier to use or more attractive. Mambots are very distinct from components and modules, whose output site visitors can see distinctly. Rather than being producers of output in and of themselves, the Mambots' functions are often unseen because they are enabling technologies. A classic example of a Mambot functioning to enhance the basic site output is the SEF Mambot, which turns a site's URLs into a format that is more search engine friendly. Mambots can also enhance the functionality of a site, for example, the MOStlyCE Mambot, which helps power the WYSIWYG content editor.

How to Handle Mambots

You typically install and publish Mambots and then leave them alone. Mambots do not provide work spaces for the Administrator, and you rarely open a Mambot to make any changes to it. Most Mambots include very limited configuration options and some have none at all; they are simply installed and published.

Core Mambots

The default Mambo installation includes a variety of Mambots that provide functionality throughout the front end and back end of the site. Mambots are divided into five types: authenticator, content, editors, editors-xtd, and search. To help you get started, the following table lists all the Mambots in a default Mambo site with a short synopsis of each Mambot's function.

MAMBOT NAME	DESCRIPTION
User Authenticator	Provides validation of the Administrators and registered users of your Mambo site.
MOS Image	Enables the MOSimage function that inserts images alongside the text in Content Items. Disabling this Mambot denies the administrators access to the function.
Legacy Mambot Includer	Provides support for outdated Mambo 4.5 Mambots. The Mambot is unpublished by default. If you attempt to install an older Mambot on your site and then experience trouble with it, try enabling this Mambot.
Code Support	Allows you to display lines of formatted code inside of Content Items. The Mambot is disabled by default. Once enabled, you can insert code lines between the tags `{moscode}` and `{/moscode}` into a Content Item. The code is rendered on the page, rather than executed.
SEF	Enables the use of Search Engine Friendly URLs for your site. The Mambot is enabled by default, but in order to activate SEF URLs, you must select the options in the Global Configuration Manager. For more on how to use the Global Configuration Manager, see Chapter 2.
MOS Rating	Provides the optional Content Item Voting functionality. The Mambot is enabled by default, but in order to activate the voting function, you must select the option in the Global Configuration Manager. For more on how to use the Global Configuration Manager, see Chapter 2.
Email Cloaking	Hides all email addresses located inside content items from automated SPAMbots.
GeSHi	Similar to the Code Support Mambot, the GeSHi Mambot allows you to insert code into Content Items for display on the site. Unlike the Code Support Mambot, the GeSHi function highlights the code in color, using various colors to denote different types of code, such as HTML, HTML, PHP, and so on.

Core Mambots *(continued)*

MAMBOT NAME	DESCRIPTION
Load Module Positions	Allows you to insert module positions within Content Items. By inserting the command `{mosloadposition positionname}` within a Content Item, you can load modules assigned to that position into your Content Items, all without having to define the position in the Template file. Note that in the example above, you must substitute the name of the position where it says *positionname*, such as `{mosloadposition banner}`.
MOS Pagination	Enables the automated production of a Table of Contents for multi-page content.
MOStlyCE	Loads the default WYSIWYG editor for editing your Content Items.
No WYSIWYG Editor	Allows for the use of a plain text editor when the WYSIWSYG editor is disabled.
TinyMCE WYSIWYG Editor	Loads the optional TinyMCE WYSIWYG editor.
MOS Image Editor Button	Provides the button to insert the `{mosimage}` tag into a Content Item.
MOS Pagebreak Editor Button	Provides the button to insert the `{mospagebreak}` tag into a Content Item.
Search Content	Enables site search within the Content Items. Disable to block the items from the search functionality.
Search Weblinks	Enables site search within the Weblinks. Disable to block the items from the search functionality.
Search Contacts	Enables site search within the Contact Items. Disable to block the items from the search functionality.
Search Categories	Enables site search within the categories. Disable to block the items from the search functionality.
Search Sections	Enables site search within the Content Sections. Disable to block the items from the search functionality.
Search Newsfeeds	Enables site search within the Newsfeeds. Disable to block the items from the search functionality.

Third Party Mambots

Of all the extensions available for Mambo, the category with the fewest options is Mambots. There are large numbers of components, modules, and templates that can be downloaded and installed, but relatively fewer Mambots. Many of the third-party Mambots that do exist are ancillary to components or modules, which they assist. The few stand alone Mambots in existence typically offer variations on content functionality, for example, increased formatting options or enhanced display. The widest assortment of third party Mambots can probably be found at www.mamboxchange.com.

An Introduction to the Mambot Manager

You can use the Mambot Manager to create, publish, and configure the Mambots for your site. The Mambot Manager interface gives you access to all the Mambots in the system, along with a quick overview of the status of the Mambots. The system allows you to reorder, publish, or unpublish Mambots directly from the main Mambot Manager screen. Tools on the Mambot Manager page allow you to create new Mambots or delete unwanted ones from the system.

The Mambot Manager is located inside the admin interface, under the Mambots menu. Only users who belong to either the Super Administrator or the Administrator User Groups can access the tool.

A Mambot Manager Toolbar

Icons to publish or unpublish one or more Mambots; to create, edit, or delete a Mambot; or to access the Help files for the screen.

B Mambot Name

Lists all the Mambots in the system. Click the name to open the Mambot Editing page.

C Published

Shows the Mambot's publication state. The icon toggles the state.

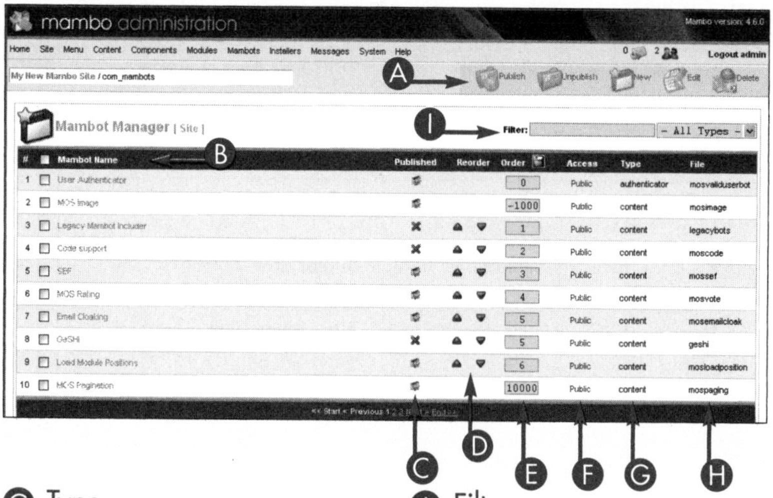

D Reorder

The arrows reorder the Mambots by moving a Mambot up or down relative to the others on the list of Mambot names.

E Order

Reorder the entire list by changing the numerical sequence of Mambots and clicking the Save icon.

F Access

Shows the current access state of the Mambot. The icon toggles the state.

G Type

Indicates the type of Mambot. Types include authenticator, editors, content, editors-xtd, and search.

H File

The name of the PHP file related to this Mambot.

I Filters

Search through the list of Mambots or use the combo box to sort by type.

Publish Mambots

You must publish a Mambot before you can enjoy the benefits of its functionality on your site. Once published, an Administrator can use a Mambot immediately, and the output that the Mambot affects immediately appears to site visitors.

You can publish a Mambot either directly from the Mambot Manager, or by opening the editing screen for an individual Mambot and setting the Published option to Yes. In the default deployment of Mambo, a number of Mambots are published, while a number of others remain unpublished. Although the default configuration is what Mambo site administrators most commonly use, your needs may vary. The section "Understanding Core Mambots" gives you some idea of what you do or do not need on your site. You can also install Mambots from third-party developers to extend the functionality of your site.

For some Mambots, the simple act of publishing is not sufficient to bring about a change in the site's appearance. The output of Mambots, like the MOS Rating Mambot or the SEF Mambot, only becomes apparent when options that are selected elsewhere trigger the functionality. Other Mambots, like Code Support or Load Module Positions, require that the administrator add special codes to the Content Items before these Mambots output. It is the nature of Mambots: they enable functionality, but rarely does publishing a Mambot alone cause a result to occur.

Note that if you unpublish a Mambot, this immediately cancels the Mambot's output, although it does not affect the Mambot in any other way; unpublishing essentially suspends a Mambot's performance, nothing more. When you republish the Mambot, its functionality returns.

Publish Mambots

1. Click Mambots.
2. Click Site Mambots.

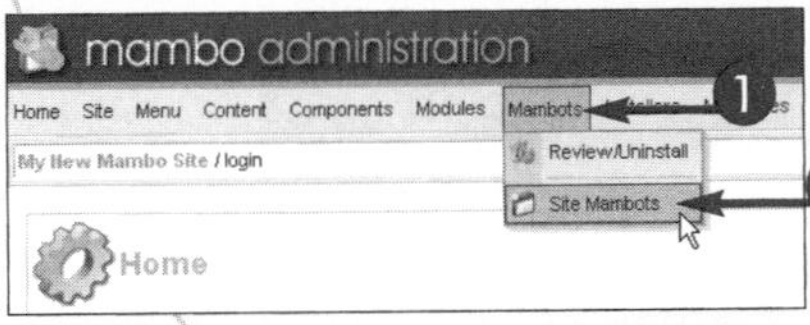

The Mambot Manager page loads.

3. Select the Mambot you want to publish.
4. Click the Edit icon.

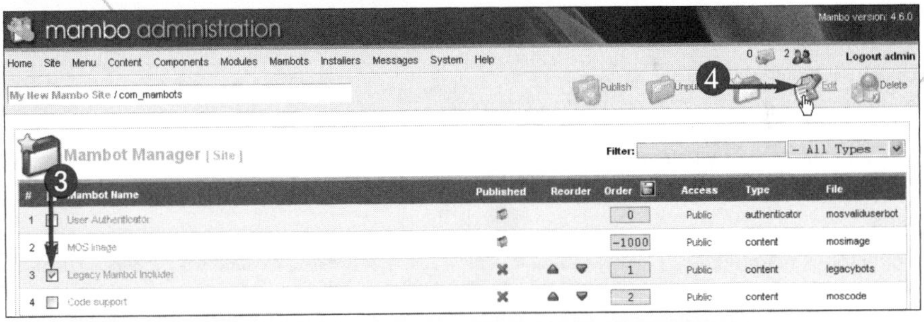

The Mambot Editing page loads.

5. Click Yes for the Published option.
6. Click the Save icon.

The Mambot becomes active.

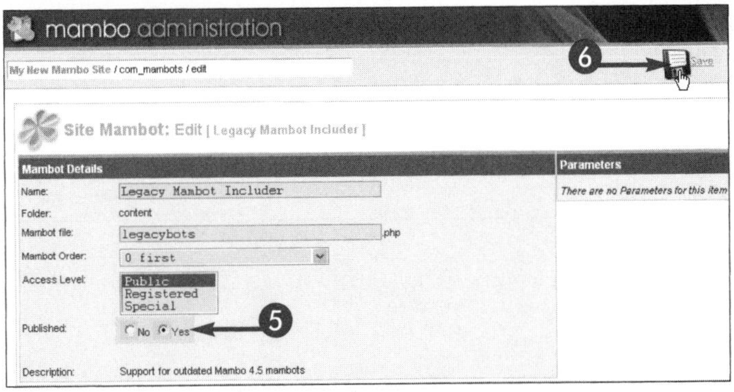

Install a New Mambot Automatically

You can install additional Mambots using the automatic installer to upload a zip file archive. When you obtain a preconfigured Mambot for your Mambo site, it is delivered in the form of a zip file archive. The archive should contain all the files necessary to install and use the new Mambot. If the Mambot has been created properly, you should not need to make any additional changes, although, of course, you may want to customize it somewhat to fit your needs.

You can use the Universal Installer to automatically install new Mambots for your Mambo site. The Installer presents three options: Upload Package File, Install from HTTP URL, and Install From Directory.

The Upload Package File option provides for automatic installation of a zip archived template file. Note that this first method functions properly only if your server supports GZip or a similar utility that enables extraction of zip file archives. If your server lacks this ability, you must use the Install From Directory option. This option is the most commonly used and accordingly this method is demonstrated in the steps below.

The second option, Install from HTTP URL also provides automatic installation and you use it when you can obtain the Mambot package directly from a URL. This method is very convenient because you do not have to download it first, then upload it. Unfortunately, some Web servers do not support the Install from HTTP URL and it is of no use if your server is not connected to the Internet.

The third option, Install From Directory, is a manual installation technique, covered in the next section, "Install a New Template Manually."

Once you install your Mambot package, you can test the new Mambot after publishing it. For more on publishing a new Mambot, see the section "Publishing a Mambot."

Install a New Mambot Automatically

1. Select Installers.
2. Click Universal.

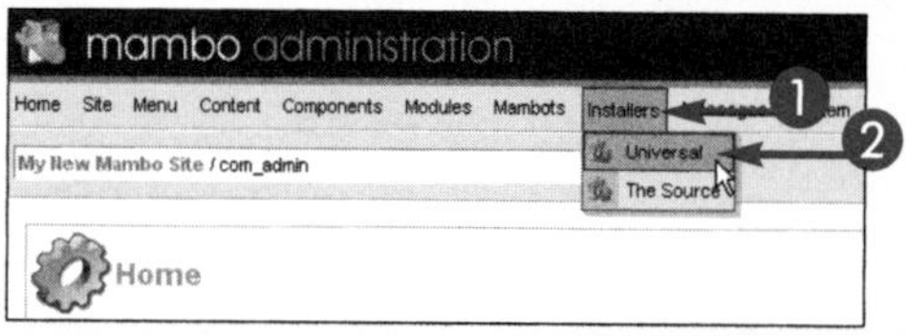

The Universal Installer loads.

- A list of directories, along with an indication of whether they are writeable, appears here.

If the directories mambots/, mambots/content, mambots/editors, mambots/editors-xtd or mambots/search show as unwriteable, you must change the permissions (read/write status) of the directory.

Note: For more on how to change file permissions, see Chapter 1.

3. Click Browse.

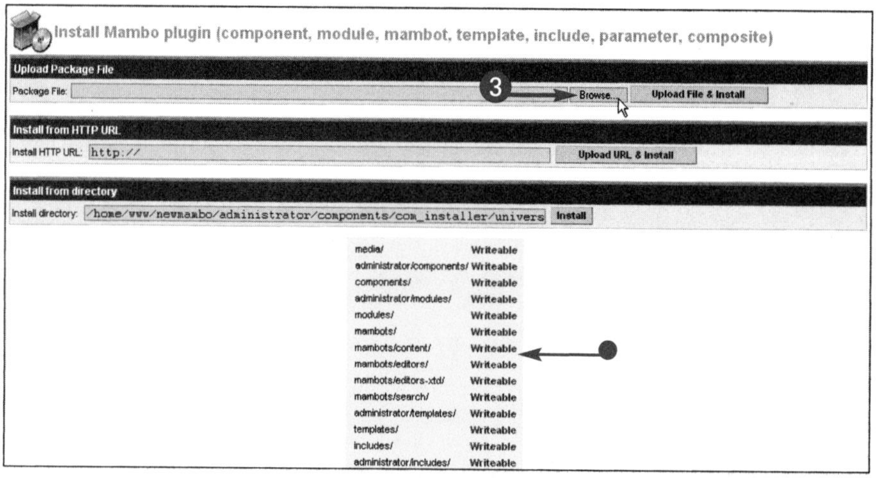

The Choose file dialog box opens.

4. Navigate to the location of the Mambot archive.
5. Select the file.
6. Click Open.

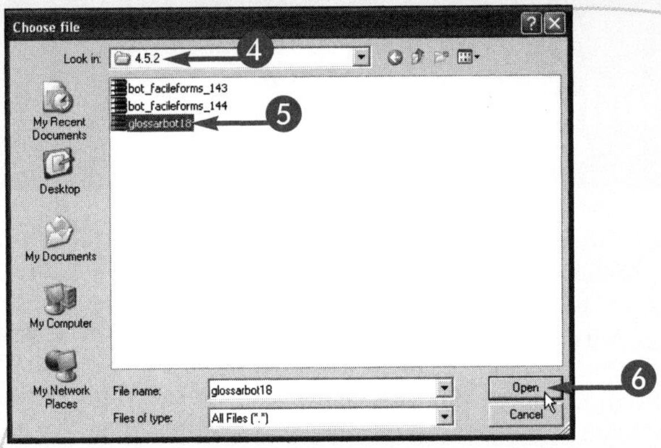

7. Click Upload File & Install.

If you are successful, you see a confirmation message when the screen reloads.

If you are not successful, you see a message indicating failure.

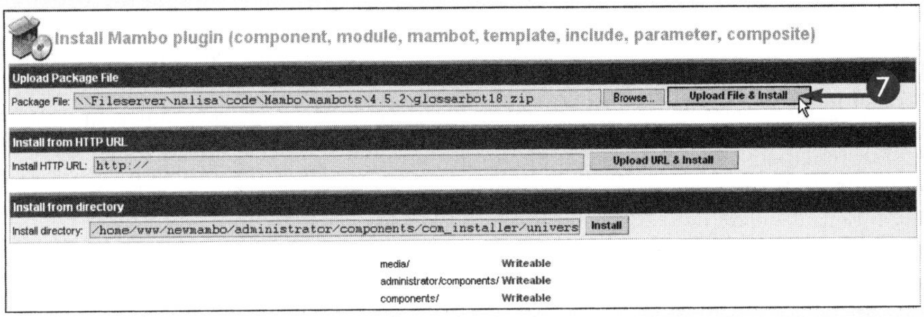

Extra

When you acquire a Mambo Mambot from a third-party developer, make sure to verify that it contains all the elements that are necessary for automatic installation. A proper Mambot package is delivered as a zip archive file and should contain at least a PHP file and an XML file. While best practices dictate that a developer create the package in a standard format that allows for easy installation, experience indicates that this is not always the case.

If all the elements are in place and properly formed, the installer will work as described in this section and all the Mambot features should work without the need for adjusting the Mambot files. If elements are missing or contain errors, you may need to manually install, as outlined in the next section, "Install a New Mambot Manually." Note that sometimes even an incorrectly created Mambot installs; but once installed, it may not have all features available.

Install a New Mambot Manually

You can install Mambots without the use of the automatic installer described in the previous section, "Install a New Mambot Automatically." Manual installation is required if your server does not support GZip or another utility for extracting file archives. In certain other circumstances you may want to install a Mambot manually, such as if you have some, but not all, of the various Mambot files.

You have two options for performing manual installation. You can either use the Install From Directory option in the Universal Installer, or you can simply copy the files to the server via FTP and bypass the Install From Directory function. Both methods require that you move files up to the server outside of the Mambo system. The choice of which method to use depends largely on the nature of the Mambot with which you are working.

If you have a proper Mambot package — that is, a Mambot that contains a complete set of properly formed files — you should use the Install From Directory option outlined in this section. If your Mambot files are incomplete, you cannot use this option; instead, you must transfer the Mambot files to the Mambo Mambot directory on the server. Note, however, that installing a Mambot without the use of the Install From Directory function means that you cannot automatically uninstall the Mambot, and you are forced to uninstall the files one by one should you decide at some point in the future to delete them from your system. Accordingly, the preferred practice, and the easiest, is to use the Install From Directory function.

You can access the Mambot Installer either through direct links under the Mambots and Installers menus.

Install a New Mambot Manually

1. If they are zipped, extract the Mambot files from the zip archive.

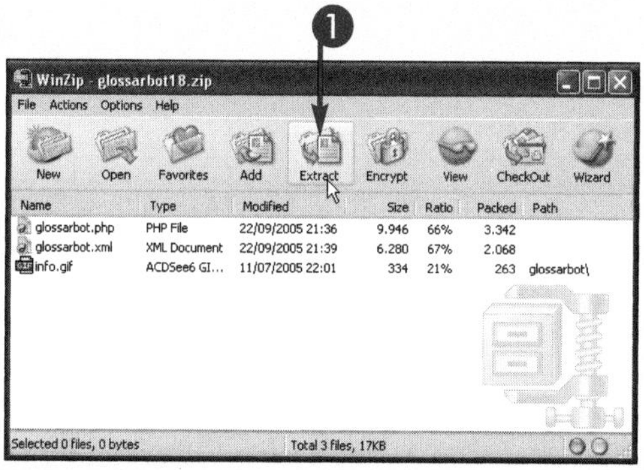

2. Access your server via FTP.

3. Move the Mambot files into a directory and note the location.

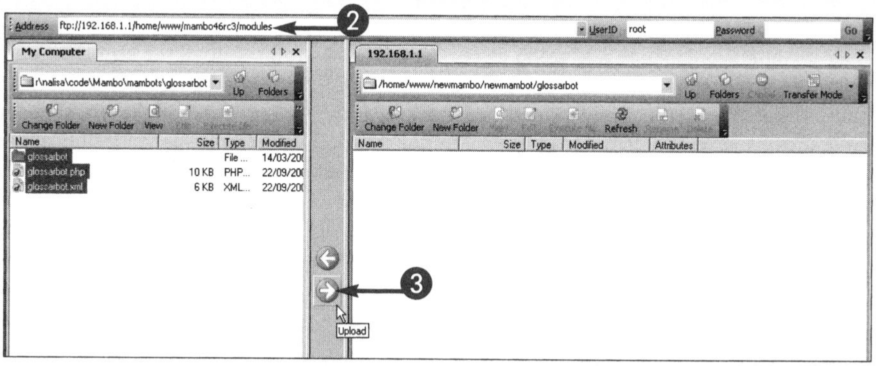

4 Click Installers.

5 Click Universal.

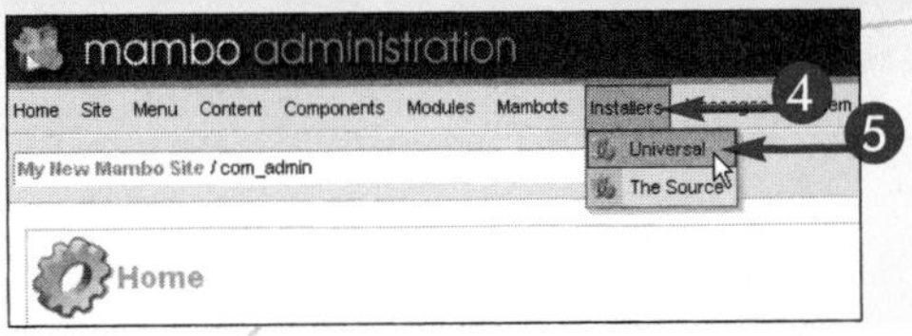

The Universal Installer loads.

6 Type the full path to the directory containing the files here.

7 Click Install.

If you are successful, you see a confirmation message when the screen reloads.

If you are not successful, you see a message indicating failure.

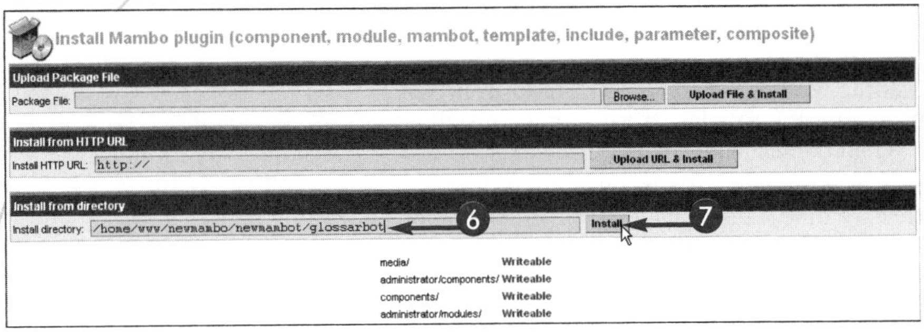

Extra

If you are inclined to build your own Mambots from scratch, the system provides a very easy way to test out a new Mambot without having to go through all the work of creating a complete installation package. After you progress with the basic files to the point where you can test them, move them onto the server and into the Mambots directory. The next step is to go to the Mambots Manager and click the New icon. In the new screen that appears, use the combo box to select the directory where you placed the Mambot files, and enter the name of the primary Mambot PHP file in the blank names Mambot file. Once you click the Save or Apply icon, you can test your Mambot.

Mambots are sometimes delivered bundled with components or modules. When a Mambot is bundled with something else, there is no point trying to install the Mambot individually because it does not add to the functionality of your site. You should install bundled packages only via the Universal Installer.

Uninstall a Mambot

You can install a Mambot automatically and remove all the files from your server. You may want to remove a Mambot to clean up your server and remove unnecessary files, or if you must install an updated version of the same Mambot.

If you have used the Universal Installer or the Install From Directory functionality, the removal of a Mambot is easy and automatic. If, on the other hand, you have installed the Mambot manually via FTP and without using the Install From Directory functionality, you must uninstall the Mambot manually by accessing the server via FTP and deleting the files you previously moved to the server. A discussion of the Universal Installer is included in the previous section "Install a New Mambot Automatically." Manual installation by way of the Install From Directory functionality is covered in the section "Install a New Mambot Manually."

Unlike Content Items or Menu Items, the system does move Mambots to the Trash Manager upon deletion. Therefore, think carefully before you confirm deletion, because Mambo completely deletes the Mambot and all its associated files from your system. The only way to get the Mambot back is to reinstall it from scratch.

Because you cannot undo a Mambot deletion, you may want to leave the Mambot in the system, unused. If you do not publish the unused Mambot, the files are completely inactive and do not impair your site's performance.

Alternatively, you can back up the files prior to deletion by accessing the Mambo Mambots directory on the server and copying the files to your local machine. Note the default Mambots have no separate installation package, and therefore reinstallation from a backup is the only way to restore them once you delete them. For more information on backing up your Mambo files, see Chapter 14.

Uninstall a Mambot

1. Load the Mambot Manager.

Note: To Load the Mambot Manager, see the section "Publish a Mambot."

2. Select the Mambot you want to uninstall.

3. Click the Delete icon.

A confirmation dialog box appears.

4. Click OK.

- You can click Cancel to cancel.

Mambo deletes the Mambot and all its parts from the system.

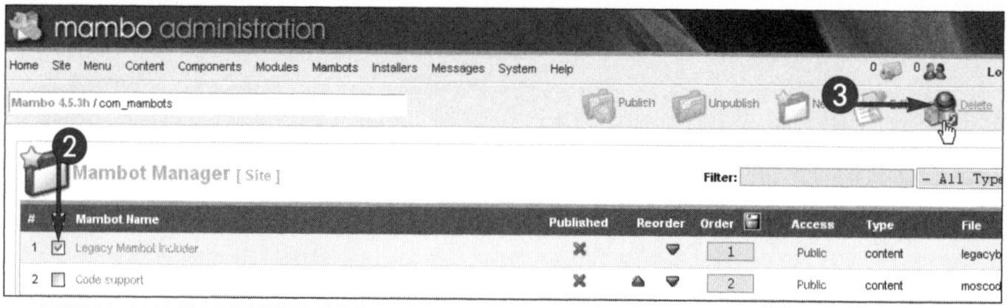

Configure MOS Image

You can configure the display of images inserted with the MOSimage command by setting options in the MOSimage Mambot. The configuration options for the MOSimage Mambot are useful for formatting the spacing around images. You can find more formatting choices on the MOS Image Editing tab inside the Content Item Editing screen. For more information about using the MOSimage command, see Chapter 7.

The MOSimage Mambot is published in the default installation of Mambo. If you unpublish the Mambot, the MOSimage functionality ceases on the front end of the site, although the MOSimage button and the MOSimage editing tab continue to appear inside the Content Item Editing screen.

The two parameters that Mambo provides with this Mambot are Margin and Padding. Note that the options affect only images that you insert with the MOSimage function, and even then, only those images that include captions. Margin and Padding are both very similar in function: they both add space between the image with its caption and the surrounding items or text. Margin is a numerical value representing the number of pixels of space between the image with its border and the surrounding objects or text. Padding is a numerical value representing the number of pixels of space between the image and its border. The only real difference between the two is seen when you use a background for the image, in which case the background appears when you use padding, but does not appear in the area denoted by Margin. To make it all the more confusing, this rule tends to vary somewhat between browsers!

The default values for both the parameters is 5, giving a total space of 10 pixels between the image with its caption and the surrounding text or objects.

Configure MOS Image

1. Load the Mambot Manager.

Note: To Load the Mambot Manager, see the section "Publish a Mambot."

2. Select MOS Image.
3. Click Edit.

   The MOS Image editing screen opens.

4. Type the Margin.
5. Type the Padding.
6. Click the Save icon.

   Mambo saves the changes and returns you to the Mambot Manager.

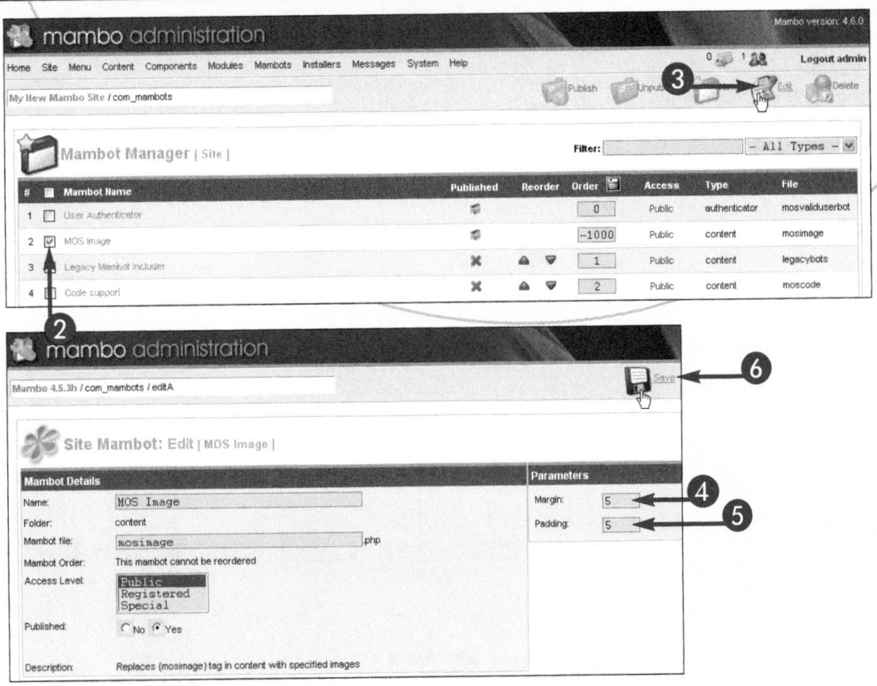

Configure Email Cloaking

You can configure the functionality attached to email addresses that appear in your Content Items. Mambo includes a very handy Mambot that automatically screens email addresses from the prying eyes of SPAMbots — those automated programs that scour the Web in search of email addresses to harvest and add to SPAM lists. The tool that provides you with protection from the SPAMbots is the Email Cloaking Mambot. The Mambot includes a configurable option that controls the functionality and allows you to decide whether links in your Content Items are clickable.

The Email Cloaking Mambot is published by default. You do not want to unpublish the Mambot unless you suspect for some reason that it is giving you problems. If you unpublish the Email Cloaking Mambot, all email addresses in your Content Items become exposed to the SPAMbots.

The Email Cloaking Mambot works by using JavaScript to hide the email addresses from the SPAMbots. The JavaScript renders the email address unrecognizable and hence avoids the entire problem by cloaking the email addresses. The cloaking does not, however, impair the functionality of the system because you can still click the email addresses. The Mambot protects both email addresses typed directly into the Content Items without links, and those entered as active mailto links.

The single configuration option presented in the Email Cloaking Mambot determines whether site visitors can click the email addresses. The default setting, "As linkable mailto address," makes the email addresses clickable. You can, however, disable the option and force all email addresses to become static items by changing the Mode setting to nonlinkable text.

Note that you should not change the Access settings for this Mambot because it may leave some of your Content Items unprotected. The default Access setting is Public, and you should leave it that way.

Configure Email Cloaking

1. Load the Mambot Manager.

Note: To Load the Mambot Manager, see the section "Publish a Mambot."

2. Click the Email Cloaking option.
3. Click the Edit icon.

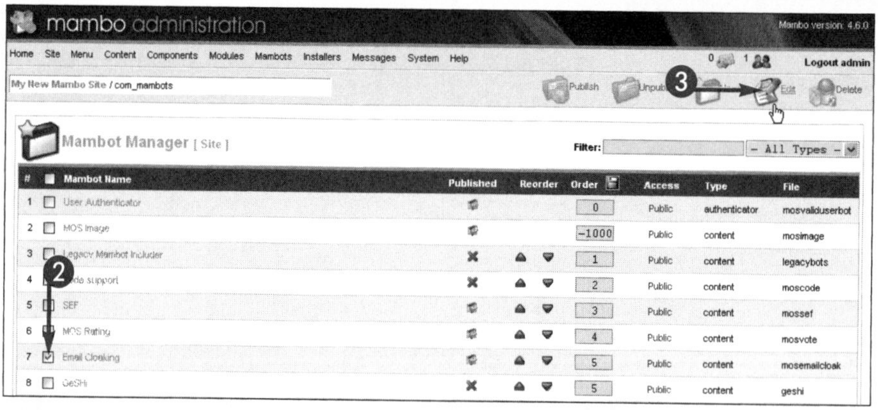

The Email Cloaking Editing screen opens.

4. Click the desired mode.
5. Click the Save icon.

Mambo saves your changes and returns you to the Mambot Manager.

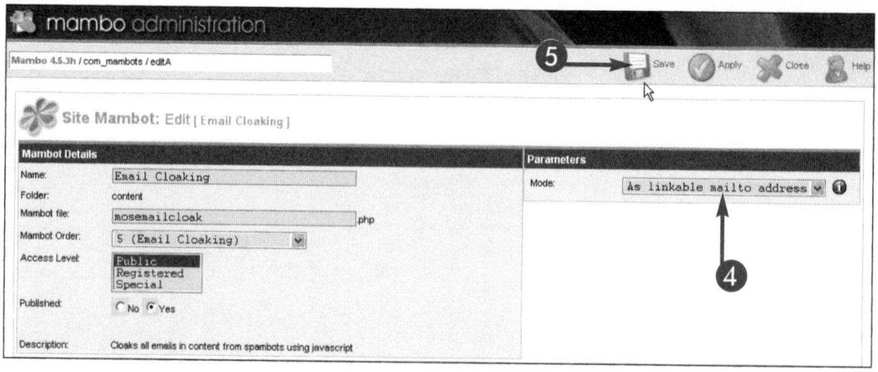

Configure Load Module Positions

You can control the formatting of modules inserted into your Content Items. The Load Module Positions Mambot gives you the ability to insert Module position holders into your Content Items and the parameters attached to the Mambot control how you format the module.

The Load Module Positions Mambot is published by default. The Mambot only affects modules that you insert using the `{mosloadposition}` command; it does not affect modules that are hard coded into the templates. If you intend to use the Mambot's functionality, you should leave it published. If you do not want to use the feature, you can unpublish the Mambot without impact on your site. For more on how to insert a module within a Content Item, see Chapter 12.

Only the Style parameter is available for the Load Module Positions Mambot. This parameter relates to how Mambo formats the modules when it inserts the Module with the `{mosloadposition}` command. The parameter includes four options: Wrapped by Table–Column, Wrapped by Table–Horizontal, Wrapped by Divs, and No Wrapping–Raw Output. The default setting is Wrapped by Table–Column, which presupposes that you want to output the module similar to how it appears in a side column position. The best way to find the right setting for your site is to experiment with the different settings to see which gives you the best result.

If you want to wrap your module in a table, you should select either of the Table options, depending on which fits best within your template and Content Item. To use a CSS approach, choose the Wrapped by Divs option. If you want to use the Module's formatting without any additional code, select the No Wrapping–Raw Output option.

Configure Load Module Positions

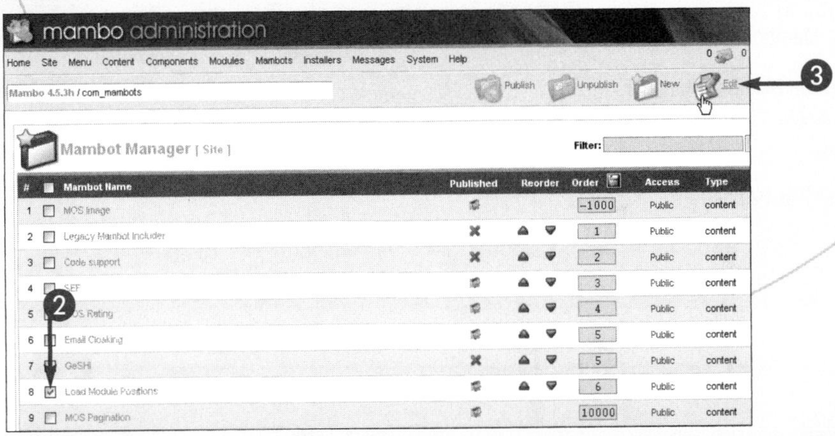

1. Load the Mambot Manager.

Note: To Load the Mambot Manager, see the section "Publish a Mambot."

2. Click the Load Module Positions option.
3. Click the Edit icon.

The Load Module Positions editing screen opens.

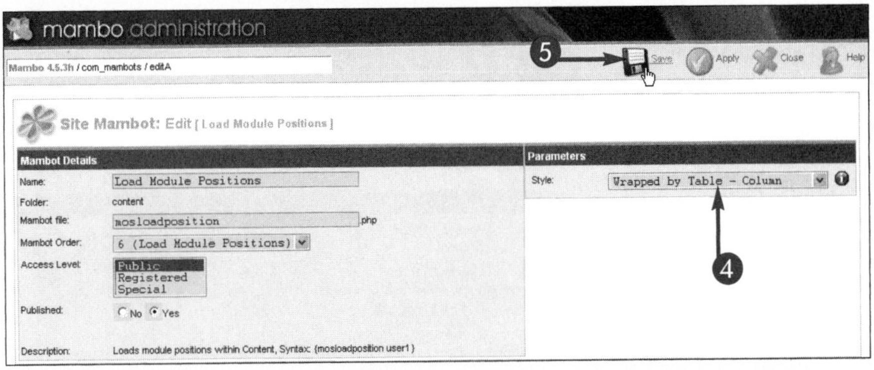

4. Click the desired style.
5. Click the Save icon.

Mambo saves the changes and returns you to the Mambot Manager.

Configure MOS Pagination

You can configure the MOS Pagination Mambot to include additional information in your page titles. The parameter included with the MOS Pagination Mambot allows you to improve your search engine optimization by creating unique page titles for each page of the multi-page content items that employ the `{mospagebreak}` command. For more on creating multi-page content items, see Chapter 6.

The MOS Pagination Mambot is published by default. The Mambot makes it possible to create multi-page Content Items through the use of the `{mospagebreak}` command. You must publish the Mambot for the `{mospagebreak}` command to function. If your site does not employ `{mospagebreak}`, you can unpublish the Mambot without impact to your site.

The MOS Pagination Mambot includes only one Parameter entitled Site Title, which determines whether the individual page titles of the pages that you created with the `{mospagebreak}` command are appended to the page titles of the site. Including additional page information with your page titles can help distinguish the individual pages for both your users' ease of use and to improve your search engine's placement of these individual pages. If you are concerned with search engine optimization, it is recommended that you employ this option.

To make the most of the Site Title parameter, you must not only use the `{mospagebreak}` command, but you should also include either one or both of the parameters that are available for the command. The Title parameter allows you to give an individual page a separate title, such as `{mospagebreak title=introduction}`. You use the other optional parameter, Heading, in a similar fashion `{mospagebreak heading=overview}`. You can use Heading and Title together so that both are appended to the page title when you set the Site Title parameter to Yes.

Configure MOS Pagination

1. Load the Mambot Manager.

Note: To Load the Mambot Manager, see the section "Publish a Mambot."

2. Click the MOS Pagination option.
3. Click the Edit icon.

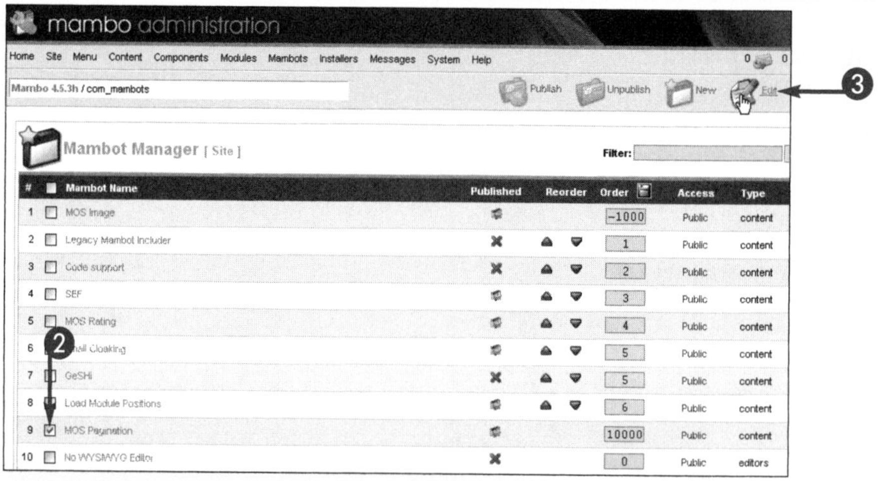

The MOS Pagination editing screen opens.

4. Click the desired site title option.
5. Click the Save icon.

Mambo saves the changes and returns you to the Mambot Manager.

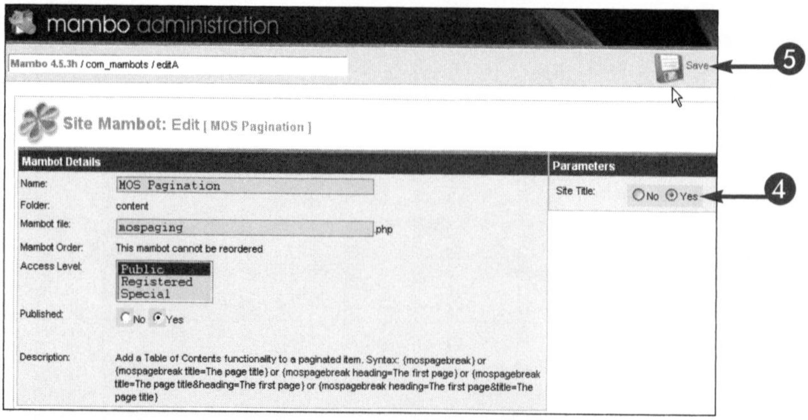

Configure the TinyMCE WYSIWYG Editor

You can customize the interface and functionality of the TinyMCE WYSIWYG Editor. Mambo comes bundled with two WYSIWYG Editors: MOStlyCE and TinyMCE. The MOStlyCE Editor is set as the default editor. Users who choose to use the TinyMCE editor instead can configure the editor through the TinyMCE WYSIWYG Editor Mambot.

The Functionality parameter has a global impact on the editor. It allows you to select between Simple and Advanced interfaces. The Advanced interface is the default setting and displays all the tools and options available. The Simple interface reduces the number of tools visible and present users with a more basic interface.

The next group of parameters affects specific functions. The Text Direction parameter dictates whether the text flows from left to right, like this text, or from right to left that some non-English languages use. The Prohibited Elements list is a text field into which you can type the names of script elements that you do not want to permit into the Content Items. The field gives you some basic security by preventing users from including potentially vulnerable script commands. Template CSS Classes determines whether the editor will rely on the template's CSS file or use a custom CSS file. If you disable this value, you must input the URL of the CSS file you want for your Content Items on the next line.

The final grouping of parameters affects the layout of the tool itself. The first option allows you to position the editor's toolbar relative to the text box where you enter the content. The next two fields determine the size of the HTML mode pop-up that the editor uses.

Configure the TinyMCE WYSIWYG Editor

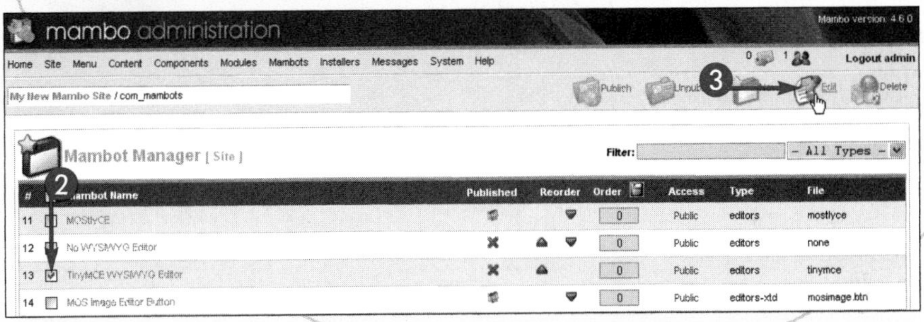

1. Load the Mambot Manager.

Note: To Load the Mambot Manager, see the section "Publish a Mambot."

2. Select TinyMCE WYSIWSYG Editor.

3. Click the Edit icon.

   The TinyMCE WYSIWSYG Editor editing screen opens.

4. Select the desired parameters.

5. Click the Save icon.

   Mambo saves the changes and returns you to the Mambot Manager.

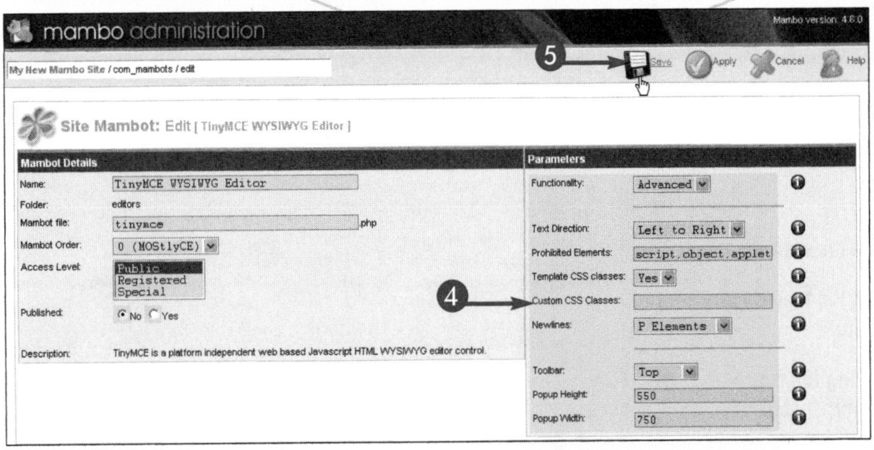

Back Up a Mambo Site

You can back up both your Mambo files and the database for your site by using a combination of tools. As a practical safeguard, you should take steps to periodically back up the data in your site. This protects you from complete loss of your site in the event of a problem with the server at your Web host or a hack attack or defacement.

The Mambo database contains all your Content Items as well as your site's configuration settings and parameters. About the only site data kept in the directories with your Mambo files are the images. Accordingly, backing up the database is the key to maintaining the safety of your content. You can back up your Mambo Web site's database with the MOStlyDBAdmin DB Tools component. The component gives you the option to back up all or part of the database tables. The tool also gives you a choice of file formats for the backup and a choice of locations. You can even use the tool to view the database tables online in HTML format from inside the admin interface. You should keep copies of the data exported from the database locally in case you need to restore the data later.

The files contained in the directories on your Mambo site relate to the code that is executed, and includes the files that power your components, modules, Mambots, and templates. Making a backup copy of the directory contents is necessary where you want to protect files you have modified, or when you want to protect your templates or your image files.

BACK UP A DATABASE

1. Click Components.
2. Click MOStlyDBAdmin DB Tools.
3. Click Backup Database.

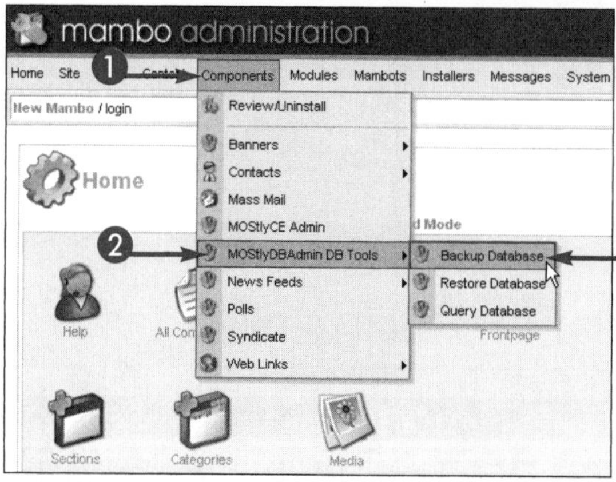

The MOStlyDBAdmin Backup screen loads.

4. Select where you want to save the backup.

Note: Downloading the file to your local computer is recommended.

5. Select the nature of the backup.
6. Select the file format you want.
7. Select the tables you want to backup.

Note: Backing up all is recommended.

8. Click Backup the Selected Tables.

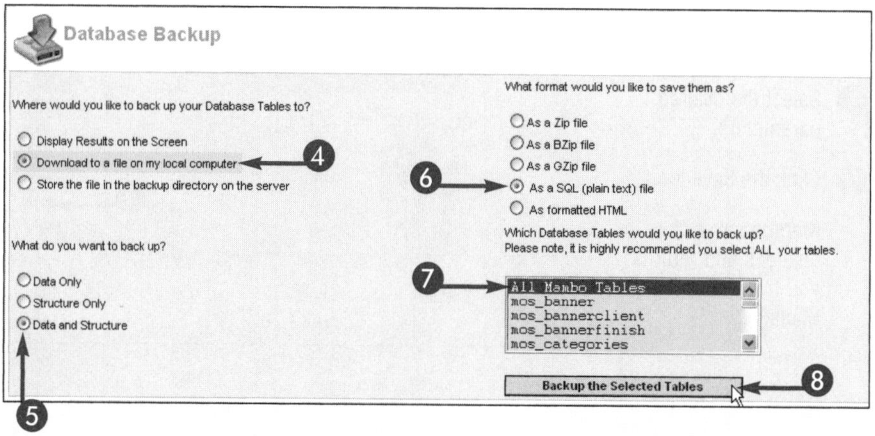

A confirmation dialog box appears.

9. Click Save.

   A dialog box appears asking for a location to save the file.

10. Select a location.

11. Click Save.

   A backup of the database is created and saved to the location you specified.

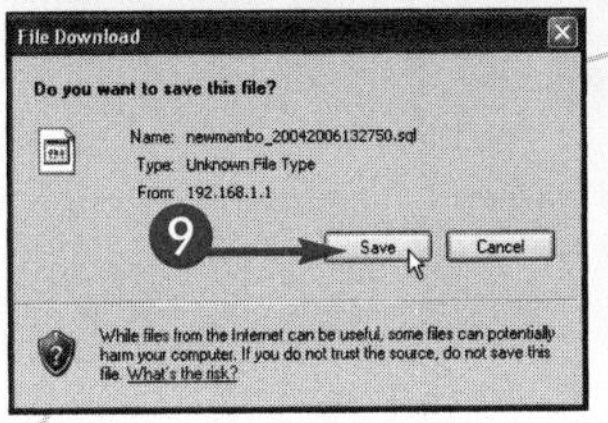

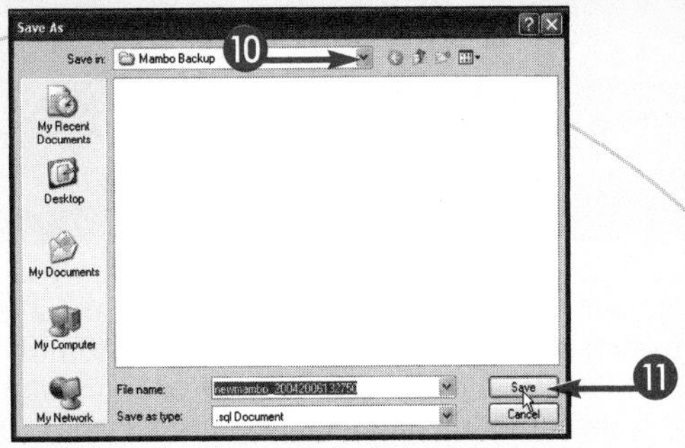

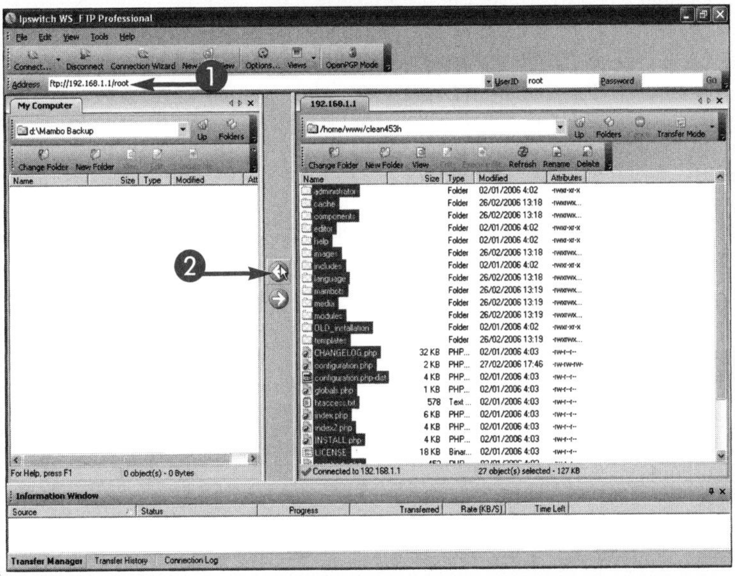

BACK UP SITE FILES

1. Access your server via FTP.

   A list of directories appears in the FTP program.

2. Copy all files to your local machine.

   Your site files are now backed up.

Extra

Keeping a local copy of your live Web site can make development and site maintenance a much easier and more predictable task. While it may not be possible or practical to keep the local offline database synchronized with the live Web site, having a local copy that serves as a test bed for new modifications or components is a great way to try things out without creating problems on your live site. Additionally, if you want to add new Content Items, sometimes it is faster to build them locally, view and test them locally, and then copy the HTML code for the Content Item and paste it into the live site.

You should regularly and locally back up your live site's database. Even if your system gives you the option to store the backups on the server, do not do it; rather, download the backups and keep them in a safe place. You should back up busy sites at least once per week. You should back up sites that change infrequently once a month. Periodically test your backups, because one of the keys to any successful backup strategy is an occasional test of the backup. Also remember that if worse comes to worst, there is always a chance your Web host has a backup of your site.

Restore a Mambo Database

You can restore all or part of a Mambo database from a backup by using the MOStlyDBAdmin component. The ability to restore your Mambo database from within the admin system is a timesaver because you no longer need to access the database using a separate tool.

The MOStlyDBAdmin tool includes three options: Backup the Database, Restore the Database, and Query the Database. The Restore functionality can work from either files stored locally on your machine or from files you have stored on the server. The system works most smoothly using files created with the MOStlyDBAdmin backup tool, but it will work with any properly formatted backup file. For more on how to back up your database using MOStlyDBAdmin, see the section "Back Up a Mambo Site."

When the Restore tool loads, you see at the top of the page a list of available backup files stored on the server, if any. You can restore from files on the server by simply selecting the file you want to restore and then clicking the Perform the Restore button.

If the files are stored on your local machine, you need to first browse your local machine to locate the file and then click Perform the Restore. Because it is advisable to store your backups on your local machine rather than on the server, this latter method of restoring the backup files is described below.

You cannot specify which data you restore with this tool. The system will restore all the data contained in the backup file; therefore, you are restricted to whatever is contained in that file. If you have only a partial backup, you will have only a partial restore.

Restore a Mambo Database

1. Click Components.
2. Click MOStlyDBAdmin DB Tools.
3. Click Restore Database.

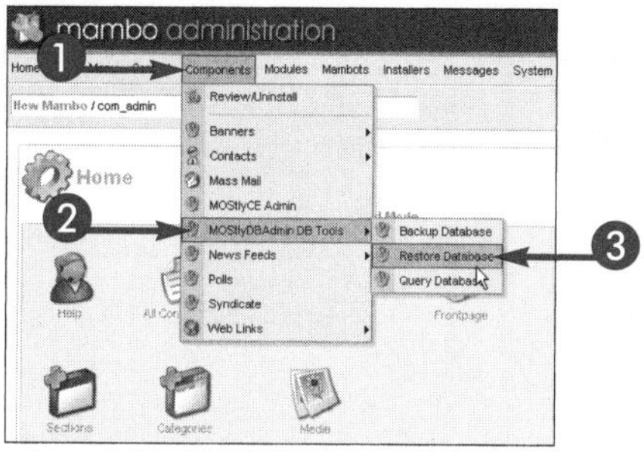

The Restore Database screen loads.

4. Click Browse.

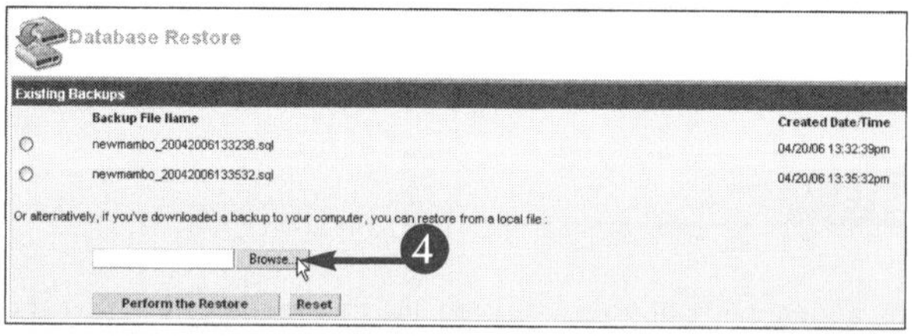

The Choose file dialog box appears.

5. Select the backup file.
6. Click Open.

The dialog box closes and takes you back to the Restore Database screen.

7. Click Perform the Restore.

Mambo performs the restore and displays a confirmation message if you were successful.

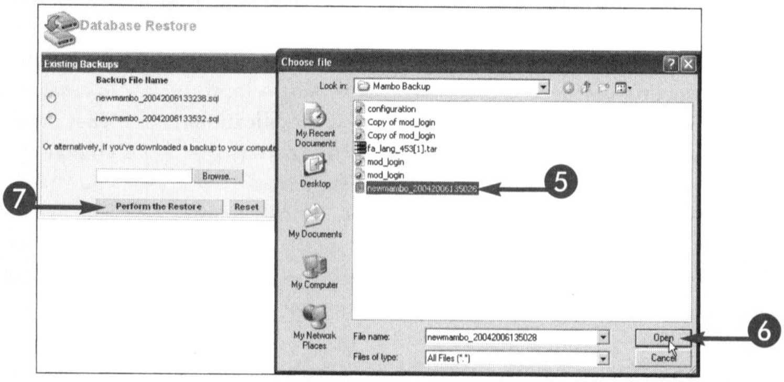

Query a Mambo Database

You can execute queries against your Mambo database from within the admin system. The ability to launch queries without having to leave the Mambo system is a convenient timesaving tool. The MOStlyDBAdmin component provides the interface for entering and executing the queries.

Executing queries from within Mambo is a simple matter. You need only access the Query Database functionality of the MOStlyDBAdmin tool on the Components menu. You enter queries directly into the textbox that appears on the Query screen. You can enter more than one query at a time and execute all in sequence by selecting the Batch Mode checkbox that appears on the Query screen. Once you click the Execute Query button, Mambo runs the queries immediately and you are informed of the success or failure of the process.

The Query function, though undoubtedly useful, is one of those Mambo features that must be used with care. Misuse of this tool can cause your site to crash and has the potential to cause serious harm to your database. This tool should be used with caution by any user and should never be used on a live site by anyone but the most experienced of users.

Before you execute a query, always back up your database. In the event something goes wrong, you may be able to restore your database from the fresh backup, either by using the MOStlyDBAdmin Restore function or by accessing your database with a third-party tool, like phpMyAdmin. To learn how to back up your database, see the section "Back Up a Mambo Site." To learn how to restore your Mambo database, see the section "Restore a Mambo Database."

Query a Mambo Database

1. Click Components.
2. Click MOStlyDBAdmin DB Tools.
3. Click Query Database.

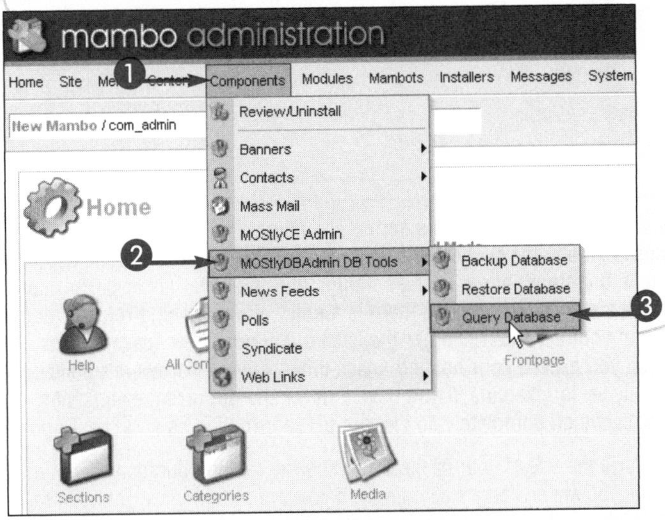

The Query Database screen loads.

4. Type your query.
5. Click Execute Query.

The system executes your query on the database and returns a confirmation message if you were successful.

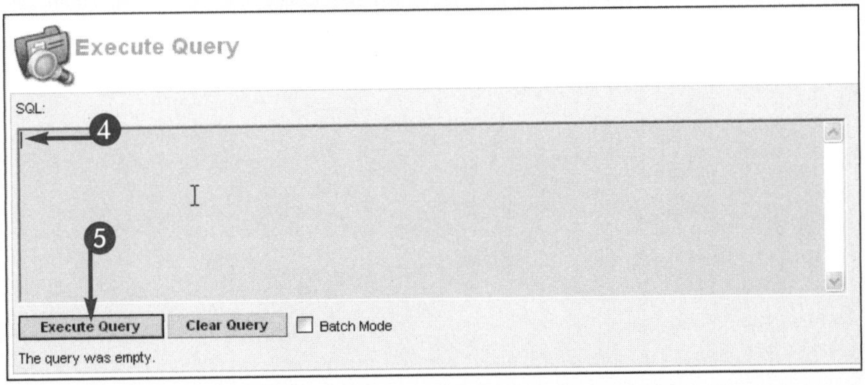

Optimize Performance Settings

You can improve your Mambo site's performance by managing its caching options. Caching makes your Web server respond more quickly to site visitors. It increases performance by temporarily holding in storage some of the files necessary for your content items to display. When a visitor requests a cached item, the system produces it immediately, rather than going back to the database to retrieve it and then display it. Although sites with a large amount of graphical content or media files benefit most from caching, all sites can see performance gains with proper cache management. Mambo generally gives you two caching controls: enabling or disabling the caching function, and changing the caching time. Mambo includes caching options in several locations, from global settings to caching specific component or module content. You can select the options that fit your site needs and traffic patterns.

Enabling or Disabling Caching

This is the first and most fundamental option. To improve performance by caching content, enable the cache. If your e-commerce site features a catalog with inventory tracking, you should disable caching for that portion of the site because it may cause inaccurate inventory figures and may lead to ordering errors.

Cache Option Location

The global caching options in Mambo are located in the Cache tab of the Global Configuration Manager. For more on accessing those controls, see Chapter 2. Some individual components, like the Syndicate component, and some modules, like those used to acquire RSS content, also have independent caching controls. For more on how to use the caching options for individual components and modules, refer to chapter 11.

Changing Cache Time

This relates to the length of time that the cache holds items. The longer the cache time, the more items Mambo caches, and the longer Mambo holds those items in the cache. As a general rule, the longer the cache setting, the more the system relies on the cache to deliver content; therefore, longer cache settings tend to deliver faster performance for site visitors. However, in certain situations you do not see a real advantage; there is a point of diminishing returns, but exactly where that point is depends on the performance of your server. The larger the cache, the more disk space it takes. You should not increase caching times to the point that you exceed your hosting space limits or your hardware's ability. More importantly, if your content changes very frequently — for example, if you have a news site or current events site — you may want to use short cache times, or even turn the cache off completely so visitors get information as soon as it updates.

Mambo only allows you to control the size of your cache by setting the caching duration. Although this is useful, it tells you very little about the size of the cache you are creating. Accordingly, if you want to optimize your site to the greatest degree possible, the only way to find the right cache settings is to experiment by running the most demanding pages on your site with different cache sizes and observing the results.

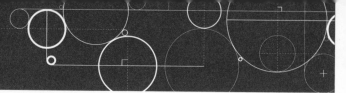

Change the Admin Template

You can change the template used by the admin system of your Mambo site. Mambo comes bundled with two admin templates. You can switch between the templates easily. You can also build and install your own template if you want. The templates bundled with the system provide a different look and feel for the admin system, and the ability to create your own template gives you the chance to personalize the appearance of the admin system to include your own choice of colors, layout, or branding.

The Mambo admin system interface is built on templates in the same manner as the front end of your Mambo Web site. Just as you can change the appearance of the front end of the Web site by changing the template, so too can you change the appearance of the admin system by changing the admin system template. Templates for the front end and the admin system work in exactly the same way and include the same required components. The admin templates are also managed in a similar fashion to the site templates. To review the discussion on front end templates, see Chapter 3.

Changing between the two installed admin templates only requires you to switch the default settings in the Admin Templates Manager. If you want to add a new template, you need to obtain or create the necessary files and then install them into the system. Admin templates can be installed either automatically or manually. To learn how to install an admin template automatically, see the next section, "Install a New Admin Template Automatically." For more on how to install a new admin template manually, see the section "Install an Admin Template Manually."

Note that only Super Administrators are allowed access to the Admin Templates menu.

Change the Admin Template

1. Click Site.
2. Click Template Manager.
3. Click Administrator Templates.

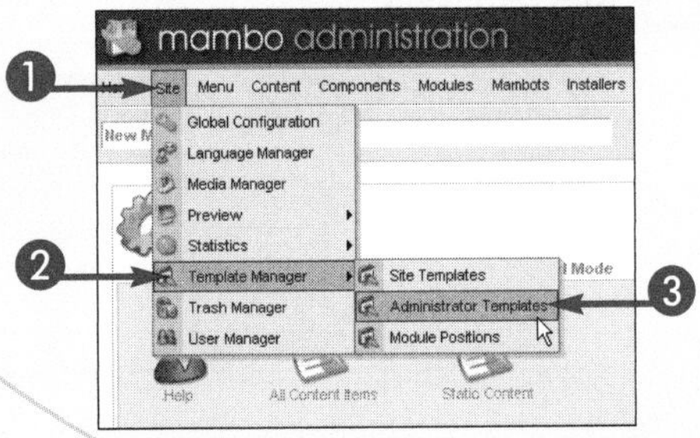

The Admin Template Manager loads.

4. Select the template you want to activate.
5. Click the Default icon.

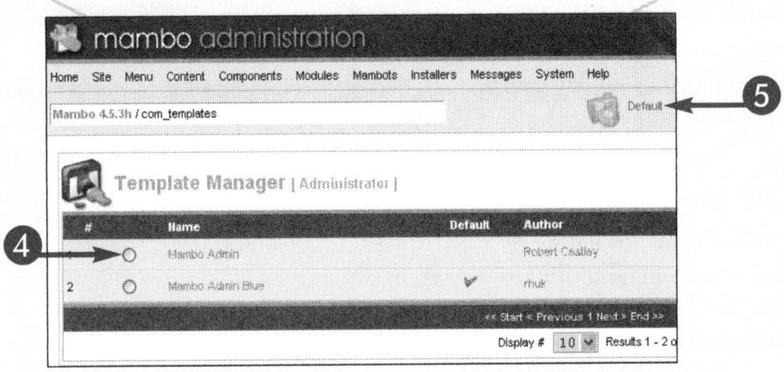

- Mambo applies the new template.

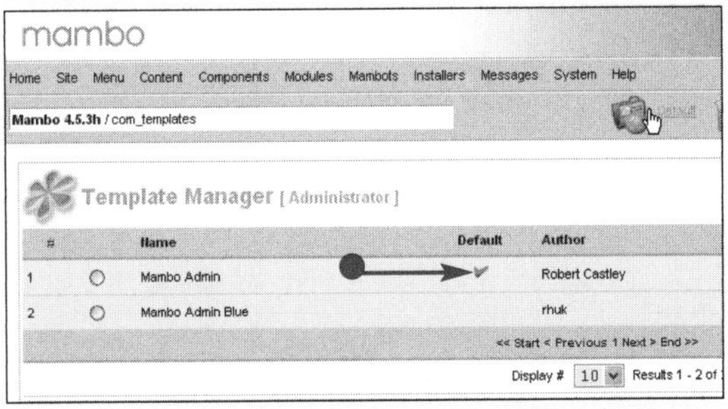

Install a New Admin Template Automatically

You can automatically install templates using the Universal Installer, and in doing so, add functionality to the Mambo core. The Universal Installer allows you to upload preconfigured template packages to your Mambo site. New templates can extend the functionality of your site and provide you alternatives for the appearance of the admin system. The Universal Installer is the easiest way to install templates to extend your Mambo site.

When you obtain a preconfigured template for your Mambo site, it is delivered in the form of a zip file archive. The archive should contain all the files necessary to install and use the new template. If the template has been created properly, you should not need to make any additional changes to get it to function properly, although you may need to configure it to fit your needs after installation.

The Universal Installer presents three options to users: Upload Package File, Install from HTTP URL, and Install From Directory. The first option provides for automatic installation of a zip-archived module file. The second allows you to input the URL of the archived file and allows the system to retrieve and install the package. The third option is a manual installation technique, covered in the section "Install an Admin Template Manually." The first method functions properly only if your server supports GZip or a similar utility that enables extraction of zip file archives. Similarly, the second option is dependent on server settings. If you do not configure your server to permit the access and installation of an archive from another server, this option will not work for you. Although the first and second options are the easiest to use, if your server does not support them, you need to use manual installation, as detailed in the next section, "Install an Admin Template Manually."

Install a New Admin Template Automatically

1. Click Installers.
2. Click Universal.

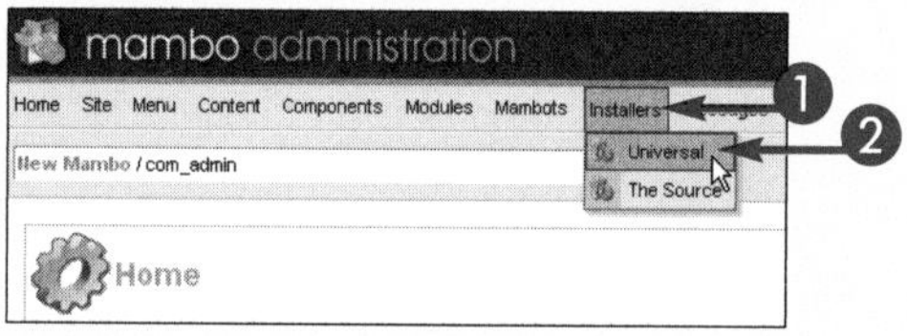

The Universal Installer loads.

- A list of directories, along with an indication of whether they are writeable, appears here.

Note: If any of the directories show as unwriteable, you must change the permissions (read/write status) of the directory. To change file permissions, see Chapter 1.

3. Click Browse.

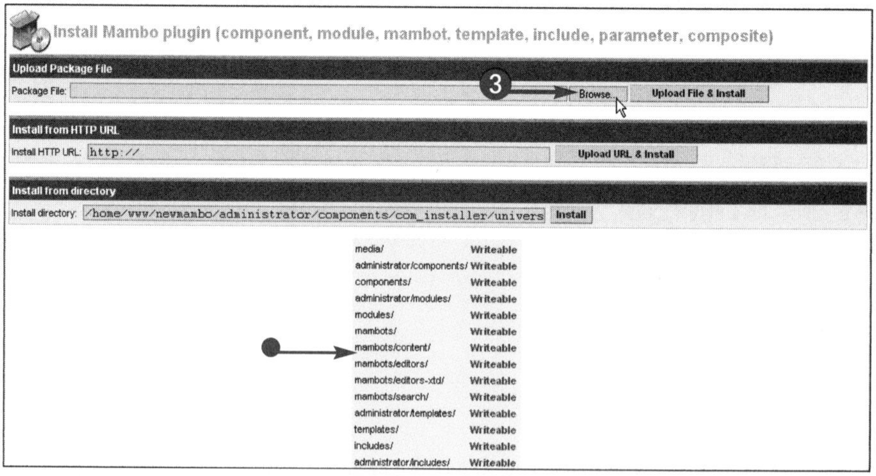

The Choose file dialog box appears.

4 Navigate to the location of the archive.

5 Select the file.

6 Click Open.

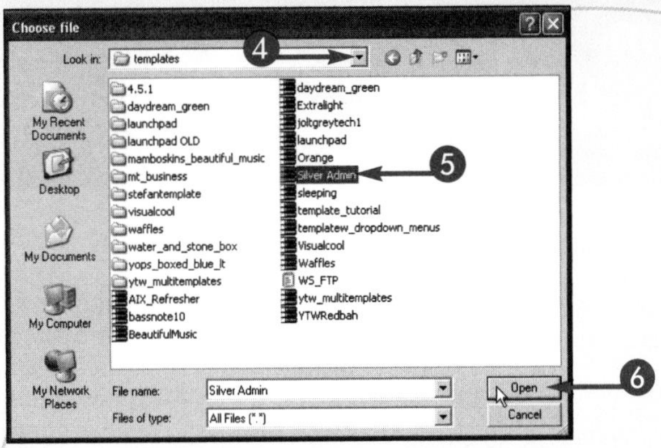

The dialog box closes and returns you to the Installer.

7 Click Upload File & Install.

Mambo displays a confirmation message when the screen reloads.

If you are not successful, a message indicates failure.

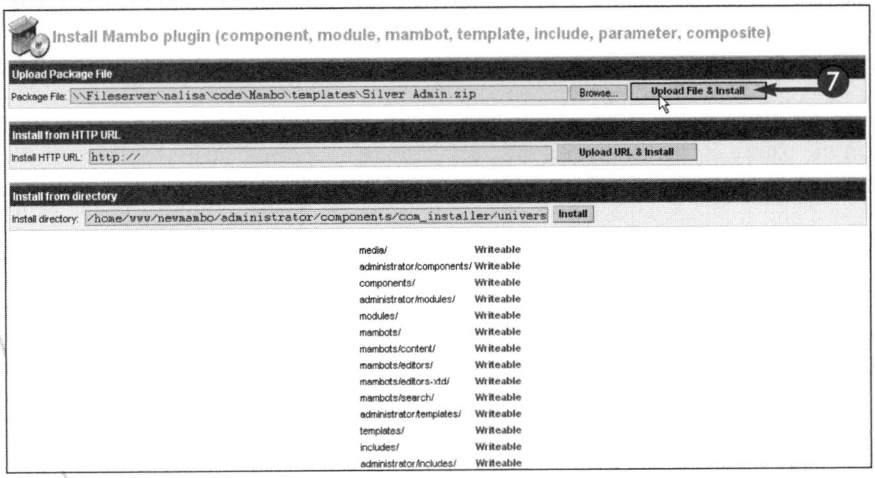

Extra

When you acquire a Mambo template from a third-party developer, make sure to verify that it contains all the elements necessary for automatic installation. A proper template package is delivered as a zip archive file and contains all of the elements outlined in Chapter 3. Although best practices dictate that a template developer create the template package in a standard format that allows for easy installation, experience indicates that this is not always the case.

If all the elements are in place and properly formed, the installer works as described here and all the template features work without the need for adjusting the template files. If elements are missing or contain errors, however, you may need to manually install, as outlined in "Install an Admin Template Manually." Sometimes even an incorrectly created template installs; but once installed, it may not have all features available.

Install an Admin Template Manually

You can install templates without the use of the automatic installer described in Chapter 2. Manual installation is required if your server does not support GZip or another utility for extracting file archives.

You can perform a manual installation by using either the Install From Directory option in the Installer, or by simply copying the files to the appropriate directory on the server. While both methods require moving files to the server outside of the Mambo system, the latter method does not rely on the Install From Directory function to activate the template. The method you use depends largely on the nature of the template with which you are working.

If you have a proper template package — that is, a template which contains a complete set of properly formed files — you should use the Install From Directory option outlined in this section. If your template files are incomplete, you cannot use this option, and instead must transfer your template files to a new directory inside the Mambo admin template directory on the server without using the Install From Directory command. Note, however, that installing a template without the Install From Directory command means that you cannot automatically uninstall the template at a later date; you must delete it manually.

Once you install your package, you can preview the new template by moving your mouse over the name of the template in the Admin Template Manager. When you mouse over a template's name, a thumbnail image appears. You can also see a template by setting the template as the Default Template and viewing the admin system of the Web site. For more on changing the default admin template, see the section "Change the Admin Template."

Install an Admin Template Manually

1. Access your server via FTP.
2. Create a directory inside the administrator/templates directory.
3. Move the template files into the new directory and note the location.

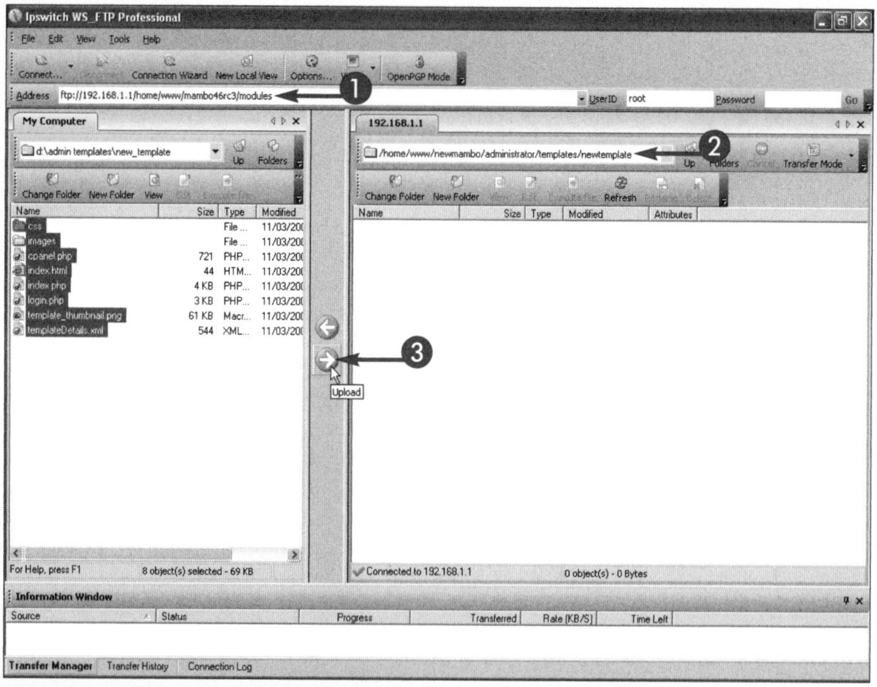

4. Click Installers.
5. Click Universal.

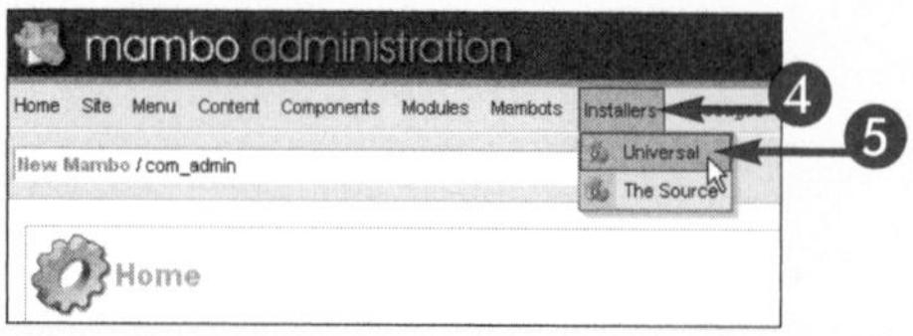

The Universal Installer loads.

6 Type the full path to the directory containing the files.

7 Click Install.

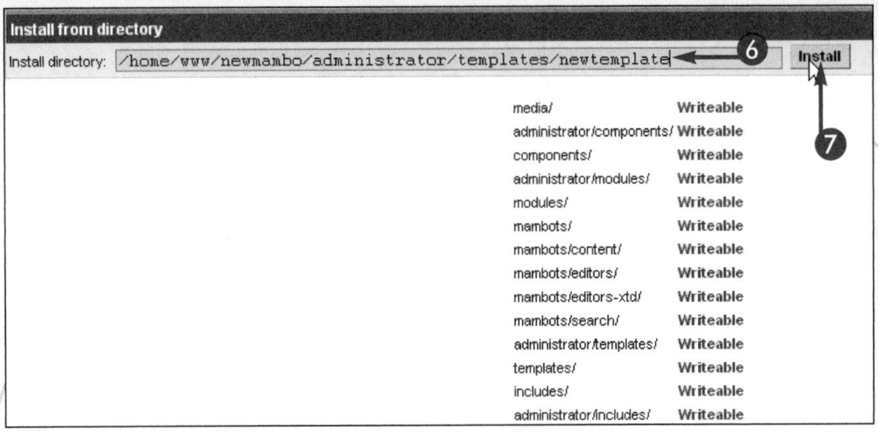

- Mambo displays a confirmation message when the screen reloads.

If you are not successful, a message indicates the failure.

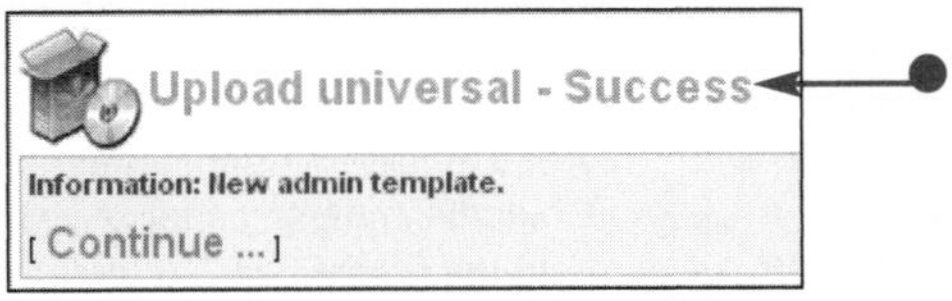

Apply It

Creating customized admin templates is particularly useful in three areas:

BRANDED ADMIN INTERFACES

If you are building a site for clients who want to maintain their brand consistency inside the admin interface, or if you are a Web developer who wants to deliver an admin interface that reflects your company's identity, creating a customized admin template can be both desirable and effective. Where the only issue is brand identity, customization can be as simple as changing the logo and the colors on the page.

ENHANCED ACCESSIBILITY

When the admin users require a more accessible admin interface, creating a custom template is an effective way to improve the usability of the Mambo system. You can use CSS to create and maintain contrast between the backgrounds and the text. You can also increase font sizes or you can introduce variable font sizes so that users can adjust the interface to their needs.

RESTRICTED ACCESS

In cases where you want to deploy a site that hides certain options from the users, creating a custom template and activating it at deployment is one way to keep users from gaining access to certain controls.

Work with Multiple Administrators

The Mambo system is designed to allow for multiple administrators on one Web site. For larger sites, multiple administrators are a way of life because it is often the only way to split up and effectively manage changing contents and users. For smaller sites, you may never use multiple administrators, or use them only sparingly. Whether your site is large or small, if you have more than one site administrator, you and your fellow administrators should agree to follow a few very basic guidelines to make the job easier and less stressful.

Stay in Touch

Use the messaging function in the administration system to leave messages for other administrators about important matters. If, for example, you suspend or restore a user's privileges, always tell your fellow administrators immediately to avoid confusion and possible misunderstanding about the user's access privileges. The messaging function is also very helpful for keeping up with small matters. With Mambo, you do not need to rely on the administrator to check his or her email account to get admin system messages because with the admin messaging system, they appear immediately if the administrator logs in. If the administrator is not logged in when you send the message, it appears the next time the administrator logs in to the admin system. For more about using the messaging function, see the sections "Send an Admin Message" and "View Admin Messages," later in the chapter.

Log Out

Always log out after you finish your work. Failure to do so properly may not only leave Content Items checked out, but it may also leave your site open to a security breach. If a log-in session attached to your user account remains active, someone can enter the system under your name and make changes to contents or components, upload materials, send emails to your users, or even cut off your access to the site. To avoid problems, log out properly every time you leave the system.

Check In What You Check Out

If you leave a Content Item checked out, other administrators cannot access the item without resorting to the Global Check In command. Always check in items you were working on before you log out of the system. If the system forces you to log out while you work on a Content Item, odds are that the item remains checked out, in which case you should log in again and check in the item as a courtesy to your fellow administrators. For more about checking in Content Items, see the section "Check In Items," later in the chapter.

Grant Few Privileges

Do not grant your users more privileges than they need to do the jobs assigned to them. Sites, for example, should have only one, or at most two, Super Administrators. Super Administrator accounts give the highest level of privileges to users. Once you create these users, you cannot delete them. Giving users more power than they need is a recipe for problems because users invariably test the limits of their powers and experiment with different things. Restrict their ability to dabble in areas outside their sphere of responsibility to prevent undesired results. For more about users and user privileges, see Chapter 4.

An Introduction to the Administrators' Messaging Manager

The Mambo administration system includes a messaging function that makes it easier for multiple administrators to communicate with each other. When administrators log in to the admin system, they can send and view messages. The personal messaging feature is a convenient way to leave notes about tasks or issues or simply to communicate a personal greeting. When users log in to the admin system, they see a notice on the screen that they have messages for viewing. Alternatively, you can configure the system to notify administrators when they receive a message. Although the personal messaging function is like email in the sense that you can send text messages back and forth quickly and easily, the messages exist only within the system. You cannot forward or view messages outside the system.

A Messages Notice

Indicates how many unread messages are in your inbox.

B Message Manager Icons

Icons that create a new message, delete messages from the system, and give access to the Help file about this screen.

C Search Box

Type a word or phrase and hit Enter to search the subject lines of the messages. Leave this box blank and press Enter to display all messages.

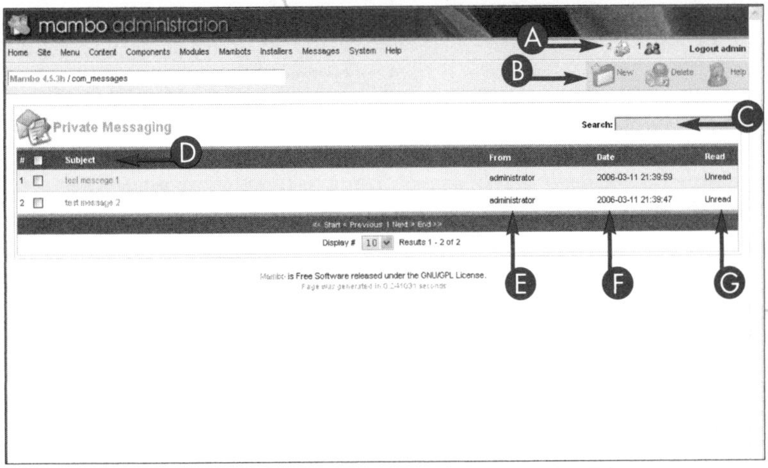

D Subject

The subject line of the messages sent to you.

E From

The sender of the messages.

F Date

The date the message was sent.

G Read Status

Shows whether you have read a message.

Configure the Administrators' Messaging Feature

Although Mambo provides only two options for the administrators' messaging feature, you can configure them to notify you of new messages and to prevent your inbox from becoming clogged with too many messages.

The configuration options, Lock Inbox and Mail me on new Message, are located on the Messaging menu, under the subheading Configuration.

The Lock Inbox function blocks your mailbox from receiving messages. This option is useful where you are receiving too many messages and need to stop them, or where you plan to suspend the use of your administrator account for a period and do not want people to send you messages during your absence. When you set the option to the default position, No, your box receives messages as it always does. When you set the option to Yes, users who try to send you a message see the error message "The user has locked their mailbox. Message failed." Your inbox does not accept any messages until you change the setting to No.

The Mail me on new Message function is an automatic alert. When a fellow administrator sends you a message by way of the messaging system, Mambo automatically sends you an email indicating that a new message is waiting for you and advising you to visit the site and log in to view the message. Note that the email does not contain the message itself; it simply tells you there is a new message. You still must visit the site and log in to see it or reply to it. Note also that the system sends the email to the address associated with your Mambo administrator's account.

Configure the Administrators' Messaging Feature

1. Click Messages.
2. Click Configuration.

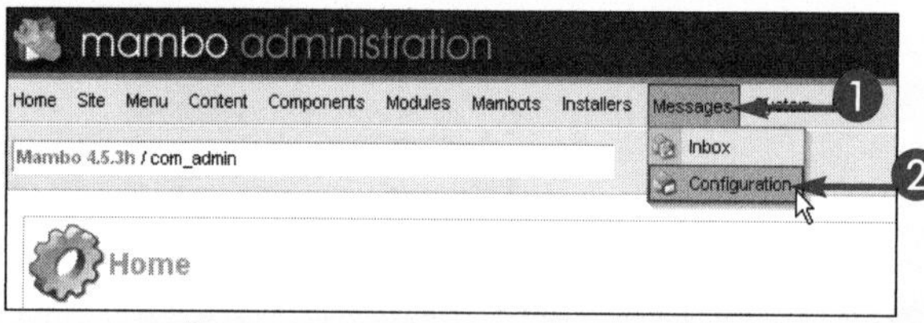

The Private Messaging Configuration screen loads.

3. Click here to change either the Lock Inbox or the Mail me on new Message option.
4. Click the Save Icon.

A message dialog box appears.

5. Click OK.

Mambo saves the changes and returns you to Private Messaging Manager.

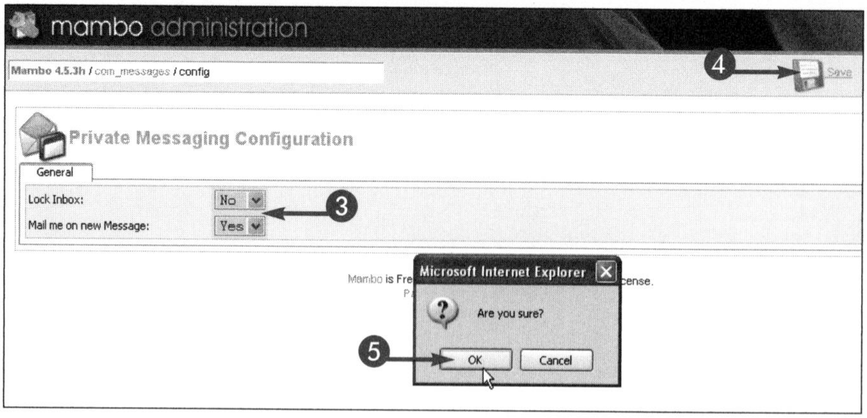

Send an Admin Message

You can use the administrators' messaging function to send messages to other administrators. Mambo's messaging system gives the site administrators an easy way to communicate with each other from inside the admin system interface. The messaging function is built into the Mambo system and deployed by default. Administrators have limited configuration options available to them, and the entire system essentially revolves around one or two basic commands. To review the configuration choices, see the section "Configure the Administrator's Messaging Feature," earlier in the chapter.

Because the messaging function does not rely on email, it is a near instantaneous method of communication. In fact, the whole system is slightly more complicated than using an IM (Instant Messaging) client, but slightly easier than sending emails.

You send messages from within the Private Messaging Manager. You use the New icon to load the New Message screen, where you select a user, enter your message, and then send it. For more on the various options and details of this interface, see the section "An Introduction to the Administrators' Messaging Manager," earlier in the chapter.

The system is purely internal, meaning that the only people to whom you can send messages are other administrators. When you compose a message, the To field restricts you to a list containing only names of the other administrators. You do not need to remember anyone's email address, or the spelling of his or her username; the system handles it all for you.

Once you activate the Send icon, Mambo immediately sends the message so that the recipient can view it if he or she is online and logged in to the administrator system at the time. If the user is not logged in to the system, the message remains in the user's inbox until the next time the user logs in.

Send an Admin Message

1. Click Messages.
2. Click Inbox.

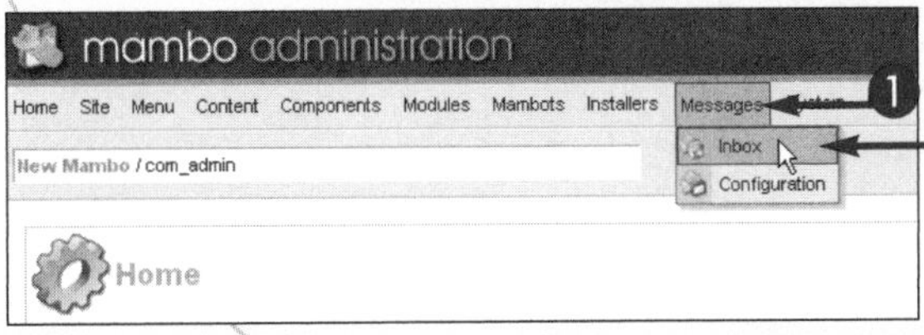

- The Private Messaging Manager loads.

3. Click the New icon.

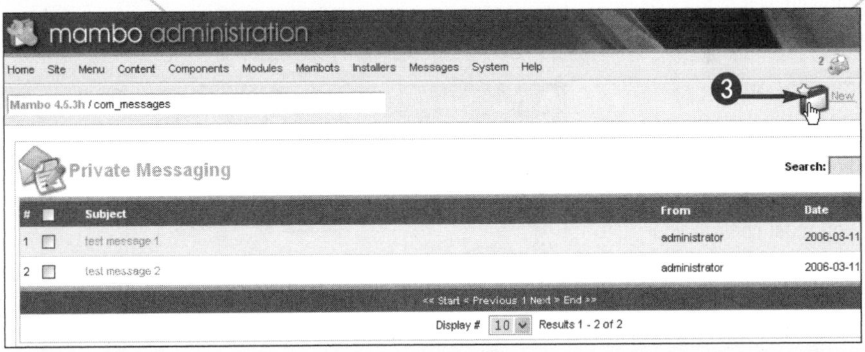

- The New Message screen loads.

4. Click here and select the recipient.
5. Type the subject.
6. Type the message.
7. Click the Send icon.

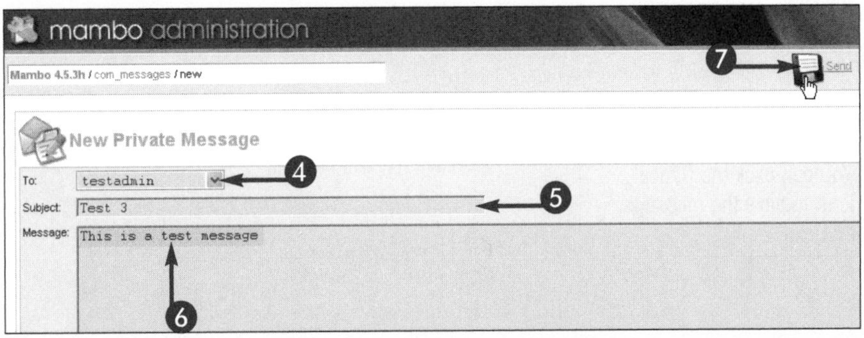

- Mambo sends the message and returns you to the Administrators' Messaging Manager.

View Admin Messages

You can use Mambo's messaging system to view and reply to messages that other administrators send to you. When you log in to the admin system, Mambo notifies you if any messages are waiting for you. You can view the messages from within the admin interface via the Private Messaging Manager. The Messaging Manager indicates which messages you have read and which remain unread. To review the functions in the Administrators' Messaging Manager, see the section "An Introduction to the Administrators' Messaging Manager," earlier in this chapter.

If you are logged in to the system at the time another administrator sends you a message, Mambo sends you a notification within the admin interface. If you are not logged in, Mambo does not notify you until you log in to the admin system. The only exception to this is when you set the Mail me on new Message option in the configuration settings to Yes. For more on how to turn on the automatic email notifications, see the section "Configure the Administrators' Messaging Feature," earlier in the chapter.

After you read a message, you have three options: you can reply to the message via the Reply icon, you can delete the message using the Delete icon, or you can exit the messaging system without taking any action. If you exit without taking action, the system saves your message indefinitely. You can view a message again at any time by logging in and accessing the Private Messaging Manager. Note that the system does not keep a record of sent messages, nor does the text of the original message appear in replies; therefore, if you reply to a message, you do not have a copy of your response, nor does the recipient have a copy of the text of the original message to which you are replying.

View Admin Messages

1. Load the Administrators' Messaging Manager.

Note: To load the Administrators' Messaging Manager, see the section "Send an Admin Message."

2. Click the subject of the message you want to read.

- The message appears.
- You can click the Delete icon to delete the message.

  If you click the Delete icon, you must confirm your deletion in the dialog box that appears.
- Alternatively you can click the Reply icon to enter a new message.

Note: For more on replying to a message, see the section "Send an Admin Message."

- You can click the Cancel icon to save the message and exit.

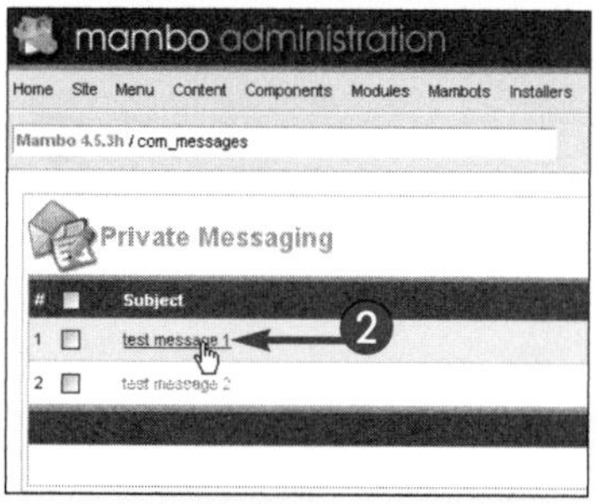

Check In Items

You can check in Content Items to unlock them and make them viewable and editable to other administrators. When you work on a Content Item, Mambo automatically locks the item from others in order to prevent two administrators from accidentally overwriting each other's work. You must either save or cancel this action to unlock the item. If, while working on a file, you utilize the Back button, close your browser window, or if connection problem logs you off, the system keeps the Content Item checked out, thereby blocking others from working with the item. Mambo provides the Global Checkin command to give Super Administrators a way to unlock checked out Content Items. Any administrator can execute this command from within the administration interface.

After you execute the Global Checkin command, a screen appears containing a list of all the Database Tables in the system and a confirmation that the system has checked items in.

Make proper Content Item handling part of your regular work habits. Always exit Content Items properly, using either the Save or Cancel icons. In the event you are disconnected unexpectedly, log back in to the system and close your Content Items properly. By checking in your content, you free up the items for other people to edit.

Be aware that choosing the Global Checkin option causes the system to check in all open Content Items, both yours and anyone else's. Use this command carefully if others are working in the system at the same time because the command may cause them to lose data if they have any Content Items open at the time you execute the command.

Check In Items

1. Click System.
2. Click Global Checkin.

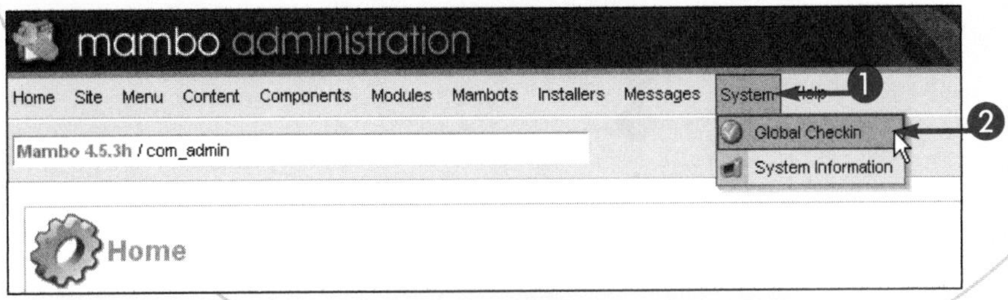

- The Checkin Confirmation screen loads, indicating which, if any, items were checked in.

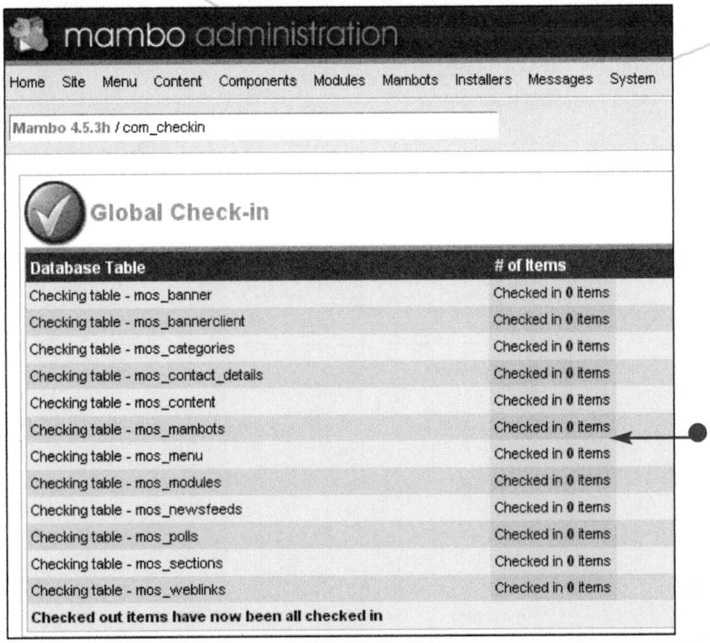

Edit the Language File

You can customize many of the messages and labels that appear on your site by editing the Mambo language file. For ease of operation and maintenance, Mambo keeps all system-generated messages and labels in one file. You can access this file from within the admin interface and make changes in your Web browser window. Being able to make changes easily allows you to customize your site's error messages and to further personalize your site to meet your needs.

You access the language file via the Language Manager, which is located inside the Site menu. The Language Manager displays a list of all the languages installed on your site. By default, Mambo is deployed with only the English language pack. You can add other language packs easily using the Global Installer. For more on additional language packs, see Chapter 15.

To make your changes, select the active language pack and edit the words or phrases you want. No special tools are required and you can make and save changes from within the admin system. Once you save your work, the changes are immediately visible on the front end of the Web site.

Although editing the language file is very useful, it opens up the possibility of entering improper syntax or accidentally deleting something you need, which can lead to errors on your site. Be careful here: if you do not know what you are doing, do not try this. Regardless of your experience level, maintain good work habits and back up the language file by copying the contents of the file and storing it on your local computer. If something goes wrong as a result of your changes, you can restore the original unchanged file.

Edit the Language File

1. Click Site.
2. Click Language Manager.

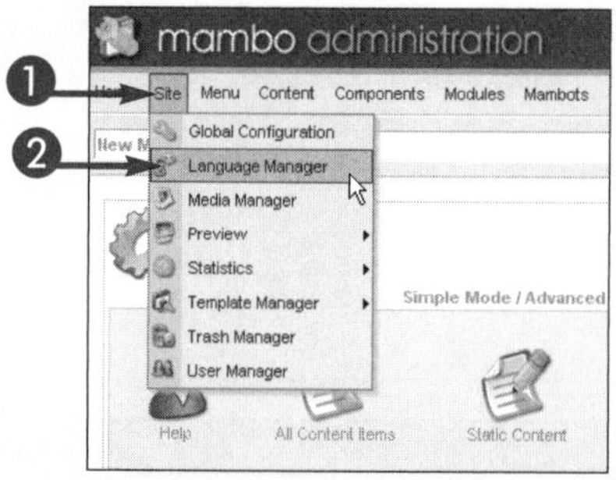

The Language Manager loads.

3. Select the language file you want to edit.
4. Click the Translate icon.

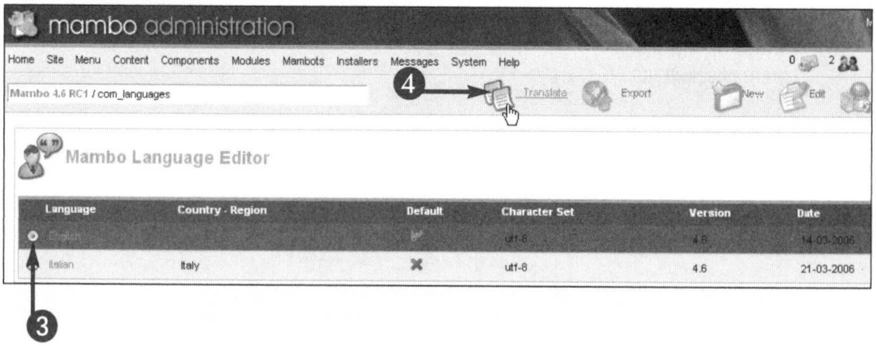

The Language editing screen loads.

5. Select the catalog you want to edit.

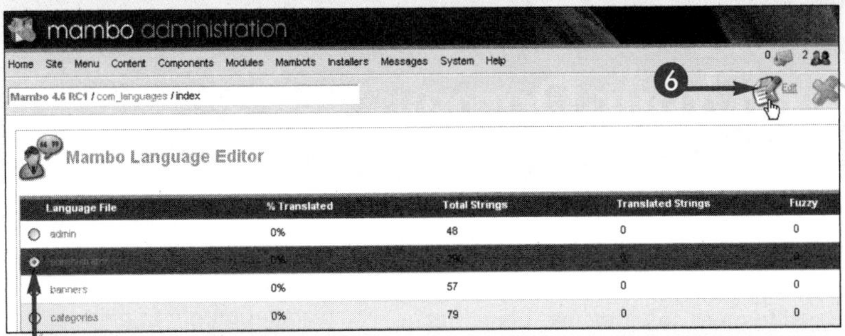

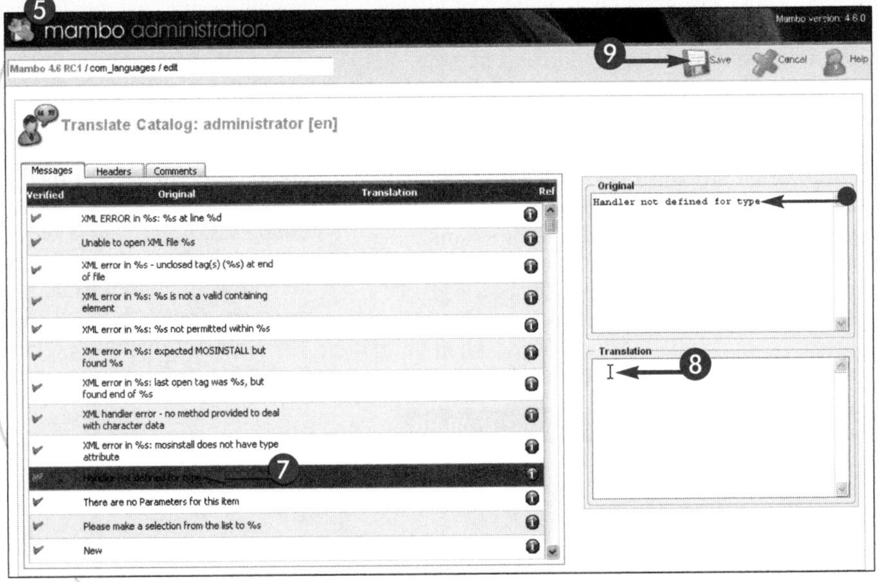

6. Click the Edit icon.
7. Select the phrase you want to edit.

- The phrase appears in this box.

8. Type your new text.
9. Click the Save icon.

Mambo makes the changes and returns you to the Language editing screen.

Extra

The default Mambo installation places all the necessary language options in one central file. Unfortunately, many third-party components and modules include separate language files applicable to their particular piece of code. If you have installed a third-party component and you want to make changes to its system-generated messages, data labels, button text, and so on, you may have to explore the files that relate to that component or module to find what you need.

If the component or module does not have a separate language file and is not drawing on Mambo's common language file, it is likely that the word or phrase you want to change has actually been hard coded into the component or module. In this case, you must open the files that were bundled with the component or module and search for occurrences of the word or phrase you want to replace.

Always start your search by first looking for a language directory, or an individual file named english.php or something similar. If you cannot find dedicated language files, open the individual component files and search their contents.

Install a Second Mambo System on Your Domain

Mambo gives you the flexibility to install more than one version of the system on a single domain, or to place one on the main domain and subsequent versions into subdomains. Installing more than one copy of Mambo on a single host enables you to create closely related sites or sub-sites on one hosting account, saving you both time and money.

In certain situations you may want to run two or more discreet Web sites on the same Web address. For example, a multinational company may want separate sites for each country of operation but still keep them all on one domain. Using Mambo, the company can create their main Mambo site on their primary domain — for example, www.globalcorp.com — and then create subdirectories for each country, installing in each subdirectory a separate copy of Mambo, such as www.globalcorp.com/brazil, or www.globalcorp.com/trinidad. Alternatively, when your Web host supports it, you can solve the same challenge by setting up each country in subdomains, such as brazil.globalcorp.com or trinidad.globalcorp.com. In the latter example, each subdomain features a separate installation of Mambo.

Installing multiple versions of Mambo is not difficult, but the process does vary depending on the approach you select for the site structure. If you use the directory approach, you must create the directory, copy all of the files into the directory, and then run the installation routine. During installation you need to set a different database prefix and/or pick a different database for each site. For more on how to change the database prefix, see Chapter 2. If you chose the subdomain approach, all you need to do is copy the files to the subdomain and install as you would any normal Mambo installation. The directory approach is outlined in the steps that follow. The steps for installing a normal Mambo site are included in Appendix A.

Install a Second Mambo System on Your Domain

INSTALL IN A SUBDIRECTORY

1. Access your site by FTP.

   The site's directories appear.

2. Create a new directory.

   The new directory appears.

3. Copy a complete set of Mambo core files into the directory.

4. Run the installer, but when prompted to input a database prefix for the new installation, replace the default MOS with a different prefix, or point the second installation to a second database.

Note: You must perform Step 4 to avoid overwriting your existing Mambo site data. For more on running the installer, see Appendix A.

5. Complete the installation steps outlined in Appendix A.

   Mambo sets up the new site in the subdirectory.

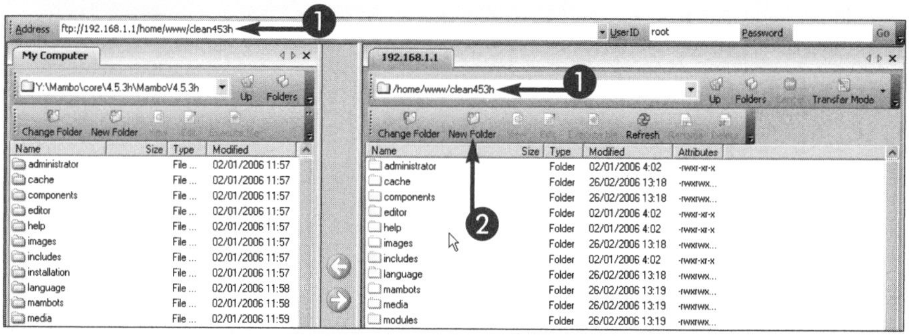

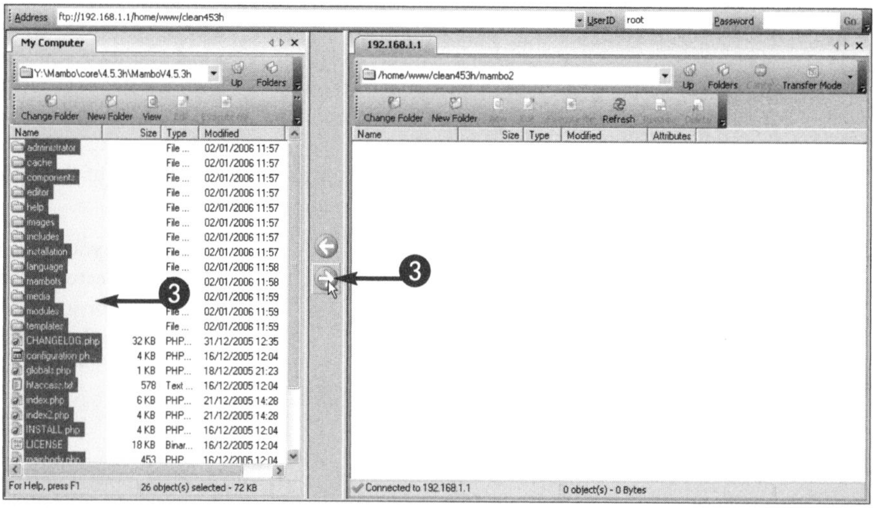

INSTALL A SECOND SITE ON A SUBDOMAIN

1. Access the subdomain on your site by FTP.

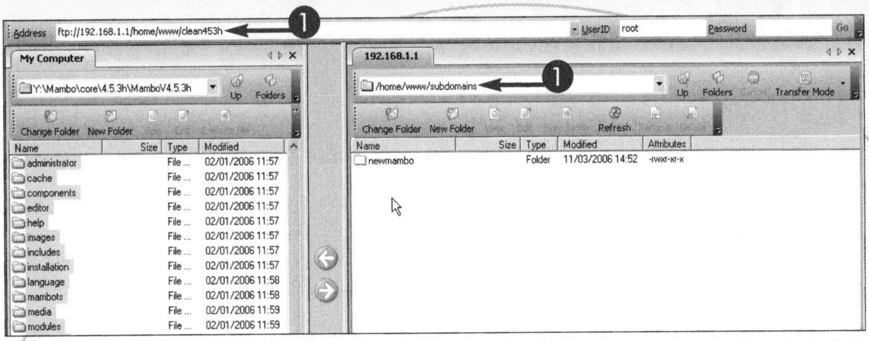

The site's directories appear.

2. Copy a complete set of Mambo core files into the directory.
3. Run the installer, following the steps outlined in Appendix A.

Mambo sets up a new site on your subdomain.

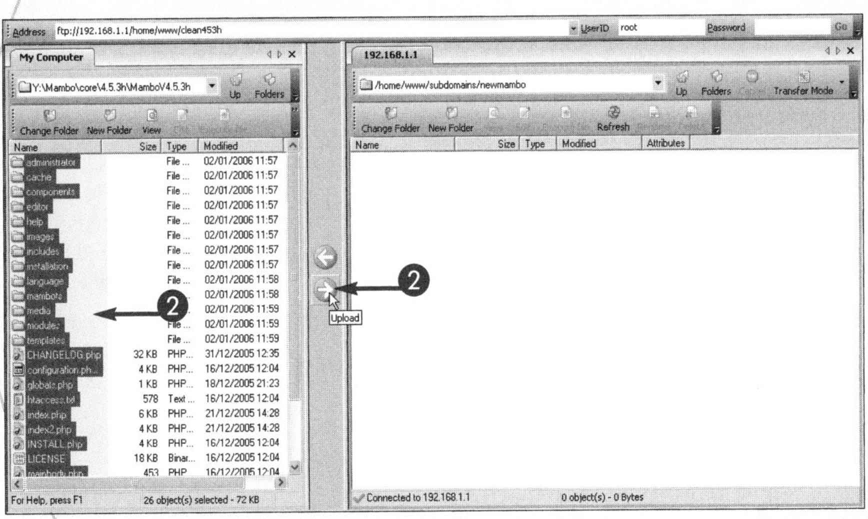

Extra

Although there is no theoretical limit to the number of Mambo sites you can place on one installation, you want to avoid stacking too many sites into one hosting account because it places a strain on the server if the sites are very large or very busy. Similarly, sites can share a single MySQL database only up to a certain point before performance issues start to appear in the form of slower response times. There is no set rule for how many sites you can place on one server or on one MySQL installation. If you feel the need to experiment, be mindful that eventually performance will suffer.

One of the downsides of running multiple installations is that you cannot share administration systems. Each of your Mambo sites has a completely separate administration system. Each of your sites also has a completely discreet set of users. Users cannot share accounts or logins among sites. Also, you cannot share components and modules. If you want to run the same functionality on more than one site, you must install and configure it multiple times.

Find New Components, Modules, and Mambots

You can use the Mambo system's large number of components, modules, and templates to extend your Web site. Just like Mambo itself, many of the extensions are released free of charge and under an Open Source license, allowing you to use the extensions freely for your sites.

You can find extensions for your Mambo system on a number of different Web sites, including the official download sites maintained by the Mambo Foundation and their partners, and a significant number of fan sites in various languages. The fan sites often contain download links and many times components and modules with regional language variations. A list of the most popular sites follow, as well as warnings about downloads and upgrades.

Words of Warnings for Downloads and Upgrades

Take caution when downloading components and modules. Due to changes in the Mambo code set and site architecture over time, extensions written for older versions of Mambo may not work properly on newer versions. Templates rarely cause compatibility problems, but occasionally problems may arise with modules or components. Check version compatibility before installing an extension. If you have not previously used the extension with your current version of Mambo, do not install the extension on a live production site. The safest course is to install all new extensions in a nonpublic environment for testing prior to deployment. Once you install, configure, and test the extension, you can move it to the live site without fear of disruption.

If you are upgrading an extension to a newer version, you should uninstall the old extension before installing the new version. If you are concerned with the loss of data or configuration parameters, you should contact the developers of the extension and seek their advice.

MamboXchange

www.mamboxchange.com

MamboXchange is run by Mambo Communities, the same company that runs MamboServer.com and the Mambo Forums. The MamboXchange is a home for developers who are maintaining extension projects premised on the Mambo system. The Xchange is the largest repository of Mambo extensions, with hundreds of projects underway at any one time. Although you may find the site a bit difficult to browse, it is worth the effort due to the wealth of options contained inside.

The Source

source.mambo-foundation.org

The Source is run by the Mambo Foundation and the members of the Mambo Steering Committee. The Source is the official site for distribution of the Mambo core files. Updates, upgrades, and patch files are usually released first on this site. The Source also includes an archive of old versions of the Mambo core in the event you need to patch an older site or upgrade to the current version. This site also has resources to assist developers who are promoting Mambo-based goods or services.

Mambo Extensions

www.mamboextensions.com

This is a directory of Mambo components, modules, and templates, with information on compatibility, known issues, and user comments and ratings. It includes listings of both free and commercial extensions.

MamboView

www.mamboview.com

The MamboView site is a repository of free templates, components, and modules, supplemented with tutorials and other related content. The site includes an extensive template preview feature and a limited live demo section for components and modules.

Display Google AdSense Ads

You can use a specialized module to manage and display Google AdSense ads on your site. Google AdSense is great way to help you earn revenue from your site. The program is free to join and open to virtually any type of site. The ads you display on your site are generated based on the content of the page on which they appear. You earn money when visitors click on the ads.

The Google AdSense administration system provides you with an automated tool for generating the code you need to insert in your Web pages. The problem with AdSense and Mambo is that you must paste the code into your template file; pasting the code directly into the template is not only too difficult for many novice users, but also robs you of positioning the ads from page to page. The Advanced Google AdSense module for Mambo solves both of the problems because it allows you to input the information from your Google AdSense into a module that you can position wherever you want it to appear. You can then create multiple versions of the module and thereby vary the placement from page to page. For more information on working with multiple modules, see Chapter 12.

You can download the Advanced Google AdSense module free of charge from MamboXchange.com. The module installs through the Universal Installer and you can configure it by directly editing the module through the Module Manager. Among the options the module offers is the ability to specify alternative ads that appear in the event the Google AdSense service is not available. Note that on some download sites the module is referred to as "Mambospan Google Ads."

Display Google AdSense Ads

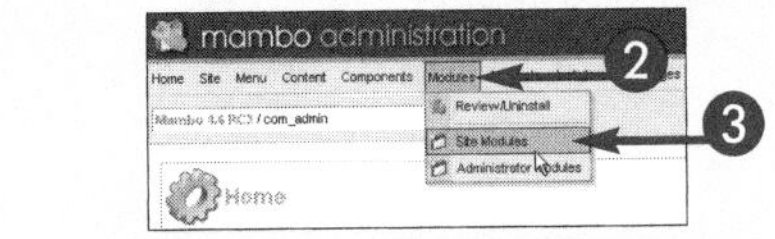

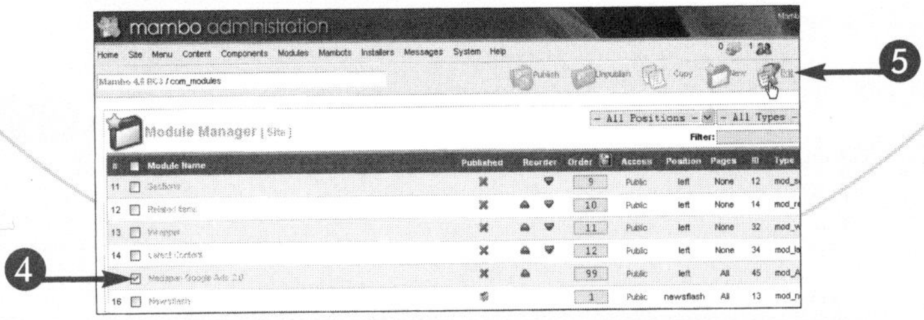

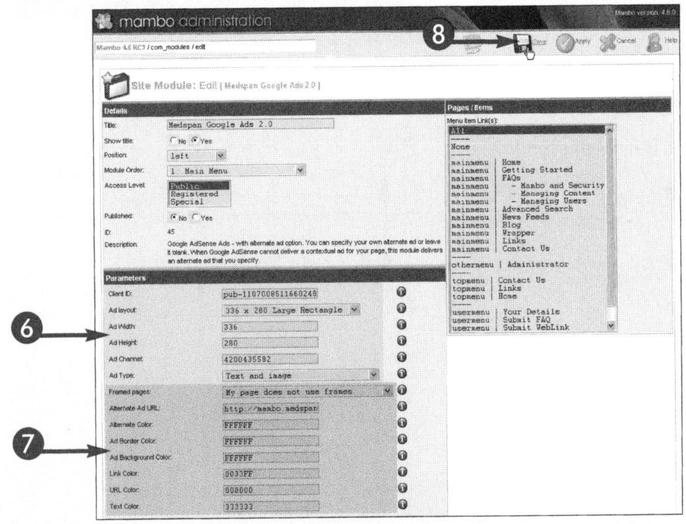

1. Install the Advanced Google AdSense Module.

Note: To install a module, see Chapter 11.

2. Click Modules.
3. Click Site Modules.

   The Module Manager loads.

4. Select the AdSense Module.
5. Click the Edit icon.

   The Module Editing screen loads.

6. Type your Google AdSense account information.
7. Select the parameters you want.

Note: You may need to scroll down to view and select these parameters.

8. Click the Save icon.

   Mambo saves the module and activates it, returning you to the Module Manager.

Add a Custom Menu with TransMenu

If you want an interactive custom menu, you can add the TransMenu module to your site. Although the default Mambo installation allows you to create several menu styles, if you want to have more-advanced menu styling, you need to add an extension that grants greater flexibility. The TransMenu module is one of the simplest and easiest-to-use third-party menu extensions. When used properly, TransMenu can help you create advanced menu effects like a subnavigation that slides out smoothly, transparent submenus, drop shadows, and other common effects.

You can download the TransMenu module free of charge from the D4M Web site at www.designformambo.com. The extension is a single module file that you install with the Universal Installer. After installation, you can access and set up the functionality by editing the module from the Module Manager. The module contains a large number of parameters that define the shape, color, orientation, and positioning of the menu. Note that this module works in conjunction with the Individual Menu Managers. You cannot manage Menu Items from the TransMenu module; you can manage only the menu's placement and appearance. For more information on working with the Individual Menu Manager and Menu Items, see Chapter 9.

To create a custom menu with TransMenu, set up your menu as you would normally, using the Menu Managers in the Mambo Core. Then, open the TransMenu module and select the menus to which you want to apply the module. Configure the layout and positioning of the module and test on the front end of the Web site. Note that you must unpublish the Mambo Menu module for the menu or it will conflict with the TransMenu module for the menu.

Add a Custom Menu with TransMenu

1. Install the TransMenu module.

Note: To install a module, see Chapter 11.

2. Click Modules.
3. Click Site Modules.

The Module Manager loads.

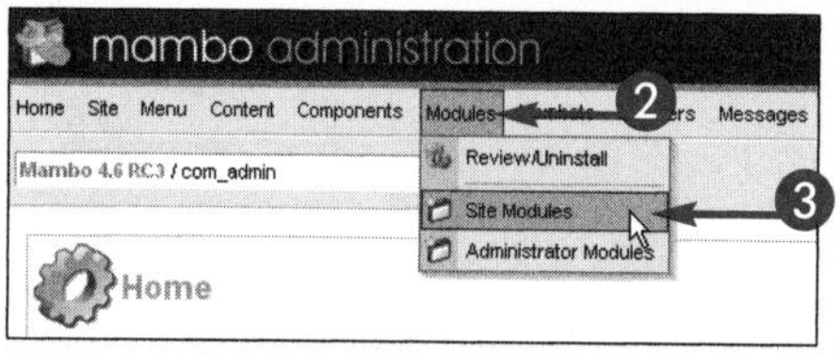

4. Select the TransMenu module.
5. Click the Edit icon.

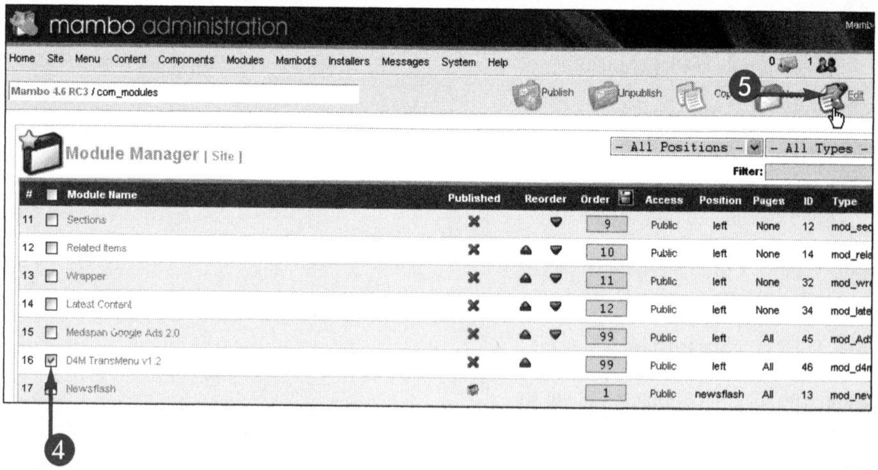

The Module Editing screen loads.

6 Select the menu to which you want TransMenu to apply.

7 Configure the look and feel by editing the parameters.

8 Assign the module to a page it.

9 Publish the module.

Note: For more on assigning and publishing publishing modules, see Chapter 11.

10 Click the Save icon.

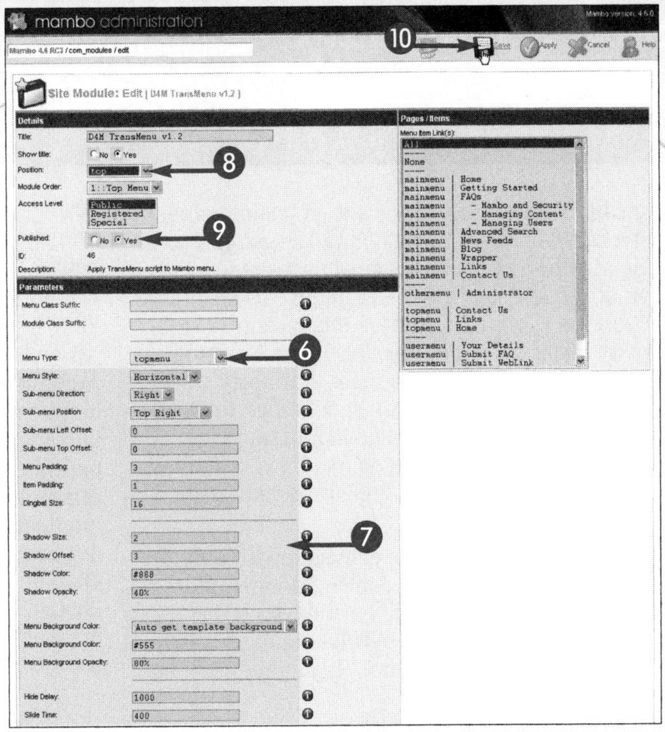

Mambo publishes the module and returns you to the Module Manager.

11 Unpublish the Mambo Menu module.

Note: For more on unpublishing modules, see Chapter 11.

The TransMenu functionality is now visible on the selected menu.

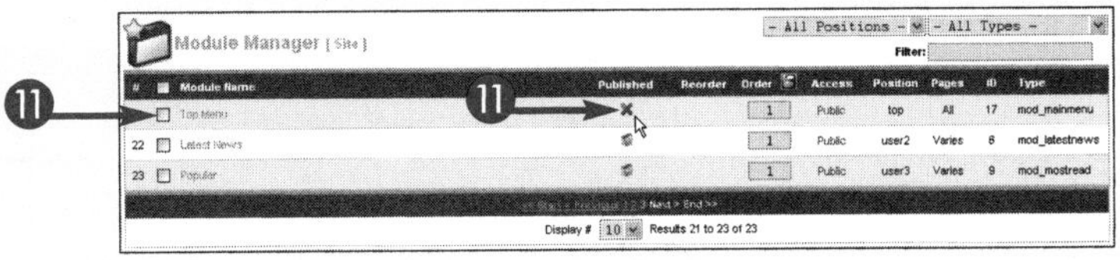

Extra

There are at least two versions of the Open Source TransMenu extension. The other popular version of the menu system is known as "MBT TransMenu." The MBT version of TransMenu has some interesting additional options, including Flash, but at the time of this writing the various pieces of the system have not been updated in many months. You can download the MBT TransMenu system free of charge from MamboXchange.com.

Note hat the default Mambo system is actually quite flexible when it comes to the subject of menus. If you are skilled with CSS, there is little you cannot do with the default system. The Module Class Suffix command, located in the Menu modules, lets you use custom classes tailored to specific menus. If you combine the Module Class Suffix option with use of `divs` within the template to define the module position holders, you can create a rich variety of menu styles that you can administer from within Mambo without adding third-party extensions to the site.

Install a Language Pack

You can extend your Mambo site to include other interface languages by installing Language Packs. The Mambo system is designed to make translation of the interface easy. Language Packs contain all of the various words and phrases the system automatically displays for buttons, labels, and controls. At the time of writing, there were more than forty translations of the Mambo system, from French to Farsi and everything in between. By installing a Language Pack, you make the system easier to use for non-native speakers, and in particular, non-English-speaking site administrators.

The default Mambo installation is delivered with only the English Language Pack installed. Super Administrators of a Mambo site can add a Language Pack through the automatic installer and switch between languages easily. The first step is to identify the proper Language Pack you need and download a copy. Language Packs are free of charge and released under the GNU GPL, the same Open Source license that applies to the Mambo Core files. The Language Pack is delivered as a zip file and you can upload and install it via the Universal Installer.

After you install a new Language Pack, the Super Administrator can use the Language Manager to switch between languages. Upon activation, the change is immediate and affects system messages and labels on both the front end and the back end of the Web site. You can also edit the language files inside the browser interface to customize them for your particular site's needs. For more about the Language Editing screen, see Chapter 14. For serious modification of the language files, it is probably best to download the file via FTP, make your changes locally, and then restore the file to the system.

Install a Language Pack

❶ Click Install.

❷ Click the Universal Installer.

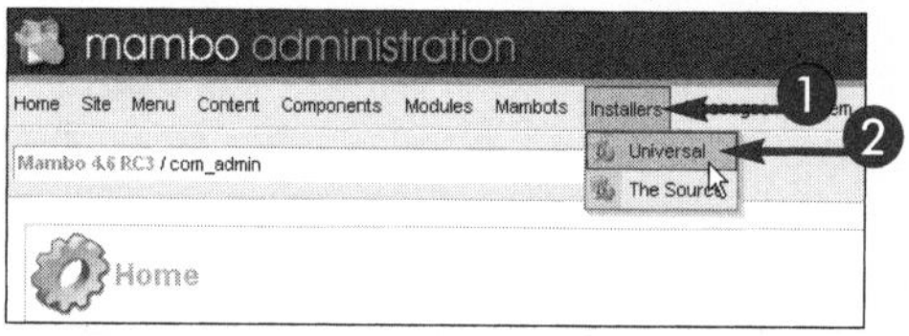

The Universal Installer loads.

- A list of directories, along with an indication of whether they are writeable, appears here.

Note: If any of the directories show as "unwriteable," you must change the permissions (read/write status) of the directory. For more on how to change file permissions, see Chapter 1.

❸ Click Browse.

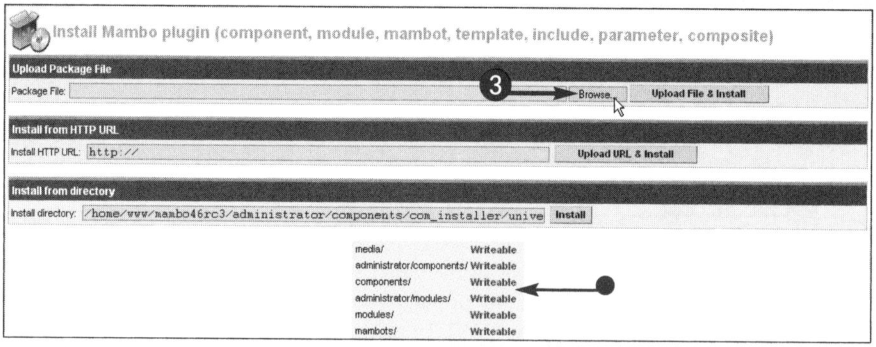

The Open File dialog box appears.

4. Navigate to the location of the archive.
5. Select the file.
6. Click Open.

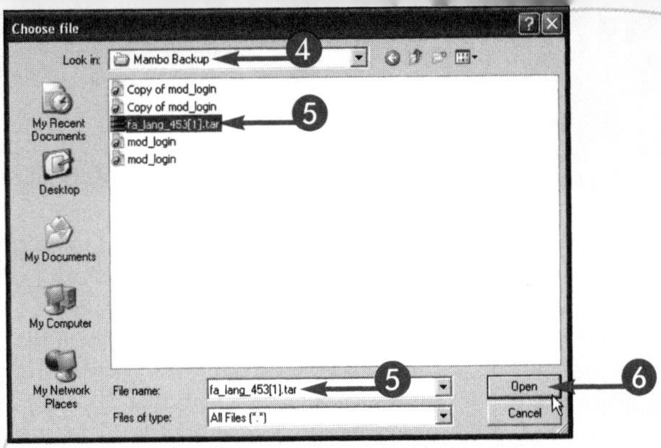

The dialog box closes and returns you to the Installer.

7. Click Upload File and Install

If you are successful, you see a confirmation message when the screen reloads.

If you are not successful, you see a message indicating failure.

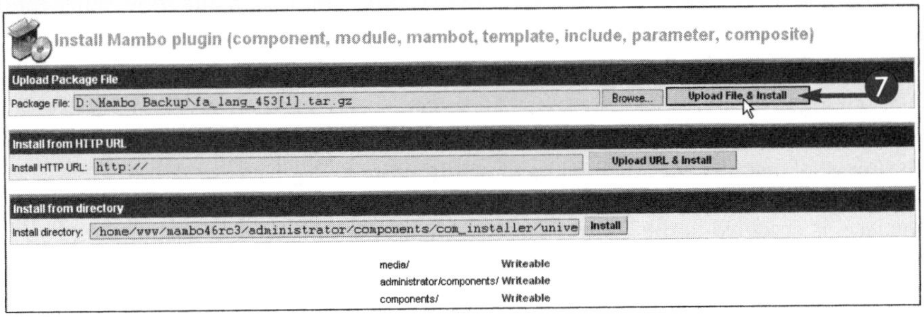

Extra

Although it is not the preferred practice, some third-party modules and components include their own language files. When you install a non-core module or component, consider checking whether the plug-in is delivered with a language file. If the plug-in is distributed with its own language file, you need to open that file to edit at least some of the words and phrases the plug-in uses. There is no way to edit the plug-in's language file within the Mambo system. You may find independent language files problematic when you want to localize the plug-in — that is, customize it for a language other than the one it was delivered with. If you need a different language than the one distributed with the plug-in, try visiting the plug-in's home page.

If you are searching for, but cannot find, a particular Language Pack for Mambo, visit the Mambo Forums and post a request. You should also visit The Source to check for the most recent Language Packs. The forums are located at forum.mamboserver.com. You can find the Source at source.mambo-foundation.org.

Add Comment Threads to Your Content

You can add functionality to your Content Items so users can submit their own comments, and thus interact with your site resulting in more dynamic and up-to-date content. Adding comments to Content Items while keeping those comments in logical threads is one of the most commonly requested additional functionalities.

Although the Mambo core does not provide for threaded comments, there is a third-party component — MOSCom — that does. The component is available free of charge from the MamboXchange Web site.

Note that you must first install the component package using the Universal Installer, and then make a modification to your template file. The required steps and the code you need to replace, is specified in the Instructions page, which you can access from the Components–MOSCom menu after installing the component.

You can configure the Comments functionality under the MSCom heading on the Components menu. The configuration settings allow you to determine the Content Sections in which the comment form appears. You can also configure the positioning of the comments and some other basic options, such as the use of BBCode and smileys (emoticons). The most important configuration options relate to whether the system accepts anonymous submissions and whether the submissions are published automatically.

Once the system is up and running, you can view all comments via the component interface. If you have the component configured to require review before publication, you must perform that task from the component interface. Note that the system is flexible and you can update or modify your settings or the page assignments at any time.

Add Comment Threads to Your Content

1. Install the MOSCom component.

Note: To install a component, see Chapter 10.

2. Click Components.
3. Click MOSCom.
4. Click Instructions.

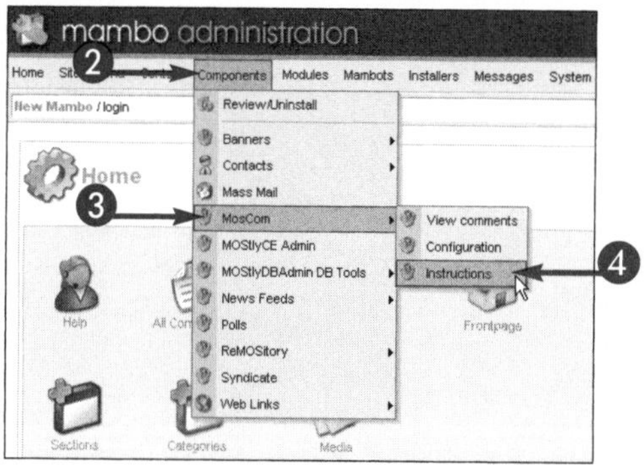

The MOSCom Instructions page loads.

5. Follow the directions on this page to modify your template file.

Note: To learn how to edit a template files HTML code, see Chapter 3.

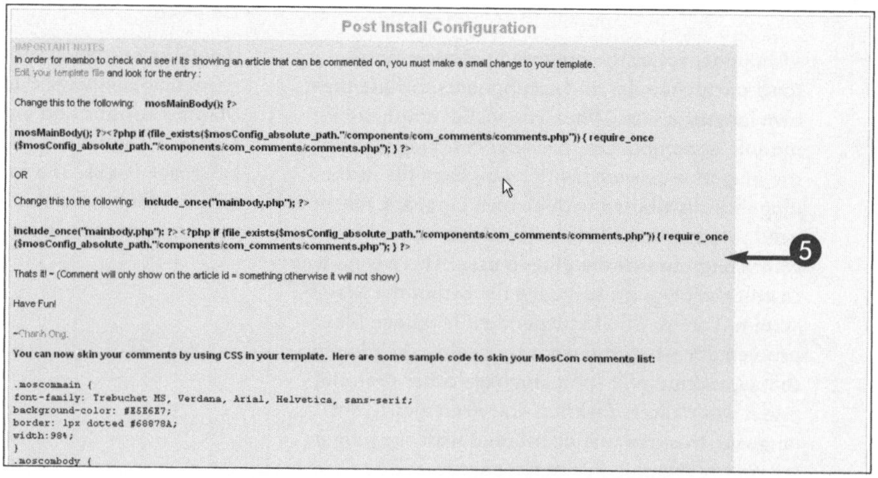

6 Click Components.

7 Click MOSCom.

8 Click Configuration.

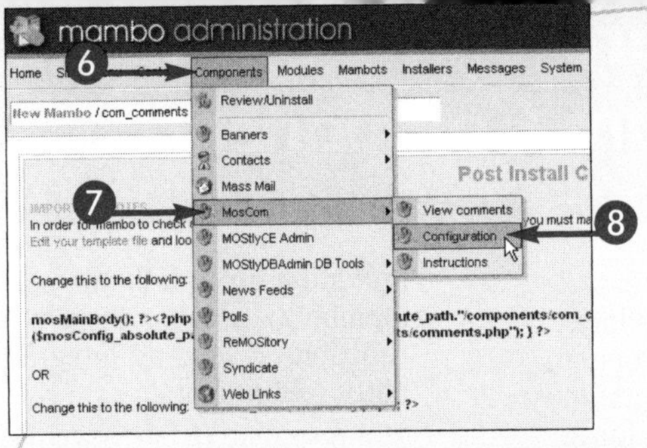

The MOSCom configuration screen loads.

9 Select the configuration options you desire.

10 Click the Save icon.

The Comments function is now active.

	Current Setting	Explanation
Admin Email	changeme@mail.com	If email is switched on, an email will be sent to this address when a new comment is entered
Exclude Section		Use to exclude section not to show comments form by default, eg: 0,1
Comments per page	3	Use to show number of comments per page, eg: 3
Admin Email Alerts	No ○ Yes ●	Enable/Disable emails to Admin
Visitor Email Alerts	No ● Yes ○	Enable/Disable emails to the person who submitted the comment
Review Submissions	No ○ Yes ●	If you set this to yes then comments will be added to the database and will wait for you to review and publish them before showing. You will receive an email **only** if there is a value in "Email Alerts" set to "yes"
Registered Users Only	No ● Yes ○	Set "Yes" to allow only registered users to leave comments but anyone can see comments, Set "No" to allow any visitor to comment
Notify if new version available	No ● Yes ○	If set to "Yes" you will be shown a dialog on the main screen when an update is available to this component (*NOTE: The only data sent to the update server is your version number*)
Have you Donated?	No ● Yes ○	Please consider make a donation throught paypal. This will inspire me to improve this script more! :-)
Force a preview	No ○ Yes ●	Set this to yes to force your visitors to preview their comments before final submission
Hide Comments	No ● Yes ○	Show (Comments (x) - Add Comments) instead of the comments and form by default
Hide URL	No ● Yes ○	Hide URL - Use to hide URL on the comments form by default
Email Required	No ○ Yes ●	Use to set either email is required or not on the comments form by default
New Comments First	No ○ Yes ●	List new comment entries first
Comment Form Above	No ● Yes ○	Show comment form above comment entries

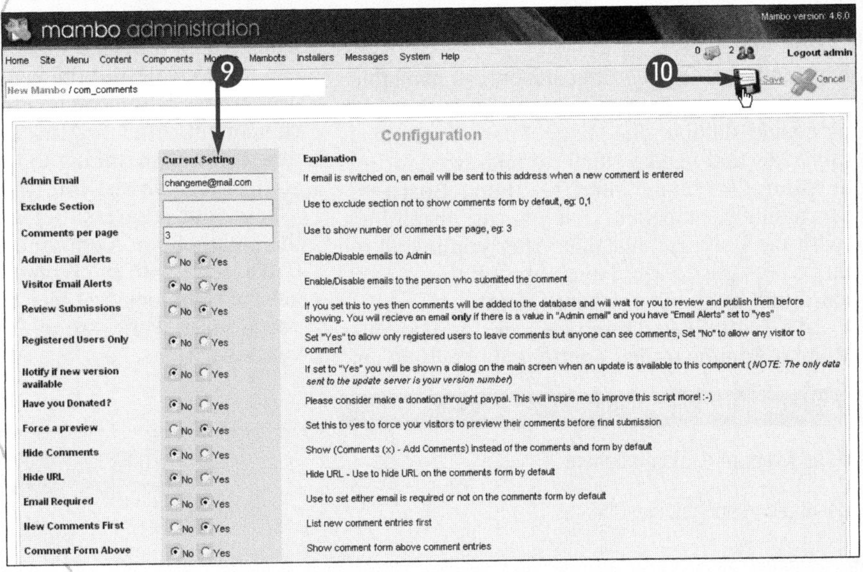

Extra

Be advised that allowing anonymous comments may be the best way to gather comments, but it also opens your system up to SPAMbots and link SPAM. If you auto-publish comments, you may soon find a wide variety of often questionable products and services promoting themselves on your site. The strictest application is to prohibit anonymous comments and disable automatic publication. If you do not want to be quite so extreme, the middle course is to disable automatic publication and enable the system to send notices of new submissions; you can then review the comments, delete the link SPAM, and keep the valid comments. Eventually you may find yourself giving some thought to prohibiting anonymous submissions.

MOSCom comes with its own language file, which contains the text and phrases the component uses in producing the comment box. The component's developer provides access to the language file from within the Admin interface, allowing you to edit the file using just your Web browser. To access and edit the language file, select the Edit Language option under MOSCom heading on the Components menu.

Install and Configure Mamboboard Forum Component

You can add a discussion forum to your site, enabling site visitors to discuss and share information. Discussion forums are popular, useful, and are particularly well suited to community sites. When administered properly, an active forum provides a very compelling reason for visitors to return to your site again and again.

There are a number of free Forum components available for Mambo and several commercial components that you can run alongside Mambo. The MamboBoard Forum is designed for sites that need a small- to mid-sized forum integrated within the Mambo interface. MamboBoard is delivered as a single component that you can install in one step with the Universal Installer. After you install the component, access the Control Panel through the MamboBoard link on the Components Menu. MamboBoard's Control Panel interface looks and operates like the Mambo Administration Control Panel with icons providing quick links to various functionalities. MamboBoard has a large number of features and functions, including integrating with additional third-party components.

The best way to get started with MamboBoard is to select the Load Sample Data option on the Control Panel. The sample data provides some very basic content that you can use to work out the layout of the front-end appearance of the comments and the configuration of the component. After you install the sample data, create a new Menu Item linking to the MamboBoard component so that you can see your changes to the layout and assess your progress. Begin customization by selecting the MamboBoard Configuration option on the Control Panel. Start with the Frontend tab, using the options to get the right look and feel. After you have the layout like you want it, work through the other tabs to explore the various options.

Install and Configure Mamboboard Forum Component

1. Install the MamboBoard component.

Note: To install a component, see Chapter 10.

2. Click Components.
3. Click MamboBoard Forum.

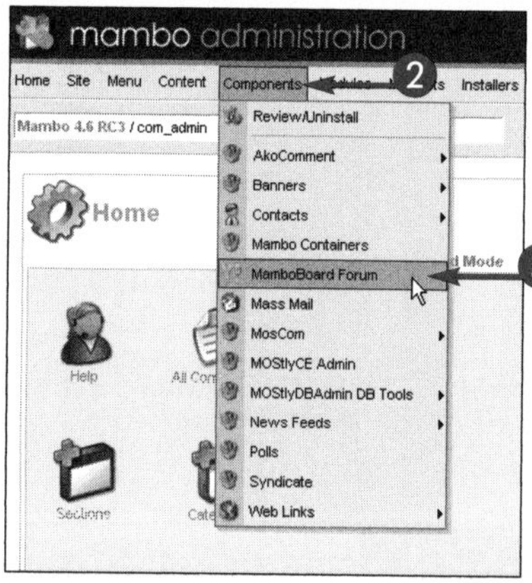

The MamboBoard Control Panel loads.

4. Select Load Sample Data.

Sample data loads.

5. Select MamboBoard Configuration.

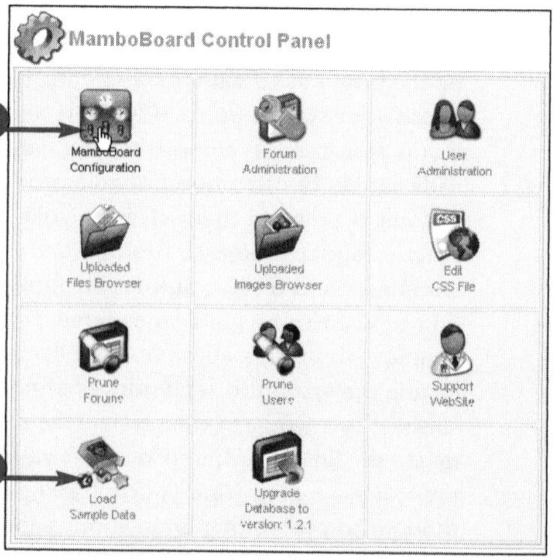

The MamboBoard Configuration Manager loads.

6. Select the parameters you want on the Basics tab.

7. Click the Frontend tab.

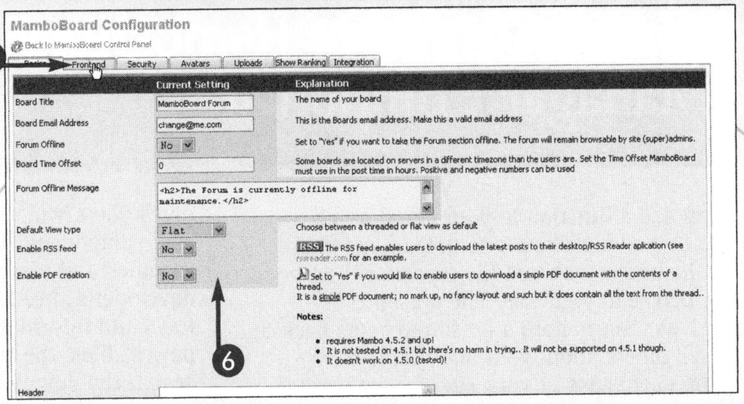

The Frontend configuration screen loads.

8. Select the parameters you want on the Frontend tab.

9. Click the Save icon.

Mambo saves the configuration changes and returns you to the MamboBoard Control Panel.

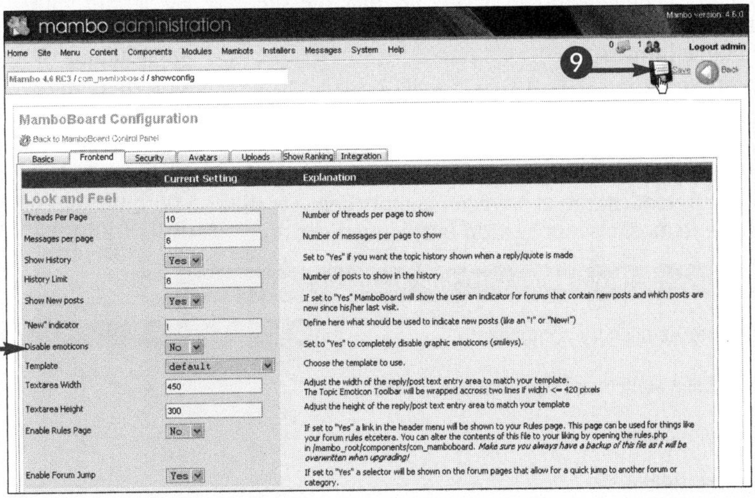

Extra

The success of an online forum is largely a byproduct of the activity on the forum. Forms with few users and few posts tend not to entice people to browse and post. It creates essentially a circular argument: to have activity on a forum you need activity. On the other hand, forums that contain too many entries and are poorly organized tend to turn people away because they cannot find what they want on the site. Forum administration is a challenge because you must work to build community and sufficient traffic to keep the forums vital and interesting, but you must also work to manage your growth so that the site remains a useful resource.

The MamboBoard component is not designed for heavy traffic. Though the component is capable of handling a significant number of threads, if you are planning to have a heavily trafficked forum with a large number of simultaneous users, you should look at some of the larger forum systems, like phpBB or the Simple Machines Forum (SMF). Both phpBB and SMF integrate well with Mambo and you can administer them easily.

Install and Configure Remository File Manager Component

You can add a function to your site that allows users and administrators to upload and share files. Installing a shared file repository is a good way to draw people to your site. The presence of downloads gives visitors both a reason to come back and a reason to tell others about your site. Aside from enhancing the usefulness of your site, for many sites a file repository is an absolute necessity because the site administrators need a way to distribute information in downloadable formats.

The default Mambo system does not include a file repository, but there are several available for no charge from third parties. One of the most popular systems is the Remository component. You can download Remository free of charge at www.remository.com. At the heart of the Remository application is a component that gives you a wide range of functionality. In addition to the core component, there is a wide range of additional modules and Mambots you can download from the developer's site. The modules and Mambots provide more tools and information for your site visitors, such as the newest files, the most popular downloads, the ability to search the downloads, and so on.

By default, either visitors or administrators can add files to the Remository archives. You can configure with a great degree of precision the permissions for the system as well as the type of files that you can add to the system. After you upload the files, you can edit the details concerning the file or expand them to include quite a bit of detail that is useful to site visitors. Configuration options are extensive and provide a great deal of information for both visitors and administrators.

Install and Configure Remository File Manager Component

1. Install the Remository component.

Note: To install a component, see Chapter 10.

2. Click Components.
3. Click ReMOSitory.
4. Click Configuration.

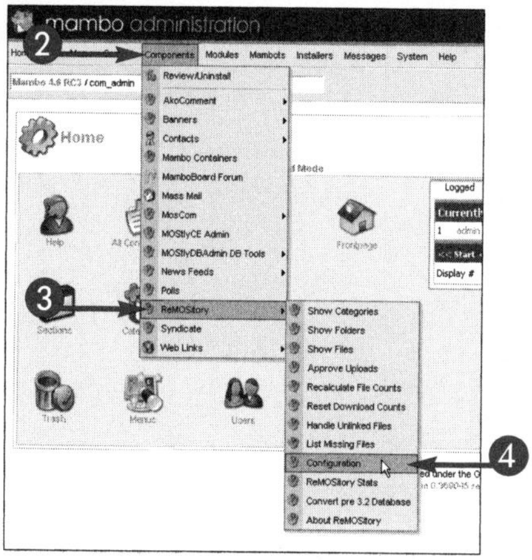

The ReMOSitory Configuration screen loads.

5. Select the parameters you want.
6. Click the Save Config icon.

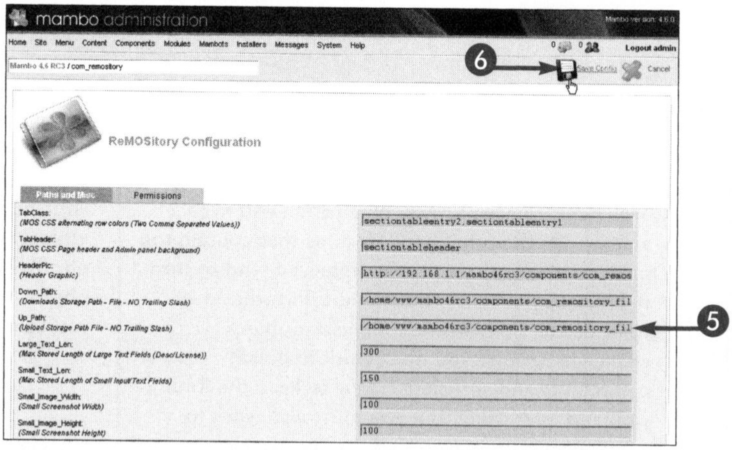

The changes are saved and you are taken to the ReMOSitory Categories Manager.

7 Click the Add Cat icon.

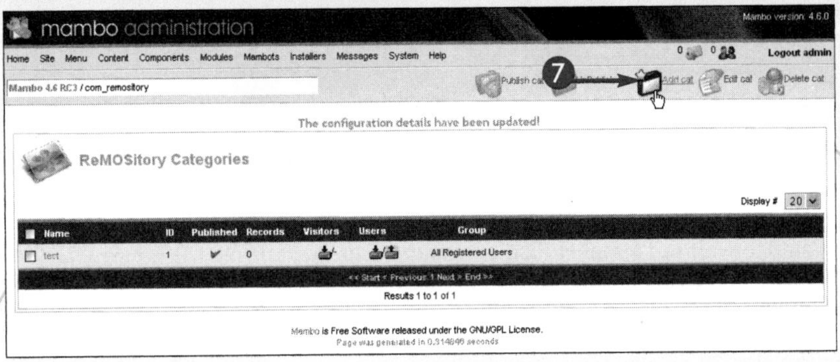

The New Category screen loads.

8 Type a category name.

9 Type a description.

10 Set access permissions.

11 Click the Save Category icon.

Mambo create the category and returns you to the Categories Manager.

You are now ready to upload your first files.

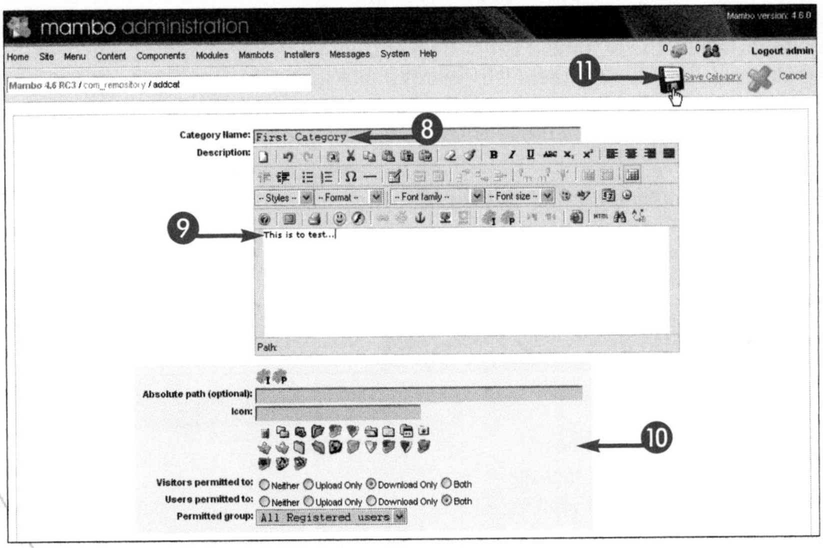

Extra

You can control the look and feel of the Remository component to a certain extent through the configuration options attached to the component. It is possible, for example, to specify which CSS classes apply to various portions of the interface and to specify some of the images to use. However, to really customize this component extensively you need to access the component's files on the server. Although the Remository code is clean and easy to work with, you should always make backups of any file before you make changes.

Remository in many ways is easier to use from the front end of the Web site than from the back end. The developer chose to focus on how site users might use the functionality to upload files and tailored much of the functionality to accommodate user interactivity. This is both good and bad because administrators who are less interested in user uploads have to adjust their work habits somewhat and explore some of the alternative methods for uploading files in bulk in order to populate the component quickly.

Create Multilingual Content with Mambel Fish

You can create multilingual content items for your Web site with the Mambel Fish extension. The Mambo Language Packs changes the language of the administration interface and the system-generated text on the front end, but do nothing for the Content Items on the site. To display your Content Items in more than one language, you must add an additional extension to your site, of which the Mambel Fish system is the most popular and flexible. Mambel Fish creates a site that displays content in several languages, with a language flag option that lets your site visitors switch between languages with ease.

The Mambel Fish is named after the Babelfish — a fictional creature from Douglas Adams's *The Hitchhiker's Guide to the Galaxy* series — that when placed in your ear, would allow you to understand any language. Although the Babelfish is a fictional translation system, the Mambel Fish is an actual tool where you to input the text in whatever language you desire. The tool does not translate your text; it only presents whatever you input for your site visitors. In other words, it is nothing more than an extension of the administration interface that manages and maintains multiple language versions of Content Items.

You may find Mambel Fish installation a bit of a chore because you must carefully check that you have the most current version of its parts and pieces, and any necessary patches. The Universal Installer greatly simplifies the Mambel Fish set-up process, but you still need the most current version that it is compatible with your version of Mambo. To install a component, module, or Mambot, see Chapters 10, 11, and 13, respectively. To install a Language Pack, see the section "Install a Language Pack." If you have the integrated package, you only need to install one time.

Create Multilingual Content with Mambel Fish

INSTALL THE MAMBEL FISH

1. Install the Mambel Fish component, modules, Mambot, and the Language Packs for each language you want to add to your site.
2. Click Components.
3. Click Mambel Fish.
4. Click Language Configuration.

   The Mambel Fish Language Activation screen loads.

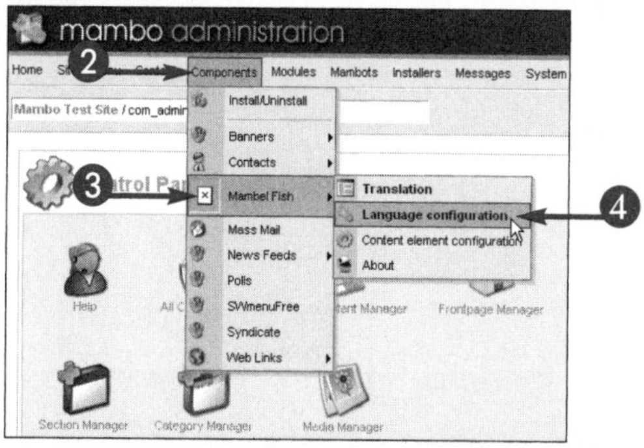

5. Type each language's name.
6. Type the ISO for each language as well as its file name.
7. Select the active option to activate the language.
   - You can type the location of the image to used as a language flag.
8. Click the Save icon.

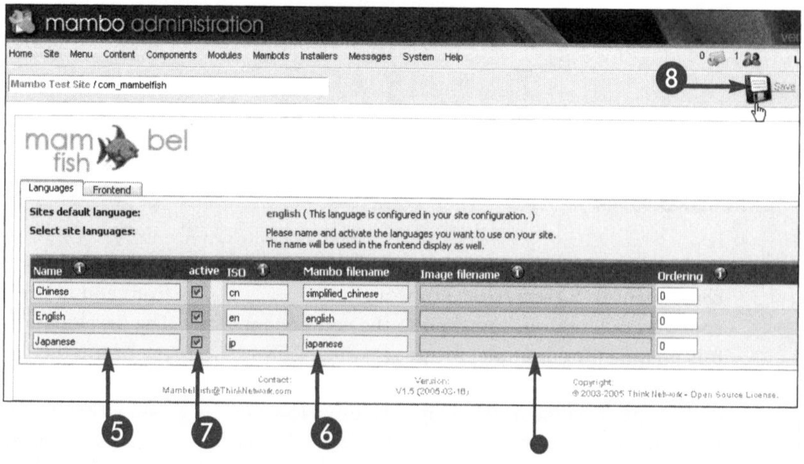

The language set up is now complete.

9. Click the Frontend tab.

10. Select the configuration options you desire.

11. Click the Save icon.

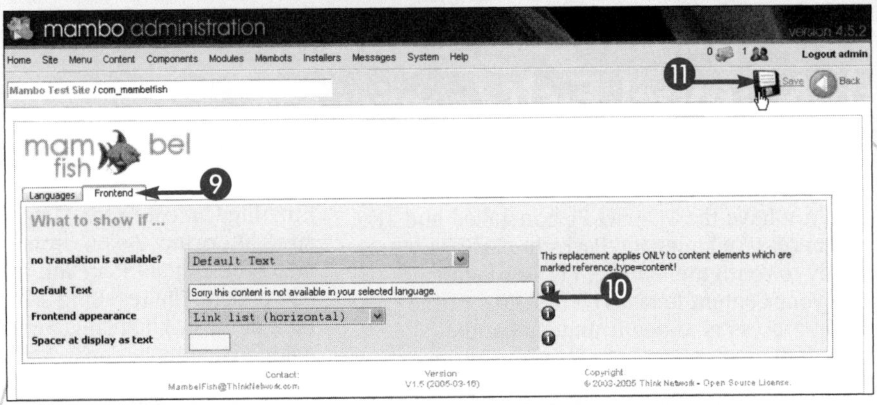

12. Publish the Mambel Fish modules.

Note: For more on how to publish a module, see Chapter 11.

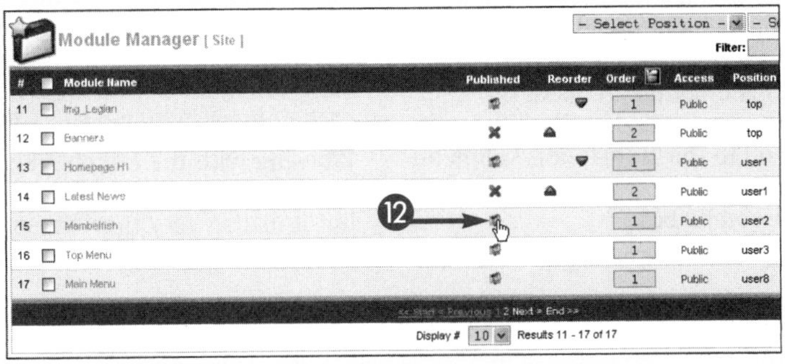

Extra

Half of the battle in dealing with multilingual sites is good planning. If you are like most site administrators, you may find that the amount of translation you have to do for the various languages is always greater than your original estimation. If you do not plan to input the translations of all the site's Content Items at one time, it is generally best to work either downwards from the top levels of the site, or to work from section to section. An ad hoc approach can result in an unpredictable selection of available items in a particular language, which is hard on your site visitors.

Customization of the Mambo system's language files is also an important part of your planning. Generally it is best to start with the English language files that are the default in the Mambo system. Get the English language copy exactly like you want it and then translate everything else to match. Do not forget that some third-party extensions may have their own language files, and you need to track those down and coordinate the consistent translation of them as well.

continued

Create Multilingual Content with Mambel Fish (continued)

After you have the Mambel Fish installed and all the necessary Language Packs in place, you are ready to configure Mambel Fish and start working on your Content Items. The first step of the configuration process is to define and enable the languages you plan to use and to set up the various language flags for your users to switch between the languages. Note also that you must select the system options that define what happens in the event that you do not enter a translation for a particular Content Item. Next, enable the Mambel Fish module to make the language flags accessible to your visitors. The final step in the setup process is to go to the Translation submenu under Mambel Fish on the Components Menu and select the Content Type from the combo box.

Entering content in the Mambel Fish is very straightforward. Again, from the Translation submenu, you select the Content Item you want to translate and select the edit option. The resulting screen shows you the Content Item in the original language and gives you a content editing window beside it. You enter your translated text into the content editing window, using the original text for your reference. The content editing window is served by an instance of the system's WYSIWYG editor. After you have typed your content, click the Save icon, and your work on the Content Item is done. Repeat the process with each Content Item and each different language.

Working with the Mambel Fish and the Language Packs is a necessary process for internationalizing your site, but it is also very time consuming. It requires planning and an attention to detail to get it right.

Create Multilingual Content with Mambel Fish *(continued)*

INPUT CONTENT WITH THE MAMBEL FISH

13 Click Components.

14 Click Mambel Fish.

15 Click Translation.

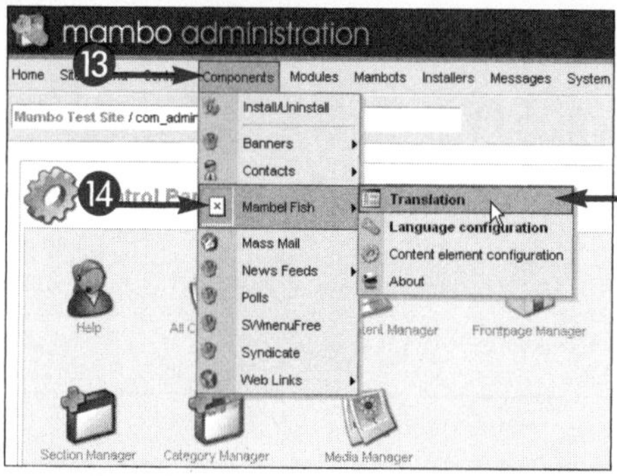

The Translation Manager loads.

16 Click here and select the Content Elements you want to translate.

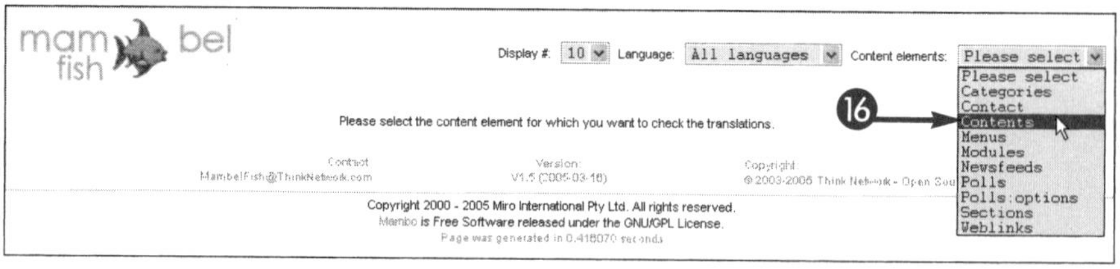

The list of items loads.

17. Select the item you want to translate.
18. Click the Edit icon.

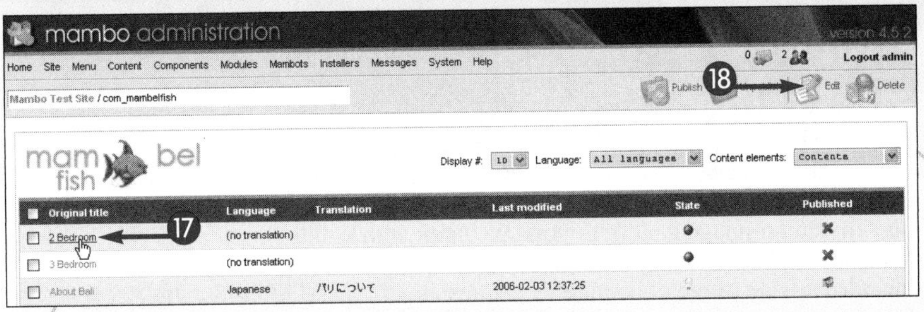

The Translation screen loads.

19. Type the content.
20. Click the Save icon.

Mambo saves the translation and you can view it from the front end.

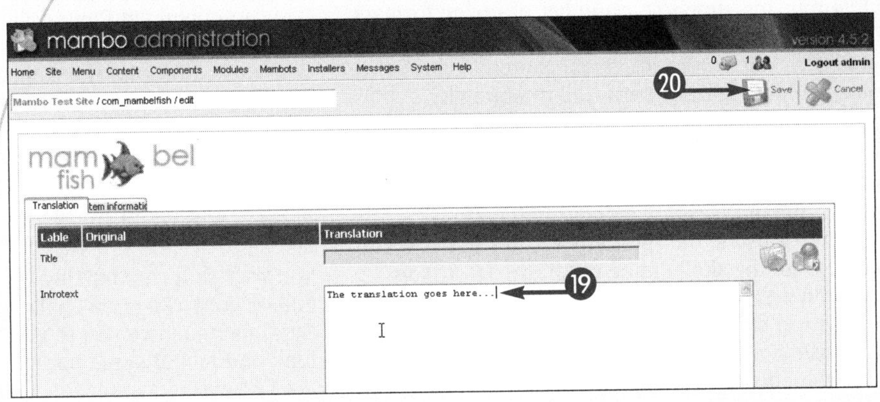

Extra

The Mambel Fish includes a Search Mambot that you should be certain to install and publish. The Mambot is necessary to enable full searching of the various multilingual Content Items. If you used a single package for the installation of Mambel Fish, the Mambot should have been installed along with the component and various dependent modules. If, on the other hand, you installed things individually, do not overlook this handy tool if you want the site to remain searchable across languages.

The Mambel Fish is distributed with basic Help files embedded in the system. To access the Help files, go to the Components Menu and look under the About section of the Mambel Fish component. Additional help regarding the use of this extension can be found on the Mambo Forums. The Mambel Fish is frequently a topic of discussion as various people work through their various problems with the rather complex system. You can visit the Mambo Forums at forum.mamboserver.com.

Install and Configure Pony Gallery

You can add an image gallery to your Web site with the Pony Gallery component. Pony Gallery includes a wide range of commonly requested gallery features and supports a number of image formats. Installing a gallery on your site is a great communication tool that allows you to present visual content for your site visitors, adding both interest and interactivity.

Image galleries are one of the most popular Web site extensions. There is a significant number of gallery options for Mambo, ranging from very basic solutions like SPGM to the professional standard Menalto G2 bridge. For most users, the right answer lies in between the extremes. As the site administrator, the trick is to find a component that you can install and customize with relative ease, yet still have it deliver enough features to satisfy the users' needs. One of the best answers to the problem is the Pony Gallery component. Pony Gallery is an updated version of the old AkoGallery component, tailored for Mambo. The Gallery supports the most commonly requested features, including thumbnails, captioning, slideshow, and comments.

You can download Pony Gallery at www.mamboy.com site and install it using the Universal Installer. Once installed, you must configure the component to suit your site's needs and to format you size your images. There are quite a few choices in the configuration screens, and probably the best course is to turn off most of the options at first to achieve a basic display with some sample images, and then turn the features on one by one to assess their impact and desirability.

You may find customizing the appearance of the front end of Pony Gallery a challenging experience. Although the Gallery allows you to edit the CSS that controls the look and feel of some portions of the system through your browser, customization beyond that is difficult.

Install and Configure Pony Gallery

1. Install the Pony Gallery component.

Note: To install a component, see Chapter 10.

2. Click Components.
3. Click Pony Gallery.
4. Click Edit Settings.

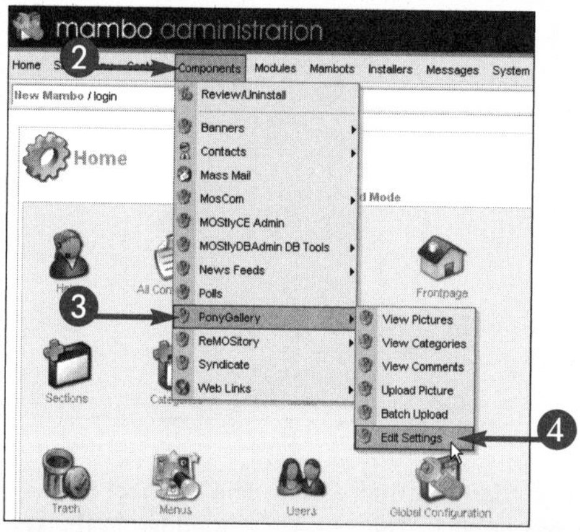

The Pony Gallery Settings Page loads.

5. Select the Settings you desire for the front end and the back end.
6. Click Save Settings.

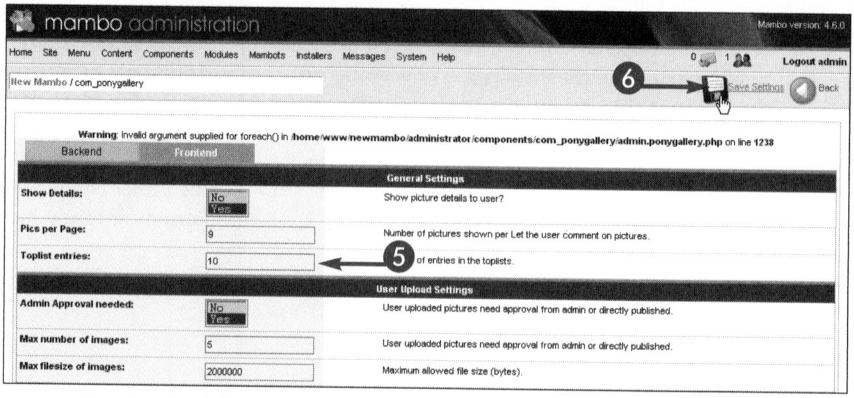

7. Click Components.
8. Click Pony Gallery.
9. Click View Categories.

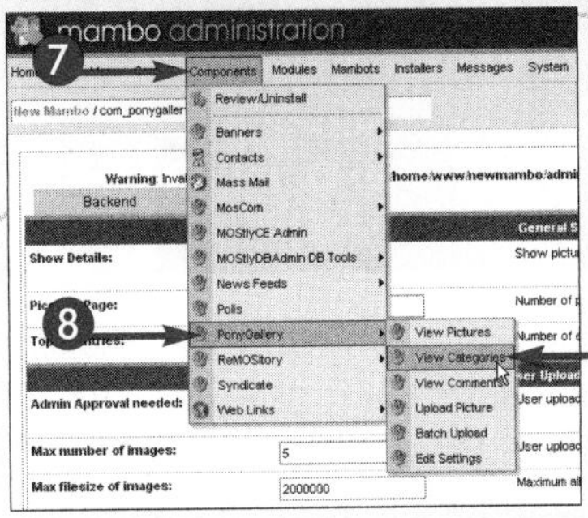

The Category Manager page loads.

10. Click the New icon.

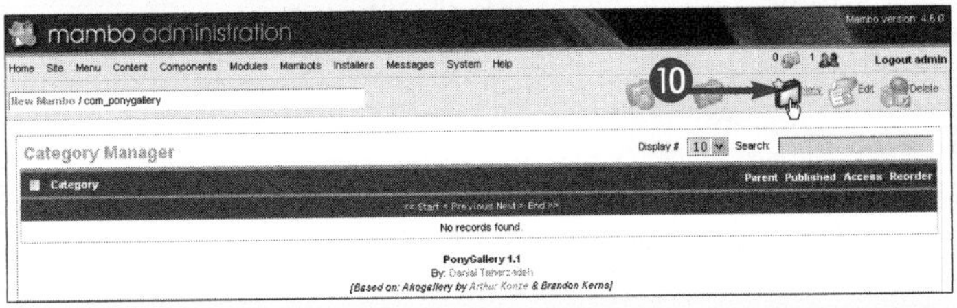

The Add Category page loads.

11. Type a title.
    - Optionally, you can add a description.
12. Click the Save icon.

Mambo creates the gallery and returns you to the Gallery Manager.

You are now ready to begin uploading images.

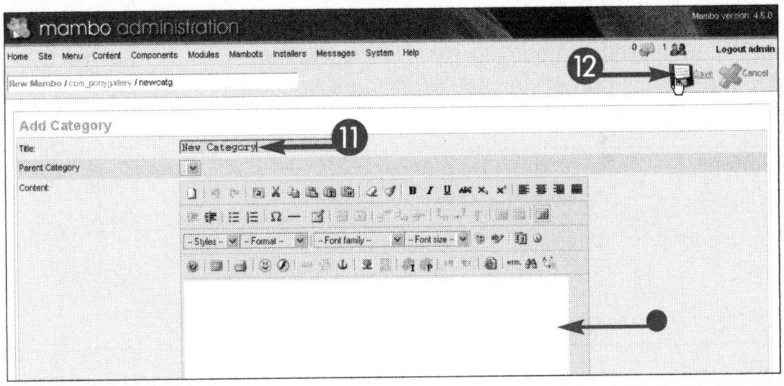

Extra

One of the most common errors made with online galleries is to make the image file sizes too large. Very large image files take a long time to download and display and can slow your site significantly. In particular, it is important to keep thumbnail file sizes down in order to allow people to get the thumbnails quickly and to decide if they want to click and wait for the larger images. Pony Gallery can create thumbnails automatically, but you should strive to keep the large image sizes under 100K so that the gallery loading speeds stay reasonable for users on slower connections.

The Pony Gallery automatically categorizes collections of images into galleries and albums. The categorization is useful for larger image collections, but the structure may be more than you need. If you want to jump directly to one album and avoid the hierarchy, create the gallery and album and publish it, and then capture the URL and create a new Menu Item linking directly to the URL of the target album. After you have your new Menu Item, remove the first Menu Item that links to the Gallery component.

Understanding Mambo Installation

The installation of a Mambo site is a straightforward matter. The technical requirements are not demanding and the actual installation process is controlled and guided by a step-by-step wizard-type interface. Once the site is installed you need to take some basic steps to secure the installation, and once completed you are ready to begin the customization of your site and the input of your contents. For more on installing Mambo on Linux, see the next section "Manual Installation of Mambo on Linux."

What You Need to Run Mambo

The two sets of technical requirements you must be concerned with are those for the server upon which you will install Mambo, and those that you, as an administrator, need to manage and maintain your Mambo site after installation.

Web Server Requirements

Mambo is not dependent upon any particular operating system. It functions properly on any operating system that satisfies the minimum requirements outlined below.

Minimum	Any Web server that supports PHP (Apache, IIS, Zeus)
Recommended	Apache 1.3.x or greater with mod_rewrite for search-engine-friendly URLs

Database Server

At present Mambo functions only on the MySQL database. The requirements below spell out minimum acceptable versions of MySQL. The system also operates on newer versions of MySQL, up to and including MySQL 5.

Minimum	MySQL 3.23.x
Recommended	MySQL 4.x or greater

PHP

The requirements below spell out minimum acceptable versions of PHP. The system also operates on newer versions of PHP, up to and including PHP 5.

Minimum	PHP 4.3.x with extensions: mySQL, xml, zlib, ftp
Recommended	PHP 4.4.x or greater with extensions: mySQL, xml, zlib, ftp, gd, gettext, iconv, mbstring

A Special Note on Shared Hosting Environments

Shared Web hosts sometimes run their machines in Safe Mode. It is recommended that you disable Safe Mode for Mambo to work optimally. Although you can make the system function in Safe Mode, it is often problematic and sometimes also causes difficulties with third-party extensions.

Mambo Site Administrator Requirements

Mambo is viewed by site visitors and managed by the administrators through a Web browser. Few limitations exist for site visitors; Mambo Web sites are cross-platform, cross-browser compatible. Users who experience problems with the front end of a Mambo Web site are most likely seeing template problems, not Mambo problems.

For site administrators, there are fewer choices. Although the administration system supports all browsers, Firefox and Internet Explorer tend to give the best results because they fully support the WYSIWYG editor functionality.

Installing Mambo on Windows

You can run Mambo on a Windows system, as long as you have installed the Apache Web server, MySQL, and PHP. You can set up the necessary tools in several ways. If you are a purist, you can download and install individually all the needed parts, but that tends to be time-consuming and rather too difficult for many people. If you are looking for a faster and easier solution, try XAMPP from Apache Friends. You can download the XAMPP package from www.apachefriends.org.

XAMPP is a bundle containing Apache, MySQL, PHP, phpMyAdmin, and a number of other related tools and services. The package is released free of charge. Apache Friends offers the package in several configurations, but the easiest path is to select the installer option and let it do the work for you.

To get started, download the Installer and run it on the Windows machine where you want to set up Mambo. Follow the steps in the installer and you will be set up and ready to run shortly. After completing the installation, you will find XAMPP under Start/Programs/XAMPP. The XAMPP Control Panel enables you to start and stop all services. Test the installation by starting Apache and MySQL. If you have installed successfully you will see confirmation messages.

The next step is to obtain the Mambo core files and copy the extracted files to the htdocs subdirectory inside the xampp directory. After you have copied the files into the htdocs directory, run the Mambo installer by directing your browser to the location of the Mambo files. (Make sure Apache and MySQL are running!)

The Mambo Installer follows the same steps as described in the section "Manual Installation of Mambo on Linux" and completes your installation. Thereafter, whenever you want to run Mambo, first start Apache and MySQL, and then direct your browser to the URL of the site.

Securing the Installation

A full treatise on managing the security of Web servers is beyond the scope of this appendix; however, there are several basic steps that you should take to secure your Mambo installation.

The first and most important line of defense is good work habits on the part of your system administrators. The vast majority of hacks and defacements are brought about through weak passwords and obvious logins. Human engineering is still the most effective tool in the hackers' toolkit. As discussed in Chapters 1 and 4 of the main text, you should encourage users to select secure passwords and adopt safe work habits.

The second most common error with Mambo sites is the failure to completely delete the installation directory. Leaving the installation directory intact gives users intent on mischief the ability to wipe out your Mambo installation completely. Do not simply rename the installation directory — delete it.

Another common source of problems is failing to keep up with security announcements, patches, and new releases. Keep your Mambo site up to date. Although in the past the Mambo team tended to release new versions with disturbing frequency, the project has matured and release cycles are more predictable and measured. Do not fall behind in your upgrades because missing one makes the next more difficult to complete, requiring you to step through two — or more! — upgrades, thereby compounding the time required and the potential for difficulties.

Team Mambo maintains a security mailing list to keep users advised of updates and security issues. You can subscribe to the mailing list by sending an email to security-notification@mambo-foundation.org. Mambo news and release information is always released on The Source, at http://source.mambo-foundation.org.

Manual Installation of Mambo on Linux

Because Mambo was originally designed for implementation in the LAMP environment — that is, on Linux, Apache, MySQL and PHP — installation on a typical Web host running a LAMP package is one of the simplest ways of getting a Mambo site running quickly.

Before installing Mambo, you must obtain the core Mambo files at the official Web site for Mambo code distributions: The Source — http://source.mambo-foundation.org. Here, you can download the current core files, which are in one archived file in either ZIP or TAR.GZ format. Choose the desired format; both archives contain the same collection of files.

Next, you extract the archive locally and then move the files to your server via FTP. Alternatively, if your Web host permits you to extract archives on the server, you can move the archive to the server by FTP and extract the files there. You then prepare a MySQL database for Mambo to use during installation, typically with a database administration tool like phpMyAdmin. Note the name you give the database, your database username, and your database password because you need this information later in the installation process.

Next, you run the installer, directing your browser to the location of the Mambo files on your Web server. The Installer's first screen contains the Pre-Install Checklist for you to review and resolve. You next see the Mambo license, which you can view in full in Appendix B. On the step 1 screen, you input the information you wrote down when you created your MySQL database. The bottom of this screen has an option to install the Mambo Sample Data. You can also clear the database tables in the event you are installing into a database that already contains tables and data. After you enter the required information and advance to the next screen, the system makes the connection with the database and populates the tables and fields.

Manual Installation of Mambo on Linux

1. Move the files to your server.
2. After accessing your MySQL database, create a new database.

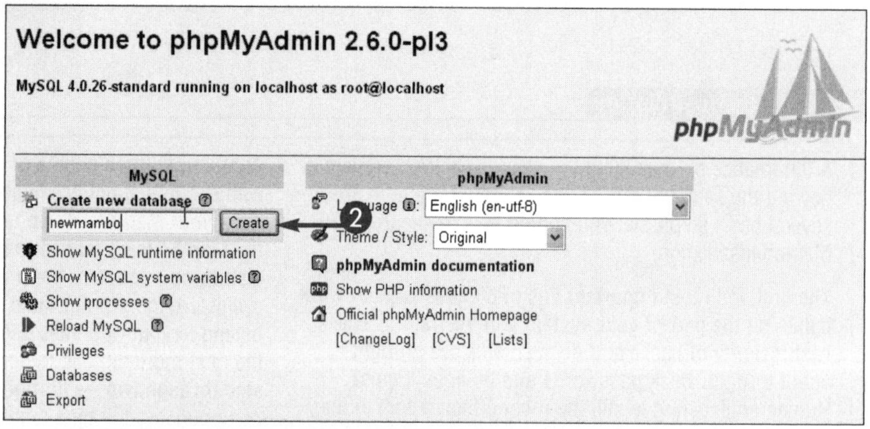

- The program you are using to create the database verifies that the database is created.

3. Note the following information for the installation process: the name you give to the database, your database username, and your database password.

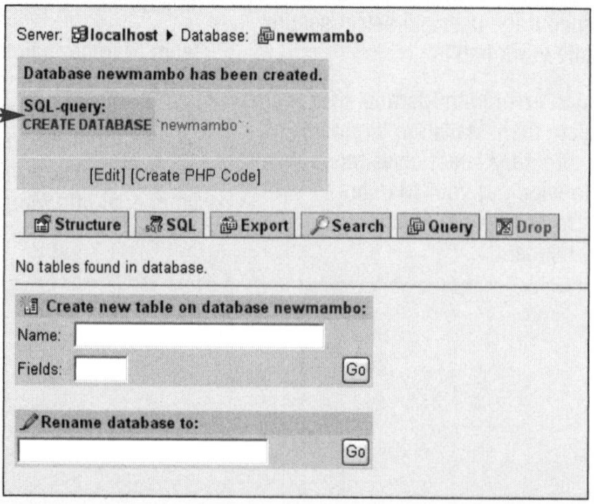

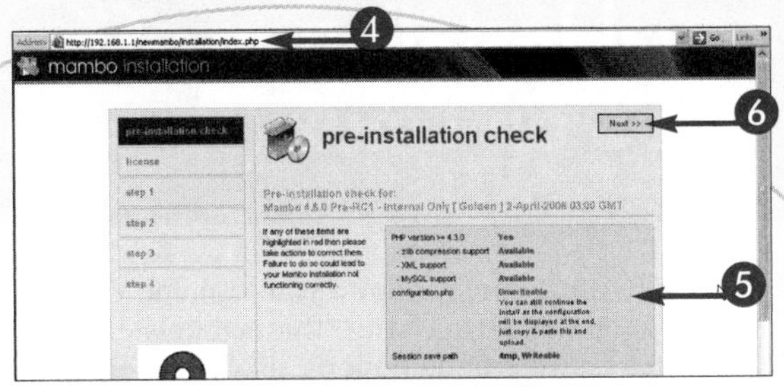

4. Direct your browser to the location of the Mambo files on your Web server.

   You should see the first installer screen, which is the Pre-Installer Checklist.

5. Resolve critical issues on the list, if any.

6. Click Next.

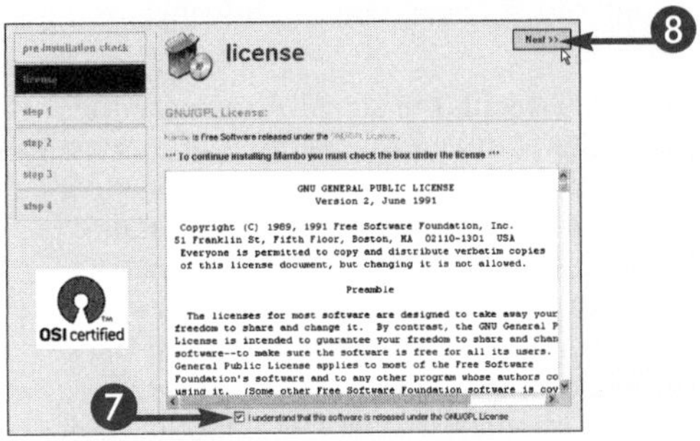

The license screen appears and shows the terms of the GNU GPL.

Note: For more on the Mambo license, see Appendix B.

7. Click the check box at the bottom of the screen to accept the license.

8. Click Next.

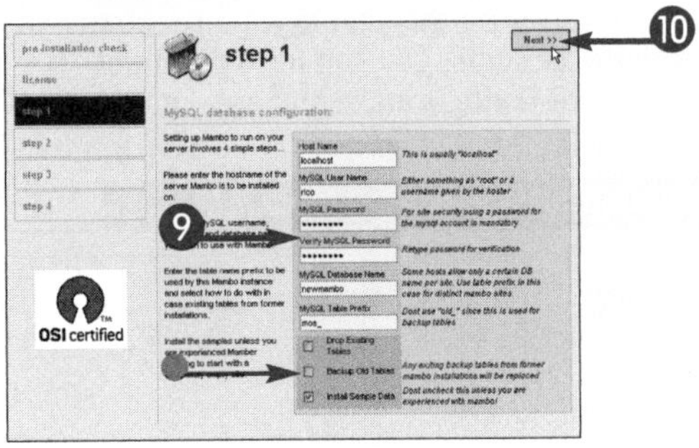

The step 1 screen appears, allowing you to configure the database.

9. Type the requested information.

   - You can select options to install the Mambo sample data, to clear the database tables, or to backup old tables.

10. Click Next.

Extra

The key task associated with the pre-installation check is to confirm that your system has everything it needs to run Mambo and that the file permissions are set to the right levels to allow full installation. Look down the columns to check for items highlighted in red. If you see items in red, check the instructions to determine whether the items require action before you can proceed. After you have resolved any critical issues, click the Next button to advance to the license screen.

continued →

Manual Installation of Mambo on Linux (continued)

The step 2 screen simply allows you to name your site. Note that you can change this name later via the Global Configuration options, as discussed in Chapter 2. After entering a name, you can advance to the step 3 screen.

The key tasks associated with the step 3 screen are the confirmation of the site path and the addition of an email address and password for the Super Administrator. Note that the site path information displayed by the installer is most probably correct, but if you are not sure, contact your Web host. You can change the email address and password for the Super Administrator later via the User Manager. For information on the User Manager, see Chapter 4. The step 3 screen also contains options to set CHMOD for the directories on the site. If you are unsure what to set, leave the defaults; you can always adjust this later via the Global Configuration Manager, as discussed in Chapter 2.

You next advance to the step 4 screen. At the top of the step 4 screen are two buttons: The View Site button takes you to the home page of your new site. The Administration button takes you to the administration login page of your new site. Clicking either button takes you to a screen that is a security reminder.

If your system was unable to automatically create the configuration.php file, then this step require one bit of additional work: You must capture the data you need to create your configuration.php file. Capture the data by clicking in the window containing the code and copying the information to the Notepad application or to an HTML editing program. Save the file with the name "configuration.php," then move it to the server via FTP and place it in the root directory where your Mambo site is located. After you have created the configuration.php file, you are ready to exit the installer.

Manual Installation of Mambo on Linux *(continued)*

The system creates the database as per your instructions.

The step 2 screen appears.

11 Type a name for your site.

12 Click Next.

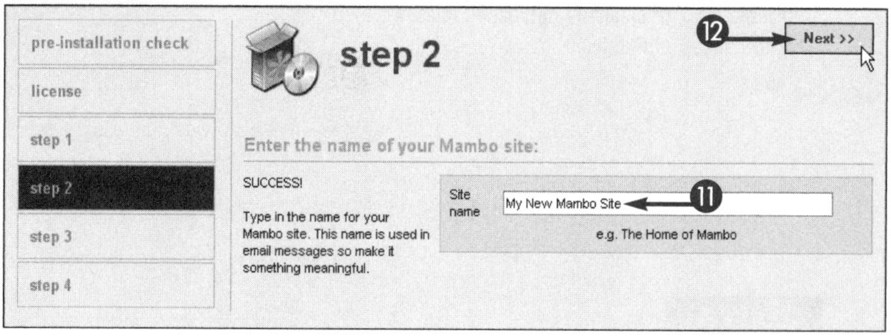

The step 3 screen appears.

13 Confirm the information in these fields.

14 Click Next.

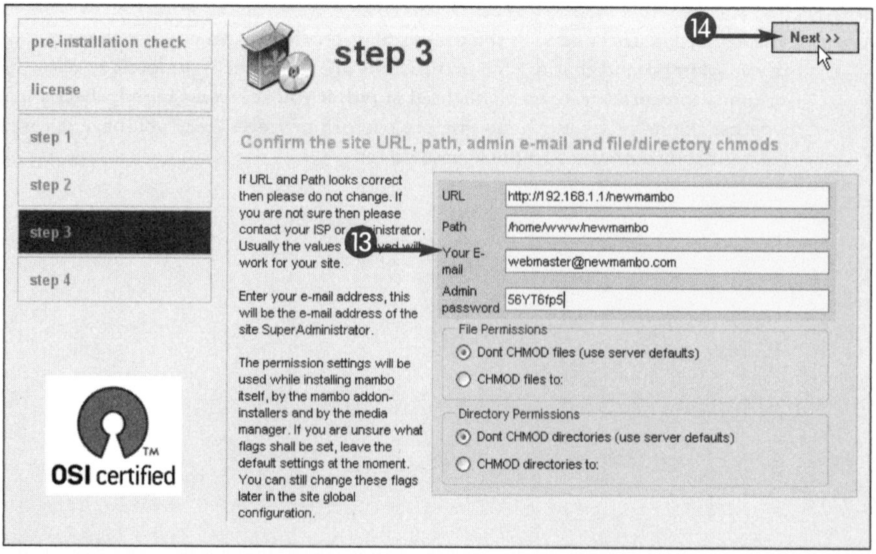

The step 4 screen appears.

Note: If the system indicates that it was unable to create the configuration.php file, click in the window containing the code.

⑮ Copy the information to the Notepad application or to an HTML editing program.

⑯ Save the file with the name "configuration.php".

⑰ Move the file to the server via FTP and place it in the root directory where your Mambo site is located.

⑱ Click either View Site or Administration.

You exit the installer and see a security screen.

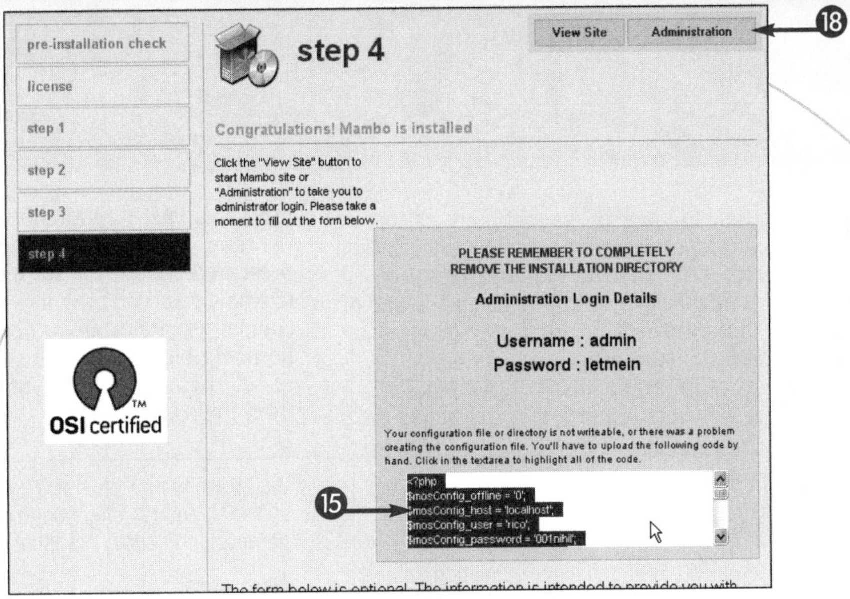

Extra

At the bottom of the step 4 screen you can find a short user survey for the benefit of the Mambo development team. The survey is optional. The information requested is very basic and is intended to give the Mambo development team basic insight into how the system is being used. There is also a checkbox where you can request additional information becoming involved in the Mambo Open Source Project.

The screen that you see when you exit the installer is a security reminder. To prevent this screen from showing, you can delete or rename the directory named "installation" inside the root of your Mambo site. Deleting or renaming the directory prevents someone from running the installation routine again and thereby damaging or destroying your site. After you have renamed or deleted the directory, refresh the browser to see your new Mambo site.

The Mambo License

Mambo, its language packs and many of its related components and modules, are released under the GNU General Public License, commonly known as the GNU GPL. The license is one of the most liberal of the Open Source software licenses. There are few restrictions on usage and additional software programs can even be based on the Mambo code and used for a variety of purposes, so long as the programs based on Mambo are also distributed under the terms of the GPL. The entire text of the license is presented, below, but for most users it is simply enough to know that you may use Mambo for your site, your company's site or any other purpose without paying licensing fees or facing legal threat, so long as you do not re-sell the program or remove the copyright statements from the code.

GNU General Public License

Version 2, June 1991

Copyright © 1989, 1991 Free Software Foundation, Inc.

51 Franklin Street, Fifth Floor, Boston, MA 02110-1301, USA

Everyone is permitted to copy and distribute verbatim copies of this license document, but changing it is not allowed.

Preamble

The licenses for most software are designed to take away your freedom to share and change it. By contrast, the GNU General Public License is intended to guarantee your freedom to share and change free software — to make sure the software is free for all its users. This General Public License applies to most of the Free Software Foundation's software and to any other program whose authors commit to using it. (Some other Free Software Foundation software is covered by the GNU Lesser General Public License instead.) You can apply it to your programs, too.

When we speak of free software, we are referring to freedom, not price. Our General Public Licenses are designed to make sure that you have the freedom to distribute copies of free software (and charge for this service if you wish), that you receive source code or can get it if you want it, that you can change the software or use pieces of it in new free programs; and that you know you can do these things.

To protect your rights, we need to make restrictions that forbid anyone to deny you these rights or to ask you to surrender the rights. These restrictions translate to certain responsibilities for you if you distribute copies of the software, or if you modify it.

For example, if you distribute copies of such a program, whether gratis or for a fee, you must give the recipients all the rights that you have. You must make sure that they, too, receive or can get the source code. And you must show them these terms so they know their rights.

We protect your rights with two steps: (1) copyright the software, and (2) offer you this license which gives you legal permission to copy, distribute and/or modify the software.

Also, for each author's protection and ours, we want to make certain that everyone understands that there is no warranty for this free software. If the software is modified by someone else and passed on, we want its recipients to know that what they have is not the original, so that any problems introduced by others will not reflect on the original authors' reputations.

Finally, any free program is threatened constantly by software patents. We wish to avoid the danger that redistributors of a free program will individually obtain patent licenses, in effect making the program proprietary. To prevent this, we have made it clear that any patent must be licensed for everyone's free use or not licensed at all.

The precise terms and conditions for copying, distribution and modification follow.

Terms and Conditions for Copying, Distribution and Modification

0. This License applies to any program or other work which contains a notice placed by the copyright holder saying it may be distributed under the terms of this General Public License. The "Program", below, refers to any such program or work, and a "work based on the Program" means either the Program or any derivative work under copyright law: that is to say, a work containing the Program or a portion of it, either verbatim or with modifications and/or translated into another language. (Hereinafter, translation is included without limitation in the term "modification".) Each licensee is addressed as "you".

   Activities other than copying, distribution and modification are not covered by this License; they are outside its scope. The act of running the Program is not restricted, and the output from the Program is covered only if its contents constitute a work based on the

Program (independent of having been made by running the Program). Whether that is true depends on what the Program does.

1. You may copy and distribute verbatim copies of the Program's source code as you receive it, in any medium, provided that you conspicuously and appropriately publish on each copy an appropriate copyright notice and disclaimer of warranty; keep intact all the notices that refer to this License and to the absence of any warranty; and give any other recipients of the Program a copy of this License along with the Program.

   You may charge a fee for the physical act of transferring a copy, and you may at your option offer warranty protection in exchange for a fee.

2. You may modify your copy or copies of the Program or any portion of it, thus forming a work based on the Program, and copy and distribute such modifications or work under the terms of Section 1 above, provided that you also meet all of these conditions:

   a) You must cause the modified files to carry prominent notices stating that you changed the files and the date of any change.

   b) You must cause any work that you distribute or publish, that in whole or in part contains or is derived from the Program or any part thereof, to be licensed as a whole at no charge to all third parties under the terms of this License.

   c) If the modified program normally reads commands interactively when run, you must cause it, when started running for such interactive use in the most ordinary way, to print or display an announcement including an appropriate copyright notice and a notice that there is no warranty (or else, saying that you provide a warranty) and that users may redistribute the program under these conditions, and telling the user how to view a copy of this License. (Exception: if the Program itself is interactive but does not normally print such an announcement, your work based on the Program is not required to print an announcement.)

   These requirements apply to the modified work as a whole. If identifiable sections of that work are not derived from the Program, and can be reasonably considered independent and separate works in themselves, then this License, and its terms, do not apply to those sections when you distribute them as separate works. But when you distribute the same sections as part of a whole which is a work based on the Program, the distribution of the whole must be on the terms of this License, whose permissions for other licensees extend to the entire whole, and thus to each and every part regardless of who wrote it.

   Thus, it is not the intent of this section to claim rights or contest your rights to work written entirely by you; rather, the intent is to exercise the right to control the distribution of derivative or collective works based on the Program.

   In addition, mere aggregation of another work not based on the Program with the Program (or with a work based on the Program) on a volume of a storage or distribution medium does not bring the other work under the scope of this License.

3. You may copy and distribute the Program (or a work based on it, under Section 2) in object code or executable form under the terms of Sections 1 and 2 above provided that you also do one of the following:

   a) Accompany it with the complete corresponding machine-readable source code, which must be distributed under the terms of Sections 1 and 2 above on a medium customarily used for software interchange; or,

   b) Accompany it with a written offer, valid for at least three years, to give any third party, for a charge no more than your cost of physically performing source distribution, a complete machine-readable copy of the corresponding source code, to be distributed under the terms of Sections 1 and 2 above on a medium customarily used for software interchange; or,

   c) Accompany it with the information you received as to the offer to distribute corresponding source code. (This alternative is allowed only for noncommercial distribution and only if you received the program in object code or executable form with such an offer, in accord with Subsection b above.)

   The source code for a work means the preferred form of the work for making modifications to it. For an executable work, complete source code means all the source code for all modules it contains, plus any associated interface definition files, plus the

continued →

scripts used to control compilation and installation of the executable. However, as a special exception, the source code distributed need not include anything that is normally distributed (in either source or binary form) with the major components (compiler, kernel, and so on) of the operating system on which the executable runs, unless that component itself accompanies the executable.

If distribution of executable or object code is made by offering access to copy from a designated place, then offering equivalent access to copy the source code from the same place counts as distribution of the source code, even though third parties are not compelled to copy the source along with the object code.

4. You may not copy, modify, sublicense, or distribute the Program except as expressly provided under this License. Any attempt otherwise to copy, modify, sublicense or distribute the Program is void, and will automatically terminate your rights under this License. However, parties who have received copies, or rights, from you under this License will not have their licenses terminated so long as such parties remain in full compliance.

5. You are not required to accept this License, since you have not signed it. However, nothing else grants you permission to modify or distribute the Program or its derivative works. These actions are prohibited by law if you do not accept this License. Therefore, by modifying or distributing the Program (or any work based on the Program), you indicate your acceptance of this License to do so, and all its terms and conditions for copying, distributing or modifying the Program or works based on it.

6. Each time you redistribute the Program (or any work based on the Program), the recipient automatically receives a license from the original licensor to copy, distribute or modify the Program subject to these terms and conditions. You may not impose any further restrictions on the recipients' exercise of the rights granted herein. You are not responsible for enforcing compliance by third parties to this License.

7. If, as a consequence of a court judgment or allegation of patent infringement or for any other reason (not limited to patent issues), conditions are imposed on you (whether by court order, agreement or otherwise) that contradict the conditions of this License, they do not excuse you from the conditions of this License. If you cannot distribute so as to satisfy simultaneously your obligations under this License and any other pertinent obligations, then as a consequence you may not distribute the Program at all. For example, if a patent license would not permit royalty-free redistribution of the Program by all those who receive copies directly or indirectly through you, then the only way you could satisfy both it and this License would be to refrain entirely from distribution of the Program.

If any portion of this section is held invalid or unenforceable under any particular circumstance, the balance of the section is intended to apply and the section as a whole is intended to apply in other circumstances.

It is not the purpose of this section to induce you to infringe any patents or other property right claims or to contest validity of any such claims; this section has the sole purpose of protecting the integrity of the free software distribution system, which is implemented by public license practices. Many people have made generous contributions to the wide range of software distributed through that system in reliance on consistent application of that system; it is up to the author/donor to decide if he or she is willing to distribute software through any other system and a licensee cannot impose that choice.

This section is intended to make thoroughly clear what is believed to be a consequence of the rest of this License.

8. If the distribution and/or use of the Program is restricted in certain countries either by patents or by copyrighted interfaces, the original copyright holder who places the Program under this License may add an explicit geographical distribution limitation excluding those countries, so that distribution is permitted only in or among countries not thus excluded. In such case, this License incorporates the limitation as if written in the body of this License.

9. The Free Software Foundation may publish revised and/or new versions of the General Public License from time to time. Such new versions will be similar in spirit to the present version, but may differ in detail to address new problems or concerns.

Each version is given a distinguishing version number. If the Program specifies a version number of this License which applies to it and "any later version", you have the option of following the terms and conditions either of that version or of any later version published by the Free Software Foundation. If the Program does not specify a version number of this License, you may choose any version ever published by the Free Software Foundation.

10. If you wish to incorporate parts of the Program into other free programs whose distribution conditions are different, write to the author to ask for permission. For software which is copyrighted by the Free Software Foundation, write to the Free Software Foundation; we sometimes make exceptions for this. Our decision will be guided by the two goals of preserving the free status of all derivatives of our free software and of promoting the sharing and reuse of software generally.

NO WARRANTY

11. BECAUSE THE PROGRAM IS LICENSED FREE OF CHARGE, THERE IS NO WARRANTY FOR THE PROGRAM, TO THE EXTENT PERMITTED BY APPLICABLE LAW. EXCEPT WHEN OTHERWISE STATED IN WRITING THE COPYRIGHT HOLDERS AND/OR OTHER PARTIES PROVIDE THE PROGRAM "AS IS" WITHOUT WARRANTY OF ANY KIND, EITHER EXPRESSED OR IMPLIED, INCLUDING, BUT NOT LIMITED TO, THE IMPLIED WARRANTIES OF MERCHANTABILITY AND FITNESS FOR A PARTICULAR PURPOSE. THE ENTIRE RISK AS TO THE QUALITY AND PERFORMANCE OF THE PROGRAM IS WITH YOU. SHOULD THE PROGRAM PROVE DEFECTIVE, YOU ASSUME THE COST OF ALL NECESSARY SERVICING, REPAIR OR CORRECTION.

12. IN NO EVENT UNLESS REQUIRED BY APPLICABLE LAW OR AGREED TO IN WRITING WILL ANY COPYRIGHT HOLDER, OR ANY OTHER PARTY WHO MAY MODIFY AND/OR REDISTRIBUTE THE PROGRAM AS PERMITTED ABOVE, BE LIABLE TO YOU FOR DAMAGES, INCLUDING ANY GENERAL, SPECIAL, INCIDENTAL OR CONSEQUENTIAL DAMAGES ARISING OUT OF THE USE OR INABILITY TO USE THE PROGRAM (INCLUDING BUT NOT LIMITED TO LOSS OF DATA OR DATA BEING RENDERED INACCURATE OR LOSSES SUSTAINED BY YOU OR THIRD PARTIES OR A FAILURE OF THE PROGRAM TO OPERATE WITH ANY OTHER PROGRAMS), EVEN IF SUCH HOLDER OR OTHER PARTY HAS BEEN ADVISED OF THE POSSIBILITY OF SUCH DAMAGES.

END OF TERMS AND CONDITIONS

How to Apply These Terms to Your New Programs

If you develop a new program, and you want it to be of the greatest possible use to the public, the best way to achieve this is to make it free software which everyone can redistribute and change under these terms.

To do so, attach the following notices to the program. It is safest to attach them to the start of each source file to most effectively convey the exclusion of warranty; and each file should have at least the "copyright" line and a pointer to where the full notice is found.

```
one line to give the program's name and an idea of
what it does.

Copyright (C) yyyy name of author

This program is free software; you can redistribute
it and/or modify it under the terms of the GNU
General Public License as published by the Free
Software Foundation; either version 2 of the
License, or (at your option) any later version.

This program is distributed in the hope that it
will be useful, but WITHOUT ANY WARRANTY; without
even the implied warranty of MERCHANTABILITY or
FITNESS FOR A PARTICULAR PURPOSE. See the GNU
General Public License for more details.

You should have received a copy of the GNU General
Public License along with this program; if not, write
to the Free Software Foundation, Inc., 51 Franklin
Street, Fifth Floor, Boston, MA 02110-1301, USA.
```

Also add information on how to contact you by electronic and paper mail.

If the program is interactive, make it output a short notice like this when it starts in an interactive mode:

```
Gnomovision version 69, Copyright (C) year name of
author

Gnomovision comes with ABSOLUTELY NO WARRANTY; for
details type 'show w'. This is free software, and
you are welcome to redistribute it under certain
conditions; type 'show c' for details.
```

The hypothetical commands 'show w' and 'show c' should show the appropriate parts of the General Public License. Of course, the commands you use may be called something other than 'show w' and 'show c'; they could even be mouse-clicks or menu items--whatever suits your program.

You should also get your employer (if you work as a programmer) or your school, if any, to sign a "copyright disclaimer" for the program, if necessary. Here is a sample; alter the names:

```
Yoyodyne, Inc., hereby disclaims all copyright

interest in the program 'Gnomovision'(which makes
passes at compilers) written by James Hacker.

<signature of Ty Coon>, 1 April 1989

Ty Coon, President of Vice
```

This General Public License does not permit incorporating your program into proprietary programs. If your program is a subroutine library, you may consider it more useful to permit linking proprietary applications with the library. If this is what you want to do, use the GNU Lesser General Public License instead of this License.

Configure MOStlyCE WYSIWYG Editor

This Appendix contains a listing of all the parameters available in the MOStlyCE Component, with a short synopsis of each parameter's function. The parameters provide a great deal of flexibility for customizing the WYSIWYG editor's functions and tailoring it to your needs.

Gen Options Tab

PARAMETER	DESCRIPTION
Editor Themes	Choose between a simple and advanced interface. The advanced interface shows all the tools available; the simple mode reduces the number of options to present a more basic interface.
Editor Compression	Enabling the Compression setting improves editor performance significantly. Disable it if you are experiencing problems with the editor.
Editor Language	Select the language you want from the drop-down menu. If your language does not appear, you must add a language file to the system.
List of supported languages	If you add an additional language file to the editor, add the language code to this field.
Override Template CSS	If you want to use a separate CSS file specifically for your Content Items, enable the option and then set the name of the CSS file in the next field. If you disable the option, the editor and your Content Items use the template CSS.
Custom CSS File	Input the name of the CSS file you want to use for MOStlyCE and your Content Items. Make sure the file is placed in the template's CSS directory. Only applicable if you select the Yes option in the Override Template CSS field.
Newlines	Determines the code that results when you hit Return while editing a Content Item. Select whether you want the editor to use a line break ` ` or a new paragraph `<p>`.
Convert Absolute URLs	Determines whether the system uses absolute or relative URLs inside of Content Items. For the SEF option to work to its best effect, enable this option.
Allow script elements	Determines whether you allow script elements to be used inside Content Items. The field immediately after the combo box allows you to specify which script elements are permitted. Use only what you need because misuse of this parameter can compromise site security.
Allow iFrame elements	Determines what elements can be associated with iFrames. The field immediately after the combo box allows you to specify which elements are permitted.
Extended Elements List	Allows you to specify additional elements permitted for use inside your Content Items. List only what you need because this parameter can compromise site security if misused.
Supported Onclick elements	Determines which elements can support Onclick events.
Path to HTML Template Directory	Specifies where you can find HTML templates. The default directory is created at the time of the Mambo installation. If you change this parameter, make sure the directory you specify exists.
Directionality	Set the direction that the text flows.

The Layout Tab

Use this tab to control the appearance of the MOStlyCE editor controls. You can rearrange the elements or hide unneeded elements.

Plugins Tab

Use this tab to specify which of the MOStlyCE plugins you want to activate. By default, all are on, but if you do not need some of these options, disable them to improve performance. The Time Format and Date Format fields let you specify the appearance of the time and date inserted into Content Items by the Time and Date controls.

Editor Info Tab

This tab contains credits related to MOStlyCE and some basic directions concerning the setup.

INDEX

Symbols and Numbers

& (ampersand) operator, omitting from URLs, 35
= (equals sign) operator, omitting from URLs, 35
? (question mark) operator, omitting from URLs, 35
one-column layouts, 91
two-column layouts, 91
two-tier content hierarchy, 67
three-tier content hierarchy, 67
four-tier content hierarchy, 67, 136–137
five-tier content hierarchy, 137
404 error message when accessing Help, 10

A

<a> tag (HTML), 125
access levels. *See also* access privileges; security
  content hierarchies and, 81, 107
  for menus, 212
  Public, 81, 107
  Registered, 63, 81, 107
  restricting for Content Items, 107
  restricting for Menu Items, 165
  restricting for menus, 164
  restricting for modules, 205
  restricting for sections or categories, 81
  Special, 81, 107
access privileges. *See also* access levels; security; user groups
  keeping to a minimum, 56
  multiple administrators and, 274
  for Template Manager, 38
  for user groups (table), 51
  for users, 56
accessibility, enhancing, 273
Admin interface. *See* Control Panel; *specific interfaces*
Admin Messaging System
  configuring, 276
  interface, 275
  multiple administrators and, 274
  number of messages listed on Control Panel, 7
  overview, 275
  sending admin messages, 277
  viewing admin messages, 278
admin modules. *See* administrator modules
admin system. *See also* Control Panel; *specific interfaces*
  accessing, 6
  Admin Templates for, 36, 232, 269–273
  interface, 7
  linking contact forms to users, 55
  logging out, 7
  Simple Mode versus Advanced Mode, 7, 9
  System Information option, 11
  toggling between Simple and Advanced Mode, 9
Admin Templates. *See also* Site Templates; Template Manager
  changing, 269
  creating custom, 273
  defined, 36
  installing automatically, 270–271
  installing manually, 272–273
  for modules, 232
  Super Administrator account required for access, 269
  third-party, 271
administering sites
  backing up, 264–265
  changing the Admin Template, 269
  checking in Content Items, 279
  editing the language file, 280–281
  installing Admin Template automatically, 270–271
  installing Admin Template manually, 272–273
  installing second Mambo system on domain, 282–283
  messaging feature configuration, 276
  messaging feature overview, 275
  multiple administrators for, 274
  optimizing performance settings, 268
  querying a database, 267
  requirements for Mambo, 302
  restoring a database, 266
  sending admin messages, 277
  unpublishing items for maintenance, 72, 73, 100
  viewing admin messages, 278
Administrator Menu Item, 145
administrator modules. *See also* modules; *specific modules*
  adding to the database, 231
  Admin Template for, 233
  changing position on template, 237
  customizing the admin interface for, 232
  default deployment, 232, 233
  deleting instances, 235
  directory for, 230, 240
  duplicating, 238
  further information, 239
  linking folder for images to, 231
  modifying, 240–241

B

INDEX

INDEX

INDEX

duplicating
  administrator modules, 238
  Archived Items (not allowed), 114
  categories, 78
  Content Items, 109
  local copy of live Web site, 265
  Menu Items, 158
  menus, 149
  before modifying modules, 229, 240
  sections, 77
  site modules, 208, 248–249
  Wrapper module, 132
Dynamic Page Titles, 31

E

editing
  Archived Items (not allowed), 114
  categories, 73, 75
  Content Items from the front end, 60–61, 140
  CSS files for templates, 48
  language file, 280–281
  links between contact forms and users, 55
  Menu Item parameters, 90, 91
  Menu Items, limitations on, 146, 151
  sections, 72, 74
  site modules, changing position on page, 202
  templates, 47
Editor User Group
  creating users in, 61
  front end content management by, 138, 139, 140
  front end only access for, 60
  rights and privileges (table), 51
  uses for, 61
email
  activating the Email to a Friend feature, 27
  configuring options for, 32
  default address for sent mail, 32
  hiding addresses in Content Items from SPAMbots, 250, 260
  Mass Mail component for, 182
Email Cloaking Mambot, 250, 260
enabling. *See also* caching; disabling
  Content Item rating, 24
  Dynamic Page Titles, 31
  links between Intro Text and Main Text, 23
  Login Form module, 60–61, 63
  MOStlyCE Editor, 20
  RSS feed options, 244
  Search Engine Friendly URLs, 35
  Site Statistics, 34
  User Registration feature, 62–63
  user to receive system notifications, 53
  write permissions for files, 13
equals sign (=) operator, omitting from URLs, 35
erasing. *See* deleting; Trash Manager; uninstalling
error messages
  diagnostic error reporting, 30
  404, when accessing Help files, 10
extensibility of Mambo, 3. *See also* third-party extensions

F

FAQs Menu Item, 144
favicon (Favorites Icon), 18–19
file management, Remository component for, 294–295
files. *See also* directories; images; *specific kinds*
  enabling write permissions, 13
  Help, viewing, 7, 10
  language, in third-party extensions, 281, 289, 291, 297
  linking to Content Items, 124–125
  media, 117–119
  unused, performance not impaired by, 46
finding. *See also* Internet resources
  Advanced Search tool for, 130
  language files, 281
  Language Packs, 289
  Mambots for, 251
  module placeholders, 209
  multilingual Content Items, 299
  path to media files, 119
  RSS feeds, 245
  third-party extensions, 284
Firefox browser (Mozilla)
  checking site display on, 14
  Web Developer extension, 49
  WYSIWYG editor suited to, 14
five-tier content hierarchy, 137
flat content hierarchy, 66–67, 97
flexibility of Mambo, 3
folders. *See* directories
forcing user to log out, 58
foreign languages. *See* languages

G

H

INDEX

L

INDEX

INDEX

N

INDEX

Q

R

S

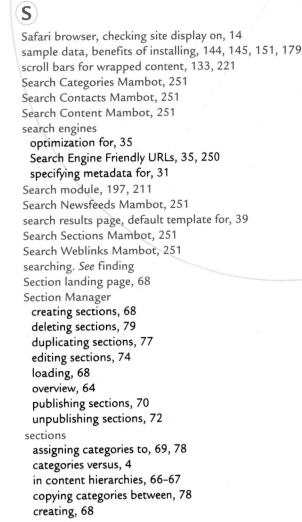

INDEX

U

...all designed for visual learners—just like you!

Master VISUALLY®

Step up to intermediate-to-advanced technical knowledge. Two-color interior.

- 3ds max
- Creating Web Pages
- Dreamweaver and Flash
- Excel VBA Programming
- iPod and iTunes
- Mac OS
- Optimizing PC Performance
- Photoshop Elements
- QuickBooks
- Quicken
- Windows Server
- Windows

Visual Blueprint™

Where to go for professional-level programming instruction. Two-color interior.

- Excel Data Analysis
- Excel Programming
- HTML
- JavaScript
- PHP

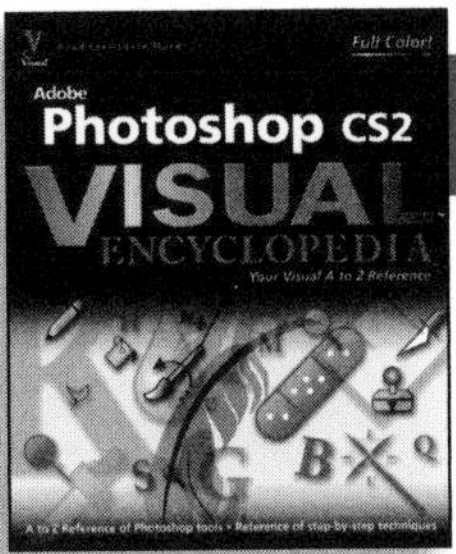

Visual Encyclopedia™

Your A to Z reference of tools and techniques. Full color.

- Dreamweaver
- Photoshop
- Windows

For a complete listing of Visual books, go to wiley.com/go/visualtech

Visual
An Imprint of WILEY
Now you know.